1998 UPDATE
ABNORMAL PSYCHOLOGY AND MODERN LIFE

TENTH EDITION

ROBERT C. CARSON
Duke University

JAMES N. BUTCHER
University of Minnesota

SUSAN MINEKA
Northwestern University

LONGMAN

An imprint of Addison Wesley Longman, Inc.

New York • Reading, Massachusetts • Menlo Park, California • Harlow, England
Don Mills, Ontario • Sydney • Mexico City • Madrid • Amsterdam

Editor-in-Chief: Priscilla McGeehon
Acquisitions Editor: Eric Stano
Developmental Editor: Betty Gatewood
Marketing Manager: Jay O'Callaghan
Supplements Editor: Cyndy Taylor
Project Coordination, Text and Cover Design: York Production Services
Photo Researcher (interior): Roberta Knauf
Photo Researcher (cover): Nina Page
Full Service Production Manager: Valerie Zaborski
Manufacturing Manager: Hilda Koparanian
Electronic Page Makeup: York Production Services
Printer and Binder: R.R. Donnelley & Sons Company
Cover Printer: Phoenix Color Corp.
Cover Illustration: Gorky, Arshile (Vosdanig Manoog Adoian). *Agony. 1947.* Oil on canvas, 40 x 50 ½" (101.5 x 128.3 cm). The Museum of Modern Art, New York. A. Conger Goodyear Fund. Photograph © 1995 The Museum of Modern Art, New York.

Library of Congress Cataloging-in-Publication Data
Carson, Robert C., 1930–
    Abnormal psychology and modern life / Robert C. Carson, James N. Butcher, Susan Mineka.—10th ed., 1998 update.
        p. cm.
    Includes bibliographical references and index.
    ISBN 0-321-01681-5
    ISBN 0-321-01830-3 (paper)
    1. Psychiatry.   2. Psychology, Pathological.   I. Butcher, James Neal, 1933–.   II. Mineka, Susan.   III. Title
RC454.C275   1997
616.89—dc20   95-21468
                                                                            CIP

987654311—DOW—97989900
ISBN 0-321-01681-5

BRIEF CONTENTS

DETAILED CONTENTS

PART ONE

PERSPECTIVES ON ABNORMAL BEHAVIOR 1

■ CHAPTER 1
ABNORMAL BEHAVIOR IN OUR TIMES 2

■ CHAPTER 2
HISTORICAL VIEWS OF ABNORMAL BEHAVIOR 30

PART TWO

PATTERNS OF
ABNORMAL (MALADAPTIVE)
BEHAVIOR   117

■ CHAPTER 4

STRESS AND ADJUSTMENT
  DISORDERS   118

PART THREE

ASSESSMENT, TREATMENT,
AND PREVENTION   565

■ CHAPTER 16
BIOLOGICALLY BASED
        THERAPIES   600

■ CHAPTER 17
PSYCHOLOGICALLY BASED
        THERAPIES   624

UPDATE PREFACE

The field of abnormal psychology moves at a fast pace. Broad-based research findings in psychology, psychiatry, genetics, imaging technology, and a host of other areas accumulate with a rapidity that seems breathtaking when compared with the more restrained rate of progress characteristic of the field's earlier history. Abnormal psychology textbook authors and publishers are faced with difficult choices about how to ensure that current students will be provided with an overview of the field that truly represents its contemporary state of development.

The problem is particularly acute in the case of *Abnormal Psychology and Modern Life,* whose authors take pride in their text's reputation for unsurpassed currency. As a consequence, the normal four-year textbook revision cycle no longer seems adequete for achieving our objectives, and yet more frequent full-scale revisions would incur enormous practical, logistic, and production cost (and therefore book pricing) problems. In mulling over this intimidating dilemma among ourselves and with our publisher, we arrived at what we believe to be a satisfactory solution—that of selectively updating in certain areas of especially rapid and important recent advances by adding supplementary material to the 10th edition.

While the decisions about which Cutting Edge issues to include were not easy to make and involved much intensive discussion, in the end we were somewhat surprised to discover a high concordance in our judgments regarding emerging "center stage" trends. We list these topics here, together with the chapters to which they pertain:

- Unpredictable and Uncontrollable Stress and PTSD (Chapter 4)
- New Findings on an "Anxiety Gene" and on Anxiety Sensitivity (Chapter 5)
- Depression and Domestic Violence (Chapter 6)
- Recovered Memories of Abuse and Dissociative Disorders: Continuing Controversy (Chapter 7)
- Depression and Coronary Heart Disease (Chapter 8)
- Functional Magnetic Resonance Imaging (Chapter 15)
- New Developments in the Treatment of Depression (Chapter 16)
- A Ray of Hope in Preventing Alcohol and Other Drug Problems (Chapter 18)
- The Crisis in Mental Health Care (Chapter 18)

These Cutting Edge highlights appear at the ends of Parts Two and Three. Within the main text each relevant chapter has a tab and the text is highlighted at the point related to the Cutting Edge piece.

We are also pleased to announce with the appearance of the 1998 Update the availability of the *Internet Companion* by Cheryl J. Hamel and David Ryan-Jones, which is a manual for facilitating independent student research in abnormal psychology using the World Wide Web.

Sometimes, the wealth of information on the Internet can be overwhelming, and the excitement of this new medium quickly wears off after long search times and many dead ends. *The Internet Companion* provides direct routes to research on a particular mental disorder, contacts with support services, and locations of mental health/professional organizations. The guide makes searches on the Internet more efficient by taking users directly to reputable sites containing scholarly and pertinent information written by or intended for the academic community and professionals in the field. The gudie also explains many types of information provided by various sources on the Net so that findings can be evaluated in terms of the sources.

The manual will come shrinkwrapped with all new copies of the text and will provide to the high-tech inclined student a survival guide for using the enormous potential of the Web to expand their horizons in the area of mental health and disorder.

R.C.C.
J.N.B.
S.M.

PREFACE

In preparing the new tenth edition of *Abnormal Psychology and Modern Life,* we enthusiastically welcome a new co-author, Professor Susan Mineka of Northwestern University, who adds a significant increment of breadth in our attempt to make accessible to students the latest and best of available research in the ever-expanding field of abnormal psychology. Dr. Mineka, herself a noted researcher and former editor of the *Journal of Abnormal Psychology,* has brought new expertise, broad knowledge of the research literature, and great energy to her work on this edition. We think readers familiar with former editions of this work will appreciate that the results speak for themselves.

The discipline of abnormal psychology has undergone many dramatic changes since this text first appeared, under the inspired authorship of James Coleman, in the early 1950s. However, our goals for this tenth edition remain unchanged from that first successful effort: to provide the reader with a comprehensive, searching, and engaging overview of the field. Over the course of nine editions, *Abnormal Psychology and Modern Life* has given generations of psychology students a thorough and rigorous grounding in abnormal psychology. In each edition, the authors have sought continually to incorporate current research and to examine critically its contribution to advancing knowledge, while retaining a focus on rich clinical description. In this tenth edition, as in the past, we have balanced the enormous challenge of including the latest developments in a constantly changing field with a judicious reevaluation and streamlining of the wide variety of topics covered by our text. We believe that the tenth edition is as thorough, timely, and dynamic as the ground-breaking first edition was in its time.

Highlights of the New Edition

Presenting in concise and pedagogically mindful fashion the wealth of exciting new research in abnormal psychology has challenged us to reevaluate each chapter from the ninth edition and, in a few cases, to completely rework chapter content. We've made a number of organizational changes in the book to accommodate the new material we've included. Among the changes in the new edition are the following:

- The new edition of the *Diagnostic and Statistical Manual of Mental Disorders* (DSM-IV) has appeared since the publication of the ninth edition of this book. Accordingly, we have integrated the DSM-IV taxonomy and diagnostic criteria into our discussion of the various types of disorder, noting changes in terminology as appropriate.

- We have updated all major topics with relevant new research where it was available. In so doing, we have sometimes found it necessary to present a complex and detailed picture. Sometimes the addition of new research, particularly from biologically oriented investigators, will pose a challenge to students unfamiliar with the methods and terminology involved. Within the context of our aims, this is largely unavoidable; the field itself is challenging, and we believe that occasional complexity is to be preferred to oversimplification. We also believe that complexity does not in and of itself preclude clarity, nor excuse unintelligible writing, and we have tried hard to present complicated systems in a manner that facilitates understanding and mastery. We have not hesitated, for example, to lay out the complex developmental pathway thought to underlie a progression from early, mild neuropsychological deficit through early-onset conduct disorder to adult antisocial personality disorder.

- In response to consistent reviewer recommendations, we have combined the ninth edition chapters on causal factors and theoretical viewpoints into a single integrated chapter.

- The anxiety disorders are now covered in a chapter of their own.

- Somatoform and dissociative disorders are also covered in a chapter of their own.

- Autism has been moved into the chapter on childhood disorders.

- Mental retardation and learning disorders have been moved into a chapter covering brain disorders and other cognitive impairments.

- We have done a considerable amount of overall trimming and reduction to essentials, largely by purging discussions of older studies and of peripheral issues.

- The use of illustrative case material has always been an important and integral component of this textbook. We have added substantial amounts of new case material at critical points in various chapters, and additional examples are provided to illustrate the procedural aspects of treatments found to be especially effective in various disorders.

Significant Changes in this Edition

The tenth edition represents an extensive reorganization and revision of the text. Some of the more important specific changes include the following.

- In our new Chapter 3, "Causal Factors and Viewpoints in Abnormal Psychology," the coverage of nonspecific causal or "risk" factors in psychopathology has been thoroughly updated to reflect a number of important findings from the expanding field of developmental psychopathology. For example, there is enhanced coverage of the concepts of vulnerability and resilience. In addition, the importance of the development of schemas and self-schemas in childhood and the role they play in vulnerability to psychopathology is emphasized.

- Our new Chapter 5, "Panic, Anxiety, and Their Disorders," has been very substantially updated and expanded. This chapter now surveys the very latest thinking on research and treatment of anxiety disorders, including the role of biological and cognitive factors in causing and maintaining these conditions. Many new case studies are also presented.

- Our new Chapter 6, "Mood Disorders and Suicide," has been heavily revised to reflect the wealth of new research in this field. We review recent biological research, including work on disturbed biological rhythms, and we also highlight important new research on psychosocial factors in the context of several prominent

and competing vulnerability-stress causal models. We discuss bipolar disorders separately from unipolar disorders, reflecting an increasing tendency, supported by research, in favor of emphasizing a distinction between the two.

- Somatoform and dissociative disorders now have their own chapter, Chapter 7, which has allowed us to expand our coverage of the fascinating issues raised by these types of phenomena, including purported basic linkages they may share. We also discuss the debate over whether "multiple personalities" really exist, and we review the controversy over what have been called "created memories."

- In Chapter 9, "Personality Disorders," we have expanded coverage about recent controversies regarding dimensional versus categorical approaches to understanding these types of exaggerations of normal personality traits. The new cognitive approaches to understanding personality disorders and their treatment are also discussed. We have also expanded our coverage of the causal factors in psychopathy and antisocial personality disorder, including, as noted above, a developmental pathway involving childhood conduct disorder.

- In Chapter 11, "Sexual Variants, Abuse, and Dysfunctions," we have added coverage of the issue of sexual abuse of children and the reliability of their memories. We also discuss historical and cross-cultural issues that affect society's views on what are normal and psychopathological variants of sexual behavior. Also examined are the methodological issues surrounding the question of childhood sexual abuse as a cause of adult psychopathology.

- We have updated our coverage of the schizophrenic disorders (Chapter 12), incorporating much new research deriving from the high level of investigative activity in this domain. For example, a recently published and exceptionally searching study of discordance for schizophrenia in identical twins is carefully examined for what it can yield in enhanced understanding of the sources of psychotic functioning.

- Chapter 15, "Clinical Assessment," now includes discussion of the new and rapidly expanding area of forensic assessment, where psychological testing is employed in the resolution of questions involving an interface between the law and psychological states or characteristics of litigants in both civil and criminal proceedings.

- In Chapter 16, "Biologically Based Therapies," we have expanded and updated our coverage of drug treatment, including the controversy concerning the new and widely used antidepressant Prozac. Also included is a contemporary review of two traditional somatic therapies, electroconvulsive therapy (ECT), and psychosurgery.

- Chapter 18, "Contemporary Issues in Abnormal Psychology," features a considerably expanded and updated treatment of the insanity defense in criminal law and undertakes a detailed examination of the often perplexing legal theories determining courtroom practices in this very controversial area.

Organization of the Text

Throughout the previous nine editions, the organization of *Abnormal Psychology and Modern Life* has to a large extent set the organizational standard for the study of abnormal psychology. Although some chapters have been rearranged, as described above, the basic organization of the tenth edition remains familiar.

- Part One, "Perspective on Abnormal Behavior," sets forth a framework for understanding abnormal behavior, beginning with discussions of classification and scientific research in abnormal psychology (Chapter 1). A brief historical overview traces the changing views of mental disorder from ancient to modern times and includes a discussion of the difficulties of interpreting historical events over time (Chapter 2). This leads to a discussion of causal factors and viewpoints (Chapter 3). Throughout, the reader will be aware of the diversity of the field and the interaction of biological, psychosocial, and sociocultural factors. The ideal of achieving a biopsychosocial integrative approach to understanding the causes of the different disorders is emphasized.

- Part Two, "Patterns of Abnormal (Maladaptive) Behavior," can be considered the core of the text. Here the clinical pictures, causal factors, and treatment and outcomes of maladaptive behavior patterns are examined individually. This section begins with an examination of stress and adjustment disorders, followed by chapters on panic- and anxiety-based disorders, mood disorders, somatoform and dissociative disorders, psychological factors and physical illness, personality disorders, sub-stance-use disorders, sexual variants and dysfunctions, schizophrenic and delusional disorders, brain insult and other cognitive impairments, and disorders of childhood and adolescence. As already noted, these chapters have been extensively revised and updated throughout.

- Finally, Part Three is a more comprehensive look at the clinical assessment, treatment, and prevention of disorders. It includes chapters on assessment, biological therapies, psychosocial therapies, and contemporary social issues pertaining to abnormalities of behavior.

Pedagogical Aids

Many features have been incorporated into this book to aid students in their understanding of abnormal psychology.

- A **chapter outline** introduces each chapter and provides an overview of what is to come. **Chapter summaries** at the end of each chapter also provide an overview, and can be read as an introduction to the chapter or as a review after reading the chapter.

- **Key terms** appear in boldface type when first introduced and defined in the text. For each chapter, these terms are also listed after the summary. At the end of the text, the terms are included and defined in a glossary.

- **Highlight boxes** expand on or summarize important text content.

- The essential features of **DSM-IV** are printed for ready reference on the endpapers of the book.

- **Case studies** of individuals with various disorders appear throughout the book. These cases provide real-life examples of the clinical pictures of many disorders covered in the text. Some are brief excerpts; others are detailed analyses. These cases serve not only to make what the student is reading about more real but also to remind students of the human factor that is so intimately a part of the subject matter of this text. Cases are set off from the text in tinted areas. They also sometimes appear in Highlight boxes. Numerous new case examples are provided for the anxiety disorders, sexual disorders, and personality disorders.

- **Patient art** appears in the chapter openers, with a brief biographical sketch of the artist.

Photos, too, are used throughout to enhance the concepts of the text visually. In some cases, these photos are of people who have been diagnosed as having the disorder in question. The art and the photos will serve not only to instruct but to humanize the study of abnormal behavior.

- At the end of the book is a **glossary** that contains definitions of key terms that appear in boldface type in the text and other terms that appear in the text.
- A **subject index** and a **name index** at the end of the book provide ready reference to any topic or person discussed in the book. The boldface page numbers in the subject index indicate where key terms are first discussed in depth.
- A list of **references** appears at the end of the text; it gives complete information on the citations that appear in the text proper.

Ancillaries

Here is an overview of the ancillaries that accompany this text.

For the Student
A *Study Guide* by Don Fowles (University of Iowa) includes learning objectives, study questions, quizzes, and key terms. New to the tenth edition of the study guide is a feature to prompt critical thinking on the part of the student (1998 Update included).

SuperShell II Computerized Study Guide by Suzanne de Beaumont is an interactive text-related program for IBM and compatible machines. It features multiple-choice, true-false, and short-answer questions as well as chapter outlines and a complete text glossary.

For the Instructor
An *Instructor's Manual* by Frank Prerost (Wesleyan Illinois University) gives overviews, learning objectives, lists of key terms, abstracts with discussion questions, suggested readings, discussion and lecture ideas, suggested films, and ideas for activities and projects. (Update by Steven Rouse.)

Videos from "The World of Abnormal Psychology," a telecourse produced by the Annenberg/CPB Project in conjunction with Toby Levine Communications, Alvin H. Perlmutter, and Longman, are available to qualified adopters. Contact your Longman sales representative for more information. The videos are accompanied by literature on how to incorporate the videos into classroom lectures.

A *Test Bank* by Gerald Metalsky (Lawrence University) and Rebecca Laird contains over 100 multiple-choice questions per chapter as well as 15 essay questions and 20 short-answer questions per chapter. (Update by Steven Rouse.)

TestMaster, the computerized version of the test bank, is also available for IBM PC and Macintosh machines and compatibles. The program allows you to customize your own tests on a built-in word processor that lets you delete, add, and revise questions as necessary.

Acknowledgments

We want here to single out for a special note of praise and appreciation our developmental editor, Betty Gatewood. For one of us, this was a first attempt at writing a textbook, and Betty showed enormous patience and wisdom in passing on the skills necessary to write at the appropriate level. For all of us, her editorial experience was evident in the great editorial wisdom that she showed in helping us with each chapter. This editorial wisdom, combined with her great organizational skills, personal warmth, and enthusiasm for the project, were central to whatever success the current edition enjoys.

We are greatly indebted to Dr. J. Michael Bailey of Northwestern University for his enormous help in revising and updating the coverage of material regarding sexual variants and abuse in Chapter 11. As a researcher in this important and controversial area, his advice on what to include in such a chapter and how to cover it in an interesting and sensitive fashion was invaluable. Dr. Steve Finn of the Center for Therapeutic Assessment (Austin, Texas) also provided important advice on how to address some of the sensitive topics raised in this chapter.

Numerous reviewers also contributed comments on the previous edition as well as on the manuscript for the current edition. These include: Norman Anderson, Duke University Medical Center; John Bates, Indiana University; Alfred Baumeister, Vanderbilt University; Ira Bernstein, University of Texas—Arlington; Bruce Bongar, Pacific Graduate School of Psychology; Linda Bosmajian, Hood College; Kenneth Bowers, University of Waterloo; Wolfgang Bringmann, University of Southern Alabama; Alan Butler, University of Maine; James Calhoun, University of Georgia; Caryn Carlson, University of Texas at Austin; Alan Carr, University College Dublin; Kathleen Carroll, Yale School of

Medicine; Lee Anna Clark, University of Iowa; David Cole, University of Notre Dame; Bruce Compas, University of Vermont; Eric Cooley, Western Oregon State; Robert Deluty, University of Maryland Baltimore County; Joan Doolittle, Anne Arundel Community College; John Exner, Rorschach Workshops; Gary Ford, Stephen F. Austin State University; Don Fowles, University of Iowa; Sol Garfield, Washington University; Carlton Gass, Veterans Administration Medical Center–Miami, Florida; Paul Goldin, Metropolitan State of Denver; Ethan Gorenstein, Columbia University; Lisa Green, Baldwin-Wallace College; Susan Hardin, University of Akron; Marc Henley, Delaware County Community College; Karen Horner, Ohio State University; William Iacono, University of Minnesota; Ira Iscoe, University of Texas at Austin; Fred Johnson, University of the District of Columbia; Gary Johnson, Normandale Community College; John Junginger, State University of New York at Binghamton; John Kihlstrom, Yale University; Marlyne Kilbey, Wayne State University; David Kosson, Chicago Medical School; Dennis Kreinbrook, Westmoreland County Community College; Gerard Lenthall, Keene State College; Gloria Leon, University of Minnesota; Arnold LeUnes, Texas A&M University; Richard Lewine, Emory University; Patrick Logue, Duke University Medical Center; Lester Luborsky, University of Pennsylvania; Edwin Megargee, Florida State University; Linda Montgomery, University of Texas of the Permian Basin; Eileen Palace, University of Minnesota; John Poppleston, Akron University; Charles Prokop, Florida Institute of Technology; Paul Retzlaff, University of Northern Colorado; Clive Robins, Duke University Medical Center; Kenneth Sher, University of Missouri; Gregory Smith, University of Kentucky; Kathleen Stafford, Court Diagnostic Clinic; Brian Stagner, Texas A&M University; Louis Stamps, University of Wisconsin–La Crosse; Veronica Stebbing, University College Dublin; Patricia Sutker, Veterans Medical Center–New Orleans; Alexander Troster, University of Kansas Medical Center; Samuel Turner, Medical University of South Carolina; Linda Van Egeren, Department of Veterans Affairs Medical Center–Minneapolis; Charles Wenar, Ohio State University; Fred Whitford, Montana State University; Jennifer Wilson, Duke University Medical Center; Richard Zinbarg, University of Oregon.

Within the former HarperCollins organization, Art Pomponio, Marcus Boggs, Susan Driscoll, Lisa Pinto, and Priscilla McGeehon performed important management roles in shepherding this large and complex project through the contemporary publishing maze. Catherine Woods was continuously ready at a moment's notice to provide backup resources and unfailing support to the authors through the inevitable but often unpredictable crises encountered in the planning, writing, and production of the revision. Diane Wansing, Supplements Editor, Mark Paluch, Marketing Manager, Erica Smith, Editorial Assistant, and Diane Kraut, who coordinated our permissions, also made significant contributions in their respective areas of expertise.

We are extremely pleased with the high quality of our text supplements for this edition, and we sincerely thank those involved. They are: Don Fowles (Study Guide), Frank Prerost (Instructor's Manual), Jerry Metalsky and Rebecca Laird (Test Bank), Suzanne de Beaumont (Supershell), and Toby Levine (Video/Telecourse materials).

Finally, we thank the staff of York Production Services, particularly Kevin Bradley, for their superbly performed role of transforming our often decidedly imperfect "copy" into what we perceive as a textbook of uncommon accuracy and attractiveness.

We suspect that only other authors of textbooks fully comprehend the disruptions and deprivations of family life entailed in a project of this magnitude. For their patience and forebearance in undergoing once again these frustrations, we acknowledge with gratitude these special contributions of Tracey Potts Carson, Kelly Carson, Carolyn Williams, and Holly Butcher.

Robert C. Carson
James N. Butcher
Susan Mineka

ABOUT THE AUTHORS

Robert Carson, a native New Englander, received his undergraduate degree in psychology at Brown University. His graduate training, culminating in the PhD in clinical psychology, occurred at Northwestern University. He has been a member of both the Medical and Arts and Sciences faculties at Duke University since 1960. In the course of that tenure he served as Head of Duke Medical Center's Division of Medical Psychology and, in the Department of Psychology, as Director of its doctoral clinical program and as Chair. He has taught psychology to undergraduates virtually uninterruptedly since his senior year at Brown, and in 1993-94 was named a Distinguished Teacher in Duke University's Trinity College. Also, partly in recognition of his teaching contributions, he was appointed a G. Stanley Hall Lecturer by the American Psychological Association for 1989. Dr. Carson's scholarly interests are focused on the interpersonal dimensions of psychopathology, although he claims to work hard at remaining a generalist and avoiding excessive specialization.

James N. Butcher was born in West Virginia. He enlisted in the Army at 17 years of age and served in the airborne infantry for three years, including a one-year tour in Korea during the Korean War. After military service, he attended Guilford College, graduating in 1960 with a BA in psychology. He received an MA in experimental psychology in 1962 and a PhD in clinical psychology from the University of North Carolina at Chapel Hill. He was awarded Doctor Honoris Causa from the Free University of Brussels, Belgium, in 1990.

He is currently Professor of Psychology in the Department of Psychology at the University of Minnesota and was Associate Director and Director of the Clinical Psychology Program at Minnesota for 19 years. He was a member of the University of Minnesota Press' MMPI Consultive Committee that undertook the revision of the MMPI in 1989. He is currently the editor of Psychological Assessment, a journal of the Amercian

Psychological Association, and serves as consulting editor or reviewer for numerous other journals in psychology and psychiatry. Dr. Butcher has been actively involved in developing and organizing disaster response programs for dealing with human problems following airline disasters. He organized a model crisis intervention disaster response for the Minneapolis-St. Paul Airport, and organized and supervised the psychological services offered fol-lowing two major airline disasters: Northwest Flight 255 in Detroit, Michigan, and Aloha Airlines on Maui.

He is a fellow of the American Psychological Association and the Society for Personality Assessment. He has published 34 books and more than 150 articles in the fields of abnormal psychology, cross-cultural psychology, and personality assessment.

Susan Mineka, born and raised in Ithaca, New York, received her undergraduate degree magna cum laude in psychology at Cornell University. She received a PhD in experimental psychology from the University of Pennsylvania in 1974, and later completed a formal clinical retraining program from 1981-1984. She taught at the University of Wisconsin-Madison and at the University of Texas at Austin before moving to Northwestern University in 1987. She has taught a wide range of undergraduate and graduate courses, including introductory psychology, learning, motivation, abnormal psychology, and cognitive-behavior thera-py. Her current research interests include cognitive and behavioral approaches to understanding the etiology, maintenance, and treatment of anxiety and mood disorders. She has served as editor of the Journal of Abnormal Psychology (1990-1994), as President of the Society for the Science of Clinical Psychology (1994-1995), and is President of the Midwestern Psychological Association (1997). She also served on the American Psychological Association's Board of Scientific Affairs (1992-1994, Chair 1994) and on the Executive Board of the Society for Research in Psychopathology (1992-1994).

A Visual Guide To: **1998 UPDATE:**

ABNORMAL PSYCHOLOGY AND MODERN LIFE

Tenth Edition

Robert C. Carson
Duke University

James N. Butcher
University of Minnesota

Susan Mineka
Northwestern University

ISBN 0-321-01681-5

The 1998 Update of *Abnormal Psychology and Modern Life, Tenth Edition* continues the text's tradition of offering the most authoritative survey of abnormal psychology, providing students with a thorough and rigorous study of the field. The classic elements of the text remain—it is serious, comprehensive, and includes unbiased, balanced discussions of psychodynamic, behavioral, cognitive-behavioral, humanistic, and interpersonal views of mental disorders and treatments. The 1998 Update now provides coverage of key, "Cutting Edge" topics that have taken center stage in the field of psychopathology since the publication of the tenth edition. These highlights can be found at the ends of Parts Two and Three and are cited within appropriate chapters with tabs and shaded text to indicate where they are most relevant.

Perspectives on Prevention 673

...nd alcohol on heart rate. In the ..t, several sessions are aimed at ...nts how to make effective deci- ...component, sessions focus on aid- ...in understanding their self-image ... self-esteem. In the fourth com- ...e taught to deal with anxiety, ...xiety. Finally, the fifth compo- ...h involves training the teens in ...nication and assertiveness, thus ...ective peer group interaction.

...are primary prevention programs ...verall impact of adolescent drug ...It is difficult to say. Some re- ...luded that drug and alcohol edu- ...ve only limited success (Tobler, ...rigorous research in primary ...problematic because the inter- ...y remotely connected to the be- ...ted for change. Moreover, it is ...e to ...

CUTTING EDGE TABS AND SHADED TEXT

Within appropriate chapters, numbered tabs act as easy-to-use guides between the "Cutting Edge" highlights and related chapter material. Shaded text passages demonstrate the exact points within the chapters where "Cutting Edge" highlights are most relevant.

CUTTING EDGE 8

See Chapter 18, page 673

A RAY OF HOPE IN PREVENTING ALCOHOL AND OTHER DRUG PROBLEMS

Prominent social forces such as attractive advertising, the influence of peer groups, negative parental role models, and the ready availability of many drugs are instrumental in promoting the early use of alcohol, tobacco, and illegal drugs in young people. Because these factors influence adolescents to begin using alcohol and drugs, it might appear reasonable to think that if these forces could be counterbalanced with equally powerful alternative influences, substance use might be delayed or even blocked altogether. This is easier said than done, and social efforts to alleviate the substance abuse problem have proved insufficient. Recent years have witnessed a sharp increase in marijuana, alcohol, and tobacco use among adolescents (Johnston, O'Mally, & Bachman, 1995). The extent and often dramatic impact of alcohol and drug use among adolescents are alarming, particularly that for binge drinking (National Institute on Drug Abuse, 1996). A recent survey found that 55% of 8th graders, 71% of 10th graders, 81% of 12th graders, and 90% of college students have tried alcohol. Heavy drinking, defined as five or more drinks in a row, has shown an alarming rate of incidence (15% for 8th graders, 24% for 10th graders, 30% for 12th graders, and 40% for college students). Heavy alcohol use among young people can lead to tragic consequences such as motor vehicle accidents involving emergency room admissions (National Clear-

inghouse for Alcohol and Drug Information, 1996) or in which several young people die as a result of drinking and driving (National Highway Traffic Safety Administration, 1990).

The federal government has approached the drug abuse problem with three broad strategies:

1. *Interfering with and reducing the supply of drugs available.* Policing our borders to intercept shipments of drugs has had little impact on their availability. The supply of illegal drugs seems to be endless. Even when drug agents know a shipment of illegal drugs is bound for the United States from suppliers in South America, they are often unable to stop it. Moreover, drug interception programs do little to affect the supply of alcohol and tobacco—the two drugs most abused by adolescents. These drugs are, of course, available in corner stores and even in the adolescent's home. Reducing the supply of these drugs to adolescents is extremely difficult.

2. *Providing treatment services for those who develop drug problems.* Although much money is spent each year on amelioration efforts, the treatment of substance abuse is perhaps the least effective avenue to reducing the problem. Addictive disorders are very intractable, and treatment failures are the rule rather than the exception. Therapeutic

programs for those addicted to drugs or alcohol, though necessary, are not the answer to eliminating or even reducing the problems in our society.

3. *Encouraging prevention.* By far the most desirable and potentially most powerful means of reducing the drug problem in our country is through prevention methods aimed at alerting citizens to the problems of drugs and teaching young people ways to avoid using them (Botvin & Botvin, 1992; Botvin et al., 1995). Several past efforts have had limited success in resolving the adolescent drug abuse crisis. As noted in the text, the lackluster performance of prevention programs has provided little reason for optimism. Initially promising prevention efforts have often failed to show the desired reduction in substance use for a number of reasons. The intervention typically has not been conducted long enough to show the desired effect; the intervention efforts have not

CS-1

CUTTING EDGE TOPICS

Following Parts Two and Three, these highlights provide rigorous, in-depth, and up-to-date coverage of key issues and concepts that have taken center stage in the field of abnormal psychology within the last two years.

DSM-IV INCORPORATED THROUGHOUT

DSM-IV has been integrated into the discussion of all disorders to familiarize students with the current standard diagnostic criteria and taxonomy. Changes in terminology are clearly noted throughout.

DSM Classification of Mental Disorders

We have already introduced the *Diagnostic and Statistical Manual of Mental Disorders* (DSM). We return to it here because, in addition to defining what is to be considered a mental disorder, this manual specifies what subtypes of mental disorder are currently officially recognized and provides for each a set of defining criteria. These criteria consist for the most part of symptoms and signs. By "symptoms" is usually meant the patient's subjective description, his or her complaints about what is wrong; "signs," on the other hand, refer to objective observations the diagnostician may make either directly or indirectly (e.g., the results of pertinent tests administered by a psychological examiner). For a given diagnosis to be made, the diagnostician *must* observe the particular criteria—the symptoms and signs asserted to define that diagnosis—to be met.

As we have seen, the DSM is currently in its fourth edition (**DSM-IV**), this version having been published in May 1994. The first edition of the manual appeared in 1951, with successive editions appearing in 1968 (II), 1980 (III), 1987 (III-R, a revision of DSM-III), and the current one in 1994. The number of officially recognized mental disorders has increased enormously from DSM-I to DSM-IV, mostly for reasons that will shortly become ap̲̅ ̲̅ ̲̅ ̲̅ ̲̅a worldwide men-

Many clinical situations require a rapid determination of the main characteristics of the presenting problem as well as assessment of any risk (e.g., suicide) involved. Diagnostic guidelines aid clinicians in making such judgments.

Biological Causal Factors

This set of identical twins from Bouchard's University of Minnesota study of the relative roles of genetics and environment provides some striking support for the prominence of genetic influences on personality traits and attitudes (Bouchard et al., 1990). Jim Springer (left) and Jim Lewis (right) were separated four weeks after their birth in 1940. They grew up 45 miles apart in Ohio. After they were reunited in 1979, they discovered they had some eerie similarities: Both chain-smoked Salems, both drove the same model blue Chevrolet, both chewed their fingernails, and both had dogs named Toy. Further, they had both vacationed in the same neighborhood in Florida. When tested for such personality traits as sociability and self-control, they responded almost identically.

manifest its effect on the phenotype until much later in life. In many other cases, the genotype may shape the environmental experiences a child has, thus affecting the phenotype in yet another way. For example, a child who may be genetically predisposed to aggressive behavior may be rejected by his or her peers in early grades because of aggressive behavior. Such rejection may lead the child to go on to associate with similarly aggressive and delinquent peers in later grades, leading to a increased likelihood of developing a full-blown pattern of delinquency in adolescence.

Researchers have found three ways in which an individual's genotype may shape his or her environment (Hetherington & Parke, 1993; Scarr, 1992). First, the genotype may have what has been termed a passive effect on the environment resulting from the genetic similarity of parents and children. Such genetic similarity is likely to result in the parents automatically creating an environment compatible with the child's predisposition. For example, highly intelligent parents may provide a highly stimulating environment for their child, thus creating an environment that will interact in a positive way with the child's genetic endowment for high intelligence. Second, the child's genotype may evoke particular kinds of reactions from the social and physical environment. For example, active, happy babies evoke more positive responses from others than do passive, unresponsive infants (Lytron, 1980). Finally, the child's genotype may play a more active role in shaping the environment. In this case the child seeks out or builds an environment which is congenial. Extraverted children may seek the company of others,

for example, thereby enhancing their own tendencies to be sociable (Baumrind, 1991; Hetherington & Parke, 1993).

The few instances in which relatively straightforward predictions of mental disorders can be made on the basis of known laws of inheritance invariably involve gross neurological impairment. In such cases, abnormal behavior arises in part as a consequence of a central nervous system malfunction, such as occurs in Huntington's disease; such conditions will be discussed in Chapter 13.

It appears likely that many of the most interesting (if still largely obscure) genetic influences in normal and abnormal behavior typically operate polygenically, that is, through the action of many genes together in some sort of additive or interactive fashion (e.g., Plomin, 1990; Torgersen, 1993). A genetically vulnerable person has inherited a large number of these genes that collectively represent faulty heredity. These faulty genes, in turn, may lead to structural abnormalities in the central nervous system, to errors in the regulation of brain chemistry, or to excesses or deficiencies in the reactivity of the autonomic nervous system, which is involved in mediating many of our emotional responses. These various processes serve to predispose the person to later difficulties.

Methods for Studying Genetic Influences. Although advances have been made in identifying faulty genetic endowment (including locating genes responsible for certain physical anomalies), we are not yet able to isolate specific defects on the genes themselves. Therefore most of the information we have

---

NEW EXAMINATION OF CAUSAL FACTORS

This vastly updated chapter thoroughly explores nonspecific developmental psychopathological causal factors as well as the latest, most significant findings in this expanding field.

Packed with new case studies to support lively discussion of the latest research, this substantially expanded and updated chapter provides an even-handed survey of viewpoints on the role of biological and cognitive factors as causal and maintaining factors for each disorder.

of these patients refuse to take the drug or stop taking the drug because of the side effects (Barlow, 1988; Mavissakalian & Perel, 1989; Wolfe & Maser, 1994).

Psychopharmacological treatment of social phobia has also received some attention in the past decade. Although there have been some promising results with the use of beta-blockers such as Inderal, which help control peripheral autonomic arousal symptoms (Barlow, 1988), it appears that monoamine oxidase inhibitors are significantly more effective (Liebowitz et al., 1992).

Recently the drug Anafranil (clomipramine) has been approved for use in the United States as an effective biological treatment for obsessive-compulsive disorder (e.g., Benkelfat et al., 1989; DeVeaugh-Geiss, 1991). It appears to reduce the intensity of this disorder's symptoms, with OCD patients showing a mean improvement of 40–45 percent (relative to 4–5 percent on placebo). Some patients may show greater improvement than this, but approximately 40 percent do not show significant improvement (Greist, 1990; McCarthy & Foa, 1990). In addition, some of the newer antidepressants that also affect serotonin activity, such as Prozac, have also been shown to be useful in the treatment of OCD (DeVeaugh-Geiss, 1991; Riggs & Foa, 1993).

A major disadvantage of all drug treatments for anxiety disorders is that relapse rates range from moderate to very high following discontinuation of the drug (see Clum et al., 1993, for panic disorder). Thus many patients who do not seek alternative forms of psychotherapy that have more long-lasting benefits may have to stay on these drugs indefinitely given that most of the anxiety disorders tend to be chronic conditions if left untreated. This problem can often be overcome through combining drug and psychosocial treatments, with the goal being to withdraw patients from the drug after they have gained the skills from psychotherapy necessary to deal with their panic or anxiety symptoms directly.

Causal Factors in Mood Disorders

Stress as a Causal Factor. Psychosocial stressors are known to be involved in the onset of a variety of disorders, ranging from some of the anxiety disorders to schizophrenia, but nowhere has their role been more carefully studied than in the case of unipolar depression. Indeed, many investigators have been impressed with the high incidence of stressful life events that apparently serve as precipitating factors for unipolar depression, and Harder and colleagues (1989) did not even find a difference between more and less severely depressed patients in regard to the magnitude of prior life stressors. Based on clinical observations, Beck (1967) provided a broad classification of the most frequently encountered precipitating circumstances in depression: (a) situations that tend to lower self-esteem; (b) the thwarting of an important goal or the posing of an insoluble dilemma; (c) a physical disease or abnormality that activates ideas of deterioration or death; (d) single stressors of overwhelming magnitude; (e) several stressors occurring in a series; and (f) insidious stressors unrecognized as such by an affected person. Paykel (1982b) comprehensively reviewed the research literature available at that time on life events occurring before episodes of mood disorder and arrived at conclusions generally in agreement with Beck's. In particular, and perhaps not surprisingly, he concluded that separations from people important in one's life (through death, for example) are strongly associated with depression, although such losses tend to precede other disorders as well. Another serious stressor that has been the focus of study only fairly recently is caregiving to a spouse with a debilitating disease such as Alzheimer's (for-

merly known as senility), which is known to be associated with the onset of both major depression and generalized anxiety disorder for the caregiver (e.g., Russo et al., 1995).

Research on stress and the onset of depression is complicated by the fact that depressed people have a distinctly negative view of themselves and the world around them (Beck, 1967), and so at least to some extent their perceptions of stress may *result* from the cognitive symptoms of their disorder rather than causing their disorder (Monroe & Simons, 1991). That is, because of their pessimistic outlook, they may evaluate events as stressful that an independent evaluator (or a nondepressed friend) would not. This is why both George Brown and Bruce Dohrenwend—two leading stress researchers—have developed more complex and sophisticated measures of stress that involve either the use of independent evaluators or of questionnaires with specific narrowly defined stressors with objectively determined weights. Therefore, both measures do not rely on the depressed person's appraisal of an event as stressful. But because relatively few studies have used these more sophisticated strategies, much of the research literature on the association of depression and life stress as assessed by self-report is difficult to evaluate.

In several studies using these sophisticated measurements of life stress, Brown and Harris (1978, 1986, 1989) have concluded that depression often follows from one or more severely stressful events, usually involving some loss or exit from one's social sphere. (Interestingly, events signifying danger or threat were found more likely to precede the onset

Physical illness and physical disability are stressors that may precipitate major depres-

This heavily revised chapter amply reflects the recent surge in biological and psychosocial causal factor research. Following the lead of current research, the authors address bipolar disorders separately from "regular" depression along with detailed examinations of depression-anxiety comorbidity and depression in women.

FULL-CHAPTER TREATMENT OF SOMATOFORM AND DISSOCIATIVE DISORDERS

Now featured is expanded coverage of the controversy and debates surrounding multiple personalities and "created memories." Fascinating case material is employed to illustrate and clarify various viewpoints.

---

if cooperative, may be a valuable consultant for the therapist.

Dual and multiple personalities have received a great deal of attention and publicity in fiction, television, and motion pictures. Actually, however, they were rare in clinical practice until relatively recently. Until approximately the last quarter-century, in fact, only slightly more than 100 cases could be found in the psychological and psychiatric literature worldwide. Their occurrence seems to have increased dramatically in recent years. No wholly complete or satisfactory explanation exists for such a change in the occurrence base rate. Some of the increase, however, is almost certainly artifactual, the product of increased acceptance of the diagnosis by clinicians, who traditionally have been somewhat skeptical of the astonishing behavior these patients often display—such as undergoing sudden and dramatic shifts in personal identity before one's eyes. More females than males are diagnosed as having the disorder, with the ratio being about nine to one (Ross, 1989).

A more substantive and disturbing reason for the apparent increase in cases of DID is offered by Ross (1989), who attributes it in part to an increasingly "sick" society in which child abuse, especially sexual abuse by adults, has become rampant. If Ross's suggestion about the deterioration of society is arguable, his observation that DID is commonly accompanied by reports of childhood abuse is not. While it is surprising that this connection was not generally recognized until about 1980, there is now no reasonable doubt about its reality. Serious questions remain, as we shall see, about the magnitude of this association, about the trustworthiness of memories of abuse, and indeed about the clinical validity of DID diagnoses. Since childhood sexual abuse is a far more common occurrence for females than for males (Trickett & Putnam, 1993), there may be a relationship here with the gender discrepancy in incidence/prevalence.

As already suggested, the question of malingering has dogged the diagnosis of DID for at least a century. These doubts are reinforced by the suspicion that clinicians, by virtue of undue fascination with the clinical phenomena and unwise use of hypnosis, are themselves responsible for eliciting this disorder in highly suggestible patients (Spanos & Burgess, 1994). The latter criticism has a ring of truth, but it fails to account convincingly for all of the observations reported—such as the elaborate pretreatment personal histories with which alternate personalities are commonly endowed. Cynicism about the concept of DID has also been encouraged by the frequency with which it is used by defendants and their

attorneys to escape punishment for crimes ("My other personality did it"). This defense was used, unsuccessfully, in the famous case of the "Hillside Strangler," Kenneth Bianchi (Orne, Dinges, & Orne, 1984).

It is also true, as Spanos, Weekes, and Bertrand (1985) have demonstrated, that normal college students can be induced by suggestion to exhibit some of the phenomena seen in DID, including the adoption of a second personality. Such role-playing demonstrations are interesting, but they do not answer, nor even convincingly address, the question of the reality of DID. That college student subjects might be able to give a convincing portrayal of a person with a broken leg would not, after all, establish the nonexistence of broken legs.

Our own view of the controversy surrounding DID is that it is too often formulated in terms of an absolute dichotomy: It is viewed either as a completely genuine disorder affecting a helpless and passive victim, or as a completely dissembled fabrication orchestrated by an unscrupulous person seeking unfair advantages. There is of course a wide range of possibilities between these two extreme positions. Our increasing knowledge, earlier alluded to, concerning widespread evidence of separate (dissociated) memory subsystems and nonconscious active mental processing, indicates that much highly organized mental activity is *normally* carried on in the "background," outside of awareness. This is analogous in some ways to computer multitasking, where the same machine may simultaneously carry on several complex activities other than the one in which its keyboard operator is currently fully engaged. Accordingly, questions about whether a given behavior is consciously or unconsciously motivated, genuine or feigned, intended or unintended, deliberate or spontaneous, and so on, are as a general rule oversimplified. So far as we can tell, the human mind does not operate in these dichotomous ways, and undue preoccupation with unanswerable questions can distract us from the task of understanding the adaptational processes in which the patient is engaged.

Is DID "real?" Our answer here is perhaps already implied in the foregoing. Addressing the question directly, Horevitz (1994), following a thorough review of the evidence, was unable to offer an unequivocal answer. The deceptive simplicity of the question is belied by a number of serious evidential and methodological issues. Do we, the authors, believe that elements of theatrical pretense are never a part of dissociative identity disorder? Not by any means, but neither are we prepared to dismiss DID as simply unqualified fakery.

Much less is known about sexual deviations, abuse, and dysfunctions than is known about many of the other disorders we have considered thus far in this book, such as anxiety and depression. The major clinical psychology and psychiatry journals have relatively few articles related to sexual dysfunctions and deviations, and there are also many fewer sex researchers than depression and anxiety researchers. One major reason is the sex taboo. Although sex is an important concern for most people, many have difficulty talking about it openly. This makes it difficult to obtain knowledge about even the most basic facts, such as the frequency of various sexual practices, feelings, and attitudes. This is especially true when the relevant behaviors are socially ostracized, such as homosexuality. It is difficult both to ask people about such behaviors and to trust their answers.

A second reason why sex research has progressed less rapidly is that many issues related to sexuality—including homosexuality, teenage sexuality, abortion, and childhood sexual abuse—are among our most divisive and controversial. In fact, sex research is itself controversial. Two large-scale sex surveys were halted because of political opposition even after being officially approved and deemed scientifically meritorious (Udry, 1993). Fortunately, one of these was funded privately, although on a much smaller scale, and it is now considered the definitive study for the 1990s (Michael et al., 1994). Senator Jesse Helms and others had argued that sex researchers tended to approve of premarital sex and homosexuality, and that this would likely bias the re-

sults of the surveys. Perhaps in part because of the controversial nature of sex research, it is not well funded. For example, although sex offenders are widely feared and millions of dollars are spent keeping convicted sex offenders behind bars every year, the National Institute of Mental Health spent only $1.2 million on sex offender research in 1993, compared with $125.3 million on depression (Goode, 1994).

Despite these significant barriers, we do know some things about sexual variants and dysfunctions. Clinical investigations have provided rich descriptions of many sexual variants. Etiological research on sexual dysfunctions and deviations, although in its infancy, has shown promise for some disorders, and we discuss these developments.

Before we turn to specific disorders, we examine sociocultural influences on sexual behavior and attitudes in general. We take this excursion first in order to provide some perspective about cross-cultural variability in standards of sexual conduct, and to encourage special caution in classifying sexual practices as "abnormal" or "deviant."

SOCIOCULTURAL INFLUENCES ON SEXUAL PRACTICES AND STANDARDS

Although some aspects of sexuality and mating are cross-culturally universal (Buss, 1989), others are quite variable. For example, all known cultures have taboos against sex between close relatives, but attitudes toward premarital sex vary considerably (Frayser, 1985). Ideas about acceptable sexual behavior also change over time. Sexual standards have changed tremendously in our own culture, especially over the past century. Less than 100 years ago, for example, sexual modesty was such that women's arms and legs were always hidden in public. Nowadays, actors are shown nude in movies and sometimes even on television.

Despite the substantial variability in sexual attitudes and behavior in different times and places, people typically behave as if the sexual standards of their time and place were obviously correct, and they are intolerant of sexual nonconformity. Sexual nonconformists are often considered evil or sick. We do not mean to suggest that such judgments are always arbitrary. There has probably never existed a society in which Jeffrey Dahmer, who was sexually aroused by killing men, having sex with them, storing their corpses, and sometimes eating them,

Recent evidence has suggested that the use of anatomically correct dolls to question young children about where they may have been touched in alleged incidents of sexual abuse does not improve the accuracy of their

---

EXPANDED COVERAGE OF SEXUAL DISORDERS

This significantly revised chapter now addresses the sexual abuse of children and the reliability of their memories, as well as historical and cross-cultural issues that affect societal views of normal and psychopathological variants of sexual behavior.

"UNRESOLVED ISSUES" SECTIONS

Provide students with a thought-provoking sampling of key debates at the end of each chapter.

UNRESOLVED ISSUES

on Containing the AIDS Epidemic

As we have seen, many of the remaining problems pertaining to the interface between psychology and physical health involve voluntary choices people make regarding their own behavior. While potential applications of this general principle are widespread, the record of success among our species in eradicating behaviors determined to be risky or dangerous to health and survival must be considered on the whole to be far less than adequate. Our accomplishments respecting the spread of the deadly HIV-1 (AIDS) virus, to date, are no exception.

As of early 1995, the cumulative number of cases of AIDS diagnosed in the United States is nearly one-half million; there may be as many as 1.5 million more persons infected, but as yet asymptomatic. Because of the nature of this virus and its profile of transmission from a carrier to the next victim, the rate of development of new cases of full-blown AIDS is expected to continue to accelerate geometrically, as it has since the disease was first recognized among a small group of gay men only a few short years ago. In the absence of some astounding biomedical breakthrough, or what would constitute an at least equally astounding social revolution in the manner in which Americans deal with sexuality, a health catastrophe will shortly be upon us.

The extent of this challenge is made clear in recent reviews of the evidence provided by Kelly and Murphy (1992) and Fisher and Fisher (1992). Kelly and Murphy note that real progress has been made in the reduction of risky sexual behavior among gay men in larger cities, especially among those who acknowledge their homosexuality and identify with the gay subculture. Yet even in this group, they report, excessive numbers of "relapses" (20–40 percent) occur where alcohol is abused or under conditions of "affectional bonding." Consistent attention to preventive measures (e.g., use of a condom in anal intercourse) is greatest among white, middle-aged, well-educated men of high socioeconomic status; risky behavior continues to be frequent among the young, among minority gays, and among those who do not identify themselves as homosexuals. In smaller cities, where the gay community is likely to be less well organized, neglect of preventive measures continues to be alarmingly high.

There is some evidence in the data reviewed by Kelly and Murphy (1992) that intravenous drug users, as a group, have become more cautious about sharing needles and syringes, thus decreasing the likelihood that they will become infected; unfortunately, there is little evidence that, as a group, they are showing a similar concern for their sexual partners.

There remains a threatening and escalating problem with heterosexual transmission of HIV-1 (Fisher & Fisher, 1992), and the "second wave" of AIDS deaths will probably first affect inner-city heterosexuals (Kelly & Murphy, 1992). Seemingly in confirmation of this projection, Kalichman, Hunter, and Kelly (1993) interviewed 272 women at large city mass transit terminals, reporting that 22 percent of them, overall, admitted recently engaging in high-risk sexual behavior. The nonminority women who had done so tended to acknowledge concern about their risk; high-risk minority women, on the other hand, expressed no more concern than did the women reporting low-risk status. In general, there is very little evidence of altered sexual practices among sexually active heterosexual adults (Kelly & Murphy, 1992), a conclusion that also seems to hold for high school and college students (Fisher & Fisher, 1992).

The facts are abundantly and frighteningly clear. Short of some sort of striking scientific triumph in biomedical research, the devastation that has already exacted an excruciating toll in the male homosexual community will become commonplace in the heterosexual population; estimates indicate that well over a million members of this much larger population are already infected and will die, on average, eight years following their encounter with the HIV-1 retrovirus. New infections, the evidence shows, continue to escalate even though the means of prevention are known and readily available. These require modest levels of forethought, judgment, restraint, and perhaps the risk of embarrassment; given the stakes involved, which include a protracted, agonizing, and as of now (with infection) certain death, they would not appear excessively demanding in terms of self-discipline. What, then, has gone wrong?

We do not pretend to have a comprehensive answer to this vital question. Undoubtedly we need a much-enhanced effort to find ways to penetrate into less advantaged high-risk groups with the life-saving information that has already had favorable effects on the behavior of the more advantaged, such as well-educated gay men. We strongly suspect, however, that exposure to and even assimilation of relevant preventive information will not in itself assure behavioral compliance. Some people will continue to engage in high-risk behavior while "knowing" that is what they are doing. Personality

---

The patient is a 32-year-old unmarried, unemployed woman on welfare who complains that she feels "spacey." Her feelings of detachment have gradually become stronger and more uncomfortable. For many hours each day she feels as if she were watching herself move through life, and the world around her seems unreal. She feels especially strange when she looks into a mirror. For many years she has felt able to read people's minds by a "kind of clairvoyance I don't understand." According to her, several people in her family apparently also have this ability. She is preoccupied by the thought that she has some special mission in life, but is not sure what it is; she is not particularly religious. She is very self-conscious in public, often feels that people are paying special attention to her, and sometimes thinks that strangers cross the street to avoid her. She has no friends, feels lonely and isolated, and spends much of each day lost in fantasies or watching TV soap operas.

The patient speaks in a vague, abstract, digressive manner, generally just missing the point, but she is never incoherent. She seems shy, suspicious, and afraid she will be criticized. She has no gross loss of reality testing, such as hallucinations or delusions. She has never had treatment for emotional problems. She has had occasional jobs, but drifts away from them because of lack of interest. (Spitzer et al., 1989, pp. 173–174).

and emotional, as well as sexually provocative and seductive. Their style of speech may be dramatic but is also quite impressionistic and lacking in detail. They are often highly suggestible and consider relationships to be closer than they are. Their sexual adjustment is usually poor and their interpersonal relationships are stormy because they may attempt to control their partner through seductive behavior and emotional manipulation, but also show a good deal of dependence. Usually they are considered to be self-centered, vain, and overconcerned about the approval of others, who see them as overly reactive, shallow, and insincere. The prevalence in the general population is estimated at 2–3 percent (DSM-IV, 1994). The following case illustrates the histrionic personality pattern:

Pam, a 22-year-old secretary, was causing numerous problems for her supervisor and coworkers. According to her supervisor, Pam was unable to carry out her duties without constant guidance. Seemingly helpless and dependent, she would overreact to minor events and job pressures with irritability and occasional temper tantrums. If others placed unwanted demands on her, she would complain of physical problems, such as nausea or headaches; furthermore, she frequently missed work altogether. To top it off, Pam was flirtatious and often demandingly seductive toward the men in the office.

CASE STUDIES THROUGHOUT

These fascinating real-life examples illustrate the clinical pictures of many disorders discussed within the text and emphasize the human side of psychological disorders and treatments.

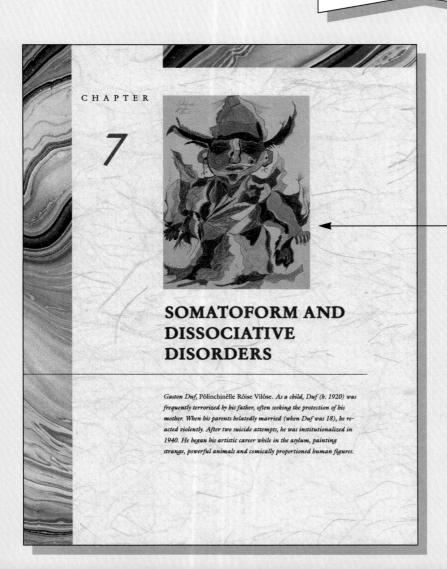

HIGHLIGHT 10.5

Biological Factors in Addiction to Psychoactive Drugs

How do substances such as alcohol, cocaine, or opium come to have such powerful effects on some people—an overpowering hold that sometimes occurs in some people after only a few uses of some drugs? Although the exact mechanisms are not fully agreed on by experts in the field, two important factors are apparently involved. One factor involves the person's biological makeup or constitution, which includes both genetic inheritance and the environmental influences (learning factors) that enter into the need to seek mind-altering substances to an increasing degree. The other important factor in the equation is the ability of some drugs to activate areas of the brain that produce intrinsic pleasure and immediate, powerful reward. Let's examine each of these elements in more detail.

Constitutional Factors

Research has begun to accumulate that genetic factors contribute substantially to the development of alcohol preference. Research with animals, for example, has shown that strains of animals can be bred to have very high preference for alcohol (McBride et al., 1992). Moreover, genetic factors are likely to be involved in increased susceptibility or sensitivity to the effects of drugs. For example, low doses of alcohol or other addictive substances might be more stimulating to some people as a result of inherited differences in the *mesocorticolimbic dopamine pathway* or *system* often referred to as the MCLP (Liebman and Cooper, 1989). It seems increasingly likely that inherited factors affect an individual's response to psychoactive drugs.

Nevertheless, genetics alone are not the whole story. The genetic mechanism or model for the generally agreed upon observation that alcoholism is familial is insufficient to explain the behavior fully (Schuckit & Irwin, 1990). That is, genetic transmission in the case of alcoholism does not follow the hereditary pattern found in other genetic disorders.

When we talk about familial or constitutional differences we are not strictly limiting our explanation to genetic inheritance. Rather, learning factors appear to play an important part in the development of constitutional reaction tendencies. Having a genetic predisposition or biological vulnerability to alcoholism, of course, is not a sufficient cause of the disorder. The person must be exposed to the substance to a sufficient degree for the addictive behavior to appear. In the case of alcohol, almost everyone in America becomes exposed to the drug to some degree through such means as peer pressure, parental example, and advertising. The development of alcoholism involves living in an environment that promotes initial as well as continuing use of the substance. People become conditioned to stimuli and tend to respond in particular ways as a result of learning. Learning appears to play an important part in the development of substance abuse and antisocial personality disorders (see Chapter 9). There clearly are numerous reinforcements for using alcohol in our social environments and everyday lives. Furthermore, the use of alcohol in a social context is often a sufficient reason for many people to continue using the drug. However, research has also shown that psychoactive drugs such as alcohol contain *intrinsic* rewarding properties that provide pleasure in and of itself—apart from the social context or its operation to diminish worry or frustration. The drug stimulates pleasure centers in the brain.

Drug Action

Let's examine the role that drugs themselves play in the process of addiction. Drugs differ in terms of their biochemical properties as well as how rapidly they enter the brain. There are several routes of administration—oral, nasal, and intravenous. Alcohol is usually drunk, the slowest route, while cocaine is often self-administered by injection or taken nasally. Central to the neurochemical process underlying addiction is the role the drug plays in activating the

CHAPTER

7

SOMATOFORM AND DISSOCIATIVE DISORDERS

Gaston Duf, Pôlinchinêlle Rôise Vilôse. *As a child, Duf (b. 1920) was frequently terrorized by his father, often seeking the protection of his mother. When his parents belatedly married (when Duf was 18), he reacted violently. After two suicide attempts, he was institutionalized in 1940. He began his artistic career while in the asylum, painting strange, powerful animals and comically proportioned human figures.*

THE SCHIZOPHRENIAS
    A Case Study
    The Clinical Picture in Schizophrenia
    Problems in Defining Schizophrenia
    Subtypes of Schizophrenia
    Causal Factors in Schizophrenia
    Treatment and Outcomes
DELUSIONAL (PARANOID) DISORDER
    The Clinical Picture in Delusional Disorder
    Causal Factors in Delusional Disorder
    Treatments and Outcomes
UNRESOLVED ISSUES ON SCHIZOPHRENIA
SUMMARY
KEY TERMS

With the schizophrenias, we move into a realm of disorder that represents in many ways the ultimate in psychological breakdown. These disorders include some of the most extreme of human behaviors, the ultimate in **"psychosis,"** a term referring to pervasive loss of contact with reality. The hallmark of **the schizophrenias** is thus a more or less sharp break with the world in which most less disturbed people live, a world that is rooted in a basic consensus about what is true and real in our shared experience. The typical schizophrenic person is thus someone who has lost or become detached from a set of anchoring points fundamental to adequate integration and communication with the surrounding human environment. To those around the schizophrenic he or she appears incomprehensible, perhaps even frightening.

If we look more closely, trying to identify the component processes underlying this detachment from reality, we observe in schizophrenics many psychological abnormalities. These include peculiarities in action, thinking, perception, feeling, sense of self, and manner of relating to others, with the features displayed varying from one patient to another. As is implied here, the group is a heterogeneous one, and this heterogeneity extends well beyond differences in current behavior. As we shall see, it includes as well marked variations in associated background features, in the course of the disorder in different people, and in the variety of outcomes they experience.

In the face of this heterogeneity, many clinicians and researchers have concluded that "schizophrenia" will probably someday be recognized as consisting of several separate and distinct conditions. We share that expectation, which explains our choice of the plural form in the title of this chapter.

As that title also indicates, we will in addition consider in this chapter the condition the DSM-IV calls *delusional disorder,* whose main features were formerly included under the classic rubric *paranoia,* or *"true" paranoia* (to distinguish it from the paranoid subtype of schizophrenia, described below). Patients with delusional disorders, like many schizophrenics, nurture, give voice to, and sometimes take actions based on, beliefs that are considered completely false and absurd by those around them. Unlike schizophrenics, however, persons with delusional disorders may otherwise behave quite normally. Their behavior does not show the gross disorganization and fragmentation characteristic of schizophrenia, and general behavioral deterioration

13

SUMMARY

Traditionally, diagnosing behavior problems of children and adolescents has been a rather confused practice, in part because children have sometimes been viewed as "miniature" adults. It was not until the second half of the twentieth century that a diagnostic classification system focused clearly on the special problems of children.

Two broad approaches to the classification of childhood and adolescent behavior problems have been undertaken: a categorical approach, reflected most extensively in the DSM-IV, and a dimensional approach. Both classification approaches involve organized classes of observed behaviors. In the categorical approach, symptoms of behavior problems are grouped together as syndromes based on clinical observations. In the dimensional approach, a broad range of observed behaviors are submitted to multivariate statistical techniques; the symptoms that group together make up the diagnostic classes referred to as "dimensions."

In this chapter, the DSM-IV classification system is followed in order to provide clinical descriptions of a wide range of childhood behavior problems. Attention-deficit hyperactivity disorder is one of the more frequent behavior problems of childhood. In this disorder, the child shows impulsive, overactive behavior that interferes with his or her ability to accomplish tasks. There is some controversy over the explicit criteria used to distinguish hyperactive children from "normal" children or from children who exhibit other behavior disorders, such as conduct disorders. This lack of clarity in defining hyperactivity increases the difficulty of determining causal factors for the disorder. The major approaches to treating hyperactive children have been medication and behavior therapy. Using medications, such as amphetamines, with children is somewhat controversial. Behavior therapy, particularly cognitive-behavioral methods, has shown a great deal of promise in modifying the behavior of hyperactive children.

Another common behavior problem among children is that of conduct disorder. In this disorder, a child engages in persistent aggressive or antisocial acts. In cases where the child's misdeeds involve illegal activities, the terms *delinquent* or *juvenile delinquent* may be applied. A number of potential causes of conduct disorder or delinquent behavior have been determined, ranging from biological factors to personal pathology to social conditions. Treatment of conduct disorders and delinquent behavior is often frustrating and difficult; treatment is likely to be

ineffective unless some means can be found for modifying a child's environment.

Another group of disorders, the childhood anxiety disorders, are quite different from the conduct disorders. Children who suffer from these disorders typically do not cause difficulty for others through their aggressive conduct. Rather they are fearful, shy, withdrawn, insecure, and have difficulty adapting to outside demands. The anxiety disorders may be characterized by extreme anxiety, withdrawal, or avoidance behavior. A likely cause for these disorders is early family relationships that generate anxiety and prevent the child from developing more adaptive coping skills. Behavior therapy approaches—such as assertiveness training and desensitization may be helpful in treating this kind of disorder.

Several other disorders of childhood involve behavior problems centering on a single outstanding symptom rather than pervasive maladaptive patterns. The symptoms may involve enuresis, encopresis, sleepwalking, or tics. In these disorders, treatment is generally more successful than in the other disorders just described.

Finally, this chapter addressed one of the most severe and inexplicable childhood disorders—autism. In this disorder, extreme maladaptive behavior occurs during the early years and prevents affected children from developing psychologically. Autistic children, for example, seem to remain aloof from others, never responding to or seemingly not caring about what goes on around them. Many never learn to speak. These disorders likely have a biological basis, although definite proof of such a basis has proven elusive. Neither medical nor psychological treatment has been notably successful in fully normalizing the behavior of autistic children, but newer instructional and behavior-modification techniques have sometimes scored significant gains in improving their ability to function. In general, at present the long-term prognosis in autism appears discouraging.

A number of potential causal factors were considered for the disorders of childhood and adolescence. Although genetic predisposition appears to be important in several disorders, parental psychopathology, family disruption, and stressful circumstances, such as parental death or desertion and child abuse, can have an important causal influence. Recent research has underscored the importance of multiple risk factors in the development of psychopathology.

There are special problems, and special opportunities, involved in treating childhood disorders. The need for preventive and treatment programs for children is always growing, and in recent years the

CHAPTER

1

ABNORMAL BEHAVIOR
IN OUR TIMES

Paul Goesch, Kopf mit Farbteilung. *Goesch, a German artist and
highly successful architect, was hospitalized at the age of 36 after suffering mental problems for some years. He lived in an institution near
Berlin until 1940, when he was removed by the Nazis to Austria, where
he was murdered along with other mental patients.*

Aberrations of behavior occupy a central place in human history, with consequences on a vast scale. These consequences range from establishment of many of the major religions of the world to the extremes of human depravity and suffering. The study of behavioral deviance and our attempts to understand it are thus critical to a full appreciation of the human condition. The traditional focus of the field of abnormal psychology has been the analysis of problematic behavior, of behavior that somehow fails to meet the requirements of adaptation and of social acceptability. This is a book about the nature of the conditions producing these unfortunate outcomes, and about the possibilities of reversing them.

During our own lifetimes all of us will experience repeated confrontations with behaviors in others, or in ourselves, that fail to meet a minimal standard of rationality or enlightened appreciation of probable consequences. In fact, most of us spend a significant proportion of our time and our cognitive resources in efforts to understand the behavior of others—and sometimes to puzzle out our own behavior, including our reactions to the behavior of others. In either case we are usually able to come up with plausible explanations of why they, or we, are behaving in the manner observed.

In studying abnormal psychology, we set our sights squarely on conditions that are often less easy to understand. Here the behaviors are not part of the fabric of everyday life; they are unusual, unexpected, or perhaps even frightening. The unstated rules of behavior that we take for granted are in these cases seemingly suspended or violated, and in our perplexity we grasp for some sort of way to "make sense" out of the seemingly irrational behavior confronting us. Consider the following cases, all from the authors' files, with slight alterations to preserve anonymity.

Albert G., a 62-year-old professor at a small college in the Midwest, was immensely popular and well regarded by everyone who knew him. Students flocked to his classes; his professional colleagues sought his consultation and scholarly views; and he wrote, when his moods permitted, with penetrating insight and unusual candor. With such high praise and with obvious success, why did he kill himself—a victim of deep personal despair? He had lived a very organized and conscientious life, always concerned about how he was viewed by others. Although dwelling alone, he had had several close friends, yet no one knew of the personal plight he apparently

3

Many people live their lives, or episodes of their lives, in suffering and desperation, unable to cope with challenges that are too great. Abnormal psychology is concerned with these difficulties of human adaptation and with investigating ways in which they may be prevented or reversed.

had experienced. No one around him, even his closest associates, had been aware of the depth of his despondent moods. The suicide left everyone in the community wondering about the psychological forces that could prompt someone as seemingly well-adjusted as Albert to end his life.

Sue D., a 38-year-old attorney, acknowledged to her treatment group that she did not know how long she had had a problem with alcohol and tranquilizer abuse. She had become painfully aware of her problems when she had "hit bottom." She described the evening when she had gone to dinner with some friends and had lingered afterward in the restaurant bar to have a few drinks. She had drunk a great deal more than she had intended (as was often the case) and had gotten into a heated argument with other patrons and the manager of the bar. Sue explained how the situation had deteriorated. Objects had been thrown, the police had been called, and she had been arrested for public drunkenness and abuse of police officers. The police then had taken her to a detoxification center at the county hospital— the same hospital where she served as chief counsel for the law firm at which she worked. Sue told her group that the hospital administrator had been incensed, and the law firm partners had been embarrassed and outraged. Sue had been given the option of leaving the law firm or seeking treatment; she had chosen the latter and had begun a new phase of her life. She had entered a treatment program and was trying to understand how she had allowed her life to shatter as it had.

Donald G., 33 years of age and of relatively high measured intelligence, has never been gainfully employed for more than a few days at a time and now lives in a sheltered community setting, except for brief but frequent periods of re-hospitalization occasioned by marked agitation and the hearing of "voices" said to heap insulting and abusive comments upon him. Donald is awkward, moderately inappropriate in introducing extraneous content into his conversations, and painfully unsure of himself in most social situations. The voices had made their appearance quite suddenly and without obvious provocation at age 17 after a brief period of social withdrawal. At that time he was stubbornly insistent that the voices were emanating, with malicious intent, from within a neighbor's house and were transmitted electronically to the speakers of the family television set; more recently he has conceded that he somehow produces them within himself. During periods of deterioration he may be heard arguing vehemently with the voices, but for the most part he is now able to ignore them; apparently, they are never entirely absent for sustained periods. Prior to his breakdown, Donald had lived a relatively normal middle-class life, was reasonably popular among peers, had maintained passing grades in school, and had shown considerable athletic prowess, although his parents and teachers had often complained that he seemed inattentive and preoccupied. There is no evidence of his ever having abused drugs. Donald's "prognosis" (the likelihood that he will ever regain a full measure of functioning) is considered "guarded" by his professional caregivers.

Manuel D., a 22-year-old Hispanic American, lived in a predominantly Spanish community in a large California city. One evening, after four teenagers in another car on the highway had allegedly made obscene gestures to him, he followed their car for some distance until they stopped. He then accosted the group and, with a revolver, killed one youth and wounded another. What prompted him to engage in such destructive behavior? Although he lived in a tough neighborhood in which youth gangs were prominent, he was not a gang member. He had acted alone in the shooting. Drug and alcohol screening, conducted shortly after the incident, was negative. A search of his background showed that he had had several previous incidents of personal violence, a record of arrests, and a previous commitment to a psychiatric hospital for suspicious and threatening behavior. What factors underlay his lack of impulse control and his violent acts toward other people?

More generally, how shall we account for *any* of the seemingly senseless behavioral distortions depicted in these accounts, all of which represent recognized patterns of deviance and none of which, unfortunately, can reasonably be considered rare? As will be seen throughout this text, there is no shortage of ideas competing for our attention that purport to explain the unexplained. Some of these ideas are promising, in the sense of having considerable scientific support, and some are far less so.

Unfortunately, the substrates of human behavior are enormously complex and our understanding of them imperfect. This means that we will often be unable, as in the above cases, to determine precisely what has gone wrong in the brains or the psyches of affected persons. That is, we cannot yet give a detailed and accurate explanation for many behavioral abnormalities. Indeed, a fundamental goal of this text is to aid the student in making discriminations among multiple conceptions of disordered behavior. As we shall see, these conceptions often vary widely in their philosophic sophistication, their scientific adequacy, and their practical utility in terms of providing effective treatments.

Acknowledging the serious conceptual problems confronting the student of abnormal behavior, it is important to note as well the more positive side of the journey on which he or she is about to embark. To an extent, when we study cases such as those presented above we see a distorted picture of human adaptation, one emphasizing the failings of psychological resourcefulness rather than the inspiring heights it often attains. But in looking at these failings, we may also overcome our probably oversimplified notions about how they come about and thus learn to appreciate more the richness and variety of the sources of human personality—perhaps even to understand that, but for some as yet largely unidentified good fortune, any of us might fall prey to abnormalities as distressing as those described.

Looking even more deeply, we may be able to discern the vague outlines of regularity, of a pattern, of a certain lawfulness, in many instances of abnormal behavior. And as our scientific understanding increases, we may reasonably hope that these perhaps somewhat vague hunches may yield explicit formulations that will stand the test of scientific proof. Indeed, as will be seen, one can discern a fair number of hypotheses that may be approaching that status. With continuing progress we may some day even reach the point where irrational behavior that leads to persistent self-defeat and threatens group survival is more or less completely understood. But before we reach that point we have much to learn. We will begin our search here by examining some popular views on the psychology of individuals whose behavior indicates disordered functioning.

POPULAR VIEWS OF ABNORMAL BEHAVIOR

Examples of mental disorders that we have heard or read about are apt to give us a distorted, perhaps even a chamber-of-horrors, impression of abnormal behavior. In truth, less spectacular maladjustments are far more common. Popular beliefs about abnormal behavior thus tend to be based on atypical, exaggerated, and often unscientific descriptions.

Mental disorders of one kind or another have been a favorite topic of writers for many centuries, and the public's changing conceptions of mental disorders have been strongly influenced by popular literary and dramatic works. Though certainly not the first to explore this area, William Shakespeare is especially notable for having created a number of characters whose actions resemble certain behaviors we now associate with officially recognized clinical patterns—characters such as Lady Macbeth (obsessive-compulsive behavior), King Lear (paranoia), Iago (antisocial personality), Ophelia (depression/melancholy), and Othello (obsessive, paranoid jealousy).

The fascination with abnormal behavior has continued in modern writing, often in autobiographies. Examples include Mark Vonnegut's *The Eden Express* (1975), in which the author describes his own acute schizophrenic breakdown, and Hannah Green's *I Never Promised You a Rose Garden* (1964), which describes her treatment by a gifted therapist for a more chronic form of the same type of disorder. Stuart Sutherland, a distinguished British psychologist, presents an account of his own psychotic episode in *Breakdown* (1977); and more recently Norman Endler, another noted psychologist, has published *Holiday of Darkness* (1990), which is in part a description of his struggles with a recurrent form of severe mood disorder. An earlier autobiographical account of psychosis, *A Mind That Found Itself* (1908/1970) by Clifford Beers, played a significant role in the development of the mental hygiene movement in the United States. The Beers book, in part a chilling account of the conditions in mental hospitals around the turn of the century, foreshadowed equally disturbing but more modern accounts by Mary Jane Ward in *The Snake Pit* (1946) and by Ken Kesey in his fictionalized (but in many ways poignantly accurate) *One Flew Over the Cuckoo's Nest* (1962). Fortunately, the horrible con-

In Shakespeare's play "Hamlet" the heroine Ophelia—driven mad with grief upon learning of the death of her father—drowns herself in a pond. Ophelia is one of a number of Shakespeare's memorable characters who suffer greatly from mental disorder and confusion.

ditions described by these writers have been eliminated in many contemporary mental hospitals, although the mentally disordered who once suffered in hospitals often now live in deplorable conditions in substandard community-based boarding facilities or are homeless.

We seem to have an insatiable curiosity about abnormal behavior, and—in addition to accounts we read in books—most of us avidly seek and devour newspaper, radio, and TV accounts on the subject. The hosts of television talk shows, in particular, parade before us an endless series of behavioral oddities, seeming to compete with one another to explore the limits of the behaviorally bizarre. Though we surely learn some things from these accounts, we also may be narrowing our perspective because the popular media typically simplify issues, appearing to give answers when, in fact, they barely succeed in posing the more significant questions. "Pop psychology," whose intellectual content only occasionally exceeds the level of clever cartoons, is today a multibillion-dollar industry. The daily press regularly carries stories about seemingly demented people and often seeks to legitimize these stories by citing mental health professionals who more often than not have never examined these people. Such armchair diagnoses are virtually useless (and probably unethical) in the majority of cases.

As a result of such exposure in literature and the media, you are likely to have a more than passing acquaintance with abnormal behavior. You may already have reached conclusions about its causes and its proper treatment. In most instances, however, we simply do not yet have sufficient information to per-

mit valid conclusions about causal factors and treatment options, and the misinformation that is readily available can cloud one's perspective. It is wise therefore to suspend any preconceived beliefs about abnormal psychology until we consider the evidence. Look, too, at HIGHLIGHT 1.1 for an overview of the more common misconceptions people are likely to have about abnormal behavior.

WHAT DO WE MEAN BY ABNORMAL BEHAVIOR?

To assess, treat, and prevent abnormal behavior, it is important to develop definitions of normal and abnormal and to specify criteria for distinguishing one from the other. Unfortunately, making such distinctions is often far from easy to do. The word *abnormal* literally means "away from the normal," but note that we do not usually employ the term for those high-end behaviors that are better than, or superior to, "normal" performance. Genius is rarely if ever addressed in textbooks of abnormal psychology; mental retardation almost always is.

Even where we attempt to restrict consideration to the "subnormal" range, however, there remains the implication of deviation from some specified norm. But what is the norm? In the case of physical illness, the norm is the structural and functional integrity of the body as a workable biological system; here, the boundary lines between normality and pathology are usually (but not always) clear. For psychological disorder, however, we have no ideal, or

Some Popular Myths and Misconceptions Concerning Mental Disorder and Abnormal Behavior

Myth	Fact
Abnormal behavior is invariably bizarre.	The behavior of most individuals diagnosed with a mental disorder is usually indistinguishable from that of "normal" people.
Normal and abnormal behavior are different in kind.	Few if any types of behavior displayed by mental patients are unique to them. Abnormality consists largely of a poor fit between behavior and the situation in which it is enacted.
As a group, former mental patients are unpredictable and dangerous.	A typical former mental patient is no more volatile or dangerous than a "normal" person. The exceptions to this rule generate much publicity and give a distorted picture.
Mental disorders are associated with fundamental personal deficiencies and hence they occur because individuals fail to have a mental deficit corrected.	So far as we know, everyone shares the potential for becoming disordered and behaving abnormally.
Appropriate attitudes toward mental disorder include awe and fearfulness about one's own foibles and vulnerability.	Most mental disorders are natural adaptive processes that are comprehensible within this context. The majority of people have an excellent chance of never becoming disordered and of recovering completely should the unlikely happen.

even universally "normal," model of human mental and behavioral functioning to use as a base of comparison. Thus we find considerable confusion and disagreement as to just what is or is not normal, a confusion aggravated by changing values and expectations in society at large. As recently as two decades ago in our culture, the wearing of earrings by male persons regularly inspired questions about their mental health; now such adornments are quite routine and, among some groups of youths, virtually a requirement for social acceptance, for being considered "normal."

Dilemmas of Definition

Consider once again the four cases introduced earlier. Albert G., a successful and highly respected professor, committed suicide during the last of a series of despondent moods. Sue D., a capable attorney, risked her professional reputation and a promising career by overindulging in alcohol. Donald G., after an unremarkable start in life, seemed to undergo unexplained but profoundly disabling mental changes, culminating in persistent complaints of voices unheard by others and in beliefs unsupported by either physical evidence or social consensus. And Manuel D., by young manhood, had become sufficiently suspicious, threatening, and violent as to involve himself in both the mental health and criminal justice systems as a potentially dangerous person well before, finally, he fatally attacked another youth. What is common to all of these diverse behaviors that justifies their inclusion within the rubric *abnormal*, or, more specifically, on what basis do we conclude that each of these individuals is suffering from a mental disorder?

What is considered abnormal or deviant behavior in one society may be quite normal in another. We might consider this Arab woman's style of dress to be abnormal, but in her society it is the norm. What we consider normal may not be normal for everyone.

Any reader who seriously ponders these questions will discover that explicit, unequivocal answers to them are by no means obvious. Moreover, issues of value are inextricably linked to the problem. As Ethan Gorenstein (1992) has noted in a searching analysis of the concept of mental illness, the scientific and the valuational are "hopelessly intertwined" (p. 11). Thus, we think it *wrong* that Albert G. was despondent enough to kill himself, and we are *distressed* that Donald G. responds to imaginary voices, quite apart from more technical issues pertaining to their mental health status. In short, virtually all of what we regard as "abnormal" in behavior we also regard as undesirable, although in a strict and literal sense undesirability is not a necessary attribute of behaviors that may deviate from some normative expectation. We can readily think of statistically infrequent (hence literally abnormal) behaviors, such as extraordinary heroism, that most people would regard as praiseworthy. Society has no stake in changing, or "treating," abnormalities of this sort—quite the contrary. From the standpoint of political democracy, society also has no "right" to treat or otherwise seek to change abnormal behavior unless that behavior can be deemed undesirable, that is, contrary to the public interest. As you will see, the problem of values will never be far beneath the surface as you proceed through the pages of this text.

Despite the evident difficulties, the arguments for having a consensus understanding about what is to be considered abnormality, or more precisely mental disorder, are in certain contexts—for example, legal ones, matters concerning health insurance coverage, and abnormal psychology textbooks—quite compelling. We need, in other words, some sort of working definition of the subject matter that is to occupy our attention. The "gold standard" for defining mental disorder and its subclasses in the United States as well as many other parts of the world has become the American Psychiatric Association's *Diagnostic and Statistical Manual of Mental Disorders* (DSM), whose fourth edition (DSM-IV) was published in 1994. Here is how the DSM defines mental disorder:

> "[A mental disorder] is conceptualized as a clinically significant behavioral or psychological syndrome or pattern that occurs in an individual and that is associated with present distress (a painful symptom) or disability (impairment in one or more areas of functioning) or with a significantly increased risk of suffering death, pain, disability, or an important loss of

Statistical infrequency of behavior does not usually in itself raise a question of abnormality. Here a Habitat for Humanity worker volunteers his labor to build a house in which someone else will live. Few would regard his selflessness as a symptom of mental disorder.

freedom. In addition, this syndrome or pattern must not be merely an expectable and culturally sanctioned response to a particular event, for example, the death of a loved one. Whatever its original cause, it must currently be considered a manifestation of a behavioral, psychological, or biological dysfunction in the individual. Neither deviant behavior (e.g., political, religious, or sexual) nor conflicts that are primarily between the individual and society are mental disorders unless the deviance or conflict is a symptom of a dysfunction in the individual, as described above" (American Psychiatric Association, 1994, pp. xxi–xxii).

Note: The term **syndrome** refers to a group of clinical observations or symptoms that tend to co-occur. For example, feelings of despondency, lowered self-esteem, and suicidal preoccupation constitute important parts of a *depressive* syndrome.

A noteworthy characteristic of this DSM definition is that it is by no means a casually constructed statement. It carefully rules out, among other things, certain otherwise questionable behaviors that are culturally sanctioned, and it is careful also to assert that mental disorders are always the product of "dysfunctions," ones that in turn always reside in individuals; in other words, there are no mentally disordered groups per se, although such a concept might arguably apply where some significant proportion of a group's members *individually* qualify as mentally disordered. It is unfortunate and puzzling, in light of the central role of the notion of "dysfunction" (a given pattern of behavior might or might not be declared mentally disordered depending on whether or not it is due to "dysfunction"), that this term is itself left undefined in the DSM manual (see Wakefield, 1992a, 1992b, for important discussion of this omission).

It may be a useful exercise at this point for you to review the cases of Albert, Sue, Donald, and Manuel in light of the DSM definition, and to try to identify possible underlying mental mechanisms whose natural functions may have been compromised in such a manner as to account for the problematic behavior each displays. We recommend, however, that you not be unduly distressed should this exercise prove frustrating. Your future reading in this text should provide you with a much expanded range of potential approaches for grappling with the problem than you are now likely to have available. We suggest the exercise primarily because it illustrates the kind of puzzle routinely confronting mental health professionals in their daily work of trying to understand what has gone wrong with their patients.

The widely accepted DSM definition of abnormality or mental disorder is thus not so clear, precise, or objective as one might wish. It is in fact extremely difficult to formulate a definition having all of these characteristics. In the final analysis, as you may already have discerned, any definition of abnormality or mental disorder must be somewhat arbitrary. Historically, attempted definitions have tended to represent either of two broad perspectives, as follows.

One such perspective is that the concepts of normal and abnormal are meaningful only with reference to a given culture: abnormal behavior is behavior that deviates from the norms of the society in which it is enacted (see, e.g., Ullmann & Krasner, 1975; Scheff, 1984). A critical case would be the Nazi concentration camp commandant of the early 1940s who, on orders from his superiors, willingly and without remorse presided over the deliberate and cold-blooded murders of tens of thousands of innocent victims, many of them children. A strict version of the cultural relativist position would hold that such a person is not, by virtue of that behavior, mentally disordered; from this point of view, in fact, actions in the prisoners' behalf might be taken as pathological. The not-mentally-disordered verdict would presumably be required by the DSM definition, which incidentally (because of its individual focus) would also exclude from considerations of mental disorder the politico/military system that issued the commandant's orders.

Cultural relativists maintain that behavior cannot be considered abnormal as long as society accepts it. In this context, is the behavior of a concentration camp guard—such as these German guards leading Jewish prisoners to a Nazi concentration camp—abnormal if he is conforming to the norms of his environment?

The other general viewpoint—toward which we incline favorably—is one that acknowledges the critical significance of context (including that pertaining to prevailing social norms) in trying to understand behavior, but that attempts a less culturally variable position regarding what is to be considered abnormal or disordered in behavior. In principle, at least, such a position need not be any more arbitrary than its conceivable alternatives. And although it is likely to involve value choices, such choices are at present central to the concept of mental disorder. Everything considered, it is probably better that these choices be explicitly stated rather than covertly embedded in a purportedly "objective" and value-free format.

Mental Disorder as Maladaptive Behavior

Although some measure of social conformity is essential to group life, we suggest that the best criterion for determining the normality of behavior is not whether society accepts it, but rather whether it is inimical to individual and group well-being. According to this perspective, **abnormal behavior** *is maladaptive behavior*. Even behavior that conforms strictly to contemporary societal values is abnormal, mentally disordered, if it seriously interferes with functioning and is self-defeating in its consequences.

In keeping with the above perspective as well as with the comprehensive aims of this text, *we hold that behavior is abnormal, a manifestation of mental disorder, if it is both persistent and in serious degree contrary to the continued well-being of the individual and/or that of the human community of which the individual is a member.* This "working definition" contains, of course, an explicit value judgment that ties the definition of mental disorder to the persistent enactment of behavior that produces harmful consequences for self and/or others.

So defined, abnormal or disordered behavior includes the more traditional categories of mental disorders—such as alcoholism and schizophrenia—as well as, for example, promotion of intergroup hostility, destructive assaults on the environment in which all of us must live, irrational violence, and political corruption, regardless of whether such actions are condemned or condoned by a given society or subculture. All of these actions represent maladaptive behavior that impairs individual or group well-being. Typically they lead to personal distress among those victimized, and often they bring about destructive group conflict as well.

We also intend to imply that mental disorder is by no means limited to individuals; groups as groups, and even couples as couples, may behave in what we would regard as a mentally disordered fashion, without any necessary implications concerning the mental health status of individual members. Every experienced child clinician, for example, has seen couples who function well, perhaps even in superior fashion, in their roles outside of the home, but who create, in their interactions as partners, an interpersonal environment that has devastating effects on the well-being of both themselves and their children. Sometimes, in other words, seriously maladaptive outcomes are primarily the product of the particular "mix" of personalities involved in some relationship to each other, rather than of notable individual abnormalities.

In assessing, treating, and preventing abnormal behavior, mental health personnel are concerned not only with the maladaptive behavior itself, but also with the family, community, and society in which it occurs. From this perspective, therapy is defined not solely in terms of helping individuals adjust to their personal situations—no matter how frustrating or abnormal in themselves—but also in terms of alleviating group and societal conditions that may be causing or maintaining the maladaptive behavior.

Before we move on, you should have some introduction to the main personnel who labor in this rather complex mental health arena. Represented here are several distinct but closely related professional fields involved with the study of abnormal behavior and mental health. The distinction among them is often hard to draw precisely, for even though each has its own special functions and areas of work there is considerable overlapping of responsibilities, and the discoveries in one field are constantly influencing and contributing to the thinking and work in others.

Abnormal psychology, or **psychopathology,** has long been referred to as that part of the field of psychology concerned with the understanding, treatment, and prevention of abnormal behavior. Within the area of applied psychology, **clinical psychology** is the discipline broadly concerned with the study, assessment, treatment, and prevention of abnormal behavior. **Psychiatry** is the corresponding field of medicine; it is thus closely related to clinical psychology, the chief difference being that psychiatrists tend to conceptualize abnormal behavior and its treatment in medical rather than behavioral and cognitive terms. **Psychiatric social work** is concerned with the analysis of social environments and with providing services that help individuals adjust in both family and community settings. **Psychiatric nursing** is a specialized branch of the nursing profession whose work setting is typically that of hospital wards devoted to the care of mental patients, thus demanding skills that are quite different from those required of the nurse caring for medical and surgical patients.

Most research on abnormal behavior is conducted by psychologists, in keeping with their primarily academic roots—the Ph.D. continues to be the most common degree among clinical psychologists, although the alternate Psy. D. (doctor of psychology, a more practice-oriented, less research-oriented degree) has become increasingly popular. A relatively small proportion of psychiatrists, chiefly those in academic settings (such as medical schools), also do research, typically after obtaining specialized research training. Research is not usually conducted by social workers or other types of mental health professionals.

CLASSIFYING ABNORMAL BEHAVIOR

Traditionally, the study of abnormal behavior focuses on three distinct but often overlapping concerns: (a) the nature of the abnormality, (b) the factors that cause or influence its occurrence, and (c) the methods developed for reducing or eliminating the behavior.

Describing the nature of any abnormal behavior, also known as defining its **clinical picture,** is critical to the search for understanding the cause and treatment of the behavior. Considerable attention has been paid to obtaining accurate clinical pictures because they serve as scientific guideposts, often pointing to important areas of needed research. For these descriptions to be helpful, they must organize the observed data in a systematic way, one that enables us to use the descriptions as diagnostic and treatment tools. In other words, good clinical pictures allow us to sort various forms of abnormal behavior into potentially revealing subvarieties, to *classify* them.

Classification is important in any science, whether we are studying plants, planets, or people. With an agreed-upon classification system, we can be confident that we are communicating clearly. If someone says to you, "I saw a dog running down the street," you can probably produce a reasonably accurate mental image of what the dog may have looked like—not from seeing it but rather from your knowledge of animal classifications. There are of course many breeds of dogs that vary widely in their configurations of size, color, appearance, etc., and yet we have little difficulty in recognizing the essen-

tial features of "dogness." It is unlikely, for example, that your mental image of the dog in the street would resemble a cat, a beaver, or a donkey. "Dogness" is an example of what psychologists refer to as a cognitive prototype, about which we shall have more to say later.

In abnormal psychology, classification involves the attempt to delineate in a meaningful fashion various subvarieties of maladaptive behavior. Classification of some kind is the necessary first step toward introducing order into our discussion of the nature, causes, and treatment of such behavior. It enables communication about particular clusters of behavior in agreed-upon and meaningful ways. For example, we cannot conduct research on background causal factors for a given form of behavioral abnormality unless we begin with a more or less clear definition of the behavior under examination. We need that clarity first of all to select proper research subjects. There are other reasons for "diagnostic" classifications, too, such as gathering statistics on the incidence of various disorders or meeting the needs of medical insurance companies (which insist on having formal diagnoses before they will authorize payment of claims).

It is of crucial importance to keep in mind that all classification is the product of human invention—it is, in essence, a matter of making generalizations based on what has been observed. Even when observations are precise and carefully made, the particular generalizations arrived at go beyond them by making inferences about underlying similarities and differences. In fact, it is not unusual for a classification system to require revision as new knowledge demonstrates an earlier generalization to be faulty; this has been the case on numerous occasions in the history of abnormal psychology, and we have no doubt that additional revisions will be necessary in the future. In this field, too, it is important to bear in mind that formal classification is successfully accomplished only through precise techniques of psychological, or clinical, assessment—techniques that have been increasingly refined over the years. We will examine these techniques in Chapter 15, after we have looked thoroughly at the kinds of abnormal behavior thus far discriminated by judicious application of these observational methods.

Granting that all classification systems are in some fundamental sense arbitrary, some of them are much better than others in helping us organize and discuss our observations. We base a classification system's usefulness largely on its reliability and validity. **Reliability** is the degree to which a measuring device produces the same result each time it is used to measure the same thing. In the context of classification, it is an index of the extent to which different observers can agree that a person's behavior "fits" a given diagnostic category. If observers cannot agree, it may mean that the classification criteria are not precise enough to determine whether the imputed disorder is present or absent. In contrast, **validity** refers to the extent to which a measuring instrument actually measures what it claims to measure. In the case of classification, validity is determined by the degree to which the diagnostic category accurately conveys to us something clinically important or basic about the person whose behavior fits the category. If, for example, a person is diagnosed as having schizophrenia, as was Donald G. (p. 4), we should be able to infer from that classification the precise characteristics that differentiate the person from others considered normal, or from those suffering from other types of mental disorder—characteristics that in turn go beyond the observations leading to the diagnosis.

Normally, validity presupposes reliability. If a person's behavior cannot be reliably assigned to a given class of disorder, the validity of that class will prove difficult to establish and will as a practical matter be irrelevant, regardless of any intuitive appeal the proposed diagnostic category may have. In fact, before 1980 (when DSM-III was introduced) the diagnosis of schizophrenia in the United States, based as it was on quite vague criteria, suffered from exactly this deficiency. We will encounter the important concepts of reliability and validity again when we discuss psychological assessment techniques in Chapter 15.

DSM Classification of Mental Disorders

We have already introduced the *Diagnostic and Statistical Manual of Mental Disorders* (DSM). We return to it here because, in addition to defining what is to be considered a mental disorder, this manual specifies what subtypes of mental disorder are currently officially recognized and provides for each a set of defining criteria. These criteria consist for the most part of symptoms and signs. By "symptoms" is usually meant the patient's subjective description, his or her complaints about what is wrong; "signs," on the other hand, refer to objective observations the diagnostician may make either directly or indirectly (e.g., the results of pertinent tests administered by a psychological examiner). For a given diagnosis to be made, the diagnostician *must* observe the particular criteria—the symptoms and signs asserted to define that diagnosis—to be met.

As we have seen, the DSM is currently in its fourth edition (**DSM-IV**), this version having been

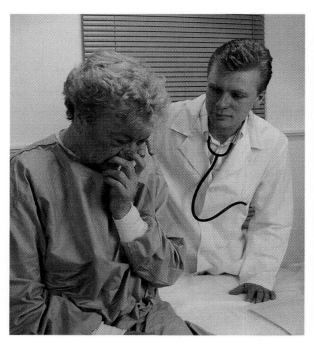

Many clinical situations require a rapid determination of the main characteristics of the presenting problem as well as assessment of any risk (e.g., suicide) involved. Diagnostic guidelines aid clinicians in making such judgments.

published in May 1994. The first edition of the manual appeared in 1952, with successive editions appearing in 1968 (II), 1980 (III), 1987 (III-R, a revision of DSM-III), and the current one in 1994. The number of officially recognized mental disorders has increased enormously from DSM-I to DSM-IV, mostly for reasons that will shortly become apparent. There also exists a worldwide mental disorder classification system, a subsection of the International Classification of Diseases (ICD), that is sponsored by the World Health Organization. In recent editions of both the DSM and the ICD there has been some attempt to integrate the two, or at least to ensure that they do not flatly contradict one another. The mental disorders subsection of the 10th edition of the ICD (ICD-10) was published in 1992 (World Health Organization, 1992), having completed extensive multinational field trials (Sartorius et al., 1993). As was intended, the mental disorders section of the ICD-10 does indeed appear to overlap considerably with the DSM-IV. The classes of mental disorder recognized in the DSM-IV are reproduced on this book's endsheets.

Each successive edition of the DSM has sought to improve its precision, which enhances both its clinical and its scientific effectiveness. Efforts have been directed specifically at overcoming the weaknesses in reliability and validity encountered with its predecessors. A distinctive innovation since the DSM-III of 1980 has been an attempt to use only "operational" criteria for defining the different disorders included in the classification system. This innovation means that the DSM system now specifies the exact behaviors that must be observed for a given diagnostic label to be applied, as already noted. In a typical case, a specific number of signs or symptoms from a designated list must be present before a diagnosis can properly be assigned. In other words, efforts have been made to remove as far as possible subjective elements from the diagnostic process; to the extent that goal is achieved, diagnostic reliability is almost necessarily enhanced, thereby also improving the accuracy with which the validity of the resultant diagnostic categories can be assessed.

On the other hand, it must be acknowledged that the real problems of real patients show a stubborn tendency at times to resist neat accommodations to the precise lists of signs and symptoms that are the heart of the modern DSM effort. How should we deal, for example, with the patient who meets three of the criteria for a particular diagnosis where four is the minimum threshold for rendering the diagnosis? Conscientious use of stricter criteria can and does cause some abnormal behavior to be assigned to "wastebasket" or residual categories, such as "psychotic disorder not otherwise specified" (NOS). When this occurs, validity suffers, since a category so broad can give only vague hints as to the nature of the disorders within it.

More generally, the demand for the use of very precise criteria so as to enhance interdiagnostician agreement (reliability) by clearly separating one class of disorder from another has certain limits. The clinical reality is that the disorders people actually suffer are often not as finely differentiated as is the DSM grid on which they must be mapped. Increasingly fine differentiation also produces, of course, more and more recognized types of disorder. Too often, we believe, the unintended effect is to sacrifice validity in an effort to maximize reliability, which makes little sense. For example, blends of anxiety *and* depression are extremely common in a clinical population, and they typically show much overlap (correlation) in quantitative scientific investigations as well. Nevertheless, the DSM treats the two as generically distinct forms of disorder, with the consequence that a person who is clinically both anxious and depressed may receive two diagnoses, one for each of the supposedly separate conditions. There is no official category for "mixed" anxiety-depression, although the DSM-IV mentions such a syndrome in

an appendix set aside for conditions proposed for further study. Perhaps future research will demonstrate them to be in fact uniformly separate and distinct classes of disorder, but the scientific evidence supporting that hypothesis is at present less than wholly convincing.

The anxiety-depression example also points up another problem deriving from what may be a too fine-grained DSM taxonomic or classificatory approach. That is, the tendency to inflate artificially the occurrence of "comorbidity," instances in which two or more supposedly separate disorders are found regularly to occur together in the same persons (Frances, Widiger, & Fyer, 1990). Anxiety and depressive disorders, for example, are frequently found to be comorbid. In fact, a burgeoning research literature pertaining to the "discovery" of new comorbidities between disorders alleged to be distinct from one another has reached unprecedented proportions in recent years, suggesting that the spurious effect predicted has indeed occurred (Carson, 1994a, 1994b).

In making these critical observations regarding contemporary DSM efforts we do not intend to suggest we are unrespectful or unappreciative of either the difficulties of the task or the considerable advances in understanding those efforts have produced. Rather, our intent is to alert the thoughtful reader to the many perplexing problems of classification that remain to be solved. We would be uncomfortable with an approach that glossed over difficulties and said, in effect, "This is the way it is; learn it." Should you become puzzled and confused about particular issues of classification as we proceed, therefore, do not assume that the difficulty resides in you; it may, instead, reflect continuing problems in developing the basic taxonomy, or classification system, of the field.

As has been the case since the advent of DSM-III in 1980, DSM-IV evaluates an individual according to five dimensions, or "axes." The first three axes assess an individual's present clinical status or condition:

I. The particular clinical syndromes or other conditions that may be a focus of clinical attention, such as schizophrenia.
II. Personality disorders. Any long-standing personality problems that meet diagnostic criteria for one or more of these problematic ways of relating to the world, such as antisocial personality disorder. The latter diagnosis, for example, refers to an early-developing and persistent pattern of disregard for accepted standards of conduct, including legal ones;

Manuel D. (p. 4) qualified for this diagnosis. (Note: In contrast to its immediate predecessors, DSM-IV does not code childhood developmental disorders on Axis II, but rather on Axis I.)

III. General medical conditions. Listed here are any general medical conditions potentially relevant to understanding or management of the case.

Axis III of DSM-IV may where justified be used in conjunction with an Axis I diagnosis qualified by the phrase, "Due to a [specifically designated] General Medical Condition," as, for example, where a major depressive disorder is conceived as resulting from the chronic pain associated with some serious medical disease.

More than one diagnosis is permissible on any of these axes. That is, a person may be diagnosed as having multiple psychiatric syndromes, disorders of personality, or potentially relevant medical problems.

The last two DSM-IV axes are used to assess broader aspects of an individual's situation, one dealing with the stressors that may have contributed to the current disorder and the other dealing with how well the individual is coping at the present time.

IV. Psychosocial and environmental problems.
V. Global assessment of functioning.

For Axis IV the diagnostician is invited to use a checklist approach for various categories of impinging life problems, such as family, economic, occupational, legal, etc. For Axis V a 100-point rating scale, the Global Assessment of Functioning (GAF) Scale, is provided for the examiner to assign a number summarizing the patient's overall functionability. The GAF Scale is reproduced in HIGHLIGHT 1.2.

As an example of an extended DSM-IV diagnosis, let us consider the case of Albert G., the college professor described at the beginning of this chapter. Immediately before his suicide, his multiaxial diagnosis might have looked like this:

Axis I

Major depressive disorder

Axis II

Compulsive personality disorder

Axis III

None

Axis IV

No primary support group

Social environment problem: living alone

Axis V

Global functioning: 20 (some danger of hurting self)

Axes IV and V are significant additions. Knowing the frustrations and demands a person has been facing is important for understanding the problem behavior that has developed. Knowing someone's general level of functioning conveys important information not necessarily contained in the entries for other axes and indicates how well the individual is coping with the problems indicated. Some clinicians, however, object to the routine use of these axes for insurance forms and the like on the grounds that such use unnecessarily compromises a patient's right to privacy. Because of such concerns, Axes IV and V are now considered optional for diagnosis and in fact are rarely used in most clinical settings.

The different Axis I and II disorders are identified in the previously noted listing of DSM-IV categories of mental disorder appearing on the endsheets of this book. These categories may be regarded for purposes of clarity as fitting into several broad groupings, each containing several subgroupings:

1. Disorders secondary to gross destruction or malfunctioning of brain tissue, as in Alzheimer's dementia and a wide range of other conditions based on permanent or reversible organic brain pathology. These disorders are described in Chapter 13.

2. Substance-use disorders involve problems such as habitual drug or alcohol abuse. These are discussed in Chapter 10.

3. Disorders of psychological or sociocultural origin having no known brain pathology as a primary causal factor, as in anxiety (Chapter 5), somatoform and dissociative (Chapter 7), psychosomatic (Chapter 8), psychosexual (Chapter 11), and most Axis II personality (Chapter 9) disorders. The "functional" psychoses—that is, severe mental disorders for which a specific organic pathology has not been demonstrated—such as major mood disorders (Chapter 6) and schizophrenia (Chapter 12), are also traditionally included here, although it appears increasingly likely that certain types of brain dysfunction often help cause them.

4. Disorders usually arising during childhood or adolescence include cognitive impairments such as mental retardation and specific learning disabilities (Chapter 13), and a large variety of behavioral problems that constitute deviations from the expected or normal path of development (Chapter 14).

In referring to mental disorders, several qualifying terms are commonly used. **Acute** is a term used to describe disorders of relatively short duration, usually under six months. In some contexts, it also

Global Assessment of Functioning (GAF) Scale

Consider psychological, social and occupational functioning on a hypothetical continuum of mental health illness. Do not include impairment in functioning due to physical (or environmental) limitations. (**Note:** Use intermediate codes when appropriate, e.g., 45, 68, 72.)

Code	
100 | 91	Superior functioning in a wide range of activities, life's problems never seem to get out of hand, is sought out by others because of his or her many positive qualities. No symptoms.
90 | 81	Absent or minimal symptoms (e.g., mild anxiety before an exam), good functioning in all areas, interested and involved in a wide range of activities, socially effective, generally satisfied with life, no more than everyday problems or concerns (e.g., an occasional argument with family members).
80 | 71	If symptoms are present, they are transient and expectable reactions to psychosocial stressors (e.g., difficulty concentrating after family argument; no more than slight impairment in social, occupational, or school functioning (e.g., temporarily falling behind in school work).
70 | 61	Some mild symptoms (e.g., depressed mood and mild insomnia) OR some difficulty in social, occupational, or school functioning (e.g., occasional truancy or theft within the household), but generally functioning pretty well, has some meaningful interpersonal relationships.
60 | 51	Moderate symptoms (e.g., flat affect and circumstantial speech, occasional panic attacks) OR moderate difficulty in social, occupational, or school functioning (e.g., few friends, conflicts with peers or co-workers).
50 | 41	Serious symptoms (e.g., suicidal ideation, severe obsessional rituals, frequent shoplifting) OR any serious impairment in social, occupational, or school functioning (e.g., no friends, unable to keep a job).
40 | 31	Some impairment in reality testing or communication (e.g., speech is at times illogical, obscure, or irrelevant) OR major impairment in several areas, such as work or school, family relations, judgment, thinking or mood (e.g., depressed man avoids friends, neglects family, and is unable to work; child frequently beats up younger children, is defiant at home, and is failing at school).
30 | 21	Behavior is considerably influenced by delusions or hallucinations OR serious impairment in communication or judgment (e.g., sometimes incoherent, acts grossly inappropriately, suicidal preoccupation) OR inability to function in almost all areas (e.g., stays in bed all day; no job, home, or friends).
20 | 11	Some danger of hurting self or others (e.g., suicide attempts without clear expectation of death; frequently violent; manic excitement) OR occasionally fails to maintain minimal personal hygiene (e.g., smears feces) OR gross impairment in communication (e.g., largely incoherent or mute).
10 | 1	Persistent danger of severely hurting self or others (e.g., recurrent violence) OR persistent inability to maintain minimal personal hygiene OR serious suicidal act with expectation of death.
0	Inadequate information.

(American Psychiatric Association, 1994, p. 32)

connotes behavioral symptoms of high intensity. **Chronic** refers to long-standing and usually permanent disorders, but the term can also be applied generally to low-intensity disorders, since long-term difficulties are often of this sort. **Mild, moderate,** and **severe** are terms relating to varying points on a dimension of severity or seriousness. **Episodic** and **recurrent** are used to describe unstable disorder patterns that tend to come and go, as with some mood and schizophrenic conditions.

The Problem of Labeling

It is important to note that psychiatric diagnoses of the sort typified by the DSM-IV system are not uniformly revered among mental health professionals, not even in fact among all psychiatrists (see, e.g., Lidz, 1994; Wilson, 1993). One important and frequently voiced criticism is that a psychiatric diagnosis is little more than a label applied to a defined category of socially disapproved or otherwise problematic behavior. The label does not describe a person, nor necessarily any pathological condition the person harbors, but rather some behavioral pattern associated with that person's current level of functioning. Yet once a label has been assigned, it may close off further inquiry. It is all too easy—even for professionals—to accept a label as an accurate and complete description of an individual rather than of that person's behavior. It is hard then to look at the person's behavior objectively, without preconceptions about how he or she will act. These expectations can influence even the simplest interactions and treatment choices.

Once an individual is labeled, he or she may accept a redefined identity and play out the expectations of that role. ("I'm a substance abuser, therefore everyone expects me to take drugs. Furthermore, since this is a certifiable disease and hence out of my control, I expect myself to take drugs and should not be held accountable for doing so.") This tendency can be harmful for a variety of reasons, not least because of the pejorative and stigmatizing implications of many psychiatric labels—implications that have the power to transform social identities and "mark" people as second-class citizens with severe limitations, often presumed to be permanent (Jones et al., 1984). Obviously, the effects on a person's morale and self-esteem can be devastating.

Interestingly, other researchers have concluded that "labeling," per se, does not necessarily imply that people are going to act negatively toward a former patient simply because he or she has been mentally ill (Cockerham, 1981; Rabkin, 1972). In fact,

Gladys Burr (shown here with her attorney) is a tragic example of the dangers of labeling. Involuntarily committed by her mother (apparently because of some personality problems) in 1936 at the age of 29, Ms. Burr was diagnosed as psychotic and was later declared to be mentally retarded. Though a number of IQ tests administered from 1946 to 1961 showed her to be of normal intelligence, and though a number of doctors stated that she was of normal intelligence and should be released, she was confined in a residential center for the mentally retarded or in a state boarding home until 1978. Though a court did give her a financial reward in compensation, surely nothing can compensate for 42 years of unnecessary and involuntary commitment.

some writers have stated that former mental patients can avoid negative reactions from people by simply behaving differently. In this view, labeling actually has little impact on people's attitudes toward mental illness (Segal, 1978). In opposition to this view and reaffirming the role of labeling on the social rejection of former mental patients, Link and colleagues (1987) found that placing labels of mental illness on a person did influence others to judge that individual as "dangerous" and to seek social distance from the individual. The relative impact of labeling on views toward mental illness is an active debate within the field of abnormal psychology, and one can find considerable research and emotional commitment to both sides of the argument.

Clearly, it is important for professionals to be very cautious and circumspect in the diagnostic process, in their use of labels, and in ensuring confidentiality with respect to both. A related change has developed over the past 50 years regarding the person who goes to see a mental health professional. For years the traditional term for such a person has been *patient,* which is closely associated with a medically "sick" person and a passive stance, waiting for a doctor's cure. Today many such professionals, especially those trained in nonmedical settings, prefer the term *client* because it implies more responsibility and participation on the part of an individual for bringing about his or her own recovery.

THE EXTENT OF ABNORMAL BEHAVIOR

What is the rate of mental disorder in society today? Or, to put it another way, how many people actually have psychological disorders? The frequency or infrequency of particular disorders is an important consideration for a number of reasons. For one, researchers in the mental health field need to have a clear understanding of the nature and extent of abnormal behaviors in various groups because this may provide clues about their causes. In addition, mental health practitioners need to know whether the problems they are dealing with are relatively common or rare in order to evaluate the appropriateness of available treatment measures. Finally, mental health planners need to have a clear picture of the nature and extent of psychological problems being faced by society in order to determine how resources can be most effectively allocated.

Before we can discuss the extent of mental disorders in society we must clarify how psychological problems are counted. **Epidemiology** is the study of the distribution of diseases, disorders, or health-related behaviors in a given population. Mental health epidemiology refers to the study of the distribution of mental disorders. A key component of an epidemiological survey is determining the magnitude of the problem being studied. There are several ways of doing this. The term **prevalence** refers to the relative proportion of active cases that can be identified at a given point in, or during a given period of, time. For example, "point prevalence" refers (as the term implies) to the estimated proportion of actual, active cases in a given population at any instant in time. It is to be distinguished from the term **incidence,** which is the occurrence (onset) rate of a given disorder in a given population, often expressed as a cumulative ratio of onsets per unit population over some time period—say one year. Incidence rates include recovered cases as well as people who may have died. Increasingly employed in the contemporary literature is a measure termed

lifetime prevalence, which is the total proportion of living persons in a population ever having had the disorder up to the time of epidemiologic assessment; it too includes recovered cases.

A large-scale epidemiological study sponsored by the National Institutes of Mental Health (NIMH), still ongoing at this writing, has provided us with perhaps the most reliable and valid information about the prevalence of mental disorders in contemporary society (Regier et al., 1988). The original NIMH catchment area epidemiological study surveyed 18,571 adults from five communities: Baltimore, New Haven, St. Louis, Durham (NC), and Los Angeles. It found that about 15.4 percent of the population, overall, suffer from substance abuse or other diagnosable mental health problems in any given month.

These data were recently updated (Regier et al., 1993) with a new sample of 20,291 persons from the same areas who were contacted on two occasions one year apart. The figures for the first contact (wave 1, also involving one-month prevalence) are, as might be expected, quite comparable to the earlier ones, with an overall one-month prevalence rate of mental disorder or substance abuse of 15.7 percent (13.0 percent for non-substance-abusing mental disorder alone). Within the year, however (as determined at wave 2), there was an occurrence of new cases at a rate of 12.3 percent, for an overall one-year prevalence of 28 percent. This translates to a U.S. population one-year prevalence of over 44 million persons. Correcting for the estimated U.S. population increase in the interim since the survey, we calculate that the comparable 1996 figure would be in excess of 56 million persons. That is, at some time during 1996 the behavior of more than 56 million American adults will have met criteria for a diagnosable mental disorder or substance abuse problem.

These figures are roughly confirmed in an independent national epidemiological study reported by Kessler and colleagues (1994), who found an overall 12-month prevalence rate for 14 major mental and substance abuse disorders of 29.5 percent. Nearly 50 percent of the 15- to 54-year-olds in this survey reported at least one diagnosable disorder during their lifetimes up to the point of the study (i.e., lifetime prevalence).

The NIMH (Myers et al., 1984; Robins et al., 1984; Regier et al., 1988) study also provided information of a more detailed sort. Among the more interesting findings were the following:

1. There appear to be substantial differences in the lifetime prevalence for various disorders in the five sites studied. For example, the prevalence rate for simple phobia in Baltimore was more than twice

Appearances are sometimes deceiving. Much real mental disorder is not obvious, and the frankly bizarre does not always signify abnormality. Modern epidemiologic researchers employ trained interviewers and refined assessment techniques to determine the presence or absence of various mental disorders in the population of interest.

the rate in St. Louis and three times the rate in New Haven.

2. One-month prevalence studies, not surprisingly, show that disorders vary considerably in frequency of occurrence. The most common specific disorders were phobia (6.2 percent), moderate but persistent depression—called "dysthymia" (3.3 percent), major depressive episode (2.2 percent) and alcohol abuse or dependence (2.8 percent).

3. Rates of disorder (one-month prevalence) differ between men and women. Men have a greater preponderance of substance abuse disorder (6.3 as opposed to 1.6 percent in women) and antisocial personality disorder (0.8 as opposed to 0.02 percent in women); women appear to develop relatively more mood disorders (6.6 as opposed to 3.5 percent

in men), anxiety disorders (9.7 as opposed to 4.7 percent in men), and somatization disorder (0.2 percent as opposed to a negligible occurrence in men).

These more detailed findings were also generally confirmed in the more recent work of Kessler and colleagues (1994). By any measure, these epidemiologic findings, taken together, represent a problem of astounding magnitude.

Most people with significant psychological problems do not now get hospitalized in a large state or county psychiatric institution. Of those who are hospitalized, most receive these services in other types of inpatient settings (Narrow et al., 1993). Information from the U.S. Department of Health and Human Services (1990) indicates that admission to mental hospitals has decreased substantially over the past 40 years. Inpatient hospitalization constituted 77 percent of all mental health episodes in 1955 but only 27 percent in 1986. The dramatic declines in the use of public mental hospitals have been accompanied by a steady rise in admissions to private psychiatric hospitals and to psychiatric facilities in general hospitals, most of them also privately sponsored (Lee & Goodwin, 1987). This trend, often referred to as deinstitutionalization, will be discussed more extensively in Chapter 18. People with psychological problems are now more likely to receive treatment in outpatient facilities (Narrow et al., 1993). However, evidence suggests that only about 25 percent of those with psychological problems actually receive any professional treatment at all (Regier et al., 1993; Robins et al., 1984). Of persons receiving any kind of help for their problems, about 40 percent rely on voluntary support networks (Narrow et al., 1993).

RESEARCH IN ABNORMAL PSYCHOLOGY

The facts and ideas presented in this book are products of the powerful methods of science as used to study maladaptive human behavior. You are probably already familiar with scientific methods in general and their uses in various areas of psychology. Certain issues and problems arise in applying these methods to understanding the nature, causes, and treatment of abnormal behavior; thus some review is appropriate before we move on. Our review will be organized around (a) direct observation of behavior, (b) sampling and generalization, (c) correlation and causation, (d) experimental strategies, (e) case studies, and (f) retrospective and prospective strategies.

This space served as a kitchen/dining and barber shop area of the Central Islip State Hospital on Long Island, where 10,000 mental patients and employees once lived and worked. Like many other old and outmoded public mental hospitals, Central Islip did not survive the era of deinstitutionalization.

Observation of Behavior

As in all other sciences, the bedrock of psychological knowledge is observation, and what psychologists observe is the behavior of organisms. The focus of such observations is variable and includes the overt actions of an organism, certain of its measurable internal behaviors (e.g., its physiological processes), and at the human level verbal reports about inner processes or events. It is the last of these sources of information that is by far the most troublesome and yet often the most interesting and potentially useful. Of course, all of us observe our own overt behavior and certain of our inner events, such as thoughts and feelings. But self-observation of one's inner processes has distinct limits as a database for psychological science, in part because much important mental activity is carried on automatically, so to speak, outside of the range of a person's awareness (see, e.g., Nisbett & Wilson, 1977). In addition, mental events are in their fundamental nature *private* events, forever inaccessible to confirmation by anyone else. Science normally demands such confirmation (intersubjective reliability) by others as a means of assuring accuracy in the observations made. This constraint has been a source of considerable difficulty for the discipline of psychology throughout its history.

Scientific observational methods employ systematic techniques by which observers are trained to watch and record behavior without bias. Such methods have helped to ensure the scientific integrity of observational research, but obstacles still remain.

In the field of abnormal psychology, researchers must inevitably make use of a subject's verbal reports or "observations" of his or her inner experience because only the subject has observational access. In most situations, a subject will be cooperative and truthful. But even assuming a sincere attitude, often a subject will be unable to make crucial observations. The determinants of behavior are many, and as already noted a substantial proportion of them do not enter conscious experience.

To make sense of observed behavior, researchers (as do people in general) generate **hypotheses,** more or less plausible ideas to explain something—in this case, behavior. All empirical sciences use hypotheses, although these hypotheses appear to be more closely tied to observable phenomena in the more established physical sciences. For example, the concept of electricity is actually hypothetical. Scientists have only observed the effects of this presumed entity, but these effects are extremely reliable and predictable; hence we believe in the real existence of electricity. Most people have less confidence in a construct such as borderline personality disorder.

These considerations are particularly important in the study of abnormal behavior. For the most part, as already noted, we understand the behavior of the people we meet, at least to the extent necessary to carry on ordinary social interactions. Even when we observe something unexpected in a person's behavior, we can usually empathize enough to have a sense of "where they're coming from," of the factors that have contributed to the behavior. Almost by definition, abnormal behavior is far more opaque. It is extraordinary, and our minds are therefore attracted to extraordinary explanations of it—to extraordinary hypotheses. Whether these hypotheses can account satisfactorily for abnormal behavior is open to question, but it is clear that we need them in order to begin to understand. Behavior never explains itself, whether it is normal or abnormal.

Several competing hypotheses typically exist to explain the complex patterns we find in abnormal behavior. In fact, these hypotheses tend to cluster together in distinctive approaches or viewpoints. These general viewpoints are addressed in Chapter 3. For now, we merely wish to emphasize that all forms of psychological inquiry begin with observations of behavior, and that much of the subject matter of abnormal psychology is built on hypotheses that account more or less adequately for observed behavior declared to be disordered.

These hypotheses are important because they frequently determine the therapeutic approaches

Many persons with psychological problems, including most young children, are unable to formulate and express clearly the nature of their difficulties. In these instances careful and reliable observations of behavior become especially critical in developing accurate diagnostic assessments.

used to treat an abnormality. For example, suppose we are confronted with someone who washes his or her hands 60 to 100 times a day, causing serious injury to the skin and underlying tissues. If we conclude that this behavior is a result of subtle neurological damage, we would try to discover the nature of the individual's disease in the hope of administering a cure. If we view the behavior as the symbolic cleansing of sinful thoughts, we would try to unearth and address the sources of the person's excessive scrupulousness. If we regard the handwashing symptom as merely the product of unfortunate conditioning or learning, we would devise a means of counterconditioning to eliminate the problematic behavior. These different approaches are based on different concepts of the causes of the abnormal behavior. Without such concepts—if we are limited merely to observing behavior itself—we would be left with no means of grasping abnormal behavior, and few clues as to what should be done to change it.

Sampling and Generalization

Research in abnormal psychology is concerned with gaining enhanced understanding and, where possible, control of abnormal behavior. Although we can occasionally get important leads from the intensive study of a single case of a given disorder, such a strategy rarely yields enough information to allow us to reach firm conclusions. The basic diffi-

culty with this strategy is that we cannot know whether our observations pertain to the disorder, to unrelated characteristics of the person with the disorder, to some combination of these factors, or even to characteristics of the observer. It is also possible that the particular abnormality might arise from different internal sources in different people, a circumstance that could be detected only by studying a number of people who exhibit the behavior.

For these reasons, we generally place greater reliance on research studies using groups of individuals who show roughly equivalent abnormalities of behavior. Typically, several people in such studies share one characteristic (the problematic behavior) while varying widely on others. We can then infer that anything else they have in common, such as having a chronically depressed parent, may be related to the behavioral abnormality—provided, of course, that the characteristic is not widely shared by people who do not have the abnormality. If the abnormality arises from different sources in different people (which might in itself be an important finding), we would probably have considerable difficulty identifying with precision the patterns underlying the abnormality. In fact, difficulties of this sort appear to be impeding our progress in respect to several of the disorders we will consider in later chapters.

If we wanted to research the problem of major psychological depression, for example, a first step would be to determine criteria for identifying persons affected with the condition. DSM-IV provides an officially adopted set of such criteria, so that part of our problem is solved. We would then need to find people who fit our criteria. Obviously, we could never hope to study all of the people in the world who meet our criteria; we would use instead a technique called **sampling,** in which we would select as subjects a limited number of depressed persons who appear to be representative of the much larger group of individuals having major depressive disorders. From our study of this group, we would hope to generalize our findings to the larger group. To ensure validity, it is important that every person in the larger group have an equal chance of being included in the group we intend to study. Usually, we can only approximate this degree of rigor in choosing research samples.

As we have learned from the results of poorly designed public opinion polls, nonrepresentative sampling can produce erroneous conclusions about the larger group we wish to study. For example, if our research group of depressed people did not adequately represent the socioeconomic statuses of persons in general who suffer from major depression, we might attribute some characteristic to such sufferers that is in fact more true of persons in a given socioeconomic group.

Even if our study group were thoroughly representative, there would always be the possibility that our findings about, for example, the levels of prior stress experienced by our depressed subjects would be similar to findings about other selected groups, or even about persons in general. If such were the case, it would not be particularly interesting. Thus researchers use a **control group,** a sample of people who do not exhibit the disorder being studied but who are comparable in all other respects to the **criterion group,** members of which do exhibit the disorder. Typically, the control group is psychologically "normal" according to specified criteria. We can then compare the two groups in certain areas—such as reported prior stress experienced—to determine if they differ. They would in fact almost certainly differ because of chance factors, but we have powerful statistical techniques to determine whether or not such observed differences are truly significant. If we found, for example, that major depressives had significantly more prior stress, as reported, than the "normals," we might be tempted to hypothesize that the experience of unusual stress is associated with later onset of major depression. Entertaining this hypothesis assumes, of course, that the people in our study have reported their stressful experiences accurately, a sometimes dubious assumption.

Correlation and Causation

The mere **correlation,** or association, of two or more variables can never by itself be taken as evidence of **causation,** that is, a relationship in which a preceding variable causes other variables. This is an important distinction to bear in mind, especially so in the field of abnormal psychology. Returning to our hypothetical depression study, for instance, we could not legitimately conclude from our findings alone that the experience of severe prior stress is a causal factor in the onset of major depression. There are simply too many alternative ways to account for such an association, including the possibility that depressed persons are more prone than others to remember stressful events in their immediate pasts. In this instance, we would need at a minimum to seek corroborating evidence that prior excessive stress did, in fact, occur.

Many studies in abnormal psychology show that two (or more) things regularly occur together, such as poverty and retarded intellectual development or depression and reported prior stressors. Such variables may well be related to one another in some kind of causal context, but the relationship could take a variety of forms:

Variable *a* causes variable *b* (or vice versa).

Variable *a* and variable *b* are both caused by variable *c*.

Variables *a* and *b* are both involved in a complex pattern of variables influencing *a* and *b* in similar ways.

Coming from a broken home, for instance, has been established as a significant correlate of many forms of abnormal behavior. Yet we cannot conclude that such families cause abnormality because many other potential causes of abnormality are statistically associated with parental separation or divorce—socioeconomic stress, family disharmony, alcoholism in one or both parents, a move to a new neighborhood or school, the effort to adjust to a single parent's new love relationships, and so forth. Unfortunately, such complexity is the rule rather than the exception when attempting to understand how abnormal behavior becomes established.

Statistical techniques of relatively recent development (such as path analysis) that take into account how variables "predict" and are related to one another through time are frequently helpful in disentangling correlated factors. These techniques give us much greater confidence in our causal inferences. A relatively simple application of path analysis was made in a study by Mednick (1978) of high-risk children. The study found that an adult

Though a dysfunctional family relationship may be a correlate of some form of abnormal behavior, this is not necessarily a causal factor because there may be many other ways of accounting for a particular mental disorder.

outcome of schizophrenia was statistically linked (correlated) with both obstetrical complications at birth and the presence of subtle autonomic nervous system impairment. Path analysis confirmed that the impact of the birth complications was dependent on the influence of the nervous system damage. In other words, obstetrical complications were involved with schizophrenia only to the extent that they were accompanied by nervous system impairment observed in childhood. This study strongly suggested a causal chain beginning with birth difficulties and leading to neurological dysfunction, which in turn increased the likelihood of schizophrenia.

However great their problems in pinning down causal relations, correlational studies can be a powerful and rich source of inference. They often suggest causal hypotheses and occasionally provide crucial data that confirm or refute these hypotheses. As a measure of their usefulness, we need only reflect on what the science of astronomy would be without correlational studies, since astronomers cannot manipulate the variables they study, such as the relative positions and movements of stars and planets.

Correlational studies have been useful in many areas of abnormal psychology but especially so in determining epidemiological patterns. Epidemiological research attempts to establish the pattern of occurrence of certain disorders (in our case, mental disorders) in different times, places, and groups of people. Where we find significant variations in the incidence or prevalence of a disorder, we ask why. In some cases, the answer will be obvious or trivial, as in the observation that the diagnosis of mental retar-

dation increases suddenly among six-year-olds (i.e., children facing their first real intellectual challenge, in school). But in other cases, the question leads, if not to the unequivocal identification of causal factors, at least to promising avenues for investigation.

Observations that, for example, a particular disorder is highly associated with a particular potentially causal factor but is uncorrelated with certain others may help us narrow our field of search. Such observations make certain hypotheses more likely and others less so and thus maximize the efficiency with which the search for understanding continues. In the next section, we review methodological approaches that have a higher promise of exactitude than correlational studies, as well as the enhanced problems and risks of actively intervening in people's lives.

Experimental Strategies

Scientific research is most rigorous, and its findings most reliable, when it employs the full power of the **experimental method.** In such cases, scientists control all factors, except one, that could have an effect on a variable or outcome of interest; then they actively manipulate that one factor. If the outcome of interest is observed to change as the manipulated factor is changed, that factor can be regarded as a cause of the outcome.

Unfortunately, the experimental method cannot be applied to many problems of abnormal psychology because of practical and ethical constraints. Suppose, for example, we wanted to use the experimental method to evaluate the hypothesis that prior stressful events are a cause of major depression. But for ethical constraints, our ideal approach would be to choose at random two groups of normal adults for a longitudinal study (a study in which the same subjects are followed over some time period). The individuals in one group would be subjected in systematic fashion to a rigorous program of contrived (but believable) stressful harassment. Subjects in the other (control) group would spend the same amount of time in some emotionally neutral activity. Naturally occurring stressors in both groups would be monitored to ensure that expected comparable levels in fact obtained. Some days or weeks hence the subjects of both groups would receive thorough, systematic assessments as to their levels of depression and in particular the proportions meeting DSM-IV criteria for Major Depressive Episode. Our causal hypothesis would be confirmed if the group of stressed subjects significantly exceeded controls in occurrences of major depressive episodes. Such a study would be good science, but it would of course be ethically unacceptable to treat people in this deliberately callous, destructive, and potentially dangerous (depressive episodes enhance the risk of suicide) manner.

The ethical and procedural constraints on using the experimental method to search for causes can sometimes be circumvented or reduced by employing models of abnormal behavior. Experiments of this kind are generally known as **analogue studies**—studies in which a researcher attempts to simulate the conditions under investigation. These experiments establish the causes of maladaptive behavior by (a) inducing the behavior in subhuman species or (b) inducing the behavior in humans, if the behavior has a very high likelihood of being temporary or reversible (for example, inducing temporary depression by having normal subjects concentrate on negative thoughts). Apart from what some would regard as continuing ethical problems in research of this sort, the major scientific problem is, of course, to establish major commonality between the contrived behavior and the real thing as it occurs "naturally." Many such analogue studies have failed to make convincing connections.

A case in point is the hypothesis that learned helplessness is a cause of depression in humans (Seligman, 1975). Laboratory experiments with dogs had demonstrated that, when subjected to repeated experiences of painful, unpredictable, inescapable electric shock, these animals lost their ability to learn a simple escape routine to avoid further shock; they just sat and endured the pain. Seligman

Analogue studies in which generalizations are made from laboratory models to the real world may fail to make convincing connections. Results of testing—using rats, mice, dogs, or monkeys, for example, in a laboratory setting—may not hold up when extended to humans.

argued from this observation that human depression (which he equated with the reaction of the "helpless" dogs) is a reaction to the experience of noncontingency between one's behavior and the outcomes of that behavior—that is, to learned helplessness. There ensued a large number of learned helplessness experiments on normal human subjects, all attempting to induce learned helplessness and to determine if that state would produce mild and reversible depressions. The results were generally disappointing. Human subjects often did not respond with helplessness to noncontingency situations, many of them actually showing enhanced effort (facilitation, also called reactance) following the frustrating experiences (see the February 1978 issue of *Journal of Abnormal Psychology,* Volume 87).

Reacting to these disappointing results, Seligman and his colleagues (Abramson, Seligman & Teasdale, 1978) modified the learned helplessness theory of depression. They suggested that a noncontingency experience should have a depression-inducing effect only on those persons prone to interpret failure-to-cope experiences in a negative way—specifically by attributing them to personal (internal) characteristics that are pervasive (global) and relatively permanent (stable). This idea has fared considerably better in subsequent research, which will be reviewed in Chapter 6. Curiously, the original learned helplessness notion may be a better model of human anxiety disorders than of depression, as will be seen in Chapter 5.

In this case, despite the earlier disappointment, which does illustrate the hazards involved in generalizing too readily from laboratory models to the real world, the learned helplessness analogue generated much research and thereby clarified certain aspects of an important psychopathological problem relating to depression. In addition, its range of application has turned out to be probably considerably broader than was originally anticipated. We count that as a successful outcome.

If the role of the experimental method in establishing the causes of abnormal behavior must necessarily be a limited one, no such restriction applies to its role in the evaluation of treatment approaches. On the contrary, the sophisticated use of experimental techniques in determining the efficacy of different therapies for a given disorder remains an indispensable tool.

It is a relatively simple and straightforward matter to set up a study in which a purportedly effective treatment is given to a designated group of patients and withheld from a similar group of patients. Should the former group show significantly more improvement than the latter, we can have confidence in the treatment's effectiveness, although—as is distressingly common—we may still lack knowledge as to *why* the treatment works. Of course, special techniques must usually be employed in such treatment research to ensure that the two groups are in fact comparable in every respect except the presence or absence of the active treatment agent. Once a treatment has proved effective, it can subsequently be employed for members of the original control group, leading to improved functioning for everyone. When this waiting list control group strategy is deemed inadvisable, as it sometimes is for ethical and other reasons (Imber et al., 1986), a research design may call for a comparison of two or more treatments in different equivalent groups. Such comparative outcome research has much to recommend it (VandenBos, 1986) and is being utilized increasingly.

Many variables of potential importance in abnormal behavior cannot readily be manipulated in the active way the experimental method demands, quite apart from the constraints ethical considerations may impose. Fortunately, we have made great progress in the statistical control of variables that do not yield to the classic form of experimental control. Statistical controls, in effect, allow us to adjust for otherwise uncontrolled (or uncontrollable) variables. For example, the incidence of certain mental disorders appears to vary with socioeconomic status. Using statistical controls, we can "correct" our results for any differences in socioeconomic status existing between our experimental and control groups. The same effect could be achieved by experimental control if we could ensure that socioeconomic statuses in our control group existed in exactly the same proportions as those in the pathological group we wish to study, but such a proportional distribution might be difficult to achieve. And we might thereby also inadvertently create an additional problem: If we insist that socioeconomic statuses in our control group exactly mirror those in the experimental group rather than those in the general population, then our control group may no longer be representative of the general population. As this example shows, considerable knowledge and expertise are required in the proper design of research studies in abnormal psychology.

Clinical Case Studies

Despite the growing use of representative group research methods, most instances of a given disorder are still studied individually, using the traditional clinical case study method. A **case study** is an indepth examination of an individual or family that draws from a number of data sources, including interviews and psychological testing. The clinical investigator, who is usually also a patient's therapist, intensively observes an individual's behavior and marshals background facts that may be pertinent when attempting to formulate the case. A case study includes a set of hypotheses about what is causing the problem and a guide to treatment planning. These hypotheses and therapies may be revised as necessary based on a patient's response to treatment interventions. This strategy is sometimes called an *N = 1 experiment,* especially when the precise relationships between treatment interventions and patient responses are systematically monitored. While much can be learned when skilled clinicians use the case study method, the information thus acquired can also be seriously flawed, especially if one seeks to apply it to other cases involving an apparently similar abnormality. When there is only one observer, and when the observations are made in a relatively uncontrolled context, there is a distinct possibility that erroneous conclusions will be drawn.

Retrospective Versus Prospective Strategies

In one of the most important developments in recent years, the more or less standard **retrospective research** (research that looks backward from the present) has been supplemented by **prospective research** that focuses, before the fact, on individuals who have a higher-than-average likelihood of becoming psychologically disordered. As we saw in our example of major depressives, there are certain difficulties in attempting to reconstruct the pasts of people already experiencing a disorder. It is hard to disentangle the effects of the present disorder from the effects of past events, or the memory of them, and to trace a clear cause-and-effect relationship. Nevertheless, this has been the standard method of causal investigation: We observe the behavioral abnormality and then comb the backgrounds of afflicted individuals for shared factors that might have caused it. Apart from the fact that a disordered person may not be the most accurate or objective source of information, such a strategy invites investigators to discover what they expect to discover about the background factors theoretically linked to a disorder. One way around these difficulties is to utilize documents and records dated before the emergence of the disorder. While this strategy has on occasion been productively employed, it obviously depends on the accidental availability of the precise information needed.

We can have much more confidence in our causal hypotheses when they look ahead instead of backward and when they correctly predict the individuals in a group who will develop a particular form of disordered behavior—or, alternatively, which of two or more groups will prove to have been at risk. It is, of course, sobering from a logistical standpoint to contemplate following various unselected groups from childhood into adulthood in the numbers required to produce a suitable "yield" of various adult disorders. Hence, in a typical instance, children sharing a risk factor known to be associated with relatively high rates of subsequent breakdown are studied over the course of years. Those who do break down are compared with those who do not in the hope that crucial differentiating factors will be discovered.

Today, serious researchers in abnormal behavior are aware of the magnitude of the challenges facing them, and as a group they have learned there are few easy answers lying about ready to be discovered by enterprising but impatient investigators. In fact, the study of behavioral abnormalities has enriched the entire discipline of psychology by contributing to an enhanced understanding of the enormously complex organization of the origins of human behavior.

THE ORIENTATION OF THIS BOOK

Psychology is an unusual science in that the human mind is both the agent and the object of study. We employ the mind as an instrument to try to understand the mind. Keeping a proper perspective in such a situation presents special challenges. Can we fashion an approach to abnormal behavior that is scientific and humanistic in the best senses of both of these terms? We hope so, and this book is an attempt at that objective.

Our intent is to introduce you to the sophisticated examination of abnormal behavior and its place in contemporary society. Although we will deal with all the major categories of mental disorders, we will focus on those patterns that seem most relevant to a broad, basic understanding of maladaptive behavior. While we will not hesitate to include the unusual or bizarre, our emphasis will be on the unity of human behavior, ranging from normal to abnormal.

Throughout this text we assume that a sound and comprehensive study of abnormal behavior should be based on the following concepts:

1. *A scientific approach to abnormal behavior.* Any comprehensive view of human behavior must draw upon concepts and research findings from a variety of scientific fields. Of particular relevance are genetics, biochemistry, neurophysiology, sociology, an-

thropology, and of course psychology. Common scientific concepts, such as causal processes, control groups, dependent variables, placebos, and theories, will figure in our discussion. Special emphasis will be placed on the application of learning principles to the understanding and treatment of mental disorders.

In this general context, you are encouraged to take a critical and evaluative attitude toward the research findings presented in this text and in other sources. When properly conducted, scientific research provides us with information that has a high probability of being accurate, but many research findings are subject to various sorts of errors and unintended biases and are thus open to serious questions. We intend to show you some of the recurrent sources of these errors and to some extent teach you how to evaluate and interpret research outcomes in this field. We think the benefits of acquiring such skills will persist long after your course in abnormal psychology will have ended, and will make it possible for you to understand and appreciate at perhaps a somewhat advanced level the research the field produces on into the future.

2. *An awareness of our common human concerns.* Science cannot effectively address many of the experiences and problems common to human existence. Insights into hope, faith, courage, love, grief, despair, death, and the quest for values and meaning are not readily obtainable in a laboratory. Rather, we must supplement what science with its present methods can teach by turning to literature, drama, autobiographical accounts, and even art, history, and religion to seek a greater understanding of these aspects of human psychological functioning. Although these sources of insight strike a common chord in all of us, it is important to distinguish the information gained through them from the information obtained through scientific observation. The latter, while limited, is apt to be quite precise; the former, while limitless, will normally be less so.

3. *Respect for the dignity, integrity, and growth potential of all persons, notably including those individuals whose current functioning may be compromised by psychological problems mild or severe in magnitude.* Implicit in this statement is a view of individuals not merely as products or victims of their past conditioning and present situation, but as potentially active agents as well—people who can develop and use their capacities for building the kind of life they choose and for contributing to a psychological environment in which all others can flourish as well.

In attempting to provide a perspective on abnormal behavior, we will focus not only on how maladaptive patterns are perceived by clinical psychologists and other mental health personnel, but also on how such disorders feel to and are perceived by the individuals experiencing them. In dealing with the major patterns of abnormal behavior, we will focus on four significant aspects of each: the clinical picture, causal factors, treatments, and outcomes. In each case, we will examine the evidence for biological, psychosocial (psychological and interpersonal), and sociocultural (the broader social environment of culture and subculture) influencing factors.

Since this is a psychology book, much of our focus will be on the psychosocial factors involved in abnormal behavior. This focus is apt as well because it is the psychosocial area that presents especially challenging adaptational problems for the future. We are less well equipped for rapid advance in this area than in the biomedical arena, which continues to develop at a rate more equal to that of technological advance in the culture generally. Yet even in respect to our physical health, there are increasing signs that ultimate solutions will depend on a far greater sophistication about ourselves as psychosocial, as well as biological, entities. The truly amazing advances in medicine to which we have become accustomed will almost certainly prove to have substantial limits—at least for the foreseeable future—in managing or overcoming ineffective, self-defeating, or dangerous behavior patterns. For example, it is not presently even conceivable that a prescription medication or a brain operation might be fashioned that will convert a person lacking a myriad of essential skills into one capable of effectively negotiating the complexities of modern life. Accomplishing this will require both an enhanced understanding of the psychosocial underpinnings of social competence and the development of remedial techniques of unprecedented power. The challenge is very great, but also we think very exciting.

Most of this book will be devoted to a presentation of well-established patterns of mental disorder and to special problem behaviors of our time that are more controversial but directly relevant. Initially, however, we will trace the development of contemporary views of abnormal behavior from early beliefs and practices, outline several attempts to explain what makes human beings tick, and review the general causes of abnormal behavior in modern life.

Later, after a series of chapters on various problem behaviors, we will devote four chapters to modern methods of assessment and treatment and to problems in the wider social context on which mental disorders impinge. These chapters will include a discussion of the potential of modern psychology and allied sciences for preventing mental disorders and for helping us achieve a more sane and harmonious world.

At the close of his journeys, Tennyson's Ulysses says, "I am part of all that I have met." It is the authors' hope that, at the end of your journey through this book, you will have a better understanding of human experience and behavior—and that you will consider what you have learned to be a meaningful part of your own life experience.

UNRESOLVED ISSUES

on Classification

As we have seen, the standard for classifying abnormalities of behavior or mental disorders, the DSM-IV, is not an entirely satisfactory system. Although, like its immediate predecessors, the DSM-IV has evidently made it possible to achieve respectable levels of reliability in the diagnostic process, the validity of the diagnoses it officially identifies and recognizes in many instances remains suspect and the subject of controversy. According to some accounts, in fact, recent editions of the DSM have tended to sacrifice validity in attempts to improve interdiagnostician agreement, or reliability. Diagnostician agreement on assignment of patients to a diagnosis of questionable validity or meaning would clearly not constitute an exceptional level of progress.

The difficulties of simultaneously satisfying the dual requirements of reliability and validity in diagnosing mental disorders are unquestionably due in no small part to the enormous complexity of the factors underlying and determining human behavior. But they are also due, according to some observers, to our having chosen an inadequate model for organizing our observations of behavioral abnormalities. This model is essentially a medical or disease metaphor, imported as it were into the domain of abnormal behavior. By this we mean that identified types of abnormal behavior have been conceptualized in the DSM framework as the outward manifestation of a corresponding type of illness or disease ("dysfunction"). But we run the risk here of taking the metaphor too literally and thereby of being misled as to the nature of abnormality. While we are not troubled by the notion of a diseased brain, what possible meaning, on close examination, can we assign to the concept of a diseased mind? They are not, after all, the same thing.

Consistent with the adopted medical disease metaphor, the DSM-IV attempts to treat mental disorder as consisting of a large number of discrete (discontinuous) categories. Implicit in this approach is the idea that each of the categories has a unique underlying core and a definable boundary separating it from other categories, as in the case of true diseases (Millon, 1991). The fact that we cannot identify the features of the core except by uncertain inference from surface characteristics is attributed to a temporary lack of knowledge, a lack that supposedly will be overcome by future research. Meanwhile, the exact boundary of each category will remain uncertain and will have to be approximated by somewhat arbitrary rules to achieve a satisfactory separation from other categories. The latter is what justifies the highly explicit lists of criteria for applying DSM diagnoses.

There is considerable disagreement and doubt about the possibility of our ever finding such a precisely definable and constant array of causal factors at the core of each mental disorder included in the DSM classification. The only exceptions may be those relatively few disorders that are in fact related to independently diagnosable brain diseases. Thus, lacking a constant core for each purported disorder, it becomes difficult to know if our efforts to differentiate one sort of disorder from another are in fact correct or even meaningful.

As noted by Widiger and Frances (1985), there appear to be three basic approaches currently possible to classify abnormal behavior: the categorical, the dimensional, and the prototypal. A **categorical approach,** which is the one we have described as deriving from physical medicine, assumes that (a) all human behavior can be sharply divided into the categories normal and abnormal, and (b) there exist discrete, nonoverlapping classes or types of abnormal behavior, often referred to as "mental" illnesses or diseases. As already suggested, many professionals believe that this approach is inappropriate for most recognizable types of mental disorder, which seem to be neither discrete (i.e., their boundaries routinely blend with those of other categories) nor always the manifestation of a common set of underlying factors.

The dimensional and prototypal approaches differ fundamentally in the assumptions they make, particularly in respect to the requirement of discrete classes of behavior. In a **dimensional approach,** it is assumed that a person's typical behavior is the product of differing strengths or intensities of behavior along several definable dimensions, such as mood, emotional stability, aggressiveness, gender identity, anxiousness, interpersonal trust, clarity of thinking and communication, social introversion, and so on. The important dimensions, once established, would be the same for everyone. In this conception, people differ from one another in their configuration or profile of these dimensional traits (each ranging from very low to very high), not in terms of surface indications of some presumed disease. Normal could be discriminated from abnormal, then, by precise statistical criteria applied to dimensional intensities.

There have been numerous discussions in the recent literature seriously proposing the abandonment of the categorical in favor of a dimensional approach to the notoriously intermingled ("comorbid") DSM Axis II personality disorders, including one by Widiger (1993), a principal architect of DSM-IV. Some (e.g., Carson, 1993) have suggested that this proposal is too limited and should be extended as well to the Axis I disorders, a position supported by increasing evidence that even the distinction between Axis I and Axis II disorders is rationally and empirically untenable (Benjamin, 1994; Livesley et al., 1994). This debate will doubtless continue, but in the meantime the DSM-IV retains its disease-like categorical format for both Axes I and II. DSM Axis V is, as we have seen, a dimensional scale. However, this axis is not concerned with the organization of psychopathology, but rather with its effects in terms of disrupted functioning.

Of course, in taking a dimensional approach it would be possible—perhaps even likely—to discover that such profiles tend to cluster together in types, and even that some of these types are correlated, though imperfectly, with recognizable sorts of gross behavioral malfunctions, such as anxiety disorders or depression. It is highly unlikely, however, that any individual's profile would exactly fit a narrowly defined type, or that the types identified will not have some overlapping features. This brings us to the matter of a prototypal approach.

A *prototype* (as the term is used here) is a conceptual entity depicting an idealized combination of characteristics, ones that more or less regularly occur together in a less perfect or standard way at the level of empirical reality. Recall our earlier example of the "dogness" prototype. Prototypes, as that example demonstrates, are actually an aspect of our everyday thinking and experience. We can all readily generate in our mind's eye an image of a dog, while recognizing we have never seen nor ever will see two identical dogs. Thus no item in a prototypally defined group may actually have all of the characteristics of the defining prototype, although it will have many of the more central of them. It is also possible that a certain item may be an exemplar, in part at least, of more than one prototype within a given domain. A dog whose parents are, let us say, a purebred collie and a purebred golden retriever will show both prototypal organizations in its appearance. Unlike the often forced categorical separations of the DSM, prototypes are not mutually exclusive. A given prototype may blend into another with which it shares many characteristics, perhaps especially its more peripheral ones, such as muzzle length in dogs.

Some psychologists believe that by adopting a **prototypal approach** we could wed some of the advantages of the categorical and the dimensional approaches while avoiding the disadvantages of each (the dimensional approach, for example, is cumbersome and inconvenient for routine clinical use). Use of such a "hybrid" (Millon, 1991) approach implies, however, that we should expect to find few if any pure exemplars of diagnostic groupings, as well as much blurring of the boundaries between them. This might make communication for researchers and clinicians somewhat more difficult. For advocates of a prototypal approach, however, any such drawback is tolerable if it helps attain the more desirable goals of enhanced validity and a classification system more representative of the empirical realities of mental disorder (see, e.g., Cantor et al., 1980).

Though many psychologists have reservations about the prevailing classificatory and diagnostic procedures, most do not recommend that these procedures be summarily abandoned or ignored. While far from ideal, they constitute the standard language of the field for both formal (especially research-based) and informal communication. Familiarity with the system in use is thus vital for the serious student. We hope, however, that this discussion has given you a more sophisticated perspective on the classificatory issues facing the field.

SUMMARY

Far from being separate and distinct from the events shaping human history, mental disorders and other aberrations of behavior have often played central roles in the drama. If considered in terms of numbers of citizens affected, they continue to do so. Nevertheless, students beginning serious study of abnormal psychology are likely to hold mistaken preconceptions about the field, ones widely shared by people in general. In part, this is due to certain popular images of mental disorders that have persisted over time, but it is also due to the great attention that the media has focused on the subject in recent years and to the willingness of mental health professionals to supply offhand accounts of behavior disorders and their treatment. Much of this exposure has accurately depicted limited aspects of the field, but some of it has distorted other aspects, causing widespread misconceptions about mental disorders and the people who suffer from them.

The most certain way to avoid misconception and error is to adopt a scientific attitude and approach to the study of abnormal behavior. This involves, among other things, the habit of suspending judgment until pertinent facts are known, the employment of objective and reliable methods of observation, and the development of a valid system for classifying the phenomena being studied. Progress

has been made in all these areas, but abnormal psychology continues to be a complex and challenging field. Much work remains to be done, even in so basic an area as classification. We still lack even a universally accepted definition of abnormality, although we, the authors, argue for one that emphasizes evaluating behavior in terms of the goodness of its outcomes for an individual or group.

A scientific approach to abnormal behavior also involves a focus on research and research methods, including an appreciation of the distinction between what is observable and what is hypothetical or inferred. Much of the content of abnormal psychology falls into the latter category. Research on abnormal conditions, if it is to produce valid results, must be done on people who are truly representative of the pathological groups to which they purportedly belong—a requirement that is often difficult to satisfy. We must also remain alert to the fact that mere correlation does not establish a causal relationship between the variables in question. Researchers use experimental methods and prospective research designs to resolve questions of causality, but these approaches are not always appropriate and may not always be effective. The individual case study method, despite its weaknesses, remains a frequently used investigative technique.

Science, of course, does not have all the answers. Any approach to the field must also recognize the significance of more simply human concerns, such as the feelings of despair or of hope that are such crucial elements in the total picture of normal and abnormal functioning.

KEY TERMS

syndrome (p. 9)	epidemiology (p. 17)
abnormal behavior (p. 10)	prevalence (p. 17)
abnormal psychology (p. 10)	incidence (p. 17)
psychopathology (p. 10)	lifetime prevalence (p. 17)
clinical psychology (p. 10)	hypotheses (p. 19)
psychiatry (p. 10)	sampling (p. 21)
psychiatric social work (p. 10)	control group (p. 21)
psychiatric nursing (p. 10)	criterion group (p. 21)
clinical picture (p. 11)	correlation (p. 21)
reliability (p. 11)	causation (p. 21)
validity (p. 12)	experimental method (p. 22)
DSM-IV (p. 12)	analogue studies (p. 23)
acute (p. 14)	case study (p. 24)
chronic (p. 16)	retrospective research (p. 24)
mild (p. 16)	prospective research (p. 24)
moderate (p. 16)	categorical approach (p. 27)
severe (p. 16)	dimensional approach (p. 27)
episodic (p. 16)	prototypal approach (p. 27)
recurrent (p. 16)	

CHAPTER

2

HISTORICAL VIEWS OF ABNORMAL BEHAVIOR

J. Richardson, Tennessee Confederates. *Very little is known about Richardson, whose drawings were discovered in a wooden box sold at a country auction. It is believed that he worked in the town of New Bedford, Massachusetts, around 1917–1922. Experts think that his drawings may have been done as part of a program of art therapy, which was beginning to be used to treat traumatized soldiers after World War I. Richardson chose historical subjects for many of his artworks.*

The history of our efforts to understand abnormal behavior is a fascinating one. Certainly, many of our misconceptions about mental disorders have their roots in the past, but it is equally true that many modern scientific concepts and treatments have their counterparts in approaches tried long ago. For example, free association—a technique used in twentieth-century psychoanalytic therapy to allow repressed conflicts and emotions to enter conscious awareness—is described by the Greek playwright Aristophanes in his play *The Clouds* (423 B.C.). Interestingly enough, the scene in which Socrates tries to calm and bring self-knowledge to Strepsiades is complete with a couch. In addition, nineteenth-century psychiatrists attempted to use electricity to cure mental disorders almost a century before electroconvulsive therapy became an accepted form of biologically based treatment. (See Chapter 16 for more on early electrical stimulation instruments.)

In this chapter, we will trace the evolution of views and treatments of psychopathology from ancient times to the twentieth century. In a broad sense, we will see an evolution from beliefs we consider today as superstition to those based on scientific awareness—from a focus on supernatural causes to a knowledge of natural causes. The course of this evolution has not been a steady movement forward. On the contrary, it has often been marked by periods of advancement or unique individual contributions followed by long years of inactivity or unproductive backward steps. (A summary of many of the historical figures we will discuss and their contributions appears later in this chapter.)

As we will see, current views of abnormal behavior have been shaped by the prevailing attitudes of past times and the advances of science. Each has contributed to the growth—and often the stagnation—of the other. For example, during certain periods in ancient Greece, the human body was considered sacred. Since autopsies on human beings were not performed, the understanding of human anatomy or biological processes was impeded. Much later, during the nineteenth and early twentieth centuries, the belief that a biological (medical) solution was needed to cure mental disorders frustrated investigation into psychological causes. Even today, with renewed emphasis on biological causes and treatments, the focus on psychological causation and treatment is sometimes undervalued.

The advances in understanding and treatment of abnormal behavior are all the more remarkable when viewed against a persistent resurfacing of ignorance, superstition, and fear. And if we think that we have today arrived at a knowledgeable and humane approach to treating the mentally ill, we should think again. We are still bound by culturally conditioned constraints and beliefs. For many, attitudes toward people who are different are still formed, at least in part, by superstition and fear.

ABNORMAL BEHAVIOR IN ANCIENT TIMES

Although human life presumably appeared on earth some 3 million or more years ago, written records extend back only a few thousand years. Thus our knowledge of our early ancestors is limited.

Two Egyptian papyri dating from the sixteenth century B.C. have provided some clues into the earliest interest in the treatment of diseases and behavior disorders. The Edwin Smith papyrus (named after its nineteenth-century discoverer) contains detailed descriptions of the treatment of wounds and other surgical operations. In it, the brain is described—possibly for the first time in history—and the writing clearly shows that the brain was recognized as the site of mental functions. We may think this remarkable for the sixteenth century B.C.; it becomes even more remarkable once we realize that this papyrus is believed to be a copy of an earlier work from about 3000 B.C. The Ebers papyrus provides another perspective on treatment. It covers internal medicine and the circulatory system but relies more on incantations and magic for explaining and curing diseases that had unknown causes. Although surgical techniques may have been used, they were probably coupled with prayers and the like that reflected the prevailing view of the origin of behavior disorders, to which we now turn.

Demonology, Gods, and Magic

References to abnormal behavior in the early writings of the Chinese, Egyptians, Hebrews, and Greeks show that they often attributed such behavior to a demon or god who had taken possession of a person. This belief is not surprising if we remember that "good" and "bad" spirits were widely used to explain lightning, thunder, earthquakes, storms, fires, sickness, and many other events that otherwise seemed incomprehensible. It was a simple and logical step to extend this theory to peculiar and incomprehensible behavior as well.

The decision as to whether the "possession" involved good spirits or evil spirits usually depended on an individual's symptoms. If a person's speech or behavior appeared to have a religious or mystical significance, it was usually thought that he or she was possessed by a good spirit or god. Such people were often treated with considerable awe and respect, for it was thought that they had supernatural powers.

Most possessions, however, were considered to be the work of an angry god or an evil spirit, particularly when a person became excited or overactive and engaged in behavior contrary to religious teachings. Among the ancient Hebrews, for example, such possessions were thought to represent the wrath and punishment of God. Moses is quoted in the Bible as saying, "The Lord shall smite thee with madness." Apparently this punishment was thought to involve the withdrawal of God's protection and the abandonment of the person to the forces of evil. In such cases, every effort was made to rid the person of the evil spirit. Jesus reportedly cured a man with an "unclean spirit" by transferring the devils that plagued him to a herd of swine who, in turn, became possessed and "ran violently down a steep place into the sea" (Mark 5:1–13).

The primary type of treatment for demonic possession was **exorcism,** which included various techniques for casting an evil spirit out of an afflicted person. These techniques varied considerably but typically included magic, prayer, incantation, noise-making, and the use of various horrible-tasting concoctions, such as purgatives made from sheep's dung and wine. More severe measures, such as starving or flogging, were sometimes used in extreme cases to make the body of a possessed person such an unpleasant place that an evil spirit would be driven out. We will look more closely at exorcism as a treatment in the Middle Ages later in this chapter. The continuing popularity of movies and books on possession and exorcism suggests, and recent newspaper accounts of animal sacrifices and witchcraft preoccupation confirm, that these primitive ideas still have appeal even today.

Exorcism was originally the task of shamans, but it was eventually taken over in Egypt and Greece by priests, who apparently served as holy people, physicians, psychologists, and magicians. Many of their cures remained based in magical rites. Although these priests typically believed in demonology and used established exorcistic practices, many of them began to treat people with mental disturbances in a more humane way. For example, in the temples of the god Asclepius in ancient Greece, the priests had patients sleep in the temple. Supposedly, the dreams they had there would reveal what they needed to do to get better. The priests supplemented prayer and incantation with kindness, suggestion, and recreational measures, such as plays, riding, walking, and harmonious music.

Early Philosophical and Medical Concepts

The Greek temples of healing ushered in the Golden Age of Greece under the Athenian leader Pericles (461–429 B.C.). During this time, considerable progress was made in the understanding and treatment of mental disorders. Interestingly, this progress was made in spite of the fact that Greeks of this time considered the human body sacred and thus little could be learned of human anatomy or physiology. During this period the Greek physician Hippocrates (460–377 B.C.), often referred to as the father of modern medicine, received his training and made substantial contributions to the field.

Hippocrates Hippocrates denied that deities and demons intervened in the development of illnesses and insisted that mental disorders had natural causes and required treatments like other diseases. His position was unequivocal: "For my own part, I do not believe that the human body is ever befouled by a God" (in Lewis, 1941, p. 37). Hippocrates believed that the brain was the central organ of intellectual activity and that mental disorders were due to brain pathology. He also emphasized the importance of heredity and predisposition and pointed out that injuries to the head could cause sensory and motor disorders.

Hippocrates classified all mental disorders into three general categories—mania, melancholia, and phrenitis (brain fever)—and gave detailed clinical descriptions of the specific disorders included in each category. He relied heavily on clinical observation, and his descriptions, which were based on daily clinical records of his patients, were surprisingly thorough. Hippocrates considered dreams to be important in understanding a patient's personality. On this point, he not only elaborated on the thinking set forth by the priests in the temples of Asclepius, but also was a harbinger of a basic concept of modern psychodynamic psychotherapy.

The treatments advocated by Hippocrates were far in advance of the exorcistic practices then prevalent. For the treatment of melancholia, for example, he prescribed a regular and tranquil life, sobriety and abstinence from all excesses, a vegetable diet, celibacy, exercise short of fatigue, and bleeding if indicated. He also believed in the importance of the

Hippocrates' (460–377 B.C.) belief that mental disease was the result of natural causes and brain pathology was revolutionary for its time.

environment and often removed his patients from their families.

Hippocrates' emphasis on the natural causes of diseases, clinical observation, and brain pathology as the root of mental disorders was truly revolutionary. Like his contemporaries, however, Hippocrates had little knowledge of physiology and could still be far from the truth. He wrongly believed that hysteria (the appearance of physical illness in the absence of organic pathology) was restricted to women and was caused by the uterus wandering to various parts of the body, pining for children. For this "disease," Hippocrates recommended marriage as the best remedy. He also wrongly believed in the existence of four bodily fluids or *humors*—blood, black bile, yellow bile, and phlegm. In his work *On Sacred Disease,* he stated that when the humors were adversely mixed or otherwise disturbed, physical or mental disease resulted: "Depravement of the brain arises from phlegm and bile; those made from phlegm are quiet, depressed and oblivious; those from bile excited, noisy and mischievous" (in Lewis, 1941, p. 37). Although the concept of humors went far beyond demonology, it was too crude physiologically to be of much therapeutic value. Yet in its emphasis on the importance of bodily balances to mental health, it may be seen as a precursor of today's focus on the need for biochemical balances to maintain normal brain functioning and good health.

Plato and Aristotle The problem of dealing with mentally disturbed individuals who have committed criminal acts was studied by the Greek philosopher Plato (429–347 B.C.). He wrote that such persons were in some "obvious" sense not responsible for their acts and should not receive punishment in the same way as normal persons: ". . . someone may commit an act when mad or afflicted with disease. . . . [If so,] let him pay simply for the damage; and let him be exempt from other punishment." Plato also made provision for mental cases to be cared for in the community as follows: "If anyone is insane, let him not be seen openly in the city, but let the relatives of such a person watch over him in the best manner they know of; and if they are negligent, let them pay a fine. . . " (Plato, n.d., p. 56). In making these humane suggestions, Plato was addressing issues with which we are still grappling today—for example, the issue of insanity as a legal defense. **Insanity** is a legal term for mental disorder that implies a lack of understanding as required by law and therefore a lack of responsibility for one's acts and an inability to manage one's affairs. Even today the question of whether a person's mental condition at the time of a crime is relevant to a legal defense is widely debated. (We will return to this issue in Chapter 18.)

In addition to his emphasis on the humane treatment of the mentally disturbed, Plato contributed to a better understanding of human behavior by pointing out that all forms of life, human included, were motivated by physiological needs, or "natural appetites." He viewed psychological phenomena as responses of the whole organism, reflecting its internal state. He also seems to have anticipated Freud's insight into the functions of fantasies and dreams as substitute satisfactions. He concluded that in dreams, a person could satisfy desires through imagery because the higher faculties no longer inhibited the "passions." In his *Republic,* Plato emphasized the importance of individual differences in intellectual and other abilities, pointing to the role of sociocultural influences in shaping thinking and behavior. He also included a provision for "hospital" care for individuals who developed beliefs that were contrary to the broader social order. These antagonistic individuals would be removed and housed separately so that their minds could be altered. They would have periodic conversations analogous to psychotherapy to promote the health of their souls

(Milns, 1986). Despite these modern ideas, however, Plato shared the belief of his time that mental disorders were in part divinely caused.

The celebrated Greek philosopher Aristotle (384–322 B.C.), who was a pupil of Plato, wrote extensively on mental disorders. Among his most lasting contributions to psychology are his descriptions of consciousness. He, too, anticipated Freud in his view of "thinking" as directed striving toward the elimination of pain and the attainment of pleasure. On the question of whether mental disorders could be caused by psychological factors such as frustration and conflict, Aristotle discussed the possibility and rejected it; his lead on this issue was widely followed. Aristotle generally believed the Hippocratic theory of disturbances in the bile. For example, he thought that very hot bile generated amorous desires, verbal fluency, and suicidal impulses.

Later Greek and Roman Thought Hippocrates' work was continued by some of the later Greek and Roman physicians. Particularly in Alexandria, Egypt (which became a center of Greek culture after its founding in 332 B.C. by Alexander the Great), medical practices developed to a high level, and the temples dedicated to Saturn were first-rate sanatoriums. Pleasant surroundings were considered of great therapeutic value for mental patients, who were provided with constant activities, including parties, dances, walks in the temple gardens, rowing along the Nile, and musical concerts. Physicians of this time also used a wide range of therapeutic measures, including dieting, massage, hydrotherapy, gymnastics, and education, as well as some less desirable practices, such as bleeding, purging, and mechanical restraints.

One of the most influential Greek physicians was Galen (A.D. 130–200), who practiced in Rome. Although he elaborated on the Hippocratic tradition, he did not contribute much that was new to the treatment or clinical descriptions of mental disorders. Rather, he made a number of original contributions concerning the anatomy of the nervous system. (These findings were based on dissections of animals because human autopsies were still not allowed.) Galen also maintained a scientific approach to the field, dividing the causes of psychological disorders into physical and mental categories. Among the causes he named were injuries to the head, alcoholic excess, shock, fear, adolescence, menstrual changes, economic reverses, and disappointment in love.

Roman medicine reflected the characteristic pragmatism of the Roman people. Roman physicians wanted to make their patients comfortable and thus

Galen (A.D. 130–200) believed that psychological disorders could have either physical causes, such as injuries to the head, or mental causes, such as disappointment in love.

Islamic physician Avicenna (980–1037) approached the treatment of mental disorder with humane practices unknown to Western medical practitioners of the time.

used pleasant physical therapies, such as warm baths and massage. They also followed the principle of *contrariis contrarius* (opposite by opposite)—for example, having their patients drink chilled wine while they were in a warm tub.

Although historians generally consider the fall of Rome at the end of the fifth century to be the dividing line between ancient and medieval times, the "Dark Ages" in the history of abnormal psychology began much earlier, with Galen's death in A.D. 200. The contributions of Hippocrates and the later Greek and Roman physicians were soon lost in the welter of popular superstition, and though some exceptions can be found, most of the physicians of Rome returned to some sort of belief in demonology as an underlying factor in abnormal behavior.

Views During the Middle Ages

In Islamic countries of the Middle East during medieval times, the more scientific aspects of Greek medicine survived. The first mental hospital was established in Baghdad in 792 A.D.; it was soon followed by others in Damascus and Aleppo (Polvan, 1969). In these hospitals, the mentally disturbed in-

dividuals received humane treatment. The outstanding figure in Islamic medicine was Avicenna (c. A.D. 980–1037), called the "prince of physicians" (Campbell, 1926) and author of *The Canon of Medicine,* perhaps the most widely studied medical work ever written. In his writings, Avicenna frequently referred to hysteria, epilepsy, manic reactions, and melancholia. The following story shows his unique approach to the treatment of a young prince suffering from a mental disorder:

> A certain prince was afflicted with melancholia, and suffered from the delusion that he was a cow . . . he would low like a cow, causing annoyance to everyone, . . . crying "Kill me so that a good stew may be made of my flesh," finally . . . he would eat nothing. . . . Avicenna was persuaded to take the case. . . . First of all he sent a message to the patient bidding him be of good cheer because the butcher was coming to slaughter him, whereat . . . the sick man rejoiced. Some time afterwards Avicenna, holding a knife in his hand, entered the sickroom saying, "Where is this cow that I may kill it?" The patient lowed like a cow to indicate where he was. By Avicenna's orders he was laid on the ground bound hand and foot. Avicenna then felt him all over and said, "He is too lean, and not ready to be killed; he

must be fattened." Then they offered him suitable food of which he now partook eagerly, and gradually he gained strength, got rid of his delusion, and was completely cured. (Browne, 1921, pp. 88–89)

Unfortunately, most Western medical practitioners of Avicenna's time dealt with mental patients in a far different way. The advances made by the thinkers of antiquity had little impact on the ways most people approached abnormal behavior.

During the Middle Ages in Europe (about A.D. 500–1500), scientific inquiry into abnormal behavior was limited, and the treatment of psychologically disturbed individuals was more often characterized by ritual or superstition than by attempts to understand an individual's condition. In contrast to Avicenna's era in the Islamic countries of the Middle East or to the period of enlightenment during the seventeenth and eighteenth centuries, the Middle Ages in Europe can largely be characterized as void with respect to scientific thinking and the humane

treatment of the mentally disturbed. A similar sequence of events occurred in other parts of the world, as can be seen in HIGHLIGHT 2.1.

Mental disorders were quite prevalent throughout the Middle Ages in Europe, especially so toward the end of the period, when medieval institutions, social structures, and beliefs began to change drastically. During this time, supernatural explanations of the causes of mental illness grew in popularity. Within this environment, it obviously was difficult to make great strides in the understanding and treatment of abnormal behavior. However, as Schoeneman (1984) puts it, "Demonology did not triumph as a theory of insanity, but coexisted with naturalistic etiologies and treatments derived from Galenic humoural theory and folk medicine" (p. 301). Although the influence of theology was growing rapidly, "sin" was not always cited as a causal factor in mental illness. For example, Kroll and Bachrach (1984) examined 57 episodes of mental illness, ranging from madness and possession to alcohol and

HIGHLIGHT 2.1

Early Views of Mental Disorders in China

Tseng (1973) traced the development of Chinese concepts of different mental disorders by reviewing their descriptions and recommended treatments in historical medical documents. For example, the following passage is taken from an ancient Chinese medical text supposedly written by Huang Ti (c. 2674 B.C.), the third legendary emperor. Historians now believe that the text was written at a later date, possibly during the seventh century B.C.:

The person suffering from excited insanity initially feels sad, eating and sleeping less; he then becomes grandiose, feeling that he is very smart and noble, talking and scolding day and night, singing, behaving strangely, seeing strange things, hearing strange voices, believing that he can see the devil or gods. . . . (p. 570)

Even at this early date, Chinese medicine was based on a belief in

natural rather than supernatural causes for illnesses. For example, in the concept of Yin and Yang, the human body, like the cosmos, is divided into positive and negative forces that both complement and contradict each other. If the two forces are balanced, the result is physical and mental health; if they are not, illness will result. Thus treatments focused on restoring balance: "As treatment for such an excited condition withholding food was suggested, since food was considered to be the source of positive force and the patient was thought to be in need of a decrease in such force" (p. 570).

Chinese medicine reached a relatively sophisticated level during the second century, and Chung Ching, who has been called the Hippocrates of China, wrote two well-known medical works around A.D. 200. Like Hippocrates, he based his views of physical and mental disorders on

clinical observations, and he implicated organ pathologies as primary causes. However, he also believed that stressful psychological conditions could cause organ pathologies, and his treatments, like those of Hippocrates, utilized both drugs and the regaining of emotional balance through appropriate activities.

As in the West, Chinese views of mental disorders regressed to a belief in supernatural forces as causal agents. From the later part of the second century through the early part of the ninth century, ghosts and devils were implicated in "ghost-evil" insanity, which presumably resulted from possession by evil spirits. The "Dark Ages" in China, however, were not as severe—in terms of the treatment of mental patients—nor as long lasting as in the West. A return to biological, somatic (bodily) views and an emphasis on psychosocial factors occurred in the centuries that followed.

epilepsy. They found sin implicated in only 9 cases (16 percent).

To understand better this elusive period of history, let us look at two events of the times—mass madness and exorcism—to see how they relate to views of abnormal behavior.

Mass Madness During the last half of the Middle Ages in Europe, a peculiar trend emerged in abnormal behavior. It involved the widespread occurrence of group behavior disorders that were apparently cases of hysteria. Whole groups of people were affected simultaneously.

Dancing manias (epidemics of raving, jumping, dancing, and convulsions) were reported as early as the tenth century. One such episode, occurring in Italy early in the thirteenth century, was recorded by physicians of the time whose records were reviewed by medical historian H. E. Sigerist. He wrote the following:

> [It] occurred at the height of the summer heat. . . . People, asleep or awake, would suddenly jump up, feeling an acute pain like the sting of a bee. Some saw the spider, others did not, but they knew that it must be the tarantula. They ran out of the house into the street, to the market place, dancing in great excitement. Soon they were joined by others who like them had been bitten, or by people who had been stung in previous years. . . .
>
> Thus groups of patients would gather, dancing wildly in the queerest attire. . . . Others would tear their clothes and show their nakedness, losing all sense of modesty. . . . Some called for swords and acted like fencers, others for whips and beat each other. . . . Some of them had still stranger fancies, liked to be tossed in the air, dug holes in the ground, and rolled themselves into the dirt like swine. They all drank wine plentifully and sang and talked like drunken people. . . . (1943, pp. 103, 106–107)

Known as **tarantism** in Italy, this dancing mania later spread to Germany and the rest of Europe, where it was known as **St. Vitus's dance.** The behavior was similar to the ancient orgiastic rites by which people had worshiped the Greek god Dionysus. These rites had been banned with the advent of Christianity, but they were deeply embedded in the culture and were apparently kept alive in secret gatherings (which probably led to considerable guilt and conflict). Then, with time, the meaning of the dances changed. The old rites reappeared, but they were attributed to symptoms of the tarantula's bite. The participants were no longer sinners but the unwilling victims of the tarantula's spirit. The dancing became the "cure" and is the source of the dance we know today as the *tarantella.*

This fifteenth-century engraving shows peasant women overcome by St. Vitus's dance.

Isolated rural areas were also afflicted with outbreaks of **lycanthropy**—a condition in which people believed themselves to be possessed by wolves and imitated their behavior. In 1541 a case was reported in which a lycanthrope told his captors, in confidence, that he was really a wolf but that his skin was smooth on the surface because all the hairs were on the inside (Stone, 1937). To cure him of his delusions, his extremities were amputated, following which he died, still uncured.

Mass madness occurred periodically into the seventeenth century but apparently reached its peak during the fourteenth and fifteenth centuries—a period noted for oppression, famine, and pestilence. During this period, Europe was ravaged by a plague known as the Black Death, which killed millions (some estimates say 50 percent of the population of Europe died) and severely disrupted social organization. Undoubtedly, many of the peculiar cases of mass madness were related to the depression, fear, and wild mysticism engendered by the terrible events of this period. People simply could not believe that frightening catastrophes such as the Black Death could have natural causes and thus could be within our power to control, prevent, or even create.

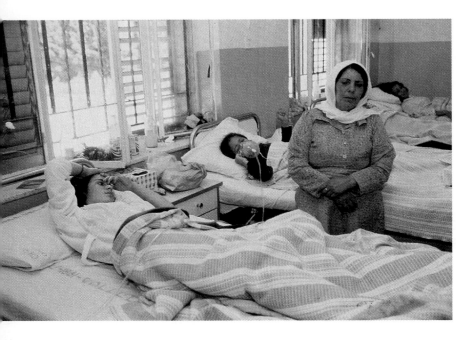

Mass disorders seem to occur during periods of widespread public fear and stress, such as that felt by these West Bank Palestinian schoolgirls, who developed the same mysterious physical symptoms in April 1983. Although Arab leaders at first suspected the girls had been the victims of an Israeli poison plot, it was later thought that psychological factors had played an important role in the appearance of their symptoms.

So-called mass hysteria occasionally occurs today; the affliction usually mimics some type of physical disorder, such as fainting spells or convulsive movements. In 1982, after a nationwide story about some Chicago-area residents poisoned by Tylenol capsules, California health officials reported a sudden wave of illness among some 200 people who drank soda at a high school football game. No objective cause for the illness could be found, and officials speculated that most sufferers had been experiencing a kind of mass hysteria related to the Tylenol incident (United Press International, 1982). Another case of apparent mass hysteria occurred among hundreds of West Bank Palestinian girls in April 1983. This episode threatened to have serious political repercussions because some Arab and Israeli leaders initially thought that the girls had been poisoned by Israelis; health officials later concluded that psychological factors had played a key role in most of the cases. As in many such instances, the initial failure to control inflammatory reactions to the incident was due to a communications breakdown (Hefez, 1985; *Time,* April 18, 1983, p. 52).

Exorcism In the Middle Ages in Europe, management of the mentally disturbed was left largely to the clergy. Monasteries served as refuges and places of confinement. During the early part of the medieval period, the mentally disturbed were, for the most part, treated with considerable kindness. "Treatment" consisted of prayer, holy water, sanctified ointments, the breath or spittle of the priests, the touching of relics, visits to holy places, and mild forms of exorcism. In some monasteries and shrines, exorcisms were performed by the gentle "laying on of hands." Such methods were often joined with vaguely understood medical treatments derived mainly from Galen, which gave rise to prescriptions such as the following: "For a fiend-sick man: When a devil possesses a man, or controls him from within with disease, a spewdrink of lupin, bishopswort, henbane, garlic. Pound these together, add ale and holy water" (Cockayne, 1864–1866).

As exorcistic techniques became more fully developed, emphasis was placed on Satan's pride, which was believed to have led to his original downfall. Hence, in treating persons possessed by a devil, the first goal was to strike a fatal blow to the devil's pride—to insult him. This strategy involved calling the devil some of the most obscene epithets that imagination could devise, and the insults were usually supplemented by long litanies of cursing.

This procedure was considered highly successful in the treatment of possessed persons. A certain bishop of Beauvais in France claimed to have rid a person of five devils, all of whom signed an agreement stating that they and their subordinate imps would no longer persecute the possessed individual (White, 1896).

Interestingly, there has been a resurgence of superstition in contemporary society. Today one can find those who believe that supernatural forces cause psychological problems and that "cures" should involve exorcism to rid people of unwanted

As the notion spread in the Middle Ages that madness was caused by Satanic possession, exorcism became the treatment of choice.

characteristics or "spells." Occasionally exorcism is still practiced.

Witchcraft and Mental Illness: Fact or Fiction?

Fifteenth- and sixteenth-century Europe witnessed extensive witch-hunts in which many people (primarily women) were accused of and punished for deviating from the Christian faith. Possessed people were supposed to have made a pact with the devil, consummated by signing in blood a book presented to them by Satan, which gave them certain supernatural powers. It was believed that these people could cause pestilence, storms, floods, sexual impotence, and injuries to their enemies; could turn milk sour; and could rise through the air, ruin crops, and turn themselves into animals. In short, they were witches.

These beliefs were not confined to simple peasants but were held and elaborated on by most of the important clergy of the period. No less a man than Martin Luther (1483–1546), the German leader of the Protestant Reformation, came to the following conclusions:

> The greatest punishment God can inflict on the wicked . . . is to deliver them over to Satan, who with God's permission, kills them or makes them to undergo great calamities. Many devils are in woods, water, wildernesses, etc., ready to hurt and preju-

dice people. When these things happen, then the philosophers and physicians say it is natural, ascribing it to the planets.

> [People] are possessed by the devil in two ways; corporally or spiritually. Those whom he possesses corporally, as mad people, he has permission from God to vex and agitate, but he has no power over their souls. (*Colloquia Mensalia* [Table Talk])

It has long been thought that during this period, many mentally disturbed people were accused of being witches and thus were punished and often killed (e.g., Zilboorg & Henry, 1941). But more recent interpretations have questioned the extent to which this situation was so. Schoeneman (1984), for example, in a review of the literature, points out that "the typical accused witch was not a mentally ill person but an impoverished woman with a sharp tongue and a bad temper. . . " (p. 301). He goes on to say that "witchcraft was, in fact, never considered a variety of possession either by witch hunters, the general populace, or modern historians. . . " (p. 306). To say "never" may be overstating the case; clearly, some mentally ill people were punished as witches. Otherwise, as you will see in the next section, why did some physicians and thinkers go to great lengths to expose the fallacies of the connection? In the case of witchcraft and mental illness, the confusion may be due, in part, to a confusion about demonic possession. As can be seen in the quote from Luther's *Colloquia Mensalia*, there were two types of demonically possessed people—those corporally possessed were considered mad; those spiritually possessed were likely considered witches. With time, the distinctions between these two categories may have blurred in the eyes of historians, thus resulting in a less-than-accurate perception that witchcraft and mental illness were connected more frequently than was the case.

The changing view of the relationship between witchcraft and mental illness points up an even broader issue—the difficulties of interpreting historical events accurately. We will discuss this issue in more depth in the "Unresolved Issues" section at the end of the chapter.

THE GROWTH TOWARD HUMANITARIAN APPROACHES

During the latter part of the Middle Ages and the early Renaissance, scientific questioning reemerged and a movement emphasizing the importance of specifically human interests and concerns began—a movement (still with us today) that can be loosely referred to as *humanism*. Consequently, the superstitious beliefs that had retarded the understanding and therapeutic treatment of mental disorders began to be challenged.

The Resurgence of Scientific Questioning in Europe

Paracelsus, a Swiss physician (1490–1541), was an early critic of superstitious beliefs about possession. He insisted that the dancing mania was not a possession but a form of disease, and that it should be treated as such. He also postulated a conflict between the instinctual and spiritual nature of human beings, formulated the idea of psychic causes for mental illness, and advocated treatment by "bodily magnetism," later called hypnosis (Mora, 1967). Although Paracelsus rejected demonology, his view of abnormal behavior was colored by his belief in astral influences (lunatic is derived from the Latin word *luna* or "moon"). He was convinced that the moon exercised a supernatural influence over the brain—an idea, incidentally, that persists among some people today. Paracelsus defied the medical and theological traditions of his time; he often burned the works of Galen and others of whom he disapproved. Had he been more restrained and diplomatic in his efforts, he might have exerted more influence over the scientific thinking of his day. Instead, he became known more for his arrogance than for his scientific advances.

During the sixteenth century, Teresa of Avila, a Spanish nun who was later canonized, made an extraordinary conceptual leap that has influenced thinking to the present day. Teresa, in charge of a group of cloistered nuns who had become hysterical and were therefore in danger from the Spanish Inquisition, argued convincingly that her nuns were not possessed but rather were "as if sick" (*comas enfermas*). Apparently, she did not mean that they were sick of body. Rather, in the expression "as if," we have what is perhaps the first suggestion that a mind can be ill just as a body can be ill. It was a momentous suggestion, which apparently began as a kind of metaphor but was, with time, accepted as fact: People came to see mental illness as an entity, and the "as if" dropped out of use (Sarbin & Juhasz, 1967).

Johann Weyer (1515–1588), a German physician and writer who wrote under the Latin name of Joannus Wierus, was so deeply disturbed by the imprisonment, torture, and burning of people accused of witchcraft that he made a careful study of the entire

Teresa of Avila, a sixteenth-century Spanish nun, had a major influence on the conception of mental illness in her era when she insisted that the hysterical nuns in her care were not possessed, but were "as if sick." This argument paved the way for the view that the mind can be sick like the body.

problem. About 1563 he published a book, *The Deception of Demons*, which contains a step-by-step rebuttal of the *Malleus maleficarum*, a witch-hunting handbook published in 1486 for use in recognizing and dealing with those suspected of being witches. In his book, Weyer argued that a considerable number, if not all, of those imprisoned, tortured, and burned for witchcraft were really sick in mind or body, and consequently that great wrongs were being committed against innocent people. Weyer's work received the approval of a few outstanding physicians and theologians of his time. Mostly, however, it met with vehement protest and condemnation.

Weyer was one of the first physicians to specialize in mental disorders, and his wide experience and progressive views justify his reputation as the founder of modern psychopathology. Unfortunately, however, he was too far ahead of his time. He was scorned by his peers, many of whom called him

"Weirus Hereticus" and "Weirus Insanus." His works were banned by the Church and remained so until the twentieth century.

Perhaps there is no better illustration of the developing spirit of scientific skepticism in the sixteenth century than the works of the Oxford-educated Reginald Scot (1538–1599). Scot devoted his life to exposing the fallacies of witchcraft and demonology. In his book *Discovery of Witchcraft,* published in 1584, he convincingly and daringly denied the existence of demons, devils, and evil spirits as the cause of mental disorders:

> These women are but diseased wretches suffering from melancholy, and their words, actions, reasoning, and gestures show that sickness has affected their brains and impaired their powers of judgment. You must know that the effects of sickness on men, and still more on women, are almost unbelievable. Some of these persons imagine, confess, and maintain that they are witches and are capable of performing extraordinary miracles through the arts of witchcraft; others, due to the same mental disorder, imagine strange and impossible things which they claim to have witnessed. (In Castiglioni, 1946, p. 253)

King James I of England, however, came to the rescue of demonology, personally refuted Scot's thesis, and ordered his book seized and burned.

The clergy, however, were beginning to question the practices of the time. For example, St. Vincent de Paul (1576–1660), at the risk of his life, declared: "Mental disease is no different to bodily disease and Christianity demands of the humane and powerful to protect, and the skillful to relieve the one as well as the other."

In the face of such persistent advocates of science, who continued their testimonies throughout the next two centuries, demonology and superstition gave ground. These advocates gradually paved the way for the return of observation and reason, which culminated in the development of modern experimental and clinical approaches.

The Establishment of Early Asylums and Shrines

From the sixteenth century on, special institutions called **asylums,** meant solely for the care of the mentally ill, grew in number. The early asylums were begun as a way of removing from society troublesome individuals who could not care for themselves. Although scientific inquiry into understanding abnormal behavior was on the increase, most early asylums, often referred to as madhouses, were not much better than concentration camps. The unfortunate residents lived and died amid conditions of incredible filth and cruelty.

Early Asylums In 1547 the monastery of St. Mary of Bethlehem at London was officially made into an asylum by Henry VIII. Its name soon was contracted to Bedlam, and it became widely known for its deplorable conditions and practices. The more violent patients were exhibited to the public for one penny a look, and the more harmless inmates were forced to seek charity on the streets of London in the manner described by Shakespeare: "Bedlam beggars, who, with roaring voices . . . Sometimes with lunatic bans, sometime with prayers enforce their charity" (*King Lear,* Act II, Scene iii).

Such asylums for the mentally ill were gradually established in other countries. The San Hipolito, established in Mexico in 1566 by philanthropist Bernardino Alvares, was the first asylum established in the Americas. The first such hospital in France, La Maison de Charenton, was founded in 1641 in a suburb of Paris. An asylum was established in Moscow in 1764, and the notorious Lunatics' Tower in Vienna was constructed in 1784. This structure was a showplace in Old Vienna, an ornately decorated round tower within which were square rooms. The doctors and "keepers" lived in the square rooms, while the patients were confined in the spaces between the walls of the rooms and the outside of the tower. The patients were put on exhibit to the public for a small fee.

These early asylums were primarily modifications of penal institutions, and the inmates were treated more like beasts than like human beings. The following passage describes the treatment of the chronically insane in La Bicêtre, a hospital in Paris. This treatment was typical of the asylums of the period and continued through most of the eighteenth century.

> The patients were ordinarily shackled to the walls of their dark, unlighted cells by iron collars which held them flat against the wall and permitted little movement. Ofttimes there were also iron hoops around the waists of the patients and both their hands and feet were chained. Although these chains usually permitted enough movement that the patients could feed themselves out of bowls, they often kept them from being able to lie down at night. Since little was known about nutrition, and the patients were presumed to be animals anyway, little attention was paid to whether they were adequately fed or to whether the food was good or bad. The cells were furnished only with straw and were never swept or cleaned; the patient remained in the midst of all the

accumulated odor. No one visited the cells except at feeding time, no provision was made for warmth, and even the most elementary gestures of humanity were lacking. (Modified from Selling, 1943, pp. 54–55)

In the United States, the Pennsylvania Hospital at Philadelphia, completed under the guidance of Benjamin Franklin in 1756, provided some cells or wards for mental patients. The Public Hospital in Williamsburg, Virginia, constructed in 1773, was the first hospital in the United States devoted exclusively to mental patients. The treatment of mental patients in the United States was no better than that offered by European institutions. Zwelling's (1985) review of Public Hospital's treatment methods shows that, initially, the philosophy of treatment involved the view that patients needed to choose rationality over insanity. Thus the treatment techniques were aggressive, aimed at restoring a "physical balance in the body and brain." These techniques were designed to intimidate patients. They included powerful drugs, water treatments, bleeding and blistering, electrical shocks, and physical restraints. For example, a violent patient might be plunged into ice water or a listless patient into hot water; frenzied patients might be administered drugs to exhaust them; or any patient might be bled in order to drain their system of "harmful" fluids. Early estimates of the cure rate for patients at the hospital were only about 20 percent.

Even as late as 1830, new patients had their heads shaved, were dressed in straitjackets, put on sparse diets, compelled to swallow some active purgative, and placed in dark cells. If these procedures did not quiet unruly or excited patients, more severe measures, such as starvation, solitary confinement, cold baths, and other torture-like methods, were used (Bennett, 1947).

The Geel Shrine There were a few bright spots in this otherwise bleak situation. Out of the more humane Christian tradition of prayer, laying on of hands (or holy touch), and visits to shrines, there arose several great shrines where treatment by kindness and love stood out in marked contrast to prevailing conditions. The shrine at Geel in Belgium, visited since the thirteenth century, is probably the most famous. Legend has it that hidden in the forest of Geel is the body of a young princess who, upon the death of her mother, had dedicated her life to the poor and mentally disturbed. She was later slain by her incestuous father. Years later, five lunatics who spent the night in the forest recovered their mental health. Villagers believed that the princess, reincar-

nated as St. Dymphna, was responsible for the cures. Pilgrimages to Geel were organized for the mentally sick; many of the patients stayed on to live with the local inhabitants (Karnesh & Zucker, 1945). The colony of Geel has continued its work into modern times (Aring, 1974, 1975a; Belgian Consulate, 1994). Today, a new psychiatric hospital has been built in Geel, and nearly 1000 mental patients live in private homes with "foster families," work in community-based centers, and suffer few restrictions other than not drinking alcohol. Many types of mental disorders are represented, including schizophrenia, mood disorder, antisocial personality, and mental retardation. Ordinarily, patients remain in Geel until they are considered recovered by a supervising therapist. It is unfortunate that the great humanitarian work of this colony—and the opportunity it affords to study the treatment of patients in a family and community setting—has received so little recognition.

Humanitarian Reform

Clearly, by the late eighteenth century, most mental hospitals in Europe and America were in great need of reform. The humanitarian treatment of patients received great impetus from the work of Philippe Pinel (1745–1826) in France.

Pinel's Experiment In 1792, shortly after the first phase of the French Revolution, Pinel was placed in charge of La Bicêtre in Paris. In this capacity, he received the grudging permission of the Revolutionary Commune to remove the chains from some of the inmates as an experiment to test his views that mental patients should be treated with

Geel, a city in Belgium, known for its humane care of the mentally ill in a homelike setting.

kindness and consideration—as sick people and not as vicious beasts or criminals. Had his experiment proved a failure, Pinel might have lost his head, but fortunately it was a great success. Chains were removed; sunny rooms were provided; patients were permitted to exercise on the hospital grounds; and kindness was extended to these poor beings, some of whom had been chained in dungeons for 30 years or more. The effect was almost miraculous. The previous noise, filth, and abuse were replaced by order and peace. As Pinel said: "The whole discipline was marked with regularity and kindness which had the most favorable effect on the insane themselves, rendering even the most furious more tractable" (Selling, 1943, p. 65).

Interestingly, a newly discovered historical document, found in the French Archives, raises some question about the beginning of humanitarian reforms in France. The document provided by Jean-Baptiste Pussin (Pinel's predecessor at the Bicêtre) indicated that he had been the head of the hospital beginning in 1784 and had removed some of the chains from patients and employed more humane straitjackets instead. He also pointed out in the document that he had issued orders forbidding the staff from beating patients (Weiner, 1979).

Regardless of whether Pussin or Pinel began the reform at the Bicêtre, Pinel is nevertheless given the credit for carrying out the extensive humanitarian effort (Reisman, 1991). The reactions of these patients when all their chains were removed for the first time was telling. One patient, an English officer who had years before killed a guard in an attack of fury, tottered outside on legs weak from lack of use, and for the first time in some 40 years saw the sun and sky. With tears in his eyes he exclaimed, "Oh, how beautiful!" (Zilboorg & Henry, 1941, p. 323). When night came, he voluntarily returned to his cell, which had been cleaned during his absence, to fall peacefully asleep on his new bed. After two years of orderly behavior, including helping to handle other patients, he was pronounced recovered and permitted to leave the hospital. Pinel himself was once saved from a mob that accused him of antirevolutionary activities by a soldier whom he had freed from asylum chains.

Pinel was later given charge of La Salpêtrière hospital, where the same reorganization was instituted with similar results. La Bicêtre and La Salpêtrière hospitals thus became the first modern hospitals for the care of the insane. Pinel's successor, Jean Esquirol (1772–1840), continued Pinel's good work at La Salpêtrière and, in addition, helped establish ten new mental hospitals. Incidentally, in his classic textbook *Mental Maladies,* Esquirol attributes the origin of the humane treatment at La Bicêtre to Pinel and makes no mention of Pussin as having initiated reforms

. . . but Pinel made himself master of it, and changed the lot of the insane. The chains were broken, the insane were treated with humanity, hope gained hearts, and a more rational system of therapeutics, directed to the treatment. (1845, p. 10)

This painting shows Philippe Pinel supervising the unchaining of inmates at La Bicêtre hospital. Pinel's experiment represented both a great reform and a major step in devising humanitarian methods of treating mental disorders.

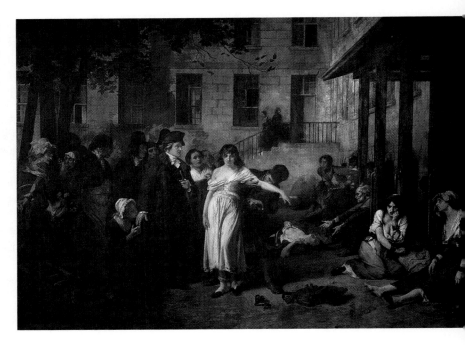

Viewed from a contemporary perspective the scene depicted in this nineteenth-century drawing appears inhumane and degrading. However, hydrotherapy treatment, as shown here at St. Anne's Hospital in Paris in 1868, was considered a standard treatment method.

These hospitals put France in the forefront of humane treatment for the mentally disturbed and "signalled the end of the indiscriminate mixture of paupers and criminals, the physically sick, and the mentally deranged" (Rosenblatt, 1984, p. 246).

Tuke's Work in England   At about the same time that Pinel was reforming La Bicêtre, an English Quaker named William Tuke (1732–1822) established the York Retreat, a pleasant country house where mental patients lived, worked, and rested in a kindly religious atmosphere (Narby, 1982). This retreat represented the culmination of a noble battle against the brutality, ignorance, and indifference of his time. Some insight into the difficulties and discouragements he encountered may be gleaned from a simple statement he made in a letter regarding his early efforts: "All men seem to desert me." This statement is not surprising when we remember that the belief in demonology was still widespread and that as late as 1768 Protestant leader John Wesley declared that "the giving up of witchcraft is in effect the giving up of the Bible." The belief in demonology was too strong to be conquered overnight.

As word of Pinel's amazing results spread to England, Tuke's small force of Quakers gradually gained support from John Connolly, Samuel Hitch, and other great English medical psychologists. In 1841 Hitch introduced trained nurses into the wards at the Gloucester Asylum and put trained supervisors at the head of the nursing staffs. These innovations, quite revolutionary at the time, were of great importance not only in improving the care of mental patients but also in changing public attitudes toward the mentally disturbed.

Rush and Moral Management in America   The success of Pinel's and Tuke's humanitarian experiments revolutionized the treatment of mental patients throughout the Western world. In the United States, this revolution was reflected in the work of Benjamin Rush (1745–1813), the founder of American psychiatry, who incidentally had earlier been one of the signers of the Declaration of Independence. While associated with the Pennsylvania Hospital in 1783, Rush encouraged more humane treatment of the mentally ill; wrote the first systematic treatise on psychiatry in America, *Medical Inquiries and Observations upon the Diseases of the Mind* (1812); and was the first American to organize a course in psychiatry. But even he did not escape entirely from established beliefs of his time. His medical theory was tainted with astrology, and his principal remedies were bloodletting and purgatives. In addition, he invented and used a device called "the tranquilizer," which was probably more torturous than tranquil for patients. Despite these limitations, we can consider Rush an important transitional figure between the old era and the new.

During the early part of this period of humanitarian reform, the use of **moral management**—a wide-ranging method of treatment that focused on a patient's social, individual, and occupational needs—became relatively widespread. This approach, which stemmed largely from the work of Pinel and Tuke, began in Europe during the late eighteenth century and in America during the early nineteenth century. As Rees (1957) has described the approach:

> The insane came to be regarded as normal people who had lost their reason as a result of having been exposed to severe psychological and social stresses. These stresses were called the moral causes of insanity, and moral treatment aimed at relieving the patient by friendly association, discussion of his difficulties, and the daily pursuit of purposeful activity; in other words, social therapy, individual therapy, and occupational therapy. (pp. 306–307)

Changes at Williamsburg's Public Hospital reflected this change in attitude. First, the hospital was renamed the Williamsburg Lunatic Asylum to reflect "the view that the mentally ill were innocent victims who required protection from society" (Zwelling,

Benjamin Rush (1745–1813) founded American psychiatry and encouraged more humane treatment of the mentally ill. He was the first American to write a systematic treatise on psychiatry and to organize a course on the subject.

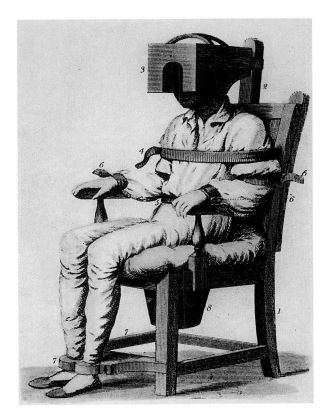

Early engraving depicting a chair similar to the "tranquilizing chair" developed by Benjamin Rush around 1800. An agitated patient was strapped in and then whirled around rapidly until he or she became more docile.

1985, p. 30). Treatment regimens were also changed. There were fewer physical restraints, more open wards, and opportunities to practice positive activities such as farming and carpentry. Social activities, some involving members of the opposite sex, were incorporated into the daily activities of the patients.

Moral treatment in asylums was actually part of a broader movement in which more humane treatment of physical illness in hospitals was being provided for patients, usually people from the poorer classes (Luchins, 1990). (See HIGHLIGHT 2.2.) A great deal more emphasis was placed in both the general hospitals and asylums on the patients' moral and spiritual development and on rehabilitation of their "character" than on their physical or mental disorders, perhaps because very little effective treatment was available for these conditions at the time. The treatment or rehabilitation of the physical or mental disorders was usually through manual labor and spiritual discussion along with humane treatment.

Moral management achieved a high degree of effectiveness—all the more amazing because it was done without the benefit of the antipsychotic drugs used today and because many of the patients were probably suffering from syphilis, the then-incurable disease of the central nervous system. In the 20-year period between 1833 and 1853, Worcester State Hospital's discharge rate for patients who had been ill less than one year before admission was 71 percent. Even for patients with a longer preadmission disorder, the discharge rate was 59 percent (Bockhoven, 1972).

Despite its relative effectiveness, moral management was nearly abandoned by the latter part of the nineteenth century. The reasons were many and varied. Among the more obvious ones were the ethnic and racial prejudice that came with the rising immigrant population, leading to tension between staff and patients; the failure of the movement's leaders to train their own replacements; and the overextension of hospital facilities, reflecting the misguided belief that bigger hospitals would differ from smaller ones only in size.

Two other reasons for the demise of moral management are, in retrospect, truly ironic. One was the rise of the **mental hygiene movement,** which advocated a method of treatment that focused almost ex-

Moral management involved less use of restraint and more positive activities and socializing. This photo from the turn of the century shows male patients taking their leisure. Moral management had profoundly positive effects on a great many patients, and it was certainly a more humanitarian practice than the methods that had preceded it.

clusively on the physical well-being of hospitalized mental patients. Although the creature comforts of patients may have improved under the mental hygienists, the patients received no help for their mental problems and thus were condemned subtly to helplessness and dependency.

Advances in biomedical science also contributed to the demise of moral management and the rise of the mental hygiene movement. These advances fostered the notion that all mental disorders would eventually yield to biological explanations and biologically based treatments (Luchins, 1990). Thus the psychological and social environment of a patient was considered largely irrelevant; the best one could do was keep the patient comfortable until a biological cure was discovered. Needless to say, the anticipated biological cure-all did not arrive, and by the late 1940s and early 1950s discharge rates were down to about 30 percent. We do better today, with discharge rates above 90 percent, but these improved rates are a recent development due to many factors, including advances in drug therapy and a trend to release many patients for continued care in their communities. The fact that the care in the community often does not

meet acceptable standards is an issue we will address in Chapter 18.

Notwithstanding its negative effects on the use of moral management, the mental hygiene movement has accounted for many humanitarian accomplishments.

Dix and the Mental Hygiene Movement Dorothea Dix (1802–1887) was an energetic New England schoolteacher forced into early retirement because of recurring attacks of tuberculosis. In 1841 she began to teach in a women's prison. Through this contact she became acquainted with the deplorable conditions in jails, almshouses, and asylums. In a "Memorial" submitted to the Congress of the United States in 1848, she stated that she had seen

more than 9000 idiots, epileptics and insane in the United States, destitute of appropriate care and protection . . . bound with galling chains, bowed beneath fetters and heavy iron bails attached to drag-chains, lacerated with ropes, scouraged with rods and terrified beneath storms of execration and cruel blows; now subject to jibes and scorn and torturing

Nineteenth Century Views of the Causation and Treatment of Mental Disorders

Most of us hold some views or attitudes, not because we have thought them through carefully or molded them out of our experiences, but because they were imparted to us through family, school, or broader social influences. We are influenced to believe certain things or react in certain ways by broader cultural and societal pressures that remain hidden until long after these influential factors cease to exert their influence. It often takes decades or longer for well-ingrained cultural viewpoints to be amenable to objective interpretation from a different perspective.

Viewed from our contemporary vantage point, for example, well-meaning professionals during the nineteenth century were often quite naive and inaccurate in the ways they conceptualized mental health problems and generally ineffective in their attempts to treat them. Our understanding of the impact of broader cultural influences in understanding nineteenth-century concepts of mental disorder has recently been illuminated by a historical analysis of the period by Janet Oppenheim (1991). In an interesting and informative discussion, Oppenheim provides a view of how Victorian notions of morality influenced doctors' attempts to understand and treat depression during this "socially repressive" period in England's history.

In the early part of the nineteenth century, mental hospitals were controlled essentially by lay persons because of the prominence of moral management in the treatment of "lunatics." Medical professionals, or *alienists* as psychiatrists were called at this time, had a rela-

Cocaine was the active ingredient of a "digestive tonic" promoted as a beauty secret in this late-1800s French poster. While it renders a euphoric state of mind, cocaine can also confer a powerful addiction, paranoid psychosis, and fatal convulsions.

tively inconsequential role in the care of the insane and management of the asylums of the day. Moreover, effective treatments for mental disorders were unavailable, with the only measures being such procedures as drugging, bleeding, or purging, which produced little objective results. However, during the latter part of the century, alienists gained control of the insane asylums and incorporated the traditional moral management therapy into their other rudimentary physical-medical procedures.

Over time, the alienists came to have more status and influence in society and during the latter part of the century were influential as purveyors of morality, touting the benefits of Victorian morality as important to good mental health.

In this era mental disorders were only vaguely understood, and conditions such as depression were considered to be the result of nervous exhaustion—that is, psychiatrists of the time thought that emotional problems were caused by the expenditure of energy or depletion of bodily energies as a result of excesses in living. The condition of mental deterioration or "shattered nerves" that supposedly resulted from a person's using up precious nerve force came to be referred to as *neurasthenia*. Neurasthenia involved pervasive feelings of low mood, lack of energy, and physical symptoms that were considered to be, in part, related to "life style" problems brought on by the demands of civilization. These vague symptoms, viewed by the alienists as a definable medical condition, were then considered

2.2

Continued from page 47

treatable by medical men of the times.

Victorian prejudices underlay the notion of depression as a result of energy-depleting activities. In men, for example, the nerve force was thought to be easily depleted through such activities as work, sexual intercourse, or even excessive study. Many famous historical figures, such as John Stuart Mill, Charles Dickens, William James, and Herbert Spencer, to mention only a few, were considered to be affected by "nerves" or neurasthenia at some point. They were treated by Victorian physicians by such means as long vacations, rest, hydrotherapy, and tonics such as laudanum (an opiate), mercury, and barbiturates in an effort to restore their depleted nerve force.

The Victorian view of women was even more negative—they were seen as extremely fragile, cursed by their biological nature, and especially vulnerable to emotional illness. Nineteenth-century doctors believed that women's nervous problems were tied to their uterus, and signs of anxiety or depression were routinely attributed to uterine disturbances. Interestingly, apparently Victorian men (especially doctors and husbands) "expected women to experience neither sexual desire nor pleasure, and that, owing in part to utter ignorance about their own bodies, women did, in fact, go through life in a state of sexual anaesthesia" (p. 200). Oppenheim points out that Victorian society, with its view that women were inferior to men (biologically, intellectually, and morally) served to keep women out of academic and occupational roles. She points out:

"There is no doubt that, generally speaking, the nineteenth-century medical profession considered women's bodies to be defective—suitable companions for their inadequate minds" (p. 190).

The perspective on the powerful and pervasive influence of Victorian thinking provided by Oppenheim gives us more than an interesting picture of the workings of the nineteenth-century mind. It causes us to wonder about the resiliency and veracity of our present-day views. How will our current explanatory views and treatments stand up against viewpoints that will emerge over the coming generations? In a hundred years, will our contemporary views appear as biased and narrow as do those of the medical practitioners of the nineteenth century when viewed from our present perspective?

---

tricks; now abandoned to the most outrageous violations. (Zilboorg & Henry, 1941, pp. 583–584)

As a result of her findings, Dix carried on a zealous campaign between 1841 and 1881 that aroused people and legislatures to do something about the inhuman treatment accorded the mentally ill. Through her efforts, the mental hygiene movement grew in America: millions of dollars were raised to build suitable hospitals, and 20 states responded directly to her appeals. Not only was she instrumental in improving conditions in American hospitals, but she directed the opening of two large institutions in Canada and completely reformed the asylum system in Scotland and several other countries. She is credited with establishing 32 mental hospitals, an astonishing record considering the ignorance and superstition that still prevailed in the field of mental health. She rounded out her career by organizing the nursing forces of the northern armies during the Civil War. A resolution presented by the United States Congress in 1901 characterized her as "among the noblest examples of humanity in all history" (Karnesh & Zucker, 1945, p. 18).

Retrospective criticism of Dix's work has questioned the importance of her contributions and has attributed several negative consequences to her efforts (Bockhoven, 1972; Dain, 1964). Later critics have claimed that establishing hospitals for the mentally ill and increasing the number of people in them created overcrowded facilities and custodial care. Housing patients in institutions away from society, these critics have claimed further, interfered with the treatment of the day (moral therapy) and deferred the search for more appropriate and effective treatments for mental disorders (Bockhoven, 1972). These criticisms, however, do not consider the context in which Dix's contributions were made (see the "Unresolved Issues" discussion on pages 58–60). Dix's advocacy of the humane treatment of the mentally ill should be considered in light of the cruel treatment common at the time (Viney & Bartsch, 1984), and we believe her efforts warrant considerable praise for their results.

Dorothea Dix (1802–1887) was a tireless reformer who made great strides in changing public attitudes toward the mentally ill.

THE FOUNDATIONS OF TWENTIETH-CENTURY VIEWS

It is difficult to partition modern views of abnormal behavior into discrete, uniform attitudes or to trace their historical precedents without appearing arbitrary and overly simplistic. However, a brief, selective overview here will bring us into the twentieth century and set the scene for our discussion of the major viewpoints and causal considerations in Chapter 3.

Changing Attitudes Toward Mental Health

By the end of the nineteenth century, the mental hospital or asylum—"the big house on the hill"—with its fortresslike appearance, had become a familiar landmark in America. In it, mental patients lived under very harsh conditions. To the general public, however, the asylum was an eerie place, and its occupants a strange and frightening lot.

Clifford Beers (1876–1943) used his own experiences of incarceration in mental institutions to wage a campaign of public awareness about the need for changes in attitudes toward and treatment of mental patients.

Little was done by the resident psychiatrists—then called alienists, in reference to treating the "alienated," or insane—to educate the public to reduce the general fear and horror of insanity. A principal reason for this silence, of course, was that early psychiatrists had little actual information to impart.

Gradually, however, important strides were made toward changing the general public's attitude toward mental patients. In America, the pioneering work of Dix was followed by that of Clifford Beers (1876–1943), whose book *A Mind That Found Itself* was published in 1908. Beers, a Yale graduate, described his own mental collapse and told of the bad treatment he received in three typical institutions of the day. He also explained his eventual recovery in the home of a friendly attendant. Although chains and other torture devices had long since been given up, the straitjacket was still widely used as a means of "quieting" excited patients. Beers experienced this treatment and supplied a vivid description of what such painful immobilization of the arms means to an overwrought mental patient:

No one incident of my whole life has ever impressed itself more indelibly on my memory. Within one hour's time I was suffering pain as intense as any I ever endured, and before the night had passed that pain had become almost unbearable. My right hand was so held that the tip of one of my fingers was all but cut by the nail of another, and soon knife-like pains began to shoot through my right arm as far as the shoulder. If there be any so curious as to wish to get a slight idea of my agony, let him bite a finger tip as hard as he can without drawing blood. Let him continue the operation for two or three minutes. Then let him multiply that effect, if he can, by two or three hundred. In my case, after four or five hours the excess of pain rendered me partially insensible to it. But for nine hundred minutes—fifteen consecutive hours—I remained in that strait-jacket; and not until the twelfth hour, about breakfast time the next morning, did an attendant so much as loosen a cord. (Beers, 1970, pp. 127–128)

After Beers recovered, he began a campaign to make people realize that such treatment was no way to handle the sick. He soon won the interest and support of many public-spirited individuals, including the eminent psychologist William James and the "dean of American psychiatry," Adolf Meyer.

THE GROWTH OF SCIENTIFIC RESEARCH

While the mental hygiene movement was gaining ground in the United States during the latter years of the nineteenth century, great technological discoveries were occurring both at home and abroad. These advances helped begin what we know today as the scientific, or experimentally oriented, view of abnormal behavior and the application of scientific knowledge to the treatment of disturbed individuals.

The Roots of the Biological Viewpoint

The most immediately apparent advances were in the study of the biological and anatomical factors underlying both physical and mental disorders. A major biomedical breakthrough, for example, came with the discovery of the organic factors underlying general paresis—syphilis of the brain—one of the most serious mental illnesses of the day. General paresis produced paralysis and insanity and typically caused death within two to five years. The investigation into the causes of paresis and the finding of a

cure—in essence, infecting a sufferer with malaria the high fevers of which killed the syphilis organism—stretched over a period of nearly 100 years, as outlined in HIGHLIGHT 2.3. Though today we have penicillin as an effective, simpler treatment of syphilis, the early malarial treatment represented, for the first time in history, a clear-cut conquest of a mental disorder by medical science. The field of abnormal psychology had come a long way—from superstitious beliefs to scientific proof of how brain pathology can cause a specific disorder. This breakthrough raised great hopes in the medical community that organic bases would be found for many other mental disorders—perhaps for all of them.

The Establishment of Brain Pathology as a Causal Factor

With the emergence of modern experimental science in the early part of the eighteenth century, knowledge of anatomy, physiology, neurology, chemistry, and general medicine increased rapidly. These advances led to the gradual identification of the biological, or organic, pathology underlying many physical ailments. Scientists began to focus on diseased body organs as the cause of physical ailments. It was only another step for these people to assume that mental disorder was an illness based on the pathology of an organ—in this case, the brain. In 1757 Albrecht von Haller (1708–1777), in his *Elements of Physiology,* emphasized the importance of the brain in psychic functions and advocated post-mortem dissection to study the brains of the insane. The first systematic presentation of this viewpoint, however, was made by the German psychiatrist Wilhelm Griesinger (1817–1868). In his textbook *The Pathology and Therapy of Psychic Disorders,* published in 1845, Griesinger insisted that all mental disorders could be explained in terms of brain pathology.

Following the discovery that brain pathology resulted in general paresis, other successes followed. The brain pathology in cerebral arteriosclerosis and in the senile mental disorders was established by Alois Alzheimer and other investigators. Eventually, the organic pathologies underlying the toxic mental disorders (disorders caused by toxic substances such as lead), certain types of mental retardation, and other mental illnesses were discovered.

It is important to note here that although the discovery of the organic bases of mental disorders may have addressed the *how* behind causation, it did not, in most cases, address the question of *why*. This situation is sometimes true to this day. For example, although we know what causes certain "presenile"

Events Leading to the Discovery of Organic Factors in General Paresis

Scientific discoveries do not occur overnight; usually they require the combined efforts of many scientists over extended periods of time. In addition, such discoveries rarely proceed sequentially from point *a* to point *z*. Rather, they often result from an uncoordinated process in which many scientists pursue dead-end hypotheses, go off on tangents, refuse to accept "evidence," experience crises in their thinking, and so on.

Abbreviated descriptions of the events leading to scientific discoveries often fail to capture the excitement, intrigue, and frustration that enter the process. With this caution in mind, we identify here ten key steps in the long effort to find a cure for general paresis.

1. In 1825 French physician A. L. J. Bayle differentiated general paresis as a specific type of mental disorder. Bayle gave a complete and accurate description of the symptom pattern of paresis and convincingly presented his reasons for believing paresis to be a distinct disorder.

2. In 1857 Esmarch and Jessen reported on paretic patients known to have had syphilis and concluded that the syphilis caused the paresis.

3. In 1869 Argyll-Robertson in Scotland described the failure of the pupillary reflex (failure of the pupil to narrow under bright light) as diagnostic of the involvement of the central nervous system in syphilis.

4. In 1897 Viennese psychiatrist Krafft-Ebing conducted experiments involving the inoculation of paretic patients with matter from syphilitic sores. None of the patients developed secondary symptoms of syphilis, which led to the conclusion that they must previously have been infected. This crucial experiment established the relationship of general paresis to syphilis.

5. In 1905 Schaudinn discovered that *Spirochaeta pallida* is the cause of syphilis.

6. In 1906 von Wassermann developed a blood test for syphilis. This development made it possible to check for the presence of the deadly spirochetes in the bloodstream of an individual before the more serious consequences of infection appeared.

7. In 1908 Plant applied the Wasserman test to the cerebrospinal fluid to indicate whether or not the

spirochete had invaded a patient's central nervous system.

8. In 1909 Ehrlich, after 605 failures, developed the arsenical compound arsphenamine (which he thereupon called 606) for the treatment of syphilis. Although 606 proved effective in killing the syphilitic spirochetes in the bloodstream, it was not effective against the spirochetes that had penetrated the central nervous system.

9. In 1913 Noguchi and Moore verified that the syphilitic spirochete was the brain-damaging agent in general paresis. They discovered these spirochetes in a postmortem study of the brains of patients who had suffered from paresis.

10. In 1917 Wagner-Jauregg, chief of the psychiatric clinic of the University of Vienna, introduced the malarial fever treatment of syphilis and paresis because the high fever associated with malaria killed off the spirochete. He inoculated nine paretic patients with the blood of a soldier who was ill with malaria and found marked improvement in three patients and apparent recovery in three others.

mental disorders—brain pathology—we do not yet know why some individuals are afflicted and others not. Nonetheless, we can predict quite accurately the courses of these disorders. This ability is due not only to a greater understanding of the organic factors involved, but also, in large part, to the work of a follower of Griesinger, Emil Kraepelin (1856–1926).

The Beginnings of a Classification System

Kraepelin played a dominant role in the early development of the biological viewpoint. His textbook

Lehrbuch der Psychiatrie, published in 1883, not only emphasized the importance of brain pathology in mental disorders but also made several related contributions that helped establish this viewpoint. The most important of these contributions was his system of classification, which became the forerunner of today's DSM-IV (discussed in Chapter 1). Kraepelin noted that certain symptom patterns occurred regularly enough to be regarded as specific types of mental disease. He then proceeded to describe and clarify these types of mental disorders, working out a scheme of classification that is the basis of our present system. The integration of the clinical material underlying this classification was a

Emil Kraepelin (1856–1926), by integrating clinical data, worked out one of the first systematic classification systems, a forerunner of the modern DSM-IV.

herculean task and represented a major contribution to the field of psychopathology.

Kraepelin saw each type of mental disorder as distinct from the others and thought that the course of each was as predetermined and predictable as the course of measles. Thus the outcome of a given type of disorder could presumably be predicted even if it could not yet be controlled. Such conclusions led to widespread interest in the accurate description and classification of mental disorders.

Advances Achieved as a Result of Early Biological Views

Although early biologically based thinking was perhaps too widely adopted before its limitations were recognized, it represented the first great advance of modern science toward the understanding and treatment of mental disorder. In turn, there was an enormous research effort to discover specific causes of disorders that would yield to specific medical treatments; researchers looked for damage or disease in particular sections of the brain to find the causes un-

derlying different disorders. Such efforts necessarily involved differentiating various forms of abnormality, leading to a promising system for classifying separate disorders. These were substantial accomplishments. Not all of the consequences of this early thinking were positive, however. Because the disorders best understood in terms of then-available knowledge were ones in which brain damage or deterioration was a central feature (as in general paresis), there naturally developed an expectation that all abnormal behavior would eventually be explained by reference to gross brain pathology. To be sure, organic mental disorders do occur (and we will describe them in Chapter 13), but the vast majority of abnormal behavior is not clearly associated with physical damage to brain tissue. Nonetheless, the medical model—a conceptual model that is inappropriate for much abnormal behavior—became stubbornly entrenched by these early but limited successes.

It is important to note that a medical-model orientation is not limited to biological viewpoints on the nature of mental disorder. It has also extended into psychosocial theorizing by adopting a *symptom/underlying-cause* point of view. This point of view assumes that abnormal behavior, even though it may be psychological (rather than biological) in nature, is a symptom of some sort of underlying, internal pathology or "illness"—just as a fever is a symptom of an underlying infection. As we will discuss shortly, Freud, who was a physician, took this approach in developing his psychoanalytic theory of abnormal behavior.

Advances in Psychological Understanding of Mental Disorders: The Psychodynamic Perspective

Despite the emphasis on biological causation, the scientific investigation into psychological factors and human behavior was progressing, too. The first steps toward understanding psychological factors in mental disorders were taken by Sigmund Freud (1856–1939). During five decades of observation, treatment, and writing, Freud developed a theory of psychopathology that emphasized the inner dynamics of unconscious motives, called the **psychoanalytic perspective.** The methods he used to study and treat patients are called **psychoanalysis.** Over the last half century, to be discussed in Chapter 3, other clinicians have modified and revised Freud's theory, resulting in new **psychodynamic perspectives.** These perspectives contain many of the same assumptions and viewpoints as Freud's original theory, but they differ from classical psychoanalysis in some important respects (for example, Adler rejected Freud's emphasis on sexuality in favor of social motivation).

The Roots of the Psychodynamic Viewpoint We find the roots of psychoanalysis in a somewhat unexpected place—the study of hypnosis, especially in its relation to hysteria. Hypnosis, an induced state of relaxation in which a person is highly open to suggestion, first came into widespread use in late eighteenth- and early nineteenth-century France.

Mesmerism. Our story starts with Franz Anton Mesmer (1734–1815), an Austrian physician who further developed Paracelsus' ideas about the influence of the planets on the human body. Mesmer believed that the planets affected a universal magnetic fluid in the body, the distribution of which determined health or disease. In attempting to find cures for mental disorders, Mesmer concluded that all people possessed magnetic forces that could be used to influence the distribution of the magnetic fluid in other people, thus effecting cures.

Mesmer attempted to put his views into practice in Vienna and various other towns, but it was in Paris in 1778 that he gained a broad following. There he opened a clinic in which he treated all kinds of diseases by "animal magnetism." In a dark room, patients were seated around a tub containing various chemicals, and iron rods protruding from the tub were applied to the affected areas of the patients' bodies. Accompanied by music, Mesmer appeared in a lilac robe, passing from one patient to another and touching each one with his hands or his wand. By this means, Mesmer was reportedly able to remove hysterical anesthesias and paralyses. He also demonstrated most of the phenomena later connected with the use of hypnosis.

Eventually branded a charlatan by his medical colleagues, Mesmer was forced to leave Paris and he quickly faded into obscurity. His methods and results, however, were at the center of scientific controversy for many years—in fact, **mesmerism,** as his technique

Mesmer believed that the distribution of magnetic fluid in the body was responsible for determining health or disease. He further thought that all people possessed magnetic forces that could be used to influence the distribution of fluid in others, thus effecting cures. In this painting of his therapy, Mesmer stands at the back, on the right, holding a wand. Mesmer was eventually branded a fraud by his colleagues, but he did demonstrate most of the phenomena later connected with the use of hypnosis.

came to be known, was as much a source of heated discussion in the early nineteenth century as psychoanalysis became in the early twentieth century. This discussion led to a renewed interest in hypnosis itself as an explanation of the "cures" that took place.

The Nancy School. Liébeault (1823–1904), a French physician who practiced in the town of Nancy, used hypnosis successfully in his practice. Also in Nancy at the time was a professor of medicine, Bernheim (1840–1919), who became interested in the relationship between hysteria and hypnosis. His interest was the result of Liébeault's success in curing by hypnosis a patient who Bernheim had been treating unsuccessfully by more conventional methods for four years (Selling, 1943). Bernheim and Liébeault worked together to develop the hypothesis that hypnotism and hysteria were related and that both were due to suggestion (Brown & Menninger, 1940). Their hypothesis was based on two lines of evidence: (a) phenomena observed in hysteria, such as paralysis of an arm, inability to hear, or anesthetic areas in which an individual could be stuck with a pin without feeling pain (all of which occurred when there was apparently nothing organically wrong), could be produced in normal subjects by means of hypnosis; and (b) the same symptoms also could be removed by means of hypnosis. Thus it seemed likely that hysteria was a sort of self-hypnosis. The physicians who accepted this view ultimately came to be known as the **Nancy School.**

Meanwhile, Jean Charcot (1825–1893), who was head of the Salpêtrière Hospital in Paris and the leading neurologist of his time, had been experimenting with some of the phenomena described by the mesmerists. As a result of his research, Charcot disagreed with the findings of the Nancy School and insisted that degenerative brain changes led to hysteria. In this, Charcot was eventually proved wrong, but work on the problem by so outstanding a scientist did a great deal to awaken medical and scientific interest in hysteria.

The dispute between Charcot and the Nancy School was one of the major debates of medical history, during which many harsh words were spoken on both sides. The adherents of the Nancy School finally triumphed, representing the first recognition of a psychologically caused mental disorder. This recognition spurred more research on the behavior underlying hysteria and other disorders. Soon it was suggested that psychological factors were also involved in anxiety states, phobias, and other psychopathologies. Eventually, Charcot himself was won over to the new point of view and did much to promote the study of psychological factors in various mental disorders.

The debate over whether mental disorders are caused by biological or psychological factors continues to this day. The Nancy School/Charcot debate represented a major step forward for psychology, however. Toward the end of the nineteenth century, it was clear that mental disorders could have either psychological bases or biological bases, or both. With this recognition, a major question remained to be answered: How do the psychologically based mental disorders actually develop?

It took some time before Jean Charcot (1825–1893), the leading neurologist of his time, believed that there might be a causal relationship between self-hypnosis and hysteria. Once convinced, however, he did much, through research and lectures about hypnosis, such as the one shown here, to promote interest in the role psychological factors may play in mental disorders.

The Beginnings of Psychoanalysis The first systematic attempt to answer this question was made by Sigmund Freud (1856–1939). Freud was a brilliant young Viennese neurologist who received an appointment as lecturer on nervous diseases at the University of Vienna. In 1885 he went to study under Charcot and later became acquainted with the work of Liébeault and Bernheim at Nancy. He was impressed by their use of hypnosis with hysterical patients and came away convinced that powerful mental processes could remain hidden from consciousness.

On his return to Vienna, Freud worked in collaboration with another physician, Josef Breuer (1842–1925), who had introduced an interesting innovation in the use of hypnosis with his patients. Unlike hypnotists before him, he directed his patients to talk freely about their problems while under hypnosis. The patients usually displayed considerable emotion, and on awakening from their hypnotic states felt significantly relieved. Because of the emotional release involved, this method was called **catharsis.** This simple innovation in the use of hypnosis proved to be of great significance: It not only helped patients discharge their emotional tensions by discussing their problems, but it also revealed to the therapist the nature of the difficulties that had brought about certain symptoms. The patients, on awakening, saw no relationship between their problems and their hysterical symptoms.

Thus was made the discovery of the unconscious—that portion of the mind that contains experiences of which a person is unaware—and with it the belief that processes outside of a person's awareness can play an important role in the determination of behavior. In 1893 Freud and Breuer published their joint paper *On the Psychical Mechanisms of Hysterical Phenomena*, which was one of the great milestones in the study of psychodynamics. Freud soon discovered, moreover, that he could dispense with hypnosis entirely. By encouraging patients to say whatever came into their minds without regard to logic or propriety, Freud found that patients would eventually overcome inner obstacles to remembering and would discuss their problems freely. Two related methods allowed him to understand patients' conscious and unconscious thought processes. One method, **free association,** involved having patients talk freely about themselves, thereby providing information about their feelings, motives, and so forth. A second method, **dream analysis,** involved having patients record and describe their dreams. These techniques helped analysts and patients gain insights and achieve a more adequate understanding of emotional problems. Freud devoted the rest of his long and energetic life to the development and elaboration of psychoanalytic principles. His views were formally introduced to American scientists in 1909, when he was invited to deliver a series of lectures at Clark University by the eminent psychologist G. Stanley Hall, who was then president of the university. These lectures created a great deal of controversy and helped popularize psychoanalytic concepts to scientists as well as the general public. We will return to a more complete discussion of the psychoanalytic viewpoint in Chapter 3. Next, we will discuss the early developments of psychological research and the evolution of the behavioral perspective in viewing abnormal behavior.

Sigmund Freud (1856–1939), the founder of psychoanalysis, emphasized the role of unconscious processes in the determination of behavior. He abandoned the use of hypnosis for the techniques of free association and dream analysis to help patients achieve insight into their problems.

Advances in Psychological Research

In 1879 Wilhelm Wundt (1832–1920) established the first experimental psychology laboratory at the University of Leipzig. While studying the psycho-

Psychoanalysis was introduced to North America at a famous meeting at Clark University, Worcester, Massachusetts, in 1908. Among those present were (back row) A. A. Brill, Ernest Jones, and Sandor Ferenczi; (front row) Sigmund Freud, G. Stanley Hall, and Carl Jung.

logical factors involved in memory and sensation, Wundt and his colleagues devised many basic experimental methods and strategies. Early contributors to the empirical study of abnormal behavior were directly influenced by Wundt; they followed his experimental methodology and also used some of his research strategies to study clinical problems. For example, a student of Wundt's, J. McKeen Cattell (1860–1944), brought Wundt's experimental methods to the United States and used them to assess individual differences in mental processing. He and other students of Wundt's work established research laboratories throughout the United States.

It was not until 1896, however, that another of Wundt's students, Lightner Witmer (1867–1956), combined research with application and established the first American psychological clinic at the University of Pennsylvania. Witmer's clinic focused on the problems of mentally deficient children, in terms of both research and therapy. Other clinics were soon established. One clinic of note was the Chicago Juvenile Psychopathic Institute (later called the Institute of Juvenile Research), established in 1909 by William Healy (1869–1963). Healy was the first to describe juvenile delinquency as a symptom of urbanization and not as a result of inner psychological problems. In so doing, he was among the first to seize upon a new area of causation—environmental, or sociocultural, factors.

By the first decade of the twentieth century, psychological laboratories and clinics were burgeoning, and a great deal of research was being generated (Reisman, 1991). The rapid and objective communication of scientific findings was perhaps as important in the development of modern psychology (or any science) as the collection and interpretation of

research findings. This period saw the origin of many scientific journals for the dissemination of research and theoretical discoveries. Two notable publications in the field of abnormal psychology were the *Journal of Abnormal Psychology,* founded by Morton Prince in 1906, and *The Psychological Clinic,* founded by Lightner Witmer in 1907. (Interestingly, Prince was a psychiatrist who created an outlet for papers on abnormal psychology that were not biological in nature.) As the years have passed, the number of journals has grown. The American Psychological Association now publishes 29 scientific journals, many of which focus on research into abnormal behavior and personality functioning.

The Behavioral Perspective While psychoanalysis dominated thought about abnormal behavior at the end of the nineteenth and in the early twentieth century, another school—behaviorism—was emerging to challenge its supremacy. Behavioral psychologists believed that the study of subjective experience—through the techniques of free association and dream analysis—did not provide acceptable scientific data, because such observations were not open to verification by other investigators. In their view, only the study of directly observable behavior and the stimuli and reinforcing conditions that "control" it could serve as a basis for formulating scientific principles of human behavior.

The **behavioral perspective** is organized around a central theme: the role of learning in human behavior. Although this perspective was initially developed through research in the laboratory rather than through clinical practice with disturbed individuals, its implications for explaining and treating maladaptive behavior soon became evident.

Roots of the Behavioral Perspective The origins of the behavioral view of abnormal behavior and its treatment are tied to experimental work on the form of learning known as **classical conditioning.** This work began with the discovery of the conditioned reflex by Russian physiologist Ivan Pavlov (1849–1936). Around the turn of the century, Pavlov demonstrated that dogs would gradually begin to salivate to a nonfood stimulus, such as a bell, after the stimulus had been regularly accompanied by food.

Pavlov's discovery, which came to be known as classical conditioning, excited a young American psychologist, John B. Watson (1878–1958), who was searching for objective ways to study human behavior. Watson reasoned that if psychology was to become a true science, it must abandon the subjectivity of inner sensations and other "mental" events and limit itself to what could be objectively observed. What better way to do this than to observe systematic changes in behavior brought about simply by rearranging stimulus conditions? Watson thus changed the focus of psychology to the study of overt behavior, an approach he called **behaviorism.**

Watson, a man of impressive energy and demeanor, saw great possibilities in behaviorism, and he was quick to point them out to his fellow scientists and a curious public. He boasted that, through conditioning, he could train any healthy child to become whatever sort of adult one wished. He also challenged the psychoanalysts and the more biologically oriented psychologists of his day by suggesting that abnormal behavior was the product of unfortunate, inadvertent earlier conditioning and could be modified through reconditioning.

By the 1930s Watson had made an enormous impact on American psychology. Watson's approach placed heavy emphasis on the role of the social environment in conditioning personality development and behavior, both normal and abnormal. Today's behaviorally oriented psychologists still accept many of the basic tenets of Watson's doctrine, although they are more cautious in their claims.

While Watson was studying stimulus conditions and their relation to behavioral responses, E. L. Thorndike (1874–1949) and subsequently B. F. Skinner (1904–1990) were exploring the other side of the conditioning coin—the fact that, over time, the consequences of behavior tend to influence behavior. Behavior that *operates* on the environment is *instrumental* in producing certain outcomes, and those outcomes, in turn, determine the likelihood that the behavior will be repeated on similar occasions. This type of learning came to be called **instrumental** or **operant conditioning.**

In this chapter we have touched upon several important trends in the evolution of the field of abnormal psychology and have recounted the contributions of numerous individuals from history that brought us to our current prevailing views. The very amount of information available can cause confusion and controversy when it comes to obtaining an integrated

Ivan Pavlov (1849–1936), a pioneer in demonstrating the part conditioning plays in behavior, is shown here with his staff and some of the apparatus used to condition reflexes in dogs.

John B. Watson (1878–1958) changed the focus of psychology from the study of inner sensations to the study of observable behavior, an approach called behaviorism.

E. L. Thorndike (1874–1949) formulated the law of effect—that rewarded responses are strengthened and unrewarded responses are weakened—which had implications for controlling human behavior.

B. F. Skinner (1904–1990) formulated the concept of operant conditioning, in which reinforcers could be used to make a response more or less probable and frequent.

view of behavior and causation. We may have left supernatural beliefs behind, but we have moved into something far more complex in trying to determine the role of natural factors—be they biological, psychological, or sociocultural—in abnormal behavior. For a recap of some of the key contributors to the field of abnormal psychology, see HIGHLIGHT 2.4.

UNRESOLVED ISSUES

on Interpreting Historical Events

One would think that trying to look back in history to get a picture of events that occurred long ago would not be a difficult task—that it would be a simple matter of reviewing some history books and some publications from the time in question. However, our views of history and our "collective memory" of events are constantly open to re-interpretation. As Schudson (in press) recently pointed out: "Collective memory, more than individual memory, at least in liberal pluralistic societies, is provisional. It is always open to contestation" (p. 16).

Any number of obstacles can stand in the way of our gaining an accurate picture of the attitudes and behaviors of people who lived hundreds of years ago. This has certainly been the case with our views of the Middle Ages. The foremost problem in retrospective psychological analysis is that we cannot rely on direct observation, a hallmark of psychological research. In-

stead, we must turn to written documents or historical surveys of the times. Though these sources are often full of fascinating information, they may not reveal directly the information we seek; we must therefore extrapolate "facts" from the information we have, which is not always an easy task. We are restricted in our conclusions by the documents or sources available to us. Attempting to learn about a people's subtle social perceptions hundreds of years ago by examining surviving church documents or biographical accounts is less than ideal. First, we inevitably view these documents out of the context in which they were written. Second, we do not know whether the authors had ulterior motives or what they were—that is, what the real purposes were behind the documents. Kroll and Bachrach (1984), in their review of historical misinterpretations of the Middle Ages, point to the "propaganda element" that existed during the Middle Ages (as it still does today). For example, many historians have concluded erroneously that people of the Middle Ages considered sin to be a major causal factor in mental illness. This wrong conclusion may have been due in part to writings that invoked God's punishment if the victims of illnesses were enemies of the authors. Apparently, historians did not take note of the fact that if the victims were friends of the authors, sin was typically not mentioned as a causal factor (Kroll & Bachrach, 1984). Such writings, of course, are biased, but we may have no way of knowing this. The fewer the sources surveyed, the more likely that any existing bias will go undetected.

Major Figures in the Early History of Abnormal Psychology

The Ancient World

Hippocrates (460–377 B.C.) A Greek physician who believed that mental disease was the result of natural causes and brain pathology rather than demonology.

Plato (429–347 B.C.) A Greek philosopher who believed that mental patients should be treated humanely and should not be held responsible for their actions.

Aristotle (384–322 B.C.) Greek philosopher and pupil of Plato who believed in the Hippocratic theory that various agents, or humors, within the body, when imbalanced, were responsible for mental disorders. Aristotle rejected the notion of psychological factors as causes of mental disorders.

Galen (A.D. 130–200) A Greek physician and advocate of the Hippocratic tradition who contributed much to our understanding of the nervous system. Galen divided the causes of mental disorders into physical and mental categories.

The Middle Ages

Avicenna (980–1037) An Islamic physician who adopted principles of humane treatment for the mentally disturbed at a time when Western approaches to mental illness were the opposite.

Martin Luther (1483–1546) A German theologian and leader of the Reformation who held the belief, common to his time, that the mentally disturbed were possessed by the devil.

Paracelsus (1490–1541) A Swiss physician who rejected demonology as a cause of abnormal behavior. Paracelsus believed in psychic causes of mental illness.

The Sixteenth Through the Eighteenth Centuries

Teresa of Avila (16th century) A Spanish nun who argued that mental disorder was an illness of the mind.

Johann Weyer (1515–1588) A German physician who argued against demonology and was ostracized by his peers and the Church for his progressive views.

Reginald Scot (1538–1599) An Englishman who refuted the notion of demons as the cause of mental disorders and was castigated by King James I.

Robert Burton (1576–1640) An Oxford scholar who wrote a classic, influential treatise on depression, *Anatomy of Melancholia,* in 1621.

William Tuke (1732–1822) An English Quaker who established the York Retreat, where mental patients lived in humane surroundings.

Philippe Pinel (1745–1826) A French physician who pioneered the use of moral management in La Bicêtre and La Salpêtrière hospitals in France, where mental patients were treated in a humane way.

Benjamin Rush (1745–1813) An American physician and founder of American psychiatry who used moral management, based on Pinel's humanitarian methods, to treat the mentally disturbed.

The Nineteenth and Early Twentieth Centuries

Dorothea Dix (1802–1887) An American teacher who founded the mental hygiene movement in the United States, which focused on the physical well-being of mental patients in hospitals.

Clifford Beers (1876–1943) An American who campaigned to change public attitudes toward mental patients after his own experiences in mental institutions.

Franz Anton Mesmer (1734–1815) An Austrian physician who conducted early investigations into hypnosis as a medical treatment.

Sigmund Freud (1856–1938) The founder of the school of psychological therapy known as psychoanalysis.

Wilhelm Wundt (1832–1920) A German scientist who established the first experimental psychology laboratory in 1879 and subsequently influenced the empirical study of abnormal behavior.

J. McKeen Cattell (1860–1944) An American psychologist who adopted Wundt's methods and studied individual differences in mental processing.

Lightner Witmer (1867–1956) An American psychologist who established the first psychological clinic in the United States, focusing on problems of mentally deficient children. He also founded the journal *The Psychological Clinic* in 1907.

Ivan Pavlov (1849–1936) A Russian physiologist who published classical studies in the psychology of learning.

William Healy (1869–1963) An American psychologist who established the Chicago Juvenile Psychopathic Institute and advanced the idea that mental illness was due to environmental or sociocultural factors.

John B. Watson (1878–1958) Conducted early research into learning principles and came to be known as the father of behaviorism.

In other cases, concepts important to historical interpretation may have quite a different meaning to us today than they did in the past. Or the meaning may simply be unclear. Kroll and Bachrach (1984) point out that the concept of "possession"—so critical to our views of the Middle Ages—is

> a very vague and complex concept for which we have no helpful natural models. Our language fails us, except for colourful analogies and metaphors. Just as the term "nervous breakdown" means different things to different people, so too "possession" means and meant many different things, and undoubtedly had a different range of meanings to medieval persons from what it has to us. (p. 510)

This kind of uncertainty can make definitive assessments of the happenings during the Middle Ages difficult—if not impossible.

Bias can come into play during interpretation, also. Our interpretations of historical events or previously held beliefs can be colored by our own views of normal and abnormal. In fact, it is difficult to conduct a retrospective analysis without taking current perspectives and values as a starting point. For example, our modern beliefs about the Middle Ages have led, says Schoeneman (1984), to our contemporary misinterpretation that, during the fifteenth and sixteenth centuries, the mentally ill were typically accused of being witches. For most of us, this interpretation—albeit a wrong one—makes sense simply because we do not understand the medieval perspective on witchcraft.

Although reevaluations of the Middle Ages have minimized the views that demonology, sin, and witchcraft played a key role in the medieval understanding of mental illness, it is also clear that in some cases, these concepts were associated with mental illness. Wherein lies the truth? It appears that the last word has not been written on the Middle Ages, nor on any period of our history, for that matter. At best, historical views—and, therefore, retrospective psychological studies—must be held as working hypotheses that are open to change as new perspectives are applied to history or "new" historical documents are discovered.

On a related topic, some authorities interested in the area of applying psychological thought to the interpretation of historical events have proposed a field of study, **psychohistory** (DeMause, 1984), which according to Lawton (1990) involves "the interdisciplinary study of why man has acted as he has in history, prominently utilizing psychoanalytic principles" (p. 353). This approach to history (which is not without its critics; see Shephard, 1979) has attempted to provide penetrating analyses of historical figures or historical events using psychological theory, particularly psychoanalysis, to explain events.

This approach to studying or re-interpreting historical events is fraught with validational problems and may be viewed as providing "plausible" applications of the particular theory in question rather than as revelations of fact about the event itself.

Historical events, of course, are often ambiguous and open to considerable interpretation and re-interpretation before they become "written history." The final version of a particular event is often debated long after the ink has dried on the historical tomes reporting and interpreting it. Even when historical events are relatively recent it may not be an easy task for well-meaning individuals to accurately reconstruct what actually happened. A recent example of the difficulties of conducting a psychological reconstruction of historical events, or "psychological autopsy," can be found in the highly publicized case of the explosion aboard the United States Navy ship the USS *Iowa*. In 1989, an explosion in a gun emplacement on the ship killed 47 people on board and led to the retirement of the famous battleship. Investigation of the incident by the Navy and the FBI initially ruled out the possibility of accident or sabotage and placed the blame for the accident on a sailor who was alleged to be a psychologically disturbed homosexual who was thought to have intentionally caused the accident in an effort to commit suicide. A controversy followed, prompting a congressional investigation into the accident and the Navy's attribution of blame to the sailor. As part of the congressional panel to evaluate the potential cause of the accident and evaluate whether the sailor being accused of creating the accident had done so, 14 noted psychologists were asked to review the existing information about the sailor in question and develop a psychological autopsy concerning the sailor's psychological state at the time of the incident. Eleven of the 14 panelists were critical of the Navy's conclusions and raised doubts about the FBI's report on the sailor's mental health status at the time of the accident. Considerable disagreement was found in the expert opinion reports, especially for detailed judgments, and agreement was obtained for only the broad categories. Recently, Otto, Poythress, Starr, and Darkes (1993) suggested caution in the use of psychological autopsies for such cases because the expert reviewers were quite inconsistent in their judgments.

SUMMARY

The development of modern views on psychopathology has not followed a straight evolutionary path. We can, however, trace a general movement away from superstitious and "magical" explanations of abnormal behavior toward more reasoned, scientific explanations.

Early superstitions were followed by the emergence of medical concepts in many places, such as Egypt and Greece; many of these concepts were developed and refined by Roman physicians. With the fall of Rome near the end of the fifth century A.D., most Europeans turned to superstitious views, which dominated popular thinking about mental disorders for over 1000 years. In the fifteenth and sixteenth centuries, it was still widely believed, even by scholars, that mentally disturbed people were possessed by a devil.

During the latter stages of the Middle Ages and early Renaissance, a spirit of scientific questioning reappeared in Europe, and several noted physicians spoke out against inhumane treatments, arguing that "possessed" individuals were actually "sick of mind" and should be treated as such. With this recognition of a need for the special treatment of disturbed people came the founding of various "asylums" toward the end of the sixteenth century. However, with institutionalization came the isolation and maltreatment of mental patients; slowly, this situation was recognized, and in the eighteenth century, further efforts were made to help afflicted individuals by providing them with better living conditions and kind treatment.

The nineteenth and early twentieth centuries witnessed a number of scientific and humanitarian advances. The work of Philippe Pinel in France, William Tuke in England, and Benjamin Rush and Dorothea Dix in the United States prepared the way for several important developments in contemporary abnormal psychology. Among these developments were the gradual acceptance of mental patients as afflicted individuals who needed and deserved professional attention; the success of biomedical methods as applied to disorders; and the growth of scientific research into the biological, psychological, and sociocultural roots of abnormal behavior.

In the nineteenth century great technological discoveries and scientific advancements were made in the biological sciences that aided in the understanding and treatment of disturbed individuals. A major biomedical breakthrough, for example, came with the discovery of the organic factors underlying general paresis—syphilis of the brain—one of the most serious mental illnesses of the day.

Additionally, in the early part of the eighteenth century, knowledge of anatomy, physiology, neurology, chemistry, and general medicine increased rapidly. These advances led to the identification of the biological, or organic, pathology underlying many physical ailments.

The development of a psychiatric classification system by Kraepelin played a dominant role in the early development of the biological viewpoint. Kraeplin's work helped to establish the importance of brain pathology in mental disorders and made several related contributions that helped establish this viewpoint.

The scientific investigation into psychological factors and human behavior began to make progress in the later part of the nineteenth century also. The first steps toward understanding psychological factors in mental disorders were taken by Sigmund Freud. During five decades of observation, treatment, and writing, he developed a theory of psychopathology, known as psychoanalysis, that emphasized the inner dynamics of unconscious motives. Over the last half century, other clinicians have modified and revised Freud's theory, evolving into new psychodynamic perspectives.

Finally, the end of the nineteenth and the early twentieth centuries saw another school, behaviorism, emerge as an explanatory model in abnormal psychology. The behavioral perspective is organized around a central theme—that learning plays an important role in human behavior. Although this perspective was initially developed through research in the laboratory, unlike psychoanalysis, which emerged out of clinical practice with disturbed individuals, it has been shown to have important implications for explaining and treating maladaptive behavior.

Understanding the history of viewpoints on psychopathology, with its forward steps and reverses, helps us understand the emergence of modern concepts of abnormal behavior. This knowledge also provides us with a perspective for understanding new and future advances.

KEY TERMS

exorcism (p. 32)

insanity (p. 34)

tarantism (p. 37)

St. Vitus's dance (p. 37)

lycanthropy (p. 37)

asylums (p. 41)

moral management (p. 44)

mental hygiene
   movement (p. 45)

psychoanalytic perspective
   (p. 52)

psychoanalysis (p. 52)

psychodynamic perspectives
   (p. 52)

mesmerism (p. 53)

Nancy School (p. 54)

catharsis (p. 55)

free association (p. 55)

dream analysis (p. 55)

behavioral perspective (p. 56)

classical conditioning (p. 57)

behaviorism (p. 57)

instrumental (operant)
   conditioning (p. 57)

psychohistory (p. 60)

CHAPTER

3

CAUSAL FACTORS AND VIEWPOINTS IN ABNORMAL PSYCHOLOGY

Adolf Wölffli, General-Ansicht der Insell Niezohrn. *Wölffli (1864–1930), born in Bern, Switzerland, was abandoned by his father in early childhood and at the age of eight was removed from the care of his mother—occurrences that marked the beginning of violent, erratic behaviors that finally culminated in a schizophrenic breakdown. Wölffli created an imaginary world in much of his artwork, one in which elements and symbols are arranged according to his paranoid thinking.*

We saw in the last chapter that speculation about the causes of abnormal behavior goes back very far in human history. From early times those who observed disordered behavior grappled with the question of its cause. Hippocrates, for example, suggested that imbalance in bodily humors produced abnormal behavior. To other observers the cause was possession by demons or evil spirits. Later, bodily dysfunction was suggested as a cause.

Each attempt at identifying a cause brought with it a theory, or model, of abnormal behavior. Hippocrates' theory, a type of disease model, posited the existence of four bodily humors that were connected with certain kinds of behavior. Other theories similarly grew out of attempts to identify causes.

Today we are still puzzling over the causes of abnormal behavior, and speculation about causes continues to give rise to new models of abnormality. Since the beginning of this century, several important schools of thought developed elaborate models to explain abnormal behavior and to suggest how it might be treated. We will discuss each of these theoretical perspectives in this chapter, giving attention to the causal factors each has identified. First, however, we need to address the question of causation itself.

WHAT CAUSES ABNORMAL BEHAVIOR?

Central to the field of abnormal psychology are questions about what causes people to behave maladaptively. Equipped with a knowledge of the causes for given disorders, we might be able to prevent conditions that lead to them and perhaps reverse those that maintain them. We could also classify and diagnose disorders better if we clearly understood their causes rather than relying on clusters of symptoms, as we usually do now.

Although understanding the causes of abnormal behavior is clearly a desirable goal, it is enormously difficult to achieve because human behavior is so complex. Even the simplest human behavior, such as speaking or writing a word, is the product of thousands of prior events—the connections among which are not always clear. Attempting to understand a person's life in causal terms, even an "adaptive" life, is a task of enormous magnitude; when the life is a maladaptive one, it is even more difficult. As a result, many investigators now prefer to speak of risk factors (variables correlated with an abnormal outcome) rather than of causes. Nevertheless, understanding causes remains the ultimate goal.

In analyzing causal factors of abnormal behavior, it is helpful to consider (a) the distinctions between necessary, sufficient, and contributory causes; (b) the problem of feedback and circularity in abnormal behavior; and (c) the concept of diathesis-stress as a broad causal model of abnormal behavior.

Necessary, Sufficient, and Contributory Causes

Regardless of one's theoretical perspective, several terms can be used to specify the role a factor plays in the **etiology,** or causal pattern, of abnormal behavior. A **necessary cause** is a condition that *must* exist for a disorder to occur. For example, general paresis cannot develop unless a person has previously contracted syphilis. A necessary cause, however, is not always sufficient by itself to cause a disorder—other factors may also be required. Many mental disorders do not seem to have necessary causes, although there continues to be a search for such causes. A **sufficient cause** of a disorder is a condition that guarantees the occurrence of a disorder. For example, one current theory hypothesizes that hopelessness is a sufficient cause of depression (Abramson, Metalsky & Alloy, 1989). According to this theory, if you are hopeless enough about your future, you will become depressed. However, a sufficient cause may not be a necessary cause. Continuing with the depression example, Abramson and colleagues (1989) acknowledge that hopelessness is not a necessary cause of depression—there are other causes of depression as well. Finally, what we study most often in psychopathology research are contributory causes. A **contributory cause** is one that increases the probability of developing a disorder but that is neither necessary nor sufficient for the disorder to occur. A contributory cause may be a condition that comes before and paves the way for a later occurrence of disorder under certain conditions. For example, parental rejection could increase the probability that a child may have difficulty in handling close personal relationships later or may increase the probability that being rejected in a relationship in adulthood might precipitate depression. We say here that parental rejection is a contributory cause for the person's later difficulties, but it is neither necessary nor sufficient (Abramson et al., 1989).

In addition to distinguishing between necessary, sufficient, and contributory causes of abnormal behavior, we must also consider the time frame under which the different causes operate. Some causal factors occurring relatively early in life may not show their effects for many years; these would be considered *distal causal factors* that may contribute to a predisposition to develop a disorder. By contrast, other causal factors operate shortly before the occurrence of the symptoms of a disorder; these would be considered *proximal causal factors.* A proximal causal factor may be a condition that proves too much for a person and triggers a disorder. Examples are a crushing disappointment at work or school, or loss of a loved one. Sometimes proximal or precipitating causes may seem insignificant and related only slightly, if at all, to the more distal causes. In short, it is the straw that breaks the camel's back. For example, leaving dirty clothes lying on the bathroom floor may be a minor annoyance in a basically well-adjusted family, but the same act can cause a heated argument in a family already experiencing major difficulties.

A *reinforcing cause* is a condition that tends to maintain maladaptive behavior that is already occurring. An example is the extra attention, sympathy, and removal from unwanted responsibility that may come when a person is ill; these pleasant experiences may discourage recovery. Another example occurs in cases of severe depression where the depressed person's behavior may alienate friends and family, leading to a greater sense of rejection that reinforces the existing depression (Hammen, 1991; Monroe & Simons, 1991).

For many forms of psychopathology we do not yet have a clear understanding of whether there are necessary or sufficient causes, although this remains the goal of much current research. However, we do have a good understanding of many of the contributory causes for most forms of psychopathology. Some of these contributory causes, to be discussed later in this chapter, operate in a distal manner, setting up vulnerability during childhood for disorder later in life. Other contributory causes have a more proximal relationship to the onset of a disorder and yet others may contribute to the maintenance of a disorder. This complex causal picture is further complicated by the fact that what may be a proximal cause for a problem at one stage in life may also serve as a distal contributory cause, setting up a predisposition for another disorder later in life. For example, the death of a parent can be a proximal necessary causal factor for a child's subsequent grief reaction that might last a few months or a year; however, the parent's death may also serve as a distal contributory factor that increases the probability that when the child grows up he or she may become depressed in response to certain stressors.

Feedback and Circularity in Abnormal Behavior

Traditionally in the sciences, the task of determining cause-and-effect relationships has focused on isolating the condition X (cause) that could be demonstrated to lead to condition Y (effect). For example, when the alcohol content of the blood reaches a certain level, alcoholic intoxication occurs. Where more than one causal factor is involved, the term *causal pattern* has been used. Here conditions A, B, C, etc. lead to condition Y. In either case, this concept of cause follows a simple linear model in which a given variable or set of variables leads to a result either immediately after or later in time.

In the behavioral sciences, and particularly in abnormal psychology, such simple cause-and-effect sequences are very rare. This happens not only because we usually deal with a multitude of interacting causes, but also because we often have difficulty distinguishing between what is cause and what is effect. In abnormal behavior, the effects of feedback and the existence of mutual, two-way influences must be taken into account. Consider the following situation:

A husband and wife are undergoing counseling for difficulties in their marriage. The husband accuses his wife of drinking excessively, while the wife accuses her husband of rejecting her and showing no affection. In explaining her frustrations to the therapist, the wife views the situation as "I drink because my husband rejects me." The husband sees the problem differently: "I reject my wife because she drinks too much."

Over time, a vicious circle has developed in which the husband has increasingly withdrawn as his wife has increasingly lost control of her drinking. It is extremely difficult, if not impossible, to differentiate cause from effect. Rather, the problem has become a vicious circle: each person influences and maintains the behavior of the other.

Even more subtle confounding of cause and effect occurs regularly in the lives of disturbed people. Consider the following scenario:

A boy with a history of disturbed interactions with his parents routinely misinterprets the intentions of his peers as being hostile. He develops defensive strategies to counteract the supposed hostility of those around him, such as the rejection of others' efforts to be friendly, which

In abnormal psychology, we often have difficulty distinguishing between what is cause and what is effect. For example, in problems between marital partners, a vicious circle may develop in which each person influences and maintains the behavior of the other. A wife who feels her husband is rejecting her may become increasingly hostile, and the husband may become more withdrawn as his wife's hostility increases, making it virtually impossible to differentiate cause from effect.

he misinterprets as patronizing. His behavior is difficult for others to deal with, even when their intentions are benign. Confronted by the boy's prickly behavior they become defensive, hostile, and rejecting, thus confirming and strengthening the boy's distorted expectations. In this manner, each opportunity for new experience and new learning is in fact subverted and becomes another encounter with a social environment that seems perversely and persistently hostile—exactly in line with the boy's expectations.

These examples illustrate that our concepts of causal relationships must take into account the complex factors of feedback, patterns of interaction, and circularity.

Diathesis-Stress Models

A predisposition toward developing a disorder is termed a *diathesis*. It can derive from biological, psychosocial, and/or sociocultural causal factors. Most mental disorders are conceived of as the result of stress operating on a person with a diathesis for the type of disorder that emerges. Hence we will discuss what are commonly known as **diathesis-stress models** of abnormal behavior (e.g., Meehl, 1962; Metalsky et al.,

1982; Rosenthal, 1963). To translate these terms into the types of causal factors described earlier, the diathesis is a relatively distal necessary or contributory cause, but it is not sufficient to cause the disorder. Instead, there must be a more proximal cause (the stressor), which may also be contributory or necessary but is generally not sufficient by itself to cause the disorder. In the past these models often had limited use because it was impossible to identify diatheses or stressors independently of one another or of an occurrence of maladaptive behavior. However, in recent years increasingly sophisticated methods of measuring both diatheses and stressors have developed that have made many of these models more useful (e.g., Monroe & Simons, 1991; Nietzel & Harris, 1990).

Stress, the response of an individual to demands that the individual perceives as taxing or exceeding his or her personal resources (Lazarus & Folkman, 1984) will be the focus of Chapter 4. Inevitably, however, we will find ourselves referring to stress and stressors (the demands themselves) in our discussion of diatheses because these concepts are so closely related. Indeed, the presence of a diathesis is often only inferred after stressful circumstances have led to maladaptive behavior. To further complicate matters, factors contributing to the development of a diathesis are themselves highly potent stressors, as when a child experiences the death of a parent and may thereby acquire a predisposition or diathesis for becoming depressed later in life.

In recent years, attention has been focused on the concept of **protective factors,** which are influences that modify a person's response to an environmental stressor, making it less likely that the person will experience the adverse consequences of the stressor (Rolf et al., 1990; Rutter, 1985). One important protective factor is having a family environment in which at least one parent is warm and supportive (Hetherington & Parke, 1993). However, protective factors are not necessarily positive experiences. Indeed, sometimes exposure to stressful experiences that are dealt with successfully can promote a sense of self-confidence or self-esteem and thereby serve as a protective factor; thus, some stressors paradoxically promote coping. This has sometimes been referred to as a "steeling" or "inoculation" effect, and is most likely to occur with moderate rather than with mild or extreme stressors (Hetherington, 1991; Rutter, 1987). Often protective factors may not show their effects at all unless a person is faced with a stressor (Rutter, 1985). And some protective factors have nothing to do with experiences at all, but are simply some quality or attribute of a person. For example, girls are less vulnerable than boys to many psychosocial stressors and physical hazards for reasons that are not yet well understood (Rutter, 1982). In addition, other protective attributes include having an easy temperament, high self-esteem, and high intelligence (Hetherington, 1991; Hetherington & Parke, 1993; Rutter, 1987). Protective factors are likely to lead to **resilience,** which is "the process of, capacity for, or outcome of successful adaptation despite challenging or threatening circumstances" (Masten, Best, & Garmezy, 1990, p. 426). The term *resilience* has been used to describe three distinct phenomena: "(1) good outcomes despite high-risk status, (2) sustained competence under threat, and (3) recovery from trauma" (Masten et al., 1990, p. 426). A more everyday way of thinking of resilience is in terms of "overcoming the odds" against you.

A child growing up under conditions of adversity may be protected from problems later in life if he or she has a warm and supportive relationship with some adult—in this case a grandmother. Encouraging children to ask questions, taking the time to listen to their problems and concerns, and trying to understand the conflicts and pressures they face are the important elements of such a supportive and protective relationship.

In sum, we can distinguish between causes of abnormal behavior that lie within and are part of the biological makeup or prior experience of a person—diathesis, vulnerability, or predisposition—and those that pertain to current challenges in a person's life—stressors. The diathesis can involve either necessary or contributory distal causal factors, but it is not by itself sufficient to cause the disorder. The stressors are more proximal causal factors and may also be necessary or contributory but generally not sufficient by themselves to cause the disorder. In addition, we can also examine protective factors, which may derive either from particular types of experiences or from certain qualities of the person, that can promote resilience in the face of vulnerability and stress. Most protective factors are probably contributory rather than necessary or sufficient to produce resilience. Different models of abnormal behavior, as we shall see in the sections that follow, identify different diatheses and different stresses as the route to abnormality, and different protective factors as the route to resilience.

MODELS OR VIEWPOINTS FOR UNDERSTANDING ABNORMAL BEHAVIOR

In attempting to uncover the causes of abnormal behavior, we rarely find clear-cut answers as we sometimes do in the case of physical disease. In the preceding chapter, for example, we examined many interpretations developed over the centuries to explain deviant behavior, from theories of supernatural possession to naturally occurring biological causes. Alternative viewpoints of the causes of abnormal behavior have emerged because no single approach satisfactorily explains all abnormal behavior. Each different viewpoint focuses on important facets of behavior, although each falls short of providing a complete explanation. In this chapter, we will look at several models or viewpoints that dominate today's approaches to understanding the causes of abnormal behavior and that form the basis for the types of therapy we will discuss in Chapters 16 and 17. All these viewpoints derive from the events described in Chapter 2, and, because they continue to evolve to meet new ideas and discoveries, some of them may well represent tomorrow's "history."

Students are often perplexed by the fact that, in the behavioral sciences, there are several competing explanations for the same thing. In general, the more complex the phenomenon being investigated, the greater the number of viewpoints that attempt to explain it. Inevitably, not all these viewpoints are equally valid. As you will see, the applicability of a viewpoint is often determined by the extent to which it helps an observer understand a given phenomenon, and its validity is usually determined by whether it can be supported through empirical research.

The viewpoints to be discussed here help mental health professionals explain abnormal behavior. They help us understand disorders on three broad fronts: their clinical pictures (the symptoms of the disorders), their causal factors, and their treatments. In each case, these viewpoints help professionals organize the observations they have made, provide a system of thought in which to place the observed data, and suggest areas of focus. Unfortunately, they can also blind us to evidence that may call for a change of orientation. This is because theoretical orientations in science often retain a strong hold over their adherents, even in the face of disconfirming evidence and alternative explanations of observable phenomena. They do so until some new insight is achieved that resolves the problems left unsolved by the conflicting interpretations of the empirical data. These new insights constitute *paradigm shifts,* fundamental reorganizations of how people think about an entire field of science (Kuhn, 1962). For example, the sun was thought to revolve around the earth until Copernicus proposed the radical idea that the earth revolved around the sun, causing a major paradigm shift in astronomy and physics.

Sigmund Freud, as we saw in Chapter 2, was responsible for a major shift in the focus of abnormal psychology; later, major aspects of Freud's theory came under attack. In recent years there seem to have been two paradigm shifts occurring in parallel in the study of abnormal behavior. First, the newer biological viewpoint is having a significant impact and is the dominant force in psychiatry. Second, the behavioral and cognitive-behavioral viewpoints have become the dominant paradigms among most research-oriented clinical psychologists. In the long run, however, we also know from psychosocial and sociocultural research that only an integrated approach is likely to provide anything approaching a long-lasting cure for many serious forms of psychopathology.

Many researchers and practitioners do not subscribe to a single theoretical perspective. Rather, they take an eclectic approach, drawing on what they see as the best principles or techniques from several viewpoints. Some integrate these different techniques into their own somewhat unique approach, and others use different viewpoints and techniques for different kinds of psychopathology. Either of these approaches seems to work better in practice than in theory; nevertheless, it reflects a growing trend by some practitioners not to be bound to any one viewpoint. We will return to this issue in the "Unresolved Issues" section of this chapter.

But first we must understand the major viewpoints of abnormal behavior and their perspectives on the causes of such behavior. Our survey will be descriptive. We do not intend to advocate one viewpoint over another. Rather, we will present information about the key ideas of each perspective, along with information about attempts to evaluate their validity. We will also describe the kinds of causal factors that each model tends to emphasize. As we will see, different models often have different perspectives on how and why a particular causal factor is involved in a given disorder.

We will first consider biological viewpoints. These emphasize organic conditions that impair brain and bodily functioning and lead to psychopathology. From there we will move on to psychosocial approaches. Of the psychosocial viewpoints, the psychodynamic focuses on intrapsychic conflicts that lead to anxiety; the behavioral, on faulty learning; the cognitive, on types of information processing that lead to distorted thinking; the humanistic, on blocked or distorted personal growth; and the interpersonal, on unsatisfactory relationships. We will look briefly, too, at the sociocultural viewpoint, which focuses on pathological social conditions and the importance of differing cultural backgrounds in shaping both vulnerability to psychopathology and the form psychopathology may take. Finally, in the "Unresolved Issues" section, we will investigate avenues leading toward the integration of theories.

THE BIOLOGICAL VIEWPOINTS

Many professionals in the field with biological backgrounds focus on the biological processes that have gone awry in affected people. As discussed in Chapter 2, in its most extreme form, the biological viewpoint, also referred to as the medical model, focuses on mental disorders as medical *diseases,* the primary symptoms of which are behavioral rather than physiological or anatomical. Mental disorders are thus viewed as diseases of the central nervous system, the autonomic nervous system, or the endocrine system, that are either inherited or caused by some pathological process. Neither psychological factors nor a person's psychosocial environment is believed to play a causal role in the mental disorder. Moreover, in its extreme form the medical model uses a strictly categorical approach for studying psychopathology. That is, it assumes, for example, that one has anxiety or depression or schizophrenia and that these are distinct disease entities. As we will see, however, these assump-

tions are not well supported by the study of these disorders given that there are many points of overlap among these and other disorders. A less extreme version of the biological viewpoint—the biopsychological model—allows for other causal factors but focuses on the genetic, biochemical, and other biological processes that have become imbalanced (for whatever reason) and are disrupting normal behavior.

As discussed in Chapter 2, the disorders first recognized as having biological or organic components were those associated with gross destruction of brain tissue. These disorders were neurological diseases—that is, they resulted from the disruption of brain functioning by physical or chemical means and often involved a psychological or behavioral aberration. We should distinguish between neurological diseases and the abnormal mental states (such as delusions) that sometimes accompany them, because neurological damage does not necessarily result in abnormal behavior.

Likewise, the bizarre thought content of delusions and other abnormal mental states is probably never, in itself, the direct result of brain damage. Clearly, a person's behavioral impairment (such as memory loss) may be readily accounted for by structural damage to the brain, but it is not so apparent how such damage produces the sometimes bizarre content of the person's thoughts or behavior. For example, we can understand how the loss of neurons in general paresis can lead to difficulties in executing certain tasks, but the fact that a person claims to be Napoleon is not likely to be the result simply of a loss of neurons. Such behavior must be the product of some sort of functional integration of different neural structures, some of which have been "programmed" by personality and and learning based on past experience.

Today we know that many conditions temporarily disrupt the information-processing capabilities of the brain without inflicting permanent damage or death to the neural cells involved—for example, brain inflammation or high fever. In these cases, normal functioning is altered by the context (especially the chemical context) in which the neural cells operate. The most familiar example is alcohol intoxication. In this condition, behavior is sometimes indulged in that would normally be inhibited. In sum, many processes short of brain damage can affect the functional capacity of the brain and thus change behavior.

BIOLOGICAL CAUSAL FACTORS

In this section we will focus on five categories of biological factors that seem particularly relevant to the development of maladaptive behavior: (a) biochemical imbalances in the brain, (b) genetic defects, (c) constitutional liabilities, (d) brain dysfunction, and (e) physical deprivations or disruptions. Each of these categories encompasses a number of conditions that influence the quality and functioning of our bodies. They are not necessarily independent of each other, and they often occur in varying combinations in different people.

Neurotransmitter and Hormonal Imbalances

Adequate brain functioning depends on the efficiency with which an excited nerve cell, or neuron, can transmit its "message" across a synapse to the next neuron in an established pathway in the brain. These interneuronal (or transsynaptic) transmissions are accomplished by chemicals called **neurotransmitters** that are released into the synaptic gap by the presynaptic neuron (see HIGHLIGHT 3.1 on page 70). There are many different kinds of neurotransmitters; some increase the likelihood that the postsynaptic neuron will "fire" (produce an impulse), while others inhibit the impulse. Whether the neural message is successfully transmitted to the postsynaptic neuron depends on the concentration of certain neurotransmitters within the synaptic cleft. This situation can be complicated by the fact that the cleft is normally bathed in various other biochemical substances that may or may not have transmitter properties. The belief that *biochemical imbalances* in the brain can result in abnormal behavior is one of the basic tenets of the biological perspective today. Some adherents of this view even suggest that psychological stress can bring on biochemical imbalances.

These biochemical imbalances can be created in a variety of ways. For example, there may be excessive production and release of the neurotransmitter substance into the synapses, causing a functional excess in levels of that neurotransmitter. Alternatively, there may be dysfunctions in the normal processes by which neurotransmitters, once released into the synapse, are deactivated. Ordinarily this occurs in one of two ways. After being released into the synaptic cleft, the neurotransmitter substance either is deactivated by enzymes present in the synapse or is reabsorbed into the presynaptic axon button, a process called *re-uptake*. Dysfunctions can create biochemical imbalances either when the deactivation enzymes present in the synapse are deficient, or when there is a slowing of the ordinary process of re-uptake.

Finally, there may also be problems with the receptors in the postsynaptic neuron, which may be either abnormally sensitive or abnormally insensitive. As we will see, different disorders are thought to stem from different patterns of neurotransmitter imbalances.

Some forms of psychopathology have also been linked to *hormonal imbalances*. **Hormones** are chemical messengers secreted by a set of endocrine glands in our bodies. They travel through our blood stream and affect various parts of our brain and body. Our central nervous system is linked to the endocrine system by the effects of the hypothalamus on the pituitary gland, which in turn controls the other endocrine glands. As we will see, malfunction of the hypothalamic-pituitary-adrenal-cortical axis has been implicated in various forms of psychopathology. Imbalances in sex hormones such as the male hormones—the androgens—can also contribute to maladaptive behavior.

Hormonal influences on the developing nervous system also seem to contribute to some of the differences in behavior between men and women. Although we know that sex-typing and other social learning experiences can sometimes override such influences, some biological influence still shows up in gender-related differences in behavior (Ehrhardt & Meyer-Bahlburg, 1981; Money & Ehrhardt, 1972; Rubin, Reinisch, & Haskett, 1981). For example, girls who were exposed prenatally to high levels of male hormones are likely to show higher levels of tomboyism and a preference for toys usually preferred by boys (trucks versus dolls) (Berenbaum & Hines, 1992; Money & Ehrhardt, 1972). In adulthood, males clearly show more aggressive behavior, with evidence coming from evolutionary, cross-cultural, developmental, and biological-hormonal sources (e.g., Eagly & Steffen, 1986; Hyde, 1984).

Genetic Defects

Genes affect biochemical processes and thereby the structure and physiological functioning of organisms. Although behavior is never determined exclusively by genes, organisms are genetically programmed through biochemical processes to adapt, physically and behaviorally, to their environments. Substantial evidence shows that some mental disorders have a hereditary component. The genetic transmission of traits or vulnerabilities from one generation to the next is, by definition, a biological process. Thus, the many recent studies suggesting

HIGHLIGHT   3.1

Neurotransmission and Abnormal Behavior

A nerve impulse, which is electrical in nature, travels from the cell body of a neuron down the axon. Although there is only one axon for each neuron (nerve cell), axons have branches at their end, called axonal endings or terminal buttons. These are the sites where neurotransmitter substances get released into a synapse—a tiny fluid-filled gap between the axon endings of one neuron (the presynaptic neuron) and the dendrites or cell body of another neuron (the postsynaptic neuron). The synapse is the site of neural transmission between neurons; that is, it is the site of communication between neurons. The neurotransmitter substances are contained within synaptic vesicles near the axon endings. When a nerve impulse reaches the axon endings, the synaptic vesicles travel to the presynaptic membrane of the axon and release the neurotransmitter substance into the synapse. The neurotransmitter substances released into the synapse then act on the postsynaptic membrane of the dendrite of the receiving neuron, which has specialized places called *receptor sites* where the neurotransmitter substances pass on their message. The receptor sites then initiate the receiving cell's response. The neurotransmitters can either stimulate that postsynaptic neuron to initiate an impulse or can inhibit impulse transmission. The message transmitted is thus a chemical one, and it may be either excitatory or inhibitory in nature—that is, it may either cause the postsynaptic neuron to fire or it may inhibit its firing. Some important neurotransmitters deliver inhibitory messages and others deliver excitatory messages. Both kinds of messages are important. Once the neurotransmitter substance is released into the synapse it does not stay around indefinitely (so that the second neuron does not continue firing in the absence of a real impulse). Sometimes the neurotransmitters are quickly destroyed by an enzyme, such as monoamine oxidase,

or sometimes they are returned to storage vesicles in the axonal button by a "re-uptake" mechanism.

Given that many forms of psychopathology have been associated with various imbalances in neurotransmitter substances, and with altered sensitivities of receptor sites, it is not surprising that many of the medications used to treat various disorders have as their site of action the synapse. For example, certain medications act to increase or decrease the concentrations of pertinent neurotransmitters in the synaptic gap. They may do so by affecting the actions of the enzymes that ordinarily break down the neurotransmitter substances in the synapse, or by blocking the re-uptake process, or by altering the sensitivity of the receptor sites.

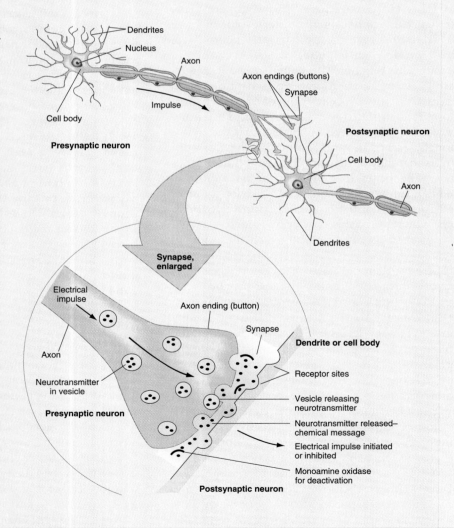

that heredity is an important predisposing causal factor in several disorders—particularly depression, schizophrenia, and alcoholism—support the biological viewpoint (Cloninger et al., 1986; Gottesman, 1991; Plomin, 1991; Torgersen, 1993). In these cases it is important to note that the genetic source of vulnerability does not manifest itself until later in life—adolescence or adulthood. It also seems possible that many broad temperamental features of newborns and children are genetically influenced—for example, behavioral inhibition and social introversion (Matheny, 1989), neuroticism and extraversion (Carey & DiLalla, 1994; Plomin, 1991).

The essential characteristics of human inheritance are basically the same for all people, although the specific features of genetic endowment vary widely. Except for identical twins, no two humans ever begin life with the same endowment. Thus heredity not only provides the potentialities for development and behavior typical of the species but is also an important source of individual differences. Heredity determines not the specifics of human behavior but rather the ranges within which characteristic behavior can be modified by environmental or experiential influences. For example, a child born with an introverted disposition may become more or less introverted depending on various experiences growing up, but it is unlikely that he or she will ever be truly extraverted.

Inheritance begins at conception, when a female's egg cell is fertilized by a male sperm cell. The resulting embryo receives a genetic code that provides potentialities for development and behavior throughout a lifetime. Because our behavior is inevitably influenced by our biological inheritance, it should hardly be surprising that certain vulnerabilities have their sources at this basic level. Some inherited defects interfere directly with the normal development of the brain. Other more subtle defects can leave a person susceptible to severe mental disorders. These subtle influences are usually transmitted in the genetic code itself, showing up as metabolic or biochemical variations from an ideally functional norm. The form of mental retardation known as phenylketonuria (PKU), for example, is produced by a genetically determined deficiency that makes the body unable to adequately metabolize a chemical compound present in many foods (phenylalanine) (see Chapter 13). (But see also HIGHLIGHT 3.2.) Other genetic defects are believed to affect adversely the delicate regulation of brain biochemistry.

Chromosomal Anomalies The chainlike structures within a cell nucleus that contain the genes are chromosomes. Advances in research have enabled us to readily detect *chromosomal anomalies*—irregularities

in the chromosomal structure—even before birth, thus making it possible to study their effects on future development and behavior. Normal human cells have 46 chromosomes containing the genetic materials in which the hereditary plan is encoded. When fertilization takes place, the normal inheritance consists of 23 pairs of chromosomes, one of each pair from the mother and one from the father. Twenty-two of these chromosome pairs are called *autosomes;* they determine by their biochemical action general anatomical and physiological characteristics. The remaining pair, the *sex chromosomes,* determine an individual's sex. In a female both of these sex chromosomes—one from each parent—are designated as X chromosomes. In a male, the sex chromosome from the mother is an X, but that from the father is a Y chromosome.

Research in developmental genetics has shown that abnormalities in the structure or number of the chromosomes are associated with a wide range of malformations and disorders. For example, Down syndrome is a type of mental retardation in which there is a trisomy (a set of three chromosomes instead of two) in chromosome 21. Here the extra chromosome is the primary cause of the disorder. Anomalies may also occur in the sex chromosomes, producing a variety of complications that may predispose a person to develop abnormal behavior.

Faulty Genes Genes are the long molecules of DNA (deoxyribonucleic acid) that are present at various locations on a chromosome. Genes could be likened to beads on a necklace (the chromosome). Individual genes may contain information that causes bodily processes to malfunction, although we cannot yet predict with any great certainty the occurrence of most such malfunctions.

In the field of abnormal psychology, genetic influences rarely express themselves in a simple and straightforward manner. This is because behavior, unlike some physical characteristics such as eye color, is not determined exclusively by genetic endowment: It is a product of the organism's interaction with the environment. In other words, genes can affect behavior only indirectly. Gene "expression" is normally not a simple outcome of the information encoded in DNA, but is rather the end product of an intricate process that may be influenced by the internal and external environment. A person's total genetic endowment is referred to as his or her **genotype**. The observed structural and functional characteristics that result from an interaction of the genotype and the environment are referred to as a person's **phenotype.** In some cases the genotypic vulnerability present at birth will not manifest its effect on the phenotype until much later in life. In many other cases, the genotype may shape the environmental experiences a child has, thus affecting the phenotype in yet another way. For example, a child who may be genetically predisposed to aggressive behavior may be rejected by his or her peers in early grades because of aggressive behavior. Such rejection may lead the child to go on to associate with similarly aggressive and delinquent peers in later grades, leading to an increased likelihood of developing a full-blown pattern of delinquency in adolescence.

Researchers have found three ways in which an individual's genotype may shape his or her environment (Hetherington & Parke, 1993; Scarr, 1992). First, the genotype may have what has been termed a passive effect on the environment resulting from the genetic similarity of parents and children. Such genetic similarity is likely to result in the parents automatically creating an environment compatible with the child's predisposition. For example, highly intelligent parents may provide a highly stimulating environment for their child, thus creating an environment that will interact in a positive way with the child's genetic endowment for high intelligence. Second, the child's genotype may evoke particular kinds of reactions from the social and physical environment. For example, active, happy babies evoke more positive responses from others than do passive, unresponsive infants (Lyton, 1980). Finally, the child's genotype may play a more active role in shaping the environment. In this case the child seeks out or builds an environment which is congenial. Extraverted children may seek the company of others, for example, thereby enhancing their own tendencies to be sociable (Baumrind, 1991; Hetherington & Parke, 1993).

The few instances in which relatively straightforward predictions of mental disorders can be made on the basis of known laws of inheritance invariably involve gross neurological impairment. In such cases, abnormal behavior arises in part as a consequence of a central nervous system malfunction, such as occurs in Huntington's disease; such conditions will be discussed in Chapter 13.

It appears likely that many of the most interesting (if still largely obscure) genetic influences in normal and abnormal behavior typically operate polygenically, that is, through the action of many genes together in some sort of additive or interactive fashion (e.g., Plomin, 1990; Torgersen, 1993). A genetically vulnerable person has inherited a large number of these genes that collectively represent faulty heredity. These faulty genes, in turn, may lead to structural abnormalities in the central nervous system, to errors in the regulation of brain chemistry, or to excesses or deficiencies in the reactivity of the autonomic nervous system, which is involved in mediating many of our emotional responses. These various processes serve to predispose the person to later difficulties.

Methods for Studying Genetic Influences. Although advances have been made in identifying faulty genetic endowment (including locating genes responsible for certain physical anomalies), we are not yet able to isolate specific defects on the genes themselves. Therefore most of the information we have on the role of genetic factors in mental disorders is based not on studies of genes, but on studies of people who are related to one another. This *pedigree,* or *family history,* method requires that an investigator observe samples of relatives of each *proband* or *index case* (the subject, or carrier, of the trait or disorder in question) in order to see whether the incidence increases in proportion to the degree of hereditary relationship. In addition, the incidence of the trait in a normal population is compared (as a control) with its incidence among the relatives of the index cases.

Another important method used to study genetic influences on abnormal behavior involves the study of twins. Identical or monozygotic twins share the same genetic endowment because they develop from a single zygote, or fertilized egg, so if a given disorder or trait were completely heritable, one would expect 100 percent *concordance* rates for the disorder. That is, if one identical twin had a particular disorder, the other twin would as well. There are virtually no forms of psychopathology where the concordance rates for identical twins are this high, and so we can safely conclude that virtually no disorders are completely heritable. However, as we will see, there are relatively high concordance rates for identical twins in some common and severe forms of psychopathology. Nevertheless, these concordance rates are only meaningful when they differ from those found for *nonidentical* twins. Nonidentical or dizygotic twins do not share any more genes than do siblings from the same parents because they develop from two different fertilized eggs. One would therefore expect concordance rates for a disorder to be much lower for dizygotic than for monozygotic twins if the disorder had a strong genetic component. That is, evidence for genetic transmission of a trait or a disorder can be obtained by comparing the concordance rates between identical and nonidentical twins. For most of the disorders we will discuss, concordance rates are much lower for nonidentical twins than for identical twins.

Some researchers have argued that higher concordance rates for a disorder in monozygotic twins

This set of identical twins from Bouchard's University of Minnesota study of the relative roles of genetics and environment provides some striking support for the prominence of genetic influences on personality traits and attitudes (Bouchard et al., 1990). Jim Springer (left) and Jim Lewis (right) were separated four weeks after their birth in 1940. They grew up 45 miles apart in Ohio. After they were reunited in 1979, they discovered they had some eerie similarities: Both chain-smoked Salems, both drove the same model blue Chevrolet, both chewed their fingernails, and both had dogs named Toy. Further, they had both vacationed in the same neighborhood in Florida. When tested for such personality traits as sociability and self-control, they responded almost identically.

than in dizygotic twins do not provide conclusive evidence for a genetic contribution because the possibility always remains that identical twins are treated more similarly by their parents than are nonidentical twins (Baker & Daniels, 1990; Torgersen, 1993). However, recent studies that have examined this possibility have provided reasonably strong evidence that this is not the case; in other words, it seems to be the genetic similarity that is more important than the similarity of the parents' behavior (e.g., Kendler, 1993). Nevertheless, the ideal study of genetic factors involves identical twins who have been reared apart in significantly different environments. Obviously, finding such twins is extremely difficult (there are probably only a few hundred in the United States), and only a few such studies with small numbers have been conducted. For example, Gottesman (1991) notes that only 14 pairs of identical twins reared apart where one has a diagnosis of schizophrenia have ever been studied. Although this sample is too small to be definitive, it is of interest to note that the concordance rates for schizophrenia for these identical twins reared apart was very similar to that reported for identical twins reared together.

The third important method used to study genetic influences is the *adoption* method. In one variation on this method, the biological and adoptive parents of individuals who have a given disorder are studied to determine their rates of disorder. If there is a genetic influence, one expects to find higher rates of the disorder in the biological than in the adoptive relatives. Although each of these methods alone has its pitfalls of interpretation, if the results from studies using all three strategies converge, one can draw reasonably strong conclusions about the

genetic influence on a disorder (Rutter, 1991a). In HIGHLIGHT 3.2 various misconceptions about studies of genetics and psychopathology are discussed (Rutter, 1991a).

Heritability studies, because they separate heredity from environment to some extent, also allow for testing the influence of environmental factors, and even for differentiating "shared" and "nonshared" environmental influences (Plomin & Daniels, 1987; Plomin, 1989). *Shared environmental influences* are those that would affect all children in a family similarly, such as overcrowding or poverty, and sometimes family discord. *Nonshared environmental influences* are those in which different children in a family differ. These would include experiences at school, but also some features of upbringing in the home that may not be the same for all children, as when a parent treats one child in a qualitatively different way from another. For many important psychological characteristics and forms of psychopathology, nonshared influences appear to be more important—that is, experiences that are specific to a child may do more to influence his or her behavior and adjustment than experiences shared by all children in the family (Rutter, 1991a).

Constitutional Liabilities

The term *constitutional liability* is used to describe any detrimental characteristic that is either innate or acquired so early—often prenatally—and in such strength that it is functionally similar to a genetic characteristic. Physical handicaps, basic reaction tendencies, and temperament are among the many

"Nature, Nurture, and Psychopathology: A New Look at an Old Topic"

Michael Rutter, one of the world's most prominent developmental psychopathologists, discussed in a 1991 article some mistaken stereotypes that people have about studies of genetic influences on behavior and psychopathology. Several of the more important misconceptions he identified (Rutter, 1991a) are:

1. *Strong genetic effects mean that environmental influences must be unimportant.* Even if we are discussing a trait or disorder that has a strong genetic influence, environmental factors can have a major impact on the level of that trait. Height, for example, is strongly genetically determined and yet nutritional factors have a very large effect on the actual height a person attains. Between 1900 and 1960 the average height of boys reared in London increased about 10 cm due to improvements in diet, in spite of the fact that there were not genetic changes in the same time period (Tizard, 1975).

2. *Genes provide a limit to potential.* One's potential can change if one's environment changes, as the above example illustrates. Another example comes from children born to socially disadvantaged parents who are adopted and reared with socially advantaged parents. These children have a mean IQ about 12 points higher than those reared in the socially disadvantaged environment (Capron & Duyme, 1989).

3. *Genetic strategies are of no value for studying environmental influences.* The opposite is true because genetic research strategies provide critical tests of the influence of environmental factors. For example, because monozygotic twins have identical genes, concordance rates of less than 100 percent clearly illustrate the importance of environmental influences, particularly those of the nonshared environment.

4. *Nature and nurture are separate.* Throughout this chapter and the book we try to emphasize that this is not so. Genetic effects "operate mainly through their effect on susceptibility to environmental influences" (Rutter, 1991a, p. 129). For example, babies born with the genetic defect causing phenylketonuria, a metabolic disease, only develop the disease if they are exposed to diets with phenylalanine. In addition, genes affect the kinds of experiences people have, as is immediately evident if one thinks about the effects that gender, IQ, and temperament have on one's life experiences. Another example comes from examining the effects of the aggressive behaviors shown by young delinquents, which tend to lead to rejections, broken friendships, and ultimately poor marriages; thus their own behavior (partially genetically determined) affects the

amount and kinds of stressors they later encounter.

5. *Genetic effects diminish with age.* Although many people assume that genetic effects should be maximal at birth, with environmental influences getting stronger with increasing age, it is now evident that this is not true (Plomin, 1986). For height, weight, and IQ, dizygotic twins are more alike than are monozygotic twins at birth, but over time dizygotic twins show greater differences than monozygotic twins. For whatever the reasons, many genetic effects on psychological characteristics increase with age up to at least middle childhood. Of course, other genetic effects do not appear until much later in life, as in cases like Huntington's disease, to be discussed in Chapter 13.

6. *Disorders that run in families must be genetic and ones that do not run in families must not be genetic.* Many examples contradict these misconceptions. For example, juvenile delinquency and conduct disorder tend to run in families, and yet this does not seem to be due primarily to genetic, but rather to environmental influences (McGuffin & Gottesman, 1985). Conversely, autism is such a rare disorder that it doesn't appear to run in families (only about 3 percent of siblings have the disorder), and yet there seems to be a very powerful genetic effect (Rutter, 1991b).

traits included in this category. We will briefly explore the role of these constitutional factors in the etiology of maladaptive behavior.

Physical Handicaps Embryologic abnormalities or environmental conditions operating before or after birth may result in physical defects. The most common birth difficulty associated with later mental disorders (including mental retardation, hyperactivity, and emotional disturbances) is low birth weight (5

pounds or less); approximately 6–7 percent of all babies born in this country in 1985 were of low birth weight (Kopp & Kaler, 1989) and current projections are that this will still be true in the year 2000 (Barnard, Morisett, & Spieker, 1993). This problem is most often a factor in premature births, but can also occur in full-term births. Prenatal conditions that can lead to premature birth and to low birth weight include nutritional deficiencies, disease, exposure to radiation, drugs, severe emotional stress, or the mother's excessive use of alcohol or tobacco. As might be expected, socioeconomic status is related to fetal and birth difficulties, the incidence being several times greater among mothers of lower socioeconomic levels (Kopp & Kaler, 1989). Fortunately, early intervention programs for the mothers of low birth weight infants, as well as for the infants, can be quite effective in preventing some of the problems often associated with low birth weight (e.g., Hetherington & Parke, 1993; Rauh et al., 1988).

Thus, a variety of biological and psychological conditions affecting a mother during pregnancy can have profound effects on a child's development and adjustment. Considerable evidence suggests that children whose earliest development is thus compromised are at significant risk for a variety of later maladaptive behaviors (e.g., Rutter, Tizard, & Whitmore, 1970). Such difficulties may be the direct result of impaired brain function (Breslau, 1990), or they may reflect diminished abilities to handle life challenges. For example, children with fetal alcohol syndrome (whose mothers consumed excessive alcohol in pregnancy) not only have stunted growth, impaired intellectual development, and abnormal facial features (Abel et al., 1993); they also show a wide range of psychopathological outcomes into adolescence, including emotional disorders, sleep disorders, hyperactivity, and abnormal habits (Steinhausen, Williams, & Spohr, 1993). (See Chapter 10 for further discussion.)

Primary Reaction Tendencies and Temperament
Newborns differ in how they react to particular kinds of stimuli. Some are startled by slight sounds or cry if sunlight hits their faces; others are seemingly insensitive to such stimulation. These reactions differ from baby to baby and are examples of *primary reaction tendencies,* characteristic behaviors that appear to have been established before any extensive interaction with the environment. These behaviors are regarded as constitutional rather than genetic because they are probably due to more than genetic influences alone; prenatal environmental factors may also play a role in their development. Primary reaction tendencies are one component of **temperament,** which involves not only reactivity but also characteristic ways of self-regulation. When we say that babies differ in temperament, we mean that they differ in systematic ways in their emotional and arousal responses to various stimuli, and in their tendency to approach, withdraw, or attend to various situations (Rothbart & Ahadi, 1994). Our early temperament is thought to be the substrate from which our personality develops. Starting at about 2–3 months of age, approximately five dimensions of temperament can be identified: fearfulness, irritability and frustra-

tion, positive affect, activity level, and attentional persistence, although some of these emerge later than others. These seem to be related to the three important dimensions of adult personality, which are neuroticism or negative emotionality, extraversion or positive emotionality, and constraint (conscientiousness and agreeableness) (Rothbart & Ahadi, 1994; Watson, Clark, & Harkness, 1994). The infant dimensions of fearfulness and irritability correspond to the adult dimension of neuroticism (disposition to experience negative affect). The infant dimensions of positive affect and possibly activity level seem related to the adult dimension of extraversion, and the infant dimension of attentional persistence seems related to the adult dimension of constraint or control. At least some aspects of temperament show a moderate degree of stability from late in the first year of life through at least middle childhood (e.g., Kagan et al., 1984; Kagan et al., 1990).

The temperament of an infant or young child has profound effects on a variety of important developmental processes (Rothbart & Ahadi, 1994). For example, someone with a fearful temperament has many opportunities for the classical conditioning of fear to situations in which fear is provoked; later avoidance learning may operate to keep the older child from entering those feared situations. A child with a low threshold for distress may also learn to regulate distress by keeping the level of stimulation low, whereas a child with a high need for stimulation may do things to increase excitement. In addition, a child who is prone to distress may have trouble forming a secure attachment relationship because caretakers find dealing with a distressed infant distressing to themselves. This can sometimes lead the caregiver to avoid the child, thereby creating a tendency for the child to develop an avoidant style of attachment in which he or she is unlikely to turn to the mother when upset (Rothbart & Ahadi, 1994).

Given these profound effects on various basic developmental processes, it is not surprising that temperament may also set the stage for the development of various forms of psychopathology later in life. For example, children who are fearful in many situations have been labelled *behaviorally inhibited* by Kagan and his colleagues. This trait has a significant heritable component (Kagan et al., 1990; Matheny, 1989), and when it is stable, it is a risk factor for the development of anxiety disorders later in childhood and probably in adulthood (Biederman et al., 1990; Hirshfeld et al., 1992; Kagan et al., 1990). Conversely, a child who is highly *uninhibited,* showing little fear of anything, may have difficulty internalizing moral standards for behavior (Rothbart & Ahadi, 1994). If these personality ingredients were combined with high levels of hostility, the stage could be set for the development of conduct disorder and antisocial personality disorder (Harpur, Hart, & Hare, 1993).

Brain Dysfunction

As we discussed in Chapter 2, a major scientific breakthrough in psychopathology came when researchers proved that general paresis was related to destruction of brain tissue by neurosyphilis. We now know that significant damage of brain tissue places a person at risk for psychopathology, but brain damage is rarely a cause of psychiatric disorder (Eisenberg, 1990). The incidence of such damage increases notably among the elderly, mostly because of the aging process itself (often resulting in Alzheimer's disease) or associated cardiovascular insufficiency, both of which will be discussed in Chapter 13. Brain damage in the elderly sometimes leads to abnormal behavior. In addition, it also increases vulnerability by making a person less able to cope.

Clearly then, gross brain pathology, in which there are observable defects in brain tissue, occurs in only a small percentage of people with abnormal behavior. However, more subtle deficiencies of brain function, such as those involved in attention deficit disorders and specific learning disabilities in children (see Chapters 13 and 14), may enhance vulnerability to more serious disorders later, particularly when a child's difficulties remain undiagnosed and remedial efforts are not undertaken.

Physical Deprivation or Disruption

Although we do not fully understand the processes involved, we do know that digestive, circulatory, and other bodily functions work to maintain the body's physiological equilibrium and integration. The mechanisms for ensuring normal blood chemistry, for maintaining constant body temperature, and for combating invading microorganisms strive to preserve steady states—to maintain physiological activity within a range essential to efficient functioning and survival. This process is referred to as *homeostasis*. For example, if we are cold, we shiver; if we are too hot, we sweat.

Injuries and diseases strike all of us from time to time and upset our normal equilibrium. The psychological repercussions from such events, often underestimated, can be profound. Depressions, for example, frequently accompany significant physical illnesses, in part because illnesses painfully remind us of the limits of our control over our lives. Also, obvious physical disabilities may result in social stigmatization that is itself demoralizing and destabilizing, leaving a person vulnerable to still other types of stress (Jones et al., 1984). Even without serious illness or disability people may experience challenges to their equilibriums. In the following sections, we deal with two such situations: deprivation of basic physiological needs and nonoptimal levels of stimulation.

Basic Physiological Needs   The most basic human requirements are those for food, oxygen, water, sleep, and the elimination of wastes. In order to survive, people must constantly renew themselves through rest and take in food and water. Insufficient rest, inadequate diet, or attempts to carry a full work load under the handicap of a severe cold, fatigue, or emotional strain may interfere with a person's ability to cope and predispose him or her to a variety of problems. Prisoners have sometimes been "broken" by nothing more persuasive than the systematic prevention of sleep or deprivation of food over a period of several days. Experimental studies of volunteers who have gone without sleep for periods of 72 to 98 hours show increasing psychological problems as the sleep loss progresses—including disorientation for time and place and feelings of depersonalization.

It is also now recognized that chronic but relatively mild sleep deprivation can have adverse emotional consequences in children and adolescents. For example, in an extensive review of the empirical literature Carskadon (1990) demonstrated that over the course of adolescence there is a pattern of decreasing total sleep time. This pattern was associated with a good deal of daytime sleepiness. She argued that the performance lapses that are associated with excessive sleepiness can in turn lead to an increased vulnerability to accidents and to the use of caffeine and alcohol, and to mood and behavior problems. In an interesting case study, a ten-year-old girl with attention-deficit disorder and a five-year history of sleep difficulties was treated for her sleep problem; associated with the improvement in sleep was a significant improvement in the symptoms of her attention-deficit disorder (Dahl, Pelham, & Wierson, 1991).

Studies of dietary deficiencies have also found effects on psychological functioning, the exact changes depending largely on the type and extent of the deficiencies. Some of these effects were demonstrated in a pioneering study of semistarvation carried out by Keys and his associates (1950) during World War II. Thirty-two conscientious objectors served as volunteer subjects and were put on low-calorie diets characteristic of European famine areas for a period of six months, followed by a three-month period of nutritional rehabilitation. The men had an average weight loss of 24 percent and showed dramatic personality and behavioral changes. They became irritable, unsociable, and increasingly unable to concentrate on anything but food, sometimes lying and stealing food to obtain additional food. By the close of the experiment, the men's predominant mood was one of gloom and depression, accompanied by apathy, feelings of inadequacy, and loss of interest in sex. Hunger and food dominated the men's thoughts, conversations, and even daydreams. There may also be some very long-term consequences of such severe weight loss. For example, when a group of former World War II and Korean War POWs who had lost 35 percent or more of their original body weight while in captivity were tested more than 30 years later, they performed more poorly on a variety of tests of cognitive functioning than did other former POWs who had not lost this much weight (Sutker, Galina, & West, 1990). In addition, Polivy and colleagues (1994) found that former POWs who had lost a great deal of weight reported higher than expected levels of binge eating in the interim years.

Perhaps the most tragic deprivation is seen in young children who are malnourished, with estimates by the World Health Organization being that 40–60 percent of the world's children suffer from mild to moderate malnutrition (Lozoff, 1989). In some parts of the world 3–7 percent may be severely malnourished. If these children survive, the scars of vulnerability are likely to remain for life. Severe malnutrition, which is associated with a host of other potentially damaging variables such as parental neglect and limited access to health care (Brozek & Schurch, 1984; Lozoff, 1989), not only impairs physical development and lowers resistance to disease, but also stunts brain growth and results in markedly lowered intelligence (Amcoff, 1980; Lozoff, 1989). In a postmortem study of infants who had died of malnutrition during their first year of life, Winick (1976) found the total brain cell content to be 60 percent below that of normal infants. Babies who undergo severe malnutrition but survive suffer the permanent stunting of brain growth because the brain's fastest growth occurs from about five months before until ten months after birth. In one important longitudinal study, 129 children in Barbados who had been severely undernourished dur-

During the semistarvation period in the Keys and colleagues (1950) experiment, the hunger drive became the most important factor affecting the subjects' behavior. The men became unsociable, frequently ignoring such amenities as table manners.

ing infancy, but who had caught up in physical growth later, were compared with 129 classmates of similar backgrounds for the first 18 years of life (Galler, 1984). Although their physical growth was normal, they showed major deficits in cognitive and behavioral functioning. Their IQ was an average of 12 points lower than that of the control group, and fully 60 percent suffered from attention-deficit disorder, which leads to attentional problems and increased distractibility and interferes with school performance. In this and other studies like it, not all of the effects are necessarily due to the early malnutrition per se because in many cases the families are impoverished in terms of social stimulation as well, sometimes simply because the mother is depressed (Lozoff, 1989).

Stimulation and Activity We have known for some time that healthy mental development depends on a child's receiving adequate amounts of stimulation from the environment. In addition to psychological vulnerabilities that can be induced by too little stimulation, and which will be discussed later, the physical development of the brain is adversely affected by an unstimulating environment. Conversely, many animal studies demonstrate enhanced biological development produced by conditions of special stimulation, including positive changes in brain chemistry and anatomy (Diamond, 1988; Swain et al., in press).

On the other hand, there are limits to how much stimulation is beneficial to a developing organism. We know that sensory overload can impair adult functioning (Gottschalk et al., 1972), and although we do not yet have evidence on this, one might assume that infants and children are similarly affected. In general, each person seems to have an optimal level of stimulation and activity that may vary over time, but that must be maintained for normal psychological functioning. Under excessive pressure, we may strive to reduce the level of input and activity. On the other hand, under some conditions—such as boredom—we may strive to increase the level of stimulation by doing something engaging. In Chapter 9, we will see that certain personality types, such as antisocial personalities, have higher-than-average needs for excitement.

The Impact of the Biological Viewpoint

Biological discoveries have profoundly affected the way we think about human behavior. We now recognize the important role of biochemical factors and innate characteristics, many of which are genetically determined, in both normal and abnormal behavior. In addition, since the 1950s we have witnessed many new developments in the use of drugs that can dramatically alter the severity and course of certain mental disorders—particularly the more severe ones. We know to some extent what biochemical changes are caused by taking these drugs, and we can evaluate their effects by noting behavioral, cognitive, and emotional changes in a patient. The host of new drugs has brought a great deal of attention to the biological viewpoint, not only in scientific circles but also in the popular media. Biological treatments seem to have more immediate results than other available therapies, and the hope is that they may in most cases lead to a "cure-all"—immediate results with seemingly little effort.

However, as Gorenstein (1992) has recently argued, there are several common errors in the way many people interpret the meaning of recent biological advances. For example, some prominent biological psychiatrists have suggested that "if we can show that a particular biological attribute is causally related to a particular abnormal mental condition, then that

mental condition can objectively be considered an illness (e.g., Andreason, 1984; Kety, 1974)" (Gorenstein, 1992, p. 119). But as Gorenstein argues, it is illusory to think that establishing biological differences between, for example, schizophrenics and nonschizophrenics in and of itself substantiates that schizophrenia is an illness. All behavioral traits such as introversion and extraversion, or high and low sensation seeking, are characterized by distinctive biological characteristics—and yet we do not label these traits as illnesses. Thus, the decision about what constitutes a mental illness or disorder ultimately still rests on subjective opinion regarding the functional effects of the disordered behavior. Establishing the biological substrate does not bear on this issue because all behavior—normal and abnormal—has a biological substrate. The second important misconception discussed by Gorenstein (1992) concerns the idea that most, if not all, mental disorders are biological conditions with biological causes (Andreason, 1984; Kety, 1974). Given that all of our cognitions and behavior are ultimately reducible to a set of biological events occurring in the brain, it is a mistake to distinguish between psychological and biological causes in this way. As Gorenstein argues, psychological causes can be distinguished from biological causes "only *prior* to their entry into the central nervous system" (p. 123). This is because once a psychological cause has had its effect on a person, the effect of that psychological event is also mediated through the activities of the central nervous system. In actuality then, if we find some dysfunction of the nervous system, this dysfunction could as well have arisen from psychosocial as from biological causes.

At a more general level we must remind ourselves again that few, if any, mental afflictions are independent of people's personalities or of the problems they face in trying to live their lives. We will examine viewpoints that emphasize these psychosocial and sociocultural considerations in the pages that follow. The challenge remains to integrate these varying perspectives into a theoretically consistent general system of psychopathology. We will return to this challenge in more depth in this chapter's "Unresolved Issues" section.

THE PSYCHOSOCIAL VIEWPOINTS

There are many more psychosocial interpretations of abnormal behavior than biological ones, reflecting a wider range of opinions regarding how to best understand humans as people rather than just as biological organisms. We will examine five perspectives on human nature and behavior: psychodynamic, humanistic, behavioral, cognitive-behavioral, and interpersonal. Although these viewpoints represent distinct and sometimes conflicting orientations, they are in many ways complementary. All of them emphasize the importance of early experience and an awareness of social influences and psychological processes within an individual—hence the term *psychosocial viewpoints* as a descriptive label. After describing these different psychosocial models we will consider a variety of psychosocial causal factors known to be associated with abnormal behavior and discuss how some of the psychosocial models would explain their effects.

The Psychodynamic Perspectives

Basics of Psychoanalysis As discussed in Chapter 2, Sigmund Freud founded the psychoanalytic school, which emphasized the role of unconscious processes in the determination of both normal and abnormal behavior. The actual techniques of psychoanalysis are based on the general principles underlying Freud's theory of personality. They are very complex and will not be dealt with in detail here. For our purposes, a general overview of the principles of classical psychoanalytic theory will suffice. For those wishing more information, good resources include Alexander's (1948) *Fundamentals of Psychoanalysis* and any of Freud's original works.

Id, Ego, and Superego. Freud theorized that a person's behavior results from the interaction of three key components of the personality or psyche: the id, ego, and superego.

The **id** is the source of instinctual drives. These are inherited and considered to be of two opposing types: (a) *life instincts,* which are constructive drives primarily of a sexual nature and which constitute the **libido,** the basic energy of life; and (b) *death instincts,* which are destructive drives and tend toward aggression, destruction, and eventual death. Freud used the term *sexual* in a broad sense to refer to almost anything pleasurable, from eating to painting. The id is completely selfish and pleasure-oriented, concerned only with the immediate gratification of instinctual needs without reference to reality or moral considerations. Hence it operates on the **pleasure principle.** Although the id can generate mental images and wish-fulfilling fantasies, referred to as **primary process thinking,** it cannot undertake the realistic actions needed to meet instinctual demands.

Consequently, after the first few months of life a second part of the personality, as viewed by Freud,

develops—the ego. The **ego** mediates between the demands of the id and the realities of the external world. The basic purpose of the ego is to meet id demands, but in such a way as to ensure the well-being and survival of the individual. This role requires the use of reason and other intellectual resources in dealing with the external world, as well as the exercise of control over id demands. The ego's adaptive measures are referred to as **secondary process thinking,** and the ego operates on the **reality principle.** Freud viewed id demands, especially sexual and aggressive strivings, as inherently in conflict with the rules and prohibitions imposed by society.

As a child grows and gradually learns the rules of parents and society regarding right and wrong, Freud postulated that a third part of the personality gradually emerges from the ego—the **superego.** The superego is the outgrowth of internalizing the taboos and moral values of society. It is essentially what we refer to as the *conscience;* it is concerned with right and wrong. As the superego develops, it becomes an inner control system that deals with the uninhibited desires of the id. The superego operates through the ego system and strives to compel the ego to inhibit desires that are considered wrong or immoral. Because the ego mediates between fulfilling the desires of the id, the demands of reality, and the moral constraints of the superego, it is often called the *executive branch of the personality.*

Freud believed that the interplay of id, ego, and superego is of crucial significance in determining behavior. Often inner conflicts arise because the three subsystems are striving for different goals. These conflicts are called **intrapsychic conflicts** and, if unresolved, lead to mental disorder.

Anxiety, Defense Mechanisms, and the Unconscious. The concept of anxiety—generalized feelings of fear and apprehension—is prominent in the psychoanalytic viewpoint. Freud distinguished three types of anxiety, or "psychic pain," that people can suffer: (a) *reality anxiety,* arising from dangers or threats in the external world; (b) *neurotic anxiety,* caused by the id's impulses threatening to break through ego controls into behavior that will be punished in some way; and (c) *moral anxiety,* arising from a real or contemplated action that is in conflict with an individual's superego and arouses feelings of guilt.

Anxiety is a warning of impending danger as well as a painful experience, and forces an individual to take corrective action. Often, the ego can cope with anxiety through rational measures. If these do not suffice, however, the ego resorts to irrational protective measures that are referred to as **ego-defense mechanisms** and are described in HIGHLIGHT 3.3. These defense mechanisms discharge or soothe

Ego-Defense Mechanisms

Mechanism	Example
Denial of reality. Protecting the self from an unpleasant reality by the refusal to perceive or face it.	A smoker concludes that the evidence linking cigarette use to health problems is scientifically worthless.
Fantasy. Gratifying frustrated desires by imaginary achievements.	A socially inept and inhibited young man imagines himself chosen by a group of women to provide them with sexual satisfaction.
Repression. Preventing painful or dangerous thoughts from entering consciousness.	A mother's occasional murderous impulses toward her hyperactive two-year-old are denied access to awareness.
Rationalization. Using contrived "explanations" to conceal or disguise unworthy motives for one's behavior.	A fanatical racist uses ambiguous passages from Scripture to justify his hostile actions toward minorities.
Projection. Attributing one's unacceptable motives or characteristics to others.	An expansionist-minded dictator of a totalitarian state is convinced that neighboring countries are planning to invade.
Reaction formation. Preventing the awareness or expression of unacceptable desires by an exaggerated adoption of seemingly opposite behavior.	A man troubled by homosexual urges initiates a zealous community campaign to stamp out gay bars.
Displacement. Discharging pent-up feelings, often of hostility, on objects less dangerous than those arousing the feelings.	A woman harassed by her boss at work initiates an argument with her husband.
Emotional insulation. Reducing ego involvement by protective withdrawal and passivity.	A child separated from her parents because of illness and lengthy hospitalization becomes emotionally unresponsive and apathetic.
Intellectualization (isolation). Cutting off affective charge from hurtful situations or separating incompatible attitudes by logic-tight compartments.	A prisoner on death row awaiting execution resists appeals on his behalf and coldly insists that the letter of the law be followed.
Undoing. Atoning for or magically trying to dispel unacceptable desires or acts.	A teenager who feels guilty about masturbation ritually touches a doorknob a prescribed number of times following each occurrence of the act.
Regression. Retreating to an earlier developmental level involving less mature behavior and responsibility.	A man whose self-esteem has been shattered reverts to childlike "show-off" behavior and exhibits his genitals to young girls.
Identification. Increasing feelings of worth by affiliating oneself with a person or institution of illustrious standing.	A youth-league football coach becomes excessively demanding of his young players in emulation of an authoritarian pro football coach.
Overcompensation. Covering up perceived weaknesses by emphasizing a desirable characteristic or making up for frustration in one area by overgratification in another.	A dangerously overweight woman goes on eating binges when she feels neglected by her husband.
Acting out. Engaging in antisocial or excessive behavior without regard to negative consequences as a way of dealing with emotional stress.	An unhappy, frustrated man has several indiscriminate affairs without regard to the negative effects of the behavior.
Splitting. Viewing oneself or others as all good or bad without integrating positive or negative qualities into the evaluations; reacting to others in an "all or none" manner rather than considering the full range of their qualities.	A conflicted manager does not recognize individual qualities or characteristics of her employees. Instead, she views them as all good or all bad, seeing most of them as all bad.
Sublimation. Channeling frustrated sexual energy into substitutive activities.	A sexually frustrated artist paints wildly erotic pictures.
Fixation. Attaching oneself in an unreasonable or exaggerated way to some person, or arresting emotional development on a childhood or adolescent level.	An unmarried, middle-aged man still depends on his mother to provide his basic needs.

Based on A. Freud (1946); American Psychiatric Association (1994, pp. 751–753).

The demands of the id are evident in early childhood. According to Freud, babies pass through an oral stage, in which sucking is a dominant pleasure.

anxiety, but they do so by helping a person push painful ideas out of consciousness rather than by dealing directly with the problem. This results in a distorted view of reality.

A key concept of psychoanalytic principles is the *unconscious.* Freud thought that the conscious part of the mind represents a relatively small area, while the unconscious part, like the submerged part of an iceberg, is the much larger portion. In the depths of the unconscious are the hurtful memories, forbidden desires, and other experiences that have been repressed—that is, pushed out of consciousness. Unconscious material continues to seek expression when ego controls are temporarily lowered under hypnosis, or in fantasies, dreams, slips of the tongue, and so forth. Until such unconscious material is brought to awareness and integrated into the ego structure—for example, through psychoanalysis—it may lead to irrational and maladaptive behavior.

Psychosexual Stages of Development. Freud conceptualized five **psychosexual stages of development.** Each stage is characterized by a dominant mode of achieving libidinal (sexual) pleasure:

The oral stage. During the first two years of life, the mouth is the principal erogenous zone; an infant's greatest source of gratification is sucking.

The anal stage. From age 2 to age 3, the anus provides the major source of pleasurable stimulation during the time when toilet training is often going on and there are urges both for retention and elimination.

The phallic stage. From age 3 to age 5 or 6, self-manipulation of the genitals provides the major source of pleasurable sensation.

The latency stage. In the years from 6 to 12, sexual motivations recede in importance as a child becomes preoccupied with developing skills and other activities.

The genital stage. After puberty the deepest feelings of pleasure come from heterosexual relations.

Freud believed that appropriate gratification during each stage is important if a person is not to be *fixated* at that level. For example, he maintained that an infant who does not receive adequate oral gratification may be prone to excessive eating or drinking in adult life.

In general, each stage of development places demands on an individual and arouses conflicts Freud believed must be resolved. One of the most important conflicts occurs during the phallic stage, when the pleasures of self-stimulation and accompanying fantasies pave the way for the **Oedipus complex.** Oedipus, according to Greek mythology, unknowingly killed his father and married his mother. Each young boy, Freud thought, symbolically relives the Oedipus drama. He longs for his mother and views his father as a hated rival; however, he also fears his father and is especially afraid that his father may remove his penis. This **castration anxiety** forces the boy to repress his sexual desire for his mother and his hostility toward his father. Eventually, if all goes well, the boy identifies with his father and comes to have only harmless affection for his mother.

The **Electra complex** is the female counterpart of the Oedipus complex and is also drawn from a Greek tragedy. It is based on the view that each girl experiences penis envy and wants to possess her father and replace her mother. While the boy renounces his lust out of fear of castration, no such threat can realistically be posed for the girl. Her emergence from the complex is milder and less complete than the boy's. She essentially settles for a promissory note: One day she will have a man of her own who can give her a baby—which unconsciously serves as a type of penis substitute.

For either sex, resolution of this conflict is considered essential if a young adult is to develop satisfactory heterosexual relationships. The psychoanalytic perspective holds that the best we can hope for is a compromise among our warring inclinations, and to realize as much instinctual gratification as possible with minimal punishment and guilt. This perspective thus presents a pessimistic and deterministic view of human behavior that minimizes rationality and freedom of self-determination. On a group level, it interprets violence, war, and related phenomena as the inevitable products of the aggressive and destructive instincts present in human nature.

Newer Psychodynamic Perspectives In seeking to understand his patients and develop his theories, Freud was chiefly concerned with the workings of the id, its nature as a source of energy, and the manner in which it could be channeled or transformed. Later theorists, notably including his daughter Anna Freud (1895–1982), were much more concerned with how the ego performed its central functions as the "executive" of personality. This second generation of psychodynamic theorists refined and elaborated on the ego-defense reactions.

Contemporary approaches focus neither on the nature of the id nor the ego, but rather on the objects toward which the child has directed these impulses and which the child has introjected (incorporated) into his or her own personality. *Object* in this context refers to the symbolic representation of another person in the child's environment, most often a parent. The concept of **introjection** refers to an internal process in which the child incorporates symbolically, through images and memories, some person viewed with strong emotion. For example, the child might internalize the image of a parent's scowling face. Later, this symbol, or object, can influence how a person experiences events and behaves.

The earliest development of this *object-relations* emphasis in psychodynamic thought took place in the 1930s in England under the leadership of Melanie Klein, W. R. D. Fairbairn, and D. W. Winnicott. These theorists developed the general notion that internalized objects could have various conflict-

ing properties—such as exciting or attractive versus hostile, frustrating, or rejecting—and moreover that these objects could split off from the central ego and maintain independent existences, thus giving rise to inner conflicts. For example, a child might internalize images of a punishing father; that image would then become a harsh self-critic. An individual experiencing such splitting among internalized objects is, so to speak, "the servant of many masters" and cannot therefore lead an integrated, orderly life.

The work of Margaret Mahler (1897–1985) in the United States complemented and added additional insights to this approach (see, for example, Mahler, 1976). Mahler pointed out that a very young child does not differentiate between self and object. Only gradually does a child gain an internal representation of self as distinct from representations of other objects. Only gradually is object constancy achieved (in which, for instance, the mother of yesterday is seen as the same object as the mother of today). This process involves a developmental phase of *separation-individuation,* the successful completion of which is essential for the achievement of personal maturity.

In recent years many other American analysts have become advocates of the object-relations point of view. Among them is Otto Kernberg, noted especially for his studies of both borderline and narcissistic personalities (see Chapter 9). Kernberg's view is that the borderline personality, whose chief characteristic is instability (especially in personal relationships), is an individual who is unable to achieve a full and stable personal identity (self) because of an inability to integrate and reconcile pathological internalized objects. These newer developments in psychodynamic theory emphasize interpersonal relationships and how the quality of early relationships

Anna Freud (1895–1982) elaborated the theory of ego-defense mechanisms and pioneered the psychoanalytic treatment of children.

Margaret Mahler (1897–1985) elaborated the object-relations approach, which many see as the main focus of contemporary psychoanalysis.

affects a person's subsequent ability to achieve fulfilling adult interactions. They will be addressed further in a later section on the interpersonal perspective.

Impact of the Psychodynamic Perspectives In historical perspective, Freudian psychoanalysis can be seen as the first systematic approach to show how human psychological processes can result in mental disorders. Much as the biological perspective had replaced superstition with organic pathology as the suspected cause of mental disorders, the psychoanalytic perspective replaced brain pathology with intrapsychic conflict and exaggerated ego defenses as the suspected cause of at least some mental disorders.

Freud greatly advanced our understanding of both normal and abnormal behavior. Many of his original concepts have become fundamental to our thinking about human nature and behavior. Two of Freud's contributions stand out as particularly noteworthy:

1. He developed techniques such as free association and dream analysis for becoming acquainted with both the conscious and unconscious aspects of mental life. The results thus obtained led Freud to emphasize (a) the extent to which unconscious motives and defense mechanisms affect behavior, (b) the importance of early childhood experiences in later personality adjustment and maladjustment, and (c) the importance of sexual factors in human behavior and mental disorders. Although, as we have said, Freud used the term *sexual* in a much broader sense than usual, the idea struck a common chord, and the role of sexual factors in human behavior was finally brought out into the open as an appropriate topic for scientific investigation.

2. He demonstrated that certain abnormal mental phenomena occur in the attempt to cope with difficult problems and are simply exaggerations of normal ego-defense mechanisms. This realization that the same psychological principles apply to both normal and abnormal behavior dissipated much of the mystery and fear surrounding mental disorders.

The psychodynamic perspective has come under attack from many directions—from other perspectives as well as from theorists within the psychodynamic tradition. Two important criticisms of psychoanalytic theory center on its failure as a scientific theory to explain abnormal behavior. First, it fails to recognize the scientific limits of personal reports of experience as the primary mode of obtaining information. Second, there is a lack of scientific evidence to support many of its explanatory assumptions or the effectiveness of its therapy. Freudian theory in

particular has been criticized for an overemphasis on the sex drive, for its demeaning view of women, for undue pessimism about basic human nature, for exaggerating the role of unconscious processes, and for failing to consider motives toward personal growth and fulfillment. The second generation of psychodynamic theorists did much to overcome these objections. Criticisms surrounding the scientific validity of psychodynamic approaches remain, however. In addition, psychodynamic theory has been criticized for neglecting the role of cultural differences in shaping behavior.

The Behavioral Perspective

Although psychoanalysis dominated thought about abnormal behavior in the early part of this century, another school—behaviorism—was emerging to challenge its supremacy. Behavioral psychologists believed that the study of subjective experience—through the techniques of free association and dream analysis—did not provide acceptable scientific data, because such observations were not open to verification by other investigators. In their view, only the study of directly observable behavior and the stimuli and reinforcing conditions that control it could serve as a basis for understanding human behavior, normal or abnormal.

The behavioral perspective is organized around a central theme: the role of learning in human behavior. Although this perspective was initially developed through research in the laboratory rather than through clinical practice with disturbed patients, its implications for explaining and treating maladaptive behavior soon became evident. As discussed in Chapter 2, the roots of the behavioral perspective came from the study of classical conditioning by Ivan Pavlov and from the study of instrumental conditioning by Edward Thorndike (later renamed operant conditioning by B. F. Skinner). In the United States, John Watson did much to promote the behavioral approach to psychology with his book *Behaviorism* (1924).

Basics of the Behavioral Perspective As we have noted, *learning*—the modification of behavior as a consequence of experience—provides the central theme of the behavioral approach. Because most human behavior is learned, the behaviorists addressed themselves to the question of how learning occurs. They focused on the effects of environmental conditions (stimuli) on the acquisition, modification, and possible elimination of various types of response patterns—both adaptive and maladaptive.

Classical and Operant Conditioning. A specific stimulus may come to elicit a specific response through the process of **classical conditioning.** For example, although food naturally elicits salivation, a stimulus that reliably precedes the presentation of food will also come to elicit salivation. In this case, food is the *unconditioned stimulus* (US), and salivation is the *unconditioned response* (UR). A stimulus that precedes food delivery and eventually elicits salivation is called a *conditioned stimulus* (CS). Conditioning has occurred when presentation of the conditioned stimulus alone elicits salivation (called the *conditioned response*—CR). Pavlov, for instance, sounded a tone (the soon-to-be conditioned stimulus) just before he presented food (the unconditioned stimulus) to his dogs (Pavlov, 1927). After a number of tone-food pairings, the dogs salivated (the conditioned response) to the tone (the conditioned stimulus) alone. The dogs learned that the tone was a reliable predictor of food delivery and came to respond to it in a similar fashion. The hallmark of classical conditioning is that a formerly neutral stimulus—the CS—acquires the capacity to elicit biologically adaptive responses through repeated pairings with the US. However, we also now know that this process of classical conditioning is not as blind or automatic as once thought. Rather, it seems that animals (and people) actively acquire information about what CSs allow them to predict, expect, or prepare for a biologically significant event (the US). Indeed, only CSs that provide reliable and nonredundant information about the occurrence of a US will acquire the capacity to elicit CRs (Rescorla, 1988). For example, if USs occur as often without being preceded by a CS as they do with the CS, conditioning will not occur because the CS in this case does not provide reliable information about the occurrence of the US.

Classically conditioned responses are well maintained over time, that is, they are not simply forgotten. However, if a CS is repeatedly presented without the US the conditioned response will gradually extinguish. This gradual process, known as **extinction,** should not be confused with the idea of unlearning because we know that the response may return at some future point in time (a phenomenon Pavlov called **spontaneous recovery**). Moreover, the CR may also still be elicited in different environmental contexts than that in which the extinction process took place (Bouton, 1994). Thus, any extinction of fear that has taken place in a therapist's office may not necessarily generalize automatically to other contexts outside the therapist's office. As we will see, these principles of extinction and spontaneous recovery have important implications for many forms of behavioral treatment.

The chief importance of classical conditioning in abnormal psychology is the fact that many physiological and emotional responses can be conditioned, including those relating to fear, anxiety, sexual arousal, and those stimulated by drugs or abuse. Thus, for example, one can learn a fear of the dark if fear-producing stimuli (such as frightening dreams or fantasies) occur regularly during conditions of darkness, or one can acquire a fear of snakes if bitten by a snake.

In **operant (or instrumental) conditioning,** an individual learns how to achieve a desired goal. The goal in question may be to obtain something that is rewarding or to escape from something that is unpleasant. Essential here is the concept of **reinforcement,** which refers to the delivery of a reward or a pleasant stimulus, or to escape from an aversive stimulus. New responses are learned and tend to recur if they are reinforced. Although it was originally thought that operant conditioning, like classical conditioning, consisted of simple strengthening of a stimulus-response connection, it is now believed that the person learns a *response-outcome expectancy* (Mackintosh, 1983), and if sufficiently motivated for that outcome (e.g., being hungry) the person will make the response that it has learned produces the outcome (e.g., opening the refrigerator).

Initially a high rate of reinforcement may be necessary to establish an operant response, but lesser rates are usually sufficient to maintain it. In fact, an operant response appears to be especially persistent when reinforcement is intermittent—when the reinforcing stimulus does not invariably follow the response—as demonstrated in gambling when occasional wins seem to maintain high rates of response. However, when reinforcement is consistently withheld over time, the conditioned response—whether classical or operant—gradually extinguishes. In short, the subject eventually stops making the response.

A special problem arises in extinguishing a response in situations in which a subject has been conditioned to anticipate an aversive event and to make an instrumental response to avoid it. For example, a boy who has nearly drowned in a swimming pool may develop a fear of water and a *conditioned avoidance response* in which he consistently avoids all large bodies of water. When he sees a pond, lake, or swimming pool, he feels anxious; running away and avoiding contact lessens his anxiety and is thus reinforcing. As a result, his avoidance response is highly resistant to extinction. It also prevents him from having experiences with water that could bring about extinction of his fear. In later discussions, we will see that conditioned avoidance responses play a role in many patterns of abnormal behavior.

As we grow up, operant learning becomes an important mechanism for discriminating between what will prove rewarding and what will prove unrewarding—and thus for acquiring the behaviors essential for coping with our world. Unfortunately, there is no guarantee that what we learn will always be useful. We may learn to value things that seem attractive in the short run, such as cigarettes or alcohol, but that can actually hurt us in the long run, or we may learn coping patterns such as helplessness, bullying, or other irresponsible behaviors that are maladaptive rather than adaptive in the long run.

Generalization and Discrimination. In both classical and operant conditioning, when a response is conditioned to one stimulus or set of stimulus conditions, it can be evoked by other, similar stimuli; this process is called **generalization.** A person who fears bees, for example, may generalize that fear to all flying insects.

A process complementary to generalization is **discrimination,** which occurs when a person learns to distinguish between similar stimuli and to respond differently to them. The ability to discriminate may be brought about through *differential reinforcement.* For example, because red strawberries taste good and green ones do not, a conditioned discrimination will occur if a person has experience with both. According to the behavioral perspective, complex processes like perceiving, forming concepts, and solving problems are all based on this basic discriminative process.

The concepts of generalization and discrimination have many implications for the development of maladaptive behavior. Although generalization enables us to use past experiences in sizing up new situations, the possibility always exists of making inappropriate generalizations—as when a troubled youth fails to discriminate between friendly and hostile "joshing" from peers. In some instances, a vital discrimination seems to be beyond an individual's capability—as when a bigoted person deals with others as stereotypes rather than as individuals—and may lead to inappropriate and maladaptive behavior.

Impact of the Behavioral Perspective The principles of conditioning had been fairly well worked out by 1950 when John Dollard and Neal Miller published their classic work *Personality and Psychotherapy,* which reinterpreted psychoanalytic theory in the terminology of learning principles. They asserted that the ungoverned pleasure-seeking impulses of Freud's id were merely an aspect of the principle of reinforcement (the behavior of organisms being generally determined by the maximiza-

tion of pleasure and minimization of pain); that anxiety was merely a conditioned fear response; that repression was merely conditioned thought-stoppage reinforced by anxiety reduction; and so on. The groundwork was thus laid for a behavioral assault on the prevailingly psychodynamic doctrines of the time. Early efforts to apply learning principles in the treatment of abnormal behavior, such as those by Salter (1949) and Wolpe (1958), were met with much resistance by the well-entrenched supporters of psychoanalysis; it was not until the 1960s and 1970s that behavioral therapy became established as a powerful way of viewing and treating abnormal behavior.

By means of relatively few basic concepts, behaviorism attempts to explain the acquisition, modification, and extinction of nearly all types of behavior. Maladaptive behavior is viewed as essentially the result of (a) a failure to learn necessary adaptive behaviors or competencies, such as how to establish satisfying personal relationships; or (b) the learning of ineffective or maladaptive responses. Maladaptive behavior is thus the result of learning that has gone awry and is defined in terms of specific, observable, undesirable responses.

For the behaviorist, the focus of therapy is on changing specific behaviors and emotional responses—eliminating undesirable reactions and learning desirable ones. For example, therapists can have considerable impact with the application of learning principles in the area of social skills training (Liberman, Mueser, & DeRisi, 1989). A number of *behavioral techniques* have been developed, based on the systematic application of learning principles, many of which are described in HIGHLIGHT 3.4. Additional examples of these techniques will be given in later chapters.

The behavioral approach has been heralded for its precision and objectivity, for its wealth of research, and for its demonstrated effectiveness in changing specific behaviors. A behavior therapist specifies what behavior is to be changed and how it is to be changed. Later, the effectiveness of the therapy can be evaluated objectively by the degree to which the stated goals have been achieved. On the other hand, the behavioral perspective has been criticized for being concerned only with symptoms (a criticism considered unfair by many contemporary behavior therapists), and for ignoring the problems of value, meaning, and self-direction that may be important for those seeking help.

Whatever its limitations, the behavioral perspective has had and continues to have a tremendous impact on contemporary views of human nature, behavior, and psychopathology.

Some Behavior-Modification Techniques Based on Learning Principles

Learning Principle	Technique	Example
Behavior patterns are developed and established through repeated association with positive reinforcers.	Use of **positive reinforcement** to establish desired behavior	A group of chronic mental patients were successfully rehabilitated by being provided with tokens as rewards for desirable behavior. The tokens could subsequently be used to "purchase" food, pleasant surroundings, etc. (Paul & Lentz, 1977).
The association of a behavior pattern with aversive stimuli (**punishment**) results in suppression of that behavior pattern.	Use of **aversive stimuli** to eliminate undesirable behavior (punishment)	Tantrums in a five-year-old psychotic boy and inappropriate behavior in a ten-year-old retarded boy were suppressed through use of a delayed punishment procedure. Parents tape-recorded tantrums or inappropriate behavior that occurred in daily school settings, then later played back portions of the tape while administering punishment. Punishment consisted of response suppression (holding the child in a corner) and firm verbalizations. The tape recorder–mediated procedure produced greater reductions in tantrums than verbal punishment alone (Rolider & Van Houten, 1985).
When a behavior is no longer reinforced, it tends to extinguish.	**Withdrawal of reinforcement** for undesirable behavior	Depression was alleviated when family members of depressed patients were told to provide attention for constructive behavior but to ignore depressive behavior (Liberman & Raskin, 1971).
Avoidance behavior will be inhibited or reduced if the conditions that provoke it are repeatedly paired with positive stimuli.	**Desensitization** to conditions that elicit unreasonable fear or anxiety	A 45-year-old veteran was successfully treated for phobias concerning loud noises and high places. The treatment, known as systematic desensitization, consisted of having the man repeatedly imagine fearful scenes relating to his phobias while in a state of deep relaxation (Rimm & Lefebvre, 1981).
A behavior can be established gradually if successive approximations of the behavior are reinforced.	**Shaping of desired behavior**	Shaping and modeling procedures were used to teach children to swallow pills required for their treatment. Five out of six children successfully learned to take their medications (Blount et al., 1984).
Reinforcement can operate to modify covert behavior (cognitions) as well as overt behavior.	**Cognitive restructuring**	Highly anxious subjects were asked to imagine being in an anxiety-arousing test situation and were then presented with instructions for reducing their anxiety. Subjects not only learned to react to test situations with less anxiety but responded to other social circumstances with more adaptive attitudes (Goldfried, Linehan, & Smith, 1978).

John Dollard (1900–1980) was a pioneer in shifting the focus on the nature of psychological functioning from overt behavior to the underlying cognitions assumed to be producing that

Neal Miller (b. 1909), along with John Dollard, reinterpreted psychoanalytic theory into the language of learning principles in their classic work Personality and Psychotherapy.

The Cognitive-Behavioral Perspective

The behavioral perspective was a reaction to the subjectivism of an earlier era in psychology. It sought to banish private mental events from psychological study because they were unobservable and therefore deemed unsuitable for scientific research. Some proponents of behaviorism even refused to use such terms as *mind* and *thought*. Behaviorism quickly gained wide acceptance among psychologists, but ironically just as it was at the peak of its influence as a theoretical school, it was challenged by members of its own ranks, as well as by psychologists and psychiatrists originally trained in the psychodynamic tradition.

The Basics of the Cognitive-Behavioral Perspective Since the 1950s psychologists, including some learning theorists, have focused on *cognitive processes* and their impact on behavior. Cognitive psychology involves the study of basic information-processing mechanisms, such as attention and memory, as well as higher mental processes such as thinking, planning, and decision making. In many respects, the current emphasis within psychology as a whole on understanding all of these facets of normal human cognition was originally a reaction against the relatively mechanistic nature of the traditional behavioral viewpoint, including its failure to attend to the importance of mental processes—both in their own

right and because of their influence on emotions and behavior.

Developments in clinical psychology have paralleled this reorientation in psychology as a whole. In many instances, the developments in this area were led by individuals who were formerly identified with the behavioral tradition in clinical psychology. The **cognitive** or **cognitive-behavioral perspective** on abnormal behavior focuses on how thoughts and information processing can become distorted and lead to maladaptive emotions and behavior. Unlike behaviorism's focus on overt behavior, the cognitive view treats thoughts as "behaviors" that can be studied empirically and that can become the focus of attention in therapy. In addition, by studying the patterns of distorted information processing exhibited by people with various forms of psychopathology, the mechanisms that may be involved in the maintenance of certain disorders have been illuminated. Today the cognitive-behavioral perspective is highly influential, both because of the successes it has had in developing effective treatments for many disorders and because of the insights it has provided into the importance of distorted cognitions in understanding abnormal behavior.

One pioneering theorist, George Kelly (1905–1966), contributed substantially to the cognitive viewpoint by developing a personality theory in which he postulated that people build *personal constructs*—uniquely individual ways of perceiving

Albert Bandura (b. 1925) stressed that people learn more by internal than external reinforcement. They can visualize the consequences of their actions rather than rely exclusively on environmental reinforcements.

Aaron Beck (b. 1921) pioneered the development of cognitive theories of depression, anxiety, and personality disorders. He also developed highly effective cognitive-behavioral treatments for these disorders.

Before the turn of the twentieth century, William James (1842–1910) set the stage for the humanistic perspective by discussing the concept of self in his book Principles of Psychology.

other people and events. People then use these personal constructs to interpret events around them. For example, the way a person interprets a comment made by an acquaintance can produce emotional upset even though the comment was neutral and not intended to hurt. Thus, it is the meaning an individual attaches to a stimulus, filtered through his or her own personal constructs, that results in negative feelings and an emotional reaction.

A learning theorist, Albert Bandura (b. 1925), placed considerable emphasis on the cognitive aspects of learning. Bandura stressed that human beings regulate their behavior by internal symbolic processes—thoughts. That is, they learn by *internal reinforcement*. We prepare ourselves for difficult tasks, for example, by visualizing what the consequences would be if we did not perform them. Thus we take our automobiles to the garage in the fall and have the antifreeze checked because we can "see" ourselves stranded on a road in winter. We do not always require external reinforcement to alter our behavior patterns; with our cognitive abilities we can solve many problems internally. Bandura (1974) has gone so far as to say that human beings have "a capacity for self-direction" and that recognition of this capacity "represents a substantial departure from exclusive reliance upon environmental control" (pp. 861, 863).

Attribution theory has also contributed significantly to the cognitive-behavioral approach (Bem, 1972; Fiske & Taylor, 1991; Heider, 1958; Weary & Mirels, 1982). **Attributions** simply refer to the process of assigning causes to things that happen. We may attribute causes to external events, such as rewards or punishments; or we may assume that the causes are internal—that they derive from traits within ourselves or others. Causal attributions help us explain our own or other people's behaviors and make it possible to predict what we or others are likely to do in the future. For example, if a person does something mean, we may assume that he or she has a quality of meanness and expect it to cause mean behavior in the future. Or if someone fails a test, he or she may attribute the failure to lack of intelligence (a personal trait) or to ambiguous test questions or unclear directions (environmental causes).

Attribution theorists have been interested in whether different forms of psychopathology are associated with characteristic attributional styles. *Attributional style* refers to a characteristic way that an individual may tend to make attributions for bad events or for good events. For example, depressed people tend to attribute bad events to internal, stable, and global causes ("I failed the test because I'm stupid" as opposed to "I failed the test because the teacher was in a bad mood and graded it unfairly"). However inaccurate our attributions may be, they become important parts of our view of the world and can have significant effects on our emotional well-being. They can also make us see other people and ourselves as unchanging and unchangeable, leading us to be inflexible in our relationships.

Another pioneering cognitive theorist, Aaron Beck (b. 1921), adapted the concept of schemas from cognitive psychology (e.g., Neisser, 1967, 1982). *Schemas* are underlying representations of knowledge that guide the current processing of information and often lead to distortions in attention, memory, and comprehension. According to Beck (1967, 1976), different forms of psychopathology are characterized by different maladaptive schemas that have developed as a function of adverse early learning experiences and that lead to the distortions in thinking characteristic of certain disorders such as anxiety, depression, and personality disorders.

The development of a cognitive-behavioral viewpoint distinct from behaviorism is not surprising. A hallmark of clinical behavioral practice has always been the precise identification of specific problem behaviors, followed by techniques directed specifically at those behaviors. Indeed, some behaviorally oriented therapies, such as *systematic desensitization* (described in Chapter 17), have always relied on asking clients to conjure up images in their minds, certainly a cognitive process. Cognitive-behavioral theoreticians and clinicians have simply shifted their focus from overt behavior itself to the underlying cognitions assumed to be producing that behavior. The issue then becomes one of altering the maladaptive cognitions. This is in contrast to, for example, psychodynamic practice, which assumes that diverse problems are due to a limited array of intrapsychic conflicts (such as an unresolved Oedipus complex) and tends not to focus treatment techniques directly on a person's particular problems or complaints.

In sum, cognitive-behavioral clinicians are concerned with their clients' self-statements—with what people say to themselves by way of interpreting their experiences. For example, people who interpret what happens in their lives as a negative reflection of their self-worth are likely to feel depressed; people who interpret a sensation that their heart is racing as meaning they may have a heart attack and die are likely to have a panic attack. Cognitive-behavioral clinicians use a variety of techniques designed to alter whatever negative cognitive bias the client harbors (see, for example, Beck et al., 1985; Hollon & Beck, 1994). The most widely used cognitive-be-

havioral therapies, Ellis's rational-emotive therapy and Beck's cognitive-behavioral treatment, will be described in greater detail in Chapter 17.

The Impact of the Cognitive-Behavioral Perspective The cognitive-behavioral viewpoint has had a powerful impact on contemporary clinical psychology. Many researchers and clinicians have found support for the principle of altering human behavior through changing the way people think about themselves and others. Many traditional behaviorists, however, are skeptical of the cognitive-behavioral viewpoint. Skinner (1990), in his last major address, remained true to behaviorism. He questioned the move away from principles of operant conditioning and toward cognitive behaviorism. He reminded his audience that cognitions are not observable phenomena and, as such, cannot be relied on as solid empirical data. Although Skinner is gone, this debate will surely continue. Indeed, Wolpe (1988), who was another founder of behavior therapy, remains highly critical of the cognitive perspective even today.

The Humanistic Perspective

The humanistic perspective focuses on freeing people from disabling assumptions and attitudes so that they can live fuller lives. Its emphasis is thus on growth and self-actualization rather than on curing diseases or alleviating disorders; its practitioners do not typically treat persons suffering from serious mental disorders.

The humanistic perspective has been influenced by both the behavioral and the psychodynamic perspectives, but it is in significant disagreement with both. The behavioral perspective, with its focus on the stimulus situation and observable behavior, is seen as an oversimplification that underrates the importance of a person's psychological makeup, inner experience, and potential for self-direction. Humanistic psychologists also disagree with the negative picture of human nature presented by psychoanalytic theory and its stress on the overwhelming power of irrational, unconscious impulses. Instead, the **humanistic perspective** views basic human nature as "good," emphasizes present conscious processes—paying less attention to unconscious processes and past causes—and places strong emphasis on people's inherent capacity for responsible self-direction. Humanistic psychologists think that much of the empirical research designed to investigate causal factors is too simplistic to uncover the complexities of human behavior. Thus the humanistic perspective tends to be as much a statement of values—how we ought to view the human condition—as it is an attempt to account for human behavior, at least among persons beset by personal problems.

The Roots of the Humanistic Perspective The humanistic approach emerged as a major perspective in psychology during the 1950s and 1960s when many middle-class Americans began to feel materially affluent and spiritually empty. (A related movement—the existential perspective—is described in HIGHLIGHT 3.5.) The humanistic approach recognizes the importance of learning and other psychological processes that have traditionally been the focus of research, but, as noted above, it is optimistically concerned with an individual's future rather

---

HIGHLIGHT   3.5

The Existential Perspective

During the middle part of this century, as the humanistic perspective was becoming an influential force in the field of psychology, a related intellectual movement (centered in Europe) was also beginning to have a notable impact. This movement was called existentialism, a philosophical outlook with roots in the work of such existential thinkers as Martin Heidegger and Søren Kierkegaard. The existential perspective resembles humanism in its emphasis on the uniqueness of each individual, the quest for values and meanings, and the existence of freedom for self-direction and self-fulfillment.

The existential perspective, however, represents a less optimistic view of human beings and places more emphasis on the irrational tendencies and the difficulties inherent in self-fulfillment—particularly in a modern, bureaucratic, and dehumanizing mass society. In short, living is much more of a "confrontation" for the existentialists than for the humanists. Existential thinkers are especially concerned with the inner experiences of an individual in his or her attempts to understand and deal with the deepest human problems. The following paragraphs summarize some of the basic tenets of existentialism:

1. *Existence and essence.* A basic theme of existentialism is that our

existence is a given, but what we make of it—our essence—is up to us. An adolescent boy who defiantly blurts out, "Well, I didn't ask to be born," is stating a profound truth, but in existential terms it is completely irrelevant. Whether he asked to be born or not, he is in the world and answerable for himself—for one human life. It is his responsibility to shape the kind of person he is to become and to live a meaningful and constructive life.

2. *Choice, freedom, and courage.* Our essence is created by our choices, because our choices reflect the values on which we base and order our lives. As Sartre said, "I am my choices." In choosing what sort of people to become, we have absolute freedom; even refusing to choose represents a choice. Thus the locus of value is within each individual. We are inescapably the architects of our own lives.

3. *Meaning, value, and obligation.* A central theme in the existential perspective is the will-to-meaning. This trait is considered a basic human characteristic and is primarily a matter of finding satisfying values and guiding one's life by them. As we have noted, this is a difficult and highly individual matter. Each of us must find our own pattern of values. This orientation should not be interpreted as purely nihilistic or selfish. Existen-

tialism also places strong emphasis on our obligations to each other. The most important consideration is not what we can get out of life but what we can contribute to it. Our lives can be fulfilling only if they involve socially constructive values and choices.

4. *Existential anxiety and the encounter with nothingness.* A final existential theme, nonbeing, or nothingness, adds an urgent and painful note to the human situation. In its ultimate form, nothingness is death, which is the inescapable fate of all human beings. The awareness of our inevitable death and its implications for our living can lead to existential anxiety—a deep concern over whether we are living meaningful and fulfilling lives. We can overcome our existential anxiety and deny victory to nothingness by living a life that counts for something.

This philosophy has clear implications for students of abnormal psychology. Existential psychologists focus on the importance of establishing values and acquiring a level of spiritual maturity worthy of the freedom and dignity bestowed by one's humanness. It is the avoidance of such central issues that creates corrupted, meaningless, and wasted lives. Much abnormal behavior, therefore, is seen as the product of a failure to deal constructively with existential despair and frustration.

Carl Rogers (1902–1987) contributed significantly to the humanistic perspective with his systematic formulation of the concept of self, which emphasizes the importance of individuality and a striving towards what Rogers called self-actualization.

Abraham H. Maslow (1908–1970) devoted more than two decades to showing the potentialities of human beings for higher self-development and functioning.

Alfred Adler (1870–1937) was a student of Freud who took issue with psychoanalytic theory for its neglect of social factors as determinants of behavior. Adler believed that people were inherently social beings motivated primarily by the desire to belong to and participate in a group. His work laid the foundation for the interpersonal perspective.

than his or her past. This perspective is also concerned with processes about which we have as yet little scientific information—love, hope, creativity, values, meaning, personal growth, and self-fulfillment.

Basics of the Humanistic Perspective Although not readily subject to empirical investigation, certain underlying themes and principles of humanistic psychology can be identified. These views are described in the following sections.

The Self as a Unifying Theme. In the first comprehensive textbook on psychology, published in 1890, William James included a discussion of the consciousness of self. This concept was later dropped by the behaviorists because the self could not be observed by an outsider. Although the cognitive-behaviorists have again incorporated cognitive aspects of human behavior into their perspective, it was the humanists of the 1950s and 1960s who focused their perspective on the concept of self.

Among humanistic psychologists, Carl Rogers (1902–1987) developed the most systematic formulation of the *self-concept,* based largely on his pioneering research into the nature of the psychotherapeutic process. Rogers (1951, 1959) stated his views in a series of propositions that may be summarized as follows:

- Each individual exists in a private world of experience of which the I, me, or myself is the center.
- The most basic striving of an individual is toward the maintenance, enhancement, and actualization of the self.
- An individual reacts to situations in terms of the way he or she perceives them, in ways consistent with his or her self-concept and view of the world.
- A perceived threat to the self is followed by a defense—including a tightening of perception and behavior and the introduction of self-defense mechanisms.
- An individual's inner tendencies are toward health and wholeness; under normal conditions, a person behaves in rational and constructive ways and chooses pathways toward personal growth and self-actualization.

In using the concept of self as a unifying theme, humanistic psychologists emphasize the importance of individuality. In studying human nature, psychologists are thus faced with the dual task of describing the uniqueness of each person and identifying the characteristics that all people share.

A Focus on Values and Personal Growth. Humanistic psychologists emphasize values and the process of choice in guiding our behavior and achieving meaningful and fulfilling lives. They consider it crucial that each of us develop values based on our own experiences and evaluations rather than blindly accepting the values of others; otherwise, we deny our own experiences and lose touch with our own feelings. To evaluate and choose for ourselves requires a clear sense of our own identity—the discovery of who we are, what sort of person we want to become, and why. Only in this way can we become **self-actualizing,** meaning that we are achieving our full potential.

According to the humanistic view, psychopathology is essentially the blocking or distortion of personal growth and the natural tendency toward physical and mental health. Such blocking or distortion is generally the result of one or more of these causal factors: (a) the exaggerated use of ego-defense mechanisms that leave an individual increasingly out of touch with reality, (b) unfavorable social conditions and faulty learning, and (c) excessive stress.

Impact of the Humanistic Perspective   The major impact of the humanistic perspective has been its emphasis on our capacity for full functioning as human beings; it has thus introduced a new dimension to our thinking about abnormal behavior. Abnormality is seen as a failure to develop our tremendous potentials as human beings—as a blocking or distortion of our natural tendencies toward health and personal growth rather than as abnormality or deviance. In fact, Maslow (1962, 1969) even expressed concern about the disappointing and wasteful failure of so many "normal" people to realize their potentialities as human beings. Therapy, according to this way of thinking, is not a means of moving a person from maladjustment to adjustment, but of fostering growth toward a socially constructive and personally fulfilling way of life.

The humanistic perspective has been criticized for its diffuseness, for its lack of scientific rigor, and for its high expectations. Although some psychologists view its goals as grandiose, others see them as useful descriptions of the challenging long-range tasks that confront psychology today.

The Interpersonal Perspective

We are social beings, and much of what we are is a product of our relationships with others. It is logical to expect that much of psychopathology reflects this fact—that psychopathology is rooted in the unfortunate tendencies we have developed while dealing with our interpersonal environments. Abnormal be-

Erich Fromm (1900–1980) focused on the orientations that people adopt in their interactions with others. He believed that these basic orientations to the social environment were the bases of much psychopathology.

havior has a great deal of impact on our relationships with other people. Hence it should not be surprising that many theorists conclude that abnormal behavior is best understood by analyzing our relationships, past and present, with other people. This is the focus of the **interpersonal perspective.**

Roots of the Interpersonal Perspective   The roots of the interpersonal perspective lie in the psychodynamic movement. The defection in 1911 of Alfred Adler (1870–1937) from the psychoanalytic viewpoint of his teacher, Freud, grew out of Adler's emphasis on social rather than inner determinants of behavior. Adler objected to the prominence Freud gave to instincts as the basic driving forces of personality. In Adler's view, people were inherently social beings motivated primarily by the desire to belong to and participate in a group.

Over time, a number of other Freudian theorists took issue with psychoanalytic theory for its neglect of crucial social factors. Among the best known of these theorists were Erich Fromm (1900–1980) and Karen Horney (1885–1952). Fromm focused on the orientations, or dispositions (exploitive, for example), that people adopted in their interactions with others. He believed that these orientations to the social environment were the bases of much psychopathology. Horney independently developed a similar view and, in particular, vigorously rejected Freud's demeaning psychoanalytic view of women (for instance, the idea that women experience penis envy). According to Horney, "femininity" was a

Karen Horney (1885–1952) was trained in Freudian theory, but she rejected Freud's demeaning psychoanalytic view of women. She believed that "femininity" was a product of the culturally determined social learning that most women experience.

Erik Erikson (1902–1994) elaborated and broadened Freud's psychosexual stages into more socially oriented concepts. Erikson described conflicts that occurred at eight stages, each of which could be resolved in a healthy or unhealthy way.

The interpersonal model is based largely on the work of Harry Stack Sullivan (1892–1949), who believed that personality had meaning only in relation to interaction with others.

product of the culturally determined social learning that most women experienced.

Erik Erikson (1902–1994) also extended the interpersonal aspects of psychoanalytic theory. He elaborated and broadened Freud's psychosexual stages into more socially oriented concepts, describing conflicts that occurred at eight stages, each of which could be resolved in a healthy or unhealthy way. For example, during what Freud called the oral stage, when a child is preoccupied with oral gratification, Erikson believed that a child's real development centered on learning either "basic trust" of his or her social world or "basic mistrust." Although these conflicts are never fully resolved, failure to develop toward the appropriate pole of each conflict handicaps an individual during later stages. Trust, for instance, is needed for later competence in many areas of life. A clear sense of identity is necessary for a satisfying intimacy with another person; such intimacy, in turn, is important for becoming a nurturing parent.

Sullivan's Interpersonal Theory Until recently the dominant interpersonal theory was that developed by Harry Stack Sullivan (1892–1949), an American psychiatrist. Sullivan offered a comprehensive and systematic theory of personality that was explicitly interpersonal. Sullivan (1953) maintained that the concept of personality had meaning only when defined in terms of a person's characteristic ways of relating to others. He argued that personality development proceeded through various stages involving different patterns of interpersonal relationships. Early in life, for example, a child becomes socialized mainly through interactions with parents, and somewhat later peer relationships become increasingly important. In young adulthood, intimate relationships are established, culminating typically in marriage. Failure to progress satisfactorily through these various stages paves the way for maladaptive behavior.

Sullivan was concerned with the anxiety-arousing aspects of interpersonal relationships during early childhood. Because an infant is completely dependent on parents and siblings for meeting all needs, a lack of love and care leads to insecurity and anxiety. Sullivan emphasized the role of early childhood relationships in shaping the self-concept. For example, if a little girl perceives that others are rejecting her, she may view herself in a similar light and develop a negative self-image that almost inevitably leads to maladjustment.

The pressures of the socialization process and the continual appraisals by others lead a child to label some personal tendencies as the *good-me* and others as the *bad-me*. It is the bad-me that is associated with anxiety. With time, an individual develops a *self-system* that protects him or her from such anxiety through the control of awareness—the person simply does not attend to elements of experience that cause anxiety. If severe anxiety is aroused by some especially frightening aspect of self-experience, the individual perceives it as the *not-me,* totally screening it out of consciousness or even attributing it to someone else. Such actions, however, lead to an incongruity between the person's perceptions and the world as it really is, which may result in maladaptive behavior. Here we can see a similarity between Sullivan's views and those of Freud, Rogers, and the cognitive-behavioral psychologists.

The good-me and bad-me constructs are especially important aspects of a much broader idea—that all mental processing concerning ourselves, others, and our relationships is influenced by precedents, or prototypes, established in earlier relationships. These mental prototypes, which Sullivan called *personifications,* determine how we perceive current relationships. We each have our own ideas about the characteristics, behaviors, and interactions we expect of our moms, teachers, lovers, and friends. Unfortunately, this means that we may distort events involving important current relationships. For example, if our parents were highly critical, we may see criticism in the innocent actions and comments of others. When such distortions are severe (such as when every harmless remark—"when will dinner be ready?"—is misinterpreted as critical and hostile) relationships become complicated and confusing. Because these distortions shape our behavior toward other people, they tend to become self-fulfilling. The result can be anxiety and, ultimately, dissolution of certain relationships.

Contemporary psychodynamic thought has partially responded to the challenges leveled by Sullivan, Erikson, Fromm, Horney and Adler—all socially oriented theorists. The psychodynamic tradition has become much more interpersonal in focus, largely due to the influence of the object-relations approach (see page 82). In fact many foresee the possibility of an integration of the psychodynamic with the more distinctly social and interpersonal viewpoints (Fine, 1979). Nevertheless, differences remain because classical psychodynamic theory continues to emphasize the primacy of libidinal energies and intrapsychic conflicts, an emphasis that many interpersonally oriented theorists find objectionable.

Features of the Interpersonal Perspective Many subdisciplines of the social sciences and psychiatry have contributed to the interpersonal perspective in recent years. Some of these contributions are described briefly in the following sections.

Social Exchange and Roles. Two ways of viewing our relationships with other people can help illuminate both satisfying and hurtful interactions. First, the **social-exchange view,** developed largely by Thibaut and Kelley (1959) and Homans (1961), is based on the premise that we form relationships with each other to satisfy our needs. Each person in a relationship wants something from the other, and the exchange that results is essentially like trading or bargaining. When we feel that we have entered into a bad bargain—that the rewards are not worth the costs—we may attempt to work out some compromise or simply terminate the relationship.

A second way of viewing interpersonal relationships is in terms of *social roles.* Whether we are teachers, or doctors, or patients, we exhibit certain characteristic behaviors. Although we each lend a personal interpretation to our roles, there are usually limits to the "script," beyond which we are not expected to go. Similarly, in intimate personal relationships, each person has certain role expectations—in terms of obligations, rights, duties, and so on—that the other person is expected to meet. If one spouse, for example, fails to live up to the other's role expectations, or if the husband and wife have different conceptions of what a "wife" or "husband" should be or do, serious complications are likely to occur.

Communication and Interpersonal Accommodation. **Interpersonal accommodation** is the process in which two people develop patterns of communication and interaction that enable them to attain common goals, meet mutual needs, and build a satisfying relationship. People use many cues, both verbal and nonverbal, to interpret what is really being said to them. When communication and interpersonal accommodation fail and a relationship does not meet the needs of one or both partners, it is likely to be characterized by conflict, dissension, and eventually dissolution. The principles of interpersonal behavioral accommodation have been analyzed at length by Benjamin (1982, 1993), Carson (1979), Kiesler (1983), Leary (1957), and Wiggins (1982).

Impact of the Interpersonal Perspective The interpersonal perspective views unsatisfactory relationships in the past or present as the primary causes of many forms of maladaptive behavior. In the area of diagnosis, many supporters of the interpersonal perspective believe that the reliability and validity of psychological diagnoses could be improved if a new system based on interpersonal functioning were developed and some progress has been made toward developing such a system (e.g., Benjamin, 1982, 1993). The focus of *interpersonal therapy* is on alleviating problem-causing relationships and on helping people achieve more satisfactory relationships.

Such therapy is concerned with verbal and nonverbal communication, social roles, processes of accommodation, causal attributions (including those supposedly motivating the behavior of others), and the general interpersonal context of behavior. The therapy situation itself can be used as a vehicle for learning new interpersonal skills. In recent years, major progress has been made in documenting the effectiveness of interpersonal psychotherapy in the treatment of disorders such as depression and bulimia, an eating disorder discussed in Chapter 8 (Fairburn et al., 1993; Klerman et al., 1994).

Although the interpersonal approach of Sullivan and others lacks a fully adequate scientific grounding, it has generated considerable enthusiasm among researchers in recent years and has far more potential in this regard than does the humanistic approach, which does not promote empirical testing of its basic ideas. The major impact of the interpersonal perspective has been its focus on the key role a person's close relationships play in determining whether behavior will be effective or maladaptive.

Summary

Each of the psychosocial perspectives on human behavior—psychodynamic, behavioral, cognitive-behavioral, humanistic, and interpersonal—contributes to our understanding of psychopathology, but none alone can account for the complex variety of human maladaptive behaviors. Each perspective depends on generalizations from limited observations and research. In attempting to explain a complex disorder such as alcoholism, for example, the psychodynamic viewpoint focuses on intrapsychic conflict and anxiety; the behavioral viewpoint focuses on faulty learning and environmental conditions that may be exacerbating or maintaining the condition; the cognitive-behavioral viewpoint focuses on maladaptive thinking, including deficits in problem solving and information processing; the humanistic viewpoint focuses on the ways in which a person's struggles with values, meaning, and personal growth may be contributing to the problem; and the interpersonal viewpoint focuses on difficulties in a person's past and present relationships.

Thus adopting one perspective or another has important consequences: It influences our *perception* of maladaptive behavior, the *types of evidence* we look for, and the *way in which we are likely to interpret data*. In the following section we will discuss a range of psychosocial causal factors which have been implicated in the origins of maladaptive behavior. We will also illustrate how some of these different

viewpoints would provide contrasting (or some complementary) explanations for how the their effects. In later chapters, we will discuss relevant concepts from all these viewpoints as they relate to different forms of psychopathology, and in many instances, we will contrast different ways of explaining and treating the same disorder.

PSYCHOSOCIAL CAUSAL FACTORS

We begin life with few built-in patterns and a great capacity to learn from experience. What we do learn from our experiences may help us face challenges resourcefully and resiliently. Unfortunately, some of our experiences may be much less helpful in our later lives, and we may be deeply influenced by factors in early childhood over which we have no control. In this section we will examine the psychosocial factors that make people vulnerable to disorder or that may precipitate disorder. Psychosocial factors are those developmental influences that may handicap a person psychologically, making him or her less resourceful in coping with events.

We begin this section with a brief examination of the central role played by our perceptions of ourselves and our world which derive from our schemas and self-schemas. Then we will review specific influences that may distort the cognitive structures on which good psychological functioning depends. We will focus on four categories of psychosocial causal factors that exemplify the range of factors that have been studied: early deprivation and trauma, inadequate parenting, pathogenic family structures, and maladaptive peer relationships. Such factors typically do not operate alone. They interact with each other and with other psychosocial factors, with particular genetic and constitutional factors, and with particular settings or environments.

Schemas and Self-Schemas

Fundamental to determining what we know, want, and do are some basic assumptions that we make about ourselves, our world, and the relationship between the two. Using terminology from the cognitive perspective, these assumptions make up our frames of reference—our *schemas* about other people and the world around us, and our *self-schemas* or ideas that we have about our own attributes. Because what we can learn or perceive directly through our senses can provide only an approximate representation of "reality," we need cognitive frameworks to fill in the gaps and make sense out of what we can observe and experience. A **schema** is an organized representation of prior knowledge about a concept or about some stimulus that helps guide our processing of current information (Alloy & Tabachnik, 1984; Fiske & Taylor, 1991). Our schemas about the world around us and about ourselves are our guides, one might say, through the complexities of living in the world as we understand it. We all have schemas about other people (for example, expectations about their traits and goals), as well as schemas about social roles (for example, expectations about what appropriate behaviors for someone in that role are) and about events (for example, what appropriate sequences of events are for particular situations) (Fiske & Taylor, 1991). Our **self-schemas** include our views on what we are, what we might become, and what is important to us. Other aspects of our self-schema concern our notions of the various roles we occupy or might occupy in our social environment, such as woman, man, student, parent, physician, American, older person, and so on. The various aspects of a person's self-schema also can be construed as his or her *self-identity* (similar to Rogers' self-concept and Sullivan's self-system). Most people have clear ideas about at least some of their own personal attributes, and less clear ideas about other attributes (Fiske & Taylor, 1991).

Schemas about the world and self-schemas are vital to effective and organized behavior, but they are also sources of psychological vulnerabilities. This is because some of our schemas or certain aspects of our self-schema may be distorted and inaccurate. In addition, some schemas—even distorted ones—may be held with conviction, making them resistant to change. We are usually not completely conscious of our schemas. Although our daily decisions and behavior are largely shaped by these frames of reference, we may be unaware of the assumptions on which they are based—or even of having made assumptions at all. We think that we are simply seeing things the way they are and often do not often consider the fact that other pictures of the "real" world might be possible or that other rules for "right" might exist.

On the one hand, the self-schema can be seen as a set of rules for processing information and for selecting behavior alternatives; on the other hand, it can be seen as the product of those rules—a sense of selfhood, or self-identity (Vallacher, Wegner, & Hoine, 1980). Deficiencies or deviations in either aspect of the development of the self can make one vulnerable to disorder. For example, if a person's information-processing rules differ in major respects from those of his or her peers, then that person's

Our self-schemas—our frames of reference for what we are, what we might become, and what is important to us—influence our choice of goals and our confidence in being able to attain them. A key element of this older woman's self-schema was that she could accomplish her lifelong goal of obtaining a college education once her children were grown in spite of the fact that she was nearly 40 years older than the average college student.

"reality" will be correspondingly different and may lead to rejection, isolation, despair, and disorder.

As Vallacher and colleagues (1980) have put it, we look *through* the rules of the self—rarely at them. For this reason, the rules, once established, may be hard to identify, and it may be difficult to change them deliberately. New experiences tend to be worked into our existing cognitive frameworks, even if the new information has to be reinterpreted or distorted to make it fit—a process known as **assimilation.** We tend to cling to existing assumptions and reject or change new information that contradicts them. **Accommodation**—changing our existing frameworks to make it possible to incorporate discrepant information—is more difficult and threatening, especially when important assumptions are challenged. Accommodation is, of course, a basic goal of psychosocial therapies—explicitly in the case of the cognitive and cognitive-behavioral variants, but deeply embedded in virtually all other approaches as well. This process makes major therapeutic change a difficult task.

A person's failure to acquire appropriate principles or rules in cognitive organization can make him or her vulnerable to psychological problems later in life. Mischel (1973, 1990, 1993) has identified five learning-based differences that become apparent early in childhood: (a) children acquire different levels of competency in different areas; (b) they learn different concepts and strategies for encoding and categorizing their experiences, and they thus "process" new information differently; (c) although they all learn that certain things follow from certain others, what they learn to expect is quite different, depending on their unique experiences; (d) they learn different subjective values and goals, which lead to their finding different situations attractive or disagreeable; and (e) they learn different ways of coping with impulses and regulating their behavior—they develop a characteristic "style" of dealing with life's demands. Differences in these general areas continue through childhood and into the adult years and help shape later learning.

These learned variations make some children far better prepared than others for further learning and personal growth. The ability to make effective use of new experience depends very much on the degree to which past learning has created cognitive structures that facilitate the integration of the novel or unexpected. A well-prepared child will be able to assimilate or when necessary accommodate new experience in ways that will enhance growth; a child with less adequate cognitive foundations may be confused, unreceptive to new information, and psychologically vulnerable. It is mainly for this reason that most theories of personality development, and all of the psychosocial viewpoints of abnormal behavior just described, emphasize the importance of early experience in shaping the main directions that a person's coping style will take.

A good example is afforded by modern research on the cognitive antecedents of psychological depression. As discussed in Chapter 6, the onset of many cases of depression, including severely incapacitating depression, has been linked repeatedly with the prior occurrence of negative life events, such as illness, divorce, or a serious financial setback. Some evidence shows that people who respond to such events with clinically diagnosable depressions are in some sense "primed" to respond in this way because of the ways in which they process the negative happenings. Although the details of such a negative "set" are still being studied, they seem to involve a kind of overreaction to and overgeneralization of the meaning of negative events, one that was learned much earlier and may have remained dormant for many years (Beck 1967, 1987). Some evidence suggests that traumatic experiences, such as the death of

a parent in childhood, may encourage the acquisition of such maladaptive self-schemas (Bowlby, 1980).

The example just given reminds us that the events making up one child's experiences may be vastly different from those of another, and that many such events are neither predictable nor controllable. At one extreme are children who grow up in stable and lovingly indulgent environments, buffered to a large extent from the harsher realities of the world; at the other extreme are children whose experiences consist of constant exposure to frightening events or unspeakable cruelties. Such different experiences have corresponding effects on the schemas about the world and about the self of adults: Some suggest a world that is uniformly loving, unthreatening and benign, which of course it is not; others a jungle in which safety and perhaps even life itself is constantly in the balance. Given a preference in terms of likely outcomes, most mental health professionals would opt for the former of these sets of experiences. However, these may not be the best blueprint for engaging the real world, because it may be important to encounter some stresses and learn ways to deal with them in order to gain a sense of control (Seligman, 1975) or self-efficacy (Bandura, 1977a, 1986).

Exposure to multiple uncontrollable and unpredictable frightening events is likely to leave a person vulnerable to *anxiety,* a central problem in a number of the mental disorders to be discussed in this book. For example, Barlow's (1988) and Mineka's (1985a) models acknowledge some biological vulnerability to stressful circumstances in creating anxiety, but they also stress the importance of experience with negative outcomes perceived to be unpredictable and uncontrollable, based on a review of pertinent research (see also Mineka & Zinbarg, 1991; in press-b). A clinically anxious person is someone whose schemas include strong possibilities that terrible things over which he or she has no control may happen unpredictably, and that the world is a dangerous place. It is not difficult to imagine developmental scenarios that would lead a person to have schemas with these elements as prominent characteristics.

Finally, it appears that some uncontrollable experiences to which children are subjected are so overwhelming that they do not develop a coherent self-schema. This situation is perhaps seen most clearly in cases of dissociative identity disorder, where separate personalities have developed separate self-schemas that may be completely walled off from one another. We have learned in recent years that dissociative identity disorder (formerly called "multiple personality disorder"; see Chapter 7) may be associated with repeated, traumatic sexual and physical abuse in childhood. The main point here is that a fragmented sense of identity, whatever its origin—and it is frequently traumatic—invites the development of abnormal behaviors. On this the psychosocial viewpoints all concur; they differ primarily in the mechanisms through which they hypothesize these abnormal behaviors develop.

Early Deprivation or Trauma

Fortunately, experiences of the intensity and persistence just noted, although more common than was thought only a decade ago, are nevertheless relatively rare. There are, however, other kinds of experiences that, while less dramatic and chilling, may leave children with deep and sometimes irreversible psychic scars. The deprivation of needed resources normally supplied by parents or parental surrogates is one such circumstance.

Parental deprivation refers to an absence of adequate care from and interaction with parents or their substitutes during the formative years. It can occur even in intact families where, for one reason or another, parents are unable (for instance, because of mental disorder) or unwilling to provide for a child's needs for close and frequent human contact. The most severe manifestations of deprivation are usually seen among abandoned or orphaned children who may either be institutionalized or placed in a succession of unwholesome foster homes.

We can interpret the consequences of parental deprivation from several psychosocial viewpoints. Such deprivation might result in fixation at the oral stage of psychosexual development (Freud); it might interfere with the development of basic trust (Erikson); it might retard the attainment of needed skills because of a lack of available reinforcements (Skinner); it might preempt self-actualizing tendencies with maintenance and defensive requirements (Rogers, Maslow); or it might stunt the development of the child's capacity for relatively anxiety-free exchanges of tenderness and intimacy with others (Sullivan). Any of these viewpoints might be the best way of conceptualizing the problems that arise in a particular case, or some combination of them might be superior to any one. From the cognitive perspective, which we have been focusing on, we see the victims of such experiences as acquiring dysfunctional schemas and self-schemas in which relationships are represented as unstable, untrustworthy, and without affection.

Institutionalization In an institution, compared with an ordinary home, there is likely to be less warmth and physical contact; less intellectual, emotional, and social stimulation; and a lack of encour-

Success at school—such as winning a spelling bee—may be a protective factor that helps a child overcome disadvantages such as parental deprivation or institutionalization.

agement and help in positive learning. A much-referenced study by Provence and Lipton (1962) compared the behavior of infants living in institutions with that of infants living with families. At one year of age, the institutionalized infants showed general impairments in their relationships to people, rarely turning to adults for help, comfort, or pleasure and showing no signs of strong attachments to any person. These investigators also noted a marked retardation of speech and language development, emotional apathy, and impoverished and repetitive play activities. With more severe and pervasive deprivation, development may be even more retarded.

The long-range prognosis for children suffering early and prolonged parental deprivation through institutionalization is considered unfavorable (Quinton & Rutter, 1988; Quinton, Rutter, & Little, 1984; Rutter, 1990; Rutter & Quinton, 1984a; Tizard & Hodges, 1978). It is clear that many children deprived of normal parenting in infancy and early childhood show maladaptive personality development and are at risk for psychopathology. Institutionalization later in childhood in a child who has already had good attachment experiences is not so damaging (Rutter, 1987). However, even among those institutionalized at an early age, some show resilience and do well in adulthood. One important protective factor found to influence this was whether the child went from the institution into a harmonious family or a discordant one, with better outcomes among those who entered harmonious homes (Rutter, 1990). Another influential protective factor was having some good experiences at school, whether in the form of social relationships, or athletic or academic success; these successes probably contributed to a better sense of self-esteem or self-efficacy (Quinton & Rutter, 1988; Rutter, 1985, 1990).

Deprivation and Abuse in the Home Most infants subjected to parental deprivation are not separated from their parents, but rather suffer from inadequate care at home. In these situations parents typically neglect or devote little attention to their children and are generally rejecting. Parental rejection of a child is closely related to deprivation and may be demonstrated in various ways—by physical neglect, denial of love and affection, lack of interest in the child's activities and achievements, harsh or inconsistent punishment, failure to spend time with the child, and lack of respect for the child's rights and feelings. In a minority of cases, it also involves cruel and abusive treatment. Parental rejection may be partial or complete, passive or active, or subtly or overtly cruel.

The effects of such deprivation and rejection may be very serious. For example, Bullard and his colleagues (1967) delineated a "failure to thrive" (FTT) syndrome that "is a serious disorder of growth and development frequently requiring admission to the hospital. In its acute phase it significantly compromises the health and sometimes endangers the life of the child" (p. 689). The problem is fairly common in low-income families, with estimates at about 6 percent of children born at medical centers serving low-income families (Lozoff, 1989). Some have suggested that it may occur in a child who has become severely depressed (because of the deprivation and/or abuse) and has developed a neuroendocrine problem stunting growth (Ferholt et al., 1985), but it is also now clear that this syndrome often has prenatal origins, with a disproportionate number having had low birth weights (Lozoff, 1989).

Outright parental abuse of children has also been associated with many other negative effects on the development of its victims, although some studies have suggested that, at least among infants, gross neglect may be worse than having an abusive relationship. Abused children often have a tendency to be overly aggressive and prone to impulsive behavior (Emery, 1989). Researchers have also found that maltreated children have difficulties in linguistic development and significant problems in emotional and social functioning, including depression and impaired relationships with peers (Cicchetti, 1990; Emery, 1989). In addition, abused children are at heightened risk for later aggressive behavior (Dodge, Bates, & Pettit, 1990). Abused and maltreated infants and toddlers are likely to develop a pattern of disorganized and disoriented style of attachment (Crittenden & Ainsworth, 1989), characterized by bizarre, disorganized, and inconsistent behavior with the mother. A recent review of re-

search in this area concluded that "maltreatment by the primary caregiver in early childhood appears to jeopardize the organization and development of the attachment relationship, the self, and the regulation and integration of emotional, cognitive, motivational, and social behavior" (Masten et al., 1990, p. 437).

Nevertheless maltreated children—whether the maltreatment comes from abuse or from deprivation—can improve when the caregiving environment improves (Crittenden, 1985; Farber & Egeland, 1987; Masten & O'Connor, 1989; Rutter, 1979). Yet even though subsequent experiences may have a moderating influence, for some children the detrimental effects of such early traumas may never be completely overcome, partly because experiences that would provide the necessary relearning may be selectively avoided. A child whose schemas do not include the possibility that others can be trusted may not venture out toward others far enough to learn that some people in the world are in fact trustworthy. This idea is supported by the findings of Dodge and colleagues (1990) who found that abused children tend to attribute hostile intent to negative interactions with peers. Moreover, this tendency to attribute hostile intent seemed to mediate the development of aggressive behavior. That these effects may be enduring is supported by a recent review of the long-term consequences of physical abuse (into adolescence and adulthood) which concluded that childhood physical abuse predicts both familial and nonfamilial violence in adolescence and adulthood, especially in abused men (Malinosky-Rummell & Hansen, 1993). Physical abuse was also found to be associated with self-injurious behaviors and suicidal behavior, as well as anxiety, depression, and psychosis, especially in women.

A significant proportion of parents who reject or abuse their children have themselves been the victims of parental rejection. Their early history of rejection or abuse would clearly have had damaging effects on their schemas and self-schemas, and probably resulted in a failure to internalize good models of parenting. Kaufman and Zigler (1989) estimated that there is about a 30 percent chance of this pattern of intergenerational transmission of abuse (see also Widom, 1989). Those who were least likely to show this pattern tended to have one or more protective factors, such as a good relationship with some adult during childhood, higher IQ, positive school experiences, or physical attractiveness, among others.

Childhood Trauma Most of us have had one-time traumatic experiences that temporarily shattered our feelings of security, adequacy, and worth and influenced our perceptions of ourselves and our environment. The term **psychic trauma** is used to describe

In February 1994 during a drug raid, Chicago police discovered 19 children in this freezing, squalid cockroach-infested apartment. The stove in the kitchen did not work, and children were found sharing food with dogs off the floor. The six adults in the apartment were charged with child neglect, and child abuse charges were also considered. Growing up in such a setting may predispose children to later psychological problems.

any aversive (unpleasant) experience that inflicts serious psychological damage on an individual. The following illustrates such an incident:

> I believe the most traumatic experience of my entire life happened one April evening when I was 11. I was not too sure of how I had become a member of the family, although my parents had thought it wise to tell me that I was adopted. That much I knew, but what the term adopted meant was something else entirely. One evening after my step-brother and I had retired, he proceeded to explain it to me—with a vehemence I shall never forget. He made it clear that I wasn't a "real" member of the family, that my parents didn't "really" love me, and that I wasn't even wanted around the place. That was one night I vividly recall crying myself to sleep. That experience undoubtedly played a major role in making me feel insecure and inferior.

Traumas of this sort are apt to leave psychological wounds that may never completely heal. As a result, later stress that reactivates these wounds may be particularly difficult for an individual to handle; this often explains why one person has difficulty with a problem that is not especially stressful to another. Psychic traumas in infancy or early childhood are especially damaging because children have limited coping resources and are relatively helpless in the face of threat. They are therefore more readily overwhelmed by traumas than an older person would be. Conditioned responses, which in cognitive terms are acquired expectancies that a particular event will follow from another, are readily established in situations that evoke strong emotions; such responses are often highly resistant to extinction. Thus one traumatic experience of almost drowning in a deep lake may be sufficient to establish a fear of water that en-

dures for years or a lifetime. Conditioned responses stemming from traumatic experiences may also generalize to other situations. For example, the child who has learned to fear water may also come to fear riding in boats and other situations associated with even the remotest possibility of drowning. Young children are thus especially prone to acquiring intense anxieties that remain resistant to modification even as their coping resources develop over time.

Bowlby (1960, 1973) has summarized the traumatic effects for children from two to five years old of being separated from their parents during prolonged periods of hospitalization. First, there are the short-term or acute effects of the separation, which can include significant despair during the separation and detachment from the parents upon reunion; Bowlby considers this to be a *normal* response to prolonged separation, even in securely attached infants. Children who undergo such separations may develop an insecure attachment. In addition, there can be longer-term effects of early separation from one or both parents. For example, such separations can cause an increased vulnerability to stressors in adulthood, making it more likely that the person will become depressed (Bowlby, 1980). As with other early traumatic experiences, the long-term effects of separation depend heavily on the support and reassurance given a child by parents or other significant people, which is most likely if the child has a secure relationship with at least one parent (Lease & Ollendick, 1993; Main & Weston, 1981).

Many psychic traumas in childhood, although highly upsetting at the time, probably have minor long-term consequences. Some children are less vulnerable than others and show more resilience and ability to recover from hurt (Crittenden, 1985). For example, not all children who experience a trauma—even a parent's death—exhibit discernible long-term effects (Barnes & Prosen, 1985; Brown, Harris, & Bifulco, 1985; Crook & Eliot, 1980; Rutter, 1985).

Inadequate Parenting

Even in the absence of severe deprivation, neglect, or trauma, many kinds of deviations in parenting can have profound effects on a child's subsequent ability to cope with life's challenges, and thus create vulnerability to various forms of psychopathology. Therefore, although their explanations vary considerably, the psychosocial viewpoints on abnormal behavior all focus attention on the behavioral tendencies a child acquires in the course of early social interaction with others—chiefly parents or parental surrogates.

You should keep in mind that a parent-child relationship is always bidirectional: As with any continuing relationship, the behavior of each person affects the behavior of the other. Some children are easier to love than others; some parents are more sensitive than others to an infant's needs. In occasional cases, we are able to identify characteristics in an infant that have been largely responsible for an unsatisfactory relationship between parent and child. A common example occurs in parents who have babies with high levels of negative emotionality. For example, Rutter and Quinton (1984b) found that parents tended to react with irritability, hostility, and criticism to children who were high in negative mood and low on adaptability. This in turn may set such children at risk for psychopathology because they become "a focus for discord" in the family (Rutter, 1990, p. 191). Because parents find it difficult and stressful to deal with babies who are high on negative emotionality, many of these infants may be more prone to developing avoidant styles of attachment than are infants who are not high on negative emotionality (Rothbart & Ahadi, 1994). Although these examples illustrate that characteristics of an infant can contribute to unsatisfactory attachment relationships, in most cases the influence of a parent on his or her child is likely to be more important in shaping a child's behavior, as we will see in the following sections.

Parental Psychopathology In general, it has been found that parents who have various forms of psychopathology, including schizophrenia, depression, antisocial personality disorder, and alcoholism, tend to have children who are at heightened risk for a wide range of developmental difficulties. Although some of these effects may have a genetic component, many researchers believe that genetic effects cannot account for all of the adverse effects that parental psychopathology has on children. For example, the children of seriously depressed parents are at enhanced risk for disorder themselves

(Downey & Coyne, 1990; Gotlib & Avison, 1993), at least partly because depression makes for unskillful parenting—notably including inattentiveness to a child's needs (Gelfand & Teti, 1990). Not only do depressed mothers rate their children as having more psychological and physical problems than do nondepressed mothers, but independent observers also rate infants of depressed mothers as more unhappy and tenser than infants of nondepressed mothers. Slightly older children of depressed mothers have also been rated as having a wide range of problems (see Gotlib & Avison, 1993). In addition, children of alcoholics have elevated rates of truancy and substance abuse and a greater likelihood of dropping out of school, as well as higher levels of anxiety and depression and lower levels of self-esteem (Chassin, Rogosch, & Barrera, 1991; Gotlib & Avison, 1993), although many children of alcoholics do not have difficulties. Although most research on this topic has focused on the effects of disordered mothers on their children, recently attention has been drawn to the fact that disordered fathers also make significant contributions to child and adolescent psychopathology, especially to problems such as conduct disorder, delinquency, and attention deficit disorder (Phares & Compas, 1992).

In spite of the profound effects that parental psychopathology can have on children, it should also be noted that many children raised in such families do just fine because of a variety of protective factors that may be present. For example, a child living with a parent with a serious disorder who also has a warm and nurturing relationship with the other parent, or with another adult outside the family, has a significant protective factor. Other important protective factors that promote resilience include having good intellectual skills and being appealing to adults (Masten et al., 1990).

Although not associated with any particular form of parental psychopathology, several specific patterns of parental influence appear in the backgrounds of children who show certain types of faulty development that may increase their risk for psychopathology. Some of these patterns will be discussed in the following sections.

Parental Warmth and Control In the past, discipline was conceived of as a method for both punishing undesirable behavior and preventing or deterring such behavior in the future. Discipline is now thought of more positively as providing needed structure and guidance for promoting a child's healthy growth. Such guidance provides a child with schemas similar to outcomes actually meted out by the world, contingent on a person's behavior. The person thus informed has a sense of control over these outcomes and is free to make deliberate choices. When coercion or punishment is deemed necessary, it is important that a parent make clear exactly what behavior is considered inappropriate. It is also important that the child know what behavior is expected, and that positive and consistent methods of discipline be worked out for dealing with infractions. In general, a child should be allowed independence in keeping with his or her level of maturity. As competent parents would doubtless agree, this judgment is not always easy to make.

Researchers have been interested in the degree to which *parenting styles*—including their disciplinary styles—affect children's behavior over the course of development. Four different types of parenting styles have been identified that seem to be related to different developmental outcomes for the children: authoritative, authoritarian, indulgent, and neglecting. These styles vary in the degree of *parental warmth* (amount of support, encouragement, and affection versus shame, rejection, and hostility) and in the degree of *parental control* (extent of discipline and monitoring versus being largely unsupervised) (Maccoby & Martin, 1983). First, the *authoritative style* is one in which the parents are both very warm and very careful to set clear limits and restrictions regarding certain kinds of behaviors, but also allow considerable freedom within certain limits. This style of parenting is associated with the most positive early social development, with the children tending to be energetic and friendly and showing development of general competencies for dealing

with others and with their environments (Baumrind, 1967, 1975, 1993). When followed into adolescence in a longitudinal study, children of authoritative parents continued to show positive outcomes. This parenting style was particularly predictive of competence in sons (Baumrind, 1991).

Parents with an *authoritarian style* are high on control but low on warmth, and their children tend to be conflicted, irritable, and moody (Baumrind, 1967). When followed into adolescence these children had more negative outcomes, with the boys doing particularly poorly in social and cognitive skills. If such authoritarian parents also use overly *severe discipline* in the form of physical punishment—as opposed to the withdrawal of approval and privileges—the result tends to be increased aggressive behavior on the part of a child (Eron et al., 1974; Faretra, 1981; Patterson, 1979). Apparently, physical punishment provides a model of aggressive behavior that the child emulates and incorporates into his or her own self-schema.

A third parenting style is the *permissive-indulgent style,* in which parents are high on warmth but low on discipline and control. This style of parenting is associated with impulsive and aggressive behavior in children (Baumrind, 1967; Hetherington & Parke, 1993). Overly indulged children are characteristically spoiled, selfish, inconsiderate, and demanding. In a classic study Sears (1961) found that much permissiveness and little discipline in a home were correlated positively with antisocial, aggressive behavior, particularly during middle and later childhood. Unlike rejected and emotionally deprived children,

This father, who is helping his child with homework, has an authoritative parenting style. He has a warm and supportive relationship with his son, but also sets clear limits and restrictions—for example, about how much homework must be done before his son is allowed to watch TV.

indulged children enter readily into interpersonal relationships, but they exploit people for their own purposes in the same way that they have learned to exploit their parents. Overly indulged children also tend to be impatient, and to approach problems in an aggressive and demanding manner (Baumrind, 1971, 1975). In short, they have self-schemas with significant "entitlement" features. Confusion and adjustive difficulties may occur when "reality" forces them to reassess their assumptions about themselves and the world.

Finally, there are parents who are low both on warmth and on control—the *neglecting-uninvolved style*. This latter style of parental uninvolvement is associated with disruptions in attachment during childhood (Egeland & Sroufe, 1981), and with moodiness, low self-esteem, and conduct problems later in childhood (Baumrind, 1991; Hetherington & Parke, 1993). These children of uninvolved parents also have problems with peer relations and with academic performance (Hetherington & Parke, 1993).

When just examining the effects of restrictiveness (ignoring the warmth variable), research has shown that restrictiveness can serve as a protective factor for children growing up in high-risk environments, as defined by a combination of family occupation and education level, minority status, and absence of a father (Baldwin, Baldwin, & Cole, 1990). Among high-risk children, those who did well in terms of cognitive outcome (IQ and school achievement) tended to have more restrictive and less democratic parents. Indeed, restrictiveness was positively related to cognitive outcome only among high-risk children and not among low-risk children. Restrictiveness was also particularly helpful for families living in areas with high crime rates.

Inadequate, Irrational, and Angry Communication Parents sometimes discourage a child from asking questions and in other ways fail to foster the information exchange essential for helping the child develop essential competencies. Inadequate communication may take a number of forms. Some parents are too busy or preoccupied with their own concerns to listen to their children and to try to understand the conflicts and pressures they are facing. As a consequence, these parents often fail to give needed support and assistance, particularly when there is a crisis. Other parents have forgotten that the world often looks different to a child or adolescent—rapid social change can lead to a communication gap between generations. In other instances, faulty communication may take more deviant forms in which messages become completely garbled because a listener distorts, disconfirms, or ignores a speaker's intended meaning.

Not uncommonly children are exposed to high levels of anger and conflict. The anger can occur in the context of marital discord, abuse, or parental psychopathology, and is often associated with psychological problems in children (Emery, 1982; Porter & O'Leary, 1980; Schneider-Rosen & Cicchetti, 1984). That there are psychological problems is not surprising given findings that children experience such background anger, like abuse, as emotionally arousing and distressing (Cummings, 1987; Emery, 1989).

Pathogenic Family Structures

The pathogenic parent-child patterns so far described, such as parental rejection, are rarely found in severe form unless the total familial context is also abnormal. Thus pathogenic family structure is an overarching risk factor that increases an individual's vulnerability to particular stressors. We will distinguish between intact families where there is significant marital discord and families that have been disrupted by divorce or separation.

Marital Discord In some cases of marital discord, one or both of the parents is not gaining satisfaction from the relationship. One spouse may express feelings of frustration and disillusionment in hostile ways such as nagging, criticizing, and doing things purposely to annoy the other person. Whatever the reasons for the difficulties, seriously discordant relationships of long standing are likely to be frustrating, hurtful, and generally pathogenic in their effects on the adults and their children.

In more severe cases of marital discord, one or both of the parents behave in grossly eccentric or abnormal ways and may keep the home in constant emotional turmoil. Such families differ greatly, but it is common to find (a) parents who are fighting to maintain their own equilibrium and are unable to give children the love and guidance they need, (b) grossly irrational communication patterns, and (c) entanglement of children in the parents' emotional conflicts. In all these cases, the children are caught up in an unwholesome and irrational psychological environment and as they grow up they may find it difficult to establish and maintain marital and other intimate relationships.

Divorced Families In many cases a family is incomplete as a result of death, divorce, separation, or some other circumstance. Due partly to a growing cultural acceptance of divorce, more than a million divorces now occur yearly in the United States (U.S. Bureau of the Census, 1989). Estimates are that about 20 percent of children under the age of 18 are living in a single-parent household—some with un-wed parents and some with divorced parents. About 40–50 percent of marriages end in divorce and about 60 percent of these divorces involve children (Hetherington & Parke, 1993). Unhappy marriages are difficult, but ending a marital relationship can also be enormously stressful for the adults, both mentally and physically. Divorced and separated persons are overrepresented among psychiatric patients, although the direction of the causal relationship is not always clear. In their comprehensive review of the effects of divorce on adults, Bloom, Asher, and White (1978) concluded that it is a major source of psychopathology, as well as physical illness, death, suicide, and homicide.

Divorce can have traumatic effects on children, too. Feelings of insecurity and rejection may be aggravated by conflicting loyalties and, sometimes, by the spoiling the children receive while staying with one of the parents. Not surprisingly, some children do develop serious maladaptive responses. Temperamentally difficult children are likely to have a more difficult time adjusting than are temperamentally easy children (Hetherington, Stanley-Hagan, & Anderson, 1989). Somewhat ironically, these also may be the children whose parents are more likely to divorce, perhaps because having difficult children is likely to exacerbate marital problems (Block, Block, & Gjerde, 1986). Delinquency and other abnormal behaviors are much more frequent among children and adolescents from divorced families than among those from intact families, although it is likely that a contributing factor here is prior or continuing parental strife (Rutter, 1971, 1979). Moreover, given that both broken homes and delinquency are more common among families in lower socioeconomic circumstances, it may be that disrupted homes and childhood deviance are both largely caused by the stresses of poverty and exclusion from society's mainstream. Finally, Amato and Keith (1991; Amato, 1988) also note that there may well be long-term effects of divorce on adaptive functioning in early adulthood in as much as some studies have found lower educational attainment, lower incomes, increased probability of being on welfare and having children out of wedlock in young adults from divorced families.

Nevertheless, many children adjust quite well to the divorce of their parents. Indeed, a recent quantitative review of 92 studies conducted on 13,000 children since the 1950s on parental divorce and the well-being of children concluded that the average negative effects of divorce on children are actually quite modest (Amato & Keith, 1991). They also found that the effects seem to be decreasing over the past four decades (particularly since 1970), perhaps because the stigma of divorce is decreasing. The domains of well-being that were examined included school achievement, conduct problems, psychological and social adjustment, self-concept, and parent-child relations. Children in the middle-age range (grade school to high school) had slightly worse outcomes than preschool-age and college-age children (Amato & Keith, 1991).

The effects of divorce on children have been compared with the effects of remaining in a home torn by marital conflict and dissension, and the effects of divorce are often more favorable (Hetherington et al., 1989). The Amato and Keith review (1991) also demonstrated that children who were in intact but high-conflict families were worse off than children in divorced families. At one time it was thought that detrimental effects of divorce might be minimized if a successful remarriage provided an adequate environment for child rearing. Unfortunately, however, the Amato and Keith review revealed that such children living with a stepparent were no better off than children living with a single parent, although this was more true for girls than for boys. Indeed, some studies have found that the period of adjustment to remarriage may be longer than that for divorce (Hetherington et al., 1989). Other studies have shown that children—especially very young children—living with a stepparent are at increased risk for physical abuse and even death by the stepparent, relative to children living with two biological parents (Daly & Martin, 1988).

Maladaptive Peer Relationships

Another important set of relationships outside the family usually begins in the preschool years—those involving age-mates, or peers. Normally, these neighborhood or school relationships involve a much broader range of possible experiences than do the more constrained and established relationships within families. When a child ventures into the world independently, he or she is faced with a number of complicated and unpredictable challenges. The potential for problems and failure is considerable.

Children at this stage are hardly masters of the fine points of human relationships or diplomacy. Empathy—the appreciation of another's situation, perspective, and feelings—is at best only primitively developed, as can be seen in a child who turns on and rejects a current playmate when a more favored candidate arrives. The child's own immediate satisfaction tends to be the primary goal of any interaction, and there is only an uncertain recognition that cooperation and collaboration may bring even greater benefits. A substantial minority of youngsters seems somehow ill-equipped for the rigors and competition of the school years, most likely by virtue of constitutional factors and deficits in the psychosocial climate of their families. A significant number of them withdraw from their peers; a large number of others (especially among males) adopt physically intimidating and aggressive lifestyles. The neighborhood bully and the menacing schoolyard loner are examples. Neither of these routes bode well for good mental health outcomes (e.g., Coie et al., 1992; Coie & Cillessen, 1993; Hartmann et al., 1984; Kupersmidt, Coie, & Dodge, 1990).

Fortunately, there is another side to this coin. If peer relations have their developmental hazards, they can also be sources of key learning experiences that stand an individual in good stead for years, perhaps for a lifetime. For a resourceful youngster, the give-and-take, the winning and losing, the successes and failures of the school years provide superb training in coming to grips with the real world and with his or her developing self—its capabilities and limitations, its attractive and unattractive qualities. The experience of intimacy with another, a friend, has its beginning in this period of intense social involvement. If all has gone well in the early juvenile years, a child emerges into adolescence with a considerable repertoire of social knowledge and skills. Such an adolescent can effectively adapt his or her behavior to the requirements of a situation and communicate, as appropriate, his or her thoughts and feelings to others. Practice and experience in intimate communication with others makes possible a transition from attraction, infatuation, and mere sexual curiosity to genuine love and commitment. Such resources can be strong protections against frustration, demoralization, despair, and mental disorder.

Although the scenario just outlined seems reasonable, it lacked until recently a strong empirical research foundation. In fact, the developmental period it addresses had been largely ignored by the major personality theorists, Erikson and Sullivan being notable exceptions. In the last 20 years, however, research into risk factors associated with children's peer relations has been accelerating. Some of the more important of these findings are briefly summarized in the following section.

Sources of Popularity Versus Rejection What determines which children will be popular and which

will be rejected? By far the most consistent correlate of popularity among juveniles is being seen as friendly and outgoing (Hartup, 1983). The causal relationship between popularity and friendliness is indeterminate and probably complexly involved with other variables, such as intelligence and physical attractiveness.

Far more attention has been devoted to identifying why some children are persistently rejected by their peers. One large factor is an excessively demanding or aggressive approach to ongoing peer activities, but this factor by no means characterizes the behavior of all children rejected by their peers. A smaller group of children is apparently rejected because of their own social withdrawal. The remaining large group is rejected for unknown reasons; evidently some reasons are quite subtle (Coie, 1990).

Many rejected children have poor entry skills in seeking to join ongoing group activities: They draw attention to themselves in disruptive ways; make unjustified aversive comments to others; and frequently become the focal point of verbal and physical aggression (Coie & Kupersmidt, 1983; Coie & Dodge, 1988; Putallaz & Gottman, 1983). Indeed, approximately half of rejected boys are highly aggressive (Coie & Cillessen, 1993). More generally, Dodge and colleagues (1980; Dodge & Newman, 1981; Dodge & Frame, 1982; Dodge, Murphy, & Buchsbaum, 1984) have described these children as taking offense too readily and as attributing hostile intent to the teasing of their peers, escalating confrontations to unintended levels. They also tend to take a more punitive and less forgiving attitude toward such situations (Coie et al., 1991). In the end, rejection leads to social isolation, often self-imposed (Dodge, Coie, & Brakke, 1982; Hymel & Rubin, 1985; Ladd, 1983). Coie (1990) pointed out that such isolation is likely to have serious consequences because it deprives a child of further opportunities to learn the rules of social behavior and interchange, rules that become more sophisticated and subtle with increasing age. Repeated social failure is the usual result, with further damaging effects on self-confidence and self-esteem. Kupersmidt and Coie (1990) reported that boys who were rejected by their peers in the fifth grade were more likely to have nonspecific negative outcomes seven years later than were average, popular, or neglected boys. Aggression toward peers in the fifth grade was the best predictor of juvenile delinquency and school dropout seven years later (see also Coie et al., 1992; Coie & Cillessen, 1993). One causal pathway for this association has been supported by Patterson, Capaldi, and Bank (1991; see also Dishion, 1994). Building on the finding that aggression is the best predictor of

Juvenile socializing is a risky business in which a child's hard-won prestige in a group is probably perceived as being constantly in jeopardy. Actually, reputation and status in a group tend to be stable, and a child who has been rejected by peers is likely to continue to have problems in peer relationships.

peer rejection (Coie et al., 1990), they found that peer rejection often leads a child to associate with deviant peers several years later, which in turn is associated with a tendency toward juvenile delinquency.

A child's position in a group tends, in the absence of intervention, to remain stable, especially by the fifth grade and beyond. On average, "stars" tend to remain stars and "rejects," rejects. For example, in one study almost half of the fifth graders who were rejected by their peers continued to be rejected over the next five years (Coie & Dodge, 1983). Some of this happens because other children tend to explain the behavior of the rejected child in terms of stable characteristics of the child. Because they have negative expectations of the rejected child, they act more negatively toward the child, thus setting up a kind of self-fulfilling prophecy for the interaction between the rejected child and his peers.

In summary, both logic and research findings lead to a similar conclusion: A child who fails to establish a satisfactory relationship with peers during the developmental years is deprived of a crucial set of background experiences and is at higher-than-average risk for a variety of negative outcomes in adolescence and adulthood (Kupersmidt et al., 1990). Peer social problems in childhood have been linked to a variety of breakdowns in later adaptive functioning, including schizophrenia, school dropout, and crime. Although these correlational data do not in themselves permit strong causal inferences, they constitute important links in a highly plausible causal chain.

THE SOCIOCULTURAL VIEWPOINT

By the beginning of the twentieth century, sociology and anthropology had emerged as independent scientific disciplines and were making rapid strides toward understanding the role of sociocultural factors in human development and behavior. Early sociocultural theorists included such notables as Ruth Benedict, Ralph Linton, Abram Kardiner, Margaret Mead, and Franz Boas. Their investigations and writings showed that individual personality development reflected the larger society—its institutions, norms, values, ideas, and technologies—as well as the immediate family and other groups. Studies also made clear the relationship between sociocultural conditions and mental disorders—between the particular stressors in a society and the types of mental disorders that typically occur in it. Further studies showed that the patterns of both physical and mental disorders in a given society could change over time as sociocultural conditions changed. These discoveries have added another dimension to modern perspectives on abnormal behavior.

Uncovering Sociocultural Factors Through Cross-Cultural Studies

The sociocultural viewpoint is concerned with the impact of the social environment on mental disorder, but the relationships between maladaptive behavior and sociocultural factors such as poverty, discrimination, or illiteracy are complex. It is one thing to observe that a person with a psychological disorder has come from a harsh environment. It is quite another thing, however, to show empirically that these circumstances were either necessary or sufficient conditions for producing the disorder. Part of the problem relates to the impossibility of conducting controlled experiments. Investigators cannot ethically rear children with similar genetic or biological traits in diverse social or economic environments in order to find out which variables affect development and adjustment.

Nevertheless, natural occurrences have provided laboratories for researchers. Groups of human beings have been exposed to very different environments, from the Arctic to the tropics to the desert. These societies have developed different means of economic subsistence and different types of family structures. Accordingly, highly diverse social and political systems have developed. Nature has indeed done social scientists a great favor by providing such a wide array of human groups for study.

In the earliest cross-cultural studies, Western-trained anthropologists observed the behavior of "natives" and considered those behaviors in the context of Western scientific thought. One of the earliest attempts to apply Western-based concepts in other cultures was the classic study of Malinowski (1927), *Sex and Repression in Savage Society*. In this work, he attempted to explain the behavior of "savages" through the use of the then-dominant principles of psychoanalysis. Malinowski found little evidence among the Trobriand Islanders of any Oedipal conflicts as described by Freud. He concluded that the sexually based behavior postulated by psychoanalytic theory was not universal but rather was a product of the patriarchal family structure in Western society.

Shortly thereafter, Ruth Benedict (1934) pointed out that even the Western definitions of abnormality might not apply to behavior in other cultures. Citing various ethnographic reports, she indicated that behavior considered abnormal in one society was sometimes considered normal in another. For example, she noted that some cultures valued trancelike states. Thus she concluded that normality was simply a culturally defined concept.

Early research also found that some types of abnormal behavior occurred only in certain cultures. Several of these "culture-related" behaviors are described in HIGHLIGHT 3.6. These and other early anthropological findings led many investigators to take a position of cultural relativism concerning abnormal behavior. According to this view, one cannot apply universal standards of normality or abnormality to all societies. In fact, for a time many people accepted the anthropologist's veto: Any general principle could be rejected if a contrary instance somewhere in the world could be demonstrated. For example, schizophrenia would no longer be viewed as abnormal if its symptoms were somewhere accepted as normal behavior.

This extremely relativistic view of abnormal behavior is not widely held today (Strauss, 1979). It is generally recognized that the more severe types of mental disorder described in Western psychology are found and considered maladaptive in societies throughout the world. When people become so mentally disordered that they can no longer control their behavior, perform their expected roles, or even survive without special care, their behavior is considered abnormal in any society.

Research supports the view that many psychological disturbances are universal, appearing in most

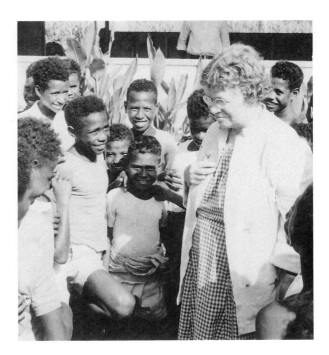

Margaret Mead (1901–1978), the world-famous anthropologist, spent years studying other societies and amassing cross-cultural data. Her Coming of Age in Samoa *(published in 1928) gave a favorable picture of many aspects of life in a "primitive" society and was influential in establishing an attitude of cultural relativism among many scientists and thinkers. Here she is pictured meeting with schoolchildren in New Guinea.*

cultures studied (Al-Issa, 1982; Carpenter & Strauss, 1979; Cooper et al., 1972; Murphy, 1976; World Health Organization, in press). For example, although the incidences and symptoms vary, the behaviors we call schizophrenia (Chapter 12) can be found among almost all peoples, from the most primitive to the most technologically advanced. Recent studies have also shown that certain psychological symptoms, as measured by the Minnesota Multiphasic Personality Inventory (MMPI-2; see Chapter 15), were consistently found among similarly diagnosed clinical groups in other countries (in Turkey by Savacir & Erol, 1990; in China by Cheung & Song, 1989; Butcher, 1995).

Nevertheless, although some universal symptoms appear, cultural factors do influence abnormal behavior. Human biology does not operate in a vacuum; cultural demands serve as causal factors and modifying influences in psychopathology. Sociocultural factors often create stress for an individual (Al-Issa, 1982; Sue & Sue, 1987). For example, children growing up in an oppressive society that offers few rewards and many hassles are likely to experi-

HIGHLIGHT   3.6

Unusual Patterns of Behavior Considered to Be Culture-Related Disorders

Name of Disorder	Culture	Description
Amok	Malaya (also observed in Java, Philippines, Africa, and Tierra del Fuego)	A disorder characterized by sudden, wild outbursts of homicidal aggression in which an afflicted person may kill or injure others. This rage disorder is usually found in males who are rather withdrawn, quiet, and inoffensive prior to the onset of the disorder. Stress, sleep deprivation, extreme heat, and alcohol are among the conditions thought to precipitate the disorder. Several stages have been observed: Typically in the first stage the person becomes more withdrawn; then a period of brooding follows in which a loss of reality contact is evident. Ideas of persecution and anger predominate. Finally, a phase of automatism or Amok occurs, in which the person jumps up, yells, grabs a knife, and stabs people or objects within reach. Exhaustion and depression usually follow, with amnesia for the rage period.
Anorexia nervosa	Western nations (particularly the U.S.)	A disorder occurring most frequently among young women in which a preoccupation with thinness produces a refusal to eat. This condition can result in death (see Chapter 8).
Latah	Malay	A fear reaction often occurring in middle-aged women of low intelligence who are subservient and self-effacing. The disorder is precipitated by the word *snake* or by tickling. It is characterized by echolalia (repetition of the words and sentences of others) and echopraxia (repetition of the acts of others). A disturbed individual may also react with negativism and the compulsive use of obscene language.
Koro	Southeast Asia (particularly Malay Archipelago)	A fear reaction or anxiety state in which a person fears that his penis will withdraw into his abdomen and he will die. This reaction may appear after sexual overindulgence or excessive masturbation. The anxiety is typically very intense and of sudden onset. The condition is "treated" by having the penis held firmly by the patient or by family members or friends. Often the penis is clamped to a wooden box.
Windigo	Algonquin Indian hunters	A fear reaction in which a hunter becomes anxious and agitated, convinced that he is bewitched. Fears center on his being turned into a cannibal by the power of a monster with an insatiable craving for human flesh.
Kitsunetsuki	Japan	A disorder in which victims believe that they are possessed by foxes and are said to change their facial expressions to resemble foxes. Entire families are often possessed and banned by the community. This reaction occurs in rural areas of Japan where people are superstitious and relatively uneducated.
Taijin kyofusho (TKS)	Japan	A relatively common psychiatric disorder in Japan in which an individual develops a fear of offending or hurting other people through being awkward in social situations or because of an imagined physical defect or problem. The excessive concern over how a person presents himself or herself in social situations is the salient problem.

Based on Kiev (1972), Kirmayer (1991), Lebra (1976), Lehmann (1967), Simons and Hughes (1985), and Yap (1951).

ence more stress and thus be more vulnerable to disorder than children growing up in a society that offers ample rewards and considerable social support. Growing up during a period of great fear, such as during a war, a famine, or a period of persecution, can make a child vulnerable to psychological problems.

Sociocultural factors also appear to influence what disorders develop, the forms that they take, and their courses. A good example of this point is a comparison study of psychiatric patients from Italy, Switzerland, and the United States carried out by Butcher and Pancheri (1976). Patients grouped according to diagnostic categories produced similar general personality patterns on the MMPI. However, the Italian patients also showed an exaggerated pattern of physical complaints significantly greater than that of the Swiss and the American patients, regardless of clinical diagnosis. This finding was consistent with earlier work by Opler and Singer (1959) and Zola (1966). Zola attributed this difference to a defense mechanism, which he called dramatization, that led the Italian patients, once identified as ill, to exaggerate or dramatize their physical problems to a greater extent than the Irish patients.

In another example, Kleinman (1986) traced the different ways that Chinese people (in Taiwan and in the People's Republic of China) deal with stress compared with Westerners. He found that in Western societies depression was a frequent reaction to individual stress. In China, on the other hand, he noted a relatively low rate of reported depression. Instead, the effects of stress were more typically manifested in physical problems, such as fatigue, weakness, and other complaints. Moreover, Kleinman and Good (1985) surveyed the experience of depression across cultures. Their data show that important elements of depression in Western societies—for example, the acute sense of guilt typically experienced—do not appear in other cultures. They also point out that the symptoms of depression (or dysphoria), such as sadness, hopelessness, unhappiness, lack of pleasure in the things of the world and in social relationships, have dramatically different meanings in different societies. For Buddhists, seeking pleasure from things of the world and social relationships is the basis of all suffering; a willful disengagement is thus the first step on the road to salvation. For Shi'ite Muslims in Iran, grief is a religious experience, associated with recognition of the tragic consequences of living justly in an unjust world; the ability to experience dysphoria fully is thus a marker of depth of personality and understanding.

Fascinating issues are also raised by recent studies of childhood psychopathology in different cultures. In certain cultures like that of Thailand, adults are highly intolerant of undercontrolled behavior such as aggression, disobedience, and disrespectful acts in their children. Children are taught to be polite and deferential and to inhibit any expression of anger. This raises interesting questions about whether childhood problems of undercontrolled behavior would be lower in Thailand than in the United States where such behavior is tolerated to a greater extent. Conversely it also raises the question of whether overcontrolled behavior problems such as shyness, anxiety, and depression would be overrepresented in Thailand relative to the United States. Two recent cross-national studies (Weisz et al., 1987, 1993) have confirmed that Thai children and adolescents do indeed have a greater prevalence of overcontrolled problems than do American children. Although there were no differences in the rate of undercontrolled problems between the two countries, there were differences in the kind of undercontrolled behavior problems reported. For example, Thai adolescents had higher scores than American adolescents on indirect and subtle forms of undercontrol not involving interpersonal aggression, such as having difficulty concentrating or being cruel to animals; American adolescents on the other hand had higher scores than Thai adolescents on behaviors like fighting, bullying, and disobeying at school (Weisz et al., 1993). Related findings have also emerged from studies comparing Jamaican and American children. Jamaicans come from an Afro-British tradition that is also intolerant of acting out behavior and that promotes politeness and respectfulness. Accordingly, it is not surprising that Jamaican children were more likely to be referred to a clinic for overcontrolled behavior than were American children, whereas American children were more likely to be referred for undercontrolled behavior than were Jamaican children (Lambert, Weisz, & Knight, 1989).

All of these findings illustrate an important point—the need for greater study of cultural influences on psychopathology. This neglected area of research may yet answer many questions about the origins and courses of behavior problems (Draguns, 1979; Marsella et al., 1985). Yet even with strong evidence of cultural influences on psychopathology, many professionals may fail to adopt an appropriate cultural perspective when dealing with mental illness. Clark (1987) notes a reluctance of "mainstream" psychologists and psychiatrists to incorporate the cross-cultural perspective in their research and clinical practices even when their patients or subjects are from diverse cultures. In a shrinking world, with instant communication and easy transportation, it is crucial for our sciences and professions to take a world view. In fact, Kleinman and Good consider cultural factors so important to our understanding of depressive disorders that they have urged the psychiatric community to incorporate another axis in the DSM diagnostic system to reflect cultural factors in psychopathology.

Sociocultural Influences in Our Own Society

As was noted in Chapter 1, the study of the incidence and distribution of physical and mental disorders in a population (as in the research just cited) is called epidemiology. The epidemiological approach implicates not only the social conditions and high-risk areas that are correlated with a high incidence of given disorders, but also the groups for whom the risk of pathology is especially high—for example, refugees from other countries (Vega & Rumbaut, 1991). Throughout this text we will point out many high-risk groups with respect to suicide, drug dependence, and other maladaptive behavior patterns. This information provides a basis for formulating prevention and treatment programs; in turn, the effectiveness of these programs can be evaluated by means of further epidemiological studies.

With the gradual recognition of sociocultural influences, what was previously an almost exclusive concern with individual patients has broadened to include a concern with societal, communal, familial, and other group settings as factors in mental disorders. Sociocultural research has led to programs designed to improve the social conditions that foster maladaptive behavior and to community facilities for the early detection, treatment, and long-range prevention of mental disorder. In Chapter 18 we will examine some clinical facilities and other programs—both governmental and private—that have been established as a result of community efforts.

SOCIOCULTURAL CAUSAL FACTORS

We will begin our discussion of the sociocultural causal factors that increase our vulnerability to the development of abnormal behavior by considering the role of culture in determining an individual's behavior patterns. For reasons of temperament, conditioning, and other individual factors, not all people

adopt the prevailing cultural patterns. This situation is especially common in Western society, where we are exposed to many competing values and patterns. We will also examine the particular factors in the social environment that may increase vulnerability: low socioeconomic class, disorder-engendering social roles, prejudice and discrimination, economic and employment problems, and social change and uncertainty.

The Sociocultural Environment

In much the same way that we receive a genetic inheritance that is the end product of millions of years of biological evolution, we also receive a sociocultural inheritance that is the end product of thousands of years of social evolution. The significance of this inheritance was well pointed up by Aldous Huxley (1965):

> The native or genetic capacities of today's bright city child are no better than the native capacities of a bright child born into a family of Upper Paleolithic cave-dwellers. But whereas the contemporary bright baby may grow up to become almost anything—a Presbyterian engineer, for example, a piano-playing Marxist, a professor of biochemistry who is a mystical agnostic and likes to paint in water colours—the paleolithic baby could not possibly have grown into anything except a hunter or food-gatherer, using the crudest of stone tools and thinking about his narrow world of trees and swamps in terms of some hazy system of magic. Ancient and modern, the two babies are indistinguishable. . . . But the adults into whom the babies will grow are profoundly dissimilar; and they are dissimilar because in one of them very few, and in the other a good many, of the baby's inborn potentialities have been actualized. (p. 69)

Because each group fosters its own cultural patterns by systematically teaching its offspring, all its members tend to be somewhat alike—to conform to certain basic personality types. Children reared among headhunters become headhunters; children reared in societies that do not sanction violence learn to settle their differences in nonviolent ways. In New Guinea, for example, Margaret Mead (1949) found two tribes—of similar racial origin and living in the same general geographical area—whose members developed diametrically opposed characteristics. The Arapesh were a kindly, peaceful, cooperative people, while the Mundugumor were warlike, suspicious, competitive, and vengeful. Such differences appear to be social in origin.

The more uniform and thorough the education of the younger members of a group, the more alike they will become. Thus in a society characterized by a limited and consistent point of view, there are not the wide individual differences typical in a society like ours, where children have contact with diverse, often conflicting, beliefs. Even in our society, however, there are certain core values that most of us consider essential.

Subgroups within a general sociocultural environment—such as family, sex, age, class, occupational, ethnic, and religious groups—foster beliefs and norms of their own, largely by means of social roles that their members learn to adopt. Expected role behaviors exist for a student, a teacher, an army officer, a priest, a nurse, and so on. Because most people are members of various subgroups, they are subject to various role demands, which also change over time. In fact, an individual's life can be viewed as a succession of roles—child, student, worker, spouse, parent, and senior citizen. When social roles are conflicting, unclear, or uncomfortable, or when an individual is unable to achieve a satisfactory role in a group, healthy personality development may be impaired—just as when a child is rejected by juvenile peer groups.

The extent to which role expectations can influence development is well illustrated by masculine and feminine roles in our own society and their effects on personality development and on behavior. In recent years, a combination of masculine and feminine traits (androgyny) has often been claimed to be psychologically ideal for both men and women. Many people, however, continue to show evidence of having been strongly affected by traditional assigned masculine and feminine roles. Moreover, there is accumulating evidence that the acceptance of gender-role assignments has substantial implications for mental health. In general, studies show that low "masculinity" is associated with maladaptive behavior and vulnerability to disorder for either biological sex, possibly because this condition tends to be strongly associated with deficient self-esteem (Carson, 1989). Baucom (1983), for example, has shown that high-feminine-sex-typed (low masculinity) women tend to reject opportunities to lead group problem-solving situations. He likens this effect to learned helplessness, which, as we have seen, has in turn been suggested as a causal factor in anxiety (Barlow, 1988; Mineka, 1985a) and depression (Abramson et al., 1978). Given findings like these, it should not be too surprising that women show much higher rates of anxiety and depressive disorders (see Chapters 5 and 6).

Pathogenic Societal Influences

There are many sources of pathogenic social influences, some of which stem from socioeconomic factors, and others of which stem from sociocultural factors regarding role expectations and the destructive forces of prejudice and discrimination. Some of the more important ones will be examined in the following sections.

Low Socioeconomic Status In our society, an inverse correlation exists between socioeconomic status and the prevalence of abnormal behavior—the lower the socioeconomic class, the higher the incidence of abnormal behavior (e.g., Eron & Peterson, 1982). The strength of the correlation seems to vary with different types of disorder, however. Some disorders may be related to social class only minimally or perhaps not at all. For example, the incidence of schizophrenia is inversely correlated with social class, while that of mood disorders bears a less distinct relationship to class.

We do not understand all the reasons for the more general inverse relationship. There is evidence that some people with mental disorders slide down to the lower rungs of the economic ladder and remain there because they do not have the economic or personal resources to climb back up (Gottesman, 1991). These people will often have children who also show abnormal behavior for a whole host of reasons, including increased risk for prenatal complications leading to low birth weight. At the same time, more affluent people are better able to get prompt help or to conceal their problems. In addition, it is almost certainly true that people living in poverty encounter more, and more severe, stressors in their lives than do people in the middle and upper classes, and they usually have fewer resources for dealing with them. As Kohn (1973) pointed out, the conditions under which lower-class children are reared tend to inhibit the development of the coping skills needed in our increasingly complex society. Thus the tendency for some forms of abnormal behavior to appear more frequently in lower socioeconomic groups may be at least partly due to increased stress in the people at risk (Gottesman, 1991). Nevertheless, findings from a longitudinal study of inner-city children in Boston showed that in spite of coming from high-risk socioeconomic background, many of the boys did very well and showed upward mobility. Resilience here was best indicated by childhood IQ and having adequate functioning as a child in school, family, and peer relationships (Long & Valliant, 1984; Felsman & Valliant, 1987).

In our society the lower the socioeconomic class, the higher the incidence of abnormal behavior. The conditions under which lower-class youngsters are reared tend to inhibit the development of coping skills. Many individuals, however, emerge from low socioeconomic environments with strong, highly adaptive personalities and skills.

Disorder-Engendering Social Roles An organized society, even an "advanced" one, sometimes asks its members to perform roles in which the prescribed behaviors either are deviant themselves or may produce maladaptive reactions. A soldier who is called upon by his superiors (and ultimately by his society) to deliberately kill and maim other human beings may subsequently develop serious feelings of guilt. He or she may also have latent emotional problems resulting from the horrors commonly experienced in combat and hence be vulnerable to disorder. As a nation, we are still struggling with the many problems of this type that have emerged among veterans of the Vietnam War (Kulka et al., 1990). The diagnosis of posttraumatic stress disorder was added to DSM-III (1980) largely in response to the problems of Vietnam veterans. Although this condition can occur following a range of highly traumatic events (such as rape, torture, and natural disasters), as discussed in Chapter 4, the feeling of guilt over atrocities committed were especially pronounced in Vietnam veterans.

Militaristic regimes and organizations are especially likely to foster problematic social roles. Military and civilian officials in Germany during the Nazi Holocaust and in the Soviet Union during Stalin's collectivization of rural areas in the 1930s (Conquest, 1986) willingly participated in history's most heinous and cold-blooded mass murders. Some American street gangs demand extreme cruelty and callousness on the part of their members. Well-organized terrorist groups, feeling that the world is ignoring their just claims, train their members for taking hostages, mass destruction, and murder.

There is, of course, no easy answer to the problems of violence and coercion in the modern world; people will often resort to force when other remedies fail. As long as such actions are taken, many people will be subjected to conditions of extraordinary stress and will feel compelled to enact difficult and painful social roles. In some cases, the end result will be psychological disorder.

Prejudice and Discrimination Vast numbers of people in our society have been subjected to demoralizing stereotypes and overt discrimination in areas such as employment, education, and housing. We have made progress in race relations since the 1960s, but the lingering effects of mistrust and discomfort among various ethnic and racial groups can be clearly observed on almost any college campus. For the most part, students socialize informally only with members of their own subcultures, despite the attempts of many well-meaning college administrators to break down the barriers. The tendency of students to avoid crossing these barriers needlessly limits their educational experiences and probably contributes to continued misinformation about, and prejudice toward, others.

We have also made progress in recognizing the demeaning and often disabling social roles our society has historically assigned to women. Again, though, much remains to be done. As already noted, many more women than men seek treatment for various emotional disorders, notably depression and many anxiety disorders. Mental health professionals believe this is a consequence both of the vulnerabilities (such as passivity and dependence) intrinsic to the traditional roles assigned to women, and possibly of the special stressors with which many modern women must cope (being full-time mothers, full-time homemakers, and full-time employees) as their traditional roles rapidly change. However, it should also be noted that working outside the home has also been shown to be a protective factor against depression under at least some circumstances (e.g., Brown & Harris, 1978).

Economic and Employment Problems Economic difficulties and unemployment have repeatedly been linked to enhanced vulnerability and thus to elevated rates of abnormal behavior (Dew, Penkower, & Bromet, 1991; Dooley & Catalano, 1980). Recession and inflation coupled with high unemployment are sources of chronic anxiety for many people. Unemployment has placed a burden on a sizable segment of our population, bringing with it both financial hardships, self-devaluation, and emotional distress. In fact, unemployment can be as damaging psychologically as it is financially. Research on the effects of unemployment was intense in the 1930s (Eisenberg & Lazarsfeld, 1938), but during the period of economic prosperity following World War II interest in the topic waned. However, interest was rekindled in the 1970s and 1980s when severe economic recessions were experienced worldwide and moderately high rates of employment became a seemingly permanent part of modern society. We certainly have not come close to solving the human problems such major economic shifts entail. The philosophies of free enterprise and rugged individualism run deep in American culture and politics, and they are shared by many unemployed people. The result is self-blame and personal demoralization.

Periods of extensive unemployment are typically accompanied by adverse effects on mental and physical health. In particular, rates of depression, marital problems, and somatic complaints increase during periods of unemployment, but usually normalize following reemployment (Dew et al., 1991; Jones, 1992). These effects occur even when mental health status before unemployment is taken into account; thus, it is not simply that those who are mentally unstable tend to lose their jobs. The psychological and physical health problems are more severe in lower socioeconomic groups (Jones, 1992). It also seems that physical violence among couples is associated with unemployment, although the causal direction is unclear (Dew et al., 1991). Not surprisingly, the wives of unemployed men also are adversely affected, with higher levels of anxiety, depression, and hostility. These effects appear to be mediated by the distress of the unemployed husband (Dew, Bromet, & Schulberg, 1987). In addition, children can be seriously affected. In the worst cases, the unemployed fathers engage in child abuse, with many studies documenting an association between child abuse and father's unemployment (Dew et al., 1991). In one prospective study, all the children born on Kauai, Hawaii, in 1955 were followed until age 18 (Werner & Smith, 1982). One of the best predictors distinguishing children (especially boys) who experienced significant problems with mental health or delinquency from those who did not was whether the father had lost his job when his children were small.

Social Change and Uncertainty The rate and pervasiveness of change today are different from anything our ancestors ever experienced. All aspects of our lives are affected—our education, our jobs, our families, our leisure pursuits, our finances, and our beliefs and values. Constantly trying to keep up with the numerous adjustments demanded by these changes is a source of constant and considerable stress. Simultaneously, we confront inevitable crises as the earth's consumable natural resources dwindle and as our environment becomes increasingly noxious with pollutants. Certain neighborhoods have increasing problems with drugs and crime. No longer are Americans confident that the future will be better than the past or that technology will solve all our problems. On the contrary, our attempts to cope with existing problems increasingly seem to create new problems that are as bad or worse. The resulting despair, demoralization, and sense of helplessness are well-established predisposing conditions for abnormal reactions to stressful events (Dohrenwend et al., 1980; Frank, 1978).

UNRESOLVED ISSUES

on Theoretical Viewpoints and Causation of Abnormal Behavior

The viewpoints described in this chapter are theoretical constructions devised to orient psychologists in the study of abnormal behavior. As a set of hypothetical guidelines, each viewpoint speaks to the importance and integrity of its own position to the exclusion of other explanations. Most psychoanalytically oriented clinicians, for example, value those traditional writings and beliefs consistent with Freudian or later psychodynamic theory, and they minimize or ignore the teachings of opposing viewpoints. They usually adhere to prescribed practices of psychoanalytic therapy and do not use other methods, such as desensitization therapy.

Theoretical integrity and adherence to a systematic viewpoint has a key advantage: It provides a consistent approach to orient one's practice or research efforts. Once mastered, the methodology can guide a practitioner or researcher through the complex web of human problems. Theoretical adherence has its disadvantages, however. By excluding other possible explanations, it can blind researchers to other factors that may be equally important.

The fact is that none of the theories to date addresses the whole spectrum of abnormality—each is limited in its focus. Two general trends have occurred as a result. The first involves revisions of an original theoretical doctrine by expanding or modifying some elements of the system. The second involves making use of two or more diverse approaches in a more general, eclectic approach. We will now examine how effectively each of these trends brings order to theoretical complexity.

1. *The revision of theoretical viewpoints.* The emergence of diverse viewpoints to explain abnormal behavior has led to criticisms of each viewpoint and thus to attempts to accommodate these criticisms. There are many examples of such corrective interpretations, such as Adler's or Jung's modification of Freudian theory or the more recent cognitive-behavioral approach in behavior therapy. But many of the early Freudian theorists did not accept the neo-Freudian additions, and many classical behavior therapists today do not accept the revisions proposed by cognitive behaviorists. Therefore, theoretical viewpoints tend to multiply and coexist—each with its own proponents—rather than being assimilated into previous views. In effect, at least some "revisions" of an original doctrine tend to survive as new, alternative interpretations of psychopathology. The result is a cumbersome backdrop of many theoretical viewpoints from which to study abnormal behavior. This situation also complicates communication among psychologists who may adhere to different perspectives, and with so many different perspectives, it is nearly impossible to have a clear grasp of them all.

2. *The eclectic approach.* As already noted, explanations based on single viewpoints are likely to be incomplete. In practice, many psychologists have responded to the existence of many perspectives by adopting an eclectic stance—that is, they accept working ideas from several existing viewpoints and use whichever they find to be useful. For example, a psychologist using an eclectic approach might accept causal explanations from psychoanalytic theory while applying techniques of anxiety reduction derived from behavior therapy. Another psychologist might combine techniques from the cognitive-behavioral approach with those from the interpersonal approach. Purists in the field—those advocates of a single viewpoint—are skeptical about eclecticism, claiming that the eclectic approach tends to lack integrity and produces a "crazy quilt" of activity with little rationale and inconsistent practice. This criticism may be true, but the approach certainly works for many psychologists.

Typically, those using an eclectic approach make no attempt to synthesize the theoretical perspectives. Although the approach can work in practical settings, it is not successful at a theoretical level because the underlying principles of many of the theoretical perspectives are incompatible as they now stand. Thus the eclectic approach still falls short of the final goal, which is to tackle the theoretical clutter and develop a single, comprehensive, internally consistent viewpoint that accurately reflects what we know empirically about abnormal behavior. It may be unrealistic to expect a single theoretical viewpoint to be broad enough to explain abnormal behavior in general and specific enough to accurately predict the symptoms and causes of specific disorders. Nevertheless, such a unified viewpoint is the challenge for the next generation of theorists in the field of abnormal psychology.

At present the one attempt at such a unified viewpoint is called the *biopsychosocial viewpoint*. This viewpoint acknowledges the interaction of biological, psychosocial, and sociocultural causal factors in the development of abnormal behavior. The biopsychosocial model was first articulated in order to account for the effects of psychological and sociocultural factors in physical health and has now become the dominant viewpoint in the fields of health psychology and behavioral medicine (see Chapter 8). However, it has also now been extended to the study of many other disorders as well.

The biopsychosocial viewpoint fits well with the conclusion that most disorders, especially beyond childhood, are the result of many causal factors—biological, psychosocial, and sociocultural. Moreover, for any person the particular combination of causal factors may be relatively unique, or at least not widely shared by large numbers of people with the same disorder. For example, some children may become delinquents because of having a heavy genetic loading for antisocial behavior, while others may become delinquent more because of environmental influences such as living in an area with a large number of gangs. Nevertheless, we can still have a scientific understanding of many of the causes of abnormal behavior even if we cannot predict such behavior with exact certainty in each individual case. However, there may also remain a rather large array of "unexplained" influences.

SUMMARY

In most instances the occurrence of abnormal or maladaptive behavior is the joint product of a person's vulnerability (diathesis) to disorder and of certain stressors that challenge his or her coping resources. Such vulnerabilities may be necessary or contributory causal factors, but they are not generally sufficient to cause disorder. Some of the major contributory causal influences are reviewed in this chapter. We also distinguished between relatively distal causal factors and more proximal causal factors. There are also a variety of protective factors that can promote more positive developmental outcomes even in persons who have the diathesis for a disorder.

Both the distal and the proximal causes of mental disorder may involve biological, psychosocial, and sociocultural factors. These three classes can interact with each other in complicated ways. At present there are many different points of view on the interpretation and treatment of abnormal behavior. We discussed biological, psychosocial, and sociocultural viewpoints, each of which tends to emphasize the importance of causal factors of the same type.

The early biological viewpoint focused on brain damage as a model for the understanding of abnormality. Modern biological thinking about mental disorders has focused more on the biochemistry of brain functioning, as well as other more subtle forms of brain dysfunction. In examining biologically based vulnerabilities, we must consider genetic endowment (including chromosomal irregularities), physical deprivation, primary reaction tendencies, and temperament. Investigations in this area show much promise for advancing our knowledge of how the mind and the body interact to produce maladaptive behavior.

The psychosocial viewpoints on abnormal behavior, dealing with human psychology rather than biology, necessarily are more varied than the biological perspective. The oldest of these perspectives is Freudian psychoanalytic theory. For many years this view was preoccupied with questions about libidinal energies and their containment, but more recently it has shown a distinctly social or interpersonal thrust under the direction of object-relations theory. Psychoanalysis and closely related approaches are termed *psychodynamic* in recognition of their attention to inner, often unconscious forces. An integration of psychodynamic and interpersonal perspectives (as suggested by Sullivan's work) would seem possible as we move into the future.

The behavioral perspective on abnormal behavior, which was rooted in the desire to make psychology an objective science, was slow in overcoming a dominant psychodynamic bias, but in the last 30 years it has established itself as a significant force. Behaviorism focuses on the role of learning in human behavior. It views maladaptive behavior either as a failure of learning appropriate behaviors, or learning maladaptive behaviors. Its therapeutic methods have achieved excellent results, and its ability to accommodate itself to the current dominance of cognitive thinking in psychology ensures its continued growth and importance.

Initially a spinoff from (and in part a reaction against) the behavioral perspective, the cognitive-behavioral viewpoint attempts to incorporate the complexities of human cognition in a rigorous, information-processing framework. This viewpoint attempts to alter maladaptive thinking and improve people's abilities to solve problems and to plan. As we will discuss in Chapter 17, the treatment procedures incorporating cognitive processes are highly effective in treating a variety of disorders.

The humanistic perspective does not chiefly concern itself with the origins and treatments of severe mental disorders. Rather, it focuses on the conditions that can maximize functioning in individuals who are just "getting along." It views abnormality as a failure to develop individual human potential. As such, it has to do with personal values and personal growth.

The originators of the interpersonal perspective were defectors from the psychoanalytic ranks who took exception to the Freudian emphasis on the internal determinants of motivation and behavior. As a group, interpersonal theorists have emphasized that important aspects of human personality have social or interpersonal origins. This viewpoint sees unsatisfactory relationships in the past or present as the primary causes of maladaptive behaviors.

For psychosocially determined causes or sources of vulnerability, the situation is somewhat more complicated than for biological causes. It is clear, however, that people's schemas and self-schemas play a central role in the way that they process information and in the kinds of attributions and values concerning the world that they have. The efficiency, accuracy, and coherence of a person's schemas and self-schemas appear to provide an important protection against breakdown. Sources of psychosocially determined vulnerability include early social deprivation, severe emotional trauma, inadequate parenting, and dysfunctional peer relationships.

Any comprehensive approach to the study of human behavior—normal or abnormal—must take account of the sociocultural context in which a given behavior occurs. Cultural influences on psychopathology are important in understanding the origin and course of a behavioral problem. The sociocultural viewpoint is concerned with the social environment as a contributor to mental disorder because sociocultural variables are also important sources of vulnerability, or, conversely, of resistance to it. The incidence of particular disorders varies widely among different cultures. Unfortunately, we know little of the specific factors involved in these variations. In our own culture, certain prescribed roles, such as those relating to gender, appear to be more predisposing to disorder than others. Low socioeconomic status is also associated with greater risk for various disorders, possibly because it is often difficult for economically distressed families to provide their offspring with sufficient coping resources. Additionally, certain roles evolved by given cultures may in themselves be maladaptive, and certain large-scale cultural trends, such as rapid technological advance, may increase stress while lessening the effectiveness of traditional coping resources.

Finally, we are still a long way from the goal of a complete understanding of abnormal behavior. The many theoretical perspectives that exist have given us a start, and a good one at that—but they fall short. To obtain a more comprehensive understanding of mental disorder, we must draw on a variety of sources, including the findings of genetics, biochemistry, psychology, sociology, and so forth. The biopsychosocial approach comes closest, but in many ways it is merely a descriptive acknowledgment of these complex interactions rather than a clearly articulated theory of how they interact. It is the task of future generations of theorists to devise a general theory of psychopathology, if indeed one is possible.

KEY TERMS

etiology (p. 64)
necessary cause (p. 64)
sufficient cause (p. 64)
contributory cause (p. 64)
diathesis-stress models (p. 65)
protective factors (p. 66)
resilience (p. 66)
neurotransmitters (p. 69)
hormones (p. 69)
genotype (p. 71)
phenotype (p. 71)
temperament (p. 75)
id (p. 79)
libido (p. 79)
pleasure principle (p. 79)
primary process thinking (p. 79)
ego (p. 79)
secondary process thinking (p. 79)
reality principle (p. 79)
superego (p. 79)
intrapsychic conflicts (p. 79)
ego-defense mechanisms (p. 79)
psychosexual stages of development (p. 81)
Oedipus complex (p. 81)

castration anxiety (p. 81)
Electra complex (p. 81)
introjection (p. 82)
classical conditioning (p. 84)
extinction (p. 84)
spontaneous recovery (p. 84)
operant (or instrumental) conditioning (p. 84)
reinforcement (p. 84)
generalization (p. 85)
discrimination (p. 85)
cognitive-behavioral perspective (p. 87)
attributions (p. 88)
humanistic perspective (p. 89)
self-actualizing (p. 92)
interpersonal perspective (p. 92)
social-exchange view (p. 94)
interpersonal accommodation (p. 94)
schema (p. 96)
self-schema (p. 96)
assimilation (p. 96)
accommodation (p. 96)
psychic trauma (p. 99)

PATTERNS OF ABNORMAL (MALADAPTIVE) BEHAVIOR

CHAPTER

4

STRESS AND ADJUSTMENT DISORDERS

Gaston Duf, Rinocerose. *As a child, Duf (b. 1920) was frequently terrorized by his father, often seeking the protection of his mother. When his parents belatedly married (when Duf was eighteen), he reacted violently. After two suicide attempts, he was institutionalized in 1940. He began his artistic career while in the asylum, painting strange, powerful animals and comically proportioned human figures.*

Any one of us may break down if the going gets tough enough. Under conditions of overwhelming stress, even a previously stable person may develop temporary (transient) psychological problems and loss of the capacity to gain pleasure from life (Berenbaum & Connelly, 1993). That is, a person may experience a lowering or breakdown of integral, adaptive functioning. This breakdown may be sudden, as in the case of a person who has gone through a severe accident or fire, or it may be gradual, as for a person who has been subjected to prolonged periods of tension and self-esteem loss culminating in a marital breakup. Usually a person recovers once a stressful situation is over, although in some cases there may be long-lasting damage to his or her self-concept and an increased vulnerability to certain types of stressors—today's stress can be tomorrow's vulnerability. In the case of a person who is quite vulnerable to begin with, of course, a stressful situation may precipitate more serious and lasting psychopathology.

In Chapter 3 we focused on the diathesis, or vulnerability, half of the diathesis-stress model of abnormal behavior. We saw that our vulnerabilities can predispose us to develop abnormal behavior. In this chapter we will focus on the role of stress as a precipitating causal factor in abnormal behavior. We will see that, at times, the impact of stress depends not only on its severity, but on a person's preexisting vulnerabilities as well. It is important to remember here that many of the factors that contribute to diatheses are also sources of stress. This is especially true of psychosocial factors, such as emotional deprivation, inadequate parenting, and the like. In this chapter our focus will be on the precipitating nature of stress; in Chapter 3 we focused on its predisposing nature.

We will first look at what stress is, the factors that affect it, and how we react to it. Then we will turn to some specific situations that result in severe stress and consider their effects on adjustment. We will then examine severe, catastrophic stress situations that precipitate the development of posttraumatic stress disorders. In the last part of the chapter, we will look at attempts made by mental health workers to intervene in the stress process—either to prevent stress reactions or to limit their intensity and duration once they have developed.

STRESS AND STRESSORS

Life would be simple indeed if our needs were automatically gratified. As we know, many obstacles, both personal and environmental, prevent this ideal situation. Such obstacles place adjustive demands on us and can lead to stress. The term *stress* has typically been used to refer both to the adjustive demands placed on an organism and to the organism's internal biological and psychological responses to such demands. To avoid confusion, we will refer to adjustive demands as **stressors,** to the effects they create within an organism as **stress,** and to efforts to deal with stress as **coping strategies.** Note that separating these constructs is a somewhat arbitrary action; as Neufeld (1990) has pointed out, stress is a by-product of poor or inadequate coping. For the purpose of study, however, making the distinction can be of help. What is important to remember in the long run is that the two concepts—stress and coping—are interrelated and dependent on each other.

All situations, positive and negative, that require adjustment can be stressful. Thus, according to Canadian physiologist Hans Selye (1956, 1976a), the notion of stress can be broken down further into positive stress, **eustress,** and negative stress, **distress.** (In most cases, the stress experienced during a wedding would be eustress; during a funeral, distress.) Both types of stress tax a person's resources and coping skills, though distress typically has the potential to do more damage. In the following sections, we will look at (a) categories of stressors, (b) factors predisposing a person to stress, and (c) the unique and changing stressor patterns that characterize each person's life.

Categories of Stressors

Adjustive demands, or stressors, stem from a number of sources. These sources represent three basic categories: frustrations, conflicts, and pressures.

Though we will consider these categories separately, they are closely interrelated.

Frustrations When a person's strivings are thwarted, either by obstacles that block progress toward a desired goal or by the absence of an appropriate goal, frustration occurs. Frustrations can be particularly difficult for a person to cope with because they often lead to self-devaluation, making the person feel that he or she has failed in some way or is incompetent.

A wide range of obstacles, both external and internal, can lead to frustration. Prejudice and discrimination, unfulfillment in a job, and the death of a loved one are common frustrations stemming from the environment; physical handicaps, lack of needed competencies, loneliness, guilt, and inadequate self-control are sources of frustration based on personal limitations.

Conflicts In many instances stress results from the simultaneous occurrence of two or more incompatible needs or motives: The requirements of one preclude satisfaction of the others. In essence we have a choice to make, and we experience conflict while trying to make it. Conflicts with which everyone has to cope may be classified as approach-avoidance, double-approach, and double-avoidance types:

1. *Approach-avoidance conflicts* involve strong tendencies to approach and to avoid the same goal. Perhaps a person wants to join a high-status group but can do so only by endorsing views contrary to his or her personal values. Approach-avoidance conflicts are sometimes referred to as mixed-blessing dilemmas because some negative and some positive features must be accepted regardless of which course of action is chosen.

Selye distinguished between two types of stress: eustress (positive stress) and distress (negative stress). The stress experienced during a wedding is eustress; during a funeral, distress. In general, distress has greater potential for causing difficulties in adjustment.

2. *Double-approach conflicts* involve choosing between two or more desirable goals, such as which of two movies to see on one's only free night of the week. To a large extent, such simple positive conflicts result from the inevitable limitations in one's time, space, energy, and resources; they are usually handled in stride. In more complex cases, however, as when a person is torn between two good career opportunities or between present satisfactions and future ones, decision making can be difficult and stressful. Though the experience may cause more eustress than distress, the stress is still real and the choice difficult. In either case, the person gives up something.

3. *Double-avoidance conflicts* are those in which the choices are between undesirable alternatives, such as either going to a party when you would rather stay home versus being considered impolite if you cancel at the last moment. Neither choice will bring satisfaction, so the task is to decide which course of action will be least disagreeable—that is, least stressful.

Classifying conflicts in this manner is somewhat arbitrary, and various combinations among the different types are perhaps the rule rather than the exception. Thus a double-approach conflict between alternative careers may also have its approach-avoidance aspects because of the responsibilities that either will impose. Regardless of how we categorize conflicts, they represent a major source of stress that can often become overwhelming in intensity.

Pressures Stress may stem not only from frustrations and conflicts, but also from pressures to achieve specific goals or to behave in particular ways. In general, pressures force a person to speed up, intensify effort, or change the direction of goal-oriented behavior. All of us encounter many everyday pressures, and we often handle them without undue difficulty. In some instances, however, pressures seriously tax our coping resources, and if they become excessive, they may lead to maladaptive behavior.

Pressures can originate from external or internal sources. Students may feel under severe pressure to make good grades because their parents demand it, or they may submit themselves to such pressure because they want to get into graduate school. The long hours of study, the tension of examinations, and the sustained concentration of effort over many years result in considerable stress for many students. Many students preparing for important, career-determining examinations, such as the Graduate Record Exam (GRE) or the Medical College Admissions Test (MCAT), experience considerable anxiety as the examination date approaches. Bolger (1990)

obtained self-reported anxiety ratings on 50 premedical students for 17 days before and 17 days after the MCAT examination. The experience of anxiety was clearly greater in the days preceding the examination—with peak anxiety occurring as the examination day approached. People who were prone to using maladaptive coping mechanisms, such as wishful thinking or self-blame, tended to show increased maladaptive behavior and increased anxiety under high stress. Performance on the examination, however, did not appear to be related to the use of various coping strategies to deal with the stress—that is, those students who used maladaptive behaviors did not appear to do worse on the exam.

Occupational demands can also be highly stressful, and many jobs make severe demands in terms of responsibility, time, and performance (Snow & Kline, 1995). Carruthers (1980) has noted that some occupations, such as coal mining, airplane flying, or auto racing, apparently place people under unusually high levels of stress, which result in vulnerabilities to heart disease. Carruthers has pointed out that our "stone-age biochemistry and physiology has in several important respects failed to adapt to [our] present-age situation" (p. 11).

Although we have arbitrarily separated stress into three categories, it appears that a given situation may involve elements of all three categories. The following case illustrates this point:

Pressure is a significant source of stress. Certain occupations make severe demands in terms of responsibility, time, and performance. Workers who experience unusually high degrees of stress, such as air-traffic controllers, may have an increased vulnerability to disease or disorder.

A premed student whose lifelong ambition was to become a doctor received rejection letters from all the medical schools to which he had applied. This unexpected blow left him feeling depressed and empty. He felt extreme frustration over his failure and conflict over what his next steps should be. He was experiencing pressure from his family and peers to try again, but he was also overwhelmed by a sense of failure. He felt so bitter that he wanted to drop everything and become a beach bum or a blackjack dealer in Las Vegas. The loss of self-esteem he was experiencing left him with no realistic backup plans and little interest in pursuing alternative careers.

Although a particular stressor may predominate in any situation, we rarely deal with an isolated demand. Instead, we usually confront a continuously changing pattern of interrelated and sometimes contradictory demands.

Factors Predisposing a Person to Stress

The severity of stress is gauged by the degree to which it disrupts functioning. The actual degree of disruption that occurs or is threatened depends partly on a stressor's characteristics and partly on a person's resources—both personal and situational—and the relationship between the two. Everyone faces a unique pattern of adjustive demands. This fact is partly due to differences in the way people perceive and interpret similar situations, but also, objectively, no two people are faced with exactly the same pattern of stressors. The following sections examine the factors that predispose us to react poorly to external demands.

The Nature of a Stressor The impact of a stressor depends on many factors such as its importance to the person, the duration of the stress, the "cumulative effect" of stressors in the person's life, whether the stressor appears along with other stressors, and its prominence in the person's life and whether or not that stressor is seen by the victim as within or outside his or her own control. Although most minor stressors are dealt with as a matter of course, stressors that involve important aspects of a person's life—such as the death of a loved one, a divorce, a job loss, or a serious illness—tend to be highly

stressful for most people. Furthermore, the longer a stressor operates, the more severe its effects. Prolonged exhaustion, for example, imposes a more intense stress than does temporary fatigue. Also, stressors often appear to have a cumulative effect (Singer, 1980). A married couple may maintain amicable relations through a long series of minor irritations or frustrations only to dissolve the relationship in the face of one "last straw"—a precipitating stressor. Sometimes, key stressors in a person's life center on a continuing, difficult life situation. These stressors are considered chronic, or long-lasting. A person may be frustrated in a boring and unrewarding job from which there is seemingly no escape, suffer for years in an unhappy and conflictful marriage, or be severely frustrated by a physical handicap or a long-term health problem.

Encountering a number of stressors at the same time also makes a difference. If a man has a heart attack, loses his job, and receives news that his son has been arrested for drug abuse—all at the same time—the resulting stress will be more severe than if these events occurred separately.

In difficult situations, including those involving conflicts, the severity of stress usually increases as the need to deal with the demand approaches. For example, in a study of sports parachutists, jumpers became more anxious as the hour of their next jump approached (Epstein & Fenz, 1962, 1965). People anticipating other stressful situations—such as major surgery—have found that the severity of stress increased as the time for the ordeal approached (Janis & Leventhal, 1965).

Finally, the symptoms of stress intensify when a person is more closely involved in a traumatic situation. Pynoos and colleagues (1987) conducted an extensive investigation of children's symptoms and behavior one month after a shooting incident in a schoolyard (one child was killed and several others wounded when a sniper randomly fired into the playground). A total of 159 children from the school were interviewed. Depending on where they were—on the playground, in the school, in the neighborhood, on the way home, absent from school, or out of the vicinity—the children experienced different stress levels. Children on the playground, closest to the shooting, had the most severe symptoms, whereas children on vacation or who were not at school during the shooting experienced no symptoms.

A Person's Perception and Tolerance of Stress Most of us are well aware that, in some cases, one person's stressor is another person's "piece of cake."

The different reactions can be due to both a person's perception of threat and his or her stress tolerance.

Perception of Threat. If a situation is seen as threatening—whether or not the threat is real—it is highly stressful. A person who feels overwhelmed or is concerned that he or she will be unable to deal with the threat is more likely to experience negative consequences from the situation than a person who feels able to manage it.

Often, new adjustive demands that have not been anticipated and for which no ready-made coping strategies are available will place a person under severe stress. To avoid this stress, the training of emergency workers, such as police and firefighters, normally involves repeated exposure to controlled or contrived stressors until coping patterns have become second nature—until they have confidence that they can deal with extreme circumstances. Likewise, recovery from the stress created by major surgery can be markedly facilitated when a patient is given realistic expectations beforehand (MacDonald & Kuiper, 1983). The same sense of adequacy and control can be achieved by choosing a stressful situation voluntarily, rather than having it imposed by others or occur unexpectedly (Averill, 1973). The importance of having a sense of control has been noted by Paterson and Neufeld (1987): "Control appears to moderate the effects of stress by allowing the person to alter the stress response directly or to select a response that will alter or avert the threatened event" (p. 413).

Understanding the nature of a stressful situation, preparing for it, and knowing how long it will last—all lessen the severity of the stress when it does come. Of course, new stressors constantly appear that make preparation and anticipation difficult at best. Two major nuclear accidents the world has witnessed are cases in point: the Chernobyl nuclear disaster in the Soviet Union in 1986 and the 1979 nuclear accident at Three Mile Island in Pennsylvania. Koscheyev (1990) reported high levels of stress and lowered psychological functioning among workers at the plant following the Chernobyl accident. Sixty percent of the workers were experiencing psychological symptoms a year after the accident. Victims of the Three Mile Island nuclear accident were showing physical effects from the experience, such as high blood pressure, more than a year after its occurrence (Baum, Gatchel, & Schaeffer, 1983). (See HIGHLIGHT 4.1.)

Stress Tolerance. If a person is marginally adjusted, the slightest frustration or pressure may be highly stressful. A person who is generally unsure of his or her adequacy and worth is much more likely to experience threat than a person who feels generally confident and secure. The term **stress tolerance** refers to a person's ability to withstand stress without becoming seriously impaired.

Both biologically and psychologically, people vary greatly in overall vulnerability to stressors. In addition, different people are vulnerable to different stressors. Emergencies, disappointments, and other problems that one person can take in stride may prove incapacitating to another. Early traumatic experiences can leave a person especially vulnerable to certain stressors.

External Resources and Social Supports Considerable evidence suggests that positive social and family relationships can moderate the effects of stress on a person and can reduce illness and early death (Monroe & Steiner, 1986). Conversely, the lack of external supports—either personal or material—can make a given stressor more potent and weaken a person's capacity to cope with it. A recent nationwide survey of stressful life events in mainland China found that problems with interpersonal relationships were the most commonly reported stressor in daily life (Zheng & Lin, 1994). A divorce or the death of a person's mate evokes more stress if he or she is left feeling alone and unloved than if the person is surrounded by people he or she cares about and feels close to. Siegel and Kuykendall (1990), for example, found that widowed men who attended church or temple experienced less depression than those who did not. This study found that men who had lost a spouse were more often depressed than women who had done so. The reasons for this finding remain unclear, though others have found similar results as well (e.g., Stroebe & Stroebe, 1983). It could be that the women had more social resources available to them from the outset, which may have reduced their vulnerability to depression.

In other situations, a person may be adversely affected by other family members who are experiencing problems. The level of tension for all family members can be increased if one member experiences extreme difficulty, such as a chronic or life-threatening illness or a psychiatric disability. Yager, Grant, and Bolus (1984) concluded that the intensity of a person's own psychological symptoms was related to that of his or her spouse; a person showed more emotional symptoms if his or her spouse was psychologically disturbed.

Often the culture offers specific rituals or courses of action that support people as they attempt to deal

Long-Term Follow-Up of Nuclear Disaster Victims

In April 1986, an accident at the Chernobyl nuclear power plant in the Ukraine produced a radiation leak that was 65,000 times greater than the accident at the Three Mile Island nuclear plant in the United States. In greatest jeopardy were the power plant employees and the disaster response team that worked to seal off the damaged reactor building and to secure the other reactors to prevent further damage. The power plant operators, several of whom were among the over 200 lives claimed by the accident, were especially vulnerable to radioactivity exposure.

In a major study of the long-term consequences of radioactivity exposure, physicians and psychologists from the Specialized Center for Disaster Medicine Protection of the Russian Ministry of Health have conducted follow-up

studies of the survivors of the accident. Operators who were working at Chernobyl during the accident were evaluated four times over a 20-month period. The evaluations involved about 100 employees at each testing time. The research team also tested a control group of nuclear plant operators from plants that were some distance from the Chernobyl site. In addition to the physical examinations, each employee was also given a battery of psychological tests, including the Russian language version of the Minnesota Multiphasic Personality Inventory (MMPI) (see Chapter 15 for discussion of the MMPI).

The postdisaster evaluation demonstrated significant increases in symptoms of stress such as physical problems, depression, interpersonal conflict, social alienation, and lack of concern for others. Those tested also showed an increase in mistrust of information being provided by the government (Koscheyev et al., 1993).

with certain types of stress. For example, most religions provide rituals that help the bereaved through their ordeals, and in some faiths, confession and atonement help people deal with stresses related to guilt and self-recrimination.

In sum, the interaction between the nature of a stressor and a person's resources for dealing with it largely determines the severity of stress. However great a challenge, it creates little stress if a person can easily handle it.

Intense Stress and the Experience of Crisis From time to time, most of us experience periods of especially *acute* (sudden and intense) *stress*. The term **crisis** is used to refer to times when a stressful situation approaches or exceeds the adaptive capacities of a person or group. Crises are often especially stressful because the coping techniques we typically use do not work.

A crisis may center on a traumatic divorce, an episode of depression in which a person seriously considers suicide, or the aftermath of an injury or disease that forces difficult readjustments in a person's self-concept and way of life. Estimates of how often such crises occur in the life of the average person range from about once every ten years to about once every two years. In view of our complex and rapidly changing society, the latter estimate may be more realistic.

The outcome of such crises has a profound influence on a person's subsequent adjustment. An effective new method of coping developed during a crisis

Emotional support can be powerfully expressed by actions as well as words. The boys shown in this photograph, who referred to themselves as the "Bald Eagles," shaved their heads so that their classmate who lost his own hair during chemotherapy for cancer would not feel alone.

may be added to the person's repertoire of coping behaviors; the inability to deal adequately with the crisis may impair the person's ability to cope with similar stressors in the future because of the expectation of failure. For this reason **crisis intervention**—providing psychological help in times of severe and special stress—has become an important element in contemporary treatment and prevention approaches. We will discuss such intervention in more detail in Chapter 18.

It is important to remember that life changes, even some positive ones, place new demands on us and thus may be stressful. The faster the changes, the greater the stress. Early research efforts on life changes focused on developing scales that could measure the relationship between stress and possible physical and mental disorders. Holmes and his colleagues (Holmes & Rahe, 1967; Rahe & Arthur, 1978), for example, developed the Social Readjustment Rating Scale, an objective method for measuring the cumulative stress to which a person has been exposed over a period of time. This scale measures life stress in terms of "life change units" (LCU): The more stressful the event, the more LCUs assigned to it. At the high end of the scale, "death of a spouse" rates 100 LCUs and "divorce" rates 73 LCUs; at the low end of the scale, "vacation" rates 13 LCUs and "minor violations of the law" rates 11 LCUs. Holmes and his colleagues found that people with LCU scores of 300 or more for recent months were at significant risk for getting a major illness within the next two years. In another effort, Horowitz and his colleagues (Horowitz, Wilner, & Alvarez, 1979) developed the Impact of Events Scale. This scale measures a person's reaction to a stressful situation by first identifying the stressor and then posing a series of questions to determine how he or she is coping.

These life stress scales have been criticized for numerous methodological problems. For example, a number of criticisms have targeted the items selected for different scales, the subjectivity of the scoring, the failure to take into account the relevance of items for the populations studied, and the reliance on subjects' memory of events (Monroe, 1983; Monroe & Simons, 1991; Zimmerman, 1983). Perhaps the most problematic aspect of life events scales is that they provide only a general indicator of distress and do not assess specific types of disorders. Another significant limitation of life event scales is that they tend to measure chronic problems rather than reactions to specific environmental events (Depue & Monroe, 1986). Despite the limitations of scales devised to measure life stressors, however, the weight of evidence supports the stressfulness of life changes (Maddi, Bartone, & Puccetti, 1987).

Another approach to the assessment of significant life events that has been receiving a great deal of attention among researchers is the *Life Event and Difficulty Schedule* by Brown and Harris (1989) and Brown (1995). This approach involves a semistructured interview that places the life event rating variables in a clearly defined context in order to increase rater reliability. This approach allows for the "meaning" of the event to the individual to be assessed more directly. Although this approach is more time-

Relaxation therapy group session for stroke victims. Participating in a group with other people coping with similar problems can be helpful in reducing stress.

consuming and costly, in terms of professional time to administer, the resulting ratings are more reliable than other life event approaches.

With an awareness that research in this area is sometimes flawed, let us examine, in the following sections, some of the ways people cope with stressful events.

COPING STRATEGIES

Evidence suggests that some particularly hardy individuals may be relatively immune to stressors that would impair most people's functioning (Kobasa, 1979). In general, however, increased levels of stress threaten a person's well-being and produce automatic, persistent attempts to relieve the tension. Stress forces a person, in short, to do something. What is done depends on many influences. Sometimes inner factors—such as a person's frame of reference, motives, competencies, or stress tolerance—play the dominant role in determining his or her coping strategies. At other times, environmental conditions—such as social demands and expectations—are of primary importance. Any stress reaction, of course, reflects the interplay of inner strategies and outer conditions—some more influential than others, but all working together to make the person react in a certain way. Ironically, some people create stress for themselves rather than coping. Recent research has shown that stressful situations might be, in part, related to or produced by the person's cognitions. For example, if you're depressed or anxious, you may perceive events as more stressful than if you are not depressed or anxious. That is, people may *generate* the life events that in turn produce their psychological adjustment problems (Simons et al., 1993).

In the following section, we will consider some general principles of adjustive behavior and coping; then we will examine some characteristic stages that occur when an individual's adaptive functioning is threatened.

General Principles of Coping with Stress

In reviewing certain general principles of coping with stress, it is helpful to conceptualize three interactional levels. On a biological level, there are immunological defenses and damage-repair mechanisms; on a psychological and interpersonal level, there are learned coping patterns, self-defenses, and support from family and friends; and on a sociocultural level, there are group resources, such as labor unions, religious organizations, and law-enforcement agencies.

The failure of coping efforts on any of these levels may seriously increase a person's vulnerability on other levels. For example, a breakdown of immunological defenses may impair not only bodily functioning, but psychological functioning as well; chronically poor psychological coping patterns may lead to other diseases; or the failure of a group on which a person depends may seriously interfere with his or her ability to satisfy basic needs.

In coping with stress, a person is confronted with two challenges: (a) to meet the requirements of the stressor, and (b) to protect the self from psychological damage and disorganization. When a person feels competent to handle a stressful situation, a **task-oriented response** is typical—that is, behavior is directed primarily at dealing with the requirements of the stressor. Typically, this response means the person objectively appraises the situation, works out alternative solutions, decides on an appropriate strategy, takes action, and evaluates feedback. The steps in a task-oriented response—whether the actions turn out to be effective or ineffective—are generally flexible enough to enable a person to change course.

Task-oriented responses may involve making changes in one's self, one's surroundings, or both, depending on the situation. The action may be overt—as in showing one's spouse more affection—or it may be covert—as in lowering one's level of aspiration. The action may involve retreating from the problem, attacking it directly, or trying to find a workable compromise. Any of these actions are appropriate under certain circumstances. For instance,

if one is faced with a situation of overwhelming physical danger, such as a forest fire, the logical task-oriented response might well be to run.

When a person's feelings of adequacy are seriously threatened by a stressor, a **defense-oriented response** tends to prevail—that is, behavior is directed primarily at protecting the self from hurt and disorganization, rather than at resolving the situation. Typically, the person using defense-oriented responses has forsaken more productive task-oriented action in favor of an overriding concern for maintaining the integrity of the self, however ill-advised and self-defeating the effort may prove to be.

There are two common types of defense-oriented responses. The first consists of responses such as crying, repetitive talking, and mourning that seem to function as psychological damage-repair mechanisms. The second type consists of the so-called ego- or self-defense mechanisms introduced in Chapter 3 (pp. 79–80). These mechanisms, including such responses as denial and repression, relieve tension and anxiety and protect the self from hurt and devaluation. They protect a person from external threats, such as failures in work or relationships, and from internal threats, such as guilt-arousing desires or actions. They appear to protect the self in one or more of the following ways: (a) by denying, distorting, or restricting a person's experience; (b) by reducing emotional or self-involvement; and (c) by counteracting threat or damage. Often, of course, a given defense mechanism may offer more than one kind of protection.

These defense mechanisms are ordinarily used in combination rather than singly, and often they are

Two ways that we may choose to deal with a stressful situation are through task-oriented behavior, in which we try to resolve the situation, or through defense-oriented behavior, in which we protect ourselves from psychological damage and disorganization. The couple weeping and holding each other in this photo have witnessed a fire in a Bronx discotheque that left 87 dead. They cannot change or resolve the situation. Their reactions are defense-oriented, used to help them cope with the hurt of an overwhelming stressor.

combined with task-oriented behavior. We all use them to some extent for coping with the problems of living. In fact, Gleser and Sacks (1973) have concluded that we tend to be fairly consistent in the particular mechanisms we use. Ego-defense mechanisms are considered maladaptive when they become the predominant means of coping with stressors, and are applied in excess.

Decompensation Under Excessive Stress

As we have seen, stressors challenge a person's adaptive resources, bringing into play both task- and defense-oriented reactions. Most of the time these varied reactions are successful in containing a threat. When stressors are sustained or severe, however, a person may not be able to adapt and may experience lowered integrated functioning and eventually a breakdown. This lowering of adaptive functioning is referred to as **decompensation.**

The Effects of Severe Stress Our reactions to stress can give us competencies we need and would not develop without being challenged to do so. Stress can be damaging, however, if certain demands are too severe for our coping resources or if we believe and act as if they are. Severe stress can exact a high cost in terms of lowered efficiency, depletion of adaptive resources, wear and tear on the system, and, in extreme cases, severe personality and physical deterioration—even death.

Lowering of Adaptive Efficiency. On a physiological level, severe stress may result in alterations that can impair the body's ability to fight off invading bacteria and viruses. On a psychological level, the perception of threat leads to an increasingly narrow perceptual field and rigid cognitive processes. It thus becomes difficult or impossible for the person to see the situation objectively or to perceive the alternatives actually available. This process often appears to be part of suicidal behavior.

Depletion of Adaptive Resources. In using its resources to meet one severe stressor, an organism may suffer a lowering of tolerance for other stressors. Selye (1976b) demonstrated that successions of noxious stimuli can have lethal effects on animals. It appears that an organism's coping resources are limited: If they are already mobilized against one stressor, they are less available against others. This finding helps explain how sustained psychological stress can lower biological resistance to disease and vice versa. Interestingly, prolonged stress may lead to either pathological overresponsiveness to stressors—as illustrated by the "last straw" response—or

to pathological insensitivity to stressors, as shown by a loss of hope or extreme apathy. In general, severe and sustained stress on any level leads to a serious reduction in an organism's overall adaptive capacity.

Wear and Tear on the System. Most of us probably believe that even after a very stressful experience, rest can completely restore us. In his pioneering studies of stress, however, Selye has found evidence to the contrary:

> Experiments on animals have clearly shown that each exposure leaves an indelible scar, in that it uses up reserves of adaptability which cannot be replaced. It is true that immediately after some harassing experience, rest can restore us almost to the original level of fitness by eliminating acute fatigue. But the emphasis is on the word almost. Since we constantly go through periods of stress and rest during life, even a minute deficit of adaptation energy every day adds up—it adds up to what we call aging. (1976, p. 429)

When pressure is severe and long-lasting, adjustment problems such as excessive worry may become chronic and eventually lead to physical changes such as high blood pressure. Davidson and Baum (1986) studied the effects of stress over a five-year period. In a follow-up to the study mentioned earlier on p. 123, they found that people exposed to the March 1979 nuclear accident at Three Mile Island, even five years after the incident, showed symptoms of high stress such as elevated blood pressure and the presence of urinary noradrenaline (often associated with a persistent arousal state). These people also reported more intense psychological symptoms of stress, such as intrusive thoughts, than residents in the control community.

Biological Decompensation. It is difficult to specify the exact biological processes underlying an organism's response to stress. A model that helps explain the course of biological decompensation under excessive stress is the **general adaptation syndrome,** introduced by Selye (1956, 1976b) has been supported by recent research in the field (Chrousos & Gold, 1992; Mazure & Druss, 1995). Selye found that the body's reaction to sustained and excessive stress typically occurs in three major phases: (a) *alarm reaction,* in which the body's defensive forces are "called to arms" by the activation of the autonomic nervous system; (b) *stage of resistance,* in which biological adaptation is at the maximum level in terms of bodily resources used; and (c) *exhaustion,* in which bodily resources are depleted and the organism loses its ability to resist so that further exposure to stress can lead to illness and death. A diagram of this general adaptation syndrome is shown in HIGHLIGHT 4.2.

HIGHLIGHT 4.2

Selye's General Adaptation Syndrome (GAS)

The general adaptation syndrome (GAS), shown in the diagram below, graphically illustrates a typical person's general response to stress. In the first phase (alarm reaction), the person shows an initial lowered resistance to stress or shock. If the stress persists, the person shows a defensive reaction or resistance (resistance phase) in an attempt to adapt to stress. Following extensive exposure to stress, the energy necessary for adaptation may be exhausted, resulting in the final stage of the GAS—collapse of adaptation (exhaustion phase).

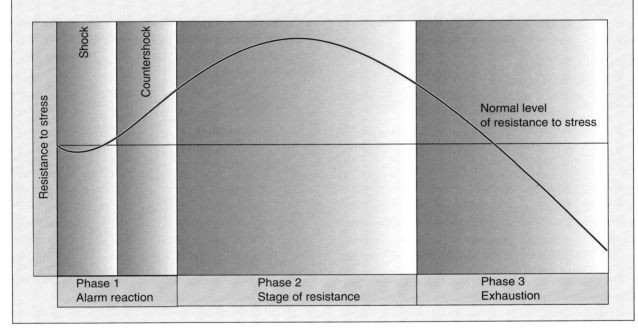

When decompensation does not run its entire course (resulting in the death of an organism), maintenance mechanisms attempt to repair damage and reorganize normal functioning. If the stress has resulted in extensive damage, this restorative process is often a matter of reorganizing remaining resources, but a permanent lowering of the previous level of integration and functioning remains.

Psychological Decompensation. Personality decompensation under excessive stress is somewhat easier to specify. It appears to follow a course resembling that of biological decompensation and may, in fact, involve specific biological responses:

1. *Alarm and mobilization.* First a person's resources for coping with a stressor are alerted and mobilized. Typically involved at this stage are emotional arousal, increased tension, heightened sensi-

tivity, greater alertness (vigilance), and determined efforts at self-control. At the same time, the person undertakes various coping measures—which may be task-oriented or defense-oriented or a combination of the two—in attempts to meet the emergency. During this stage, symptoms of maladjustment may appear, such as continuous anxiety and tension, gastrointestinal upset or other bodily diseases, and lowered efficiency—signs that the mobilization of adaptive resources is inadequate.

2. *Resistance.* If stress continues, a person is often able to find some means for dealing with it and thus to resist psychological disintegration. Resistance may be achieved temporarily by concerted, task-oriented coping measures; the use of ego-defense mechanisms may also be intensified during this period. Even in the resistance stage, however, indications of strain may exist, including psychophysio-

Police officer assisting an office worker who fled from the World Trade Center terrorist explosion in New York City in 1993 that killed two people and injured over 200. The initial stages of such a disaster typically provoke an alarm reaction in those involved.

logic symptoms and mild reality distortions. During the late phases of this stage, the person tends to become rigid and to cling to previously developed defenses rather than trying to reevaluate the stressor situation and work out more adaptive coping patterns.

3. *Exhaustion.* In the face of continued excessive stress, a person's adaptive resources are depleted and the coping patterns called forth in the stage of resistance begin to fail. As the stage of exhaustion begins, integration is lowered and exaggerated and inappropriate defensive measures are introduced. The latter reactions may be characterized by psychological disorganization and a break with reality, involving delusions and hallucinations. These delusions appear to represent increasingly disorganized thoughts and perceptions along with desperate efforts to salvage psychological integration and self-integrity by restructuring reality. Metabolic changes that impair normal brain functioning may also be involved in delusional and hallucinatory behavior. Eventually, if the excessive stress continues, the process of decompensation proceeds to a stage of complete psychological disintegration—perhaps involving continuous uncontrolled violence, apathy, stupor, and eventually death. Siegel (1984) found this pattern among 31 hostage victims whose cases he analyzed. Those who had been held under conditions of isolation, visual deprivation, physical restraint, physical abuse, and threat of death typically experienced hallucinations.

Over the past 20 years a great deal of research has been devoted to exploring the link between stress and physiological changes in human beings that result in organic disorders such as heart disease and cancer. An increasing number of studies is showing that severe stress, particularly in the case of young children where the person's brain is developing, influences the biological organizing processes and development. Schwartz and Perry (1994) point out:

> Evidence is accumulating that the alarm reaction initiates a cascade of cellular and molecular processes that alter brain structure and function to create an adaptive record of survival-related information. Intense danger activates the neurosensory apparatus and alters the pattern of neurotransmitter release throughout neuronal systems responsible for sensation, perception, and processing of survival information. Neurotransmitter receptor/effector activation then alters intracellular chemical constituents. . . . (p. 372)

The activation of the organism in the alarm reaction appears to be initiated by norepinephrine from the noradrenergic brain systems. However, other endocrine action is initiated as well, for example, the hormone cortisol is hypothesized to operate to preserve the metabolic reaction, and endogenous opiates serve an analgesic function involved in the "numbing effect" common to the disaster response (Pitman et al., 1990; Pitman, 1993; Falsetti, 1995).

Numerous studies have shown a link between stress related to grief (Irwin et al., 1987), separation and divorce (Kiecolt-Glaser et al., 1988), and examination stress (Workman & La Via, 1987). In their evaluation of research on how changes in the immune system could affect health, Zakowski, Hall, and Baum (1992) noted:

> The importance of the immune system cannot be overstated. Its organs and cells provide the major defense the body has against foreign organisms, pathogens, inert material, and other potential dangers. The skin stops much of what is virtually an onslaught of microbes and molecules in the air and water around us, and the rest of the immune system is a major factor in combatting diseases such as cancer or immunodeficiency virus (HIV) disease. Regulation by the immune system protects us against autoimmune diseases and maintains a balance of cells that maximizes survival. (p. 1)

Stress resulting from situations or events that are out of our control, in all likelihood, elevates corticosteroid levels which decreases lymphocyte metabolism and reduces the organism's immunity to disease, although the mechanisms by which this comes about are by no means clear (Mazure & Druss, 1995). As we will see, relatively severe psychological decompensation may be precipitated by sudden and extreme stress; but more often, decompensation is a gradual, long-term process. Typically, of course, treatment measures are instituted before decompensation runs its course. Such measures may increase a person's adaptive capabilities or alleviate a stressor situation so that the process of decompensation is reversed.

ADJUSTMENT DISORDER: REACTIONS TO COMMON LIFE STRESSORS

Research literature and clinical observations on the relationship between stress and psychopathology are so substantial that the role of stressors in symptom development is now formally emphasized in diagnostic formulations. In DSM-IV (American Psychiatric Association, 1994), for example, a diagnostician can specify on Axis IV the specific psychosocial stressors facing a person. The Axis IV scale is particularly useful in relation to three Axis I categories: adjustment disorder, acute stress disorder, and posttraumatic stress disorder (acute, chronic, or delayed). These disorders involve patterns of psychological and behavioral disturbances that occur in

response to identifiable stressors. The key differences between them lie not only in the severity of the disturbances, but also in the natures of the stressors and the time frames during which the disorders occur. In these disorders, the stressors supposedly can be identified as causal factors and specified on Axis IV.

A person whose response to a common stressor—such as marriage, divorce, childbirth, or losing a job—is maladaptive and occurs within three months of the stressor can be said to have an **adjustment disorder.** The person's reaction is considered maladaptive if he or she is unable to function as usual or if the person's reaction to the particular stressor is excessive. Usually, the person's maladjustment lessens or disappears when (a) the stressor has subsided or (b) the individual learns to adapt to the stressor. Should the symptoms continue beyond six months, DSM-IV recommends that the diagnosis be changed to some other mental disorder. As will be evident, the reality of adjustment disorders does not always adhere to such a strict time schedule.

We might well ask here, "What would be considered a normal response to a stressor?" The answer seems a bit elusive by DSM criterion. Clearly, not all reactions to stressors are adjustment disorders. What seems to push a reaction into this category is the inability to function as usual—and yet this criteria is true for many other disorders as well. We will not resolve this uncertainty any time soon; it is perhaps more important to recognize that adjustment disorder is probably the least stigmatizing and mildest diagnosis a therapist can assign to a client, and it is frequently used by therapists for insurance purposes even though a more debilitating disorder might also be considered.

We will look now at some of the stressor situations that typically cause adjustment disorders: unemployment, bereavement, and divorce or separation. We will then turn to stressor situations that can lead to posttraumatic stress disorder: major life problems such as life-threatening traumatic events, rape, military combat, imprisonment, being held hostage, and forced relocation.

Stress from Unemployment

Managing the stress associated with unemployment requires great coping strength, especially for people who have previously earned an adequate living. The misfortune of losing one's job and being unable to find suitable employment has been common in the last decade. The decline of the automobile, steel, oil, gas, electronics, and small-scale farming industries especially has transformed many thriving communities into depressed areas and many industrious employees into unemployed or underemployed people. In almost any community one can find numerous workers who have been laid off from jobs they had held for many years and who are facing the end of their unemployment compensation. The following case is typical of the problems that unemployment can bring:

David C., a 49-year-old construction foreman who was married and had two children attending college, had worked for a large building construction firm since he graduated from high school. One afternoon in May of 1982, his company, without warning, filed for bankruptcy, closed down its remaining job sites, and began to liquidate its resources.

David was stunned. The unexpected changes in his life were not easy for him to face. Early efforts to find other employment were met only with frustration because other construction companies were experiencing similar economic problems and layoffs.

After a few weeks his savings were depleted, and he took a step he never dreamed possible: He applied for unemployment compensation. This action was a tremendous blow to his self-esteem. He had always been self-sufficient and had taken great pride in being a hard worker and a good provider for his family. He was particularly upset at not being able to pay the tuition and living costs for his two sons in college and he felt a great sense of failure when they remained on their summer jobs rather than returning to school. His wife, who had never worked outside the home since their marriage, took a job in a local department store to meet some of the family's living expenses.

After some searching David seemingly gave up on finding a job and began to spend more time in bars. His drinking problems intensified. When he returned home in the evenings he sulked around the house and rebuffed most attempts by other family members to socialize or communicate. During this period family arguments were so frequent that Joel, his eldest son, felt that he couldn't tolerate the tension any more and enlisted in the army. In February, eight months after he lost his job, David saw a notice in the newspaper indicating that a local company was taking applications for 25 construction jobs the following Monday. He arrived at the company's employment office early on Monday morning only to

find that there were about 3000 other applicants ahead of him—some who had arrived the day before and had stood in line all night in the bitter cold. He left the lot dejected. That same week the bank initiated foreclosure proceedings on his house because he had not made a mortgage payment in seven months. He was forced to sell his house and move into an apartment.

For the next year David still could not find work in his community. Finally, after he had exhausted his unemployment benefits, he and a fellow employee left their families and moved to another city in the Southeast to find work. David planned to have his wife follow him when he got settled. She, however, had by that time been enjoying some success on her job and refused to move away. After several months of living apart, David's wife filed for a divorce. No further information is available on David.

Unemployment, a common experience in today's society with corporate restructuring, plant closings, and layoffs, results in work-force reductions, often in management-level positions. Some population subgroups—especially young minority males—live in a permanent economic depression, more pervasive and just as debilitating as the Great Depression was for the white majority. Unemployment among blacks (12.2 percent) is almost twice that among whites (6.3 percent) (Department of Labor, 1991). Indeed, for young black men, rates of unemployment are greater than 50 percent, over twice those for whites during the 1930s (Lebergott, 1964). The long-range psychological consequences of unemployment can be great. Some people can deal with setbacks such as David experienced and can adapt without suffering long-range adjustment difficulties once the initial stressful situation has ended. For others, however, unemployment can have serious long-term effects.

The impact of chronic unemployment on a person's self-concept, sense of worth, and feeling of belongingness is shattering—especially in an affluent society. The vulnerability of our population's lower socioeconomic segment to unemployment helps explain why this segment contributes a disproportionately high number of people to penal institutions and mental hospitals.

A number of employee-based intervention programs have been initiated to counsel and assist displaced workers. Maida, Gordon, and Farberow (1989) provide a valuable survey of the issues that affect these newly unemployed people and describe many problems resulting from transitional stress and chronic unemployment. They also explore several

Managing the stress associated with unemployment requires great coping strength. Some people can deal with setbacks and can adapt without suffering long-range adjustment difficulties once the initial stressful situation has ended. The impact of chronic unemployment, however, can be shattering and can have serious long-term effects. People shown here are waiting in line to file for unemployment at the New York State Department of Labor at a time when the unemployment rate rose to a three-year high of 5.9 percent in November 1990.

intervention strategies—such as increasing support networks, out-placement counseling, stress counseling, and more—that can reduce the psychological impact of job loss and promote more effective coping strategies.

Stress from Bereavement

When someone close to us dies, we are psychologically upended. Often the first reaction is disbelief. Then, as we begin to realize the significance of the death, our feelings of sadness, grief, and despair (even, perhaps, anger at the departed person) frequently overwhelm us.

Grief over the loss of a loved one is a natural process that allows the survivors to mourn their loss and then free themselves for life without the departed person. Some people do not go through the typical process of grieving, perhaps because of their personality makeups or as a consequence of their particular situations. A person may, for instance, be expected to be stoical about his or her feelings or may have to manage the family's affairs. Other people may develop exaggerated or prolonged depressions after their normal grieving processes should have ended (a normal grieving process should last no longer than about one year). Complicated or prolonged bereavement is often found in situations where there has been an untimely or unexpected death (Kim & Jacobs, 1995). Pathological reactions to death are also more likely to occur in people who have a history of emotional problems or who harbor a great deal of resentment and hostility toward the deceased, thus experiencing intense guilt. They are usually profoundly depressed and may, in some instances, be suffering from major depression (see Chapter 6). The follow-

ing case illustrates an extreme adjustment disorder with withdrawal or pathological grief reaction (and, in this instance, a positive outcome):

Nadine, a 66-year-old former high school teacher, lived with Charles, age 67, her husband of 40 years (also a retired teacher). The couple had been nearly inseparable since they met—they even taught at the same schools during most of their teaching careers. They lived in a semirural community where they had worked and had raised their three children, all of whom had married and moved to a large metropolitan area about 100 miles away. For years they had planned their retirement and had hoped to travel around the country visiting friends. A week before their fortieth anniversary, Charles had a heart attack and, after five days in the intensive care unit, had a second heart attack and died.

Nadine took Charles's death quite hard. Even though she had a great deal of emotional support from her many friends and her children, she had great difficulty adjusting. Elaine, one of her daughters, came and stayed a few days and encouraged her to come to the city for a while. Nadine declined the persistent invitation even though she had little to do at home. Friends called on her frequently, but she seemed almost to resent their presence. In the months following the funeral, Nadine's reclusive behavior persisted. Several well-wishers reported to Elaine that her mother was not doing well and was not even leaving the house to go shopping. They reported that Nadine sat alone in the darkened

Loss of a loved one is one of the most intense stressors experienced by people. These Bosnians grieving at a new grave site show the powerful emotions experienced during grief.

house—not answering the phone and showing reluctance to come to the door. She had lost interest in activities she had once enjoyed.

Greatly worried about her mother's welfare, Elaine organized a campaign to get her mother out of the house and back to doing the things she had formerly enjoyed. Each of Nadine's children and their families took turns visiting and taking her places until she finally began to show interest in living again. In time, Nadine agreed to come to each of their homes for visits. This proved a therapeutic step since Nadine had always been fond of children and took pleasure in the time spent with her eight grandchildren—she actually extended the visits longer than she had planned.

Stress from Divorce or Separation

The deterioration or ending of an intimate relationship is a potent stressor and a frequent reason why people seek psychological treatment. Divorce, though more generally accepted today, is still a tragic and usually stressful outcome to a once close and trusting relationship. We noted in Chapter 3 that marital disruption is a major source of vulnerability to psychopathology: People who are recently divorced or separated are markedly overrepresented among people with psychological problems.

Many factors make a divorce or separation unpleasant and stressful for everyone concerned: the acknowledgment of failure in a relationship impor-

tant both personally and culturally; the necessity of "explaining" the failure to family and friends; the loss of valuable friendships that often accompanies the rupture; the economic uncertainties and hardships that both partners frequently experience; and, when children are involved, the problem of custody—including court battles, living arrangements, and so on.

After the divorce or separation, new problems typically emerge. The readjustment to a single life, perhaps after many years of marriage, can be a difficult experience. Since in many cases it seems that friends as well as assets have to be divided, new friendships need to be made. New romantic relationships may require a great deal of personal change. Even when the separation has been relatively agreeable, new strength to adapt and cope is needed. Thus it is not surprising that many people seek counseling after the breakup of a significant relationship.

ACUTE STRESS DISORDER AND POSTTRAUMATIC STRESS DISORDER: REACTIONS TO SEVERE LIFE STRESSORS

In **acute** and **posttraumatic stress disorders** (PTSD), the stressor is unusually severe, involving intense fear, and is psychologically traumatic—for example, a life-threatening situation, the destruction of one's home, seeing another person mutilated or killed, or being the victim of physical violence. Posttraumatic stress disorder includes the following symptoms:

1. The traumatic event is persistently reexperienced by the person—he or she may have intrusive, recurring thoughts or repetitive nightmares about the event. A recent study of college students who experienced the Loma Prieta earthquake in 1989 confirmed this long-held belief about traumatic events influencing the experience of nightmares. Wood and colleagues (1992) found that students who experienced the earthquake had substantially more nightmares and more nightmares about earthquakes than students who did not experience the earthquake.

2. The person persistently avoids stimuli associated with the trauma; for example, he or she tries to avoid activities related to the incident or blocks out the memory of certain aspects of the experience. Situations that recall the traumatic experience provoke anxiety.

3. The person may experience persistent symptoms of increased arousal, such as chronic tension and irritability, often accompanied by insomnia, the inability to tolerate noise, and the complaint that "I just can't seem to relax."

4. The individual may experience impaired concentration and memory.

5. The person may experience feelings of depression. In some cases he or she may withdraw from social contact and avoid experiences that might increase excitation—commonly manifested in the avoidance of interpersonal involvement, loss of sexual interest, and an attitude of "peace and quiet at any price."

In DSM-IV no separate category exists for stress disorders, and acute stress disorder and posttraumatic stress disorder are categorized under the anxiety disorders. Clearly, PTSD includes elements of anxiety—generalized feelings of fear and apprehension—but since PTSD bears such a close relationship to the experience of stress, we cover it here and follow in Chapter 5 with coverage of the other anxiety disorders.

Acute stress disorder occurs within four weeks of the traumatic event and lasts for a minimum of two days and a maximum of four weeks. If the symptoms last longer the appropriate diagnosis is posttraumatic stress disorder. The diagnosis of posttraumatic stress disorder is not given unless the symptoms last for at least one month. The diagnosis can be further specified in terms of when the symptoms begin. If the symptoms begin within six months of the traumatic event, then the reaction is considered to be acute. If symptoms begin more than six months after the traumatic situation, the reaction is considered to be delayed. The delayed version of PTSD is less well defined and more difficult to diagnose than disorders that emerge shortly after the precipitating incident. Some authorities have questioned whether a delayed reaction should be diagnosed as a posttraumatic stress disorder at all; instead, some would categorize such a reaction as some other anxiety-based disorder. It is important to keep in mind that the criteria for posttraumatic stress disorder specify that the reaction last for at least one month.

We will look now at some general principles underlying reactions to catastrophic events. Then we will turn to some specific stressor events that can cause posttraumatic stress.

Reactions to Catastrophic Events

Many people who are exposed to plane crashes, automobile accidents, explosions, fires, earthquakes, tornadoes, sexual assaults, or other terrifying experiences show psychological "shock" reactions—transient personality decompensation. The symptoms may vary greatly, depending on the nature and severity of the terrifying experience, the degree of surprise, and the personality makeup of the person. Consider the following examples: over half of the survivors of the disastrous Coconut Grove nightclub fire—which took the lives of 492 people in Boston in 1942—required treatment for severe psychological shock (Adler, 1943). Psychological evaluations of 8 of the 64 survivors of the collision of two jet planes on Santa Cruz de Tenerife Island in 1977, in which 580 people died, indicated that all eight suffered from serious emotional problems stemming directly from the accident (Perlberg, 1979).

A **disaster syndrome** has been described that appears to characterize the reactions of many victims of such catastrophes (see HIGHLIGHT 4.3). This syndrome may be described in terms of the reactions during the traumatic experience, the initial reactions after it (the acute posttraumatic stress), and the long-lasting or late-arising complications (the chronic or delayed posttraumatic stress).

The Disaster Syndrome A victim's initial responses following a disaster typically involve three stages: (a) *the shock stage,* in which the victim is stunned, dazed, and apathetic; (b) *the suggestible stage,* in which the victim tends to be passive, suggestible, and willing to take directions from rescue

Problems of Recovery in the Aftermath of a Killer Hurricane

In September 1989 one of the most powerful and destructive hurricanes of all times, Hurricane Hugo, came ashore in the vicinity of Charleston, South Carolina, bringing with it winds that were estimated at 175 miles per hour and a tidal wave ranging from 12 to 23 feet high. Over 35 people were killed and hundreds of houses and buildings were destroyed, leaving tens of thousands of people homeless. Hundreds of thousands of people were without services such as electricity, and nearly 300,000 people were left without work.

Among the most seriously affected victims of Hugo were young children. Belter and Shannon (1993) found that children showed a significant increase in the number and severity of problem behaviors after the hurricane, including dependent and demanding behavior, frustration, irritability, temper tantrums, and sleep difficulties (p. 97).

Symptoms of posttraumatic stress disorder in children continued to persist even months after the hurricane. Swenson and colleagues (1991) reported that 28 percent of the children they examined had displayed emotional and behavioral problems immediately after the hurricane, 29 percent continued to have problems three months after the hurricane; 16 percent showed problems at seven to nine months following the hurricane; and 6 percent still had problems one year later.

In another study, Garrison and colleagues (1993) followed up 1264 adolescents between the ages of 11 and 17 who lived in three South Carolina communities hit by Hurricane Hugo and administered a 174-item questionnaire. The extent of the stress from the hurricane is reflected in the fact that 12 percent of the youngsters reported that they had to move out of their homes and 4 percent reported that someone close to them was injured in the hurricane, 10 percent were actually injured themselves, and 71 percent reported experiencing fear of being injured. The most frequent PTSD symptoms reported by the adolescents were detachment (36 percent), avoidance of feelings or thoughts related to the hurricane (36 percent), irritability and anger (25 percent), and physiological arousal (20 percent). The total number of reported PTSD symptoms was associated with severity of exposure to the hurricane. Overall, 5 percent of the adolescents in the study reported severe and extensive enough symptoms to receive a PTSD diagnosis.

The recovery process following the disaster was sped up considerably by several community-based programs aimed at helping victims deal with the immediate crisis and to readjust to a difficult set of environmental circumstances following the disaster. Crisis intervention services were made available immediately following the disaster to provide brief counseling and outreach programs to needy victims (Joyner & Swenson, 1993). In addition, school-based social support programs were provided to assist the children in their reentry to school (Stewart et al., 1992).

workers or others; and (c) the *recovery stage,* in which the victim may be tense and apprehensive and show generalized anxiety, but gradually regains psychological equilibrium—often showing a need to repeatedly tell about the catastrophic event. It is in the third stage that posttraumatic stress disorder may develop.

In some cases, the clinical picture may be complicated by intense grief and depression. When a person feels that his or her own personal inadequacy contributed to the loss of loved ones in a disaster, the picture may be further complicated by strong feelings of guilt, and the posttraumatic stress may last for months. This pattern is well illustrated in the following case of a husband who failed to save his wife in the jet crash at Tenerife in 1977:

Martin's story is quite tragic. He lost his beloved wife of 37 years and blames himself for her death, because he sat stunned and motionless for some 25 seconds after the [other plane] hit. He saw nothing but fire and smoke in the aisles, but he roused himself and led his wife to a jagged hole above and behind his seat. Martin climbed out onto the wing and reached down and took hold of his wife's hand, but "an explosion from within literally blew her out of my hands and pushed me back and down onto the wing." He reached the runway, turned to go back after her, but the plane blew up seconds later.

[Five months later] Martin was depressed and bored, had "wild dreams," a short temper and

The aftermath of catastrophic events, such as the destruction of one's home by a tornado, may bring about psychological reactions including initial shock, passivity, repetitive retelling of the experience, and sometimes long-lasting or delayed symptoms of stress, such as recurrent nightmares.

became easily confused and irritated. "What I saw there will terrify me forever," he says. He told [the psychologist who interviewed him] that he avoided television and movies, because he couldn't know when a frightening scene would appear. (Perlberg, 1979, pp. 49–50).

In some instances the guilt of the survivors seems to center on the belief that they deserved to survive no more or perhaps even less than those who died. As one flight attendant explained after the crash of a Miami-bound jet in the Florida Everglades that took many lives, "I kept thinking, I'm alive. Thank God. But I wondered why I was spared. I felt, it's not fair. . ." (*Time,* Jan. 15, 1973, p. 53).

Extreme posttraumatic symptoms are not uncommon. One month after a mass-murder spree by a gunman in Texas, psychologists interviewed 136 survivors who had been terrorized. They diagnosed 20 percent of the men and 36 percent of the women as having PTSD. In a recent review and comparison of all published disaster research in which estimates of postdisaster psychopathology were included, on average 17 percent of victims showed psychological adjustment problems in the aftermath of the disaster (Rubonis & Bickman, 1991). Green and colleagues (1992) and Green and Lindy (1994) followed up 193 victims of the tragic Buffalo Creek flood 14 years later, finding that symptoms of past and present PTSD were diagnosable in a significant portion of the sample. Shore, Vollmer, and Tatum (1989) studied the prevalence rates of posttraumatic stress disorder in two northwestern communities and found the lifetime prevalence rate of posttraumatic stress reaction, according to diagnostic criteria, to be about 3 percent for both men and women.

Recurrent nightmares and the typical need to tell the same story about the disaster again and again appear to be mechanisms for reducing anxiety and desensitizing the self to the traumatic experience. Tension, apprehensiveness, and hypersensitivity appear to be residual effects of the shock reaction and to reflect the person's realization that the world can become overwhelmingly dangerous and threatening. As we have seen, feelings of guilt about having failed to protect loved ones who perished may be quite intense, especially in situations where some responsibility can be directly assigned.

The person's traumatic reaction to disaster stress may be more complicated in cases of physical mutilation that necessitate changes in one's way of life. It may also be complicated by the psychological effects of disability compensation or personal damage law suits, which tend to prolong posttraumatic symptoms (Egendorf, 1986; Okura, 1975).

Many potential sources of trauma exist in contemporary society, and posttraumatic stress disorder symptoms are by no means rare in the general population. Accidents, for example, are quite common. One recent study in Israel found that 10 percent of survivors of serious traffic accidents suffered symptoms of PTSD one to six months after the accident (Brom, Kleber, & Hofman, 1993). Another source of trauma in contemporary society is violence, which often results in long-term adjustment problems for victims (Norris & Kaniasty, 1994; Falsetti et al., 1995). General population surveys have recently shown that we live in a violent and dangerous world. Breslau and colleagues (1991) reported that four out of ten Americans have been exposed to significant traumatic events before the age of 30 and 9 percent of young adults met the diagnostic criteria for PTSD. Women are especially vulnerable to victimization, as shown in a recent study on the prevalence of civilian trauma in a representative sample of women conducted by Resnick and colleagues (1993). These investigators surveyed 4008 women in the United States to determine the extent to which women have experienced traumatic events in their lives. Consistent with the study described above, the majority of respondents (69 percent) reported experiencing at least one type of traumatic event in their lifetime. Fully one-third reported a crime such as a sexual or physical assault. Of the women who reported having been the victim of a crime, over half reported multiple incidents. Resnick and colleagues found the lifetime prevalence of PTSD in their sample of women to be 12.3 percent, which is consistent with the other recent community-based estimates of PTSD that placed the lifetime prevalence between 8 and 15 percent (Davidson et al., 1991; Helzer, Robins, & McEvoy, 1987).

Causal Factors in Posttraumatic Stress Most people function relatively well in catastrophes, and, in fact, many behave with heroism (Rachman, 1990). Whether someone develops posttraumatic stress disorder or not depends on a number of factors. Some research suggests that preexisting personality factors are more relevant at low and moderate levels of stress, and less relevant for more extreme traumatic experiences (Clark, Watson, & Mineka, 1994). For the latter, the nature of the traumatic stressor itself appears to account for most of the stress-response variance (e.g., Ursano, Boydstun, & Wheatley, 1981). In other words, everyone has a breaking point, and at sufficiently high levels of stress the average person can be expected to develop some psychological difficulties (which may be either short-lived or long-term) following a traumatic event. Other researchers suggest that preexisting factors may play a greater role even at high levels of stress. For example, McFarlane (1988) studied fire fighters over a period of months after an intensely traumatic experience fighting a brushfire. He concluded that though an extremely traumatic event can trigger multiple psychiatric problems, the trauma is insufficient to explain the onset of disorder. The existence of posttraumatic symptoms can only be explained by considering the person's biological makeup; preexisting psychological problems, such as low self-esteem; emotional insecurity; interpersonal skill deficits; and the social context of recovery.

In all cases of posttraumatic stress, conditioned fear—the fear associated with the traumatic experience—appears to be a key causal factor. Thus prompt psychotherapy following a traumatic experience is considered important in preventing conditioned fear from establishing itself and becoming resistant to change.

We will explore now several instances of posttraumatic stress disorder, examining both the immediate and long-range effects of several debilitating situations: rape, military combat, imprisonment as a POW or in a concentration camp, detainment as a hostage, and displacement from one's homeland.

The Trauma of Rape

In our society rape occurs with an alarming frequency. Using a fairly broad definition of rape (see chapter 11), Koss (1993) estimated that one woman in five will experience rape in her lifetime. This crime inflicts severe trauma on a victim. Rape is an act of violence in which sexual relations, typically intercourse, are forced on one person by another. In most cases, the victim is a woman.

Our concern here is with a victim's response to rape, which can vary depending on a number of factors. In a "stranger" rape—one in which the victim does not know the offender—the victim is likely to experience strong fear of physical harm and death. In an "acquaintance" rape the reaction is apt to be slightly different (Ellison, 1977; Frazier & Burnett, 1994). In such a situation the victim not only may feel fear, but also may feel that she has been betrayed by someone she had trusted. She may feel more responsible for what happened and experience greater guilt. She may also be more hesitant to seek help or report the rape to the police out of fear that she will be held partially responsible for it.

The age and life circumstances of a victim may also influence her reaction (Adam, Everett, & O'Neal, 1992). For a young child who knows nothing about sexual behavior, rape can lead to sexual scars and confusion, particularly if the child is encouraged to forget about the experience without thoroughly talking it over first (Browne & Finkelhor, 1986). For young adult women, rape can increase the conflicts over independence and separation that are normal in this age group. In an effort to be helpful, parents of these victims may encourage various forms of regression, such as moving back to the family home, which may prevent mastery of this developmental phase. Married rape victims with children face the task of explaining their experience to their children. Sometimes the sense of vulnerability that results from rape leaves a woman feeling temporarily unable to care for her children.

Husbands and boyfriends can also influence rape victims' reactions by their attitudes and behavior. Rejection, blaming, uncontrolled anger at the offender, or insistence on a quick resumption of sexual activity can increase victims' negative feelings.

In an informative formulation of the stress women experience following rape, McCann (1988) found empirical evidence of problems in five areas of functioning: (a) physical disturbances, including hyperarousal; (b) emotional problems, such as anxiety, depressed mood, and low self-esteem; (c) cognitive dysfunction, including disturbed concentration and the experience of intrusive thoughts; (d) atypical behavioral acts, such as aggressive, antisocial actions and substance abuse; and (e) interference in social relationships, including sexual problems, intimacy problems, and further victimization. Two recent studies have reported a high incidence of women experiencing symptoms of anxiety or panic disorder following victimization. Fierman and colleagues (1993) found that prior trauma, particularly sexual abuse, physical abuse, and rape were prominent in the life histories of patients seeking treatment at an anxiety clinic. Falsetti and colleagues (1995) reported that 94 percent of their sample of women with panic disorders had histories of criminal victimization.

Coping Behavior of Rape Victims Research on rape victims soon after their rapes has provided clear insights into the emotional turmoil and psychological processes they go through in coping with their experiences (Burgess & Holmstrom, 1974, 1976; Frazier & Schauben, 1994; Frazier & Burnett, 1994; McCombie, 1976; Meyer & Taylor, 1986; Roth & Lebowitz, 1988). The following sections summarize these findings and integrate the feelings and problems women experience at different points of their traumas.

Anticipatory Phase. This period occurs before an actual rape when an offender "sets up" a victim and the victim begins to perceive that a dangerous situation exists. In the early minutes of this phase, the victim often uses defense mechanisms such as denial to preserve an illusion of invulnerability. Common thoughts are "Rape could never happen to me" or "He doesn't really mean that."

Impact Phase. This phase begins with a victim's recognition that she is actually going to be raped and ends when the rape is over. The victim's first reaction is usually intense fear for her life, a fear much stronger than her fear of the sexual act itself. Symonds (1976) has described the paralytic effect of intense fear on victims of crime, showing that this fear usually leads to varying degrees of disintegration in the victim's functioning and possibly to complete inability to act. Roth and Lebowitz (1988) found that the sexual trauma "confronts the individual" with emotions and images that are difficult to manage and may have long-term adjustment consequences. When the victim later recalls her behavior during the assault, she may feel guilty about not reacting more efficiently, and she needs to be reassured that her actions were normal. Major physiological reactions such as vomiting sometimes occur during this phase, but victims who try to simulate such reactions in order to escape generally discover that they cannot produce them voluntarily.

Posttraumatic Recoil Phase. This phase begins immediately after a rape. Burgess and Holmstrom (1974, 1976) observed two emotional styles among the rape victims they interviewed in hospital emergency rooms. Some victims exhibited an expressed style where feelings of fear and anxiety were shown through crying, sobbing, and restlessness. Others demonstrated a controlled style in which feelings appeared to be masked by a calm, controlled, subdued facade. Regardless of style, most victims felt guilty about the way they had reacted to the offender and wished that they had reacted faster or fought harder. (Excessive self-blame has been associated with poor long-term adjustment [Meyer & Taylor, 1986].) Feelings of dependency were increased, and victims often had to be encouraged and helped to call friends or parents and make other arrangements. Physical problems, such as general tension, nausea, sleeplessness, and trauma directly related to the rape were common and resulted in greater use of medical services (Kimerling & Calhoun, 1994).

Reconstitution Phase. This phase begins as a victim starts to make plans for leaving the emergency room or crisis center. It ends, often many months later, when the stress of the rape has been assimilated, the experience shared with significant others, and the victim's self-concept restored. Certain behaviors and symptoms are typical during this phase:

1. Self-protective activities, such as changing one's telephone number and moving to a new residence, are common. The victim's fear is often well justified at this point because, even in the unlikely event that the offender has been arrested and charged with rape, he is often out on bail.

2. Frightening nightmares in which the rape is relived are common. As the victim moves closer toward assimilating the experience, the content of the dreams may gradually shift until the victim successfully fights off the assailant.

Emotional support can be an important element in recovery from psychological adjustment problems following rape. The young woman in this picture is being counseled in a rape trauma center. Rape crisis centers provide both psychological counseling and advocacy services with the intent of helping rape victims cope with their crisis and its aftermath. Such intervention can have a significant impact on psychological recovery from rape.

3. Phobias—including fear of the indoors or outdoors (depending on where the rape took place), fear of being alone, fear of crowds, fear of being followed, and sexual fears—are often observed to develop immediately following rape.

Counseling Rape Victims The women's movement has played a crucial role in establishing specialized rape counseling services, such as rape crisis centers and hotlines. Rape crisis centers are often staffed by trained paraprofessionals who provide general support for victims, both individually and in groups. Many crisis centers also have victim advocacy services in which a trained volunteer accompanies a woman to a hospital or police station, helps her understand the procedures, and assists her with red tape. The advocate may also accompany the person to meetings with legal representatives and to the trial—experiences that tend to temporarily reactivate the trauma of the rape.

In a study of the counseling needs of rape victims, Meyey and Taylor (1988) reported that rape victims needed to better understand the trauma situation and desired information about how they could cope with their dramatically altered lives. They also found that rape victims wanted to talk with other women who had gone through similar experiences.

Long-Term Effects Whether a rape victim will experience serious psychological decompensation depends to a large extent on her past coping skills and level of psychological functioning. A previously well-adjusted woman usually will regain her prior equilib-

rium, but rape can precipitate severe pathology in a woman with psychological difficulties (Atkeson et al., 1982; Meyer & Taylor, 1986; Santiago et al., 1985). Keep in mind that this general finding is not true in every case—clearly the nature of the crime and the adequacy of therapy are critical factors contributing to a victim's recovery. What we are saying is that research does point to a correlation between previous psychological functioning and recovery from a rape experience. Frazier and Schauben (1994), in their study of recovering rape victims, found that victims' causal attributions about whether they were able to control future circumstances influenced the recovery process. Women who tended to blame themselves or thought more about "why" the rape occurred were slower to recover from the trauma than those who believed that future assaults were less likely.

As for long-term effects, comparisons of women who have been raped with those who have not indicate that although victims feel that their rapes have had and continue to have an effect on them, in many cases no significant differences in overall psychological adjustment exist between victims and nonvictims (Oros & Koss, 1978). More adjustment difficulties, of course, are likely to occur in situations when the rape victim has a prior psychological adjustment problems and is more vulnerable to stress. When problems do continue, or when they become manifest later in a delayed posttraumatic stress disorder, they are likely to involve anxiety, depression, withdrawal, and heterosexual relationship difficulties (Gold, 1986; Koss, 1983; Meyer & Taylor, 1986; Santiago et al., 1985).

The Trauma of Military Combat

"War is a constant of history" as Shaw (1990) recently noted. War continues to take an incredible toll on human lives and economic resources, often leaving large numbers of civilian and military victims in its wake. Many people who have been involved in the turmoil of war experience devastating psychological problems for months or even years afterward.

During World War I, traumatic reactions to combat conditions were called *shell shock,* a term coined by a British pathologist, Col. Frederick Mott (1919), who regarded these reactions as organic conditions produced by minute brain hemorrhages. It was gradually realized, however, that only a small percentage of such cases represented physical injury. Most victims were suffering instead from the general combat situation, with its physical fatigue, ever-present threat of death or mutilation, and severe psychological shocks. During World War II traumatic reactions to combat passed through a number of classifications, such as *operational fatigue* and *war neuroses,* before finally being termed *combat fatigue* or *combat exhaustion* in the Korean and Vietnam wars.

Even the latter terms were none too aptly chosen, because they implied that physical exhaustion played a more important role than was usually the case. They did, however, serve to distinguish such disorders from other psychological disorders that happened to occur under war conditions but might well have occurred in civilian life—for example, among people showing histories of maladaptive behaviors that were aggravated by the stress of combat. Most soldiers who became psychological casualties because of combat had adjusted satisfactorily to civilian life and to prior military experiences.

It has been estimated that in World War II, 10 percent of Americans in combat developed combat exhaustion. However, the actual incidence is not known because many soldiers received supportive therapy at their battalion aid stations and were returned to combat within a few hours. Records were kept mainly on soldiers evacuated from the front lines who were considered the most seriously disturbed cases. Of the just over 10 million people accepted for military service during World War II, approximately 530,000—a little over 5 percent—were given medical discharges for neuropsychiatric reasons (including combat exhaustion, psychosis, neurosis, and other personality disorders that made them unsuitable for military life). In fact, combat exhaustion caused the single greatest loss of personnel during that war (Bloch, 1969). During the Ko-

rean War the incidence of combat exhaustion dropped from an initial high of over 6 percent to 3.7 percent; 27 percent of medical discharges were for psychiatric reasons (Bell, 1958). In the Vietnam War the figure dropped to less than 1.5 percent for combat exhaustion, with a negligible number of discharges for psychiatric disorders (Allerton, 1970; Bourne, 1970).

Reasons advanced to explain the decrease in combat exhaustion during the Vietnam War include (a) better medical care near the front lines; (b) the sporadic nature of the fighting, in which brief intensive encounters were followed by periods of relative calm and safety—as contrasted with the weeks and months of prolonged combat that many soldiers went through in World War II and the Korean War; and (c) a policy of rotation after 12 months of service (13 months for Marines).

However, research has shown a high prevalence of posttraumatic stress disorder for Vietnam veterans. Though combat exhaustion was not as great a factor as in previous wars, combat-related stress apparently manifested itself later. Adopting research methodology developed in the study of genetic inheritance, Goldberg and colleagues (1990) studied identical twins who were in the military during the Vietnam War but who experienced different degrees of combat exposure. Some members of the twin pairs had served in Southeast Asia (SEA) and others had not; the latter served as the control group. Using military service records, the researchers identified 2092 pairs of male identical twins who agreed to cooperate in the study. These twins were surveyed to determine their exposure to stressful combat situations using an objective demographic and

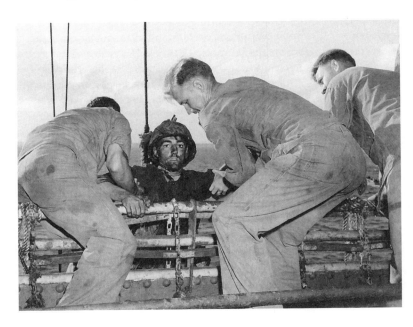

It has been estimated that in World War II, 10 percent of Americans in combat developed combat exhaustion. The stress of combat clearly took its toll on this Marine who had just finished two days of heavy fighting in the Pacific.

experience questionnaire. The researchers placed subjects into combat-exposure groups as follows: 950 twin pairs had not served in SEA; 427 twin pairs included two individuals who had served in SEA; 715 twin pairs included one twin who had served in SEA and one who had not.

Marked differences in the prevalence of PTSD were found between the groups that had served in SEA and those that had not. The twin pair group that had not served in SEA reported low rates of PTSD symptoms (4.3 to 12.3 percent) compared with the group in which both pairs had served in SEA (14.4 to 28.2 percent). The most interesting comparison was in the discordant group in which one twin had served in SEA and the other had not. In this group the twins not serving in SEA reported low rates of PTSD (from 4.8 to 12.2 percent), similar to the group of twins that had not served in SEA. Those twins from the discordant pair who had actually served in SEA reported high rates of PTSD (from 15.8 to 30.6 percent), similar to the twin group in which both pairs had served in SEA.

A further analysis was conducted to assess the relationship between the degree of combat exposure and the later development of posttraumatic stress disorder. The researchers found a clear intensity effect in the later development of PTSD symptoms. Men who had experienced high levels of combat had a greater prevalence of posttraumatic stress symptoms than those who had had lower levels of combat exposure (Bremner, Southwick, & Charney, 1995).

Clinical Picture in Combat-Related Stress The specific symptoms of combat-related stress vary considerably, depending on the type of duty, the severity and nature of the traumatic experience, and the personality of the person. Just being in a war zone with the ever-present possibility that a shell can explode and kill or injure anyone around it is a frightening experience (Zeidner, 1993). Two recent studies provide strong evidence of the impact of war on civilian populations. Schwarzwald and colleagues (1993) studied 492 Israeli elementary school children who were exposed to SCUD missile attacks during the war with Iraq and determined that higher stress responses were found in areas that were hit by missiles, and stress was related to proximity to the damage sites. In another study, Weizman and colleagues (1994) measured psychological and physiological stress among Israeli civilians who lived in cities subject to missile attacks during the war. The anxiety levels of the civilians exposed to the threat of attack were significantly higher during the war than when retested when the war was over. Moreover, anxiety

was higher during the evenings (when the SCUD attacks usually occurred) than during the day. In another study, Lomranz and colleagues (1994) surveyed 3204 Israelis on four occasions: before the Gulf War crisis, as the war approached, during the SCUD missile attacks, and after the hostilities ceased. They found an increase in depressive mood during the SCUD attacks and a "quick return to baseline" following the hostilities.

One study evaluating different dimensions of posttraumatic stress disorder according to the type of war-related stress experienced was conducted by Laufer, Brett, and Gallops (1985). They surveyed 251 Vietnam veterans, and on the basis of the veterans' self-reports, grouped them according to three levels of experienced stress: (a) exposed to combat; (b) exposed to abusive violence in combat; and (c) participated in abusive violence in combat. They found that different degrees of stress symptoms were reported by people who had been exposed to different types of war trauma. Exposure to combat and exposure to violence were found to be associated with later experiences of posttraumatic symptoms, including intrusive imagery, hyperarousal, numbing, and cognitive disruption. Participation in abusive violence was most highly associated with more severe pathologies marked by cognitive disruptions, such as depression. The authors concluded that the clinical picture of posttraumatic stress disorder varies depending on the stressors experienced. Patients who have experienced particular types of war stress are likely to present specific types of symptoms, and not all PTSD patients present identical symptoms. Combat involvement is also not the only stressor in a war zone. Sutker and colleagues (1994) found that soldiers involved in graves registration duties (i.e., handling corpses) had high rates of PTSD symptoms such as anger, anxiety, and somatic complaints compared with soldiers not assigned to such duties. Moreover, some people entering the military are more vulnerable to developing stress-related symptoms than others. During World War II, for example, "total mobilization" efforts brought a great deal more older men into the service. Recent research has shown that older mobilized men were at greater risk for developing health-related problems than younger men (Elder, Shanahan, & Clipp, 1994).

Despite variations in experience, however, the general clinical picture was surprisingly uniform for soldiers who developed combat stress in different wars. The first symptoms were a failure to maintain psychological integration, with increasing irritability and sensitivity, sleep disturbances, and often recurrent nightmares. In the Vietnam War, soldiers were seldom exposed to prolonged periods of shelling and bombardment; combat reactions were typically more sudden and acute as a result of some particularly overwhelming combat experience. A recent empirical study of the emotional components of PTSD in combat veterans found anger and anger-control problems to be a strong component in posttraumatic stress among combat veterans (Chemtob et al., 1994).

The recorded cases of combat-related stress among soldiers in various wars show that the common symptom usually has been overwhelming anxiety. In comparison, it is interesting to note that most wounded soldiers have shown less anxiety or fewer combat exhaustion symptoms—except in cases of permanent mutilation. Apparently a wound, in providing an escape from a stressful combat situation, removes the source of anxiety. A similar finding was reported among Israeli soldiers hospitalized during the five-to-six-week Yom Kippur War in 1973 when Egyptian and Syrian forces attacked Israel. Those soldiers hospitalized for physical injuries—even severe ones such as paralysis or loss of limb—showed no appreciable psychological disturbances. In contrast, those hospitalized because of psychiatric problems—such as severe depression, thought disorders, and obsessiveness—were quite disturbed about their physical symptoms, even minor ones (Merbaum & Hefez, 1976).

In fact, it is not unusual for soldiers to admit that they have prayed to be hit or to have something "honorable" happen to them to remove them from battle. When approaching full recovery and the necessity of returning to combat, injured soldiers sometimes show prolonged symptoms or delayed traumatic reactions of nervousness, insomnia, and other symptoms that were nonexistent when they were first hospitalized.

Causal Factors in Combat Stress Problems In a combat situation, with the continual threat of injury or death and repeated narrow escapes, a person's ordinary coping methods are relatively useless. The adequacy and security the person has known in the relatively safe and dependable civilian world are completely undermined. However, we must not overlook the fact that most soldiers subjected to combat have not become psychiatric casualties, although most of them have evidenced severe fear reactions and other symptoms of personality disorganization that were not serious enough to be incapacitating. In addition, many soldiers have tolerated almost unbelievable stress before they have broken, while others have become casualties under conditions of relatively slight combat stress or even

Many factors may contribute to traumatic reactions to combat—constitutional predisposition, personal immaturity, compromised loyalty to one's unit, diminished confidence in one's officers, as well as the actual stress experienced. Thus, although combat situations completely undermine a person's ordinary coping methods, some soldiers can tolerate great stress without becoming psychiatric casualties, while others may break down under only slight combat stress.

as noncombatants—for example, during basic training.

In order to understand traumatic reactions to combat, we need to look at factors such as constitutional predisposition, personal maturity, loyalty to one's unit, and confidence in one's officers—as well as at the actual stress experienced.

Biological Factors. Do constitutional differences in sensitivity, vigor, and temperament affect a soldier's resistance to combat stress? They probably do, but little actual evidence supports this assumption. We have more information about the conditions of battle that tax a soldier's emotional and physical stamina. Add other factors that often occur in combat situations—such as severe climatic conditions, malnutrition, and disease—to the strain of continual emotional mobilization, and the result is a general lowering of a person's physical and psychological resistance to all stressors.

Psychosocial Factors. A number of psychological and interpersonal factors may contribute to the overall stress experienced by soldiers and predispose them to break down under combat. Such factors include reductions in personal freedom, frustrations of all sorts, and separation from home and loved ones. Central, of course, are the many stresses arising from combat, including constant fear, unpredictable circumstances, the necessity of killing, and prolonged harsh conditions.

Personality is an important determinant of adjustment to military experiences. Personality characteristics that lower a person's resistance to stress or to particular stressors may be important in determining his or her reactions to combat. Personal immaturity—sometimes stemming from parental overprotection—is commonly cited as making a soldier more vulnerable to combat stress. Worthington (1978) found that American soldiers who experienced problems readjusting after they returned home from the Vietnam War also tended to have had greater difficulties before and during their military service than soldiers who adjusted readily. Clark and colleagues (1994) provide an informative discussion of the role of personality and temperament in the development of anxiety symptoms.

In their study of the personality characteristics of Israeli soldiers who had broken down in combat during the Yom Kippur War, Merbaum and Hefez (1976) found that over 25 percent reported having had psychological treatment prior to the war. Another 12 percent had experienced difficulties previously in the six-day Israeli-Arab war of 1967. Thus about 37 percent of these soldiers had clear histories of some personality instability that may have predisposed them to break down under combat stress. On the other hand, the other soldiers who broke down—over 60 percent—had not shown earlier difficulties and would not have been considered to be at risk for such breakdown.

A background of personal maladjustment does not always make a person a poor risk for withstanding combat stress. Some people are so accustomed to anxiety that they cope with it more or less automatically, whereas soldiers who are feeling severe anxiety for the first time may be terrified by the experience, lose their self-confidence, and go to pieces. It has also been observed that psychopaths (antisocial personalities, according to DSM criteria), though frequently in trouble during peacetime service for disregarding rules and regulations, have of-

ten demonstrated good initiative and effective combat aggression against the enemy. This observation has recently been questioned by Clark and colleagues (1994) who point out that antisocial personality can actually be a risk factor for development of PTSD. Most authorities agree that the soldiers who function most effectively and are most apt to survive combat usually come from backgrounds that fostered self-reliance, the ability to function in a group, and ready adjustment to new situations (Borus, 1974; Grinker, 1969; Lifton, 1972).

Sociocultural Factors. Several sociocultural factors play an important part in determining a person's adjustment to combat. These general factors include clarity and acceptability of war goals, identification with the combat unit, esprit de corps, and quality of leadership.

An important consideration is how clear and acceptable the war's goals are to a person. In general, war goals have a supportive effect on a soldier if they can be concretely integrated into the soldier's values in terms of his or her "stake" in the war and the worth and importance of what he or she is doing. Another important factor is a person's identification with the combat unit. The soldier who is unable to identify with or take pride in his or her group lacks the feeling of "we-ness" that helps maintain stress tolerance. Lacking this identity, a soldier stands alone, psychologically isolated and less able to withstand combat stress. In fact the stronger the sense of group identification, the less chance that a soldier will break down in combat. Feelings of esprit de corps influence a person's morale and adjustment to extreme circumstances. Finally, the quality of leadership and confidence in one's unit are of vital importance in a soldier's adjustment to combat. If a soldier respects his or her leaders, has confidence in their judgment and ability, and can accept them as relatively strong parental or sibling figures, the soldier's morale and resistance to stress are bolstered. On the other hand, lack of confidence or dislike of leaders is detrimental to morale and to combat stress tolerance.

It also appears that returning to an unaccepting social environment can increase a soldier's vulnerability to posttraumatic stress. For example, in a one-year follow-up of Israeli men who had been psychiatric war casualties during the Yom Kippur War, Merbaum (1977) found that they not only continued to show extreme anxiety, depression, and extensive physical complaints, but in many instances they appeared to have become more disturbed over time. Merbaum hypothesized that their psychological deterioration had probably been due to the unaccepting attitudes of the community; in a country so reliant on the strength of its army for survival, considerable stigma is attached to psychological breakdown in combat. Because of the stigma, many of the men were experiencing not only isolation within their communities, but also self-recrimination about what they perceived as failure on their own parts. These feelings exacerbated the soldiers' already stressful situations.

Long-Term Effects of Posttraumatic Stress In some cases, soldiers who have experienced combat exhaustion may show symptoms of posttraumatic stress for sustained periods of time. In cases of delayed posttraumatic stress, some soldiers who have stood up exceptionally well under intensive combat situations have experienced posttraumatic stress only upon their return home, often in response to relatively minor stresses that they had handled easily before. Evidently, these soldiers have suffered long-term damage to their adaptive capabilities, in some cases complicated by memories of killing enemy soldiers or civilians that are tinged with feelings of guilt and anxiety (Haley, 1978; Horowitz & Solomon, 1978).

In a study of Vietnam returnees, Strange and Brown (1970) compared combat and noncombat veterans who were experiencing emotional difficulties. The combat group showed a higher incidence of depression and of difficulties in close interpersonal relationships. They also showed a higher incidence of aggressive and suicidal threats but did not actually carry them out. In a later study of Vietnam veterans who were making a satisfactory readjustment to civilian life, DeFazio, Rustin, and Diamond (1975) found that the combat veterans still reported certain symptoms twice as often as the noncombat veterans. Based on a questionnaire obtained from 207 veterans who had been out of the armed forces for over five years, DeFazio and colleagues found the following percentages of combat veterans still reporting symptoms: (a) frequent nightmares—68 percent; (b) quick temper—44 percent; (c) many fears—35 percent; (d) worries about employment—35 percent; (e) difficulties with emotional closeness—35 percent; and (f) quick fatigue—32 percent. In a more recent study of veterans from World War II, the Korean War, and Vietnam, symptoms of PTSD were found to diminish somewhat with age (Fontana & Rosenheck, 1994). The researchers also reported that PTSD symptoms were similar across the three wars, suggesting that the relationship between trauma and symptoms was generally the same across wars.

The nature and extent of delayed posttraumatic stress disorder are somewhat controversial (Burstein, 1985). Reported cases of delayed stress syndrome among Vietnam combat veterans are often difficult to relate explicitly to combat stress because these people may also have other significant adjustment problems. People with adjustment difficulties may erroneously attribute their present problems to specific incidents from their past, such as experiences in combat. The wide publicity recently given to delayed posttraumatic stress disorder has made it easy for clinicians to "find" a precipitating cause in their patients' backgrounds. Indeed, the frequency with which this disorder has recently been diagnosed in some settings suggests that its increased use is as much a result of its plausibility and popularity as of its true incidence.

The Trauma of Being a Prisoner of War or in a Concentration Camp

Although some people adjust to the stress of being a prisoner of war or in a concentration camp (especially if part of a supportive group), the past shows us that the toll on most prisoners is great. About half of the American prisoners in Japanese POW camps during World War II died during their imprisonment; an even higher number of prisoners of Nazi concentration camps died. Those who survived the ordeal often sustained residual organic and psychological damage along with a lowered tolerance to stress of any kind.

Without question, reentry to society is difficult for former POWs and concentration camp survivors. They must adjust to the sudden and major changes in their lives and to the social changes that took place during their imprisonments.

The residual damage to survivors of Nazi concentration camps was often extensive and commonly included anxiety, insomnia, headaches, irritability, depression, nightmares, impaired sexual potency, and "functional" diarrhea (which occurs in any situation of stress, even relatively mild stress). Such symptoms were attributed not only to the psychological stressors but also to biological stressors, such as head injuries, prolonged malnutrition, and serious infectious diseases (Sigal et al., 1973; Warnes, 1973).

Among returning POWs, psychological problems were often masked by the feelings of relief and jubilation that accompanied release from confinement. Even when there was little evidence of residual physical pathology, however, survivors of prisoner-of-war camps commonly showed impaired resistance to physical illness, low frustration tolerance, frequent dependence on alcohol and drugs, irritability, and other indications of emotional instability (Chambers, 1952; Goldsmith & Cretekos, 1969; Hunter, 1978; Strange & Brown, 1970; Wilbur, 1973). In a

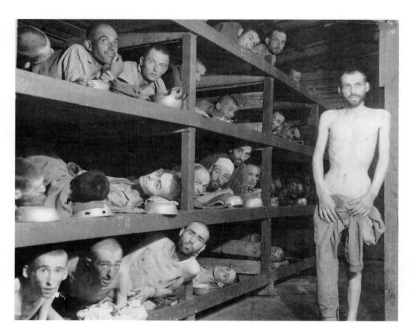

The physical and psychological stresses of life in Nazi concentration camps left permanent scars on many of those who survived the ordeal. When samples of concentration camp survivors who did not undergo psychotherapy have been studied, however, they have been shown to be resilient and well-functioning over time. Elie Wiesel, pictured here on the second tier of prisoners (the second man behind the man with the bandaged head), was liberated from Buchenwald and went on to win the Nobel Peace Prize in 1986.

retrospective study of psychological maladjustment symptoms following repatriation, Speed and colleagues (1989) interviewed a large sample of former POWs and found that half of them reported symptoms that met DSM-III criteria for PTSD in the year following their releases from captivity.

Another measure of the toll taken by the prolonged stress of being in a POW or concentration camp is the higher death rate after return to civilian life. Among returning World War II POWs from the Pacific area, Wolff (1960) found that within the first six years, nine times as many died from tuberculosis as would have been expected in civilian life, four times as many from gastrointestinal disorders, over twice as many from cancer, heart disease, and suicide, and three times as many from accidents. Many problems of adjustment and posttraumatic symptoms can be found in POWs many years after their release (Sutker & Allain, 1995). Engdahl and colleagues (1993) followed up 402 Pacific War and 509 Korean War veterans and found symptoms of depression and somatic complaints prominent even 40 years after imprisonment. Some of the lingering problems experienced by former POWs might be a direct result of harsh treatment and starvation during captivity. Sutker and colleagues (1992) conducted a study of memory and cognitive performance of POW survivors and found that those who experienced the greatest trauma-induced weight loss, defined as greater than 35 percent of their precaptive weight, performed significantly worse on memory tasks than POWs who experienced less malnutrition.

Aware that problems may show up years after release, military psychologists and psychiatrists have

been following representative groups of Vietnam War POWs on a long-term basis with yearly checkups. These former POWs differ from those in earlier wars in that they were almost all flight crew personnel, which meant that they were officers and somewhat older than the rank-and-file combat personnel. In the examination made two years after their return, it was found that the longer the imprisonment, the more likely a person was to develop psychiatric problems (O'Connell, 1976). Other factors that seemed to predispose people to later problems were harsh treatment and isolation while captured (Hunter, 1976). The most frequent problems requiring psychological help were depression and marital difficulties (Hunter, 1978, 1981).

A great deal has been written about the long-term adjustment problems of concentration camp survivors. Some writers, for example Krystal (1968) and Niederland (1968) (who based their views on the survivors of death camps who later sought psychological treatment), have contended that concentration camp survivors carry psychological scars with them for the rest of their lives. Other writers have concluded that these emotional scars are so profound that they can be transmitted to the survivors' children (Epstein, 1979; Schneider, 1978). We must bear in mind, however, that most of the conclusions about the psychopathologies of concentration camp survivors and their children are based on people who are undergoing or have undergone psychotherapy. The observations that long-term adjustment problems persist, as noted by some writers, may be valid for particular people and may support the idea that some people do not deal effectively with life after experiencing severe life stress. These clinical studies, however, cannot be viewed as representative. The biased nature of their samples (psychotherapy patients) precludes generalizations about concentration camp survivors as a whole. In fact, when community (nonpsychiatric) samples of concentration camp survivors are studied they have been shown to be remarkably resilient and well functioning over time (Kahana, Harel, & Kahana, 1988; Leon et al., 1981).

The Trauma of Being Held Hostage

Hostage-taking seems to increase each year. Not only are politically driven hostage-taking situations becoming more frequent, but kidnappings in the United States for economic or other motives also seem on the rise. Clearly such situations can produce disabling psychological symptoms in victims (Allodi, 1994). The following case reported by Sonnenberg (1988) describes a man who experienced a horrifying ordeal that left him with intense symptoms of anxiety and distress for months following the incident:

> Mr. A. was a married accountant, the father of two, in his early thirties. One night, while out performing an errand, he was attacked by a group of youths. These youngsters made him get into their car, and took him to a deserted country road.
>
> There they pulled him from the car and began beating and kicking him. They took his wallet,

began taunting him about its contents (they had learned his name, his occupation, and the names of his wife and children), and threatened to go to his home and harm these family members. Finally, after brutalizing him for several hours, they tied him to a tree, one youth held a gun to his head, and after he begged and pleaded for his life, the armed assailant pulled the trigger. The gun was empty, but at the moment the trigger was pulled this victim defecated and urinated in his pants. Then the youths untied him and left him on the road.

This man slowly made his way to a gas station he had seen during his abduction, and called the police. I was called to examine him, and did so at intervals for the next 2 years. The diagnosis was PTSD. He had clearly experienced an event outside the range of normal human experience, and was at first re-experiencing the event in various ways: intrusive recollections, nightmares, flashbacks, and extreme fear upon seeing groups of unsavory looking youths. He was initially remarkably numb in other respects: he withdrew from the members of his family and lost interest in his job. He felt generally estranged and detached. He expected to die in the near future. There were also symptoms of increased psychophysiologic arousal: poor sleeping, difficulty concentrating, exaggerated startle response, and when we first spoke about his abduction in detail, he actually soiled himself at the moment he described doing so during the original traumatic experience.

Being held hostage, like this blindfolded American in Iran, and subjected to both physical and mental abuse is an experience that seems to be on the rise. Victims of other traumatic situations outside the range of normal human experience may exhibit disabling psychological symptoms months and years after the ordeal is over.

This man received treatment during the next 2 years from another psychiatrist, consisting of twice-weekly intensive individual psychotherapy sessions and the concurrent administration of a tricyclic antidepressant. The individual psychotherapy consisted of discussions that focused on the sense of shame and guilt this man felt over his behavior during his abduction. He wished he had been more stoic and had not pleaded for his life. With the understanding help of his psychotherapist, he came to see that he could accept responsibility for his behavior during his captivity, that his murderous rage at his abductors was understandable, as was his desire for revenge and that his response to his experience was not remarkable compared with what others might have done and felt. Eventually he began to discuss his experience with his wife and friends, and by the end of the 2 years over which I followed him, he was essentially without symptoms, although he still became somewhat anxious when he saw groups of tough-looking youths. Most importantly, his relationship with his wife and children was warm and close, and he was again interested in his work. (p. 585)

A common problem among hostage victims is their response to being tortured while being held prisoner. A recent series of articles by Başoğlu and his colleagues provide empirical verification of the long-term consequences of torture (see HIGHLIGHT 4.4).

The Trauma of Forced Relocation

Being uprooted from home is a threatening event that violates a person's sense of security. In recent years a hazardous substance fire in Canada forced 1663 families to evacuate their homes for 18 days (Breton, Valla, & Lambert, 1993) and 24,000 people were killed and hundreds left homeless in a volcano/mudslide in South America. It is not surprising that, in such circumstances, the accompanying stress can be severe.

Imagine, then, the trauma of refugees who are forced not only to leave their homes but also their homelands and to face the stress of adapting to a new and unfamiliar culture. For those who come to the United States, the "land of opportunity" may seem a nightmare rather than a haven. Such was the case for Pham, a 34-year-old Vietnamese refugee who killed his sons and himself. Because Pham had no past history of mental disorder and seemed to function reasonably well, it is likely that he was experiencing symptoms of poor adaptation to his new environment:

Pham's ordeal began with a comfortable life in a wealthy Vietnamese family and a good job as a Saigon pharmacist. It ended after six months in the United States in a small two-bedroom apartment in Washington, D.C. The county police called it a murder-suicide.

Police believe that the refugee, a lab technician in a local community college's work-study program, administered the poison to his own

Being forced out of one's home is a threatening event that violates one's sense of security. The suffering of the Bosnian refugees shown in this photograph shows the psychological trauma people experience in being uprooted from their homes.

HIGHLIGHT 4.4

Psychological Trauma Among Victims of Torture

Among the most highly stressful experiences human beings have reported have been those inhuman acts perpetrated upon them by other human beings—torture. From the beginning of human history to the present, some people have been subjecting other people to pain, humiliation, and degradation for political or inexplicable personal reasons. History and literature are full of personal accounts of intense suffering and lifelong dread resulting from maltreatment by ruthless captors. Psychological symptoms experienced after torture have been well documented and involve a range of problems including physical symptoms (such as pain, nervousness, insomnia, tremors, weakness, fainting, sweating, and diarrhea); psychological symptoms (such as night terrors and nightmares, depression, suspiciousness, social withdrawal and alienation, irritability, and aggressiveness); cognitive impairments (such as concentration problems, disorientation, confusion, and memory deficits); and unacceptable behaviors (such as aggressiveness, impulsivity, and suicidal attempts) (see Başoğlu & Mineka, 1992; Goldfeld et al., 1984; Mollica et al., 1990).

Most of what we know about the psychological consequences of torture comes from anecdotal reports by victims. More recently, the experiences of torture victims have been empirically evaluated in a well-controlled study of victims by Metin Başoğlu and his colleagues in an effort to understand the psychological factors involved, the long-term consequences of torture, and possible rehabilitation strategies. Başoğlu and colleagues (1994) report the results of a unique empirical study in which 55 former Turkish political prisoners were compared with 55 political activists who were not tortured. The torture victims and control subjects were identified through articles and ads in newspapers and political journals. The investigators were able to closely match the victims and controls on a number of variables including, age, gender, education level, ethnic status, and occupation. They used a number of standard assessment techniques to obtain an objective picture of each person's adjustment and psychological symptoms—psychiatric interview and a number of standardized psychological tests including the Turkish language MMPI, the Beck Depression Scale, and the State-Trait Anxiety Inventory.

Although the victims of torture were for the most part not found to be extremely psychiatrically disturbed compared with the controls, the victims of imprisonment and torture were found to experience significant symptoms of posttraumatic stress disorder related to being uprooted, being a refugee, living in a repressive political environment, and living through related traumatic events. Moreover, Başoğlu and his colleagues also found evidence sufficient to conclude that "torture induces psychological effects independent of other stressors" (Başoğlu et al., 1994). Interestingly, the authors found that traumatic experience from torture had a differential impact depending on the manner in which torture was applied, that is, whether the torture was perceived by the victim as uncontrollable and unpredictable (Başoğlu & Mineka, 1992). Victims who were able to assert some element of cognitive control over the circumstances (for example, who were able to predict and ready themselves for the pain they were about to experience) tended to be less affected over the long term. They concluded:

Prior knowledge of and preparedness for torture, strong commitment to a cause, immunization against traumatic stress as a result of repeated exposure, and strong social supports appear to have protective value against PTSD in survivors of torture. (p. 76)

family and then took his own life. Only Pham's wife survived the administration of the poison. Two seven-page suicide notes, one in Vietnamese and one in English, began, "To whom it may concern. We committed suicide by cyanide. The reason is that I lost my mind I cannot live here like a normal person. . . ."

Pham, according to relatives, had been depressed over what he considered his financial and social failures in America. He was despondent over having to study five years to become a pharmacist here and about his difficulties communicating in English.

Pham was a dutiful son who had never been away from home before leaving for Thailand. He was homesick for his native country and for the parents who remained behind.

"He had a lot of expectations about America," said one relative, "he just could not cope." (Adapted from the *Washington Star*, December 8, 1980)

Pham's suffering is not unique. It is estimated that more than 16 million refugees exist in today's world, mostly from third-world or developing countries, with only about 11 percent of them relocating in developed nations like the United States and Canada (Brandel, 1980). Most refugees move between third-world countries. For example, more than 1.5 million Kurdish refugees from Iraq have either fled to Iran or live near the Iraq-Turkey border in makeshift living quarters, and there are countless numbers of Rwandan refugees living in Zaire.

In the United States, recent refugees have come from many countries—Poland, the Soviet Union, Iran, Cuba, Haiti, Laos, Vietnam, and Cambodia. The Southeast Asians who began arriving in America after 1975 perhaps had the most difficult adjustment. Although many of these people were functioning well in their homeland and in time became successful and happy American citizens, others have had difficulty adjusting (Carlson & Rosser-Hogan, 1993; Clarke, Sack, & Goff, 1993; Westermeyer, Williams, & Nguyen, 1991). For example, in a ten-year longitudinal study of Hmong refugees from Laos, Westermeyer, Neider, and Callies (1989) found that many refugees had made considerable progress in their acculturation. Many had improved economically—about 55 percent were employed, with incomes approaching those of the general population. The percentage of people initially living on welfare had dropped from 53 to 29 percent after ten years. As a group, psychological adjustment had also improved, with symptoms of phobia, somatization, and low self-esteem showing the most positive changes. Considerable problems remain, however. Many refugees still have not learned the language, some seemingly have settled permanently onto the welfare rolls, and some show symptoms—such as anxiety, hostility, and paranoia—that have changed little over the period studied. Although many refugees have adapted to their new culture, many are still experiencing considerable adjustment problems even af-

ter ten years in the United States (Westermeyer, 1989) or in other refugee countries such as Norway (Hauff & Vaglum, 1994).

TREATMENT AND PREVENTION OF STRESS DISORDERS

Treatment After Severe Trauma

Supportive therapy and proper rest (induced by sedatives if necessary) usually can alleviate symptoms that lead to posttraumatic stress disorder. Repetitive talking about the experience and constantly reliving it in fantasies or nightmares may serve as built-in repair mechanisms to help a person adjust to the traumatic event.

In general, the more stable and better-integrated a personality and the more favorable a person's life situation, the more quickly he or she will recover from a severe stress reaction. Many people who experience a disaster benefit from at least some psychological counseling, no matter how brief, to begin coping with their experiences. Brom, Kleber, and Defares (1989) conducted a controlled study of the effectiveness of brief therapy with people experiencing PTSD and found that treatment immediately following the traumatic event significantly reduced the PTSD symptoms. Sixty percent of the treated persons showed improvement while only 26 percent of the untreated group improved. They also found, however, that treatment did not benefit everyone and that some people maintained their PTSD symptoms even after therapy was terminated.

Treatment is often required, too, for disaster area workers, as can be seen in HIGHLIGHT 4.5. Many people called to the scene of a disaster to assist victims later experience posttraumatic stress disorder themselves. Bartone and colleagues (1989) found that workers who provide support to bereaved families of disaster victims are at risk for increased illness, psychiatric symptoms, and negative psychological well-being for up to a year following the disaster. They also reported a dose-response effect relating disaster intensity with later psychological symptoms in assistance workers following an air disaster. (That is, the closer one is to the disaster, the more intense and disabling the reaction is.) They found that social supports, including high morale and cohesive group relationships, lessen the amount and intensity of posttraumatic symptoms among disaster workers.

Counseling for Disaster Workers

In September 1978 an airliner collided with a private airplane in the vicinity of the San Diego airport, killing all 137 passengers aboard the two planes and 7 people on the ground. Unlike many other air disasters, the wreckage and remains of the victims were not scattered widely but were instead concentrated in an area smaller than a city block. The force with which the planes struck the ground left few recognizable aircraft parts or human beings.

Disaster workers called to the scene to give aid and clear away the debris were generally unprepared for the calamity they witnessed. One police officer reported that "it was like stepping suddenly into hell. . . . We were standing in a pile of human tissue mixed with tiny pieces of airplane" (Davidson, 1979a). Several hundred police officers and fire fighters worked five days in temperatures that soared over 100 degrees to clean up the area. Most of the people involved in the cleanup operation— even veterans of many years of police work—were stunned by the horrible circumstances. Apparently one reason why such experienced people were so adversely affected by the situation was that "it looked very different from what people expected a plane crash to look like—they had no frame of reference for such a calamity and really lost their equilibrium" (Davidson, 1979b). Many developed psychological symptoms—depression, loss of appetite, inability to sleep, and anxiety.

To help the disaster workers, a group of psychologists from the San Diego area offered free psychological counseling. Within a few days of the accident, over 30 police officers and fire fighters along with about 50 civilians sought counseling. Interestingly, few relatives or friends of people who perished in the crash sought help, presumably because many of the victims were not San Diego residents. Several reasons were given for why so many police officers—a group traditionally skeptical of mental health

professionals and wary of being viewed by their superiors as "weird"—sought help: (a) Many officers developed unexpected problems as a result of this experience; (b) these officers had no effective outlet for the feelings of anger and frustration they were experiencing; (c) their superior officers indicated that it would be appropriate for them to discuss their feelings with professional psychologists; and (d) the counseling was set up outside of the police department's influence, thus assuring anonymity.

The counseling—crisis intervention therapy (see Chapter 18)—focused on providing support and reassurance and allowing people to vent their pent-up or unmanageable emotions. For most of the persons involved, this brief crisis intervention was effective in providing symptom relief. A few individuals, however, required more extensive, long-term psychotherapy. The following description is of a 42-year-old police officer who suffered a severe reaction to the stress of the San Diego air crash:

Don had been a model police officer during his 14 years on the force. He was highly evaluated by his superiors, had a master's degree in social work, and had attained the rank of sergeant. While patrolling in a squad car, he heard that there had been an accident, and he quickly drove to the

scene to give aid to any survivors. When he arrived he wandered around "in a daze" looking for someone to help—but there was only destruction. He later remembered the next few days as a bad dream.

He was quite depressed for several days after the cleanup, had no appetite, couldn't sleep, and was impotent. Images and recollections of the accident would come to him "out of nowhere." He reported having a recurring dream in which he would come upon an airplane crash while driving a car or flying a plane. In his dream, he would rush to the wreckage and help some passengers to safety.

Don decided that he needed help and sought counseling. Because of his deteriorating mood and physical condition, he was placed on medical leave from the police force. Eight months after the accident he was still in therapy and had not returned to work. During therapy it became apparent that Don had been experiencing a great deal of personal dissatisfaction and anger prior to the crash. His prolonged psychological disorder was not only a result of his anguish over the air crash but also a vehicle for expressing other problems. (Davidson, 1979a)

(Based on Davidson, 1979a, 1979b; O'Brien, 1979.)

Stress Prevention or Reduction

If we know that extreme or prolonged stress can produce maladaptive psychological reactions that have predictable courses, is it possible to intervene early in the process to prevent the development of emotional disorder? When an unusually stressful situation is about to occur, is it possible to "inoculate" a person by providing information about likely stressors ahead of time and suggesting ways of coping with them? If preparation for battle stressors can help soldiers avoid breakdowns, why not prepare other people to effectively meet anticipated stressors?

One researcher, Janis, did just this with patients about to undergo dangerous surgery. His findings provide a substantial base for preventive efforts aimed at reducing the emotional problems of patients following their surgery (Janis, 1958; Janis et al., 1969).

Janis (1958) conducted interviews before and after surgery to determine the relationship between preoperative fear and adjustment after surgery. He found that patients with moderate fear did better than those with either extreme or little fear. Those who greatly worried about suffering pain or being mutilated by the surgery exhibited, after surgery, extreme anxiety, emotional outbursts, and fearfulness about participating in postoperative treatment. Those who showed very little anticipatory fear displayed afterward an acute preoccupation with their vulnerability and were often angry and resentful toward the staff for being "mistreated." Those patients who were moderately fearful before surgery were the most cheerful and cooperative during the postoperative treatment.

An important finding in Janis's work is that people who are outwardly calm and appear to feel invulnerable to real danger are likely to have more post-crisis problems than people who have been "part-time worriers" beforehand. Janis suggested that the "work of worrying" may involve processes similar to the "work of mourning" following bereavement. In this case, however, it is accomplished before a trauma, helping a person understand and work through the dangerous and aversive situation and be emotionally ready to adjust to it when it comes. Later studies, too, have shown that when patients are prepared for surgery by being given accurate information about the procedures and a warning about the pain they will experience, they are less likely to have severe emotional reactions following surgery (Egbert et al., 1964).

The use of cognitive-behavioral techniques to help people manage potentially stressful situations or difficult events has been widely explored (Beech, Burns, & Sheffield, 1982; MacDonald & Kuiper, 1983; Meichenbaum & Cameron, 1983). This preventive strategy, often referred to as **stress-inoculation training,** prepares people to tolerate an anticipated threat by changing the things they say to themselves before the crisis. A three-stage process is employed. The first stage provides information about the stressful situation and about ways people can deal with such dangers. In the second stage, self-statements that promote effective adaptation— for example, "Don't worry, this little pain is just part of the treatment"—are rehearsed. In the third stage, the person practices making such self-statements while being exposed to a variety of ego-threatening or pain-threatening stressors, such as unpredictable electric shocks, stress-inducing films, or sudden cold. This last phase allows the person to apply the new coping skills learned earlier. We shall discuss stress-inoculation training and the use of self-statements in greater detail in Chapter 17.

Treatment of Posttraumatic Stress Symptoms

The treatment of stress-related psychological problems is most effective when intervention is applied early or as soon following the traumatic events as possible. We will describe some medications that have been considered useful in providing relief from the symptoms of posttraumatic stress disorder; however, psychopharmacotherapy works best in the context of psychological treatment. We will also describe effective approaches to reduction of symptoms related to stress.

Medications Several medications are used to provide relief for intense PTSD symptoms. However, since the symptoms can fluctuate over a brief period of time, careful monitoring of medications or dosage is required. The use of medication tends to be focused on specific symptoms; for example, intrusive distressing symptoms or nightmares, images of horrible events, startle reaction, and so forth can be reduced by the MAO inhibitor phenelzine; avoidance symptoms can be improved by fluoxetine and amitriptyline (see Chapter 16). Vargas and Davidson (1993) concluded that psychotherapy along with medications were more effective in improving PTSD symptoms than medications taken alone.

Crisis Intervention Therapy A brief problem-focused counseling approach referred to as crisis intervention (see Chapter 18) may aid a victim of a traumatic event in readjusting to life after the stressful situation has ended. In some situations it may be possible to prevent maladaptive responses to stress by preparing a person in advance to deal with the stress. This approach to stress management has been shown to be effective in cases where the person is facing a known traumatic event, such as major surgery or the breakup of a relationship. In these cases a professional attempts to prepare the person in advance to cope better with the stressful event through developing more realistic and adaptive attitudes about the problem.

Direct Therapeutic Exposure One behaviorally oriented treatment strategy that has been used effectively with posttraumatic stress disorder clients has been called the "direct therapeutic exposure" approach (Fairbank et al., 1992). In this approach, the client is exposed or re-introduced to stimuli that have come to be feared or associated with the traumatic event. This procedure involves "repeated or extended exposure, either *in vivo* or in imagination, to objectively harmless but feared stimuli for the purpose of reducing anxiety" (Fairbank et al., 1992).

Exposure to stimuli that have come to be associated with fear-producing situations might also be supplemented by other behavioral techniques in an effort to reduce the symptoms of PTSD. For example, the use of traditional behavioral therapy methods such as relaxation training and assertiveness training might also be found to be effective in helping a client deal with the anxiety following a traumatic event.

UNRESOLVED ISSUES

on the Politics of Posttraumatic Stress Disorder

This chapter has addressed the role of stress in producing psychological disorders. A considerable amount of research has substantiated the link between severe stress or trauma and subsequent psychological problems. People may react to stressful situations in ways that are quite disabling. Many symptoms of posttraumatic stress disorder can interfere with psychological functioning, at least for a time, and can require considerable adaptive effort to overcome.

In recent years, for better or for worse, alleged psychological disability as a result of posttraumatic stress disorder has been used in both civil and criminal cases (Slovenko, 1994). Posttraumatic stress has been used as a defense in court cases to justify criminal acts according to the "not guilty by reason of insanity" plea (see Chapter 18). A recent case illustrates the sometimes loose connection between PTSD and deviant behavior.

In January 1987 an employee of an air cargo company, who had been fired from his job the day before, returned to the office dressed in army fatigues and carrying a sawed-off shotgun. He chased several employees away from the office and took his former supervisor hostage. He held his supervisor at gunpoint for about 1½ hours, making him beg for his life. During this time he fired about 21 shots at desks, computers, and windows, destroying a great deal of property. Once the hostage-taking situation ended, the former employee was arrested on charges of property destruction and assault with a deadly weapon. He reportedly claimed that he was extremely distraught and was suffering a posttraumatic stress disorder. He explained that he had just seen the movie *Platoon*, which brought back horrible memories of Vietnam and had resulted in his becoming enraged. However, a check of his background and military records showed that he had never been in Vietnam and had actually spent his service time in a low stress, noncombat environment.

The ofttimes sensational nature and resulting publicity of some cases may give the impression that the use of the PTSD defense is on the increase. A recent study of insanity plea defendants showed that concerns over widespread abuse of the PTSD insanity defense are unfounded because the defense is not used as frequently as is often supposed. Appelbaum and colleagues (1993) found that in 8163 defendants pleading insanity between 1980 and 1986 only 28 (0.3%) had been given PTSD diagnoses. People employing the insanity defense were, however, more likely to be able to avoid pre-trial detention than those in the control group of non-PTSD defendants (Appelbaum et al., 1993).

The posttraumatic syndrome is more frequently being used in civil court cases, such as those involving compensation and personal injury. For example, in one case (*Albertson's Inc.* v. *Workers' Compensation Appeals Board of the State of California,* 1982), a bakery employee was awarded damages because her boss's comments to her caused her great embarrassment. The court concluded that job harassment was a sufficient cause of psychological damage and stress, and it was thus compensable. In another case a police officer filed a compensation claim because his job had created a great deal of stress for him. The police officer was not awarded a stress-related disability; the court ruled that when a person accepts a job as a police officer, he or she accepts the stress that accompanies it. The court did, however, award compensation payments for his physical disability (ulcers) as a result of the stressful job (*Egeland* v. *City of Minneapolis,* 1984).

Establishing legal justification for the "stress defense" is an interesting exercise, often involving considerable imagination if not out-and-out mythmaking. Whether a stressor is causally linked to a specific psychological disorder—thereby warranting compensation in disability cases or commanding leniency in criminal trials—is often difficult to substantiate and usually involves expert witness testimony by psychiatrists or psychologists. In most situations both sides in a case rely on expert testimony to support their side. However, the most important factor, from the standpoint of legal precedent, is that there must be sufficient evidence that the alleged stressor was clearly related to the behavior in question.

When circumstances clearly involve a significant psychological stressor, the opposing side may attempt to lessen the perception of its responsibility for stress effects in order to reduce liability in the case. The most dramatic example of this tactic involves the litigation following a 1985 Delta Airlines crash in Dallas, which resulted from the pilot's inability to control the aircraft because of wind shear. In an apparent effort to limit the amount of claims against the airline, the legal staff employed by the airline's insurer conducted private investigations on many of the victims and survivors to show that their problems actually preceded the crash. For example, in the case of one passenger who was killed, the insurer's attorneys argued that the man and his wife had been having marital problems and that the baby born to his wife four days after the crash was not actually his. The lawyers concluded that, because the man's marriage was on the rocks, they shouldn't have to pay much for his death. In another trial the attorneys argued that another passenger who was killed in the crash was a homosexual who probably would have died of AIDS anyway—thus limiting their liability (*60 Minutes,* February 15, 1987). These tactics are certainly questionable, but we must keep in mind that our legal system requires a lawyer to do everything legally possible to defend his or her client. In the Delta Airlines cases, the lawyers' tactics may be more indicative of the fact that definitively proving the existence of posttraumatic stress disorder remains exceedingly difficult.

Seeking psychological damages for alleged stress, whether justified or contrived, will probably continue as a legal strategy in court cases. Because symptoms of stress disorders are not uniform, and disabilities following stressful events are not easily predictable, it is likely that the problem of clearly establishing causal links between stressors and claimed symptoms will continue to plague our courts.

SUMMARY

Many factors influence a person's response to stressful situations. The impact of stress depends not only on its severity, but also on the person's preexisting vulnerabilities. A person's response to conflict situations may be viewed differently depending on whether the conflicts are approach-avoidance, double-approach, or double-avoidance. A wide variety of psychosocial stressors exists, and a person can respond to them in different ways. In attempting to deal with stressful events, for instance, a person may react with task-oriented or defense-oriented responses. The effects of extreme or prolonged stress on a person can bring about extensive psychological problems.

The DSM-IV classifies people's problems in response to stressful situations under two categories: adjustment disorders and posttraumatic stress disorder (included with the anxiety disorders). Several relatively common stressors (prolonged unemployment, loss of a loved one through death, and marital separation or divorce) may produce a great deal of stress and psychological maladjustment, resulting in adjustment disorder. More intense psychological disorders in response to trauma or excessively stressful situations (such as rape, military combat, imprisonment, being held hostage, relocation, or other disasters) may be categorized as posttraumatic stress disorder. These disorders may involve a variety of symptoms, including intrusive thoughts and repetitive nightmares about the event, intense anxiety, avoidance of stimuli associated with the trauma, increased arousal manifested as chronic tension, irritability, insomnia, impaired concentration and memory, and depression. If the symptoms begin six months or more after the traumatic event, the diagnosis is delayed posttraumatic stress disorder. Many factors contribute to breakdown under excessive stress, including the intensity or harshness of the stress situation, the length of the traumatic event, the person's biological makeup and personality adjustment before the stressful situation, and the ways in which the person manages problems once the stressful situation is over. In many cases the symptoms recede as the stress diminishes, especially if the person is given supportive psychotherapy. In extreme cases, however, there may be residual damage or the disorder may be of the delayed variety, not actually occurring until some time after the trauma.

Posttraumatic stress disorder has been used in recent criminal and, more frequently, civil court cases to explain deviant behavior or to justify compensation for perceived damages. The extent to which this psychological disorder has been successfully used in court has varied. In some situations, especially when extreme trauma has been involved, the maladaptive behavior is readily explainable in terms of the traumatic event. In other situations, however, a causal link between maladaptive behavior and a traumatic event has been difficult to establish.

KEY TERMS

stressors (p. 120)
stress (p. 120)
coping strategies (p. 120)
eustress (p. 120)
distress (p. 120)
stress tolerance (p. 123)
crisis (p. 124)
crisis intervention (p. 125)
task-oriented response (p. 127)
defense-oriented response
    (p. 127)
decompensation (p. 128)
general adaptation syndrome
    (p. 128)
adjustment disorder (p. 131)
acute stress disorder (p. 134)
posttraumatic stress disorder
    (PTSD) (p. 134)
disaster syndrome (p. 135)
stress inoculation training
    (p. 152)

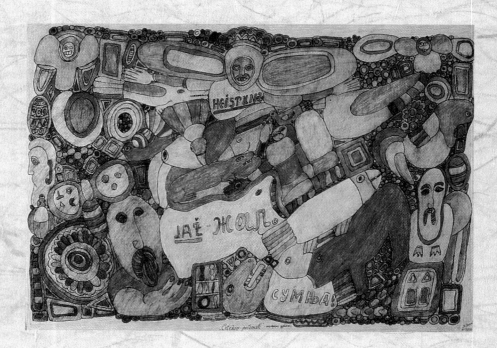

PANIC, ANXIETY, AND THEIR DISORDERS

Vojislav Jakic, Les Descendants du Dessin-Dessin Insolite. *Jakic (b. 1932) was born in Macedonia and grew up in Serbia. His position as the son of an Orthodox priest at a time of social transformation when traditional institutions were mocked caused Jakic to be teased mercilessly by other children. At the urging of an art professor, Jakic attended art school in Belgrade, where he studied drawing and sculpture. His work encompasses a variety of media, including drawing, sculpture, collages, and painting.*

Overwhelming stress, as we noted in the last chapter, can produce psychological problems in anyone. Even stable, well-adjusted people may break down if forced to face extensive combat stress, torture, or devastating natural disaster, for example. But for some people, even everyday problems can be disturbing. Faced with the normal demands of life—socializing with friends, waiting in line for the bus, taking an airplane trip, touching a doorknob—they experience serious fear or anxiety. In the most severe cases, people with anxiety problems may be unable even to leave the safety of their home or may spend much of their time in maladaptive behavior, such as constant handwashing.

Historically, anxiety disorders were considered to be examples of **neurotic behavior,** which involved the exaggerated use of avoidance behaviors (such as not leaving home) or defense mechanisms (such as rationalizing that making a trip by car is "more convenient" than confronting the feared airplane ride). Although neurotic behavior is maladaptive and self-defeating, a neurotic person is not out of touch with reality, incoherent, or dangerous; but such a person's social relations and work performance are likely to be impaired.

As we shall see, although DSM-IV now calls this group of disorders *anxiety disorders,* not neuroses, the idea of "neurosis" has a long history. (And indeed it is still used in psychoanalytic professional circles, and in casual conversation by the general public.) The term **neurosis** was first coined in 1769 by an Englishman, William Cullen, to refer to disordered sensations of the nervous system. It reflected the long-held belief that neurological malfunction must be involved in neurotic behavior. This belief was challenged by Freud, who believed that neurosis was caused not by a disruption of the nervous system but by intrapsychic conflict. To Freud, neurosis was a *psychological disorder* that resulted when there was an internal conflict between some primitive desire (from the id) and prohibitions against its expression (from the ego and superego). **Anxiety**—a general feeling of apprehension about possible danger—was in Freud's formulation a sign of this inner battle. Sometimes this anxiety seemed evident to him in patients who were obviously fearful and nervous. To complicate matters, however, he also believed that the anxiety might *not* be obvious, either to the person involved or to others, if psychological defense mechanisms were able to deflect or mask it. Yet, in his view, it still was causing the neurotic behavior in such cases.

In recent years, Freud's views on the nature of neurosis have been criticized as too theoretical and not sufficiently tied to the real world. This is because he believed anxiety to be key not only to disorders where anxiety symptoms are obvious, but also to many disorders in which there are few, if any, actual symptoms of anxiety. For these latter disorders, Freud's ideas required inferring that anxiety somehow existed "in the mind" and caused neurotic behavior even though it could not be observed or measured. The approach of editions of the DSM since 1980 has been to avoid such inferences about the causes of disorders. Therefore, although we still hear and use the term *neurosis,* the DSM has separated what used to be officially called neuroses into different categories based on their symptom picture. (Symptoms *can* be observed and measured.) People with anxiety disorders, which we shall be considering in this chapter, show prominent symptoms of anxiety. Other disorders that Freud considered neuroses, but that did not involve obvious anxiety symptoms, have been reclassified and will be discussed in Chapter 7 (the dissociative and somatoform disorders). One other category of neurotic disorders (depressive neurosis) is now included with the other mood disorders which will be discussed in Chapter 6.

Although the new DSM classification has provoked some disagreement among those committed to a psychodynamic position (because the concept of neurosis as anxiety-based is central to Freud's theory), the grouping of disorders that share obvious symptoms and features has allowed major advances to be made in understanding their causes and treatment. One reason for this is that the diagnostic criteria for the different disorders are now much more clearly defined. The diagnostician or therapist need not make inferences about underlying unobservable inner states, such as anxiety that is present but not observable because it is "defended against." As a consequence, the reliability of the diagnosis is higher than it was previously, allowing investigators to study much more homogeneous groups of people who share a common diagnosis. This greatly facilitates our ability to understand what causes the disorders and how best to treat them.

We now begin by discussing the nature of fear and anxiety as emotional states both of which have an extremely important adaptive value, but to which humans at times seem all too vulnerable. We will then move to a discussion of the anxiety disorders as described in DSM-IV and of causal factors and optimal modes of treatment for each disorder.

THE FEAR AND ANXIETY RESPONSE PATTERNS

The task of defining *fear* and *anxiety* is difficult; there has never been complete agreement whether the two emotions are indeed distinct from each other. Historically, the most common way of distinguishing between fear and anxiety has been whether there is a clear and obvious source of danger that would be regarded as real by most people. When the source of danger is obvious, the experienced emotion has been called fear. With anxiety, however, we frequently cannot specify clearly what the danger is. Intuitively, anxiety seems to be experienced as an unpleasant inner state in which we are anticipating some dreadful thing happening that is not predictable from our actual circumstances. The term *anxious apprehension* is often used to describe this state (Barlow, 1988, 1991a).

In recent years, many prominent researchers have proposed a more fundamental distinction between fear or panic, and anxiety (Barlow, 1988, 1991a; Gray, 1982, 1991; Lang, 1985). According to these theorists, **fear** or **panic** is a basic emotion that involves the activation of the "fight or flight" response of the sympathetic nervous system, allowing us to respond quickly when faced with any imminent threat. Such threats range from dangerous predators who preyed on our early ancestors, and which may still be encountered (for example, by hikers in wilderness areas), to threats that derive from more modern sources of danger such as facing someone with a loaded gun, or being in an airplane that has started to plunge earthward. Fear has cognitive/subjective components ("I feel afraid"), physiological components (such as increased heart rate and heavy breathing), as well as behavioral components (a strong urge to escape) (Lang, 1968, 1971). The three components of fear are only "loosely coupled" (Lang, 1985), meaning that someone might show, for example, physiological and behavioral indications of fear without much of the subjective component, or vice versa. For the fear response to serve its adaptive purpose of enabling us to escape or avoid danger, it must be activated with great speed. Indeed, subjectively we often seem to go from a normal state to a state of intense fear almost instantaneously. Not surprisingly, given its adaptive value for helping us escape from sources of danger, this is not a uniquely human emotion but one that is shared by many higher animals.

Although these theorists share the view that fear and panic differ in a number of ways from anxiety, they differ somewhat in their characterization of anxiety. For our purposes, we will follow David Barlow, who argues that anxiety, in contrast to fear, is best thought of as a complex blend of emotions and cognitions that is much more diffuse than fear. At the cognitive/subjective level, anxiety involves negative mood, worry about possible future threat or danger, self-preoccupation, and a sense of being unable to predict the future threat or to control it if it occurs (Barlow, 1988, 1991a). Rather than involving the activation of the fight or flight response itself, as we see with fear, anxiety involves preparing for that response should it become necessary ("Something awful may happen and I had better be ready for it if it does"). As with fear, anxiety involves not only cognitive/subjective components, but also physiological and behavioral components. At a physiological level, anxiety involves a state of chronic overarousal which may reflect the state of readiness for dealing with danger should it occur (preparation for, or priming of, the fight-or-flight response). At a behavioral level anxiety may involve a strong tendency to avoid situations where the danger or threat might be encountered, but there is no immediate urge to flee associated with anxiety as there is with fear (Barlow, 1988, 1991a). The adaptive value of anxiety may derive from the fact that it helps us plan for and prepare for possible threat, and in mild to moderate degrees, anxiety actually enhances learning and performance. But although anxiety is often adaptive in mild or moderate degrees, it is maladaptive when it becomes chronic and severe, as we generally see in people diagnosed with anxiety disorders.

Animal experimentation going back many decades has established that the basic fear and anxiety response patterns are highly conditionable. That is, previously neutral and novel stimuli that are repeatedly paired with, and reliably predict, aversive events (such as electric shocks) can acquire the capacity to elicit fear or anxiety themselves. Of course, few human infants or children are subjected to electric shocks, but many have experiences that are inherently aversive or painful. And, as we have increasingly discovered in recent years, some have unspeakably cruel and terrifying experiences visited upon them by disturbed parents or other adults. For example, a girl who sees and hears her father physically abuse her mother in the evening may become anxious as soon as she hears her father's car arrive in the driveway at the end of the day. In such situations a wide variety of initially neutral stimuli may accidentally come to serve as cues that something threatening and unpleasant is about to happen. These neutral stimuli may consist not only of external cues, but also of internal bodily sensations such as stomach or intestinal contractions or heart palpitations. As a result of such pairings, these conditioned stimuli can themselves become fear- or anxiety-provoking. In addition, we as humans have a richly elaborate mental life, such that thoughts and images become capable of eliciting the fear or anxiety response pattern. In this scenario virtually any type of novel stimulus (external, mental, or internal bodily sensations) that reliably precedes and predicts an aversive event would be expected to acquire the tendency to elicit fear or anxiety. For example, the girl described above whose father beats her mother in the evening might well come to feel anxious even when thinking about her father.

When the source of danger involves a real physical threat such as this snarling dog, the fight-or-flight response of the sympathetic nervous system is activated.

ANXIETY DISORDERS

An **anxiety disorder,** as the term suggests, has an unrealistic, irrational fear or anxiety of disabling intensity at its core and also as its principal and most obvious manifestation. DSM-IV recognizes seven primary types of anxiety disorder: phobias of the "specific" or of the "social" type, panic disorder with or without agoraphobia, generalized anxiety disorder, obsessive-compulsive disorder, and post-traumatic stress disorder. The last of these, basically a prolonged reaction to traumatic stressors, was discussed in the preceding chapter and will not be considered here.

Anxiety disorders are relatively common. In the New Haven–Baltimore–St. Louis Epidemiologic Catchment Area (ECA) program sponsored by the National Institute of Mental Health, phobias were the most common psychiatric disorder reported for women and the second-most common (behind alcohol abuse or dependence) for men. Among women, generalized anxiety disorder and agoraphobia had a prevalence rate exceeded only by phobias and certain mood disorders (Robins & Regier, 1991). For all the anxiety disorders combined, six-month prevalence rates were about 9 percent, and lifetime prevalence rates were nearly 15 percent (Robins & Regier, 1991).

It is also very common for a person diagnosed with one anxiety disorder to be diagnosed with one or more additional anxiety disorders, as well as with a mood disorder (discussed in Chapter 6; see HIGHLIGHT 6.3 for a discussion of anxiety/depression comorbidity). For example, in the ECA study about 21 percent of those with an anxiety disorder also had an affective disorder in a six-month period; lifetime prevalence rates suggested that 25 percent of those with an anxiety disorder had an affective disorder at some point (Robins & Regier, 1991). However, other reviews of the literature have estimated that as many as 50 percent of those receiving an anxiety disorder diagnosis will also receive a depressive diagnosis at some point (e.g., Clark & Watson, 1991a, 1991b).

Phobic Disorders

A **phobia** is a persistent and disproportionate fear of some specific object or situation that presents little or no actual danger to a person. When a person with a phobia encounters a feared object, he or she will often experience the fight-or-flight response discussed earlier, which prepares the person to escape from the situation. Thus, physiologically and behaviorally the phobic response is often identical to that which would occur in an encounter with an objectively terrifying situation such as being chased down a hiking trail by a grizzly bear. Phobics go to great lengths to avoid such encounters with their phobic stimulus, or often even seemingly innocent reminders of it such as pictures. In DSM-IV there are three main categories of phobias—specific phobia, social phobia, and agoraphobia. **Specific phobias** (formerly known as *simple phobias*) may involve fears of other species (snake and spider phobias being the most common) or fears of various aspects of the environment, such as water or heights. **Social phobias** involve fears of social situations in which a person is

There are many different types of phobias. Fear of flying is such a common phobia that a number of classes and programs have been developed to help airplane phobics, such as the man shown here, to overcome their fears.

exposed to the scrutiny of others and is afraid of acting in a humiliating or embarrassing way. Social phobias may be circumscribed (as in fear of public speaking) or generalized (as in fear of many different sorts of social interactions). Traditionally, *agoraphobia* was thought to involve, somewhat paradoxically, a fear of both open and enclosed spaces. However, as discussed later, it is now understood that agoraphobia most often stems from fears of having a panic attack in situations where escape might prove difficult or embarrassing. The apparent paradox is resolved in this view because escape is difficult from both open and enclosed spaces. Because it is no longer considered to be closely related to the specific phobias, we will discuss agoraphobia in the context of panic disorder, as is done in DSM-IV.

Specific Phobia
Specific phobia is diagnosed if a person shows "marked and persistent fear that is excessive or unreasonable, cued by the presence or anticipation of a specific object or situation" and when "exposure to the phobic stimulus almost invariably provokes an immediate anxiety response" that resembles a panic attack except for the existence of a clear external trigger (DSM-IV, p. 410). The avoidance of the feared situation, or the distress experienced in the feared situation, must also interfere significantly with normal functioning or produce

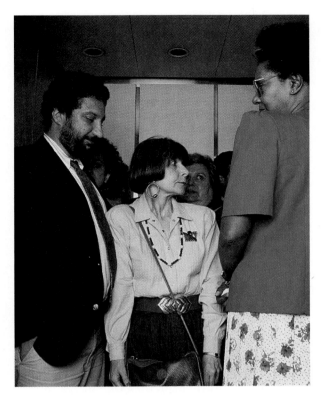

People with claustrophobia may find elevators so frightening that they go to great lengths to avoid them. If for some reason they have to take an elevator, they will be very frightened and may have thoughts about the elevator falling, the doors never opening, or there not being enough air to breathe.

marked distress. The following list of the common phobias and their objects will give some hint of the variety of situations and events around which specific phobias may be centered:

Acrophobia—heights

Algophobia—pain

Astraphobia—thunderstorms, lightning

Claustrophobia—enclosed places

Hydrophobia—water

Monophobia—being alone

Mysophobia—contamination or germs

Nyctophobia—darkness

Ochlophobia—crowds

Pathophobia—disease

Pyrophobia—fire

Zoophobia—animals or some particular animal

Some of these specific phobias involve exaggerated fears of things that most of us fear to some extent, such as darkness, fire, disease, spiders, and snakes. Others, such as phobias of water or crowds, involve situations that do not elicit fear in most people. Of course, most of us have minor irrational fears, but in phobic disorders such fears are intense and often interfere significantly with everyday activities. For example, claustrophobic persons may go to great lengths to avoid entering a small room or an elevator, even if this means climbing many flights of stairs or turning down jobs that might require them to take an elevator. This avoidance is a cardinal characteristic of phobias; it occurs both because the phobic response itself is so unpleasant and because of phobics' irrational appraisals of the likelihood that something terrible will happen to them. People who suffer from phobias usually admit that their fears are somewhat irrational, but they say that they cannot help themselves. If they attempt to approach the phobic situation, they are overcome with fear or anxiety, which may vary from mild feelings of apprehension and distress (usually while still at some distance) to a full-fledged activation of the fight-or-flight response very similar to a panic attack.

One category of specific phobias has a number of interesting and unique characteristics. In **blood-injury phobia** the afflicted person shows a unique physiological response when confronted with the sight of blood or injury. Rather than showing the simple increase in heart rate and blood pressure that is seen when most phobics encounter their phobic object, these people show an initial acceleration, followed by a *drop* in both heart rate and blood pressure. This is often accompanied by nausea, dizziness, and fainting. Indeed it has been estimated that about 75 percent of people with blood-injury phobia have a history of fainting in these situations (DSM-IV, 1994). Interestingly, blood-injury phobics only show this unique physiological response pattern in the presence of blood and injury stimuli; in the presence of other feared objects they show the more typical physiological response pattern characteristic of the fight-or-flight response (see Öst, 1985). This category of phobia also has a strong familial component, with as many as two-thirds of blood-injury phobics having at least one first-degree relative who is also blood phobic. This is three to six times the number of affected first-degree relatives seen with all other phobias, including animal, social, dental, and agoraphobia (Marks, 1987). From an evolutionary and functional standpoint, this unique physiological response pattern may have evolved because it would have been adaptive for an injured person to experience a drop in heart rate and blood pressure so as to minimize blood loss. Moreover, if a person had been attacked, fainting might inhibit further attack (Marks & Nesse, 1991).

People with blood-injury phobia are terrified of being confronted with scenes involving blood or injury and often faint if they do encounter such a scene. Such people go to great lengths to avoid doctors and hospitals, sometimes to the extent of avoiding necessary medical treatments.

Specific phobias are quite common, especially in women. Results of the Epidemiological Catchment Study conducted in the early 1980s revealed a lifetime prevalence rate of over 14 percent for women and nearly 8 percent for men (Robins & Regier, 1991). The relative sex ratios vary considerably according to the type of specific phobia. For example, about 95 percent of people with animal phobias are women, but the sex ratio is less than two to one for blood-injury phobia. The average age of onset for different types of specific phobias also varies widely. Animal phobias usually begin in childhood (where they are actually equally common in boys and girls, but boys tend to "outgrow" them), as do blood-injury phobias and dental phobias. However, other phobias, such as claustrophobia and agoraphobia, tend to begin in adolescence and early adulthood (Öst, 1987).

The following case is typical of specific phobia:

Mary, a married mother of three, was 47 at the time of her first seeking treatment for both claustrophobia and acrophobia. She reported having been intensely afraid of enclosed spaces and of heights since her teens. She remembered having been locked in closets by her older siblings when she was a child; the siblings also confined her under blankets to scare her, and added to her fright by showing her pictures of spiders after releasing her from under the blankets. She traced the onset of her claustrophobia to those traumatic incidents, but she had no idea why she was afraid of heights. While her children had been growing up she had been a housewife and had managed to live a fairly normal life in spite of her two specific phobias. However, her children were now grown and she wanted to find a job outside her home. This was proving to be very difficult, however, because she could not take elevators and was not comfortable being on anything other than the first floor of an office building because of her fear of heights. Moreover, her husband had for some years been working for an airline, which entitled him to free airline tickets for himself and his wife. The fact that she could not fly (primarily because of her claustrophobia and but to some extent because of her acrophobia as well) had become a sore point in her marriage because they both wanted to be able to take advantage of these free tickets to see far away parts of the United States and Europe. Thus, although she had had these phobias for many years, they had only become truly disabling in recent years as her life circumstances had changed and she could no longer easily avoid heights or enclosed spaces.

Treatment consisted of 13 sessions of graduated exposure exercises in which the therapist first accompanied Mary into mildly fear-provoking situations, and then gradually into more and more fear-provoking situations. She also engaged in homework doing these exposure exercises by herself. The prolonged in vivo ["real life"] exposure sessions lasted as long as necessary for her anxiety to subside. Initial sessions focused on her claustrophobia and getting her to be able to ride for a few floors in an elevator, first with the therapist and then alone. Later she took longer elevator rides in taller buildings. Exposure for the acrophobia consisted of walking around the periphery of the inner atrium on the top floor of a tall hotel, and later spending time at a mountain vista overlook spot. The top of the claustrophobia hierarchy consisted of taking a tour of an underground cave. After 13 sessions Mary successfully took a flight with her husband to Europe and climbed to the top of many tall tourist sites there.

Regardless of how it begins, phobic behavior tends to be reinforced by the reduction in anxiety that occurs each time a feared situation is avoided. In addition, phobias may sometimes be maintained in part by secondary gains (benefits derived from being disabled), such as increased attention, sympathy, and some control over the behavior of others. For example, a phobia for driving may result in a homemaker being able to escape from responsibilities outside the home, such as grocery shopping or transporting children to and from school. Phobias, then, in addition to being primary manifestations of irrational, acquired fears, may sometimes serve the interests of seemingly remote objectives, although usually without the sufferer's awareness.

Psychosocial Causal Factors. According to the *psychoanalytic* view of the origins of phobias, phobias represent a defense against anxiety that stems from repressed impulses from the id. Because it is too dangerous to "know" the repressed id impulse, the anxiety is displaced onto some external object or situation that has some symbolic relationship to the real object of the anxiety. For example, in his classic case of Little Hans, Freud (1909) postulated that five-year-old Hans had developed a phobia for horses as a result of anxiety stemming from a repressed Oedipal conflict. Specifically, Freud believed that Hans unconsciously desired his mother and was so jealous of his father that he wanted to kill him. According to Freud, this led Hans to fear that his father would castrate him. The intense internal conflict created by all these unconscious feelings was not acceptable to Hans's conscious mind, and so the anxiety was displaced onto horses, which supposedly bore some symbolic relationship to his father.

Although widely accepted among psychoanalytic theorists as a prototypical case of phobia, this account has also been severely criticized as being far too speculative (e.g., Wolpe & Rachman, 1960). Moreover, an alternative and much simpler account of the origins of Hans's phobia for horses derives from learning theory. In particular, when Hans was four years old he had witnessed an accident with a horse in which the horse was badly hurt; Hans had become very upset at witnessing this incident and had later begun to avoid leaving the house so as to not encounter horses in the street. So according to Wolpe and Rachman, Hans's phobia can be seen as having originated from an instance of traumatic classical conditioning.

More generally, there are many instances in which the principles of *classical conditioning* appear to account for the acquisition of irrational fears and phobias. As noted earlier, the fear response has been shown in countless experiments to be readily conditioned to previously neutral stimuli when they are paired with traumatic or painful events. Moreover, from the principles of classical conditioning we would also expect that once acquired, phobic fears

would *generalize* to other similar objects or situations. The powerful role of classical conditioning in the development of phobias was supported in a survey by Öst and Hugdahl (1981). These investigators administered questionnaires to 106 adult phobic patients concerning, among other things, the purported origins of their fears. In describing the situations they considered as sources of their phobias, 58 percent cited traumatic conditioning experiences.

Direct traumatic conditioning is not the only way in which people can learn irrational fears. Indeed, much human learning, including the learning of fears, is *observational*. Simply watching a frightening event can be distressing, and this includes watching a phobic person behaving fearfully with his or her phobic object. In this case, fears can be transmitted from one person to another through a process of *vicarious* or *observational classical conditioning*. Merely observing the fear of another in a given situation may cause the observer to acquire a fear of that situation. Indeed, the Öst and Hugdahl study mentioned earlier found that 17 percent of their phobic patients described their phobias as having originated from instances of vicarious conditioning.

Just as much of our knowledge about classical conditioning of fear comes from research with animals, vicarious conditioning of intense fears has also been demonstrated in animal research, using rhesus monkey subjects. In these experiments, Mineka and Cook and their colleagues (e.g., 1984, 1987, 1993) showed that laboratory-reared monkeys who were not initially afraid of snakes rapidly developed a phobic-like fear of snakes simply through observing a wild-reared monkey behaving fearfully with snakes. Significant fear was acquired after only 4–8 minutes of exposure to the wild-reared monkey, and there were no signs that the fear had diminished three months later. Moreover, the fear could also be learned simply through watching a videotape of the wild-reared model monkey behaving fearfully with snakes—suggesting that the mass media may play a role in vicariously conditioning fears and phobias in people (Cook & Mineka, 1990).

Conditioning models of phobia acquisition have often been criticized because at first glance they do not appear to account for why so many people who undergo traumatic experiences do *not* develop intense or persistent fears or phobias. In other words, given all the traumas some people undergo, why don't more people develop phobias (Rachman, 1990)? Much of the answer to this question seems to stem from differences in life experiences that affect the outcome of a given conditioning experience. The traditional view was that phobias originate from simple instances of traumatic conditioning or avoidance learning occur-

*Monkeys who watch a model monkey (such as the one il-
lustrated here) behaving fearfully with a live boa con-
strictor will rapidly acquire an intense fear of snakes
themselves. Fears can thus be learned vicariously, without any direct traumatic experience.*

*A person who has good experiences with a potentially
phobic stimulus, such as the young woman romping here
with her dog, is likely to be immunized from later acquiring a fear of dogs even if she has a traumatic encounter
with one.*

ring more or less in a vacuum in a person's life. Instead, we now know that many experiences that occur
before, during, and after a given traumatic or observational conditioning experience affect the fear that is
experienced, conditioned, or maintained over time.
For example, years of positive experiences with
friendly dogs before experiencing a dog bite will probably keep the bite victim from developing a dog phobia. So to understand individual differences in the development and maintenance of phobias, it is
important to understand the role of different life experiences, or experiential variables, in which persons
undergoing the same trauma may differ (Mineka,
1985a, 1985b; Mineka & Zinbarg, in press-b).

The example of good "dog experience" immunizing one from developing a dog phobia after a
dog bite shows that one important variable that affects the amount of fear conditioned is the amount
of prior exposure a person has had with a conditioned stimulus. Indeed, Mineka and Cook (1986)
showed that monkeys who simply *watched* nonfearful monkeys behaving nonfearfully with snakes were
immunized against acquiring a fear of snakes when
subsequently exposed to fearful monkeys behaving
fearfully with snakes. Thus direct experience with an
object may not even be necessary for immunization
to occur. By analogy, if a child has extensive exposure to a nonfearful parent or peer behaving nonfearfully with the phobic object or situation of his or
her other parent, this may immunize the child
against the effects of later seeing the phobic parent
behaving fearfully with that object.

Events that occur *during* a conditioning experience, as well as before it, are also important in determining the level of fear that is conditioned. For ex-

ample, experiencing an inescapable and uncontrollable trauma seems to condition fear much more
powerfully than experiencing the same intensity of
trauma that one can escape from or to some extent
control (Mineka, 1985a, 1985b; Mineka & Kelly,
1989). In addition, the experiences that a person
has *after* a conditioning experience may affect
whether the conditioned fear is maintained or
strengthened. A person who is exposed to a more
intense traumatic experience (not paired with the
conditioned stimulus) after the first may be likely to
become more fearful of the conditioned stimulus
(Rescorla, 1974). This so-called inflation effect suggests that a person who acquired a mild conditioned
fear might be expected to develop a full-blown phobia if a later traumatic experience occurred even
without the conditioned stimulus being present
(Mineka, 1985a, 1985b; Mineka & Zinbarg, 1991,
in press-b). These examples show that the factors involved in the origins and maintenance of fears and
phobias are more complex than suggested by the
traditional conditioning view.

Recently it has been suggested that *cognitive* variables may help maintain phobias once they have been acquired. It is now well known that our cognitions or thoughts have a powerful influence on our emotional state, as well as vice versa. Recent research suggests that people with phobias are constantly on the alert for their phobic stimuli or other stimuli relevant to their phobia. Nonphobic persons, on the other hand, tend to direct their attention away from threatening stimuli (see Mineka, 1992, for a review). In addition, phobics also markedly overestimate the probability that feared objects have been or will be followed by aversive events. This bias may help maintain or strengthen phobic fears with the passage of time (Mineka, 1992; Tomarken, Mineka, & Cook, 1989).

Biological Causal Factors. Two very different types of biological variables may affect the acquisition of phobias. First, genetic and temperamental or personality variables are known to affect the speed and strength of conditioning of fear (Pavlov, 1927; Eysenck, 1965; Gray, 1982, 1987). That is, people are more or less likely to acquire phobias depending on their temperament or personality. Indeed, Kagan and his colleagues have found that children defined as *behaviorally inhibited* (excessively timid, shy, etc.) at 21 months of age were at higher risk for the development of multiple specific phobias at 7–8 years of age than were uninhibited children (32 vs. 5 percent). The average number of reported fears in the inhibited group was three to four per child (Biederman et al., 1990).

Second, our evolutionary history has affected which stimuli we are most likely to come to fear. Human fears and phobias do not tend to occur to an arbitrary group of objects or situations that may have been associated with trauma (Marks, 1969; Seligman, 1971). For example, people are much more likely to have phobias of snakes, water, heights, and enclosed spaces than of bicycles, knives, or cars, even though the latter objects may be at least as likely to be associated with trauma. These observations are contrary to what would be expected from traditional conditioning theory, which held that all objects associated with trauma would be equally likely to become objects of fear. Accordingly, some theorists have argued that primates and humans may have a biologically based *preparedness* to rapidly associate certain kinds of objects—such as snakes, spiders, water, and enclosed spaces—with aversive events (e.g., Öhman, 1986; Seligman, 1971). They have argued that this is because there may have been a selective advantage in the course of evolution for primates and humans who rapidly acquired fears of certain objects or situations that

posed threats to our early ancestors. Thus *prepared fears* are not inborn or innate but rather easily acquired or especially resistant to extinction.

Two lines of evidence now support the preparedness theory of phobias. In one important series of experiments using human subjects, Arne Öhman and his colleagues (e.g., Öhman, Dimberg, & Öst, 1985; Öhman, 1986) found that fear was conditioned more effectively to fear-relevant stimuli (slides of snakes and spiders) than to fear-irrelevant stimuli (slides of flowers and mushrooms). The responses conditioned to the fear-relevant stimuli were more resistant to extinction than were those conditioned to the fear-irrelevant stimuli. This is important support for classical conditioning models of phobia acquisition, because they have traditionally been criticized in part because most responses conditioned in laboratory settings (to fear-irrelevant stimuli) extinguish quite readily, unlike phobias (Seligman, 1971).

The experimenters also found that once the subjects acquired the conditioned responses, these could be elicited even when the subjects' exposure to the fear-relevant stimulus was subliminal (that is, presentation was so brief that it was not consciously perceived). By contrast, subliminal presentations of fear-irrelevant conditioned stimuli did not elicit conditioned responses. This subliminal activation of responses to phobic stimuli may help to account for certain aspects of the irrationality of phobias. That is, phobics may not be able to control their fear because the fear may arise from cognitive structures that are not under conscious control (Öhman & Soares, 1993).

Other experiments that support these general ideas on preparedness and phobias were conducted with rhesus monkeys as subjects and used a variant on the observational fear conditioning procedure with videotapes described earlier. In these experiments it was shown that monkeys can easily acquire fears of fear-relevant stimuli such as toy snakes and toy crocodiles, but not of fear-irrelevant stimuli such as flowers or a toy rabbit (Cook & Mineka, 1989, 1990, 1991). This was so even though monkeys on the videotapes behaved identically in the presence of the fear-relevant and the fear-irrelevant stimuli (this was possible through splicing the videotape). Thus, both monkeys and humans seem to selectively associate certain fear-relevant stimuli such as snakes or crocodiles with threat or danger. It is also noteworthy that these laboratory-reared monkeys had no prior exposure to or experience with any of the fear-relevant or fear-irrelevant stimuli before participating in these experiments. Thus these results are particularly important because they clearly support the preparedness hypothesis, which implicates evolutionary factors as being responsible for these biased

People are more likely to acquire fears of objects or situations that once posed a threat to our evolutionary ancestors than of objects that did not exist in our early evolutionary history (such as cars and knives). Such prepared fears include a fear of heights.

associations. The same is not true of the human subjects who participated in Öhman's experiments, all of whom had prior experiences with, and associations to, the stimuli used in these experiments. In other words, it remains possible that human subjects showed superior conditioning to snakes or spiders because they had preexisting negative associations based on prior experiences with snakes or spiders, rather than because of evolutionary factors.

Social Phobia Social phobia was only identified as a distinct form of phobia in the late 1960s (Marks, 1969). Fear of negative evaluation by others may be the hallmark of social phobia (Hope & Heimberg, 1993). As currently conceptualized in DSM-IV there are two subtypes of social phobia—specific and generalized. People with *specific social phobias* have disabling fears of one or more discrete social situations in which they fear they may be exposed to the scrutiny of others and may act in an embarrassing or humiliating manner (e.g., public speaking, urinating in a public bathroom, or eating or writing in public). Intense fear of public speaking is the single most common specific social phobia. Individuals

with *generalized* social phobia have significant fears of most social situations (including both public performance situations *and* situations requiring social interactions), and often also share a diagnosis of avoidant personality disorder (see Chapter 9) (Turner, Beidel, & Townsley, 1992). That these are truly *social* phobias becomes clear when one observes that these people have no difficulty performing the same acts (e.g., speaking, urinating, or eating) when alone.

The diagnosis of social phobia is quite common, with estimates that approximately 2 percent of the population may qualify for the diagnosis of social phobia in any six-month period. Unlike specific phobias, which most often originate in childhood and are more common in women than in men, social phobias typically begin during adolescence or early adulthood and occur about equally often in men and women (Hope & Heimberg, 1993; Marks, 1987). Persons with social phobia often suffer from one or more additional anxiety disorders (e.g., panic disorder, generalized anxiety disorder, or simple phobia) and/or a depressive disorder (Hope & Heimberg, 1993). Many also abuse alcohol in order to reduce their anxiety and help them face their feared situations (for example, drinking *before* going to a party).

The case of Paul is typical of social phobia (except that not all social phobics have full-blown panic attacks, as Paul did, in their social phobic situations):

Paul was a single white male in his mid-30s when he first presented for treatment at an anxiety clinic. He was a surgeon who practiced at a large local hospital. He reported a 13-year history of social phobia. He had very few social outlets because of his persistent concerns that people would notice how nervous he was in social situations, and he had not dated in many years for the same reasons. He was convinced that people would perceive him as foolish or crazy, and particularly worried that people would notice how his jaw tensed up when around other people. He frequently chewed gum in public situations because he thought that this kept his face from looking distorted. Importantly, he had no particular problems talking with people in professional situations. He was, for example, quite calm talking with patients before and after surgery. During surgery when his face was covered with a mask, he also had no trouble carrying out surgical tasks and no trouble interacting with the other surgeons and nurses in the room. The trouble began when he left the operating room and had to make small talk with the other doctors and nurses, or with the patient's family. He frequently had panic attacks in these social situations where he had to make eye contact and social chit-chat. During the panic attacks he experienced heart palpitations, fears of going crazy, and a sense of his mind "shutting down." The most specific trigger for these fears and panic attacks was making eye contact in social situations. Because the panic attacks occurred *only* in social situations he was diagnosed as having social phobia rather than panic disorder.

Paul reported that his social phobia and panic had begun about 13 years earlier at a time when he was under a great deal of stress. His family's business had failed, his parents had divorced, and his mother had a heart attack. It was in this context of multiple stressors that a personally traumatic incident probably triggered the onset of his social phobia. One day he had come home from medical school to find his best friend in bed with his fiancée. It was about one month later that he had his first panic attack and started avoiding social situations.

Over the intervening 13 years, Paul had taken a tricyclic antidepressant at one point, which had helped stop his panic attacks, although he continued to fear them intensely and still avoided social situations. He had also been in supportive psychotherapy, which helped his depression at the time but not his social phobia or his panic. At the time he came for treatment at our anxiety clinic he was not on any medication or in any other form of treatment. Treatment consisted of 14 weeks of cognitive-behavior therapy. By the end of treatment he was not panicking at all and was quite comfortable in most social situations he had previously avoided. He was seeing old friends that he had avoided for years because of his anxiety, and was beginning to date. Indeed, he even asked his female therapist for a date during the last treatment session!

Interaction of Psychosocial and Biological Causal Factors. Social fears and phobias by definition involve fear of members of one's own species; this is in contrast, for example, to animal fears and phobias, which involve fear of potential predators. The latter probably evolved to help activation of the fight-or-flight response as a reaction to threat from potential predators and may be most likely to originate early in development because the young are most vulnerable to predation. Öhman and his colleagues have theorized that social fears and phobias, by contrast,

evolved as a by-product of dominance hierarchies that are a common social arrangement among animals like primates (Öhman et al., 1985). Dominance hierarchies are established through aggressive encounters between members of a social group, and a defeated individual typically displays fear and submissive behavior but only rarely attempts to escape the situation completely. Thus, they argue, it is not surprising that social phobics are more likely to endure being in their feared situation than to run away and escape it as animal phobics are likely to do. They further note that it is probably not coincidental that social phobias most often originate in adolescence and early adulthood, which is also when dominance conflicts are most prominent.

Like specific phobias, social phobias seem to often originate out of simple instances of direct or vicarious classical conditioning, such as experiencing or witnessing a perceived social defeat or humiliation, or being or witnessing the target of anger or criticism. In one study, 58 percent of social phobics recalled direct traumatic conditioning experiences as having been involved in the origin of their social phobia (Öst & Hugdahl, 1981); another study found that this was true for 56 percent of specific social phobics and 44 percent of generalized social phobics (Townsley, 1992). Öst and Hugdahl also reported that another 13 percent of their subjects recalled vicarious conditioning experiences of some sort as having been involved in the origin of their social phobia.

Öhman and his colleagues have extended the preparedness theory of specific phobias discussed above to the understanding of social phobia. Earlier we presented the theory that humans may have an evolutionarily based preparedness to acquire fears of certain objects or situations that may once have posed a threat to our early ancestors. But it seems that we also have an evolutionarily based predisposition to acquire fears of social stimuli signaling dominance and aggression from other humans. These social stimuli include facial expressions of anger or contempt. In a series of experiments paralleling those described for specific phobias, Öhman and his colleagues have demonstrated that subjects develop stronger conditioned responses when slides of angry faces are paired with mild electric shocks than when happy or neutral faces are paired with the same shocks. Moreover, they also demonstrated that this superior conditioning only occurs when the angry facial expression is directed at the subject (Dimberg & Öhman, 1983). Finally, they have also demonstrated that even very brief presentations of the angry face that are not consciously perceived are sufficient to activate the conditioned responses (Öhman, Dimberg, & Esteves, 1989). Such results may help to account for the seemingly irrational quality of social phobia, in that the emotional reaction can be activated without a person's awareness of any threat.

As with specific phobias, not all persons who undergo or witness traumatic social humiliation or defeat go on to develop full-blown social phobia. Recent results from a very large study of female twins suggests that there is a modest genetic contribution to social phobia; estimates were that the proportion of variance due to genetic factors was about 30 percent (Kendler et al., 1992b). Such results are also consistent with the results of a family study that found that the first-degree relatives of social phobics were more than three times as likely to also share a diagnosis of social phobia as were the relatives of normal controls (Fyer et al., 1993). Nevertheless, more research is needed before the exact contribution of genetic and environmental variables can be disentangled.

It also seems that a similar range of individual differences in temperament and experience that make an individual vulnerable to developing specific phobias are also likely to affect a person's vulnerability for developing social phobia (see Barlow, 1988; Mineka & Zinbarg, in press-a). These individual differences include behavioral inhibition and exposure to uncontrollable events. For example, perceptions of uncontrollability often lead to submissive and unassertive behavior such as is characteristic of socially anxious or phobic persons. This may be especially likely if the perceptions of uncontrollability stem from an actual social defeat, which is known in animals to lead to both increased submissive behavior and to increased fear (Mineka & Zinbarg, in press-a). Consistent with this, it has also been found that social phobics have a diminished sense of personal control over events in their lives; they are particularly prone to beliefs that control over events is primarily determined by "powerful others" (Cloitre et al., 1992).

In recent years increased attention has also been paid to the role that cognitive factors play in the onset and maintenance of social phobia. Beck and colleagues (1985) suggest that social phobics have danger schemas about other people (latent expectations that other people will reject or negatively evaluate them—see Chapter 3), leading to a sense of vulnerability in the presence of other persons who might potentially pose a threat. The danger schemas of social phobics lead them to be hypervigilant to cues that people around them are negative or critical. Research has confirmed that social phobics do seem to spend a great deal of their time paying attention to and evaluating possible negative evaluations by others (Hope et al., 1990; Mattia, Heimberg, & Hope,

Fear of public speaking is the most common social phobia. It can be effectively treated, however, with cognitive-behavior therapy.

1993). In a recent elaboration of this theory, Clark and Wells (in press) have argued that the schemas of social phobics also include expectations that they will behave "in an inept and unacceptable fashion *and* that such behavior will have disastrous consequences" (p. 2). Clark and Wells have also observed that such expectations lead social phobics to be preoccupied with their bodily responses in social situations, as well as with their negative self-evaluative thoughts. Such intense preoccupation during social situations interferes with their actual ability to interact in as skillful a fashion as they might if they were not so preoccupied. This in turn may lead to a vicious circle in which their somewhat awkward behavior may indeed lead others to react to them in a less friendly fashion, thus confirming their expectations (Clark & Wells, in press).

Panic Disorder and Agoraphobia

Diagnostically, **panic disorder** is defined and characterized by the occurrence of "unexpected" panic attacks that often seem to come "out of the blue." According to the DSM-IV definition, the person must have experienced recurrent unexpected attacks and must have been persistently concerned about having another attack or worried about the consequences of having an attack (e.g., of "losing control" or "going crazy") for at least a month. To qualify as a full-blown panic attack, there must be abrupt onset of at least 4 of 13 symptoms (such as shortness of breath, heart palpitations, sweating, dizziness, depersonalization or derealization, fear of dying, of "going crazy," or of "losing control"). Such attacks are normally unexpected in the sense that they do not appear to be provoked by identifiable aspects of the immediate situation. Indeed, they sometimes occur in situations in which they might be least expected, such as during relaxation or during sleep (known as *nocturnal panic*). The stark terror of a panic attack typically subsides within a matter of minutes. Many people experiencing such an attack do not identify it as a panic attack, and instead think that they are, for example, having a heart attack. These people may show up repeatedly at emergency rooms or at their physicians' offices for what they are convinced is a medical problem. Unfortunately, a correct diagnosis of the problem is often not made for years in spite of numerous medical tests that produce normal results. Such delays in correct diagnosis are avoided if the person sees a physician who is familiar with the condition or one who refers the person to a mental health professional.

The two features of panic attacks that distinguish them from other types of anxiety are their characteristic brevity and their intensity. In a panic attack the symptoms develop abruptly and usually reach a peak intensity within 10 minutes; the attacks usually subside in 20–30 minutes and rarely last more than an hour. Periods of anxiety, by contrast, do not usually have such an abrupt onset, are more long-lasting, and the symptoms are not as intense. If we go back to the distinction drawn at the beginning of the chapter between fear and anxiety, it is important to note that a number of influential contemporary researchers of panic believe that a panic attack is simply the activation of the fight-or-flight response of the sympathetic nervous system (Gray, 1987, 1991), which is identified with the emotion of fear for some theorists (e.g., Barlow, 1988, 1991a). For example, Barlow refers to the activation of the fight-or-flight response as a "true alarm" when there is an identifiable trigger in the form of a real and present danger (such as an encounter with a grizzly bear on a hiking path). When the fight-or-flight response is activated by a phobic object, it is referred to as a "learned alarm." Barlow refers to the same response as a "false alarm" when there is no obvious trigger, as in the case of a panic attack. Thus for Barlow the primary feature that distinguishes the panic attacks occurring in panic disorder from the phobic responses seen when specific and social phobics encounter their phobic object or situation is simply whether there is an identifiable external trigger (see also Marks, 1987). As discussed earlier, anxiety, in contrast to phobic fear and panic, is a more complex and diffuse blend of emotions and cognitions, including high levels of negative affect, worry about future threat, and a sense of preparation for dealing with danger should it occur.

Historically, agoraphobia was thought to involve a fear of the "agora"—the Greek word for public places of assembly (Marks, 1987). And indeed the most commonly feared and avoided situations for agoraphobics include streets and crowded places such as shopping malls, movie theaters, and sports arenas. Standing in line can be particularly difficult. However, agoraphobics also usually fear one or more forms of travel, and commonly avoid cars, buses, airplanes, and subway trains. What is the common theme that underlies this seemingly diverse cluster of fears? Today it is thought that **agoraphobia** involves fear of being in places or situations from which escape would be physically difficult or psychologically embarrassing, or in which immediate help would be unavailable in the event that something bad happened, such as getting sick or having a panic attack (DSM-IV, 1994). In cases of moderate severity these people may even be uncomfortable venturing outside their homes alone, doing so only with significant anxiety. In very severe cases agoraphobia is a terribly disabling disorder in which a person cannot go beyond the narrow confines of home, or even particular parts of the home.

Agoraphobia is a frequent complication of panic disorder, but it can also occur in the absence of prior full-blown panic attacks. In the latter instance a common pattern is that of a gradually spreading fearfulness in which more and more aspects of the environment outside the home acquire threatening properties. Cases of agoraphobia without panic are extremely rare in clinical settings, and when they are seen there is often a history of limited symptom attacks (with fewer than four symptoms) or of some other unpredictable somatic ailment such as epilepsy or colitis where the person may fear sudden physical incapacitation (Barlow, 1988; McNally, 1994). However, cases of agoraphobia without panic are not uncommon in epidemiological studies (Eaton & Keyl, 1990; Weissman et al., 1986). The reasons for this are unclear at the present time and little research attention has yet been directed toward understanding agoraphobia without panic. Some believe that in many cases where this disorder has been diagnosed, it would more appropriately be characterized as a kind of specific phobia if correct diagnostic procedures were used (McNally, 1994).

We consider panic disorder and agoraphobia together because accumulating research evidence suggests that they share some basic properties, including a possible genetic linkage (e.g., Noyes et al., 1986, 1987). Many people with an agoraphobic pattern report a history of repeated panic attacks, and it appears that in most cases agoraphobia develops as a secondary reaction to the experience of panic. That is, after having experienced a few panic attacks, the person begins to develop a fear of the situations in which the attacks have occurred, which gradually spreads to involve fear of other situations where attacks *might* occur. The person experiences this anticipatory anxiety much of the time when he or she thinks about having to leave home for any reason.

Panic disorder with and without agoraphobia affects many people. For example, a large epidemiological study conducted in the early 1980s found approximately 1.5 percent of the adult population had pure panic disorder at some time in their life (Eaton, Dryman, & Weissman, 1991), with approximately another 5 percent qualifying for a diagnosis of agoraphobia (Bourdon et al., 1988). However, there have been many criticisms of the way this study diagnosed panic disorder and agoraphobia, and there is good reason to believe that estimates of pure panic disorder were too low and estimates of agoraphobia without panic were too high (McNally, 1994). A more recent and carefully conducted study of panic disorder estimated lifetime prevalence of panic disorder to be nearly 4 percent (Katerndahl & Realini, 1993).

The age of onset for panic disorder with or without agoraphobia is typically in the 20s, although it is quite common for these disorders to begin in late adolescence or not until the 30s. Once it begins, it tends to have a chronic course, although the intensity of symptoms often waxes and wanes over time (Ehlers, 1995; Wolfe & Maser, 1994). One interesting fact is that although many studies find panic disorder without agoraphobia is about as common in men as in women, the same is not true of agoraphobia, which occurs much more frequently in women than in men. Indeed, the percentage of women increases as the extent of agoraphobic avoidance increases, and among severe agoraphobics approximately 80 percent are female (Barlow, 1988; Reich, Noyes, & Troughton, 1987). The most common explanation of this finding is a sociocultural one. That is, in our culture (and many others as well), it is more acceptable for women experiencing panic to avoid the situations they fear, or to depend on having a trusted companion accompany them when they enter their feared situations. Men who experience panic are more prone to "tough it out" because of societal expectations. Supporting this idea, Chambless and Mason (1986) administered a sex-role scale to both male and female agoraphobics and found that the more "feminine" one scores on the scale, the more extensive the agoraphobic avoidance, for both males and females.

The case of Anne Watson is in many respects typical of panic disorder with agoraphobia:

Ms. Watson, married mother of two and age 45 at her first clinic contact, experienced her first panic attack some two years earlier, several months after the sudden death of an uncle to whom she had been extremely close while growing up. While returning home from work one evening she had the feeling that she couldn't catch her breath. Immediately thereafter her heart began to pound, she broke out in a cold sweat, and she had a sense of unreality. Feeling immobilized by a leaden quality in her legs, she became certain she would pass out or die before she could reach home. Soliciting help from a passerby, she was able to engage a cab, directing the driver to take her to the nearest hospital emergency room. Her ensuing physical examination revealed no abnormalities apart from a slightly elevated heart rate, which subsided to normal limits before the examination was completed. She regained composure rapidly and was able to return home on her own.

Four weeks later, after the incident had been all but forgotten, Ms. Watson had a second similar attack while at home preparing a meal. Four more occurred in the next several weeks, all of them surprises, and she began to despair about discovering their source. She also noticed that she was becoming anxious about the probability of additional attacks. Consultation with the family physician yielded a diagnosis of "nervous strain" and a prescription for antianxiety medication. The medication made Ms. Watson calmer, but seemed to have no effect on the continuing panics. She discovered alcohol was even more effective than the medication in relieving her tension and began to drink excessively, which only increased the worry and concern of her husband.

As the attacks continued, Ms. Watson began to dread going out of the house alone. She feared that while out she would have an attack and would be stranded and helpless. She stopped riding the subway to work out of fear she might be trapped in a car between stops when an attack struck, preferring instead to walk the 20 blocks between her home and work. She also severely curtailed her social and recreational activities—previously frequent and enjoyed—because an attack might occur, necessitating an abrupt and embarrassing flight from the scene. When household duties and the like required brief driving excursions, she surreptitiously put these off until she could be accompanied by one of the children or a neighbor. Despite these drastic alterations of lifestyle and her growing unhappiness and desperation, however, she remained her normal self when at home or when her husband accompanied her away from home. (Adapted from Spitzer et al., 1983)

The case of Mindy Markowitz is typical of someone who has panic disorder without agoraphobia:

Mindy Markowitz is an attractive, stylishly dressed 25-year-old art director for a trade magazine who comes to an anxiety clinic after reading about the clinic program in the newspaper. She is seeking treatment for "panic attacks" that have occurred with increasing frequency over the past year, often 2 or 3 times a day. These attacks begin with a sudden intense wave of "horrible fear" that seems to come out of nowhere, sometimes during the day, sometimes waking her from sleep. She begins to tremble, is nauseated, sweats profusely, feels as though she is choking, and fears that she will lose control and do something crazy, like run screaming into the street.

Mindy remembers first having attacks like this when she was in high school. She was dating a boy her parents disapproved of, and had to do a lot of "sneaking around" to avoid confrontations with them. At the same time, she was under a lot of pressure as the principal designer of her high school yearbook, and was applying to Ivy League colleges. She remembers that her first panic attack occurred just after the yearbook went to press and she was accepted by Harvard, Yale, and Brown. The attacks lasted only a few minutes, and she would just "sit through them." She was worried enough to mention them to her mother; but because she was otherwise perfectly healthy, she did not seek treatment.

Mindy has had panic attacks intermittently over the 8 years since her first attack, sometimes not for many months, but sometimes, as now, several times a day. There have been extreme variations in the intensity of the attacks, some being so severe and debilitating that she has had to take a day off from work.

Mindy has always functioned extremely well in school, at work, and in her social life, apart from her panic attacks and a brief period of depression at age 19 when she broke up with a boyfriend. She is a lively, friendly person who is respected by her friends and colleagues both for her intelligence and creativity and for her ability to mediate disputes.

Mindy has never limited her activities, even during the times that she was having frequent, severe attacks, although she might stay home from work for a day because she was exhausted from multiple attacks. She has never associated the attacks with particular places. She says, for example, that she is as likely to have an attack at home in her own bed as on the subway, so there is no point in avoiding the subway. Whether she has an attack on the subway, in a supermarket, or at home by herself, she says, "I just tough it out." (Spitzer et al., 1994)

Persons with panic disorder often have one or more additional diagnoses, including generalized anxiety, social phobia, simple phobia, depression, and alcohol abuse (Craske & Barlow, 1993). Not uncommonly they may also meet criteria for dependent or avoidant personality disorder (a personality disorder is diagnosed when a person has personality traits that are inflexible and maladaptive and that cause significant impairment or distress—see Chapter 9) (Craske & Barlow, 1993). There is also considerable recent controversy over whether patients with panic disorder show an increased risk of suicidal ideation and suicide attempts. A recent review concluded that there is little evidence that panic disorder, by itself, increases the risk for suicide, although it may do so indirectly by increasing risk for depression and substance use, both of which are risk factors for suicide (Hornig & McNally, 1995; McNally, 1994).

It is also important to note that occasional panic attacks occur in many people who do not have panic disorder or agoraphobia. Indeed, current estimates are that 20–30 percent of adults have experienced at least one panic attack in their lifetime, but have not gone on to develop full-blown panic disorder. Occasional panic attacks also commonly occur in persons who have other anxiety disorders and/or major depression (Barlow, 1988). Given that panic attacks occur much more commonly than does panic disorder, this leads us to the important question: What causes full-blown panic disorder to develop in only a subset of these people?

Although panic attacks themselves appear to come "out of the blue," their initial appearance frequently follows feelings of distress (Lelliott et al., 1989) or some highly stressful life circumstance, such as the loss of a loved one, loss of an important relationship,

Agoraphobics may be frightened about walking in the street, and if they are, some will experience a panic attack.

or loss of a job (Foa, Steketee, & Young, 1984; Polland, Pollard, & Corn, 1989). Indeed, estimates are that approximately 80 percent of patients report their first panic attack as having occurred after one or more negative life events (Barlow, 1988). Thus, the timing of the initial attacks is usually not random but rather associated with generally stressful life circumstances. Nevertheless, not all people who have a panic attack following a stressful event go on to develop full-blown panic disorder. Several very different prominent theories about the causes of panic disorder have addressed this question.

Biological Causal Factors A variety of research findings have led biological psychiatrists to hypothesize that panic disorder results from a biochemical abnormality in the brains of patients with the disorder. Donald Klein first argued in the 1960s that panic was qualitatively different from generalized anxiety—not just a more severe form of anxiety, as was previously thought. This was based on his apparent finding that imipramine (a tricyclic antidepressant drug) appeared to block panic attacks in agoraphobics without affecting their anticipatory anxiety. He reasoned that if imipramine affected panic but not anxiety, then panic must not simply be a more severe form of anxiety. Klein (1981) and others (Sheehan, 1982, 1983) argue that panic attacks are alarm reactions that are caused by biochemical dysfunctions.

The biochemical dysfunction hypothesis also appears to be supported by numerous studies over the past 30 years that have shown that panic patients are much more likely to experience panic attacks in response to a variety of biological challenge procedures than are normal people or other psychiatric controls. These *biological challenge procedures* put stress on certain neurobiological systems, which in turn produce intense physical symptoms often culminating in a panic attack for patients with panic disorder. For example, infusions of sodium lactate, a substance that resembles the lactate produced by our bodies during exercise (e.g., Gorman et al., 1989; Hollander et al., 1989; Liebowitz et al., 1984, 1985), or the inhalation of carbon dioxide (e.g., Woods et al., 1986, 1987), or the ingestion of caffeine or a chemical compound called yohimbine (Charney et al., 1987; Uhde, 1990) can produce panic attacks in panic disorder patients at a much higher rate than in normal subjects. Unfortunately, as Barlow (1988, 1991a) and van den Hout (1988) have argued, there is such a broad range of pharmacological agents that provoke panic (hence the term *panic provocation agents*), some of which are associated with quite different and even mutually exclusive neurobiological processes, that no single neurobiological mechanism could possibly be implicated. Moreover, as discussed below in the section on cognitive causal factors, there does seem to be a simpler psychological account of this pattern of results.

One prominent theory about the neurobiology of panic implicates a particular area of the brain—the locus coeruleus in the brain stem—and a particular neurotransmitter—norepinephrine—which is centrally involved in brain activity in this area. For example, Redmond (1985) has shown that electrical stimulation of the locus coeruleus in monkeys leads to a response that strongly resembles a panic attack; moreover, destruction of this area leaves the monkey seemingly unable to experience fear even in the presence of real danger. In addition, some of the drugs most commonly used in the treatment of panic disorder—the tricyclic antidepressants such as imipramine and the monamine oxidase inhibitors—are also known to reduce norepinephrine function (Redmond, 1985). Thus, it is possible that abnormal norepinephrine activity in the locus coeruleus may play a causal role in panic attacks (e.g., Gorman et al., 1989). More research is certainly needed before we have a complete understanding of the neurobiology of panic, however. At present the evidence for this theory is mixed, and it is not likely to explain all cases of panic disorder (McNally, 1994).

But panic attacks are only one component of panic disorder. As we have seen, persons with panic disorder also experience anticipatory anxiety about the possible occurrence of another attack, and those with agoraphobia also engage in phobic avoidance behavior. Gorman and colleagues (1989) have proposed that different brain areas are involved in these different aspects of panic disorder. The panic attacks themselves arise from activity in the locus coeruleus in the brain stem and involve "storms of autonomic nervous system activity" (p. 150). For people who have one or more panic attacks and who go on to develop significant anticipatory anxiety about having another, the limbic system (a part of the brain below the cortex that is very involved in emotional behavior) generates this anxiety, which often involves a vague sense that future attacks may occur and be dangerous. Because there are well-defined pathways between the locus coeruleus and the limbic system, Gorman and colleagues propose that panic attacks may produce generalized or anticipatory anxiety through a kind of *kindling* phenomenon: Repeated stimulation of the limbic system by discharges from the locus coeruleus (panic attacks) might lower the threshold for stimulation of anxiety from the limbic system. Finally, they argue that the phobic avoidance seen with agoraphobia is truly a learned phenomenon that is controlled by the prefrontal cortex, which is the part of the brain involved in learning (see Figure 5.1).

There is also evidence that panic disorder tends to run in families. Many studies have shown that first-degree relatives of panic patients are more likely to experience panic disorder than are relatives of controls (Barlow, 1988; McNally, 1994), and monozygotic twins are somewhat more likely to be concordant for the diagnosis than are dizygotic twins (Torgersen, 1983; Kendler et al., 1992b, 1993a). Some studies have suggested that this heritability is specific for panic disorder and does not occur for generalized anxiety disorder (e.g., Crowe et al., 1983; Noyes et al., 1986, 1987). However, Barlow (1988) has pointed out major methodological shortcomings in the studies drawing these conclusions about genetic specificity and has concluded that it is likely that the heritability is more nonspecific. Moreover, it should also be emphasized that what heritability does exist is modest. For example,

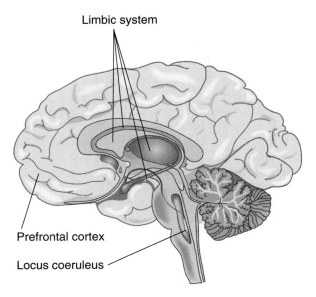

Figure 5.1 *Panic attacks may arise from abnormal activity in the locus coeruleus, a small area in the brain stem. The anticipatory anxiety that people develop about having another panic attack is thought to arise from activity in the limbic system. Phobic avoidance, a learned response, involves activity of the prefrontal cortex (Gorman et al., 1989).*

in Torgersen's study of monozygotic twins, only 30 percent were concordant, suggesting that environmental factors play a very important role in determining who develops the disorder among those with the genetic predisposition. More recently Kendler and colleagues (1992b), in a very large female twin study, estimated that 39 percent of the variance in liability to agoraphobia was due to genetic factors.

Cognitive and Behavioral Causal Factors One early hypothesis about the origins of panic and agoraphobia was the "fear of fear" hypothesis (Goldstein & Chambless, 1978). According to this hypothesis, agoraphobics come to fear the experience of a panic attack because it is so terrifying. They become hyperalert to their bodily sensations and begin to interpret mild signs of anxiety as a signal that a panic attack may occur; they then react with anxiety to their anxiety. If they gradually also come to fear a range of places in which panic might occur, they develop agoraphobic avoidance. Relatedly, van den Hout (1988) has argued that panic disorder involves **interoceptive fears,** that is, fear of various internal bodily sensations. These fears may have come about through a process of interoceptive conditioning in which various internal bodily sensations that have been associated with panic attacks acquire the capacity to provoke panic themselves. For example, heart palpitations may occur at the beginning of a full-blown attack and because they become predictors of the rest of the attack, they may acquire the capacity to provoke panic.

Building on these behavioral hypotheses, Beck and Emery (1985) and Clark (1986, 1988) have proposed a cognitive model of panic. According to this model, panic patients are hypersensitive to their bodily sensations and are very prone to giving them the direst possible interpretation. Clark refers to this as a tendency to catastrophize about the meaning of their bodily sensations. For example, a panic patient might notice that his heart is racing and conclude that he is having a heart attack. That very frightening thought causes many more physical symptoms of fear or anxiety, which provides further fuel for the catastrophic thoughts, leading to a vicious cycle culminating in a panic attack. Or if someone feels dizzy and interprets this as meaning that she is going to faint or that she may have a brain tumor, this could culminate in a panic attack through the same kind of vicious cycle (see Figure 5.2). It should be noted that the person is often not aware of making these catastrophic interpretations; rather the thoughts are often just barely out of the realm of their awareness. These "automatic thoughts," as Beck calls them are in a sense, however, the triggers of panic. Taken literally, then, this model suggests that panic attacks don't really "come out of the blue" but rather are triggered by these automatic thoughts, which may or may not be conscious (although they can be brought into awareness through cognitive therapy).

The key difference between the cognitive model and the interoceptive or "fear of fear" models is the importance for the cognitive model of the *meaning* the person places on bodily sensations. For example, the interoceptive or "fear of fear" models would predict that a man with panic disorder who fears having a heart attack would always respond with fear or panic when his heart races, but the cognitive model would predict panic only if this patient makes catastrophic interpretations about what it means that his heart is racing on a particular occasion. According to the cognitive model, he might not panic if he attributed his heart racing to the fact that he had just climbed three flights of stairs or had just finished exercising. In other words, Clark (1988) argues that the "fear of fear" and interoceptive conditioning models overpredict panic relative to the cognitive model.

At present the cognitive model of panic does not specify what factors lead a person to develop this

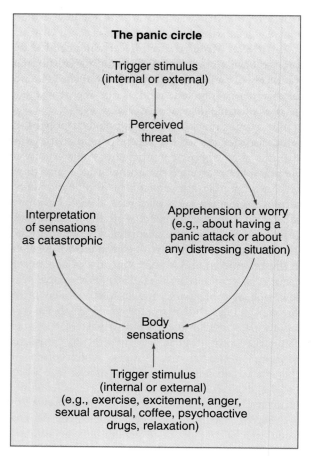

Figure 5.2 *Any kind of perceived threat may lead to apprehension or worry, which is accompanied by various bodily sensations. According to the cognitive model of panic, if a person then catastrophizes about the meaning of his or her bodily sensations, this will raise the level of perceived threat, thus creating more apprehension and worry, as well as more physical symptoms, which fuel further catastrophic thoughts. This vicious cycle can culminate in a panic attack. The initial physical sensations need not arise from the perceived threat (as in the top of the circle), but may come from other sources (such as exercise, anger, or psychoactive drugs). (Adapted from Clark, 1986.)*

tendency to catastrophize about his or her bodily sensations. What it hypothesizes is that among the people who have had at least one panic attack (possibly 30 percent of the population), it is those who have this tendency to catastrophize who will be the ones likely to go on to develop panic disorder. Thus, the cognitive model may not always adequately explain why an initial panic attack occurs, but it does provide a plausible account of why only a small subset of people who have experienced one or more panic attacks go on to develop panic disorder. Obviously, however, longitudinal prospective studies will be needed to provide definitive tests of this aspect of the theory.

In spite of the fact that we still lack such prospective studies, several lines of evidence are consistent with the cognitive model of panic. For example, many studies have demonstrated that panic patients are more likely to interpret their bodily sensations in a catastrophic manner (e.g., Hibbert, 1984; see Clark, 1988, for a review). Moreover, even indirect and false information about feared bodily sensations can lead to increases in anxiety in panic patients but not in normal controls (Ehlers et al., 1988). In particular, panic patients given false feedback that their heart rate was surging showed increases in anxiety. The model also predicts that changing patients' cognitions about their bodily symptoms should reduce or prevent panic. Evidence from cognitive therapy for panic is consistent with this prediction (D.M. Clark et al., 1994—see below). In addition, however, Clark, Salkovskis, and Anastasiades (1990) have shown that a brief explanation of what to expect in a panic provocation study can prevent panic. Patients with panic disorder were either given a brief but detailed explanation of what physical symptoms to expect from their infusion of sodium lactate, along with a rationale for why they should not worry about these symptoms, or they were given minimal explanation. Patients with the cognitive rationale did not show as strong physiological responses to the lactate infusion (for example, their heart rate did not increase as much as did that of control patients). Moreover, the patients with the cognitive rationale about what to expect were significantly less likely to panic in response to the lactate (30 percent) than were control patients (90 percent).

Indeed, these findings lead us to the point made earlier that there is a simpler psychological explanation of the common mechanism underlying the effects of all the various panic provocation agents. This simple explanation pertains to the subjective effects produced by all these procedures, as well as their physiological effects, which include an overall heightening of arousal in both normals and panic patients (Margraf, Ehlers, & Roth, 1986a, 1986b). Because these agents produce arousal, they mimic the physiological cues that normally precede a panic attack or serve as a sign of some other impending catastrophe. Panic disorder patients, who already start at a higher level of arousal and who are very familiar with these early warning cues, apparently frequently misinterpret these symptoms as the beginning of a panic attack. As proposed by Clark and Beck, such a misinterpretation would be expected often to lead to a full-blown panic attack in panic patients but not in normal controls

who do not make such misinterpretations. In other words, sensitivity to lactate or carbon dioxide or other panic provocation agents probably occurs as a *consequence* of having panic disorder.

The cognitive model does not deny a role for biological or genetic factors in producing a vulnerability to panic, but it asserts that such factors cannot account for why simple cognitive manipulations could block panic. It asserts that cognitive variables play a much more immediate and prominent causal role in initiating panic attacks. The power of psychological manipulations to block panic was also demonstrated in an important study by Sanderson, Rapee, and Barlow (1989). In this study the psychological manipulation involved perceptions of control over the rate of infusion of carbon dioxide. Patients with perceived control were told that while they were inhaling the carbon dioxide, if a light was on they could turn a dial to reduce the rate of infusion if they were anxious; patients without perceived control were given the same instructions, but the light was never turned on and so they had no opportunity to experience perceived control. In fact, none of the patients in the perceived control group ever turned the dial and so the control that they experienced was only perceived control and not actual control. Nevertheless, patients with perceived control showed lower levels of physiological arousal in response to the carbon dioxide and were significantly less likely to panic than patients without perceived control. These findings are consistent with Barlow's (1988, 1991a) proposal that the psychological vulnerability to panic stems from experiences with uncontrollable and unpredictable aversive events, and that panic disorder is maintained, in part, by the fact that patients experience the panic attacks themselves as largely unpredictable and uncontrollable (see Mineka & Zinbarg, in press-b).

Another possible explanation for why only some people develop catastrophic misinterpretations of their bodily sensations may be that people who are prone to developing panic disorder have previously developed beliefs that their bodily sensations are harmful or dangerous. Reiss and McNally (1985; McNally, 1990, 1994) have proposed that people prone to developing panic are those who have high levels of preexisting *anxiety sensitivity* (a high level of belief that certain bodily symptoms may have harmful consequences). For example, someone high on anxiety sensitivity would endorse statements like: "When I notice that my heart is beating rapidly, I worry that I might have a heart attack." At present we know that people with panic disorder score higher on a measure of anxiety sensitivity than do

CUTTING
EDGE
2

patients with other anxiety disorders, but this could be a consequence of having panic disorder rather than a cause. Thus what is needed are good prospective studies showing that people high in anxiety sensitivity are indeed more prone to developing panic disorder; this certainly seems like an important area for future research. An initial naturalistic study of this type followed four groups of people for a year: one group with panic disorder, one group with infrequent panic attacks, one group with specific phobias, and one nonanxious control group. Anxiety sensitivity was a significant predictor of the maintenance of panic attacks for the group with panic disorder and for the group of infrequent panickers. Anxiety sensitivity also predicted the first occurrence of panic attacks for the combined group of simple phobics and nonanxious controls (Ehlers, 1995).

Finally, there are also many studies that underscore the fact that people with panic disorder are biased in the way they process threatening information. Such people are more prone to interpreting ambiguous bodily sensations as threatening, and they seem to show a bias to remember threatening information (McNally, 1990, 1994; see also Becker, Rinck, & Margraf, 1994). There is also evidence that their attention is particularly drawn to threatening information, especially information about physical threat. Whether these information-processing biases play a causal role in panic disorder is unclear, but they are certainly likely to help maintain the disorder once it has begun.

In summary, research into both biological and psychological factors involved in panic disorder has provided important insights into this disorder in the 15 years since it was first identified as a distinct disorder. It seems unlikely that research from either tradition alone will ever be able to provide a complete account of this disorder, and we eagerly await more attempts at synthesizing and integrating findings from these different traditions (McNally, 1994).

Generalized Anxiety Disorder

People with generalized anxiety disorder, unlike those with other anxiety disorders, do not have any very effective anxiety-avoidance mechanisms. Thus, although victims of other anxiety disorders can to some extent allay their anxieties through avoidance behavior, seemingly unavoidable feelings of threat and anxiety are the central feature of this disorder.

Generalized anxiety disorder (GAD) is characterized by chronic excessive worry about a number of events or activities. This state was traditionally de-

scribed as *free-floating anxiety* because it was not anchored to a specific object or situation as with specific or social phobias. DSM-IV criteria (1994) specify that the worry must occur more days than not for at least six months and that it must be experienced as difficult to control. Its content may not be exclusively related to the worry associated with another concurrent Axis I disorder, such as the possibility of having a panic attack. The subjective experience of excessive worry must also be accompanied by at least three of the following six symptoms: (a) restlessness or feelings of being keyed up or on edge, (b) a sense of being easily fatigued, (c) difficulty concentrating or mind going blank, (d) irritability, (e) muscle tension, and (f) sleep disturbance. In previous DSMs, symptoms of autonomic hyperactivity were also included (such as shortness of breath, rapid pulse, sweating, dizziness, nausea, etc.), but these were dropped from DSM-IV when it was found in a multisite study that none of these symptoms were endorsed with much frequency in patients diagnosed with GAD (Brown, O'Leary, Barlow, 1993). Indeed, Brown and colleagues review evidence that these patients respond to laboratory stressors with less autonomic responding than do nonanxious controls. Instead, they respond to such stressors with high levels of psychic and muscle tension.

Thus, the general picture of people suffering from generalized anxiety disorder is that they live in a relatively constant state of tension, worry, and diffuse uneasiness. Barlow (1988, 1991a, 1991b; Brown et al., 1993) refers to the fundamental process as one of *anxious apprehension, which is defined as a future-oriented mood state in which a person attempts to be constantly ready to deal with upcoming negative events.* This mood state is characterized by high levels of negative affect, chronic overarousal, and a sense of uncontrollability (Barlow, 1991b). Although anxious apprehension also is part of other anxiety disorders (e.g., the agoraphobic is anxious about future panic attacks and about dying; the social phobic is anxious about possible negative social evaluation), it is the essence of GAD, leading Barlow to refer to GAD as the "basic" anxiety disorder.

In addition to their excessive levels of worry and anxious apprehension, people with generalized anxiety disorder often have difficulty concentrating and making decisions, dreading to make a mistake. They may engage in certain subtle avoidance activities such as procrastination or checking, but these are generally not very effective in reducing anxiety. They also tend to show a marked vigilance for possible signs of threat in their environment. Their high level of tension is often reflected in strained postural

Frequency of Symptoms in 100 Cases of Generalized Anxiety Disorder

Affective/Somatic	%	Cognitive/Behavioral	%
Unable to relax	97	Difficulty concentrating	86
Tense	86	Fear losing control	76
Frightened	79	Fear being rejected	72
Jumpy	72	Unable to control thoughts	72
Unsteady	62	Confusion	69
Weakness all over	59	Mind blurred	66
Hands (only) sweating	52	Inability to recall	55
Terrified	52	Sentences disconnected	45
Heart racing	48	Blocking in speech	45
Face flushed	48	Fear of being attacked	35
Wobbly	45	Fear of dying	35
Sweating all over	38	Hands trembling	31
Difficult breathing	35	Body swaying	31
Urgent need to urinate	35	Stuttering	24
Nausea	31		
Diarrhea	31		
Faint/dizzy feeling	28		
Face is pale	24		
Feeling of choking	14		
Actual fainting	3		

Adapted from Beck and Emery (1985, pp. 87–88).

movements and overreaction to sudden or unexpected stimuli. Commonly, they complain of muscle tension, especially in the neck and upper shoulder region, and sleep disturbances including insomnia and nightmares. (See HIGHLIGHT 5.1 for the frequency of different symptoms in GAD.)

No matter how well things seem to be going, people with generalized anxiety disorder are apprehensive and anxious. Their nearly constant worries leave them continually upset, uneasy, and discouraged. In one study their most common spheres of worry were found to be family, finances, work, and personal illness (Sanderson & Barlow, 1990). Not only do they have difficulty making decisions, after they have managed to make a decision they worry endlessly over possible errors and unforeseen circumstances that may prove the decision wrong and lead to disaster. Even after going to bed, people suffering from GAD are not likely to find relief from their worries. Often, they review each mistake, real or imagined, recent or remotely past. When they are not reviewing and regretting the events of the past, they are anticipating all the difficulties that may arise in the future. They have no appreciation of the logic most of us use in concluding that it is pointless to torment ourselves about possible outcomes over which we have no control. Although it may seem at times that they are actually looking for things to worry about, it is their feeling that they cannot control their tendency to worry.

Generalized anxiety disorder is a relatively common condition, with current estimates that it is experienced by approximately 4 percent of the population in any one-year period (Robins & Regier, 1991). This makes it about as common as panic disorder with agoraphobia or major depression. However, perhaps because most people with GAD do manage to function in spite of their high levels of worry and anxiety, they are less likely to come to clinics for treatment than are people with panic disorder or major depression, which are frequently more debilitating conditions. GAD is somewhat more common in women than in men, although not as much so as severe agoraphobia or many simple phobias. Age of onset is often difficult to determine, with a large proportion of patients reporting that they remember having been anxious nearly all their lives; many others report a slow and insidious onset (Barlow, 1988; Rapee & Barlow, 1993). In recent years this has led many to suggest that GAD might be reconceptualized as a personality disorder (see Chapter 9) given its lifelong presentation, unlike that of most of the other anxiety disorders, which have a more acute onset (Rapee & Barlow, 1993; Sanderson & Wetzler, 1991).

Generalized anxiety disorder often cooccurs with other Axis I disorders, especially other anxiety and mood disorders. The most common additional anxiety disorders are panic disorder with agoraphobia, social phobia, and simple phobia (Barlow, 1988). In addition, many people with GAD experience occasional panic attacks without qualifying for a full-blown diagnosis of panic disorder (Barlow, 1988). Many of these people show mild depression as well as chronic anxiety (Barlow, 1988; Brown et al., 1993). This finding is not unexpected in view of their generally gloomy outlook on the world. Nor is it surprising that excessive use of tranquilizing drugs, sleeping pills, and alcohol often complicates the clinical picture in generalized anxiety disorder.

The following case is fairly typical of generalized anxiety disorder:

John was a 26-year-old single graduate student in the social sciences at a prestigious university. Although he reported that he had had problems with anxiety nearly all his life, including as a child, the past 7–8 years since he had left home and gone to college had been worse. During the past year his anxiety had seriously interfered with his functioning. He reported worries about several different spheres of his life. He was very concerned about his own health and that of his

parents. During one incident a few months earlier he had thought that his heart was beating slower than usual and he had experienced some tingling sensations; this led him to worry that he might die. In another incident he had heard his name being paged over a loudspeaker in an airport and worried that someone at home must be dying. He was also very worried about his future because he had had trouble completing his Master's thesis on time given his high level of anxiety. He also worried excessively about getting a bad grade even though he had had never had one during four years at a prestigious Ivy League university or at his equally prestigious graduate institution. In classes he worried excessively about what the professor and other students thought of him and tended not to talk unless the class was small and he was quite confident about the topic. Although he had a number of friends, he had never had a girlfriend because of his shyness about dating. He had no problem talking or socializing with women as long as it was not defined as a dating situation. He worried that he should only date a woman if he was quite sure it could be a serious relationship from the outset. He also worried excessively that if a woman did not want to date him that it meant that he was boring.

In addition to his worries, John reported muscle tension and easy fatiguability. He also reported great difficulty concentrating and a considerable amount of restlessness and pacing. When he couldn't work he spent a great deal of time daydreaming, which worried him because he didn't seem able to control it. At times he had difficulty falling asleep if he was particularly anxious, but at other times he slept excessively, in part to escape from his worries. He frequently experienced dizziness and palpitations, and in the past had had full-blown panic attacks. Overall, he reported frequently feeling paralyzed and unable to do things.

Both of John's parents were professionals; his mother was also quite anxious and had been treated for panic disorder. He was obviously extremely bright and had managed to do very well in school in spite of his lifelong problems with anxiety. But as the pressures of finishing graduate school and starting his career loomed before him, and as he got older and still had never dated, the anxiety became severe enough that he sought treatment. He had seen someone at a student counseling center for several months the previous year but hadn't found the "talk therapy" very useful. He had heard from his mother that cognitive-behavior therapy might be useful and had sought a referral for such treatment. He was in treatment for about six months, during which time he found training in deep muscle relaxation helpful in reducing his overall level of tension. In addition, cognitive restructuring helped reduce his worry levels considerably; indeed, he reported that he was worrying much less about all spheres of his life. He still had problems with procrastinating when he had deadlines, but this too was improving. He also began socializing more frequently and had tentatively begun dating when treatment ended for financial reasons. He was better able to see that if a woman didn't wish to go out with him again, this did not mean that he was boring but simply that they might not be a good match.

Psychosocial Causal Factors According to the psychoanalytic viewpoint, generalized or free-floating anxiety results from an unconscious conflict between ego and id impulses that is not adequately dealt with because the person's defense mechanisms have broken down. Freud believed that it was primarily sexual and aggressive impulses that had been either blocked from expression or punished upon expression that led to free-floating anxiety. Defense mechanisms may become overwhelmed when a person experiences frequent and extreme levels of anxiety, as might happen if expression of id impulses were frequently blocked from expression (e.g., under periods of prolonged sexual deprivation). In other cases adequate defense mechanisms may never have developed. According to the psychoanalytic view, the primary difference between simple phobias and free-floating anxiety is that in the phobias defense mechanisms of repression and displacement are operative, whereas in free-floating anxiety these defense mechanisms are not operative. For example, we saw in the case of Little Hans that Freud believed that he repressed his Oedipal impulses and displaced his fear of his father onto horses. Thus he only experienced fear in the presence of horses. Persons with generalized anxiety disorder, by contrast, have not succeeded in repressing their anxiety and have not displaced it onto some external object; thus they are anxious nearly all the time and unaware of the real source of their anxiety.

According to early behavioral formulations, generalized anxiety stems from classical conditioning of anxiety to many environmental cues in the same general way that phobias are conditioned. In effect, this formulation sees generalized anxiety disorder as in-

volving phobic-like responses to many aspects of the external environment, ranging from light and shade contrasts to amorphous noises and the passage of time (Wolpe, 1958, p. 83). Thus the primary difference between phobias and generalized anxiety is simply in the number and kind of environmental cues that have become sources of anxiety. Wolpe hypothesized that such conditioning of anxiety to many stimuli might be especially likely to occur when a person experiences extremely intense anxiety, or if there is a lack of clearly defined environmental stimuli during the conditioning of anxiety (e.g., if it occurs during the night when the room is dark). This account can be amplified by postulating that interoceptive conditioning of anxiety to internal bodily cues may also occur (Razran, 1961; Mineka, 1985a). Nonetheless, this purely behavioral formulation has not fared well as our understanding of generalized anxiety has evolved. The essence of GAD is now thought to be anxious apprehension or worry about a variety of negative things that may happen, rather than a fear of many external or internal stimulus situations as the purely behavioral view would have us believe (Barlow, 1988; Borkovec, 1985, 1988).

In recent years, attention has turned to several different cognitive processes that seem to play important roles in the etiology of generalized anxiety disorder. One prominent theme of research on fear and anxiety for the past 25 years has been the importance of uncontrollability and unpredictability. Uncontrollable and unpredictable aversive events are much more stressful than are controllable and predictable aversive events, and so it is perhaps not surprising that they also create more fear and anxiety (Barlow, 1988, 1991a; Mandler, 1964, 1972; Mineka, 1985a; Mineka & Kelly, 1989). This has led researchers to hypothesize that people with GAD may have a history of experiencing many important events in their lives as unpredictable and/or uncontrollable. Perhaps this history of uncontrollability contributes to their seeming inability to control their worries. Conversely, it would be expected that a history of experience with controlling important aspects of one's life may immunize us against developing generalized anxiety (Mineka & Kelly, 1989; Mineka & Zinbarg, in press-b).

In addition, perhaps some of the tension and hypervigilance that persons with generalized anxiety disorder experience may stem from their lacking *safety signals* in their environment. If a person has primarily had experience with predictable stressors (e.g., on Mondays the boss is always in a bad mood and is likely to be highly critical), he or she can predict when something bad is likely to happen through the occurrence of a cue or signal (Mondays at work); for such a person the absence of that signal implies *safety* (e.g., Tuesday through Friday at work). But if another person has experienced many unpredictable or unsignalled stressors (e.g., the boss is in a bad mood and highly critical on random days of the week), he or she will not have developed safety signals for when it is appropriate to relax and feel safe, leading to a sense of relatively chronic anxiety (Mineka, 1985a; Seligman, 1975; Seligman & Binik, 1977). Thus a relative lack of safety signals may help account for why people with GAD feel constantly tense and vigilant for possible threats.

Although many of these ideas about unpredictability and uncontrollability as they apply specifically to our understanding of generalized anxiety disorder are somewhat speculative at this point, they have received a great deal of attention in recent years and provide many ideas for future research (Barlow, 1988, 1991; Mineka & Kelly, 1989). One inherent difficulty in this research is that we cannot directly manipulate the controllability and predictability of people's life experiences. Therefore we must rely more on laboratory analogue studies than is desirable. However, there is one longitudinal experiment with infant rhesus monkeys that does provide support for the hypothesized role of experiences with control in immunizing individuals against fear and anxiety (Mineka, Gunnar, & Champoux, 1986). In this experiment two groups of infant monkeys were reared in peer groups in which they had extensive experience with control and mastery over appetitive reinforcers in their environment (pressing bars, pulling chains, etc., to obtain food, water, and treats). These monkeys were called "Masters." Two other groups of monkeys (called "Yoked" monkeys) were reared in identical environments but had no control over their reinforcers; instead, they received reinforcers when a member of the Master group exerted control. Thus the Master and Yoked groups were equated on exposure to reinforcers; they only differed in whether they controlled access to the reinforcers. Between 7 and 11 months of age, all monkeys were tested for their responses to a variety of fear- and anxiety-provoking situations. Master monkeys habituated more rapidly to the presence of a fear-provoking toy monster than did Yoked monkeys. Moreover, relative to Yoked monkeys, Master monkeys were bolder and more willing to enter a novel, somewhat frightening playroom situation, and once in the playroom they explored it more freely. There was also suggestive evidence that Master monkeys coped better when they were separated from their peers and placed as an intruder in the Yoked group than vice versa. Thus, it appears that early experiences with control and mastery can im-

munize to some extent against the harmful effects of exposure to stressful situations, and by analogy perhaps against the development of generalized anxiety.

The second prominent line of research on cognitive factors involved in generalized anxiety disorder focuses both on the content of anxious cognitions and on the effects that anxiety has on our processing of threatening information. Beck and Emery (1985) summarized evidence showing that patients with GAD tend to have images and automatic thoughts revolving around physical injury, illness or death, loss of control, failure and inability to cope, rejection, and mental illness. Common automatic thoughts included "I will make a fool of myself," "People will laugh at me," "What if I fail?" "I won't have time to do a good job," and "I'll never be as capable as I should be" (Beck & Emery, 1985, p. 106). It is generally thought that these negative automatic thoughts are fueled by underlying maladaptive assumptions or schemas about the world that these people have developed in the course of growing up. Common maladaptive assumptions that patients with GAD may have are "Any strange situation should be regarded as dangerous," "It is always best to assume the worst," "My survival depends on my always being competent and strong," and "My security and safety depend on anticipating and preparing myself at all times for any possible danger" (Beck & Emery, 1985, p. 63).

In addition to having frequent thoughts with threatening content, people with GAD process threatening information in a biased way. Many studies have shown that generally anxious people tend to have their attention drawn toward threat cues when there is a mixture of threat and nonthreat cues in the environment. Nonanxious people show, if anything, the opposite bias, tending to have their attention drawn away from threat cues (see MacLeod & Mathews, 1991; Mathews, 1993; Mineka, 1992, for reviews). Moreover, this different perception of threat cues occurs at a very early stage of information processing, even before the information has even entered the person's conscious awareness. This automatic, unconscious attentional bias would seem to have the effect of reinforcing or even enhancing the person's current emotional state. That is, if when one is already anxious, one's attention is automatically drawn toward threat cues in the environment, this would only seem to make the anxiety worse. In addition, this automatic drawing of attention to threat cues may help account for why people with GAD experience much of their worry as intrusive and uncontrollable. Generally anxious people also have a much stronger tendency to interpret ambiguous information in a threatening way than do nonanxious individuals. For example, when clinically anxious subjects read a series of ambiguous sentences (e.g., "The men watched as the chest was opened," "The doctor examined little Emma's growth," "They discussed the priest's convictions," or "The farmer gave Dave the sack"), they are more likely to remember the threatening meaning of the sentences than are nonanxious controls (Eysenck et al., 1991; see also MacLeod & Cohen, 1993).

Given these strong attentional and interpretive biases for threat cues, one might well expect that anxious persons would also be especially likely to remember the threat cues they have encountered. However, the weight of the evidence at present suggests that this is not the case (MacLeod & Mathews, 1991; Mathews, 1993; Mineka & Nugent, in press). Although some studies have found results suggesting the presence of such a memory bias, at least as many have not, and some have even found a memory bias *against* threatening cues. It seems that the vigilance for threat cues that underlies the attentional bias is also somewhat paradoxically associated with *avoidance* of further elaboration of those threat cues; such elaboration would be necessary to show a memory bias.

In summary, several cognitive variables seem to promote the onset of generalized anxiety as well as its maintenance. Experience with unpredictable and/or uncontrollable life events may promote both current anxiety as well as a vulnerability to anxiety in the presence of future stressors (Barlow, 1988, 1991b; Mineka, 1985a; Mineka & Kelly, 1989). In addition, schemas that one develops early in life about how to cope with strange and dangerous situations and about how to survive may leave one prone to developing automatic thoughts focused on possible threats. The content of such thoughts surely helps to maintain anxiety. Finally, for anxiety-prone people, anxiety affects the processing of threatening information in such a way that they automatically pay attention to threatening cues in their environment. Moreover, they are prone to interpret ambiguous information in a threatening manner. Yet they do not seem to have especially good memory for the threatening cues they encounter.

Biological Causal Factors Although evidence regarding genetic factors in GAD is mixed, it does seem likely that there is a modest heritability, as for the other anxiety disorders (Barlow, 1988; Kendler et al., 1992a; Rapee & Barlow, 1993). Part of the problem for research in this area has been the evolving nature of our understanding of GAD and what

its diagnostic criteria are. GAD was only introduced as a diagnostic category in 1980. Thus many of the people participating in studies before that who had been diagnosed with "anxiety states" may have included a mixture of GAD and panic disorder patients. But even since 1980 the diagnostic criteria for GAD have changed significantly with each revision of the DSM, making it difficult to compare the results of studies done at different times (Barlow, 1988). A recent large twin study reveals exactly how heritability estimates vary as a function of one's definition of GAD (Kendler et al., 1992a).

Another important line of neurobiological research on generalized anxiety dates back to the discovery in the 1950s of the effects of certain drugs on reducing anxiety. This category of drugs, the benzodiazepines, includes some of today's most prescribed psychoactive drugs (e.g., Valium, Librium, and most recently Xanax). Discovery of the marked effects that these drugs have on generalized anxiety was followed in the 1970s by the finding that the drugs probably exert their effects through stimulating the action of GABA, a neurotransmitter now strongly implicated in generalized anxiety (Redmond, 1985). It appears that highly anxious people have a kind of functional deficiency in GABA (*gamma aminobutyric acid*)—a neurotransmitter that ordinarily plays an important role in the way our brain inhibits anxiety in stressful situations. The benzodiazepine drugs appear to reduce anxiety by increasing GABA activity in certain parts of the brain known to be implicated in anxiety, such as the limbic system. Whether the functional deficiency in GABA in anxious people causes their anxiety or occurs as a consequence of it is not yet known, but it does appear that this functional deficiency would promote the maintenance of anxiety.

It is also important to reemphasize here that the neurobiological factors implicated in panic attacks and generalized anxiety are *not* the same. As we noted at the outset of this chapter, contemporary theorists are drawing a distinction between fear, or panic, and anxiety that is far more fundamental than the old one that anxiety is simply fear without a known source. Fear and panic involve the activation of the fight-or-flight response, and the brain area and neurotransmitters that seem most strongly implicated in these emotional responses are the locus coeruleus in the brain stem and the neurotransmitter norepinephrine. Generalized anxiety or anxious apprehension is a more diffuse emotional state involving arousal and a preparation for possible impending threat, and the brain area and neurotransmitters that seem most strongly implicated are the limbic system and GABA (Gorman et al., 1989; Redmond, 1985).

Obsessive-Compulsive Disorder

Diagnostically **obsessive-compulsive disorder** (OCD) is defined by the occurrence of unwanted and intrusive obsessive thoughts or distressing images; these are usually accompanied by compulsive behaviors designed to neutralize the obsessive thoughts or images or to prevent some dreaded event or situation. More specifically, according to DSM-IV **obsessions** involve "recurrent and persistent thoughts, impulses or images that are experienced, at some time during the disturbance, as intrusive and inappropriate. . . . The person attempts to ignore or suppress such thoughts, impulses or images, or to neutralize them with some other thought or action." **Compulsions** involve "repetitive behaviors (e.g., handwashing, ordering, checking) or mental acts (e.g., praying, counting, repeating words silently) that the person feels driven to perform in response to an obsession, or according to rules that must be applied rigidly. . . . The behaviors or mental acts are aimed at preventing or reducing distress or preventing some dreaded event or situation; however, these behaviors either are not connected in a realistic way with what they are designed to neutralize or prevent or are clearly excessive" (DSM-IV, 1994, p. 422–23). In addition, the person must recognize that the obsession is the product of his own mind rather than being imposed from without (as might occur in schizophrenia). It is also now recognized that there is a continuum of "insight" among obsessive-compulsives about exactly how senseless and excessive their obsessions and compulsions are (Riggs & Foa, 1993). In most cases these people do have some recognition that their behavior is irrational, but they cannot seem to control it; in a minority of cases this insight is absent for most of the time. Finally, the DSM-IV diagnosis requires that this seemingly involuntary behavior cause a person marked distress, consume excessive time (over an hour a day), or interfere with occupational or social functioning.

Although once thought to be an extremely rare disorder (e.g., Black, 1974, reviewed studies estimating the prevalence at 0.05 percent), estimates from the Epidemiologic Catchment Area study indicate that obsessive-compulsive disorder is much more prevalent than was once thought. Specifically, the average one-year prevalence rate of OCD in this composite sample was 1.6 percent, and the average lifetime prevalence was 2.5 percent (Robins & Regier, 1991). Similar results were obtained in an epidemiological study conducted in Canada (Bland, Orn, & Newman, 1988). Divorced (or separated) and unemployed people were somewhat overrepresented (Karno et al., 1988), which is not surprising given the difficulties this disorder creates for interpersonal and occupational functioning. Contrary to earlier reports suggesting a preponderance of OCD among females, these newer figures show little or no gender difference. Although the disorder generally begins in late adolescence or early adulthood, it is not uncommon in children, where its symptoms are strikingly similar to those of adult cases (Rapoport, 1989; Swedo et al., 1989). In most cases the disorder has a gradual onset, but once it becomes a serious condition it tends to be chronic, although the severity of symptoms usually waxes and wanes in intensity over time (e.g., Rasmussen & Eisen, 1991).

Most people with obsessive-compulsive disorder experience both obsessions and compulsions. Although earlier estimates were that as many as 25 percent experienced pure obsessional disorder without any compulsive rituals (Rachman & Hodgson, 1980), recent estimates from research conducted in the development of the DSM-IV are that over 90 percent experience both obsessions and compulsions. When mental rituals or compulsions such as counting are also included as compulsive behaviors, this figure jumps to 98 percent. In 90 percent of cases the compulsions are seen as functionally related to the obsessions (Riggs & Foa, 1993).

Most of us have experienced minor obsessive thoughts, such as whether we remembered to lock the door or turn the stove off. In addition, most of us occasionally engage in repetitive or stereotyped behavior, such as checking the stove or the lock on the door, or stepping over cracks on a sidewalk. In the case of obsessive-compulsive disorder, however, the thoughts are much more persistent and distressing, they generally appear irrational to the individual, and along with the associated compulsive acts they interfere considerably with everyday behavior. Nevertheless, research indicates that normal and abnormal obsessions and compulsive behaviors exist on a continuum (Rachman & De Silva, 1978; Rachman & Hodgson, 1980), with the primary difference being in the frequency and intensity of the obsessions and in the degree to which the obsessions and compulsions are troubling and to which they are resisted (see also Salkovskis & Harrison, 1984).

Obsessive thoughts may center on a variety of topics. In one study the most frequent themes of obsessions were contamination (55 percent), aggressive impulses (50 percent), the need for symmetry (37 percent), somatic concerns (35 percent), and sexual content (32 percent) (Jenike et al., 1986). A study of OCD conducted in India revealed a similar range of themes, although the proportions showing obsessions about aggression and sex were somewhat smaller (Akhtar et al., 1975).

Obsessive thoughts involving themes of violence or aggression might include a wife being obsessed with the idea that she might poison her husband, or a daughter constantly imagining pushing her mother down a flight of stairs. Even though such obsessive thoughts are only *very* rarely carried out in action, they remain a source of often excruciating torment to a person plagued with them. This pattern is well illustrated in a classic case described by Kraines (1948) of a woman who

> complained of having "terrible thoughts." When she thought of her boyfriend she wished he were dead; when her mother went down the stairs, she "wished she'd fall and break her neck"; when her sister spoke of going to the beach with her infant daughter, the patient "hoped that they would both drown." These thoughts "make me hysterical. I love them; why should I wish such terrible things to happen? It drives me wild, makes me feel I'm crazy and don't belong to society; maybe it's best for me to end it all than to go on thinking such terrible things about those I love." (p. 183)

As is the case with obsessive thoughts, many of us show some compulsive behavior—stepping over cracks in sidewalks, checking to see that a door is locked immediately after having locked it, or making multiple backups of our computer files—but without the degree of compulsiveness of people with OCD, who feel compelled to perform repeatedly acts that seem pointless and absurd even to them and that they in some sense do not want to perform. These compulsive acts are of three primary types: cleaning, checking, and counting (Barlow, 1988), with many people showing multiple kinds of rituals. For a smaller number the compulsions are to perform various everyday acts such as eating or dressing extremely slowly (primary obsessional slowness), and for others the compulsions are to have things exactly symmetrical or "evened up" (Rasmussen & Eisen, 1991). Washing rituals vary from relatively mild ritual-like behavior, such as spending 15 to 20 minutes washing one's hands after going to the bathroom, to more extreme behavior, such as washing one's hands with disinfectants for hours every day to the point that the hands bleed. Checking rituals also vary from relatively mild, such as checking all the lights, appliances, and locks two or three times before leaving the house, to very extreme, such as going back to an intersection where one thinks one may have run over

a pedestrian and spending hours checking for any sign of the imagined accident. Both cleaning and checking rituals are often performed a specific number of times and thus also involve counting. Compulsive rituals are sometimes covert or cognitive in nature, involving feelings and thoughts (see HIGHLIGHT 5.2). The performance of the compulsive act or the ritualized series of acts usually brings a feeling of reduced tension and satisfaction (Carr, 1971; Rachman & Hodgson, 1980).

Given the range of content of both obsessions and compulsive rituals, considerable attention has been devoted to the issue of whether OCD is a homogeneous disorder, or rather several different disorders. For example, a distinction is often made between "cleaners" and "checkers," with the former having obsessions about contamination accompanied by cleaning rituals, and the latter having obsessions about causing harm to others, leading to checking rituals. However, problems with this distinction arise when one notes that many people with OCD have both cleaning and checking rituals, and the primary type of ritual may change over time (Barlow, 1988; Rapoport, 1989). Moreover, a recent study comparing different possible subgroups on a host of demographic variables and clinical features found very few differences. Thus, the disorder seems more homogeneous than one might guess given the many different ways in which it presents itself (Rasmussen & Eisen, 1991). What seems consistent across nearly all the different clinical presentations is: (a) anxiety is the affective symptom (except with primary obsessional slowness); (b) nearly all people afflicted with OCD fear that something terrible will happen to themselves or others for which they will be responsible; and (c) compulsions usually reduce the anxiety, at least in the short term.

Another consistent theme across different cases of obsessive-compulsive disorder lies in its characterization as a "what if" illness (Rasmussen & Eisen, 1991). Most patients with obsessive-compulsive disorder are continually worried about the possibility that something terrible will happen. "If there is a one in a million chance that something terrible will happen, they somehow convince themselves that it will happen to them ... [e.g.] 'The very fact that it is within the realm of possibility, however unlikely, that I will stab my baby, or poison my child, is enough to terrify me so that I can think of nothing else no matter how hard I try.'" (Rasmussen & Eisen, 1991, p. 37). This tendency to judge risks unrealistically seems to be a very important feature of OCD.

As with all of the anxiety disorders, obsessive-compulsive disorder frequently co-occurs with other mood and anxiety disorders. Depression is especially

HIGHLIGHT 5.2

Cognitive and Motor Behavior Patterns in Obsessive-Compulsive Disorder

	Symptoms	Examples
Cognitive	**Obsessions.** Recurrent, persistent ideas, thoughts, images, or impulses involuntarily coming to awareness.	A person has ideas of contamination, dread, guilt; urges to kill, attack, injure, confess, or steal.
	Ruminations. Forced preoccupation with thoughts about a particular topic, associated with brooding, doubting, and inconclusive speculation.	A person spends several hours per day in worried anticipation that a former lover may attempt to reestablish contact.
	Cognitive rituals. Elaborate series of mental acts the patient feels compelled to complete. Termination depends on proper performance.	Before retiring for the evening, a patient feels required to recite mentally a long series of prayers learned in childhood.
Motor	**Compulsive motor rituals.** Elaborate, often time-consuming activities frequently associated with everyday functions such as eating, toileting, grooming, dressing, and sexual activity.	A patient evidences hand washing (sometimes reaching 400 or more washes per day), compulsive counting (e.g., of passersby), or "checking" of objects.
	Compulsive avoidances. Substitute actions performed instead of appropriate behavior that induces anxiety.	A student becomes involved in several distracting activities before exams, leaving no time to study.

common, with estimates suggesting that as many as 80 percent of those with OCD may experience major depression at some time in their life (Barlow, 1988). Given the chronic and debilitating nature of this disorder, it may not be surprising that many develop depression at least partly in response to having OCD. Nevertheless, this high degree of comorbidity has led some to question whether OCD is really a mood disorder rather than an anxiety disorder. However, current evidence suggests that there are enough important differences between OCD and depression (including at the biological marker level), and enough similarities with other anxiety disorders to continue to classify it as an anxiety disorder (e.g., Barlow, 1988; Sturgis, 1993; Weizman, Zohar, & Insel, 1991).

The anxiety disorders with which OCD most often co-occurs include panic disorder, specific phobia, and social phobia. The most common personality disorders (see Chapter 9) in people with OCD are dependent and avoidant (indeed Baer et al., 1992, found that about 25 percent of 55 OCD patients met criteria for either avoidant and dependent personality disorders, with a subset having both).

Given that these two personality disorders also commonly occur in people with other anxiety disorders, this suggests some degree of shared vulnerability (Rasmussen & Eisen, 1991; Sturgis, 1993).

The following is a fairly typical case of severe obsessive-compulsive disorder:

Mark was a 28-year-old single male with severe obsessions about causing harm to others, including committing crimes. The obsessions were accompanied by lengthy and excessive checking rituals. At the time he came to an anxiety disorder clinic, he was no longer able to live by himself, and had been forced to move back home with his parents after having lived for several years on his own since college. His obsessions about harming others or confessing to crimes were so severe that he was virtually confined to his room and could only leave it if he had a tape recorder with him so that he would have a record of any crimes he confessed to. The clinic was several hours' drive

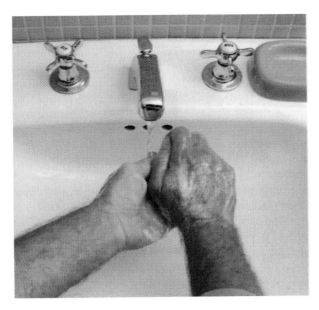

Many of us show some compulsive behavior, but people with obsessive-compulsive disorder feel compelled to repeatedly perform some act in response to an obsession in order to reduce the anxiety or discomfort created by the obsession. Although the person may realize that the behavior is excessive or unreasonable, he or she does not feel able to control the urge. Obsessive-compulsive washers may spend hours a day washing, and may even use abrasive cleansers to the point that their hands bleed.

from his home; his mother usually had to drive. One day when he drove he began obsessing that he had caused an accident at an intersection and felt compelled to spend several hours driving and walking around all parts of that intersection to find evidence of the accident. He could not speak on the phone for fear of confessing to a crime, and he could not mail a letter for the same reason. He also could not go into a store alone or into public bathrooms, where he feared he might write a confession on the wall.

Mark was a very bright young man with considerable artistic talent. He had finished college at a prestigious school for people interested in the arts and had begun a successful career as a young artist when the obsessions began in his early 20s. At first they were focused on the possibility that he would be implicated in some crime that he had not committed; only later did they evolve to the point that he was actually afraid that he might commit a crime and confess to it. The checking rituals and avoidance of all places where such confessions might occur eventually led to his having to give up his career and his own apartment and move back in with his family.

Mark was treated with medication and with exposure and response prevention. He found the side effects of the medication (clomipramine) intolerable and gave it up within a few weeks. For the behavioral treatment he was directed to get rid of the tape recorder and was given a series of exercises in which he exposed himself to feared situations where he might confess to a crime or cause harm to others. Checking rituals (including the tape recorder) were prevented. Although the initial round of treatment was not especially helpful, in part because of the distance and difficulty of getting to treatment, he did eventually commit to more intensive treatment by moving to a small apartment closer to the clinic and did quite well.

Psychosocial Causal Factors Until recently the dominant theories of the origins of obsessive-compulsive disorder were the psychoanalytic and behavioral views. According to Freud's psychoanalytic view, a person with OCD has been unable to cope with the instinctual conflicts of the Oedipal stage and has either never advanced beyond this stage or has regressed back to an earlier stage of psychosexual development. Specifically, such a person is thought to be fixated in the anal stage of development (about two years of age) when children are thought to derive psychosexual pleasure from defecating. This is also the time at which parents are often attempting to toilet train their children, which involves learning to control and delay these urges. If parents are too harsh, they may instill rage in the child, as well guilt and shame about these drives. According to this theory, the intense conflict that may develop between impulses from the id and the ego leads to the development of defenses that may ultimately produce obsessive-compulsive symptoms. The four primary defense mechanisms thought to be used are isolation, displacement, reaction formation, and undoing (Nemiah, 1975; Sturgis, 1993). With isolation, the associations between a blasphemous thought and the affect that would ordinarily be associated with it are disconnected. Thus, the person might think about violence without experiencing anger, isolating himself from the affect associated with the distressing situation. With displacement, the person substitutes one thought or activity for another that is more frightening or threatening. With reaction formation, the person thinks and acts in a fashion that is opposite to his or her true impulses. For example, someone who was obsessed with thoughts of harming her children might become a "supermom." Finally, with undoing the person tries to obtain forgiveness for some imagined transgression through some magical compulsive behavior. For example, someone with blasphemous thoughts might engage in extensive praying and cleaning rituals (see Sturgis, 1993). Unfortunately, there has been virtually no empirical research documenting any of the major tenets of this theory, and the treatment that stems from it has not proved to be useful in treating OCD.

The dominant behavioral view of obsessive-compulsive disorder derives from O. H. Mowrer's two-process theory of avoidance learning (1947). According to this theory, neutral stimuli become associated with aversive stimuli through a process of classical conditioning and come to elicit anxiety. For example, touching a doorknob or shaking hands might become associated with the "scary" idea of contamination. Once having made this association, the person may discover that the anxiety produced by shaking hands or touching a doorknob may be reduced by an activity like hand washing. By washing his or her hands extensively the anxiety would be reduced and the washing response would be reinforced, making it more likely to occur again in the future when anxiety about contamination was evoked in other situations. Once learned, such avoidance responses are extremely resistant to extinction.

Several experiments conducted by Rachman and Hodgson (1980) supported these ideas. They found that for most patients with OCD, exposure to a situation that provoked their obsession (e.g., a doorknob or toilet seat for someone with obsessions about contamination) did indeed produce distress, which would continue for a moderate amount of time and then gradually dissipate. If the patient was allowed to engage in the compulsive ritual immediately after the provocation, however, his or her anxiety would generally decrease rapidly. This model predicts then that exposure to feared objects or situations should be useful in treating OCD if the exposure is followed by prevention of the ritual, allowing the patient to see that the anxiety will subside naturally in time without the ritual. And this is indeed the core of the most effective form of behavior therapy for OCD (see below and HIGHLIGHT 5.3). Thus, the behavioral model has been very useful in helping us understand what factors may help to maintain obsessive-compulsive behavior, and it has also been useful in generating an effective form of treatment. However, it has not been helpful in explaining why people with OCD develop obsessions in the first place, and why they have such abnormal assessments of risk.

Just as the conditioning view of phobias has been revitalized through the addition of the preparedness concept, which puts phobias in the evolutionary context of what fears may have been adaptive for our early ancestors, so too has our understanding of obsessive-compulsive disorder increased through looking at it in an evolutionary context. For example, one group of researchers found that the preparedness concept as applied to phobias was also relevant to understanding the nonrandom distribution of obsessive thoughts and compulsive rituals (De Silva, Rachman, & Seligman, 1977). For example, thoughts about dirt and contamination associated with compulsive washing are so common as to make their occurrence seem nonrandom. The researchers developed a rating system for the "preparedness" of different kinds of objects or situations based on estimates of the level of probable danger that they posed to pretechnological humans. Ratings of preparedness of compulsive behaviors were based on estimates that those behaviors almost certainly defended pretechnological people against danger. These ratings were applied to the content of the obsessions, compulsions, and phobias for 82 cases of OCD and 69 cases of phobia. The contents of the great majority of both obsessions and phobias were rated as highly prepared, as were the ratings of most compulsive behaviors (such as washing off animal feces or checking fire hazards). The overall consensus seems to be that humans' obsessions with dirt and contamination and certain other potentially dangerous situations did not arise out of a vacuum but rather have deep evolutionary roots (Mineka, 1993).

In addition, some theorists have argued that the displacement activities that many species of animals engage in under situations of conflict or high arousal bear a significant resemblance to the compulsive rituals seen in obsessive-compulsive disorder (Holland, 1974; Mineka, 1985a, 1993; Winslow & Insel, 1991). Displacement activities often involve grooming or nesting under conditions of high conflict or frustration, and may therefore be related to the grooming or tidying rituals seen in obsessive-compulsives, which are often provoked by anxiety, discomfort, or distress brought about by obsessive thoughts or images. Rapoport (1989) has argued even more generally that the rituals of OCD may be instinctive behaviors that have been released inappropriately, noting that "the behaviors in OCD resemble misplaced grooming and/or protective rituals" (p. 193).

Cognitive factors have also been implicated in obsessive-compulsive disorder. Sher, Frost, and Otis (1983; see also Sher et al., 1989), for example, have shown that people with checking compulsions show poor memory for their behavioral acts, such as "Did

Treatment of Obsessive-Compulsive Disorder with Exposure and Response Prevention

Steketee and Foa (1985) present the following case as an illustration of their recommended approach to the treatment of obsessive-compulsive disorders. The patient, June, was a 26-year-old recently married nursing graduate who complained of washing and cleaning problems so severe that she was unable to seek work in her profession. On initial evaluation she was agitated and distressed, feeling helpless to control her need to take at least two 45-minute showers daily and, in addition, to wash her hands some 20 times a day for 5 minutes. She also spent a great deal of time wiping various objects with alcohol. Inquiry soon determined that she was terrified of becoming "contaminated," particularly by bird, animal, or human feces, which she took great pains to avoid. She also had problems with garbage and with dead animals on the road. Previous treatment by systematic desensitization, tranquilizing drugs, and "cognitive restructuring" had been ineffective. Her marriage was now threatened owing to her husband's frustration with her excessive cleanliness.

Exposure Treatment

The therapist and patient worked together to create a hierarchy of upsetting stimuli, rating them on a scale of 1 through 100 according to their capacities to evoke disgust and the impulse to wash. For example, the patient gave ratings of 100 to touching dog feces (if unable to wash immediately), 90 to automobile tires (which may have contacted a dead animal), and 40 to the outside doorknob of a public bathroom (the inside doorknob rated 80). Subsequently, in treatment sessions three times weekly,

June was instructed to expose herself deliberately to these stimuli either in guided fantasy (in vitro) or directly (in vivo), beginning with those rated relatively low in the hierarchy and moving gradually to the more severely threatening ones.

In addition to the exposures conducted during therapy sessions, "homework" was liberally assigned. Subjective ratings of discomfort were carefully monitored during these encounters. On one occasion well into treatment, the therapist drove with the patient to a place where she had observed a dead cat on the roadside and insisted that the patient approach the "smelly" corpse and touch it with a stick. The stick and a pebble lying close by were presented to the patient with the instruction that she keep them in her pocket and touch them frequently throughout the day. The patient was also told to drive her car past the spot on subsequent days.

The therapist made "home visits" to assist the patient in facing her problems in that setting touching contaminated objects and places (such as a porch railing soiled with pigeon droppings) and contaminating (by unwashed touch) clean ones. Systematic exposure continued until the patient appeared at ease with a particular confrontation and her discomfort rating concerning it dropped to the 40–50 range.

Response Prevention

After obtaining June's commitment to the full treatment procedure (which had previously been explained) in the fourth session, the therapist instituted a no-washing rule. Specifically, the patient was to remain unwashed for a period of five days, after which she

could take a 10-minute shower to be followed by another wash-free five days. As anticipated, June was notably upset by this proposed regimen and strongly doubted she could carry it off. The therapist was encouraging but insistent, promising support through the hard times, and the patient was successful in curbing her frequent impulses to wash. A transition to "normal washing and cleaning behavior" was instituted shortly before the end of the planned 15 therapy sessions. This plan consisted of one 10-minute shower per day and hand washings not to exceed six per day at mealtimes, after bathroom use, and after touching clearly soiled or greasy objects.

Because June's discomfort ratings remained somewhat high (maximum 70, but only briefly) following the planned 15 sessions, a few additional follow-up sessions were given. In an evaluation nine months following the initiation of treatment, June described herself as "definitely a lot better . . . maybe 80 percent." She acknowledged that she still had obsessions "once every week or two" (such as "driving over someone"), but she was now employed and her relationship with her husband was much improved. She felt she was living a "normal life."

As Steketee and Foa pointed out, obsessive-compulsive disorders rarely remit completely; even a successfully treated patient will usually have some residual obsessive problems or rituals, as in June's case. The treatment undertaken here was of course direct and rigorous and was based on a behavioral formulation. It appears to have been the treatment of choice.

I check to see if the stove was off?" Having a poor memory for one's actions could easily be seen as contributing to the repetitive nature of checking rituals. In addition, it has now been shown that when normal people attempt to suppress unwanted thoughts, they may find a paradoxical increase in those thoughts later (Wegner, Wegner, & Klein, 1987; Wegner, 1989). Moreover, two other studies with normal subjects showed that thought suppression during a negative mood produced a connection between the thought and the negative mood. When the negative mood occurred again later the thought was more easily experienced, or when the thought was later experienced the mood returned (Wenzlaff, Wegner, & Klein, 1991). They concluded that if people try not to think of something, "unintentionally they bond that thought to their mood such that each will later make the other return" (p. 507). Given the findings of Rachman that people with normal and abnormal obsessions differ primarily in the degree to which their thoughts are resisted and found unacceptable, it may be that a major factor contributing to the frequency of obsessive thoughts and negative moods may be these attempts to suppress them, leading to paradoxical increases.

Biological Causal Factors In the past 15 years there has been an explosion of research investigating the possible biological basis for obsessive-compulsive disorder. Some studies have sought to discover whether there is a genetic contribution to this disorder. Others have explored whether there are structural brain abnormalities associated with OCD, and yet others whether there are abnormalities in specific neurotransmitter systems associated with OCD. The accumulating evidence from all three kinds of studies is that biological causal factors are probably more clearly implicated in the causes of OCD than in any of the other anxiety disorders.

Genetic studies have included both twin studies and family studies. Evidence from twin studies reveals a moderately high concordance rate for monozygotic twins (about 65 percent averaged across the studies reviewed by Rasmussen & Tsuang, 1986), but these results are somewhat difficult to interpret given the failure to include dizygotic twins (Pauls, Raymond, & Robertson, 1991). As discussed in Chapter 3, high concordance rates in monozygotic twins only suggest a genetic influence if the concordance rate is significantly lower in dizygotic twins. One small study by Carey and Gottesman (1981) did include dizygotic twins and found that concordance rates were smaller, although not significantly so, perhaps because of the small sample sizes. Most family studies have also found substan-

tially higher rates of OCD in first-degree relatives of OCD patients than would be expected based on current estimates of the prevalence of OCD, with estimates that about 15–20 percent of first-degree relatives have diagnosable OCD (Pauls et al., 1991). With both twin and family studies, estimates of a genetic contribution go up if twins or family members who have some obsessive-compulsive symptoms (but not full-blown OCD) are included (Pauls et al., 1991). Finally, there is also quite convincing evidence of a genetic contribution to some forms of OCD given that OCD is linked to another disorder—Tourette's syndrome (TS), which is known to have a genetic basis. For example, one study found that 23 percent of first-degree relatives of patients with Tourette's syndrome had diagnosable OCD (Pauls et al., 1986, 1991). In general, it seems that there is probably a moderate genetic contribution to OCD, although it may be a rather nonspecific "neurotic" predisposition (Black et al., 1992). However, more research is needed with new genetic methodologies before the exact nature of this contribution will be completely understood.

The search for structural abnormalities in the brains of OCD patients has also been intense in the past decade as major advances have been made in techniques used to study the functioning of brain structures in living patients. Findings from studies using positron emission tomography (PET) scans have shown that patients with OCD have abnormally active metabolic levels in the orbital prefrontal cortex and caudate nucleus (Baxter, Schwartz, & Guze, 1991; Liebowitz & Hollander, 1991). Other studies have shown some normalization of at least some of these abnormalities with successful treatment (Baxter et al., 1992; Insel, 1992; Swedo et al., 1992). Rapoport's findings also implicate abnormalities in the functioning of the basal ganglia (Rapoport & Wise, 1988; Insel, 1992; Liebowitz & Hollander, 1991).

Exactly how these areas are implicated is unclear as yet, although several different theories are currently being tested. For example, Baxter et al. (1991) have speculated that the primary dysfunction in OCD may be in an area of the brain called the striatum, which is involved in the preparation of appropriate behavioral responses. They cite evidence that when this area is not functioning properly inappropriate behavioral responses may occur, including repeated behaviors such as occur in OCD. They further hypothesize that in OCD there is a dysfunctional interaction of this area with certain areas of the cortex, leading those higher brain areas to become abnormally active. This causes sensations, thoughts, and behaviors that would normally be inhibited (if the striatum were functioning properly) to not be inhibited in patients with OCD. In this case impulses toward aggression, sex, hygiene, and danger ("the stuff of obsessions," p. 116) that most people keep under control with relative ease "leak through" as obsessions in the patient with OCD and lead to distractions from ordinary goal-directed behavior. This would in turn cause the cortex to "cope" through the use of mechanisms such as compulsive rituals in order to dampen the concerns raised by the obsessive thoughts (Baxter et al., 1991, 1992).

Pharmacological studies of obsessive-compulsive disorder intensified with the discovery that a drug called Anafranil (clomipramine) is often effective in the treatment of obsessive-compulsive disorder. Although the drug was first discovered to be useful in the treatment of OCD in the late 1960s, double-blind placebo-controlled studies clearly documenting its effectiveness in the treatment of OCD did not begin to appear until the 1980s (see DeVeaugh-Geiss, 1991). Clomipramine is closely related to other tricyclic antidepressants (see Chapter 6) but is more effective than they are in the treatment of OCD. It seems very likely that clomipramine is more effective with OCD than the other tricyclics because it has greater effects on the neurotransmitter serotonin, which is now strongly implicated in OCD. This is also in keeping with the fact that several other antidepressant drugs such as fluoxetine (Prozac) that also affect serotonin have also been shown to be useful in the treatment of OCD.

The exact nature of the dysfunction in serotonergic systems in OCD is as yet unclear (see Goodman et al., 1991; Liebowitz & Hollander, 1991). Clomipramine, like Prozac, is known to inhibit the re-uptake of serotonin after it has been released into the synapse. This would seem to suggest that it operates through increasing the availability of serotonin, which in turn would suggest that OCD may be characterized by *deficiencies* in serotonin levels. Unfortunately, however, the story is much more complicated because it is also known that administration of a drug that is a serotonin-agonist (causing release of serotonin) results in *increases* in obsessive-compulsive symptoms (Zohar et al., 1987), suggesting that OCD is characterized by excessively *high* levels of serotonin. The complex picture that seems to be emerging is that increased serotonin activity and increased sensitivity of some brain structures to serotonin may be involved in OCD symptoms. In this view, long-term administration of clomipramine causes a down-regulation of certain serotonin receptors. That is, although the immediate effect of clomipramine may be to increase serotonin levels, the long-term effects are quite different. This is con-

sistent with the finding that clomiprimine must be taken for at least 8–12 weeks before significant improvement in OCD symptoms occurs (Liebowitz & Hollander, 1991). However, it is also becoming clear that dysfunction in serotonergic systems cannot by itself fully explain this complex disorder. Other neurotransmitter systems and structural brain abnormalities also seem to be involved (Hollander et al., 1992).

In summary, there is now a substantial body of evidence implicating biological causal factors in OCD. This evidence comes from genetic studies, from studies of structural brain functioning, and from psychopharmacological studies. Although the exact nature of these factors and how they are interrelated is not yet understood, major research efforts are currently underway and are sure to enhance our understanding of this very serious and disabling disorder in the next decade.

General Sociocultural Causal Factors for all Anxiety Disorders Cross-cultural research suggests that although anxiety disorders probably exist in all human societies, there are many differences in prevalence and in the form of expression of the different disorders in different cultures (Good & Kleinman, 1985). For example, in the Yoruba culture of Nigeria, there are three primary clusters of symptoms associated with generalized anxiety: worry, dreams, and bodily complaints. The sources of worry are very different than in Western society, however, and focus on creating and maintaining a large family, and on fertility. Dreams are a major source of anxiety because they are thought to indicate that one may be bewitched. Somatic complaints are also unusual from a Western standpoint. Common ones include "Occasionally I experience heat sensation in my head," I have the feeling of something like water in my brain," "Things like ants keep on creeping in various parts of my brain," and "I am convinced some types of worms are in my head" (Ebigbo, 1982; Good & Kleinman, 1985). In India as well there are many more worries about being possessed by spirits and about sexual inadequacy than are seen in generalized anxiety in Western cultures (Carstairs & Kapur, 1976; Good & Kleinman, 1985).

There is also some evidence that the form that certain anxiety disorders take has actually evolved so as to fit within certain cultural patterns. A good example is the Japanese disorder *taijin kyofusho (TKS)*, which is related to the Western diagnosis of social phobia. Like social phobia it refers to a fear of interpersonal relations or a fear of social situations (Kirmayer, 1991; Tseng et al., 1992). Most people with this disorder have a single dominant symptom, which in the past was a fear of blushing but currently seems to be most often a phobia about eye contact—symptoms not mentioned in the DSM-IV description of social phobia (Kirmayer, 1991). Dysmorphophobia—the fear that some part of the body is defective or malformed—is also commonly associated with this disorder. People with this disorder also believe that they are harming others through their inappropriate behavior or their deformed body; that is, they may think that their blushing or eye contact or imagined deformity is causing others significant discomfort. Kirmayer (1991) has argued that the pattern of symptoms that occurs in *taijin kyofusho* has clearly been shaped by cultural factors. Japanese children are raised to be highly dependent on their mothers and to have a fear of the outside world, especially strangers. As babies and young children they are praised for being obedient and docile. There is also a great deal of emphasis on implicit communication—being able to guess another's thoughts and feelings and being sensitive to them. People who make too much eye contact are likely to be considered to be aggressive and insensitive, and children are taught to look at the throat of people with whom they are conversing rather than into their eyes. The society is also very hierarchical and structured, and many subtleties in language and facial communication are used to communicate one's response to social status. Kirmayer compares the effects of such Japanese cultural patterns on the symptoms seen in *taijin kyofusho* with the effects of Western cultural patterns on the symptoms seen in social phobia:

> The delusional fear of harming others through one's tense or inappropriate social behavior is rooted in Japanese concerns about the social presentation of self. Other-centered group conformity puts the individual on stage at all times and transforms ordinary awkwardness into a more serious social or moral failing. In Western society, where individuality is emphasized, concern with the feelings of the other does not reach a comparable intensity and so does not promote the formation of rigid preoccupations with injuring or offending others. (Kirmayer, 1991, p. 24)

At a more general level, Good and Kleinman (1985) have noted that recognition of the cognitive component of most anxiety disorders leads one to expect many cross-cultural variations in the form that different anxiety disorders take. Anxiety disorders can be considered to be, at least in part, disorders of the interpretive process. Because cultures influence the categories and schemas that we use to interpret our symptoms of distress, there are bound to be significant differences in the form that anxiety disorders take in different cultures.

TREATMENTS AND OUTCOMES

The treatment of anxiety disorders may involve a wide range of goals and procedures. Treatment may be aimed at alleviating distressing symptoms such as generalized anxiety or panic, at changing a person's basically defensive and avoidant lifestyle, or both; it may include drug therapy or psychotherapy, or some combination of these approaches. Most people with anxiety disorders respond quite well to at least certain forms of treatment, although the prognosis may be less favorable when the person has comorbid depression or personality disorders. For present purposes, we shall keep our discussion brief and focused on the aspects of treatment that are particularly relevant to anxiety disorders. These therapies will be more thoroughly examined in Chapters 16 and 17.

Pharmacological (Drug) Therapies

"Psychopharmacological agents are the most widely prescribed, widely misprescribed, most frequently abused, and probably the most advertised of all the pharmaceuticals available to the practicing clinician. They clearly occupy a role at or near the center of medical practice" (Levenson, 1981, p. xi). This statement was made 15 years ago and unfortunately the situation is perhaps even worse today. Probably a majority of the misprescribed and abused drugs referred to here are those used in the treatment of anxiety disorders.

Many patients with anxiety disorders are seen by medical practitioners rather than by mental health professionals; they are seeking relief from their "nerves" or anxieties and/or their various functional (psychogenic) physical problems. Most often in such cases drugs from the benzodiazepine category such as Valium or Xanax are prescribed. These drugs (known as *minor tranquilizers* or *anxiolytics*) are used—and misused—for tension relief and for relaxation; they also reduce subjective anxiety and may reduce emotional reactivity to new stressors. People with anxiety disorders also frequently attempt to control their anxiety or other symptoms by self-medication with nonprescription drugs, especially alcohol.

Many patients with anxiety disorders (especially generalized anxiety disorder and panic disorder) show some symptom relief with anxiolytic therapy, and some are able to function more effectively. However, the effects are generally much smaller (when compared with the effects of placebo) than is generally recognized by the public. These drugs also tend to lose their effectiveness after several weeks (Barlow, 1988). Moreover, the anxiolytic drugs can also have quite undesirable side effects such as drowsiness and sedation, which lead to impaired cognitive and motor performance. Furthermore, not uncommonly a patient develops an increasing tolerance for and persistent dependence on a drug—these drugs have considerable addictive potential. Withdrawal from these drugs can be slow and difficult, and often precipitates relapse. With panic disorder, if the withdrawal is not done very gradually the patient is likely to experience what has been called "rebound panic," which may be worse than the original panic. In addition, many people expect too much of a treatment that merely reduces symptoms without affecting the underlying problem, and the masking of their symptoms may discourage them from seeking needed psychotherapy that may have more long-lasting effects.

Two other classes of drug that are useful in the treatment of panic disorder and agoraphobia are the tricyclic antidepressants and the monoamine oxidase inhibitors; they may also be useful in the treatment of generalized anxiety disorder (Barlow, 1988; Rickels et al., 1993). These drugs have both advantages and disadvantages when compared with anxiolytics. One major advantage is that they are not addictive. However, one disadvantage is that they take several weeks before they have any beneficial effects and so are not useful in the acute situation that a person having a panic attack or extreme anxiety may come to a doctor with. Troublesome side effects (such as dry mouth and blurred vision) can also be a serious problem with the antidepressants, in part because many of the side effects involve the creation of physical symptoms that patients with panic disorder fear. Thus, a large number of these patients refuse to take the drug or stop taking the drug because of the side effects (Barlow, 1988; Mavissakalian & Perel, 1989; Wolfe & Maser, 1994).

Psychopharmacological treatment of social phobia has also received some attention in the past decade. Although there have been some promising results with the use of beta-blockers such as Inderal, which help control peripheral autonomic arousal symptoms (Barlow, 1988), it appears that monoamine oxidase inhibitors are significantly more effective (Liebowitz et al., 1992).

Recently the drug Anafranil (clomipramine) has been approved for use in the United States as an effective biological treatment for obsessive-compulsive disorder (e.g., DeVeaugh-Geiss, 1991). It appears to reduce the intensity of this disorder's symptoms, with OCD patients showing a mean improvement of 40–45 percent (relative to 4–5 percent on placebo). Some patients may show greater improvement than this, but approximately 40 percent do not show significant improvement (Greist, 1990; McCarthy & Foa, 1990). In addition, some of the newer antidepressants that also affect serotonin activity, such as Prozac, have also been shown to be useful in the treatment of OCD (DeVeaugh-Geiss, 1991; Riggs & Foa, 1993).

A major disadvantage of all drug treatments for anxiety disorders is that relapse rates range from moderate to very high following discontinuation of the drug (see Clum, Clum, & Surls, 1993, for panic disorder). Thus many patients who do not seek alternative forms of psychotherapy that have more long-lasting benefits may have to stay on these drugs indefinitely given that most of the anxiety disorders tend to be chronic conditions if left untreated. This problem can often be overcome through combining drug and psychosocial treatments, with the goal being to withdraw patients from the drug after they have gained the skills from psychotherapy necessary to deal with their panic or anxiety symptoms directly.

Psychological Therapies

Traditional psychotherapies, behavior therapy, cognitive-behavior therapy, and multimodal therapy have all been used to treat anxiety disorders.

Traditional Psychotherapies In general, these therapies do not distinguish between the ways to treat the different anxiety disorders, which are still considered under the general rubric of neurotic disorders. Traditional psychotherapies are oriented toward helping clients achieve greater understanding of themselves, their problems, and their relationships, and toward helping clients develop healthier attitudes and better coping skills. The various types of therapy included in this general category differ somewhat in their specific goals and procedures—each reflecting the particular psychosocial perspective on which it is based—but all stress the need for self-understanding, a realistic frame of reference, a satisfying pattern of values, and the development of effective techniques for coping with adjustive demands. The psychodynamic approach is specifically directed at helping the patient uncover the repressed conflict that is thought to underlie the symptoms of the disorder; there is little if any focus on the symptoms themselves.

These objectives sound deceptively easy to achieve, but actually they share a number of stumbling blocks. First is the problem of creating a therapeutic situation in which anxious persons feel safe enough to lower their defenses; explore their innermost feelings, thoughts, and assumptions; and begin to recognize the possibility of other options. Second is the problem of providing opportunities for anxious persons to learn new ways of perceiving themselves and their world, and to see new ways of coping. Third is the problem of helping them transfer what they have learned in therapy to real life. Even when they understand the nature and causes of their self-defeating behavior and have learned that more effective coping techniques are available, they may still have difficulty confronting the situations they have avoided. Freud was among the first to recognize the importance of this in noting that at a certain point the analyst must encourage patients to confront the situations they have been avoiding. Fourth is the problem of changing the conditions in their life situations that may be reinforcing and thus maintaining the problem behavior. For example, a domineering and egocentric husband who will not participate in a therapy program may tend to block his wife's efforts toward self-direction and make it more difficult for her to give up her anxious and avoidant behavior. He may even manage to sabotage the entire treatment program.

Although traditional psychodynamic psychotherapy may be useful in treating many of the general life problems that a person with an anxiety disorder may have, it does not have an impressive record for helping reduce the prominent symptoms of the anxiety disorder itself. For example, there is no clear documented efficacy of psychodynamic psychotherapy for the treatment of panic attacks or agoraphobia (Wolfe & Maser, 1994), or for obsessive-compulsive disorder.

Behavior and Cognitive-Behavior Therapies As we have seen, behavior therapies focus on (a) removing specific symptoms or maladaptive behaviors, (b) developing needed competencies and adaptive behaviors, and (c) modifying environmental conditions that may be reinforcing and maintaining maladaptive behaviors. In general, behavior therapy approaches have an excellent record of efficacy in the treatment of anxiety disorders (Barlow, 1988, 1993; Marks, 1987; McNally, 1994).

The behavior therapy most commonly used in the treatment of many anxiety disorders involves controlled *exposure* to anxiety-producing circumstances. Here clients are gradually placed—symbolically or increasingly under "real life" conditions—in those situations they find most threatening. In the

During exposure therapy for phobias, the therapist may guide the client through various anxiety-provoking exercises. Here someone with claustrophobia and a fear of heights is being coaxed up a stairway by the therapist.

variant known as *systematic desensitization,* patients are first trained in the techniques of deep muscle relaxation and asked to develop a hierarchy of situations they fear, ranging at the bottom from only mildly anxiety-provoking to the top at maximally fear-provoking. Then, while remaining in a state of relaxation, they are asked to imagine their fear-producing situations, starting with those lowest in a hierarchy and gradually moving up the hierarchy as the fear of the scenes lower in the hierarchy extinguishes (Wolpe, 1958, 1988; O'Leary & Wilson, 1987).

Other more efficient forms of treatment involving graded exposure to fear-producing stimuli do not rely on the use of relaxation or imaginal exposure but rather on encouraging patients to expose themselves (either with the aid of a therapist or friend, or alone) to their actual feared situations for long enough periods of time that their anxiety begins to subside. This enables them to learn that these situations are not as frightening as they had thought and that their anxiety, albeit unpleasant, is not harmful and will gradually dissipate (Foa & Kozak, 1986).

Exposure-based treatments are the treatment of choice for specific phobias (Butler, 1989; Marks, 1987) and form a core part of most behavioral treatments for agoraphobia (Craske & Barlow, 1993), social phobia (Hope & Heimberg, 1993), and OCD. With OCD, a combination of exposure and (compulsive) response prevention, illustrated in HIGHLIGHT 5.3 on page 187, may be the most effective approach to the difficult problem of obsessive-compulsive disorders (Riggs & Foa, 1993). In addition, Klosko and colleagues (1990) have recently shown that a particular behavior therapy program emphasizing exposure is significantly superior to antianxiety medication in the treatment of panic disorder. This treatment for panic disorder includes a new variant on exposure known as *interoceptive exposure*. Given the prominent fears that people with panic disorder have of their bodily sensations, the idea is that fear of these internal sensations should be treated in the same way that fear of external situations is treated—namely, through prolonged exposure to those internal sensations so that the fear may extinguish. Thus, panic patients are asked to do a variety of exercises (such as hyperventilating, shaking their head from side to side, running in place, holding their breath, etc.) that bring on physical sensations they may fear. Whichever exercises bring on the symptoms that most resemble the symptoms they experience during panic are then targeted for practice so that extinction of the anxiety that accompanies these physical sensations may occur.

As noted in Chapter 3, in recent years many behavior therapists have been adding *cognitive* therapy techniques to their repertoire for the treatment of their patients with anxiety disorders. As we have seen, many people who have an anxiety disorder may be viewed as behaving anxiously in response to internal thoughts and beliefs (cognitions). Here a therapist attempts to help clients identify their underlying automatic thoughts, which are often irrational and generally involve discrete predictions about frightening or dangerous things that may happen to them. After helping clients understand that these automatic thoughts often involve cognitive distortions, the therapist then helps the clients change these inner thoughts and beliefs through logical reanalysis. Although these techniques were first developed by Beck for the treatment of depression, they have now been successfully applied to the treatment of panic disorder, social phobia, and generalized anxiety disorder (Barlow, 1993; Hollon & Beck, 1994). Adding a cognitive therapy component to the already established behavioral treatments of these three disorders seems to enhance treatment

efficacy. By contrast, it does not seem to enhance the efficacy of exposure treatments for specific phobias or OCD. HIGHLIGHT 5.4 illustrates one kind of cognitve-behavioral treatment approach for panic disorder. We will discuss cognitive-behavior therapy in more detail in Chapter 17.

Although behavior therapy is usually directed toward changing specific "target behaviors"—such as removing phobias—it often seems to have more far-reaching positive results (Barlow, 1988, 1993; Marks, 1987). For example, a client who overcomes a specific phobia may gain confidence in his or her ability to overcome other problems. Ultimately, the person learns that coping effectively with adjustive demands is more rewarding than trying to avoid them. Cognitive-behavioral therapies that focus on modifying a patient's internal cognitions as well as behavior also have far-reaching positive results.

Multimodal Therapy As this term, coined by Lazarus (1981, 1985), implies, a combination of varied approaches may be used in the treatment of clients with an anxiety disorder. In fact increasing evidence (see, for example, Goldfried, 1980; Goldfried & Safran, 1986) shows that professional therapists are lessening their strong allegiances to particular therapies and are increasingly willing to learn and to employ techniques they formerly criticized. For example, a therapist could use an interpersonal therapeutic strategy to defeat a client's maladaptive style of interacting with others while employing behavior therapy techniques such as exposure to eradicate phobic avoidance behavior. In our judgment, this "ecumenical" trend in psychosocial treatment represents a maturing of the field, and we strongly applaud it.

No matter which therapeutic techniques are employed, it often requires a great deal of courage and persistence of a person with an anxiety disorder to face problems realistically and give up the avoidant lifestyle that has helped alleviate feelings of inadequacy, anxiety, and even stark terror. For some, this seems too great a task, and they present themselves in such a way as to put the whole responsibility for their immediate well-being and happiness on their therapists. Moreover, they may be unwilling to practice the exercises that are necessary to overcome their anxiety and avoidance behavior. For these people, drug therapy that reduces anxiety symptoms may be the only recourse.

Despite the difficulties involved, however, powerful forces are aligned on the side of psychotherapy. For one thing, anxious persons who seek help are usually experiencing considerable inner distress, so they are motivated to change. When helped, in a supportive environment, to understand current ways

Cognitive-Behavior Therapy for Panic Disorder

The cognitive model of panic disorder has been responsible for the formulation of a new treatment that has been shown to be highly effective in over a dozen different studies in at least four countries (Wolfe & Maser, 1994). Although the treatments used in the different research studies vary somewhat, there are many common threads that identify each as a form of cognitive-behavior therapy. In one version of the treatment used at a panic disorder treatment clinic co-directed by one of the authors, a 14-session treatment format is used (modified from Barlow & Cerny, 1988).

There are three aspects to the treatment. First, clients are taught about the cognitive model of panic through the use of numerous examples from their own experiences with panic, as well as the experiences of other people with the disorder. Through learning about the panic circle (Figure 5.2, p. 174), they come to see how their tendency to catastrophize about the meaning of their bodily sensations is likely to spiral initially low levels of anxiety into full-blown panic. Over the first three or four sessions clients are taught to identify their own automatic thoughts during panic attacks, as well as during anxiety-provoking situations. They are then taught about the logical errors that people who have panic are prone to making and to subject their own automatic thoughts to a logical reanalysis. For example, a person who fears having a heart attack is asked at the first sign of heart palpitations to examine the *evidence* that this might be true (e.g., when did the doctor last tell him that his heart was perfectly healthy?), and what the *likelihood* is of having a heart attack at age 30, etc. Alternatively, if someone is afraid of making a fool of herself in a restaurant if she has a panic attack and has to leave, she is asked not only to evaluate the

evidence that her friends would think this made her look foolish, but also to examine her *standards* for her own behavior and whether they are higher than the standards she has for other people (e.g., would *she* think other people were foolish if they had to leave a restaurant during a panic attack?), as well as whether she is engaging in *all-or-none* thinking (e.g., her friends might be concerned about her without thinking she was a fool).

In later sessions the cognitive part of the treatment is focused on teaching people how to *decatastrophize,* that is, to learn how to think through what the worst possible outcome might be if they did have a panic attack (e.g., if they had a panic attack while driving they might have to pull their car over to the side of the road until the attack subsided). Usually once they learn to decatastrophize, the entire experience of panic becomes less terrifying, although still quite unpleasant (and no attempts are made to decatastrophize death!).

The second part of the treatment involves teaching people with panic disorder two techniques that lower their overall level of physical arousal and tension. This includes training in deep muscle relaxation, followed by training in how to breathe from the diaphragm. By learning how to relax they reduce the number of physical symptoms of anxiety from which panic attacks tend to spiral. The breathing retraining is important not only as a relaxation tool, but also because many people with panic disorder have a chronic tendency to *hyperventilate* (to overbreathe, which is adaptive during exercise but not at other times). Hyperventilation is known to create a variety of unpleasant physical sensations such as lightheadedness, dizziness, and tightness of the chest, which often occur during panic at-

tacks. (You can see this for yourself by breathing very fast and deeply for 1–2 minutes.) By learning how to counteract this tendency to hyperventilate, these clients have a new coping tool to use that will reduce the likelihood that they are themselves creating some of the symptoms they are so frightened of.

The third part of the treatment involves exposure to feared situations and feared bodily sensations. Because of the importance of interoceptive fears (fears of bodily sensations), clients are asked to do a variety of exercises with the therapist that bring on different bodily sensations. These include hyperventilating, breathing through a straw, shaking one's head from side to side, jogging in place, holding one's breath for a minute, etc. After each exercise, clients describe the sensations produced, how similar these sensations are to those that they experience during panic, and how scary those sensations are. Whichever exercises produce symptoms most similar to their own during panic attacks are targeted for practice. The idea is that if clients practice these exercises, their anxiety about these sensations will gradually extinguish. Moreover, they will also learn a sense of control over producing the sensations, which may help reduce the anxiety the sensations create when they appear to come out of the blue. Finally, clients who also have extensive agoraphobic avoidance begin by about session 9 to expose themselves to their feared situations for long enough so that their anxiety comes down. This part of the treatment is delayed until this point so that clients have a variety of coping skills (cognitive techniques, and relaxation and breathing skills) that should help them deal better with these feared situations than they have been able to do in the past.

One variation on exposure therapy is called participant modeling. Here the therapist models how to touch and pick up a live tarantula and encourages the spider-phobic client to imitate her behavior. This treatment is graduated, with the client's first task being simply to touch the tarantula from the outside of the cage, then to touch the tarantula with a stick, then with a gloved hand, then with a bare hand, and finally to let the tarantula crawl over his hand. This is a highly effective treatment, with most spider-phobic clients being able to reach the top of the hierarchy within 60 to 90 minutes.

of viewing their problems and to learn more effective and satisfying ways of coping with them, they usually find the courage to see it through. Although outcomes vary considerably, it appears that from 70 to 90 percent of the people who receive appropriate kinds of help for their anxiety disorder obtain substantial benefit from it (Barlow, 1993).

UNRESOLVED ISSUES

on the Anxiety Disorders

As we have seen, research on the anxiety disorders has expanded at a rapid pace since they became a separate category of disorder 15 years ago in DSM-III (1980). Progress had been relatively slow until that point in part because of the lumping together of the anxiety disorders with the other "neurotic" disorders. This tended to blur the distinctions among the different anxiety disorders discussed in this chapter, as well as the distinctions of these disor-

ders from the other so-called neurotic disorders (to be discussed in Chapters 6 and 7). Many of the advances in our understanding of anxiety disorders that have occurred since 1980 have been made by biological psychiatrists and psychologists who search for the genetic vulnerabilities, as well as for the biochemical and structural abnormalities, that underlie them. Progress in understanding the neurobiology of the anxiety disorders has occurred in parallel with increased understanding of which drug therapies are most effective in treating them. This is because insights derived from neurobiology often lead to new ideas for drugs that may work, and new findings about drugs that are effective often provide new insights about what the neurobiology of a disorder may be.

Over the same time period many other advances have been made by cognitive and behaviorally oriented psychologists and psychiatrists who search for the psychological vulnerabilities and causes of anxiety disorders. Progress in understanding the cognitive and behavioral factors involved has also occurred in parallel with increased understanding of how best to treat anxiety disorders with cognitive and behavioral therapies. Again, research in this area is a two-way street, with findings about the psychopathology of the disorders giving new insights into possible new effective treatments and vice versa.

What is unfortunate is that these two different lines of research have so often proceeded along relatively independent and unrelated paths. All too often these approaches are pitted against each another as if a disorder has either biological *or* psychological causes, or as if drugs *or* psychotherapeutic treatments always constitute the best approach. Clearly this is not generally the case with most forms of psychopathology. As discussed in Chapter 3, all of our cognitions and behaviors are ultimately reducible to a set of biological events occurring in the brain. What we need to understand is how the events occurring at one level of analysis (cognitive or behavioral) affect events occurring at another level of analysis (physiological) and vice versa. Adding another layer of complexity, we also need to examine the sociocultural context in which disorders arise and how this can affect the way in which the disorder manifests itself. This is important because there certainly seem to be more cultural variations in the manifestations of disorders such as the anxiety disorders than probably exist for most medical disorders such as pneumonia, colds, or cancer. This leads us to the importance of developing a coherent *biopsychosocial* approach to understanding these disorders. Yet progress in this regard for anxiety disorders has been minimal.

What are the impediments to this kind of progress? Some seem to stem simply from difficulties mental health professionals with the different orientations have in communicating with one another because of lack of knowledge and understanding of other approaches. For most psychologists reading and understanding the research reports regarding the neurobiology of these disorders is a difficult task because of their relative lack of knowledge of neuroscience—a field that is advancing at a rapid rate. And for many neuroscientists and biological psychiatrists, reading and understanding the research reports regarding cognitive and behavioral factors associated with these disorders is also difficult because of their lack of training in these areas. But lack of knowledge is not the only, or necessarily even the major impediment to progress in developing a biopsychosocial approach to understanding these disorders. Many of the problems stem from the fact that many of these mental health professionals are simply entrenched in their beliefs about the superiority of one approach relative to the other. Yet there is hope that this situation may change. Today

there are more interdisciplinary research teams consisting of people trained in all of these perspectives than there ever been in the past. They are working on both the psychopathology and the treatment of anxiety disorders. The work of such interdisciplinary teams will be critical to the advancement of a biopsychosocial integrative perspective on these disorders.

SUMMARY

This chapter has been concerned with maladaptive behavior patterns that appear to have anxiety or panic or both at their core. Formerly the anxiety disorders were officially a subset of the neuroses, but recent versions of the DSM-III and DSM-IV have largely abandoned this term. Fear or panic is a basic emotion that involves activation of the fight-or-flight response of the autonomic nervous system. Anxiety is a more diffuse blend of emotions that includes high levels of negative affect, worry about possible threat or danger, and sense of being unable to predict threat or control it if it occurs. Although we all have identifiable, rational, realistic sources of anxieties at times, people with anxiety disorders, by definition, have irrational sources of, and unrealistic levels of, anxiety.

As we have seen, anxiety and panic are each associated with a number of distinct anxiety disorder syndromes. With specific phobias, there is an intense and irrational fear of specific objects or situations; when confronted with a feared object, the phobic person often shows activation of the fight-or-flight response also associated with panic. In social phobia, a person has disabling fears of one or more social situations usually because of fears of negative evaluation by others or of acting in an embarrassing or humiliating manner; in some cases a social phobic may actually experience panic attacks in social situations. In panic disorder, a person experiences unexpected panic attacks that often create a sense of stark terror, which usually subsides in a matter of minutes. Many people who experience panic attacks develop anxious apprehension about experiencing another one because the attacks can be so terrifying. Many also develop agoraphobic avoidance of situations in which they fear that they might have an attack and would find it difficult to escape or would be especially embarrassed. In cases of severe agoraphobia the person may become housebound except perhaps when accompanied by a spouse or trusted companion. In generalized anxiety disorder a person has chronic and excessively high levels of worry about a number of events or activities, and responds to stress with high levels of psychic and muscle tension. In obsessive-compulsive disorder a person experiences unwanted and intrusive distressing thoughts or images that are usually accompanied by compulsive behaviors designed to neutralize those thoughts or images. Checking and cleaning rituals are most common.

Many of the sources of fear and anxiety are believed to be acquired through conditioning or other learning mechanisms, although some people are more constitutionally predisposed to acquire such responses than are others. Specific phobias do not tend to occur to a random or arbitrary group of objects or situations associated with trauma. Instead, we seem to have a biologically based preparedness to acquire fears of objects or situations that posed a threat to our early ancestors. For social phobias we also seem to have an evolutionarily based predisposition to acquire fears of social stimuli signaling dominance and aggression from other humans, including facial expressions of anger or contempt. Social phobics are also preoccupied with negative self-evaluative thoughts that tend to interfere with their ability to interact in a socially skillful fashion. For panic disorder one prominent theory is that this condition may develop in people who have panic attacks if they are prone to making catastrophic misinterpretations of their bodily sensations. Other biological theories of panic disorder emphasize that the disorder may result from biochemical abnormalities in the brains of people with the disorder; abnormal activity of the neurotransmitter norepinephrine in the brain area called the locus coeruleus may play a causal role in panic attacks. Generalized anxiety disorder may occur in people who have had extensive experience with unpredictable and/or uncontrollable life events. In addition, people with generalized anxiety seem to have schemas about how to cope with strange and dangerous situations that promote automatic thoughts focused on possible threats. The neurobiological factors implicated in generalized anxiety are a functional deficiency in the neurotransmitter GABA, which is involved in inhibiting anxiety in stressful situations; the limbic system is the brain area most involved. Thus different neurotransmitters and brain areas are involved in panic attacks and generalized anxiety. Biological causal factors are clearly involved in obsessive-compulsive disorder, with evidence coming from genetic studies, studies of structural brain functioning, and psychopharmacological studies. Once this disorder begins, the anxiety-reducing qualities of the compulsive behaviors may help to maintain the disorder. For all the anxiety disorders, once a person has the disorder, mood-congruent information processing, such as attentional and interpretive biases, seems to help maintain them.

Many people with anxiety disorders are treated by physicians, often with drugs designed to allay anxiety. Such treatment focuses on suppressing the symptoms, and it is not without dangers. A number of alternative means of achieving anxiety reduction are available. In general, psychosocial treatments (especially the cognitive and behavioral therapies) have a very good track record with the anxiety disorders. Behavior therapies focus on prolonged exposure to feared situations to allow fear or anxiety to habituate; with obsessive-compulsive disorder the rituals also must be prevented following exposure to the feared situations. Cognitive therapies focus on getting clients to understand their underlying automatic thoughts, which often involve cognitive distortions such as unrealistic predictions of catastrophes that in reality are very unlikely to occur. Once clients can identify these automatic thoughts, therapy focuses on helping them change these inner thoughts and beliefs through a process of logical reanalysis known as cognitive restructuring.

 ## KEY TERMS

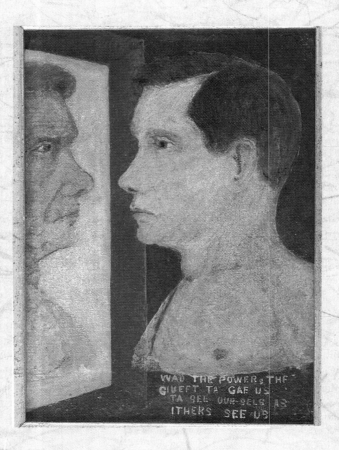

WHAD THE POWER THE
GIUEFT TA GAE US
TA SEE OUR SELS AS
ITHERS SEE US

MOOD DISORDERS AND SUICIDE

John Kane, Seen in the Mirror. Kane (1860–1934) was born in Scotland and moved to the United States in 1879. He traveled and worked as a laborer until he lost a leg in an accident, thereafter settling in Pittsburgh. Kane married and had three children, but after his youngest child died he became despondent and withdrew from his family. Obtaining work painting freight cars, he began to paint his own images on the sides of cars. He continued painting and eventually had some recognition as an artist before his death from tuberculosis in 1934.

Mood disorders have as their most prominent features disturbances of mood that are intense and persistent enough to be clearly maladaptive. Consider the following case:

A prominent businesswoman in her middle years, noted for her energy and productivity, was unexpectedly deserted by her husband for a younger woman. Following her initial shock and rage, she began to have uncontrollable weeping spells and doubts about her business acumen. Decision making became an ordeal. Her spirits rapidly worsened, and she began to spend more and more time in bed, refusing to deal with anyone. Her alcohol consumption increased to the point that she was seldom entirely sober. Within a period of weeks, serious financial losses were incurred owing to her inability, or refusal, to keep her affairs in order. She felt she was a "total failure," a self-attribution that was entirely resistant to alteration by a review of her considerable achievements; indeed, her self-criticism gradually spread to all aspects of her life and her personal history. Finally, members of her family, having become alarmed, essentially forced her to accept an appointment with a clinical psychologist.

How was the psychologist to deal with this situation? Was something "wrong" with the woman, or was she merely experiencing normal human emotions due to her husband's departure? The psychologist concluded that the woman was suffering from a mood disorder and initiated treatment. The diagnosis, based on the severity of the symptoms and the degree of impairment, was major depressive disorder.

When significant mood change brings about behavior that seriously endangers a person's welfare, psychologists and other mental health professionals conclude that the person has a mood disorder. Mood disorders are diverse in nature, as is illustrated by the many types of depression recognized in the DSM-IV, listed in HIGHLIGHT 6.1. Nevertheless, in all mood disorders (formerly called affective disorders), extremes of emotion or *affect*—soaring elation or deep depression—dominate the

Varieties of Depression According to DSM-IV

	Diagnosis	Main Features
Unipolar Disorders	**Dysthymia**	For at least the past two years, the person has been bothered for most of the day, for more days than not, by a depressed mood, and at least two other depressive symptoms, but not of sufficient persistence or severity to meet the criteria for major depression. The person cannot have had any manic or hypomanic episodes.
	Adjustment disorder with depressed mood	The person reacts with a maladaptively depressed mood to some identifiable stressor occurring within the past three months. Symptoms stemming from bereavement do not qualify. Once the stressor has terminated, the symptoms must remit within six months.
	Major depressive disorder	The person has one or more major depressive episodes in the absence of any manic or hypomanic episodes. Symptoms of a major depressive episode include prominent and persistent depressed mood or loss of pleasure for at least two weeks, accompanied by four or more symptoms such as poor appetite, insomnia, psychomotor retardation, fatigue, feelings of worthlessness or guilt, inability to concentrate, and thoughts of death or suicide.
Bipolar Disorders	**Cyclothymia, depressed**	At present or during the past two years, the person has experienced episodes resembling dysthymia, but also has had one or more periods of hypomania—characterized by elevated, expansive, or irritable mood not of psychotic proportions.
	Bipolar I disorder, depressed	The person experiences a major depressive episode (as in major depressive disorder) and has had one or more manic episodes.
	Bipolar II disorder, depressed	The person experiences a major depressive episode and has had one or more hypomanic episodes.
Other Mood Disorders	**Mood disorder due to a general medical condition**	The person has notably depressed mood, including symptoms associated with major depression, whose primary cause is considered to be the direct physiological effects of a general medical condition. The medical conditions include degenerative neurological conditions such as Parkinson's disease, stroke, various metabolic and endocrine conditions, viral infections (including HIV), and certain cancers.
	Substance-induced mood disorder	The person has a prominent and persistent depression that is judged to be due to the direct physiological effects of some drug. The drug may be a drug of abuse, or a medication. The depression may occur in association with intoxication by the drug, or in association with withdrawal from the drug.

clinical picture. Other symptoms are also present, but the abnormal mood is the defining feature.

The two key states of mood disorder are **mania,** characterized by intense and unrealistic feelings of excitement and euphoria, and **depression,** which involves feelings of extraordinary sadness and dejection. These states are often conceived to be at opposite ends of a mood continuum, with normal mood in the middle. Although this concept is accurate to a degree, it cannot explain every instance of mood disorder, because in rare cases a patient may have symptoms of mania and depression at the same time. In these rare cases, the person experiences rapidly alternating moods such as sadness, euphoria, and irritability, all within the same episode of illness.

Our discussion will be organized around the distinction between unipolar and bipolar forms of the mood disorders. In the **unipolar** form of disorder, which is much more frequent, the person experiences only depressive episodes. In the **bipolar** form of disorder, the person experiences both manic and depressive episodes. This distinction is prominent in DSM-IV, and although the unipolar and bipolar forms of mood disorder may not be wholly separate and distinct, there are sufficient differences in symptoms, causal factors, and treatments that it is useful to make this distinction. It is also customary to differentiate the mood disorders by (a) *severity*—the number of dysfunctions experienced in various areas of living and the relative degree of impairment evidenced in those areas; and (b) *duration*—whether the disorder is acute, chronic, or intermittent (with periods of relatively normal functioning between the episodes of disorder). The following discussion reflects these customary divisions that are seen in the DSM-IV categories.

Within each of these general categories of unipolar and bipolar disorders, our discussion will start with the milder mood disturbances. From there, we will move to disorders in which a person's functioning is moderately to severely impaired. Research suggests that we can conceive of mild mood disturbances as being largely on the same continuum, at least at the clinical level (what we can actually observe), as the more severe disorders on which this chapter will focus. The differences seem chiefly to be of degree, not of kind, a conclusion supported in several recent reviews of the evidence (Free & Oei, 1989; Vredenburg, Flett, & Krames, 1993; Watson et al., 1995b). At some point along this continuum, however, as we encounter more extreme or even psychotic symptoms (such as delusions), significant biological changes often occur, sometimes rendering a person less amenable to psychological treatment.

Mild depressions are so much a part of our lives that incidence and prevalence figures for them would be difficult to estimate and would probably be meaningless anyway. But major mood disorders also occur with alarming frequency—at least ten times more frequently than schizophrenia, for example, and at about the same rate as the anxiety disorders taken together. Of the two types of serious mood disorders, *unipolar major depression* is much more frequent, and its occurrence has apparently increased in recent years (Lewinsohn et al., 1993). The most recent results from the National Comorbidity Survey (Kessler et al., 1994) found lifetime prevalence rates of major depression for males at nearly 13 percent, and lifetime prevalence rates for females at 21 percent (12-month prevalence rates were nearly 8 percent for men and nearly 13 percent for women). These figures illustrate the nearly universal observation that unipolar depression is much more common in women than in men; this difference is similar to the sex differences for many anxiety disorders (see Chapter 5). The issue of sex differences in unipolar depression will be discussed in detail later in the chapter. The other type of mood disorder, *bipolar disorder* (in which both manic and depressive episodes occur), is much less common. Estimates of lifetime risk range from 0.4–1.6 percent, and there is no discernible difference in the prevalence rates between sexes. Similar rates were found in the recent National Comorbidity Survey (Kessler et al., 1994).

Although most mood disorder cases occur during early and middle adulthood, such reactions may occur anytime from early childhood to old age. For example, in a recent study Sorenson, Rutter, and Aneshensel (1991) found that about one-quarter of adults reported the first onset of unipolar depression in childhood or adolescence. Depression was once thought not to occur in childhood, but we now know that this is not the case. Although relatively rare, major depressions have been observed in preadolescent youngsters (Puig-Antich et al., 1985, 1989), with estimates that about 2 percent of school age children meet criteria for some form of unipolar disorder (see Gotlib & Hammen, 1992). Even infants may experience a form of depression (commonly known as anaclitic depression or despair) if they are separated for a prolonged period from their attachment figure (usually their mother) (Bowlby, 1973, 1980). Although there is not universal agreement about whether this is simply a "normal" depressive response to loss, Bowlby (1980) has made a persuasive case that this form of depression observed in infants is at least a "prototype" for depression seen in adulthood. Although significant depressions do occur in infancy and childhood, the incidence of depression rises sharply during adolescence—a period of great turmoil for many people. It is also during this time period that sex differences in rates of depression first emerge (Nolen-Hoeksema, 1990). (See Chapter 14 for further discussion of childhood and adolescent depression.)

Suicide is a distressingly frequent outcome (and always a potential outcome) of significant depressions, both unipolar and bipolar. In fact, depressive episodes are undoubtedly the most common of the predisposing causes leading to suicide. The latter part of this chapter includes a discussion of the causes and prevention of suicide.

UNIPOLAR MOOD DISORDERS

Sadness, discouragement, pessimism, and hopelessness about being able to improve matters are familiar feelings to most people. Depression is unpleasant when we are in it, but it usually does not last long. Sometimes it seems almost to be self-limiting, turning off after a period or after it has reached a certain intensity level. Sometimes we may experience it as having been in some sense useful: We were stuck, and now we can move on; what bothered us was easier to get out of than we thought it could be, and our new perspective may offer new possibilities.

This scenario contains hints that may be significant to our understanding of depression generally. For example, that mild depression may actually be adaptive in the long run; that much of the "work" of depression seems to involve facing images, thoughts, and feelings that one would normally avoid; and that depression may sometimes be self-limiting. These considerations suggest that the capacity to experience depression may be normal—even desirable—if the depression is brief and mild. They also suggest the idea of normal depressions—depressions we would expect to occur in anyone undergoing painful but common life events, such as significant personal, interpersonal, or economic losses.

Normal Depression

Normal depressions are almost always the result of recent stress. In fact, some depressions are considered adjustment disorders (those that develop in response to stressors) rather than mood disorders. We discuss such reactions here because such sharp demarcations may not be justified. Indeed, many depressions meeting criteria as "major" are also clearly related to the prior occurrence of stress (Brown & Harris, 1978; Gotlib & Hammen, 1992; Harder et al., 1989; Hirschfeld et al., 1985; Monroe & Simons, 1991; Shrout et al., 1989; Winokur, 1985). We will consider some of the milder forms of normal depression in the following sections.

Grief and the Grieving Process We usually think of grief as the psychological process one goes through following the death of a loved one—a process that appears to be more damaging for men than women (Stroebe & Stroebe, 1983). Although this may be the most common and intense cause of grieving, many other types of loss will give rise to a similar state. Loss of a favored status or position, separation or divorce, financial loss, the breakup of a romantic affair, retirement, separation from a friend, absence from home for the first time, or even the loss of a cherished pet may all give rise to symptoms of acute grief.

Whatever its source, grief has certain characteristic qualities. Indeed, Bowlby (1980) has observed that there are usually four phases of response to the loss of a spouse or close family member: (a) a phase of numbing and disbelief that may last from a few hours to a week and which may be interrupted by outbursts of intense distress, panic, or anger; (b) a phase of yearning and searching for the dead person, which may last for months or occasionally for years; (c) a phase of disorganization and despair; and finally (d) a phase of some level of reorganization. In the second phase (which resembles anxiety more than depression), the grieving person may show great restlessness, insomnia, and preoccupation with the dead person; anger is also very common in this phase and is entirely normal. The intensity of the yearning and search gradually diminishes. The third phase of despair sets in when the person finally accepts the loss as permanent and finds it is necessary to discard old patterns of thinking, feeling, and acting, including establishing a new identity (e.g., as a widow or widower). During this phase the person may meet the criteria for a major depression. Gradually, however, most people pass into the fourth phase and begin to rebuild their lives. The ability to respond to the external world is gradually regained, sadness abates, zest returns, and a person emerges into a more productive engagement with the challenges of life. This is the *normal* pattern. Clayton (1982) estimated that the process of grieving following bereavement is normally completed within one year. Some people, however, become stuck somewhere in the middle of the sequence, and if depressive symptoms persist beyond the first year after loss, therapeutic intervention may be called for.

Ignoring for the moment such potential complications, it is easy to see grief as having an adaptive

We usually think of grief as the psychological process a person goes through following the death of a loved one. We see here a man grieving at his wife's grave. Grief may accompany other types of loss as well, including separation or divorce, or loss of a pet.

function (Bowlby, 1980). In fact, the lack of grief under conditions in which it seems warranted would generally be of concern. On the other hand, as we will discuss in Chapter 8, a prolonged sense of hopelessness may endanger physical health, and eventual recovery and resolution following loss is not a guaranteed outcome (Wortman & Silver, 1989).

Other Normal Mood Variations Many situations other than obvious loss can provoke depressive feelings, and as we will see, some people seem especially prone to develop depression. It is a common observation, for example, that some doctoral candidates become depressed after completing their final oral exams. Other kinds of "success" depressions have also been observed following election to public office after a difficult campaign, and in successful novelists and actors.

A seemingly similar phenomenon is the so-called postpartum depression of some new mothers (and sometimes fathers) on the birth of a child. Until recently, it was believed that postpartum depression was a relatively common form of clinical depression (i.e., not a normal mood variation). However, recent evidence suggests that some depressive feelings

in the postpartum period are within the normal range of mood variation. O'Hara and colleagues (1990, 1991) conducted an important prospective study on this topic in which nearly 200 pregnant women, each with a matched partner who was one of their nonpregnant close friends, were followed for nine weeks following delivery. O'Hara and colleagues (1990) found that as many as 42 percent of the pregnant women experienced at least a mild attack of "the blues" following childbirth (similar to the 50 percent rate observed by Pitt [1982]), while only about 10 percent of their nonpregnant matched friends showed a similar mood state. By contrast, the two groups did not differ significantly in their rates of clinically diagnosable major or minor depression, and these rates of diagnosable clinical depression were in the range of the one-month prevalence rates reported from epidemiological studies. So although postpartum blues are common, the once firmly held notion that women were at especially high risk for significant depression in the postpartum was not upheld. Gotlib and colleagues (1989) reached similar conclusions, and in a recent review Whiffen (1992) concluded that postpartum depression is best understood as an adjustment disorder because it tends to be relatively mild and is resolved rather quickly.

Hormonal readjustments may play a role in postpartum blues and depression, although the evidence on this issue is mixed (O'Hara et al., 1991). It is obvious that a psychological component is present as well: Postpartum blues or depression may reflect a letdown after sustained effort and anticipation; or perhaps a new mother's expectations had failed to include the more challenging and sometimes seemingly overwhelming aspects of infant care and dependency, leading to depression rather than to joy; or the woman may be feeling loss—that is, missing the constant companion in the womb who is now a separate entity.

Many students also experience mild or serious depression during their college years of supposed freedom and carefree personal growth. Normal depressions among college students were studied by Blatt, D'Afflitti, and Quinlan (1976) in an effort to determine the basic dimensions of the experience. In brief, they found that depression was similar for males and females, and that it mainly involved three psychological variables: (a) dependency, the sense that one is in dire need of help and support from others; (b) self-criticism, the tendency to exaggerate one's faults and to engage in self-devaluation; and (c) inefficacy, the sense that important events in the world are happening independent of—not contingent on—one's own actions or efforts.

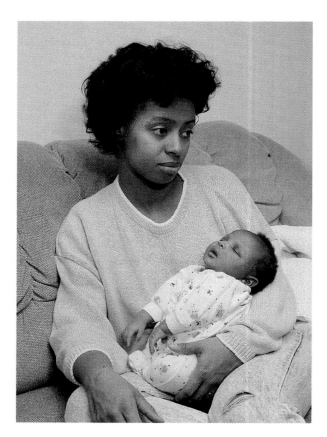

Many women experience postpartum "blues" following the birth of a child, but these depressive symptoms do not usually reach the severity required for a diagnosis of major depression. It is now understood that the experience of clinically significant postpartum depression is much less common than it was once thought to be.

Mild to Moderate Depressive Disorders

The point at which mood disturbance becomes mood disorder is a matter of clinical judgment. Unfortunately, although criteria exist for exercising this judgment, they are not precise enough for complete consensus among different clinicians. Even if criteria permitted a sharp demarcation, they might not meet the requirement of validity—in other words, they might not actually reflect a meaningful point of transition between clinical and nonclinical depression. Although severe mood disorders are obviously abnormal, a gray area exists where a distinction between normal and abnormal is difficult to establish.

DSM-IV includes two main categories for depressions of mild to moderate severity: dysthymia and adjustment disorder with depressed mood. These are both considered in the following sections.

Dysthymia To qualify for a diagnosis of **dysthymia,** a person must have a persistently depressed mood, more days than not, for at least two years. In addition, dysthymics must have at least two of the following six symptoms when depressed: poor appetite or overeating, sleep disturbance, low energy level, low self-esteem, difficulties in concentration or decision making, and feelings of hopelessness. That is, they experience moderate, nonpsychotic levels of depression over a chronic period of at least two years (one year for children and adolescents). Normal moods may briefly intercede, but they last at most from a few days to a few weeks. Indeed, this quality of intermittently normal moods seems to be the primary characteristic distinguishing dysthymia from major depression in that the average number of symptoms endorsed by patients from the two categories do not appear to differ (Klein, Riso, & Anderson, 1993). Thus, dysthymics do not really show less severe symptoms than do major depressives; the difference is simply that the dysthymics do not necessarily have the symptoms every day. No identifiable precipitating event or condition need be present, although such circumstances are frequently observed for depressions of this general type. Indeed, a dysthymic person may elicit reactions from the social environment that will bring about "bad" feelings on a continuous basis (Strack & Coyne, 1983). The following case, which includes obvious self-sustaining features, is typical of this disorder:

A 28-year-old junior executive was referred by a senior psychoanalyst for "supportive" treatment. She had obtained a master's degree in business administration and moved to California a year and a half earlier to begin work in a large firm. She complained of being "depressed" about everything: her job, her husband, and her prospects for the future.

She had previously had extensive psychotherapy. She had seen an "analyst" twice a week for three years while in college, and a "behaviorist" for a year and a half while in graduate school. Her complaints were of persistent feelings of depressed mood, inferiority, and pessimism, which she claims to have had since she was 16 or 17 years old. Although she did reasonably well in college, she constantly ruminated about those students who were "genuinely intelligent." She dated during college and graduate school, but claimed that she would never go after a guy she thought was "special," always feeling inferior and intimidated. Whenever she saw or met such a man, she acted stiff and aloof, or actually walked away as quickly as possible, only to berate herself afterward and then fantasize about him for many months. She claimed that her therapy had helped, although she still could not remember a time when she didn't feel somewhat depressed.

Just after graduation, she married the man she was going out with at the time. She thought of him as reasonably desirable, though not "special," and married him primarily because she felt she "needed a husband" for companionship. Shortly after their marriage, the couple started to bicker. She was very critical of his clothes, his job, and his parents; and he, in turn, found her rejecting, controlling, and moody. She began to feel that she had made a mistake in marrying him.

Recently she has also been having difficulties at work. She is assigned the most menial tasks at the firm and is never given an assignment of importance or responsibility. She admits that she frequently does a "slipshod" job of what is given her, never does more than is required, and never demonstrates any assertiveness or initiative to her supervisors. She views her boss as self-centered, unconcerned, and unfair, but nevertheless admires his success. She feels that she will never go very far in her profession because she does not have the right "connections" and neither does her husband, yet she dreams of money, status, and power.

Her social life with her husband involves several other couples. The man in these couples is usually a friend of her husband. She is sure that the women find her uninteresting and unimpressive, and that the people who seem to like her are probably no better off than she.

Under the burden of her dissatisfaction with her marriage, her job, and her social life, feeling tired and uninterested in "life," she now enters treatment for the third time. (Spitzer et al., 1994, pp. 110–11)

Adjustment Disorder with Depressed Mood
Basically, **adjustment disorder with depressed mood** is behaviorally indistinguishable from dysthymia. It differs from dysthymia in that it does not exceed six months in duration, and it requires the existence of an identifiable (presumably precipitating) psychosocial stressor in the client's life within three months before the onset of depression. The justification for making a clinical diagnosis is that the client is experiencing impaired social or occupational functioning, or that the observed stressor would not normally be considered severe enough to account for the client's depression. There is a difficulty here, of

course, because assessing the severity of a stressor is a highly subjective matter. Also, the diagnosis assumes that the person's problems will remit when the stressor ceases or when a new level of adjustment is achieved. Presumably, chronic cases of this sort would need to be rediagnosed as dysthymia.

Despite some problems with the formal diagnostic criteria, there are doubtless many cases of relatively brief but moderately serious depression (involving definite maladaptive behavior) that occur in reaction to stressful circumstances. (Uncomplicated bereavement following loss of a loved one, by the way, would not be included under this diagnosis.) The following excerpt from a clinical interview illustrates an adjustment disorder with depressed mood:

Patient: Well, you see, doctor, I just don't concentrate good, I mean, I can't play cards or even care to talk on the phone. I just feel so upset and miserable, it's just sorta as if I don't care any more about anything.

Doctor: You feel that your condition is primarily due to your divorce proceedings?

Patient: Well, doctor, the thing that upset me so, we had accumulated a little bit through my efforts—bonds and money—and he (sigh) wanted one half of it. He said he was going to San Francisco to get a job and send me enough money for support. So (sigh) I gave him a bond, and he went and turned around and went to an attorney and sued me for a divorce. Well, somehow, I had withstood all the humiliation of his drinking and not coming home at night and not knowing where he was, but he turned and divorced me and this is something that I just can't take. I mean, he has broken my health and broken everything, and I've been nothing but good to him. I just can't take it, doctor. There are just certain things that people—I don't know—just can't accept. I just can't accept that he would turn on me that way.

It should be noted that few, if any, depressions—including milder ones—occur in the absence of significant anxiety. As discussed later in this chapter, the issues surrounding the cooccurrence of depression and anxiety, which have received an enormous amount of attention in recent years, are very complex.

Major Depressive Disorder

The diagnostic criteria for **major depressive disorder** require that the person exhibit more symptoms than are required for dysthymia and the symptoms be more persistent (not interwoven with periods of normal mood). An affected person must experience either markedly depressed mood or marked loss of interest in pleasurable activities most of every day for at least two weeks. In addition, the person must experience at least four more of the following symptoms during the same period: fatigue or loss of energy; insomnia or hypersomnia (that is, too little or too much sleep); decreased appetite and significant weight loss without dieting (or, much more rarely, their opposites); psychomotor agitation or retardation (a slowdown of mental and physical activity); diminished ability to think or concentrate; self-denunciation to the point of claiming worthlessness or guilt out of proportion to any past indiscretions; and recurrent thoughts of death or suicidal ideation. Most of these symptoms (at least five, including either sad mood, or loss of interest or pleasure) must be present all day and nearly every day for two consecutive weeks before the diagnosis is applicable. The diagnosis of major depression is not made if a patient has ever experienced a manic or hypomanic episode; in such a case, the current depression is viewed as a depressive episode of bipolar disorder, which is discussed in the next section.

The following conversation between a therapist and a patient illustrates a major depression of moderate severity:

Therapist: Good morning, how are you today?

Patient: (Pause) Well, okay I guess, doctor.... I don't know, I just feel sort of discouraged.

Therapist: Is there anything in particular that worries you?

Patient: I don't know, doctor ... everything seems to be futile ... nothing seems worthwhile any more. It seems as if all that was beautiful has lost its beauty. I guess I expected more than life has given. It just doesn't seem worthwhile going on. I can't seem to make up my mind about anything. I guess I have what you would call the "blues."

Therapist: Can you tell me more about your feelings?

Patient: Well ... my family expected great things of me. I am supposed to be the outstanding member of the family ... they think because I went through college everything should begin to pop and there's nothing to pop. I ... really don't expect anything from anyone. Those whom I have trusted proved themselves less than friends should be.

Therapist: Oh?

Patient: Yes, I once had a very good girlfriend with whom I spent a good deal of time. She was very important to me.... I thought she was my friend but now she treats me like a casual acquaintance (tears).

Therapist: Can you think of any reason for this?

Patient: Yes, it's all my fault. I can't blame them—anybody that is.... I am not worthy of them ... I am worthless ... nobody can love me. I don't deserve friends or success....

Therapist: You don't deserve friends?

Patient: Well ... I am just no good. I am a failure. I was envious of other people. I didn't want them to have more than I had and when something bad happened to them I was glad.... All my flaws stand out and I am repugnant to everyone. (Sighs) I am a miserable failure.... There is no hope for me.

As this conversation between a person with major depressive disorder and her therapist illustrates, a person with this disorder not only shows mood symptoms of sadness, but also shows a variety of cognitive and motivational symptoms. In this case the person shows various cognitive distortions, including being firmly convinced that she is a failure and that her family also thinks so. She vacillates between anger at her friends and family for not being trustworthy, and self-hatred and self-blame. Because of her sense of hopelessness about her future, she shows no motivation to try to improve her situation. Her problems with friends who appear to no longer be close to her occur commonly with depression because, as we will see, most people find it aversive to be around depressed persons.

Psychotic symptoms, characterized by loss of contact with reality, and including delusions (false beliefs) or hallucinations (false sensory perceptions), may sometimes accompany the other symptoms of major depression. In such cases a diagnosis of **severe**

major depressive episode with psychotic features is made. Ordinarily, any delusions or hallucinations present are **mood-congruent;** that is, they seem in some sense "appropriate" to serious depression because the content is negative in tone. Additional examples of mood-congruent delusions might involve themes of personal inadequacy, guilt, deserved punishment, death, disease, and so forth. For example, the delusional idea that one's internal organs have totally deteriorated—an idea sometimes held by severely depressed people—ties in with the mood of a despondent person. In contrast, the idea that one has been chosen by the Deity for a special mission to save humankind is inconsistent with the self-abnegation normally seen in depression. The latter type of disordered thinking is termed **mood-incongruent** delusional thinking, which means that it is inconsistent with the predominant mood, and is usually associated with a poorer prognosis.

In addition to major depression with psychotic features, several other subcategories of major depression have been defined. There has been considerable interest recently in attempting to differentiate various possible types of depression—especially major depression—according to the particular symptom patterns displayed. Such efforts are driven mostly by the hope of distinguishing causes and effective treatments for the different subtypes.

One such subcategory in DSM-IV is major depression of the **melancholic type.** This designation is applied when, in addition to meeting the criteria for major depression, a patient has either loss of interest or pleasure in almost all activities, or does not react to usually pleasurable stimuli or desired events. In addition, the patient must also experience at least three of the following: early morning awakenings, depression being worse in the morning, marked psychomotor retardation or agitation, significant loss of appetite and weight, inappropriate or excessive guilt, or the depressed mood has a qualitative difference from the sadness experienced following a loss or during a nonmelancholic depression. It has also been found that patients with this subtype of depression are more likely to respond to antidepressant medications or electroconvulsive treatment. The chief theoretical importance of the melancholia concept is that it is strongly linked in the psychiatric literature to the idea of *endogenous* causation—that is, to the notion that certain depressions are caused "from within," so to speak, and are unrelated to any stressful events in a patient's life. We will have more to say about this in a later section.

Discriminating major depression from other forms of depressive disorder is not always easy. Ma-

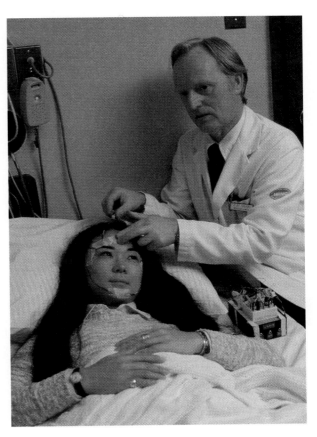

Sleep disturbances are common in dysthymia, major depression, and bipolar disorders. Studying the brainwave patterns of patients with mood disorders has helped researchers discover some of the basic patterns underlying these disorders.

jor depression may coexist with dysthymia in some people, a condition given the designation "double depression" (Keller & Shapiro, 1982; Keller et al., 1983). Double depressives are people who are moderately depressed on a chronic basis and who undergo increased problems from time to time, during which they manifest "major" symptoms. Among dysthymics, the experience of double depression appears to be common. For example, in one sample of dysthymics studied by Klein, 54 percent were in a major depressive episode at the time they sought treatment, and 75 percent reported a lifetime history of one or major depressive episodes; other studies have found comparable high rates of double depression in dysthymics (Klein et al., 1993).

When a diagnosis of major depression is made, it is usually also specified whether this is a *single* (initial) episode or a *recurrent* episode (one or more previous episodes have already occurred). This reflects the fact that depressive episodes are usually time-limited (with the average duration of an untreated episode being about six months according to DSM-IV), but often recur following a period of remission of symptoms for at least two months. In recent years **recurrence** has been distinguished from **relapse,** where the latter term refers to the return of symptoms within a fairly short period of time and probably reflects the fact that the underlying episode of depression has not yet run its course (Frank et al., 1991; Keller et al., 1982). Relapse may commonly occur, for example, when pharmacotherapy is terminated prematurely after symptoms have remitted but before the underlying episode is really over (Shelton et al., 1991).

The proportion of patients who will exhibit a recurrence of major depression is difficult to estimate reliably; studies have found wide variations. Based on an extensive review of nearly all studies done between 1970 and 1993, Piccinelli and Wilkinson (1994) estimated that 26 percent of patients experienced a recurrence within one year of recovery and 76 percent experienced a recurrence within ten years of recovery. The same review estimated that approximately 10–12 percent show persistent depression over five- and ten-year follow-up. There is also evidence that the probability of recurrence increases with the number of prior episodes. Conversely, the probability of recurrence seems to decrease the longer the person remains symptom free (see Belsher & Costello, 1988).

Persons who experience recurrent depressions can be distinguished from those who experience only a single episode in a number of ways. Merikangas, Wicki, and Angst (1994) followed a sample of nearly 600 young adults for ten years and subdivided them into five groups: no depression, one episode of major depression, more than one episode of major depression, recurrent brief depressions, and major depression plus recurrent brief depressions. They found that the latter three groups with some form of recurrent depression showed not only greater severity in terms of number and frequency of symptoms, but also many more suicide attempts, a much higher proportion with a family history of depression, more work and social impairment, and higher divorce rates.

Most of these estimates of recurrence rates come from samples of treated patients, and it is also important to determine whether comparable rates of recurrence occur in untreated samples. Probably the best data we have on the question of recurrence and relapse come from a large community sample (which included 1003 subjects with at least one prior episode of major or minor depression—some treated and some untreated). In this study Lewin-

sohn, Zeiss, and Duncan (1989) found the probability of relapse or recurrence was 46 percent over the lifetime. Among the 469 subjects with two prior episodes, the probability of having a third over the lifetime was 33 percent. These recurrence rates are somewhat lower than those reported in most other studies for treated patients, but nonetheless are still very high. Factors that may increase the probability of recurrence include age, with younger subjects being more prone to have a recurrence, and the occurrence of stressful life events (see Gotlib & Hammen, 1992).

Some people who experience recurrent depressive episodes show a seasonal pattern, commonly known as **seasonal affective disorder.** To meet DSM-IV criteria for recurrent major depression with a seasonal pattern, the person must have had at least two episodes of depression in the past two years occurring at the same time of the year (most commonly the fall or winter), and full remission must also have occurred at the same time of the year (most commonly the spring). In addition, the person cannot have had other nonseasonal depressive episodes in the same two-year period, and most of their lifetime depressive episodes must have been of the seasonal variety. Prevalence rates suggest that winter seasonal affective disorder is more common in people living at higher latitudes (northern climates) and in younger people. As will be discussed later, there has been a great deal of interesting research on this relatively recently identified subtype of depression.

The traditional view has been that between episodes, a person suffering from a recurrent major mood disorder is essentially normal. This view has been increasingly called into question as more research data have become available (Coryell & Winokur, 1982, 1992), and some have raised the possibility that major depressive episodes may leave "scars" after the episode that may leave a person at risk for future recurrences. Evidence of the scar hypothesis at this point is mixed (Rohde, Lewinsohn, & Seeley, 1990). The probability of depression leaving scars may be especially likely in younger persons and in those who have experienced multiple episodes (Gotlib & Hammen, 1992).

Given the relatively high probability that people who have experienced one episode of major depression will have a recurrence at some point, increasing attention is being directed toward finding possible ways of limiting both the severity and the duration of depressive episodes, and also for preventing recurrences. For example, we now know that marital distress—especially as manifested in perceived criticism from the spouse—is a substantial predictor of short-term relapse (Hooley & Teasdale, 1989), and intervention techniques have been developed that lessen the impact of such risk factors.

BIPOLAR DISORDERS

As we have seen, depression and mania—despite their seeming opposition—are sometimes closely related and some people experience both states. As with the unipolar disorders, the severity of disturbance in bipolar disorder ranges from mild to moderate to severe. In the mild to moderate range the disorder is known as **cyclothymia,** and in the moderate to severe range the disorder is known as *bipolar disorder.*

Cyclothymia

As we have noted, mania is in some ways the opposite of depression. It is a state involving excessive levels of excitement, elation, or euphoria, often liberally mixed with inflated self-esteem or grandiosity and the assumption of great powers. In its milder forms it is known as **hypomania.** It has long been recognized that some people are subject to cyclical mood changes with relative excesses of hypomania and depression that, though substantial, are not disabling. These, in essence, are the symptoms of cyclothymia.

Changes in the DSM classification reflect current thinking about cyclothymia. In DSM-I and DSM-II, this pattern was included under the category of personality disorders (see Chapter 9). By contrast, the DSM-III-R and DSM-IV definitions of cyclothymia make the pattern sound like a less serious version of major bipolar disorder, minus certain extreme symptoms and psychotic features, such as delusions, and minus the marked impairment caused by full-blown manic or depressive episodes. In the depressed phase of cyclothymia, a person's mood is dejected, and he or she experiences a distinct loss of interest or pleasure in usual activities and pastimes. In addition, the person may exhibit sleep irregularity (too much or too little); low energy levels; feelings of inadequacy; decreased efficiency, productivity, talkativeness, and cognitive sharpness; social withdrawal; restriction of pleasurable activities, including a relative lack of interest in sex; a pessimistic and brooding attitude; and tearfulness. A cyclothymic does not, however, experience enough of the symptoms, or experience them persistently enough, to qualify for a diagnosis of major depression.

Symptoms of the hypomanic phase of cyclothymia are essentially the opposite of the symptoms of dysthymia, except that the sleep disturbance is invariably one of an apparent decreased need for sleep. As in the case of bipolar disorder, no obvious precipitating circumstance may be evident, and an affected person may have significant periods between episodes in which he or she functions in a relatively adaptive manner. In cyclothymia, however, the diagnostic criteria for adults specify at least a two-year span during which there are numerous periods with hypomanic and depressed symptoms (only one year is required for adolescents and children).

As already noted, many clinicians feel that cyclothymia is but a milder variant of bipolar disorder, and evidence for this view has in recent years become quite compelling. For example, Depue and his colleagues have identified people with cyclothymic personality organization who have some symptoms of cyclothymia, although not enough to qualify for the diagnosis. These people were at higher-than-average risk for serious mood disorder episodes (Depue et al., 1981; Goplerud & Depue, 1985; Klein & Depue, 1984, 1985; Klein, Depue, & Slater, 1985, 1986). Specifically, these investigators, using a group of college students, developed a hypomanic personality inventory scale that postdicted (that is, identified those individuals who had had) not only hypomanic episodes but other maladaptive patterns, including depression. This study is significant because it suggests that an identifying personality component is present in cyclothymia independent of hypomanic or depressive episodes. Akiskal and his colleagues (Akiskal, Khani, & Scott-Strauss, 1979; Akiskal, 1989) have also noted the relationship of cyclothymic temperament to bipolar disorders by noting an excess of depressive and manic or hypomanic episodes during prospective follow-up.

The following case is illustrative of cyclothymia:

A 29-year-old car salesman was referred by his current girl friend, a psychiatric nurse, who suspected he had a Mood Disorder, even though the patient was reluctant to admit that he might be a "moody" person. According to him, since the age of 14 he has experienced repeated alternating cycles that he terms "good times and bad times." During a "bad" period, usually lasting four to seven days, he oversleeps 10–14 hours daily, lacks energy, confidence, and motivation—"just vegetating," as he puts it. Often he abruptly shifts, characteristically upon waking up in the morning, to a three-to-four-day stretch of overconfidence, heightened social awareness, promiscuity, and sharpened thinking—"things would flash in my mind." At such times he indulges in alcohol to enhance the experience, but also to help him sleep. Occasionally the "good" periods last seven to ten days, but culminate in irritable and hostile outbursts, which often herald the transition back to another period of "bad" days. He admits to frequent use of marijuana, which he claims helps him "adjust" to daily routines.

In school, A's and B's alternated with C's and D's, with the result that the patient was considered a bright student whose performance was mediocre overall because of "unstable motivation." As a car salesman his performance has also been uneven, with "good days" canceling out the "bad days"; yet even during his "good days" he is sometimes perilously argumentative with customers and loses sales that appeared sure. Although considered a charming man in many social circles, he alienates friends when he is hostile and irritable. He typically accumulates social obligations during the "bad" days and takes care of them all at once on the first day of a "good" period. (Spitzer et al., 1994, pp. 155–56)

In short, cyclothymia consists of mood swings that, at either extreme, are clearly maladaptive but of insufficient intensity to merit the major disorder designation.

Bipolar Disorder

Although recurrent cycles of mania and melancholia were recognized as early as the sixth century, it remained for Kraepelin, in 1899, to introduce the term *manic-depressive insanity* and to clarify the clinical picture. Kraepelin described the disorder as a series of attacks of elation and depression, with periods of relative normality in between, and a generally favorable prognosis. Today DSM-IV calls this illness **bipolar disorder.**

Bipolar disorder is distinguished from major depression by at least one episode of mania. Any given episode is classified as depressive, manic, or mixed, according to its predominant features. The depressed or manic classification is self-explanatory. A mixed episode is characterized by symptoms of both manic and major depressive episodes, whether the

symptoms are either intermixed or alternate rapidly every few days. Such cases are rare.

Even though a patient may be exhibiting only manic symptoms, it is assumed that a bipolar disorder exists and that a depressive episode will eventually occur. Thus, there are no officially recognized "unipolar" manic or hypomanic counterparts to dysthymia or major depression. The implicit assumption is that all mania-like behaviors must be part of a cyclothymic or bipolar disorder, or perhaps exist along a continuum on which these two conditions fall. This is in spite of the fact that some researchers have noted the probable existence of a unipolar type of manic disorder (Andreasen, 1982; Nurnberger et al., 1979).

The features of the depressive form of bipolar disorder are usually clinically indistinguishable from those of major depression (Perris, 1982, 1992; DSM-IV, 1994), although some studies do report higher rates of psychomotor retardation and hypersomnia in the depressed phase of bipolar disorder (Cassano et al., 1992). Nevertheless, the essential difference is that these depressive episodes alternate with manic ones. In about two-thirds of cases, the manic episodes either immediately precede or immediately follow a depressive episode; in other cases the manic and depressive episodes are separated by intervals of relatively normal functioning. DSM-IV (1994) also identified a form of bipolar disorder called Bipolar II disorder, in which the person may not experience full-blown manic episodes, but has experienced clear-cut hypomanic episodes. That this is indeed a distinct disorder is suggested by findings that Bipolar II disorder evolves into Bipolar I disorder (the type already described with full-blown manic episodes—usually simply called "bipolar disorder") in less than 5 percent of cases (Coryell, Endicott, & Keller, 1987).

Manic symptoms in bipolar disorder tend to be extreme, and there is significant impairment of occupational and social functioning. A person who experiences a manic episode has a markedly elevated, euphoric, and expansive mood, often interrupted by occasional outbursts of irritability or even violence—particularly when others refuse to go along with the manic person's antics and schemes. This mood must persist for at least a week to qualify for a diagnosis. In addition, three or more of the following symptoms must also occur in the same time period: A notable increase in goal-directed activity may occur, which sometimes may appear as an unrelievable restlessness, and mental activity may speed up, so that the person may evidence a "flight of ideas" or thoughts that "race" through the brain. Distractibility, high levels of verbal output in speech or in writing, and a severely decreased need for sleep may also occur. In addition, inflated self-esteem is common and when severe becomes frankly delusional, so that the person harbors feelings of enormous grandeur and power. Finally, personal and cultural inhibitions loosen, and the person may indulge in foolish ventures with a high potential for painful consequences, such as foolish business ventures, major spending sprees, and sexual indiscretions.

The following conversation illustrates a manic episode of moderate severity. The patient is a 46-year-old woman.

Doctor: Hello, how are you today?

Patient: Fine, fine, and how are you, Doc? You're looking pretty good. I never felt better in my life. Could I go for a schnapps now. Say, you're new around here, I never saw you before—and not bad! How's about you and me stepping out tonight if I can get that sour old battleship of a nurse to give me back my dress. It's low cut and it'll wow 'em. Even in this old rag, all the doctors give me the eye. You know I'm a model. Yep, I was number one—used to dazzle them in New York, London, and Paris. Hollywood has been angling with me for a contract.

Doctor: Is that what you did before you came here?

Patient: I was a society queen . . . entertainer of kings and presidents. I've got five grown sons and I wore out three husbands getting them . . . about ready for a couple of more now. There's no woman like me, smart, brainy, beautiful, and sexy. You can see I don't believe in playing myself down. If you are good and know you're good you have to speak out, and I know what I've got.

Doctor: Why are you in this hospital?

Patient: That's just the trouble. My husbands never could understand me. I was too far above them. I need someone like me with savoir faire you know, somebody that can get around, intelligent, lots on the ball. Say, where can I get a schnapps around here—always like one before dinner. Someday I'll cook you a meal. I've got special recipes like you never ate before . . . sauces, wines, desserts. Boy, it's making me hungry. Say, have you got anything for me to do around here? I've been showing these slowpokes how to make up beds but I want something more in line with my talents.

Doctor: What would you like to do?

Patient: Well, I'm thinking of organizing a show, singing, dancing, jokes. I can do it all myself but I want to know what you think about it. I'll bet there's some schnapps in the kitchen. I'll look around later. You know what we need here . . . a dance at night. I could play the piano, and teach them the latest steps. Wherever I go I'm the life of the party.

This case is particularly illustrative of the inflated self-esteem characteristic of a manic person. The erotic suggestiveness and impatience with routine seen here are also common features of manic episodes.

Bipolar disorder, like major depression, is typically a recurrent disorder. As with unipolar major depression, the recurrences can be seasonal in nature, in which case **bipolar disorder with a seasonal pattern** is diagnosed. Although most patients with bipolar disorder experience periods of remission when they are relatively symptom free, as many as 20–30 percent continue to experience significant impairment (occupational and/or interpersonal) and mood lability. Moreover, a few chronic patients continue to meet diagnostic criteria over long periods of time, even years, sometimes despite the successive application of all standard treatments. It is not known whether these "refractory" cases represent fundamentally different psychopathological entities (Akiskal & Simmons, 1985).

As we have seen, a person who is depressed cannot be diagnosed as bipolar unless he or she has exhibited at least one manic episode in the past. This means that many people with bipolar disorder whose initial episode or episodes are depressive will be misdiagnosed at first, and possibly throughout their lives (if no manic episodes are observed or reported, or if they die before a manic episode is experienced). Estimates are that about 18–28% of people who have an initial major depressive episode will later have a manic or hypomanic episode and will be diagnosed as having Bipolar I or II disorder (Goodwin & Jamison, 1990). On the other hand, misdiagnosis is automatically prevented if a person has manic symptoms: By DSM-IV definition, this would be a bipolar disorder even though, as already noted, some researchers believe that a very rare unipolar form of manic disorder may in fact exist.

People with bipolar disorder seem in some ways to be even more unfortunate than those who suffer from recurrent major depression. On average they suffer from more episodes during their lifetimes than do persons with unipolar disorder (although these episodes tend to be somewhat shorter). Indeed, according to DSM-IV more than 90 percent of those who have one manic episode will go on to

Many highly creative people are believed to have had bipolar disorder, going through periods of intense productivity in their creative medium during manic phases, and often through unproductive periods when clinically depressed. Two such individuals are the German composer Robert Schumann (1810–1856) and the English novelist Virginia Woolf (1882–1941). Schumann was committed to a mental asylum in 1854 and died there two years later. Woolf committed suicide by drowning herself.

have further episodes. As many as 5–10 percent of persons with bipolar disorder experience at least four or more episodes (either manic or depressive) every year, a pattern known as **rapid cycling.** (See Figure 6.1 for the different kinds of patterns of manic and depressive episodes that can be seen in bipolar disorder.) Overall, the probabilities of "full recovery" for bipolar and unipolar disorder (that is, being symptom-free for a period of five years) are about equally discouraging—about 40 percent (Coryell & Winokur, 1982, 1992). In one recent follow-up study of 73 hospitalized manic patients, 40 percent had experienced another manic episode within 1.7 years after discharge, many of them in spite of maintenance lithium therapy (Harrow et al., 1990).

Schizoaffective Disorder

Occasionally, clinicians are confronted with a patient whose mood disorder is as severe as those seen in the major depressive or bipolar disorders but whose mental and cognitive processes are so deranged as to suggest the presence of a schizophrenic psychosis (see Chapter 12). Such cases are likely to be diagnosed as **schizoaffective disorder** in the DSM-IV category. To receive this diagnosis, a person must have a period of illness during which he or she meets criteria for both a major mood disorder (unipolar or

bipolar) and at least two major symptoms of schizophrenia (such as hallucinations and delusions). However, during at least two weeks of the illness they must experience the schizophrenic symptoms in the absence of prominent mood symptoms; and they must meet criteria for a mood disorder for a substantial portion of the period of illness. In spite of its inclusion in the DSM, the diagnosis of schizoaffective disorder is a controversial one. Some clinicians believe these persons are basically schizophrenic; others believe they have primarily psychotic mood disorders; and still others consider this disorder a distinct entity (Lehmann, 1985).

The often severe disturbances of psychological functioning seen in these cases, such as mood-incongruent delusions and hallucinations, are indeed reminiscent of schizophrenic phenomena. Unlike schizophrenia, however, the schizoaffective pattern tends to be highly episodic, with a good prognosis for individual attacks and with relatively lucid periods between episodes. Although it was once thought that schizoaffective patients had a relatively good prognosis for full recovery under the five-year criterion, recently published follow-up data on these patients cast considerable doubt on such a benign outlook (Coryell et al., 1990a, 1990b). According to DSM-IV, the prognosis is probably better than that for schizophrenia but considerably worse than that for mood disorders.

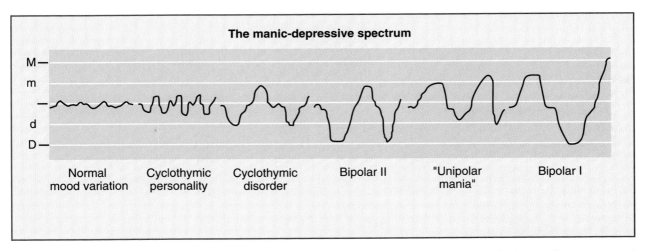

Figure 6.1   *There is a spectrum of bipolarity in moods. All of us have our ups and downs, which we refer to as normal mood variation. People with a cyclothymic personality have more marked and regular mood swings, and people with cyclothymic disorder go through periods during which they meet the criteria for dysthymia (except for the two-year duration), and other periods when they meet criteria for hypomania. People with Bipolar II disorder have periods of major depression as well as periods of hypomania. Unipolar mania is an extremely rare condition. Finally, people with Bipolar I disorder have periods of major depression and periods of mania. (Adapted from Goodwin & Jamison, 1990.)*

CAUSAL FACTORS IN MOOD DISORDERS

In considering the development of major mood disorders, we again find it useful to examine the possible roles of biological, psychosocial, and sociocultural factors. We will first examine what is known about the causes of unipolar disorders, followed by a discussion of the causes of bipolar disorders.

Unipolar Disorders

Biological Causal Factors   It has long been known that a variety of diseases and drugs can affect mood, sometimes leading to depression, and sometimes to elation or even hypomania. Indeed, this idea goes back to Hippocrates, who hypothesized that depression was caused by an excess of "black bile" in the system (c. 400 B.C.). Thus, it is not surprising that researchers have sought to determine whether there is a biological basis for at least some of the depressive disorders. Investigators attempting to establish a biological basis for unipolar disorders have considered genetic and constitutional factors as well as neurophysiological, neuroendocrinological, and biochemical alterations. A good deal of attention has also been focused on disturbances in many of our biological rhythms, including the effects of seasonal variations in light and darkness.

Hereditary Factors. The prevalence of mood disorders is higher among blood relatives of persons with clinically diagnosed mood disorders than in the population at large. For example, Perris (1992) reviewed eight studies examining the risk for mood disorders in relatives of unipolar depressives and estimated that about 15 percent of first-degree relatives had also experienced unipolar depression, substantially higher than would be expected in the general population. Some studies have suggested that this higher prevalence of mood disorders in first-degree relatives is especially true for endogenous or melancholic depression (relative to other types of unipolar depression), but other studies have not found such a difference (see Katz & McGuffin, 1993). Because of the difficulties of disentangling hereditary and environmental influences, however, a higher rate of disorder among family members can never in itself be taken as conclusive proof of genetic causation.

Twin studies have also suggested that there may be a moderate genetic contribution to unipolar depression. Katz and McGuffin (1993) reviewed evidence from four studies showing that monozygotic co-twins of a twin with unipolar major depression are about twice as likely to develop major depression as are dizygotic co-twins of a depressed twin. However, the actual rates of concordance differ widely, at least in part because of differences in diagnostic criteria used across studies—a problem that is almost inevitable as diagnostic criteria change over time as our understanding of diagnostic subtypes changes. Evidence for this point is illustrated in a recent very large population-based twin study (as opposed to a patient sample) of 1033 same-sex female twin pairs (Kendler et al., 1992c). These investigators examined concordance rates using a variety of different definitions of "major depression" that have been used over the years by different investigators. They found that for most of the different definitions of depression, heritability estimates ranged from 33–45 percent—simply resulting from the use of different definitions of depression. The evidence for a genetic contribution is much less consistent for milder forms of unipolar depression such as neurotic depression or dysthymia (Katz & McGuffin, 1993), and indeed some twin studies have not found evidence of a genetic contribution to these milder but more chronic forms of unipolar depression.

A number of years ago the adoption method of genetic research was applied to the study of mood disorders. This method involves the psychiatric evaluation of people who were adopted at an early age and the comparison of the rates of disorders in both their biological and adoptive family members. If a predisposition to develop a given disorder is heritable, it should show up (so the logic goes) more often among biological, as opposed to adoptive, relatives of the affected adoptees. However, there should be no difference in the rates of illness in the biological and adoptive relatives of control adoptees who do not experience depression.

Of the limited number of adoption studies on mood disorders published thus far, the most adequate is one conducted by Wender and colleagues (1986). Beginning with Danish samples of 71 mood-disordered adopted subjects and 71 matched normal control adoptees, the close biological and adoptive relatives of these individuals were independently assessed for psychiatric status. The researchers found that unipolar depression was eight times more likely to occur among the biological relatives of the severely depressed subjects than among the biological relatives of control cases; suicide was fifteen times more likely among biological relatives. By any standard, these are impressive figures, but unfortunately the depressed group of adoptees included 27 percent with bipolar disorder and it is well known that there is a stronger genetic contribution to bipolar than to unipolar disorder, as we will discuss below. Unfortunately, at present there are no good adoption studies focusing solely on unipolar disorder.

Based on the evidence so far, the case for some hereditary contribution in the causal patterns of unipolar major depression is quite strong, although not as strong as for bipolar disorder (Katz & McGuffin, 1993; Rifkin & Gurling, 1991). Indeed, one recent study estimated that genes contribute approximately 50 percent of the variance in the tendency to develop (that is, the liability for) unipolar major depression (McGuffin, Katz, & Rutherford, 1991). Other studies (e.g., Kendler et al., 1992c) place the estimates more in the 33–45 percent range. By contrast, the same study that estimated 50 percent of the variance was due to genetic factors for major depression estimated that less than 10 percent of the variance in liability for "neurotic depression" (a category similar to dysthymia) was due to genetic factors.

Biochemical Factors. Starting in the 1960s the view that depression may arise from disruptions in the delicate balance of neurotransmitter substances that regulate and mediate the activity of the brain's nerve cells, or neurons, has received a great deal of attention. Neurotransmitters, released by the activated presynaptic neuron, mediate the transfer of nerve impulses across the synaptic cleft from one neuron to the next in a neuronal pathway; they may either stimulate or inhibit the firing of the next neuron in the chain.

A large body of evidence suggests that various biological therapies often used to treat severe mood disorders—such as electroconvulsive therapy and antidepressant drugs—may affect the concentrations or the activity of neurotransmitters at the synapse and thus determine the extent to which particular brain pathways are relatively volatile or sluggish in conducting messages. In fact, the largely accidental discovery of these treatments (particularly the antidepressant drugs), and initial explanations of how they work, are what encouraged the development of biochemical theories of the etiology of major depression.

A bit of history is in order here. Early attention in the 1960s and 1970s focused primarily on two neurotransmitter substances of the monoamine class, norepinephrine and serotonin, because researchers observed that antidepressant medications seemed to have the effect of increasing their availability at synaptic junctions. This observation led to the monoamine hypothesis—that depression was due to a depletion of one or both of these neurotransmitters (Schildkraut, 1965). However, it is now clear, some 30 years later, that no such straightforward mechanism is likely to provide the answers we need (Goodwin & Jamison, 1990; Pryor & Sulser, 1991; Shelton et al., 1991; Siever & Davis, 1985; Thase, Frank, & Kupfer, 1985). For example, some studies have found exactly the opposite of what is predicted by the monoamine hypothesis—that is, net *increases* in norepinephrine activity in depressed patients (Koslow et al., 1983; Lake et al., 1982). In addition, it is also now known that even though the immediate short-term effects of antidepressant drugs are to increase the availability of norepinephrine and serotonin, the long-term effects of these drugs (when they actually begin to have their clinical effects two to four weeks later) are to produce functional *decreases* in available norepinephrine and serotonin.

Unfortunately, the early monoamine theory has not been replaced by a compelling alternative. Initially, research attention shifted to a concern that depression may be associated with abnormal receptor systems—that is, the large molecules on a postsynaptic neuron to which neurotransmitters bearing the appropriate chemical codes selectively bond (McNeal & Cimbolic, 1986; Sedvall et al., 1986). This shift of attention occurred because of findings that antidepressant drugs when administered for at least several weeks (long enough to have a therapeutic antidepressant effect) decrease the number and sensitivity of certain types of receptors and increase the responsiveness of others (Goodwin & Jamison, 1990; McNeal & Cimbolic, 1986; Shelton et al., 1991). Unfortunately, the yield from such studies has not yet provided any firm etiological conclusions, and as we will see, in the past decade attention has shifted toward more integrative theories that do not focus exclusively on biochemical systems.

Neuroendocrine and Neurophysiological Factors. There has also been a good deal of research on the possible neurophysiological and neuroendocrine (hormonal) correlates of some distinguishable forms of mood disorder (Checkley, 1992; Goodwin & Jamison, 1990; Shelton et al., 1991). Ideas about hormonal influences on mood have a long history. One contemporary theory (e.g., Stokes & Sikes, 1987) has focused on the hypothalamic-pituitary-adrenal axis, and in particular on the hormone cortisol, which is excreted by the outermost portion of the adrenal glands. Blood plasma levels of this substance are known to be elevated in from 50 to 60 percent of seriously depressed patients (Holsboer, 1992), suggesting a possible clue of etiological significance. Even more intriguing, however, is the finding that a potent suppressor of plasma cortisol in normal individuals, dexamethasone, either fails entirely to suppress or fails to sustain suppression of cortisol in about 45 percent of seriously depressed patients (Shelton et al., 1991).

These findings, in themselves essentially undisputed, gave rise some years ago to widespread use of the dexamethasone suppression test (DST) in assess-

ing depressed individuals. At first it was suggested that DST nonsuppressor patients constitute a distinct subgroup among depressed people, namely the group sometimes referred to as having an "endogenous" or melancholic form of depression (Carroll, 1982; Kalin et al., 1981). Consistent with this idea was evidence showing that nonsuppression is in fact correlated with clinical severity and positive response to drug treatment (Arana, Baldessarini, & Ornsteen 1985; Shelton et al., 1991). However, over time it has become apparent that several other groups of psychiatric patients exhibit high rates of nonsuppression, calling into question the specificity and hence the diagnostic utility of the DST for depression (Goodwin & Jamison, 1990; Thase et al., 1985). This suggests that nonsuppression may merely be a nonspecific indicator of generalized mental distress.

The other endocrine system that has relevance to depression is the hypothalamic-pituitary-thyroid axis, because it is known that disturbances to this axis are also linked to mood disorders (Checkley, 1992; Loosen, 1986). For example, people with low thyroid levels (a condition known as hypothyroidism) often become depressed. In addition, about 30 percent of depressed patients who have normal thyroid levels show dysregulation of this axis as evidenced through abnormal responses to thyrotropin releasing hormone (which through a complex sequence of steps leads to increased levels of thyroid hormone). In addition, administration of the same thyrotropin-releasing hormone improves the mood and sense of motivation and coping for both normal and psychiatric subjects (Loosen, 1986; Shelton et al., 1991).

Other exciting neurophysiological research in recent years has followed up on earlier neurological findings showing that lesions of the left (but not the right) anterior or prefrontal cortex (as, for example, from having a stroke in that region) often lead to depression (e.g., Robinson et al., 1984). This led to the idea that perhaps depression in people without brain lesions is nonetheless linked to lowered levels of brain activity in this same region. Several recent studies have supported this idea. When one measures the electroencephalographic (EEG) activity of both cerebral hemispheres in depressed patients, one finds that there is an asymmetry or imbalance in the EEG activity of the two sides of the anterior (prefrontal) regions of the brain. In particular, depressed persons show relatively low activity in the left hemisphere in these regions (Henriques & Davidson, 1991). It also seems that this may be a risk marker for depression, since patients in remission show the same pattern (Henriques & Davidson, 1990), as do children at risk for depression (Tomarken, Siemien, & Garber,

1994). Although this is a relatively new area of research, it seems to hold promise as a way of identifying persons at risk, both for an initial episode and for recurrent episodes.

Sleep and Biological Rhythms. Although findings of sleep disturbances in depressed patients have existed as long as depression has been studied, only recently have some of these findings been linked to more general disturbances in biological rhythms. As we will see, these links provide some of today's most interesting biologically based etiological hypotheses.

Sleep is characterized by five stages that occur in a relatively invariant sequence throughout the night (Stages 1 to 4 of non-REM sleep, and REM sleep). REM sleep (rapid-eye-movement sleep) is characterized by rapid eye movements and dreaming, as well as other bodily changes; the first REM period does not usually begin until near the end of the first sleep cycle, about 75–80 minutes into sleep. Depressed patients, especially those with melancholic features, show a variety of sleep problems, ranging from early morning awakening, periodic awakening during the night, and, for some, difficulty falling asleep. However, research using EEG recordings has found that many depressed patients also show a shorter-than-usual latency to the first period of REM sleep, as well as greater amounts of REM sleep early in the night, than are seen in nondepressed persons. Because this is the period of the night when most deep sleep (Stages 3 and 4) usually occurs, the depressed person also receives a lower than normal *amount* of deep sleep. These findings suggest disturbances in both the overall sleep-wake cycle rhythms and the REM sleep rhythm (Goodwin & Jamison, 1990; Shelton et al., 1991).

Humans have many other circadian (24-hour or daily) cycles other than sleep, including body temperature and secretion of cortisol, thyroid stimulating hormone, and melatonin (a hormone secreted by the pineal gland during the dark). These circadian rhythms are controlled by two related central "oscillators," which act like internal clocks. The strong oscillator (so named because it is relatively impervious to environmental influence) controls the regulation of body temperature, hormones such as cortisol, and REM sleep rhythms. The weak oscillator (so named because it does readily respond to environmental influence) controls the rest-activity and sleep-wake cycles (Goodwin & Jamison, 1990). Research has found some rhythmic abnormalities in all of these rhythms in depressed patients, though not all patients show abnormalities in all rhythms (Healy & Williams, 1988; Sack et al., 1987; Shelton et al., 1991). Although there is no agreement yet about the exact nature of the dysfunctions, there seems to

be increasing agreement that some kind of circadian rhythm dysfunction may account for many of the clinical features of depression.

Several theorists have indeed proposed that the primary biological disturbance in depression is in the regulation of the circadian system, with alterations in neurotransmitters occurring as a secondary consequence to the disturbed rhythms (Goodwin & Jamison, 1990; Healy & Williams, 1988). An alternative comprehensive theory is one which hypothesizes that there is a dysregulation in one or more neurotransmitter systems in depression (Siever & Davis, 1985). This theory rests on the idea that our bodies have homeostatic regulatory systems for neurotransmitters just as they do for other biological functions such as sleep, temperature, respiration, and heart rate. The central proposal is not that these neurotransmitter systems show too much or too little activity, but rather that there is a failure of *regulation* of interrelated biological systems, so that their activity may be "highly variable, unstable, inappropriately responsive to incoming information and desynchronized from normal periodicities" (Siever & Davis, 1985, p. 1017). These irregularities in neurotransmitter activity are thought in turn to be responsible for the changes in the neuroendocrine system and in the circadian rhythms. According to this theory, antidepressant drugs work by restoring efficient regulation of the dysregulated neurotransmitter systems. These theories can account for many of the seeming discrepancies of prior findings in the literature, but considerably more research is required to determine how valid they are (see Shelton et al., 1991).

Another rather different kind of rhythm abnormality or disturbance may be seen in *seasonal affective disorder*. In this subset of mood disorder, most patients seem to be responsive to the total quantity of available light in the environment (Rosenthal et al., 1984), with a majority becoming depressed in the fall and winter and normalizing in the spring and summer (Wehr et al., 1986). Research in animals has also documented that many seasonal variations in basic functions such as sleep, activity, and appetite are related to the amount of light in a day (which except near the equator is much greater in summer than in winter). For depressed patients who fit the seasonal pattern, there is now a good deal of research demonstrating the therapeutic use of controlled exposure to light, even artificial light (Blehar & Rosenthal., 1989; Goodwin & Jamison, 1990; Sack et al., 1990). The mechanisms through which light therapy works for seasonal affective disorder are still not well understood, but research in this area is giving many clues to the underlying biological dysfunctions, and it still remains possible that

Some people are especially susceptible to seasonal variation in the quantity of available light in their environment and are prone to becoming depressed in the winter when there is not much natural light available. People with this disorder, known as seasonal affective disorder, often respond well to exposure to bright artificial light.

light therapy works by reestablishing normal biological rhythms.

Summary. To summarize, although none of these approaches has established a definitive case for exactly how biological factors may be involved in causing major depression, biological causation in general remains a viable hypothesis (see Goodwin & Jamison, 1990; Pryor & Sulser, 1991; Shelton et al., 1991). The case rests essentially on five facts that are beyond reasonable dispute: (a) A predisposition to these disorders may be genetically transmitted; (b) Certain profound alterations of bodily function, such as sleep disturbance, appetite loss, reduced libido, and loss of pleasure, often accompany the mood symptoms. These biological functions are all regulated by the *limbic system* (a part of the brain below the cortex that is very involved in emotional responding) and related structures (Shelton et al., 1991); (c) Physical illnesses that affect the limbic system, hypothyroidism, and stroke to the left anterior cortex all frequently cause depression; (d) Many

of the most effective biological interventions for depression are known to affect functioning of the limbic system (Pryor & Sulser, 1991), and other agents known to deplete neurotransmitters central to limbic system functioning often cause depression; (e) The disruptions of both circadian and seasonal rhythms in depression support the role of biological factors, and there is some evidence that manipulation of these rhythms can cause symptom remission in at least some individuals (Shelton et al., 1991).

Psychosocial Causal Factors Growing awareness of biological factors in the etiology of unipolar depressive disorders does not, of course, imply that psychosocial factors are irrelevant. Indeed, evidence for important psychological causal factors in most mood disorders is at least as strong as evidence for biological factors. However, there is no inherent incompatibility between biochemical and psychosocial approaches to understanding the mood disorders because in many ways they are simply working at different levels of analysis.

Stress as a Causal Factor. Psychosocial stressors are known to be involved in the onset of a variety of disorders, ranging from some of the anxiety disorders to schizophrenia, but nowhere has their role been more carefully studied than in the case of unipolar depression. Indeed, many investigators have been impressed with the high incidence of stressful life events that apparently serve as precipitating factors for unipolar depression, and Harder and colleagues (1989) did not even find a difference between more and less severely depressed patients in regard to the magnitude of prior life stressors. Based on clinical observations, Beck (1967) provided a broad classification of the most frequently encountered precipitating circumstances in depression: (a) situations that tend to lower self-esteem; (b) the thwarting of an important goal or the posing of an insoluble dilemma; (c) a physical disease or abnormality that activates ideas of deterioration or death; (d) single stressors of overwhelming magnitude; (e) several stressors occurring in a series; and (f) insidious stressors unrecognized as such by an affected person. Paykel (1982b) comprehensively reviewed the research literature available at that time on life events occurring before episodes of mood disorder and arrived at conclusions generally in agreement with Beck's. In particular, and perhaps not surprisingly, he concluded that separations from people important in one's life (through death, for example) are strongly associated with depression, although such losses tend to precede other disorders as well. Another serious stressor that has been the focus of study only fairly recently is caregiving to a spouse with a debilitating disease such as Alzheimer's (formerly known as senility), which is known to be associated with the onset of both major depression and generalized anxiety disorder for the caregiver (e.g., Russo et al., 1995).

Research on stress and the onset of depression is complicated by the fact that depressed people have a distinctly negative view of themselves and the world around them (Beck, 1967), and so at least to some extent their perceptions of stress may *result* from the cognitive symptoms of their disorder rather than causing their disorder (Monroe & Simons, 1991). That is, because of their pessimistic outlook, they may evaluate events as stressful that an independent evaluator (or a nondepressed friend) would not. This is why both George Brown and Bruce Dohrenwend—two leading stress researchers—have developed more complex and sophisticated measures of stress that involve either the use of independent evaluators or of questionnaires with specific narrowly defined stressors with objectively determined weights. Therefore, both measures do not rely on the depressed person's appraisal of an event as stressful. But because relatively few studies have used these more sophisticated strategies, much of the research literature on the association of depression and life stress as assessed by self-report is difficult to evaluate.

In several studies using these sophisticated measurements of life stress, Brown and Harris (1978, 1986, 1989) have concluded that depression often follows from one or more severely stressful events, usually involving some loss or exit from one's social sphere. (Interestingly, events signifying danger or threat were found more likely to precede the onset of anxiety disorders [Finlay-Jones & Brown, 1981; Paykel, 1982]). Indeed, when comparing the incidence of such stressful events in depressed subjects with that in nondepressed controls, Brown and Harris (1978) estimated that stressful life events played a causal role in the depression of about 50 percent of their subjects. In another sophisticated study, Dohrenwend and colleagues (1986) found that depressed patients had more negative life events of three types in the year before the onset of their depression than did nondepressed controls: physical illness and injury, fateful loss events, and events that disrupted their social network. A study by Phifer and Murrell (1986) of a community sample of older people (ages 55 and over) that did use self-report measures of stress confirmed that loss events were associated with the onset of depressive symptoms, and like the Dohrenwend and colleagues study it also pointed to health problems and lack of social support as having depression-inducing effects.

Whether mildly stressful events and chronic strains are also associated with the onset of depression is more controversial. Using their sophisticated strategies for assessing life stress, Brown and his colleagues, and Dohrenwend and his colleagues, have not found minor stressful events, and only occasionally chronic strains, to be associated with the onset of clinical depression (e.g., Dohrenwend et al., 1995). However, Bebbington and colleagues (1988) used Brown's method for measuring life stress and did find minor events associated with the onset of both neurotic and endogenous depression. Moreover, from self-report measures of stress there is also evi-

Physical illness and physical disability are stressors that may precipitate major depression.

dence that minor events and chronic strains may be associated with the onset of depression. For example, in a rigorously conducted study of 409 matched pairs of normal and unipolar depressive subjects, Billings, Cronkite, and Moos (1983) provided evidence not only of a greater frequency of prior stressor "events" but also of more chronic sources of psychosocial strain in the depressed group. Similarly, Lewinsohn, Hoberman, and Rosenbaum (1988) also found that both major and minor life events and chronic strains such as marital or employment problems were predictors of the onset of depression in a community sample that was followed for a year. Although these are well-conducted studies, their results should be interpreted with some caution given that subjects rated stressful events at the follow-up period when they were depressed, and this may have colored their perceptions of what constituted minor life events and chronic strains. Given the dozens of studies in this area, it is perhaps best to rely on findings from a recent review of the literature that concluded that chronic stressors (such as poverty) and minor events may be associated with an increase in depressive symptoms but probably not major depression (Monroe & Simons, 1991).

For one subtype of major mood disorder that is not officially recognized in DSM-IV but is still widely discussed in the literature—endogenous depression—there is a strong implication that it occurs *de novo*—out of the blue, so to speak. If endogenous depression occurs in the absence of significant psychosocial antecedents, it must be caused entirely from within. This idea of endogenous causation is most compatible with a strong version of the biomedical model. However, there is at least some evidence that the onset of so-called endogenous depressions does not differ substantially from other forms of depression (formerly called neurotic) in terms of the frequency with which major life events are associated with their onset (e.g., Bebbington et al., 1988). Indeed, the problems in defining exactly what is meant by endogenous depression, as well as findings that it is often associated with precipitating life events, may be part of the reason why it is not officially recognized in DSM-IV.

If we take the position—and the available research data seem to justify doing so—that some people are constitutionally more prone than others to develop mood disorders, then it would seem reasonable to suppose that such high-risk persons would react more intensely to subtle, easily overlooked stressors than would persons less at risk for these disorders. Unfortunately, no data at present permit us to evaluate this hypothesis directly. Indeed, a recent critical review of the literature by Monroe and Si-

mons (1991) suggests that there is much more evidence for the idea that a large percentage of the population (perhaps half) is at risk for depression if they are exposed to one or more severe life events. They point, for example, to Brown and Harris's findings that among depressed women, more than 60 percent (compared with about 20 percent of nondepressed women) had had one or more severe life events in the past two to six months. Looked at from a different perspective, with one severe life event the odds were about 50/50 of becoming depressed, but with two severe events the odds were about 75/25 of becoming depressed, and with three or more severe events 100 percent of the women became depressed (although there was a very small sample in this category). This suggests that any person who experiences a series of misfortunes can become clinically depressed.

It is obvious from these findings, however, that not everyone with one or two severe life events becomes depressed. What makes one vulnerable or invulnerable? Brown and Harris (1978) found some interesting answers in their classic study of women living in a poor area of inner London. Of women experiencing a severe event, there were four factors associated with *not* becoming depressed: having an intimate relationship with a spouse or lover, having no more than three children still at home, having a part-time or full-time job outside the home, and having a serious religious commitment. Conversely, not having a close relationship with a spouse or lover, having three children under five at home, not having a job, and having lost a parent by death before the age of 11 were strongly associated with the onset of depression following a major negative life event.

One way in which stressors may act is through their effects on biochemical and hormonal balances, and on biological rhythms. Barchas and his colleagues (1978), in a summary of research in this area, suggest that psychosocial stressors may cause long-term changes in brain functioning and that these changes may play a role in the development of mood disorders. Essentially the same point has been made by other leading researchers in the field, including Akiskal (1979) and Thase and colleagues (1985). This may be especially true for individuals with certain vulnerability factors.

We can now turn to the more general question of how stress interacts with various types of vulnerability factors to produce depression. As noted in Chapter 3, psychopathology researchers have long advocated the use of **diathesis-stress models** for understanding the development of certain kinds of psychopathology such as schizophrenia and recently have begun to do so for depression as well. The idea is that people who eventually develop a disorder differ in some underlying way from those who do not, and this underlying difference is known as their diathesis (or predisposition). However, among those with the diathesis, only those who experience stress will actually develop the disorder. Originally it was assumed that the diathesis was constitutional or biological in origin (e.g., Meehl, 1962; Rosenthal, 1963), but more recently depression researchers have also begun to propose diatheses for depression that are cognitive and social rather than constitutional (e.g., Metalsky et al., 1982).

Types of Diathesis-Stress Models for Unipolar Depression. One kind of diathesis-stress model for depression has already been discussed in the context of biological causal factors. As we saw, there is substantial evidence for some heritability for unipolar depression. Yet even among monozygotic twins there is only about 50 percent concordance, suggesting that a large role is left for environmental factors such as stressful life events in determining which of those who inherit the predisposition will develop the disorder. Moreover, at present we do not know what the nature of this genetic predisposition is. It may be some kind of constitutional weakness, for example, or it may be a personality trait.

Another general kind of diathesis-stress model for depression indeed proposes that personality variables play a role in predisposition to depression. Early clinical observations suggested that depressive patients are very concerned about what others think of them, and they also appear to be somewhat obsessive, anxious, and self-deprecatory. However, such observations of the personalities of depressed patients unfortunately confound the disorder with the personality that may predispose to it. That is, some of these observations of the personality features of depressives may be colored by their depressive symptoms (e.g., Hirschfeld et al., 1983).

Nevertheless, some studies that have been able to make good assessments of personality before the onset of illness confirm at least some of these clinical observations. For example, recent findings of low emotional strength and resiliency, and somewhat elevated levels of neuroticism in people who later became depressed (Hirschfeld et al., 1989), suggest that prede-pressive persons tend not to take an active approach to problem resolution and are somewhat more neurotic than persons who do not become depressed. In a recent review of many studies of this type, L.A. Clark and colleagues (1994) concluded that there was good evidence that neuroticism is the primary

personality variable that serves as a vulnerability factor for depression (and anxiety as well). Neuroticism or negative affectivity is a stable and heritable personality trait that involves a temperamental sensitivity to negative stimuli (Tellegen, 1985). That is, people who are high on this trait are prone to experiencing a broad range of negative moods, including not only sadness, but also anxiety, guilt, and hostility. In addition to serving as a vulnerability factor, neuroticism is also associated with a worse prognosis for complete recovery from depression. L.A. Clark and colleagues (1994) also concluded that there is some evidence (but more limited than that for neuroticism) that low levels of extraversion or positive affectivity may also serve as a vulnerability factor for depression. Positive affectivity involves a disposition to feel joyful, energetic, bold, proud, enthusiastic, and confident; people low on this disposition tend to feel unenthusiastic, unenergetic, dull, flat, and bored. It is therefore not surprising that this might make them more prone to depression.

Two other cognitive personality dimensions have also been associated with a vulnerability to depression. Moreover, these personality dimensions are thought to be specifically associated with different types of environmental stressors. Both Blatt (1974) and Beck (1983) have identified two different types of people who may be prone to depression when negative life events occur to which their personality makes them particularly sensitive. First, there are people high on *sociotropy,* who are excessively concerned with interpersonal dependency and who are overly sensitive to interpersonal losses or rejections. Second, there are people high on *autonomy,* who are excessively concerned with achievement issues and who tend to be highly self-critical; these people are especially sensitive to achievement failures. Research on these ideas has provided reasonably good support for the hypothesis that highly sociotropic people are especially vulnerable to negative interpersonal events (relative to their sensitivity to achievement failures) and are likely to become depressed when faced with them. Evidence supporting the idea that highly autonomous or self-critical subjects are especially vulnerable to becoming depressed in response to achievement failures is less consistent, but there are some supportive findings (Blatt & Zuroff, 1992; L.A. Clark et al., 1994; Nietzel & Harris, 1990).

Two other diathesis-stress models propose that cognitive diatheses are important vulnerability factors for depression. The first was proposed by Beck (1967), who argues that psychosocial stressors provoke severe depressive reactions only in people who already have negative **dysfunctional beliefs** that are rigid, extreme, and counterproductive. According to this hypothesis, a stressor merely serves to activate these depressogenic schemas that have previously been dormant. An example of a dysfunctional belief (that the person may well not be consciously aware of) is "If everyone doesn't love me, then my life is worthless." According to Beck and others, such a belief would predispose the person holding it to develop depression if he or she perceived social rejection. Alternatively, if the dysfunctional belief was "If I'm not perfectly successful, then I'm a nobody," then the person would be likely to develop negative thoughts and depressed affect if he or she felt a failure. Research addressing this theory will be discussed below in the context of a more general discussion of Beck's theory.

The second cognitive diathesis that has been proposed as creating vulnerability to depression is one's *attributional style* for important negative events. In this theory, known as the reformulated helplessness theory, Abramson and colleagues (1978) theorized that people with a depressive or **pessimistic attributional style,** which involves a tendency to make internal, stable, and global attributions for negative life events, are prone to experience depression following negative life events. A pessimistic or depressive attribution for receiving a low grade on an exam, for example, would be "I'm stupid" (i.e., the cause is *internal*—"I," *stable* because intelligence is not likely to change much, and *global* because stupidity is likely to affect a wide range of issues in one's life). A more optimistic attribution for the same event would be "The teacher made up the test in a bad mood and made it especially difficult" (i.e., the cause is *external*—the teacher, *unstable* because the teacher hopefully isn't always in a bad mood, and *specific* because it was only this one teacher for this one course). Evidence supporting this theory will be discussed below in the context of the more general presentation of the reformulated helplessness theory.

A final diathesis-stress model is based on evidence that early parental loss through death or permanent separation can create a vulnerability for depression. Beck (1967) provided some early clinical observations on this point in the context of his cognitive model of depression, although such a diathesis can be formulated in psychodynamic terms as well. Considerable research since that time has documented such observations. For example, in the classic Brown and Harris (1978) study, 40 out of 458 women had lost their mother before the age of 11. Among those 40, 42 percent developed clinical depression in adulthood; of the other 418 women who had not lost their mother at an early age, only 14 percent

had developed clinical depression in adulthood. Thus, the incidence of depression was three times higher in women who had lost their mother before the age of 11 (see Bowlby, 1980). Moreover, Brown and Harris also found that the type of loss (by death vs. by divorce or separation) also affected the severity of the depression experienced in adulthood. Women who had experienced loss by death were more likely to develop severe psychotic depression, whereas women who had experienced loss by divorce or separation were more likely to develop less severe neurotic depression. Two additional confirmations of a link between adult depression and childhood parental loss have also been reported by Barnes and Prosen (1985) and Roy (1985). If parental loss occurs through suicide, it doubtless adds an additional layer of problems for child survivors and potentially into adulthood as well. There is some research on the subject of the effects of parental suicide on children but none on the enduring effects into adulthood (Bowlby, 1980).

However, a number of studies have *not* found any evidence that early parental loss produces a vulnerability to depression in adulthood. In a recent review, Gotlib and Hammen (1992) concluded that it seems that the contradictory findings can be resolved if one considers the quality of parental care following the loss. In cases where the child continues to receive good parental care, a vulnerability to depression may not be created. However, if parental loss is followed by poor parental care, a vulnerability to depression is likely to be created (Bifulco, Brown, & Harris, 1987; Harris, Brown & Bifulco, 1986). More generally, Gotlib and Hammen (1992) have also reviewed evidence that the early lives of depressed adults were often marked by inadequate parenting, independent of parental loss. On average, depressed adults tend to remember more strained and unhappy relationships with their parents than do nondepressed adults, and mothers and siblings have tended to corroborate the depressed patients' memories (Brewin, Andrews, & Gotlib, 1993). Thus, poor early parenting, whether or not it occurs in the context of parental loss, seems to create a vulnerability to depression in adolescence and adulthood; this may be especially true for people with dysthymia beginning in adolescence, compared with people with major depression (Lizardi et al., 1995).

In summary, several different diathesis-stress models have been proposed for depression. Some propose a genetic or constitutional diathesis, which in conjunction with stressful life events can lead to depression. Other models suggest that personality variables, such as neuroticism or high levels of sociotropy and autonomy, provide the diathesis, which in interaction with negative life events can produce depression. Recently models proposing a cognitive diathesis—either in the form of underlying dysfunctional beliefs or depressogenic schemas, or in the form of a pessimistic or depressive attributional style—have received research attention. Finally, models proposing the importance of parental loss or poor parental care, especially in early childhood, have also received a good deal of attention. It should be understood that none of these models is mutually exclusive, and some may simply be describing the same diathesis in different terms or at different levels of analysis. For example, there is probably a genetic basis for neuroticism (Carey & DiLalla, 1994), and neuroticism seems to be highly correlated with depressive attributional style (L.A. Clark et al., 1994; Luten, Ralph & Mineka, 1995), and so these two proposed diatheses may be closely interrelated. Moreover, poor early parenting and parental loss have been strongly implicated in the formation of depressogenic schemas or dysfunctional beliefs (Beck, 1967; Bowlby, 1980). Thus, these two proposed diatheses may simply differ in whether they operate distally (poor early parenting) or proximally (depressogenic schemas) in contributing to vulnerability for depression.

We now turn to five major psychological theories of depression that have received much attention in recent years.

Psychodynamic Theories. In Freud's classic paper "Mourning and Melancholia" (1917), he noted the important similarity that we discussed earlier between the symptoms of clinical depression and the symptoms seen in someone mourning a lost loved one. Freud and a colleague, Karl Abraham (1911/1960a, 1916/1960b), both hypothesized that when a loved one dies, the mourner regresses to the oral stage of development (when the infant cannot distinguish self from other) and introjects or incorporates the lost person, feeling all the same feelings toward the self as toward the lost person. These feelings were thought to include anger and hostility because Freud believed that we unconsciously hold negative feelings toward those we love, in part because of their power over us. Freud hypothesized that depression could also occur in response to imagined or symbolic losses. For example, a student who fails in school or who fails at a romantic relationship may experience this symbolically as a loss of her parents' love. The primary difference that Freud observed between mourning and depression was that depressed people show lower self-esteem and are more self-critical. He further hypothesized that these self-accusations are really unconsciously directed at the lost love object (real or symbolic), and

do not occur in normal grief if the person has had a childhood characterized by good attachment relationships. By contrast, the person who is predisposed to becoming depressed is someone who has either experienced the loss of a mother or whose parents did not fulfill the infant's needs for nurturance and love. In both cases, the infant will grow up feeling unworthy of love, have low self-esteem, and be prone to depression when faced with real or symbolic losses.

Later psychodynamic theorists such as Klein (1934) and Jacobson (1971) emphasized even more than did Freud the importance of the quality of the early mother-infant relationship in establishing a vulnerability (or invulnerability) to depression. Bowlby (1973, 1980), who started as a psychoanalyst and later developed an integrative approach known as attachment theory, also extensively documented a child's need for a secure attachment to parental figures in order to be resistant to depression (and anxiety) in later life. As we saw earlier, much research supports this position. At the same time these later theorists emphasized low self-esteem as a critical issue (Bibring, 1953) and de-emphasized the idea of regression to an oral stage of development (Jacobson, 1971). Freud's idea that depression is associated with anger turned inward has also not fared very well. For example, Beck and Ward (1961) showed that the dreams of depressed people more often reflected themes involving loss and failure rather than anger and hostility. Moreover, as noted in DSM-IV, depressed people often show high levels of anger and criticism toward those close to them.

Perhaps the most important contribution of the psychodynamic approaches to depression has been to note the importance of loss (both real, and symbolic or imagined) to the onset of depression and to note the striking similarities between the symptoms of mourning and the symptoms of depression (Bowlby, 1980). Even theorists who disagree with many of the specific details of these theories have found it imperative that their own theories also be able to account for these basic observations.

Behavioral Theories. Over the past few decades several variations on behavioral theories of depression have been proposed. For example, Ferster (1973, 1974) argued that depression could be equated with a state of extinction from positive reinforcement, that is, a state in which the person's responses no longer produce positive reinforcement. He noted that this was consistent with the idea that major losses in one's life—which we know can precipitate depression—can be associated with loss of significant sources of reinforcement. Lewinsohn (1974;

Lewinsohn et al., 1985) elaborated on this model and proposed that depression can be elicited when a person's behavior no longer brings the accustomed reinforcement or gratification. The failure to receive positive reinforcement contingent on one's responses, or an increase in the rate of negative reinforcements, in turn leads to a reduction in effort and activity, thus resulting in even less chance of coping with aversive conditions and achieving need gratification. One problem that can lead to a low rate of positive reinforcement is a deficit in social skills, which makes it difficult for a person to obtain rewards that stem from social interactions. Another problem may be the lack of reinforcers due to environmental circumstances (e.g., being sick and confined to home, or losing one's job). Finally, some people simply find more activities reinforcing than do others, and people's sensitivity to reinforcers can change as they become depressed; moreover, people also differ in sensitivity to negative reinforcers.

Lewinsohn and his colleagues conducted a significant amount of research to investigate this theory, finding, for example, that depressed persons receive fewer positive verbal reinforcements from their families than do nondepressed persons and fewer social reinforcements in their lives in general. As we have already seen, they also tend to experience more negative events. Moreover, their moods seem to vary with both their positive and their negative reinforcement rates. They also have lower levels of activity and report less pleasure from seemingly positive events (see Rehm & Tyndall, 1993).

Although much of this research is consistent with the behavioral theory, the findings only show that depressed persons may have a low rate of response-contingent positive reinforcement, or a high rate of negative reinforcement. However, they cannot demonstrate that depression is *caused* by these factors. Instead it may be that some of the primary symptoms of depression, such as low levels of energy and pessimism, instead cause the depressed person to experience these lower rates of reinforcement (Carson & Carson, 1984).

Beck's Cognitive Theory. One of the most prominent theories of depression for the past 25 years has been that of Aaron Beck—a psychiatrist who became disenchanted with psychodynamic theories of depression early in his career and developed his own cognitive theory of depression. Whereas the most prominent symptoms of depression have generally been considered to be the affective or mood symptoms, Beck hypothesized that the cognitive symptoms of depression may often precede and cause the affective or mood symptoms rather than vice versa. That is, if you think that you're a failure or that you're ugly, it would not be surprising if those thoughts led to a depressed mood. According to Beck it is these negative cognitions that are central to depression, rather than, for example, the low rates of reinforcement postulated by the behavioral view.

There are several important features of Beck's theory. First, there are the underlying *depressogenic schemas* or *dysfunctional beliefs* that we have already discussed in the context of diathesis-stress models. These depression-producing beliefs are thought to develop during childhood and adolescence as a function of one's experiences with one's parents and with significant others (teachers, peers, etc.). Children who lose a parent or who have poor parenting are prone to develop such depressogenic schemas. The schemas or beliefs are thought to serve as the underlying diathesis or vulnerability to develop depression, although they may lie dormant for years in the absence of significant stressors. However, when dysfunctional beliefs are activated by current stressors, the **negative cognitive triad** becomes apparent and is experienced by the depressed person in the form of **negative automatic thoughts.** These are thoughts that often occur just below the surface of awareness and that involve unpleasant pessimistic predictions. These pessimistic predictions tend to center on the three themes of the negative triad: (a) negative thoughts about the *self* ("I'm ugly"; "I'm worthless"; "I'm a failure"), (b) negative thoughts about one's experiences and the surrounding *world* ("No one loves me"; "People treat me badly"); and (c) negative thoughts about one's *future* ("It's hopeless because things will always be this way").

Along with the dysfunctional beliefs that fuel the negative cognitive triad once they are activated, Beck also postulates that the negative cognitive triad tends to be maintained by a variety of cognitive biases or distortions. These include:

1. *Dichotomous or all-or-none reasoning,* which involves a tendency to think in extremes. For example, someone might discount a less-than-perfect performance by saying "If I can't get it 100 percent right, there's no point in doing it at all."

2. *Selective abstraction,* which involves a tendency to focus on one negative detail of a situation while ignoring the other elements of the situation. Someone might say "I didn't have a moment of pleasure or fun today" not because this is true but because he or she selectively remembered the negative things and not the positive things that happened.

3. *Arbitrary inference,* which involves jumping to a conclusion based on minimal or no evidence. A depressed person might say after an initial homework assignment from a cognitive therapist did not work: "This therapy will never work for me."

4. *Overgeneralization,* which involves a tendency to draw a sweeping conclusion from a single, perhaps rather unimportant, event. For example, someone who makes one mistake may conclude "Everything I do goes wrong." (Examples taken from Fennell, 1989, p. 193.)

It is easy to see how each of these cognitive distortions tends to maintain the negative cognitive triad. That is, if the content of your thoughts regarding your views of your self, your world, and your future is already negative, and you tend to minimize the good things that happen to you or to draw negative conclusions based on minimal evidence, those negative thoughts are not likely to disappear. In addition, just as the underlying dysfunctional beliefs when activated elicit the negative cognitive triad, so too does the negative thinking produced by the negative triad serve to reinforce those underlying beliefs. Thus, each of these components of Beck's cognitive theory serves to reinforce the others (see Figure 6.2). Moreover, as already noted, these negative thoughts can be expected to produce some of the other symptoms of depression, such as sadness, dejection, and lack of motivation.

Over the past 20 years an enormous amount of research has been conducted testing various aspects of Beck's theory. As we will see in a later section on treatment, it has generated a very effective form of treatment for depression known as cognitive therapy. In addition, it has been well supported as a descriptive theory. Depressed patients are considerably more negative in their thinking than are nondepressed persons, and than they themselves are when they are not depressed. Moreover, there is also evidence for the negative cognitive triad—depressed persons do think more negatively about themselves and the world around them than do nondepressed persons and are quite negative about the future—especially their own future. The negative thinking that Beck describes seems to occur in all subtypes of depression studied to date (see Haaga, Dyck, & Ernst, 1991).

In addition to evidence showing that depressed people have negative automatic thoughts revolving around the themes of the negative cognitive triad, there is also some evidence supporting the existence of cognitive biases in depression. For example, depressed people show biased recall of negative information, whereas nondepressed people tend to show a bias for positive information. The bias occurs

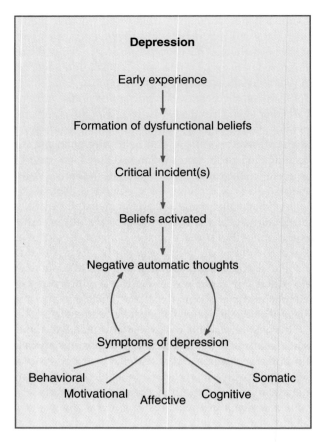

Figure 6.2 *According to Beck's cognitive model of depression, certain kinds of early experiences can lead to the formation of dysfunctional assumptions that leave the person vulnerable to depression later in life if certain critical incidents (stressors) serve to activate those assumptions. Once activated, these dysfunctional assumptions trigger automatic thoughts that in turn produce depressive symptoms. The depressive symptoms further fuel the depressive automatic thoughts. (Adapted from Fennel, 1989.)*

whether or not the information involves autobiographical material (about their own lives) or emotionally meaningful words (lonely, blue, dejected vs. confident, exuberant, outgoing) presented by an experimenter (Matt, Vazquez, & Campbell, 1992; Mathews & MacLeod, 1994; Mineka & Nugent, in press). In addition, depressed people are more likely to draw negative conclusions that go beyond the information presented in a scenario than are nondepressed people, and to underestimate the positive feedback they have received (Haaga et al., 1991). It is easy to see how these biases can play an important role in maintaining depression. For example, if you're already depressed and your memory is biased so that you primarily remember the bad things that have happened to you it is easy to see how this is likely to maintain or exacerbate the depression.

Teasdale (1988) has called this the vicious cycle of depression.

Although research supports most features of the descriptive aspects of Beck's theory, research directed toward confirming the *causal* hypotheses of Beck's theory has had more mixed findings. For example, it has been difficult to find convincing support for the hypothesis that the depressogenic schemas or dysfunctional beliefs thought to reflect the underlying vulnerability to depression are actually present when the person is not depressed (either before an episode of depression or following recovery). For example, the elevations shown on scales measuring dysfunctional beliefs seen when the person is depressed tend to disappear when the patient has recovered. There is some recent evidence that when a recovered depressed patient is in a sad mood the elevations in dysfunctional beliefs may come back (Miranda & Persons, 1988; Miranda, Persons, & Byers, 1990), suggesting that it may be best to test for vulnerability when people are in a sad mood. However, more research on this topic is necessary before strong conclusions can be drawn. In addition, tests of the causal hypothesis of Beck's theory regarding the onset of depression have also provided mixed results. That is, most studies that have measured vulnerability at Time 1 and followed subjects for one or more months, have *not* found that a measure of vulnerability, in interaction with stressful life events, predicts depression at Time 2. However, a recent review (Haaga et al., 1991) concluded that there has not yet been an adequate test of the causal aspects of the theory and that it would be premature to dismiss it at this point in time.

The Helplessness and Hopelessness Theories of Depression. A second set of interrelated cognitive theories of depression has also generated an enormous amount of research over the past 20 years. Whereas Beck's theory originated out of his clinical observations of the pervasive patterns of negative thinking seen in depressed patients, the learned helplessness theory of depression originated out of observations in an animal research laboratory. Martin Seligman (1974, 1975) first proposed that the laboratory phenomenon known as **learned helplessness** might provide a useful animal model of depression. In the late 1960s Seligman and his colleagues (Maier, Seligman, & Solomon, 1969; Overmier and Seligman, 1967) noted that laboratory dogs who were first exposed to uncontrollable shocks later showed major deficits in learning in a different situation that they could control shocks. Animals first exposed to equal amounts of *controllable* shocks showed no such deficits. Indeed, when the uncontrollably shocked animals were put in the new situation with potentially controllable shocks, they didn't even seem to try to learn whether there was some way to control the shocks; instead they seemed to simply passively accept the shocks.

Seligman and his colleagues proposed the learned helplessness hypothesis to explain these effects. This hypothesis states that when an organism learns that it has no control over aversive events such as shock, this "learned helplessness" will produce three kinds of deficits: (a) motivational deficits: if you have already learned that you have no control, why bother trying? This was consistent with observations that the helpless animals did not initiate many responses on their own, that is, they didn't even try to escape the shocks in the new situation; (b) cognitive deficits: if you've learned that you have no control, this interferes with your future ability to *learn* that you can have control. This was consistent with observations that even when a dog made an occasional response to escape the shock, it did not seem to notice that its response had brought relief and returned to passively accepting the shock on future trials; (c) emotional deficits: learning that you have no control produces passivity and perhaps depression. It was this observation (that the animals looked depressed) that captured Seligman's attention and led ultimately to his proposing a learned helplessness model of depression.

Subsequent research demonstrated that helpless animals also show lower levels of aggression, loss of appetite and weight, and a variety of physiological changes in neurotransmitter levels. After demonstrating that the learned helplessness phenomenon occurred across species, including humans (Hiroto & Seligman, 1975), Seligman went on to propose that learned helplessness may underlie some types of human depression. That is, people undergoing stressful life events over which they have little or no control develop a syndrome like the helplessness syndrome seen in animals. Seligman noted that there were many symptom similarities between helplessness and depression. For example, both helpless animals and depressed humans show lowered initiation of voluntary responses, or what is known in the depression literature as "paralysis of will." In addition, both show a negative cognitive set, and here he noted the similarities between the cognitive deficits seen in helpless animals and the pervasive negative thinking seen in depressives noted by Beck. Moreover, the lack of aggression and loss of appetite, as well as the physiological changes observed, seemed to be parallel in helplessness and depression.

The idea of helplessness being central to depression was not entirely new, as investigators of widely differing theoretical orientations had emphasized that feelings of helplessness and hopelessness are basic to depressive reactions. For example, in what is considered the original classic treatment of the subject, Bibring (1953), a psychoanalyst, held that the basic mechanism of depression is "the ego's shocking awareness of its helplessness in regard to its aspirations . . . such that the depressed person . . . has lost his incentives and gives up, not the goals, but pursuing them, since this proves to be useless" (p. 39). However, none of the earlier proposals about the role of helplessness in depression were stated in a testable form as was Seligman's helplessness model. Thus it is not surprising that the learned helplessness model of depression quickly attracted a great deal of attention and much research was devoted to testing it. HIGHLIGHT 6.2 discusses the helplessness approach, as well as other approaches to understanding sex differences in unipolar depression.

By 1978, there was both a substantial amount of evidence supporting the theory, as well as some that was critical. Indeed, an entire special issue of the *Journal of Abnormal Psychology* was devoted specifically to this topic—with arguments and evidence both pro and con. At that time, Abramson and colleagues (1978) published a major reformulation of the theory that took into account some of the critiques and better acknowledged some of the complexities of what humans do when faced with uncontrollable events (complexities that are not necessarily shared by animals). In particular, they proposed that when people (probably unlike animals) are exposed to uncontrollable negative events, they ask themselves, why? The kinds of **attributions** that people make about uncontrollable events are, in turn, central to whether they become depressed. They proposed three critical dimensions on which attributions are made: internal/external, global/specific, and stable/unstable. As noted earlier, a depressogenic or pessimistic attribution for a negative event would be an internal, stable, and global one. For example, if your boyfriend treats you badly and you conclude that "It's because I'm ugly and boring" you are much more likely to become depressed than if you conclude that "it's because he's in a bad mood today after failing his exam and he is taking it out on me." Moreover, as noted in the diathesis-stress section earlier, Abramson and colleagues also hypothesized that people have a relatively stable and consistent style for making attributions and that people who have a pessimistic or depressogenic style are at risk for depression when faced with uncontrollable negative life events. That is, the pessimistic attributional style is a diathesis for depression.

Since it was proposed in 1978, the *reformulated helplessness theory* has generated an enormous amount of research. For example, in 1986 a review of over 100 studies that had already examined whether depressed people do indeed have this kind of pessimistic attributional style concluded that there was strong evidence in support of this idea (Sweeney, Anderson, & Bailey, 1986). However, the evidence in support of the vulnerability hypothesis is much more mixed. As with Beck's vulnerability construct (dysfunctional attitudes), evidence seems to suggest that the pessimistic attributional style seems to go away when the person has recovered from depression, although no one has as yet tested whether it would be reinstated in a sad mood. In addition, studies that have examined the ability of this diathesis to predict the onset of depression in interaction with negative life events have produced mixed results (Abramson et al., 1989; Barnett & Gotlib, 1988b; Peterson, Maier, & Seligman, 1993). However, this theory, like Beck's, is sufficiently complex that it is difficult to provide a critical test of it, and probably no one study has yet done so.

In 1989, a further revision of this theory was presented—known as the *hopelessness theory* (Abramson et al., 1989). Although many elements of the earlier theory were similar, these investigators proposed that having a pessimistic attributional style in conjunction with one or more negative life events was not sufficient to produce depression unless one first experienced a state of hopelessness. A hopelessness expectancy was defined by the perception that one had no control over what was going to happen and by absolute certainty that an important bad outcome was going to occur or that a highly desired good outcome was not going to occur. So a hopelessness expectancy was proposed as a sufficient condition for depression, although Abramson and colleagues acknowledged that this may be true for only a subset of depressives—a new subtype that they defined as the hopelessness subtype of depression.

Research is currently testing this theory. One supportive study with college students found that students with a pessimistic attributional style who also had low-self esteem were likely to develop a depressed mood for several days following a poor grade on a midterm exam (Metalsky et al., 1993). In addition, this effect was related to the tendency to become hopeless, as predicted by the theory. However, much further research remains to be done to determine whether this theory can also explain the development of clinical depression. Moreover, the theory has also been criticized for proposing hopelessness as a *cause* of depression (as well as a symptom) when most investigators have considered it to be only a *symptom* of depression. This is similar to

Sex Differences in Unipolar Depression

It has long been observed that women are about twice as likely to become clinically depressed (to have dysthymia or unipolar depression) as are men. These differences occur in most countries around the world, with the few exceptions coming from developing and rural countries such as tribes in Nigeria and Iran. In the United States, this sex difference starts in adolescence (with the exception of students in college) and continues until about age 65, when it seems to disappear. Yet among school age children, boys are more likely to be diagnosed with depression than girls. Questions have been raised about whether these differences stem from some kind of artifact, such as young women in adolescence becoming more willing to report their feelings, but the data do not support this idea (Nolen-Hoeksema, 1987, 1990; Young et al., 1990). What kinds of theories have been proposed that can explain this interesting collection of observations?

One set of theories is biological— for example, suggestions have been made that hormonal factors account for the differences. Studies examining this hypothesis have not been very supportive, however. Other biological theories have proposed that among women and men sharing a common genetic diathesis, women are more likely to become depressed and men are more likely to become alcoholic. Research has also addressed the possibility that women are simply more predisposed to depression because of some kind of mutant gene on the X chromosome (of which women have two and men only one). However, research does not support any of these biological hypotheses, leading us to look at social and psychological factors (Nolen-Hoeksema, 1990).

One psychological theory has proposed that by virtue of their roles in society women are more prone to experiencing a sense of lack of control over negative life events. These feelings of helplessness might stem from any or all of the following: dis-

crimination in the workplace, the relative imbalance of power in many heterosexual relationships, high rates of sexual and physical abuse against women, and role overload (e.g., being a working wife and mother). There is at least some evidence that each of these conditions is associated with higher-than-expected rates of depression, but whether the effects involve a sense of helplessness has not been established (Nolen-Hoeksema, 1990). Nevertheless, this remains a plausible hypothesis in need of further research designed directly to test it.

Another intriguing hypothesis is that women have different responses to being in a depressed mood than do men, and it may be these different responses that lead to differences in the severity and duration of depression for women and men. In particular, it seems that women are more likely to *ruminate* when they become depressed. Rumination includes responses such as trying to figure out why you are depressed, crying to relieve tension, or talking to your friends about your depression. It is known that rumination is likely to exacerbate depression, in part by interfering with instrumental behavior (i.e., taking action). Men, by contrast, are more likely to engage in a distracting activity when they get in a depressed mood, and distraction seems to reduce depression (Nolen-Hoeksema, 1990). Distraction might include going to a movie, playing a

sport, or avoiding thinking about why you are depressed. The origin of these sex differences in response to depression is unclear, but if further research supports this hypothesis, it would certainly suggest that a prevention strategy for girls would be to teach them distraction rather than rumination as a response to depression.

Finally, we must consider why the sex differences only start in adolescence. This is a time of rapid physiological, environmental, and psychological changes known to create turmoil for many adolescents, but why are adolescent females more likely to become depressed? There is evidence that the development of secondary sexual characteristics is harder psychologically for girls than for boys. Body dissatisfaction goes up for females at this time, and down for males; moreover, body dissatisfaction is more closely related to self-esteem for girls than for boys. Much of girls' dissatisfaction with their bodies comes from their realization of the discrepancy between our society's ideal of a thin, prepubescent body shape for females and the fact that they are gaining fat as they mature sexually. In addition, this is a time of an increase in sex role socialization. Girls tend to have increased pressure to assume a feminine sex role, and if they accept this somewhat nonassertive, dependent role they may be predisposed to anxiety and depression. But if they reject this role, they may in turn be rejected by the opposite sex. One piece of evidence consistent with this hypothesis is that adolescent girls do perceive competence as a liability and tend to conceal their intelligence. Indeed, one study showed a significant positive correlation between IQ and depression in adolescent girls. For boys, by contrast, there was a small negative correlation between IQ and depression. Again, much research remains to be done to fully reveal how sex differences in depression emerge in adolescence, but these are intriguing ideas that will be pursued in the future (Nolen-Hoeksema, 1990).

the points made earlier regarding Beck's negative cognitive triad and Seligman's pessimistic attributional style, which may only be concomitants or correlates of depression rather than causes. Nevertheless, the hopelessness theory, like the other cognitive theories, is likely to remain a significant area of research for the foreseeable future. HIGHLIGHT 6.3 discusses how the hopelessness theory accounts for the high degree of comorbidity between anxiety and unipolar depressive disorders.

Interpersonal Effects of Mood Disorders. Although there is no interpersonal theory of depression that is as clearly articulated as are the cognitive theories, there has nevertheless been a considerable amount of research in the past two decades on interpersonal factors in depression. As we will see, interpersonal problems and social skills deficits may well play a causal role in at least some cases of depression. In addition, depression creates many interpersonal difficulties—with strangers and friends as well as with family members (Hammen, 1991, 1995). We will first start by discussing the way in which interpersonal problems can play a causal role in depression.

We noted earlier that Brown and Harris (1978) had found that women without a close confiding relationship were more vulnerable to depression. Since that time many more studies have supported the idea that people who lack social support are more vulnerable to depression. For example, Holohan and Moos (1991) in a four-year prospective study of 254 adults found that low family support predicted levels of depression four years later. In addition, Gotlib and Hammen (1992) reviewed a considerable amount of research showing that depressed individuals have smaller and less supportive social networks. Billings and colleagues (1983) confirmed that these findings are not just due to a negative reporting bias, because the findings were confirmed by nondepressed family members. These restricted social networks seem to precede the onset of depression, and although depressed persons may have more social contact when their symptoms remit, their social networks are still more restricted than those of never-depressed persons. In addition, Gotlib and Hammen (1992) review evidence that depressives have social skills deficits. For example, they seem to speak more slowly and monotonously and to maintain less eye contact; they are also poorer than nondepressed people at solving interpersonal problems.

As already noted, depressed people not only have interpersonal problems, but their own behavior also seems to make these problems worse. For example, the behavior of a depressed individual often places others in the position of providing sympathy, support, and care. Such positive reinforcement does not necessarily follow, however. Depressive behavior can, and frequently does, elicit negative feelings and rejection in other people, including strangers, roommates, and spouses (Coyne, 1976; Gurtman, 1986; Hammen & Peters, 1977, 1978; Hokanson et al., 1989; see Gotlib & Hammen, 1992, for a review). In fact, merely being around a depressed person may induce depressed feelings in others (Howes, Hokanson, & Loewenstein, 1985; Strack & Coyne, 1983) and may make a nondepressed person less willing to interact again with the depressed person. Moreover, such negative reactions are often correctly anticipated by a depressed person (Strack & Coyne, 1983).

Coyne (1976) suggested that the presence or absence of support may depend on whether a depressed individual is skillful enough to circumvent or turn to advantage the negative affect he or she tends to create in other people. Especially if the other people are prone to guilt feelings, a depressed person may elicit considerable sympathy and support, at least over the short term. More commonly, the ultimate result is probably a downwardly spiraling relationship from which others finally withdraw, making the depressed person worse. Indeed, this idea is supported by the findings from several longitudinal studies of college roommates. Howes, Hokanson, and Loewenstein (1985) found that the initially nondepressed roommates showed more and more depressed mood themselves over the course of a year living with a depressed roommate. Yet these roommates, even as they were showing more depressed mood themselves, also showed increasing levels of caretaking as their depressed roommates became more and more dependent (Hokanson et al., 1986). Hokanson and colleagues (1989) further reported that the depressed roommate reporting *reduced* (rather than increased) contact with the nondepressed roommate and low enjoyability of such contact. Finally, Hokanson, Hummer, and Butler (1991) found that depressed roommates perceived more hostility and lower levels of friendliness from their roommates than did nondepressed roommates.

In recent years interpersonal aspects of depression have also been carefully studied in the context of marital and family relationships. Gotlib and Hammen (1992) have reviewed evidence that between one-third and one-half of maritally distressed couples have at least one partner with clinical depression. In addition, it is known that marital distress predicts a poor prognosis for a depressed spouse whose symptoms have remitted (Hooley & Teasdale, 1989). That is, a person whose depression clears up is likely to relapse if he or she has an unsatisfying marriage.

Comorbidity of Anxiety and Mood Disorders

Questions regarding whether depression and anxiety can be differentiated in a reliable and valid way have received a good deal of attention over the years. Only recently, however, have researchers begun to make significant advances in understanding the real scope of the problem. The overlap between measures of depression and anxiety occurs at all levels of analysis—patient self-report, clinician ratings, diagnosis, and family/genetic factors (Clark & Watson, 1991a, 1991b). That is, persons who rate themselves high on a scale for symptoms of anxiety also tend to rate themselves high on a scale for symptoms of depression, and clinicians rating these same individuals do the same thing. Moreover, the overlap also occurs at the diagnostic level. One recent review of the literature estimated that approximately half of the patients who receive a diagnosis of a mood disorder also receive a diagnosis of an anxiety disorder, and vice versa (Clark & Watson, 1991a, 1991b). Finally, there is also considerable evidence from genetic and family studies of the close relationship between anxiety and depressive disorders (Clark & Watson, 1991a, 1991b; Kendler et al., 1992d; Merikangas, 1990; Weissman, 1990). Much of the genetic evidence has concerned the relationship between panic disorder and depression (Breier, Charney, & Heninger, 1984; Weissman, 1990), but one recent very large twin study has also shown that the liability for depression and generalized anxiety disorder comes from the same genetic factors, and which disorder develops is a result of what environmental experiences occur (Kendler et al., 1992d).

At present the dominant theoretical approach to understanding the overlap between depressive and anxiety symptoms is that of Watson, L. A. Clark, and Tellegen (L. A. Clark & Watson, 1991a, 1991b; L. A. Clark et al., 1994; Tellegen, 1985; Watson et al., 1995a, 1995b). They have demonstrated that the substantial overlap between various measures of anxiety and depression reflects the fact that most of the measures used tap the broad mood and personality dimension of *negative affect,* which includes affective states such as distress, anger, fear, guilt, and worry. Both depressed and anxious individuals show high levels of negative affect and cannot be distinguished on this basis. But these researchers have also shown that anxiety and depression can be distinguished on the basis of a second dimension of mood and personality known as *positive affect,* which includes affective states such as excitement, delight, interest, and pride. Depressed persons tend to be characterized by low levels of positive affect, but anxious individuals are not. That is, only depressed individuals show the signs of fatigue and lack of energy and enthusiasm characteristic of low positive affect. Clark and Watson have also shown that anxious, but not depressed people tend to be characterized by high levels of yet another mood dimension known as *anxious hyperarousal,* symptoms of which include racing heart, trembling, dizziness, and shortness of breath. This tripartite model of anxiety and depression thus explains what features for anxiety and depression are common to both (high negative affect) and what features are distinct (low positive affect for depression, and anxious hyperarousal for anxiety). Beck and D. A. Clark have presented evidence that there is also some discriminability of anxiety and depression based on the kinds of cognitions the patients show (e.g., D. A. Clark, Beck, & Beck, 1994a; D. A. Clark, Steer, and Beck, 1994b). For example, cognitions about loss, failure, and hopelessness are more common in major depression and dysthymia than in panic disorder and generalized anxiety disorder (although they are elevated in all of these disorders). Threat-related cognitions were significantly elevated in panic disorder (but not generalized anxiety disorder) relative to major depression and dysthymia.

There are also several features of comorbidity between anxiety and mood disorders at the diagnostic level that raise interesting questions about what the common and distinct causal factors may be. For example, there is usually a sequential relationship between the symptoms of anxiety and depression, both within an episode and between episodes. For example, Bowlby (1973, 1980) described a biphasic response to separation and loss in which the first phase appears to be one of agitation and anxiety, followed by despair and depression. And across a lifetime, individuals are more likely to experience an anxiety disorder first and a depressive disorder later, rather than vice versa (Alloy et al., 1990). There is also differential comorbidity between depression and the different anxiety disorders, with panic disorder and obsessive-compulsive disorder being more likely to be accompanied by depression than, for example, simple or social phobia.

Alloy and colleagues (1990) proposed an expansion of the hopelessness model of depression to account for these and other features of comorbidity. In their helplessness/hopelessness model they propose that anxiety and anxiety disorders are characterized by prominent feelings of helplessness. People with these disorders expect that they may be helpless in controlling important outcomes, but they also believe that future control might be possible and so are likely to experience increased arousal and anxiety and an intense scanning of the environment in efforts to gain control. If the person becomes convinced of his or her helplessness to control important outcomes, but is still uncertain about whether the bad outcome will actually occur, a mixed anxiety/depression syndrome is likely to emerge. And finally, if the person is convinced not only of his or her helplessness, but also becomes certain that bad outcomes will occur, helplessness becomes hopelessness and depression sets in. Alloy and colleagues show how this perspective can explain certain features of comorbidity between anxiety and depressive disorders. For example, the sequential relationship is explained by the fact that one is likely to go through a stage of feeling helpless for some time before one becomes totally hopeless. And some anxiety disorders may be more associated with depression precisely because the symptoms of the disorder themselves (for example, obsessive thoughts and compulsions, and panic attacks) are so distressing and seemingly uncontrollable as to create a more certain form of helplessness, leading to the mixed anxiety/depressive diagnostic picture.

People without social support networks are more prone to depression when faced with major stressors. Depressed people also have smaller and less supportive social support networks while they are depressed and to some extent even after their depression has remitted.

As already noted, the high cooccurrence of marital distress and depression may occur because depressed people induce negative affect in their spouses along the lines discussed above with strangers and roommates. There is good evidence that living with a depressed person is highly stressful—indeed, so stressful that it may make nearly half of nondepressed spouses candidates for psychotherapy (Coyne et al., 1987). In reviewing the literature on this topic, Gotlib and Hammen (1992) concluded that depressed people and their spouses tend to perceive their interactions as marked by tension and hostility. Moreover, these high levels of tension and hostility do not necessarily seem to remit soon after the depressed spouse recovers.

But there is also evidence that marital distress can lead to depression as well, because marital distress often precedes a depressive episode and is frequently identified as a precipitant of depression and as a reason for seeking treatment (see Gotlib & Hammen, 1992). And certainly marital distress is likely to affect the course of a depressive episode and the likelihood of relapse. Thus the evidence suggests both that marital distress can lead to depression, and that depression can lead to marital distress.

This research is consistent with the clinical impressions one often has of depressed couples. Depression can often be seen as a person's attempts to communicate feelings of angry discouragement and despair—to say, in effect, "I have needs that you are failing to meet." Too often, however, this communication goes unheeded. Thus in failing marriages we may see one partner trying to communicate his or her unmet expectations, distress, and dependency and becoming increasingly depressed and disturbed when the other partner fails to make the hoped-for response. Indeed, the nondepressed spouse may respond with increased contempt for what he or she sees as the other's "weakness," while at the same time becoming distressed because of an inability to control the situation.

The effects of depression in one family member extend to children as well. Parental depression puts children at high risk for many problems, but especially for depression (Beardslee et al., 1983; Puig-Antich et al., 1989). In addition, Keller and colleagues (1986) reported a study on 72 children from families in which at least one parent had a severe (but not psychotic) mood disorder. They found that the severity and chronicity of the parents' (especially the mothers') disorders were uniformly associated with adaptive failure and psychiatric diagnoses, including depression, among the children. These are just a handful of the findings in this extensively researched area (see Gotlib & Hammen, 1992). A skeptic may argue that such studies merely prove that these disorders are genetically transmitted. However, genetic transmission as a sole explanation becomes less likely when we consider that there are many studies documenting negative interactional patterns between depressed mothers and their children. For example, depressed mothers show more friction and have less playful, mutually rewarding interactions with their children (see Gotlib & Hammen, 1992). So although genetically determined vulnerability may be involved, psychosocial influences probably play a more decisive role.

Thus, there are many different psychological theories regarding what causes unipolar depression, ranging from the psychodynamic to the cognitive and interpersonal. Some, such as Beck's cognitive theory and the reformulated helplessness and hopelessness theories, are clearly formulated as diathesis-stress models, where in each of these the diathesis is seen as cognitive in nature. The psychodynamic and interpersonal approaches are not as clearly formulated as diathesis-stress models, although both emphasize the importance of early experiential variables (such as the quality of the parent-child relationship) in determining vulnerability to depression. Each of these theories captures interesting aspects of the causal pathways to depression, and given the probable heterogeneity of unipolar depression it is unlikely that any one theory will ever successfully explain all of the variance regarding who does and who does not become depressed when faced with comparable stressful life circumstances.

Bipolar Disorders
Biological Causal Factors

Hereditary Factors. As we have already noted, there is a significant genetic component to bipolar disorder, one that is stronger than that for unipolar disorder. A recent summary of studies using refined diagnostic procedures suggests that about 8 percent of the first-degree relatives of a person with bipolar illness can also be expected to have bipolar disorder, and another 11 percent can be expected to have unipolar disorder (Katz & McGuffin, 1993). This means that the combined risk for unipolar or bipolar disorder in first-degree relatives of a person with bipolar disorder is about 19 percent.

Although family studies cannot by themselves establish a genetic basis for the disorder, results from twin studies also point to a genetic basis. Kallmann (1958) found the concordance rate for these disorders to be much higher for identical than for fraternal twins. Other studies have supported these earlier findings (Mendlewicz, 1985; Perris, 1979), and one particularly good study by Bertelsen, Harvald, and Hauger (1977) estimated that monozygotic twins were 3 ½ times more likely to be concordant (69 percent) for a diagnosis of bipolar disorder than were dizygotic twins (19 percent). About three-quarters of the affected cotwins had the same form of the disorder (bipolar), but nearly one-quarter had unipolar disorder. Thus, the results from both family and twin studies suggest that the risk for blood relatives of people with bipolar disorders includes an enhanced risk for unipolar disorder.

There appears to be only one adoption study focusing exclusively on people with bipolar disorder (Mendlewicz & Rainer, 1977). They found that 31 percent of the biological parents of the bipolar subjects had a mood disorder (both bipolar and unipolar), compared with only 2 percent of the biological parents of controls. The rate for biological parents was very similar to that seen in the biological parents of nonadopted bipolars (26 percent). Thus the results of this one adoption study are also consistent with the conclusion that there is a strong genetic predisposition for bipolar illness. Indeed, the Bertelsen and colleagues (1977) study suggests that genes account for over 80 percent of the variance in liability for bipolar disorder—a figure that is much

higher than estimates for unipolar disorder or any of the other major adult psychiatric disorders, including schizophrenia (Torrey et al., 1994). It is of interest that Kraepelin (1922), who first identified manic-depressive illness, also estimated that about 80 percent of his cases were predisposed to the disorder by a "hereditary taint" (Katz & McGuffin, 1993).

The finding of elevated rates of both bipolar and unipolar forms of the disorder in the relatives of bipolars can be taken in one of two ways. One possibility is that bipolar disorder does not "breed true" (that is, bipolar genes do not specifically predispose for bipolar disorder, but also for unipolar disorder). This possibility would be of considerable theoretical interest given the current trend to treat unipolar and bipolar disorders as separate conditions. As discussed by Goodwin and Jamison (1990), this possibility that bipolar disorder does not breed true might occur because bipolar disorder as currently conceived is a rather different diagnostic category than Kraepelin's original manic-depressive illness. For Kraepelin, manic-depressive illness also included recurrent forms of unipolar disorder (that is, unipolar disorder that occurs over and over again). If recurrent unipolar disorder should indeed be grouped with bipolar disorder from the standpoint of etiology, this would predict that the increased risk of unipolar disorder in the relatives of bipolar patients should be accounted for by the recurrent type of unipolar disorder, which is known to be more heritable than nonrecurrent unipolar disorder (Goodwin & Jamison, 1990). Alternatively, others have noted that these elevations in rates of unipolar depression in the relatives of bipolars may not actually be much greater than would be expected by chance given that unipolar disorder is so much more prevalent in the general population than is bipolar disorder. In the latter case, the conclusion that bipolar disorder does not "breed true" would be unwarranted.

Finally, we should mention work on genetic linkage studies and attempts by gene-mapping techniques to locate the chromosomal site of the implicated gene or genes. One such study presented what appeared to be compelling evidence for the locus of genetic transmission of the diathesis for bipolar disorder. The population involved was the tightly knit Amish community of Lancaster County, Pennsylvania (Egeland et al., 1987). Identifying 32 active cases of bipolar disorder in this community of 12,500 members, all of them descendants of a small number of couples immigrating to the area in the early eighteenth century, the investigators were able to document, for every case, instances of the disorder in ancestors going back several generations. The 26 documented cases of suicide occurring since

The prevalence of mood disorders is considerably higher among the blood relatives of persons with clinically diagnosed mood disorders than in the population at large. This family has a history of bipolar disorder spanning four generations, from a woman to her daughter, granddaughter, and a great-grandson, who was diagnosed at only three years of age.

1880 were all traced to just four families. The gene involved was traced to a specific region on chromosome 11, using complicated recombinant DNA techniques. Some 63 percent of persons carrying this gene were said to show at least minimal signs of bipolar disorder.

Reactions to the publication of this study constitute a case history in the premature acceptance of preliminary scientific findings. In fact two other studies (Detera-Wadleigh et al., 1987; Hodkinson et al., 1987) published in the same issue of the same journal in which the Egeland and colleagues (1987) study was published presented data contradicting the notion of a single gene locus for bipolar disorder. These contradictory studies were almost uniformly ignored at the time. It is now clear that daunting methodological problems must be overcome before genetic linkage studies can identify specific genes for bipolar disorder, or indeed any of the mood disorders (Merikangas, Spence, & Kupfer, 1989). Most importantly, linkage studies are highly dependent on the existence of homogeneous diagnostic groupings. Of the various mood disorders, bipolar disorder is doubtless the best candidate in this respect; unfortunately, it cannot be identified with complete accuracy. Overall, no consistent support yet exists for any *specific* mode of genetic transmission of the bipolar disorders according to several recent comprehensive reviews (Faraone, Kremer, & Tsuang, 1990; Gershon, 1990; Nurnberger & Gershon, 1992).

Biochemical Factors. Kraepelin was confident that manic-depressive illness had a biological cause, and

as for unipolar disorder, much research effort in the past few decades has been directed toward finding the biological substrate of this illness. The early monoamine hypothesis for unipolar disorder discussed earlier was extended to bipolar disorder with the hypothesis being that if depression was caused by deficiencies of norepinephrine and/or serotonin, then perhaps mania is caused by excesses of these neurotransmitters. Although there is some evidence for increased norepinephrine activity during manic episodes, serotonin activity appears to be low in both phases of the illness. Moreover, one recent and influential model more strongly implicates another neurotransmitter—dopamine—rather than norepinephrine or serotonin for bipolar disorder (Depue & Iacono, 1989). However, as for unipolar disorder, there has been growing doubt in recent years that any simple biochemical deficiency or excess could cause this debilitating illness that can send its victims on an emotional roller-coaster (Goodwin & Jamison, 1990).

One of the thorniest issues that must be addressed by any theory is how the most effective and widely used drug in the treatment of bipolar disorder (lithium) can stabilize individuals from both depressive and manic episodes. We know that lithium is closely related chemically to sodium and that sodium plays a key role in the passage of the neural impulse down an axon. Therefore, questions have been raised regarding whether bipolar patients have abnormalities in the way ions (such as sodium) are transported across the neural membranes. Although the abnormality has not yet been identified, research suggests that there is indeed some such kind of abnormality in bipolar disorder (Goodwin & Jamison, 1990). One possible account of the effectiveness of lithium is that it may substitute for sodium ions.

Other Biological Causal Factors. Some hormonal research on bipolar depression has focused on the hypothalamic-pituitary-adrenal axis. Bipolar patients, when depressed, show evidence of abnormalities on the dexamathasone suppression test (DST), described earlier, at about the same rate as do unipolar depressed patients, but when manic their rate of abnormalities has generally (but not always) been found to be much lower (Goodwin & Jamison, 1990). Research has also focused on abnormalities of the hypothalamic-pituitary-thyroid axis because abnormalities of thyroid function are frequently accompanied by changes in mood. Many bipolar patients have subtle but significant abnormalities in the functioning of this axis, and administration of thyroid hormone is known at times to make antidepressant drugs work better (Goodwin & Jamison, 1990). However, thyroid hormone can also precipitate manic episodes in bipolar patients (Wehr & Goodwin, 1987). Finally, some investigators have suggested that the most effective drugs for the treatment of bipolar disorder—lithium and carbamazepine—may alter the functioning of this axis (Goodwin & Jamison, 1990).

There is also considerable evidence regarding disturbances in biological rhythms in bipolar disorder. During manic episodes, bipolar patients tend to sleep very little (seemingly by choice, not because of insomnia). During depressive episodes they tend toward hypersomnia (too much sleep), but they do not appear to show the reduced latency to REM sleep seen in unipolar patients (Goodwin & Jamison, 1990). Bipolar disorder also sometimes shows a seasonal pattern as does unipolar disorder, suggesting disturbances of different biological rhythms that may nonetheless derive from circadian abnormalities. Given the cyclic nature of the disorder itself, this focus on disturbances in biological rhythms holds promise for future integrative theories of the biological underpinnings of bipolar disorder. Indeed, Goodwin and Jamison (1990) formulated a bold hypothesis worthy of further investigation: "The genetic defect in manic-depressive illness involves the circadian pacemaker or systems that modulate it" (p. 589).

With the modern technology of positron emission tomography (PET) scans, it has even proved possible to visualize variation in brain glucose metabolic rates in depressed and manic states. In one study, Baxter and colleagues (1985) found that the

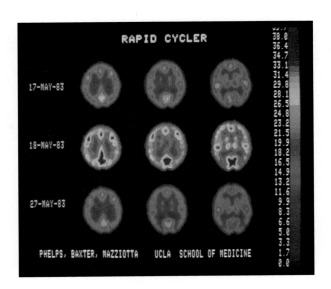

Shown here are positron emission tomographic (PET) scans of identical planes of the brain of a rapid-cycling bipolar patient. The top and bottom sets of planes were obtained on days in which the patient was depressed; the middle set was obtained on a hypomanic day. Colors of scans correspond to glucose (sugar) metabolic rates in the respective brain areas, the reds and yellows representing high rates and the blues and greens low rates.

glucose metabolic rate was lower in bipolar depressed patients than in unipolar depressed patients, manic patients, and controls, suggesting that global abnormalities in metabolism (across the whole cortex) are unique to bipolar depression (Goodwin & Jamison, 1990). Moreover, as illustrated in the photograph above, the hypometabolism in the bipolar depressed patients disappeared when their mood normalized or when they became manic. Unfortunately, research in this area has not yet inspired a coherent conceptual integration of the findings.

Psychosocial Causal Factors

Stressful Life Events. Research data on stressful life events preceding manic or depressive episodes has shown that such events are especially important as precipitants early in the course of the disorder, just as Kraepelin had noted in his clinical observations (Goodwin & Jamison, 1990). It seems that as the illness unfolds, the episodes become more autonomous and do not usually seem to be precipitated by stressful events. Some of these conclusions may be premature, however, given that most studies addressing this issue have relied on patients' memories of events before episodes, which may be unreliable (Johnson & Roberts, 1995). In the best prospective study to date using the most sophisticated stress measurement techniques, Ellicott and colleagues (1990; Hammen, 1995) followed 61 patients with established bipolar disorder for one to two years. They found a significant association between the occurrence of high levels of stress (but not low levels of stress) and the experience of manic, hypomanic, or depressive episodes. Moreover, they did not find that stress played any less important a role in precipitating episodes for people who had had more episodes of illness (Hammen, 1995).

One interesting example of the apparent role of aversive life events as precipitating causes in bipolar attacks has been described by Ellicott and colleagues (1990, p. 1197):

> Mr. A., a 30-year-old man, had been given a diagnosis of bipolar I disorder at age 21. He had had two manic episodes and multiple minor depressions and hypomanic episodes before treatment at the affective disorders clinic. After entering the study, he remained asymptomatic on a regimen of lithium carbonate and had no severely threatening life events (those rated 4 or 5 on the objective threat scale) during the first 6 months of observations. Then the patient reported a severely threatening event that involved a month-long financial investigation at his workplace. Directly afterward he experienced a mild subsyndromal depression, which spontaneously resolved after 18 days. Several weeks later, however, Mr. A reported three severely threatening events over the course of a month, two of which were employment-related changes that jeopardized his job, and one of which involved a major estrangement from his live-in girlfriend. One week after these events, he had a 2-week manic episode, which was controlled on an outpatient basis with an increased dose of lithium and which subsided into hypomania that persisted over 3 months.

As already noted, most research on diathesis-stress models for bipolar disorder focuses on the role of genetic factors as causing the predisposition for this disorder. Given the strong evidence for a constitutional basis for this disorder it is difficult to determine if personality factors may also serve as a diathesis because any personality differences seen before the onset of the disorder may simply be manifestations of the disorder itself in mild form. For this reason, attempts to delineate a typical pre-bipolar personality pattern for adults have met with limited

success. One might expect these individuals to share the personality characteristics of both groups, perhaps in alternating phases. Depue and colleagues (1981) presented strong evidence suggesting that cyclothymia does serve as a significant risk factor for bipolar disorder. However, as noted earlier, whether cyclothymia should be seen as a personality variable is now questioned by its official recognition (since DSM-III-R) as an Axis I disorder. Akiskal (1989) also argues for the existence of a cyclothymic personality that would be a risk factor for bipolar disorder. Nevertheless, it should be noted that many people who exhibit these traits will never have a serious mood disorder, and many who do not will develop such a disorder.

Psychodynamic Views. According to psychodynamic theorists, manic and depressive disorders may be viewed as two different but related defense-oriented strategies for dealing with severe stress. Manic persons try to escape their difficulties by a "flight into reality"—that is, they try to avoid the pain of their inner lives through outer-world distractions. In less severe form, hypomania, this type of reaction to stress is shown by a person who goes on a round of parties to try to forget a broken love affair or tries to escape from a threatening life situation by restless action, occupying every moment with work, athletics, sexual affairs, and countless other activities—all performed with professed gusto but not necessarily with true enjoyment. In full-blown mania, this pattern is exaggerated. With a tremendous expenditure of energy, a manic person tries to deny feelings of helplessness and hopelessness and to play a role of domineering competence. Once this mode of coping with difficulties is adopted, it is maintained until it has spent itself in emotional exhaustion, for the only other alternative is an admission of defeat and inevitable depression. Thus as a manic episode proceeds, any defensive value it might originally have had is negated, for thought processes are speeded up to a point where an individual can no longer process incoming information with any degree of efficiency. This results in behavior that is highly erratic at best and incomprehensible at the extreme.

Although a manic person may appear to have high self-esteem (and even be quite grandiose), there is one study supporting the idea that this may be a defensive posture. Winters and Neale (1985) used two measures of self-esteem in a study of normals and patients with unipolar disorder and manic disorder in remission (i.e., between episodes). In the direct measure of self-esteem, the normals and remitted manics reported higher self-esteem than did the unipolar depressives. But on another indirect task that all subjects thought was a measure of their memory, the remitted manics scored more like the unipolar depressives, revealing that they indeed had lower self-esteem than that seen in normals.

According to psychodynamic views about bipolar disorder, the shift from mania to depression may tend to occur when the defensive function of the manic reaction breaks down. Similarly, the shift from depression to mania may tend to occur when an individual, devalued and guilt-ridden by inactivity and an inability to cope, finally feels compelled to attempt some countermeasure, however desperate. Although the view of manic and depressive reactions as extreme defenses may seem plausible up to a point, it is difficult to account satisfactorily for the more extreme versions of these states without acknowledging the importance of biological causal factors. The effectiveness of biological treatment in alleviating severe episodes lends support to this hypothesis.

General Sociocultural Factors for Both Unipolar and Bipolar Disorders

Research on the association of sociocultural factors with both bipolar and unipolar mood disorders is discussed together because much of the research conducted in this area has not made clear-cut diagnostic distinctions between the two types of disorder. The prevalence of mood disorders seems to vary considerably among different societies: In some, manic episodes are more frequent, while in others, depressive episodes are more common. However, it has been difficult to provide conclusive evidence on this because of various methodological problems, including widely differing diagnostic practices in different cultures, and because the symptoms of depression also appear to vary considerably across cultures. For example, in some cultures like China, rates of depression are low but appear to be manifested as somatic symptoms (Kleinman, 1986).

In spite of the difficulties in drawing definitive conclusions about cross-cultural differences, a number of interesting cross-cultural findings raise provocative questions about the kinds of factors that promote high versus low rates of mood disorders. For example, in early studies, Carothers (1947, 1951, 1959) found manic disorders to be fairly common among the East Africans he studied, but depressive disorders relatively rare—the opposite of their incidence in the United States. He attributed the low incidence of depressive disorders to the fact that in traditional African cultures individuals have not usually been held personally responsible for fail-

ures and misfortunes. The culture of the Kenya Africans, Carothers observed, may be taken as fairly typical in this respect (1947, 1951, 1953). He noted that their behavior was largely group-determined, and that therefore they were not confronted with problems of self-sufficiency, choice, and responsibility, which are so prominent in Western cultures. Setting high achievement goals was discouraged (so there was little room for disappointment or failure in this regard). They were humble to the harsh environment they lived in and always expected the worst from it. Responsibility and blame for misfortunes were attributed to outside forces; because they weren't personally responsible there were few opportunities for self-devaluation. Needless to say, much has changed in Africa since Carothers made these observations, and more recent data suggest a quite different picture. In general, it appears that as societies take on the ways of Western culture, their members become more prone to developing Western-style mood disorders (Marsella, 1980).

Yet there are still societies relatively untouched by Western culture, such as the Kaluli—a primitive tribe in New Guinea studied by Scheiffelin (1984), where it is still very difficult to detect any sign of depression. A recent summary of Scheiffelin's work by Seligman (1990) provides interesting suggestions regarding why this might be the case:

Briefly, the Kaluli do not seem to have despair, hopelessness, depression, or suicide in the way we know it. What they do have is quite interesting. If you lose something valuable, such as your pig, you have a right to recompense. There are rituals (such as dancing and screaming at the neighbor who you think killed the pig) that are recognized by the society. When you demand recompense for loss, either the neighbor or the whole tribe takes note of your condition and usually recompenses you one way or another. The point I want to make here is that reciprocity between the culture and the individual when loss occurs provides strong buffers against loss becoming helplessness and hopelessness. I want to suggest that a society that prevents loss from becoming hopelessness, and that prevents sadness from becoming despair, breaks up the process of depression. Societies that promote, as ours does, the transition from loss to helplessness to hopelessness, promote depression. (Seligman, 1990, pp. 4–5)

Even in those nonindustrialized countries where depressive disorders are relatively common, Marsella's (1980) comprehensive review of the cross-cultural literature on depression leaves little doubt that it generally takes a different form from that customarily seen in our society. For example, in some non-Western cultures, symptoms of depression lack substantial psychological components, being limited to the so-called vegetative manifestations, such as sleep disturbance, loss of appetite, weight loss, and loss of sexual interest (see also Goodwin & Jamison, 1990). Interestingly, in some such cultures there is not even a concept of depression that would be reasonably comparable to our own. The psychological components that seem to be missing are the feelings of guilt and self-recrimination that are so commonly seen in the "developed" countries (Kidson & Jones, 1968; Lorr & Klett, 1968; Zung, 1969). In fact, among several groups of Australian aborigines, Kidson and Jones (1968) found not only an absence of guilt and self-recrimination in depressive reactions, but also no incidence of attempted or actual suicide. In connection with the latter finding, they stated, "The absence of suicide can perhaps be explained as a consequence of strong fears of death and also because of the tendency to act out and project hostile impulses" (p. 415).

In our own society, the role of sociocultural factors in mood disorders is gradually becoming evident. Results from the large Epidemiological Catchment Area study conducted at multiple sites in the United States in the early 1980s were informative. In general, this study did not find any substantial racial differences, although there were trends for the prevalence to be lower among blacks and Hispanics than among non-Hispanic whites (Robins et al., 1984). The study also failed to find significant rural/urban differences in the prevalence of mood disorders, in spite of the fact that some other research, such as that by Blazer and colleagues (1985), had found rates of depression to be much higher in urban than in rural areas.

For unipolar disorder, there are suggestions that the poor have higher rates of depressive symptoms, but not necessarily of diagnosable mood disorder (Hirschfeld & Cross, 1982). However, for bipolar disorder the findings are opposite, with a number of studies showing that bipolar disorder is more common in the higher socioeconomic classes (see Goodwin & Jamison, 1990). Moreover, some studies show that bipolars tend to have more education and that they come, on average, from families with higher socioeconomic status than do unipolar depressives. In one study, relatives of bipolars (compared with relatives of unipolars) were found to have higher levels of occupational and educational achievement, with the differences being especially striking for those who themselves had bipolar disorder (Coryell et al., 1989). Some have suggested that

this association of bipolar disorder with higher socioeconomic status might come about because some of the personality and behavioral correlates of bipolar illness, at least in hypomanic phases (such as outgoingness, increased energy, increased productivity), may lead to increased achievement and accomplishment (Goodwin & Jamison, 1990).

Other interesting findings emerged from the ECA regarding the association of marital status to depression. In general, single and divorced persons tend to have higher rates of unipolar depression than do those who are married, although as we have already seen distressed marriages are highly associated with depression. The same findings hold for bipolar disorder, with it being slightly more common in single and divorced persons (Boyd & Weissman, 1985). With bipolar disorder, perhaps even more than with unipolar disorder, there is a good chance that the disorder itself may contribute to divorce, although there is no good evidence on this point at present.

TREATMENTS AND OUTCOMES

Pharmacotherapy and Electroconvulsive Therapy

Antidepressant, antipsychotic, and antianxiety drugs are all used in the treatment of unipolar and bipolar disorders. The role of medication in mild or normal forms of depression (such as occur with a grief reaction or an adjustment disorder) is minimal, and such patients are likely to benefit more from appropriate psychological therapies (Beckham & Leber, 1985a; Klerman, 1982; Merson & Tryer, 1991).

For most moderately to seriously depressed patients, including those with dysthymia (Conte & Karasu, 1992), the drug treatment of choice until recently has been one of the standard antidepressants (called tricyclics because of their chemical structure), such as Tofranil (imipramine) (Goodwin, 1992; Shelton et al., 1991). The efficacy of the tricyclics has been demonstrated in hundreds of studies where the response of depressed patients given these drugs has been compared with the response of patients given placebo. Unfortunately, the tricyclics have unpleasant side effects, and many patients do not continue long enough with the drug for it to have its antidepressant effect. In addition, because these drugs are highly toxic when taken in large doses, there is some risk in prescribing them for suicidal patients who might use them for an overdose. (See also Chapter 16.)

For all these reasons, physicians are increasingly choosing to prescribe one of the antidepressants from a new category of drugs (the selective serotonin re-uptake inhibitors—SSRIs), which tend to have many fewer side effects and are better tolerated by patients. One of these, Prozac (fluoxetine), is now extremely popular among physicians in various specialties, not only to treat significant depression but also for people with mild depressive symptoms. Prescriptions for Prozac are being written at a rate that seems excessive; modest distress or unhappiness should not, we think, be an occasion for taking drugs but rather for seriously examining one's life and perhaps seeking psychotherapy. There are many interesting and controversial questions about the ethics of prescribing drugs to essentially healthy people because the drugs make them feel more energetic, outgoing, and productive than they have ever been. Recently these have been discussed widely in the popular media because of the the controversial best-selling book *Listening to Prozac* (Kramer, 1993) written by a psychiatrist who describes his own dilemmas in deciding when and how long to continue his patients (many of whom are not depressed) on this drug. This question is considered further in Chapter 16 (see the "Unresolved Issue" section).

Unfortunately, antidepressant drugs usually require at least several weeks to take effect. Also, discontinuing the drugs when symptoms have remitted may result in relapse—probably because the underlying depressive episode is still present and only its symptomatic expression has been suppressed (Evans et al., 1992; Montgomery, 1994). Because depression tends to be a recurrent disorder, there are also increasing trends to continue patients for very long periods of time on the drugs in order to prevent recurrence. For example, Frank and colleagues (1990) continued patients on moderate doses of imipramine for three years and found that only about 20 percent showed a recurrence, compared with about 90 percent of those maintained on placebo for the same time period. Thus, when properly prescribed, these drugs are often effective in prevention as well as treatment for patients subject to recurrent episodes (Montgomery, 1994). (See also Chapter 16.)

Because antidepressants often take three to four weeks to produce significant improvement, electroconvulsive therapy (ECT) is often used with severely depressed patients who may present an immediate and serious suicidal risk (Fink, 1992; Merson & Tryer, 1991; Weiner & Krystal, 1994). ECT is also used with patients who have not responded to other forms of pharmacological treatment; it is frequently considered the treatment of choice for the elderly who often cannot take antidepressant medications. When selection criteria for this form of treatment are carefully observed, a complete remission of symptoms occurs after about four to six treatments and usually within about two weeks in some 70–80 percent of the cases treated (Noll, Davis, & DeLeon-Jones, 1985). Maintenance dosages of antidepressant and antianxiety drugs are then ordinarily used to maintain the treatment gains achieved, until the depression has run its course. ECT is also very useful in the treatment of manic episodes, with a recent review of the evidence suggesting that it is associated with remission or marked improvement in 80 percent of manic patients (Mukherjee, Sackeim, & Schnur, 1994). (See also Chapter 16.)

Lithium therapy has now become widely used in the treatment of both depressive and manic episodes of bipolar disorder. It is often effective in preventing cycling between manic and depressive episodes (although not necessarily for patients with rapid cycling), and bipolar patients are frequently maintained on lithium therapy over long time periods. Early studies indicated that lithium was considered an effective preventive for approximately 65 percent of patients suffering repeated bipolar attacks (Prien, 1992), but other studies present a more pessimistic picture, with one large study finding only 33 percent of patients remaining free of episodes over a two-year follow-up (Prien et al., 1984). One possible explanation is that this apparent drop in efficacy does not reflect reality because the more recent studies may have treated more difficult treatment-resistant patients—leading to lower estimates of efficacy. This could occur because the easy-to-treat patients are now being successfully treated in their community (Prien & Potter, 1990).

Lithium therapy has some unpleasant side effects, such as lethargy, decreased motor coordination, and gastrointestinal difficulties in some patients. Long-term use of lithium has also been associated with kidney malfunction and sometimes permanent kidney damage (Abou-Saleh, 1992; Goodwin & Jamison, 1990). Not surprisingly these side effects, combined with the fact that many bipolar patients seem to miss the highs and the abundance of energy associated with their hypomanic and manic episodes, sometimes create problems with compliance to taking the drug. More recently there has also been emerging evidence for the usefulness of another category of drugs known as the anticonvulsants (such as carbamazepine) in the treatment of bipolar disorder (Post, 1992). These drugs may sometimes be effective in patients who do not respond well to lithium or who have unacceptable side effects from it (Goodwin & Jamison, 1990). (See also Chapter 16.)

Psychotherapy

In the best of circumstances, the treatment of depression is not confined to drugs or to drugs plus electroconvulsive therapy, but is combined with individual or group psychotherapy directed at helping a patient develop a more stable long-range adjustment. Considerable evidence, reviewed by Hollon and Beck (1994), also suggests that certain forms of psychotherapy for depression, alone or in combination with drugs, significantly decrease the likelihood of relapse within a two-year follow-up period. Although these results are encouraging, no study has as yet followed patients for long enough to know whether these treatments are also effective in preventing recurrence, that is, a new depressive episode. Studies on the efficacy of combining drugs and psychotherapy have been reviewed by Klerman and colleagues (1994), who conclude that whether combined treatment is really superior to either kind of treatment alone is as yet unclear.

Proposed psychosocial treatments for unipolar depression have proliferated at an extraordinary rate over the years. In addition to depression-focused modifications of traditional therapies, a number of specialized systems of psychotherapy have been developed that specifically address the problem of unipolar depression. By and large, these psychosocial therapies are intended for outpatient (nonpsychotic) treatment, but they are increasingly applied in inpatient settings as well (e.g., Thase et al., 1991).

Two of the best-known of these depression-specific psychotherapies are the cognitive-behavioral approach of Beck and colleagues (Beck et al., 1979) and the interpersonal therapy (IPT) program developed by Klerman, Weissman, and colleagues (Klerman et al., 1984). Both are relatively brief approaches (10–20 sessions) that focus on here-and-now problems rather than on the more remote causal issues that are often focused on in psychodynamic psychotherapy. For example, cognitive-behavioral techniques consist of highly structured, systematic attempts to teach people with unipolar depression to evaluate their beliefs and negative automatic thoughts systematically. They are also taught to identify and correct their biases or distortions of information processing, and to uncover and challenge their underlying depressogenic assumptions. Cognitive therapy relies heavily on an empirical approach, in that patients are taught to treat their beliefs as hypotheses that can be tested through the use of behavioral experiments.

An example of challenging a negative automatic thought through a behavioral experiment can be seen in the following interchange between a cognitive therapist and a depressed patient:

Patient: My husband doesn't love me any more.

Therapist: That must be a very distressing thought. What makes you think that he doesn't love you?

Patient: Well, when he comes in in the evening, he never wants to talk to me. He just wants to sit and watch TV. Then he goes straight off to bed.

Therapist: OK. Now, is there any evidence, anything he does, that goes against the idea that he doesn't love you?

Patient: I can't think of any. Well, no, wait a minute. Actually it was my birthday a couple of weeks ago, and he gave me a watch which is really lovely. I'd seen them advertised and mentioned I liked it, and he took notice and went and got me one.

Therapist: Right. Now how does that fit with the idea that he doesn't love you?

Patient: Well, I suppose it doesn't really, does it? But then why is he like that in the evening?

Therapist: I suppose him not loving you any more is one possible reason. Are there any other possible reasons?

Patient: Well, he has been working very hard lately. I mean, he's late home most nights, and he had to go in to the office at the weekend. So I suppose it could be that.

Therapist: It could, couldn't it? How could you find out if that's it?

Patient: Well, I could say I've noticed how tired he looks and ask him how he's feeling and how the work's going. I haven't done that, I've just been getting annoyed because he doesn't pay any attention to me.

Therapist: That sounds like an excellent idea. How would you like to make that a homework task for this week? (From Fennell, 1989).

Another example of trying to challenge an underlying depressogenic assumption of having to be loved (once this has been discovered in the course of treatment) occurs in the following interchange:

Patient: Not being loved leads automatically to unhappiness.

Therapist: Not being loved is a "nonevent." How can a nonevent lead automatically to something?

Patient: I just don't believe anyone could be happy without being loved.

Therapist: This is your belief. If you believe something, this belief will dictate your emotional reactions.

Patient: I don't understand that.

Therapist: If you believe something, you're going to act and feel as if it were true, whether it is or not.

Patient: You mean if I believe I'll be unhappy without love, it's only my belief causing my unhappiness?

Therapist: And when you feel unhappy, you probably say to yourself, "See, I was right. If I don't have love, I am bound to be unhappy."

Patient: How can I get out of this trap?

Therapist: You could experiment with your belief about having to be loved. Force yourself to suspend this belief and see what happens. Pay attention to the natural consequences created by your belief. For example, can you picture yourself on a tropical island with all the delicious fruits and other food available?

Patient: Yes, it looks pretty good.

Therapist: Now, imagine that there are primitive people on the island. They are friendly and helpful, but they do not love you. None of them loves you.

Patient: I can picture that.

Therapist: How do you feel in your fantasy?

Patient: Relaxed and comfortable.

Therapist: So you can see that it does not necessarily follow that if you aren't loved, you will be unhappy. (From Beck et al., 1979, p. 260.)

The usefulness of cognitive therapy has been amply documented in dozens of studies, including several studies with unipolar depressed inpatients and with patients diagnosed with depression with melancholic features (Hollon & Beck, 1994; Dobson, 1989). It may have a special advantage in preventing relapse, although evidence of whether it can also prevent recurrence is not yet available (Blackburn et al., 1981; Murphy et al., 1984; Rush et al., 1977, 1981; Simons et al., 1986). When compared with pharmacotherapy, it seems to be at least as effective (Dobson, 1989). Nevertheless, some have questioned whether adequate tests of the comparative efficacy of cognitive therapy versus pharmacotherapy have yet been adequately conducted (Hollon, Shelton, & Loosen, 1991; Hollon & Beck, 1994). (See also Chapter 17.)

The interpersonal therapy (IPT) approach, being relatively new, has not yet been subjected to as extensive an evaluation. The efficacy of this psychosocial treatment for depression (and also of cognitive therapy), however, recently received strong support from the findings of a carefully designed multisite study sponsored by the National Institute of Mental Health. When immediate posttherapy outcomes were compared, both these psychosocial treatment approaches proved as effective as antidepressant drugs for milder cases of major depression, and in some instances even severe ones (Elkin et al., 1989; this important study is further described in Chapter 17). More recently, the question has been addressed whether IPT can be useful in long-term follow-up for individuals with severe recurrent unipolar depression (Frank et al., 1990). Patients with recurrent depression who had responded well to a combination of IPT and imipramine were followed for three years; some were maintained on medication, others on placebo, and others received a session of IPT once a month. Patients who received continued treatment with IPT once a month or who received continued medication were much less likely to have a recurrence than those maintained on placebo.

Of course, in any treatment program, it is important to deal with unusual stressors in a patient's life, because an unfavorable life situation may lead to a recurrence of the depression and may necessitate longer treatment. This point has been well established in studies that extended to the mood disorders, the well-established finding that relapse in schizophrenia and bipolar disorder is correlated with certain noxious elements in family life (Hooley, 1986; Hooley, Orley, & Teasdale, 1986; Miklowitz et al., 1988). Behavior by a spouse that can be interpreted by a former patient as criticism seems especially likely to produce depression relapse (Hooley & Teasdale, 1989). Some types of couples or family intervention directed at reducing the level of expressed emotion or hostility, described in Chapter

17, have been found to be very useful in preventing relapse in these situations. In addition, for married people who are depressed and having marital discord, it has been shown that marital therapy is as effective as cognitive therapy in reducing unipolar depression for the depressed spouse. The marital therapy had the further advantage of also producing greater increases in marital satisfaction than did the cognitive therapy (Beach & O'Leary, 1992; Jacobsen et al., 1991; O'Leary & Beach, 1990).

Even without formal therapy, as we have noted, the great majority of manic and depressed patients recover from a given episode within less than a year. With modern methods of treatment, the general outlook has become increasingly favorable—so much so that most hospitalized patients can now be discharged within 30–60 days. Although relapses may occur in some instances, these can now often be prevented by maintenance therapy.

At the same time, the mortality rate for depressed patients appears to be significantly higher than that for the general population, partly because of the higher incidence of suicide, but some studies also indicate an excess of deaths due to natural causes as well (see Coryell & Winokur, 1992; Perris, 1992). Manic patients also have a high risk of death, due to such circumstances as accidents (with or without alcohol as a contributing factor), neglect of proper health precautions, or physical exhaustion (Coryell & Winokur, 1982, 1992). Thus, although the development of effective drugs and other new approaches to therapy have brought greatly improved outcomes for patients with mood disorders, the need clearly remains for still more effective treatment methods, both immediate and long-term. Also, a great need remains to study the factors that put people at risk for depressive disorders and to apply relevant findings to early intervention and prevention.

SUICIDE

The risk of **suicide**—taking one's own life—is a significant factor in all depressive states. Although it is obvious that people also commit suicide for reasons other than depression, most who complete the act do so during or in the recovery phase of a depressive episode. Paradoxically, the act often occurs at a point when a person appears to be emerging from the deepest phase of the depressive attack. The risk of suicide is about 1 percent during the year in which a depressive episode occurs, but the lifetime risk for someone who has recurrent depressive episodes is about 15 percent (Clark & Fawcett,

1992; Klerman, 1982). Compared with rates for other possible causes of death—especially in younger age groups—these are substantial figures.

Suicide now ranks among the ten leading causes of death in most Western countries. In the United States, it is the eighth leading cause of death, with current estimates of 30,000 suicides each year (Clark & Fawcett, 1992). Indeed, the problem may be much more serious than these figures suggest, because many self-inflicted deaths are attributed in official records to other "more respectable" causes. Most experts agree that the number of actual suicides is at least two and possibly several times higher than the number officially reported (Wekstein, 1979). In addition to completed suicides, estimates also suggest that more than 200,000 people attempt suicide each year and that nearly 3 percent of Americans have made a suicide attempt at some time in their lives (Clark & Fawcett, 1992).

Statistics, however accurate, cannot begin to convey the tragedy of suicide in human terms. As we will see, most people who commit suicide are ambivalent about taking their own lives. This irreversible choice is often made when they are alone and in a state of severe psychological distress, unable to see their problems objectively or to evaluate alternative courses of action. Thus a basic humanitarian problem in suicide is the seemingly senseless death of a person who may be ambivalent about living or who does not really want to die. A second tragic concern arises from the long-lasting distress among those left behind that may result from such action. As Shneidman (1969) put it, "The person who commits suicide puts his psychological skeleton in the survivor's emotional closet . . . " (p. 22). Studies of survivors show that loss of a loved one through suicide "is one of the greatest burdens individuals and families may endure" (Dunne, 1992, p. 222).

In the discussion that follows, we will focus on various aspects of the incidence and clinical picture in suicide, on factors that appear to be of causal significance, on degrees of intent and ways of communicating it, and on issues of treatment and prevention.

The Clinical Picture and Causal Pattern

Because the clinical picture and etiology of suicide are so closely interrelated, it is useful to consider these topics under one general heading. This approach will lead us to address the following questions: Who commits suicide? What are the motives for taking one's own life? What general sociocultural variables appear to be relevant to an understanding of suicide?

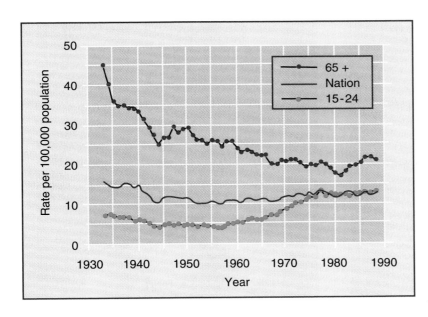

Figure 6.3 *Rates of suicide in the elderly have dropped dramatically over the past 60 years, with a slight increase in the late 1980s. By contrast, rates of suicide in the 15–24 age range have increased dramatically over the same period. (From McIntosh, 1992.)*

Who Attempts and Who Commits Suicide? Suicide *attempts* primarily are actions of young people; at least two-thirds of suicide attempters are under 35 (Hawton, 1992). Women are about three times as likely to attempt suicide as are men. Rates of suicide attempts are also about four times higher in people who are separated or divorced than for any other marital status category (Clark & Fawcett, 1992). Most attempts occur in the context of interpersonal discord or other severe life stress. The story is different, however, for completed suicides; three times more men than women die by suicide each year in the United States. The highest rate of completed suicides is in the elderly (65 and over), although these rates have been coming down since 1930, especially for elderly men (McIntosh, 1992) as shown in Figure 6.3. Unfortunately, there has also been a trend back upward during the 1980s.

For women, the most commonly used method is drug ingestion; men tend to use methods more likely to be lethal, particularly gunshot, which may be a good part of the reason that completed suicides are higher among men. There is also some evidence from various Western countries, including the United States, that suggests that the male/female ratio of 3 to 1 completed suicides may be changing, because the incidence of completed suicide has been increasing at a faster rate for women than for men in recent years. The precise reasons for these trends are unknown, but they are probably related to rapid sociocultural changes, including those relating to sex roles.

Besides the elderly, persons with mood disorders, and separated or divorced persons, there are a number of other high-risk groups among adults. These include people with alcoholism or schizophrenia,

which are the two other forms of psychopathology most commonly associated with suicide (after the mood disorders). The lifetime risk of suicide in people with mood disorders is 15 percent, in people with schizophrenia 10 percent, and in alcoholics 3 percent, relative to an average risk of 1.4 percent in the general population (Clark & Fawcett, 1992). People living alone, people from socially disorganized areas, and members of some Native American tribes are also at risk. Finally, certain professionals, such as physicians, dentists, lawyers, and psychologists are at higher-than-average risk (Wekstein, 1979). Both female physicians and female psychologists commit suicide at a rate about three times that of women in the general population; male physicians have a suicide rate about twice that of men in the general population (Ross, 1974; Schaar, 1974; Wekstein, 1979).

Another perplexing trend is that rates of completed suicide among teenagers and even children seem to be increasing at an alarming pace (Berman & Jobes, 1992; Fremouw, de Perczel, & Ellis, 1990; Sokol & Pfeffer, 1992). For children between the ages of 5 and 14, suicide is the seventh leading cause of death in the United States, and there has been a gradual increase in suicide in this age group since 1970. The trend is by no means limited to youngsters from deprived or troubled backgrounds. Children from all backgrounds and social status are vulnerable (Joffe & Orford, 1990) and suicide rates for children from affluent families are also on the increase. Children are at increased risk for suicide if their parents are divorced, dead, or separated, or if there is an abusive, neglectful, or chaotic home environment. The forms of psychopathology associated with these environmental risk factors are not surpris-

Fame is no barrier to suicide. Kurt Cobain, the rock musician, is seen here performing and as his body is removed from his home after he committed suicide. Interestingly, Cobain had communicated his contemplation of suicide in a song he had recorded called "I hate myself and I want to die." He died at 27.

ingly also known to be risk factors for suicide in children: depression, antisocial behavior, and impulsivity (Sokol & Pfeffer, 1992)

For persons between the ages of 15 and 24, the rate of successful suicides has essentially tripled since the mid-1950s, far exceeding its increase as a proportion of the total population; for those between 15 and 19, rates have quadrupled over the same time period. Suicide ranks as the second (Asarnow, 1992) or third (Frederick, 1985) most common cause of death in the United States for 15- to 24-year-olds (the first two are accidents and homicide, respectively; Frederick, 1985). Firearms, explosives, and hanging are the three most common methods used for completed suicides in this age group (Berman & Jobes, 1992). The increases in suicide rates in the United States for adolescents are not unique to this country but have been observed in 23 out of 29 countries studied (Lester, 1988). As for suicide attempts, several surveys of high school students have estimated the rate of attempted suicide at between 8 and 9 percent (Berman & Jobes, 1992); between 5 and 40 percent of these are believed to be "repeaters." A very large proportion of these attempts have very low lethality and do not require

medical attention, but they do need to be taken seriously.

Thus although the overall national suicide rate has decreased dramatically for the elderly over the past several decades, there have been disproportionate increases among adolescents. Studies attempting to distinguish who is at risk for a completed suicide, as opposed to a nonfatal attempted suicide, find that conduct disorder and substance abuse are relatively more common in the completers, and mood disorders are relatively more common among the nonfatal attempters (Berman & Jobes, 1992). However, these differences are only relative, and each of these forms of psychopathology puts an adolescent at risk for both a nonfatal attempt and a completed suicide. Data from the San Diego Suicide Study suggest that at least some of the increase in adolescent suicide may be associated with increases in drug abuse (Fowler, Rich, & Young, 1986; Rich, Young, & Fowler, 1986), and given increased rates of adolescent depression, this is also likely to play a role in the increased rates of suicide. Risk for suicide may also be increased by adolescents' exposure to other people in their social network who have shown suicidal behavior. About 6–8 percent of suicide attempters have a family history of suicide (Murphy & Wetzel, 1982). In addition, exposure to suicide through the media has led to reports of aggregate increases in adolescent suicide, perhaps because adolescents are highly susceptible to suggestion and imitative behavior (Berman & Jobes, 1992). In some examples, particular communities have seen a series of suicides or suicide attempts within a brief time period. Some years ago, for example, seven students attending the same high school in suburban Omaha made suicide attempts in rapid succession, and three of them succeeded (*Time,* February 24, 1986).

Most of us feel that there is something especially tragic when a young person—physically healthy and having seemingly unlimited potential—undertakes an irreversible self-destructive action. The motivation for suicide among adults is often related to a sense of hopelessness (Beck, Brown, & Steer, 1989; Holden, Medonca, & Serin, 1989). However, the idea that hopelessness plays a significant role in adolescent suicide is much more controversial (Cole, 1989). The motivation to "escape from self" (Baumeister, 1990), on the other hand, possibly has special relevance for this age range; it is discussed further in a later section.

Many college students seem peculiarly vulnerable to the development of suicidal motivations. The combined stressors of academic demands, social interaction problems, and career choices—perhaps interacting with challenges to their basic values—evidently make it impossible for some students to continue making the adjustments their life situations demand. Some 10,000 college students in the United States attempt suicide each year, and over 1,000 of them succeed. Reflecting the general trend, approximately three times as many female as male students attempt suicide, but more males than females succeed. For an overview of warning signs for student suicide, see HIGHLIGHT 6.4

Other Psychosocial Factors Associated with Suicide The specific factors leading a person to suicide may take many forms. For example, one middle-aged man developed profound feelings of guilt after being promoted to the presidency of the bank for which he worked; shortly after his promotion, he fatally slit his throat. Such "success suicides" are undoubtedly related to those occasional depressive episodes that seem to be precipitated by positive life events. Much more often, suicide is associated with

---

HIGHLIGHT | 6.4

Warning Signs for Student Suicide

A change in a student's mood and behavior is a significant warning of possible suicide. Characteristically, the student becomes depressed and withdrawn, undergoes a marked decline in self-esteem, and shows deterioration in personal hygiene. These signs are accompanied by a profound loss of interest in studies. Often he or she stops attending classes and stays at home most of the day. Usually, the student's distress is communicated to at least one other person, often in the form of a veiled suicide warning.

When college students attempt suicide, one of the first explanations to occur to those around them is that they may have been doing poorly in school. As a group, however, they are superior students, and though they tend to expect a great deal of themselves in terms of academic achievement, their grades and academic competition are not regarded as significant precipitating stressors. Also, although many lose interest in their studies before becoming suicidal and thus receive worse grades, the loss of interest appears to be associated with depression and withdrawal caused by other problems. Moreover, when academic failure does appear to trigger suicidal behavior—in a minority of cases—the actual cause of the behavior is generally considered to be loss of self-esteem and failure to live up to parental expectations, rather than academic failure itself.

For most suicidal students, both male and female, the major precipitating stressor appears to be either the failure to establish, or the loss of, a close interpersonal relationship. Often the breakup of a romance is the key precipitating factor. It has also been noted that significantly more suicide attempts and suicides are made by students from families that have experienced separation, divorce, or the death of a parent.

Although most colleges and universities have mental health facilities to assist distressed students, few suicidal students seek professional help. Thus it is of vital importance for those around a suicidal student to notice the warning signs and try to obtain assistance.

Sources drawn on for this description include Hendin (1975), Miller (1975), Murray (1973), Nelson (1971), Pausnau and Russell (1975), Peck and Schrut (1971), Shneidman, Parker, and Funkhouser (1970), and Stanley and Barter (1970).

negative events, such as severe financial reverses, loss of social status, imprisonment, or interpersonal crises of various sorts. The common denominator may be either that these events lead to the loss of a sense of meaning to life (Farberow, Shneidman, & Leonard, 1963) and/or to hopelessness about the future (Beck et al., 1985; Eyman & Eyman, 1992; Fawcett et al., 1987), which can both produce, independently or in combination, a mental state that looks to suicide as a possible way out. Should a person also happen to be drinking excessively at the time (or using drugs with similar effects), the danger of successful suicide is markedly increased (Murphy & Wetzel, 1990).

Historically, researchers have proposed several theoretical rationales for suicidal behavior. As a group, these theories tend to be abstract, even impersonal, and therefore to miss something in depicting the emotional charge of the suicidal act. The essential element here, it seems to us, is that a suicidal person intends—even if only at the moment of taking fatal action—to put a permanent end to conscious experience. The states of mind that might lead to such a decision are limited and have in common the quality of intolerability, of desperate need for certain and irrevocable escape. Oblivion thus becomes a positive goal. A recent theoretical analysis of suicide offered by Baumeister (1990) captures this notion of escape from intolerable experience. Baumeister conceives of suicide as basically an escape from self, or at least self-awareness. In this effort a person achieves a "cognitive deconstruction," which entails both irrationality and disinhibition, such that drastic action becomes acceptable.

General Sociocultural Factors. Suicide rates appear to vary considerably from one society to another. Hungary, with an annual incidence of 44.9 per 100,000, has the world's highest rate. Other Western countries with high rates—20 per 100,000 or higher—include Switzerland, Finland, Austria, Sweden, Denmark, and Germany. The United States has a rate of approximately 12.2 per 100,000, which is roughly comparable to that of Canada. Countries with low rates (less than 9 per 100,000) include Egypt, Greece, Italy, Israel, Spain, Mexico, and Ireland (World Health Organization, 1987). Among certain groups, such as the aborigines of the western Australian desert, the suicide rate drops to zero—possibly as a result of a strong, culturally determined fear of death (Kidson & Jones, 1968). These estimates should, however, be considered in light of the fact that there are wide differences across countries in the criteria used for determining whether a death was due to suicide (Hawton, 1992), and such differ-

ences may well contribute to the apparent differences in suicide rates.

Religious taboos concerning suicide and the attitudes of a society toward death are apparently important determinants of suicide rates. Both Catholicism and Islam strongly condemn suicide, and suicide rates in Catholic and Islamic countries are correspondingly low. In fact, most societies have developed strong sanctions against suicide, and many still regard it as a crime as well as a sin.

Japan is one of the few societies in which suicide has been socially approved under certain circumstances—for example, in response to conditions that bring disgrace to an individual or group. During World War II, many Japanese villagers were reported to have committed mass suicide when faced with imminent capture by Allied forces. There were also reports of group suicide by Japanese military personnel under threat of defeat. In the case of the kamikaze, Japanese pilots who deliberately crashed their explosives-laden planes into American warships during the war's final stages, self-destruction was a way of demonstrating complete personal commitment to the national purpose. It is estimated that 1000 young Japanese pilots destroyed themselves in this exercise of patriotic zeal. Despite the extraordinary effectiveness of this type of attack, one can hardly imagine its being ordered by an American commander, or such an order being obeyed by American pilots.

In a pioneering study of sociocultural factors in suicide, the French sociologist Emile Durkheim (1897/1951) attempted to relate differences in suicide rates to differences in group cohesiveness. Analyzing records of suicides in different countries and for different historical periods, Durkheim concluded that the greatest deterrent to committing suicide in times of personal stress is a sense of involvement and identity with other people. More contemporary studies, including an exceptionally well-designed one by Slater and Depue (1981), tend to confirm this idea.

Durkheim's views also appear relevant to understanding the higher incidence of suicide among subgroups in our society who are subjected to conditions of uncertainty and social disorganization in the absence of strong group ties. For example, there is a well-known association between unemployment and suicide, which may primarily be related to the effects that unemployment has on mental health (Hawton, 1992; Platt, 1984). Similarly, suicide rates have been found to be higher than average among people who are "downwardly mobile" (or who fear they may become so) and among groups undergoing severe social pressures.

For example, in 1932 at the height of the Great Depression in the United States, the suicide rate increased from less than 10 to 17.4 per 100,000; during the early years of the severe recession of the mid- and late 1970s, the suicide rate also increased (NIMH, 1976; Wekstein, 1979). Following the same pattern, we could point to the environmental pressures such as unemployment and alienation that appear to contribute to the high rate of suicide among black youth in our society, or to the marked increase in suicide among Eskimo teenagers in Alaska, who find themselves trapped in a sort of no-man's-land between their past culture and assimilation into the "White world" (Parkin, 1974).

Suicidal Ambivalence

From the standpoint of intent or motivation, suicide appears to be one method of obtaining relief from an aversive life situation. However, because most people undergoing severe stress do not commit suicide—only a small number of people who are depressed or who develop terminal illness take their own lives—the question arises as to why a person resorts to this method of coping rather than another. This is not an easy question to answer; it involves consideration not only of stress, but also of other aspects of an individual's psychological state at the time of a suicide attempt.

Degree of Intent The ambivalence that typically accompanies thoughts of suicide finds classic expression in Hamlet's famous soliloquy:

> To be, or not to be: that is the question:
> Whether 'tis nobler in the mind to suffer
> The slings and arrows of outrageous fortune
> Or to take arms against a sea of troubles,
> And by opposing end them? To die: to sleep;
> No more; and by a sleep to say we end
> The heart-ache and the thousand natural shocks
> That flesh is heir to, 'tis a consummation
> Devoutly to be wish'd. To die, to sleep;
> To sleep: perchance to dream: ay, there's the rub;
> For in that sleep of death what dreams may come
> When we have shuffled off this mortal coil,
> Must give us pause. . . .
> *(Hamlet, Act III, Scene I)*

Recognizing that the vast majority of people who contemplate suicide do not in fact kill themselves, some investigators have focused on analyzing the degree of intent associated with suicidal behavior.

Thus Farberow and Litman (1970)—echoing Hamlet—have classified suicidal behavior into three categories: "to be," "not to be," and "to be or not to be."

The "to be" group involves people who do not really wish to die, but instead want to communicate a dramatic message to others concerning their distress. Their suicide attempts involve nonlethal methods such as minimal drug ingestion or minor wrist-slashing. They usually arrange matters so that intervention by others is almost inevitable. This group, estimated to make up about two-thirds of the total suicidal population, is disproportionately female, perhaps because women have been socialized to feel helpless and to fantasize being rescued (Suter, 1976).

In contrast, the "not to be" group includes people who seemingly are intent on dying. They give little or no warning of their intent, and they generally rely on the more violent and certain means of suicide, such as shooting themselves or jumping from high places. Investigators have estimated that this group makes up only about 3–5 percent of the suicidal population. Successful preventive intervention with this group is extremely difficult.

The "to be or not to be" group constitutes about 30 percent of the suicidal population. These people are ambivalent about dying and tend to leave the question of death to fate. Although loss of a love relationship, financial problems, or feelings of meaninglessness may be present, a person in this group still entertains some hope of working things out. The methods used for the suicide attempt are often dangerous but moderately slow acting, such as drug ingestion. The feeling during such attempts can be summed up as, "If I die the conflict is settled, but if I am rescued that is what is meant to be." Often the people in this group lead stormy, stress-filled lives and make repeated suicide attempts.

After an unsuccessful attempt, a marked reduction in emotional turmoil usually occurs. This reduction is not stable, however, and subsequent suicidal behavior may follow. In the year following a suicide attempt, repetition of the behavior is common, with 12–25 percent of attempters being referred to the same hospital within a year. There is an increased risk that the second attempt will be fatal, especially if the first attempt was a serious one (Hawton, 1992; Rosen, 1970). Long-term follow-up of those who have made a suicide attempt show that about 7–10 percent will eventually die by suicide (Clark & Fawcett, 1992). Moreover, of people who do kill themselves, about 20–40 percent have a history of one or more previous attempts (Clark & Fawcett, 1992).

Farberow and Litman's classification is largely descriptive and has little practical value in terms of predicting suicidal behavior. As indicated, however, it does seem possible to infer the degree of intent from the lethality of the method used—a conclusion strongly supported by the findings of Beck, Beck, and Kovacs (1975). The concept of intent is also a useful reminder that most people who contemplate suicide retain at least some urge to live. Their hold on life, however tenuous, provides the key to successful suicide prevention (Fremouw et al., 1990).

Communication of Suicidal Intent Research has clearly disproved the tragic belief that those who threaten to take their lives seldom do so. A recent review of more than a half dozen studies conducted around the world that involved interviewing friends and relatives of people who had committed suicide revealed that more than 40 percent had communicated their suicidal intent in very clear and specific terms, and another 30 percent had communicated a wish to die or a preoccupation with death. These communications were usually made to several people and occurred within a few weeks or months before the suicide (Clark & Fawcett, 1992). Nevertheless, it should also be remembered that such information is always gathered after the fact and most of those interviewed say the suicide came as a surprise.

It is also interesting that most of these communications of intent are to friends and family members and *not* to mental health professionals. Indeed, nearly 50 percent of people who die by suicide have never seen a mental health professional in their lifetime, and only 25–30 percent are under the care of one at the time of their death (Clark & Fawcett, 1992). This is generally even true of those with major depression. A recent study in Finland showed that only 45 percent of individuals with a diagnosis of major depression who had committed suicide were receiving any kind of psychiatric treatment at the time of death, and it was generally minimal and inadequate (Isometsä et al., 1994).

Indirect threats to friends and family members typically include references to being better off dead, discussions of suicide methods and burial, statements such as "If I see you again. . . ," and dire predictions about the future. Whether direct or indirect, communication of suicidal intent usually represents a warning and a cry for help. The person is trying to express distress and ambivalence about suicide. Unfortunately, the message is often not received or is received with skepticism and denial. Skepticism is particularly likely when a suicidal person has given repeated warnings but has not made

an actual suicide attempt. As a consequence, those given the message may discount it. In this instance, "crying wolf" needs to be taken seriously. As several investigators have pointed out, many people who are contemplating suicide feel that living may be preferable if they can obtain the understanding and support of their family and friends. Failing to receive it after a suicidal threat, they go on to actual suicide.

Suicide Notes Several investigators have analyzed suicide notes in an effort to understand better the motives and feelings of people who take their own lives. In several large studies of completed suicides, it has been found that only about 25 percent percent left notes, usually addressed to relatives or friends (Cohen & Fiedler, 1974; Tuckman, Kleiner, & Lavell, 1959). The notes, usually coherent and legible, were either mailed, found on the person's body, or located near the suicide scene. In terms of emotional content, the suicide notes were categorized into those showing positive, negative, neutral, and mixed affect. Cohen and Fiedler found that women—especially separated and divorced women—were somewhat more likely to leave suicide notes than men. The emotional content of the notes was rated, in decreasing order of frequency, positive, neutral, mixed, and negative in content. HIGHLIGHT 6.5 provides examples of notes showing differing types of emotional content.

An understanding of the reasons for or motives underlying note writing (or its absence) could possibly help make the bases of these variations clearer. For example, the motivation for writing a note with positive content may stem from the desire to be remembered positively. More specifically, statements of love and concern may be motivated by the desire to reassure the survivor of the worth of their relationship (Cohen & Fiedler, 1974).

Suicide Prevention

The prevention of suicide is extremely difficult. One complicating factor is that most people who are depressed and contemplating suicide do not realize that their thinking is restricted and irrational and that they are in need of assistance. As we have seen, less than one-third voluntarily seek psychological help, and most of those who do probably do not receive adequate care. Others are brought to the attention of mental health personnel by family members or friends who are concerned because the person appears depressed or has made suicide threats. The vast majority, however, do not receive the assistance they desperately need. As we have seen, most people who attempt suicide do not really want to die and give prior warning of their inten-

Types of Suicide Notes

The Tuckman and colleagues (1959) study classified suicide notes by types of emotional content. A sampling of these various types appears in the following excerpts.

Positive Emotional Content

"Please forgive me and please forget me. I'll always love you. All I have was yours. No one ever did more for me than you, oh please pray for me please." (Tuckman et al., 1959, p. 60)

Negative (Hostile) Emotional Content

"I hate you and all of your family and I hope you never have a peace of mind. I hope I haunt this house as long as you live here and I wish you all the bad luck in the world." (Tuckman et al., 1959, p. 60)

Neutral Emotional Content

"To Whom It May Concern,
"I, Mary Smith, being of sound mind, do this day make my last will as follows—I bequeath my rings, Diamond and Black Opal to my daughter-in-law, Doris Jones and any other of my personal belongings she might wish. What money I might have in my savings account goes to my dear father, as he won't have me to help him. To my husband, Ed Smith, I leave my furniture and car. I would like to be buried as close to the grave of John Jones as possible." (Darbonne, 1969, p. 50)

Mixed Emotional Content

Dear Daddy, Please don't grieve for me or feel that you did something wrong, you didn't. I'll leave this life loving you and remembering the world's greatest father. I'm sorry to cause you more heartache but the reason I can't live anymore is because I'm afraid. Afraid of facing my life alone without love. No one ever knew how alone I am. No one ever stood by me when I needed help. No one brushed away the tears I cried for "help" and no one heard. I love you Daddy, Jeanne

tions; if a person's cry for help can be heard in time, it is often possible to intervene successfully.

Currently, the main thrust of preventive efforts is on crisis intervention. Efforts are gradually being extended, however, to the broader tasks of alleviating long-term stressful conditions known to be associated with suicidal behavior and trying to better understand and cope with the suicide problem in high-risk groups (Fremouw et al., 1990; Hawton, 1992).

Crisis Intervention The primary objective of crisis intervention is to help a person cope with an immediate life crisis. If a serious suicide attempt has been made, the first step involves emergency medical treatment, usually in the emergency room of a general hospital or clinic. It appears, however, that only about 10 percent of suicide attempts are considered of sufficient severity to warrant intensive medical care. Most people who attempt suicide, after initial treatment, are referred to inpatient or outpatient mental health facilities (Comstock, 1992; Kirstein et al., 1975; Paykel et al., 1974). This is important because as already noted the suicide rate for previous

attempters is much higher than that for the population in general, and so it is apparent that those who have attempted suicide remain a relatively high-risk group. (See also Chapter 18.)

When people contemplating suicide are willing to discuss their problems with someone at a suicide prevention center, it is often possible to avert an actual suicide attempt. Here the primary objective is to help these people regain their ability to cope with their immediate problems—and to do so as quickly as possible. Emphasis is usually placed on (a) maintaining contact with a person over a short period of time—usually one to six contacts; (b) helping the person realize that acute distress is impairing his or her ability to assess the situation accurately and to choose among possible alternatives; (c) helping the person see that other ways of dealing with the problem are available and preferable to suicide; (d) taking a highly directive and supportive role—for example, fostering a dependent relationship and giving specific suggestions to the person about what to do and what not to do; and (e) helping the person see that the present distress and emotional turmoil will not be endless. When feasible, counselors may elicit

In recent years, the availability of competent assistance at times of suicidal crisis has been expanded through the establishment of suicide prevention centers. These centers are geared toward crisis intervention—usually via 24-hour-a-day telephone hotlines.

the understanding and emotional support of family members or friends; and, of course, they may make frequent use of relevant community agencies. Admittedly, however, these are stopgap measures and do not constitute complete therapy.

Farberow (1974) has pointed out that it is important to distinguish between (a) individuals who have demonstrated relatively stable adjustment but have been overwhelmed by some acute stress—about 35–40 percent of people coming to the attention of hospitals and suicide prevention centers; and (b) individuals who have been tenuously adjusted for some time and in whom the current suicidal crisis represents an intensification of ongoing problems—about 60–65 percent of suicidal cases. For people in the first group, crisis intervention is usually sufficient to help them cope with the immediate stress and regain their equilibrium. For people in the second group, crisis intervention may also be sufficient to help them deal with the present problem, but with their lifestyle of "staggering from one crisis to

another," they are likely to require more comprehensive therapy.

Since the 1960s the availability of competent assistance at times of suicidal crisis has been expanded through the establishment of suicide prevention centers. At present, there are more than several hundred such centers in the United States. These centers are geared primarily toward crisis intervention, usually via the 24-hour-a-day availability of telephone contact. Some centers, however, offer long-term therapy programs, and they can refer suicidal people to other community agencies and organizations for special types of assistance. Suicide prevention centers are staffed by a variety of personnel: psychologists, psychiatrists, social workers, clergy, and trained volunteers. Although initially there was some doubt about the wisdom of using nonprofessionals in the important first-contact role, experience has shown that the empathic concern and peer-type relationship provided by a caring volunteer can be highly effective in helping a person through a suicidal crisis. Unfortunately, good information on the assessment of the effects of these centers has not revealed much impact on suicide rates, except perhaps in young women who are the primary users (Hawton, 1992; Miller et al., 1984).

One difficult problem with which suicide prevention centers must deal is that most people who use them do not follow up their initial contact by seeking additional help from the center or other treatment agencies (e.g., Sawyer, Sudak, & Hall, 1972). Therefore, some suicide prevention centers have made more systematic attempts to expand their services to better meet the needs of clients, including the introduction of long-range after-care or maintenance-therapy programs.

Focus on High-Risk Groups and Other Measures Many investigators have emphasized the need for broadly based preventive programs aimed at alleviating the life problems of people who are in high-risk groups for suicide. Few such programs have actually been initiated, but one approach has been to involve older men—a high-risk group—in social and interpersonal roles that help others. These roles may lessen their frequent feelings of isolation and meaninglessness. Among this group, such feelings often stem from forced retirement, financial problems, the death of loved ones, impaired physical health, and feeling unwanted.

Other measures to broaden the scope of suicide prevention programs include focusing efforts on the training of clergy, nurses, police, teachers, and other professional personnel who come in contact with many people in their communities. An important aspect of such training is to increase their alertness for, and sensitivity to, suicidal threats. For example, a parishioner might clasp the hand of a minister after church services and intensely say, "Pray for me." Because such a request is quite normal, a minister who is not alert to suicidal cries for help might reply with a simple, "Yes, I will" and turn to the next person in line—only to receive the news a few days later that the parishioner has committed suicide.

UNRESOLVED ISSUES

on Mood Disorders and Suicide

Most of us respect the preservation of human life as a worthwhile value. Thus in our society suicide is generally considered not only tragic but "wrong." Efforts to prevent suicide, however, also involve ethical problems. If people wish to take their own lives, what obligation—or right—do others have to interfere? Not all societies have taken the position that others should interfere when someone wishes to commit suicide. For example, the classical Greeks believed in dignity in death, and people who were extremely ill could get permission from the state to commit suicide. Officials of the state gave out hemlock (a poison) to those who received such permission (Humphry & Wickett, 1986). In certain Western European countries today, the law also allows terminally ill people to be given access to drugs that they can use to commit suicide.

By contrast, in the United States there is heated debate even today about the right of people who are terminally ill or who suffer chronic and debilitating pain to shorten their agony. One group, the Hemlock Society, supports the rights of terminally ill people to get help in terminating their own life when they wish (called assisted suicide or voluntary euthanasia); the society also provides support groups for people making this decision. Several other groups press related issues at a legislative level. One physician in Michigan, Jack Kevorkian, has helped a number of gravely ill people commit suicide, and in so doing has tried to get Michigan to pass laws permitting such acts. The state, however, has tried to block Kevorkian from assisting in any further suicides, and at one point he was even imprisoned and his medical license was revoked because he refused to obey injunctions that instructed him to not assist with any further suicides. He was also indicted on two counts of murder after assisting in two suicides of people who were not quite terminally ill, but a judge who seemed not to oppose assisted suicide later dismissed the charges. In spite of the failure to pass laws supporting assisted suicide for such gravely ill individuals (indeed, Michigan has now passed a law prohibiting assisted suicide!), there is increasing sympathy on the part of substantial numbers of people for this position. Arguments against this position have included fears that the right to suicide might be abused. For example, people who are terminally ill and severely incapacitated might feel pressured to end their own lives rather than burden their families with their care, or the cost of their care in a medical facility or hospice. However, the countries in Europe where assisted suicide is legal have not seen this happen, as advocates for this position in this country are pointing out.

But what about the rights of suicidal people who are not terminally ill and who have dependent chil-

The question of a "right to suicide" is an ethical issue with no easy answers. The issue becomes further clouded in the case of a terminal illness, where the doomed person does not want to go through the painful and extremely debilitating stages of certain diseases. The two women in this picture decided to take their own lives before becoming too incapacitated to be able to act for themselves. They enlisted the help of Dr. Jack Kevorkian, who had invented a so-called suicide machine that allows the terminally ill person to initiate his or her own suicide through fatal injection. The notion of a "suicide machine" has further complicated the issue of the right to suicide, and even some who would defend suicide as a reasonable choice under some circumstances feel that such a machine should be illegal.

dren, parents, a spouse, or other loved ones who will be adversely affected, perhaps permanently (Lukas & Seiden, 1990), by their death? Here a person's "right to suicide," reduced to such nonabstract terms, is not immediately obvious. The right to suicide is even less clear in the case of those who are ambivalent about taking their lives and who might, through intervention, regain their perspective and see alternative ways of dealing with their distress. Still, who has the right to prevent another's self-destruction?

Possibly, as has been pointed out by Nelson (1984), the early suicidologists erred in focusing on suicide "prevention." Nelson suggests suicide "intervention'" as both a more appropriate term and as descriptive of a more ethically defensible professional approach to suicidal behavior. Suicide intervention, according to this perspective, embodies a more neutral moral stance to suicide than does prevention—it means interceding without the implication of preventing the act—and, in certain circumstances, such as when people are terminally ill, may even hold out the possibility of facilitating the suicidal person's objective.

Here, however, we should reemphasize that the great majority of people who attempt suicide either do not really want to die or are ambivalent about taking their lives; and even for the minority who do wish to die, the desire is often a transient one. With improvement in a person's life situation and a lifting of depression, the suicidal crisis is likely to pass and not recur.

The dilemma becomes even more intense when prevention requires that a person be hospitalized involuntarily; when personal items, such as belts and sharp objects, are taken away; and when calming medication is more or less forcibly administered. Sometimes considerable restriction is needed to calm the individual. Not uncommonly, particularly in these litigious times, the responsible clinician feels trapped between threats of legal action on either side of the issue. Undue restriction might lead to a civil rights suit, whereas failure to employ all available safeguards could, in the case of the patient's injury or death, lead to a potentially ruinous malpractice claim initiated by the patient's family (Fremouw et al., 1990). Currently, it appears that most practitioners resolve this dilemma by taking the most cautious and conservative course. Thus many patients are hospitalized with insufficient clinical justification. Even where the decision to hospitalize is made on good grounds, however, preventive efforts may be fruitless, as truly determined persons may find a way to commit suicide even on a "suicide watch."

Thus, the vexing ethical problems of whether and to what extent one should intervene in cases of threatened suicide have now been complicated by no less vexing legal ones. As in other areas of professional practice, clinical judgment is no longer the exclusive consideration in intervention decisions. The ramifications of clinical decisions spread widely to matters that were formerly remote or irrelevant, such as the cost of malpractice insurance or the estimated likelihood that a patient or his or her family will sue. Because this is a societal problem, the solutions—if any—will have to be societal ones.

Admittedly, the preceding considerations do not resolve the issue of a person's basic right to suicide. As in the case of most complex ethical issues, no simple answer is apparent. Unless and until sufficient evidence confirms this alleged right—and society agrees on the conditions under which it may appropriately be exercised—it thus seems the wiser course to encourage existing suicide prevention (intervention) programs and to foster research into suicidal behavior with the hope of reducing the toll in human life and misery taken each year by suicide in our society.

 ## SUMMARY

Mood disorders (formerly called affective disorders) are those in which extreme variations in mood—either low or high—are the predominant feature. We all experience such variations at mild to moderate levels in the natural course of life. In some instances, however, the extremity of a person's mood in either direction is causally related to behavior that most would consider maladaptive. This chapter described the official categories of disorder associated with such maladaptive mood variations.

The large majority of people with these disorders have some form of unipolar depression—dysthymia or major depression. In these disorders the person experiences a range of affective, cognitive, and motivational symptoms including persistent sadness, negative thoughts about the self and the future, and lack of energy or initiative to engage in formerly pleasurable activities. Basic biological functioning is often also altered—for example, the sleep pattern may be dramatically altered or the person may become uninterested in food or eating. In the bipolar disorders (cyclothymia, and Bipolar I and II disorder), the person experiences episodes of both depression and hypomania or mania. During manic or hypomanic episodes the symptoms are essentially the opposite of those during a depressive episode. Unipolar disorders are much more common than bipolar disorders.

For unipolar disorders, there are both biological and psychosocial causal factors. Among biological causal factors, there is evidence of a modest genetic contribution to the vulnerability for major depression, but probably not for dysthymia. Although we do not yet understand how biological factors are involved in causing major depression, there are many reasons to think that biological factors do indeed play an important causal role. For example, many of the alterations in bodily function that accompany depression (sleep disturbance, appetite loss, and reduced libido) are regulated by the limbic system, and it is known that effective biological interventions for depression affect limbic system functioning. Disruptions in circadian and seasonal rhythms in depression also support the role of biological factors; much of the most exciting biological research on depression in recent years has focused on circadian rhythm dysfunction and how it may account for many of the clinical features of depression.

There are also many important psychosocial theories regarding what causes unipolar depression. Beck's cognitive theory and the reformulated helplessness and hopelessness theories are formulated as diathesis-stress models, where the diathesis is cognitive in nature (e.g., dysfunctional beliefs and pessimistic attributional style, respectively). Personality variables such as neuroticism, sociotropy, and autonomy may also serve as diatheses for depression. Psychodynamic and interpersonal theories emphasize the importance of early experiences (especially the quality of the parent-child relationship) as setting up a predisposition for depression. Although no one of these theories can successfully explain all of the causes of depression, it is unlikely that any one theory will ever explain all of the causal pathways to unipolar depression, which is undoubtedly multiply determined.

For bipolar disorders, biological causal factors play an even stronger role than for unipolar disorders. The genetic contribution to bipolar disorder is probably stronger than for any other major psychiatric disorder. Biochemical imbalances and abnormalities of the hypothalamic-pituitary-adrenal axis are also clearly implicated, although the exact nature of the abnormalities remains to be determined. There is also clear evidence regarding disturbances in biological rhythms in bipolar disorder. One major challenge is to determine how one drug—lithium—can play a role in reducing both manic symptoms and depressive symptoms. Stressful life events may be involved in precipitating manic or depressive

episodes, but it is unlikely that they cause the disorder, as opposed to affecting the timing and frequency of episodes of illness.

In general, biologically based treatments, such as drugs or ECT, are most often used in the treatment of the more severe or major disorders. Increasingly, however, psychosocial treatments are also being used with good effectiveness in many cases of these more severe disorders. In the milder forms of mood disorder, psychosocial treatments, of which an increasing variety are available, seem as effective as, or more effective than, drugs. Considerable evidence suggests that recurrent depression is best treated by specialized forms of psychosocial treatment or by maintenance for prolonged periods on drugs.

Suicide is a constant danger with depressive syndromes of any type or severity. Accordingly, an assessment of suicide risk is essential in the proper management of depressive disorders. A small minority of suicides appears unavoidable—chiefly those of the deliberate "not to be" type. A substantial amount of suicidal behavior (for example, taking nonlethal or slow-acting drugs where the likelihood of discovery is high) is motivated more by a desire for indirect interpersonal communication than by a wish to die. Somewhere between these extremes is a large group of people who are ambivalent about killing themselves and who initiate dangerous actions that they may or may not carry to completion, depending on momentary events and impulses. Most suicide prevention efforts are normally and properly focused on this ambivalent group.

KEY TERMS

mood disorders (p. 199)
mania (p. 201)
depression (p. 201)
unipolar disorder (p. 201)
bipolar disorder (p. 201)
dysthymia (p. 204)
adjustment disorder with
    depressed mood (p. 205)
major depressive disorder
    (p. 206)
severe major depressive
    episode with psychotic
    features (p. 207)
mood-congruent (p. 207)
mood-incongruent (p. 207)
melancholic type (p. 207)
recurrence (p. 208)
relapse (p. 208)
seasonal affective disorder
    (p. 208)

cyclothymia (p. 209)
hypomania (p. 209)
bipolar disorder with a
    seasonal pattern (p. 211)
rapid cycling (p. 212)
schizoaffective disorder
    (p. 212)
diathesis-stress models (p. 219)
dysfunctional beliefs (p. 220)
pessimistic attributional style
    (p. 221)
negative cognitive triad
    (p. 223)
negative automatic thoughts
    (p. 223)
learned helplessness (p. 225)
attributions (p. 226)
suicide (p. 240)

CHAPTER

7

SOMATOFORM AND DISSOCIATIVE DISORDERS

Gaston Duf, Pôlinchinêlle Rôise Vilôse. *As a child, Duf (b. 1920) was frequently terrorized by his father, often seeking the protection of his mother. When his parents belatedly married (when Duf was 18), he re-acted violently. After two suicide attempts, he was institutionalized in 1940. He began his artistic career while in the asylum, painting strange, powerful animals and comically proportioned human figures.*

Problems in our own lives provide most of us with ample experience of the disorganizing effects of stressful events. Most of us are also aware from time to time of temporarily disrupting levels of anxiety, depression, or perhaps even excessively euphoric self-confidence. Our personal acquaintance with such states is a considerable aid in understanding on an intuitive, empathic level those extreme and abnormal deviations discussed in the last three chapters. The disorders to be examined in this chapter will seem to most readers much less familiar and less readily grasped as merely exaggerated forms of everyday psychological phenomena. Somatoform and dissociative processes appear to involve more complex and exotic mental operations than those we have so far encountered, and to that extent they confront the field of psychopathology with some of its most fascinating and difficult challenges.

The **somatoform disorders** are conditions involving physical complaints or disabilities occurring in the absence of any physical pathology that could account for them. Although differing in clinical manifestations, they have as a common feature the expression of psychological difficulties in the "body language" of medical infirmities. The **dissociative disorders,** on the other hand, are conditions involving a disruption in the sense of a coherent and stable personal identity; included here are some of the more dramatic phenomena to be observed in the entire domain of psychopathology.

In Freudian psychodynamic theory, both of these types of disorder were considered neuroses—that is, varying manifestations of intrapsychic conflict involving defense against unacceptable sexual and aggressive impulses, deriving in turn from infantile fixations. Freud was not the only early theorist to suggest a connection between dissociative and somatoform processes, however. Other early writers, notably the French investigator Pierre Janet in the late nineteenth century, considered the somatoform symptoms of the disorder known as "hysteria" (now called *conversion disorder* and discussed below) to be basically a *dissociated* expression of memories relating to past traumatic events. Unlike Freud's notion, the trauma-dissociation-somatic symptom relationship as envisaged by Janet did not imply the presence of an active intrapsychic conflict; it was conceived instead as a more passive, almost structural, state of the central nervous system (see Frankel, 1994). The term *dissociated* in this context refers to processes that are both autonomous from and inaccessible to the conscious self. There is in fact some empirical evidence (e.g., Kihlstrom, 1994; Pribor et al., 1993; Saxe et al., 1994) indicating a close association between dissociative tendencies on the one hand and the likelihood of experiencing somatoform symptoms on the other.

Despite these scattered suggestions of some sort of shared basic properties in the underlying psychopathology of somatoform and dissociative disorders, of which more will be said in the "Unresolved Issues" section, the idea has not received prominent attention in the contemporary research literature. They are therefore addressed separately in the following sections. We begin with the somatoform.

SOMATOFORM DISORDERS

Soma means "body," and somatoform disorders involve patterns in which individuals complain of bodily symptoms that suggest the presence of physical problems, but for which no organic basis can be found that satisfactorily explains the symptoms. Such individuals are typically preoccupied with their state of health and with various presumed disorders or diseases of bodily organs.

Though no sufficient organic bases exist, these people sincerely believe their symptoms are real and serious. They should not be confused with people who feign physical illness in order to gain some specific objective (**malingering**), or those with **factitious disorders,** in which symptoms are feigned in order to satsify the psychological need to assume and maintain a sick role. Somatic symptoms in which psychological problems are manifested in sincere but factually mistaken complaints of physical dysfunction are extremely common (Kellner, 1985); they represent a large proportion of the complaints brought to primary care physicians.

In our discussion, we will focus on four more or less distinct somatoform patterns: somatization disorder, hypochondriasis, pain disorder, and conversion disorder. Although all four involve the neurotic development or elaboration of physical disabilities, the patterns of causation and the most effective treatment approaches may differ somewhat. The diagnosis of undifferentiated somatoform disorder is reserved for those persistent (i.e., a duration of at least six months) somatoform disorders of insufficient clarity or intensity to meet criteria for a more specific somatoform disorder. DSM-IV also includes a sixth syndrome, body dysmorphic disorder, in which there is a preoccupation with some imagined defect in one's physical appearance. While this problem doubtless occurs with significant frequency and

sometimes with such severity as to approach delusional proportions, it seems to be fundamentally different in character from the classic somatoform patterns. It will not be considered in this section.

Somatization Disorder

Somatization disorder is characterized by multiple complaints of physical ailments over a long period, beginning before age 30, that are inadequately explained by independent findings of physical illness or injury and that lead to medical treatment or to significant life impairment. A diagnostician need not be convinced that these claimed illnesses actually existed in a patient's background history; the mere reporting of them is sufficient. The DSM-IV provides a list of four types and levels of symptoms that, where each is present to at least a minimal degree, qualify as justifying a diagnosis of somatization disorder, as follows:

1. *Four pain symptoms:* The patient must report a history of pain experienced with respect to at least four different sites or functions—for example, head, abdomen, back, joints, rectum, or during menstruation, sexual intercourse, or urination.

2. *Two gastointestinal symptoms:* The patient must report a history of at least two symptoms, other than pain, pertaining to the gastroinestinal system—such as nausea, bloating, diarrhea, multiple food intolerances, or vomiting when not pregnant.

3. *One sexual symptom:* The patient must report at least one reproductive system symptom other than pain—as for example sexual indifference or dysfunction, menstrual irregularity, vomiting throughout pregnancy. (Note: This criterion would seem to involve the possibility of a gender bias in rendering the diagnosis.)

4. *One pseudoneurological symptom:* The patient must report a history of at least one symptom, not limited to pain, suggestive of a neurological condition—for example, various symptoms that mimic sensory or motor impairments, or symptoms involving anomalies of consciousness or memory.

The main features of somatization disorder are illustrated in the following case summary, which also involves a secondary diagnosis of depression:

This 38-year-old married woman, the mother of five children, reports to a mental health clinic with the chief complaint of depression, meeting diagnostic criteria for Major Depressive Disorder, the latest of several such episodes. Her marriage, which began at age 17, has been a chronically unhappy one; her husband is described as an alcoholic with an unstable work history, and there have been frequent arguments revolving around finances, her sexual indifference, and her complaints of pain during intercourse.

The history reveals that the patient had herself abused alcohol between ages 19 and 29, but has been abstinent since. She describes herself as nervous since childhood and as having been continuously sickly beginning in her youth; she believes she has a not yet discovered physical illness. She experiences chest pain and reportedly has been told by doctors that she has a "nervous heart." She sees physicians frequently for abdominal pain, having been diagnosed on one occasion as having a "spastic colon." In addition to M.D. physicians she has consulted chiropractors and osteopaths for backaches, pains in her extremities, and a feeling of anesthesia in her fingertips. She was recently admitted to a hospital following complaints of abdominal and chest pain and of vomiting, during which admission she received a hysterectomy. Following the surgery she has been troubled by spells of anxiety, fainting, vomiting, food intolerance, and weakness and fatigue. Physical examinations reveal completely negative findings.

The patient attributes her depression to hormonal irregularities, and she continues to seek a medical explanation of her other problems as well. (Adapted from Spitzer et al., 1994, pp. 404–405)

The somatization disorder diagnosis, new to the DSM-III of 1980, has not as yet been subjected to the extensive clinical and research scrutiny characteristic of other somatoform disorders. It is apparently based on long clinical experience with a certain group of medical patients who seem almost never to be entirely "well," even though clear, objective identification of specific organ malfunctions often (although not always) proves to be elusive. The pattern was earlier known as Briquet's syndrome.

Hypochondriasis

The differences between somatization disorder and **hypochondriasis** are none too clear in the DSM-IV diagnostic manual, apparently because the two disorders (if they are in fact distinct) are closely related (see Noyes et al., 1993). The main differences seem to be that hypochondriasis may have its onset after age 30; that the abnormal health concerns characteristic of hypochondriasis need not focus on any particular set of symptoms nor on a profusion of them; and that a hypochondriacal person mostly focuses on the idea that he or she has a serious disease, rather than claiming various symptoms or physical disabilities.

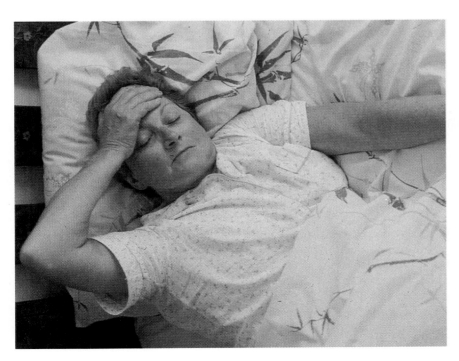

Hypochondriacal individuals are preoccupied with health matters and unrealistic fears of disease. They are convinced that they have symptoms of physical illness, but their complaints typically do not conform to any coherent symptom pattern, and they usually have trouble giving a precise description of their symptoms.

Hypochondriasis is one of the most frequently seen somatoform patterns, with a reported prevalence in general medical practice of between 4 and 9 percent. The disorder is characterized by multiple and stubbornly held complaints about possible physical illness where no evidence of such illness can be found. Hypochondriacal complaints are usually not restricted to any physiologically coherent symptom pattern; rather, they express a preoccupation with health matters and unrealistic fears of disease. Although hypochondriacal people repeatedly seek medical advice, their concerns are not in the least lessened by their doctors' reassurances—in fact they are frequently disappointed when no physical problem is found.

Individuals with this disorder may complain of uncomfortable and peculiar sensations in the general area of the stomach, chest, head, genitals, or anywhere else in the body. They usually have trouble giving a precise description of their symptoms, however. They may begin by mentioning pain in the stomach, which on further questioning is not really a pain but a gnawing sensation, or perhaps a feeling of heat, or of pressure, whose locus may now on more careful observation migrate to a neighboring portion of the abdomen, and so on. The mental orientation of these individuals keeps them constantly on the alert for new symptoms, the description of which may challenge the capacity of mere language to communicate.

Hypochondriacal patients are likely to be avid readers of popular magazines on medical topics and are apt to feel certain that they are suffering from every new disease they read or hear about. They are major consumers of over-the-counter (and often virtually worthless) remedies touted in ads as being able to heal vaguely described problems such as "tired blood" or "irregularity." Tuberculosis, cancer, exotic infections, and numerous other diseases are readily self-diagnosed by these individuals. Their morbid preoccupation with bodily processes, coupled with their often limited knowledge of medical pathology, leads to some interesting diagnoses. One patient diagnosed his condition as "ptosis of the transvex colon," and added, "If I am just half as bad off as I think, I am a dead pigeon."

This attitude appears to be typical: Such individuals are sure they are seriously ill and cannot recover. Yet—and this is revealing—despite their exaggerated concerns over their health, they do not usually show the intense fear or anxiety that might be expected of those suffering from such horrible ills. In fact they are usually in good physical condition. Nevertheless, they are not malingering, that is, consciously faking symptoms to achieve specific ends; they are sincere

in their conviction that their symptoms represent real illness, although an attentive listener may get the impression that something more is being communicated in these complaints.

A classic illustration of the shifting symptoms and complaints in a severe case of hypochondriasis is presented in the following letter that a hospitalized patient wrote to her anxious relatives:

"Dear Mother and Husband:

"I have suffered terrible today with drawing in throat. My nerves are terrible. My head feels queer. But my stomach hasn't cramped quite so hard. I've been on the verge of a nervous chill all day, but I have been fighting it hard. It's night and bedtime, but, Oh, how I hate to go to bed. Nobody knows or realizes how badly I feel because I fight to stay up and out doors if possible. . . .

"These long afternoons and nights are awful. There are plenty of patients well enough to visit with but I'm in too much pain.

"The nurses ignore any complaining. They just laugh or scold.

"Eating has been awful hard. They expect me to eat like a harvest hand. Every bite of solid food is agony to get down, for my throat aches so and feels so closed up. . . .

"My eyes are bothering me more.

"Come up as soon as you can. My nose runs terrible every time I eat.

"The trains and ducks and water pipes are noisy at night.

"Annie"
(Menninger, 1945, pp. 139–40).

Hypochondriacal persons often show a morbid preoccupation with digestive and excretory functions. Some keep charts of their bowel movements, and most are able to give detailed information concerning diet, constipation, and related matters. Many, as earlier suggested, use a wide range of self-medications of the type frequently advertised on television. However, they do not show the losses or distortions of sensory, motor, and visceral functioning that occur in conversion disorder (to be discussed in a later section); nor do their complaints have the bizarre delusional quality—such as "insides rotting away" or "lungs drying up"—that occurs in some psychotic disorders.

Most of us as children learn well the lesson that, when we are sick, special comforts and attention are provided and, furthermore, that we are excused from a number of responsibilities or at least are not expected to perform certain chores up to par. This lesson has been learned all too well by the hypochondriacal adult. Such an adult is in effect saying (a) "I deserve more of your attention and concern," and (b) "You may not legitimately expect me to perform as a well person would." Typically these messages are conveyed with more than a touch of angry rebuke or whining, inconsolable demand.

It is a reasonable assumption that these patients have, as a group, more deep-seated problems than merely a fear of disease, and most hypochondriacs also meet criteria for other Axis I psychiatric diagnoses (Barsky, Wyshak, & Klerman, 1992). Moreover, Barsky and colleagues (1994) have indicated reports of significantly elevated psychological trauma, including violence and sexual abuse, in the childhood histories of hypochondriacal patients, compared with appropriate medical-patient controls. These authors also found their hypochondriacal patients to report much childhood sickness and missing of school, suggesting that the pattern of communicating psychic distress by reference to physical malfunction was learned quite early.

In short, hypochondriasis may be viewed as a certain type of needful interpersonal communication as well as a disorder involving abnormal preoccupation with disease. Treatment of the latter in the absence of an appreciation of the former frequently produces clinical frustration, if not exasperation. In fact, it may be that the (understandable) impatience with which many physicians react to these patients has the unintended effect of maintaining or increasing their fears of abandonment and an early demise from some terrible condition that remains undetected by an insufficiently caring physician (Kirmayer, Robbins, & Paris, 1994; Noyes et al., 1993).

Pain Disorder

Pain disorder is characterized by the report of pain of sufficient duration and severity to cause significant life disruption in the absence of objective findings of medical pathology that would explain pain experience and behavior of the magnitude observed. DSM-IV specifies coded subdiagnoses of (a) pain disorder associated with psychological factors, and (b) pain disorder associated with both psychological factors and a general medical condition. The former subdiagnosis applies where any co-existing general medical condition is considered of minimal causal significance in the pain complaint; the latter applies where the experienced pain is considered to be out of proportion to the physical findings concerning an established medical condition that might cause some pain. Implicated general medical conditions are of course coded on Axis III. The DSM-IV also takes note of pain reports and behavior that *correspond* with expectancies associated with a general medical condition, but this condition (appropriately enough) is not considered a mental disorder. Medically unexplained pain associated with sexual intercourse is diagnosed as dyspareunia (see Chapter 11).

In approaching the phenomenon of pain it is important to underscore that it is *always* in essence a sensation registered in a patient's mental experience; there is no perfect correlation between the occurrence or intensity of pain (as reported in the general population) and tissue damage or irritation. This partial independence of physical damage and psychological experience evidently makes possible the considerable effectiveness of purely psychological treatment for pain that has a definite physical basis (see Keefe & Williams, 1989).

Because, like all other subjective experience, pain is ultimately always private, we have no way of gauging with certainty the actual extent of a patient's pain. This fundamental unclarity is wholly insufficient to justify the conclusion that a patient is faking or exaggerating his or her pain, although such a judgment is regrettably frequent among clinicians. Pain disorder is fairly common among psychiatric patients (Katon, Egan, & Miller, 1985) and is more often diagnosed among women. There is some evidence that, even where some physical basis for pain is present, its experienced intensity is a function of the level of stress the patient is currently undergoing. For example, Schwartz, Slater, and Birchler (1994) have reported a study in which chronic back pain patients subjected to a prior contrived stressful circumstance reported more pain and engaged in more pain behavior than a comparable group exposed to an emotionally neutral prior circumstance.

The reported pain may be vaguely located in the area of the heart or other vital organs, or it may center in the lower back or limbs. (Tension headaches and migraines are not included here, since they involve demonstrable physiological changes, such as muscle contractions.) People with psychogenic pain disorders may adopt an invalid lifestyle. They tend to "doctor-shop" in the hope of finding both a physical confirmation of their pain and some medication to relieve it. This behavior continues even if several visits to doctors fail to indicate any underlying physical problem. Sadly enough, in many cases somatoform pain patients actually wind up being

Persons having hypochondriasis or somatoform pain disorder often despair of help from physicians and become obsessed with finding the "right" medication on their own.

disabled—either through addiction to pain medication or through the crippling effects of surgery they have been able to obtain as treatment for their condition. The following case is illustrative:

An attractive, socially prominent, middle-aged woman developed a severe pain, increasing over time, in her right breast. Over a period of several years she consulted numerous physicians in various specialties, none of whom was able to establish any objective medical reason for the pain despite the employment of every known diagnostic procedure that might yield an answer; the painful breast was, so far as could be determined using the most advanced methods available, anatomically and physiologically normal. Increasingly desperate, she so pressured one of her physicians that he recommended she consider mastectomy (surgical removal of the breast), and she did in fact travel to a tertiary-care, university medical center to request this operation.

Fortunately, the surgeon to whom she was assigned was an extraordinarily compassionate and psychologically sophisticated man. He sensed that this pain was somehow associated with the woman's concerns about growing older and losing her sexual attractiveness, which had been central to her self-esteem and feelings of worth since adolescence. He skillfully diverted her to an experienced psychotherapist. In somewhat less than a year of work with this therapist the patient was free of pain and in general far more comfortable with herself and her life.

Unnecessary, mutilating surgery was in this case averted; sometimes, in pain disorder, it is not.

Conversion Disorder

Conversion disorder, earlier called *hysteria,* involves a pattern in which pseudoneurological symptoms of some physical malfunction or loss of control appear without any underlying organic pathology. It is one of the most intriguing and baffling patterns in psychopathology, and we still have much to learn about it. Nevertheless, contemporary research relating to the problem has been notably sparse.

As we mentioned in Chapter 2, the term *hysteria* was derived from the Greek word meaning "uterus." It was thought by Hippocrates and other ancient Greeks that this disorder was restricted to women, and that it was caused by sexual difficulties, particularly by the wandering of a frustrated womb to various parts of the body because of sexual desires and a yearning for children. Thus the uterus might lodge in the throat and cause choking sensations, or in the spleen, resulting in temper tantrums. Hippocrates considered marriage the best remedy for the affliction. Freud used the term *conversion hysteria* for these disorders because he believed that the symptoms were an expression of repressed sexual energy—that is, the psychosexual conflict was seen as "converted" into a bodily disturbance. For example, a conflict over masturbation might be "solved" by developing a paralyzed hand. This was not done consciously, of course, and the person was not aware of the origin or meaning of the physical symptom.

In contemporary psychopathology, reactions of this type are no longer interpreted in Freudian terms as the "conversion" of sexual conflicts or other psychological problems into physical symptoms. Rather, the physical symptoms are now usually seen as serving the rather obvious function of plausible excuse, enabling an individual to escape or avoid a stressful situation without having to take responsibility for doing so. The term *conversion* has been retained, however. Relatedly, the term **secondary gain,** which originally referred to advantages of the symptom(s) beyond the "primary gain" of neutralizing intrapsychic conflict, has also been retained. Generally, it is used to refer to any "external" circumstance, such as financial compensation, that would tend to reinforce the maintenance of disability. The distinction between primary and secondary gain has thus become rather blurred over the course of time, although the latter term retains a more pejorative connotation of active management of environmental outcomes.

Conversion disorders were once relatively common in civilian and especially in military life. In World War I, conversion disorder was the most frequently diagnosed psychiatric syndrome among soldiers; it was also relatively common during World War II. Conversion disorder typically occurred under highly stressful combat conditions and involved men who would ordinarily be considered stable. Here, conversion symptoms—such as paralysis of the legs—enabled a soldier to avoid an anxiety-arousing combat situation without being labeled a coward or being subjected to court-martial.

Today conversion disorders constitute only some 1–3 percent of all disorders referred for mental health treatment. Interestingly enough, their decreasing incidence seems to be closely related to our growing sophistication about medical and psychological disorders: A conversion disorder apparently loses its defensive function if it can be readily shown to lack an organic basis. In an age that no longer believes in such phenomena as being struck blind or suddenly afflicted with an unusual and dramatic paraplegia, the cases that do occur increasingly simulate more exotic physical diseases that are harder to diagnose, such as convulsive seizures or gastrointestinal ailments. Even psychologically sophisticated people have been known to develop conversion symptoms under stress, however, as the following case shows:

A 29-year-old physician in the first year of a psychiatric residency was experiencing a great deal of stress from problems in both his personal life and his hospital work. His marriage was deteriorating and he was being heavily criticized by the rather authoritarian chief of psychiatry for allegedly mismanaging some treatment cases. Shortly before he was to discuss his work in an important hospital-wide conference being conducted by the chief psychiatrist, he had an "attack" in which he developed difficulty in speaking and severe pains in his chest. He thought his condition was probably related to a viral infection, but physical findings were negative.

During World War I, conversion disorder was the most frequently diagnosed psychiatric syndrome among soldiers. It enabled soldiers to avoid anxiety-arousing combat situations, the severity of which is evident in this scene on the western front.

Here we see with particular clarity how a conversion symptom may serve the function of escape from unwanted responsibility.

The range of symptoms in conversion disorder is practically as diverse as for physically based ailments. In describing the clinical picture in conversion disorder, it is useful to think in terms of three categories of symptoms: sensory, motor, and visceral.

Sensory Symptoms Any of the senses may be involved in sensory conversion reactions. The most common forms are as follows:

Anesthesia—loss of sensitivity

Hypesthesia—partial loss of sensitivity

Hyperesthesia—excessive sensitivity

Analgesia—loss of sensitivity to pain

Paresthesia—exceptional sensations, such as tingling

You may be wondering why somatoform pain disorder, given its essential similarity to the symptoms just listed, is not included here as merely another form of sensory conversion disorder. Why is it a separate category? The DSM-IV offers no satisfactory answer to this question. It may be that it was given separate status because it appears to occur far more frequently than other conversion phenomena.

Some idea of the range of sensory symptoms that may occur in conversion disorders can be gleaned from Ironside and Batchelor's (1945) classic study of hysterical visual symptoms among airmen in World War II. They found blurred vision, photophobia (extreme sensitivity to light), double vision, night blindness, a combination of intermittent visual failure and amnesia, deficient stereopsis (the tendency to look past an object during attempts to focus on it), restriction in the visual field, intermittent loss of vision in one eye, color blindness, jumbling of print during attempts to read, and failing day vision. They also found that the symptoms of each airman were closely related to his performance duties. Night fliers, for example, were more subject to night blindness, while day fliers more often developed failing day vision. The results of a later study of student military aviators who developed conversion disorders are reported in HIGHLIGHT 7.1.

The other senses may also be subject to a wide range of disorders. A puzzling and unsolved question in hysterical blindness and deafness is whether affected persons actually cannot see or hear, or whether the sensory information is received but screened from consciousness (Theodor & Mandelcorn, 1973). In general, the evidence supports the latter hypothesis, that the sensory input is registered but is somehow screened from explicit conscious recognition. Numerous demonstrations of this type of phenomenon occur in the literature of hypnosis, which has, for good reason, been closely associated historically with conversion phenomena (see Hilgard, 1994). For example, hysterically blind persons rarely endanger themselves, and a normal subject hypnotically induced to be unable to "see" an object in his or her path will nevertheless avoid walking into it.

Motor Symptoms Motor conversion reactions also cover a wide range of symptoms, but only the most common need be mentioned here.

Paralysis conversion reactions are usually confined to a single limb, such as an arm or a leg, and the loss of function is usually selective. For example, in "writer's cramp," a person cannot write but may be able to use the same muscles in shuffling a deck of cards or playing the piano. Tremors (muscular shaking or trembling) and tics (localized muscular twitches) are common. Occasionally, symptoms include contractures, which usually involve flexing of the fingers and toes, or rigidity of the larger joints, such as the elbows and knees. Paralyses and contractures frequently lead to walking disturbances. A person with a rigid knee joint may be forced to throw his or her leg out in a sort of arc as he or she walks. Another walking disturbance is *astasia-abasia*, in which an individual can usually control leg movements when sitting or lying down, but can hardly stand and has a grotesque, disorganized walk, with both legs wobbling about in every direction.

The most common speech-related conversion disturbances are *aphonia*, in which an individual is able to talk only in a whisper, and *mutism*, in which he or she cannot speak at all. Interestingly enough, a person who can talk only in a whisper can usually cough in a normal manner. In true, organic laryngeal paralysis both the cough and the voice are affected. Aphonia is a relatively common conversion reaction and usually occurs after some emotional shock, whereas mutism is relatively rare. Occasionally, symptoms may involve convulsions, similar to those in epilepsy. People with such symptoms, however, show few of the usual characteristics of true epileptics—they rarely, if ever, injure themselves in falls; their pupillary reflex to light remains unaffected; they are able to control excretory functions; and they do not have attacks when alone.

Visceral Symptoms Visceral conversion reactions also cover a wide range of symptoms, including headaches, "lump in the throat" and choking sensa-

Conversion Reactions in Student Naval Aviators

Mucha and Reinhardt (1970) reported on a study of 56 student aviators with conversion reactions who were assessed at the U.S. Naval Aerospace Medical Institute in Pensacola, Florida. In the group, representing 16 percent of a total population of 343 patients at the institute, four types of symptoms were found. These were, in order of frequency: visual symptoms (most common), auditory symptoms, paralysis or paresthesias (prickling sensations) of extremities, and paresthesia of the tongue.

Generally, the 56 students came from middle-class, achievement-oriented families. The fathers of 80 percent of them were either high school or college graduates and were either professional men or white-collar workers. Interestingly enough, 89 percent of the cases had won letters in one or more sports in high school or col-

lege; all were college graduates and presently were flight students, officer candidates, or officers.

Commenting on the relatively high incidence of conversion reactions among the patients at the institute, Mucha and Reinhardt emphasized three conditions which they considered of etiological significance:

1. *Unacceptability of quitting.* In the students' previous athletic training, physical illness had been an acceptable means of avoiding difficult situations, whereas quitting was not. Moreover, the present training environment tended to perpetuate this adaptation, since the military is also achievement-oriented and does not tolerate quitting as a means of coping with stress situations.

2. *Parental models and past experience.* Seventy percent of the par-

ents of these students had had significant illnesses affecting the organ system utilized in the students' disorders; and a majority of the students had had multiple physical symptoms prior to enlistment—often as a result of athletic injuries.

3. *Sensitization to the use of somatic complaints.* As a result of their previous experience, the students were sensitized to the use of somatic complaints as a face-saving means of coping with stressful situations.

When faced with the real stress of the flight training program and with frequent life-or-death incidents they resorted to this unconscious mechanism to relieve the stress and to avoid admitting failure. To admit failure would be totally unacceptable to the rigid demands of their superegos. (p. 494)

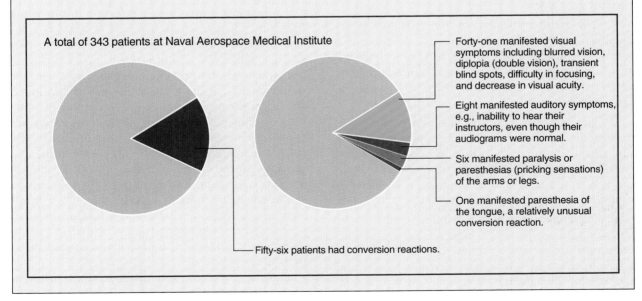

A total of 343 patients at Naval Aerospace Medical Institute

Forty-one manifested visual symptoms including blurred vision, diplopia (double vision), transient blind spots, difficulty in focusing, and decrease in visual acuity.

Eight manifested auditory symptoms, e.g., inability to hear their instructors, even though their audiograms were normal.

Six manifested paralysis or paresthesias (pricking sensations) of the arms or legs.

One manifested paresthesia of the tongue, a relatively unusual conversion reaction.

Fifty-six patients had conversion reactions.

tions, coughing spells, difficulty in breathing, cold and clammy extremities, belching, nausea, vomiting, and so on. Occasionally, persistent hiccoughing or sneezing occurs.

Actual organic symptoms may be simulated to an almost unbelievable degree. In a pseudoattack of acute appendicitis, a person not only may evidence lower-abdominal pain and other typical symptoms, but also may have a temperature far above normal. Conversion-reaction cases of malaria and tuberculosis have also been cited in the literature. In the latter, for example, an individual may show all the usual symptoms—coughing, loss of weight, recurrent fever, and night sweats—without actual organic disease. Numerous cases of pseudopregnancy (formerly called pseudocyesis) have been reported, in which menstruation may cease, the abdominal area and breasts may enlarge, and the woman may experience morning sickness.

Because the symptoms in conversion disorder can simulate almost every known disease, accurate diagnosis can be a serious problem. However, in addition to specialized medical techniques, several criteria are commonly used for distinguishing between conversion disorders and organic disturbances:

1. A certain unconcern *("la belle indifférence"),* in which the patient describes what is wrong in a rather matter-of-fact way, with little of the anxiety and fear that would be expected in a person with a paralyzed arm or loss of sight. Mucha and Reinhardt (1970) reported that all of the 56 student fliers in their study showed this pattern, seeming to be unconcerned about long-range effects of their disabilities. In itself, however, unconcernedness cannot be taken as a reliable sign of conversion; some stoic persons with genuine organic pathology show a similar disregard, and some conversion patients exhibit a level of concern "appropriate" to the disabilities they display.

2. The frequent failure of the dysfunction to conform clearly to the symptoms of the particular disease or disorder. For example, little or no wasting away or atrophy of a "paralyzed" limb occurs in paralyses that are conversion reactions, except in rare and long-standing cases.

3. The selective nature of the dysfunction. For example, in conversion blindness, an individual does not usually bump into people or objects; "paralyzed" muscles can be used for some activities but not others; and uncontrolled contractures (muscular rigidities) usually disappear during sleep.

4. The interesting fact that under hypnosis or narcosis (a sleeplike state induced by drugs) the symptoms can usually be removed, shifted, or reinduced by the suggestion of the therapist. Similarly, if the person is suddenly awakened from a sound sleep, he or she may be tricked into using a "paralyzed" limb.

Where conversion symptoms are superimposed on an actual organic disorder, a not uncommon occurrence, an accurate and unequivocal diagnosis may become extremely difficult to achieve. It is usu-

ally fairly easy, however, to distinguish between a conversion reaction and frank malingering or factitiously "sick" role-playing. Persons so engaged are consciously perpetrating frauds by faking the symptoms of diseases, and this fact is reflected in their demeanors. Individuals with conversion disorders are usually dramatic and apparently naive; they are concerned mainly with the symptoms and willingly discuss them, often in excruciating detail. If inconsistencies in their behaviors are pointed out, they are usually unperturbed. Persons who are feigning symptoms, on the other hand, are inclined to be defensive, evasive, and suspicious; they are usually reluctant to be examined and slow to talk about their symptoms, lest the pretense be discovered. Should inconsistencies in their behaviors be pointed out, deliberate deceivers as a rule immediately become more defensive. Thus conversion disorder and deliberate faking of illness are considered distinct patterns, although sometimes they overlap.

The phenomenon of mass hysteria, as typified by outbreaks of St. Vitus's dance and biting manias during the Middle Ages, is a form of conversion disorder that has become a rarity in modern times. As we saw in Chapter 2, however, some outbreaks do still occur (for recent examples, see page 38). In all cases, suggestibility clearly plays a major role—a conversion reaction in one person rapidly spreads to others for whom, one suspects, the appearance of having the imputed "condition" has some sort of psychic payoff.

In the development of a conversion disorder, the following chain of events typically occurs: (a) a desire to escape from some unpleasant situation; (b) a fleeting wish to be sick in order to avoid the situation (this wish, however, is suppressed as unfeasible or unworthy); and, under additional or continued stress, (c) the appearance of the symptoms of some physical ailment. The individual sees no relation between the symptoms and the stress situation. The particular symptoms that occur are usually those of a previous illness or are copied from other sources, such as symptoms observed among relatives, seen on television, or read about in magazines. The symptoms may also be superimposed on an existing organic ailment, associated with anticipated secondary gains, or symbolically related to major conflict situations in the individual's life.

Sometimes, conversion disorders seem to stem from feelings of guilt and the necessity for self-punishment. In one case, for example, a female patient developed a marked tremor and partial paralysis of the right arm and hand after she had physically attacked her father. During this incident she had clutched at and torn open his shirt with her right hand, and apparently the subsequent paralysis represented a sort of symbolic punishment of the "guilty party," while preventing a recurrence of her hostile and forbidden behavior.

Conversion symptoms often develop following an accident or injury from which an individual hopes to receive financial compensation. These reactions usually occur after accidents in which an individual might have been seriously injured but is actually only shaken up or slightly injured. Later, in discussions with family or friends, it may be agreed that the individual would have had a strong legal case if there had been an injury. "Are you sure you are all right? Could you possibly have injured your back? Perhaps there is something wrong with it." Indeed, the recent advertising practices of some law firms have involved precisely this approach. With the aid of a "sympathetic" lawyer (whose fee often will be determined by the size of the monetary award), the individual may proceed to file suit for injury compensation.

In such cases it is especially hard to distinguish between a malingerer's deliberate simulation of injury and the unconscious deception of an individual suffering from conversion disorder (Lewis, 1974). It may well be that this dichotomy itself is misleading. Apparently many conversion disorder cases include a combination of the two, in which conscious acting is superimposed on unconscious acting or role playing. In any event, the patient in such cases often shows an amazingly rapid recovery once there has been "proper" compensation for the "injuries."

Whatever specific causal factors may be involved, however, the basic motivational pattern underlying conversion disorder seems to be to avoid or reduce anxiety-arousing stress by getting sick—thus converting an intolerable emotional problem into a face-saving physical one. Once this response is learned, it is maintained because it is repeatedly reinforced—both by anxiety reduction and by the gains (in terms of sympathy and support or financial "compensation") that result from being disabled.

DISSOCIATIVE DISORDERS

The unity of consciousness is illusory. Man does more than one thing at a time—all the time—and the conscious representation of these actions is never complete.

(Hilgard, 1977, p. 1)

With this brief but profound statement, distinguished experimental psychologist Ernest Hilgard announced the arrival of a new era in psychologists' understanding of how the human mind operates. That new conceptualization recognizes—indeed emphasizes—that much (most?) mental activity, much processing of information, occurs outside and independent of conscious awareness. In short, much of an individual's mental life involves nonconscious processes that are to a large extent autonomous with respect to deliberate, self-aware monitoring and direction. Such unaware processing extends to the areas of memory and perception, where it can be demonstrated that persons routinely "remember" things they do not consciously remember and perceive things they cannot report they have perceived, called **implicit memory** and **implicit perception,** respectively (Kihlstrom, Tataryn, & Hoyt, 1993; Nisbett & Wilson, 1977). As we have seen, this general idea has been embraced by psychodynamically oriented clinicians for many years; that it should be adopted into the mainstream of the concerns of intellectually conservative, laboratory-based experimental psychologists is something of a momentous development.

Of course, the older, psychodynamic concept of *the unconscious* differs in important respects from the unconscious mental activity posited by contemporary cognitive psychologists. The former was conceived as an emotionally driven "experiential" system, whereas the latter is considered more or less rational, "kinder" and "gentler" (Kihlstrom, 1990), in its mode of operation. This distinction has been thoroughly analyzed by Epstein (1994), who argues that both types of automatic, unaware processing of information have evolved for sound adaptational reasons. In any event, one important result of the clinical-experimental rapprochement indicated is a resurgence of interest in the century-old clinical concept of **dissociation** (Kihlstrom, 1994). This concept, referring to the human mind's capacity to mediate complex mental activity in channels split off from or independent of conscious awareness, is clearly pertinent to the modern manner of thinking captured in Hilgard's statement quoted above.

The process of dissociation in itself is neither extraordinary nor pathological, therefore. The ability to conduct integrated and complex mental operations without the necessity of conscious control or monitoring has obvious advantages in the efficient use of whatever information-processing capacity the brain provides. In certain clinical conditions, however, this multichannel quality of human cognition appears to lose some sort of overall, integrative control. When this happens, the affected person may be unable to access information that is normally in the forefront of consciousness. In addition, the person may become subject to the influence of cognitive subsystems not normally accessible to awareness. Or, to put it another way, the normally useful capacity to maintain ongoing mental activity outside of

HIGHLIGHT 7.2

Continuum of Dissociative Processes and States

The following figure is a graphic representation of the manner in which Ross (1989, p. 80) conceives dissociation's fundamental role in mental disorders of varying types and severities. Thus a simple form of dissociative process is involved in normal dissociative states, whereas complex dissociation processes characterize DID, all the more where many and changing alter personalities are poorly integrated with one another (called "polyfragmented" DID). Notice that Ross includes conversion disorder on this continuum, the symptoms of which are also conceived to be dissociated parts of the self. While this idea is not prominent in contemporary writings on conversion disorder, much historical precedence exists for it.

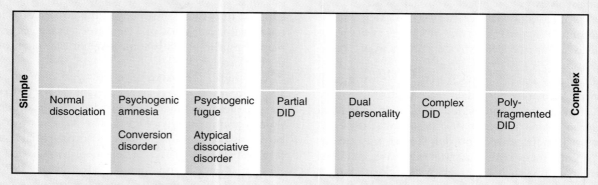

Simple — Normal dissociation | Psychogenic amnesia / Conversion disorder | Psychogenic fugue / Atypical dissociative disorder | Partial DID | Dual personality | Complex DID | Poly-fragmented DID — Complex

Note: DID = dissociative identity disorder

awareness appears to be subverted and misused for the purpose of managing severe psychological threat. When that happens we observe the behavioral outcomes known as dissociative disorders.

Like somatoform disorders, dissociative disorders appear mainly to be ways of avoiding anxiety and stress and of managing life problems that threaten to overwhelm the person's usual coping resources. Both disorders also permit a person to deny personal responsibility for his or her "unacceptable" wishes or behavior. In the case of dissociative disorders, however, the person avoids the stress by *pathologically dissociating*—in essence by escaping from his or her own autobiographical memory, or personal identity.

According to the DSM-IV, dissociative patterns include dissociative amnesia and fugue states, dissociative identity disorder (formerly called multiple personality disorder), and depersonalization disorder. A generalized conception of these patterns appears in HIGHLIGHT 7.2, where Ross (1989), originator of this graphic, also indicates his preference for including conversion disorder under the dissociative (rather than somatoform) rubric. John

Kihlstrom (1993, 1994), a major contributor to contemporary thinking in this arena, has also mounted a cogent argument in favor of considering conversion disorder to be essentially a variety of pathological dissociation. We tend to agree, but have yielded to the DSM-IV format here in an attempt to minimize confusion for the reader. The matter is addressed further in the "Unresolved Issues" section.

Dissociative Amnesia and Fugue

Amnesia is partial or total inability to recall or identify past experience. Persistent amnesia may occur in neurotic and psychotic disorders and in organic brain pathology, including traumatic brain injury and diseases of the central nervous system. If the amnesia is caused by brain pathology, it usually involves an actual retention failure. That is, either the information contained in experience is not registered and does not enter memory storage, or, if stored, it cannot be retrieved; it is truly and almost always permanently lost (Hirst, 1982).

Psychogenic or **dissociative amnesia,** on the other hand, is usually limited to a failure to recall. The "forgotten" material is still there beneath the level of consciousness, as becomes apparent under hypnosis or narcosis (sodium amytal, or so-called "truth serum") interviews, and in cases where the amnesia spontaneously clears up. Four types of psychogenic amnesia are recognized: *localized* (a person remembers nothing that happened during a specific period—usually the first few hours following some traumatic event); *selective* (a person forgets some but not all of what happened during a given period); *generalized* (a person forgets his or her entire life history); and *continuous* (a person remembers nothing beyond a certain point in the past). The latter two types occur only rarely.

As we have noted, psychogenic (or dissociative) amnesia is fairly common in initial reactions to intolerably traumatic experiences, such as those occurring during combat conditions and immediately after catastrophic events. Some troubled persons, however, develop such amnesias in the face of stressful life situations with which most people deal more effectively.

In typical dissociative amnesic reactions, individuals cannot remember their names, do not know how old they are or where they live, and do not recognize their parents, spouses, relatives, or friends. Yet their basic habit patterns—such as their abilities to read, talk, perform skilled work, and so on—remain intact, and they seem normal aside from the memory deficit. Another way of putting this is that only a particular type of memory is affected, the type of memory psychologists refer to as episodic (pertaining to events experienced), or autobiographical. The other recognized (Tulving, 1993) forms of memory—semantic (pertaining to language and concepts), procedural (how to do things), perceptual representation (imaging), and short-term storage—remain almost always intact.

In such an amnesic state, a person may retreat still further from real-life problems by going away in what is called a **fugue** state. A fugue reaction, as the term implies (*fugue* means "flight" in French), is a defense by actual flight—a person is not only amnesic, but also departs from home surroundings, often assuming a partially or completely new identity. Days, weeks, or sometimes even years later, such persons may suddenly find themselves in strange places, not knowing how they got there and with apparently complete amnesia for their fugue periods. Their activities during their fugues may vary from merely going on a round of motion pictures to traveling across the country, entering a new occupation, and starting a whole new way of life.

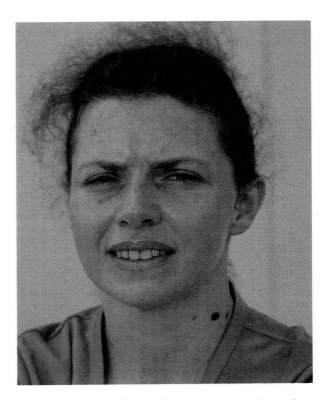

This woman, dubbed "Jane Doe," was emaciated, incoherent, partially clothed, covered by insect and animal bites, and near death when discovered by a Florida park ranger in September 1980. Her recovery was further complicated by a rare form of psychogenic amnesia, generalized amnesia, in which she had lost the memory of her name, her past, and her ability to read and write. Judging from her accent, linguistic experts said the woman was probably from Illinois. Although interviews conducted under the effect of drugs revealed that the woman had apparently had a Catholic education, her few childhood memories were so common that they were meaningless. In a dramatic attempt to recover her past, Jane Doe and her doctor appeared on Good Morning America *and appealed to her relatives to step forward. The response was overwhelming, and authorities came to believe that Jane Doe was the daughter of a couple from Roselle, Illinois, whose daughter had gone to the Ft. Lauderdale area to open a boutique. Their last contact with their daughter had been a phone call in 1976. Despite the couple's certainty, Jane Doe was never able to remember her past.*

The pattern in dissociative amnesia, it should be noted, is essentially similar to that in conversion symptoms, except that instead of avoiding some unpleasant situation by becoming physically dysfunctional, a person avoids thoughts about the situation or in the extreme leaves the scene. Apparently, virtually any type of inner conflict involving wishes that are unacceptable to a person and are therefore anxiety-arousing may serve as the basis of an amnesic reaction and its elaboration into fugue. The threatening information becomes inaccessible, owing either to some sort of automatic cognitive blockage or to deliberate suppression. In patterns involving conscious suppression, individuals apparently tell themselves that they will not remember some traumatic event or situation; subsequently they try to believe and behave as though they actually are amnesic. For example, in a study of 98 amnesia cases, primarily among military personnel, Kiersch (1962) found 41 to be of this seemingly "feigned" ("malingering" in DSM-IV terminology) type.

People experiencing dissociative amnesia are typically highly suggestible individuals who are faced with extremely unpleasant situations from which they see no escape. Often, they previously had experienced conscious impulses to "forget" and run away but were too inhibited to accept that solution. Eventually, however, the stress becomes so intolerable that they suppress large segments of their personalities and all memory for the stressful situations. As already noted, this type of amnesia is highly selective and normally involves only material that is basically intolerable or threatening to the self. During a dissociative fugue, an individual appears normal and is able to engage in complex activities. Normally the activities chosen reflect a rather different lifestyle from the previous one, the rejection of which is usually obvious. Such behavior is well illustrated in the following case:

Burt Tate, a 42-year-old short-order cook in a small-town diner, was brought to the attention of local police following a heated altercation with another man at the diner. Questioned by the police, he gave his name as Burt Tate and indicated that he had arrived in town several weeks earlier. However, he could produce no official identification and could not tell the officers where he had previously lived and worked. No charges were proffered and no arrest made, but Burt was asked to accompany the officers to the emergency room of a local hospital so that he might be examined, to which request he agreed.

Burt's physical examination was negative for evidence of recent head trauma or any other medical abnormality, and there was no indication of drug or alcohol abuse. He was oriented as to current time and place, but manifested no recall of his personal history prior to his arrival in town. He did not seem especially concerned about his total lack of a remembered past. He was kept in the hospital overnight for observation and discharged the following day.

Meanwhile, the police instituted missing-person search procedures and discovered that Burt matched the description of one Gene Saunders, a resident of a city some 200 miles away who had disappeared a month earlier. The wife of Mr. Saunders was brought to the town and confirmed the real identity of "Burt," who, now noticeably anxious, stated that he did not recognize Mrs. Saunders.

Prior to his disappearance, Gene Saunders, a middle-level manager in a large manufacturing firm, had been experiencing considerable difficulties at work and at home. A number of stressful work problems, including failure to get an expected promotion, the loss through resignation of some of his key staff, failure of his section to meet production goals, and increased criticism from his superior—all occurring within a brief time frame—had upset his normal equanimity. He had become morose and withdrawn at home, and had been critical of his wife and children. Two days before he had left he had had a violent argument with his 18-year-old son, who'd declared his father a "failure" and had stormed out of the house to go live with friends.

(Adapted from Spitzer et al., 1989, pp. 215–16.)

Dissociative Identity Disorder

Dissociative identity disorder (DID), formerly multiple personality disorder (MPD), is a dramatic dissociative pattern, usually having identifiable stressor precipitants, in which a patient manifests two or more complete systems of personality. Each system has distinct, well-developed emotional and thought processes and represents a separate, unique, and relatively stable personality. The individual may change from one personality to another at periods varying from a few minutes to several years, though shorter time frames are more common. One personality is commonly the **"host"**; other personalities are usually strikingly different from the host personality and from one another; one may be carefree and fun-loving, and another quiet, studious, and serious. Needs and behaviors inhibited in the main or host personality are usually liberally displayed by the others. The case of Mary Kendall is illustrative:

Mary, a 35-year-old divorced social worker, had a somewhat rare condition in her right forearm and hand, one of several general medical problems, that caused her chronic pain. Medical management of this pain had proven problematic, and it was decided to teach her self-hypnosis as a means whereby she might control it. She proved an excellent hypnotic subject and quickly learned effective pain-control technique.

Her hypnotist-trainer, a psychiatrist, describes Mary's life in rather unappealing terms. She is said to be competent professionally but has an "arid" personal and social life. Although her brief marriage ended some ten years ago, she evidences little interest in men and doesn't seem to have any close friends. She spends most of her free time doing volunteer work in a hospice, a type of psychologically supportive alternative care facility where terminally ill patients go to die.

In the course of the hypnotic training Mary's psychiatrist discovered that she seemed to have substantial gaps in her memory. One phenomenon in particular was very puzzling: she reported that she could not account for what seemed an extraordinary depletion of the gasoline in her car's tank. She would arrive home from work with a nearly full tank, and by the following morning as she began her trip to work would notice that the tank was now only half-full. When it was advised that she keep track of her odometer readings she discovered that on many nights on which she insisted she'd remained at home the odometer showed significant accumulations of up to 100 miles. The psychiatrist, by now strongly suspecting that Mary had a dissociative disorder, also established that there were large gaps in her memories of childhood. He shifted his focus to exploring the apparently widespread dissociative difficulties.

In the course of one of the continuing hypnotic sessions the psychiatrist again asked about "lost time," and was greeted with a response in a wholly different voice tone that said, "It's about time you knew about me." Marian, an apparently well-established alter personality, went on to describe the trips she was fond of taking at night, during which she traveled to various scenic resort areas to "work out problems." It soon became apparent that Marian was an extraordinarily abrupt and hostile personality, the epitome in these respects of everything the compliant and self-sacrificing Mary was not. Marian regarded Mary with unmitigated contempt, and asserted that "worrying about anyone but yourself is a waste of time."

In due course some six other alter personalities emerged, all rather saliently arranged in characteristic behavior along a dimension an-chored at one end by traits of marked compliance/dependency and at the other of equally marked aggressiveness/autonomy. There was notable competition among the alters for time spent "out," and Marian was often so provocative as to frighten some of the more timid others, which included a six-year-old child. When one of the hostile adult alters seriously threatened suicide, the alarmed therapist insisted on consulting the other personalities, to which the intended suicidal alter responded with charges of violation of doctor-patient confidentiality!

Mary's history, as gradually pieced together, included memories of physical and sexual abuse by her father as well as others during her childhood. She also reported considerable feelings of guilt for not having protected her siblings from similar abuse. Her mother was described as not especially physically abusive but as having abdicated to a large extent the maternal role, forcing Mary from a young age to assume these duties in the family.

Four years of subsequent psychotherapy resulted in only modest success in achieving a true "integration" of these diverse trends in Mary Kendall's selfhood. (Adapted from Spitzer et al., 1994, pp. 56–57)

The number of **alter personalities** in DID varies, but in two substantial series of cases evaluated by questionnaire it averaged an amazing 15 (Ross, 1989). The historical trend, in fact, seems to be one of increasing multiplicity, suggesting the operation of social factors, perhaps even some "competition" among victims, in their production (Spanos & Burgess, 1994). As already noted, alter personalities are usually strikingly different from the host or primary personality, leading to the inference that the alters express rejected parts of the original self. Alter characteristics are also highly varied and have been known to include nonhuman species.

Nevertheless, certain "roles" are extremely common in the alter repertoires of DID patients. These include the roles of Child, Protector, and Persecutor; an Opposite Sex alter, who may share one of these other roles, is also present in most cases (Ross, 1989). Normally, alters know of the existence of the host personality and of each other, but the host or primary personality is not "permitted" knowledge of these others occupying his or her space, time, and body. Mutual and unidirectional amnesias among the alters also sometimes occur. Interestingly, very often one alter personality knows "everything" and, if cooperative, may be a valuable consultant for the therapist.

Dual and multiple personalities have received a great deal of attention and publicity in fiction, television, and motion pictures. Actually, however, they were rare in clinical practice until relatively recently. Until approximately the last quarter-century, in fact, only slightly more than 100 cases could be found in the psychological and psychiatric literature worldwide. Their occurrence seems to have increased dramatically in recent years. No wholly complete or satisfactory explanation exists for such a change in the occurrence base rate. Some of the increase, however, is almost certainly artifactual, the product of increased acceptance of the diagnosis by clinicians, who traditionally have been somewhat skeptical of the astonishing behavior these patients often display—such as undergoing sudden and dramatic shifts in personal identity before one's eyes. More females than males are diagnosed as having the disorder, with the ratio being about nine to one (Ross, 1989).

A more substantive and disturbing reason for the apparent increase in cases of DID is offered by Ross (1989), who attributes it in part to an increasingly "sick" society in which child abuse, especially sexual abuse by adults, has become rampant. If Ross's suggestion about the deterioration of society is arguable, his observation that DID is commonly accompanied by reports of childhood abuse is not. While it is surprising that this connection was not generally recognized until about 1980, there is now no reasonable doubt about its reality. Serious questions remain, as we shall see, about the magnitude of this association, about the trustworthiness of memories of abuse, and indeed about the clinical validity of DID diagnoses. Since childhood sexual abuse is a far more common occurrence for females than for males (Trickett & Putnam, 1993), there may be a relationship here with the gender discrepancy in incidence/prevalence.

As already suggested, the question of malingering has dogged the diagnosis of DID for at least a century. These doubts are reinforced by the suspicion that clinicians, by virtue of undue fascination with the clinical phenomena and unwise use of hypnosis, are themselves responsible for eliciting this disorder in highly suggestible patients (Spanos & Burgess, 1994). The latter criticism has a ring of truth, but it fails to account convincingly for all of the observations reported—such as the elaborate pretreatment personal histories with which alternate personalities are commonly endowed. Cynicism about the concept of DID has also been encouraged by the frequency with which it is used by defendants and their attorneys to escape punishment for crimes ("My other personality did it"). This defense was used, unsuccessfully, in the famous case of the "Hillside Strangler," Kenneth Bianchi (Orne, Dinges, & Orne, 1984).

It is also true, as Spanos, Weekes, and Bertrand (1985) have demonstrated, that normal college students can be induced by suggestion to exhibit some of the phenomena seen in DID, including the adoption of a second personality. Such role-playing demonstrations are interesting, but they do not answer, nor even convincingly address, the question of the reality of DID. That college student subjects might be able to give a convincing portrayal of a person with a broken leg would not, after all, establish the nonexistence of broken legs.

Our own view of the controversy surrounding DID is that it is too often formulated in terms of an absolute dichotomy: It is viewed either as a completely genuine disorder affecting a helpless and passive victim, or as a completely dissembled fabrication orchestrated by an unscrupulous person seeking unfair advantages. There is of course a wide range of possibilities between these two extreme positions. Our increasing knowledge, earlier alluded to, concerning widespread evidence of separate (dissociated) memory subsystems and nonconscious active mental processing, indicates that much highly organized mental activity is *normally* carried on in the "background," outside of awareness. This is analogous in some ways to computer multitasking, where the same machine may simultaneously carry on several complex activities other than the one in which its keyboard operator is currently fully engaged. Accordingly, questions about whether a given behavior is consciously or unconsciously motivated, genuine or feigned, intended or unintended, deliberate or spontaneous, and so on, are as a general rule oversimplified. So far as we can tell, the human mind does not operate in these dichotomous ways, and undue preoccupation with unanswerable questions can distract us from the task of understanding the adaptational processes in which the patient is engaged.

Is DID "real"? Our answer here is perhaps already implied in the foregoing. Addressing the question directly, Horevitz (1994), following a thorough review of the evidence, was unable to offer an unequivocal answer. The deceptive simplicity of the question is belied by a number of serious evidential and methodological issues. Do we, the authors, believe that elements of theatrical pretense are never a part of dissociative identity disorder? Not by any means, but neither are we prepared to dismiss DID as simply unqualified fakery.

Depersonalization Disorder

A more common dissociative disorder that occurs mostly in adolescents and young adults is **depersonalization disorder,** in which there is a loss of the sense of self. Individuals with this disorder feel that they are, all of a sudden, different—for example, that they are other people or that their bodies have drastically changed—have become quite grotesque, for example. A related, and commonly accompanying, experience is that of **derealization,** in which the external world is perceived as distorted and as lacking a stable and palpable existence. Frequently, the altered states are reported as out-of-body experiences in which individuals feel that they are, for a time, floating above their physical bodies and observing what is going on below. Mild forms of the experience are extremely common and are no cause for alarm. Reports of out-of-body experiences have included perceptions of visiting other planets or relatives who are in other cities. The disorder is often precipitated by acute stress resulting from an infectious illness, an accident, or some other traumatic event, as in the following case:

Charlotte D., a recently separated 19-year-old woman, was referred to an outpatient mental health service by her physician because she had experienced several "spells" in which her mind left her body and went to a strange place in another state. The first instance had occurred two months earlier, a few days after her husband had left her without explanation. Since then, she had had four episodes of "traveling" that had occurred during her waking state and had lasted for about 15 to 20 minutes. She described her experiences as a dreamy feeling in which her arms and legs were not attached to her body and other people around her were perceived as zombielike. Typically she felt dizzy and had pains in her stomach for hours after each spell.

Individuals who experience depersonalized states, and they are many, are usually able to function normally between episodes. With more severe manifestations, as in the preceding case, the experience can be quite frightening and may cause a victim to become concerned about imminent mental collapse. Such fears are generally unfounded, but the seriously affected person might well profit from some

In depersonalization/derealization disorders the world is often experienced as hazy and indistinct.

professional help in dealing with the precipitating stressors and for reducing anxiety. A diagnostic problem may nevertheless arise because feelings of depersonalization sometimes are early manifestations of impending decompensation and the development of psychotic states of a schizophreniform type, discussed in Chapter 12.

CAUSAL FACTORS IN SOMATOFORM AND DISSOCIATIVE DISORDERS

In contrast to those "neurotic" disorders in which some form of anxiety is the chief and most salient manifestation, and in which we enjoy a relatively advanced level of understanding as to the causal patterns probably involved (see Chapter 5), specific causal pathways in the somatoform and dissociative disorders remain to a large extent obscure. Of course, many holding to a psychodynamic viewpoint contend that anxiety is the central problem in these disorders as well, and hence that the primary sources of somatoform and dissociative problems are probably the same as for those disorders in which anxiety is the principal feature. According to this conception, therefore, somatoform and dissociative symptoms are ultimately the products of apprehensions concerning dreadful but vaguely defined events that can be neither predicted nor controlled, with perhaps some biological contribution in terms of excessive nervous system sensitivity.

Given widespread reports of childhood abuse, it is reasonable to suppose that some form of apprehension or anxiety may be involved in the development of somatoform and dissociative symptoms. Even assuming that anxiety is somehow implicated in the etiology of these disorders, however, there is much that remains unexplained with respect to the development of these particular modes of coping. We shall try to address such questions in what follows, although the reader should be forewarned that relevant research is unevenly distributed and in certain areas quite sparse.

Biological Factors

The precise role of genetic and constitutional factors in somatoform and dissociative behavior has not been clearly delineated. Limited evidence suggests a modest genetic contribution to somatoform disorders generally (Cloninger & Guze, 1970; Cloninger et al., 1984; Guze et al., 1986; Sigvardsson et al., 1984), but observed familial associations might also be the result of learning from exposure to somatizing parents or siblings (see, Kreitman et al., 1965; Kriechman, 1987). We have found no convincing evidence of a genetic contribution to pathological dissociation, but would not be surprised if future research should uncover a modest risk from this source. Certainly we cannot rule out the possibility of an innate dissociative capacity in patients experiencing these disorders (Braun & Sachs, 1985).

Bishop, Mobley, and Farr (1978) have reported the curious observation from a large series of cases that somatoform disorders involving nervous system and musculoskeletal symptoms showed a pronounced tendency to be located on the left side of the body, a finding supported by other research as well (Galin, Diamond, & Braff, 1977; Stern, 1977). Since the right side of the brain generally controls the left side of the body, and vice versa, this would suggest that the right cerebral hemisphere (which is known to be involved chiefly with nonverbal mental processes) may have some special importance in mediating these types of disorders. Beyond that, however, the meaning of the finding remains obscure.

There has been a fair amount of research, reviewed by Brown (1994), on electroencephalographic (EEG) responses to various forms of sensory stimulation—so-called evoked potentials—as well as various other biobehavioral assays among patients with dissociative disorders. None of this research has yet revealed the biological substrate, if any, of these disorders.

Psychosocial Factors

The likely role of **traumatic childhood abuse** as a risk factor for dissociative disorders, particularly DID, and quite possibly for hypochondriasis as well, has already been mentioned. Also already noted is the substantial association between dissociation and somatoform processes in general, perhaps indicating an etiologic role for abusive childhood experience as encouraging the development of *both* dissociative and somatoform modes of coping. Most of the available research in this area has concerned DID. We begin with that problem and then move on to a brief consideration of other psychosocial etiologic hypotheses in DID and the somatoform disorders.

Wolfe, Gentile, and Wolfe (1989), in a study evaluating 71 sexually abused children, likened their reactions to posttraumatic stress disorder. Evidence is building impressively in support of the notion that DID is largely a type of posttraumatic dissociative disorder (see Brown, 1994; Zelikovsky & Lynn, 1994), although it must be emphasized that sexual abuse rarely occurs in the absence of serious overall family pathology, many aspects of which could themselves be traumatizing (Nash et al., 1993; Tillman, Nash, & Lerner, 1994). In any event, the development of partially independent (dissociated) subsystems that constitute, in themselves, coherent personality organizations may serve important adaptive and coping functions for individuals who were severely and repeatedly traumatized as children, perhaps particularly (although certainly not exclusively) by incestuous sexual abuse.

Concerning the latter, 79.2 percent of Ross, Norton, and Wozney's (1989) 236 cases, and 83.0 percent of Putnam and colleagues' (1986) 100 cases of DID reported childhood abuse of a specifically sexual nature. The figures for other types of physical abuse were not far behind, suggesting that as children most of these individuals had lived in environments characterized by marked brutality. It is thought that the tendency to dissociate as a method of coping begins while victimization is in process—"This is not happening to *me*."

If we are to believe various case reports, notably including the rather famous one of Sybil, who is re-

One of the best-known recent illustrations of dissociative identity disorder (DID) is the case of Truddi Chase, who developed 92 personalities by the time she was an adult. Truddi's history of unspeakable brutal treatment by her stepfather and the subsequent manifestation of the "troops" is in keeping with the growing evidence that severe and repeated childhood trauma, both physical and sexual, is a significant factor in the occurrence of DID.

ported to have been repeatedly tortured and nearly killed by her psychotic mother (Schreiber, 1973), the cruelty that some DID patients suffered as children is gut-wrenching in its severity. The more recently publicized case of Truddi Chase and her "troops," a total of 92 separately identifiable personalities, is more typical in involving a male stepfather as the abuser, but no less revolting in its depiction of years of sadistic cruelty and heinous sexual victimization—beginning in this case at age two (Chase et al., 1990).

As is well known, however, reports of widespread sexual and other forms of childhood abuse as causal factors in DID, as well as in certain other disorders, have become a matter of raging controversy in recent years. It is alleged, in some cases with compellingly good reason, that many of these reports derive from **false memories,** which are in turn a product of the employment of unwise, highly leading and suggestive techniques by "convinced" but inadequately trained psychotherapists. We have no

doubt that this sort of thing has happened, often with tragic consequences to innocent families. We also have no doubt, however, that brutal abuse of children too often occurs and that it can have devastating effects on normal development, among other things probably encouraging pathological dissociation (see, Nash et al., 1993; Trickett & Putnam, 1993). The issue of false memory is more extensively considered in HIGHLIGHT 7.3.

The question arises as to whether DID occurs in the absence of a history of chronic childhood trauma. Ross (1989), who has had much clinical experience with DID, allows that there may be such atraumatic cases of the disorder, but that he has personally never seen one where DID was well established and complexly organized. An unequivocal answer to the question is not easily obtained owing to the unreliability of patient memories, as discussed in HIGHLIGHT 7.3. In the absence of definitive information, our guess is that significantly disruptive DID does occur in people whose backgrounds are unremarkable with respect to abuse. We would expect in such cases, however, to see evidence of other factors encouraging the development of dissociative tendencies, such as ease of hypnotizability and a high capacity for personal absorption (inward focus of attention) and fantasy (Kihlstrom, Glisky, & Angiulo, 1994). The Dissociative Experiences Scale (Bernstein & Putnam, 1986), a self-administered questionnaire that taps into such traits as well as reports of mild dissociative episodes, has been widely used to measure and predict dissociative tendencies and has garnered considerable support as a valid indicator of this propensity (Carlson & Armstrong, 1994).

Given the heterogeneous nature of the somatoform disorders, emphasized by Iezzi and Adams (1993), it should perhaps come as no surprise that these problems are often accompanied by other psychiatric disorders as well, notably depression and anxiety disorders (e.g., Boyd et al., 1984). As a group, then, somatizing patients exhibit widespread difficulties in their emotional lives, exhibiting a pattern of negative affect and emotional vulnerability frequently referred to as **neuroticism** (Lipowski, 1988). Neuroticism as a personality trait has been shown to include "facets" of anxiety, angry hostility, depression, self-consciousness, impulsiveness, and vulnerability (Costa & Widiger, 1994)—a combination of characteristics often associated with medical complaints that prove on careful examination to be spurious (Costa & McCrae, 1987).

Another group of patients showing frequent somatoform patterns are those who seem unwilling or unable to communicate their personal distress in other than somatic language. They tend to focus

HIGHLIGHT 7.3

Recovering Memories of Childhood Trauma

As noted at varying points in this text, it has become increasingly clear that traumatic abuse in childhood, particularly sexual abuse, is a risk factor for several types of adult mental disorder. Among the disorders implicated, evidence of a connection with an abusive history is probably most robust for dissociative identity disorder (DID). The adequate assessment of past abuse, however, poses significant problems because of its central reliance on childhood memory for abusive events among patients who may have been in a traumatized state at the time of their occurrence. Even under ideal circumstances memory for long-past events is at best uncertain, and it is reasonable to assume that concurrent extreme emotional arousal would further compromise accurate remembering. The difficulties have been well stated by Kirsch, Lynn, and Rhue (1993), as follows:

A traumatic history . . . consists not only of past childhood events but also of the person's interpretations, embellishments, and distortions of those events from the perspective of recent events, accomplishments, behaviors, and relationships that constitute life in the present. . . . In short, memory is not immutable or preserved like a fly in amber, nor is the mind like a vast storehouse of indelible impressions, facts, and information. Indeed, the memory literature indicates that ordinary memory is fallible and that certain subjects

place an inordinate degree of confidence in their remembrances. . . . (p. 18)

Taking seriously this concise and accurate summary of a vast amount of information accumulated in recent years on the workings of human autobiographical memory entails the sobering conclusion that

Abuse happens, but so do false accusations.

This is the central message of a fascinating book, *Suggestions of Abuse*, recently published by clinical psychologist Michael Yapko (1994, p. 21). Yapko goes on to say, in richly illustrated fashion, that it is the responsibility of mental health professionals to sort out true from false reports of childhood traumatic abuse. Acknowledging the difficulty of the challenge, he quite rightly insists that, at the least, members of these professions should be extremely cautious to ensure that they do not, in their efforts to heal, *create* memories of childhood abuse that did not occur. His book can reasonably be described as a detailed documentation of the fact that failures to hold to this professional standard have in recent times become frequent, if not among a certain overzealous subgroup of therapists quite routine. The book is thus also a powerful indictment of serious deficiencies in professional competence among some persons holding themselves out to be psychotherapists (see Chapter 17).

There can be no reasonable doubt, and Yapko forcefully affirms it, that childhood abuse, particularly sexual abuse of girls, is widespread in our contemporary society. Perhaps it always has been, but, encouraged by Freud's assertion that most such reports by patients were merely libidinally inspired fantasies, we have somehow managed until recent years not to examine carefully either individual complaints or occasional suggestions of substantial overall incidence rates for these assaults upon children, often very young ones. Firm estimates of rates of occurrence are still hard to come by, but such data as we have suggest that the numbers could easily be in the hundreds of thousands per year for the United States alone (Loftus, 1993). Although most investigated cases of alleged sexual abuse of children prove to be unsubstantiated (Fincham et al., 1994), significant underreporting of actual abuse is widely acknowledged. Available information, in short, paints an appalling picture of adult brutality in subjecting children to traumatizing experiences known to have seriously disruptive effects on development and, as already noted, to be associated with a variety of adult psychological abnormalities. Nothing said here, therefore, should be taken as diminishing or mitigating our conviction that childhood abuse, both sexual and general, is egregiously common and is a major risk factor for adult disorder.

Nevertheless, indications are also very strong that many recent adult accusations of past abuse, particularly in the form of sexual molestation or incest/rape, are factually false. They are the products of decided imperfections in the manner in which memory functions, as well as, far too often, the misuse of therapist influence and certain technical procedures often employed by professionals working in the area of psychological trauma and the recovery of purportedly "repressed" memories. Not uncommonly, such therapists form hypotheses of childhood sexual abuse based on flimsy evidence, such as the client's complaining of symptoms from a certain list said to be indicative of past abuse (see Bass & Davis, 1988; Blume, 1990); in fact, these supposedly critical symptoms (e.g., anxiety, depression, headaches, poor self-esteem) are extremely common in a general clinical population. These overly credulous therapists then by various means proceed to persuade the client, who typically at first has *no memory of abusive experience,* that such abuse did take place—the memory trace of its occurrence, they insist, having been obliterated by repression.

As described by both Yapko (1994) and Loftus (1993), therapists of this persuasion are normally relentless in their pursuit of the supposedly buried information and in their demands that the client "remember" it. When these efforts eventually meet with success, as they often do, many of these same therapists compound the problem by insisting, in the absence of established clinical justification (Yapko, 1994), that confronta-

tion and suitable condemnation of the alleged perpetrator(s) are essential for a successful therapeutic outcome. Large numbers of astounded and eventually demoralized parents and other family members have thus had to endure vehement accusations of abuse they know nothing about and of which they are entirely innocent. A growing number have been sued by their furious alleged victims. In at least one recent case, an accused and maligned father has successfully sued the therapists involved, winning a judgment of $500,000; however, his daughter, who accuses him of raping her repeatedly between the ages of five and eight, has brought civil suit against him that is pending as of this writing (Ewing, 1994). Severely disrupted family ties, possibly permanent, have thus been a common outcome of this remarkable climate of suspicion and accusation.

As is made abundantly clear in the superb review of the problem provided by Loftus (1993), the creation of false memories is by no means as difficult a feat as the reader may imagine. Given the nature of remembering, which as noted above is a *constructive* act employing multiple associational cues of diverse origin, it is likely that most of us harbor autobiographical memories whose content departs significantly from the actual events of our lives. Again, a great deal of evidence, from both laboratory and real-life contexts, demonstrates in convincing fashion that memory is notably fallible.

This evidence includes many instances of memories for events that are known *never* to have taken place (pseudomemories). There is some evidence, in fact, that hypnosis, which is widely employed among therapists seeking to recover "repressed" memories, encourages the rich elaboration of such pseudomemories (Weekes et al., 1992). Such observations are consistent with many reports of gradually increasing bizarreness of the memories these clients report, including for example incredible tales of lengthy enforced participation in satanic cult rituals, for which no corroborating evidence can be found (Yapko, 1994). The implications of these known facts concerning the malleability of autobiographical memory are, to say the least, disturbing in the light of the psychological damage resulting from acceptance of therapy-assisted recovery of purported traumatic childhood events.

There is an even more serious cause for alarm, one eloquently voiced by Loftus (1993):

There is one last tragic risk of suggestive probing and uncritical acceptance of all allegations made by clients, no matter how dubious. These activities are bound to lead to an increased likelihood that society in general will disbelieve the genuine cases of childhood sexual abuse that truly deserve our sustained attention. (p. 534)

on and amplify body sensations almost to the exclusion of attending to their own subjective attitudes and feelings, which if negative in character (as is often the case) are referred to some supposedly malfunctioning body part. The term **alexithymia** (Sifneos, 1973) has been coined to denote this personality pattern. Contrary to common belief, the so-called hysterical (now histrionic) personality disorder pattern (see Chapter 9) is not strongly associated with risk for conversion disorder (Iezzi & Adams, 1993).

Sociocultural Factors

There are several non-Western cultures (e.g., Chinese) in which, unlike our own, frank expression of emotional distress is considered unacceptable. We would thus expect somatizing patterns to be relatively more common in these areas, and this expectation appears to be borne out (see, Katon, Kleinman, & Rosen, 1982; Kirmayer, 1984).

In regard to dissociative disorders, and especially their more dramatic forms such as DID, there seems little doubt that incidence and prevalence are strongly influenced by the degree to which such phenomena are accepted or tolerated as legitimate mental disorders by the surrounding cultural context. And, as seen in our own society, acceptance and tolerance are likely to vary over time. Spanos (1986) has been particularly sharp in his criticism of the prevailing acceptance of DID as a legitimate psychopathological phenomenon, explicitly linking the abrupt rise in incidence in recent years to what he considers the naive and unwarranted credulity of both patients and clinicians.

Krippner (1994) has broadened this general view considerably, pointing out that many seemingly related phenomena, such as spirit possession, occur in abundance in many different parts of the world where the local culture sanctions them. He also notes that instances of what we might regard as pathological dissociation are not always maladaptive and need not be construed in these negative, mental disorder terms. In his own words, "People can create personalities as required to defend themselves against trauma, to conform to cultural pressures, or to meet the expectations of a psychotherapist, medium, or exorcist. This malleability has both adaptive and maladaptive aspects" (p. 358). Considered from this perspective, we are again forcefully confronted with the stubborn problem of trying to disentangle issues of value from what we

define as mental disorder, discussed at some length in Chapter 1.

TREATMENT AND OUTCOMES

Most authorities recommend caution in using medical (e.g., drug) interventions in the treatment of somatoform disorders. Where there is no alternative (many of these patients, convinced of the "realness" of their symptoms, adamantly refuse psychosocial therapies), antianxiety and antidepressant medication are sometimes useful in making the patient more comfortable. They are rarely effective in achieving sustained relief of primary symptoms. In many instances the best treatment turns out to be no treatment at all, but rather the provision of support, reassurance, and nonthreatening explanations as to causal factors; frequent office visits and contrived medical reexaminations may be helpful in this general approach. With the exception of conversion disorder and pain syndromes, however, the prognosis for full recovery from somatoform disorders is not encouraging (Iezzi & Adams, 1993).

The development of behavior and cognitive-behavior therapies for both conversion and pain disorders (and as noted we have doubts about the validity of this distinction), and their evaluation in the relatively recent appearance of controlled clinical trials, shows some real promise (see, Blanchard, 1994; Iezzi & Adams, 1993). We suspect that the direct approach of behaviorally oriented therapies in, for example, eliminating sources of "secondary gain" would in itself hasten a positive therapeutic outcome in conversion disorders, but there exist as yet no entirely convincing data on the ultimate validity of this hypothesis.

Kluft (1993) has offered a three-stage "consensus" model for the treatment of DID, one endorsed in a more recent work on the same subject by Horevitz and Loewenstein (1994). The three stages are:

1. *Stabilization,* in which ground rules for the nature of the therapeutic relationship are established, understandings about the "problem" are shared, trust issues are explored, and preliminary stopgaps are put in place to halt further untoward reactions to impinging stressors.

2. *Working through of trauma and resolution of dissociative defenses,* which if successful leads to "integration" of the separate personality systems. This phase, obviously the critical therapeutic one, is said

to involve three essential tasks: (a) dealing effectively with amnesia and the propensity to "switch," often in the obvious service of defense, among differing identity states; (b) dealing effectively with dissociative memories, which must be "reconnected" to real life events; and (c) reestablishing connections between distinct, seemingly separarate, identity states. Clearly, successful negotiation of this critical phase of treatment requires therapeutic skills of the highest order, as well as attitudes of patience and forebearance not abundantly available in the human community. In short, the therapist *must* be strongly committed as well as professionally competent; regrettably, not all are (see Chapter 17).

3. *Postintegration therapy,* which is basically a stage of repair and compensation for the multiple deficiencies left in the wake of (often) years of pseudo-adjustment accomplished by means of dissociative strategies. Huge gaps may appear in the patient's skills, knowledge, and general functioning, and there is often a sense of profound loneliness and detachment owing to the requirement to resume living in a world that is in many respects wholly unfamiliar. Grief concerning the "loss" is frequently a complicating feature. This last phase of therapy is said to be often long (one to two years) and arduous for both patient and therapist.

The general outline of this treatment plan makes a good deal of sense to us. It deserves careful empirical evaluation. Nevertheless, it must be stressed that available controlled studies on the treatment of DID are extremely rare; most reports are case summaries of single cases, with widely varying treatment approaches employed. Where therapy for larger groups of DID patients has been studied, as in a report by Coons (1986), the outcomes have been mixed.

In closing we should also note a reservation we have about the almost standard use of hypnosis in programs of treatment for dissociative disorders, including DID. A central feature of hypnosis, it could be argued, is the deliberate induction of a dissociative state. It seems to us odd on the face of it to employ dissociation to treat dissociation, although there are, to be sure, loosely related precedents in the field of infectious diseases. Perhaps this approach will appear more rational when we more fully understand why treatment goals might require encouraging the behavior one is seeking ultimately to eliminate. For now, however, we are skeptical, and we note that few alternative therapeutic strategies have been systematically examined for their potential contribution in this field.

UNRESOLVED ISSUES

On The Somatoform/Dissociative Interface

As we have seen, there are several points of contact, of apparently shared properties, between the manifestly different somatoform and dissociative disorders. We have also noted that, historically, the somatoform pattern now known as *conversion disorder* has been conceived as a form of psychopathologic *dissociation*. The connecting link is the venerable (at least 4000 years old; Veith, 1977) concept of *hysteria,* or hysterical neurosis, which in its modern version pertains to inauthentic physical malfunction due to the operation of dissociated elements of the mind or psyche.

In fact, it was not until the DSM-III of 1980 that somatoform and dissociative syndromes were allocated to separate categories of disorder, where they remain in DSM-IV. The DSM-II of 1968 included the major category "Hysterical Neurosis," with the subdivisions "Conversion Type" and "Dissociative Type" ("Hypochondriacal Neurosis" was another major category; the present somatization and pain disorders had not yet been specifically recognized). Evidently, the intent of the DSM-III authors was to gather together under the "somatoform" category all disorders involving physical disabilities or complaints for which no organic basis could be established.

The principle of classification used in this instance might be more or less defensible depending on whether other ones better illuminate potential underlying mechanisms common to the class. If there are sound reasons to regard conversion and dissociative disorders as sharing certain basic properties, it would seem unwise to assign them to separate categories simply because of their superficial somatic vs. nonsomatic manifestations. This is the basic argument advanced by Kihlstrom (1994), who advocates including conversion syndromes under the dissociative disorders rubric, where they have been for most of the past century. Kihlstrom (1994) makes an intriguing case. In his own words,

> The conversion disorders are inherently dissociative in the descriptive sense in that they involve the exclusion of mental contents and processes from conscious awareness and control. . . . The symptoms of the conversion disorders are not physical, but mental in nature. And they do not suggest physical dis-

order, but rather a disorder in consciousness. Just as functional amnesia, fugue, and MPD [DID] are disorders of consciousness that affect memory and identity, so are functional blindness, deafness, anesthesia, and paralysis disorders of consciousness that affect sensation, perception, and voluntary action. (p. 387)

Insofar as pain disorder appears indiscriminable from the sensory forms of conversion disorder except by DSM fiat, it may be assumed that the argument holds with equal force for that type of very common disorder, although Kihlstrom does not explicitly make this extension. In our judgment, there is also a question about whether at least some of the phenomena of somatization disorder (e.g., "pseudoneurological symptoms") may fit the same pattern; Cloninger (1986), for example, has referred to somatization disorder as "chronic hysteria," and Kellner (1990) draws a similar analogy.

The reader should not mistake the issue raised here as merely semantic wordplay. It relates to the basic nature of an important class of disorders of widespread incidence and prevalence, one that consumes a substantial proportion of our national medical resources year after year. And it has significant implications for treatment planning as well as for the directions treatment research should take in attempts to discover new and more effective modes of intervention in the somatoform syndromes. Perhaps, for example, we need to revisit the possibility of traumatic childhood abuse as a risk factor in these syndromes, an idea entertained and subsequently abandoned—possibly prematurely—by Freud himself.

ease), pain disorder (experienced pain disproportional to objective findings of disease), and conversion disorder (relatively specific malfunction in the sensory, motor, or visceral apparatus. Secondary gain, or external benefits that accrue to the person by virtue of being disabled, may complicate the picture in somatoform disorders and interfere with treatment progress. While there are certain known risk factors for the development of these disorders, such as the neuroticism personality syndrome, etiologic hypotheses remain for the most part vague and nonspecific. With the exception of pain and conversion disorder, treatment prospects generally are not encouraging.

In dissociative disorders the normal processes regulating awareness and the multichannel capacities of the mind apparently become disorganized, leading to various anomalies of consciousness and personal identity. These include functional amnesic states with or without fugue, the dramatic phenomena of dissociative identity disorder (DID) in which the individual may harbor a multitude of seemingly autonomous personalities, and the far more common depersonalization disorder in which the person has a sense of lost connection with self. The incidence/prevalence of diagnosed DID has increased markedly over the last quarter-century, suggesting it is a disorder whose occurrence is strongly affected by trends in the sociocultural milieu. Certain traits of personality such as capacity for absorption appear to facilitate dissociative experiences, and there is growing evidence that traumatic abuse in childhood is a specific risk factor, especially for the development of DID. Treatment of DID is regarded as difficult and arduous, and in well-established cases the prospects for complete recovery are limited.

 ## SUMMARY

Orginally considered subvarieties of the general class known as neurotic disorders, somatoform and dissociative disorders came to be recognized as separate and distinct general types of disorder in their own right with the adoption of the DSM-III in 1980. Some controversy remains, however, as to whether this separation is wholly justified.

Somatoform disorders are those in which psychological problems are manifested in physical disorders (or complaints of physical disorders) that mimic medical conditions but for which there can be found no evidence of corresponding organic pathology. They include somatization disorder (chronic absence of a sense of physical wellness), hypochondriasis (anxious preoccupation with self-attributed dis-

 ## KEY TERMS

somatoform disorders (p. 253)
dissociative disorders (p. 253)
malingering (p. 254)
factitious disorders (p. 254)
somatization disorder (p. 254)
hypochondriasis (p. 255)
pain disorder (p. 257)
conversion disorder (p. 258)
secondary gain (p. 258)
la belle indifférence (p. 262)
implicit memory (p. 263)
implicit perception (p. 263)

dissociation (p. 263)
dissociative amnesia (p. 265)
fugue (p. 265)
dissociative identity disorder (DID) (p. 266)
host personality (p. 266)
alter personalities (p. 267)
depersonalization disorder (p. 269)
derealization (p. 269)
traumatic childhood abuse (p. 270)
false memories (p. 271)
neuroticism (p. 271)
alexithymia (p. 274)

CHAPTER

8

PSYCHOLOGICAL FACTORS AND PHYSICAL ILLNESS

Louis Soutter, L'Ascension. *Soutter (1871–1942), an educated Swiss native who was a college professor in America, began in his 30s to behave eccentrically. He lost his job and his marriage ended; returning to Geneva, he played the violin in professional orchestras until during one concert he began to play music of his own. Soutter spent most of the rest of his life in institutions. In the hospital, he filled small notebooks with hundreds of line drawings. Later, after losing most of his vision, be created artworks by rubbing ink onto the paper with his fingers.*

Traditionally, the medical profession has concentrated clinical and research efforts on understanding and controlling anatomical and physiological factors in disease. In psychopathology, on the other hand, interest has centered primarily on the discovery and remedy of psychological factors that are associated with mental disorders. Today we realize that both these approaches are limited: Although a disorder may be primarily physical or primarily psychological, it is always a disorder of the whole person—not just of the body or the psyche.

Fatigue or a bad cold may lower tolerance for psychological stress; an emotional upset may lower resistance to physical disease; maladaptive behavior, such as excessive alcohol use, may contribute to the impairment of various organs, like the brain and liver. Furthermore, a person's overall life situation has much to do with the onset of a disorder, its nature, duration, and prognosis.

Recovery from a physical or mental disorder is apt to be more rapid for a patient eager to get back to work and to accustomed interactions with family and friends than for the one who will be returning to a frustrating job or an unpleasant home. There seems little doubt, too, that sociocultural influences affect the types and incidences of disorders found in different groups. The ailments to which people are most vulnerable—whether physical, psychological, or both—are determined in no small part by when, where, and how they live. In short, an individual is a biopsychosocial unit.

Behavioral medicine is the broad interdisciplinary approach to the treatment of physical disorders thought to have psychological factors as major aspects of their causal patterns. It has been formally defined as

> the interdisciplinary field concerned with the development and integration of behavioral and biomedical science knowledge and techniques relevant to health and illness and the application of this knowledge and these techniques to prevention, diagnosis, treatment and rehabilitation. (Schwartz & Weiss, 1978, p. 250)

The field thus includes professionals from many disciplines—including medicine, psychology, and sociology—who seek to incorporate biological, psychological, and sociocultural factors into a total picture. Its emphasis, however, is essentially on the role psychological factors play in the occurrence, maintenance, and prevention of physical illness.

Because we are dealing here with largely **psychogenic illnesses** (psychologically induced or maintained diseases), it is only natural that psychologists have found this an area of major interest. **Health psychology** is the subspecialty within the behavioral medicine approach and within the generic discipline of psychology that deals specifically with psychology's contributions to the diagnosis, treatment, and prevention of these psychological components of physical illnesses (Bradley & Prokop, 1981; Weiss, Herd, & Fox, 1981). Currently developing at a rapid pace, the field has already evolved some of the trappings of a new and independent profession (Stone et al., 1987), including the establishment in 1981 of the specialized scientific journal *Health Psychology*.

A behavioral medicine approach examines the broad biopsychosocial context of the following problem areas (adapted from Gentry, 1984):

1. *Etiology*. How do critical life events, characteristic behavior, and personality organization predispose an individual to physical illness?

2. *Host resistance*. How are the effects of stress reduced by personal resources, such as coping styles, social supports, and certain personality traits?

3. *Disease mechanisms*. How is human physiology altered by stressors, particularly those arising from maladaptive behavior? What effects are produced in such systems as the immune, the gastrointestinal, and the cardiovascular?

4. *Patient decision making*. What are the processes involved in the choices individuals make with respect to such matters as hazardous lifestyles, health care decisions, and adherence to preventive regimens?

5. *Compliance*. What factors—biomedical, behavioral, self-regulative, cultural, social, and interpersonal (for example, factors in the practitioner-patient relationship)—determine compliance with sound medical advice?

6. *Intervention*. How effective are psychological measures, such as health education and behavior modification, in altering unhealthy lifestyles and in directly reducing illness and illness behavior at both individual and community levels?

From this perspective, then, *any* instance of physical illness should occasion a review of the context in which the specific pathogen or primary cause is operating. To do so is to use a behavioral medicine approach; properly applied, it multiplies the tools available for interventions whose efficacy often extends beyond any immediate crisis to conditions both prior and subsequent to such events.

We might, for example, ask whether emotional factors may have lowered the resistance of a tuberculosis patient and hence contributed to the onset of the disease. We might also ask how the individual will react to the life changes brought about by the disease. Some patients apparently give up when medically the chances seem good that they will recover. Others with objectively more serious organic pathologies recover or survive for long periods of time. Dunbar, a pioneer in the field, concluded that it is often "more important to know what kind of patient has the disease than what kind of disease the patient has" (1943, p. 23).

Before DSM-III, psychogenic illnesses were categorized as psychophysiologic disorders (and before that as psychosomatic disorders); the focus in these earlier times was on specific body system diseases, such as peptic ulcer, traditionally thought to have psychological origins. In 1980 (with the adoption of DSM-III), the category of psychophysiologic disorders was dropped (and it has remained so in DSM-III-R and DSM-IV), largely because of the newer perspective that emphasizes the psychological component of all physical illnesses. That is, the attempt to specify particular diseases as having psychological components in their etiology or maintenance came to be seen as both limiting and misleading, because it was increasingly understood that the absence of such components in any disease would in fact be quite rare. As we have seen, in DSM-IV patients are now rated separately on different axes for psychiatric symptom disorders (Axis I), personality disorders (Axis II), and accompanying physical disorders or "General Medical Conditions" (Axis III). Thus there is no place on the first two axes for the classic psychosomatic disorders.

To permit some sort of psychiatric coding for the many diseases that we now recognize may involve psychological contributions, Axis I provides a major category called Psychological Factors Affecting Medical Condition. The suspected contributing factors are specified under six subcategories: (a) mental disorder, (b) psychological symptoms, (c) personality traits or coping style, (d) maladaptive health behaviors, (e) stress-related physiological response, or (f) other/unspecified. This diagnosis is to be used when a "general medical condition," coded on Axis III, involves psychological factors that have either definitely or probably played a significant role in initiating or exacerbating the illness. Obviously, this decision is intended to be left to the diagnostician's judgment, because no sharp line of demarcation exists between a significant and a less significant role for psychological factors.

In this chapter, after a broader consideration of the role of psychological factors in both health and illness, we will look at coronary heart disease and

Persistent negative affect has been shown to be associated with health endangerment.

the eating disorders known as anorexia nervosa and bulimia nervosa, which have special contemporary significance. From there, we will move to brief consideration of other physical illnesses having strong psychological components. Then we will examine possible causal factors, and, finally, highlight several treatment approaches in this rapidly developing area.

GENERAL PSYCHOLOGICAL FACTORS IN HEALTH AND DISEASE

Research has repeatedly shown that mental and emotional processes are somehow implicated both in good health and in most physical diseases. In this section we will outline the main phenomena relating to psychosocial influences on biological health in general, specifying, where possible, the mechanisms involved. We will begin our survey with observations on health, attitudes, and coping. We move

from there to an examination of the autonomic nervous system and its potential effects on health. We then consider what may eventually be recognized as the most basic and general topic in this area—the immune system and the compromise of its functioning by psychological states and events. The section ends with a brief discussion of lifestyle and its implications for physical health maintenance.

Health, Attitudes, and Coping Resources

The sometimes devastating effects of hopeless and helpless attitudes on organic functioning have long been known, partly through anthropological research on voodoo deaths and similar phenomena. Today many surgeons will delay a major operation until they are convinced that a patient is reasonably optimistic about the outcome, and optimism in a more positive, everyday sense seems to buffer against disease (Scheier & Carver, 1987, 1992). We should also note here, however, the obvious point that one can be *too* optimistic about one's health status, perhaps leading to dangerous neglect of health care, as has been documented in a variety of ways (Fawzy et al., 1993; Fisher & Fisher, 1992; Friedman et al., 1993; Friedman, Hawley, & Tucker, 1994; Kalichman, Hunter, & Kelly, 1993; Kelly & Murphy, 1992; Tennen & Affleck, 1987).

It seems increasingly likely that the trait of optimism, as it pertains to health matters, will need to be differentiated into two types having quite different health implications. The more positive aspect appears related to a person's sense of efficacy, of being able to cope with any adversity that may arise. Its more problematic form is seen in defensive denial, an unwillingness or inability to acknowledge illness, symptoms, or potential threats to well-being. The defensive type of optimism is not only unhelpful in the health context, but actually constitutes a significantly enhanced risk for health problems (see, e.g., Shedler, Mayman, & Manis, 1993).

A deficit in optimism of the more positive kind is tantamount to a psychological sense of helplessness, and it does indeed appear that harboring an attitude of helplessness in the face of adversity is associated with poor health outcomes (e.g., Fawzy et al., 1993). This was shown in an interesting study of hall-of-fame baseball players by Peterson and Seligman (1987). In this group of athletes, negative attitudes were significantly associated with health problems following their active playing years. Similarly, a follow-up study of Harvard graduates having pessimistic attitudes at age 25 demonstrated them to have an elevated incidence of physical disease at ages

45–60 (Peterson, Seligman, & Vaillant, 1988). In the literature, too, are numerous reports of apathy deaths in situations such as concentration and prisoner-of-war camps. Every year we hear reports of "unexplained" deaths among people who believed themselves to be in hopeless circumstances—for example, after having ingested poisonous substances in dosages that were actually too small to be lethal. Such phenomena have been extensively reviewed by both Seligman (1975) and Jones (1977).

Less dramatically but in many ways of equal or greater importance, the effects of multiple life changes on a variety of illnesses have been amply documented (e.g., Elliott, 1989), as outlined in Chapter 4. To cite only two examples, Rahe (1974) reported a study on the health status of physicians that demonstrated a marked correspondence between health problems experienced and the amount of change-related stress undergone in an immediately preceding period. Similarly, in a study of 192 men between the ages of 30 and 60, Payne (1975) found that long-standing physical and psychological health problems were related to larger degrees of life changes, even when the changes had been favorable. Some evidence suggests, however, that the negative health effects of positive life changes are limited, interestingly, to individuals having prior low self-esteem (Brown & McGill, 1989). Evidently, it is the amount of adjustment required following change that overtaxes such individuals' resources, and good things happening to people who do not expect them may constitute significant adjustment challenges.

In other instances, the particular nature of a person's coping resources is itself suspect. The most familiar example here is the Type A behavior pattern. When certain ordinary frustrations of life (such as having to wait in line) habitually provoke extremes of behavior (such as rage), a person is designated "Type A." A large body of evidence, some of it reviewed later in this chapter, has implicated a component of this coping style as a significant risk factor for coronary heart disease. More generally, any type of chronic negative affect or emotion seems to enhance the risk of disease (Friedman & Booth-Kewley, 1987b), although it must also be noted that, through its association with the personality trait of *neuroticism* (see Chapter 7, page 271), negative emotion increases complaints about health problems that cannot be medically documented (Costa & McCrae, 1987; Thoreson & Powell, 1992; Watson & Pennebaker, 1989). Neuroticism, incidentally, is associated with increased occurrence of negative life events (Magnus et al., 1993), which themselves are linked with disease onset. As recently noted by Friedman, Hawley, and Tucker (1994), and as these

examples illustrate, the relationships between personality and health often prove to be very complex.

Often it appears that any severe stress serves to facilitate, precipitate, or aggravate a physical disorder in a person already predisposed to it. This assumption is in keeping with the diathesis-stress model we discussed in Chapter 3. A person with allergies may find his or her resistance further lowered by emotional tension; similarly, as we will see, when an invading virus has already entered a person's body—as is thought to be the case in multiple sclerosis, for example—emotional stress may interfere with the body's normal defensive forces or immunological system. In like manner, any stress may tend to aggravate and maintain certain disorders, such as migraine headaches (Levor et al., 1986) or rheumatoid arthritis (Affleck et al., 1994).

The relationship between psychological factors and good health has also been well documented (e.g., Jones, 1977); that is, positive emotions often seem to protect against physical disease or to be associated with speedy and uncomplicated recoveries when disease does strike (O'Leary, 1985). In fact, this reality complicates efforts to determine the true effectiveness of new treatment techniques, such as new drugs. A patient who believes a treatment is going to be effective has a much better chance of showing improvement than does one who is neutral or pessimistic—even when the treatment is subsequently shown to have no direct or relevant physiological effects. This reaction is known generally as the **placebo effect,** and it accounts in part for the controversies that arise periodically between the scientific community and the general public regarding the efficacy of certain drugs or other treatments.

It has even been suggested that, had it not been for the placebo effect, the medical profession as we know it would not have survived to the present century, because until this century practitioners had little else to offer disease sufferers; indeed, many widely employed specific treatments (e.g., bleeding) were plainly harmful. The profession's survival and prosperity from ancient times is to a large extent a demonstration of the power of "faith" in healing (Shapiro & Morris, 1978). Thus the fundamental intimacy of the mind and body is perhaps nowhere better documented than in the history of the medical profession itself.

Autonomic Excess and Tissue Damage

Our cave-dwelling ancestors needed organ systems that could rapidly prepare their bodies for the intense life-or-death struggles that were part of their daily existence. Nature provided these in the form of a rather elaborate apparatus for dramatically enhancing energy mobilization on a short-term basis. The pertinent physiological events, chiefly involving the autonomic nervous system, were termed the "fight or flight" response by Walter Cannon (1929), underscoring its apparent function either in fleeing danger or subduing an aggressor. In describing the fight-or-flight response, Cannon noted that, with the advance of civilization, it has become to a degree obsolete; in fact he referred to certain psychogenic disorders as "diseases of civilization." Because contemporary human beings are rarely able to flee or attack a threat, no effective avenue exists for the prompt discharge of high states of physiologic readiness to perform extraordinary physical feats. In Cannon's view (and the views of many contemporary investigators), this state of affairs, when unduly repetitive or long-continued, produces tissue breakdown—that is, disease, such as high blood pressure (hypertension).

Autonomic nervous system arousal involves many component processes, some of them subtle or even "silent" in terms of ready accessibility to observation. With increasing levels of arousal, we can directly observe many of the more dramatic manifestations: increased breathing and heart rate, increased sweating, increased muscle tone, and flushing; a keen observer will note pupillary dilation, enhancing vision. With adequate instrumentation, we could also observe increased blood pressure, the dumping of sugar reserves into the blood, redistribution of blood pooled in the viscera to the peripheral or "voluntary" musculature, and enhanced secretion of powerful neurotransmitters. All of these changes are sometimes referred to collectively as the alarm reaction (Selye, 1976b), the first phase of a general adaptation syndrome (Chapter 4). They are the body's response to a "battle stations" signal from the brain. Such a system was not evolved for dealing with trifling circumstances, and it is hardly surprising that such widespread and potent effects, if not permitted to subside, might over time lead to organic pathology.

Coming to a similar conclusion, the early psychosomatic theorists, notably including Flanders Dunbar (1943) and Franz Alexander (1950), reasoned that chronic *internal* sources of threat could place physical health in serious jeopardy. In other words, unremitting psychological stress of the type found in, for example, chronic anxiety disorders (Chapter 5) might actually cause physical damage to vital organs. These early theorists appear to have been largely on the right track, although—as so often happens in psychology and in science generally—

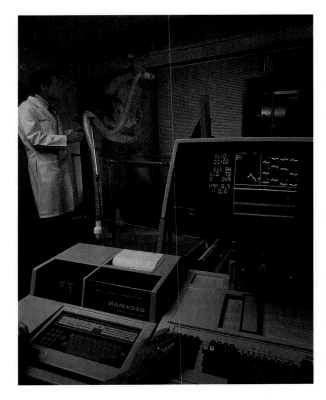

Internal bodily changes similar to those caused by stress can be induced by carefully monitored physical activity. This patient on a treadmill can be observed for such things as increased heart rate and blood pressure to determine how much arousal may be a threat to physical health.

many of their conceptions have proven inaccurate or oversimplified.

Psychosocial Factors and the Immune System

Although autonomic nervous system events often dominate the alarm stage of the general adaptation syndrome, they are often joined quite rapidly by a complex array of other bodily processes. These processes contain or, if possible, eliminate the threat posed. This reaction is the beginning of Selye's stage of resistance, where the protective resources of an organism are mobilized to detect the nature of a threat and to deploy countermeasures against it. To use a simple example, if you burn your finger while cooking, your "alarm" reaction is followed promptly by transport to the site of the injury of a variety of substances that tend to limit damage and initiate tissue repair. We say "tend" in the above sentence because in this instance, as in many other more important ones, the damage-control mechanism sometimes overshoots the mark, exceeding the requirements of adequate defense and producing new problems of its own making. Thus the recommended first aid of cold application for minor burns has as its purpose the inhibition of an excessive defense process.

The example just cited illustrates an important point: just as the psyche's defensive resources can display "adaptiveness" without "intelligence," so too can the body's defensive resources be both marvelously attuned to protection and at the same time clumsy and self-defeating. This paradox has important implications in many areas of medicine, such as organ transplantation. Here the body's defenses against invasion by "foreign" protein may actually destroy the life-sustaining new organ.

Considered biomedically, a crucial component of an organism's resistance-stage equipment is the immune system, whose basic properties are outlined in the next section.

Elements of the Human Immune System While much remains to be learned about the details of immunologic functioning, particularly in regard to psychosocial influences, certain broad outlines are now fairly well understood. What follows is a brief summary of the workings of the system insofar as they are known or strongly suspected, based on contemporary research.

The **immune system** is an organism's principal means of defending itself against the intrusion of foreign substances, such as bacteria, viruses, or tumors. The primary components of the immune system are the blood, thymus, bone marrow, spleen, and lymph nodes. Of the blood's principal components, the serum (a soluble medium) and the white blood cells are especially important in immune function. The serum is made up of large protein molecules and water; it is the medium by which the body transports its defenses.

The white blood cells, also called leukocytes, contain much of the body's defense system. They can be further divided into subpopulations (each with specialized functions) and are found in the thymus, spleen, and lymph nodes and in the blood itself. White blood cell subpopulations include B-cells, T-cells, macrophages (literally, big eaters), and natural killer cells, which have inherent properties destructive to foreign protein. While the role of these cells in immune functioning is often quite direct, certain of them also secrete various chemical substances that have a more indirect effect in regulating, orchestrating, and enhancing the total immune response.

Immune function is traditionally divided into two branches, humoral and cellular. The humoral branch

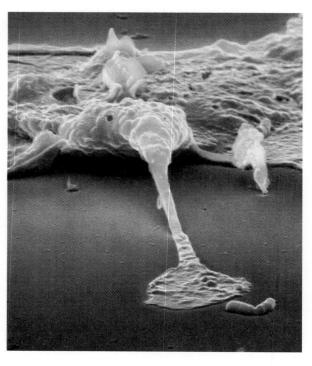

A macrophage reaches out to eat bacteria. Macrophages are important components of the immune system because they initiate the action of B-cells and T-cells against bacterial, or antigen, invasion.

refers to the activity of B-cells and the antibodies they produce. Cellular immune function, on the other hand, is mediated by T-cells, whose effects, while widespread, do not include antibody production. When an organism is invaded by an **antigen**—that is, a substance recognized as foreign—B- and T-cells become activated and multiply rapidly, deploying the various forms of counterattack mediated by each type of cell.

B-cells, which are formed in the bone marrow, perform their defensive function by producing antibodies that circulate in the blood serum. B-cell (or humoral immune) functioning is involved chiefly with protection against the more common varieties of bacterial infection. T-cells develop to maturity in the thymus and mediate immune reactions that, while slower, are far more extensive and direct in character. These cells mainly generate an attack that is highly specific to a given invading antigen.

In summary, the front line of immune defense is contained within the highly differentiated system of white cells that circulate freely in the blood or remain as resident reinforcements in the lymph nodes. One of its two main divisions, the B-cell (or humoral), mediates the production of antibodies, whose main role is detecting the presence of and destroying invading bacteria. The other and far more complicated main division—mediated by several descendant forms of the progenitor T-cell—includes the following among its functions: (a) destruction of certain types of antigens, especially nonbacterial ones; and (b) regulation and in certain instances activation of the other, antibody-based division of the defense system. The immune system's response to antigen invasion is thus generalized and intricately orchestrated, requiring the intact functioning of numerous components.

Psychosocial Compromise of the Immune Response The virulence of the virus causing AIDS (HIV-1) is such that psychosocial factors were originally thought to play little or no role in the pervasive immune breakdown characteristic of that disease. More recent research suggests that this conclusion may have been premature (Kiecolt-Glaser & Glaser, 1988, 1992). For example, Antoni and colleagues (1990) reported preliminary results indicating that behavioral interventions, such as aerobic exercise, had positive psychological and immunocompetence effects among groups of uninfected high-risk and early-stage infected gay men. More recently, Kemeny and colleagues (1994) presented evidence suggesting that a depressed mood was associated with enhanced HIV-1 activity among infected gay men, confirming in this group the more general point that psychological depression compromises immune function (Herbert & Cohen, 1993). Inasmuch as we now have effective treatments for depression, notably including nonbiological ones (e.g., Hollon et al., 1992), the stage is set for potentially important new initiatives in the area of psychological control of HIV-1 progression.

If gains such as these prove sustainable over time, they may show how to prevent HIV from gaining a sustainable foothold after exposure, or to slow the progress of the disease following established infection. In light of the serious toxicity of the antiviral drugs known to deter the progress of HIV infection, the discovery of more benign, noninvasive (and less expensive) treatment methods would be of tremendous help in containing the disease's effects and improving the quality of life of infected individuals.

The role of psychosocial factors with respect to many other less fearsome disease-producing antigens may be considerable. Recent evidence from a wide variety of sources, reviewed by Antoni and colleagues (1990), Geiser (1989), and Kiecolt-Glaser and Glaser (1992) strongly suggests that psychosocial factors can have an important effect on the functional status of the immune system at any point in time. In particular, psychosocial stressors and the mental states associated with them may depress immune function to the point of enhancing vulnerability to virtually any antigen to which a person is concurrently exposed. It seems extremely likely, for example, that some such mediating mechanism is involved in the observed relationship between stressful life changes and subsequent physical illnesses (Geiser, 1989; Kiecolt-Glaser & Glaser, 1992; Koranyi, 1989; Rogers, 1989).

Until recently, the observed relationship between stress and compromised immune function, while reliable and in most studies robust, was basically correlational and hence not necessarily causal. Two studies have now demonstrated such a linkage. Strauman, Lemieux, and Coe (1993) designed an experiment that (temporarily) manipulated the self-evaluations of their subjects. They found that natural killer cell cytotoxicity (as assessed with blood samples) was significantly diminished with induced negative self-evaluations, an effect that was especially strong for persons who were determined to be anxious and/or dysphoric in mood before the experiment. The second of these experimental demonstrations, reported by Cohen, Tyrrell, and Smith (1993), is unique in the field in deliberately exposing quarantined, healthy volunteer subjects to a common cold virus and assessing the outcome in terms of actual contraction of an upper respiratory infection. Stressful life events, self-perceived stress, and negative emotion, all assessed before exposure, *each* significantly predicted which subjects would become ill with colds.

As noted already, depression or dysphoric affect may turn out to have special significance with respect to the suppression of immunocompetence. A review of the evidence by Weisse (1992) indicates a strong association between dysphoric mood and compromised immune function, one that appears to be at least partially independent of specific situations or events that may provoke such feelings. Even more persuasive is a quantitative review of the published evidence by Herbert and Cohen (1993), one that included only studies that met certain rigorous methodological standards. These authors concluded that depressive affect was reliably associated with lowered numbers of white cells following foreign protein challenge, lowered natural killer cell activity, and lowered quantities of several varieties of circulating white cells. A possibly related finding of markedly diminished health care use with recovery from depressive disorders among members of a health maintenance organization has been reported by Von Korff and colleagues (1992).

These indications of strong relationships between certain negative psychological states and diminished immune system functioning suggest some sort of central mediating mechanism that presides over the interaction. The obvious candidate for such a role is the central nervous system, specifically the brain. Such considerations have led to the development of the field of **psychoneuroimmunology,** which explores psychological influences on the nervous system's control of immune responsiveness. Although still relatively new and hampered for obvious reasons in mounting a full-scale experimental assault on some outstanding questions (such as the risks associated with purposely introducing antigens into the bloodstreams of experimental subjects), the field has developed in a rapid and impressive manner (see Maier, Watkins, & Fleshner, 1994, for an up-to-date overview).

Fortunately for research progress, it is possible to estimate at least the earliest phases of immune responsiveness (for example, enhanced reproduction of various types of white cells) from laboratory examination of blood samples. This strategy has been used effectively in demonstrating, for example, the suppression of white blood cell reproduction following sleep deprivation, marathon running, space flight, death of a spouse, and (as we have seen) during psychological depression (Schleifer, Keller, & Stein, 1985; Schleifer et al., 1989; Vasiljeva et al., 1989). Immune responsiveness has been shown to vary with even normal, diurnal mood variations (A. A. Stone et al., 1987). A group of researchers at Ohio State University has repeatedly demonstrated the compromise of white blood cell proliferation, including diminished natural killer cell activity, among medical students undergoing the stress of academic examinations (Glaser et al., 1985, 1987). Natural killer cells are believed to play a key role in tumor surveillance and the control of viral infections.

Granting the likelihood that stressors, in particular psychosocial or "mental" ones, can impair the immune response through some type of brain mediation, a conclusion supported by the weight of evidence (Antoni et al., 1990; Jemmott & Locke, 1984; Kiecolt-Glaser & Glaser, 1992; Maier et al., 1994), intriguing questions remain about the pathway or pathways of influence that may be involved. Until fairly recently, most researchers were convinced that the primary pathway was the hypothalamic-pituitary-adrenocortical (HPA) axis. According to this hypothesis, the processing of stressful events in the brain causes hypothalamic activation of the pituitary, which in turn stimulates the adrenal cortex to secrete excessive levels of adrenocortical hormones (steroids). Certain of the latter substances are known to have negative (as well as some positive) effects on immune functioning. Hence the hypothesis, while largely speculative, remains somewhat attractive.

Nevertheless, more recent research findings and conceptual refinements have turned up a host of strong competitors to the HPA interpretation. For example, we now know that a number of other hormones, including growth hormone, testosterone, and estrogen, respond to stress and also affect immune competence. The same is true of a variety of neurochemicals, including the endorphins (endogenous peptide substances that mimic the action of opium). The link between psychosocial stressors and the immune system may be even more direct, however. The discovery of nerve endings in thymus, spleen, and lymph nodes, tissues literally teeming with white blood cells, suggests the possibility of direct neural control of the secretion of immunologic agents. It is now known that white blood cell surfaces contain receptors for circulating neurotransmitters (Rogers, 1989). We must assume that the presence of such structures on these cells is not accidental, but rather that the cells respond in some way to messages conveyed by the brain-regulated substances.

Perhaps most unexpectedly, immunosuppression can be classically conditioned (Ader & Cohen, 1984; Maier, Watkins, & Fleshner, 1994)—that is, it can come to be elicited as an acquired response to previously neutral stimuli, just as Pavlov's dogs learned to salivate to a tone. Conceivably, even mental stimuli such as thoughts could thus come to activate immunosuppression if they were regularly paired with immunosuppressive events (operating as unconditioned stimuli). Finally, the recent Maier and colleagues (1994) review emphasizes that the relationship between psychological variables and immune system events increasingly appears to be bidirectional. That is, the person's behavior and psychological states affect immune functioning, but the status of immunologic defenses also feeds back to affect current mental states and behavioral dispositions by affecting the blood levels of circulating neurochemicals.

In sum, we have a wealth of potential ways to eventually understand the relationship between psychosocial stressors and immunosuppression. It is already obvious that such an understanding will turn out to be very complicated.

You may recall from our discussion of Selye's general adaptation syndrome in Chapter 4 that the end result of unsuccessfully contained challenge was postulated to be a stage of *exhaustion*. Selye believed that the resources of the immune system and other "resistance" mechanisms are not infinitely replenishable, and there is widespread evidence he was right. In other words, these defensive resources may at times be used up at a rate faster than they can be replaced by the body's metabolism. Indeed, Selye held that this metabolic regulatory mechanism might itself become impaired as demands placed on it over a lifetime accumulate, resulting ultimately in aging and death. In any event, evidence strongly suggests that the adequacy of the immune response to a particular antigen diminishes proportionally with the quantity and intensity of other stressors simultaneously affecting an organism, including other, unrelated illnesses.

This conception nicely integrates the vast amount of data we have associating much physical illness, notably including infectious diseases, with the occurrence of antecedent stressful events (Cohen et al., 1993; Elliott, 1989; Koranyi, 1989; Maddi et al., 1987). Note that the stressful events referred to in the preceding sentence are largely psychosocial rather than physical in impact on a recipient—for example, death of a spouse, change in employment status, marital difficulties, and so on. In short, we find the evidence to be at this point beyond reasonable dispute that psychosocial stressors temporarily impair the immune response and thereby contribute substantially to the development of many physical illnesses.

While efforts to relate specific stressors to specific physical diseases have not generally been successful, stress is becoming a key underlying theme in our understanding of the development and course of virtually all organic illness. Stress may serve as a predisposing, precipitating, or reinforcing factor in the causal pattern, or it may merely aggravate a condition that might have occurred anyway. Even stress that is treatment-related, as in aggressive therapy for certain cancers, may carry its own measure of risk for compromising defensive resources by seriously diminishing the patient's "quality of life," as recently pointed out by Anderson, Kiecolt-Glaser, and Glaser (1994). Posttraumatic stress may continue to have destructive health effects long after the traumatic event, as suggested in the problematic health histories of a group of Los Angeles women who had previously been victims of sexual assault (Golding, 1994). Often stress appears to speed up the onset or increase the severity of a disorder, and to interfere with the body's immunological defenses and other homeostatic functions. Presuming that we all have one organ system in our bodies that is relatively vulnerable, a high, chronic level of stress puts us at risk for a breakdown of that organ system, and perhaps others, sooner or later.

Lifestyle as a Factor in Health Maintenance

Today a great deal of attention is being paid to the role of lifestyle in the development or maintenance of many health problems. Numerous aspects of the way we live are now considered influential in the development of some severe physical problems: diet—particularly overeating and consuming too many high-fat, low-fiber foods; lack of exercise; smoking cigarettes; excessive alcohol and drug use; constantly facing high-stress situations; and even ineffective ways of dealing with day-to-day problems are but a few of the many lifestyle patterns that are viewed as contributing causes. Growing awareness of such factors has resulted in more attention to lifestyle by both physicians and psychologists working in health care settings (Engel, 1977; O'Leary, 1985; Oldenburg, Perkins, & Andrews, 1985; Weiner, 1977). New efforts are being made to determine more precisely what role personality or lifestyle factors play in the genesis and course of disease. Finding the answers becomes all the more important when we realize that lifestyle factors—habits or behavior patterns presumably under our own control—are believed to play a major role in three of the leading causes of death in this country: coronary heart disease, automobile accidents, and alcohol-related deaths (National Center for Health Statistics, 1982).

We cannot help but be struck by the rather sobering observation of Knowles (1977), who has taken the position that most people are born healthy and suffer premature death and disability only as a result

Lifestyle is a significant factor in health maintenance.

of behavior destructive to health and unnecessarily pathogenic environmental conditions. He believes that most health problems could be drastically reduced if only no one

> smoked cigarettes or consumed alcohol and everyone exercised regularly, maintained optimal weight on a low-fat, low refined-carbohydrate, high-fiber content diet, reduced stress by simplifying their lives, obtained adequate rest and recreation, . . . drank fluoridated water, followed the doctor's orders for medication and self-care once disease was detected, and used available health resources. (p. 1104)

Before anyone rushes to alter his or her lifestyle according to the rather Spartan regimen outlined by Knowles, it should be pointed out that the connection between many lifestyle habits or patterns and physical illness may not be as strong as some advocates suggest. In many cases the statistical connection is relatively weak and usually one of correlation, with the force of the argument based more on common sense than definitive data. For example, the extent to which rates of physical diseases, such as coronary heart disease, can be controlled or reduced through reducing dietary cholesterol remains somewhat controversial. Nevertheless, the stakes are sufficiently high that it would seem imprudent to tempt fate by ignoring one's cholesterol intake.

Even in cases where virtual proof of causation exists, it is difficult for many people to change their lifestyles to reduce their risk of disease—an incentive that may be remote for healthy people. Significant and lasting change is generally hard to accomplish, and this is especially true where available rewards are immediate and powerful, as in the case of addictions (Chapter 10). The high and sustained motivation necessary to achieve reliable self-control often proves fragile. Some of the best established risk factors, such as cigarette smoking, are thus not easy habits to alter, even when the connection between the habit and the disease is direct and seemingly evident. After having two heart attacks and surgery to remove a cancerous lung, one man continued to smoke two and a half packs of cigarettes a day even though he frequently said, "I know these things are killing me a little at a time . . . but they have become so much a part of my life I can't live without them!"

PSYCHOSOCIAL FACTORS IN SPECIFIC DISEASE PROCESSES

The harmful effects of stressful life circumstances and destructive habits tend to be diffuse and non-specific in terms of the organ systems adversely af-

fected and the diseases for which risk is enhanced. Excessive autonomic activity, persistent negative emotional states, diminished immune competence, or even "bad habits" such as cigarette smoking typically compromise a person's functioning in several different ways and may, therefore, be implicated in a range of disease processes. A host of more specific factors help determine whether a given person will acquire a particular illness or disease at some time. Most obvious among these are certain congenital predispositions to develop a disease, often inherited ones, and levels of exposure to pathogenic agents, such as noxious chemicals in the workplace. In addition, contemporary research (see Friedman & Booth-Kewley's [1987b] quantitative review) increasingly implicates factors of personality and interpersonal functioning as having causal roles in the development of certain physical illnesses. This section undertakes a selective survey of apparent instances of the latter.

As we have seen, the idea that personality traits might be causally related to the development of physical illness is by no means new. Until fairly recently, however, evidence for such relationships was based mainly on unsystematic and often rather casual observations. This evidence has now been supplemented with more rigorously developed data that render the causal hypotheses highly plausible, if not compelling. In the following sections we will review in some detail certain widespread conditions that are the focus of much contemporary psychophysiologic research and theorizing—coronary heart disease and the eating disorders known as anorexia nervosa and bulimia. Then we shall move on to a brief survey of several other illnesses classically considered to have strong psychogenic aspects.

Coronary Heart Disease and the Type A Behavior Pattern

Coronary heart disease (CHD) is a potentially lethal blockage of the arteries supplying blood to the heart muscle, or myocardium. Its chief clinical manifestations are (a) angina pectoris, severe chest pain signaling that the delivery of oxygenated blood to the affected area of the heart is insufficient for its current work load; (b) myocardial infarction, functionally complete blockage of a section of the coronary arterial system, resulting in death of the myocardial tissue supplied by that arterial branch; and (c) disturbance of the heart's electrical conduction consequent to arterial blockage, resulting in disruption or interruption of the heart's pumping action, often leading to death. Many instances of sudden cardiac death, in which victims have no prior history of CHD symptoms, are attributed to "silent" CHD (see HIGHLIGHT 8.1).

While deaths from CHD have declined dramatically in recent years, this decline has occurred at the end of a long period, comprising most of the twentieth century, of rising CHD-related mortality in the United States. CHD retains today the dubious distinction of being the nation's number one killer, despite impressive advances in treatment (such as various types of coronary artery surgery) and markedly enhanced appreciation of risk factors, some of which (elevated serum cholesterol, smoking, lack of exercise, obesity, and hypertension, for example) are potentially reversible.

The known biological risk factors for CHD explain less than half of the CHD-related outcomes people actually experience. In other words, much of the causal pattern for CHD development (or, for that matter, for its failure to develop) remains a mystery. Noting this circumstance, cardiovascular researchers have increasingly turned their attention to possible nonbiological contributions to the disease's development—to psychosocial and personality factors—emulating in this respect some eminent forebears. William Harvey, the Engishman who discovered circulation of the blood, was writing of "affections of the mind" that generate problems in heart function as early as 1628. The distinguished Canadian physician Sir William Osler, in landmark lectures on cardiology published in 1892, explicitly related the development of CHD to "the worry and strain of modern life" and "the high pressure" under which people live. Attempts to refine and precisely specify the psychological contribution to the development of the disease continue to the present day, for the most part in the context of identifying the crucial components of what M. Friedman and Rosenman (1959) first labeled the **Type A behavior pattern.**

As conceptualized by Friedman and Rosenman, the Type A pattern is a complex set of behaviors that may be observed in certain people under appropriately stressful or challenging circumstances. The pattern, they said, involves excessive competitive drive in the absence of well-defined goals, impatience or time urgency, and hostility. It manifests itself in accelerated speech and motor activity. The pattern is best assessed and measured, according to these investigators, by means of a structured interview devised for this purpose (Rosenman, 1978). The contrasting Type B pattern, to which little descriptive attention has been paid, is negatively defined in terms of the absence of Type A characteristics. Various questionnaire-type approaches to the assessment of Type A behavior have also been developed, of which the Jenkins Activity Survey for Health Predic-

tion (Jenkins, Zyzansky, & Rosenman, 1971) has been most popular among researchers.

Unfortunately, the various assessment measures for the A/B typology are not as strongly intercorrelated as one might wish. This situation suggests continuing problems in the construct's definition and the likelihood that differing measurement approaches emphasize different components of the Type A pattern as originally described. This measurement problem may be the main reason why a few studies have failed to find a Type A-CHD relationship (Fischman, 1987; Thoreson & Powell, 1992). Moreover, as Krantz and Glass (1984) have noted, some evidence shows that not all components of the Type A pattern are equally predictive of CHD or even of differing pathological manifestations within the CHD syndrome (e.g., angina versus infarction). Overall, some consensus has developed that the pattern's hyperaggressivity/hostility component, perhaps in association with status insecurity and inhibition of overt expressions of anger, is the one most closely correlated with demonstrable coronary artery deterioration (M. Friedman & Ulmer, 1984; Krantz & Glass, 1984; Williams et al., 1980; Williams, Barefoot, & Shekelle, 1985; Wood, 1986).

The Type A behavior pattern may be observed in certain individuals under stressful or challenging circumstances. The pattern involves excessive competitiveness, impatience, hostility, and accelerated speech and motor activity.

Heart Attack

We have all heard the old story about the faint-hearted guard dog who, on being told "Attack," had one. Attack is now a common word in our vocabulary, as well it should be since heart attacks kill over half a million Americans each year. The incidence of heart disease among Americans is one of the highest in the world; about 30 million people are affected. (Some countries have a higher rate, including France, or a lower one, such as Japan.) But what is a heart attack? Technically, it is the result of a *myocardial infarction*—that is, a blockage of the arteries that feed the heart. (The lighter areas in the photo indicate blockage.) When such an artery is blocked, the oxygen-starved muscles of the heart begin to die. Depending on how much of the heart is damaged and how badly, the results can vary from almost complete recovery to death.

Blockage of the coronary vessels that feed the heart is usually caused by one of three things: a clot lodged in the vessel, a prolonged contraction of the vessel walls, or atherosclerosis. Atherosclerosis is the result of the buildup of a number of substances, such as fat, fibrin (formed in clots), parts of dead cells, and calcium. These substances reduce the elasticity of the vessel, and by decreasing its diameter, they raise blood pressure, just as you raise the pressure in a garden hose by holding your thumb over the end. No one knows what causes atherosclerosis, but a number of things can speed its development, such as smoking cigarettes and, probably, eating animal fat and cholesterol. Other factors include age, hypertension, diabetes, stress, heredity, gender (males have more heart attacks), and a Type A behavior pattern.

The warnings of heart attack are often (but not always) (1) a pain that spreads along the shoulders, arm, neck, or jaw; (2) sudden sweating; (3) a heavy pressure and pain in the center of the chest; and (4) nausea, vomiting, and

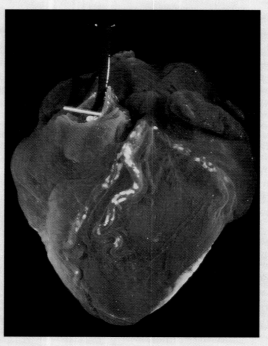

shortness of breath. The symptoms may come and go. People who have not developed a strong and efficient cardiovascular system through exercise are particularly susceptible to *angina pectoris* (chest pain), which occurs when the heart fails to receive enough blood, particularly during times of stress or exercise. It should not be confused with a true heart attack, although it may forecast one in the future. The pain may be relieved by stopping the unusual exercise or by reducing the stress

levels. Blood flow to the heart can be increased by an exercise program or by surgically inserting vessels from other parts of the body (a coronary bypass). Certain chemicals, such as nitroglycerin, also dilate the heart's vessels and increase the circulation of blood there.

Another form of heart attack results in a phenomenon called *sudden death*. The death may be due to chaotic and uncoordinated contractions of the ventricles, often brought on by an unanticipated myocardial infarction. The contractions do not move blood along and, after a few spasms, the heart may stop entirely. Many people afflicted in such a way mysteriously fall dead in their tracks. Some however, can be saved if they are helped in time. In fact, victims of any form of heart attack stand a much greater chance of surviving if they are treated immediately. In many metropolitan areas, citizens are being trained in cardiopulmonary resuscitation (CPR) to help restore a victim's circulation in such emergencies. CPR continues the flow of blood to the brain, where sensitive tissues die quickly without oxygen. In Seattle, Washington, with an extensive citizen-training program, passersby have performed about one-third of the city's resuscitations. Their success rate is higher than that of professionals because they usually reach victims sooner.

Adapted from *Biology: The world of life,* Robert A. Wallace (Glenview, IL: Scott, Foresman, 1987).

However, considerable conceptual and empirical uncertainties remain regarding the measurement of the A/B-Type variable and identification of its most significant components (Thoreson & Powell, 1992). Booth-Kewley and H. Friedman (1987), after a careful review of the pertinent evidence, have suggested that anxiety and depression are as important as anger and hostility in the correlational network that includes CHD development. Further, a longitudinal study by Hearn, Murray, and Luepker (1989) tends to negate any role for hostility. These authors contacted, in 1985 through 1986, 1313 men, or their surviving relatives, who had completed the Minnesota Multiphasic Personality Inventory, or MMPI (see Chapter 15) as university freshmen in 1953. The MMPI can be scored for a special, relatively well-validated scale measuring hostility (Ho). The subjects, divided according to those scoring high and low on the Ho scale, or their relatives were interviewed (by telephone) about their intervening health statuses. Hostility, as measured by the Ho scale, did not predict subsequent CHD-related illness, CHD mortality, or total mortality from all causes over the 33-year period involved, contrary to earlier findings.

In spite of these continuing conceptual and measurement uncertainties, it remains difficult to dispute the original evidence that the general cluster of reactions identified as the Type A pattern is a significant predictor of CHD, independent of other risk factors. While several studies support such a conclusion, two in particular stand out because their prospective designs circumvent many of the interpretation problems attending less powerful investigative strategies. (For example, inquiry about personality factors occurring after a diagnosis of CHD could lead to retrospective distortion based on preconceived notions of a coronary-prone personality type.) The first of these prospective studies is known as the Western Collaborative Group Study (WCGS) project, in which some 3150 healthy men between the ages of 35 and 59 on entry were typed as to A or B status and followed for a period of eight and a half years. Type As were found to be approximately twice as likely as Type Bs to have developed CHD (angina or myocardial infarctions) during the follow-up period. This differential remained even when other risk factors were statistically eliminated from consideration. When the data for a younger group of men (ages 39 to 49 on entry into the project) were considered separately, CHD was proportionately six times more prevalent among Type As than Type Bs (Rosenman et al., 1975). The findings also linked the Type A pattern to recurrent myocardial infarctions (Jenkins, Zyzanski, & Rosenman, 1976)

and to sudden cardiac death (M. Friedman et al., 1973).

We should note in passing that Ragland and Brand (1988) have called into question the WCGS study's conclusions on the basis of their finding that people who died from a heart attack subsequent to their first ones were more likely to be Bs than As. It seems to us, however, that such a finding does not negate the original conclusions. Also to be noted is that those Type As who were maximally at risk were already dead when the data on subsequent attacks was analyzed, leaving behind a sample of subjects biased in favor of CHD deaths among Bs. Nobody ever held that A or B status was the only determinant of death from CHD.

The second prospective study to be considered here was part of the well-known Framingham Heart Study, begun in 1948 and involving long-term follow-up of a large sample of men and women from Framingham, Massachusetts. Some 1700 coronary-free subjects were typed as to A or B status in the mid-1960s. Analysis of the data for CHD occurrence during an eight-year follow-up period not only confirmed the major findings of the WCGS project but extended them to women as well. In fact, the twofold increase in CHD risk reported for Type A men was almost exactly replicated for Type A women. Somewhat curiously, the CHD-Type A association among males in this study was limited to those of white-collar socioeconomic status (Haynes, Feinleib, & Kannel, 1980). Also, some question has been raised about the validity of the results for female subjects (Thoreson & Powell, 1992). See HIGHLIGHT 8.2 for a graph summarizing the Framingham results.

Taken together, these and other studies meet most of the stringent criteria established by epidemiologists to justify the assumption of a cause-effect relationship in disease genesis. That is, the evidence overall suggests that some aspect of the Type A behavior pattern, possibly one involving general negative affect that remains unexpressed (Endicott, 1989; H. Friedman & Booth-Kewley, 1987a), is implicated in the development of a potentially lethal organic deficit (CHD) among some people. Also, a recent quantitative review by Lyness (1993) has confirmed that Type A individuals do show elevated cardiovascular reactivity to a variety of stressful situations. It is important to note, too, however, that this area continues under active investigation and heated debate. Clearly, many factors are involved in the causal chain of CHD.

The theoretical importance of these findings for advancing our understanding of basic processes underlying CHD is considerable. Beyond that, they raise the possibility of saving lives by devising pre-

HIGHLIGHT   8.2

The Type A Behavior Pattern and Coronary Heart Disease

The graph below depicts the percent incidence of coronary heart disease (CHD) over an eight-year period among subjects of the Framingham Heart Study. Subjects are distinguished according to age, sex, occupation (men only), and Type A versus Type B behavior pattern. Note the substantial rise in CHD among Type A women and men of white-collar occupations over their Type B counterparts. The failure to confirm this finding among blue-collar males remains unexplained.

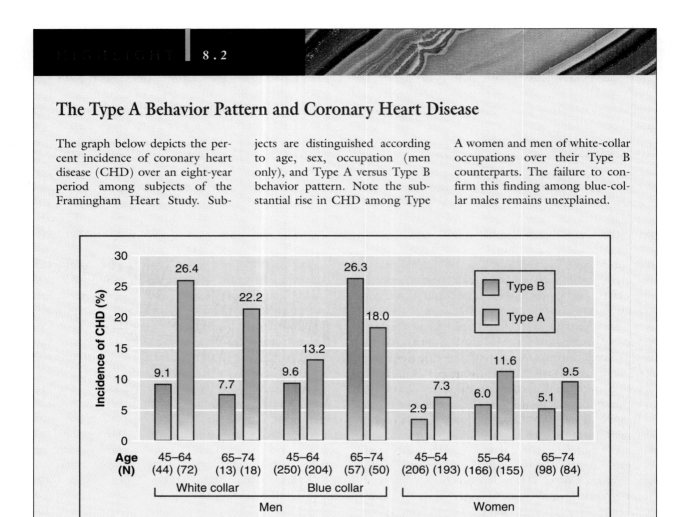

The Anorexic and Bulimic Syndromes

ventive therapeutic interventions to alter the Type A reaction pattern (or more precisely its negative affect component) in persons at risk. To date, however, work in this area has yielded inconsistent results; in general, the best-designed studies have generated the most optimistic conclusions (Thoreson & Powell, 1992).

The Anorexic and Bulimic Syndromes

Anorexia nervosa and bulimia nervosa, which historically have been considered separate syndromes, are coded (separately) as adult Eating Disorders in DSM-IV. In fact neither syndrome occurs in appreciable numbers before adolescence, and onset after age 25 is rare. Also, the overwhelming number of persons with these disorders are female—on the order of at least nine out of ten. This marked gender imbalance suggests that, for reasons not yet fully un-

derstood, "femaleness" may be an intrinsic factor in these disorders. For this reason we will confine ourselves here to typical cases involving girls or young women. Anorexia, in particular, is often a persistent and dangerous disorder, with a mortality rate near 5 percent overall (Szmukler & Russell, 1986) and perhaps twice that in the more severe and intractable cases (American Psychiatric Association, 1994).

Anorexia nervosa has been officially recognized as a distinct disorder for at least a century. The central features of the syndrome, as defined in DSM-IV, are an intense fear of gaining weight coupled with refusal to maintain adequate nutrition, often associated with the manifestly mistaken complaint of being "fat"; loss of original body weight to a level 85 percent or lower than that expected on the basis of height/weight norms (or, in those still in a period of growth, a discrepancy from average projected weight gain that constitutes a 15 percent shortfall); disturbance of body image or undue influence of the latter in determining self-evaluation; and (in post-menarchial females) absence of at least three consecutive menstrual periods. Associated features that are usually present include marked overactivity and a pattern that emphasizes either severe dietary restriction or binge-eating with or without voluntary purging; this distinction is coded diagnostically with Restricting or Binge-eating/Purging subtype designations, respectively, the latter of these constituting one of several links with bulimia nervosa.

Several characteristics of anorexic girls, apart from their eating problems, have frequently been observed in the long history of literature on this disorder. They usually describe their mothers in unflattering terms: excessively dominant, intrusive, overbearing, and markedly ambivalent. We must register caution here, however, in light of the possibility that mothers respond in these ways to the self-starvation of their children. By contrast, anorexic girls usually describe their fathers as "emotional absentees." Most clinicians who work with anorexic patients are impressed with the extent to which family dynamics seem to contribute to the disorder. Humphrey (1989) has analyzed the interactions of families with an anorexic daughter using the Structural Analysis of Social Behavior (SASB; Benjamin, 1974), a highly systematic, quantitative technique for measuring the nature of interpersonal relationships. The parents of these young women were found to communicate with their daughters in abnormally complicated ways, providing "double messages" that at once communicated both nurturant affection and disregard of the daughters' attempts to express themselves. In turn, the anorexic daughters displayed behaviors that wavered between self-expression and submission to the leads provided by parents.

Anorexia nervosa often begins when life changes require new or unfamiliar skills concerning which the person feels inadequate, such as when a person goes off to college, gets married, or even reaches puberty. Often the disorder begins as an extension of normal dieting, which is common among young women. What distinguishes the normal dieter from the one who converts dieting into a dangerous flirtation with disaster remains a mystery. The case of Mary S., including her marked activity despite dwindling energy resources and her unfailing denial of the growing seriousness of her condition, is in most respects fairly typical of the anorexic syndrome:

Mary S., aged sixteen and one-half years, grew disgusted with a close friend who began to put on weight by eating candy. The two girls agreed

Though this anorexic woman's appearance is shocking to us, she is likely convinced that she is "fat." This distorted view of the true nature of one's body weight is a central feature of anorexia nervosa, along with a refusal to maintain weight within the normal limits for age and height. Anorexia often begins as an extension of normal dieting, but what distinguishes a normal dieter from one who converts dieting into a dangerous activity remains a mystery.

to go on a reducing diet, although Mary weighed only 114 pounds. A year later she graduated from high school and obtained a job as a stenographer. She began to lead a very busy life, working every day, and going dancing at night with a young man who paid her attention. As her activities increased, her weight loss became more apparent, and soon her menses disappeared. Up to this time her dieting had been a voluntary control of eating, but now her appetite failed. Some months later one of the patient's sisters lured her boyfriend from her. Mary began to feel tired, and had to force herself to keep active. The onset of dizzy spells caused her to consult a doctor, who suggested a tonsillectomy. After the operation she refused to eat, but continued her active pace, including dancing every night. She now weighed 71 pounds. Two months later she became so dizzy and weak that she could no longer walk, and was finally brought to the hospital weighing 63 pounds. In three days, two and a half years after beginning her diet, Mary S. was dead of bronchopneumonia. (Nemiah, 1961, p. 10)

Recurrent episodes of seemingly uncontrollable binge-eating, with full awareness of the pattern's abnormality and with much secrecy, shame, guilt, and self-deprecation concerning it, are the hallmarks of bulimia, now relabeled **bulimia nervosa** since the advent of DSM-III-R in 1987. Bulimic young women normally have pronounced fears that they will be unable to stop eating voluntarily; are preoccupied with weight gain; and engage in frequent, inappropriate attempts to lose weight by severe methods, such as fasting, self-induced vomiting, and overuse of laxatives and diuretics (see HIGHLIGHT 8.3). While extreme weight fluctuations are common among bulimics, most are not obviously severely underweight and many also successfully avoid obvious obesity; they are thus often able to conceal their problems from families, associates, and friends. Bulimia nervosa is therefore a quite specific and distinctive syndrome and should be distinguished from the more common and demographically far less specific problem of overeating and obesity per se, which is discussed in Chapter 10. Unlike anorexia nervosa, its specific recognition as a psychiatric syndrome is relatively recent—it is not mentioned in the DSM-II of 1968. In DSM-IV, Purging and Nonpurging subtypes are recognized based on whether or not, in the current episode, the person has employed purgative methods of neutralizing food intake, such as vomiting or inappropriate use of laxatives, diuretics, or enemas.

As a group, bulimic young women seem to be more heterogeneous with regard to both eating habits and personality than do anorexics, particularly the restricting ones, who generally appear markedly constricted and obsessional. Vitousek and Manke (1994), in a study of the personality organizations of both groups, noted this heterogeneity among bulimics but did identify a subgroup sharing characteristics of emotional instability and impulsivity. A similar subgroup was identified by Gleaves and Eberenz (1993) among binge-eating women who met diagnostic criteria for anorexia nervosa, one that gave indications of having suffered traumatic childhood

abuse. The question of childhood sexual abuse as a background factor in bulimia, incidentally, has been studied by Pope and colleagues (1994) and by Welch and Fairburn (1994), neither of whom found convincing evidence of its making a specific contribution to the development of an eating disorder. Overall, Gleaves and Eberenz (1993) were impressed by the basic similarities of personality organization in bulimic and anorexic eating disorder patterns. This issue will be further addressed in what follows.

Both anorexia nervosa (Strober, 1986) and bulimia nervosa (Boskind-White & White, 1986) have become markedly more common in the United States over the past 35 years. Because of this changing rate of occurrence, reliable estimates of incidence/prevalence are difficult to pin down. For females, onset of an eating disorder within the age range of 12 to 18 is probably in excess of 1 in 250. Foreyt (1986) estimates the point prevalence of bulimia to be "as high as" 15 percent in college-age women.

Most authorities agree that these eating disorders have their origins in psychological problems that somehow become focused on food ingestion and body proportions. Many believe that our contemporary cultural preoccupation with an ideal of thinness has encouraged the rise in eating disorders we seem to be experiencing. The fact that these syndromes are overwhelmingly more common in females than males is explained, in part, by the greater pressure for thinness experienced by females, as demonstrated in a clever study by Fallon and Rozin (1985). Using figure drawings as stimuli, these authors found that (a) most women judged their "current figure" as too heavy; (b) most men believed women liked heavier female figures than they in fact did; and (c) most women believed men liked thinner female figures than they in fact did. Overall, men were satisfied and women dissatisfied with their own current figures as personally judged. While this self-devaluating perceptual bias in women hardly seems a complete explanation for their markedly disproportionate vulnerability to serious eating disorders, the likelihood is high of its making some contribution to that outcome (Hsu, 1989). Leon and colleagues (1993), for example, found body dissatisfaction to be unusually high among a group of seventh- to tenth-grade girls considered at high risk for eating disorders. Fashion magazines and the like, with their depictions of the ideal woman as malnourished in appearance, undoubtedly exacerbate the effect.

As Garner (1986a) convincingly argues, the current trend of considering anorexia and bulimia to be psychologically dissimilar disorders may be seriously misleading. Not only do anorexic and bulimic individuals typically share many psychological traits,

A Bulimic's Morning

Nicole awakens in her cold dark room and already wishes it was time to go back to bed. She dreads the thought of going through this day, which will be like so many others in her recent past. She asks herself the same question every morning: "Will I be able to make it through the day without being totally obsessed by thoughts of food, or will I blow it again and spend the day binge-ing?" She tells herself that today she will begin a new life, today she will start to live like a normal human being. However, she is not at all convinced that the choice is hers.

She feels fat and wants to lose weight, so she decides to start a new diet: "This time it'll be for real! I know I'll feel good about myself if I'm thinner. I want to start my exercises again because I want to make my body more attractive." Nicole plans her breakfast, but decides not to eat until she has worked out for a half hour or so. She tries not to think about food since she is not really hungry. She feels anxiety about the day ahead of her. "It's this tension," she rationalizes. That is what is making her want to eat.

Nicole showers and dresses and plans her schedule for the day—classes, studying, and meals. She plans this schedule in great detail, listing where she will be at every minute and what she will eat at every meal. She does not want to leave blocks of time when she might feel tempted to binge. "It's time to exercise, but I don't really want to; I feel lazy. Why do I always feel so lazy? What happened to the will power I used to have?" Gradually, Nicole feels the binge-ing signal coming on. Halfheartedly she tries to fight it, remembering the promises she made to herself about changing. She also knows how she is going to feel at the end of the day

if she spends it binge-ing. Ultimately, Nicole decides to give into her urges because, for the moment, she would rather eat.

Since Nicole is not going to exercise, because she wants to eat, she decides that she might as well eat some "good" food. She makes a poached egg and toast and brews a cup of coffee, all of which goes down in about thirty seconds. She knows this is the beginning of several hours of craziness!

After rummaging through the cupboards, Nicole realizes that she does not have any binge food. It is cold and snowy outside and she has to be at school fairly soon, but she bundles up and runs down the street. First she stops at the bakery for a bagful of sweets—cookies and doughnuts. While munching on these, she stops and buys a few bagels. Then a quick run to the grocery store for granola and milk. At the last minute, Nicole adds several candy bars. By the time she is finished, she has spent over fifteen dollars.

Nicole can hardly believe that she is going to put all of this food, this junk, into her body; even so, her adrenaline is flowing and all she wants to do is eat, think about eating, and anticipate getting it over with. She winces at the thought of how many pounds all of this food represents, but knows she will throw it up afterward. There is no need to worry.

At home Nicole makes herself a few bowls of cereal and milk, which she gobbles down with some of the bagels smothered with butter, cream cheese, and jelly (not to mention the goodies from the bakery and the candy bars which she is still working on). She drowns all of this with huge cups of coffee and milk, which help speed up the process

even more. All this has taken no longer than forty-five minutes, and Nicole feels as though she has been moving at ninety miles an hour.

Nicole dreads reaching this stage, where she is so full that she absolutely has to stop eating. She will throw up, which she feels she has to do but which repels her. At this point, she has to acknowledge that she's been binge-ing. She wishes she were dreaming, but knows all too well that this is real. The thought of actually digesting all of those calories, all of that junk, terrifies her.

In her bathroom, Nicole ties her hair back, turns on the shower (so none of the neighbors can hear her), drinks a big glass of water, and proceeds to force herself to vomit. She feels sick, ashamed, and incredulous that she is really doing this. Yet she feels trapped—she does not know how to break out of this pattern. As her stomach empties, she steps on and off the scale to make sure she has not gained any weight.

Nicole knows she needs help, but she wants someone else to make it all go away. As she crashes on her bed to recuperate, her head is spinning. "I'll never do this again," she vows. "Starting tomorrow, I'm going to change. I'll go on a fast for a week and then I'll feel better." Unfortunately, deep inside, Nicole does not believe any of this. She knows this will not be the last time. Reluctantly, she leaves for school, late and unwilling to face the work and responsibilities that lie ahead. She almost feels as though she could eat again to avoid going to school. She wonders how many hours it will be until she starts her next binge, and she wishes she had never gotten out of bed this morning.

Boskind-White and White (1983, pp. 29–32).

such as perfectionism and dysfunctional thought processes, they also share the same goal of maintaining suboptimal body weights. Moreover, a given patient may often move between the two syndromes at different times in her quest for ultimate thinness. Most anorexic and bulimic individuals come from socioeconomically advantaged backgrounds. The perfectionism and overachievement typical of anorexic patients were illustrated in a study by Dura and Bornstein (1989), who showed the school achievements of a group of hospitalized anorexic adolescents to be well above those predicted from their IQ scores.

Comparable underlying psychodynamics have also been described for anorexic and bulimic patients. The Humphrey (1989) study on family interactions in anorexia mentioned earlier contained a bulimic subject group. Disturbed family dynamics involving an undercutting of the daughter's autonomy (here within a context of excessive family enmeshment) were also observed for these young women. The general picture of family dysfunction in bulimia was also confirmed by Scalf-McIver and Thompson (1989) in a questionnaire study of college women with bulimic eating patterns. In short, both anorexic and bulimic individuals seem deeply but ambivalently involved with their parents in power struggles concerning autonomy and identity.

Bruch (1986), who until her death was generally considered the world's leading authority on anorexia, saw the anorexic person as attempting to camouflage an undeveloped and amorphous selfhood by being different, even unique, in a special and fiercely "independent" way. She reportedly doubted that bulimia existed as an entity independent of anorexia (Foreyt, 1986). Boskind-White and White (1983, 1986), although seeing anorexic and bulimic individuals as struggling with similar personal and family issues, consider the typical bulimic person to be at a relatively more advanced stage of identity development, having achieved a measure of independence from family and succeeded at least minimally in peer relations. The establishment of a truly autonomous selfhood, including a mature approach to sexuality, however, remains difficult for both groups of women—although bulimic women as a group may be more likely to have had extensive sexual experience (Coovert, Kinder, & Thompson, 1989).

Granting apparent psychological origins, persistent anorexia or bulimia leads eventually to serious physical problems relating both to starvation and to the dire methods often employed to purge food following a binge. These patients routinely suffer from anemia; dehydration; deficiencies in essential vitamins, minerals, and electrolytes; chronic urinary and bowel difficulties; hypoglycemia; endocrine abnor-

malities; and potentially serious alterations in cardiovascular functioning. Amenorrhea is virtually always present in anorexia and is common in bulimia as well. At some point in the process, biological factors seem to develop their own demands, taking the behavior beyond conscious control and making it exceedingly difficult to reverse, as we will see later in the chapter in our discussion of treatment measures. One school of thought holds that hypothalamic functioning is altered by deliberate self-starvation, resulting finally in autonomous dysregulation of both appetite and menstruation, and yielding the typical advanced clinical picture (Bemis, 1978; Walsh, 1980).

Like CHD, these disorders of the basic drive for food are dangerous and have become commonplace in modern American society. Also like CHD, we have yet to devise a reliably effective means of preventing or reversing the psychological factors that encourage their development and maintenance. As we will see later, however, progress is being made on both these fronts.

The main issues addressed thus far in this chapter have had a decidedly contemporary focus, and deliberately so. We have sought to introduce the topic of psychological influences on health by discussing some currently high-profile concerns in both the public and professional sectors. We have also tried to give due attention to the contextual, system-level thinking that is growing in the health field (for example, organ failure is not a discrete, isolated event). As we have seen, the behavioral medicine approach explicitly embodies such a far-reaching perspective, calling into question much of traditional medicine's exclusive concern with the pathophysiology of individual organs after disease strikes (Weiner & Fawzy, 1989).

We have also seen, however, that various medical pioneers have from time to time called attention to the influence of psychosocial factors, chiefly emotional ones, in causing or maintaining physical illness. By the 1950s this thinking had become strongly wedded to the psychoanalytic tradition. As was noted earlier, these ideas involved quite specific causal hypotheses concerning certain diseases that came to be considered "psychosomatic" in nature—organic dysfunctions produced by aberrant emotional processes.

As a group, these early notions were both too specific and too general. They frequently specified the exact type of psychological "conflict" presumed to underlie a given disease, and they tended to assume that this alleged conflict was both necessary and sufficient in causing any instance of the disease. For example, asthma was conceived as "suppressed crying" caused by an impulse to cry joined with a need to inhibit it, both propensities relating in turn to a fear of abandonment. We now know that asthma can have many causes, that it probably does not occur in the absence of a biologically based predisposition, and that any emotional factors involved in precipitating an attack tend to be quite idiosyncratic to the person (A.B. Alexander, 1977, 1981; Knapp, 1989). Comparable ideas relating a number of other illnesses to rather fanciful and specific psychogenic hypotheses also lost credibility when evaluated empirically.

Despite the general failure of this "psychosomatic specificity" approach, there were some exceptions. Modest associations were established between certain illnesses and certain emotional states (much as in the more recent case of CHD and some still imprecisely identified aspect of the Type A pattern). We will now briefly examine two illnesses that have continued to attract attention in this regard: essential hypertension or high blood pressure, and persistently recurrent headaches.

Essential Hypertension

When a person is calm, heartbeat is regular, pulse is even, blood pressure is relatively low, and visceral organs are well supplied with blood. With stress, however, the vessels of the visceral organs constrict, and blood flows in greater quantity to the muscles of the trunk and limbs—part of the flight-or-fight pattern described earlier. With the tightening of the tiny vessels supplying the visceral organs, the heart must work harder. As it beats faster and with greater force, the pulse quickens and blood pressure mounts. Usually, when the crisis passes, the body resumes normal functioning and the blood pressure returns to normal. Under continuing emotional strain, however, high blood pressure may become chronic.

About 12 percent of Americans suffer from chronically high blood pressure, or **hypertension.** Preexisting organic factors account for only some 5–10 percent of hypertension cases (Byassee, 1977); the large remainder are given the designation **essential hypertension,** meaning no physical cause is known. Although Wing and Manton (1983) have reported a decline in deaths due to hypertension, it is nevertheless the primary cause of more than 60,000 deaths each year and a major predisposing factor in another 1 million or more deaths a year from strokes and cardiovascular diseases, including CHD (Coates et al., 1981). It is also a risk factor in kidney failure, blindness, and a number of other physical ailments. For reasons that are not entirely clear but may relate in part to diet, the incidence of hypertension is about twice as high among blacks as among whites (Anderson & Jackson, 1987; Edwards, 1973; Mays, 1974), making it a more serious health problem in this population than even sickle-cell anemia (a serious malformation of red blood cells that mainly affects blacks).

Unlike the other disease states we have dealt with, there are usually no symptoms to signal high blood pressure. Sufferers experience no personal distress. In severe cases, some people complain of headaches, tiredness, insomnia, or occasional dizzy spells—symptoms often easy to ignore—but most people suffering from hypertension receive no warning symptoms. In fact, Nelson (1973) reported on one survey encompassing three middle-class neighborhoods in Los Angeles that revealed a third of the adults tested to have high blood pressure; only half of them had been aware of it. As Mays (1974) has described the situation, "In most instances . . . the disease comes as silently as a serpent stalking its prey. Someone with high blood pressure may be unaware of his affliction for many years and then, out of the blue, develop blindness or be stricken by a stroke, cardiac arrest or kidney failure" (p. 7).

Since there is no such thing as benign hypertension, high blood pressure is an insidious and dangerous disorder. Ironically, it is both simple and painless to detect by means of the familiar inflated arm cuff, automatic versions of which are now widely available for self-testing at shopping centers and the like.

In some cases a physical cause of hypertension can be identified. For example, it may be attributable to a narrowing of the aorta or one of its artery branches, to the excessive use of certain drugs, or to dietary factors. The normal regulation of blood pressure, however, is so complex that when it goes awry in a particular case, identifying the causal factors can be extremely difficult (Herd, 1984). Kidney dysfunction, for example, may be a cause or an effect of dangerously elevated pressures—or both.

A number of investigators have shown that chronic hypertension may be triggered by emotional stress. For example, a highly stressful job markedly increases the risk of high blood pressure (Edwards, 1973). The stresses of inner-city life—as well as dietary factors such as excessive salt intake—have been identified as probably playing a key role in the high incidence of hypertension among black people (Anderson & Jackson, 1987; Mays, 1974). Too, some people "carry their stress around with them," as in the Type A behavior pattern, which is associated with elevated systolic (beat) and diastolic (between beat) blood pressure (Lyness, 1993).

The classical psychoanalytic interpretation of hypertension is that affected people suffer from "suppressed rage," and scattered evidence supports this

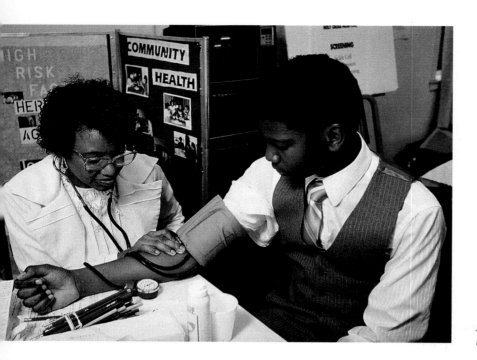

African Americans as a group are at exceptionally high risk for hypertension.

hypothesis (Gentry et al., 1982; Spielberger et al., 1985; Stone & Hokanson, 1969). Although there is a high incidence of hypertension in the black inner-city population, among whom suppressed hostility might be expected to run high (Harburgh et al., 1973), the suppressed-rage hypothesis cannot be said to be firmly established with respect to all, or even necessarily a majority, of affected persons. Findings by Esler and colleagues (1977) suggest that, in the subgroup of hypertensive people who do show suppressed hostility, it is often accompanied by high levels of submissiveness, overcontrol, and guilt.

A variant of the suppressed-rage hypothesis has been proposed by McClelland (1979). According to this view, an affected individual is driven not so much by rage and the need to suppress it as by power motives and the need to inhibit their expression. Unexpressed anger is then a frequent accompaniment. In a well-conceived study designed to test these ideas, McClelland found that personality measures of "need for power" and "activity inhibition" were indeed jointly associated with elevated blood pressures. Moreover, he demonstrated that this inhibited power motive syndrome in men in their 30s significantly predicted elevated blood pressure and signs of hypertensive disease in these same men 20 years later.

Perhaps we will find that neither rage nor power motives per se are critical elements in essential hypertension. What is common to the findings of McClelland and earlier work is the inhibition or suppression of strong urges to perform acts that are poorly tolerated by polite society. The common factor, in other words, might be that of a poor match between individual drives and internalized societal restraints. Conflictual states of this sort are by no means unusual and, as noted in earlier chapters, are at the conceptual center of certain psychodynamic notions pertaining to "neurotic" processes.

Recurrent Headaches

Although headaches can result from a wide range of organic conditions, most of them seem to be related to emotional tension, as many sufferers confirm. More than 50 million Americans suffer from frequent tension or migraine headaches, with the overall incidence apparently being higher among women than men. In one survey, Andrasik, Holroyd, and Abell (1979) found that 52 percent of a large group of college students reported headaches at least once or twice a week.

Research in this area has focused primarily on **migraine,** an intensely painful headache that recurs periodically. Although typically involving only one side of the head, migraine is sometimes more generalized; it may also shift from side to side. Migraine was described extensively by medical writers of antiquity, but the cause of the pain remained a mystery until the 1940s, when interest was focused on pain-sensitive structures of the head. The *"classic" migraine* occurs in two phases. First, there is an *aura,* a variably experienced but painless disturbance having odd sensory (particularly visual), motor, and/or mood components. Once thought to be primarily the subjective effects of sudden changes in vascular diameter and hence blood flow to the brain, modern researchers tend to emphasize alterations in the brain's electrical activity. The two conceptions are not, of course, mutually exclusive. In any event, when the involved pathophysiology reaches pain-sensitive tissues, it is thought, the second phase of intense pain (often experienced as "throbbing") begins. Frequently excruciating in severity, it may last for hours, days, or in rare cases weeks. Nausea and vomiting sometimes accompany this dire experience in classic migraine attacks.

The *"common" migraine,* whose prevalence is actually higher than the classic variety (about 70 vs. 30 percent), is distinguished chiefly by the absence of an aura. Onset is often experienced, therefore, as abrupt and unpredictable. As in the classic type, the pain is likely to be localized to a particular region of the head, and it is also commonly of excruciating intensity. Fortunately for the sufferer, common migraines tend to resolve themselves within one to several hours. They may, however, recur within relatively brief intervals. Sometimes confused with common migraine (and sometimes called "migrainous neuralgia") are *cluster headaches,* short periods

Simple tension headaches are extremely common, impairing both productivity and personal well-being.

of severe, "stabbing" pain usually centered over one eye. Cluster headaches are most often observed in men.

It seems increasingly likely that the tendencies to be subject to migraine and cluster headaches are related to primary causes involving variants of normal physiology, some of them probably inherited. Cluster headaches, for example, are now thought due to a disorder of histamine metabolism. In individual instances of migraine or cluster headaches, therefore, the role of stress in provoking attacks of pain may be minimal to nonexistent.

The vast majority of headaches—almost 90 percent of those treated by physicians—are so-called **simple tension headaches.** They appear to be particularly common as accompaniments of depressed mood, but generally the role of emotional upset in contributing to their onset is fairly obvious. With these headaches, emotional stress seems to lead to contraction of the muscles surrounding the skull; these contractions may be painful in themselves, but in addition may result in vascular constrictions that also cause headache pain. Regarding the latter, it may be noted that, with the more precise measurement techniques now available, the evidence for the physiological differences between migraine and tension headaches has been called into question (Blanchard & Andrasik, 1982). Though further studies are needed, it may be that the physiological processes are similar for the two types of headaches and that the difference is rather one of degree, with migraine involving greater vascular (or other central physiologic) disruption. Certainly it is true that many people suffer headaches that appear to have both vascular and muscular origins.

Both tension and migraine headaches usually appear during adolescence and recur periodically during stressful times. The pain can often be relieved with analgesics, with muscle-relaxant drugs, or with certain relaxation-inducing psychological procedures (Blanchard, 1994; Blanchard et al., 1990a; Carlson & Hoyle, 1993). These latter procedures include **biofeedback,** a technique in which a person is taught to influence his or her own physiological processes (Blanchard, 1992; Blanchard et al., 1990b). Of the two types, migraine headaches are usually more painful and slower to respond to treatment than simple tension headaches. Overall, however, these psychological techniques for headache control have amassed an impressive record, and done so with "side effects" (e.g., decreased anxiety and depression) that are generally positive in nature (Blanchard, 1992).

The presumed psychological predispositions for psychogenic headaches are less clear than in the case of other disorders considered in this chapter. Also, the interaction of personality factors with particular types of stressors appears to be especially important for headache sufferers (Levor et al., 1986). However, clinicians historically have held the view that it is important to the typical headache-prone person to feel in control of events impinging on him or her. Such individuals have usually been described as highly organized and perfectionistic (Williams, 1977).

In a study by Andrasik and colleagues (1982), the traditional belief that migraine sufferers show higher levels of depression, passivity, nonassertiveness, hostility, and high-achievement strivings was not supported. Psychological tests of migraine sufferers revealed psychologically normal profiles. Instead, the tension headache sufferers showed the greatest psychopathology. There is also some independent evidence (Lehrer & Murphy, 1991) that tension headache sufferers are unusually reactive to stress and to the experience of pain. These findings support the suggestion already made that tension headaches might be more indicative of psychological problems per se than migraine headaches.

In focusing, as we have in this section, on certain diseases in which a psychogenic contribution to etiology seems especially likely, we do not intend to exclude by omission the possibility—indeed likelihood—that other specific diseases may sometimes have identifiable psychogenic roots. As in all such cases, however, we suspect that some sort of biological predisposition will turn out to be a necessary element in the total causal pattern. Within this constraint, the literature indicates several additional candidates for continued scrutiny in search of specific psychogenic mediators. These diseases include peptic ulcers; certain allergies and skin eruptions; chronic diarrhea and ulcerative colitis; rheumatoid arthritis; Raynaud's disease (a potentially serious local vasoconstriction that may interrupt the blood supply to certain body parts); diabetes; menstrual irregularities and other endocrine disturbances (see Levitan, 1989; Sandhu & Cohen, 1989); and chronic disturbances of the sleep cycle.

PSYCHOGENIC PHYSICAL DISEASE: ADDITIONAL ETIOLOGIC CONSIDERATIONS

In the foregoing pages we have explored at a general level the manner in which negative thinking and attitudes, autonomic excess, stressor-induced immunosuppression, and health-endangering lifestyles can compromise a person's biological integrity.

From there, we proceeded to discuss apparently specific psychogenic contributions, insofar as these are known, to the etiology of four extremely common and sometimes life-threatening physical conditions: coronary heart disease, eating disorders (anorexia and bulimia), essential hypertension, and recurrent headaches. We also noted that this listing is by no means exhaustive in cataloging the physical ills that may have psychogenic roots.

In this section we return to a more general level of analysis to complete our picture of psychological causation in physical illness. We will be particularly concerned with the problem of specificity—of why, under stress, one person develops anorexia, another hypertension, and still another tension headaches. For the sake of economy and convenience, we will generally refer to such stress-related conditions as psychogenic illnesses or diseases, even though it should be clear that other etiological factors, particularly predisposing biological ones, are inevitably involved. We begin the discussion at the level of biological predisposition.

Biological Factors

Obviously, biological factors are involved in all disease. We focus here on those factors likely to have a role in determining the adequacy of a person's response to stressor circumstances.

Genetic Factors   In general, understanding of genetic contributions to diseases believed to have strong psychogenic origins remains limited (Kidd & Morton, 1989). The field involves many complexities, including the extreme difficulty of differentiating genetic contributions to (a) an underlying physical vulnerability for acquiring the disease in question; (b) the psychological makeup of the individual and his or her stress tolerance; and (c) the nature of any interaction between (a) and (b). Despite these difficulties of interpretation, nearly all diseases of multifactor origin can be shown to "run in families" to at least some extent. Although social learning (for example, children modeling the inadequate coping skills of their parents) could be a factor in such family resemblances, research evidence on this point is equivocal, and genetic factors cannot usually be ruled out.

An interesting separation of genetic and psychological influences is contained in the findings of Liljefors and Rahe (1970), who studied the role of life stress in coronary heart disease among twins. The subjects consisted of 32 pairs of identical male twins between 42 and 67 years of age, in which only one twin in each pair suffered from coronary heart disease. The genetic contribution in such twinships is of course constant for each pair, thus controlling for this factor. The investigators found that the twins suffering from heart disease were more work-oriented, took less leisure time, had more home problems, and in general experienced greater dissatisfactions in their lives than their healthier twin brothers. Such a finding represents a rather compelling case for psychosocial contribution to the development of CHD, but the study's design cannot rule out a genetic contribution as well. The latter could still be a necessary, but not sufficient, condition for CHD pathology. According to this scenario, both twins may have been at genetic risk for CHD—its actual "expression" then being determined by an excess of psychosocial disorganization in one of the pair's members. Interpretive complexities of this sort are the rule rather than the exception in trying to estimate the magnitude of genetic influences here as well as in other areas of psychopathology.

Differences in Autonomic Reactivity and Somatic Weakness In our earlier discussion (Chapter 3) of vulnerability and causal factors, we noted that individuals vary significantly in primary reaction tendencies and temperament. Even very young infants reveal marked differences in their sensitivities to aversive stimuli; some infants react to such stressors by developing fevers, others by digestive upsets, and still others by sleep disturbances. Such differences in reactivity continue into adult life and presumably help account for individual differences in susceptibility to psychogenic diseases and for the types of diseases a given person is most likely to develop.

In connection with the latter point, Wolff (1950) suggested that people can be classified as "stomach reactors," "pulse reactors," "nose reactors," and so on, depending on what kinds of physical changes stress characteristically triggers in them. For example, a person who has an inherited tendency to respond to stressors with increased cardiac output and vasoconstriction may be at special risk for chronic hypertension (Friedman & Iwai, 1976). A person who reacts with increased secretion of stomach acids will be more likely to develop peptic ulcers (Strang, 1989), although an infectious microorganism, *Helicobacter pylori*, is now considered to be the primary cause in most instances of this problem.

Sometimes a particular organ is especially vulnerable because of heredity, illness, or prior trauma. A person who has inherited or developed a "weak" stomach will be prone to gastrointestinal upsets during anger or anxiety. Presumably, the weakest link in the chain of visceral organs will be the organ affected. Caution must be exercised, however, to avoid *ex post facto* reasoning, because it would not

be safe to conclude that when a particular organ system is affected it must have been weak to begin with. Also, as we will see, conditioning may play a key role in determining which organ system is involved.

Disruption of Corticovisceral Control Mechanisms The human organism is an extremely complex biological system whose adequate functioning and survival depend on an elaborate network of monitors and feedback mechanisms to maintain vital processes within certain quantitative limits. The site of most of this "homeostatic" regulation is the brain itself, although many of the details of how it performs these functions remain quite speculative. The term *corticovisceral control mechanisms* is loosely employed as a general rubric to refer to these equilibrium-maintaining systems. According to one hypothesis, the corticovisceral control mechanisms of the brain may fail in their regulation of autonomic nervous system arousal, so that an individual's emotional response is exaggerated in intensity and his or her physiological equilibrium is not regained within normal time limits following the occurrence of stressful events (Halberstam, 1972; Lebedev, 1967; Schwartz, 1989). Such control failures might then lead to chronically excessive autonomic activation, as appears to be the case in essential hypertension, for example. In addition, excessive hypothalamic activation may be associated with attendant dysregulation of circulating adrenocortical hormones, which are involved in the body's immunity to disease. More generally, we have seen that breakdowns in a number of different pathways can compromise immune competence during the brain's processing of stressor events.

In assessing the role of biological factors in psychogenic diseases, most investigators would take into consideration each of the factors we have described. Perhaps the greatest emphasis at present would be placed on a person's characteristic autonomic activity, the vulnerability of affected organ systems, and possible constitutionally based or acquired alterations in the control mechanisms of the brain that normally regulate autonomic nervous system and hormonal functioning.

Psychosocial Factors

Though evidence suggests that psychological factors play a prominent role in causing many diseases, it is still not clear what factors are involved or how they exert their effects. Factors that investigators have emphasized include personality characteristics (including failure to learn adequate coping patterns), interpersonal relationships, and the learning of biological dysfunctions.

Personality Characteristics The work of Dunbar (1943, 1954) and a number of other early investigators raised the hope of identifying specific personality factors associated with certain psychophysiologic disorders—for example, noting that rigidity, high sensitivity to threat, and chronic underlying hostility are typical among those who suffer from hypertension. The ability to delineate hypertensive characters and those linked to other diseases would be of great value in understanding, assessing, and treating the pertinent illnesses—and perhaps even in preventing them.

As we have seen, however, later research evidence has suggested that such an approach is oversimplified. For example, although Kidson (1973) found hypertensive patients as a group to be significantly more insecure, anxious, sensitive, and angry than a nonhypertensive control group, a sizable number of the control-group members also showed these characteristics. Similarly, the association of Type A behavior (or some limited component of it) with CHD and heart attacks must be tempered with the observation that most Type As do not have coronary problems, and some Type Bs do (see the graph in HIGHLIGHT 8.2 on page 292). As we have emphasized, the relationships between particular personality variables and disease processes, while often clearly important, tend to be complex and difficult to pin down (see Friedman et al., 1994).

So even though personality makeup seems to play an important role, we still do not know why some people with "predisposing" personality characteristics do not develop a particular disease, nor can we account adequately for the wide range of personality types among people who suffer from the same condition. Usually, we can only conclude that particular personality factors are weakly but significantly correlated with the occurrence of certain illnesses.

Normally, when people are subjected experimentally to frustrating experiences, their blood pressures rise and their hearts beat more rapidly. If they are then given an opportunity to express physical or verbal aggression against the frustrator, their blood pressures and heart rates rapidly return to normal. If they are permitted only fantasy aggression or no aggression at all, however, their bodies return much more slowly to normal physiological functioning (Hokanson & Burgess, 1962). Thus, besides looking at people's abilities to cope with the stress of frustrations or conflicts or whatever, it seems necessary to consider their abilities to deal adequately with the accompanying emotional tensions.

Interpersonal Relationships In our previous discussions we have repeatedly noted the destructive effects that stressful interpersonal patterns—including marital unhappiness and divorce—may have on personality adjustment. Such patterns may also influence physiological functioning. In fact, death rates from varied causes, including physical disease, are markedly higher in people who have recently undergone marital problems or divorce than in the general population (Bloom et al., 1978).

Loss of a spouse through death also puts the survivor at risk. In an extensive review of the literature, Stroebe and Stroebe (1983) concluded that men are slightly more adversely affected by the death of their wives than women are by the death of their husbands. For example, in an earlier study of widowers, Parkes, Benjamin, and Fitzgerald (1969) reported

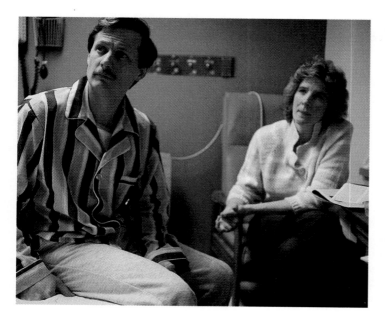

Stressful relationships may contribute to the development or maintenance of illness.

HIGHLIGHT 8.4

The Health Costs of Bereavement

A recent comprehensive review of the contemporary literature by Aiken (1994) indicates that bereavement is quite often followed by compromised health and increased risk of death among survivors. The idea of this association is hardly new, however. Reportedly, grief was a legally accepted cause of death, and could be so indicated on official death certificates, as early as the fifteenth century.

The nature of the physical pathology described as causing the death of loved ones goes well beyond cardiovascular effects and appears to encompass virtually all of the major body organs and systems. Infectious diseases and can-

cer are included, suggesting that at least some of these adverse health effects are due to compromised immune functioning. Also reported are symptoms of apparently pseudoneurological (conversion) origin, such as muscle weakness, visual difficulties, and choking sensations, thus indicating that not all of the physical symptoms experienced are necessarily related to organic pathology.

Some of the reported data suggest that the risk of adverse health effects among survivors may be influenced by the degree of suddenness of their loss, but there are some inconsistencies in the findings. A lengthy terminal illness provides survivors with an oppor-

tunity to prepare themselves for the fatal outcome, but may also entail chronic exposure to an emotionally debilitating situation. Wholly unanticipated sudden death, it would appear, is notably health-endangering for survivors.

Survivor mortality is influenced by several demographic variables, including age, sex, and ethnicity. Bereavement is especially likely to have a fatal outcome among survivors in the 55–65 age range, decreasing after age 65. Men are substantially more likely to succumb than women, and nonwhites more than whites. Remarriage after widowhood dramatically reduces the death rate for both men and women.

that during the six-month period following the death of their wives, the widowers' death rate was 40 percent above the expected rate. In fact, the incidence of cardiac deaths among these men was so high that the investigators referred to this pattern as "the broken-heart syndrome."

Lynch (1977), in a book entitled *The Broken Heart,* argues convincingly that the relatively high incidence of heart disease in industrialized communities stems in part from the absence of positive human relationships. He notes that heart disease and other illnesses are more prevalent among people who lack human companionship and for whom loneliness is common. This group includes not only those people who have recently lost a spouse through death but also single or divorced persons. See HIGHLIGHT 8.4 for more on the health endangering effects of bereavement.

Other studies have focused on the role of pathogenic family patterns. For example, studies have found that the mothers of asthmatic patients have in many cases felt ambivalent toward these children and tended to reject them, while at the same time being overprotective and unduly restrictive of the children's activities (Lipton, Steinschneider, & Richmond, 1966; Olds, 1970). Because individuals coming out of such family backgrounds tend to be overdependent and insecure, it would hardly be surprising if they should react with chronic emotional

mobilization to problems that do not seem threatening to most people. On the other hand, a strictly psychogenic interpretation of asthma is questionable. Severe asthma is a terrifying and life-threatening disorder. It would not be surprising on this basis alone to discover that asthmatic children are overdependent and insecure, or that their mothers tend to become ambivalent, protective, and restrictive after the asthma appears.

Complementing the work of Humphrey (1989) mentioned earlier, Kog and Vandereycken (1985) found substantial evidence of controlling relationships and parental discord in the families of eating disorder patients. They also noted a high incidence of physical illness, mood disorder (see Chapter 6), and alcoholism (Chapter 10) in these families.

The Learning of Illnesses Although Pavlov and many subsequent investigators have demonstrated that autonomic responses can be conditioned—as in the case of salivation—it was long assumed that people could not learn to control such responses "voluntarily." We now know that this assumption was wrong. Not only can autonomic reactivity be conditioned involuntarily via the classical Pavlovian model, but operant conditioning of the autonomic nervous system can also take place.

Thus the hypothesis has developed that certain physical disorders may arise through accidental rein-

Warm and loving relationships are a protective factor in health maintenance.

forcement of symptom and behavioral patterns. "A child who is repeatedly allowed to stay home from school when he has an upset stomach may be learning the visceral responses of chronic indigestion" (Lang, 1970, p. 86). Similarly, an adolescent girl may get little or no attention from being "good," but if she starves herself to the point of severe weight loss she may become the center of attention. If this pattern is continued, she might learn to avoid weight gain at all costs and correspondingly learn a profound aversion to food. The increasing alarm of her parents and others would presumably serve as a potent reinforcement for her to continue avoiding food.

Although causal factors other than conditioning are now thought to play a role in most cases of psychogenic illness, it seems clear that regardless of how a physical symptom may have developed, it may be elicited by suggestion and maintained by the reinforcement provided by **secondary gains,** indirect benefits derived from the illness behavior. The role of suggestion was demonstrated by a study in which 19 of 40 volunteer asthmatic subjects developed asthma symptoms after breathing the mist of a salt solution that they were told contained allergens, such as dust or pollen. In fact, 12 of the subjects had full-fledged asthma attacks. When the subjects then took what they thought was a drug to combat asthma (actually the same salt mist), their symptoms disappeared immediately (Bleeker, 1968). This study clearly shows the effect of suggestion on an autonomically mediated response. Why the other 21 subjects remained unaffected is not clear.

In short, it appears that some physical disorders may be acquired, maintained, or both in much the same way as other behavior patterns. Indeed, this finding is a basic tenet of behavioral medicine and health psychology, one aspect of which examines how various behavior modification and psychotherapeutic techniques can alter overt and covert reactions to physical disease processes (Blanchard, 1994; Bradley & Prokop, 1982; Gentry, 1984; G. C. Stone et al., 1987; Williams & Gentry, 1977; see also the August 1992 [Vol. 60, No. 4] special issue of the *Journal of Consulting and Clinical Psychology*). This approach includes the psychological assessment and management of pain (Keefe, Dunsmore, & Burnett, 1992), which is of course a serious complication of many medical diseases. Severe or chronic pain diminishes the patient's "quality of life" beyond any impediments caused by the disease itself, and may therefore impair immune function and the body's own resources for healing.

Sociocultural Factors

As we have seen, the incidence of specific disorders, both physical and mental, varies in different societies, in different strata of the same society, and over time. In general, what Cannon (1929) called diseases of civilization do not occur among nonindustrialized societies like the aborigines of the Australian Western Desert (Kidson & Jones, 1968), the Navajo Indians of Arizona, or certain isolated groups in South America (Stein, 1970). As these societies are exposed to social change, however, gastrointestinal, cardiovascular, and other psychogenic diseases begin to make their appearances. There is evidence of change in the nature and incidence of such disorders in Japan paralleling the tremendous social changes that have taken place there since World War II (Ikemi et al., 1974). For example, the incidence of hypertension and coronary heart disease has increased markedly with the postwar westernization of Japanese culture.

The Westernization of Japanese culture has brought with it an increase in stress-related diseases.

The phenomenon of eating disorders poses fascinating sociocultural questions for which answers are largely lacking. We still have no entirely satisfactory explanation of the seeming epidemic of eating disorders recently among young American women, although it appears likely that changing sociocultural factors are implicated. It seems doubtful that the cultural preference for thinness, which for women was well established at a time when eating disorders were rare, provides a complete answer. Although the combination of high achievement striving and middle-class socioeconomic origins is consistent from a sociocultural standpoint, it is not clear what role that combination, or either factor separately, plays in the increasing incidence and prevalence of these disorders among young females. For that matter, we do not yet understand the tremendous gender imbalance in the occurrence of these syndromes, although again sociocultural factors are likely to be involved. As many commentators have noted, the expectations our culture now imposes on young women about to assume adult status are intimidating as well as conflictual.

In general, it appears that any sociocultural conditions that markedly increase life stress tend to play havoc with the human organism and lead to an increase in disease as well as other physical and mental problems.

TREATMENTS AND OUTCOMES

Though a particular environmental stressor may have been a key causal factor in the development of a physical illness, removal of this stressor, even com-

bined with learning more effective coping techniques, may be insufficient for recovery if organic changes have taken place; such changes may have become chronic and irreversible.

Treatment therefore begins by assessing the nature and severity of the organic pathology as well as the roles of psychosocial and organic factors in the total causal pattern. In hypertension, for example, the role of dietary factors may far outweigh that of current psychosocial stressors in causation and maintenance. Dietary patterns, however, reflect cultural patterns and attitudes—that all-important lifestyle—that also may have to be reckoned with. Thus a thorough assessment involving the past and present roles of biological, psychosocial, and sociocultural factors is essential to the development of an effective treatment program.

Except for conditions involving serious organic pathology, treatment methods are similar to those for mental disorders in general, discussed in Chapters 16 and 17; the outcomes are likewise reasonably favorable. Instead of going into detail concerning the methods of treatment and the outcomes for each type of disorder, we shall briefly summarize the general treatment measures currently used. More detailed discussion of these therapies can be found in the chapters mentioned.

Biological Measures

Aside from immediate and long-range medical measures, such as emergency care for a hypertensive crisis or bypass surgery for coronary heart disease, biological treatment often involves the use of tranquilizer medications aimed at reducing emotional tension. Such drugs, of course, do not deal with the stressful situation or the coping reactions involved. By alleviating emotional tension and distress symptoms, however, they may provide a person with an opportunity to regroup his or her coping resources. Of course, health professionals must guard against too readily prescribing tranquilizers to insulate patients against everyday stress that they might be better off facing and resolving in some manner. Some patients may also come to rely too much on their prescriptions for easy "cures," and such palliative, symptomatic treatment may divert needed attention from a persistently destructive lifestyle. The development of physiologic dependence on these medications is also a very real danger to be considered.

Other drugs, such as those used to control high blood pressure, are prescribed on a more specific basis. The recent development of the nicotine-delivering skin patch has been a boon to many persons seeking to overcome the smoking habit. There have been reports suggesting that antidepressant medication may have a modest role in the treatment of bulimia nervosa (Hughes et al., 1986; Mitchell et al., 1990), although there are often troublesome side effects (Fluoxetine Bulimia Nervosa Collaborative Study Group, 1992). A change of diet may be indicated in certain diseases, including CHD, migraine headaches, and hypertension. Acupuncture is still considered a largely experimental approach for alleviating certain types of symptoms (such as the pain of tension and migraine headaches) because of problems in disentangling specific therapeutic from nonspecific placebo effects.

Psychosocial Measures

In treating psychosocially mediated physical diseases, one-on-one, nonspecific, verbally oriented psychotherapies—aimed at helping patients understand their personality problems—have been, with certain exceptions, relatively ineffective. The most notable of the exceptions concerns the cognitive-behavioral therapy (CBT) variant, considered below.

It is interesting to note here that, although classical psychoanalytic theory has emphasized associations between emotions and pathological visceral states, it has had little impact on the treatment of psychogenic physical disorders (Agras, 1982). That is, psychoanalytic approaches have not derived treatment methods that can reverse or prevent the disease process in reliable and predictable ways. Also somewhat ironically (in light of its focus on altering physiological states), biofeedback treatment for psy-

chogenic diseases, though showing modest success (for example, in treating headache [Blanchard, 1992, 1994; Blanchard et al., 1990b]), had until recently generally failed to live up to the enthusiasm it generated when first introduced some 25 years ago. In general, its effects proved so small and transient as to lack substantial clinical significance, and they rarely exceeded those that could be obtained in simpler (and cheaper) ways, as by providing systematic relaxation training (Carlson & Hoyle, 1993; Reed, Katkin, & Goldband, 1986).

That situation may now be changing, although it is still not entirely clear that biofeedback is anything more than an elaborate means to teach patients to relax. In any event, biofeedback practitioners and their equipment have become much more sophisticated in the interim, and there have been increasingly favorable reports in recent years regarding efficacy in the behavioral medicine area. For example, Flor and Birbaumer (1993) have reported impressive effectiveness, especially in long-term follow-up, for electromyographic (muscle tonus) biofeedback in the control of musculoskeletal pain. Similarly, some work on biofeedback in respect to the muscle tonus of air passageways in cases of asthma looks promising (Lehrer, Sargunaraj, & Hochron, 1992).

Behavior Therapy Behavior-modification techniques are based on the assumption that because autonomic responses can be learned, they can be unlearned. In one now classic case, the patient, June C., was a 17-year-old girl who had been sneezing every few seconds of her waking hours for a period of five months. Medical experts had been unable to help her, and Kushner, a psychologist, volunteered to attempt treatment by behavior therapy.

Dr. Kushner used a relatively simple, low power electric-shock device, activated by sound—the sound of June's sneezes. Electrodes were attached to her forearm for 30 minutes, and every time she sneezed she got a mild electric shock. After a ten-minute break, the electrodes were put on the other arm. In little more than four hours, June's sneezes, which had been reverberating every 40 seconds, stopped. Since then, she has had only a few ordinary sneezes, none of the dry, racking kind that had been draining her strength for so long. "We hope the absence of sneezes will last," said Dr. Kushner cautiously. "So do I," snapped June. "I never want to see that machine again." (*Time,* June 17, 1966, p. 72)

In a follow-up report, Kushner (1968) stated that a program of maintenance therapy had been instituted, and at the end of 16 months the intractable sneezing had not recurred.

Many studies have examined the effects of various behavioral relaxation techniques on selected stress-related illnesses (Carlson & Hoyle, 1993). Results obtained have been variable, though generally encouraging. For example, simple tension headaches have proved quite amenable to general relaxation treatment procedures (Blanchard, 1992; Blanchard et al., 1990a; Cox, Freundlich, & Meyer, 1975; Tasto & Hinkle, 1973). The same kinds of procedures have not been quite as effective when used to treat essential hypertension (Blanchard et al., 1979; Schwartz, 1978; Surwit, Shapiro, & Good, 1978), especially compared with medication (Wadden et al., 1985).

The potential of behavior therapy alone in treating psychogenic physical disorders remains to be established. A great deal of research is continuing in this area, and it looks promising (Epstein, 1992). It may turn out that the greatest contribution of behavioral approaches will be in the area of altering self-injurious "habits," such as smoking and excessive alcohol use, in systematic programs that teach self-control and lifestyle alteration (Blanchard & Andrasik, 1982; Goldfried & Merbaum, 1973; Weisenberg, 1977). Such programs may have particular importance in recovery from heart attack (Oldenburg et al., 1985). Relatedly, some success has been reported in modifying Type A lifestyles (Thoreson & Powell, 1992).

Cognitive-Behavioral Treatment Cognitive-behavioral therapy (CBT) has shown striking success in the treatment of bulimia nervosa (Agras et al., 1989; Fairburn et al., 1993; Thackwray et al., 1993; Wilfley et al., 1993; Wilson & Fairburn, 1993). Similarly, CBT has proven an effective intervention for headache (Blanchard, 1992; Blanchard et al., 1990a, 1990b) as well as other types of pain (Keefe et al., 1992). CBT-oriented family therapy was markedly more successful than routine pediatric care in alleviating children's complaints of recurrent abdominal pain, as reported in a study by Sanders and colleagues (1994).

Some CBT techniques have also been used for the general purpose of stress reduction. In one study, these techniques were shown to be effective at reducing maladaptive behaviors—such as rushing, impatience, and hostility—characteristic of Type A personalities (Jenni & Wollersheim, 1979). In two studies designed to teach patients how to cope better with life stresses that precipitated headaches, researchers showed that stress-management techniques could decrease the frequency of headaches (Holroyd & Andrasik, 1978; Holroyd, Andrasik, & Westbrook, 1977). More generally, Kobasa (1985) and colleagues have experimented with cognitive-behavioral methods to increase "hardiness," the ability to withstand stressful circumstances and remain healthy. Though we will look at these techniques in more detail in Chapter 17, they basically involve teaching people to use more effective coping skills to lower their experiences of stress and

In sports, behavioral relaxation techniques are used as a means of reducing stress and enhancing performance. Here the University of Wisconsin football team goes through a relaxation exercise before a game.

thus reduce the occurrence of physical symptoms and illness.

Combined Treatment Measures To be treated successfully, psychogenic diseases usually require prompt medical attention for physical symptoms combined with psychosocial therapy to alter or reduce the maladaptive behavioral factors underlying the disorder. The treatment for anorexia nervosa clearly illustrates the need for combined medical and psychological measures. If an anorexia patient's condition becomes life-threatening, extreme measures must be taken to provide nourishment. Typically, hospitalization is necessary. The patient may initially be fed intravenously, but because the disorder is apparently under voluntary control, therapy must ultimately focus not only on weight gain but also on the psychological factors underlying the patient's refusal to eat.

This conclusion seems related to an earlier finding by Halmi, Falk, and Schwartz (1981) in which data suggested that treatment choice did not seem to be a factor in successful weight gain for hospitalized patients: They typically gained weight regardless of the treatment technique employed. Though the obvious goal, both short- and long-term, is to get an anorexic patient to gain weight, therapy for psychological adjustment may be far more important and far more elusive for long-term success. Cognitive-behavioral approaches would seem to hold much promise here, especially in light of their demonstrated success with the related bulimic syndrome, but for some reason they have not been adequately explored in this context (Wilson & Fairburn, 1993). In the end, as Bruch (1988) has noted, lasting therapeutic results in anorexia may involve nothing less than a patient's rediscovery of herself. Such a goal is unlikely to be achieved by merely technical interventions that cause the patient temporarily to put on a few pounds.

Lucas, Duncan, and Piens (1976), in an influential report, described a therapeutic setting developed at the Mayo Clinic and designed to deal with both the physiological and psychological needs of an anorexic patient. Their approach was a combined medical-psychiatric effort, with a coordinated team of professionals who focused on the problems of malnutrition as well as on the psychological family problems in each case. The first step in their treatment efforts was to remove the anorexic person from the home. The individual was placed in an inpatient ward where the nutritional problems were dealt with by staff members who monitored food intake. The patient was given social rewards—such as

time with peers—for appropriate food consumption. Group psychological treatment with a supportive orientation was provided, in which the patient was allowed to express her thoughts, concerns, and fears. While the inpatient treatment program was in progress, the staff also worked with the family in an effort to resolve the family behaviors that might be encouraging the patient's anorexic behavior. This approach thus combined medical efforts with individual and family therapy.

That family therapy should prove an important component in the treatment of anorexia should hardly come as a surprise. More than two decades ago, Minuchin (1974) reported on the apparent effectiveness of family therapy in gaining control over this potentially lethal disorder. Rather than singling out the individual, family therapy examines the whole family structure and patterns of communication. Those structures that are thought to be preventing the patient from developing positive relationships within the family (resulting in anorexia and other types of personal maladjustment) are then targeted for change.

Sociocultural Measures

Sociocultural treatment measures are targeted more toward preventive efforts and are typically applied to selected populations or subcultural groups thought to be at risk for developing disorders. Within these groups, efforts are made to alter certain lifestyle behaviors to reduce the overall level of susceptibility to a disorder. For example, cigarette smoking is associated with increased risk for lung cancer and heart disease; to reduce the general risk of these scourges, persistent efforts have been made to reduce or prevent smoking. Similarly, some correlation appears to exist between high-cholesterol diets and coronary heart disease; and efforts are made to convince people to alter their diets to reduce the rate of coronary heart disease in the total population. Obviously, such intervention efforts involve substantial amounts of persuasion—often employing the media and, in the case of smoking, even restrictive changes in quasi-legal federal regulations (such as airline passenger and workplace smoking policies).

An excellent example of a community-based, prevention-oriented program aimed at reducing the incidence of atherosclerotic disease (a predisposing factor in coronary heart disease) comes from Finland. The North Karelia Project, named after the province in which it was conducted, was a large-scale effort that included 60,000 "subjects" (the province residents) and involved several types of community intervention efforts. Project staff (a) provided information through the mass media—such as a seven-session TV course aimed at reducing smoking—and through public meetings; (b) organized existing health care services and initiated new ones to focus on eliminating high-risk factors by forming self-help groups; (c) trained community leaders, such as teachers, to work on the program; (d) promoted the distribution and sale of healthy, low-fat foods; and (e) devised a method by which they could measure the effects of the program (McAlister et al., 1980; Puska, 1983; Puska et al., 1979).

Early results were encouraging. The intervention program was shown to lower the coronary heart disease risk in the population: Death from heart disease fell 27 percent for men and 42 percent for women. A self-report survey on smoking behavior indicated that participants had reduced their cigarette consumption; significant reductions were also found in population serum cholesterol levels.

As we learn more about the role of biological, psychosocial, and sociocultural factors in the etiology of disease, it becomes increasingly possible to identify high-risk persons and groups—such as heart attack–prone personalities with chronic negative affects, sexually active young singles, and groups living in precarious and rapidly changing life situations. This ability, in turn, enables treatment efforts to focus on early intervention and prevention. In this context, counseling programs—aimed at fostering changes in maladaptive lifestyles and at remedying pathological social conditions—seem eminently worthwhile, indeed life-saving.

 UNRESOLVED ISSUES

on Containing the AIDS Epidemic

As we have seen, many of the remaining problems pertaining to the interface between psychology and physical health involve voluntary choices people make regarding their own behavior. While potential applications of this general principle are widespread, the record of success among our species in eradicating behaviors determined to be risky or dangerous to health and survival must be considered on the whole to be far less than adequate. Our accomplishments respecting the spread of the deadly HIV-1 (AIDS) virus, to date, are no exception.

As of early 1995, the cumulative number of cases of AIDS diagnosed in the United States was nearly one-half million; there may be as many as 1.5 million more persons infected, but as yet asymptomatic. Because of the nature of this virus and its profile of transmission from a carrier to the next victim, the rate of development of new cases of full-blown AIDS is expected to continue to accelerate geometrically, as it has since the disease was first recognized among a small group of gay men only a few short years ago. In the absence of some astounding biomedical breakthrough, or what would constitute an at least equally astounding social revolution in the manner in which Americans deal with sexuality, a health catastrophe will shortly be upon us.

The extent of this challenge is made clear in recent reviews of the evidence provided by Kelly and Murphy (1992) and Fisher and Fisher (1992). Kelly and Murphy note that real progress has been made in the reduction of risky sexual behavior among gay men in larger cities, especially among those who acknowledge their homosexuality and identify with the gay subculture. Yet even in this group, they report, excessive numbers of "relapses" (20–40 percent) occur where alcohol is abused or under conditions of "affectional bonding." Consistent attention to preventive measures (e.g., use of a condom in anal intercourse) is greatest among white, middle-aged, well-educated men of high socioeconomic status; risky behavior continues to be frequent among the young, among minority gays, and among those who do not identify themselves as homosexuals. In smaller cities, where the gay community is likely to be less well organized, neglect of preventive measures continues to be alarmingly high.

There is some evidence in the data reviewed by Kelly and Murphy (1992) that intravenous drug users, as a group, have become more cautious about sharing needles and syringes, thus decreasing the likelihood that they will become infected; unfortunately, there is little evidence that, as a group, they are showing a similar concern for their sexual partners.

There remains a threatening and escalating problem with heterosexual transmission of HIV-1 (Fisher & Fisher, 1992), and the "second wave" of AIDS deaths will probably first affect inner-city heterosexuals (Kelly & Murphy, 1992). Seemingly in confirmation of this projection, Kalichman and colleagues (1993) interviewed 272 women at large city mass transit terminals, reporting that 22 percent of them, overall, admitted recently engaging in high-risk sexual behavior. The nonminority women who had done so tended to acknowledge concern about their risk; high-risk minority women, on the other hand, expressed no more concern than did the women reporting low-risk status. In general, there is very little evidence of altered sexual practices among sexually active heterosexual adults (Kelly & Murphy, 1992), a conclusion that also seems to hold for high school and college students (Fisher & Fisher, 1992).

The facts are abundantly and frighteningly clear. Short of some sort of striking scientific triumph in biomedical research, the devastation that has already exacted an excruciating toll in the male homosexual community will become commonplace in the heterosexual population; estimates indicate that well over a million members of this much larger population are already infected and will die, on average, eight years following their encounter with the HIV-1 retrovirus. New infections, the evidence shows, continue to escalate even though the means of prevention are known and readily available. These require modest levels of forethought, judgment, restraint, and perhaps the risk of embarrassment; given the stakes involved, which include a protracted, agonizing, and as of now (with infection) certain death, they would not appear excessively demanding in terms of self-discipline. What, then, has gone wrong?

We do not pretend to have a comprehensive answer to this vital question. Undoubtedly we need a much-enhanced effort to find ways to penetrate into less advantaged high-risk groups with the life-saving information that has already had favorable effects on the behavior of the more advantaged, such as well-educated gay men. We strongly suspect, however, that exposure to and even assimilation of relevant preventive information will not in itself assure behavioral compliance. Some people will continue to engage in high-risk behavior while "knowing" that is what they are doing. Personality factors doubtless come into play in making such decisions. We know, for example, that some people, such as those having an antisocial personality organization (Chapter 9), are far more prone to take death-defying risks than is the average person; nor is it likely that such a person, once infected, will show compassion about possibly infecting sexual partners.

There is another personality factor probably involved—the trait of optimism, specifically maladaptively excessive optimism, which, as we have already noted in this chapter, is known to be implicated in health-endangering behavior. Since infection is far from certain, even during sexual intercourse with an infected person, the risk-denial optimist manages to convince himself or herself that the real risk is low to nonexistent. Complicating this scenario is the likelihood that the denier will: (a) fail to have his or her presumed seronegativity tested, (b) fail to appreciate the significance of any early AIDS-related symp-

toms, and (c) if infected, unknowingly go on to infect subsequent sexual partners.

Excessively optimistic denial of the seriousness of the AIDS threat has not been limited to individuals. It was common among government and medical officials and agencies (e.g., blood banks), costing us much time and many lives, during the early phases of what has now, in the 1990s, become an epidemic too advanced and widespread to be satisfactorily contained by ordinary public health measures. At this stage, the challenge would appear ultimately to be one of individual choice and behavior.

 ## SUMMARY

Research has clearly established that emotional factors influence the development of many physical disorders and play an important role in the course of disease processes. The official Axis I diagnostic classification, Psychological Factors Affecting Medical Condition, is an acknowledgment of our enhanced appreciation of the widespread nature of such effects. Likewise, the relatively new field of behavioral medicine has its origins in the general recognition of these influences and seeks to extend our conception of disease beyond the traditional medical preoccupation with the physical breakdown of organs and organ systems.

At the most general level, the influence of psychological variables on health is seen in excessive autonomic nervous system responses to stressor conditions, sometimes resulting directly in organ damage. It is also seen in the increasing evidence that psychosocial challenges, including negative emotional states, can impair the immune system's ability to respond, leaving a person more vulnerable to disease-producing agents. Damaging habits and lifestyles also enhance risk for physical disease, as in the notable instance of AIDS infection, discussed in the preceding "Unresolved Issues" section.

Psychogenic vulnerability to particular diseases may be somewhat specific in nature, although not so specific as early doctrines implied. The distressingly common coronary heart disease and the increasingly common eating disorders known as anorexia nervosa and bulimia nervosa seem to be cases in point. The Type A behavior pattern, or rather one or more of its components, is now well-established as an independent risk factor for CHD, and the two eating disorders have been somewhat less compellingly associated with deficiencies in achieving autonomy. Evidence relating to specific psychosocial factors in the etiology of other physical diseases—notably hypertension and recurrent headaches—continues to show promise.

Biological factors, including genetic vulnerabilities, excessive autonomic reactivity, and possible organ weaknesses, must of course continue to be given prominent attention in the search for etiological patterns. They must also be a part of treatment considerations whenever physical disease occurs, regardless of strong evidence of psychological contributions to its development.

A common factor in much psychosocially mediated physical disease is inadequacy in an individual's coping resources for managing stressful life circumstances. Our culture seems particularly rich in providing these challenges, whereas we have made only limited progress in learning how to instill hardiness in our population and thereby prevent many needless physical breakdowns. Psychosocial treatment measures, typically used (if at all) only after illness is discovered, show considerable promise. However, the more exciting challenge will be to devise more, and more effective, psychosocial interventions that prevent breakdowns in the first place.

KEY TERMS

behavioral medicine (p. 279)
psychogenic illnesses (p. 279)
health psychology (p. 280)
placebo effect (p. 282)
immune system (p. 284)
antigen (p. 284)
psychoneuroimmunology (p. 286)
coronary heart disease (CHD) (p. 288)

Type A behavior pattern (p. 289)
anorexia nervosa (p. 292)
bulimia nervosa (p. 294)
hypertension (p. 297)
essential hypertension (p. 297)
migraine (p. 298)
simple tension headaches (p. 299)
biofeedback (p. 299)
secondary gains (p. 304)

9

PERSONALITY DISORDERS

Inez Walker, Untitled. Walker (1911–1990) was born on a farm in South Carolina. As a young woman she migrated to the North, where she worked in a pickle plant and in apple orchards. In 1970 she was convicted of criminally negligent homicide for killing a man whom she said had abused her. In prison she began to draw, primarily portraits of women. Released from prison, she was occasionally an inpatient at a New York state mental hospital. She died of cancer in 1990.

Healthy people continue to grow and change throughout their lives. Successful adjustment through the life cycle is, after all, mostly a matter of flexibly adapting to the changing demands, opportunities, and limitations associated with different stages of life. Nevertheless, a person's broadly characteristic traits, coping styles, and ways of interacting in the social environment emerge during childhood and normally crystalize into established patterns by the end of adolescence or early adulthood. These patterns constitute the individual's *personality*—the unique pattern of traits and behaviors that characterize the individual.

For most of us, our adult personality is attuned to the demands of society. In other words, we readily comply with societal expectations. In contrast, there are certain people who, although not necessarily displaying obvious symptoms of an Axis I disorder, nevertheless seem somehow ill-equipped to become fully functioning members of society. For these individuals, personality formation has led to some traits that are so inflexible and maladaptive that they are unable to perform adequately at least some of the varied roles expected of them by their societies. These people might be diagnosed as having **personality disorders,** which were formerly known as *character disorders*.

Personality disorders typically do not stem from debilitating reactions to stress, as in post-traumatic stress disorder or many cases of major depression. Rather, the disorders to be examined here stem largely from the gradual development of inflexible and distorted personality patterns, which result in persistently maladaptive ways of perceiving, thinking about, and relating to the world. These maladaptive approaches usually significantly impair at least some aspects of functioning and in some cases cause a good deal of subjective distress.

The category of personality disorders is broad, with behavioral problems that differ greatly in form and severity. In the milder cases we find people who generally function adequately but who would be described by their relatives, friends, or associates as troublesome, eccentric, or difficult to get to know. They have characteristic ways of approaching situations and people that make them either have difficulties developing close relationships with others, or have difficulties getting along with those with whom they have close relationships. However, they are often quite capable or even gifted in some ways. In more severe cases, we find people whose extreme and often unethical "acting out" against society makes them less able to function in a normal setting; many are incarcerated in prisons or maximum security hospitals, although some are able to manipulate others and keep from getting caught.

There is not a great deal of evidence on the prevalence of personality disorders, in part because many people with such disorders never come in contact with mental health or legal agencies. Many individuals with a subset of the personality disorders are identified through the correctional system or through court-ordered psychological evaluations stemming from family problems such as physical abuse. Others eventually show up in alcohol treatment programs or in psychiatric emergency rooms after a suicide attempt. Nevertheless, estimates of the prevalence of one serious personality disorder, antisocial personality, were reported in a very large epidemiological study to be between 2.1 and 3.3 percent in the three study sites (Robins et al., 1984). More recent estimates concur that about 2–3 percent of individuals in the United States and Canada have antisocial personality disorder (Weissman, 1993). Weissman's (1993) recent comprehensive summary of epidemiological studies of all the personality disorders concluded that about 10–13 percent of the population meet the criteria for a personality disorder at some point in their lifetime. Not surprisingly, personality disorders are more common among psychiatric patients.

In the 15 years since DSM-III first identified personality disorders on a separate axis of disorders, there has been a great deal of research directed at understanding their nature and some research about how they develop. In this chapter, we will consider each of the types of disordered personalities that have been identified and then examine one of them—antisocial personality—in greater detail to give you an idea of the extensive research in this area.

Personality disorders are often associated with a number of the Axis I disorders that have been and will be considered in other chapters, such as anxiety disorders (Chapters 4 and 5), mood disorders (Chapter 6), alcoholism (Chapter 10), sexual deviations (Chapter 11), and delinquency (Chapter 14). The behavioral patterns associated with personality disorders are in some cases also similar to those related to head injuries or other brain pathologies. In such cases, these behaviors are evidence of organic brain disorders, which we consider in Chapter 13. These qualifications aside, let us move on to an examination of personality disorders.

PERSONALITY DISORDERS

Clinical Features of Personality Disorders

People with personality disorders often cause at least as much difficulty in the lives of others as in their own lives. Other people tend to find the behavior of individuals with personality disorders confusing, exasperating, unpredictable, and, in varying degrees, unacceptable—although rarely as bizarre or out of contact with reality as that of people with psychotic disorders. Some people with personality disorders experience a good deal of emotional suffering, although others do not, at least not obviously. Their persistent behavioral deviations seem to be intrinsic to their personalities and they have difficulty taking part in mutually respectful and satisfying social relationships. Whatever the particular trait patterns affected individuals have developed (obstinacy, covert hostility, suspiciousness, or fear of rejection, for example), these patterns color their reactions to each new situation and lead to a repetition of the same maladaptive behaviors. For example, a dependent person may wear out a relationship with someone, such as a spouse, by incessant and extraordinary demands; after that partner leaves, the person may go immediately into another dependent relationship and repeat the behavior. Thus personality disorders are marked by considerable consistency over time, with no apparent learning from previous troubles.

In the past, these persistent disorders were thought to center on personality characteristics referred to as *temperament* or *character traits,* suggesting the possibility of hereditary or constitutional influences. The possibility of genetic transmission of a liability for some of these disorders, particularly antisocial and schizotypal personality, has been receiving strong support in the research literature. More recently, however, environmental and social factors, particularly learning-based habit patterns and maladaptive cognitive styles, have been receiving more attention as possible causal factors. Many of these maladaptive habits and cognitive styles may originate in disturbed parent-child attachment relationships. Early attachment relationships are thought by developmental psychologists to create models for children of what adult relationships should be like. If early models are not healthy, this may predispose the child to a pattern of personality development that can lead to the diagnosis of personality disorder later in life.

The definition of personality disorders in DSM-IV is as follows:

Personality traits are enduring patterns of perceiving, relating to, and thinking about the environment and oneself, that are exhibited in a wide range of important social and personal contexts. Only when personality traits are inflexible and maladaptive and cause significant functional impairment or subjective distress do they constitute Personality Disorders. The essential feature of a Personality Disorder is an enduring pattern of inner experience and behavior that deviates markedly from the expectations of the individual's culture and is manifested in at least two of the following areas: cognition, affectivity, interpersonal functioning, or impulse control (Criterion A). This enduring pattern is inflexible and pervasive across a broad range of personal and social situations (Criterion B) and leads to clinically significant distress or impairment in social, occupational, or other important areas of functioning (Criterion C). The pattern is stable and of long duration, and its onset can be traced back at least to adolescence or early adulthood (Criterion D). The pattern is not better accounted for as a manifestation or consequence of another mental disorder (Criterion E). Specific diagnostic criteria are also provided for each of the Personality Disorders. (American Psychiatric Association, 1994, p. 630)

In the DSM-IV, as in DSM-III and DSM-III-R, the personality disorders are coded on a separate axis, Axis II, because they are regarded as being different enough from the standard psychiatric syndromes (which are coded on Axis I) to warrant separate classification. As already noted, Axis II represents long-standing personality traits that are thought to be inflexible and maladaptive and that cause social or occupational adjustment problems or personal distress. These reaction patterns are so deeply embedded in the personality structure (for whatever reason) that they are extremely resistant to modification. Although a person might be diagnosed on Axis II only, he or she could instead be diagnosed on both Axes I and II, which would reflect the existence of both a currently active mental disorder and a more chronic, underlying personality disorder.

A special caution is in order regarding the personality disorders. Perhaps more misdiagnoses occur here than in any other categories. There are a number of reasons for this problem. One is that personality disorders are not as sharply defined as most Axis I diagnostic categories. Although DSM-IV includes criteria that must be met for a particular personality disorder diagnosis, these criteria are often not very precise or easy to follow in practice. For example, it may be difficult to diagnose reliably whether someone meets a criterion for dependent personality disorder such as "goes to excessive length to obtain nurturance and support from others," or "has difficulty making everyday decisions without an excessive amount of advice and reassurance from others." Because the criteria for personality disorders are defined by inferred traits or consistent patterns of behavior rather than by objective behavioral standards, more judgment is required from the clinician making the diagnosis than is the case for many Axis I disorders. Nevertheless, with the recent development of semi-structured interviews for the diagnosis of personality disorders, diagnostic reliability has increased substantially. However, because the different structured interviews often result in different diagnoses (e.g., Oldham et al., 1992; Oldham, 1991; Skodol et al., 1991), there are still substantial problems with the reliability and validity of these diagnoses (Livesley & Jackson, 1991).

A second problem is that the diagnostic categories are not mutually exclusive: People often show characteristics of more than one personality disorder (Blashfield & Breen, 1989; Gorton & Akhtar, 1990; Widiger & Rogers, 1989; Widiger, 1993; Zimmerman & Coryell, 1989). For example, someone might show the suspiciousness, mistrust, avoidance of blame, and guardedness of paranoid personality disorder, along with the withdrawal, absence of friends, and aloofness that characterize schizoid personality disorder. It should be noted, however, that this problem also occurs with Axis I disorders, where many individuals also qualify for more than one diagnosis.

A third reason for diagnostic problems is that the personality characteristics that define personality disorders are *dimensional* in nature—that is, they range from normal expressions to pathological exaggerations and can be found, on a smaller scale and less intensely expressed, in many normal people (Clark, 1992; Livesley, Jackson, & Schroeder, 1992; Livesley et al., 1994; Widiger, 1992). For example, liking one's work and being conscientious about the details of one's job does not make one an obsessive-compulsive personality, nor does being economically dependent automatically make a spouse a dependent personality. Applying diagnostic labels to people who are in some cases functioning reasonably well is always risky; it is especially so where the diagnosis involves judgment about characteristics that are also common in normal people.

These problems can lead to unreliability of diagnoses and in fact they often do (Gorton & Akhtar, 1990). Someday a more objective way of diagnosing the personality disorders may be devised. In the meantime, however, the categorical system of symptoms and traits will continue to be used with the recognition that it is more dependent on the observer's judgment than one might wish. Several theorists have attempted to deal with the problems inherent in categorizing personality disorders (Clark, 1992; Cloninger, 1987; Livesley et al., 1994; Millon, 1981; Tyrer, 1988; Widiger & Frances, 1985; Widiger, 1992); however, no clearly consistent theoretical view on the classification of personality disorders currently exists. With these cautions, we will look now at the elusive and often exasperating clinical features of the personality disorders. It is important to bear in mind, however, that we will be describing the prototype for each personality disorder. In reality, it is rare for any individual to fit these "ideal" descriptions. (See also Chapter 1.)

Types of Personality Disorders

The DSM-IV personality disorders are grouped into three clusters on the basis of similarities among the disorders. As already noted, many people meet the criteria for more than one personality disorder, including ones from different clusters.

Cluster A includes paranoid, schizoid, and schizotypal personality disorders. People with these disorders often seem odd or eccentric, with unusual behavior ranging from distrust and suspiciousness to social detachment.

Cluster B includes histrionic, narcissistic, antisocial, and borderline personality disorders. Individuals with these disorders have in common a tendency to be dramatic, emotional, and erratic. Their impulsive behavior, often involving antisocial activities, is more colorful, more forceful, and more likely to bring them into contact with mental health or legal authorities than the behaviors characterizing disorders in the first cluster.

Cluster C includes avoidant, dependent, and obsessive-compulsive personality disorders. In contrast to the other clusters, anxiety and fearfulness are often part of these disorders, making it difficult in some cases to distinguish them from anxiety-based disorders. People with these disorders, because of their anxieties, are more likely to seek help.

Two additional personality disorders—depressive and passive-aggressive personality disorders—are listed in DSM-IV in an appendix under the heading *proposed diagnostic categories needing further study.* (See HIGHLIGHT 9.1 for a summary of personality disorder diagnoses.)

Paranoid Personality Disorder Individuals with **paranoid personality disorder** have a pervasive suspiciousness and distrust of others. They tend to see themselves as blameless, instead finding fault for their own mistakes and failures in others—even to the point of ascribing evil motives to others. Such people are constantly expecting trickery and looking for clues to validate their expectations, while disregarding all evidence to the contrary. They are often preoccupied with doubts about the loyalty of friends, leading to a reluctance to confide in others. They also may be hypersensitive, as indicated by a tendency to read threatening meanings into benign remarks. They also commonly bear grudges and are unwilling to forgive perceived insults and slights. It is important to keep in mind that paranoid personalities are not usually psychotic; that is, most of the time they are in clear contact with reality, although they may experience transient psychotic symptoms (Thompson-Pope & Turkat, 1993). Another disorder, paranoid schizophrenia, to be discussed in Chapter 12, shares some symptoms found in paranoid personality. Paranoid schizophrenics have additional problems, however, including more persistent loss of reality contact and extreme cognitive and behavioral disorganization, such as delusions and hallucinations.

The following case demonstrates well the behaviors characteristic of paranoid personality disorder:

A 40-year-old construction worker believes that his coworkers do not like him and fears that someone might let his scaffolding slip in order to cause him injury on the job. This concern followed a recent disagreement on the lunch line when the patient felt that a coworker was sneaking ahead and complained to him. He began noticing his new "enemy" laughing with the other men and often wondered if he were the butt of their mockery. He thought of confronting them, but decided that the whole issue might just be in his own mind, and that he might get himself into more trouble by taking any action.

The patient offers little spontaneous information, sits tensely in the chair, is wide-eyed and carefully tracks all movements in the room. He reads between the lines of the interviewer's questions, feels criticized, and imagines that the interviewer is siding with his coworkers. He makes it clear that he would not have come to the personnel clinic at all except for his need for sleep medication.

He was a loner as a boy and felt that other children would form cliques and be mean to him. He did poorly in school, but blamed his teachers—he claimed that they preferred girls or boys who were "sissies." He dropped out of

Summary of Personality Disorders

Personality Disorder	Characteristics
Cluster A	
Paranoid	Suspiciousness and mistrust of others; tendency to see self as blameless; on guard for perceived attacks by others
Schizoid	Impaired social relationships; inability and lack of desire to form attachments to others
Schizotypal	Peculiar thought patterns; oddities of perception and speech that interfere with communication and social interaction
Cluster B	
Histrionic	Self-dramatization; overconcern with attractiveness; tendency to irritability and temper outbursts if attention seeking is frustrated
Narcissistic	Grandiosity; preoccupation with receiving attention; self-promoting; lack of empathy
Antisocial	Lack of moral or ethical development; inability to follow approved models of behavior; deceitfulness; shameless manipulation of others; history of conduct problems as a child
Borderline	Impulsiveness, inappropriate anger; drastic mood shifts; chronic feelings of boredom; attempts at self-mutilation or suicide
Cluster C	
Avoidant	Hypersensitiveness to rejection or social derogation; shyness; insecurity in social interaction and initiating relationships
Dependent	Difficulty in separating in relationships; discomfort at being alone; subordination of needs in order to keep others involved in a relationship; indecisiveness
Obsessive-compulsive	Excessive concern with order, rules, and trivial details; perfectionistic; lack of expressiveness and warmth; difficulty in relaxing and having fun
Provisional Categories	
Passive-aggressive	Negativistic attitudes and passive resistance to adequate performance expressed through indirect means, such as complaining, being sullen and argumentative, expressing envy and resentment toward those who are more fortunate.
Depressive	Pervasive depressive cognitions. Persistent unhappiness or dejection. Feeling of inadequacy, guilt, and self-criticism.

school, and has since been a hard and effective worker; but he feels he never gets the breaks. He believes that he has been discriminated against because of his Catholicism, but can offer little convincing evidence. He gets on poorly with bosses and coworkers, is unable to appreciate joking around, and does best in situations where he can work and have lunch alone. He has switched jobs many times because he felt he was being mistreated.

The patient is distant and demanding with his family. His children call him "Sir" and know that it is wise to be "seen but not heard" when he is around. At home he can never comfortably sit still and is always busy at some chore or another. He prefers not to have people visit his house and becomes restless when his wife is away visiting others. (Spitzer et al., 1981, p. 37)

This pervasive suspiciousness and mistrust of other people leave a paranoid personality prone to numerous difficulties and hurts in interpersonal relationships. These difficulties typically lead the person to be continually "on guard" for perceived attacks by others.

Schizoid Personality Disorder Individuals with **schizoid personality disorder** usually show an inability to form social relationships and a lack of interest in doing so. Consequently they typically do not have good friends, with the possible exception of close relatives. Such people are unable to express their feelings and are seen by others as cold and distant; they often lack social skills and can be classified as loners, with solitary interests and occupations. They tend not to take pleasure in many activities, including sexual activity. Commonly they may even appear indifferent to praise or criticism from others. More generally, they are not very emotionally reactive, rarely experiencing strong positive or negative emotions, which contributes to their appearing cold and aloof.

Early theorists considered a schizoid personality to be a likely precursor to the development of schizophrenia. This viewpoint has been challenged in recent times, however (Siever, 1986). Research on the possible genetic transmission of schizoid personality has failed to establish either a link between the two disorders or the hereditary basis of schizoid personality (Kety et al., 1975; Slater, 1953). Siever (1986), in his theoretical comparison of schizoid and schizotypal personality disorders (to be considered in the next section), considered the schizotypal personality to be more closely linked genetically to schizophrenia. Two more recent reviews of the literature also suggest that evidence for a genetic link between schizotypal personality disorder and schizophrenia is much stronger (Nigg & Goldsmith, 1994; Thompson-Pope & Turkat, 1993).

The following case of a schizoid personality illustrates a fairly severe personality problem in a man who had been functioning adequately as judged both by occupational criteria and by his own standards of "happiness." When he sought help, it was at the encouragement of his supervisor and his physician.

People with schizoid personality disorder are often loners interested in solitary pursuits, such as assembling odd collections of objects.

Bill D., a highly intelligent but quite introverted and withdrawn 33-year-old computer analyst, was referred for psychological evaluation by his physician, who was concerned that Bill might be depressed and unhappy. At the suggestion of his supervisor, Bill had recently gone to the physician for rather vague physical complaints and because of his gloomy outlook on life. Bill had virtually no contact with other people. He lived alone in his apartment, worked in a small office by himself, and usually saw no one at work except for the occasional visits of his supervisor to give him new work and pick up completed projects. He ate lunch by himself and about once a week, on nice days, went to the zoo for his lunch break.

Bill was a lifelong loner; as a child he had had few friends and always had preferred solitary activities over family outings (he was the oldest of five children). In high school he had never dated and in college had gone out with a woman only once—and that was with a group of students after a game. He had been active in sports, however, and had played varsity football in both high school and college. In college he had spent a lot of time with one relatively close friend—mostly drinking. However, this friend now lived in another city.

Bill reported rather matter-of-factly that he had a hard time making friends; he never knew what to say in a conversation. On a number of occasions he had thought of becoming friends with other people but simply couldn't think of the right words, so "the conversation just died."

He reported that he had given some thought lately to changing his life in an attempt to be more "positive," but it never had seemed worth the trouble. It was easier for him not to make the effort because he became embarrassed when someone tried to talk with him. He was happiest when he was alone.

In short, the central problem of the schizoid personality is an inability to form attachments to other people. It is as though the needs for love, belonging, and approval fail to develop in these people—or if they had been there earlier in development they had somehow disappeared at an early stage. The result is a profound barrenness of interpersonal experience.

Schizotypal Personality Disorder Individuals with **schizotypal personality disorder** not only have pervasive social and interpersonal deficits; they also have cognitive and perceptual distortions and eccentricities in their communication and behavior. Although both schizotypal and schizoid personalities are characterized by social isolation and withdrawal, the two can be distinguished in that schizotypal personality—but not schizoid personality—also involves oddities of thought, perception, or speech. Although reality contact is usually maintained, highly personalized and superstitious thinking are characteristic of people with schizotypal personality, and under extreme stress they may experience *transient* psychotic symptoms (Thompson-Pope & Turkat, 1993). Indeed, they often believe that they have magical powers and may engage in magical rituals. Their oddities in thinking, talking, and other behaviors are similar to those often seen in more severe forms in schizophrenic patients; in fact, they are sometimes first diagnosed as exhibiting simple or latent schizophrenia. Widiger, Frances, and Trull (1987) found that the symptoms of cognitive malfunctioning included in schizotypal personality disorder were more useful in making a clinical diagnosis than were symptoms of social isolation, inadequate rapport, and social anxiety. The cognitive symptoms that were useful in making the diagnosis included cognitive perceptual problems, magical thinking (for example, belief in telepathy and superstitions), ideas of reference (the belief that conversations or gestures of others have special meaning or personal significance), odd speech, and suspicious beliefs (see also Thompson-Pope & Turkat, 1993).

The prevalence of this disorder in the general population is estimated at about 3 percent (DSM-

IV, 1994). A genetic or biological association with schizophrenia is widely suspected (Meehl, 1990a; Nigg & Goldsmith, 1994; Siever, 1986; Siever et al., 1990; Thompson-Pope & Turkat, 1993). Indeed, several studies have documented that patients with schizotypal personality disorder (Siever et al., 1990), as well as college students with schizotypal personality disorder (Lencz et al., 1993), have deficits in smooth pursuit eye-tracking that are common in schizophrenia (see Chapter 12). In fact the term *schizotypal* is an abbreviation for "schizophrenic genotype" (Rado, 1956), and many consider it to be part of a spectrum of schizophrenia that often occurs in the first-degree relatives of schizophrenics (Nigg & Goldsmith, 1994; Thompson-Pope & Turkat, 1993). The following case is fairly typical:

The patient is a 32-year-old unmarried, unemployed woman on welfare who complains that she feels "spacey." Her feelings of detachment have gradually become stronger and more uncomfortable. For many hours each day she feels as if she were watching herself move through life, and the world around her seems unreal. She feels especially strange when she looks into a mirror. For many years she has felt able to read people's minds by a "kind of clairvoyance I don't understand." According to her, several people in her family apparently also have this ability. She is preoccupied by the thought that she has some special mission in life, but is not sure what it is; she is not particularly religious. She is very self-conscious in public, often feels that people are paying special attention to her, and sometimes thinks that strangers cross the street to avoid her. She has no friends, feels lonely and isolated, and spends much of each day lost in fantasies or watching TV soap operas.

The patient speaks in a vague, abstract, digressive manner, generally just missing the point, but she is never incoherent. She seems shy, suspicious, and afraid she will be criticized. She has no gross loss of reality testing, such as hallucinations or delusions. She has never had treatment for emotional problems. She has had occasional jobs, but drifts away from them because of lack of interest. (Spitzer et al., 1989, pp. 173–174).

The distinguishing feature of a schizotypal person is peculiar thought patterns, which are in turn associated with a loosening—although not a complete rupture—of ties to reality. The individual appears to lack some key integrative competence of the sort that enables most of us to "keep it all together" and move our lives toward some personal goals. As a result, many basic abilities, such as being able to communicate clearly, are never fully mastered, and the person tends to drift aimlessly and unproductively through the adult years.

Histrionic Personality Disorder   Individuals with **histrionic personality disorder** typically show excessive attention-seeking behavior and emotionality. They tend to feel unappreciated if not the center of attention, and their lively and dramatic styles often assure that they can charm others into attending to them. But these qualities do not lead to stable and satisfying relationships because others tire of providing this level of attention. In seeking attention, their appearance and behavior are often quite theatrical and emotional, as well as sexually provocative and seductive. Their style of speech may be dramatic but is also quite impressionistic and lacking in detail. They are often highly suggestible and consider relationships to be closer than they are. Their sexual adjustment is usually poor and their interpersonal relationships are stormy because they may attempt to control their partner through seductive behavior and emotional manipulation, but also show a good deal of dependence. Usually they are considered to be self-centered, vain, and overconcerned about the approval of others, who see them as overly reactive,

shallow, and insincere. The prevalence in the general population is estimated at 2–3 percent (DSM-IV, 1994). The following case illustrates the histrionic personality pattern:

> Pam, a 22-year-old secretary, was causing numerous problems for her supervisor and coworkers. According to her supervisor, Pam was unable to carry out her duties without constant guidance. Seemingly helpless and dependent, she would overreact to minor events and job pressures with irritability and occasional temper tantrums. If others placed unwanted demands on her, she would complain of physical problems, such as nausea or headaches; furthermore, she frequently missed work altogether. To top it off, Pam was flirtatious and often demandingly seductive toward the men in the office.
>
> As a result of her frequent absenteeism and her disruptive behavior in the office, Pam's supervisor and the personnel manager recommended that she be given a psychological evaluation and counseling in the Employee Assistance Program. She went to the first appointment with the psychologist but failed to return for follow-up visits. She was finally given a discharge notice after several incidents of temper outbursts at work.

People with histrionic personality disorder often engage in seductive and attention-seeking behavior—appearing in public in scanty clothing, for example.

Both Pam's physical complaints and her seductive behavior are examples of attention-seeking tactics commonly found in the histrionic personality pattern. When these tactics fail to bring about the desired result, irritability and temper outbursts typically follow.

Narcissistic Personality Disorder Individuals with **narcissistic personality disorder** show an exaggerated sense of self-importance, a preoccupation with being admired, and a lack of empathy for the feelings of others. Ronningstam and Gunderson (1989) reported that grandiosity was the most stable and generalizable criterion for diagnosing narcissistic patients. Their grandiosity is manifested by a strong tendency to overestimate their abilities and accomplishments, while often concurrently underestimating the abilities and accomplishments of others. Their sense of entitlement is frequently a source of astonishment to others, although they themselves seem to regard their lavish expectations as merely what they deserve. They behave in stereotypical ways (for example, with constant self-references and bragging) to gain the acclaim and recognition that feeds their grandiose expectations and their fantasies of unlimited success, power, beauty, or brilliance. Because they believe they are so special they often think they can only be understood by other high-status people, or should only associate with such people. These tactics, to those around them, appear to be excessive efforts to make themselves look good.

Narcissistic personalities share another central element—they are unable to take the perspective of others, to see things other than "through their own eyes." In more general terms, they lack the capacity for empathy, which is an essential ingredient for mature relationships. In this sense all children begin life as narcissists and only gradually acquire a perspective-taking ability. For reasons that are far from entirely understood, some children do not show normal progress in this respect, and indeed, in extreme cases, show little or none. The latter may grow up to become adult narcissistic personalities. Along with the lack of empathy, narcissistic persons not uncommonly take advantage of others to achieve their own ends and often show arrogant, snobbish, or haughty behaviors and attitudes. Finally, they are often very envious of other people (Kernberg, 1975), or believe that other people are envious of them (DSM-IV, 1994).

Most researchers and clinicians believe that people with narcissistic personality disorder have a very fragile sense of self-esteem under all their grandiosity. This may be why they are often preoccupied with what others think, why they show such a great need for admiration, and why they are so preoccupied with fantasies of outstanding achievement. Not surprisingly, they are also very sensitive to criticism, which may leave them feeling humiliated or empty. The following case is illustrative:

A 25-year-old, single graduate student complains to his psychoanalyst of difficulty completing his Ph.D. in English Literature and expresses concerns about his relationships with women. He believes that his thesis topic may profoundly increase the level of understanding in his discipline and make him famous, but so far he has not been able to get past the third chapter. His mentor does not seem sufficiently impressed with his ideas, and the patient is furious at him, but also self-doubting and ashamed. He blames his mentor for his lack of progress, and thinks that he deserves more help with his grand idea, that his mentor should help with some of the research. The patient brags about his creativity and complains that other people are "jealous" of his insight. He is very envious of students who are moving along faster than he and regards them as "dull drones and ass-kissers." He prides himself on the brilliance of his class participation and imagines someday becoming a great professor.

He becomes rapidly infatuated with women and has powerful and persistent fantasies about each new woman he meets, but after several experiences of sexual intercourse feels disappointed and finds them dumb, clinging, and physically repugnant. He has many "friends," but they turn over quickly, and no one relationship lasts very long. People get tired of his continual self-promotion and lack of consideration of them. For example, he was lonely at Christmas and insisted that his best friend stay in town rather than visit his family. The friend refused, criticizing the patient's self-centeredness; and the patient, enraged, decided never to see this friend again. (Spitzer et al., 1981, pp. 52–53)

Narcissistic personality disorder may be more frequently observed in men than in women (Akhtar & Thompson, 1982; American Psychiatric Association, 1994), although not all studies show this. Compared with some of the other personality disorders, it is thought to be relatively rare, with estimates that it occurs in about 1 percent of the population.

The term "narcissistic personality disorder" comes from the Greek legend of Narcissus. Narcissus was a beautiful boy who fell in love with his own image in the water and pined away after it. In this painting the artist Caravaggio shows Narcissus admiring himself.

Given the overlapping features between histrionic and narcissistic personality disorders, Widiger and Trull (1993) attempt to summarize the major differences in this way: "The histrionic tends to be more emotional and dramatic than the narcissist, and whereas both may be promiscuous, the narcissistic is more dispassionately exploitative, while the histrionic is more overtly needy. Both will be exhibitionistic, but the histrionic seeks attention, whereas the narcissistic seeks admiration" (p. 388).

Individuals with narcissistic personality patterns may not seek psychological treatment because they view themselves as nearly perfect and in no need of change. Those who do enter treatment often do so at the insistence of another person, such as a husband or wife, and may terminate therapy prematurely—particularly if their therapist is confrontational and questions their self-serving behavior. Most of what is known about narcissistic personality disorder has emerged from psychoanalytic therapy and later ego-analytic writings (Kernberg, 1984, 1985; Kohut & Wolff, 1978). The psychodynamic treatment approach may be the most viable therapy, because a long-term treatment relationship seems

needed to bring about changes in these patients' persistent self-oriented patterns (Kernberg, 1985). However, there are unfortunately no controlled studies to date documenting the effectiveness of this (or any other) form of treatment for narcissistic personality disorder.

Antisocial Personality Disorder Individuals with **antisocial personality disorder** continually violate and show disregard for the rights of others through deceitful, aggressive, or antisocial behavior, typically without remorse or loyalty to anyone. They tend to be impulsive, irritable, and aggressive, and show a pattern of generally irresponsible behavior. Moreover, according to the DSM, this pattern of behavior must have been occurring since the age of 15, and before age 15, the person must have had symptoms of conduct disorder. (Conduct disorder is a similar disorder occurring in children and young adolescents who show persistent patterns of aggression toward people or animals, destruction of property, deceitfulness or theft, and serious violation of rules at home or in school—see Chapter 14.) Some people with antisocial personalities have enough intelligence and social charm to devise and carry out elaborate schemes for conning large numbers of people. Impostors frequently fit into this category. Because this pattern has been studied more fully than the others, it will be examined in some detail later in this chapter. A brief clinical description should suffice here:

Mark, a 22-year-old, came to a psychology clinic on court order. He was awaiting trial for car theft and armed robbery. His case records revealed that he had a long history of arrests beginning at age 9, when he had been picked up for vandalism. He had been expelled from high school for truancy and disruptive behavior. On a number of occasions he had run away from home for days or weeks at a time—always returning in a disheveled and "rundown" condition. To date he had not held a job for more than a few days at a time, even though his generally charming manner enabled him to obtain work readily. He was described as a loner, with few friends. Though initially charming, Mark usually soon antagonized those he met with his aggressive, self-oriented behavior.

Mark was generally affable and complimentary during the therapy session. At the end of it, he enthusiastically told the therapist how much he'd benefited from the counseling and looked forward to future sessions.

Mark's first session was his last. Shortly after it, he skipped bail and presumably left town to avoid his trial.

Given that there is some overlap in the criteria for narcissistic and antisocial personality disorder, Widiger and Trull (1993) note that the most basic distinction is that "The narcissist's exploitation would be more for the purpose of demonstrating domination, prestige, and superiority rather than for the personal, material gain of the antisocial personality" (p. 388).

Borderline Personality Disorder Individuals with **borderline personality disorder** show a pattern of behavior characterized by impulsivity and instability in interpersonal relationships, self-image, and moods. The term *borderline personality* has a long and rather confusing history (Widiger & Trull, 1993). Originally it was most often used to refer to a condition that was thought to occupy the "border" between neurotic and psychotic disorders (as in the term *borderline schizophrenia*). However, this sense of the term *borderline* later became identified with schizotypal personality disorder, which as we have discussed is biologically related to schizophrenia. Since DSM-III, the term *borderline personality disorder* has been used for people who have "enduring personality features of instability and vulnerability" (Widiger & Trull, 1993, p. 372) and it is no longer considered to be biologically related to schizophrenia.

People with borderline personalities show serious disturbances in basic identity or sense of self, which is highly unstable. Given this extremely unstable self-image, it is not surprising that they also have highly unstable interpersonal relationships. For example, they may make desperate efforts to avoid real or imagined abandonment, perhaps because their fears of abandonment are so intense. Feeling slighted, they might, for example, become verbally abusive toward loved ones or might threaten suicide over minor setbacks. Given such behaviors, it is not surprising that they commonly have a history of intense but stormy relationships, typically involving overidealizations of friends or lovers that later end in bitter disillusionment and disappointment (Gunderson & Singer, 1986). Their mood is also highly unstable. For example, they may display intense anger outbursts with little provocation and have difficulty controlling their anger. They tend to have a low tolerance for frustration, as well as chronic feelings of emptiness. Associated with the sense of emptiness is a common intolerance for being alone. Their extreme affective instability is reflected in drastic mood shifts and impulsive or erratic self-destructive behaviors, such as binges of gambling, sex, substance abuse, binge-eating, or reckless driving. Suicide attempts, often flagrantly manipulative, are frequently part of the clinical picture (Fine & Sansone, 1990), and self-mutilation is one of the most discriminating signs for borderline personality (Widiger et al., 1986). In some cases the self-injurious behavior is associated with relief from anxiety or dysphoria and research has documented that it may even be associated with analgesia (absence of the experience of pain in the presence of a theoretically painful stimulus) (Russ et al., 1992, 1994). The following prototypic case illustrates the frequent risk of suicide and self-mutilation among borderline personalities:

A 26-year-old unemployed woman was referred for admission to a hospital by her therapist because of intense suicidal preoccupation and urges to mutilate herself by cutting herself with a razor.

The patient was apparently well until her junior year in high school, when she became preoccupied with religion and philosophy, avoided friends, and was filled with doubt about who she was. Academically she did well, but later, during college, her performance declined. In college she began to use a variety of drugs, abandoned the religion of her family, and seemed to be searching for a charismatic religious figure with whom to identify. At times massive anxiety swept over her and she found it would suddenly vanish if she cut her forearm with a razor blade.

Three years ago she began psychotherapy, and initially rapidly idealized her therapist as being incredibly intuitive and empathic. Later she became hostile and demanding of him, requiring more and more sessions, sometimes two in one day. Her life centered on her therapist, by this time to the exclusion of everyone else. Although her hostility toward her therapist was obvious, she could neither see it nor control it. Her difficulties with her therapist culminated in many episodes of her forearm cutting and suicidal threats, which led to the referral for admission. (Spitzer et al., 1994, pp. 233)

Clinical observation of people with borderline personality disorder points strongly to a problem of achieving a coherent sense of self as a key predisposing causal factor. These people somehow fail to complete the process of achieving an articulated self-identity, and this failure leads to complications in interpersonal relationships.

Although people with borderline personality disorder are usually aware of their circumstances and surroundings, they may have relatively short or transient episodes in which they appear to be out of contact with reality and experience delusions or other psychotic-like symptoms, such as hallucinations, paranoid beliefs, body image distortions, or dissociative symptoms. Among inpatients with severe borderline personality disorder the frequency and duration of psychotic symptoms may be greater. Indeed, one recent study found that 27 percent of 92 such inpatients were found to have hallucinations or delusions; for a majority of these the psychotic symptoms lasted 1–12 weeks (Miller et al., 1993a), although they apparently did not meet criteria for a diagnosis of schizophrenia.

Estimates are that about 2 percent of the population may qualify for the diagnosis of borderline personality disorder, although they represent a disproportionate number of patients in both inpatient and outpatient clinical settings (Widiger & Trull, 1993). There are estimates that about 8 percent of outpatients and about 15 percent of inpatients seeking treatment have borderline personality disorder. Approximately 75 percent of individuals receiving this diagnosis are women. Given their many and varied symptoms and problems with their sense of personal identity, it is not surprising that this personality disorder commonly co-occurs with a variety of Axis I disorders, ranging from mood and anxiety disorders (especially panic and PTSD), to substance use and eating disorders (Widiger & Trull, 1993). The relationship with mood disorders is especially strong, with about 50 percent also qualifying for a mood disorder diagnosis at some time (Widiger & Trull, 1993). Indeed, this has led some to suggest that borderline disorders are closer to "the border of affective [psychoses]" rather than schizophrenic psychoses (Akiskal et al., 1985, p. 45) or that borderline personality disorder may represent "a literally borderline condition of both personality and mood pathology" (Widiger & Trull, 1993, p. 377). That is, borderline personalities have both a disturbance in the ability to regulate their moods, and a pathological organization of the personality (Soloff, Cornelius, & George, 1991).

Some of the overlap between borderline personality and depression occurs because of the overlap in symptomatology required for a diagnosis of borderline personality and for mood disorders, but the consensus today is that the relationship between

these disorders is not a special or unique one (Gunderson & Philips, 1991). For example, other Axis II disorders are actually more commonly associated with depression than is borderline personality disorder. Moreover, depression as experienced by the borderline personality is apparently somewhat different from that of other depressives in that it is more often characterized by chronic feelings of loneliness (Soloff et al., 1991; Westen et al., as cited in Gunderson & Philips, 1991). In addition, borderline patients with depression do not show as good a response to the most common classes of antidepressant medication as do other depressed patients (Gunderson & Philips, 1991; Soloff et al., 1991).

There is also substantial co-occurrence of borderline personality disorder with other personality disorders—especially histrionic, dependent, antisocial, and schizotypal personality disorders. Nevertheless, Widiger and Trull (1993) note that a prototypical borderline personality can be distinguished from these other personality disorders in the following way: "The prototypic borderline's exploitative use of others is usually an angry and impulsive response to disappointment, whereas the antisocial's is a guiltless and calculated effort for personal gain. Sexuality may play a more central role in the relationships of histrionics than in borderlines, evident in the histrionic's tendency to eroticize situations, to compete with members of the same sex, and to be inappropriately seductive. The prototypic schizotypal lacks the emotionality of the borderline, and tends to be more isolated, odd and peculiar" (p. 377).

Avoidant Personality Disorder Individuals with **avoidant personality disorder** have a pattern of extreme social inhibition, leading to lifelong patterns of limited social relationships and reluctance to enter into social interactions. Because of their hypersensitivity to, and their fear of, criticism and rebuff, they do not seek out other people; yet they desire affection and are often lonely and bored. Unlike schizoid personalities, they do not enjoy their aloneness; their inability to relate comfortably to other people causes acute distress and is accompanied by low self-esteem. Because of their hypersensitivity to any sign of rejection or social derogation, they may readily see ridicule or disparagement where none was intended, as shown by the following case:

Sally, a 35-year-old librarian, lived a relatively isolated life and had few acquaintances and no close personal friends. From childhood on, she had been very shy and had withdrawn from close ties with others to keep from being hurt or criticized. Two years before she entered therapy, she had had a date to go to a party with an acquaintance she had met at the library. The moment they had arrived at the party, Sally had felt extremely uncomfortable because she had not been "dressed properly." She left in a hurry and refused to see her acquaintance again. It was because of her continuing concern over this incident that—two years later—Sally decided to go into therapy, even though she dreaded the possibility that the psychologist would be critical of her.

In the early treatment sessions, she sat silently much of the time, finding it too difficult to talk about herself. After several sessions, she grew to trust the therapist, and she related numerous incidents in her early years in which she had been "devastated" by her alcoholic father's obnoxious behavior in public. Though she had tried to keep her school friends from knowing about her family problems, when this had become impossible she instead had limited her friendships, thus protecting herself from possible embarrassment or criticism.

When Sally first began therapy, she avoided meeting people unless she could be assured that they would "like her." With therapy that focused on enhancing her assertiveness and social skills, she made some progress in her ability to approach and talk with people.

People with avoidant personality disorder are socially inhibited because of their fear of criticism and rejection. Although they do not enjoy being alone, their fear of rejection often leads to their leading rather solitary lives.

Sally's extreme need to avoid situations in which she might be embarrassed is the keynote of the avoidant personality. Life is full of risks; yet such people cannot face even the slightest risk of embarrassment or criticism. They want guarantees of success before they will participate—and if they cannot have them, they just will not play the game.

Some research (e.g., Alden & Capp, 1988) suggests that avoidant personality may be a biologically based disorder often starting in infancy or childhood that is reinforced by environmental factors to become a highly stable and chronic behavioral pattern (Kagan, Reznick, & Snidman, 1988). Nevertheless, the diagnosis of avoidant personality is not without its critics. One problem is whether it can be distinguished clearly from schizoid personality disorder (Livesley, West, & Tanney, 1985). However, Trull, Widiger, and Frances (1987) in a diagnostic study of personality disorders in an inpatient facility, found that these disorders were clearly distinguishable. The key difference is that avoidant personality is associated with being hypersensitive to criticism, shy,

and insecure, while schizoid personality is characterized by being indifferent to criticism, aloof, and cold. Another difficult distinction is between dependent and avoidant personalities. In this case, a dependent personality has great difficulty separating in relationships, while an avoidant personality has problems initiating them. In addition, the primary focus of the dependent personality is on being taken care of, whereas the primary focus of the avoidant personality is on avoidance of humiliation and rejection (DSM-IV, 1994). It should also be noted, however, these two disorders co-occur rather frequently.

Another major problem is in distinguishing avoidant personality disorder and generalized social phobia (Chapter 5). For example, three recent studies found substantial overlap between these two disorders, with a general conclusion that avoidant personality disorder may simply be a somewhat more severe manifestation of generalized social phobia (Herbert, Hope, & Bellack, 1992; Holt, Heimberg, & Hope, 1992; Turner et al., 1992). This is consistent with the finding of all three studies that there are cases of generalized social phobia without avoidant personality disorder, but very few cases of avoidant personality disorder without generalized social phobia, as well as with findings of somewhat higher levels of dysfunction and distress in the individuals with avoidant personality disorder. These findings led Widiger (1992) to suggest that these two disorders "may represent boundary conditions of the anxiety and personality disorders that involve essentially the same psychopathology" (p. 341). DSM-IV (1994) has recently come to the same conclusion, noting that they overlap so extensively "that they may be alternative conceptualizations of the same or similar conditions" (p. 663–64).

Dependent Personality Disorder Individuals with **dependent personality disorder** show extreme dependence on other people, particularly a need to be taken care of, which leads to clinging and submissive behavior. They also show acute discomfort—even panic—at the possibility of separation or sometimes of simply having to be alone. These individuals usually build their lives around other people and subordinate their own needs or views to keep these people involved with them. This means that they often fail to get appropriately angry with others because of a fear of losing their support. They have great difficulty making even simple decisions without a great deal of advice and reassurance. This may be because they lack self-confidence and feel helpless even when they have actually developed good work skills or other competencies. They function well as long as they are not required to be on their own. The following case is one in which a woman with a dependent personality experienced such distress following desertion by her husband that she sought help:

Sarah D., a 32-year-old mother of two and a part-time tax accountant, came to a crisis center late one evening after Michael, her husband of a year and a half, abused her physically and then left home. Although he never physically harmed the children, he frequently threatened to do so when he was drunk. Sarah appeared acutely anxious and worried about the future and "needed to be told what to do." She wanted her husband to come back and seemed rather unconcerned about his regular pattern of physical abuse. At the time, Michael was an unemployed resident in a day treatment program at a halfway house for paroled drug abusers that taught abstinence from all addictive substances through harassment and group cohesiveness. He was almost always in a surly mood and "ready to explode."

Although Sarah had a well-paying job, she voiced great concern about being able to make it on her own. She realized that it was foolish to be "dependent" on her husband, whom she referred to as a "real loser." (She had had a similar relationship with her first husband, who had left her and her oldest child when she was 18.) Several times in the past few months, Sarah had made up her mind to get out of the marriage but couldn't bring herself to break away. She would threaten to leave, but when the time came to do so, she would "freeze in the door" with a numbness in her body and a sinking feeling in her stomach at the thought of "not being with Michael."

As a result of their lack of confidence, dependent personalities passively allow other people to take over the major decisions in their lives—such as where they will live and work, what friends they will have, and even how they will spend their time. These individuals typically appear "selfless" and bland, since they usually feel they have no right to express even mild individuality. They are often preoccupied with a fear of being left to take care of themselves, and if one relationship ends they often will seek out a new one with great urgency.

Some features of dependent personality disorder overlap with those of borderline, histrionic, and avoidant personality disorders, but there are differences as well. For example, both borderline personalities and dependent personalities fear abandonment. However, the borderline reacts with feelings of emptiness or rage if abandonment occurs, whereas the dependent personality reacts initially with submissiveness and appeasement, and if abandonment occurs with an urgent seeking of a new relationship. Histrionic and dependent personalities both have strong needs for reassurance and approval. However, the style of the histrionic personality is much more gregarious, flamboyant, and actively demanding of attention, whereas the dependent is more docile and self-effacing. Finally, as already noted, the avoidant and dependent personalities share feelings of inadequacy and hypersensitivity, but the avoidant personality avoids relationships rather than be rejected, whereas the dependent seeks out relationships with others in spite of the fear of being rejected.

Obsessive-Compulsive Personality Disorder Individuals with **obsessive-compulsive personality disorder** show an excessive concern with maintaining order and are very perfectionistic. They are also preoccupied with maintaining mental and interpersonal control through careful attention to rules and schedules. They are very careful in what they do so as not to make mistakes, and they will often repeatedly check for possible mistakes. The details they are preoccupied with are often trivial and they therefore use their time poorly. This perfectionism is also often quite dysfunctional in that it can result in their never finishing projects. They also tend to be devoted to work to the exclusion of leisure activities and may have difficulty relaxing or doing anything just for fun.

People with obsesssive-compulsive personality disorder are often excessively conscientious and may be quite inflexible about moral or ethical issues. They may also have difficulty getting rid of old and worn out household items, and may be quite stingy or miserly as well. At an interpersonal level, they have difficulty delegating tasks to others and are quite rigid and stubborn. Not surprisingly, other people tend to view obsessive-compulsive personalities as rigid, stiff, and cold.

Although it was once thought that obsessive-compulsive personality disorder served as a diathesis for full-blown obsessive-compulsive disorder, this is generally not considered to be the case today (Sturgis, 1993), although others consider the evidence still to be inconclusive (Crino, 1991). For example, two studies by Baer and colleagues (1990, 1992) found that only 6–16 percent of patients with obsessive-compulsive disorder met criteria for obsessive-compulsive personality disorder; this figure would surely be higher if this personality disorder served as a diathesis for obsessive-compulsive disorder. Moreover, reviews of the literature suggest that about 35 percent of people with obsessive-compulsive disorder have no obsessive-compulsive personality traits whatsoever (Barlow, 1988).

To underscore the distinction between these two disorders, recall that with full-blown obsessive-compulsive disorder (Chapter 5) a person suffers from the persistent intrusion of particular undesired thoughts or images (obsessions) that are a source of extreme anxiety or distress. The anxiety or distress can only be reduced through the performance of compulsive rituals (such as cleaning or checking) and much of the person's life may be absorbed by the time taken to perform these rituals over and over again. By contrast, people with obsessive-compulsive personality disorder have lifestyles characterized by obstinacy and compulsive orderliness, but without the presence of true obsessions or compulsive rituals. Although they may be anxious about getting all their work done in keeping with their exacting standards, they are not anxious about their compulsiveness itself, as individuals with obsessive compulsive disorder usually are (Pollack, 1979). An example of obsessive-compulsive personality is reflected in the following case:

Alan appeared to be well suited to his work as a train dispatcher. He was conscientious, perfectionistic, and attended to minute details. However, he was not close to his coworkers and, reportedly, they thought him "off." He would get quite upset if even minor variations to his daily routine occurred. For example, he would become tense and irritable if coworkers did not follow exactly his elaborately constructed schedules and plans. If he became tied up in traffic, he would beat the steering wheel and swear at other drivers for holding him up.

In short, Alan got little pleasure out of life and worried constantly about minor problems. His rigid routines were impossible to maintain, and he often developed tension headaches or stomachaches when he couldn't keep his complicated plans in order. His physician, noting the frequency of his physical complaints and his generally perfectionistic approach to life, referred him for a psychological evaluation. Psychotherapy was recommended to him, although the prognosis for significant behavioral change was considered questionable. He did not follow up on the treatment recommendations because he felt that he could not afford the time away from work.

Some features of obsessive-compulsive personality disorder overlap with some features of narcissistic, antisocial, and schizoid personality disorder, although there are also distinguishing features. For example, individuals with both obsessive-compulsive and narcissistic personality disorder may be highly perfectionistic, but the narcissistic individual is more grandiose and likely to believe he or she has achieved perfection, whereas the obsessive-compulsive personality is often quite self-critical. Individuals with narcissistic and antisocial personality disorder may also share the lack of generosity toward others that characterizes obsessive-compulsive personality, but the former tend to indulge themselves, whereas obsessive-compulsives are equally unwilling to be generous with themselves and others. Finally, both the schizoid and the obsessive-compulsive personality may have a certain amount of formality and social detachment, but only the schizoid personality lacks the capacity for close relationships. The obsessive-compulsive personality has difficulty in interpersonal relationships because of excessive devotion to work and because of difficulty expressing emotions.

Passive-Aggressive Personality Disorder One of the most controversial personality disorders is **passive-aggressive personality disorder.** One reason for the controversy over this diagnosis is that empirical support for the reliability and validity of this diagnosis is limited, in part because it may be more of a situational reaction than a personality trait (Penna, 1986; Widiger & Chat, 1994). Thus, although this disorder was previously included in DSM-III and DSM-III-R, it has been placed in an Appendix in DSM-IV, with somewhat new criteria that still need further study before the new conceptualization can be validated.

As currently conceptualized, people with passive-aggressive personality disorder show a pervasive pattern of passive resistance to demands in social or work situations. They also show a strong pattern of negativistic attitudes unrelated to any concurrent diagnosis of major depressive disorder or dysthymia. Their passive resistance to demands is shown in many ways, ranging from simple resistance to fulfilling routine tasks, to being sullen or argumentative, or alternating between defiance and submission. They commonly complain of being misunderstood and unappreciated, and at the same time may be highly critical or scornful of authority. They also complain about their personal misfortunes and are envious of others who appear more fortunate.

The passive-aggressive personality pattern is shown in the following case:

A 34-year-old psychiatrist is 15 minutes late for his first appointment. He had recently been asked to resign from his job in a mental health center because, according to his boss, he had frequently been late for work and meetings, missed appointments, forgot about assignments, was late with his statistics, refused to follow instructions, and seemed unmotivated. The patient was surprised and resentful—he thought he had been doing a particularly good job under trying circumstances and experienced his boss as excessively obsessive and demanding. Nonetheless, he reported a long-standing pattern of difficulties with authority. . . .

The patient is unhappily married. He complains that his wife does not understand him and is a "nitpicker." She complains that he is unreliable and stubborn. He refuses to do anything

around the house and often fails to complete the few tasks he has accepted as within his responsibility. Tax forms are submitted several months late; bills are not paid. The patient is sociable and has considerable charm, but friends generally become annoyed at his unwillingness to go along with the wishes of the group (for example, if a restaurant is not his choice, he may sulk all night or "forget" to bring his wallet. (From Spitzer et al., 1989, pp. 107–108)

In sum, we can see in a passive-aggressive personality a pattern of never confronting a problem situation directly, but rather showing passive resistance through procrastination, forgetfulness, or sulking. These characteristic ways of reacting to problems are frustrating for others, who must deal with the inefficient behavior, and frustrating for the individual because such behavior typically does not productively resolve problems.

Depressive Personality Disorder A second provisional category in the DSM-IV Appendix is **depressive personality disorder.** People with this disorder show a pattern of depressive cognitions and behaviors that begins by early adulthood and is pervasive in nature. Their usual mood state is one of unhappiness or dejection and they tend to feel inadequate, worthless, or guilty. They tend to be highly self-critical and may be judgmental toward others as well. They also tend to be pessimistic and prone to worry. Although the emphasis here is more on cognitive and interpersonal traits than is true for dysthymic disorder (see Chapter 6), many questions remain about the validity of the distinction between these two diagnoses. In particular, it may not be possible to distinguish early-onset dysthymia from depressive personality disorder. Nevertheless, Klein (1990; Klein et al., 1993) has provided preliminary evidence that the depressive personality diagnosis is somewhat distinct and that most patients who receive the diagnosis do not meet the criteria for dysthymia; it appears to be associated with fewer depressive symptoms than dysthymia. Thus, it remains possible that the pervasive cognitive traits of pessimism, guilt, and self-criticism seen in depressive personality disorder may not be best characterized as a disorder in mood regulation, which is the way dysthymia is characterized (Widiger & Chat, 1994).

Overview of Personality Disorders Beck and Freeman (1990) have proposed a useful integrative scheme that may highlight some of the commonalties and differences among the personality disorders. In their view people with personality disorders can be characterized on several different dimensions, including what kinds of interpersonal strategies they use, what patterns of behavior they have underdeveloped or overdeveloped, and what their characteristic core dysfunctional beliefs are. Differing interpersonal strategies include different uses of interpersonal space. For example:

Individuals may move or place themselves against, toward, away from, above, or under others. The dependent moves <u>toward</u> and often <u>below</u> (submissive, subservient). Another "type" <u>stays still</u> and may obstruct others: the passive-aggressive. The narcissists position themselves <u>above</u> others. The compulsive may move

<u>above</u> in the interest of control. The schizoid moves <u>away</u>, and the avoidant moves closer and then <u>backs off</u>. The histrionic personalities use the space to <u>draw others</u> toward them.... These vectors may be regarded as the visible manifestations of specific interpersonal strategies associated with specific personality disorders. (Beck & Freeman, 1990, p. 40)

Beck and Freeman also propose that each personality disorder is characterized by a different set of behavior patterns that are overdeveloped, and another set of behavior patterns that are underdeveloped. In many cases the deficient behaviors are somehow counterparts to the overdeveloped features. These over- and underdeveloped patterns are illustrated in HIGHLIGHT 9.2.

HIGHLIGHT 9.2

Typical Overdeveloped and Underdeveloped Strategies

Personality Disorder	Overdeveloped	Underdeveloped
Obsessive-compulsive	Control Responsibility	Spontaneity Playfulness
Dependent	Help seeking Clinging	Self-sufficiency Mobility
Passive-aggressive	Autonomy Resistance Passivity Sabotage	Intimacy Assertiveness Activity Cooperativeness
Paranoid	Vigilance Mistrust	Serenity Trust
Narcissistic	Self-aggrandizement Competitiveness	Sharing Group identification
Antisocial	Combativeness Exploitativeness Predation	Empathy Reciprocity Social sensitivity
Schizoid	Autonomy Isolation	Intimacy Reciprocity
Avoidant	Social vulnerability Avoidance Inhibition	Self-assertion Gregariousness
Histrionic	Exhibitionism Expressiveness Impressionism	Reflectiveness Control Systematization

From Beck and Freeman, 1990, p. 42.

Finally, Beck and Freeman also propose that each personality disorder is characterized by different core dysfunctional beliefs that people with personality disorders have about themselves and the world around them. For example, a woman with avoidant personality disorder is likely to see herself as inept or incompetent, and to view others as potentially critical or demeaning. Her core belief is likely to be "I am no good . . . worthless . . . unlovable. I cannot tolerate unpleasant feelings" (Beck & Freeman, 1990, p. 43). A man with the related dependent personality disorder is also likely to see himself as incompetent, but also as needy and weak, and to view strong others as all-supportive and competent. His core belief is likely to be "I need other people—specifically, a strong person—in order to survive" and/or "I can never be happy unless I am loved" (Beck & Freeman, 1990, pp. 44–45). For the dramatic emotional Cluster B personality disorders, Beck and Freeman propose that people with narcissistic personality disorder see themselves as special and unique; they view others as inferior and seek admiration from them "primarily to document their own grandiosity and preserve their own superior status" (p. 49). Their core beliefs might include "Since I am special, I deserve special dispensations, privileges, and prerogatives" and "I'm superior to others and they should acknowledge this" (p. 49). Of the odd or eccentric Cluster A personality disorders, Beck and Freeman propose that people with schizoid personality disorder would tend to view themselves as self-sufficient loners, and to view others as intrusive. Their core beliefs might be "I am basically alone" or "Close relationships with other people are unrewarding and messy" (p. 51).

Causal Factors in Personality Disorders

Little is yet known about the causal factors in personality disorders, partly because such disorders have only received consistent attention since DSM-III was published in 1980 and partly because they are less amenable to thorough study. One major problem in studying the causes of personality disorders stems from the high level of comorbidity among them. For example, in a review of four studies, Widiger and Rogers (1989) found that 85 percent of patients who qualified for one personality disorder diagnosis also qualified for at least one more, and many qualified for several more. Even in a nonpatient sample, Zimmerman and Coryell (1989) found that of those with one personality disorder, almost 25 percent had at least one more. This substantial comorbidity adds to the difficulties in

studying the causes of these disorders because of the difficulty untangling which causal factors are associated with which personality disorder.

An additional problem is that many people with these disorders are never seen by clinical personnel. Typically, those who do come to the attention of clinicians or legal authorities have already developed a full-blown disorder, so that only *retrospective* study is possible—that is, going back through what records may exist in an effort to reconstruct the chain of events that may have led to the disorder. As we have seen, researchers have more confidence in *prospective* studies, in which groups of people are observed before a disorder appears and followed over a period of time to see which ones develop problems and what causal factors have been present.

Of possible biological factors, it has been suggested that the constitutional reaction tendencies that infants display (high or low vitality, behavioral inhibition, and so on) may predispose them to the development of particular personality disorders. Given that most personality traits have been found to be moderately heritable (e.g., Carey & DiLalla, 1994), it is not surprising that there is increasing evidence for genetic contributions to certain personality disorders (Livesley et al., 1994, in press; Nigg & Goldsmith, 1994; Siever & Davis, 1991). For example, some research suggests that genetic factors may be important for the development of paranoid personality (Kendler & Gruenberg, 1982), borderline personality (Loranger, Oldham, & Tulis, 1982; Torgerson, 1984; Widiger & Trull, 1993), schizotypal personality disorder (Kendler et al., 1991; Torgersen, 1984), and antisocial personality disorder (Carey, in press; Gottesman & Goldsmith, in press). In addition, some progress is being made in understanding the psychobiological substrate of at least some of the personality disorders (Siever & Davis, 1991). Nevertheless, as with the Axis I disorders, none of the personality disorders is entirely heritable and none can be understood solely from a biological perspective. Thus psychosocial and sociocultural causal factors must also play crucial roles in their origins, and our understanding of these disorders at a psychological level must supplement any understanding of their biological underpinnings. The ultimate goal would be to achieve a biopsychosocial perspective on the origins of each personality disorder, but we are far from that goal today.

Among psychological factors, early learning is usually assumed to contribute the most in predisposing a person to develop a personality disorder, yet there is little research to support this belief. Some research has suggested that abuse in childhood may be related to the development of certain personality disorders. For example, Ogata and colleagues (1990) found that 71 percent of borderline patients reported having been abused as children, while only 22 percent of depressed patients reported having been abused. Similarly, Herman, Perry, and van der Kolk (1989) found that 81 percent of borderline personality disorder patients reported a history of childhood trauma, including some combination of physical abuse, sexual abuse, or witnessing domestic violence. For 57 percent of these patients, the abuse reportedly started before age seven. This was higher than the frequency of reported abuse (52 percent) in a group of control patients with other related disorders (such as antisocial personality disorder, schizotypal personality disorder, and Bipolar II disorder). Moreover, only 13 percent of these other patients reported having experienced abuse in the first six years of life. Although these and other related studies (e.g., Zanarini et al., 1989) are suggestive that borderline personality disorder is often associated with early childhood trauma, the studies are not without their shortcomings inasmuch as they rely on retrospective self-reports of individuals who are known for their exaggerated and distorted views of other people (Widiger & Trull, 1993). Moreover, the nature of the stressors involved seems to be somewhat nonspecific (Widiger & Trull, 1993), and the evidence does not suggest that they always occur in the first few years of life as postulated by psychoanalytic theorists such as Kernberg (1984) and Masterson (1987).

Psychoanalytic theorists such as Otto Kernberg (1984) and Heinz Kohut (1977) have also written a great deal in recent years about the origins of narcissistic personality disorder. For example, Kohut argues that all children go through a phase of primitive grandiosity during which they think that all events and needs revolve around them. Kohut argues that for normal development beyond this phase to occur, parents must do some mirroring of the infant's grandiosity. This helps the child develop normal levels of self-confidence: "However grave the blows may be to which the child's grandiosity is exposed by the realities of life, the proud smile of the parents will keep alive a bit of the original omnipotence, to be retained as the nucleus of the self-confidence and inner security about one's worth that sustain the healthy person throughout his life" (Kohut & Wolff, 1978, p. 182; from Widiger & Trull, 1993). Kohut further proposed that narcissistic personality disorder is likely to develop if parents are neglectful, devaluing, or unempathetic to the child; this individual will be perpetually searching for affirmation of this idealized and grandiose sense of self. Although this theory has been very influential among psychodynamic clinicians, it unfortunately has no real empirical support. And indeed it is interesting to note that Theodore Millon—a personality disorder researcher from the social learning tradition of Bandura—has argued quite the opposite. He believes that narcissistic personality disorder comes

Otto Kernberg (b. 1928) is an influential contemporary psychoanalytic theorist who has written a great deal about borderline and narcissistic personality disorders.

Heinz Kohut (1913–1981), another contemporary psychoanalytic thinker, theorized that poor parenting can cause narcissistic personality disorder by failing to build a child's normal self-confidence.

from parental overvaluation (Widiger & Trull, 1993). For example, he has proposed that "these parents pamper and indulge their youngsters in ways that teach them that their every wish is a command, that they can receive without getting in return, and that they deserve prominence without even minimal effort" (Millon, 1981, p. 175; from Widiger & Trull, 1993). That theorists from these two very different traditions (psychoanalytic and social learning) can come to such opposite conclusions illustrates the current poverty of knowledge regarding particular antecedents for these disorders. The only disorder for which there is a good deal of research on causal factors is antisocial personality disorder, which is discussed at length below.

Sociocultural factors contributing to personality disorders are even less well defined. We do know that the incidence and form of psychopathology in general vary somewhat with time and place, and some clinicians believe that personality disorders have increased in American society in recent years (Smith, 1978). If this claim is true, we can expect to find the increase related to changes in our culture's general priorities and activities. Is our emphasis on impulse gratification, instant solutions, and pain-free benefits leading more people to develop the self-centered lifestyles that we see in more extreme forms in the personality disorders? Only further research can clarify this issue.

Treatments and Outcomes

Personality disorders seem especially resistant to therapy. For example, Valliant (1987) wrote:

> Certainly, treating personality disorder is not easy. Indeed, we often identify personality disorders precisely because they do not respond to treatment. Due to defects in genes, socialization, or maturation, personality-disordered individuals have difficulty learning what society wishes to teach them . . . individuals with personality disorder need care that is very similar to the care required by adolescents. Indeed, adolescents do not need therapy at all: they need time and space to internalize the valuable facets of their parents and their society. . . . Like adolescents, individuals with personality disorders need opportunities to internalize fresh role models and to make peace with the imperfect familial figures who are already within. (p. 154)

In addition, it is well known that people who have both an Axis I disorder and a personality disorder do not, on average, do as well in treatment for their Axis I disorders as do patients without comorbid personality disorders (e.g., Reich & Green, 1991). That is, having one or more personality disorders makes it harder to treat disorders such as major depression, panic disorder, or obsessive-compulsive disorder.

In many cases, people with personality disorders who are seen clinically are there as part of another person's treatment—as, for example, in couples counseling, where a partner identified as the "patient" has a spouse with a personality disorder. Or a child referred to a child guidance center may have a parent with a personality disorder. In these cases, of course, the problems of the so-called patient may be due in no small measure to the great strain caused by the family member with a personality disorder. A narcissistic father, who is so self-centered and demanding of attention from others that family relationships are constantly strained, leaves little room for small children to grow into self-respecting adults. Likewise, a mother with dependent personality disorder, whose typical manner of responding to others is to be highly submissive and clinging and fearful of separation, may create an unhealthy family atmosphere that distorts a child's development.

A child subjected to such extreme, inescapable, and often irrational behavior on the part of one or both parents may become the weak link that breaks, bringing the family into therapy. Many a child or family therapist has quickly concluded after seeing a child in a family context that psychological attention, if it is to be effective at all, must be focused on the parental relationships. The following case clearly illustrates this problem:

Mrs. A. brought her 7-year-old son, Christopher, to a mental health center for treatment because he was fearful of going out and recently had been having bad nightmares. Mrs. A. sought help at the recommendation of the school social worker after Chris refused to return to school. She voiced a great deal of concern for Chris and agreed to cooperate in the treatment by attending parent effectiveness training sessions. However, she seemed quite reluctant to talk about getting her husband involved in the treatment. After much encouragement, she agreed to try to bring him to the next session, but he adamantly refused to participate. Mrs. A described him as a "very proud and strong-willed man" who was quite suspicious of other people. She felt that he might be afraid people would blame him for

Chris's problems. She reported that he had been having a lot of problems lately—he had seemed quite bitter and resentful over some local political issues and tended to blame others (particularly minorities) for his problems. He refused to come to the clinic because he "doesn't like social workers."

After several sessions of therapy, Mrs. A. confessed to her therapist that her husband's rigid and suspicious behavior was disrupting the family. He would often come home from work and accuse her of, for example, "talking with Jewish men." He was a domineering person who set strict house rules and enforced them with loud threats and intimidation. Both Mrs. A. and Chris were fearful of his tyrannical demands, but his suspicious nature made it difficult for them to explain anything to him. Mrs. A. also felt a great deal of sympathy for her husband because she felt that deep down inside he was frightened; she reported that he kept numerous guns around the house and several locks on the doors for protection against outsiders, whom he feared. Thus it became clear that her husband had at least certain features of paranoid personality disorder and that this was creating a great deal of difficulty for the family.

Because many people with personality disorders—especially those from the odd/eccentric Cluster A and the erratic/dramatic Cluster B—enter treatment only at someone else's insistence, they often do not believe that they need to change. Consequently people with such personality disorders typically put the responsibility for treatment on others and are adept at avoiding the focus of therapy themselves. In addition, the difficulties they have in forming and maintaining good relationships generally tend to make a therapeutic relationship fragile or stormy. For those from the erratic/dramatic Cluster B, the pattern of acting out, typical in their other relationships, is carried into the therapy situation, and instead of dealing with their problems at the verbal level, they may become angry at their therapist and loudly disrupt the sessions. Goldberg and colleagues (1986) reported high dropout rates for patients with borderline and schizotypal personality disorder. These patients may also behave in socially inappropriate ways outside the sessions to show their therapist that the therapy is not working.

When questioned about such behavior, these people often drop out of treatment or become even more entrenched in their defensiveness. In some cases, however, confrontation can be quite effective. For individuals who become identified with their therapy group, or who are sufficiently "hooked" into couples therapy not to flee the sessions when their behavior comes under scrutiny, the intense feedback from peers or spouse often is more acceptable than confrontation by a therapist in individual treatment (Gurman & Kniskern, 1978; Lubin, 1976).

In some situations, therapeutic techniques must be modified. For example, recognizing that traditional individual psychotherapy tends to encourage dependency in people already too dependent (such as in dependent, histrionic, and borderline personality disorders), it is often useful to develop treatment strategies specifically aimed at altering a dependent person's basic lifestyle instead of fostering it. Patients from the anxious/fearful Cluster C, such as dependent and avoidant personalities, may be hypersensitive to any perceived criticism from the therapist and may quit prematurely for such reasons. In such cases the therapist has to be extremely careful to make sure that this does not happen. One approach is to ask the patient for feedback about the therapist's behavior and attitude at the end of each session day (e.g, patients can be asked to rate their therapists on qualities such as listening well, explaining homework clearly, etc.) (Beck & Freeman, 1990). By letting the patient give feedback and discussing possible changes for future sessions, the therapist appears nondefensive and yet also encourages and reinforces assertive criticism on the part of the patient.

Such specific therapeutic techniques are a central part of Beck and Freeman's (1990) new cognitive approach to personality disorders (see pages 329–330 and HIGHLIGHT 9.2). The cognitive approach assumes that the dysfunctional feelings and behavior associated with the personality disorders are largely the result of schemas that tend to produce consistently biased judgments, as well as tendencies to make cognitive errors in many types of situations. Schemas, as we saw in Chapter 3, involve specific rules that govern information processing and behavior. They are of many types—for example, we have personal, familial, cultural, religious, gender, and occupational schemas. Changing the underlying dysfunctional schemas is at the heart of cognitive therapy for personality disorders, and doing so is particularly difficult because these schemas are held in place by behavioral, cognitive, and emotional elements. Nevertheless, through the usual cognitive techniques of monitoring automatic thoughts, challenging faulty logic, and assigning behavioral tasks that hopefully help to challenge the patient's dysfunctional assumptions and beliefs, cognitive therapists may have made a significant step in advancing treatment for personality disorders. At this point, for most disorders there are only case studies rather than controlled treatment studies, but the results do seem promising.

In general, therapy for people with severe personality disorders may be more effective in situations where acting-out behavior can be constrained. Outpatient treatment is often not promising because severe acting out can disrupt the course of treatment. In addition, many patients with borderline personality disorder are hospitalized for safety reasons because of their frequent suicidal behavior.

Treatment prognosis (probable outcome) for borderline personality disorder patients is typically considered to be guarded because of their long-standing problems and extreme instability. Because borderline patients are usually difficult to manage due to their behavioral problems and acting out tendencies, treatment often involves a judicious use of both psychological and biological treatment methods (Swenson & Wood, 1990). The use of drugs is especially controversial with this disorder because it is so frequently associated with suicidal behavior. Nevertheless, Gitlin (1993) summarized the evidence for psychopharmacological treatment of borderline personality disorder and concluded that low doses of antipsychotic medication (see Chapter 16) have modest but significant effects that are broad-based; that is, patients show some improvement in depression, anxiety, suicidality, rejection sensitivity, and psychotic symptoms. Gitlin's review also concluded that tricyclic antidepressants are ineffective in the treatment of borderline personality disorder, but that antidepressant drugs from the same class as Prozac (see Chapters 6 and 16) are promising (see also Markovitz & Schulz, 1993). In general, the drugs are used as an adjunct to psychological treatment.

Traditional psychosocial treatments for borderline personality disorder involve variants of psychodynamic psychotherapy, which is adapted for the particular problems of persons with this disorder. For example, Kernberg (1985) has developed a form of psychodynamic psychotherapy for borderline personality disorder that is much more directive than is typical psychodynamic treatment. The primary goal of treatment is seen as strengthening the weak egos of these individuals, with a particular focus on their primary defense mechanism of *splitting*, which leads them to black-and-white, all-or-none thinking, as well as to rapid shifts in their reactions to other people (including the therapist)

as "all good" or "all bad." Although this treatment can be effective in some cases, it is expensive and time-consuming (often lasting a good number of years) and has not yet been subjected to controlled research.

Probably the most promising treatment for borderline personality disorder is Linehan's (1987, 1993) recently developed dialectical *behavior therapy,* which is a kind of cognitive behavior therapy specifically designed for treating borderline personality disorder. Linehan believes that it is the inability to tolerate strong states of negative affect that is central to this disorder, and one of the primary goals of treatment is to encourage patients to accept this negative affect without engaging in self-destructive or other maladaptive behaviors. Accordingly, she has developed a problem-focused treatment in which the hierarchy of goals includes: (a) decreasing suicidal behavior; (b) decreasing behaviors that interfere with therapy such as missing sessions, lying, and getting hospitalized; (c) decreasing escapist behaviors that interfere with a stable lifestyle, such as substance abuse; (d) increasing behavioral skills in order to regulate emotions, to increase interpersonal skills, and to increase tolerance for distress; (e) other goals the patient chooses. Suicidal behaviors are the first target "simply because psychotherapy is not effective with dead patients" (Linehan, 1987, p. 329) and because this indicates these behaviors are taken very seriously.

The treatment combines individual and group components, with the group setting focusing more on the skills training for interpersonal skills, emotion regulation, stress tolerance. This all occurs in the presence of a therapist who is taught to accept the patient for who he or she is (almost a client-centered focus), in spite of the very behaviors on the part of the patients that make it so difficult to do so (such as bursts of rage, suicidal behaviors, missing appointments, etc.). As did Carl Rogers, Linehan makes a clear distinction between *accepting* the patient for who he or she is, and *approving* of the patient's behavior. For example, a therapist cannot approve of self-mutilation, but he or she should indicate acceptance of that as part of a patient's problem.

Results from one important controlled treatment study using this form of treatment have been very encouraging (Linehan et al., 1991; Linehan, Heard, & Armstrong, 1993). In this study, the researchers compared borderline patients who received dialectical behavior therapy with patients receiving treatment as usual in the community over a one-year treatment period, followed by a one-year follow-up period. Patients who received dialectical behavior therapy showed greater reduction in self-destructive and suicidal behaviors than did those in the treatment-as-usual group. The patients who received dialectical behavior therapy were also more likely to stay in treatment and to require fewer days of hospitalization. At follow-up they were also doing better occupationally and were rated as better adjusted than the control group. Although these results may seem modest in some ways, they are considered extraordinary by most therapists who work with this population, and many psychodynamic therapists are incorporating important components of this treatment into their own treatment of persons with borderline personality.

Treatment of schizotypal personality disorder is not, so far, as promising as some of the recent advances that have been made in the treatment of borderline personality disorder. For example, Mehlum and colleagues (1991) compared the outcomes following inpatient treatment for schizotypal, borderline, dependent, and avoidant personality disorders. Patients with schizotypal personality disorder had the poorest outcome. That is, although there was a moderate reduction in symptoms, they were still functioning poorly. Gitlin (1993) summarized evidence from several studies showing that low doses of antipsychotic drugs may also result in modest improvements, but no treatment has yet produced anything approaching a cure for most people with this disorder.

Treatment of some of the personality disorders from Cluster C such as dependent and avoidant personality disorder has not been extensively studied but appears more promising than for many of those from Clusters A and B. For example, Mehlum and colleagues (1991) compared the outcome of inpatient treatment two to five years later for patients with borderline, schizotypal, dependent, and avoidant personality disorders. Those with Cluster C personality disorders showed marked symptom reduction and good overall outcome; patients with borderline personality disorder showed only moderate symptom reduction and fair overall outcome; and those with schizotypal personality disorder also showed moderate symptom reduction but poor overall outcome. In addition, Winston and colleagues (1994) found significant improvement in patients with Cluster C disorders using a form of short-term psychotherapy that is active and confrontational. Finally, there is also some evidence that MAO inhibitors may sometimes help in the treatment of avoidant personality disorder (Deltito & Stam, 1989), although progress in pharmacological treatment of Cluster C disorders lags behind that for the other personality disorders (Gitlin, 1993).

ANTISOCIAL PERSONALITY AND PSYCHOPATHY

As we have seen, the outstanding characteristics of people with antisocial personality disorder is their tendency to persistently disregard and violate the rights of others. They do this through a combination of deceitful, aggressive, or antisocial behavior, with little or no sign of remorse. Basically, these people have a lifelong pattern of unsocialized and irresponsible behavior, with little regard for safety—either their own or that of others. These characteristics bring them into repeated conflict with society.

Only individuals 18 or over are diagnosed as antisocial personalities. According to DSM-IV, this diagnosis is made if the following criteria are met: (a) at least three behavioral problems occurring after age 15, such as repeatedly performing acts that are grounds for arrest, repeated deceitfulness, impulsivity or failure to plan for the future, irritability and aggressiveness, disregard for safety, consistent irresponsibility in work or financial matters, and lack of remorse; (b) at least three instances of deviant behavior before age 15, such as aggression toward people or animals, destruction of property, deceitfulness or theft, and serious violation of rules (symptoms of conduct disorder—see Chapter 14); (c) the antisocial behavior is not a symptom of another mental disorder such as schizophrenia or a manic episode.

The use of the term *antisocial personality disorder* dates back only to DSM-III in 1980, but many of the central features of this disorder have long been labeled **psychopathy** or *sociopathy*. Although several investigators identified the syndrome in the nineteenth century under such labels as "moral insanity" (Prichard, 1835), psychopathy was first carefully described by Cleckley (1941, 1982) in the 1940s. In addition to the defining features of antisocial personality in DSM-III and DSM-IV, psychopathy also includes such traits as lack of empathy, inflated and arrogant self-appraisal, and glib and superficial charm. With its strong emphasis on behavioral criteria that can be measured reasonably objectively, DSM-III and IV have broken from the tradition of psychopathy researchers, in an attempt to increase the reliability of the diagnosis (whether clinicians agree on the diagnosis). However, much less attention has been paid to its validity—that is, whether it measures a meaningful construct and whether that construct is the same as psychopathy.

Research over the past 15 years by Robert Hare and his colleagues suggests that the two constructs are related but differ in significant ways. Hare (1980, 1991) developed a 20-item Psychopathy Checklist as a way for clinicians and researchers to diagnose psychopathy based on the Cleckley criteria. Extensive research with this checklist has shown that there are two related but separable dimensions of psychopathy, with each predicting different types of behavior. The first dimension involves the affective and interpersonal core of the disorder and reflects traits such as lack of remorse, callousness, selfishness, and an exploitative use of others. The second dimension reflects the aspects of psychopathy involving an antisocial, impulsive, and socially deviant lifestyle. The second dimension is much more closely related to the DSM-III and DSM-IV diagnosis of antisocial personality disorder than is the first dimension (Hare, Hart, & Harpur, 1991). Not surprisingly, therefore, when comparisons have been made in prison settings of what percentage qualify for a diagnosis of psychopathy versus antisocial personality disorder, it is typically found that a higher percentage qualify for the latter than for the former. For example, Hare (1985a) found that 49 percent of inmates received a DSM-III diagnosis of antisocial personality disorder, whereas only 33 percent received a diagnosis of psychopathy with Hare's Psychopathy Checklist (see Hare et al., 1991; Widiger & Corbitt, 1993). That is, a significant number of the inmates show the antisocial, deviant, and aggressive behaviors that result in their meeting the criteria for a diagnosis of antisocial personality disorder, but not enough of the selfish, callous, and exploitative behaviors to qualify for a diagnosis of psychopathy.

An additional concern among researchers is that the current conceptualization of antisocial personality disorder may not include what may be a substantial segment of society who show many of the features of the first affective and interpersonal dimension of psychopathy but not as many features of the second antisocial dimension, or at least few enough that they do not get into trouble with the law. Hare and colleagues (1991) recently summarized these various problems rather succinctly when they wrote:

All of those who fulfill the APD criteria may be antisocial, but they may differ greatly in their motivations for being so and in significant interpersonal, affective and psychopathological features, such as the capacity for empathy, remorse, guilt, anxiety, or loyalty. Paradoxically, the criteria for APD appear to de-fine a diagnostic category that is at once too broad, encompassing criminals and antisocial persons who are psychologically heterogeneous, and too narrow, excluding those who have the personality structure of the psychopath but have not exhibited some of the specific antisocial behaviors listed for APD (Millon, 1981) (From Hare et al., 1991, p. 393.)

These issues remain highly controversial. Although there was considerable discussion about expanding the DSM-IV criteria for antisocial personality disorder to include more of the traditional affective and interpersonal features of psychopathy, a conservative approach was taken and such changes were not made. Nevertheless, in DSM-IV it is noted that in prison and forensic settings, where by definition we are dealing with criminals (or alleged criminals) who have engaged in antisocial behavior, psychopathic traits of lack of empathy or remorse, and glib and superficial charm, may be useful in making more valid diagnoses than relying on antisocial behavioral criteria alone. In addition, many researchers are likely to continue studying the Cleckley/Hare psychopathy diagnosis rather than the DSM-IV diagnosis of antisocial personality disorder. This is both because of the long and rich research tradition on psychopathy and because the psychopathy diagnosis has been shown to be a better predictor than is the antisocial personality disorder diagnosis of a variety of important facets of criminal behavior. For example, Harris, Rice and Cormier (1991) found that levels of psychopathy as assessed by Hare's Psychopathy Checklist predicted violent offenses better after forensic patients were released from an intensive therapeutic community program than did a DSM diagnosis of antisocial personality disorder. Indeed, following release psychopaths were almost four times as likely to commit a violent offense as were nonpsychopaths (77 percent vs. 21 percent). Hare and Hart (1993) summarized evidence from numerous studies that psychopathic offenders have a great number of violent offenses during their lifetime, including during the time they are institutionalized.

The controversy over the use of a psychopathy diagnosis or antisocial personality disorder is not likely to be solved soon, and unfortunately different researchers in this area make different choices, leading to some confusion when trying to interpret the research on causal factors. In the sections that follow we will attempt to be clear which diagnostic category was being used in different studies, because the causal factors may well not be identical.

Whichever diagnosis is used, individuals with *antisocial personality disorder* or with *psychopathy* include a mixed group of individuals: unprincipled business professionals, high-pressure evangelists, crooked politicians, impostors, drug pushers, and assorted criminals. Few of these people find their way into community clinics or mental hospitals. A larger number are confined in jail, but as already noted, a history of repeated legal or social offenses is certainly not sufficient justification for assuming that an individual is psychopathic or has antisocial personality disorder. It is believed that a large number of psychopathic individuals manage to stay out of correctional institutions, although they tend to be in constant conflict with authority (see HIGHLIGHT 9.3). The prevalence of antisocial personality disorder is estimated to be about 3 percent for males and about 1 percent for females based on several large epidemiological studies (DSM-IV, 1994). There are no epidemiological studies estimating the prevalence of psychopathy as diagnosed by Hare's Psychopathy Checklist.

The Clinical Picture in Antisocial Personality and Psychopathy

Often charming, spontaneous, and likable on first acquaintance, psychopaths and antisocial personalities are deceitful and manipulative, callously using others to achieve their own ends. Often they seem to live in a series of present moments, without consideration for the past or future. The following example is illustrative:

Two 18-year-old youths went to visit a teenager at her home. Finding no one there, they broke into the house, damaged a number of valuable paintings and other furnishings, and stole a quantity of liquor and a television set. They sold the TV to a mutual friend for a small sum of money. On their apprehension by the police, they at first denied the entire venture and then later insisted that it was all a "practical joke." They did not consider their behavior particularly inappropriate, nor did they think any sort of restitution for damage was called for.

Also included in the general category of antisocial and psychopathic individuals are hostile people who are prone to acting out impulses in remorseless and often senseless violence. In other cases, antisocial or psychopathic persons show periods of reliability and are capable of assuming responsibility and pursuing long-range goals, but they do so in unethical ways with a complete lack of consideration for the rights and well-being of others.

To fill in the clinical picture, let us begin by summarizing characteristics that psychopaths and antisocial personalities tend to share. We will then describe a case that illustrates the wide range of behavioral patterns that may be involved.

Common Characteristics Although all the characteristics examined in the following sections are not usually found in a particular case, they are typical of psychopaths as described by Cleckley (1941, 1982).

HIGHLIGHT   9.3

Wanted: Everyday Psychopaths

Most studies of antisocial personalities have been conducted on institutionalized persons, leaving us ignorant about the large number who never get caught. Widom (1977) tried an ingenious approach for reaching this large group. She ran advertisements in the local newspapers which read:

Are you adventurous? Psychologist studying adventurous,

carefree people who've led exciting, impulsive lives. If you're the kind of person who'd do almost anything for a dare and want to participate in a paid experiment, send name, address, phone, and short biography proving how interesting you are to. . . . (p. 675)

Widom had hoped to attract psychopathic individuals and ap-

parently did just that. When given a battery of tests, those who responded turned out to be similar in personality makeup to institutionalized psychopathic individuals. Although she did not go further than a personality assessment of these individuals, her method suggests a way of making contact with samples of uninstitutionalized psychopaths.

Many people with antisocial personality disorder also share at least a subset of these characteristics, although they are not all criteria for the diagnosis in DSM-IV.

Inadequate Conscience Development. Psychopaths appear unable to understand and accept ethical values except on a verbal level. They glibly claim to adhere to high moral standards that have no apparent connection with their behavior. In short, their conscience development is severely retarded or nonexistent, although their intellectual development is typically normal. Nevertheless, it should be noted that intelligence is one dimension on which the two dimensions of psychopathy seem to differ. The first dimension, having to do with selfish, callous, exploitative personality features, is generally unrelated to intelligence; but the second dimension, associated with chronic antisocial behavior, is negatively related to intelligence at least among criminal psychopaths (Harpur, Hare, & Hakstian, 1989). Indeed, there is some evidence that intelligence seems to serve as a protective factor for adolescents who are at risk for psychopathy or antisocial personality in adulthood. Kandel and colleagues (1988) and White, Moffitt, and Silva (1989), for example, found that many adolescents with conduct disorder who are known to be predisposed to antisocial personality or psychopathy never get involved in criminal behavior because they are positively influenced by schooling. Thus they presumably focus their energies on more socially accepted behaviors.

Psychopaths tend to "act out" tensions and problems rather than worry them out. Their apparent lack of anxiety and guilt, combined with the appearance of sincerity and candor, may enable them to avoid suspicion and detection for stealing and other illegal activities. They often show contempt for those they are able to take advantage of—their "marks."

Irresponsible and Impulsive Behavior. Psychopaths generally have a callous disregard for the rights, needs, and well-being of others. They have learned to take rather than earn what they want. Prone to thrill seeking and deviant and unconventional behavior, they often break the law impulsively and without regard for the consequences. They seldom forego immediate pleasure for future gains and long-range goals. They live in the present, without realistically considering either past or future. External reality is used for immediate personal gratification. Unable to endure routine or to shoulder responsibility, they are often unable to hold a steady job.

Several studies have shown that antisocial personalities and psychopaths have high rates of alcoholism and other substance abuse-dependence disorders (e.g., Lewis, Robins, & Rice, 1985; Lewis, Cloninger, & Pais, 1983; Sher & Trull, 1994; Smith & Newman, 1990). In examining the relationship of substance abuse to the two different dimensions of psychopathy assessed by Hare's Psychopathy Checklist, Smith and Newman found that substance abuse was related only to the dimension reflecting antisocial deviant behavior and not to the dimension reflecting egocentric, callous, and exploitative personality traits. The relationship between antisocial behavior and substance abuse is sufficiently strong that some have questioned whether there may be a common factor leading to both alcoholism and psychopathy (e.g., Valliant, 1983). However, Valliant's own long-term prospective study of 456 disadvantaged males for 33 years suggests that the developmental precursors of psychopathy and alcoholism are quite different, although when one is present the other becomes quite probable. In his study he found that many psychopaths began to use alcohol as part of their antisocial behavior, but he noted that most alcoholics did not show antisocial behavior before they began abusing alcohol. At least some studies of genetic factors involved in the predisposition to antisocial personality and to alcoholism also support the idea that the two disorders are genetically independent (Cadoret et al., 1985; Cadoret, Troughton, & O'Gorman, 1987; Cloninger et al., 1978; Sher & Trull, 1994; Sutker, Bugg, & West, 1993).

Rejection of Authority. Psychopaths behave as if social regulations do not apply to them: They do not play by the rules of the game. Frequently they have a history of difficulties with educational and law enforcement authorities. Yet although they often drift into criminal activities, they are not typically calculating, professional criminals. Despite the difficulties they get into and the punishments they may receive, they go on behaving as if they are immune from the consequences of their actions.

Ability to Impress and Exploit Others. Often psychopaths are charming and likable, with a disarming manner that easily wins friends. Typically, they have a good sense of humor and an optimistic outlook. Although frequent liars, they usually will seem sincerely sorry if caught in a lie and promise to make amends—but will not do so. They seem to have good insight into other people's needs and weaknesses and are adept at exploiting them. For example, many psychopaths engage in unethical sales schemes in which they use their charm and the con-

Serial killer Ted Bundy exhibited antisocial behavior at its most extreme and dangerous. He showed the classic psychopathic traits of good looks, charm, and intelligence. But he was also highly manipulative and showed a total lack of remorse for his victims. Bundy's clean-cut image, which he used to get close to his victims—all young women whom he sexually abused and then murdered—was so convincing as to be chilling when the magnitude of his acts became apparent. Bundy was executed in Florida in 1989.

fidence they inspire in others to make "easy money." They readily find excuses and rationalizations for their antisocial conduct, typically projecting the blame onto someone else. Thus they are often able to convince other people—as well as themselves—that they are free of fault.

Inability to Maintain Good Relationships. Although initially able to win the liking and friendship of other people, psychopaths are seldom able to keep close friends. Irresponsible and egocentric, they are usually cynical, unsympathetic, ungrateful, and remorseless in their dealings. They seemingly cannot understand love in others or give it in return. As Horton, Louy, and Coppolillo (1974) expressed it, the psychopathic personality "continues to move through the world wrapped in his separateness as

though in an insulator, touched rarely and never moved by his fellow man" (p. 622).

Psychopaths pose a menace not only to chance acquaintances but also to their family and friends. Violence toward family members is common. Manipulative and exploitative in sexual relationships, psychopaths are irresponsible and unfaithful mates. Although they often promise to change, they rarely do so for long.

Many of the preceding characteristics may be found in varying degrees in maladjusted individuals, in those dependent on drugs, and in those showing other maladaptive behavior patterns. In the case of psychopaths, however, these characteristics are extremely pronounced and occur apart from other "symptoms" of psychopathology. Whereas most maladjusted people, for example, are beset by worry and anxiety and have a tendency to avoid difficult situations, psychopaths act on their impulses fearlessly, with little or no thought for the difficulties they may be incurring.

Patterns of Behavior Psychopathy is illustrated in the following classic case study published by Hare (1970):

Donald S., 30 years old, has just completed a three-year prison term for fraud, bigamy, false pretenses, and escaping lawful custody. The circumstances leading up to these offenses are interesting and consistent with his past behavior. With less than a month left to serve on an earlier 18-month term for fraud, he faked illness and escaped from the prison hospital. During the ten months of freedom that followed he engaged in a variety of illegal enterprises; the activity that resulted in his recapture was typical of his method of operation. By passing himself off as the "field executive" of an international philanthropic foundation, he was able to enlist the aid of several religious organizations in a fund-raising campaign. The campaign moved slowly at first, and in an attempt to speed things up, he arranged an interview with the local TV station. His performance during the interview was so impressive that funds started to pour in. However, unfortunately for Donald, the interview was also carried on a national news network. He was recognized and quickly arrested. During the ensuing trial it became evident that he experienced no sense of wrongdoing for his activities. He maintained, for example, that his passionate plea for funds "primed the pump"—that is, induced people to give to other charities as well as to the one he professed to represent. At the same time, he stated that most donations to charity are made by those who feel guilty about something and who therefore deserve to be bilked. This ability to rationalize his behavior and his lack of self-criticism were also evident in his attempts to solicit aid from the very people he had misled. Perhaps it is a tribute to his persuasiveness that a number of individuals actually did come to his support. During his three-year prison term, Donald spent much time searching for legal loopholes and writing to outside authorities, including local lawyers, the Prime Minister of Canada, and a Canadian representative to the United Nations. In each case he verbally attacked them for representing the authority and injustice responsible for his predicament. At the same time he requested them to intercede on his behalf and in the name of the justice they professed to represent.

While in prison he was used as a subject in some of the author's research. On his release he applied for admission to a university and, by way of reference, told the registrar that he had been one of the author's research colleagues! Several months later the author received a letter from him requesting a letter of recommendation on behalf of Donald's application for a job.

Donald was the youngest of three boys born to middle-class parents. Both of his brothers led normal, productive lives. His father spent a great deal of time with his business; when he was home he tended to be moody and to drink heavily when things were not going right. Donald's mother was a gentle, timid woman who tried to please her husband and to maintain a semblance of family harmony. When she discovered her children engaged in some mischief, she would threaten to tell their father. However, she seldom carried out these threats because she did not want to disturb her husband and because his reactions were likely to be dependent on his mood at the time; on some occasions he would fly into a rage and beat the children and on others he would administer a verbal reprimand, sometimes mild and sometimes severe.

By all accounts Donald was considered a willful and difficult child. When his desire for candy or toys was frustrated he would begin with a show of affection, and if this failed he would throw a temper tantrum; the latter was seldom

necessary because his angelic appearance and artful ways usually got him what he wanted. Similar tactics were used to avoid punishment for his numerous misdeeds. At first he would attempt to cover up with an elaborate facade of lies, often shifting the blame to his brothers. If this did not work, he would give a convincing display of remorse and contrition. When punishment was unavoidable he would become sullenly defiant, regarding it as an unjustifiable tax on his pleasures.

Although he was obviously very intelligent, his school years were academically undistinguished. He was restless, easily bored, and frequently truant. His behavior in the presence of the teacher or some other authority was usually quite good, but when he was on his own he generally got himself or others into trouble. Although he was often suspected of being the culprit, he was adept at talking his way out of difficulty.

Donald's misbehavior as a child took many forms including lying, cheating, petty theft, and the bullying of smaller children. As he grew older he became more and more interested in sex, gambling, and alcohol. When he was 14 he made crude sexual advances toward a younger girl, and when she threatened to tell her parents he locked her in a shed. It was about 16 hours before she was found. Donald at first denied knowledge of the incident, later stating that she had seduced him and that the door must have locked itself. He expressed no concern for the anguish experienced by the girl and her parents, nor did he give any indication that he felt morally culpable for what he had done. His parents were able to prevent charges being brought against him. Nevertheless, incidents of this sort were becoming more frequent and, in an attempt to prevent further embarrassment to the family, he was sent away to a private boarding school. . . .

When he was 17, Donald left the boarding school, forged his father's name to a large check, and spent about a year traveling around the world. He apparently lived well, using a combination of charm, physical attractiveness, and false pretenses to finance his way. During subsequent years he held a succession of jobs, never staying at any one for more than a few months. Throughout this period he was charged with a variety of crimes, including theft, drunkenness in a public place, assault, and many traffic violations. In most cases he was either fined or given a light sentence.

His sexual experiences were frequent, casual, and callous. When he was 22 he married a 41-

year-old woman whom he had met in a bar. Several other marriages followed, all bigamous. In each case the pattern was the same: he would marry someone on impulse, let her support him for several months, and then leave. One marriage was particularly interesting. After being charged with fraud Donald was sent to a psychiatric institution for a period of observation. While there he came to the attention of a female member of the professional staff. His charm, physical attractiveness, and convincing promises to reform led her to intervene on his behalf. He was given a suspended sentence and they were married a week later. At first things went reasonably well, but when she refused to pay some of his gambling debts he forged her name to a check and left. He was soon caught and given an 18-month prison term. As mentioned earlier, he escaped with less than a month left to serve.

It is interesting to note that Donald sees nothing particularly wrong with his behavior, nor does he express remorse or guilt for using others and causing them grief. Although his behavior is self-defeating in the long run, he considers it to be practical and possessed of good sense. Periodic punishments do nothing to decrease his egotism and confidence in his own abilities, nor do they offset the often considerable short-term gains of which he is capable. However, these short-term gains are invariably obtained at the expense of someone else. In this respect his behavior is entirely egocentric, and his needs are satisfied without any concern for the feelings and welfare of others. (Hare, 1970, pp. 1–4)

The repetitive behavior pattern shown by Donald is common among people diagnosed as psychopathic. Interestingly, many psychopaths and antisocial personalities do eventually settle down to responsible positions in their community. Recent evidence by Harpur and Hare (1994) shows that there seems to be a strong drop with age in the antisocial behavior associated with the second dimension of psychopathy, although the first dimension of egocentric, callous and remorseless traits appears to be fairly stable across the lifespan of the psychopath.

Causal Factors in Psychopathy and Antisocial Personality

As is the case with all the personality disorders discussed here, the causal factors in psychopathy and antisocial personality are still not fully understood. As always in the study of psychopathology, our perspective is complicated by the fact that the causal factors involved appear to differ from case to case, as well as from one socioeconomic level to another. However, more research has been conducted on the causes of psychopathy and antisocial personality than on any of the other personality disorders, so we are beginning to have a clearer picture of what some of the more important causal factors are. Contemporary research has variously stressed the causal roles of genetic factors, constitutional deficiencies, deficiencies in aversive emotional arousal, the early learning of antisocial behavior as a coping style, and the influence of particular family and environmental patterns.

Biological Factors Because an antisocial person's impulsiveness, acting out, and intolerance of discipline tend to appear early in life, several investigators have focused on the role of biological factors as causative agents in psychopathic behaviors. The following sections focus on some of these biological factors.

Genetic Influence. Most behavior genetic research has focused on genetic influences on criminality rather than on psychopathy per se. There have been many studies using the twin method of comparing concordance rates between monozygotic and dizygotic twins, as well as a number of studies using the adoption method where rates of criminal behavior in the adopted-away children of criminals are compared with the rates of criminal behavior in adopted-away children of normals. The results of both kinds of studies show a modest heritablity for antisocial or criminal behavior (Carey, 1992; Gottesman & Goldsmith, in press; Nigg & Goldsmith, 1994; Sutker et al., 1993) and at least one study reached similar conclusions for psychopathy (Schulsinger, 1972). However, researchers also note that strong environmental influences interact with genetic predispositions to determine which individuals become criminals or antisocial personalities. As reviewed by Sutker and colleagues (1993), among adopted children whose biological parents are criminals, these include unfavorable conditions in infancy, unstable adoptive placements, low social status, prolonged institutional care, and adoptive parent criminality.

Deficient Aversive Emotional Arousal and Conditioning. Research evidence indicates that psychopaths show deficient aversive emotional arousal; this condition presumably renders them less prone to fear and anxiety in stressful situations and less prone to normal conscience development and socialization. This lack of anxiety is more associated with the egocentric, callous, exploitative dimension of psychopathy rather than with the antisocial behavior dimension (which may have a slight positive association with anxiety) (Harpur et al., 1989).

In an early classic study, for example, Lykken (1957) found that psychopaths showed deficient conditioning of anxiety when anticipating punishment and also showed poor passive avoidance learning (that is, they were slow at learning to stop responding in order to avoid punishment). Similarly, Eysenck (1960) concluded that psychopaths are less sensitive to noxious stimuli and have a slower rate of conditioning than normal individuals. As a result, psychopaths presumably fail to acquire many of the conditioned reactions essential to normal passive avoidance of punishment, conscience development, and socialization (Trasler, 1978).

Hare (1970, 1978), Fowles (1993; Fowles & Missel, 1994) have reviewed an impressive array of studies that support these early ideas of Lykken and Eysenck showing that psychopaths are deficient in the conditioning of anxiety. Because such conditioning may underlie successful avoidance of punishment, this may also explain why their impulsive behavior goes unchecked. According to Fowles, the deficient anxiety conditioning seems to stem from psychopaths' having a deficient *behavioral inhibition system* (Fowles, 1980, 1993; Fowles & Missel, 1994). The behavioral inhibition system has been proposed by Gray (1975, 1987) to be the neural substrate of anxiety. It is also the neural system responsible for learning to inhibit responses to cues signalling punishment; this kind of so-called *passive avoidance learning* depends on conditioning of anxiety to the cue and the response when they will be followed by punishment. It is called *passive* avoidance learning because one learns to avoid punishment by *not* making a response (for example, by not commiting robbery). Thus, deficiences in this neural system are associated both with deficits in anxiety conditioning, and with deficits in learning to avoid punishment through passive avoidance.

The second important neural system in Gray's model is the *behavioral activation system:* This system activates behavior in response to cues for reward (positive reinforcement), as well as to cues for *active* avoidance of threatened punishment (such as in lying or running away to avoid punishment that one has been threatened with). Activation of this system is associated with positive emotions such as hope and relief. According to Fowles' theory, the behavioral activation system is thought to be normal or

possibly overactive in psychopaths, which may explain why they are quite focused on obtaining reward. Moreover, if they are caught in a misdeed, they are also very focused on actively avoiding threatened punishment (e.g., through deceit and lies, or running away). This hypothesis of Fowles that psychopaths have a deficient behavioral inhibition system and a normal or possibly overactive behavioral activation system seems to be able to account for three features of psychopathy: (a) psychopaths' deficient conditioning of anxiety to cues for punishment, (b) their difficulty learning to inhibit responses that may result in punishment (such as illegal and antisocial acts), and (c) their normal or hypernormal active avoidance of punishment (as in deceit, lies, and escape behavior when actively threatened with punishment) (Fowles, 1993, p. 9).

In a recent modification of his theory, Fowles and Missel (1994) have noted that although psychopaths do seem to be deficient in the kind of anxiety seen in anticipation of punishment, they may not be deficient in the kind of fear or panic response discussed in Chapter 5, which is driven by different neural systems, namely those responsible for the fight-or-flight response. In support of this idea, Fowles cites evidence from Schalling (1978) who distinguished between psychic anxiety (anticipatory worry and concern) and somatic anxiety (panic, cardiovascular symptoms, and muscle tenseness). Schalling found that psychopaths were low only in psychic anxiety, but not in somatic anxiety.

Researchers have also been interested in whether there are more general emotional deficits in psychopaths than simply in the conditioning of anxiety (Fowles & Missel, 1994). Several investigators have demonstrated, for example, that psychopaths show reduced responsivity to aversive visual images. Mathis (1970, cited in Hare, 1978b) found that psychopaths were less reactive than normals to pictures of severe facial injuries, suggesting a reduced sensitivity to mutilation stimuli, and perhaps in turn a reduced sensitivity to human suffering and injury. More recently, Patrick, Bradley, and Lang (1993) made an important contribution to our understanding of emotional deficits in psychopaths by taking advantage of the well-known phenomenon that both humans and animals show a larger startle response if a startle probe stimulus (such as a loud noise) is presented when the person is already in a fearful state. When comparing psychopathic and nonpsychopathic prisoners they found that the psychopaths did not show this effect, although the nonpsychopathic prisoners did. That is, the psychopaths did not show a larger startle response when watching unpleasant slides, as the nonpsychopaths did. The startle responding during neutral

Many people with antisocial personality disorder have an insatiable need for stimulation, leading them to engage in a variety of risky activities, such as playing with dangerous weapons.

and pleasant slides did not differ between the two groups. These differences in startle response during the unpleasant slides were related to the first (egocentric, remorseless, exploitative) dimension of psychopathy rather than to the second dimension of antisocial behavior. In other words, psychopaths who were more egocentric and remorseless showed the smallest startle responses during unpleasant slides. Patrick, Cuthbert, and Lang (1994) further showed that when asked to imagine frightening and neutral situations, psychopathic prisoners showed reduced physiological reactivity to the fearful imagery relative to that seen in the nonpsychopathic prisoners. Also of interest was the finding that the self-reports of emotional experience during the fearful imagery did not differ between the psychopaths and nonpsychopaths even though there were significant differences in physiological reactivity.

Stimulation Seeking and Delay of Gratification. In his study of criminal psychopaths, Hare (1968) reported that they operate at low levels of arousal and are deficient in autonomic variability (see also Fowles & Missel, 1994). He considered these characteristics—together with their lack of normal conditioning to noxious and painful stimuli—indicative of a "relative immunity" to stimulation, which in turn prompted them to seek stimulations and thrills as ends in themselves. In an early study comparing antisocial and normal persons, Fenz (1971) also found that the former seemed to have an insatiable need for stimulation. Several other investigators, using Zuckerman's sensation-seeking scale (a scale that measures such characteristics [Zuckerman,

1972, 1978]), have noted that people involved in antisocial behaviors—such as prison escapes (Farley & Farley, 1972), drug use (Kilpatrick et al., 1976), and recurrent arrests as skid-row alcoholics (Malatesta, Sutker, & Treiber, 1981)—have higher sensation-seeking scores and low tolerances for boredom (see Sutker et al., 1993). To some extent this high level of sensation seeking may also stem from the psychopath's underactive behavioral inhibition system; normal levels of activity in the behavioral inhibition system would lead a person to inhibit approach to a novel and potentially dangerous stimulus (Zuckerman, 1990).

There are also some findings supporting the idea that at least in certain situations psychopaths do have difficulty in delaying gratification (postponing immediate satisfaction in order to obtain greater rewards at a later point in time). For example, Newman, Kosson, and Patterson (1992) compared the performance of low-anxious psychopathic prisoners with nonpsychopathic prisoners on two delay-of-gratification tasks. In the first task, subjects were rewarded on some trials (by winning money) and not on others (by neither earning nor losing money). However, they were more likely to receive a reward if they delayed responding for 10 seconds than if they responded immediately. On this first task, the psychopaths showed no deficit in the ability to delay gratification. By contrast, on the second task when subjects did not receive a reward, they also received a punishment (losing money). That is, they not only did not win money; they actually lost money. In this mixed incentive condition in the second task (involving both reward and punishment) the low-anxious psychopaths delayed gratification less often than controls and earned less money than controls. Thus, the inability of psychopaths to delay gratification may be restricted to situations in which both reward and punishment are possible outcomes. This is consistent with other findings of Newman and his colleagues that psychopaths are particularly likely to perform poorly on a variety of tasks involving mixed incentive situations, where they will be rewarded for correct responses and punished for incorrect responses (e.g., Newman & Kosson, 1986). It appears that in such situations psychopaths become so focused on obtaining reward that they do not stop to reflect on the meaning of punishment and so do not learn to inhibit punished responses (Patterson & Newman, 1993).

Such findings support the earlier view of Quay (1965), who concluded that psychopathy is, in essence, an extreme form of stimulation-seeking behavior, accompanied by an inability to delay gratification under at least some circumstances:

> The psychopath is almost universally characterized as highly impulsive, relatively refractory to the effects of experience in modifying his socially troublesome behavior, and lacking in the ability to delay gratification. His penchant for creating excitement for the moment without regard for later consequences seems almost unlimited. He is unable to tolerate routine boredom. While he may engage in antisocial, even vicious, behavior, his outbursts frequently appear to be motivated by little more than a need for thrills and excitement. . . . It is the impulsivity and the lack of even minimal tolerance for sameness which appear to be the primary and distinctive features of the disorder. (p. 180)

Such extreme stimulation seeking does not bode well in the total context of a personality also characterized as impulsive, lacking in judgment, deficient in inner reality and moral controls, and seemingly unable to learn from punishment and experience. Although further investigation is needed, it seems plausible that stimulation seeking and impulsivity "unchecked by conditioned fear response is a two-edged sword for antisocial behavior" (Borkovec, 1970, p. 222).

Deficits in Cognitive Functioning. Gorenstein (1982) raised the possibility that antisocial persons have deficits in cognitive processes, such as attention to detail, reflecting dysfunctioning in the frontal-lobe area of the brain. He found that antisocial individuals tested in a psychiatric setting performed poorly on several cognitive measures of frontal-lobe functioning compared with nonantisocial individu-

als. However, Hare (1984) disputed these results on grounds that the particular procedures were inappropriate for testing frontal-lobe functioning. In an attempt to replicate the Gorenstein study using similar procedures to test frontal-lobe functioning in a prison population, Hare did not find differences between antisocial and nonantisocial individuals. More recent findings reviewed by Kandel and Fried (1989) and Sutker and colleagues (1993) highlight the difficulties in drawing definitive conclusions on this topic and concur that at present the status of evidence on frontal-lobe dysfunction in psychopathy is mixed.

Family Relationships Perhaps the most popular generalization about the development of psychopathy and antisocial personality is the assumption of some form of early disturbance in family relationships. The following sections explore some of these disturbances.

Early Parental Loss, Parental Rejection and Inconsistency. A number of early studies reported that an unusually high number of antisocial individuals had experienced the trauma of losing a parent at an early age—usually through the separation or divorce of their parents. For example, Greer (1964) found that 60 percent of one group of antisocial persons he studied had lost a parent during childhood, compared with 28 percent for a control group of other psychologically maladjusted persons and 27 percent for a control group of normal subjects. However, Hare (1970) suggested that the factor of key significance was not the parental loss per se, but rather the emotional disturbances in family relationships created before the departure of a parent; as discussed below, recent research has clearly confirmed this suggestion.

A number of early studies also attempted to relate parental rejection and inconsistent discipline to inadequate socialization and psychopathy. After an extensive review of the available literature, McCord and McCord (1964) concluded that severe parental rejection and lack of parental affection were the primary causes of psychopathy. In Chapter 3, we noted that slow conscience development and aggression are among the damaging effects of parental rejection and inconsistent discipline. We also noted that children subjected to inconsistent rewards and punishments for aggressive behavior were more resistant to efforts to extinguish the behavior than were children who experienced more consistent discipline.

However, parental rejection and inconsistency are not sufficient explanations for the origins of psychopathy or antisocial personality. On the one hand, these same conditions have been implicated in a wide range of later maladaptive behaviors, and on the other hand, many children coming from such family backgrounds do not become psychopathic or antisocial or evidence any other serious psychopathology. Thus further explanation is needed. In the following section we present an integrated developmental perspective with multiple interacting causal pathways.

A Developmental Perspective on Psychopathy and Antisocial Personality In Robins's (1978) classic prospective longitudinal studies, she concluded that these disorders generally begin early in childhood, especially for boys, and that the number of antisocial behaviors exhibited in childhood was the single best predictor of who develops an adult diagnosis of psychopathy or antisocial personality. These early antisocial symptoms included "theft, incorrigibility, running away from home, truancy, associating with other delinquent children, staying out past the hour allowed, discipline problems in school and school retardation" (Robins, 1978, p. 260), and today are associated with a diagnosis of conduct disorder. In addition, the age of onset of such antisocial symptoms was another predictor of adult antisocial personality, even when the number of childhood symptoms was controlled (Robins, 1991; Robins & Price, 1991); earlier onset was associated with greater likelihood of developing adult antisocial personality. Our understanding of the factors associated with the development of such behavior patterns in childhood, often leading to a diagnosis of conduct disorder (discussed more extensively in Chapter 14), has increased tremendously in the past 15 years. Because of its importance for understanding the causes of psychopathy and antisocial personality, it will briefly be reviewed here.

The initial problems that children who go on to develop adult antisocial personality disorder usually exhibit often lead to a diagnosis of *oppositional defiant disorder*, which is characterized by a pattern of hostile and defiant behavior toward authority figures that usually begins by the age of six years. Prospective studies have indicated a developmental sequence from oppositional defiant disorder to conduct disorder, which does not usually begin until age nine. As will be discussed more extensively in Chapter 14, it is children with this early history of oppositional defiant disorder, followed by early-onset conduct disorder, who are most likely to develop antisocial personality disorder, psychopathy, or other serious problems as adults. By contrast, those who develop conduct disorder in adolescence do not usually become psychopaths or antisocial personali-

Antisocial personality disorder in adulthood is always preceded by conduct disorder in adolescence (usually early-onset conduct disorder). However, not all adolescents with conduct disorder (especially late-onset conduct disorder) go on to become adult antisocial personalities.

ties but instead have problems limited to the adolescent years (Hinshaw, 1994; Moffitt, 1993a). As summarized by Hinshaw (1994), the typical pattern in the prepsychopath is as follows:

> For the prototypic "early onset" child, irritable, difficult temperamental style in infancy yields to harshly defiant, argumentative behavior during preschool; early indexes of fighting, lying, and petty theft by the beginning of grade school; assault and sexual precocity in preadolescence; robbery and substance abuse by midadolescence; and repetitive criminal activities, callous relationships, and spousal and child abuse in adulthood (Caspi & Moffitt, in press; Moffitt, 1993). Thus antisocial activities persist, but they change in form markedly with development. (Hinshaw, 1994, p. 21)

There is increasing evidence that genetic propensities leading to mild neuropsychological problems and difficult temperament may be important predisposing factors for early-onset conduct disorder. The behavioral problems that these predisposing factors create have a cascade of pervasive effects over time. For example, Moffitt and Lynam (1994) hypothesize:

> How might neuropsychological risk initiate a chain of events that culminates in antisocial disorders? One possibility is that such behavioral deficits evoke a chain of failed parent-child encounters. . . . Children with difficult temperaments and early behavior problems pose a challenge to even the most resourceful, loving, and patient families. . . . Even more disturbing, an infant's neurological health status has been

shown to be related to risk for maltreatment and neglect . . . a toddler's problem behaviors may affect
his parents' disciplinary strategies . . . children characterized by a "difficult temperament" in infancy are
more likely to resist their mothers' efforts to control
them . . . children's oppositional behaviors often
provoke and force adult family members to counter
with highly punitive and angry responses . . . children who coerce parents into providing short-term
payoffs in the immediate situation may thereby learn
an interactional style that continues to "work" in
similar ways in later social encounters and with different interaction partners. . . . The child with neuropsychological problems and difficult behavior may
learn early to rely on offensive interpersonal tactics.
If he generalized antisocial tactics to other settings,
his style may consolidate into a syndrome of conduct
disorder. (Moffitt & Lynam, 1994, pp. 245–247.)

In addition, many other psychosocial and sociocultural contextual variables contribute to the probability that a child with the genetic or constitutional
liabilities discussed above will develop conduct disorder, and later adult psychopathy or antisocial personality disorder. As summarized by Capaldi and
Patterson (1994), these include parental antisocial
behavior, divorce and other parental transitions,
low socioeconomic status, poor neighborhoods,
and parental stress and depression. All of these con-

tribute to poor and ineffective parenting skills—especially ineffective discipline and supervision.
"These children are trained by the family directly in
antisocial behavior by coercive interchanges and indirectly by lack of monitoring and consistent discipline" (Capaldi & Patterson, 1994, p. 169). This in
turn all too often leads to association with deviant
peers and the opportunity for further learning of
antisocial behavior. Their mediational model of
how all this occurs is illustrated in Figure 9.1.

In summary, individuals with psychopathy and antisocial personality show patterns of deviant behavior
from early on in childhood, first often in the form of
oppositional defiant disorder, and then in the form
of early onset conduct disorder. Increasingly our understanding of the causal factors suggests that varying combinations of biological, psychosocial, and sociocultural factors appear to be involved. In other
words, this is one disorder for which a biopsychosocial approach is absolutely critical.

Treatments and Outcomes in Psychopathic and Antisocial Personality

Because most people with psychopathic and antisocial personalities do not exhibit obvious psychopathology and can function effectively in many
respects, they seldom come to the attention of men-

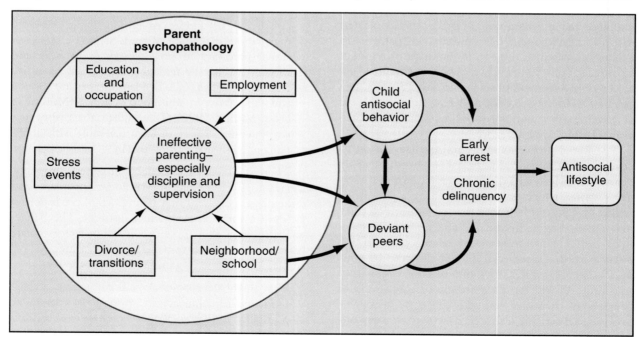

Figure 9.1   *A model for the association of family context and antisocial behavior. Each of the contextual variables in
this model has been shown to be related to antisocial behavior in boys, which in turn is related to antisocial behavior in
adults. Antisocial behavior in girls is far less common and has also been found to be less stable over time, making it more
difficult to predict (Capaldi & Patterson, 1994).*

An environment characterized by the breakdown of social norms, disorganization, undesirable peer models, and alienation may produce antisocial personalities.

tal hospitals or clinics. Those who run afoul of the law may participate in rehabilitation programs in penal institutions, but usually they are not changed by them. Even if more and better therapeutic facilities were available, effective treatment would still be a challenging task.

In general, traditional psychotherapeutic approaches have not proven effective in altering psychopathic and antisocial personalities. For example, in a treatment program for opiate addicts, those individuals with diagnosed psychopathy were the most difficult to treat and had the most negative outcomes—that is, they got worse or failed to improve (Woody et al., 1985). Factors inherent in the psychopath's personality—the inability to trust, to feel as others do, to fantasize, and to learn from experience—apparently make the prognosis for psychotherapy very poor (Charney, 1979). In addition, therapists must be vigilant for the possibility that the psychopathic patient may attempt to manipulate them, and that the information provided about the patient's life is likely to contain distortions and fabrications (Lion, 1978). Nor have biological treatment measures for psychopathic personalities—including electroconvulsive therapy or drugs—fared much better. There is some evidence that stimulant drugs that might be expected to reduce the cortical underarousal associated with psychopathy may have short-term beneficial effects on certain behavioral symptoms, but these drugs cannot be used for prolonged periods (Suedfeld & Landon, 1978). Antianxiety drugs may also have some beneficial effects in lowering hostility levels (Kellner, 1982), and drugs used to treat bipolar disorder such as lithium and carbazemine have had

some success in treating the aggressive impulsive behavior of violent aggressive criminals (Gitlin, 1993). However, none of these biological treatments have substantial impact on the disorder as a whole.

Some have considered the most promising treatment approach for psychopathic and antisocial personalities to be behavior therapy. Behavior therapists have dealt successfully with specific antisocial behaviors, and their techniques appear to offer some promise of more effective treatment (Bandura, 1969; Sutker, Archer, & Kilpatrick, 1979). On the basis of a now-classic review of research findings, Bandura (1969) suggested three steps that can be used to modify antisocial behavior through the application of learning principles: (a) the withdrawal of meaningful reinforcements for antisocial behavior, and, where appropriate, the use of punishment for such behavior; (b) the modeling of desired behavior by change agents—the therapist and other behavioral models who are admired—and the use of a graded system of rewards or reinforcers for imitating such behavior; and (c) the reduction of material incentives and rewards as the individual's behavior is increasingly brought under the control of self-administered, symbolic rewards. Essentially, the objective is to effect the gradual transfer of evaluative and reinforcement functions from the environment to the psychopathic or antisocial person by helping him or her develop inner controls that minimize the need for external ones.

An important facet of this approach is providing situations in which one individual's improved behavior becomes a model for others in treatment.

Patients can thus function as change agents for one another while furthering the long-range modification of their own behaviors. Such a program requires a controlled situation in which the therapist can administer or withhold reinforcement and the individual cannot leave treatment. The controlled situation seems necessary for treatment to succeed. When treating antisocial behavior, we are dealing with a total lifestyle rather than with a specific maladaptive behavior, like a phobia, that can be targeted for treatment. Without a controlled situation, the intermittent reinforcement of short-term gains and successful avoidance of punishments, combined with a lack of anxiety and guilt, leave an antisocial individual with little motivation to change.

Valliant (1975) has also argued that psychopaths can be effectively treated only in settings where behavioral control is possible—in other words, treating psychopaths on an outpatient basis is doomed to failure. He has found control necessary, also, to prevent self-destructive behaviors and to overcome these individuals' fears of intimacy. Like other investigators, he has concluded that by itself punishment is ineffective for controlling antisocial behavior. Vaillant also pointed out that one-to-one therapeutic relationships (even meeting several times a week) were rarely adequate to change psychopathic behavior. What seemed to work best was group membership that provided both an opportunity to learn to care for others and a place to be accepted by peers.

Beck and Freeman's (1990) more recent cognitive treatment for personality disorders also offers an interesting approach to the treatment of antisocial personality disorder by focusing on improving social and moral behavior through improvements in cognitive functioning. Beck and Freeman point to several self-serving dysfunctional beliefs that psychopaths tend to have. These include "Wanting something or wanting to avoid something justifies my actions"; "I always make good choices"; "The views of others are irrelevant to my decisions, unless they directly control my immediate consequences"; and "Undesirable consequences will not occur or will not matter to me" (Beck & Freeman, 1990, p. 154). In cognitive therapy, the therapist tries to guide the patient toward higher and more abstract kinds of thinking using principles that are based on theories of moral and cognitive development. This is done through guided discussions, structured cognitive exercises, and behavioral experiments. The following case example illustrates how a cognitive therapy session with an antisocial personality is conducted:

Therapist: How well has the "beat-the-system" approach actually worked out for you over time?

Brett: It works great . . . until someone catches on or starts to catch on. Then you have to scrap that plan and come up with a new one.

Therapist: How difficult was it, you know, to cover up one scheme and come up with a new one?

Brett: Sometimes it was really easy. There are some real pigeons out there.

Therapist: Was it always easy?

Brett: Well, no. Sometimes it was a real bitch. . . . Seems like I'm always needing a good plan to beat the system.

Therapist: Do you think it's ever easier to go with the system instead of trying to beat it in some way?

Brett: Well, after all that I have been through, I would have to say yes, there have been times that going with the system would have been easier in the long run . . . But . . . it's such a challenge to beat the system. It feels exciting when I come up with a new plan and think I can make it work. Going with the system might not even occur to me.

Therapist: So what you choose to do is dictated by how excited you feel about your idea, your plan?

Brett: Yeah.

Therapist: Yet several of your plans have actually ended up costing you and creating hassles in the long run.

Brett: Yeah.

Therapist: How does that fit with your goal of having an easy, carefree life where you don't have to work too hard?

Brett: It doesn't. (pause) So how do I get the easy life, Doc? . . .

Therapist: Do you ever think about what all your choices are and weigh them out, according to what consequences each one would have?

Brett: Not usually. Usually, I just go for beating the system.

Therapist: What do you think would happen if you thought about other options. . . .

Brett: I don't know.

Therapist: Is there some situation that you are dealing with right now in your life that you have to come up with money for, and you have to figure out how you are going to do it?

Brett: Yeah . . . how I'm going to afford to rent my apartment, the lease on the nightclub property, getting the place ready to open for business, and still pay my lawyer. . . .

[Later in the session after discussing options]

Therapist: So it sounds like you have several options for dealing with your current financial situation. Most of the time in the past, you have dealt with financial demands be getting involved in some beat-the system scheme. . . . This time, you have discussed several possibilities. Which do you think will be the easiest and best in the long run?

Brett: Fix up the space at the club and move in.

(From Beck & Freeman, 1990, pp. 171–72).

Although cognitive therapy along such lines seems quite promising, at present there are only case studies documenting its effectiveness. What will be needed in the future will be controlled trials, comparing cognitive therapy with other treatments, before we can determine if it is really more promising than other treatment modalities.

Fortunately, many psychopathic and antisocial personalities improve after the age of 40 even without treatment, possibly because of weaker biological drives, better insight into self-defeating behaviors, and the cumulative effects of social conditioning. Such individuals are often referred to as "burned-out psychopaths." Hare, McPherson, and Forth (1988) confirmed the hypothesis that psychopaths tend to burn out over time. They followed up a group of male psychopaths and tracked their criminal careers beyond age 40. They found a clear and dramatic reduction in criminal behavior after age 40. They were quick to note, however, that even with this reduction in criminal behavior, over 50 percent of these people continued being arrested after age 40. Even with the prospect that they might eventually engage in less destructive behavior, psychopaths can create a great deal of havoc before they reach 40—as well as afterward if they do not change. Moreover, Harpur and Hare (1994) have also shown that it is only the antisocial behavioral dimension of psychopathy that diminishes with age; the egocentric, callous, and exploitative affective and interpersonal dimension does not.

In view of the distress and unhappiness that psychopaths inflict on others and the social damage they cause, it seems desirable—and more economical in the long run—to put increased effort into the development of effective prevention programs. At present there is considerable ongoing longitudinal prevention research using children at risk for conduct disorder. Given that conduct disorder seems to always be a precursor of antisocial personality disorder, and that it is also very difficult to treat (e.g., Kazdin et al., 1989), the best approach seems to be a preventive one oriented both toward minimizing some of the developmental and environmental risk factors described earlier and in breaking some of the vicious cycles that these at-risk children seem to get themselves into. The early results of many of these prevention efforts seem promising (see McCord & Tremblay, 1992), but it will be many years before we understand their true potential for preventing adult psychopathy and antisocial personality disorder.

UNRESOLVED ISSUES

on Axis II of DSM-IV

While reading this chapter, you may have had some difficulty in capturing a clear, distinctive picture of each of the personality disorders. It is quite likely that as you studied the descriptions of the different disorders, the characteristics and attributes of some of them, say the schizoid personality disorder, seemed to blend with other conditions, such as the schizotypal or avoidant personality disorders. Although we attempted to highlight the apparent differences between prototypic cases of the different personality disorders with the greatest potential for overlap, in most cases people do not neatly fit these prototypes and instead qualify for more than one personality disorder. Indeed, as already noted, Widiger and Rogers (1989; Widiger et al., 1991) reported that an average of 85 percent of patients with one personality disorder also qualified for at least one other personality disorder, and Skodol and colleagues (1991) found that patients were given an average of four personality disorder diagnoses. In addition, one of the *most common* diagnoses is a grab-bag category of "Personality disorder not otherwise specified" (e.g., Morey, 1988a); this category is reserved for persons who do not cleanly fit within any of the ten categories, but rather share features from several different categories.

Further complicating matters is the fact that different semi-structured interviews and self-report inventories that have been developed to make personality disorder diagnosis more reliable tend to show only modest agreement on what personality disorder(s) a person has (Clark, 1992; Oldham et al., 1992). In other words, Axis II diagnoses are considerably less reliable than are diagnoses made for Axis I disorders. Finally, Clark (1992) has also reviewed evidence showing poor stability of personality disorder diagnoses over time, which should not be the case given the DSM definition of personality disorder as an "enduring pattern" of inflexible and maladaptive behavior.

Axis II diagnoses are unreliable (that is, there is a good deal of interrater disagreement about who qualifies for a diagnosis) for several reasons. One major difficulty stems from the assumption in DSM-IV that we can make a clear distinction between the presence and absence of a personality disorder (Widiger, 1993). In fact, some aspects of behavior are best thought of in terms of dimensions rather than categories. The personality processes classified on Axis II are dimensional in nature; that is, the data on which Axis II classifications are made are underlying personality traits that people vary on in terms of degree. For example, the trait of suspiciousness, central to paranoid personality disorder, can be viewed as a personality dimension on which essentially all people can be rated or given scores. The scores might range, on an illustrative "scale of suspiciousness," as follows:

Extremely Low	Low	Average	High	Extremely High
0 10 20	30 40 50	60	70 80	90 100

It is rather arbitrary to take the presence of a certain degree of suspiciousness as a criterion of paranoid personality disorder, because it exists to some extent as a trait in virtually everyone. Although it is possible that there might be discrete breaks in the distribution of criteria such that an extreme subgroup might be identified, many studies have now been conducted attempting to find such discrete breaks, and none have been found (Clark, 1992; Widiger, 1993). Indeed, Zimmerman and Coryell (1990) concluded that personality disorder "scores are continuously distributed without points of rarity to indicate where to make the distinction between normality and pathology" (p. 690). Moreover, Morey (1988a) showed that when changes are made in the cut-points or threshold for diagnosis of a personality disorder, as was done for several personality disorders when DSM-III was revised to DSM-III-R, this can have drastic effects in the apparent prevalence rates of a particular personality disorder diag-

nosis. For example, the revisions resulted in "an 800% increase in the rate of schizoid personality disorder and a 350% increase in narcissistic personality disorder" (Morey, 1988a, p. 575).

A second problem inherent in Axis II classifications involves the fact that there are enormous differences in the kinds of symptoms that people can have who nevertheless obtain the same diagnosis (Clark, 1992; Widiger, 1992, 1993). For example, to obtain a diagnosis of DSM-III-R borderline personality disorder, a person had to meet five out of eight possible symptom criteria (in DSM-IV it is five out of nine). Widiger (1993) calculated that this meant that there were 93 different ways (through different combinations of symptoms) to meet the DSM-III-R criteria for borderline personality disorder. Moreover, this also meant that two people *with the same diagnosis* might only share two symptoms. For example, one person might meet criteria 1–5, and a second person might meet criteria 4–8. By contrast, a third individual who met only criteria 1–4 would obtain no borderline personality diagnosis at all and yet surely would be more similar to the first person than would the first two people be to each other (Clark, 1992; Widiger, 1992, 1993).

Both researchers and clinicians are somewhat dissatisfied with Axis II. This situation is due in part to the difficulties in applying the system and to its relative unreliability. Widiger (1993), for example, has made a strong case that "categorical diagnoses of personality disorders have little to no support with respect to empirical data or rational argument. The categorical diagnoses represent instead a simplistic and presumptive understanding of personality disorder pathology that is a hindrance to empirical research and clinical practice" (p. 75). Moreover, in actual clinical practice, the multiaxial system is seldom applied to its fullest. Although information about Axis I diagnoses is usually recorded on patients' charts (because it is required for insurance and administrative purposes), information about other axes, including Axis II, is frequently omitted because their concepts are not easy to diagnose reliably. Moreover, the presence of an Axis II diagnosis is often used as a source of pessimism about the prognosis for a good response to treatment (Livesley et al., 1994).

Nevertheless, the developers of DSM-III made an important theoretical leap when they recognized the importance of weighing premorbid personality factors in the clinical picture and thus developed the second axis. Use of the Axis II concepts can lead to a better understanding of a case, particularly with regard to treatment outcomes. Strong, ingrained personality characteristics can work against treatment interventions. The use of Axis II forces a clinician to attend to these long-standing and difficult-to-change personality factors in planning treatment.

What can be done to resolve the difficulties with Axis II? The consensus today seems to be that the psychiatric community should give up on the typological approach to classification in favor of a dimensional approach and rating methods that would take into account the relative "amounts" of the primary traits shown by patients. Some of the resistance to this stems from the fact that medically oriented practitioners have a pronounced preference for categorical diagnosis. Moreover, there are fears that the dimensional approach to personality measurement might not be accepted because sound quantitative ratings might involve far too much time for most busy clinicians both to learn and to apply. Nevertheless, Widiger (1993) has also reviewed evidence showing that many clinicians are unhappy with the current categorical system, which is cumbersome when used properly because of the need to assess nearly 80 diagnostic criteria for DSM-IV. Indeed, he argued persuasively that the use of a dimensional model might require less time because it would reduce the redundancy and overlap that currently exists across the categories.

If the present categorical classification system continues to be used, a clearer set of classification rules is needed to make the categories more accurate and more mutually exclusive. The classification rules would need to be made more exhaustive and to incorporate behaviors and traits that do not overlap with other categories. However, there is little reason for optimism here because such attempts have already been made in revising DSM-III to DSM-III-R and DSM-IV. So although such an undertaking might be desirable, it may in the final analysis be scientifically impossible. There appear to be few if any "pure" clusters for grouping people's maladaptive personality traits into the type of neat pigeonholes ideally required by a categorical approach.

In sum, the ultimate status of Axis II in future editions of the DSM is uncertain. Many problems inherent in using typological classes for essentially dimensional behavior (traits) have yet to be resolved, although they are now almost universally recognized. Indeed, Allen Frances, the Chair of the DSM-IV Task Force, wrote, "Someday (perhaps in time for the fifth edition of the *Diagnostic and Statistical Manual of Mental Disorders [DSM-V]*), we will almost certainly be applying a dimensional model of personality diagnosis" (Frances, 1993, p. 110). One of the primary reasons this has not yet happened is that a number of different dimensional systems have been proposed, and there is as yet no clear evidence as to which one is best (Clark & Livesley, 1994; Frances, 1993; Widiger, 1993; Widiger & Costa, 1994). Moreover, some have argued that personality disorders should be included on Axis I along with the other Axis I disorders, saving Axis II for a description of each person's personality profile—normal or abnormal (Livesley et al., 1994).

SUMMARY

Personality disorders, in general, appear to be extreme or exaggerated patterns of personality traits that predispose an individual to maladaptive behavior. A number of personality disorders have been delineated in which there are persistent maladaptive patterns of perceiving, thinking, and relating to the environment. Three general clusters of personality disorders have been described. Individuals with paranoid, schizoid, and schizotypal personality disorders seem odd or eccentric; individuals with histrionic, narcissistic, antisocial, and borderline personality disorders share a common tendency to be dramatic, emotional, and erratic; and individuals with avoidant, dependent, and obsessive-compulsive personality disorders show fearfulness or tension as in anxiety-based disorders. Two provisional personality disorders are also listed for further study in the appendix of DSM-IV: the passive-aggressive and depressive personality disorders. The acceptability and utility of these disorders by researchers and practicing clinicians has not yet been determined.

There is as yet little research into what causes many of the personality disorders. There is some evidence for the role of constitutional and genetic causal factors in some of the personality disorders such as borderline and schizotypal personality disorders. However, none of the disorders is entirely heritable, and current work is being directed at understanding which psychological factors also play a causal role. Some evidence suggests that early childhood abuse may play a role in causing borderline personality disorder, but prospective studies are needed to draw definitive conclusions about this. In addition to the relative lack of research on causal factors for personality disorders, there is also relatively little good research about how best to treat these difficult disorders. Treatment of the Cluster C disorders such as dependent and avoidant personality disorder seems most promising, although a new form of cognitive-behavior therapy for borderline personality disorder (dialectical behavior therapy) also shows considerable promise in treating this very serious condition. Cluster A disorders such as schizotypal and paranoid are most difficult to treat.

One of the most notable of the personality disorders is the antisocial, or psychopathic, personality disorder. In this disorder, a person is callous and unethical, without loyalty or close relationships, but often with superficial charm and intelligence. Constitutional, learning, and adverse environmental factors seem to be important in causing the disorder. Some evidence suggests that genetic factors may also predispose an individual to develop this disorder. Psychopaths also show deficiencies in aversive emotional arousal and show poor conditioning of anxiety and passive avoidance, which seems to reflect an underactive behavioral inhibition system—the neural substrate for anxiety. The disorder often begins and is recognized in childhood or early adolescence, but only persons who are 18 or over are given the diagnosis of antisocial personality.

Treatment of psychopaths is difficult, because they rarely see any need for change and tend to blame other people for their problems. Traditional psychotherapy is typically ineffective, but where control is possible, as in institutional settings, methods incorporating meaningful reinforcement, behavior modification, or cognitive therapy have had some success.

Finally, there are many theoretical and practical problems with the personality disorders as currently described in the DSM-IV. One problem is that even

with the use of structured interviews the reliability of diagnosing personality disorders is less than ideal. In addition, the high number of people who are diagnosed with more than one personality disorder, or with personality disorder not otherwise specified, suggests that the categories as currently described do not really describe most people's personality problems adequately. Finally, most researchers and clinicians agree that a dimensional approach to understanding personality disorders is preferable, but as yet there has been no agreement regarding which of the possible dimensional approaches that has been studied is best.

KEY TERMS

personality disorders (p. 313)
paranoid personality disorder (p. 316)
schizoid personality disorder (p. 318)
schizotypal personality disorder (p. 319)
histrionic personality disorder (p. 320)
narcissistic personality disorder (p. 321)
antisocial personality disorder (p. 322)

borderline personality disorder (p. 323)
avoidant personality disorder (p. 324)
dependent personality disorder (p. 326)
obsessive-compulsive personality disorder (p. 326)
passive-aggressive personality disorder (p. 328)
depressive personality disorder (p. 328)
psychopathy (p. 335)

SUBSTANCE-RELATED AND OTHER ADDICTIVE DISORDERS

Alois Wey, Maisons *(1977). Wey (b. 1894) became interested in art and drawing in primary school. At the age of 14, Wey quit school and entered upon a difficult life complicated by bouts with alcoholism and by exacting toil, first as a helper in his father's roofing business, later as a master roofer, a factory worker, an electrician, a miner, and a cook. At the age of 80, living in a rest home, Wey resumed drawing. Many of his works take as their subjects exotic architectural structures, often resembling the architecture of foreign countries (though Wey's foreign travels were in fact quite limited).*

People of many ancient cultures, including the Egyptian, Greek, and Roman, made extensive and often excessive use of alcohol. Beer was first made in Egypt around 3000 B.C. The oldest surviving wine-making formulas were recorded by Marcus Cato in Italy almost a century and a half before the birth of Christ. About A.D. 800, the process of distillation was developed by an Arabian alchemist, thus making possible an increase in both the range and the potency of alcoholic beverages. Problems with excessive use of alcohol were observed almost as early as its use began. Cambyses, King of Persia in the sixth century B.C., has the dubious distinction of being one of the first alcoholics on record.

Addictive behavior, behavior based on the pathological need for a substance or activity, may involve the abuse of substances, such as alcohol or cocaine, or the excessive ingestion of high-caloric food, resulting in extreme obesity. Addictive behavior is one of the most pervasive and intransigent mental health problems facing our society today. Addictive disorders can be seen all around us: in extremely high rates of alcoholism, in tragic exposés of cocaine abuse among star athletes and entertainers, and in reports of the prevalence of pathological gambling.

The most commonly used problem substances are the **psychoactive drugs,** those drugs that affect mental functioning: alcohol, barbiturates, minor tranquilizers, amphetamines, heroin, and marijuana. Some of these drugs, such as alcohol, can be purchased legally by adults; others, such as the barbiturates, can be used legally under medical supervision; still others, such as heroin, are illegal.

The diagnostic classification of addictive or psychoactive substance-related disorders is divided into two major categories. First, psychoactive substance-induced organic mental disorders and syndromes (the latter of which are included within the organic mental disorders) are those conditions that involve *organic impairment* resulting from the ingestion of psychoactive substances. These conditions involve such factors as **toxicity,** the poisonous nature of the substance (leading to, for example, amphetamine delusional disorder, alcoholic intoxication, or cannabis delirium), or physiological changes in the brain due to vitamin deficiency (resulting in, for example, an alcohol abuse dementia disorder involving amnesia, formerly known as Korsakoff's syndrome).

A number of addictive disorders are covered in the second category, which focuses on the maladaptive behaviors resulting from regular and consistent use of a substance and includes psychoactive substance-abuse and -dependence disorders. **Psychoactive sub-**

stance abuse generally involves a pathological use of a substance resulting in potentially hazardous behavior, such as driving while intoxicated, or in continued use despite a persistent social, psychological, occupational, or health problem. **Psychoactive substance dependence** includes more severe forms of substance-use disorders and usually involves a marked physiological need for increasing amounts of a substance to achieve the desired effects. Dependence in these disorders means that an individual will show a tolerance for a drug or withdrawal symptoms when the drug is unavailable. (**Tolerance** refers to the need for increased amounts of a substance to achieve the desired effects; **withdrawal symptoms** are physical symptoms, such as sweating, tremors, and tension, that accompany abstinence from the drug.)

The increasing problem of substance abuse and dependence in our society has drawn both public and scientific attention. Although our present knowledge is far from complete, investigating these problems as maladaptive patterns of adjustment to life's demands, with no social stigma involved, has led to clear progress in understanding and treatment. Such an approach, of course, does not mean that an individual bears no personal responsibility in the development of a problem; the widespread notion that drug dependence and abuse can be viewed as forms of "disease" should not imply that the individual is a passive participant in the addiction process. Individual lifestyles and personality features are thought by many to play important roles in the development of addictive disorders and are central themes in some types of treatment.

In addition to the abuse and dependence disorders that involve particular substances, there are disorders that have all the features of an addictive condition, such as excessive eating, but do not involve substances with chemically addicting properties. Two of these disorders, excessive overeating and pathological gambling, are discussed in this chapter because the maladaptive behaviors involved and the treatment approaches shown to be effective suggest that they are quite similar to the various drug-use and drug-induced disorders.

ALCOHOL ABUSE AND DEPENDENCE

The terms *alcoholic* and *alcoholism* have been subject to some controversy and have been used differently by various groups in the past. Although these terms are widely used in practice, there is a trend today to use a more restrictive definition. The World Health Organization, for instance, no longer recommends the term *alcoholism* but prefers the term *alcohol dependence syndrome*—". . . a state, psychic and usually also physical, resulting from taking alcohol, characterized by behavioral and other responses that always include a compulsion to take alcohol on a continuous or periodic basis in order to experience its psychic effects, and sometimes to avoid the discomfort of its absence; tolerance may or may not be present" (1992, p. 4).

The term **alcoholic** is often used to refer to a person with a serious drinking problem, whose drinking impairs his or her life adjustment in terms of health, personal relationships, and occupational functioning. Likewise, the term **alcoholism** refers to a dependence on alcohol that seriously interferes with life adjustment.

However defined, alcoholism is a major problem in the United States. Helzer, Burnam, and McEvoy (1992), in a large NIMH epidemiological study, reported that the lifetime prevalence for alcoholism in the United States is 13.8 percent: One in seven people meet the criteria for alcohol abuse.

The potentially detrimental effects of excessive alcohol use—for an individual, his or her loved ones, and society—are legion. The life span of the average alcoholic is about 12 years shorter than that of the average citizen, and alcohol now ranks as the third major cause of death in the United States, behind coronary heart disease and cancer. Over 37 percent of alcohol abusers suffer from at least one coexisting mental disorder (Rovner, 1990). Organic impairment, including brain shrinkage, occurs in a high proportion of alcoholics (Lishman, Jacobson, & Acker, 1987), especially among binge drinkers, people who abuse alcohol following periods of sobriety (Hunt, 1993).

About 10 percent of alcoholics commit suicide (Miles, 1977), and over 18 percent are found to have a history of suicide attempts (Black et al., 1986). Research has reaffirmed the strong relationship found between substance abuse and suicide (Adam & Overholser, 1992; Murphy, 1988; Rich et al., 1988). The increased suicide rates among the young during the 1970s and 1980s have been tied to alcohol and drug abuse. Gomberg (1989) reported that, of women experiencing psychological difficulties, a significantly higher percentage with alcohol problems (40 percent) had attempted suicide than had women without alcohol problems (8.8 percent). In a follow-up study of mortality in psychiatric outpatients, Martin and colleagues (1985) found that alcoholics were in the group of disorders with highest mortality rates. Bengelsdorf (1970) has pointed out that ". . . its abuse has killed more people, sent more victims to hospitals, generated more police arrests, broken up more marriages and homes, and cost industry more money than has the abuse of heroin, amphetamines, barbiturates, and marijuana combined" (p. 7).

In addition to the serious problems excessive drinkers create for themselves, they also pose serious difficulties for others. About 10 percent of all deaths each year are related to alcohol abuse (Smith, 1989). Alcohol abuse is associated with over half the deaths and major injuries suffered in automobile accidents each year, and with about 50 percent of all murders, 40 percent of all assaults, 35 percent or more of all rapes, and 30 percent of all suicides. About one out of every three arrests in the United States is related to alcohol abuse. Alcohol-related accidents are, in fact, the leading cause of death among college-age people (National Institute of Drug Abuse, 1981). The financial drain imposed on the economy by alcoholism is estimated to be over $49.4 billion a year, in large part composed of losses to industry from absenteeism, lowered work efficiency, accidents, and the costs involved in the treatment of alcoholics.

Alcoholism in the United States cuts across all age, educational, occupational, and socioeconomic boundaries. It is considered a serious problem in industry, in the professions, and in the military; it is found among such seemingly unlikely candidates as priests, airline pilots, politicians, surgeons, law enforcement officers, and teenagers. The once popular image of the alcoholic as an unkempt resident of skid row is clearly inaccurate. Further myths about alcoholism are noted in HIGHLIGHT 10.1.

Most problem drinkers are men, with about five times the frequency of women (Helzer et al., 1991).

There do not appear to be important differences in rates of alcohol abuse between black and white Americans. It appears, too, that problem drinking may develop during any life period from early childhood through old age. Mann, Chassin, and Sher (1987) report that 64.9 percent of their sample of high school students indicated a moderate use of alcohol and 18.8 percent of these reported a misuse of alcohol. Helzer and colleagues (1991) reported that a lower incidence of alcoholism is associated with such factors as being married, having higher levels of education, and being older.

The Clinical Picture of Alcohol Abuse and Dependence

The Roman poet Horace, in the first century B.C., wrote lyrically about the effects of wine: "It discloses secrets; ratifies and confirms our hopes; thrusts the coward forth to battle; eases the anxious mind of its burthen; instructs in arts. Whom has not a cheerful glass made eloquent! Whom not quite free and easy from pinching poverty!" Unfortunately, the effects of alcohol are not always so benign or beneficial. According to a Japanese proverb, "First the man takes a drink, then the drink takes a drink, and then the drink takes the man."

Alcohol is a depressant that affects the higher brain centers, impairing judgment and other rational processes and lowering self-control. As behavioral restraints decline, a drinker may indulge in the satisfaction of impulses ordinarily held in check. Some degree of motor incoordination soon becomes ap-

Alcohol is associated with over half of the deaths and serious injuries suffered in automobile accidents in the United States each year.

HIGHLIGHT   10.1

Some Common Misconceptions About Alcohol and Alcoholism

Fiction	Fact
Alcohol is a stimulant.	Alcohol is actually a nervous system depressant.
You can always detect alcohol on the breath of a person who has been drinking.	It is not always possible to detect the presence of alcohol. Some individuals successfully cover up their alcohol use for years.
One ounce of 86-proof liquor contains more alcohol than two 12-ounce cans of beer.	Actually two 12-ounce cans of beer contain more than an ounce of alcohol.
Alcohol can help a person sleep more soundly.	Alcohol may actually interfere with sound sleep.
Impaired judgment does not occur before there are obvious signs of intoxication.	In fact, impaired judgment can occur long before motor signs of intoxication are apparent.
An individual will get more intoxicated by mixing liquors than by taking comparable amounts of one kind—e.g., bourbon, Scotch, or vodka.	It is the actual amount of alcohol in the bloodstream rather than the mix that determines intoxication.
Drinking several cups of coffee can counteract the effects of alcohol and enable a drinker to "sober up."	Drinking coffee does not affect the level of intoxication.
Exercise or a cold shower helps speed up the metabolism of alcohol.	Exercise and cold showers are futile attempts to increase alcohol metabolism.
People with "strong wills" need not be concerned about becoming alcoholics.	Alcohol is seductive and can lower the resistance of even the "strongest will."
Alcohol cannot produce a true addiction in the same sense that heroin can.	Alcohol has strong addictive properties.
One cannot become an alcoholic by drinking just beer.	One can consume a considerable amount of alcohol by drinking beer. It is, of course, the amount of alcohol that determines whether one becomes an alcoholic.
Alcohol is far less dangerous than marijuana.	There are considerably more individuals in treatment programs for alcohol problems than for marijuana abuse.
In a heavy drinker, damage to the liver shows up long before brain damage appears.	Heavy alcohol use can be manifested in organic brain damage before liver damage is detected.
The physiological withdrawal reaction from heroin is considered more dangerous than is withdrawal from alcohol.	The physiological symptoms accompanying withdrawal from heroin are no more frightening or traumatic to an individual than alcohol withdrawal. Actually alcohol withdrawal is potentially more lethal than opiate withdrawal.
Everybody drinks.	Actually, 28 percent of men and 50 percent of women in the United States are abstainers.

parent, and the drinker's discrimination and perception of cold, pain, and other discomforts are dulled. Typically the drinker experiences a sense of warmth, expansiveness, and well-being. In such a mood, unpleasant realities are screened out and the drinker's feelings of self-esteem and adequacy rise. Casual acquaintances become the best and most understanding of friends, and the drinker enters a generally pleasant world of unreality in which worries are temporarily left behind. Interestingly, a recent investigation by Sayette (1994) showed that when intoxicated people describe themselves they are more likely to "present negative attributes in a manner that is isolated from the self-concept" than sober subjects. That is, they tend to disclose fewer negative items in their speech in a self-protective effort.

When the alcohol content of the bloodstream reaches 0.1 percent, the individual is considered to be intoxicated, at least with respect to driving a vehicle in most states. Muscular coordination, speech, and vision are impaired, and thought processes are confused. Even before this level of intoxication is reached, however, judgment becomes impaired to such an extent that the person misjudges his or her condition. For example, drinkers tend to express confidence in their ability to drive safely long after such actions are in fact quite unsafe. When the blood-alcohol level reaches approximately 0.5 percent (although the level differs somewhat between individuals) the entire neural balance is upset and the individual passes out. Unconsciousness apparently acts as a safety device, because concentrations above 0.55 percent are usually lethal (see HIGH-LIGHT 10.2).

HIGHLIGHT | 10.2

Alcohol Levels in the Blood After Drinks Taken on an Empty Stomach by a 150-pound Male Drinking for One Hour

Effects	Time for Alcohol to Leave the Body (Hours)	Alcohol Concentration in Blood (Percent)	Amount of Beverage
Slight changes in feeling	1	0.03	1 highball (1½ oz. whiskey) *or* 1 cocktail (1½ oz. whiskey) *or* 5½ oz. ordinary wine *or* 1 bottle beer (12 oz.)
Feeling of warmth, mental relaxation	2	0.06	2 highballs *or* 2 cocktails *or* 11 oz. ordinary wine *or* 2 bottles beer
Exaggerated emotion and behavior—talkative, noisy, or morose	4	0.07	3 highballs *or* 3 cocktails *or* 16½ oz. ordinary wine *or* 4 bottles beer
Clumsiness—unsteadiness in standing or walking	6	0.12	4 highballs *or* 4 cocktails *or* 22 oz. ordinary wine *or* 6 bottles beer
Gross intoxication	10	0.15	5 highballs *or* 5 cocktails *or* 27½ oz ordinary wine *or* ½ pint whiskey

Calories
5½ oz. wine   115
12½ oz. beer   170
1½ oz. whisky   120

Note: Blood-alcohol level following given intake differs according to a person's weight, the length of the drinking time, and the person's sex.

Time, April 22, 1974, p. 77.

In general, it is the amount of alcohol actually concentrated in the bodily fluids, not the amount consumed, that determines intoxication. The effects of alcohol, however, vary for different drinkers, depending on physical condition, gender, amount of food in the stomach, and duration of the drinking. In addition, alcohol users may gradually build up a tolerance for the drug so that ever-increasing amounts may be needed to produce the desired effects. Drinkers' attitudes are important, too: Although actual motor and intellectual abilities decline in direct ratio to the blood concentration of alcohol, many people who consciously try to do so can maintain apparent control over their behavior, showing few outward signs of being intoxicated even after drinking relatively large amounts of alcohol.

Exactly how alcohol works on the brain is not yet fully understood, but several physiological effects are common. One is a tendency toward increased sexual stimulation but, simultaneously, lowered sexual performance. As Shakespeare wrote in Macbeth, alcohol "provokes the desire, but it takes away the performance."

Second, an appreciable number of alcohol abusers also experience blackouts—lapses of memory. At first these occur at high blood-alcohol levels, and a drinker may carry on a rational conversation or engage in other relatively complex activities but have no trace of recall the next day. For heavy drinkers, even moderate drinking can elicit memory lapses.

A third phenomenon associated with alcoholic intoxication is the hangover, which many drinkers experience at one time or another. Some observers consider the hangover to be a mild form of withdrawal. As yet, no one has come up with a satisfactory explanation or remedy for the symptoms of headache, nausea, and fatigue characteristic of the hangover.

Development of Alcohol Dependence Excessive drinking can be viewed as progressing insidiously from early- to middle- to late-stage alcoholism, although some alcoholics do not follow this progressively developing pattern. (HIGHLIGHT 10.3 presents some of the common early warning signs of excessive drinking.) Alcohol dependence is reached when symptoms of alcohol tolerance or alcohol withdrawal can be identified.

Chronic Alcohol Use and Dependence Although many investigators have maintained that alcohol is a dangerous systemic poison even in small amounts, in moderate amounts it is not harmful to most people. For pregnant women, however, even moderate amounts are believed to be dangerous; in fact, no safe level has been established, as is discussed in HIGHLIGHT 10.4.

For individuals who drink immoderately, the clinical picture is highly unfavorable. For one, the alcohol that is taken in must be assimilated by the body, except for about 5–10 percent that is eliminated through breath, urine, and perspiration. The work of assimilation is done by the liver, but when large amounts of alcohol are ingested, the liver may be seriously overworked and eventually suffer irreversible damage. In fact, over time, an excessive drinker has a 1-in-10 chance of developing cirrhosis of the liver,

---

10.3

Early Warning Signs of Drinking Problems

1. *Frequent desire*—increase in desire, often evidenced by eager anticipation of drinking after work and careful attention to maintaining supply.

2. *Increased consumption*—increase that seems gradual but is marked from month to month. An individual may begin to worry at this point and lie about the amount consumed.

3. *Extreme behavior*—commission of various acts that leave an individual feeling guilty and embarrassed the next day.

4. *"Pulling blanks"*—inability to remember what happened during an alcoholic bout.

5. *Morning drinking*—either as a means of reducing a hangover or as a "bracer" to help start the day.

A person who exhibits this pattern is well on the road to abusive drinking. The progression is likely to be facilitated if there is environmental support for heavy or excessive drinking from the person's spouse, job situation, or sociocultural setting.

HIGHLIGHT 10.4

Fetal Alcohol Syndrome: How Much Drinking Is Too Much?

Research indicates that heavy drinking by expectant mothers can affect the health of unborn babies. Newborn infants whose mothers drank heavily during pregnancy have been found to have frequent physical and behavioral abnormalities (Alison, 1994). For example, such infants have a growth deficiency, show facial and limb irregularities, and a central nervous system dysfunction (Jones & Smith, 1975; National Institute of Mental Health, 1978a; Jones, Smith, & Hansen, 1976; and Streissguth, 1976). In fact, *The Third Report on Alcohol and Health* (HEW, 1978) reports that alcohol abuse in pregnant women is the third-leading cause of birth defects (the first two being Down syndrome and spina bifida, the latter referring to the incomplete formation and fusion of the spinal canal and

one of the leading causes of mental retardation [Abel, 1988; Niccols, 1994] and ADHD [Nanson & Hiscock, 1990]. Although data on fetal alcohol syndrome are often difficult to obtain, current estimates range from 1 to 3 per 1,000 births (Abel, 1990) in the general population to 25 per 1,000 in women who are chronic alcoholics (Abel, 1988).

How much drinking endangers a newborn's health? The HEW report warns against drinking more than 1 ounce of alcohol per day or the equivalent (two 12-ounce cans of beer or two 5-ounce glasses of wine, for example). The actual amount of alcohol that can safely be ingested during pregnancy is not known, but it is clear that existing evidence for fetal alcohol syndrome is strongest when applied to heavy alcohol users rather

than light to moderate users (Kolata, 1981b). Nonetheless, the Surgeon General and many medical experts have concurred that pregnant women should abstain from using alcohol as the "safest course" until safe amounts of alcohol consumption can be determined (Raskin, 1993).

Unfortunately, treatment resources have traditionally been focused on and developed for men, in part because substance-abuse problems have been more common among men. However, with more women, including pregnant women developing alcohol-abuse problems, an important new need has developed for providing treatment services to future mothers and their babies. Treatment programs need to be developed that aid pregnant women and protect their children (Finkelstein, 1993).

The effects of fetal alcohol syndrome can be both dramatic and long-lasting. This child shows some of the permanent physical abnormalities characteristic of the syndrome: widely spaced eyes, short broad nose, underdeveloped upper lip, and receding chin.

a pathological condition in which liver cells are irreparably damaged and replaced by fibrous scar tissue. This results in the death of over 63,000 people each year (Smith, 1989).

Alcohol is also a high-calorie drug. A pint of whiskey—enough to make about eight to ten ordinary cocktails—provides about 1200 calories, which is approximately half the ordinary caloric requirement for a day. Thus consumption of alcohol reduces a drinker's appetite for other food. Because alcohol has no nutritional value, the excessive drinker often suffers from malnutrition (Derr & Gutman, 1994). Furthermore, heavy drinking impairs the body's ability to utilize nutrients, so the nutritional deficiency cannot be made up by popping vitamins. Alcoholics also experience increased gastrointestinal symptoms (Fields et al., 1994).

In addition to the other problems, an excessive drinker usually suffers from chronic fatigue, oversensitivity, and depression. Initially, alcohol may seem to provide a useful crutch for dealing with the stresses of life, especially during periods of acute stress, by helping screen out intolerable realities and enhancing the drinker's feelings of adequacy and worth. The excessive use of alcohol becomes counterproductive, however, resulting in lowered feelings of adequacy and worth, impaired reasoning and judgment, and gradual personality deterioration. Behavior typically becomes coarse and inappropriate, and the drinker assumes increasingly less responsibility, loses pride in personal appearance, neglects spouse and family, and becomes generally touchy, irritable, and unwilling to discuss the problem.

As judgment becomes impaired, an excessive drinker may be unable to hold a job and generally becomes unqualified to cope with new demands that arise. General personality disorganization and deterioration may be reflected in loss of employment and marital breakup. By this time, the drinker's general health is likely to have deteriorated, and brain and liver damage may have occurred. For example, Lishman (1990) has indicated that evidence is beginning to show that an alcoholic's brain could be accumulating diffuse organic damage even when no extreme organic symptoms are evident. Other researchers have found extensive alcohol consumption to be associated with an increased amount of neurological deficit in later life (Svanum and Schladenhauffen, 1986). (See Chapter 13.)

Psychoses Associated with Alcoholism Several acute psychotic reactions fit the diagnostic classification of substance-induced disorders. These reactions may develop in people who have been drinking excessively over long periods of time or who have a reduced tolerance for alcohol for other reasons—for example, because of brain lesions. Such acute reactions usually last only a short time and generally consist of confusion, excitement, and delirium. They are often called alcoholic psychoses because they are marked by a temporary loss of contact with reality. Two commonly recognized psychotic reactions will be briefly described.

Among those who drink excessively for a long time, a reaction known as *alcohol withdrawal delirium* (formerly known as *delirium tremens*) may occur. This reaction usually happens following a prolonged drinking spree when the person is in a state of withdrawal. Slight noises or sudden moving objects may cause considerable excitement and agitation. The full-blown symptoms include (a) disorientation for time and place in which, for example, a person may mistake the hospital for a church or jail, no longer recognize friends, or identify hospital attendants as old acquaintances; (b) vivid hallucinations, particularly of small, fast-moving animals like snakes, rats, and roaches, which are clearly localized in space; (c) acute fear, in which these animals may

Alcohol abuse knows no age, educational, occupational, or socioeconomic boundaries. Bill Shoemaker's outstanding career as a jockey—with the most wins in horse racing history—ended with an automobile accident that left him paralyzed. Shoemaker was alone in the car and driving drunk.

change in form, size, or color in terrifying ways; (d) extreme suggestibility, in which a person can be made to see almost any animal if its presence is merely suggested; (e) marked tremors of the hands, tongue, and lips; and (f) other symptoms, including perspiration, fever, a rapid and weak heartbeat, a coated tongue, and foul breath.

The delirium typically lasts from three to six days and is generally followed by a deep sleep. When a person awakens, few symptoms—aside from possible slight remorse—remain, but frequently the individual is badly scared and may not resume drinking for several weeks or months. Usually, however, drinking is eventually resumed, followed by a return to the hospital with a new attack. The death rate from withdrawal delirium as a result of convulsions, heart failure, and other complications once approximated 10 percent (Tavel, 1962). With drugs such as chlordiazepoxide, however, the current death rate during withdrawal delirium and acute alcoholic withdrawal has been markedly reduced.

A second alcohol-related psychosis is the disorder referred to as *alcohol amnestic disorder* (formerly known as *Korsakoff's psychosis*). This condition was first described by the Russian psychiatrist Korsakoff in 1887. The outstanding symptom is a memory defect (particularly with regard to recent events), which is sometimes accompanied by falsification of events (confabulation). Persons with this disorder may not recognize pictures, faces, rooms, and other objects that they have just seen, although they may feel that these people or objects are familiar. Such people increasingly tend to fill in their memory gaps with reminiscences and fanciful tales that lead to unconnected and distorted associations. These individuals may appear to be delirious, delusional, and disoriented for time and place, but ordinarily their confusion and disordered actions are closely related to their attempts to fill in memory gaps. The memory disturbance itself seems related to an inability to form new associations in a manner that renders them readily retrievable. Such a reaction usually occurs in older alcoholics, after many years of excessive drinking. These patients have also been observed to show other cognitive impairments such as planning deficits (Joyce & Robbins, 1991) and intellectual decline. Recent research with sophisticated brain-imaging techniques has found that patients with alcohol amnestic disorders show cortical lesions (Jernigan et al., 1991; Kopelman, 1991).

The symptoms of this disorder are now thought to be due to vitamin B (thiamine) deficiency and other dietary inadequacies. Although it has been generally believed that a diet rich in vitamins and minerals generally restores a patient to more normal physical and mental health, recent evidence suggests otherwise. Lishman (1990) reported that alcohol amnestic disorder did not respond well to thiamine replacement. Some memory functioning appears to be restored with prolonged abstinence. However, some personality deterioration usually remains in the form of memory impairment, blunted intellectual capacity, and lowered moral and ethical standards.

Causes of Alcohol Abuse and Dependence

In trying to identify the causes of problem drinking, some researchers have stressed the role of genetic and biochemical factors; others have pointed to psychosocial factors, viewing problem drinking as a maladaptive pattern of adjustment to the stress of life; and still others have emphasized sociocultural factors, such as the availability of alcohol and social approval of excessive drinking. As with most other forms of maladaptive behavior, it appears that there may be several types of alcohol dependence, each with somewhat different patterns of biological, psychosocial, and sociocultural causal factors. Recently, a committee of experts from the National Academy of Sciences (Institute of Medicine, 1990) concluded that identifying a single cause for all types of alcohol problems is unlikely.

Biological Factors In an alcohol-dependent person, cell metabolism has adapted itself to the presence of alcohol in the bloodstream and now demands it for stability. When the alcohol in the bloodstream falls below a certain level, withdrawal symptoms occur. These symptoms may be relatively mild—involving a craving for alcohol, tremors, perspiration, and weakness—or more severe—with nausea, vomiting, fever, rapid heartbeat, convulsions, and hallucinations. The shortcut to ending them is to take another drink. Once this point is reached, each drink serves to reinforce alcohol-seeking behavior because it reduces the unpleasant symptoms.

An extreme craving could result from a genetic vulnerability. The possibility of a genetic predisposition to developing alcohol-abuse problems has been widely researched. Alcoholism clearly tends to run in families (Dawson, Harford, & Grant, 1992). Cotton (1979)—in a review of 39 studies of families of 6251 alcoholics and 4083 nonalcoholics who had been followed over 40 years—reported that almost one-third of alcoholics had at least one parent with an alcohol problem. Likewise, a study of children of alcoholics by Cloninger and colleagues (1986) reported strong evidence for the inheritance of alcoholism. They found that, for males, having one alcoholic parent increased the rate of alcoholism from 11.4 percent to 29.5 percent, and having two alcoholic parents increased the rate to 41.2 percent. For females with no alcoholic parents, the rate was 5.0 percent; for those with one alcoholic parent, the rate was 9.5 percent; and for those with two alcoholic parents, it was 25.0 percent. Children of alcoholics may also develop other psychological problems. El Guebaly and colleagues (1992) reported that 38 percent of their anxiety-disordered patients were children of alcoholics. However, it should also be kept in mind that such family studies do not rule out environmental influences, such as modeling.

An interesting problem for researchers in the search for causal factors in substance abuse is how to determine if the behavior being investigated is antecedent to the drinking or caused by the drinking itself. One approach to understanding the precursors to alcoholism is to study the behavior of indi-

HIGHLIGHT | 10.5

Biological Factors in Addiction to Psychoactive Drugs

How do substances such as alcohol, cocaine, or opium come to have such powerful effects on some people—an overpowering hold that sometimes occurs in some people after only a few uses of some drugs? Although the exact mechanisms are not fully agreed on by experts in the field, two important factors are apparently involved. One factor involves the person's biological makeup or constitution, which includes both genetic inheritance and the environmental influences (learning factors) that enter into the need to seek mind-altering substances to an increasing degree. The other important factor in the equation is the ability of some drugs to activate areas of the brain that produce intrinsic pleasure and immediate, powerful reward. Let's examine each of these elements in more detail.

Constitutional Factors

Research has begun to accumulate that genetic factors contribute substantially to the development of alcohol preference. Research with animals, for example, has shown that strains of animals can be bred to have very high preference for alcohol (McBride et al., 1992). Moreover, genetic factors are likely to be involved in increased susceptibility or sensitivity to the effects of drugs. For example, low doses of alcohol or other addictive substances might be more stimulating

to some people as a result of inherited differences in the *mesocorticolimbic dopamine pathway* or *system* often referred to as the MCLP (Liebman & Cooper, 1989). It seems increasingly likely that inherited factors affect an individual's response to psychoactive drugs.

Nevertheless, genetics alone are not the whole story. The genetic mechanism or model for the generally agreed upon observation that alcoholism is familial is insufficient to explain the behavior fully (Schuckit & Irwin, 1990). That is, genetic transmission in the case of alcoholism does not follow the hereditary pattern found in other genetic disorders.

When we talk about familial or constitutional differences we are not strictly limiting our explanation to genetic inheritance. Rather, learning factors appear to play an important part in the development of constitutional reaction tendencies. Having a genetic predisposition or biological vulnerability to alcoholism, of course, is not a sufficient cause of the disorder. The person must be exposed to the substance to a sufficient degree for the addictive behavior to appear. In the case of alcohol, almost everyone in America becomes exposed to the drug to some degree through such means as peer pressure, parental example, and advertising. The development of alcoholism involves living in an

environment that promotes initial as well as continuing use of the substance. People become conditioned to stimuli and tend to respond in particular ways as a result of learning. Learning appears to play an important part in the development of substance abuse and antisocial personality disorders (see Chapter 9). There clearly are numerous reinforcements for using alcohol in our social environments and everyday lives. Furthermore, the use of alcohol in a social context is often a sufficient reason for many people to continue using the drug. However, research has also shown that psychoactive drugs such as alcohol contain *intrinsic* rewarding properties that provide pleasure in and of itself—apart from the social context or its operation to diminish worry or frustration. The drug stimulates pleasure centers in the brain.

Drug Action

Let's examine the role that drugs themselves play in the process of addiction. Drugs differ in terms of their biochemical properties as well as how rapidly they enter the brain. There are several routes of administration—oral, nasal, and intravenous. Alcohol is usually drunk, the slowest route, while cocaine is often self-administered by injection or taken nasally. Central to the neurochemical process underlying addiction is the role the drug plays in activating the

---

viduals who are at high risk for substance abuse but who are not yet affected by alcohol—prealcoholic personalities. An alcohol-risk personality has been described by Finn (1990) as an individual (usually an alcoholic's child) who has an inherited predisposition toward alcohol abuse and who is impulsive, prefers taking high risks, is emotionally unstable, has difficulty planning and organizing behavior, has problems in predicting the consequences of his or

her actions, has many psychological problems, finds that alcohol is helpful in coping with stress, does not experience hangovers, and finds alcohol rewarding.

Research has shown that prealcoholic men show different physiological patterns than nonalcoholic men in several respects (see HIGHLIGHT 10.5). Prealcoholic men are more sensitive to stress-response dampening (lessened experience of stress) with alcohol ingestion than are nonalcoholic men

"pleasure pathway." The mesocorticolimbic dopamine pathway or the MCLP is the center of psychoactive drug activation in the brain. The MCLP is made up of axons or neuronal cells in the middle portion of the brain known as the ventral tegmental area (see the figure) and connects to other brain centers such the nucleus accumbens and then to the frontal cortex. This neuronal system is involved in such functions as control of emotions, memory, and gratification. Research has shown that direct electrical stimulation of the MCLP produces great pleasure

and has strong reinforcing properties (Liebman & Cooper, 1989). Psychoactive drugs operate to change the brain's normal functioning and to activate the pleasure pathway. Drugs that activate the brain reward system obtain reinforcing action and, thereby, promote further use. The exposure of the brain to drugs changes its neurochemical structure and results in a number of behavioral effects. With continued use of the drug, neuroadaptation or tolerance and dependence develop (see p. 356).

The development of an alcohol addiction is a complex process in-

volving many elements—constitutional vulnerability and environmental encouragement as well as the unique biochemical properties of certain psychoactive substances. The exact role each of these ingredients plays in the addiction process has not been fully determined (and indeed may differ somewhat for each individual); however, each appears to contribute substantially to the process.

Sources: Kalint, 1989; Liebman & Cooper, 1989; Marlatt, 1992; Office of Technological Assessment, 1993; Tarter, 1988.

The MCLP, running from the ventral tegmental area to the nucleus accumbens to the frontal cortex, is central to the release of the neurotransmitter dopamine and in mediating the rewarding properties of drugs (Source: Office of Technology Assessment, 1993).

The mesocorticolimbic pathway

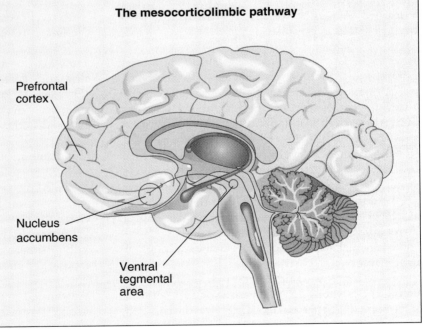

Prefrontal cortex

Nucleus accumbens

Ventral tegmental area

(Finn & Pihl, 1987; Finn, Zeitouni, & Pihl, 1990). They also show different alpha wave patterns on EEG (Stewart, Finn, & Pihl, 1990). Prealcoholic men as defined by the personality characteristics described in the preceding paragraph were found to show larger conditioned physiological responses to alcohol cues than were individuals who were considered at a low risk for alcoholism, according to Earlywine and Finn (1990). These results suggest that

prealcoholic men may be more prone to develop tolerance for alcohol than low-risk men.

In support of possible genetic factors in alcoholism, some research has suggested that certain ethnic groups, particularly Asians and American Indians, have abnormal physiological reactions to alcohol. Fenna and colleagues (1971) and Wolff (1972) found that Asian and Eskimo subjects showed a hypersensitive reaction, including flushing of the skin, a drop in blood pressure, and nausea following the ingestion of alcohol. The relatively lower rates of alcoholism among Asian groups are considered to be related to a faster metabolism of alcohol. Schaefer (1977, 1978), however, questioned these and other metabolism studies as a basis for interpreting cultural differences in alcoholism rates. Using more explicit criteria of metabolism rate, he found no differences in alcohol metabolism between a group of Reddis Indians and a group of northern European subjects. He concluded that further research into metabolism rate differences and sensitivity to alcohol needs to be integrated with studies focusing on relative stress in various cultures.

The role genetics play in the development of alcoholism remains unclear. We will return to this topic in the "Unresolved Issues" section at the end of the chapter.

Psychosocial Factors Not only do alcoholics become physiologically dependent on alcohol, they develop a powerful psychological dependence as well. Because excessive drinking is ultimately so destructive to a person's total life adjustment, the question arises as to why psychological dependence is learned. A number of psychosocial factors have been advanced as possible answers.

Failures in Parental Guidance. Stable family relationships and parental guidance are extremely important molding influences for children. The experiences and lessons we learn from important figures in our early years have a significant impact, one way or another, on us as adults. Children who are exposed to negative models early in their lives or experience other negative circumstances because the adults around them provide limited guidance often falter on the difficult steps they must take in life (Vega et al., 1993). These formative experiences can have a direct influence on whether a youngster becomes involved in maladaptive behavior such as alcohol or drug abuse.

In one recent program of research aimed at evaluating the possibility that negative socialization factors might influence alcohol use, Chassin and colleagues (1993) demonstrated that alcohol abuse in parents was associated with substance use in adolescents. They then evaluated several possible mediating factors that can influence adolescents in initiating alcohol use. They found that parenting skills or parental behavior was associated with substance use in adolescents. They reported that "alcoholic parents were less likely to monitor their adolescent's activities, and this lack of monitoring was related to the adolescent's affiliation with drug-using peers"

(p. 15). In addition, Chassin and colleagues found that stress and negative affect (more prevalent in families with an alcoholic parent) were associated with alcohol use in adolescents. They reported that "parental alcoholism was associated with increases in negative uncontrollable life events which, in turn, were linked to negative affect, to associations with drug-using peers, and to substance use" (p. 16).

Psychological Vulnerability. Is there an "alcoholic personality"—a type of character organization that predisposes a person to use alcohol rather than some other defensive pattern of coping with stress? In efforts to answer this question, investigators have found that potential alcoholics tend to be emotionally immature, to expect a great deal of the world, to require an inordinate amount of praise and appreciation, to react to failure with marked feelings of hurt and inferiority, to have low frustration tolerance, and to feel inadequate and unsure of their abilities to fulfill expected male or female roles. Morey, Skinner, and Blashfield (1984) have shown that persons at high risk for developing alcoholism were significantly more impulsive and aggressive than those at low risk for abusing alcohol.

In recent years substantial research has focused on the link between alcohol-abuse disorders and other disorders such as antisocial personality, depression, and schizophrenia. With respect to antisocial personality and alcohol abuse the relationship is strong (Harford & Parker, 1994) though by no means completely overlapping or clear in terms of which (if either) disorder causes which (Carroll, Ball, & Rounsaville, 1993). High rates of substance abuse are found among antisocial personalities (Regier, 1990).

While such findings provide promising leads, it is difficult to assess the role of specific personality characteristics in the development of alcoholism. Certainly many people with similar personality characteristics do not become alcoholics, and others with dissimilar ones do. The only characteristic that appears common to the backgrounds of most problem drinkers is personal maladjustment, yet most maladjusted people do not become alcoholics. An alcoholic's personality may be as much a result as a cause of his or her dependence on alcohol—for example, the excessive use of alcohol may lead to depression, or a depressed person may turn to the excessive use of alcohol, or both.

The two psychopathological conditions that have been most frequently linked to addictive disorders are depression (Lutz & Snow, 1985; Weissman et al., 1977) and antisocial personality (Cadoret et al., 1985; Stabenau, 1984). By far, most of the research has related antisocial personality and addictive disorders, with about 75–80 percent of the studies showing an association between the two (Alterman, 1988; Grand et al., 1985). However, other diagnostic groups have also been found to co-occur, for example, schizophrenia (Buckley et al., 1994; Mueser, Yarold, & Bellack, 1992); borderline personality (Miller et al., 1993); and anxiety disorders (Himle & Hill, 1991).

Some authorities have suggested that patients who are comorbid alcohol-depressives may be exhibiting both diseases distinctly (Coryell et al., 1992). Kushner and Mueser (1994) describe a model of comorbidity, based on common elements in the disorders, in which alcohol abuse and comorbid psychopathology share a common etiology, that is, stem from the same source.

For whatever reason they co-occur, the presence of other mental disorders in alcohol- or drug-abusing patients is a very important consideration when it comes to treatment (Mueser, Bellack, & Blanchard, 1992). McLellan and colleagues (1983) found that very troubled people showed virtually no improvement in any treatment.

Stress, Tension Reduction, and Reinforcement. A number of investigators have pointed out that the typical alcoholic is discontented with his or her life and is unable or unwilling to tolerate tension and stress. In this view, anyone who finds alcohol to be tension-reducing is in danger of becoming an alcoholic, even without an especially stressful life situation. If this were true, however, we would expect alcoholism to be far more common than it is, since alcohol tends to reduce tension for most people who use it. In addition, this model does not explain why some excessive drinkers are able to maintain control over their drinking and continue to function in society while others are not.

Cox and Klinger (1988; Cooper, 1994) describe a motivational model of alcohol use that places a great deal of responsibility on the individual. According to this view, the final common pathway of alcohol use is motivation; that is, a person decides, consciously or unconsciously, whether to consume a particular drink of alcohol. Alcohol is consumed to bring about affective changes, such as the mood-altering effects, and even indirect effects, such as peer approval. In short, alcohol is consumed because it is reinforcing to the individual.

Expectancy for Social Facilitation. In recent years a number of investigators have been exploring the idea that cognitive expectation might play an important role both in the initiation of drinking and in the maintenance of drinking behavior once adolescents have begun to use alcohol (Connors, Maisto, & Derman, 1992; Stacy, Widaman, & Marlatt, 1990). In this view, often referred to as the *reciprocal influence model*, adolescents begin drinking as a result of expectations that alcohol will increase their popularity and acceptance by their peers. Research has shown that expectancies of social benefit can influence adolescents' decisions to start drinking and predicts their consumption of alcohol (Christiansen et al., 1989).

This view that adolescents' expectancies influence the onset and pattern of drinking behavior provides professionals with an important and potentially powerful means of deterring, or at least delaying the onset of, drinking among young people. From this perspective, alcohol use in teenagers can be countered by implementing strategies to alter these expectancies before drinking begins. Smith and colleagues (1995) have suggested that prevention efforts should be targeted at children before they begin to drink to avoid the positive feedback cycle of reciprocal reinforcement between expectancy and drinking (see the discussion on prevention in Chapter 18).

Marital and Other Intimate Relationships. Excessive drinking often begins during crisis periods in marital or other intimate personal relationships, particularly crises that lead to hurt and self-devaluation. The marital relationship may actually serve to maintain the pattern of excessive drinking. Marital partners may behave toward each other in ways that promote or enable the spouse's excessive drinking. For example, a husband who lives with an alcoholic wife is often unaware of the fact that, gradually and inevitably, many of the decisions he makes every day are based on the expectation that his wife will be drinking. These expectations, in turn, may make the

The use of alcohol in convivial social settings can be highly reinforcing to drinking behavior.

drinking behavior more likely. Thus one important concern in many treatment programs today involves identifying relationship patterns that tend to foster the drinking in the alcohol-abusing person. That is, such programs try to identify the personality or lifestyle factors in a relationship that serve to promote, maintain, or to justify the drinking behavior of an alcoholic. Eventually an entire marriage may center on the drinking of an alcoholic spouse. In some instances, the husband or wife may also begin to drink excessively, possibly through the reinforcement of such behavior by the drinking mate or to blank out the disillusionment, frustration, and resentment that are often elicited by an alcoholic spouse. Of course, such relationships are not restricted to marital partners but may also occur in those involved in love affairs or close friendships.

Excessive use of alcohol is one of the most frequent causes of divorce in the United States (Fillmore et al., 1994), and often a hidden factor in the two most common causes—financial and sexual problems. The deterioration in alcoholics' interpersonal relationships, of course, further augments the stress and disorganization in their lives. The breakup of marital relationships can be a highly stressful situation for many people. The stress of divorce and the often erratic adjustment period that follows can lead to increased substance-abuse problems.

Family relationship problems have also been related to alcoholism. In a longitudinal study of alcohol abuse, Vaillant and Milofsky (1982) reported that six familial factors were significantly associated with the development of alcoholism. Six family factors—father's alcoholism, marital conflict, lax maternal supervision, many moves, no attachment to father, and no family cohesiveness—were found to be significant likely etiological sources of alcoholism.

Sociocultural Factors In a general sense, our culture has become dependent on alcohol as a social lubricant and a means of reducing tension. Thus numerous investigators have pointed to the role of sociocultural as well as physiological and psychological factors in the high rate of alcohol abuse and dependence among Americans (Vega et al., 1993). It is of interest to note here the conclusions of Pliner and Cappell (1974) concerning the reinforcing effects of social drinking in our society, in which liquor has come to play an almost ritualistic role in promoting gaiety and pleasant social interaction:

> According to the present results, if it is the case that much of the early drinking experience of . . . individuals takes place in such convivial social settings, drinking will be likely to become associated with positive

Drunken college students on spring break have become a symbol of springtime. Our society reinforces the idea that alcohol promotes gaiety and fun—witness any beer commercial—but the expectation that drinking will have social benefits can lead some people to excessive alcohol use.

affective experiences. This reinforcing consequence may in turn make drinking more probable in the future. Thus, to the extent that a social context can enhance the attraction of alcohol, for some individuals it may play a crucial role in the etiology of pathological patterns of alcohol consumption. (p. 425)

Bales (1946), in a classic study, outlined three cultural factors that play a part in determining the incidence of alcoholism in a given society: (a) the degree of stress and inner tension produced by the culture; (b) the attitudes toward drinking fostered by the culture; and (c) the degree to which the culture provides substitute means of satisfaction and other ways of coping with tension and anxiety. This outline has been borne out by cross-cultural studies. The importance of the stress level in a given culture is shown in studies of preliterate societies. Rapid social change and social disintegration also seem to foster excessive drinking.

The effect of cultural attitudes toward drinking is well illustrated by Muslims and Mormons, whose religious values prohibit the use of alcohol, and by orthodox Jews, who have traditionally limited its use largely to religious rituals. The incidence of alcoholism among these groups is minimal. In comparison, the incidence of alcoholism is high among Europeans, who comprise less than 15 percent of the world's population yet consume about half the alcohol (Sulkunen, 1976). Interestingly, Europe and six countries that have been influenced by European culture—Argentina, Canada, Chile, Japan, the

United States, and New Zealand—make up less than 20 percent of the world's population yet consume 80 percent of the alcohol (Barry, 1982). The French appear to have the highest rate of alcoholism in the world, approximately 15 percent of the population. France has both the highest per capita alcohol consumption and the highest death rate from cirrhosis of the liver (Noble, 1979). Thus it appears that religious sanctions and social customs can determine whether alcohol is one of the coping methods commonly used in a given group or society.

The behavior that is manifested under the influence of alcohol appears to be influenced by cultural factors. Lindman and Lang (1994), in a study of alcohol-related behavior in eight countries, found that most subjects expressed the view that aggressive behavior frequently followed after drinking "many" drinks; however, the expectation that alcohol leads to aggression is related to cultural traditions.

In sum, we can identify many reasons why people drink—as well as many conditions that can predispose them to do so and reinforce drinking behavior—but the combination of factors that result in a person's becoming an alcoholic are still unknown.

Treatments and Outcomes

Unfortunately, many alcoholics refuse to admit that they have a problem or seek assistance before they "hit bottom," and many who do go into treatment leave before therapy is completed. DiClemente (1993) refers to the addictions as "diseases of denial." In a survey that included more than 60,000 treated alcoholics, Booth, Cook, and Blow (1992) reported that 11 percent left treatment against medical advice. When alcoholics are confronted with their drinking problem they may react with denial or become angry at the "messenger" and withdraw from this person (Miller & Rollnick, 1991).

A multidisciplinary approach to the treatment of drinking problems appears to be most effective because the problems are often complex, requiring flexibility and individualization of treatment procedures. Also, an alcoholic's needs change as treatment progresses.

Formerly it was considered essential for the treatment of a problem drinker to take place in an institutional setting, removing the person from a probably aversive life situation and making possible more control over his or her behavior. However, an increasing number of problem drinkers are now being treated in community clinics, especially drinkers who do not require hospitalization for withdrawal treatment. In fact, one survey of treatment facilities (ADAMHA, 1982) found that most alcoholics are treated on an outpatient basis, which some authorities consider as effective as inpatient treatment (Miller & Hester, 1986). For example, McKay and associates (1994) found that patients who completed a day hospital treatment program and continued to participate in self-help groups had lower rates of cocaine or alcohol use at follow-up. When hospitalization is required, the length of the hospital stay is often short—an average of roughly 28 days. (In some treatment programs, stays are now being limited to 7–14 days.) Halfway houses are also being used increasingly to bridge the gap between institutionalization and return to the community and to enhance the flexibility of treatment programs. There is some indication that the more intensive the inpatient treatment the better the results. Bunn and colleagues (1994) reported that subsequent death rates (traditionally high among alcoholics) were significantly lower among those completing intensive inpatient treatment compared with outpatient programs.

Treatment program objectives usually include detoxification, physical rehabilitation, control over alcohol-abuse behavior, and development of an individual's realization that he or she can cope with the problems of living and lead a much more rewarding life without alcohol. Although traditional treatment programs usually include the goal of abstinence from alcohol, some current programs are attempting to promote controlled drinking as a treatment goal for some problem drinkers.

Biological Approaches Biological approaches include a variety of treatment measures ranging from detoxification procedures to medication use. In acute intoxication, the initial focus is on detoxification (the elimination of alcoholic substances from an individual's body), on the treatment of withdrawal symptoms, and on a medical regimen for physical rehabilitation. One of the primary goals in treatment of withdrawal symptoms is to reduce the physical symptoms characteristic of the syndrome such as insomnia, headache, gastrointestinal distress, and tremulousness. Central to the treatment are the prevention of heart arrhythmias, seizures, delirium, and death (Bohn, 1993). These steps can usually best be handled in a hospital or clinic, where drugs such as Valium have largely revolutionized the treatment of withdrawal symptoms (Rozdemir, Bremner, & Navanjo, 1994). Such drugs overcome motor excitement, nausea, and vomiting; prevent withdrawal delirium and convulsions; and help alleviate the tension and anxiety associated with withdrawal. Concern is growing, however, that the use of tranquilizers at this stage does not promote long-term recovery and may foster addiction to another substance. Accordingly, some detoxification clinics are exploring alternative approaches, including a gradual weaning from alcohol instead of a sudden cutoff.

Medications are also used in the treatment of alcoholism. Maintenance doses of mild tranquilizers are sometimes given to patients withdrawing from alcohol to reduce anxiety and help them sleep. Such use of tranquilizers may be less effective than no treatment at all, however. Usually patients must learn to abstain from tranquilizers as well as from alcohol, because they tend to misuse both. Further, under the influence of tranquilizers, patients may even return to alcohol use.

Disulfiram (Antabuse), a drug that causes violent vomiting when followed by ingestion of alcohol, may be administered to prevent an immediate return to drinking (Chic et al., 1992). Adelman and Weiss (1989), studying the efficacy of different treatment strategies with alcoholics, reported that alcohol treatment programs that use Antabuse may have clear advantages over programs that do not in that they usually suppress drinking when the drug is taken regularly. However, such deterrent therapy is seldom advocated as the sole approach, because pharmacological methods alone have not proven effective in treating alcoholism (Gorlick, 1993). For example, since the drug is usually self-administered, an alcoholic may simply discontinue the use of Antabuse when he or she is released from a hospital or clinic and begin to drink again. In fact, the primary value of drugs of this type seems to be their ability to interrupt the alcoholic cycle for a period of time, during which therapy may be undertaken. Uncomfortable

side effects may accompany the use of Antabuse; for example, alcohol-based after-shave lotion can be absorbed through the skin, resulting in illness. Moreover, the cost of Antabuse, since it requires careful medical maintenance, is higher than for many other, more effective treatments (Holder et al., 1991).

Psychological Treatment Approaches Detoxification is optimally followed by psychological treatment, including family counseling and the use of community resources relating to employment and other aspects of a person's social readjustment. Although individual psychotherapy is sometimes effective, the focus of psychosocial measures in the alcoholism treatment more often involves group therapy, environmental intervention, behavior therapy, and the approach used by Alcoholics Anonymous.

Group Therapy. In the rugged give-and-take of group therapy, alcoholics are sometimes forced to face their problem and recognize its possible disastrous consequences, but they also begin to see new possibilities for coping with it. Often, but by no means always, this double recognition paves the way for learning more effective methods of coping and other positive steps toward dealing with their drinking problem.

In some instances, the spouses of alcoholics and even their children may be invited to join in group therapy meetings. In other situations, family treatment is itself the central focus of therapeutic efforts. In this case, the alcoholic is seen as a member of a disturbed family in which all the members have a responsibility for cooperating in treatment. Because

Family relationships are often severely threatened by an alcoholic family member. Family-oriented counseling sessions can help alcoholics and their families gain an understanding of the nature of the alcoholism and to learn effective ways of dealing with the problems of returning to sobriety.

family members are frequently the people most victimized by the alcoholic's addiction, they often tend to be judgmental and punitive, and the alcoholic, who has already passed harsh judgment on himself or herself, tolerates this further source of devaluation poorly. In other instances, family members may unwittingly encourage an alcoholic to remain addicted, as, for example, when a man with a need to dominate his wife finds that a continually drunken and remorseful spouse best meets his needs.

Environmental Intervention. As with other serious maladaptive behaviors, a total treatment program for alcoholism usually requires measures to alleviate a patient's aversive life situation. Environmental support has been shown to be an important ingredient to an alcoholic's recovery (Booth et al., 1992a; 1992b). As a result of their drinking, alcoholics often become estranged from family and friends and either lose or jeopardize their job. Typically the reaction of those around them is not as understanding or supportive as it would be if they had a physical illness of comparable magnitude. Simply helping alcoholics learn more effective coping techniques may not be enough if their social environment remains hostile and threatening. For alcoholics who have been hospitalized, halfway houses—designed to assist them in their return to family and community—are often important adjuncts to their total treatment program.

Relapses and continued deterioration are generally associated with a lack of close relationships with family or friends, or with living in a stressful environment. In general, it appears unlikely that an alcoholic will remain abstinent after treatment unless the negative psychosocial factors that operated in the past are dealt with.

Behavior Therapy. One interesting and often effective form of treatment for alcohol-abuse disorders is behavior therapy, of which several types exist. One is *aversive conditioning,* involving the presentation of a wide range of noxious stimuli with alcohol consumption in order to suppress drinking behavior. For example, the ingestion of alcohol might be paired with an electrical shock.

A variety of pharmacological and other deterrent measures can be used in behavior therapy after detoxification. One approach involves an intramuscular injection of emetine hydrochloride, an emetic. Before experiencing the nausea that results from the injection, a patient is given alcohol, so that the sight, smell, and taste of the beverage become associated with severe retching and vomiting. That is, a conditioned aversion to taste and smell of alcohol devel-

ops. With repetition, this classical conditioning procedure acts as a strong deterrent to further drinking—probably in part because it adds an immediate and unpleasant physiological consequence to the more general socially aversive consequences of excessive drinking.

One of the most promising contemporary procedures for treating alcoholics is the cognitive-behavioral approach recommended by Marlatt (1985) and Lang and Marlatt (1983). This approach combines cognitive-behavioral strategies of intervention with social-learning theory and modeling of behavior. The approach, often referred to as a skills-training procedure, is usually aimed at younger problem drinkers who are considered to be at risk for developing more severe drinking problems because of alcoholism in their family history or their heavy current consumption level. This approach relies on such techniques as imparting specific knowledge about alcohol, developing coping skills in situations associated with increased risk of alcohol use, modifying cognitions and expectancies, and acquiring stress-management skills. This cognitive-behavioral approach clearly has intuitive appeal; however, its relative effectiveness has yet to be demonstrated. Holder and colleagues (1991) reported that this approach tends to be less effective than other behavioral methods such as social-skills training.

One promising approach to teaching alcoholics self-control over drinking was reported by Lovibond and Caddy (1970). They conducted blood-alcohol discrimination training sessions, which were aimed at getting alcoholics to control drinking by becoming aware of intoxicating levels of alcohol in their blood. Miller and Munoz (1976) and Miller (1978) used behavioral self-control training to teach alcoholics to monitor and reduce their alcohol intake. Patients kept records of their drinking behavior, and the therapy sessions focused on determining blood-alcohol concentration based on their intake. Strategies for increasing future intake control were discussed along with identifying alternatives to alcohol consumption. Self-control training techniques, in which the goal of therapy is to get alcoholics to reduce alcohol intake without necessarily abstaining altogether, have a great deal of appeal for some drinkers. It is difficult, of course, for individuals who are extremely dependent on the effects of alcohol to abstain totally from drinking. Thus many alcoholics fail to complete traditional treatment programs. The idea that they might be able to learn to control their drinking and at the same time enjoy the continued use of alcohol might serve as a motivating element (Lang & Kidorf, 1990).

Other behavioral techniques have also received attention in recent years, partly because they are based on the hypothesis that some problem drinkers need not give up drinking altogether but can learn to drink moderately (Gottheil et al., 1982; Lang & Kidorf, 1990; Miller, 1978). Several approaches to learning controlled drinking have been attempted (McMurran & Hollin, 1993), and research has suggested that some alcoholics can learn to control their alcohol intake (Miller, 1978; Miller & Caddy, 1977). Miller and colleagues (1986) evaluated the results of four long-term follow-up studies of controlled-drinking treatment programs. They reported a clear trend of increased numbers of abstainers and relapsed cases at long-term follow-up. However, a consistent percentage (15 percent) of subjects across the four studies controlled their drinking. The researchers concluded that controlled drinking was more likely to be successful in persons with less severe alcohol problems. The finding that some individuals are able to maintain some control over their drinking after treatment (and not remain totally abstinent) was also reported by Polich, Armor, and Braiker (1981). They found that 18 percent of the alcoholics they studied had reportedly been able to drink socially without problems during the six-month follow-up of treatment.

Whether alcoholics who have learned to recognize intoxicating levels of alcohol and to limit their intake to lower levels will maintain these skills in the long run has not been sufficiently demonstrated. Most workers in the field still assume that total abstinence should be the goal for all problem drinkers. Some groups, such as Alcoholics Anonymous, are adamant in their opposition to programs aimed at controlled drinking for alcohol-dependent individuals.

Alcoholics Anonymous. A practical approach to alcoholism that has reportedly met with considerable success is that of Alcoholics Anonymous (AA). This organization was started in 1935 by two men, Dr. Bob and Bill W. in Akron, Ohio. Bill W. recovered from alcoholism through a "fundamental spiritual change," and immediately sought out Dr. Bob, who, with Bill's assistance, achieved recovery. They in turn began to help other alcoholics. Since that time, AA has grown to over 10,000 groups with over 1.5 million members (AA, 1987) with an annual growth rate of about 6–7 percent (AA, 1989). In addition, AA groups have been established in many other countries.

Alcoholics Anonymous operates primarily as a nonprofessional counseling program in which both person-to-person and group relationships are emphasized. AA accepts both teenagers and adults with drinking problems, has no dues or fees, does not keep records or case histories, does not participate in political causes, and is not affiliated with any religious sect, although spiritual development is a key aspect of its treatment approach. To ensure anonymity, only first names are used. Meetings are devoted partly to social activities, but consist mainly of discussions of the participants' problems with alcohol, often with testimonials from those who have recovered from alcoholism. Recovered members usually contrast their lives before they broke their alcohol dependence with the lives they now live without alcohol. We should point out here that the term *alcoholic* is used by AA and its affiliates to refer either to persons who currently are drinking excessively or to people who have recovered from such problems but must, according to AA philosophy, continue to abstain from alcohol consumption in the future. That is, in the AA view, one is an alcoholic for life, whether or not one is drinking—one is never "cured" of alcoholism.

An important aspect of AA's rehabilitation program is that it lifts the burden of personal responsibility by helping alcoholics accept that alcoholism, like many other problems, is bigger than they are. Henceforth, they can see themselves not as weak-willed or lacking in moral strength, but rather simply as having an affliction—they cannot drink—just as other people may not be able to tolerate certain types of medication. By mutual help and reassurance through a group composed of others who have shared similar experiences, many alcoholics acquire insight into their problems, a new sense of purpose, greater ego strength, and more effective coping techniques. Continued participation in the group, of course, helps prevent the crisis of a relapse.

Affiliated movements, such as Al-Anon family groups and Ala-Teen, are designed to bring family members together to share common experiences and problems, to gain understanding of the nature of alcoholism, and to learn techniques for dealing with their own problems in the situation.

The reported success of Alcoholics Anonymous is based primarily on anecdotal information rather than objective study of treatment outcomes since AA does not participate in external comparative research efforts. Brandsma, Maultsby, and Welsh (1980), however, included an AA program in their extensive comparative study of alcoholism treatments. The success of this treatment method with severe alcoholics was quite limited. One important finding was that the AA method had high dropout rates compared to other therapies. About half of the people who come to AA drop out of the program within three months. Chappel (1993) attributes the very high dropout rate to alcoholics' denial that they have problems, resistance to external pressure, and resistance to AA itself. Apparently many alcoholics are unable to accept the quasi-religious quality of the sessions and the group testimonial format that is so much a part of the AA program. In the Brandsma study, the participants who were assigned to the AA group subsequently encountered more life difficulties and drank more than people in other treatment groups.

Results of Treatment Statistics on the long-range outcomes of alcoholism treatments vary considerably, depending on the population studied and on the treatment facilities and procedures employed. They range from low rates of success for hard-core alcoholics to recoveries of 70–90 percent where modern treatment and aftercare procedures are used. Rounsaville and colleagues (1987) reported that psychopathology was influential in treatment outcomes for alcoholics. Alcoholics who were also diagnosed as having a personality disorder or affective disorder tended to have poorer outcomes in alcohol treatment than those for whom the diagnosis was simply alcoholism.

In their extensive four-year follow-up of a large group of treated alcoholics, Polich and colleagues (1981) found that the course of alcoholism after diverse treatment methods was variable. The findings of this study were not encouraging and seemed to point to the difficulty of treating alcoholics. Only 7 percent of the total sample (922 males) abstained from alcohol use throughout the four-year period, and 54 percent continued to show alcohol-related problems. (In addition, 36 percent of the sample demonstrated alcohol-dependence symptoms, and another 18 percent showed adverse consequences—such as arrests—from drinking.)

On the positive side, however, this study can be viewed as demonstrating a clear beneficial effect of treatment for some people. Although 54 percent of the subjects showed drinking problems at follow-up, over 90 percent had had serious drinking problems at the beginning of treatment—a significant reduction. Interestingly, although only 7 percent of the alcoholics had been able to abstain from drinking for the full four-year period, others had abstained for shorter periods. For example, 21 percent had abstained for one year or more, and an additional 7 percent had abstained for six months. An impressive finding, and one that will fuel the controlled-drinking versus total-abstinence controversy, was that 18 percent of the alcoholics had been able to drink without problems during the six-month period before follow-up.

Treatment is most likely to be effective when an individual realizes that he or she needs help, when adequate treatment facilities are available, and when alcohol-use reduction (as opposed to strict abstinence) is an acceptable treatment goal. One important new treatment strategy is aimed at reinforcing treatment motivation and abstinence early in the treatment process by providing "check-up" follow-ups on drinking behavior. Miller, Benefield, and Tonigan (1993) reported that "Drinking Check-Up" sessions during the early stages of therapy resulted in a reduction of drinking in the first six weeks of therapy as compared with clients who did not have check-up sessions.

Attitudes toward alcohol-abuse problems in the workplace have undergone considerable change over the past 20 years with the introduction of employee programs in both government and industry. Such programs have proven highly effective in detecting drinking problems early, in referring drinkers for treatment, and in ensuring the effectiveness of aftercare procedures. When we realize that an estimated 5 percent of the nation's work force are severe alcoholics, and an additional 5 percent are considered alcohol abusers, it is apparent that such programs can have a major impact on coping with the alcohol problem in our society (Alander & Campbell, 1975).

As described earlier, recent years have seen a controversy develop over whether inpatient treatment for alcohol problems is required or whether alcoholics can be treated successfully as outpatients. Clearly, if outpatient therapy were as effective as inpatient treatment, several distinct advantages could be found. For example, patients could remain in the community with their families and jobs where, many would say, their ultimate adjustment needs to be made. Moreover, outpatient treatment is more cost-effective, an important factor that is a prominent issue in health care today. Unfortunately, some studies have reported a clear advantage of inpatient treatment (75 percent completion rate) over outpatient programs (18 percent completion rate) (Wickizer et al., 1994). At the present stage of research on treatment effectiveness neither inpatient nor outpatient therapy has won the majority of followers. The relative effectiveness of inpatient versus outpatient therapy for alcoholics remains controversial, and research supports both sides of the issue (Adelman & Weiss, 1993; Cocores, 1991; Collins, 1993).

In their study of various treatments of chronic, severe alcohol problems, Brandsma and colleagues (1980) found that direct treatment—whether professional or paraprofessional, insight-oriented or rational-behavior therapy—was more effective than an untreated control condition. The investigators randomly assigned chronic alcoholics to treatment groups—insight-oriented therapy, rational-behavior therapy, Alcoholics Anonymous, self-help (paraprofessional) therapy—or to a nontreatment control group. One important finding was that professional treatment was more effective than nonprofessional treatment, although either of the two major therapeutic orientations (insight-oriented versus rational-behavior therapy) was equally effective. As noted above, Alcoholics Anonymous was the least effective, partly due to a high dropout rate.

Clearly no miracle cure for alcoholism is available. Nevertheless, it appears that the great majority of alcoholics may find a treatment program that can be tailored to their needs and provide a good chance for recovery.

Relapse Prevention One of the greatest problems in the treatment of addictive disorders, such as alcoholism or any of the conditions described in this chapter, is maintaining abstinence or self-control once the behavioral excesses have been checked. Most alcohol treatment programs show high success rates in "curing" the addictive problems, but many programs show lessening rates of abstinence or controlled drinking at various periods of follow-up. Many treatment programs do not pay sufficient attention to the important element of maintaining effective behavior and preventing relapse into previous maladaptive patterns.

In recent years, some researchers have been focusing on the problem of relapse prevention by examining the thought processes that lead an abstinent person back into the self-indulgent patterns that originally got him or her in trouble. The cognitive-behavioral approach to relapse prevention by Marlatt and his colleagues (Marlatt, 1985; Marlatt & Gordon, 1980; McMurran & Hollin, 1993) shows great promise in this area (Johnson & McCown, 1993).

The cognitive-behavioral view holds that the definition of relapse behavior should be broadened beyond the previously held notion that people resume drinking because of a "craving" based on vaguely understood physiological needs. Instead, the behaviors underlying relapse are "indulgent behaviors" and are based on an individual's learning history. When an individual is abstinent or has an addiction under control, he or she gains a sense of personal control over the indulgent behavior. The longer the person is able to maintain this control, the greater the sense of achievement—the self-efficacy or confidence—and the greater the chance that he or she will be able to cope with the addiction and maintain control.

However, according to Marlatt, a person may violate this rule of abstinence through a gradual, perhaps unconscious, process rather than through the sudden "falling off the wagon" that constitutes the traditional view of craving and relapse. In the cognitive-behavioral view, a person may inadvertently make a series of minidecisions, even while maintaining abstinence, that begin a chain of behaviors making relapse inevitable. For example, an abstinent alcoholic who buys a quart of bourbon just in case his friends drop by or a dieting obese woman who changes her route to work to include a pass by the bakery are both unconsciously preparing the way for relapse. Marlatt refers to these minidecisions that place a person at risk as "apparently irrelevant decisions." These decisions are easy for the individual to make, since they do not appear to be related to the abstinent behavior; however, they lead the person into a situation in which some form of relapse is likely to occur.

Another type of relapse behavior involves the "abstinence violation effect," in which even minor transgressions are seen by the abstainer to have drastic significance. The effect works this way: An abstinent person may hold that he or she should not, under any circumstance, transgress or give in to the old habit. Abstinence-oriented treatment programs are particularly guided by this prohibitive rule. What happens, then, when an abstinent man becomes somewhat self-indulgent and takes a drink offered by an old friend? He may lose some of the sense of self-efficacy, the confidence needed to control his drinking. Since the vow of abstinence has been violated, he may feel guilty about giving in to the temptation and rationalize that he "has blown it and become a drunk again, so why not go all the way?"

Marlatt and his colleagues recommend a cognitive-behavioral treatment program for preventing relapse. Clients are taught to recognize the apparently irrelevant decisions that serve as early warning signals of the possibility of relapse. High-risk situations are targeted, and the individuals learn to assess their own vulnerability to relapse. Clients are also trained to be prepared for the abstinence violation effect, and, if they do relapse, not to become so discouraged that they lose their confidence. Some cognitive-behavioral therapists have employed a "planned relapse" phase in the treatment to supervise an individual's cognitive behavioral strategies to help the client through this important problem area.

DRUG ABUSE AND DEPENDENCE

Aside from alcohol, the psychoactive drugs most commonly associated with abuse and dependence in our society appear to be (a) narcotics, such as opium and its derivatives; (b) sedatives, such as barbiturates; (c) stimulants, such as cocaine and amphetamines; (d) antianxiety drugs, such as benzodiazepines; and (e) hallucinogens, such as LSD and PCP. (These and other drugs are summarized in HIGHLIGHT 10.6.) Caffeine and nicotine are also drugs of dependence, and disorders associated with tobacco withdrawal and caffeine intoxication are included in the DSM-IV diagnostic classification system; we will deal with them briefly in our present discussion.

Though they may occur at any age, drug abuse and dependence are most common during adolescence and young adulthood (Smith, 1989) and vary according to metropolitan area, race and ethnicity, labor force status, and other demographic characteristics (Hughes, 1992). Substance abuse problems are relatively more prominent in economically depressed minority communities (Tremble, Padillo, & Bell, 1994).

The extent that drug abuse has become a problem for society is reflected in a recent study of drug involvement among applicants for employment at a large teaching hospital in Maryland (Lange et al., 1994). Beginning in 1989, and for a two-year period, all applicants for employment were screened through a pre-employment drug screening program (individuals were not identified in the initial study). Of 593 applicants 10.8 percent were found to have detectable amounts of illicit drugs in their tests. The most frequently detected drug was marijuana (55 percent of those tested positively), followed by cocaine (36 percent) and by opiates (28 percent). In 1991, a formal drug-screening program was implemented. During the year a total of 365 applicants were screened and only 21 (5.8 percent) were found to have positive drug screens. In this study, opiates were the most frequently detected (48 percent) followed by cocaine (38 percent) and marijuana (28 percent). In both drug-testing programs, positive tests were most frequently associated with minority background and blue-collar occupational status. The drop (by nearly half) in positive drug screens over the three-year period was interpreted as reflecting the possibility that implementation of a drug-screening program can serve as a deterrent for drug-using persons applying for employment.

Among those who abuse drugs, behavior patterns vary markedly, depending on the type, amount, and duration of drug use; the physiological and psychological makeup of the individual; and, in some instances, the social setting in which the drug experience occurs. Thus it appears most useful to deal separately with some of the drugs that are more commonly associated with abuse and dependence in contemporary society.

Opium and Its Derivatives (Narcotics)

People have used opium and its derivatives for over 5000 years. Galen (A.D. 130–201) considered theriaca, whose principal ingredient was opium, to be a panacea:

> It resists poison and venomous bites, cures inveterate headache, vertigo, deafness, epilepsy, apoplexy, dimness of sight, loss of voice, asthma, coughs of all kinds, spitting of blood, tightness of breath, colic, the iliac poisons, jaundice, hardness of the spleen, stone, urinary complaints, fevers, dropsies, leprosies, the trouble to which women are subject, melancholy and all pestilences.

Even today, opium derivatives are still used for some of the conditions Galen mentioned.

Opium is a mixture of about 18 chemical substances known as alkaloids. In 1805 the alkaloid present in the largest amount (10–15 percent) was found to be a bitter-tasting powder that could serve as a powerful sedative and pain reliever; it was named **morphine** after Morpheus, god of sleep in Greek mythology. The hypodermic needle was introduced in America about 1856, allowing morphine to be widely administered to soldiers during the Civil War, not only to those wounded in battle but also to those suffering from dysentery. As a consequence, many Civil War veterans returned to civilian life addicted to the drug, a condition euphemistically referred to as "soldier's illness."

Scientists concerned with the addictive properties of morphine hypothesized that one part of the morphine molecule might be responsible for its analgesic properties (that is, its ability to eliminate pain without inducing unconsciousness) and another for its addictiveness. At about the turn of the century, it was discovered that if morphine was treated by an inexpensive and readily available chemical called acetic anhydride, it would be converted into another powerful analgesic called **heroin.** Heroin was hailed enthusiastically by its

Psychoactive Drugs Commonly Involved in Drug Abuse

Classification	Drugs	Effects
Sedatives	Alcohol (ethanol)	Reduce tension Facilitate social interaction "Blot out" feelings or events

	Barbiturates
	  Nembutal (pentobarbital)
	  Seconal (secobarbital)
	  Veronal (barbital)
	  Tuinal (secobarbital
	    and amobarbital)
		Reduce tension

Stimulants	Amphetamines
	  Benzedrine (amphetamine)
	  Dexedrine (dextroamphetamine)
	  Methedrine (methamphetamine)
	  Cocaine (coca)
		Increase feelings of alertness and confidence
		Decrease feelings of fatigue
		Stay awake for long periods
		
		Decrease feelings of fatigue
		Increase endurance
		Stimulate sex drive

Narcotics	Opium and its derivatives
	  Opium
	  Morphine
	  Codeine
	  Heroin
	Methadone (synthetic narcotic)
		Alleviate physical pain
		Induce relaxation and pleasant reverie
		Alleviate anxiety and tension
		
		Treatment of heroin dependence

Psychedelics and hallucinogens	Cannabis
	  Marijuana
	  Hashish
	Mescaline (peyote)
	Psilocybin
	  (psychotogenic mushrooms)
	LSD (lysergic acid diethylamide-25)
	PCP (phencyclidine)
		Induce changes in mood, thought, and
		  behavior
		
		"Expand" one's mind
		
		Induce stupor

Antianxiety drugs (minor tranquilizers)	Librium (chlordiazepoxide) Miltown (meprobamate) Valium (diazepam) Others, e.g., Xanax	Alleviate tension and anxiety Induce relaxation and sleep

In reviewing this list, it is important to note that it is by no means complete; for example, it does not include newer drugs, such as Ritalin, which are designed to produce multiple effects; it does not include the less commonly used volatile hydrocarbons, such as glue, paint thinner, gasoline, cleaning fluid, and nail-polish remover, which are highly dangerous when sniffed for their psychoactive effects; and it

discoverer, Heinrich Dreser (Boehm, 1968). Leading scientists of his time agreed on the merits of heroin, and the drug came to be widely prescribed in place of morphine for pain relief and related medicinal purposes. However, heroin was a cruel disappointment, for it proved to be an even more dangerous drug than morphine, acting more rapidly and more intensely and being equally if not

Medical Usage	Tolerance	Physiological Dependence	Psychological Dependence
No	Yes (reverse tolerance later)	Yes	Yes
Yes	Yes	Yes	Yes
Yes	Yes	Mixed	Yes
No	No (minimal)	Mixed	Yes
Yes, except heroin	Yes	Yes	Yes
Yes	Yes	Yes	Yes
No, except in research	No—possible reverse tolerance (marijuana)	No	Yes
No	No	No	Yes
Yes	Yes	Yes	Yes

does not include the antipsychotic and antidepressant drugs, which are abused, but relatively rarely. We shall deal with these and the antianxiety drugs in our discussion of drug therapy in Chapter 16. It also should be emphasized that abuses of various kinds can occur with both prescriptive and nonprescriptive drugs, and with both legal and illegal drugs. In all cases, drugs should be used with great care.

more addictive. Eventually, heroin was removed from use in medical practice.

As it became apparent that opium and its derivatives—including codeine, which is used in some cough syrups—were perilously addictive, the U.S. Congress enacted the Harrison Act in 1914. Under this and later acts, the unauthorized sale and distribution of certain drugs became a federal offense;

physicians and pharmacists were held accountable for each dose they dispensed. Thus, overnight, the role of a chronic narcotic user changed from that of addict—which was considered a vice, but tolerated—to that of criminal. Unable to obtain drugs through legal sources, many turned to illegal ones, and eventually to other criminal acts as a means of maintaining their suddenly expensive drug supply.

During the 1960s, there was a rapid increase in heroin use. Fortunately, the actual number of heroin users has diminished steadily since 1975 (Smith, 1989). Heroin-related hospital admissions have decreased in recent years from 47 percent of total drug-related admissions to 37 percent.

Effects of Morphine and Heroin Morphine and heroin are commonly introduced into the body by smoking, snorting (inhaling the powder), eating, "skin popping," or "mainlining," the last two being methods of introducing the drug via hypodermic injection. Skin popping refers to injecting the liquefied drug just beneath the skin, and mainlining to injecting the drug directly into the bloodstream. In the United States, a young addict usually moves from snorting to mainlining.

Among the immediate effects of mainlined or snorted heroin is a euphoric spasm (the rush) lasting 60 seconds or so, which many addicts compare to a sexual orgasm. This rush is followed by a high, during which an addict typically is in a lethargic, withdrawn state in which bodily needs, including needs for food and sex, are markedly diminished; pleasant feelings of relaxation, euphoria, and reverie tend to dominate. These effects last from four to six hours and are followed—in addicts—by a negative phase that produces a desire for more of the drug.

The use of opium derivatives over a period of time usually results in a physiological craving for the drug. The time required to establish the drug habit varies, but it has been estimated that continual use over a period of 30 days is sufficient. Users then find that they have become physiologically dependent on the drug in the sense that they feel physically ill when they do not take it. In addition, users of opium derivatives gradually build up a tolerance to the drug so that even larger amounts are needed to achieve the desired effects.

When people addicted to opiates do not get a dose of the drug within approximately eight hours, they start to experience withdrawal symptoms. The character and severity of these reactions depend on many factors, including the amount of the narcotic habitually used, the intervals between doses, the duration of the addiction, and especially the addict's health and personality.

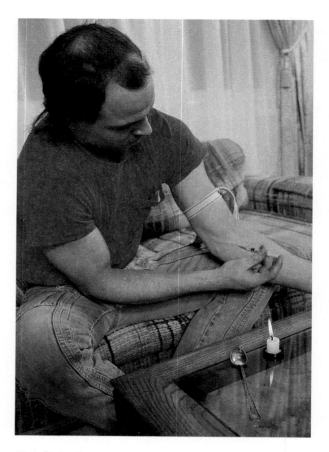

Mainlining heroin, or injecting it with a needle, gives an immediate "rush," often compared to a sexual orgasm, followed by a high lasting from 5 to 6 hours in which feelings of relaxation, euphoria, and reverie are prominent.

Contrary to what some addicts believe, withdrawal from heroin is not always dangerous or even very painful. Many addicted people withdraw without assistance. Withdrawal can, however, be an agonizing experience for some people, with symptoms of running nose, tearing eyes, perspiration, restlessness, increased respiration rate, and an intensified desire for the drug. As time passes, the symptoms may become more severe. Typically a feeling of chilliness alternates with vasomotor disturbances of flushing and excessive sweating, vomiting, diarrhea, abdominal cramps, pains in the back and extremities, severe headache, marked tremors, and varying degrees of insomnia. Beset by these discomforts, an individual refuses food and water, and this, coupled with the vomiting, sweating, and diarrhea, results in dehydration and weight loss. Occasionally, symptoms may include delirium, hallucinations, and manic activity. Cardiovascular collapse may also occur and can result in death. If morphine is administered, the subjective distress experienced by an addict ends, and physiological balance is quickly restored.

Withdrawal symptoms will usually be on the decline by the third or fourth day, and by the seventh or eighth day will have disappeared. As the symptoms subside, the person resumes normal eating and drinking and rapidly regains lost weight. An additional hazard exists now in that after withdrawal symptoms have ceased, the individual's former tolerance for the drug also disappears, and death may result from taking the former large dosage.

Typically the life of a narcotic addict becomes increasingly centered on obtaining and using drugs, so the addiction usually leads to socially maladaptive behavior as the individual is eventually forced to lie, steal, and associate with undesirable companions to maintain a supply of drugs. Many addicts resort to petty theft to support their habits, and some female addicts turn to prostitution as a means of financing their addictions.

Along with the lowering of ethical and moral restraints, addiction has adverse physical effects on an individual's well-being. An inadequate diet, for example, may lead to ill health and increased susceptibility to a variety of physical ailments. The use of unsterile equipment may also lead to various problems, including liver damage from hepatitis and transmission of the AIDS virus. In addition, the use of such a potent drug without medical supervision and government controls to assure its strength and purity can result in fatal overdosage. Injection of too much heroin can cause coma and death. In fact, over 10,000 heroin addicts have died through heroin overdose (Smith, 1989), and in one short period between January and June 1988, more than 867 deaths associated with heroin overdose were reported in the United States (Project DAWN, 1988). In the case of women who use heroin during pregnancy dire consequences can result with their children, for example, small premature babies who are themselves addicted to heroin and vulnerable to a number of diseases (Anand & Arnold, 1994; Noia et al., 1994).

Addiction to opiates usually leads to a gradual deterioration of well-being. The ill health and general personality deterioration often found in opium addiction do not result directly from the pharmacological effects of the drug, but are usually products of the sacrifice of money, proper diet, social position, and self-respect as an addict becomes more desperate to procure the required daily dosage.

Causal Factors in Opiate Abuse and Dependence
No single causal pattern fits all addictions to narcotic drugs. A study by Fulmer and Lapidus (1980)

concluded that the three most frequently cited reasons for beginning to use heroin were pleasure, curiosity, and peer pressure. Pleasure was the single most widespread reason—given by 81 percent of addicts. Other reasons, such as life stress, personal maladjustment, and sociocultural conditions, also play a part (Bry, McKeon, & Pandina, 1982).

Although the following categorization of causal factors is somewhat artificial, it does provide a convenient means of ordering our discussion.

Neural Bases for Physiological Addiction. Research teams have isolated and studied receptor sites for narcotic drugs in the brain (Goldstein et al., 1974; Pert & Snyder, 1973). Such receptor sites are specific nerve cells into which given psychoactive drugs fit like keys into the proper locks. This interaction of drug and brain cells apparently results in a drug's action, and in the case of narcotic drugs, may lead to addiction (see HIGHLIGHT 10.5 on pages 364–365).

The human body produces its own opiumlike substances, called **endorphins,** in the brain and pituitary gland. These substances are produced in response to stimulation and are believed to play a role in an organism's reaction to pain (Bolls & Fanselow, 1982). Some investigators have suspected that endorphins may play a role in drug addiction, speculating that chronic underproduction of endorphins may lead to a craving for narcotic drugs. Research on the role of endorphins in drug addiction has generally been inconclusive and disappointing.

Addiction Associated with Psychopathology. A high incidence of antisocial personality has been found among heroin addicts. In a comparison between a group of 45 young institutionalized male addicts and a control group of nonaddicts, Gilbert and Lombardi (1967) found that distinguishing features were "the addict's antisocial traits, his depression, tension, insecurity, and feelings of inadequacy, and his difficulty in forming warm and lasting interpersonal relationships" (p. 536). Meyer and Mirin (1979) found that opiate addicts were highly impulsive and showed an inability to delay gratification. Kosten and Rounsaville (1986) reported that about 68 percent of heroin abusers were also diagnosed as having a personality disorder. As in the case of alcoholism, however, it is essential to exercise caution in distinguishing between personality traits before and after addiction; the high incidence of psychopathology among narcotics addicts may in part result from, rather than precede, the long-term effects of addiction.

Addiction Associated with Sociocultural Factors. In our society a so-called narcotics subculture exists in which addicts can obtain drugs and protect themselves against society's sanctions. Apparently the majority of narcotics addicts participate in this drug culture. The decision to join this culture has important future implications, for from that point on addicts will center their activities on their drug-user role. In short, addiction becomes a way of life. In a recent survey in three large cities in Texas, Maddux and colleagues (1994) found that the majority of illicit drug injectors were predominantly undereducated and unemployed individuals from minority groups.

With time, most young addicts who join the drug culture become increasingly withdrawn, indifferent to their friends (except those in the drug group), and apathetic about sexual activity (Tremble et al., 1994). They are likely to abandon scholastic and athletic endeavors and to show a marked reduction in competitive and achievement strivings. Most of these addicts appear to lack good sex-role identification and to experience feelings of inadequacy when confronted with the demands of adulthood. While feeling progressively isolated from the broader culture, their feelings of group belongingness are bolstered by continued association with the addict milieu; at the same time, they come to view drugs both as a means of revolt against authority and conventional values and as a device for alleviating personal anxieties and tensions.

Treatments and Outcomes Treatment for heroin addiction is initially similar to that for alcoholism in that it involves building up an addict both physically and psychologically and providing help through the withdrawal period. Addicts often dread the discomfort of withdrawal, but in a hospital setting it is less abrupt and usually involves the administration of a medication that eases the distress.

After withdrawal has been completed, treatment focuses on helping a former addict make an adequate adjustment to his or her community and abstain from the further use of narcotics. Traditionally, however, the prognosis has been unfavorable. Despite the use of counseling, group therapy, and other measures, only about 13 percent of people discharged from government rehabilitation programs in England did not become readdicted (Stephens & Cottrell, 1972). These and comparable findings from studies in the United States have led to the hypothesis that withdrawal does not remove the craving for heroin and that a key target in treatment must be the alleviation of this craving.

One approach to dealing with the physiological craving for heroin was pioneered by a research team at the Rockefeller University in New York. Their approach involved the use of the drug **methadone** in conjunction with a rehabilitation program (counseling, group therapy, and other procedures) directed toward the "total resocialization" of addicts (Dole & Nyswander, 1967). Methadone hydrochloride is a synthetic narcotic that is related to heroin and is equally *addictive physiologically.* Its usefulness in treatment lies in the fact that it satisfies an addict's craving for heroin without producing serious psychological impairment, if only because it is administered as a "treatment" in a formal clinical context.

As a result of impressive preliminary findings, the federal government in 1972 agreed to a licensing program for physicians and clinics using methadone in the treatment of narcotics addicts. Research has shown the effectiveness of methadone at reducing the dependence upon heroin (Moolchan & Hoffman, 1994; Shaffer & LaSalvia, 1992); however, methadone alone may only be effective for a small minority of heroin abusers. As methadone treatment has become more widely employed, the question of whether methadone alone is sufficient to rehabilitate narcotics addicts has been questioned. Research on whether providing psychological treatment along with methadone contributes to a successful outcome has been evaluated. Woody and colleagues (1983) found that psychotherapy along with methadone increased the effectiveness of treatment. These effects were maintained over a 12-month follow-up (Woody et al., 1987). Moreover, more recent research has underscored the importance of providing psychosocial support in addition to methadone (McLellan et al., 1993).

The practice of weaning an addict from heroin only to addict him or her to another narcotic drug that may be required for life is also questionable. Methadone advocates might respond that addicts on methadone can function normally and hold jobs, which is not possible for most heroin addicts. In addition, methadone is available legally, and its quality is controlled by government standards. Nor is it necessary to increase the dosage over time. In fact, some patients can eventually stop taking methadone without danger of relapse to heroin addiction. Many heroin addicts can undergo methadone treatment without initial hospitalization, and during treatment they are able to hold jobs and function in their family and community settings (Newman & Cates, 1977).

Improvements in methadone maintenance treatment over the past few years have increased its attractiveness for treating heroin abusers and have improved its overall success rates. Milby (1988) reported that consistent gains have been made in the improvement rates for methadone maintenance over the past 20 years: from 39.7 percent reported in studies from 1970 to 1975, 54.9 percent in studies during the years between 1976 and 1980, and 76.3 percent in studies reported since 1980. The increased success rates for methadone treatment have been attributed to the use of additional drugs like clonidine (an antihypertensive drug used to treat essential hypertension and prevent headache), which aid in the detoxification process and reduce the discomfort of withdrawal symptoms.

Even though it is a clearly better alternative to continued heroin use, being in a methadone maintenance program is no picnic. Methadone patients are often viewed by themselves and others in a highly stigmatized way—"not quite a junkie, not quite a conventional person" or someone who can be trusted (Murphy & Irwin, 1992). Methadone patients often must resort to great secrecy about their program participation in an effort to accommodate to society, hold a job, and even to relate to friends and family. One crucial element in beating the drug abuse problem seems to be for the addict to develop a drug-free social network—a task that is often difficult in methadone programs.

A new medication, bupenorphine, has been used to treat heroin addiction. It promises an equally effective substitute for heroin but has fewer side effects than methadone (Blaine, 1992). Buprenorphine operates as a partial antagonist to heroin (Lewis & Walter, 1992) and produces the "feelings of contentment" associated with heroin use (Mendelson & Mello, 1992). Yet the drug does not produce the physical dependency that is characteristic of heroin (Grant & Sonti, 1994) and can be discontinued without severe withdrawal symptoms. The use of buprenorphine has not gained wide acceptance at this time, because the required controlled studies have not yet been completed. It is likely, however, that this drug will become more widely used in the future.

Cocaine and Amphetamines (Stimulants)

In contrast to narcotics, which depress or slow down the action of the central nervous system, cocaine and amphetamines stimulate or speed it up.

Cocaine Like opium, **cocaine** is a plant product discovered and used in ancient times. It was widely used in the pre-Columbian world of Mexico and Peru (Guerra, 1971). It has been endorsed by such diverse figures as Sigmund Freud and the legendary Sherlock Holmes. Because of its exorbitant price, cocaine has been considered as the "high" for the affluent. Its use increased significantly in the United States during the 1980s and 1990s to the point that its use was considered epidemic, especially among middle- and upper-income groups. Addiction to cocaine or its more recent derivative "crack," a new "supercharged" variety of the drug, has now become one of the "major public mental health problems" (Weddington, 1993).

Recent research on the extent and impact of cocaine abuse points to the prominence of the problem in today's society. Hospital admissions for cocaine abuse nearly doubled between 1978 and 1981 (National Institute of Drug Abuse, 1981). Fifty-nine percent of people arrested for reckless driving in Memphis, Tennessee tested positive for cocaine abuse (Brookoff et al., 1994). In a follow-up study of young adults (ages 15 to 16) who had been surveyed nine years earlier about drug use, Kandel and colleagues (1986) found that 37 percent of males and 24 percent of females surveyed had tried cocaine. Recent statistics (National Institute of Drug Abuse, 1990) suggest that the number of Americans who are "occasional cocaine users" is declining: 45 percent in the last two years and 72 percent since 1985. It may be that drug use is becoming unfashionable in the health-conscious middle- and upper-socioeconomic classes. A recent study reported that cocaine use in youthful arrestees in Manhattan was also on the decline (Golub & Johnson, 1994). However, according to some reports the number of hard-core cocaine users, especially those in poverty-ridden inner-city neighborhoods, is increasing, especially among the young, 18- to 25-year-olds (Hughes, 1992). In a recent survey of adults serving time in jail, the majority of inmates reported heavy drug use during the month prior to their last arrest and more than 80 percent of them had used crack cocaine (Peters & Kearns, 1992).

Like the opiates, cocaine may be ingested by sniffing, swallowing, or injecting. Also like the opiates, it precipitates a euphoric state of four to six hours' duration, during which a user experiences feelings of confidence and contentment. However, this blissful state may be preceded by headache, dizziness, and restlessness. When cocaine is chronically abused, acute toxic psychotic symptoms may occur, similar to those in acute schizophrenia—a user encounters frightening visual, auditory, and tactual hallucinations, such as the "cocaine bug" (Post, 1975).

Unlike the opiates, cocaine stimulates the cortex of the brain, inducing sleeplessness and excitement as well as stimulating and accentuating sexual feelings. Consequently, some people have been known to administer cocaine to others as an aid to seduction. To complicate matters, Rolfs, Goldberg, and Sharrar (1990) found that cocaine abusers, because of their high sexual promiscuity, were at risk for contracting syphilis.

Dependence on cocaine also differs somewhat from dependence on opiates. It was believed until recently that tolerance was not increased appreciably with cocaine use. However, acute tolerance has now been demonstrated, and some chronic tolerance may occur as well (Fischman & Schuster, 1982; Jones, 1984). The previous view that cocaine abusers did not develop physiological dependence on the drug also has been changing. Gawin and Kleber (1986) demonstrated that chronic abusers who become abstinent develop uniform, depression-like symptoms, but the symptoms are transient. These states are usually followed by a period of dysphoria. One study reported that 47 percent of cocaine abusers were found to be clinically depressed, and many also reported symptoms of phobic behavior (Kleinman et al., 1990). Certain "mild but definite" neurological symptoms such as concentration and memory deficits have also been found in cocaine abusers (O'Malley et al., 1992).

The psychological and life problems experienced by cocaine users are often great. In a 2½-year follow-up study of cocaine users and nonusers, Kosten, Rounsaville, and Kleber (1988) found that users (particularly those whose use increased over the span of the study) had significantly more psychosocial problems than nonusers. These problems included employment, family, psychological, and legal matters. Tardiff and colleagues (1994) reported that 31 percent of murder victims in New York City tested positive for cocaine. Many life problems experienced by cocaine abusers result, in part, from the considerable amounts of money that are required to support their habits. Kleinman and associates (1990) reported that most of the cocaine abusers in their sample were spending in excess of $1000 per month to buy the drug. Miller and Gold (1994) noted that daily use of crack cocaine was highly correlated with criminal activities to supply the drug.

Problems in sexual functioning have been reported to be associated with crack cocaine use. Kim and colleagues (1992) reported that most users develop a disinterest and dysfunction with prolonged sexual usage. On the other hand, Weatherby and colleagues (1992) found that increased sexual activity, particularly trading sex for drugs, was associated with crack

cocaine use, and Balshem and colleagues (1992) reported that sexual activity with anonymous partners often takes place in the context of crack cocaine use.

Women who use cocaine when they are pregnant place their babies at great risk for both health and psychological problems. Children who are born to cocaine-using mothers are at considerable risk of being maltreated as infants as well as at an increased risk of losing their mother during infancy. Wasserman and Leventhal (1993) studied a group of cocaine-exposed children and a controlled sample of nonexposed children for a 24-month period following their birth. They found that children who were regularly exposed to cocaine in utero were more likely to be mistreated (23 percent) versus only 4 percent of controls. For example, 11 percent of the exposed children had also been physically abused and 11 percent had been neglected. Moreover, the investigators found that these vulnerable children were also susceptible to losing their mothers' care during their infancy—205 had experienced a change in living circumstances, that is, placement in another home.

Finally, cocaine use can be fatal—one study showed that cocaine-related deaths almost tripled between 1985 and 1988, with a total of 1033 deaths nationwide in the first six months of 1988, excluding New York City (Project DAWN, 1988). This point was dramatically illustrated during a period of ten days in the summer of 1986 when two well-known athletes, Len Bias, an all-American basketball player, and Don Rogers, a star running back for the Cleveland Browns, died after taking cocaine.

Crack cocaine is believed to be one of the most dangerous drugs introduced to date because of its immediate addicting properties and its health risks (Smith, 1989). The devastation this drug can cause to a user is illustrated in the following case:

Eva is a 16-year-old patient at New York City's Phoenix House drug rehabilitation center who got hooked on crack two years ago. The product of a troubled middle-class family, she was already a heavy drinker and pot smoker when she was introduced to coke by her older brother, a young dope pusher. "When you take the first toke on a crack pipe, you get on top of the world," she says.

She first started stealing from family and friends to support her habit. She soon turned to prostitution and went through two abortions before she was 16. "I didn't give a damn about protecting myself," she said. "I just wanted to

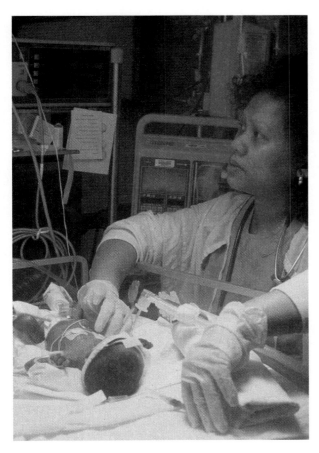

The tragedy of drug abuse can often be seen in the children of addicted mothers. This child displays many of the characteristic features of the "crack baby," such as low birth weight.

get high. Fear of pregnancy didn't cross my mind when I hit the sack with someone for drugs." (*Time*, 1986)

Our broadened knowledge about cocaine abuse, particularly with respect to the many health and social problems resulting from dependence on the drug, has resulted in considerable modification of professional views of cocaine over the past 20 years. For example, the modifications in DSM-IV diagnostic classification reflect a significant increase in our knowledge of cocaine's addictive properties. A new disorder is described, cocaine withdrawal, which involves symptoms of depression, fatigue, disturbed sleep, and increased dreaming.

Treatment for psychological dependence on cocaine does not differ appreciably from that for other drugs that involve physiological dependence. Kosten (1989) reported that effective cocaine-abuse treat-

ment includes the use of medications, such as desipramine and naltrexone (Kosten et al., 1992) to reduce cravings and the use of psychological therapy to ensure treatment compliance. The feelings of tension and depression that accompany absence of the drug have to be dealt with during the immediate withdrawal period. Some success in the treatment of cocaine abusers has been reported. Carroll and colleagues (1993a; 1993b) have shown that many cocaine abusers did well in maintaining treatment goals and one-third were abstinent at a 12-month follow-up. Several factors were associated with poorer outcomes—severity of abuse, poorer psychiatric functioning, and presence of concurrent alcoholism. One of the problems clinicians face in working with cocaine abusers is early treatment termination. Kleinman and colleagues (1992) found that 30 percent of patients dropped out after the first session and 28 percent dropped out before the third session. Only 42 percent were retained in treatment for six or more sessions. Another problem encountered in drug treatment is that many of the cocaine-dependent patients have severe antisocial personality disorders—a situation resulting in treatment resistance (Leal, Ziedonis, & Kosten, 1994). Arndt and colleagues (1994) found that cocaine-dependent patients with antisocial personality characteristics made few therapeutic gains while those without antisocial features made significant progress.

Amphetamines The earliest **amphetamine** to be introduced—Benzedrine, or amphetamine sulfate—was first synthesized in 1927 and became available in drugstores in the early 1930s as an inhalant to relieve stuffy noses. However, the manufacturers soon learned that some customers were chewing the wicks in the inhalers for "kicks." Thus the stimulating effects of amphetamine sulfate were discovered by the public before the drug was formally prescribed as a stimulant by physicians. In the late 1930s two newer amphetamines were introduced—Dexedrine (dextroamphetamine) and Methedrine (methamphetamine hydrochloride, also known as speed). The latter preparation is a far more potent stimulant of the central nervous system than either Benzedrine or Dexedrine and hence is considered more dangerous. In fact its abuse can be lethal.

Initially these preparations were considered to be "wonder pills" that helped people stay alert and awake and function temporarily at a level beyond normal. During World War II, military interest was aroused in the stimulating effects of these drugs, and they were used by both Allied and German soldiers to ward off fatigue (Jarvik, 1967). Similarly, among civilians, amphetamines came to be widely used by night workers, long-distance truck drivers, students cramming for exams, and athletes striving to improve their performances. It was also discovered that amphetamines tend to suppress appetite, and they became popular with people trying to lose weight. In addition, they were often used to counteract the effects of barbiturates or other sleeping pills that had been taken the night before. As a result of their many uses, amphetamines were widely prescribed by doctors.

Today amphetamines are used medically for curbing the appetite when weight reduction is desirable; for treating individuals suffering from narcolepsy—a disorder in which people cannot prevent themselves from continually falling asleep during the day; and for treating hyperactive children. Curiously enough, amphetamines have a calming rather than a stimulating effect on many of these youngsters (see Chapter 14). Amphetamines are also sometimes prescribed for alleviating mild feelings of depression, relieving fatigue, and maintaining alertness for sustained periods of time.

Since the passage of the Controlled Substance Act of 1970 (Drug Enforcement Administration, 1979), amphetamines have been classified as Schedule II controlled substances—that is, drugs with high abuse potential that require a prescription for each purchase. As a result, medical use of amphetamines has declined in recent years, and they are more difficult to obtain legally. Nevertheless, it is apparently easy to find illegal sources of amphetamines, which thus remain among the most widely abused drugs.

Causes and Effects of Amphetamine Abuse. Despite their legitimate medical uses, amphetamines are not a magical source of extra mental or physical energy, but rather serve to push users toward greater expenditures of their own resources—often to a point of hazardous fatigue. In fact, athletes have damaged their careers by using speed to try to improve their stamina and performance (Furlong, 1971). Amphetamines are psychologically and perhaps physiologically addictive and the body does build up tolerance to them rapidly. Thus habituated users may use the drugs in amounts that would be lethal to nonusers. In some instances, users inject the drug to get faster and more intense results.

For a person who exceeds prescribed dosages, amphetamine consumption results in heightened blood pressure, enlarged pupils, unclear or rapid speech, profuse sweating, tremors, excitability, loss of appetite, confusion, and sleeplessness. Injected in large quantities, Methedrine can raise blood pressure enough to cause immediate death. In addition,

chronic abuse of amphetamines can result in brain damage and a wide range of psychopathology, including a disorder known as amphetamine psychosis, which appears similar to paranoid schizophrenia. Suicide, homicide, assault, and various other acts of violence are associated with amphetamine abuse.

Treatments and Outcomes. Withdrawal from amphetamines is usually painless physically, because physiological addiction is often absent or minimal. In some instances, however, abrupt withdrawal from the chronic, excessive use of amphetamines can result in cramping, nausea, diarrhea, and even convulsions (American Medical Association, 1968).

Moreover, abrupt abstinence commonly results in feelings of weariness and depression. The depression usually reaches its peak in 48 to 72 hours, often remains intense for a day or two, and then tends to lessen gradually over a period of several days. Mild feelings of depression and lassitude may persist for weeks or even months. If brain damage has occurred, residual effects may also include impaired ability to concentrate, learn, and remember, with resulting social, economic, and personality deterioration.

Barbiturates (Sedatives)

In the 1930s, powerful sedatives called **barbiturates** were introduced. Although barbiturates have legitimate medical uses, they are extremely dangerous drugs commonly associated with both physiological and psychological dependence and with lethal overdoses.

Effects of Barbiturates Barbiturates were once widely used by physicians to calm patients and induce sleep. They act as depressants—somewhat like alcohol—to slow down the action of the central nervous system. Shortly after taking a barbiturate, an individual experiences a feeling of relaxation in which tensions seem to disappear, followed by a physical and intellectual lassitude and a tendency toward drowsiness and sleep—the intensity of such feelings varies depending on the type and amount of the barbiturate taken. Strong doses produce sleep almost immediately; excessive doses are lethal because they result in paralysis of the brain's respiratory centers.

Excessive use of barbiturates leads to increased tolerance as well as to physiological and psychological dependence. It can also lead to a variety of undesirable side effects, including sluggishness, slow speech, impaired comprehension and memory, extreme and sudden mood shifts, motor incoordination, and depression. Problem solving and decision making require great effort, and an individual usually is aware that his or her thinking is "fuzzy." Prolonged, excessive use of barbiturates can lead to brain damage and personality deterioration. Unlike opiates, tolerance of barbiturates does not increase the amount needed to cause death. This fact means that users can easily ingest fatal overdoses, either intentionally or accidentally.

Causal Factors in Barbiturate Abuse and Dependence Though many young people experiment with barbiturates, or downers, most do not become dependent. In fact, the people who do become dependent on barbiturates tend to be middle-aged and older people who often rely on them as "sleeping pills" and who do not commonly use other classes of drugs (except, possibly, alcohol and minor tranquilizers). Often these people are referred to as silent abusers because they take the drugs in the privacy of their homes and ordinarily do not become public nuisances.

Barbiturates are commonly used with alcohol. Some users claim they can achieve an intense high by combining barbiturates, amphetamines, and alcohol. However, one possible effect of combining barbiturates and alcohol is death, because each drug potentiates (increases the action of) the other.

Treatments and Outcomes As with many other drugs, it is often essential in treatment to distinguish between barbiturate intoxication, which results from the toxic effects of overdosage, and the symptoms associated with drug withdrawal. With barbiturates, withdrawal symptoms are more dangerous, severe, and long-lasting than in opiate withdrawal. A patient going through barbiturate withdrawal becomes anxious and apprehensive and manifests coarse tremors of the hands and face; additional symptoms commonly include insomnia, weakness, nausea, vomiting, abdominal cramps, rapid heart rate, elevated blood pressure, and loss of weight. An acute delirious psychosis may develop.

For persons used to taking large dosages, withdrawal symptoms may last for as long as a month, but usually they tend to abate by the end of the first week. Fortunately, the withdrawal symptoms in barbiturate addiction can be minimized by administering increasingly smaller doses of the barbiturate itself or another drug producing similar effects. The withdrawal program is still a dangerous one, however, especially if barbiturate addiction is complicated by alcoholism or dependence on other drugs.

LSD and Related Drugs (Hallucinogens)

The **hallucinogens** are drugs whose properties are thought to induce hallucinations. In fact, however, these preparations do not so often "create" sensory images as distort them, so that an individual sees or hears things in different and unusual ways. These drugs are often referred to as *psychedelics*. The major drugs in this category are LSD (lysergic acid diethylamide), mescaline, and psilocybin. Not long ago, PCP, or "angel dust," became popular as well. Our present discussion will be restricted largely to LSD because of its unusual hallucinogenic properties.

LSD The most potent of the hallucinogens, the odorless, colorless, and tasteless drug **LSD** can produce intoxication with an amount smaller than a grain of salt. It is a chemically synthesized substance first discovered by the Swiss chemist Albert Hoffman in 1938. Hoffman was not aware of the potent hallucinatory qualities of LSD until he swallowed a small amount. This is his report of the experience:

> Last Friday, April 16, 1943, I was forced to stop my work in the laboratory in the middle of the afternoon and to go home, as I was seized by a peculiar restlessness associated with a sensation of mild dizziness. On arriving home, I lay down and sank into a kind of drunkenness which was not unpleasant and which was characterized by extreme activity of imagination. As I lay in a dazed condition with my eyes closed (I experienced daylight as disagreeably bright) there surged upon me an uninterrupted stream of fantastic images of extraordinary plasticity and vividness and accompanied by an intense kaleidoscope-like play of colors. This condition gradually passed off after about two hours. (Hoffman, 1971, p. 23)

Hoffman followed up this experience with a series of planned self-observations with LSD, some of which he described as "harrowing." Researchers thought LSD might be useful for the induction and study of hallucinogenic states or "model psychoses," which were thought to be related to schizophrenia. About 1950, LSD was introduced into the United States for purposes of such research and to ascertain whether it might have medical or therapeutic uses. Despite considerable research, however, LSD has not proven therapeutically useful.

After taking LSD, a person typically goes through about eight hours of changes in sensory perception, mood swings, and feelings of depersonalization and detachment. The LSD experience is not always pleasant. It can be extremely traumatic, and the distorted objects and sounds, the illusory colors, and the new thoughts can be menacing and terrifying. For example, Rorvik (1970) cited the case of a young British law student who tried to "continue time" by using a dental drill to bore a hole in his head while under the influence of LSD. In other instances, people undergoing "bad trips" have set themselves aflame, jumped from high places, and taken other drugs that proved lethal in combination with LSD.

An interesting and unusual phenomenon that may occur following the use of LSD is a **flashback,** an involuntary recurrence of perceptual distortions or hallucinations weeks or even months after taking the drug. Flashbacks appear to be relatively rare among people who have taken LSD only once—although they do sometimes occur. One study found that continued effects on visual function were apparent at least two years following LSD use. In this study, Abraham and Wolf (1988) reported that individuals who had used LSD for a week were shown to have reduced visual sensitivity to light during dark adaptation and showed other visual problems compared with controls.

Despite the possibility of adverse reactions, LSD was widely publicized during the 1960s, and a number of relatively well-known people experimented with it and gave glowing accounts of their "trips." During this period, use of LSD was advocated by some, based on the conviction that the drug could "expand the mind" and enable one to use talents and realize potentials previously undetected. However, no evidence exists that LSD enhances creative activity: No recognized works of art have been produced under the influence of the drug or as a consequence of a psychedelic experience. Although several artists have claimed improved creativity stemming from their LSD experiences, objective observers recognize few, if any, improvements in the work of these artists (American Medical Association, 1968). It should also be pointed out that although users of LSD do not develop physiological dependence, some frequent users have been known to develop psychological dependence in the sense that they focus their life around LSD experiences.

For acute psychoses induced by LSD intoxication, treatment requires hospitalization and is primarily a medical matter. Often the outcome in such cases depends on a person's stability before taking the drug. Fortunately, brief psychotherapy is usually effective in treating psychological dependence on LSD and in preventing the recurrence of flashbacks. Therapy is aimed at helping the individual work through the painful experience induced by the drug and integrate it into his or her self-structure.

Mescaline and Psilocybin   Two other hallucinogens are mescaline and psilocybin. **Mescaline** is derived from the small, disclike growths (mescal buttons) at the top of the peyote cactus; **psilocybin** is obtained from a variety of "sacred" Mexican mushrooms known as *Psilocybe mexicana*. These drugs have been used for centuries in the ceremonial rites of native peoples living in Mexico, the American Southwest, and Central and South America. In fact, they were used by the Aztecs for such purposes long before the Spanish invasion. Both drugs have mind-altering and hallucinogenic properties, but their principal effect appears to be enabling an individual to see, hear, and otherwise experience events in unaccustomed ways—transporting him or her into a realm of "nonordinary reality." As with LSD, no definite evidence shows that mescaline and psilocybin actually "expand consciousness" or create new ideas; rather, they mainly alter or distort experience.

Marijuana

Although **marijuana** may be classified as a mild hallucinogen, there are significant differences in the nature, intensity, and duration of its effects as compared with those induced by LSD, mescaline, and other major hallucinogens. Marijuana comes from the leaves and flowering tops of the hemp plant, *Cannabis sativa*. The plant grows in mild climates throughout the world, including parts of India, Africa, Mexico, South America, and the United States. In its prepared state, marijuana consists chiefly of the dried green leaves—hence the colloquial name grass. It is ordinarily smoked in the form of cigarettes (reefers or joints) or in pipes. In some cultures the leaves are steeped in hot water and the liquid is drunk, much as one might drink tea. Marijuana is related to a stronger drug, **hashish,** which is derived from the resin exuded by the cannabis plant and made into a gummy powder. Hashish, like marijuana, is usually smoked.

Both marijuana and hashish use can be traced far back into history. Cannabis was apparently known in ancient China (Blum, 1969; Culliton, 1970) and was listed in the herbal compendiums of the Chinese emperor Shen Nung, written about 2737 B.C. Until the late 1960s, marijuana use in the United States was confined largely to members of lower socioeconomic minority groups and to people in entertainment and related fields. In the late 1960s, however, its use among youth dramatically increased, and during the early 1970s it was estimated that over half the teenagers and young adults in America had

Cannabis sativa, *the source of marijuana, grows wild in many parts of the world, where it is grown for the fiber known as hemp.*

experimented with marijuana in social situations, with about 10 percent presumably going from occasional to habitual use. Kandel and colleagues (1986) reported that among 24- and 25-year-old subjects, about 78 percent of males and 69 percent of females had tried marijuana.

Effects of Marijuana The specific effects of marijuana vary greatly, depending on the quality and dosage of the drug, the personality and mood of the user, the user's past experiences with the drug, the social setting, and the user's expectations. However, considerable consensus exists among regular users that when marijuana is smoked and inhaled, a state of slight intoxication results. This state is one of mild euphoria distinguished by increased feelings of well-being, heightened perceptual acuity, and pleasant relaxation, often accompanied by a sensation of drifting or floating away. Sensory inputs are intensified. Often a person's sense of time is stretched or distorted, so that an event lasting but a few seconds may seem to cover a much longer span. Short-term memory may also be affected, as when one notices a bite taken out of a sandwich but does not remember having taken it. For most users, pleasurable experiences, including sexual intercourse, are reportedly enhanced. When smoked, marijuana is rapidly absorbed and its effects appear within seconds to minutes but seldom last more than two to three hours.

Marijuana may lead to unpleasant as well as pleasant experiences. For example, if a person uses the drug while in an unhappy, angry, suspicious, or frightened mood, unsavory feelings may be magnified. With higher dosages and with certain unstable or susceptible individuals, marijuana can produce extreme euphoria, hilarity, and overtalkativeness but it can also produce intense anxiety and depression as

well as delusions, hallucinations, and other psychotic-like behavior. Recent evidence (Tien & Anthony, 1990) suggests a strong relationship between daily marijuana use and the occurrence of self-reported psychotic symptoms.

Marijuana's short-range physiological effects include a moderate increase in heart rate, a slowing of reaction time, a slight contraction of pupil size, bloodshot and itchy eyes, a dry mouth, and an increased appetite. Furthermore, marijuana induces memory dysfunction and a slowing of information processing (Mathew, Wilson, & Melges, 1992). Continued use of high dosages over time tends to produce lethargy and passivity. In such cases marijuana appears to have a depressant and a hallucinogenic effect. The effects of long-term and habitual marijuana use are still under investigation, although a number of possible adverse side effects have been related to the prolonged, heavy use of marijuana. For example, marijuana use tends to diminish self-control. One recent study exploring past substance-use history in incarcerated murderers reported that among men who committed murder, marijuana use was the most commonly used drug. One-third indicated that they used the drug before the homicide, and two-thirds were experiencing some effects of the drug at the time of the murder (Spunt et al., 1994).

Marijuana has often been compared to heroin, but the two drugs have little in common with respect either to tolerance or to physiological dependence. Marijuana does not lead to physiological dependence, as heroin does, so discontinued use is not

Group counseling is a common treatment for psychological dependence on drugs. In the give-and-take of group therapy, drug abusers may be able to face the consequences of their addiction and to see new possibilities for coping with it.

accompanied by withdrawal symptoms. Marijuana can, however, lead to psychological dependence, in which a person experiences a strong need for the drug whenever he or she feels anxious and tense.

Psychological treatment methods have been shown to be effective in reducing marijuana use in adults who are dependent on the drug (Zweben & O'Connell, 1992). One study compared the effectiveness of two treatments, Relapse Prevention (RP) and Support Group (SSP), with marijuana-dependent adults (Stephens, Roffman, & Simpson, 1994). Both treatment conditions resulted in substantial reduction in marijuana use in the 12 months following treatment. Relapse prevention and support discussion sessions were equally effective in bringing about changes in marijuana use.

Caffeine and Nicotine

Two quite common addictions to legally available and widely used substances, caffeine and nicotine, are included in the DSM-IV. Although these addictions do not represent the extensive and self-destructive problems found in the drug and alcohol disorders previously described, they are important physical and mental health problems in our society for several reasons: (a) These drugs are easy to abuse. It is easy to become addicted to them because they are widely used and most people are exposed to them early in life. (b) These drugs are readily available to anyone desiring to use them; in fact, it is usually difficult, because of peer pressure, to avoid using them in our society. (c) Both caffeine and nicotine have clearly addictive properties; use of them promotes further use, until they become a needed commodity in one's daily life. (d) It is difficult to quit using these drugs both because of their addictive properties and because they are so embedded in the social context (nicotine use, however, is falling out of favor in many settings). (e) The extreme difficulty most people have dealing with the withdrawal symptoms when trying to "break the habit" often produces considerable frustration. (f) Finally, the health problems and side effects of these drugs, particularly nicotine, have been widely noted (USDHHS, 1994). One in seven deaths in the United States is associated with cigarette consumption (USDHHS, 1988).

Because of their tenacity as habits and their contributions to many major health problems, we will examine each of these addictions in more detail.

Caffeine The chemical compound **caffeine** is found in many commonly available drinks and foods. Al-

though the consumption of caffeine is widely practiced and socially promoted in contemporary society, problems can occur as a result of excessive caffeine intake. The negative effects of caffeine involve intoxication rather than withdrawal. Unlike with other drugs, such as alcohol or nicotine, withdrawal from caffeine does not produce severe symptoms, except for headache, which is usually mild.

Caffeine-induced organic mental disorder (also referred to as Caffeinism), as described in DSM-IV, involves symptoms of restlessness, nervousness, excitement, insomnia, muscle twitching, and gastrointestinal complaints. It follows the ingestion of caffeine-containing substances, such as coffee, tea, cola, or chocolate. The amount of caffeine that results in intoxication differs among individuals; however, consumption of over 1 gram of caffeine could result in muscle twitching, cardiac arrhythmia, agitation, and rambling thinking. Consumption of 10 grams of caffeine can produce seizures, respiratory failures, and death.

Nicotine The poisonous alkaloid **nictoine** is the chief active ingredient in tobacco; it is found in such items as cigarettes, chewing tobacco, and cigars, and is even used as an insecticide.

Strong evidence exists for a nicotine dependency syndrome which almost always begins during the adolescent years and may continue into adult life as a difficult-to-break and health-endangering habit. The recent Surgeon General's report (USDHHS, 1994) estimates that there are 3.1 million adolescents and 25 percent of 17- to 18-year-olds who are current smokers. The nicotine-induced organic mental disorder, as it is called in DSM-IV, results from ceasing or reducing the intake of nicotine-containing substances after an individual has acquired physical dependence on them. The diagnostic criteria for nicotine withdrawal include (a) the daily use of nicotine for at least several weeks, and (b) the following symptoms after nicotine ingestion is stopped or reduced: craving for nicotine; irritability, frustration, or anger; anxiety; difficulty concentrating; restlessness; decreased heart rate; and increased appetite or weight gain. Several other physical concomitants are associated with withdrawal from nicotine, including decreased metabolic rate, headaches, insomnia, tremors, increased coughing, and impairment of performance on tasks requiring attention.

These withdrawal symptoms usually continue for several days to several weeks, depending on the extent of the nicotine habit. Some individuals report a desire for nicotine continuing for several months after they have quit smoking. In general, nicotine withdrawal symptoms operate in a manner similar to other addictions—they are "time limited and abate with drug replacement or gradual reduction" (Hughes, Higgins, & Hatsukami, 1990, p. 381).

Treatment of Nicotine Withdrawal Over the past 25 years, since the Surgeon General's report that detailed the health hazards of smoking cigarettes, numerous treatment programs have been developed to aid smokers in quitting (Curry, 1993; Gruder et al., 1993; Orleans, Kristeller, & Gritz, 1993). Quit-smoking programs use many different methods, including social support groups; various pharmacologic agents, which replace cigarette consumption with other safer forms of nicotine, such as candy or gum; self-directed change, which involves giving individuals guidance as to how they can change their own behaviors; and professional treatment using psychological procedures such as behavioral or cognitive-behavioral interventions.

In general, tobacco dependency can be successfully treated (USDHHS, 1989), and most of the quit-smoking programs enjoy some success, averaging about a 20–25 percent success rate, when evaluated by objective criteria.

OTHER ADDICTIVE DISORDERS: HYPEROBESITY AND PATHOLOGICAL GAMBLING

Not all addictive disorders involve the use of substances with chemical properties that induce dependency. People can develop "addictions" to certain activities that can be just as life-threatening as severe alcoholism and just as damaging, psychologically and socially, as drug abuse. We include two such disorders in this chapter—hyperobesity and pathological gambling. They are similar to other addictions in their behavioral manifestations, their etiologies, and their resistance to treatments.

Hyperobesity

To get an idea of how extensive the problem of obesity is, just look around and count the number of people who are seriously overweight. Weiss (1984), defining hyperobesity as 20 percent in excess of desirable weight, estimates that from 15 to 16 million Americans fall into this category. Recently it was reported that 24 percent of men and 27 percent of women were obese, that is, were 20 percent or more above the desirable weight (Kuczmarski, 1992). Moreover, obesity appears to be a problem that per-

sists over time. DiPietro, Mossberg, and Stunkard (1994) reported on a 40-year follow-up of 504 overweight children, the majority of whom remained overweight as adults.

In this discussion, we are concerned with **hyperobesity**—often called morbid obesity—which we define as being 100 pounds or more above ideal body weight. Such obesity is not simply unattractive; it can be a dangerous, life-threatening disorder, resulting in such conditions as diabetes, musculoskeletal problems, high blood pressure, and other cardiovascular diseases that may place a person at high risk for a heart attack. Although some cases of extreme obesity result from metabolic or hormonal disorders, most obese persons simply take in more calories than they burn.

Obesity, as a disorder, may be placed in several diagnostic categories, depending on which characteristics are emphasized. If we focus on the physical changes, for example, we may view obesity as having both psychological and physical components. Many clinicians, however, view the central problem not as the excessive weight itself, but as the long-standing habit of overeating. Thus obesity resulting from gross, habitual overeating is considered to be more like the problems found in the personality disorders—especially those involving loss of control over an appetite of some kind (Leon et al., 1978; Orford, 1985).

Causes of Persistent Overeating What prompts people to overeat to the point of obesity, despite an awareness of the detrimental health effects and a consciousness of the strong social prejudice in favor of the "body beautiful"? Several potential causal factors have been explored; although results are not conclusive, biological and learning factors seem to be of great importance.

Biological Factors. Some people seem able to eat high-calorie foods without significant weight gain, while others become overweight easily and engage in a constant struggle to maintain their weight. Most people gain weight with advancing age, but this gain could be related to reduced activity and to the fact that older people are likely to continue their earlier eating habits even though they need fewer calories. As already indicated, some people have metabolic or endocrine anomalies that can produce obesity at any age, though these cases seem to be relatively rare.

Genetic inheritance contributes substantially to the tendency for some people to become obese, or alternatively to remain thin. Findings in a study of twins reared apart have shown that genetics plays an important part in body weight (Stunkard et al., 1990). Adult obesity is related to the number and size of the adipose cells (fat cells) in the body (Weiss, 1984). People who are obese have markedly more adipose cells than do people of normal weight. When weight is lost, the size of the cells is reduced, but not their number. Some evidence suggests that the total number of adipose cells stays the same from childhood on (Crisp et al., 1970). It is possible that overfeeding infants and young children may cause them to develop more adipose cells and may thus predispose them to weight problems in adulthood.

Psychosocial Factors. Factors other than biological endowment play an important role in obesity (Newman et al., 1990; Button, 1993). In many cases the key determinants of excessive eating and obesity appear to be family behavior patterns. In some families, the customary diet or an overemphasis on food may produce obesity in many or all family members. In such families, a fat baby may be seen as a healthy baby, and there may be great pressure on infants and children to eat more than they want. In other families, eating (or overeating) becomes a habitual means of alleviating emotional distress.

Several psychological views address the causes of gross habitual overeating. According to the psychodynamic view, obese individuals are fixated at the oral stage of psychosexual development (Bychowski, 1950). They are believed to orient their lives around oral gratification (through excessive eating) because their libidinal energies and psychological growth have not advanced to a more mature level. This view has been elaborated by Bruch (1973), who distinguishes between developmental obesity and reactive obesity. She sees developmental obesity as a childhood response to parental rejection or other severe disturbances in the parent-child relationship. Supposedly, the parents compensate for their emotional rejection by overfeeding and overprotecting the child. Such children never learn to distinguish different internal signals because their parents respond to all signs of distress by giving them food. Bruch sees this pattern as leading to a distorted perception of internal states—that is, not knowing when enough food has been ingested.

Reactive obesity is defined by Bruch as obesity that occurs in adults as a reaction to trauma or stress. Here, overeating is thought to function as a defense mechanism to lessen feelings of distress or depression. There is evidence to support the idea that many obese people experience other psychological problems. For example, one study reported that 26 percent of patients seeking weight-loss treatment were diagnosed as having an affective disorder and 55 percent had at least one lifetime diagnosis of affective disorder (Goldsmith et al., 1992). Other research has found that a striking percentage of eating-disorder subjects also had one of the anxiety disorders (Schwalberg et al., 1992). However, the extent to which feelings of depression or anxiety lead to obesity has not been determined.

The simplest explanation—and therefore the easiest to accept—seems to be found in the behavioral view and more recently the cognitive-behavioral viewpoint. According to this view, a person's weight gain and his or her tendency to maintain excessive weight can be explained quite simply in terms of learning principles (Leon & Chamberlain, 1973; Stuart, 1971).

For all of us, eating behavior is determined in part by conditioned responses to a wide range of environmental stimuli. For example, people are encouraged to eat at parties and movies, while watching TV, and even at work. Eating is reinforced in all these situations, and it is difficult to avoid the many inducements to eat. Thus a wide assortment of seemingly avoidable reinforcers and conditioned stimuli enter the lives of most Americans.

Obese people, however, have been shown to be conditioned to more cues—both internal and external—than people of normal weight. Anxiety, anger, boredom, and social inducements all may lead to overeating. Eating in response to such cues is then reinforced because the taste of good food is pleasurable and the individual's emotional tension is reduced. This reinforcement increases the probability that overeating will continue and worsen. Binge-eating is a prominent factor in obesity in some individuals. Many people entering into weight-control programs report engaging in binge-eating (Marcus, Wing, and Hopkins, 1988).

With such frequent overfeeding, obese people may then learn not to respond to satiety cues, no longer feeling full when they have had enough. Meanwhile, physical activity, because its short-term effects are often aversive rather than pleasant, tends not to be reinforced, especially as pounds accumulate. Thus obese individuals may become less and less active.

Sociocultural Factors. Different cultures have different concepts of human beauty. Some value slimness; others, a rounded contour. In some cultures, obesity is valued as a sign of social influence and power. However, within our own society, obesity seems to be related to social class, occurring six times as often in lower-class adults and nine times more often in lower-class youngsters (Ernst & Harlan, 1991).

Obesity may be related to high-carbohydrate diets in lower-class families, however. Lissau and Sorenson (1994) found that children who were seriously neglected as children had a greater risk of obesity in young adulthood than well-cared for children.

Treatment of Hyperobesity Losing weight is a preoccupation of many Americans; diet books, dietary aids, and weight-loss programs are big business. Diet plans abound, with new programs emerging as often as clothing fads. The success rates of most of these devices and programs are quite low (Brownell & Wadden, 1992). In fact one study reported that the average outcome from diets is a regaining of 105 percent of the weight lost (Stuart, 1967). Cyclic loss and regaining can even be dangerous because it may do serious damage to the cardiovascular system, further compounding the problem.

A number of weight-loss group programs are conducted by organizations like TOPS (Take Off Pounds Sensibly) and Weight Watchers (Bumbalo & Young, 1973). These programs provide strong group pressures to reduce weight by public praise of weight losses and public disapproval and "punishments" for failures. Thus they provide community support and encouragement to maintain better eating habits.

Fasting or starvation diets under medically controlled conditions generally produce weight losses in hyperobese patients, with some studies reporting losses of over 100 pounds. This method of rapid weight loss, however, may involve several dangerous potential complications, such as hypertension, gout, and kidney failure (Munro & Duncan, 1972). Two eating disorders, anorexia nervosa and bulimia (discussed in Chapter 8), involve an excessive preoccupation with weight loss.

Another questionable medical treatment of hyperobese patients has centered on the use of anorexigenic drugs to reduce appetite. Diet pills, such as amphetamines, suppress the desire for food and, as a result, have been used extensively. Again, however, maintenance of weight loss once the diet pills are gone often becomes a problem.

Moreover, diet pills often present an additional problem of their own. As we have seen, amphetamines are addicting substances and are particularly dangerous when used in combination with other substances, such as alcohol. The general ineffectiveness of amphetamines for long-term weight control plus their high abuse potential has made these drugs of doubtful value in weight-reduction programs.

The most effective psychological treatment procedures for extremely obese patients are behavioral management methods, which teach people to take off weight gradually through reduced food intake and exercise (Jeffrey, Wing, & Stunkard, 1978). A number of methods using positive reinforcement, self-monitoring, and self-reward can produce moderate weight loss over time (Kern et al., 1994). In general these procedures, based on positive reinforcement, are more effective than classical conditioning procedures, such as aversive conditioning in which shock or unpleasant thoughts may be paired with eating behavior. Recently, some support for

Some of the most successful dietary programs are the self-control behavioral management programs, conducted in groups. Here dieters show how much weight they have lost by proudly displaying pants they can no longer wear. Programs like this provide strong group pressures to lose weight through public praise of successes and support and encouragement for maintaining better eating habits.

treatment of binge-eating using cognitive-behavioral methods has been found (Thackwray et al., 1993; Wilson & Fairburn, 1993). However, the effectiveness of behavior management programs has been questioned. Garner and Wooley (1991) reviewed the literature on treatment effectiveness of behavioral and dietary treatments and concluded that the evidence is overwhelming that most approaches are ineffective at producing weight loss. Wadden, Foster and Letizia (1994) showed that obese people undergoing very low calorie diets that produce dramatic weight loss during the program tend to gain back the weight and are higher at follow-up than those on a gradual (balanced diet) weight-loss program. Garner and Wooley (1991) concluded that there is evidence that high but stable weight maintenance is preferable to the weight fluctuation that commonly results from most treatment and dietary programs. Interestingly, some researchers have raised the possibility that dieting can actually play a causal role in the development of eating disorders (French & Jeffery, 1994).

Apparently, the jury is still out on the value of dieting in the treatment of hyperobesity and no firm conclusions on its effectiveness can be made at this time. Recently, concerned over the health problems obesity presents, Brownell and Rodin (1994) examined the controversy over dieting and called for more research into the reasons why some people cannot lose weight and what the health consequences of dieting versus not dieting might be.

The treatment of extremely obese patients is often a difficult and frustrating task for all concerned. Even with the most effective treatment procedures, failures abound, partly due to the necessity of self-motivation in treatment.

Impact of Failed Weight-Loss Treatment Programs. Most obese patients who seek professional help have failed on many diets in the past and tend to experience a "rollercoaster" effect rather than stabilizing at a lower, more desired weight. The weight-fluctuation effect, so much a part of most weight-loss programs, has prompted some authorities to rethink the weight-loss program goals in order to avoid both the rollercoaster effect and to prevent the negative self-views so prominent among individuals who start out with great and noble intentions and high expectations only to fail and then appear to themselves and others as a "failure." Brownell and Wadden (1991) pointed out:

Obese persons may also bear a legacy of shame and failure from cycles of weight loss and regain. Our patients have undertaken an average of five major

diets on which they lost (and eventually regained) a total of 56 kg. Despite their efforts, they have watched their weight increase from 70 kg at age 17 to 100 kg at age 40 (Wadden et al., in press). Regrettably, these failed efforts have occurred in full view of family, friends, and employers, not to mention health care practitioners. Few other conditions occur in such public view or are thought by lay persons to result from personal weakness. (p. 513.)

Brownell and Wadden propose a rather different model which includes establishing a "reasonable weight" which may differ somewhat from what the person might consider desirable but which is more obtainable and more readily maintained through such means as low-fat diets. Important to any weight-loss treatment is the awareness that obese persons are subjected to extensive prejudice and discrimination. They point out that the "psychosocial perils of obesity may well exceed its medical complications" (p. 513.)

Pathological Gambling

Gambling is usually defined as wagering on games or events in which chance largely determines the outcome. In modern societies, money is typically the item of exchange; in other societies, seashell currency, beads, jewelry, and food are often used. The ancient Chinese frequently wagered hairs of their heads—and sometimes even fingers, toes, and limbs—on games of chance (Cohen & Hansel, 1956). Regardless of the item of exchange, gambling seems to be an enduring human proclivity. Judging from written history and the studies of anthropologists, gambling has occurred and continues to occur almost universally and among all social strata. In the United States today, with the legalized and widely promoted government gambling enterprises problems of pathological gambling are increasing (Politzer, Yesalis, & Hudak, 1992; Volberg, 1994). Recent estimates place the number of pathological gamblers in the United States at between 1.2 and 2.3 percent of the adult population (Volberg, 1990; Volberg & Steadman, 1989).

Pathological gambling, also known as compulsive gambling, is a progressive disorder characterized by continuous or periodic loss of control over gambling; a preoccupation with gambling and obtaining money for gambling; irrational behavior; and continuation of the gambling behavior in spite of adverse consequences (Rosenthal, 1992). Although this behavior pattern does not involve a chemically addictive substance, it can be considered an addictive disorder because of the personality factors that tend to characterize compulsive gamblers, the difficulties attributable to compulsive gambling, and the treatment problems involved. Like other addictions, pathological gambling involves behavior maintained by short-term gains despite long-term disruption of an individual's life.

Clinical Picture in Pathological Gambling Gambling in our society takes many forms, including casino gambling, betting on horse races (legally or otherwise), numbers games, lotteries, dice, bingo, and cards. The exact sums that change hands in legal and illegal gambling are unknown, but it has been estimated that habitual gamblers in the United States lose more than $20 billion each year.

If one were to define gambling in its broadest sense, even investing in the stock market might be considered a game of chance. Sherrod (1968) has pointed to the need for a clearer definition of terms: "If you bet on a horse, that's gambling. If you bet you can make three spades, that's entertainment. If you bet cotton will go up three points, that's business. See the difference?" (p. 619).

In any event, gambling appears to be one of our major national pastimes, with some 50 percent of the population gambling at one time or another on anything from Saturday night poker games to the outcome of sporting events. Usually, such gambling is a harmless form of social entertainment; an individual places a bet and waits for the result. Win or lose, the game is over. But while most people can gamble and then get on with their life, an estimated 6 to 10 million Americans get "hooked" on gambling. The following case is illustrative:

John was a handsome 40-year-old man with slightly graying hair who managed an automobile dealership for his father. For the previous two years, he had increasingly neglected his job and was deep in debt as a result of gambling. He had gambled heavily since his twenties. Gambling had caused quarrels in his first marriage and finally a divorce. He had married his second wife without telling her of his problem, but it eventually created such difficulty that she had left him.

John joined an encounter group in the stated hope that he might be helped with his problem. In early group sessions, he proved to be an intelligent, well-educated man who seemed to understand his gambling problem and its self-defeating nature. He stated that he had started gambling after winning some money at the horse races. This experience convinced him that he could supplement his income by gambling judiciously. However, his subsequent gambling—which frequently involved all-night poker games, trips to Las Vegas, and betting on the races—almost always resulted in heavy losses.

In the group, John talked about his gambling freely and coherently—candidly admitting that he enjoyed the excitement of gambling more than sexual relations with his wife. He was actually glad his family had left because it relieved

Gambling can be a powerful, irresistible behavioral pattern similar to other addictions described in this chapter. Pathological or compulsive gamblers will often persist in their behavior, even at risk of personal disasters.

him of responsibility toward them and alleviated his guilt for neglecting them. He acknowledged that his feelings and behavior were inappropriate and self-defeating, but he stated that he was "sick" and that he desperately needed help.

It soon became apparent that although John was willing to talk about his problem, he was not prepared to take constructive steps to deal with it. He wanted the group to accept him in the role of a pathological gambler who could not be expected to "cure" himself. At the group's suggestion, he attended a few meetings of Gamblers Anonymous but found them "irrelevant." It was also suggested that he try aversive therapy, but he felt this would not help him.

While attending the group sessions, John apparently continued to gamble and to lose. After the eighth encounter group session, he did not return. Through inquiry by one of the members, it was learned that he had been arrested for embezzling funds from his father's business, but that his father had somehow managed to have the charges dropped. John reportedly then left for another state and his subsequent history is unknown.

Whatever an individual gambler's situation, compulsive gambling significantly affects the social, psychological, and economic well-being of the gambler's family (Lorenz & Shuttlesworth, 1983). In fact, one study found that a high proportion of pathological gamblers commit crimes that are related to gambling (Blaszczynski, McConaghy, & Frankova, 1989).

Causal Factors in Pathological Gambling Little systematic research on pathological gambling has been done, and the causal factors behind it are not yet well understood. Pathological gambling seems to be a learned pattern that is highly resistant to extinction. Often a person who becomes a pathological gambler won a substantial sum of money the first time he or she gambled; chance alone would dictate that a certain percentage of people would have such "beginner's luck." The reinforcement a person receives during this introductory phase may be a significant factor in later pathological gambling (Bolen & Boyd, 1968). Because anyone is likely to win from time to time, the principles of intermittent reinforcement could explain an addict's continued gambling despite excessive losses.

Despite their awareness that the odds are against them, and despite the fact that they rarely or never repeat their early success, compulsive gamblers continue to gamble avidly. To "stake" their gambling,

they often dissipate their savings, neglect their families, default on bills, and borrow money from friends and loan companies. Eventually, they may resort to embezzlement, writing bad checks, or other illegal means of obtaining money, feeling sure that their luck will change and that they will be able to repay what they have taken. Whereas others view their gambling as unethical and disruptive, they are likely to see themselves as taking "calculated risks" to build a lucrative business. Often they feel alone and resentful that others do not understand their activities.

In a pioneering and well-controlled study of former pathological gamblers, Rosten (1961) found that as a group they tended to be rebellious, unconventional individuals who did not seem to fully understand the ethical norms of society. Half of the group described themselves as "hating regulations." Of 30 men studied, 12 had served time in jail for embezzlement and other crimes directly connected with their gambling. Rosten also found that these men were unrealistic in their thinking and prone to seek highly stimulating situations. In the subjects' own words, they "loved excitement" and "needed action." Although the men admitted that they had known objectively the all-but-impossible odds they faced while gambling, they had felt that these odds did not apply to them. Often they had the unshakable feeling that "tonight is my night"; typically, they had also followed the so-called Monte Carlo fallacy—that after so many losses, their turn was coming up and they would hit it big. Many of the men discussed the extent to which they had "fooled" themselves by elaborate rationalizations. For example, one gambler described his previous rationalizations as covering all contingencies: "When I was ahead, I could gamble because I was playing with others' money. When I was behind, I had to get even. When I was even, I hadn't lost any money" (Rosten, 1961, p. 67).

It is of interest to note that within a few months after the study, 13 of Rosten's 30 subjects either had returned to heavy gambling, had started to drink excessively, or had not been heard from and were presumed to be gambling again.

Later studies strongly support Rosten's findings. They describe pathological gamblers as typically immature, rebellious, thrill-seeking, superstitious, and basically psychopathic (Bolen & Boyd, 1968; Bolen, Caldwell, & Boyd, 1975; Custer, 1982; and Graham, 1978a). The most comprehensive study is that of Livingston (1974), who observed, interviewed, and tested 55 mostly working-class men who had joined Gamblers Anonymous to try to stop gambling. Livingston found that these men often referred to their "past immaturity" in explaining their habitual gambling. They also described themselves as having a "big ego" and acknowledged a strong need for recognition and adulation from others.

Although these men had usually been able to cover their losses early in their gambling careers, the course was downhill, leading to financial, marital, job, and often legal problems. Eventually, things got so bad that it seemed the only way out of their difficulties was the way they got into them—by gambling.

Cultural factors also appear to be important in developing gambling problems. Research with Southeast Asian refugee populations highlights the role of cultural influences in gambling. Pathological gambling is a particular problem among Southeast Asian refugees, particularly those from Laos. Surveys of mental health problems have reported almost epidemic problems with gambling among such groups (Aronoff, 1987; Ganju & Quan, 1987). For example, Aronoff (1987) reported that 54 percent of informants in the Laos group reported gambling as a significant problem. This causes serious adaptation difficulties for refugees because family members who gamble away the limited resources available to them (for example, food stamps) can place additional stress on those facing the challenge of adapting to a new culture.

Pathological gambling problems are not new to Southeast Asians because gambling is reportedly common within their own cultures. However, these problems have apparently become more serious and more widespread in this country. Reasons for these increased gambling problems include the following: (a) The social sanctions that worked to control excessive gambling in Southeast Asia are absent. (b) Refugees experience considerable stress, and gambling serves temporarily to relieve cares; reportedly, when they are in their "casinos," many refugees feel, at least temporarily, as though they are still in their native lands. (c) Many refugees are unable to find employment, and gambling helps pass the time. And (d) finally, of course, gambling lures refugees with the possibility of great rewards and the opportunity to regain all they lost during migration.

Treatments and Outcomes Treatment of pathological gamblers is still a relatively unexplored area. However, Boyd and Bolen (1970) reported on a study in which eight pathological gamblers and their spouses were treated together through group psychotherapy—an approach based on the finding that a pathological gambler's marital relationship is generally chaotic and turbulent, with the spouse frequently showing seriously maladaptive behavior patterns also. Gambling ceased in three of these cases and almost completely stopped in the other five. The extent to which changes in the gamblers' marital relationships influenced the treatment outcomes

can only be surmised—six of the eight couples showed significant improvements. Other treatment approaches, including aversion therapy and covert sensitization (Cotler, 1971) and cognitive-behavioral therapy (Bannister, 1975) have been tried with individual cases, but further studies are needed before we can evaluate the potential effectiveness of psychotherapy in treating this disorder.

Some pathological gamblers who want to change find help through membership in Gamblers Anonymous. This organization was founded in 1957 in Los Angeles by two pathological gamblers who found that they could help each other control their gambling by talking about their experiences. Since then, groups have been formed in most major American cities. The groups are modeled after Alcoholics Anonymous, and they view those who gamble as personally responsible for their own actions. The only requirement for membership is an expressed desire to stop gambling. In group discussions, members share experiences and try to gain insights into the irrationality of their gambling and to realize its inevitable consequences. As with Alcoholics Anonymous, members try to help each other maintain control and prevent relapses. Unfortunately, only a small fraction of pathological gamblers find their way into Gamblers Anonymous. Of those who do, only about one in ten manages to overcome the addiction to gambling (Strine, 1971).

A novel inpatient treatment program for pathological gamblers has been developed at the Brecksville, Ohio, Veterans' Administration Medical Center (1981). This program, initiated in 1972, has helped many gamblers and has served as a model for many other hospitals. The Brecksville treatment program, which lasts for a minimum of 28 days, is integrated into the alcohol treatment program. Five inpatient beds in the 55-bed unit are set aside for pathological gamblers. Alcoholics and gamblers are housed together and share many common program elements because their problems are viewed as similar. The treatment goals for gamblers include abstinence from gambling, major lifestyle changes, participation in Gamblers Anonymous programs, and the acquisition of more adaptive forms of recreation.

Pathological gambling is on the increase in the United States (Custer, 1982). Furthermore, liberalized gambling legislation has permitted state-operated lotteries, horse racing, and gambling casinos in an effort to increase state tax revenues. In the context of this apparent environmental support and "official" sanction for gambling, it is likely that pathological gambling will increase substantially as more and more people "try their luck." Given that pathological gamblers are resistant to treatment, it is likely, too, that our future efforts toward developing more effective preventive and treatment approaches will need to be increased as this problem continues to grow.

UNRESOLVED ISSUES

on the Genetics of Alcoholism

Several recent research efforts suggest a possible genetic predisposition toward alcoholism (Dinwiddie, 1992; Finn, Earleywine, & Pihl, 1992; Tarter, 1988). One source of evidence has come from studies of alcoholics' children who were placed for adoption early in life and did not come under the environmental influences of their biological parents. Several such studies can be found to support the genetic viewpoint. For example, Goodwin and colleagues (1973) found that children of alcoholic parents who had been adopted by nonalcoholic foster parents had nearly twice the number of alcohol problems by their late 20s as did a control group of adopted children whose real parents were not alcoholics. In another study, Goodwin and colleagues (1974) compared the sons of alcoholic parents who were adopted in infancy by nonalcoholic parents with those raised by their alcoholic parents. Both adopted and non-adopted sons later evidenced high rates of alcoholism—25 percent and 17 percent, respectively. These investigators concluded that being born to an alcoholic parent, rather than being raised by one, increased the risk of a son's becoming an alcoholic.

Another approach to exploring a possible genetic basis in alcoholism has focused on finding underlying mechanisms for the transmission of alcohol abuse or susceptibility to alcoholism. For example, researchers have attempted to determine if individuals who have a genetic "risk" for alcoholism—such as children of alcoholics—show signs of a predisposition toward alcoholism. Evidence for increased alcoholism risk includes such factors as a decreased intensity of subjective feelings of intoxication, a decrease in motor performance, and less body sway after alcohol ingestion. Along with these behavioral indices, increases in prolactin (a pituitary hormone) levels after low doses of alcohol have been thought to occur in individuals with a predisposition to alcohol-abuse disorders. Research into these risk factors in alcohol predisposition typically involves obtaining a sample of highly susceptible individuals, such as children of alcoholics, and a sample of controls, and then determining if certain variables (one or more of the risk factors) distinguish the groups. Research by Schuckit and Gould (1988) has shown that alcohol susceptibility indicators significantly separate sons of alcoholics from matched controls.

The evidence on the genetic basis of alcoholism continues to be debated, however, and other experts are not convinced of the primary role of genetics in alcoholism. Searles (1991) points to the ambiguous evidence for the genetics of alcoholism and cautions against interpreting genetics as a causal factor in the development of alcoholism. Negative results have been found in both adoptive studies and in studies designed to follow up the behavior of high-risk individuals. It is clear that the great majority of children who have alcoholic parents do not themselves become alcoholics—whether or not they are raised by their real parents. The successful outcomes—that is, children of alcoholics who make successful life adjustments—have not been sufficiently studied (Heller, Sher, & Benson, 1982). In one study of high-risk children of alcoholics, a group of young men 19 to 20 years of age who were presumably at high risk for developing alcoholism were carefully studied for symptoms of psychopathology. Schulsinger and colleagues (1986) found no differences in psychopathology or alcohol-abuse behavior from a control sample similar to the general population. In another study of high-risk individuals, Alterman, Searles, and Hall (1989) failed to find differences in drinking behavior or alcohol-related symptoms between a group of high-risk subjects (those who had alcoholic fathers) and a group of non-high-risk subjects.

We do not know the possible role genetic factors play in the etiology of alcoholism. Available evidence suggests that they might be important as predisposing causes, or that they might contribute to constitutional factors in alcoholism development. Of course, a constitutional predisposition to alcoholism could be acquired as well as inherited. It is not known whether acquired conditions, such as endocrine or enzyme imbalances, increase an individual's vulnerability to alcoholism.

The evidence for a genetic basis of alcoholism is ambiguous at best. At present, it appears that the genetic interpretation of alcoholism remains an attractive hypothesis; however, additional research is needed for us to hold this view with confidence.

SUMMARY

Addictive disorders—such as alcohol or drug abuse, extreme overeating, and pathological gambling—are among the most widespread and intransigent mental health problems facing us today. Alcohol- and drug-abuse problems can be viewed as psychoactive substance-induced organic mental disorders and syndromes or as psychoactive substance-abuse and substance-dependence disorders. Many problems of alcohol or drug use involve difficulties that stem solely from the intoxicating effects of the substances. Dependence occurs when an individual develops a tolerance for the substance or exhibits withdrawal symptoms when the substance is not available. Several psychoses related to alcoholism have been identified: idiosyncratic intoxication, withdrawal delirium, chronic alcoholic hallucinosis, and dementia associated with alcoholism.

Drug-abuse disorders may involve physiological dependence on substances, such as opiates—particularly heroin—or barbiturates; however, psychological dependence may occur with any of the drugs that are commonly used today—for example, marijuana or cocaine.

A number of factors are considered important in the etiology of alcoholism. Although the data are not conclusive, it appears that genetic factors may play some role in causing susceptibility, as may other biological factors, such as metabolic rates and sensitivity to alcohol. Psychological factors—such as psychological vulnerability, stress, and the desire for tension reduction—and marital and other relationships are also seen as important etiologic elements in alcohol-use disorders. Although the existence of an "alcoholic personality type" has been disavowed by most theorists, personality factors apparently play an important role in the development and expression of addictive disorders. Finally, sociocultural factors, such as attitudes toward alcohol, may predispose individuals to alcoholism.

Possible causal factors in drug abuse include the influence of peer groups, the existence of a so-called drug culture, and the availability of drugs as tension reducers or as pain relievers. Some recent research has explored a possible physiological basis for drug abuse. The discovery of endorphins, morphine-like substances produced by the body, has raised speculation that a biochemical basis to drug addiction may exist.

The treatment of individuals who abuse alcohol or drugs is generally difficult and often fails. Many reasons can be found for this poor prognosis: The abuse may reflect a long history of psychological difficulties; interpersonal and marital distress may be involved; and financial and legal problems may be present. In addition, all such problems may be operating on an individual who denies that problems exist and is not motivated to work on them.

Several approaches to the treatment of chronic alcoholism or drug abuse have been developed. Frequently, the situation requires biological or medical measures—for example, medication to deal with withdrawal symptoms and withdrawal delirium, or dietary evaluation and treatment for malnutrition.

Psychological therapies, such as group therapy and behavioral interventions, may be effective with some alcoholic or drug-abusing individuals. Another source of help for alcoholics is Alcoholics Anonymous; however, the extent of successful outcomes with this program has not been sufficiently studied.

Most treatment programs show reasonably high success rates in "curing" addictive problems, but show lowered success rates at follow-up. Recent research on relapse prevention has contributed new insights into the problems of self-control once addictive behaviors have been checked. Part of this approach involves making a person aware of factors that can lead to relapse and preparing him or her to deal with these phenomena. Most treatment programs require abstinence; however, over the past 15 years, research has suggested that some alcoholics can learn to control their drinking while continuing to drink socially. The controversy surrounding controlled drinking continues.

Not all addictive disorders involve the use of substances such as alcohol or drugs. Some people eat to excess, endangering their health. Others gamble to such an extent that they wreck their lives and damage or destroy their family relationships. These disorders—hyperobesity and pathological gambling—involve many of the same psychological mechanisms that seem to underlie chronic alcoholism or drug addiction. Treatment approaches found to be effective for alcoholism and drug abuse appear to work about as well with obese clients and pathological gamblers. Many of the same difficulties, especially concerning response to treatment and relapse, also plague the treatment of hyperobese persons and compulsive gamblers.

KEY TERMS

addictive behavior (p. 355)
psychoactive drugs (p. 355)
toxicity (p. 355)
psychoactive substance abuse (p. 356)
psychoactive substance dependence (p. 356)
tolerance (p. 356)
withdrawal symptoms (p. 356)
alcoholic (p. 356)
alcoholism (p. 356)
opium (p. 375)
morphine (p. 375)
heroin (p. 375)
endorphins (p. 379)

methadone (p. 380)
cocaine (p. 381)
amphetamine (p. 383)
barbiturates (p. 384)
hallucinogens (p. 385)
LSD (p. 385)
flashback (p. 386)
mescaline (p. 386)
psilocybin (p. 386)
marijuana (p. 386)
hashish (p. 386)
caffeine (p. 388)
nicotine (p. 388)
hyperobesity (p. 389)
pathological gambling (p. 392)

CHAPTER

11

SEXUAL VARIANTS, ABUSE, AND DYSFUNCTIONS

Dwight Mackintosh, Three Figures. *Mackintosh (b. 1906), a native of California, was admitted to a mental institution at the age of 16 after having become "unmanageable at home." He remained in state mental hospitals until the deinstitutionalization movement inspired his release in 1978. His brother, Earl, remembered that Dwight had been interested in art as a boy and took him to the Creative Growth Art Center in Oakland, California, where he began to draw and paint earnestly. People are the primary subject of his art, and drawing his only way of expressing his interest in them; otherwise, he is deeply withdrawn.*

Sexuality is a central concern of our lives, influencing with whom we fall in love and mate, and how happy we are with them and with ourselves. Loving, sexually satisfying relationships contribute a great deal to our happiness, and if we are not in such relationships, we are apt to spend a great deal of time, effort, and emotional energy looking for them. If despite searching we cannot find satisfying sexual relationships, many of us will feel unfulfilled.

Few people are always happy with their sex lives, but a significant minority have psychological problems that make sexual fulfillment especially difficult. Three general sets of difficulties will be considered in this chapter: problematic sexual variants (deviations), sexual abuse, and sexual dysfunctions. First, some people—the vast majority of them men—develop unusual sexual interests that are difficult to satisfy in a socially acceptable manner. For example, exhibitionists are sexually aroused by showing their genitals to strangers, who are likely to be disgusted and frightened. Thus, exhibitionists' sexual expression often requires the unwilling discomfort of others, clearly a problematic situation. The pattern of sexual arousal and behavior known as pedophilia, sexual attraction to children, also involves inappropriate choice of sexual objects. Other sexual variants may be problematic primarily to the individual: Transsexualism, for example, is a disorder involving feelings of discomfort with one's biological sex and a strong desire to be of the opposite sex. Still other variants, such as fetishism, in which sexual interest centers on some inanimate object or anatomical part, involve behaviors that, although bizarre and unusual, do not clearly harm anyone. It might seem that the latter category of sexual deviations—those that result in neither harm nor psychological pain—should not be considered psychopathological. Perhaps no other area covered in this book exposes the difficulties in defining boundaries between normality and psychopathology as clearly as variant sexuality does. Later, we address this issue explicitly and in greater detail, focusing especially on homosexuality, which illustrates the influence of cultural norms on what is classified as psychopathological.

The second general category of problems, **sexual abuse** (which involves pressured or forced sexual contact), has especially devastating social effects. We will therefore focus special attention on this topic. During the past decade or so, there has been a tremendous increase in attention to the problem of sexual abuse of both children and adults (most adult victims being women). Research has addressed both the causes and consequences of sexual abuse. As we shall see, some related issues, such as the reality of "repressed memories of sexual abuse" are extremely controversial.

The third general set of sexual difficulties examined in this chapter, sexual dysfunctions, include problems that impede satisfactory performance of sexual acts. Premature ejaculation, for example, causes men to reach orgasm much earlier than they and their partners find satisfying. Vaginismus, which affects women, is an involuntary contraction of vaginal muscles that makes penile penetration impossible. The question of what is normal and what is not, which often appears in discussions of variant sexuality, is much less of an issue with sexual dysfunctions because people who have sexual dysfunctions (or their partners) typically view them as problems. Nevertheless, questions do arise concerning realistic expectations. Few people function ideally all the time, and many less-than-ideal conditions are common. For example, many young men ejaculate more rapidly than they would like but slow down as they age. Many women do not have orgasms during sexual intercourse, yet find intercourse enjoyable and satisfying.

Much less is known about sexual deviations, abuse, and dysfunctions than is known about many of the other disorders we have considered thus far in this book, such as anxiety and depression. The major clinical psychology and psychiatry journals have relatively few articles related to sexual dysfunctions and deviations, and there are also many fewer sex researchers than depression and anxiety researchers. One major reason is the sex taboo. Although sex is an important concern for most people, many have difficulty talking about it openly. This makes it difficult to obtain knowledge about even the most basic facts, such as the frequency of various sexual practices, feelings, and attitudes. This is especially true when the relevant behaviors are socially ostracized, such as homosexuality. It is difficult both to ask people about such behaviors and to trust their answers.

A second reason why sex research has progressed less rapidly is that many issues related to sexuality—including homosexuality, teenage sexuality, abortion, and childhood sexual abuse—are among our most divisive and controversial. In fact, sex research is itself controversial. Two large-scale sex surveys were halted because of political opposition even after being officially approved and deemed scientifically meritorious (Udry, 1993). Fortunately, one of these was funded privately, although on a much smaller scale, and it is now considered the definitive study for the 1990s (Michael et al., 1994). Senator Jesse Helms and others had argued that sex researchers tended to approve of premarital sex and

homosexuality, and that this would likely bias the results of the surveys. Perhaps in part because of the controversial nature of sex research, it is not well funded. For example, although sex offenders are widely feared and millions of dollars are spent keeping convicted sex offenders behind bars every year, the National Institute of Mental Health spent only $1.2 million on sex offender research in 1993, compared with $125.3 million on depression (Goode, 1994).

Despite these significant barriers, we do know some things about sexual variants and dysfunctions. Clinical investigations have provided rich descriptions of many sexual variants. Etiological research on sexual dysfunctions and deviations, although in its infancy, has shown promise for some disorders, and we discuss these developments.

Before we turn to specific disorders, we examine sociocultural influences on sexual behavior and attitudes in general. We take this excursion first in order to provide some perspective about cross-cultural variability in standards of sexual conduct, and to encourage special caution in classifying sexual practices as "abnormal" or "deviant."

SOCIOCULTURAL INFLUENCES ON SEXUAL PRACTICES AND STANDARDS

Although some aspects of sexuality and mating are cross-culturally universal (Buss, 1989), others are quite variable. For example, all known cultures have taboos against sex between close relatives, but attitudes toward premarital sex vary considerably (Frayser, 1985). Ideas about acceptable sexual behavior also change over time. Sexual standards have changed tremendously in our own culture, especially over the past century. Less than 100 years ago, for example, sexual modesty was such that women's arms and legs were always hidden in public. Nowadays, actors are shown nude in movies and sometimes even on television.

Despite the substantial variability in sexual attitudes and behavior in different times and places, people typically behave as if the sexual standards of their time and place were obviously correct, and they are intolerant of sexual nonconformity. Sexual nonconformists are often considered evil or sick. We do not mean to suggest that such judgments are always arbitrary. There has probably never existed a society in which Jeffrey Dahmer, who was sexually aroused by killing men, having sex with them, storing their corpses, and sometimes eating them, would be considered psychologically normal. Nevertheless, it is useful to be aware of historical and cultural influences on sexuality. When the expression or the acceptance of a certain behavior varies considerably across eras and cultures, we should at least pause to consider whether our own stance is the most appropriate one.

Because the influence of time and place are so important in shaping sexual behavior and attitudes, we begin by exploring three cases that illustrate how opinions about "acceptable" and "normal" sexual behavior may change dramatically over time, and may differ dramatically from one culture to another. In the first case, America during the mid-1800s, a set of beliefs about sexuality, "degeneracy theory," led to highly conservative sexual practices and dire warnings about most kinds of sexual "indulgence." In the second case, we look briefly at the Sambia tribe in New Guinea, in which a set of beliefs about sexuality has led to sexual practices unknown in Western culture. In Sambian society, all normal adolescent males go through a stage of homosexuality before switching rather abruptly to heterosexuality in adulthood. Finally, in the third case, we consider the status of homosexuality in Western culture. We focus here on the mental health profession's decision in the 1970s to change its view of homosexual behavior.

Case 1: Degeneracy and Abstinence Theory

During the 1750s the Swiss physician Simon Tissot developed degeneracy theory, the central belief of which was that semen is necessary for physical and sexual vigor in men and for masculine characteristics such as beard growth (Money, 1985, 1986). He based this theory on observations about human eunuchs and castrated animals. Of course, we now know that the loss of the male hormone testosterone, and not of semen, is responsible for relevant characteristics of eunuchs and castrated animals. Based on his theory, however, Tissot asserted that two practices were especially harmful: masturbation and patronizing prostitutes. Both of these practices wasted the vital fluid, semen, as well as (in his view) overstimulating and exhausting the nervous system. Tissot also recommended that married people engage solely in procreative sex to avoid the waste of semen. (See HIGHLIGHT 2.2 for further discussion of nineteenth century views on abnormal behavior.)

A descendant of degeneracy theory, abstinence theory, was advocated in America during the 1830s

by the Rev. Sylvester Graham (Money, 1985, 1986). The three cornerstones of his crusade for public health were healthy food (Graham crackers were named for him), physical fitness, and sexual abstinence. Graham's most famous successor, Dr. John Harvey Kellogg, began practicing medicine in the 1870s. He ardently disapproved of masturbation and urged parents to be wary of signs that their children were indulging in it. He published a paper on the 39 signs of "the secret vice," which included, among others, weakness, early symptoms of consumption (TB), sudden change in disposition, lassitude, dullness of the eyes, premature and defective development, sleeplessness, fickleness, untrustworthiness, bashfulness, love of solitude, unnatural boldness, mock piety, and round shoulders. Given his status as a physician, Kellogg was professionally admired and publicly influential, earning a fortune publishing books discouraging masturbation. His recommended treatments for "the secret vice" were quite extreme. For example, he advocated that especially persistent masturbation in boys be treated by sewing the foreskin with silver wire, or as a last resort, circumcision without anesthesia. Female masturbation was to be treated by burning the clitoris with carbolic acid. Besides deploring masturbation, Kellogg, like Graham, was especially concerned with dietary health. He urged people to eat more cereals and nuts and less meat, because he believed that eating meat increased sexual desire. Thus, Kellogg's cornflakes were invented "almost literally, as antimasturbation food" (Money, 1986, p. 186). Although Kellogg married, it appears that he slept alone and never consummated his marriage.

Given the influence of physicians like Kellogg, it should perhaps come as no surprise that many people believed that masturbation caused insanity (Hare, 1962). This hypothesis had started with the anonymous publication in the early eighteenth century in London of a book entitled *Onania, or the Heinous Sin of Self-Pollution*. It asserted that masturbation was a common cause of insanity. This idea probably arose from observations that many patients in mental asylums masturbated openly (unlike sane people, who are more likely to do it in private) and that the age at which masturbation tends to begin (at puberty in adolescence) precedes by several years the age when the first signs of insanity often begin (late adolescence and young adulthood) (Abramson & Seligman, 1977). The idea that masturbation may cause insanity appeared in some psychiatry textbooks as late as the 1940s.

The most influential American political opponent of sexual expression was Anthony Comstock. A contemporary of Kellogg, he formed the Society for the

Suppression of Vice and in 1873 successfully lob-
bied Congress to pass laws against "obscenity,"
which he construed quite broadly. As an inspector
with the post office, he became, in effect, the national censor. His targets included female nudity in
art classes and medical books pertaining to sexuality.
He believed that lust led to psychological degeneracy (Money, 1985, 1986).

Although abstinence theory and associated attitudes seem highly puritanical by today's standards,
they have had a long-lasting influence on attitudes
toward sex in American and other Western cultures.
It was not until 1972 that the American Medical Association declared: "Masturbation is a normal part
of adolescent sexual development and requires no
medical management" (American Medical Association Committee on Human Sexuality, 1972, p. 40).
Around the same time, the Boy Scout Manual
dropped its antimasturbation warnings. John Money
(1985), a prominent researcher in the field, has argued that the belief that sex is in some way physically and morally unhealthy continues to influence
public policy regarding sex education and sex research, leading to less of both.

Case 2: Ritualized Homosexuality in Melanesia

Melanesia is a collection of islands in the South Pacific that has been intensively studied by anthropologists, who have uncovered cultural influences on
sexuality unlike any known in the West. Between 10
and 20 percent of Melanesian societies practice a
form of homosexuality within the context of male
initiation rituals that all male members of society
must experience.

The best studied society has been the Sambia of
Papua New Guinea (Herdt & Stoller, 1990). Two
beliefs are related to Sambian sexual practices: *semen
conservation* and *female pollution*. Like Tissot, the
Sambians believe that semen is important for many
things, including physical growth, strength, and
spirituality. Furthermore, they believe that it takes
many inseminations (and much semen) to impreg-
nate a woman. Finally, they believe that semen cannot easily be replenished by the body and so must
be conserved or obtained elsewhere. The female
pollution doctrine refers to the belief that the female
body is unhealthy to males, primarily due to menstrual fluids. At menarche Sambian women are secretly initiated in the menstrual hut forbidden to all
males.

In order to obtain or maintain adequate amounts
of semen, young Sambian males practice semen exchange with each other. Beginning as boys, they

learn to practice fellatio (oral sex) in order to ingest
sperm. At first, they take only the oral role, but after
puberty they can take the penetrative role, insemi-
nating younger boys. Ritualized homosexuality
among the Sambian men is seen as an exchange of
sexual pleasure for vital semen. (It is ironic that although both the Sambian and Victorian-era Americans believed in semen conservation, their solutions
to the problem were radically different.) When Sambian males are well past puberty, they begin the
transition to heterosexuality. At this time the female
body is thought to be less dangerous because the
males have ingested protective semen over the previous years. For a time, they may begin having sex
with women and still participate in fellatio with
younger boys, but homosexual behavior stops after
the birth of a man's first child. Most of the Sambian
men make the transition to exclusive adult heterosexuality without problems. Those few who do not
are somewhat ironically considered misfits.

An interesting evolutionary hypothesis notes that
the Melanesian societies practicing ritualized homosexuality have highly male-biased sex ratios, probably due to what is suspected to be a high incidence
of female infanticide (Oles, 1994). According to this
hypothesis, requisite homosexuality is a tactic used
by older males to limit the arena of mate competition by channeling potential rivals' (i.e., young
men's) sexuality into homoerotic behavior, making
adolescent and young women exclusively available
to older males. By this hypothesis, the female pollution ideology is a scare tactic used for the same end.

Whatever its explanation, ritualized homosexuality among the Melanesians is a striking example of
the influence of culture on sexual attitudes and behavior. A Melanesian adolescent who refused to
practice homosexuality would be viewed as abnormal, and such adolescents are apparently absent or
rare. Homosexuality among the Sambia is not the
same as homosexuality in contemporary America,
with the possible exception of those Sambian men
who have difficulty making the heterosexual transition.

Case 3: Homosexuality and American Psychiatry

During the past half century the status of homosexuality has changed enormously both within psychiatry and psychology, and for society generally. In the
not-too-distant past, homosexuality was a taboo
topic. Now, movies, talk shows, and television sit-
coms and dramas address the topic explicitly by including gay men and lesbians in leading roles. As we
shall see, developments in psychiatry and psychology

have played an important role in these changes. Homosexuality was officially removed from the DSM (where it had previously been classed as a sexual deviation) in 1973 and today is no longer regarded as in any sense a psychological disorder. A brief survey of attitudes toward homosexuality within the mental health profession itself again illustrates how attitudes toward various expressions of human sexuality may change over time.

Homosexuality as Sickness Reading the medical and psychological literature on homosexuality written before 1970 can be a jarring experience, especially if one subscribes to views prevalent today. Relevant articles included "Effeminate homosexuality: A disease of childhood" and "On the cure of homosexuality." It is only fair to note, however, that the view that homosexual people are mentally ill was relatively tolerant compared with some earlier views. During the first half of this century, those who did not believe that homosexual people were mentally ill and in need of treatment tended to believe that they were criminals in need of incarceration (Bayer, 1981). British and American cultures had long taken punitive approaches to homosexual behavior. In the sixteenth century King Henry VIII of England declared "the detestable and abominable vice of buggery [anal sex]" a felony punishable by death, and it was not until 1861 that the maximum penalty was reduced to ten years' imprisonment. Similarly, in the United States laws were very repressive until recently, and even now homosexual behavior continues to be a criminal offense in some states. Thus the belief that homosexuality is an illness seems somewhat less intolerant in historical context.

During the late nineteenth and early twentieth centuries, several prominent theorists suggested that

Homosexuality has existed throughout history. This ancient Greek wall art showing two male lovers at a drinking party is from the tomb of the Diver, at Paestum, near the Gulf of Salerno.

homosexuality was consistent with psychological normality. The famous sexologists Havelock Ellis and Magnus Hirshfeld believed that homosexuality is natural and nonpathological. Although, as we shall see, psychoanalysts became the most vigorous proponents of the disease position, Freud's own attitude toward homosexual people was remarkably progressive for the time, and is well expressed in his touching "Letter to an American Mother" (1935):

Dear Mrs. . . . .

I gather from your letter that your son is a homosexual. I am most impressed by the fact that you do not mention this term yourself in your information about him. May I question you, why you avoid it? Homosexuality is assuredly no advantage, but it is nothing to be ashamed of, no vice, no degradation, it cannot be classified as an illness; we consider it to be a variation of the sexual function produced by a certain arrest of sexual development. Many highly respectable individuals of ancient and modern times have been homosexuals, several of the greatest men among them (Plato, Michelangelo, Leonardo da Vinci, etc.). It is a great injustice to persecute homosexuality as a crime, and cruelty too. . . .

By asking me if I can help, you mean, I suppose, if I can abolish homosexuality and make normal heterosexuality take its place. The answer is, in a general way, we cannot promise to achieve it. . . .

Sincerely yours with kind wishes,

Freud

Beginning in the 1940s, psychoanalysts, led by Sandor Rado, began to take a more pessimistic view of the mental health of homosexual people, and a more optimistic view of the likely success of therapy to induce heterosexuality. In contrast to Freud's view that homosexual impulses were universal, Rado (1962) believed that homosexuality was found only in people whose heterosexual desires were too psychologically threatening. He viewed homosexuality as an escape from heterosexuality and therefore incompatible with mental health. This general view was adopted and articulated further by Irving Bieber and Charles Socarides, who stressed the role of "highly pathologic parent-child relationships" (Bieber et al., 1962). They believed that in the case of male homosexuality, domineering, emotionally smothering mothers, and detached, hostile fathers prevented boys from identifying closely with the fathers, a step they hypothesized was necessary to normal psychological development. It may have been important that these psychoanalysts based their opinions primarily on their experiences seeing gay men in therapy, who are likely to be more psychologically troubled than other gay men.

Even in the 1990s homosexual people continue to have very large marches to promote their rights in a society that continues to practice discrimination based on sexual orientation. This picture was taken at a march held in New York City to commemorate the 25th anniversary of the Stonewall riot in 1969 that was provoked by a police

Homosexuality as Nonpathological Variation
Around 1950, the view of homosexuality as sickness began to be challenged by both scientists and homosexual people themselves. Scientific blows to the pathology position included Alfred Kinsey's finding that homosexual behavior was much more common than had been previously believed, although as we shall see, we now know that his estimates were too high (Kinsey, Pomeroy, & Martin, 1948; Kinsey et al., 1953). Perhaps the most influential studies were performed by Evelyn Hooker (1957). She demonstrated that trained psychologists could not distinguish the psychological tests of homosexual and heterosexual subjects.

Gay men and lesbians also began to challenge psychiatric orthodoxy. Beginning in the 1950s, homophile organizations encouraged frank discussion of the status of homosexuality and spawned committed opponents of the homosexuality-as-illness position. The 1960s saw the birth of the radical gay liberation movement, which took the more uncompromising stance that "gay is good." The decade closed with the famous Stonewall riot in New York City, sparked by police mistreatment of gay men, which provided a clear signal that homosexual people would no longer passively accept their status as second-class citizens. By the 1970s, openly gay psychiatrists and psychologists were working from within the mental health profession to change the orthodox position. Specifically, they wished to have homosexuality removed from the *Diagnostic and Statistical Manual of Psychiatric Disorders* (*DSM-II*).

In 1973, after acrimonious debate, the Board of Trustees of the American Psychiatric Association

(APA) voted to remove homosexuality from *DSM-II*. This move was opposed by some APA members, who argued that the board abandoned scientific principles because of political pressure. They prevailed on the APA to put the matter before its membership in a referendum, and in 1974 the membership voted 5,854 to 3,810, to remove homosexuality from *DSM-II*. This episode was both a milestone for gay rights and an embarrassment for psychiatry, and more generally, for advocates of psychodiagnosis. The spectacle of the psychiatric nomenclature being modified on the basis of a *vote* rather than the scientific consensus of experts appeared to confirm what psychodiagnosis' harshest critics, such as Thomas Szasz (1974), had been saying, that the label "mental illness" merely reflects the values of mental health professionals.

We believe the APA made a correct decision in removing homosexuality from *DSM-II* because the vast majority of evidence shows that homosexuality is compatible with psychological normality. Furthermore, we do not find the resolution of this issue by vote to be especially problematic. The classification of any behavior as psychopathology necessitates a value judgment that the behavior is undesirable (see also Chapter 1). This value judgment is usually implicit and unchallenged—for example, few people deny the impairment and pain caused by schizophrenia, even among schizophrenic patients themselves. Challenges by gay and lesbian people forced mental health professionals to confront the values question explicitly, and they made the correct determination that homosexuality is not a psychological disorder. See HIGHLIGHT 11.1 for further discussion of homosexuality as a normal sexual variant.

SEXUAL VARIANTS

We now turn to the problematic sexual variants included in DSM-IV. There are two general categories: paraphilias and gender identity disorders.

The Paraphilias

The **paraphilias** are a group of persistent sexual behavior patterns in which unusual objects, rituals, or situations are required for full sexual satisfaction. Although mild forms of these conditions probably have occurred in the lives of many normal people, a paraphilic person is distinguished by the insistence and relative exclusivity with which his or her sexuality focuses on the acts or objects in question—without which orgasm is often impossible. Paraphilias

Homosexuality as a Normal Sexual Variant

Although its current status as a nonpsychopathological sexual variant rather than a disorder might suggest that no further mention of homosexuality is warranted in an abnormal psychology textbook, we have provided a more extensive discussion, for two reasons. First, American attitudes toward homosexuality remain highly ambivalent, and at least part of this ambivalence reflects uncertainty about the causes and correlates of sexual orientation (Schmalz, 1993). Thus, one goal is to review what is known about homosexuality to clarify why we believe it is not pathological. Second, although homosexuality is not pathological, it is sometimes related to a condition that remains in DSM-IV: gender identity disorder. Thus, some findings about homosexuality may apply to gender identity disorder as well.

First, we address the question of how common homosexuality is. Kinsey's (Kinsey et al., 1948, 1953) monumental studies found that approximately 10 percent of men and women had had a significant adult homosexual relationship. However, Kinsey's samples were highly self-selected (Michael et al., 1994), and it is now clear that his estimates were much too high. Recent large, carefully selected samples from the United States (Billy et al., 1993; Michael et al., 1994), France (ACSF Investigators, 1992), and England (Johnson et al., 1992) suggest that the rate of adult homosexual behavior is between 2 and 6 percent, with the rate of exclusive male homosexuality between 1 and 2 percent. The analogous rates for female homosexuality are approximately half of those for males. The fact that homosexuality appears to be rarer than formerly believed has no implications

for its status as a nonpathological sexual variant (Herek, 1989). Moreover, according to a recent study approximately 20 percent of men and women may report having had at least one instance of sexual attraction to a member of their own sex after the age of 15 (Wypij, in press). There are also some people who are bisexual, although estimates are that this may be even less common than exclusive homosexuality, especially since the onset of the AIDS epidemic in the mid-1980s (Masters, Johnson, & Kolodny, 1992). One recent intensive study of bisexuals found that for many bisexuals, their homosexuality came after they had established a heterosexual orientation (Weinberg, Williams, & Pryor, 1994).

The second question we address is what causes some people to become homosexual and others heterosexual? An important study by the Kinsey Institute for Sex Research examined the psychoanalytic hypothesis that homosexuality is associated with dysfunctional parent-child relationships (Bell, Weinberg, & Hammersmith, 1981). The study found only very limited support for the hypothesis. For example, gay men did recall relatively distant relationships with their fathers. However, the differences observed were so small that they could not account for development of sexual orientation. The most striking finding of the study concerned childhood behavior. On average (although not in every case), homosexual adults recalled substantially more sex-atypical behavior than did heterosexual adults. For example, gay men were more likely than heterosexual men to recall playing with girls, cross-dressing, shunning sports, and wishing they were girls. Lesbians were more likely than heterosexual

women to recall enjoying sports and wishing they were boys. Large differences in recalled sex-atypical behavior have been found in many other studies (Bailey & Zucker, 1995). Of course, adults' memories of their childhood may be biased. However, prospective studies of very feminine boys have supported the retrospective findings. Most such boys have become gay men (Green, 1987; Zuger, 1984). To date, there have been no prospective studies of masculine girls. Nevertheless, it should also be emphasized that many gay men and lesbians appear to have been sex-typical as children.

The observations that homosexual people have sexual orientations and other behaviors more typical of the opposite sex are consistent with the most influential current etiological model of sexual orientation: Homosexual people have been subjected to early, possibly prenatal, hormonal influences more typical of the opposite sex. Studies of rats, mice, and some primate species have clearly shown that early exposure to androgens (male-typical hormones) for a female can induce male mating behavior during adulthood. Conversely, early androgen deprivation for a male can induce female sexual behavior in adulthood (Goy & McEwen, 1980). Of course, humans are not rats or monkeys and thus the animal studies are at best suggestive. Available evidence for the biological model of human sexual orientation is intriguing but not overwhelming (LeVay, 1993). The most important study, by Simon LeVay (1991), found gay men to be different from heterosexual men and similar to heterosexual women in the size of one region

Continued on Page 406

HIGHLIGHT   11.1

Continued from page 405

of the hypothalamus, a part of the brain that affects sexual behavior. Like all important findings, LeVay's need to be replicated, and to date no one has attempted to do so. Genetic factors have also been implicated in both male (Bailey & Pillard, 1991; Hamer et al., 1993) and female (Bailey et al., 1993) sexual orientation. For example, concordance rates for homosexuality were 52 percent for male monozygotic twins, compared with 22 percent for male dizygotic twins; the comparable figures for female homosexuality were 48 percent and 16 percent. The genetic evidence is not yet definitive because of methodological problems such as volunteer bias (Bailey & Pillard, 1991), but it is consistent with a substantial role for heredity.

Because approximately half of the monozygotic twin pairs in the genetic studies were discordant for sexual orientation, environmental factors are clearly also important (Bailey & Pillard, 1991; Bailey et al., 1993). The nature of the environmental influences is uncertain; these could include either biological (e.g., prenatal stress) or social (e.g., parental child-rearing philosophy) factors. One erroneous

environmental hypothesis is that homosexual adults seduce and "recruit" younger individuals to homosexuality. There is no scientific evidence for this belief and much against it. For example, the large majority of gay men and lesbians had homosexual feelings at least one year before their first homosexual experience (Bell et al., 1981).

Finally, we address the question of mental health and homosexuality. Nonpatient samples of homosexual and heterosexual subjects typically show little if any difference in psychological adjustment (Siegelman, 1979; Gagnon & Simon, 1973). One study found gay men to be somewhat less self-accepting and more lonely than heterosexual men, but this was attributable to the higher percentage of gay men who were not in stable relationships (Bell & Weinberg, 1978). Some writers have pointed to the high number of sexual partners reported by gay men (especially before the AIDS epidemic) as evidence that they are abnormally impulsive and promiscuous. However, a more parsimonious explanation is that both homosexual *and* heterosexual men have an elevated desire for casual sex, but that

homosexual men have more casual sex opportunities because they interact sexually with other men (Symons, 1979). One study supporting this interpretation found that gay men and heterosexual men reported similar levels of interest in casual sex (Bailey et al., 1994).

Although nonpatient samples of homosexual and heterosexual subjects typically do not differ in psychological adjustment, there is some evidence that homosexual people do have higher rates of alcoholism and depression (Mosbacher, 1988; Saghir & Robins, 1973; Pillard, 1988). However, it is likely that these elevated rates of alcoholism and depression are a consequence of the prejudice and stigmatization that they often still experience rather than being a consequence of having a homosexual orientation per se.

In summary, most research suggests that homosexuality is compatible with psychological normality. The exact causes of sexual orientation remain unclear, although recent evidence has increasingly implicated genetic and other biological variables. Researchers are actively pursuing these questions.

also frequently have a compulsive quality, with some paraphilic individuals requiring orgasmic release as often as four to ten times per day (Money, 1986, p. 133). Paraphilic individuals may or may not have persistent desires to change their sexual preferences. Some paraphilias require a partner, and a fortunate paraphilic individual may discover another person with a reciprocal paraphilia—as in sexual sadomasochism discussed below—which may then lead to a lasting although by conventional standards somewhat bizarre love affair. Fairly common is a situation in which a sexually normal person becomes unwittingly involved in a paraphilic person's ritual-

ized sexual program, only gradually discovering that he or she is a mere accessory, a sort of stage prop, in the latter's sexual drama. Because nearly all paraphilic persons are male (a fact whose etiological implications we consider later), we use masculine pronouns to refer to them.

The DSM-IV recognizes eight specific paraphilias: fetishism, transvestic fetishism, voyeurism, exhibitionism, sexual sadism, sexual masochism, pedophilia, and frotteurism (rubbing against a nonconsenting person). Additionally, the category "Paraphilias Not Otherwise Specified" includes several rarer disorders such as telephone scatologia (obscene phone calls), necrophilia (sexual desire for corpses), and coprophilia (sexual arousal to feces). Of the specified paraphilias, we will discuss all but frotteurism, a category that is relatively new and not yet satisfactorily researched. Our discussion of pedophilia is postponed, however, until a later section concerning sexual abuse.

Fetishism In **fetishism,** sexual interest typically centers on some inanimate object, such as an article of clothing, or some body part. (DSM-IV states that a fetish is diagnosed only when the object is inanimate, but most sex researchers have not traditionally made this distinction.) As is generally true for the paraphilias, males are most commonly involved in cases of fetishism; reported cases of female fetishists are extremely rare. The range of fetishistic objects includes hair, ears, hands, underclothing, shoes, perfume, and similar objects associated with the opposite sex. The mode of using these objects to achieve sexual excitation and gratification varies considerably, but it commonly involves kissing, fondling, tasting, or smelling the objects. Fetishism does not normally interfere with the rights of others, except in an incidental way such as asking the partner to wear the object during sexual encounters. Many men have a strong sexual fascination for paraphernalia such as brassieres, garter belts, hose, and high heels. Although such men do not typically meet diagnostic criteria for fetishism, because the paraphernalia are not necessary or strongly preferred for sexual arousal (as is required to be diagnosed as having a fetish), they do illustrate the high frequency of fetish-like preferences among men.

To obtain the required object, a fetishistic person may commit burglary, theft, or even assault. Probably the articles most commonly stolen by fetishistic individuals are women's undergarments. One young boy was found to have accumulated over 100 pairs of underpants from a lingerie shop when he was apprehended. In such cases the excitement and suspense of the criminal act itself typically reinforce the sexual stimulation and sometimes actually constitute the fetish—the stolen article being of little importance. For example, one adolescent admitted entering many homes in which the entering itself usually sufficed to induce an orgasm. When it did not, he was able to achieve sexual satisfaction by taking some "token," such as money or jewelry.

Frequently, fetishistic behavior consists of masturbation in association with a fetishistic object. Here, of course, it is difficult to draw a line between fetishistic activity and the effort to increase the sexual excitation and satisfaction of masturbation through the use of pictures and other articles associated with a desired sexual object. Using such articles in masturbation is a common practice and not usually considered pathological. Where antisocial behavior, such as breaking and entering, is involved, however, everyone can agree that the practice is fetishistic. For example, Marshall (1974) reported a rather unusual case of a young university student who had a "trouser fetish"; he would steal the trousers of teenagers and then use them in physical contact during masturbation. A somewhat different, but not atypical, pattern of fetishism is illustrated by the case of a man whose fetish was women's shoes and legs:

> The fetishist in this case was arrested several times for loitering in public places, such as railroad stations and libraries, watching women's legs. Finally he chanced on a novel solution to his problem. Posing as an agent for a hosiery firm, he rented a large room, advertised for models, and took motion pictures of a number of women walking and seated with their legs displayed to best advantage. He then used these pictures to achieve sexual satisfaction and found that they continued to be adequate for the purpose. (Adapted from Grant, 1953)

Most theories of fetishism emphasize the importance of classical conditioning. It is not difficult to imagine how women's underwear might become eroticized by its close association with sex and the female body. Rubber fetishism may depend on the fact that training pants are made of rubber. If so, then as plastic replaces rubber, plastic fetishes may become more common (Money, 1986, p. 65). It is important to emphasize that differential experiences do not seem sufficient to explain why some men develop fetishes. Although perhaps most rubber fetishists wore rubber training pants, most men who wore such pants do not develop fetishes. It seems likely that this is because there are individual differences in conditionability of sexual responses. Men high in sexual conditionability would be prone to developing one or more fetishes. We will later return to the role of conditioning in the development of paraphilias, in general.

Transvestic Fetishism The achievement of sexual arousal and satisfaction by "cross-dressing," that is, dressing as a member of the opposite sex, is called

transvestic fetishism. It is an uncommon condition in which an individual, usually a male, enjoys excursions into the social roles of the other sex or is markedly distressed by urges to do so. Although a transvestic male regards himself as a man when dressed as a man, he may have feelings of being a woman when dressed in women's clothing. A medical researcher and transvestite himself for 35 years expressed it this way: "The transvestite finds that he is both a 'he' and 'she' together—at the same time or alternating from one to the other when opportunity permits or desire compels" (*Los Angeles Times,* September 30, 1973). Although some gay men dress "in drag" on occasion, they do not typically do this for sexual pleasure and hence are not transvestic fetishists. The vast majority of transvestites are heterosexual (Talamini, 1982). Buckner (1970) formulated a description of the "ordinary" male transvestite from a survey of 262 transvestites conducted by the magazine *Transvestia:*

> He is probably married (about two-thirds are); if he is married he probably has children (about two-thirds do). Almost all of these transvestites said they were exclusively heterosexual—in fact, the rate of "homosexuality" was less than the average for the entire population. The transvestic behavior generally consists of privately dressing in the clothes of a woman, at home, in secret. . . . The transvestite generally does not run into trouble with the law. His cross-dressing causes difficulties for very few people besides himself and his wife. (p. 381)

The most extensive studies to date of male transvestites' personalities were conducted some time ago (Bentler & Prince, 1969, 1970; Bentler, Sherman, and Prince, 1970). These investigators obtained replies to a standardized psychological inventory from a large sample of transvestic people through the cooperation of a national transvestite organization. The transvestic individuals, compared with matched control groups, showed no gross differences on neurotic or psychotic inventory scales. They did, however, present themselves as being more controlled in impulse expression, less involved with other people, more inhibited in interpersonal relationships, and more dependent.

Interestingly, it appears that cross-dressing may reduce the strength of some of these negative tendencies. Gosslin and Eysenck (1980) asked transvestic males to take a personality test while functioning in regular male clothing and while cross-dressed. "Neuroticism" and "introversion" both declined in the cross-dressed condition. This finding was consistent with subjects' reports of less anxiety and shyness when in their female roles.

The following is a fairly typical case of transvestic fetishism and illustrates both the typical early onset of transvestic fetishism and the difficulties the condition may raise in marriage:

Mr. A., a 65-year-old security guard, formerly a fishing-boat captain, is distressed about his wife's objections to his wearing a nightgown at home in the evening, now that his youngest child has left home. His appearance and demeanor, except when he is dressing in women's clothes, are always appropriately masculine, and he is exclusively heterosexual. Occasionally, over the past 5 years, he has worn an inconspicuous item of female clothing even when dressed as a man, sometimes a pair of panties, sometimes an ambiguous pinkie ring. He always carries a photograph of himself dressed as a woman.

His first recollection of an interest in female clothing was putting on his sister's bloomers at age 12, an act accompanied by sexual excitement. He continued periodically to put on women's underpants—an activity that invariably resulted in an erection, sometimes a spontaneous emission, sometimes masturbation, but never accompanied by fantasy. Although he occasionally wished to be a girl, he never fantasized himself as one. He was competitive and aggressive with other boys and always acted "masculine." During his single years he was always attracted to girls, but was shy about sex. Following his marriage at age 22, he had his first heterosexual intercourse.

His involvement with female clothes was of the same intensity even after his marriage. Beginning at age 45, after a chance exposure to a magazine called *Transvestia,* he began to increase his cross-dressing activity. He learned there were other men like himself, and he became more and more preoccupied with female clothing in fantasy and progressed to periodically dressing completely as a woman. More recently he has become involved in a transvestite network, writing to other transvestites contacted through the magazine and occasionally attending transvestite parties. Cross-dressing at these parties has been the only time that he has cross-dressed outside his home.

Although still committed to his marriage, sex with his wife has dwindled over the past 20 years as his waking thoughts and activities have become increasingly centered on cross-dressing. Over time this activity has become less eroticized and more an end in itself, but it still is a source of some sexual excitement. He always has an increased urge to dress as a woman when under stress; it has a tranquilizing effect. If particular circumstances prevent him from cross-dressing, he feels extremely frustrated.

The patient's parents belonged to different faiths, a fact of some importance to him. He was the eldest of three children, extremely close to his mother, whom he idolized, and angry at his "whoremaster, alcoholic" father. The parents fought constantly. He is tearful, even now at age 65, when he describes his mother's death when he was 10. He was the one who found her dead (of pleurisy), and he says he has been "not the same from that day . . . always (having) the feeling something's not right." The siblings were reared by three separate branches of the family until the father remarried. When the patient was 20, his father died, a presumed suicide; but Mr. A believes he may have been murdered, as he could not figure out a suicide motive. His brother also died traumatically, drowned in his teens.

Because of the disruptions in his early life, the patient has always treasured the steadfastness of his wife and the order of his home. He told his wife about his cross-dressing practice when they were married, and she was accepting so long as he kept it to himself. Nevertheless, he felt guilty, particularly after he began complete cross-dressing, and periodically he attempted to renounce the practice, throwing out all his female clothes

and makeup. His children served as a barrier to his giving free rein to his impulses. Following his retirement from fishing, and in the absence of his children, he finds himself more drawn to cross-dressing, more in conflict with his wife, and more depressed. (Spitzer et al., 1994)

As we have indicated, transvestic fetishism may complicate a relationship. However, like other kinds of fetishism, it causes overt harm to others only when accompanied by such illegal acts as theft or destruction of property. This is not always the case with the other paraphilias, many of which do contain a definite element of injury or significant risk of injury—physical or psychological—to one or more of the parties involved in a sexual encounter. Typically these practices have strong legal sanctions against them. We shall consider only the most common forms of these paraphilias: voyeurism, exhibitionism, sadism, and masochism.

Voyeurism The synonymous terms **voyeurism,** *scotophilia,* and *inspectionalism* refer to the achievement of sexual pleasure through clandestine peeping. It occurs as a sexual offense primarily among young men. These Peeping Toms, as they are commonly called, usually observe females who are undressing or couples engaging in sexual relations. Frequently they masturbate during their peeping activity.

How do young men develop this pattern? First, viewing the body of an attractive female seems to be quite stimulating sexually for many, if not most,

Studies have shown that men who cross-dress may actually feel less anxiety and shyness when in their female roles. Although a transvestic man may therefore enjoy excursions into the social roles of the other sex, he may also be markedly distressed by urges to do so, and, if married, his transvestism may also cause difficulties for his wife. Cross-dressers are seeking out others of their kind to deal with their special problems in support groups like the one shown

men. In addition, the privacy and mystery that have traditionally surrounded sexual activities tend to increase curiosity about them. Second, if a young man with such curiosity feels shy and inadequate in his relations with the other sex, it is not too surprising for him to accept the substitute of voyeurism. In this way he satisfies his curiosity and to some extent meets his sexual needs without the trauma of actually approaching a female, and thus without the failure and lowered self-status that such an approach might bring. In fact voyeuristic activities often provide important compensatory feelings of power and secret domination over an unsuspecting victim, which may contribute to the maintenance of this pattern. Also, of course, the suspense and danger associated with voyeurism may lead to emotional excitement and a reinforcement of the sexual stimulation. A voyeur does not normally seek sexual activity with those he observes. If a voyeur manages to find a wife in spite of his interpersonal difficulties, as many do, he is rarely well-adjusted sexually in his relationship with his wife, as the following case illustrates:

A young married college student had an attic apartment that was extremely hot during the summer months. To enable him to attend school, his wife worked; she came home at night tired and irritable and not in the mood for sexual relations. In addition, "the damned springs in the bed squeaked." In order "to obtain some sexual gratification" the youth would peer through his binoculars at the room next door and occasionally saw the young couple there engaged in erotic activities. This stimulated him greatly, and he thus decided to extend his peeping to a sorority house. During his second venture, however, he was reported and apprehended by the police. This offender was quite immature for his age, rather puritanical in his attitude toward masturbation, and prone to indulge in rich but immature sexual fantasies.

Although more permissive laws concerning "adult" movies, videos, and magazines have probably removed much of the secrecy from sexual behavior and also have provided an alternative source of gratification for would-be voyeurs, their actual effects on the incidence of voyeurism is a matter of speculation. For many voyeurs these movies and magazines probably do not provide an adequate substitute for secretly watching the sexual behavior of an unsuspecting couple or the "real-life" nudity of a woman who mistakenly believes she enjoys privacy.

Although a voyeur may become reckless in his behavior and thus may be detected and assaulted by his victims, voyeurism does not ordinarily have any serious criminal or antisocial aspects. In fact many people probably have some voyeuristic inclinations, which are checked by practical considerations, such as the possibility of being caught, and ethical attitudes concerning the right to privacy. On the other hand, strong voyeuristic tendencies are sometimes accompanied by other, more bizarre elements in a peeper's sexual arousal pattern that might signal deeper and far more serious problems.

Exhibitionism The word **exhibitionism** (indecent exposure in legal terms) describes the intentional exposure of the genitals to others (generally strangers) in inappropriate circumstances and without their consent. The exposure may take place in some secluded location, such as a park, or in a more public place, such as a department store, church, theater, or bus. In cities an exhibitionist often drives by schools or bus stops, exhibits himself while in the car, and then drives rapidly away. In many instances the exposure is repeated under fairly constant conditions, such as only in churches or buses, or in the same general vicinity and at the same time of day. In one case, a youth exhibited himself only at the top of an escalator in a large department store. The type of victim too is usually fairly consistent for an individual exhibitionist. For a male offender, this ordinarily involves a young or middle-aged female who is not known to the offender.

Exhibitionism is most common during the warm spring and summer months, and most offenders are young adult males. Practically all occupational groups are represented. Often exhibitionism by males in public or semipublic places is reported to the police, although some women simply ignore such incidents. In some instances, exposure of the genitals is accompanied by suggestive gestures or masturbation, but more often there is only exposure. Although it is considered relatively rare, a hostile exposer may accompany exhibitionism with aggressive acts and may assault a victim. Some research indicates a subclass of exhibitionists who may best be considered antisocial personalities, as described in Chapter 9 (Forgac & Michaels, 1982).

Despite the rarity of assaultive behavior in these cases, and the fact that most exhibitionists are not aggressive and dangerous criminals, an exhibitionistic act nevertheless takes place without the viewer's consent and may be emotionally upsetting, as is indeed the perpetrator's intent. This intrusive quality of the act, together with its explicit violation of propriety norms respecting "private parts," assures condemnation. Thus society considers exhibitionism a criminal offense.

Exhibitionism is the most common sexual offense reported to the police in the United States, Canada, and Europe, accounting for about one-third of all sexual offenses (Rooth, 1974). One American survey found that approximately one-third of college women had been victimized by exhibitionists (Cox, 1988). Curiously enough, it is rare in most other countries. For example, in Argentina only 24 people were convicted of exhibitionism during a five-year period; in Japan only about 60 men are convicted of this offense each year. In still other countries, such as Burma and India, it is practically unheard of (Rooth, 1974).

Sadism The term **sadism** is derived from the name of the Marquis de Sade (1740–1814), who for sexual purposes inflicted such cruelty on his victims that he was eventually committed as insane. Although the term's meaning has broadened to denote cruelty in general, we will use it in its restricted sense to mean the achievement of sexual stimulation and gratification by inflicting physical or psychic pain or humiliation on a sexual partner. A closely related pattern is the practice of "bondage and discipline" (B & D), which may include tying a person up, hitting or spanking, and so on, to enhance sexual excitement. These elements of a sadist's erotic interest suggest a psychological association with rape (Marshall & Barbaree, 1990a), discussed in a later section. The arousal of sadistic individuals thus heavily depends on the infliction of suffering, or the appearance of it, on their partners.

The pain may be inflicted by such means as whipping, biting, or pinching; the act may vary in intensity, from fantasy to severe mutilation and even murder. Mild degrees of sadism (and masochism) are involved in the sexual foreplay customs of many cultures, and some couples in our own society—both heterosexual and homosexual—regularly engage in such practices. It is important to distinguish transient or occasional interest in sadomasochistic practices from sadism as a paraphilia. Surveys have found that 5–10 percent of men and women enjoy sadistic or masochistic activities occasionally (Hunt, 1975; Barbach & Levine, 1980). Paraphilic sadism and masochism, in which sadomasochistic activities are the preferred or exclusive means to sexual gratification, appear to be rare, and like all paraphilias, occur almost exclusively in men.

In some cases, sadistic activities lead up to or terminate in actual sexual relations; in others, full sexual gratification is obtained from the sadistic practice alone. A sadist, for example, may slash a woman with a razor or stick her with a needle, experiencing an orgasm in the process. The peculiar and extreme associations that may occur are shown by the case of a young man who entered a strange woman's apartment, held a chloroformed rag to her face until she lost consciousness, and branded her on the thigh with a hot iron. She was not molested in any other way.

Sometimes sadistic activities are associated with animals or with fetishistic objects instead of other human beings. East (1946) cited the case of a man who stole women's shoes, which he then slashed savagely with a knife. When he was in prison, he was found mutilating photographs that other prisoners kept in their cells by cutting the throats of the women in them. He admitted that he derived full sexual gratification from this procedure.

In other instances, gratification is achieved only if mutilation is performed directly on a victim. Chesser (1971) refers to such offenders as pathological sadists and notes that they are often extremely dangerous. The following is such a case:

> The offender, Peter Kursten, was 47 years old at the time of his apprehension in Dusseldorf, Germany, for a series of lust murders. He was a skilled laborer, well groomed, modest, and had done nothing that annoyed his fellow workers.
>
> Peter came from a disturbed family background, his father having been an alcoholic who had been sent to prison for having intercourse with Peter's older sister. Peter's own earliest sexual experiences were with animals. When he was about 13 years old, he attempted to have intercourse with a sheep, but the animal would not hold still, and he stabbed her with a knife. At that moment he had an ejaculation.
>
> After this experience, Peter found the sight of gushing blood sexually exciting, and he turned from animals to human females. Often he first choked his victim, but if he did not achieve an orgasm, he then stabbed her. Initially he used scissors and a dagger, but later he took to using a hammer or an axe. After he achieved ejaculation, he lost interest in his victim, except for taking measures to cover up his crime.
>
> The offender's sexual crimes extended over a period of some 30 years and involved over 40 victims. Finally apprehended . . . he expressed a

Mild degrees of sadism and masochism are involved in the sexual customs of many cultures, and some people in our own society—both heterosexual and homosexual—regularly engage in such practices. In some cases sexual gratification is obtained from the sadistic practice alone. Sadomasochistic equipment is sold in places like the one shown here, complete with racks, pillories, cages, whipping posts, and shackles.

sense of injustice at not being like other people who were raised in normal families. (Adapted from Berg, 1954)

The news media have reported more recent cases in which victims have been mutilated and killed in association with sadistic sexual practices. For example, in 1989, Ted Bundy was executed after having been convicted of sexually abusing and murdering numerous young women. Jeffrey Dahmer was convicted in 1992 of having mutilated and murdered 15 boys and young men, generally having sex with them after death; some of the corpses were stored and eaten later. Unfortunately, we do not have a good understanding of the causal factors involved in these extreme cases of sadism.

Masochism The term **masochism** is derived from the name of the Austrian novelist Leopold V. Sacher-Masoch (1836–1895), whose fictional characters dwelt lovingly on the sexual pleasure of pain. As in the case of the term *sadism,* the meaning of masochism has been broadened beyond sexual connotations, so that it includes deriving pleasure from self-denial, from expiatory physical suffering, such as that of the religious flagellants, and from hardship and suffering in general. Here we restrict our discussion to the sexual aspects of masochistic behavior.

The clinical picture of masochism is similar to that in sadistic practices, except that the pain is inflicted on the self instead of on others (Sack & Miller, 1975). Such sayings as "crushed in his arms" or "smothered with kisses" may reveal the associa-

tion commonly made between erotic arousal and pain or discomfort. If so, it is less surprising that some people resort to mild sadomasochistic acts, such as biting, in an attempt to increase sexual excitement. For most people, however, such behavior does not result in serious physical injury, nor does it serve as a substitute for normal sexual relations. In actual masochism, by contrast, a person experiences sexual stimulation and gratification from the experience of pain and degradation in relating to a lover. In the case of both sadism and masochism, it should be noted that gratification in many instances requires a shared, complementary interpersonal relationship: one sadist and one masochist or, in milder forms, one superior "disciplinarian" and one obedient "slave." Such arrangements are not uncommon in either heterosexual or homosexual relationships (Tripp, 1975).

One particularly dangerous form of masochism, called *autoerotic asphyxia,* involves self-strangulation to the point of oxygen deprivation. Coroners in most major U.S. cities are familiar with cases in which the deceased is found hanged next to masochistic pornographic literature or other sexual paraphernalia. Accidental deaths attributable from this practice have been estimated to range between 250 and 1000 per year in the United States (Innala & Ernuff, 1989). The following is a case of autoerotic asphyxia with a tragic ending:

A woman heard a man shouting for help and went to his apartment door. Calling through the door, she asked the man inside if he needed help.

"Yes," he said. "Break the door down."

"Is this a joke?"

"No."

The woman returned with her two sons, who broke into the apartment. They found the man lying on the floor, his hands tied behind him, his legs bent back, and his ankles secured to his hands. A mop handle had been placed behind his knees. He was visibly distraught, sweating, and short of breath, and his hands were turning blue. He had defecated and urinated in his trousers. In his kitchen the woman found a knife and freed him.

When police officers arrived and questioned the man, he stated that he had returned home that afternoon, fallen asleep on his couch, and awakened an hour later only to find himself hopelessly bound. The officers noted that the apartment door had been locked when the neighbors broke in. The man continued his story. As far as he knew, he had no enemies, and certainly no friends capable of this kind of practical joke. The officers questioned him about the rope. The man explained that, because he had considered moving in the near future, he kept a bag of rope in his bedroom. Near the couch lay a torn bag, numerous short lengths of thin rope, and a steak knife.

When the officers filed their report, they noted that "this could possibly be a sexual deviation act." Interviewed the next day, the man confessed to binding himself in the position in which he was found.

A month later, the police were called back to the same man's apartment. A building manager had discovered him face down on the floor in his apartment. A paper bag covered his head like a hood. When the police arrived, the man was breathing rapidly with a satin cloth stuffed in his mouth. Rope was stretched around his head and mouth and wrapped his chest and waist. Several lengths ran from his back to his crotch, and ropes at his ankles had left deep marks. A broom handle locked his elbows behind his back. Once freed, the man explained, "While doing isometric exercises, I got tangled up in the rope."

Police interviewed the man's employer, and the employer subsequently advised him to seek counseling. When the man agreed to follow through on a referral to a private psychiatrist, his boss supported his assertion that the incident, although unfortunate, had been unique and would not recur.

Two years passed and the man moved on to another job. He failed to appear for work one Monday morning. A fellow employee found him dead in his apartment. During their investigation, police were able to reconstruct the man's final minutes. On the preceding Friday, he had bound himself in the following manner: sitting on his bed and crossing his ankles, left over right, he had bound them together with twine. Fastening a tie around his neck, he then secured the tie to an 86-inch pole behind his back. Aligning the pole with his left side, the upper end crossing the front of his left shoulder, he placed his hands behind his bent legs and there, leaving his wrists 4 inches apart, secured them with a length of rope. He then tied the rope that secured his wrists to the pole and to an electric cord girdling his waist. Thus bound, he lay on his bed on his back and stretched his legs. By thus applying pressure to the pole, still secured to the tie around his neck, he strangled himself. In order to save himself, he might have rolled over onto his side and drawn up his legs; but the upper end of the pole pressed against the wall. He was locked into place. (Spitzer et al., 1994)

Causal Factors for Paraphilias

Many paraphilic individuals have explanations for their unusual sexual preferences. For example, an amputee paraphilic (whose preference is a partner with a missing limb) recalled that his fascination with female amputees originated during adolescence. He was neglected emotionally by his cold family but heard a family member express sympathetic feelings for an amputee. He developed the wish that he would become an amputee and thus earn their sympathy. This story raises many questions. Emotionally cold families are not uncommon, and sympathy for amputees is nearly universal. Surely, not every male in a cold family who detects sympathy for amputees develops an amputee paraphilia. Such stories do not necessarily have any validity. We are often unaware of the forces that shape us (Nisbett & Wilson, 1977).

At least two facts about paraphilia are likely to be etiologically important. First, as we have already noted, almost all paraphilics are male. Indeed, females with paraphilias are so rare that they are found in the literature only as case reports. Second, people with paraphilias often have more than one (Abel & Rouleau, 1991). For example, the corpses of men who died accidentally in the course of autoerotic asphyxia are partially or fully cross-dressed in 25–33 percent of cases (Blanchard & Hucker, 1991). There is no obvious reason for the association between masochism and transvestism. Why should it be so?

Money (1986) has noted that visual sexual stimuli are much more important for males than females, a fact supported by recent research (Bailey et al., 1994). He has suggested that male vulnerability to paraphilias is closely linked to their greater dependency on visual sexual imagery. Perhaps sexual arousal in men depends on physical stimulus features to a greater degree than in women, whose arousal may depend more on emotional context, such as being in love with a partner. If so, men may be more vulnerable to forming sexual associations to nonsexual stimuli.

The fact that men with one paraphilia often have others suggests that such men are especially vulnerable. Freund and Blanchard (1993) have suggested that the vulnerability is to errors in what they call *erotic target location*. According to this theory, although most men become heterosexual, they are not born with that orientation but instead must learn which stimuli together constitute a female sex partner, who is their target stimulus. This is the process of erotic target location. Perhaps certain men have nervous systems prone to errors in targeting, which might also help to explain the incidence of multiple paraphilias. (An analogous process may be hypothesized to cause the development of paraphilias in homosexual persons.) This theory is somewhat more useful in explaining paraphilias such as transvestism and certain fetishes (e.g., for women's underwear), in which the sexual stimuli are related to feminine characteristics, than it is for explaining others, such as masochism, in which the paraphilic target has no obvious association with normal sexual activities.

Gender Identity Disorders

"Gender identity" refers to one's sense of maleness or femaleness and may be distinguished from "gender role," which refers to the masculinity and femininity of one's overt behavior (Money, 1988, p. 77). Of all behavioral traits, gender identity may have the strongest correlation with biological sex, but the correlation is imperfect. Some rare individuals feel extreme discomfort with their biological sex and strongly desire to change to the opposite sex. Indeed, some adults with gender identity disorders, often called transsexuals, do opt for expensive and complicated surgery to accomplish just that. In DSM-IV **gender identity disorder** is characterized by two components: a strong and persistent **cross-gender identification**—that is the desire to be, or the insistence that one is, of the opposite sex—and **gender dysphoria**—persistent discomfort about one's biological sex or the sense that the gender role of that sex is inappropriate (American Psychiatric Association, 1994). The disorder may occur in children or adults, and in males or females.

Gender Identity Disorder of Childhood Boys with gender identity disorder often show a marked preoccupation with traditionally feminine activities. They may prefer to dress in female clothing. They enjoy stereotypical games of girls, such as playing dolls, house (in which they usually play the mother), drawing pictures of beautiful girls, and watching television programs with favorite female characters. They usually avoid rough-and-tumble play. They may express the desire to be a girl. Girls with gender identity disorder typically balk at parents' attempts to dress them in traditional feminine clothes such as dresses. They prefer boys' clothing and short hair, and they may be misidentified by strangers as boys. Fantasy heroes typically include powerful male figures like Batman and Superman. They show little interest in doll playing or dressing up, and increased interest in sports. Although mere tomboys frequently have many or most of those traits, girls with gender identity disorder are distinguished by their desire to be a boy, or to grow up as a man. Boys with gender identity disorder are often ostracized as "sissies" by their peers. Young girls with gender identity disorder are treated better by their peers, as cross-gender behavior in girls is better tolerated (Martin, 1990). In clinic-referred gender identity disorder, boys outnumber girls five to one. An appreciable percentage of that imbalance may reflect greater parental concern about femininity in boys than masculinity in girls.

The most common adult outcome of boys with gender identity disorder appears to be homosexuality rather than transsexualism (Green, 1987; Zuger, 1984). In Richard Green's (1987) study of fifty very feminine boys, only one sought sex change surgery as an adult. About three-quarters became gay or bisexual men evidently satisfied with their biological sex. There have been no prospective studies of girls with gender identity disorder. A recent analysis of retrospective reports of lesbians' sex-atypical behavior suggests that very masculine girls are more likely than other girls to become homosexual, but that most of them probably grow up as heterosexual women (Bailey & Zucker, 1995). Thus, the vast majority of children with gender identity disorder probably become homosexual or heterosexual adults, with only a small minority becoming transsexuals. If such children typically adjust well in adulthood, should they be considered to have a mental disorder?

One argument for considering children with atypical childhood gender identity to be disordered is that such children are often greatly distressed and thus should receive treatment. They suffer for two general reasons. First, by definition (i.e., current diagnostic criteria) they are unhappy with their biological sex. Second, as we have noted, they are likely to be mistreated by their peers and to have strained relations with their parents. An argument against considering such children "disordered" is that the primary obstacle to their happiness is a society that is intolerant of cross-gender behavior. Moreover, unlike some other behaviors that society stigmatizes, such as criminality and cruelty, cross-gender behavior harms no one. Thus, labeling children with atypical gender identity as "sick" shifts the blame from society, where it belongs. The diagnostic status of gender identity disorder of childhood therefore deserves serious debate.

Children with gender identity disorder are often brought by their parents for psychotherapy. Specialists attempt both to treat the child's unhappiness with his or her biological sex and to ease strained relations with parents and peers. Therapists try to improve peer and parental relations by teaching such children how to reduce their cross-gender behavior, especially in situations where it might cause interpersonal problems. Gender dysphoria is typically treated psychodynamically, that is, by examining inner conflicts. Controlled studies evaluating such treatment remain to be conducted.

Transsexualism Transsexuals are adults with gender identity disorder. Many, perhaps most, transsexuals desire to change their sex, and surgical advances have made this goal partially feasible, although expensive. **Transsexualism** is apparently a very rare disorder. European studies suggest that approximately 1 per 30,000 adult males and 1 per 100,000 adult females seek sex reassignment surgery. Until recently, most researchers assumed that transsexualism was the adult version of childhood gender identity disorder, and indeed this is often the case. That is, many transsexuals had gender identity disorder as children (despite the fact that most children with gender identity disorder do not become transsexual), and their adult behavior is analogous. However, there now appear to be two kinds of transsexuals, with very different causes and developmental courses: homosexual and nonhomosexual transsexuals (Blanchard, 1989). A homosexual transsexual is attracted to members of his or her biological sex, and a heterosexual transsexual is attracted to members of the opposite biological sex. For example, a homosexual female transsexual is biologically a female who describes herself as a man trapped in a woman's body and who feels sexually attracted to women. A homosexual male transsexual is a biological male who describes himself as a woman trapped in a man's body and who is sexually attracted to men. Such men seek a sex change operation in part so that as women they will have the ability to attract heterosexual male partners (Freund et al., 1974). Although homosexual transsexuals are attracted to members of their own biological sex, they resent being labelled gay because they do not feel that they *belong* to their biological sex (Adams & McAnulty, 1993).

Homosexual transsexuals generally have gender identity disorder from childhood. One adult homosexual male-to-female transsexual recalled:

> I used to like to play with girls. I never did like to play with boys. I wanted to play jacks. I wanted to jump rope and all those things. The lady in the schoolyard used to always tell me to go play with the boys. I found it distasteful. I wanted to play with the girls. I wanted to play the girl games. I remember one day the teacher said, "If you play with the girls one more day, I am going to bring a dress to school and make you wear it all day long. How would you like that?" Well, I would have liked it. (Green, 1992, p. 101)

Similarly, a homosexual female-to-male transsexual recalled analogous childhood behaviors:

> [I have felt different] as far as I can remember. Three years old. I remember wanting to be a boy. Wearing boy's clothes and wanting to do all the things boys do. I remember my mother as I was growing up saying, "Are you ever going to be a lady? Are you ever going to wear women's clothing?" These kind of things as far back as I can remember. I can remember as I got a little older always looking at women, always wanting a woman . . . I feel like a man, and I feel like my loving a woman is perfectly normal. (Green, 1992, p. 102)

Because most children with gender identity disorder do not become transsexual adults, there must be other important determinants of transsexualism. One study of men found that being raised in a religious Catholic family where homosexuality was condemned, coupled with cross-gender behavior in boyhood, was related to transsexual rather than homosexual outcomes (Hellman et al., 1981). These investigators suggested that for these men, transsexualism was a way of being sexually involved with males while still avoiding homosexuality per se. If this is true, then homosexual transsexualism should become rarer as homosexuality becomes less stigmatized. The difference between homosexual transsexualism and cross-gendered homosexuality (that is, homosexuality accompanied by behavior more typical of the opposite sex) is probably more in degree than in kind. The documentary film *Paris Is Burning* depicts gay African American men who devote a considerable amount of time, money, and energy trying to look like beautiful women. One of the men in that film described how he had considered but decided against a sex change operation. Another man intended to obtain the operation when he could afford it. Although probably only the second of these two men would merit the diagnosis of transsexualism, they are clearly very similar.

Nonhomosexual transsexuals include transsexual individuals who are bisexual, heterosexual, or asexual. Research has shown that the subtypes of nonhomosexual transsexuals are very similar to each other and differ from homosexual transsexuals in important respects beyond their sexual orientations (Blanchard, 1985, 1989, 1991). Unlike homosexual transsexuals, nonhomosexual transsexuals are not especially feminine in childhood or adulthood. Although an appreciable percentage of homosexual transsexuals are biologically female, nearly all nonhomosexual transsexuals are men. These are biological males who believe that they are a woman trapped in a man's body; they may be sexually attracted to women, or to both women and men. Nonhomosexual transsexuals typically seek sex reassignment surgery much later than homosexual transsexuals (Blanchard, 1994). Most important, nonhomosexual gender dysphoria (distress about being a man) is usually associated with *autogynephilia,* a paraphilia characterized by sexual arousal by the thought or fantasy of being women (Blanchard, 1989, 1992). The great sexologist Magnus Hirschfeld first identified a class of cross-dressing men who are sexually aroused by the image of themselves as women: "They feel attracted not by the women outside them, but by the woman inside them" (Hirschfeld, 1948, p. 167). Nonhomosexual transsexuals may fuse the idea of being a woman with their sexual attractions toward real women in fantasies in which they are engaging in lesbian interactions (Blanchard, 1991).

Treatment Psychotherapy is usually not helpful in helping transsexuals resolve their gender dysphoria (Tollison & Adams, 1979). The only treatment that has been shown to be effective is surgical sex reassignment. Initially, transsexuals awaiting surgery are given hormone treatment. Biological men are given estrogens to facilitate breast growth, skin softening, and shrinking of muscles. Biological women are given testosterone, which suppresses menstruation, increases facial and body hair, and deepens the voice. Typically, transsexuals must live for a lengthy period with hormonal therapy, and they generally must live for at least a year as the gender they wish to become. If they successfully complete the trial period, they undergo surgery. In male-to-female transsexuals, this entails removal of the penis and testes and the creation of an artificial vagina. Female-to-male transsexuals typically are given mastectomies and hysterectomies. Because relevant surgical techniques are still rather primitive, only a minority of female-to-male transsexuals are given an artificial penis; the rest function sexually without a penis. A recent review of the outcome literature found that 87 percent of 220 male-to-female transsexuals had satisfactory outcomes (meaning that they did not regret their decisions), and that 97 percent of 130 female-to-male transsexuals had successful outcomes (Green & Fleming, 1990). Blanchard (1985) also reported that the majority of transsexuals are satisfied with the outcome of sex reassignment surgery, although there is variability in the degree of satisfaction. In general, those who were reasonably well adjusted before surgery do better following surgery, and those with preexisting psychopathology are less likely to do well. In spite of the reasonably good success record for transsexual patients who are carefully chosen, such surgery remains controversial because some professionals continue to maintain that it is inappropriate to treat psychological disorders through drastic anatomical changes (e.g., McHugh, 1992).

SEXUAL ABUSE

Sexual abuse, including pedophilia, rape, and incest, concerns society more than any other sexual problem. It is somewhat ironic, then, that of these, only pedophilia is included in DSM-IV. (Furthermore, the restrictive definition of pedophilia employed there probably excludes most cases of childhood sexual abuse, because many of the victims have gone through puberty and pedophilia only applies to abuse of prepubertal children.) This partly reflects the seriousness with which society views these offenses and its preference for treating coercive sex offenders as criminals rather than patients. However, the fact that rape, for example, is not included as a DSM-IV category need not deter us. The research literature of abnormal psychology is increasingly ad-

Dr. Richard Raskin, a physician and professional tennis player, became Renee Richards through transsexual surgery.

dressing topics related to sexual abuse of both children and adults. Because of this and because sexual abuse is an extremely important social problem, we have included a thorough treatment here.

Childhood Sexual Abuse

The past decade has seen intense concern about childhood sexual abuse, with an accompanying increase in relevant research. A search of the electronic database *Medline* found only 72 articles about childhood sexual abuse from 1975 to 1984. The number of relevant articles published during the next decade grew nearly tenfold, to 693. (In contrast, the number of articles about schizophrenia only doubled during that same time period.) One of the most frequently cited articles in psychology during the past decade concerned the impact of childhood sexual abuse on psychological functioning (Browne & Finkelhor, 1986).

There are at least three reasons for the marked increase in interest in childhood sexual abuse. First, much evidence suggests that, broadly defined, childhood sexual abuse is common, much more so than was once assumed. Second, several mental disorders have been linked to childhood sexual abuse; thus, such abuse may be important in the etiology of some disorders. Third, some dramatic and well-publicized cases involving allegations of childhood sexual abuse have raised very controversial issues, such as the validity of children's testimony and recovered memories of sexual abuse. We shall consider all three of these factors in turn.

Prevalence of Childhood Sexual Abuse The prevalence of childhood sexual abuse depends on its definition. For example, different studies use different definitions of "childhood," with the upper age limit ranging from age 12 to as high as 19 (Finkelhor et al., 1990). The definition of sexual abuse also varies across studies, with most studies using rather broad, inclusive criteria. For example, in a survey of 800 American college students, 19 percent of women and 9 percent of men reported "sexual involvement" with an adult between early childhood and adolescence (Finkelhor, 1979). In a probability sample of 3000 persons in one city, 7 percent of women and 4 percent of men reported forced sexual contact during childhood (Russell, 1983, 1984). In a sample of 900 women, 12 percent reported having been sexually abused by a relative and 20 percent by a nonrelative before age 14, but fewer than 5 percent had reported the incident to police. Studies using similar definitions have generally yielded similar rates across time, with approximately 10–12 percent of women recalling unwanted sexual contact when they were younger than 14 years old (Feldman et al., 1991). Clearly, even the lowest plausible figures are sufficiently high to concern us.

Consequences of Childhood Sexual Abuse Childhood sexual abuse may have both short-term and long-term consequences. The most common short-term consequences include fears, posttraumatic stress disorder, sexual acting out, and poor self-esteem (Kendall-Tackett, Williams, & Finkelhor, 1993). Approximately one-third of sexually abused children show no symptoms. Thus, there is no single "sexual abuse" syndrome.

A number of studies have found associations between reports of childhood sexual abuse and adult psychopathology, including borderline personality disorder (Herman et al., 1989; Ogata et al., 1990), somatization disorder (Morris, 1989), dissociative symptoms (Chu & Dill, 1990), chronic pelvic pain (Walker et al., 1988), and dissociative identity disorder (Coons, 1986). A very wide variety of sexual symptoms have been alleged to result from early sexual abuse (Bass & Davis, 1986; Browne & Finkelhor, 1986), ranging, for example, from sexual withdrawal to sexual promiscuity. Knowledge about the long-term consequences of childhood sexual abuse is more uncertain than about the short-term consequences, primarily due to the difficulties of establishing causal links between early experiences and adult behavior (discussed more fully in the "Unresolved Issues" section).

Controversies Concerning Childhood Sexual Abuse Several high-profile criminal trials have highlighted the limitations of our knowledge concerning questions of great scientific and practical importance. Two general types of cases have been prosecuted. In the first, children have accused adults working in daycare settings of extensive, often bizarre, sexual abuse. The most controversial aspect of these cases has been the degree to which children's accusations could be trusted. The second type of case concerns adults who claim to have repressed and completely forgotten memories of early sexual abuse and who then "recovered" the memories during adulthood, typically while seeing a therapist who believes that re-

Recent evidence has suggested that the use of anatomically correct dolls to question young children about where they may have been touched in alleged incidents of sexual abuse does not improve the accuracy of their testimony relative to verbal interviews alone.

pressed memories of childhood sexual abuse are a very common cause of adult psychopathology. The most controversial aspect of these cases is the validity of the "recovered" memories.

Children's Testimony. Several cases involving alleged sexual abuse in daycare settings shocked the country during the past decade. The most notorious was the McMartin preschool case in California (see HIGH-LIGHT 11.2); the similar case of Kelly Michaels, in New Jersey, also attracted immense media and public attention (Rabinowitz, 1990). In these and similar cases, the initial public reaction was one of shock and fear that children in seemingly good daycare centers had been brutally sexually abused. However, as the trials progressed and allegations became increasingly difficult to believe, many observers began to question the truth of children's accusations and to suggest that something akin to mass hysteria was operating. For example, Michaels, a young woman employee of Wee Care Day Nursery, was accused of raping and assaulting children with knives, forks, a wooden spoon, and Lego blocks; of licking peanut butter off children's genitals; of playing the piano in the nude, and of making the children drink her urine and eat a feces "cake"—all during daycare hours and unnoticed by her coworkers. Although pedophilia is extremely rare in women, Michaels was nevertheless convicted in 1988 and sentenced to 47 years in prison. This is in spite of the fact that the nature of the accusations was extremely bizarre and that there was no corroborating testimony from other employees. Her conviction was finally overturned on appeal in 1993 due to concerns about the manner in which child abuse "experts" elicited children's testimony, especially the concern that the adults asked leading questions and otherwise encouraged reports of abuse.

Because children are susceptible to the influence of others and cannot always distinguish fact from fantasy, the accuracy of their testimony is a crucial issue. Sexually anatomically correct dolls have often been used during interviews to explore allegations of sexual abuse in young children. As discussed in HIGH-LIGHT 11.3, the few empirical studies investigating their use have shown that young children questioned with an anatomically correct doll may allege that they have been touched in places that they were not touched, and more generally that the use of such dolls does not improve the accuracy of the reports of where (or even if) they were touched (Ceci, in press).

Recovered Memories of Sexual Abuse. In 1990 a young woman named Eileen Franklin testified in court that she had seen her father rape and murder an eight-year-old playmate 20 years earlier. Remarkably,

The McMartin Preschool Case

In August 1983, a woman named Judy Johnson complained to police in Manhattan Beach, California, that her son had been molested by Raymond Buckey, who helped run the McMartin Preschool, which her son attended. Johnson's complaints grew increasingly bizarre. For example, she accused Buckey of sodomizing her son while he stuck the boy's head in a toilet and of making him ride naked on a horse. She made similar allegations about her estranged husband and three health-club employees. In 1985 Johnson was diagnosed with acute paranoid schizophrenia, and she died of alcohol-related liver disease in 1986, but not before she was called as the first witness for the prosecution in a preliminary hearing in 1984. By the time she died, prosecutors no longer needed her. Children at the preschool who were interviewed by therapist Kee MacFarlane began to tell fantastically lurid stories, for example, that children were forced to dig up dead bodies at cemeteries, jump out of airplanes, and kill animals with bats. Nevertheless, prosecutors and many McMartin parents believed the children (Carlson, 1990), and seven defendants were charged including Buckey, his mother, and five daycare employees.

Charges were eventually dropped against the five employees. Raymond Buckey and his mother were tried in the lengthiest and most expensive U.S. trial to that time: two and a half years and $15 million. The jury acquitted Ms. Buckey on all counts, and failed to convict Raymond Buckey on any; however, he was freed only after a retrial, having spent five years in jail. The jurors' principal reason for not finding the defendants guilty was their concern that interviewers had coaxed the children into telling stories of abuse. The following transcript raises the strong suspicion that this occurred in at least some cases. It involves the "naked movie star game," which defendants were accused of playing with the children.

Interviewer (Int.): I thought that was a naked game.
Boy: Not exactly.
Int.: Did somebody take their clothes off?
Boy: When I was there no one was naked.
Int.: Some of the kids were told they might be killed. It was a trick. All right . . . are you going to be stupid, or are you smart and can tell? Some think you're smart.
Boy: I'll be smart.
Int.: [The puppet you used earlier in the play interview] is chicken. He can't remember the games, but you know the naked movie star game, or is your memory bad?
Boy: I haven't seen the naked movie star game.
Int.: You must be dumb.
(Green, 1992)

despite her claim to have witnessed the murder, she had no memory of the event until she "recovered" the memory by accident in adulthood. (Franklin's father was convicted and given a life sentence, although in 1995 the conviction was overturned because of two serious constitutional errors made during the original trial that might have affected the jury's verdict.) In 1993, Steven Cook accused Chicago Roman Catholic Cardinal Joseph Bernardin and another priest of sexually abusing Cook 17 years earlier, when Cook was 17 years old. Cook also claimed he had forgotten the abuse for many years, recovering the memory only during therapy. Cook later withdrew his charges against Bernardin because of concern that his own "recovered memory" may have been invalid, and even later he made a personal apology to Bernadin for having made the accusation.

The possibility that traumatic experiences can be utterly forgotten due to repression and then somehow recovered intact years later has been heatedly debated during the past few years. Some have argued that repressed memories are common (Herman, 1993) and are responsible for a great deal of psychopathology. In a controversial but popular book, *The Courage to Heal,* journalists Ellen Bass and Laura Davis asserted: "If you are unable to remember any specific instances [of sexual abuse] . . . but still have the feeling that something abusive happened to you, it probably did" (1988, p. 21). Some therapists routinely give this book to their clients, and those clients often do report "recovering" such memories. Those skeptical about recovery of repressed memories point out that even normal unrepressed memories can be highly inaccurate and that false memories can be induced experimentally (Loftus, 1993, in press). A particularly dramatic case suggesting that false memories can be induced is that of Paul Ingram, a Washington state sheriff accused by his adult daughters of severe sexual abuse when they were young:

The Reliability of Children's Reports of Past Events

In recent years, as more and more children are being brought forward to testify in court about alleged physical and sexual abuse by parents or other adults, researchers have become increasingly concerned about determining how reliable we can expect the testimony of children—especially that of *young* children—to be. Because abuse of children is distressingly common, children's reports of such abuse must always be taken seriously. Increasingly, however, doubt is being cast on the accuracy of young children's testimony, especially when they have been subjected to repeated interviews over many months with highly leading questions, sometimes in a coercive atmosphere. Unfortunately, this appears to be the way in which such children are sometimes treated before the trials in which they testify.

Stephen Ceci, a leading developmental psychologist studying this problem, has recently summarized a series of experiments that casts grave doubt on young children's testimony if they have been exposed repeatedly to suggestive interviews over long intervals of time (Ceci, in press). For example, Ceci has summarized evidence that preschoolers have greater difficulty distinguishing between real and imagined acts (such as deciding whether they really touched their nose or only imagined touching it) than do older children or adults (Foley et al., in press). Younger children are not deficient at distinguishing between whether they performed an act or whether someone else performed

the act; the deficit is in distinguishing between *real* versus *imagined* acts when both were done by themselves, or when both were done by others (Lindsay, Johnson, & Kwon, 1991). In one of his own experiments, Ceci and his colleagues had an adult interview young children weekly for ten weeks about whether certain actual events (e.g., getting in an accident that required stitches) and certain fictitious events (e.g., getting their hand caught in a mousetrap and having to go to the hospital to get it removed) had occurred. In one version of this experiment, each week interviewers asked the children to think hard about whether the event had happened and prompted the children to visualize the scene. After ten such weekly interviews, children were given a forensic interview by a new adult (in a forensic interview, the interviewer first tries to make the child comfortable, then elicits a free narrative about what the child remembers happening, and then asks probing questions). All interviews were videotaped. The results were very striking. Over half the preschool children (58 percent) claimed that at least one of the fictitious events had actually happened to them, and 27 percent of the children claimed that nearly all of the fictitious events had happened to them. Their narratives describing these fictitious events were often elaborate, embellished, and coherent, and the children generally showed emotion appropriate to the event. Moreover, it appeared that the children actually believed these events had happened

to them, because Ceci and the children's parents were sometimes unable to talk them out of their false reports, with the children often protesting "but it really did happen. I remember it" (Ceci, in press, p. 17). When Ceci showed these videotapes to many psychologists who specialize in interviewing children, the psychologists' accuracy at detecting real events from fictitious events was no better than chance. Similar results have been obtained for judges, social workers, and psychiatrists. Ceci concluded: "Repeatedly thinking about a fictitious event can lead some preschool children to produce vivid, detailed reports that professionals are unable to discern from their reports of actual events" (in press, p. 17).

In another important study called the "Sam Stone Study," Leichtman and Ceci (in press) interviewed preschool children four times over ten weeks for details about a previously staged 2-minute visit by a stranger named Sam Stone to their daycare center. Some of the children were given no prior information about Sam Stone before his visit and were never asked suggestive questions during the four interviews; other children were given a stereotype about Sam Stone before his visit (e.g., that he was clumsy: "That Sam Stone is always getting into accidents and breaking things") and were also given leading questions during the four interviews (e.g., "Remember that time Sam Stone . . . spilled chocolate on that white teddy bear? Did he do it on purpose or by accident?"). One

Ingram admitted to a number of dramatic and bizarre acts of abuse against his two daughters, including forcing them to engage in anal and vaginal sex since they were young children, encouraging his friends to have sex with

the daughters during poker nights, murdering 25 babies during satanic rituals, and forcing his daughters to have abortions with coathangers. There was no independent evidence for any of these accusations, and the daugh-

month later, after the four subsequent interviews were completed (about 14 weeks after Sam Stone's visit), all children were interviewed with forensic procedures by a new interviewer, who asked about two events that had *not* happened during Sam Stone's visit—whether he had soiled a teddy bear and/or ripped a book. For the children given no prior stereotype about Sam Stone and no leading questions during the initial four interviews, only 10 percent of the youngest preschoolers claimed that Sam Stone had done either of these two nonevents, and when gently challenged about this, only 2.5 percent stuck to the story that Sam had done these things. (Older preschoolers seldom committed such errors.) By contrast, for the younger preschoolers who were given a prior stereotype that Sam Stone was clumsy and who had been asked leading questions during the four interviews, a startling 72 percent of the youngest children claimed that Sam Stone had either soiled the teddy bear or ripped the book, or both. When gently challenged, 44 percent continued to claim that they had seen him do these things. Leichtman and Ceci tested the believability of these reports by showing the videotapes of some of the forensic interviews to over 1000 researchers and clinicians who work with children. When asked about which events actually occurred during Sam Stone's visit and to rate the children for the accuracy of their testimony, the majority of the professionals were

highly inaccurate. Indeed, the videotape of the child who was *least* accurate was rated as being most credible, and the videotape of the child who was *most* accurate was rated as least credible. Leichtman and Ceci (in press) concluded: "It is not that the members of these audiences were worse than anyone else at assessing which children gave accurate accounts, but that the accuracy of children's reports is extremely difficult to discern when children have been subjected to repeated erroneous suggestions over long retention intervals, especially when coupled with the induction of stereotypes" (p. 20).

Finally, Ceci's work also challenges the use of anatomically correct dolls (dolls with bodies showing the sex organs) to symbolically represent actions, at least for very young children. Bruck and colleagues (1995) studied 70 three-year-old boys and girls who were visiting their pediatrician, 35 of whom were given a genital exam (which involved touching of the genital area but no genital insertions) and 35 of whom were not given a genital exam. Mothers were present during these exams. Five minutes later, with the mother still present, the children were asked to describe where the doctor had touched them. They were then presented anatomical dolls and asked to point on the dolls where the doctor had touched them. When interviewed verbally, most of the children who had not received a genital exam correctly refrained from stating that their genitals had

been touched. However, when given the anatomical doll, nearly 60 percent of those who had *not* received a genital exam claimed that the doctor had made genital and/or anal insertions and done other acts to be concerned about. On the other hand, just over half of the children who had been given a genital exam claimed that their genitals had *not* been touched, even though they had. Thus, it seemed that the *use of anatomical dolls failed to improve the accuracy of the three-year-olds' reports of what happened or did not happen.* A previous study by Goodman and Aman (1990) of five-year-olds also did not find that the use of anatomical dolls was useful in eliciting information, although their subjects rarely reported genital contact that had not actually been made. This and other studies have led Ceci and his colleagues to conclude that "although older children do make fewer errors, there is still no convincing evidence that dolls improve their reporting" (Bruck et al., 1995).

In summary, although young children are capable of correct recall of what happened to them, they are also susceptible to a greater variety of sources of postevent distortion than are older children and adults. Nevertheless, even adults are also susceptible to a variety of sources of post-event distortion to a lesser degree (Loftus, Feldman, & Dashiell, in press; see HIGHLIGHT 7.3), and so the differences should be seen as a matter of degree rather than of kind (Ceci, in press).

ters showed no signs of scarring that either sexual abuse or forced abortions would surely have caused. An expert on cults, Dan Ofshe, showed that Ingram was highly suggestible and could easily be persuaded

of his own guilt. Ingram eventually agreed with Ofshe's interpretation and recanted, but it was too late. He was sentenced to twenty years imprisonment. (Adapted from Wright, 1994.)

At the time of this writing, the validity of memories of childhood sexual abuse that arise during therapy remains a scientifically open question. The issue is not merely scientific, however. Many parents have been accused by their children of early sexual abuse due to recovered memories. Some children have sued their parents for damages, and some courts have ruled that the Statute of Limitations applies from the date at which an offense is remembered, not from the date it occurred (Green, 1992). Recently, a father successfully sued his daughter's therapist for inducing what he claimed were false memories that he had abused her. A large group of parents who say that they were falsely accused by their children of sexual abuse has organized as The False Memory Syndrome Foundation (Gardner, 1993). (Actually, the founder of the organization is a woman who accused her parents of sexual abuse and then recanted because she came to the realization that the abuse had never happened.) The foundation has been accused by others as a front for shielding pedophiles (Herman, 1994). The debate concerning recovered memories of sexual abuse is one of the most important and interesting contemporary controversies in the domains of psychopathology and mental health (see also HIGHLIGHT 7.3).

Pedophilia

Pedophilia is a paraphilia in which an adult's preferred or exclusive sexual partner is a prepubertal child. It is important to emphasize that pedophilia is defined by the bodily maturity, not the age, of the preferred partner. Thus, studies of childhood sexual abuse, which typically define childhood based on an age range that may extend well into adolescence, do not necessarily concern pedophilia. Nearly all pedophiles are male (Finkelhor, 1984), and about two-thirds of their victims are girls (typically between the ages of 8 and 11). The proportion of pedophilic interactions that are technically homosexual is much higher than the rate of homosexuality in the general population. This does not, however, mean that homosexual men have a greater propensity to become sexually involved with children than do heterosexual men (Freund, Watson, & Rienzo, 1989). Rather, it reflects that fact that many pedophiles are relatively indifferent to the sex of their victim, provided that he or she is a certain age (Freund & Kuban, 1993).

The common image of the pedophile is a stranger who lures children to an isolated spot to molest them. However, one study found that in cases of child molestation, the perpetrator was a stranger to the children in only approximately 10 percent of cases (Mohr, Turner, & Jerry, 1964). In another 15 percent, he was a relative. Pedophilia frequently involves manipulation of the child's genitals. It used to be thought that sexual penetration was rare; however, one study found that such penetration occurred in more than half of cases and that use of physical force or violence occurred in 89 percent (Stermac, Hall, & Henskens, 1989). Although penetration and associated violence are often injurious to the child, injuries are usually a by-product rather than a goal, as would be true with a sadist.

Studies investigating the sexual responses of pedophiles have achieved quite consistent results (Barbaree, 1990). Such studies tend to use a *penile phlethysmograph* in order to directly measure erectile responses to sexual stimuli rather than relying on self-report. (A plethysmograph consists of an expandable band placed around the penis, connected to a recording device.) In general, men who have molested nonfamilial female children have shown greater sexual arousal to pictures of nude or partially clad girls than have matched nonoffenders. Interestingly, however, as a group the offenders also responded strongly to adult women. Men who have molested nonfamilial male children have tended to respond sexually to both adult men and women. Thus, although pedophiles show deviant sexual arousal patterns, they also appear capable, under some circumstances, of arousal to adults. Thus, deviant sexual preference alone may not explain why some men become pedophiles. Other factors include cognitive and nonsexual motivational factors. As an example of the former, child molesters are more likely than nonoffenders to believe that children will benefit from sexual contacts with adults and that children often initiate such contact (Segal & Stermac, 1990). Motivationally, many pedophiles appear to desire mastery or dominance over another individual, and some idealize aspects of childhood such as innocence, unconditional love, or simplicity. Indeed, perhaps the most common type of pedophile is someone who is an interpersonally unskilled man drawn to children because he feels in control in relationships with them.

Some researchers have attempted to categorize pedophiles into subtypes. For example, one group of investigators distinguished between *fixated pedophiles* and *regressed pedophiles* (Groth, Hobson, & Gary, 1982). The fixated pedophiles are those who have arrested psychosexual development; they have been attracted to children since their adolescence. They also tend to be childlike and may take pride in their immaturity. The regressed pedophiles are not generally attracted to children, but during certain times of stress (such as a divorce) they may turn to female children as substitutes for adult women.

There has been a rash of pedophilia among a group long considered to be highly trustworthy: the Catholic clergy. Although the majority of priests are innocent of sexual wrongdoing, the Catholic Church has admitted that a significant minority have committed sexual abuse, including pedophilia. At least 400 priests were charged with sexual abuse during the 1980s, and $400 million has been paid in damages since 1985 (Samborn, 1994). The most serious scandal to date involved James R. Porter, a 57-year-old father of four who is alleged to have sexually abused as many as 100 children when he was a priest in Massachusetts during the 1960s. The case was complicated by the fact that his initial accuser claimed to have recovered memories of sexual abuse. Porter has since admitted to his offenses and was recently convicted of molesting his children's baby sitter in 1987. The Church settled a multimillion-dollar suit with 25 men whom Porter had abused while a priest. Because of the scandals, there have been calls for the Church to take more aggressive steps to find, isolate, and treat abusive priests (Greeley, 1993).

Incest

Culturally prohibited sexual relations (up to and including coitus) between family members, such as a brother and sister or a parent and child, are known as **incest**. Although a few societies have approved incestuous relationships—at one time it was the established practice for Egyptian pharaohs to marry their sisters to prevent the royal blood from being "contaminated"—the incest taboo is virtually universal among human societies. An indication of the risks involved in such inbreeding has been provided by Adams and Neel (1967), who compared the offspring of 18 nuclear-incest marriages—12 brother-sister and 6 father-daughter—with those of a control group matched for age, intelligence, socioeconomic status, and other relevant characteristics. At the end of six months, five of the infants of the incestuous marriages had died, two were severely mentally retarded and had been institutionalized, three showed evidence of borderline intelligence, and one had a cleft palate. Only 7 of the 18 infants were considered normal. In contrast, only two of the control-group infants were not considered normal—one showing indications of borderline intelligence and the other manifesting a physical defect. These consequences of matings between close relatives reflect the action of rare recessive genes with negative effects. Close relatives are much more likely than nonrelatives to share the same bad genes, and hence to have children with two of them. Presumably for this reason, many nonhuman animal species, and all known primates, avoid matings between close relatives. The mechanism for human incest avoidance appears to be lack of sexual interest in people to whom one is continuously exposed from an early age. For example, when they become adults, biologically unrelated children who were raised together in Israeli kibbutzim rarely marry or have affairs with others from their rearing group (Shepher, 1971). Evolutionarily, this makes sense. In most cultures, chil-

James R. Porter, a former Roman Catholic priest, was convicted of pedophilia that had been committed many years earlier. His conviction occurred after a number of persons came forward with reports of his earlier abuse when they were members of his church as children.

dren reared together will be biologically related siblings.

Incest is traditionally defined as sex between biological relatives. Recent trends toward nontraditional family compositions such as stepparents and stepchildren have led some researchers to expand the definition of incest to legal relatives. There are no adverse genetic consequences of matings between relatives-in-law, and thus the incest taboo might be expected to operate less effectively between them. On the other hand, it is conceivable that a young woman who is sexually molested by her stepfather could suffer every bit as much, psychologically, as one who is molested by her biological father. At present there are no relevant studies examining this question.

In our own society, the actual incidence of incest is difficult to estimate because it usually comes to light only when reported to law enforcement or other agencies. It is almost certainly more common than is generally believed, in part because many victims are reluctant to report the incest or do not consider themselves victimized (De Young, 1982; Maisch, 1972). The incidence of "intrafamilial sexual abuse" coming to the attention of professionals approached 100,000 in 1985 (Williams & Finkelhor, 1990). Brother-sister incest is clearly the most common form of incest, even though it is rarely reported (Masters et al., 1992). Indeed in two studies, brother-sister incest was reported as being five times more common than the next most common pattern—father-daughter incest (Gebhard et al., 1965; Kinsey et al., 1948, 1953). Mother-son incest is thought to be relatively rare. In a study of 78 cases of incest, which excluded the brother-sister variety, Maisch (1972) found that the father-daughter and stepfather-stepdaughter varieties accounted for fully 85 percent of the sample; mother-son incest accounted for only 4 percent. It seems that girls living with stepfathers are at especially high risk for incest, perhaps because there is less of an incest taboo among nonblood relatives (Finkelhor, 1984; Masters et al., 1992; Russell, 1986). In occasional cases, multiple patterns of incest may exist within the same family, and some incestuous fathers involve all of their daughters serially as they become pubescent.

Incestuous fathers tend to be of lower intelligence than other fathers, but they do not typically evidence serious psychopathology (Williams & Finkelhor, 1990). Indeed, they are often shy, conventional and claim devotion to their families (Masters et al., 1992). Most incestuous offenders are not pedophiles; only one-fifth to one-third have pedophilic arousal patterns (Langevin et al., 1985; Marshall, Barbaree, & Christophe, 1986). Most in-

The drawings shown here are all the work of incest victims. Top: a seven-year-old girl engulfed by a maelstrom. Middle: a teenage girl threatened by a snake. Bottom: a nine-year-old boy caught in a trap in the middle of a country landscape.

cestuous fathers have experienced substantial sexual dysfunction with their wives or adult partners. They have also tended to avoid child-care or nurturing activities that may otherwise have led them to treat their children as children, rather than sexual objects. Although not especially nurturant, incestuous fathers tend to be overprotective of their victims, which might represent an attempt to isolate and monopolize them. Incestuous families tend to be low in community involvement and high in conflict avoidance. The wives of men who commit incest were often sexually abused themselves as children, and in more than two-thirds of such cases the wife often does not help or protect her child even if she knows about the incest (Masters et al., 1992). Despite these associations, no one pattern adequately describes all incestuous fathers and families.

Rape

The term **rape** describes sexual activity that occurs under actual or threatened forcible coercion of one person by another. In most states, legal definitions restrict forcible rape to forced intercourse or penetration of a bodily orifice by a penis or other object. Statutory rape is sexual activity with a person who is legally defined (by *statute* or law) to be under the age of consent (18 in most states). Statutory rape is considered to have occurred regardless of the apparent willingness of an underage partner. In the vast majority of cases, rape is a crime of men against women, although in prison settings it is often men against men. As with childhood sexual abuse, several issues related to rape are scientifically and politically controversial. Two especially controversial questions are how frequently rape occurs, and whether rape is primarily motivated by sex or aggression.

Prevalence The prevalence of rape depends on its precise definition, and this has provoked considerable controversy during the past few years (Gilbert, 1992; Koss, Gidcyz, & Wisniewski, 1987; Koss et al., 1988; Roiphe, 1993). Some studies have yielded chillingly high figures. For example, Russell (1984) found that 24 percent of a sample of 930 randomly selected women from San Francisco had been raped, and an additional 20 percent had experienced attempted rape. Koss and colleagues (1987) found that 15 percent of 3187 randomly selected college women had been raped, and an additional 12 percent had experienced attempted rape. These studies suggest that at least one in four women will be the victim of rape or attempted rape during her lifetime.

These figures have been criticized as misleading, however (Gilbert, 1992). The definitions of "rape" employed in the studies are much broader than that often assumed. For example, Russell (1984) defined rape as "forced intercourse (i.e., penile-vaginal penetration), or intercourse obtained by threat or force, or intercourse when the woman was drugged, unconscious, asleep, or otherwise totally helpless and hence unable to consent" (p. 35). Similarly, Koss and colleagues (1987) counted as rape victims any women who had given in to a man's continual arguments and pressure, or who had been too intoxicated to consent, as well as those who fit the more conventional criteria in which a man threatened or used some degree of physical force. Other evidence that Koss's definition may be too broad includes the fact that 73 percent of the women she classified as having been raped did not perceive of themselves as victims. Furthermore, 42 percent of the women defined as having been raped had sex again with the men who had raped them (using this broad definition of rape).

Data on reported and unreported criminal offenses tell a different story. The FBI routinely gathers statistics on most major crimes reported to local law enforcement agencies throughout the country. The incidence of unreported rapes can be estimated from the National Crime Survey of the Bureau of Justice Statistics (BJS), which draws on a probability sample of 59,000 households. The incidence of reported rapes between 1979 and 1990 was fairly stable, at between 70 and 80 rapes per 100,000 women, per year (Federal Bureau of Investigation, 1991). The incidence of total (reported and unreported) rapes was approximately double these. Projecting to lifetime risk, most reasonable assumptions lead to estimates that are an order of magnitude less than those obtained by Koss and Russell, with approximately 5–7 percent of women the victim of rape or attempted rape (Gilbert, 1992) during the course of their lives.

Which numbers are correct, Koss's and Russell's or the crime statistics? The answer, probably, is "both." Koss and Russell have carefully assessed the prevalence of various coercive sexual behaviors. It is important to know the percentage of women who have had those negative experiences, whether or not we agree with the classification of a specific experience as "rape." The FBI and BJS statistics probably adhere more closely to the conventional understanding of "rape" as a criminal offense. No woman desires either to be used sexually while she is intoxicated or to be physically forced to have intercourse. We suspect, however, that many women would distinguish between these experiences and wish to know their probabilities separately. Thus, in general, we suggest that it is less useful to argue over whether specific experiences should be classified as instances of rape than it is to have detailed information about the rates of specific negative sexual experiences.

Is Rape Motivated by Sex or Aggression? Traditionally, rape has been classified as a sex crime, and society has assumed that the rapist was motivated by lust. However, some feminist scholars have challenged this view, arguing instead that rape is motivated by the need to dominate, to assert power, and to humiliate a victim rather than by sexual desire for her (Brownmiller, 1975; Groth, 1979). Before evaluating the argument that rape is about aggression and not about sex, it is important to emphasize one undeniable fact. Whatever motivates the rapist, rape victims do not find rape to be sexually pleasurable. The myth that they sometimes do is dangerous and probably has encouraged some men to rape and some juries to excuse rapists. Rape is among women's worst fears (Gordon, 1992). Even in the context of a romantic relationship, women rate forced sex as the most destructive act a partner can perform (Buss, 1994). Moreover, from the perspective of the victim, rape is always an act of violence, whatever the rapist's motivation.

One researcher, Craig Palmer (1988), has evaluated some of the reasons offered by those who believe rape is not sexually motivated, and found them unconvincing. He notes, for example, that although many rapists have stable sexual partners, it is not uncommon for men to desire multiple sexual outlets. Brownmiller (1975) noted that rape victims include females of all ages and degrees of physical attractiveness. Although this is true, the age distribution of rape victims is not random but includes a very high proportion of women in their teens and early twenties. This age distribution is quite different from the distribution of other violent crimes, in which the elderly are overrepresented because of their vulnerability. In contrast, less than 5 percent of rape victims are over the age of 50 (Groth, 1979). The fact that older women are raped very rarely despite their increased vulnerability to violent crime in general supports the interpretation that rapists prefer younger (and more attractive) victims. Rapists themselves have described their preferred victims as the "'American dream ideal'—a nice, friendly, young, pretty, middle-class, white female" (Geis, 1977, p. 27). Furthermore, rapists usually cite sexual motivation as a very important cause of their actions (Smithyman, 1978, p. iv). Finally, as we shall see, at least some rapists share features of paraphiliacs, such as a characteristic arousal pattern to abnormal (in their case, rape) stimuli, and multiple paraphilias (Abel & Rouleau, 1990). Paraphiliacs are typically highly sexually motivated. Thus, in our view, sexual desire is a factor in motivating many rapists. At the same time we agree with David Finkelhor, who states that "The debate about the sexual motivation of sexual abuse is something of an unfortunate red herring" (1984, p. 34), and who suggests that "the goal should be to explain how the sexual component fits in" (1984, pp. 34–35).

Recently some progress has been made toward Finkelhor's goal. Two prominent researchers studying sex offenders, Raymond Knight and Robert Prentky, have developed a classification system for rapists that shows all rapists have both aggressive and sexual motives, but to varying degrees. Two of the subtypes they have identified are motivated primarily by aggression, and two of the subtypes are motivated primarily by distorted sexual motives (1990; Knight, Prentky, & Cerce, 1994). In a study validating this classification system, Barbaree and colleagues (1994) found that the rapists of the sexual subtypes showed greater sexual arousal to taped scenes of rape than did rapists of the aggressive subtypes. Further research validating this classification system should be useful in helping to design better treatments for the different subtypes of rapists.

Rape and Its Aftermath   Rape tends to be a repetitive activity rather than an isolated act, and most rapes are planned events. About 80 percent of rapists commit the act in the neighborhoods in which they reside; most rapes take place in an urban setting at night. The specific scene of the rape varies greatly, however. The act may occur on a lonely street after dark, in an automobile in a large shopping center's parking lot, in the elevator or hallway of a building, and in other situations where a victim has little chance of assistance. Rapists have also entered apartments or homes by pretending to be deliverers or repairmen. In fact, rapes most often occur in the victim's home.

About a third or more of all rapes involve more than one offender, and often they are accompanied by beatings. The remainder are single-offender rapes in which the victim and the offender may know each other; the closer the relationship, the more brutally the victim may be beaten. When a victim struggles against her attacker, she is likely to receive more severe injuries or in rare cases to be killed. On the other hand, one study found that when the victim was able to cry out and run away, she was more likely to be successful in avoiding the rape (Selkin, 1975).

In addition to the physical trauma inflicted on a victim, the psychological trauma may be severe (see Chapter 4), leading to what has been called a rape trauma syndrome (Burgess & Holmstrom, 1974) or PTSD (Becker & Kaplan, 1991). One especially unfortunate factor in rape is the possibility of pregnancy; another is the chance of contracting a sexually transmitted disease. A rape may also have a negative impact on a victim's marriage or other intimate relationships. The situation is likely to be particularly upsetting to a husband or boyfriend if he has been forced to watch the rape, as is occasionally the case when a victim is raped by the members of a juvenile gang.

The concept of "victim-precipitated" rape, a favorite of defense attorneys and of some police and court jurisdictions, turns out on close examination to be a myth. According to this view, a victim, although often bruised both psychologically and physically—if not worse—is regarded as the cause of the crime, often on such grounds as the alleged provocativeness of her clothing, her past sexual behavior, or her presence in a location considered risky

In an effort to raise awareness about date rape and sexual harassment on college campuses, schools are beginning to offer rape-prevention programs, such as this one at Hobart College in New York State, in which young men and women are counseled on understanding and avoiding sexual victimization.

(Stermac, Segal, & Gillis, 1990). The attacker, on the other hand, is treated as unable to quell his lust in the face of such irresistible provocation—and therefore not legally responsible for the act. A society as troubled as is ours by sexual assault can ill-afford this type of nonsensical and myth-based jurisprudence; in more than 70 years of combined clinical practice none of the authors has ever encountered a woman who desired to be raped, nor have we ever heard a convincing account of any such case. Despite evidence to the contrary, however, the harmful and dangerous concept that women want to be forced into sex is persistent and widespread (Segal & Stermac, 1990).

Women who are repeated victims of rape are especially likely to be suspected of provoking the attacks. In fact such women tend to be significantly dysfunctional in many areas of their lives, and they also tend to be victims in situations other than rape, perhaps including other forms of sexual traumatization (Koss & Dinero, 1989). Far from being the seductresses of popular folklore, they are often quite ineffectual and inadequate (sometimes because of the effects of a prior history of abuse) with insufficient personal resources to fend off those who would exploit them (Ellis, Atkeson, & Calhoun, 1982; Myers et al., 1985).

Rape, even at its least violent, is a bullying, intrusive violation of another person's integrity, selfhood, and personal boundaries that deserves to be viewed with more gravity—and its victims with more compassion and sensitivity—than is usually the case.

Much still remains to be done in providing services to these victims (Koss, 1983), many of whom suffer from moderately severe posttraumatic stress disorder (see Chapter 4).

Rapists Based on information gathered by the FBI about arrested and convicted rapists, rape is usually a young man's crime. According to FBI Uniform Crime Reports, about 60 percent of all rapists arrested are under 25 years of age, with the greatest concentration in the 18-to-24 age group. Of the rapists who get into police records, about 30–50 percent are married and living with their wives at the time of the crime. As a group, they come from the low end of the socioeconomic ladder and commonly have a prior criminal record (Masters et al., 1992). Typically they are unskilled workers with low intelligence, low education, and low income. How representative they are of all rapists we do not know. The substantial numbers of a certain type of college male who is excessively and sometimes physically coercive (Cate & Lloyd, 1992; Kanin, 1985; Koss et al., 1987; Koss & Oros, 1982; Lisak & Roth, 1988; Rapaport & Burkhart, 1984) suggest that the basic propensity to rape is not limited to the disadvantaged. One of the authors has assisted in the college expulsion of a student with a history of four documented date rapes; as is apparently typical of the type, he saw nothing wrong with these acts.

A strong case can be made that rape should be considered a category of paraphilia—not different in its essentials from the paraphilias already discussed

(Abel & Rouleau, 1990). Rapists have many features of paraphiliacs: For example, they often report having recurrent, repetitive, and compulsive urges to rape. They typically try to control the urges, but the urges eventually become so strong that they act on them. Many rapists have other paraphilias. In one study of 126 rapists, for example, 28 percent had interest in exhibitionism and 18 percent in voyeurism (Abel & Rouleau, 1990). Most important, rapists have a characteristic pattern of sexual arousal (Abel et al., 1977; Abel & Rouleau, 1990). Most rapists are similar to normal nonoffending men in being sexually aroused to depictions of mutually satisfying, consensual intercourse. However, in contrast to normal men, many rapists are also sexually aroused to depictions of sexual assaults. A small minority of rapists, characterized by very violent assaults, are aroused more to assault than to sexual stimuli. They appear to be sexual sadists.

Rapists also show some deficits in their cognitive appraisals of women's feelings and intention (Segal & Stermac, 1990). For example, they have difficulty decoding women's negative cues during social interactions. This could lead to inappropriate behaviors that women would experience as sexually intrusive. In one study, for example, rapists and nonrapist offenders were shown a series of vignettes of heterosexual couples interacting, and subjects were asked to guess which emotional cues were being portrayed. Rapists were significantly less accurate than the control groups (violent nonrapists and nonviolent nonrapists) in interpreting cues. Moreover, rapists were especially bad at reading women's cues, and errors associated with negative cues were most common (Lipton, McDonel, & McFall, 1987).

It might seem from the preceding descriptions that rapists as a group are a disturbed segment of the population and that potential rapists should therefore be easy to recognize. This would be an erroneous and possibly dangerous conclusion, however. Although it is true that some rapists are obviously abnormal—a few even blatantly psychotic—the literature abounds with instances of rape in which, before an attack, the rapist had given no hint to the victim of being a sexually assaultive person (Gager & Schurr, 1976; Medea & Thompson, 1974). The apparently widespread occurrence of attempted (and completed) date rape, particularly on college campuses, underscores this point (Kanin, 1985; Koss et al., 1987; Koss & Oros, 1982; Rapaport & Burkhart, 1984). Whatever rape prevention involves, it is not a matter of informal psychodiagnostic predictions. Conviction rates for rape are low, and most men who have raped are free in the community. In fact one study of rapists who were in the

community found that the men had raped anywhere from 5 to 100 times (Abel et al., 1978). In a more recent study, Abel and colleagues (reported in Abel & Rouleau, 1990) found that 907 separate acts of rape were reported by only 126 nonincarcerated offenders, an average of 7 per offender.

In recent years, new rape laws have been adopted by a majority of states, many of them based on the "Michigan model," which describes four degrees of criminal sexual conduct, with different punishment levels for different degrees of seriousness. In calling the offense criminal sexual conduct rather than rape, the Michigan law also appropriately places the emphasis on the offender rather than the victim. Unfortunately, most sexual assaults are not reported, and of those that are, less than 10 percent result in conviction (Darke, 1990). Convictions often bring light sentences, and a jail term does not dissuade a substantial number of offenders from repeating their crimes (Furby, Weinrott, & Blackshaw, 1989). The upshot, we reiterate, is that the large majority of rapists are not in prison but out among us.

Treatment and Recidivism of Sex Offenders

Soon after his release from prison, convicted sex offender Earl Shriner forced a seven-year-old boy off his bike in the woods near Tacoma, Washington, then raped and stabbed him before cutting off the boy's penis. Just before his release from prison, Shriner had confided to a cellmate that he still had fantasies of molesting and murdering children (Popkin, 1994). In another case convicted pedophile Jesse Timmendequas has been accused of luring seven-year-old Megan Kanka into his house in Hamilton Township, New Jersey, then sexually assaulting her and strangling her to death with a belt. No one had notified anyone in Megan's neighborhood that a convicted child molester had moved there. As a result of cases such as these, there has been considerable concern among communities that they be notified when "sexual predators" are allowed to move there (Popkin, 1994). There is growing intolerance about sex offenders who repeat their crimes. The case of Willie Horton, who sexually assaulted a woman while out on parole, figured prominently in the defeat of Michael Dukakis in the 1988 presidential election (Dukakis was accused of permitting the parole). But are such stories representative? Are sex offenders typically incurable? Should they receive life sentences on the presumption that they are bound to offend again? Or have they been unfairly singled out due to media sensationalism when they are really responsive to treatment (Berlin & Malin, 1991)? The efficacy of treatment for sex offenders is controversial—as, it seems, are so many issues related to sexual abuse (Furby, Weinrott, & Blackshaw, 1989; Marshall, 1993; Marshall & Pithers, 1994; Quinsey et al., 1993; Rice, Quinsey, & Harris, 1991).

Therapies for sex offenders typically have at least one of the following three goals: to modify patterns of sexual arousal, to modify cognitions and social skills to allow more appropriate sexual interactions with adult partners, or to reduce sexual drive. Attempts to modify sexual arousal patterns usually involve aversion therapy. In aversion therapy a paraphilic stimulus, such as a slide of a nude prepubescent girl for a pedophile, is paired with an aversive event, such as forced inhalation of noxious odors or a shock to the arm. Alternatively, inhalation of the noxious odors or delivery of the shock may be conditional on penile response; if penile erection exceeds some minimum criterion, shock occurs; otherwise, no shock occurs. An alternative to electric aversion therapy is covert sensitization, in which the patient imagines a highly aversive event while viewing a paraphilic stimulus. Another method for reducing deviant arousal is satiation, in which the patient first masturbates to orgasm while fantasizing about sexually appropriate scenes, then continues masturbating after switching to his paraphilic fantasies. The deviant fantasy is continued for an hour each session, the goal being to produce boredom.

Reduction of deviant sexual arousal is probably insufficient. Deviant arousal patterns need to be replaced by arousal to acceptable stimuli (Quinsey & Earls, 1990). Most often investigators have attempted to pair the pleasurable stimuli of orgasm with sexual fantasies involving sex between consenting adults. Patients are asked to masturbate while thinking of deviant fantasies. At the moment of ejaculatory inevitability, the patient switches his fantasy to a more appropriate theme. The moment of switching themes is gradually moved backward in time until, ideally, the patient can rely entirely on appropriate themes. Both therapies intended to reduce inappropriate sexual arousal and those intended to increase nondeviant sexual arousal have been shown to be somewhat effective in the laboratory (Quinsey & Earls, 1990). However, there are at least two concerns about their practical effectiveness. First, some sex offenders can fake phallometric measurements of sexual preference by inhibiting their attention to the deviant stimuli (Quinsey & Earls, 1990). Thus their actual sexual preferences may not change despite apparent progress. Second, the laboratory is an artificial setting, and it is important to demonstrate that therapeutic change generalizes to the patient's outside world, which may be especially problematic if his motivation wanes following treatment.

Cognitive restructuring attempts to eliminate sex offenders' cognitive distortions, because these play a role in sexual abuse (Murphy, 1990). For example, an incest offender who stated "If my ten-year-old daughter had said no I would have stopped," might be challenged about a number of implied distortions. For example, he has implied that a child can consent to have sex with an adult, that if a child does not say no she has consented, and that it is the child's responsibility to stop sexual contact. Another approach is to have offenders who have been sexually abused themselves recount their experience, and then link these experiences with those of the offenders' victims. Social-skills training aims to help sex offenders (especially rapists) learn to process social information from women more effectively (McFall, 1990). For example, some men read positive sexual connotations into women's neutral or negative messages, or believe that women's refusals of sexual advances reflect "playing hard to get." Training typically involves interaction of patients and female partners, who can give the patients feedback on their response to their interaction. Cognitive treatment of sex offenders has shown some promise (Marshall & Barabaree, 1990b), although relevant studies have some important limitations, which we shall consider later. Social-skills training has not yet received solid empirical support (McFall, 1990).

Although some reviews of the treatment literature have reached positive conclusions (e.g., Marshall et al., 1991), some studies have also provided rather disturbing results about the long-term effectiveness of such treatments (Rice et al., 1991; Emmelkamp, 1994). For example, in one important study Quinsey and colleagues (1991) followed 136 child molesters for an average of six years following their release from imprisonment. Nearly half had committed another violent or sexual offense, and this rate of recidivism did not differ among the 50 men who had received aversion therapy and the 86 men who had not. Moreover, the degree of aversion that was conditioned during treatment was not a significant predictor of recidivism. Although some studies have had somewhat more promising results, it is probably most accurate to say that at the present time we simply do not know how likely it is that various treatments will significantly reduce sex offenders' likelihood of recidivism (Quinsey et al., 1993).

The most controversial treatment for sex offenders involves castration, either surgical removal of the testes or the hormonal treatment sometimes called "chemical castration" (Besharov, 1992; Bradford, 1990; Money, 1986, pp 135–45). Chemical castration involves the administration of antiandrogen steroid hormones such as Depo-Provera (technically, medroxyprogesterone acetate or MPA). Both surgical and chemical castration lower the testosterone level, which in turn lowers the sex drive. Although outcome studies of surgical and chemical castration have appeared to be quite promising (Berlin, 1994; Bradford, 1990; Green, 1992), many feel that the treatment is brutal and dehumanizing (Gunn, 1993). Interestingly, most recent cases have involved a request by the sex offender himself to be castrated in exchange for a lighter sentence.

The single most important defect of available studies is the lack of randomly assigned controls who were equally motivated for treatment. Some have argued that denying treatment to sex offenders is unethical (e.g., Marshall et al., 1991). However, this could only be true if the treatment were effective, and it is unclear at this point if it is. Research in this area is further complicated by the fact that the outcome variable in most studies is whether the man is reconvicted for another sex offense during the follow-up period. Because most sex offenses go unpunished (the offender is often never even caught, let alone convicted), this will exaggerate the apparent effectiveness of treatment, and underestimate the dangerousness of sex offenders. Given the social importance of the questions of whether sex offenders can be helped and how likely they are to reoffend, we hope that society will devote the resources necessary to answer them.

It is possible both to acknowledge that sex offenders cause immense human suffering and to feel sympathy for their plight. Many sex offenders have been burdened with a deviant sexual arousal pattern that has caused them great personal and legal trouble. Consider the case of Scott Murphy, a convicted pedophile:

> He lives alone with a friend, works odd hours and doesn't go out of his way to meet neighbors. Ironically, Murphy has never been prouder of his behavior. He admits he'll never be cured and will always be attracted to young boys. But he says he is now making every attempt to steer clear of them: "I went from constantly living my whole life to molest kids to now living my whole life to not molest kids." It's a 24-hour-a-day job. On the highway, Murphy keeps at a distance to guarantee he makes no eye contact with the young passengers in school buses. When the Sunday paper arrives at home, he immediately throws out the coupon section because the glossy ads often depict attractive boy models. He

> refuses to leave the office when kids might be walking to or from school and got rid of his television so the sit-com images of young boys wouldn't distract him. (Popkin, 1994, p. 67)

Society cannot allow Murphy to act on his sexual preference; nor can his past crimes be forgotten. Nevertheless, in deciding how to treat people like Scott Murphy, it is humane to remember that many of them have a tormented inner life.

SEXUAL DYSFUNCTIONS

The term **sexual dysfunction** refers to impairment either in the desire for sexual gratification or in the ability to achieve it. With some exceptions, such impairments occur in the absence of anatomical or physiological pathology and are based on dysfunctional psychosexual adjustment and learning. They vary markedly in degree, and regardless of which partner is alleged to be dysfunctional, the enjoyment of sex by both parties in a relationship is typically adversely affected.

Like sexuality in general, sexual dysfunctions were until recently either ignored entirely by polite society or—if discussed at all—were the subject of medical treatises written by authors who were usually as ill-informed and prejudiced as their readers. Then, with the popularization of Freudian thought, an era gradually developed in which all manner of difficulties in sexual functioning (and some that were not even "difficulties" in the normally accepted sense) were said to be the result of unconscious conflicts of childhood origin requiring years of psychoanalytic treatment to resolve. We now know, thanks again to precedent-breaking and courageous research—much of it by Masters and Johnson (1966, 1970, 1975)—that the common sexual dysfunctions are both more numerous and less complex and mysterious than was once believed. They occur in both heterosexual and homosexual couples (McWhirter & Mattison, 1978).

Today we understand that there are four relatively distinct phases of the human sexual response. Disorders can occur in any of the first three phases (DSM-IV, 1994). The first phase is the **desire phase,** which consists of fantasies about sexual activity or a sense of desire to have sexual activity. The second phase is the **excitement phase,** during which there is generally

HIGHLIGHT | 11.4

Sexual Dysfunctions

Dysfunctions	Characteristics
Dysfunctions of Sexual Desire	
Hypoactive sexual desire disorder	Little or no sexual drive or interest
Sexual aversion disorder	Total lack of interest in sex and avoidance of sexual contact
Dysfunctions of Sexual Arousal	
Male erectile disorder	An inability to achieve or maintain an erection (formerly known as impotence)
Female sexual arousal disorder	Nonresponsiveness to erotic stimulation both physically and emotionally (formerly known as frigidity)
Dysfunctions of Orgasm	
Premature ejaculation	An unsatisfactorily brief period between the beginning of sexual stimulation and the occurrence of ejaculation
Male orgasmic disorder	An inability to ejaculate during intercourse (also known as retarded ejaculation)
Female orgasmic disorder	A difficulty in achieving orgasm, either manually or during sexual intercourse
Sexual Pain Disorders	
Vaginismus	An involuntary muscle spasm at the entrance to the vagina that prevents penetration and sexual intercourse
Dyspareunia	Painful coitus—may have either an organic or psychological basis

both a subjective sense of sexual pleasure and physiological changes that accompany this subjective pleasure, including penile erection in the male and vaginal lubrication and enlargement in the female. The third phase is **orgasm,** during which there is a release of sexual tension and a peaking of sexual pleasure. The final phase is **resolution,** during which the person has a sense of relaxation and well-being. We will first describe the most common dysfunctions that accompany the first three phases and then discuss issues of causation and treatment. HIGHLIGHT 11.4 summarizes the dysfunctions we will be covering here.

Dysfunctions of Sexual Desire

Sexual Desire Disorders Researchers have delineated two types of sexual desire disorders. The first is **hypoactive sexual desire disorder.** It is a dysfunction in which either a man or a woman shows little or no sexual drive or interest. It is assumed in most cases that the biological basis of the sex drive remains unimpaired (see Schreiner-Engel et al., 1989), but that for some reason sexual motivation is blocked. These people usually come to the attention of clinicians only at the request of their partners, who typically complain of insufficient sexual interaction. This fact exposes one problem with the diagnosis, because it is known that preferences for frequency of sexual contact vary widely among otherwise normal individuals. Who is to decide what is "not enough"? DSM-IV explicitly indicates that this judgment is left to the clinician, taking into account the person's age and the context of his or her life. Nevertheless, there do appear to be some people who are almost totally lacking in sexual desire. In extreme cases, sex actually becomes psychologically aversive, and warrants a diagnosis of **sexual aversion disorder,** the second type of sexual desire disorder.

With this disorder the person shows extreme aversion to, and avoidance of, all genital sexual contact with a partner. Formerly considered rare and largely limited to women, sexual desire disorder diagnoses have in recent years become fairly common and are applied perhaps equally often to men (Malatesta & Adams, 1993; Rosen & Leiblum, 1989). Doubtless this change is due at least in part to changing role expectations, of which more will be said later.

Dysfunctions of Sexual Arousal

Male Erectile Disorder Inability to achieve or maintain an erection sufficient for successful sexual intercourse was formerly called *impotence*. It is now known as **male erectile disorder** or *erectile insufficiency*. In lifelong erectile disorder a man has never been able to sustain an erection long enough to accomplish a satisfactory duration of penetration. In acquired or situational erectile disorder, a man has had at least one successful experience of coitus but is presently unable to produce or maintain the required level of penile rigidity. Lifelong insufficiency is a relatively rare disorder, but it has been estimated that half or more of the male population has had some experiences of erectile insufficiency on at least a temporary basis.

Prolonged or permanent erectile disorder before the age of 60 is relatively rare and is often due to psychological factors, notably anxiety-induced interference by distracting, dysfunctional thoughts concerning "performance" (Barlow, 1986, 1988). According to the findings of Kinsey and his associates, only about one-fourth of men had serious erectile insufficiency by the age of 70, but a more recent study found that more than half of married men over 70 had some erectile difficulties (Diokno, Brown, & Herzog, 1990). Studies have indicated that men and women in their 80s and 90s are often quite capable of enjoying intercourse (Burros, 1974; Kaplan, 1975; Malatesta & Adams, 1993; Masters et al., 1992). For example, in one study of 202 healthy men and women between ages 80 and 102, it was found that nearly two-thirds of the men and one-third of the women were still having sexual intercourse, although this was not generally their most common form of sexual activity (Bretschneider & McCoy, 1988). It appears that in some cases men who experience difficulties in their later years may simply be complying with the societal expectation of declining performance (Masters et al., 1992; Tollison & Adams, 1979). On the other hand, the vascular, neurological, and hormonal factors that support adequate erectile functioning do undergo impair-

ment with advancing age in many men (Mohr & Beutler, 1990). The lessened reliability of the erectile response may lead to the type of dysfunctional cognitions already noted, thus exacerbating the difficulty. Erectile problems are notoriously self-perpetuating, with every "failure" psychologically enhancing the likelihood of further ones.

We have probably underestimated in recent years the proportion of erectile problems having some organic involvement, formerly considered to be as low as 15 percent (Kaplan, 1975). More recent data suggest that the figure may actually be close to 50 percent (Mohr & Beutler, 1990; Tiefer & Melman, 1989), which suggests that a thorough medical evaluation is important (Beck, 1992). A diagnosis of psychogenic causation does not by itself rule out an element of physiologic malfunction, or vice versa. Many organic conditions may be involved in erectile problems, including certain types of vascular disease, diabetes, neurological disorders, kidney failure, hormonal irregularities, and excess blood levels of certain drugs, including alcohol (Tiefer & Melman, 1989; Wagner & Green, 1981).

Distinguishing between psychogenic and organically caused erectile disorder for diagnostic purposes is at best a complicated process. The normal man has several erections per night, associated with periods of REM (rapid eye movement) sleep. Some researchers have suggested that organically based erectile disorder can be distinguished from psychogenically based erectile disorder by noting an absence of these nocturnal erections. However, it now appears that many other factors must also be evaluated in order to establish a proper diagnosis (Malatesta & Adams, 1993), because the nocturnal penile erection procedure has been found, by itself, to produce unreliable results (Mohr & Beutler, 1990; Wagner, 1981). An important implication of these assessment difficulties is that we have probably again made the common error of assuming a mutually exclusive dichotomy (organic versus psychogenic), where such pure cases may in fact be the exception rather than the rule (Tiefer & Melman, 1989).

Female Sexual Arousal Disorder **Female sexual arousal disorder** consists of an absence of sexual arousal feelings and an unresponsiveness to most or all forms of erotic stimulation. Formerly and somewhat pejoratively referred to as *frigidity*, it is in many ways the female counterpart of erectile disorder. Its chief physical manifestation is a failure to produce the characteristic swelling and lubrication of the vulva and vaginal tissues during sexual stimulation, a condition that may make intercourse quite uncomfortable. To be diagnosed the disturbance must cause the woman marked distress or interpersonal difficulty.

Fortunately, true primary nonresponsiveness to erotic stimuli (where a woman has never experienced arousal to any form of stimulation) is rare. Most often, then, we are dealing here with a dysfunction that, although it may be stubbornly entrenched, is at least to some minimal extent situational. The possible reasons for this inhibition range from early sexual traumatization to excessive and distorted socialization about the evils of sex to dislike of, or disgust with, a current partner's sexuality.

Orgasmic Disorders

Premature Ejaculation Premature ejaculation refers to persistent and recurrent onset of orgasm and ejaculation with minimal sexual stimulation. It may occur before, on, or shortly after penetration and before the man wants it to. The consequences include failure of the partner to achieve satisfaction and, often, acute embarrassment for the prematurely ejaculating man, with disruptive anxiety about recurrence on future occasions. It is also thought to sometimes be a precursor to erectile disorder. An exact definition of prematurity is necessarily somewhat arbitrary. LoPiccolo (1978) suggested that an inability to tolerate as much as 4 minutes of stimulation without ejaculation is a reasonable indicator that a man may be in need of sex therapy. Such guidelines are not included in DSM-IV and have generally been discarded because they are subject to numerous qualifications (Masters et al., 1992). For example, the age of a client must be considered—the alleged "quick trigger" of the younger man being more than a mere myth (McCarthy, 1989). Approximately half of young men complain of early ejaculation (Frank, Anderson, & Rubenstein, 1978). Not surprisingly, premature ejaculation is most likely when previous abstinence has been lengthy (Malatesta & Adams, 1993; Spiess, Geer, & O'Donohue, 1984). DSM-IV acknowledges these many factors that may affect time to ejaculation by noting that the diagnosis is only made if ejaculation occurs before, on, or shortly after penetration and before the man wants it to.

In sexually normal men the ejaculatory reflex is to a considerable extent under voluntary control. They monitor their sensations during sexual stimulation and are somehow able, perhaps by judicious use of distraction, to forestall the point of ejaculatory inevitability until they decide to "let go" (Kaplan, 1987). Premature ejaculators are for some reason unable to use this technique effectively, probably in many cases because their anxiety prevents adequate monitoring of their current stage in the sexual response buildup leading to orgasm. As in the case of erectile disorder, failures in control lead to increased anxiety during subsequent sexual encounters, and thus increased likelihood of failures. Although premature ejaculation is not the problem seen most frequently in clinical settings, Masters and Johnson estimate that it is the most common one in the male population. Indeed they estimate that 15–20 percent of American men have at least a moderate degree of difficulty in controlling rapid ejaculation (Masters et al., 1992).

Male Orgasmic Disorder It is interesting that, although problems of female orgasmic dysfunction have received wide attention in the popular press, one rarely hears public mention of the corresponding problem in men. It is not a topic high on the locker room agenda, and indeed sexually active women seem to have a more realistic appreciation of its prevalence than do most men. As a result, many men suffering from **male orgasmic disorder** (formerly called *inhibited male orgasm*)—that is, retarded ejaculation or the inability to ejaculate during intercourse—are condemned to worry needlessly about their supposedly unique defect, a type of worry likely to worsen the problem. In fact, relatively few cases of inhibited male orgasm are seen by sex therapists, but our own clinical experience suggests that the problem is much more widespread than this observation would seem to indicate, a conclusion shared by Apfelbaum (1989) and by Kaplan (1974). It appears that many men are too embarrassed by the problem even to contemplate therapy for it.

Men who are completely unable to ejaculate are rare. About 85 percent of men who have difficulty ejaculating during intercourse can nevertheless achieve orgasm by other means of stimulation, notably through solitary masturbation (Masters et al., 1992). In milder cases a man can ejaculate in the presence of a partner, but only by means of manual or oral stimulation (Kaplan, 1987). On rare occasions retarded ejaculation may be partner-specific; that is, it occurs only with a particular partner but not with others (Apfelbaum, 1989). The problem is therefore largely one of psychological inhibition or overcontrol, and it thus seems that substantial "symbolic" and interpersonal elements may exist in this dysfunction.

Female Orgasmic Disorder Many women who are readily sexually excitable and who otherwise enjoy sexual activity nevertheless experience **female orgas-**

mic disorder (formerly *inhibited female orgasm*)—persistent or recurrent delay in or absence of orgasm following a normal sexual excitement phase. Of these women, many do not routinely experience orgasm during sexual intercourse without direct supplemental stimulation of the clitoris; indeed this pattern is so common that it is not generally considered dysfunctional. A small percentage of women are able to achieve orgasm only through direct mechanical stimulation of the clitoris, as in vigorous digital manipulation, oral stimulation, or the use of an electric vibrator. Even fewer are unable to have the experience under any known conditions of stimulation; this condition is called lifelong orgasmic dysfunction, analogous to lifelong erectile insufficiency in males.

The diagnosis of orgasmic dysfunction is complicated by the fact that the subjective quality of orgasm varies widely among women, within the same woman from time to time, and depending on mode of stimulation. Thus precise evaluations of occurrence and quality are difficult (Malatesta & Adams, 1993; Singer & Singer, 1978). The criteria to be applied are also unclear in the vast middle range of orgasmic responsiveness. Most clinicians agree that a woman with lifelong orgasmic disorder needs treatment if she is to become orgasmic, and that a woman at the other extreme who routinely climaxes with relatively brief intercourse, or perhaps even with only breast stimulation or fantasy, does not. Differences of opinion become notable, however, as we move away from these extremes into the range in which most women's experiences actually fall (Kaplan, 1987; Masters et al., 1992). Our own view is that this question is best left to a woman herself to answer; if she is dissatisfied about her responsiveness, and if there is a reasonable likelihood that treatment will help, then she should seek it.

Dysfunctions Involving Sexual Pain

Vaginismus An involuntary spasm of the muscles at the entrance to the vagina (not due to a physical disorder) that prevents penetration and sexual intercourse is called **vaginismus.** Evidently these muscles are readily conditionable to respond with intense contraction to stimuli associated with impending penetration. In some cases, women who suffer from vaginismus also have sexual arousal disorder, possibly as a result of conditioned fears associated with earlier traumatic sexual experiences. In most cases, however, they show normal sexual arousal, but are still afflicted with this disorder (Masters et al., 1992). It is not always possible to identify the "un-

conditioned stimuli" presumed to have been involved in the acquisition of vaginismus (Kaplan, 1987), probably because the disorder is sometimes "overdetermined" in the sense of having multiple causal links (Leiblum, Pervin, & Campbell, 1989). This form of sexual dysfunction is relatively rare, but, when it occurs, it is likely to be extremely distressing for both an affected woman and her partner (Leiblum et al., 1989; Tollison & Adams, 1979).

Dyspareunia Painful coitus, or **dyspareunia,** can occur in men but is far more common in women (Lazarus, 1989). This is the form of sexual dysfunction most likely to have an organic basis—for example, in association with infections or structural pathology of the sex organs. It often has a psychological basis, however, as in the case of a woman who has an aversion to sexual intercourse and experiences her displeasure as intense physical discomfort; in such cases the designation "functional" is used. Understandably, dyspareunia is often associated with vaginismus. This form of sexual dysfunction is rare.

Causal Factors in Sexual Dysfunctions

Both sexual desire and genital functioning may be affected by a wide range of organic conditions, including injuries to the genitals, disease, fatigue, excessive alcohol consumption, and abuse of certain drugs, such as tranquilizers. Most cases of sexual dysfunction, however, are more likely due to psychosocial rather than physical causes. Although specific causal factors may vary considerably from one type of sexual dysfunction to another, the following psychosocial factors are commonly found.

Dysfunctional Learning In some nonindustrialized societies, older members of a group instruct younger members in sexual techniques before marriage. In our society, although we recognize that sexual behavior is (with certain proscriptions) an important aspect of life, the learning of sexual techniques and attitudes is too often left to chance. The result is that many young people start out with faulty expectations and a lack of needed information or harmful misinformation that can impair their sexual adequacy and enjoyment. In fact, Kaplan (1974) concluded that couples with sexual problems are typically practicing insensitive and ineffective sexual techniques. In the 1970s when sex therapy was relatively new, this conclusion was readily endorsed by most investigators in the field (Leiblum & Rosen, 1989a; LoPiccolo & LoPiccolo, 1978; Tollison &

In our society, the learning of sexual techniques and attitudes is too often left to chance, which may include such sources as X-rated films. As a result, a great number of people acquire faulty information and expectations that can impair their sexual enjoyment and adequacy.

Adams, 1979). Today, however, the story is somewhat more complicated because many people with these disorders are more sophisticated about sexuality than was true 20–30 years ago, in part because of things they have read in the popular press and in self-help books.

However, even today in our society, many people have been subjected to early training that depicts sexual relations as lustful, dirty, and evil (Masters et al., 1992). This early learning, which often takes place within the context of a strict religious upbringing, may have a particular impact on women, who are repeatedly reminded of the risk of pregnancy. The attitudes and inhibitions thus established can lead to a great deal of anxiety, conflict, and guilt about sexual relations, whether in or out of marriage. Such early conditioning may also have taken the form of indoctrination in the idea that a woman has a primary responsibility to satisfy a man sexually—and therefore to suppress her own needs and feelings. Masters and Johnson (1970) considered such conditioning to be the primary cause of orgasmic dysfunction in females (Masters et al., 1992). In vaginismus, a somewhat different conditioning patterning has occurred, leading a woman to associate vaginal penetration with pain—either physical, psychological, or both. This conditioned defensive reflex comes into operation when penetration is attempted by a sexual partner (Kaplan, 1975; Leiblum et al., 1989).

Although men may also be subjected to early training emphasizing the evils of sex, such training apparently is in general a far less important factor for them. However, another type of early conditioning may be a key factor in premature ejaculation: Men typically have their first and often extensive sexual

experiences in solitary masturbation, and such masturbatory sessions are likely to be highly efficient in the achievement of orgasm and ejaculation. A young man may thus train his sexual response cycle in this mode of rapid, direct, and altogether "impersonal" discharge, thereby paving the way for premature ejaculation in his later sexual encounters (McCarthy, 1989). In addition, having intercourse with prostitutes, who often encourage early ejaculation, or having intercourse in situations where there is a fear of detection (such as in a car) may also condition a pattern of early ejaculation (Malatesta & Adams, 1993).

Researchers have also observed the seemingly opposite pattern, in which premature ejaculators report little or no youthful masturbation because of moral or religious inhibition. Such young men are also unlikely to have alternative outlets other than involuntary nocturnal emissions, and may thus experience lengthy periods of ejaculatory inactivity. Because it is known that a lengthy interval following the last ejaculation increases the likelihood of a rapid emission, these men are at high risk for premature ejaculation when they do attempt sex. In other instances, difficulties in sexual functioning have led to conditioned anxieties that in turn have impaired later performances. We consider this point in the section that follows.

Feelings of Fear, Anxiety, and Inadequacy In a study of 49 adult men with erectile disorders, Cooper (1969) found anxiety to be a contributing factor in 94 percent of the cases and the primary problem for those whose erectile problems had started early in adult life. Many subsequent investigators have confirmed this essential observation. Similarly, Kaplan (1974) concluded from her studies that "a man who suffers from impotence is often almost unbearably anxious, frustrated, and humiliated by his inability to produce or maintain an erection" (p. 80). (As discussed later, for men with late-onset erectile disorder, medical problems also play an important role [Mohr & Beutler, 1990]). Men who suffer from premature ejaculation may also experience acute feelings of inadequacy—and often feelings of guilt as well—stemming from their lack of control and inability to satisfy their sexual partners via intercourse.

Women may also feel fearful and inadequate in sexual relations. A woman may be uncertain whether her partner finds her sexually attractive, and this may lead to anxiety and tension that interfere with her sexual enjoyment. Or she may feel inadequate because she is unable to have an orgasm or does so infrequently. Sometimes a nonorgasmic

Masters and Johnson, pioneers in the treatment of sexual dysfunction, emphasize the importance of removing crippling fears, misconceptions, and inhibitions about sex and fostering attitudes toward and participation in sexual behavior as a pleasurable, natural, and meaningful experience.

woman will pretend to have orgasms to make her sexual partner feel fully adequate. The longer a woman maintains such a pretense, however, the more likely she is to become confused and frustrated; in addition, she is likely to resent her partner for being insensitive to her real feelings and needs. This in turn only adds to her sexual difficulties.

From a more general viewpoint, Masters and Johnson (1975; Masters et al., 1992) concluded that most sexual dysfunctions are due to crippling fears, attitudes, and inhibitions concerning sexual behavior, often based on dysfunctional early learning and then exacerbated by later aversive experiences. In another review of the accumulated evidence, however, Beck and Barlow (1984) played down the role of anxiety per se—which under some circumstances can actually enhance sexual performance in normally functioning men and women (Barlow, Sakheim, & Beck, 1983; Hoon, Wincze, & Hoon, 1977; Palace & Gorzalka, 1990). For example, when Barlow and colleagues (1983) told sexually functional male subjects in a laboratory experiment that there was a 60 percent chance of receiving electric shock while watching an erotic film unless they had an average-sized erection, these men actually showed *more* sexual arousal to the film than did men who were not threatened with shock. Instead of anxiety per se, Beck and Barlow emphasized that it is the cognitive distractions frequently associated with anxiety in dysfunctional people that seem to interfere with their sexual arousal. For example, Abrahamson and colleagues (1985) found that nondysfunctional men who were distracted by material they were listening to on earphones while watching an

erotic film showed *less* sexual arousal than did men who were not distracted. The distraction in this study had nothing to do with anxiety but it nonetheless interfered with sexual arousal in normal men. Barlow and colleagues believe that sexually dysfunctional men and women get distracted by negative thoughts about their performance during a sexual encounter (such as "I'll never get aroused" or "She will think I'm inadequate"). It seems to be this preoccupation with negative thoughts, rather than anxiety per se, that is responsible for inhibiting sexual arousal. Thus, cognitive factors such as negative thoughts about performance have powerful effects on the physiology of sexual arousal. Another study consistent with this theory (Abrahamson, Barlow, & Abrahamson, 1989) confirmed that dysfunctional men with erectile problems differ from functional men in being more easily distracted by cues about their performance, resulting in smaller erections during erotic stimulation. Such self-defeating thoughts not only decrease his pleasure, but also can increase his anxiety if the erection does not happen (Malatesta & Adams, 1993), and this in turn can fuel further negative self-defeating thoughts.

Interpersonal Problems Interpersonal problems may cause a number of sexual dysfunctions (Malatesta & Adams, 1993; Masters et al., 1992). Lack of emotional closeness and poor communication can lead to erectile or orgasmic problems. An individual may be in love with someone else, may find his or her sexual partner physically or psychologically repulsive, or may have hostile feelings from prior misunderstandings, quarrels, and conflicts. A one-sided interpersonal relationship—in which one partner does most of the giving and the other most of the receiving—can lead to feelings of insecurity and resentment with resulting impairment in sexual performance (Friedman, 1974; Leiblum & Rosen, 1989a; Lobitz & Lobitz, 1978; Simon, 1975).

For a woman, lack of emotional closeness often appears to result from intercourse with a partner who is a sexually selfish and insensitive—rough, unduly hasty, and concerned only with self-gratification. As Kaplan (1974) pointed out, "Some persons have as much difficulty giving pleasure as others do in receiving it. These individuals don't provide their partners with enough sexual stimulation because they lack either the knowledge and sensitivity to know what to do, or they are anxious about doing it" (p. 78). In other instances, an individual may be hostile toward and not want to please his or her sexual partner. This situation seems to occur rather frequently in unhappy marital or other intimate relationships. In such relationships, channels of communication have largely broken down and sexual relations continue as a sort of habit or duty or simply to gratify one's own sexual needs.

Changing Male-Female Roles and Heterosexual Relationships An increase in erectile problems was reported during the 1970s, and a number of investigators hypothesized that this was related to two phenomena occurring during that period: (a) the increasing changes being achieved by the women's movement in our society, and (b) the growing awareness of female sexuality (Burros, 1974; Heiman & Grafton-Becker, 1989; Leiblum & Rosen, 1989b). These trends have led women to want and expect more from their lives, including their sexual relationships. Women no longer accept the older concept of being the passive partner in sex, and many are taking a more assertive and active role in sexual relations. This new role appears to threaten the image some men have of themselves as the supposedly "dominant" partner who takes the initiative in sexual relations (Steinmann & Fox, 1974). Some men appear to regard sexually assertive women who play an active role in sex as "castrating females" (Kaplan, 1974). In addition, there was speculation that women's greater assertiveness and higher expectations make many men feel that they are under pressure to perform. In spite of all this speculation about the effects of changes in women's roles on male sexual dysfunction, it should be noted that there is no good research supporting these hypotheses.

Changing male-female roles in heterosexual relationships also place greater demands on women. The expectation of taking an active rather than a passive role may cause a woman to make unrealistic demands on her own sexual responsiveness. Such demands may lead to some degree of unfulfilled desires, confusion, and self-devaluation, which in turn impair actual sexual performance. This situation seems especially true when a woman assumes a "spectator role" and almost literally monitors her own sexual performance, thus depriving it of spontaneity and naturalness.

Finally, our enhanced awareness of sexually transmitted diseases—fueled by the AIDS epidemic—has added an increment of anxiety to many sexual encounters both casual and otherwise (Katz, Frazer, & Wilson, 1993; Leiblum & Rosen, 1989b). The relatively carefree sexuality of the 1960s and 1970s has increasingly given way to concerns about "safe sex" with partners whose sexual (and drug-use) histories place them outside of the known high-risk groups. Several recent surveys in the United States and several European countries suggest that monogamy is the norm for most. For example, each found that between two-thirds and three-quarters of men reported having no more than one sexual partner in the past year, and only 3 percent of men reported five or more partners in the past year (9 percent of never married men had five or more partners in the past year) (Michael et al., 1994). In addition, the condom, once widely rejected as inhibiting spontaneity (or the appearance of it) and decreasing pleasure, is now heralded as essential equipment for many prudent adolescents and young adults—men and women—who are not in committed monogamous relationships. One study of college-age women reported that the percentage of women reporting that their partners used condoms during sex increased from 12 percent in 1975 to 41 percent in 1989 (Debuono et al., 1990). This was in spite of the fact that over the same time period the average number of sex partners for these college-age women did not change. In short, we are clearly in the midst of a new sexual revolution, one involving life and death decisions. It is still too early to tell what effect these dramatic changes will have on the incidence and prevalence of sexual dysfunctions. Conceivably, the added anxiety and suspicion created by the AIDS epidemic will be counterbalanced by the positive effects that may come with expectations of more enduring and committed relationships.

Treatments and Outcomes

The treatment of sexual dysfunctions, too, has undergone nothing less than a revolution in the past 25 years. Once regarded as difficult and intractable therapeutic challenges, most sexual dysfunctions are now readily treated. Modern techniques include direct methods of attack on the dysfunctions themselves, usually with high levels of gentle and affectionate partner participation. For example, a couple may be given instruction and guided practice in overcoming, by vigorous stimulation, orgasmic inhibition in one of the partners; or vaginismus may be treated with intravaginal insertion, by the partner, of cylindrical objects of gradually increasing circumference until the excessive vaginal contractions cease. As a result of these newer approaches, success rates approaching 90 percent or more for some dysfunctions have become quite routine (Kaplan, 1987; Leiblum & Rosen, 1989a; LoPiccolo & Stock, 1986; Masters et al., 1992; Tollison & Adams, 1979; Wincze & Carey, 1991; Zilbergeld & Kilmann, 1984).

The turning point in sex therapy is uniformly considered to be the publication in 1970 of Masters and Johnson's *Human Sexual Inadequacy,* the product of an 11-year search to develop truly effective

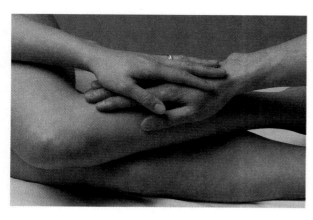

Sensate focus exercises are commonly used in the treatment of several different types of sexual dysfunction. In the first stage of such exercises, couples are instructed to touch any part of their partner's body except for the genital or breast areas. The goal at this stage is not to be sexual but rather to become aware of a wide range of touch sensations, both while touching and while being touched. At a later stage these exercises are expanded to include touching breasts and genitals, although sexual intercourse is still prohibited.

treatment procedures for the common dysfunctions, both male and female. The success rates claimed by this team of dedicated clinical researchers astonished the professional community and rapidly led to the widespread adoption of their general approach, which combined elements of traditional therapy and behavior therapy in a framework emphasizing, as already noted, direct intervention aimed at the dysfunctions themselves.

Although the early confidence inspired by Masters and Johnson's reported results has waned somewhat (Beck, 1992; Leiblum & Pervin, 1980; Leiblum & Rosen, 1989b; LoPiccolo & Stock, 1986; Vandereycken, 1982; Wincze & Carey, 1991; Zilbergeld & Evans, 1980), their work has unquestionably encouraged a host of new therapeutic techniques. Despite differences in emphasis and methods, there seems to be general agreement on the importance of removing crippling misconceptions, inhibitions, and fears, and on fostering attitudes toward sexual behavior as a pleasurable, natural, and meaningful experience.

Because of the manner in which sexual dysfunctions are presented and described by those suffering from them, it is easy to lose sight of a crucial issue emphasized by Masters and Johnson and by virtually all those who have followed in their footsteps: Most sexual dysfunctions are not normally disorders of individuals, but rather of relationships between individuals. Thus the new treatments for sexual dysfunc-

tions typically involve both partners. Joseph LoPiccolo (1978) put it this way:

> It must be stressed that all sexual dysfunctions are shared disorders; that is, the husband of an inorgasmic woman is partially responsible for creating or maintaining her dysfunction, and he is also a patient in need of help. Regardless of the cause of the dysfunction, both partners are responsible for future change and the solution of their problems. (p. 3)

With competent treatment, success rates vary between approximately 30 and 100 percent, depending in part on the individual or couple and on the nature of the problem. For example, Masters and Johnson (1970) and Kaplan (1975) reported success rates approaching 100 percent for the treatment of premature ejaculation and vaginismus, but considerably lower rates for male erectile and female orgasmic dysfunctions. More recent reviews (Andersen, 1983; Leiblum & Rosen, 1989a; LoPiccolo & Stock, 1986; Zilbergeld & Kilmann, 1984) essentially confirm these relative outcome expectancies, with one recent study suggesting that approximately 70 percent of men with erectile disorder show significant improvement with treatment (Hawton, Catalan, & Fagg, 1992). Moreover, there is an important distinction between lifelong and situational female orgasmic dysfunction. Treatment of the former, typically beginning with instruction and guided practice in masturbating to orgasm, has a high likelihood of success, while "situational" anorgasmia (where a woman may experience orgasm in some situations, with certain kinds of stimulation, or with certain partners, but not under the precise conditions she desires) often proves more difficult to treat, perhaps in part because it is often associated with relationship difficulties that may also be difficult to treat (Beck, 1992).

The somewhat more treatment-resistant erectile disorders probably reflect underlying contributory medical problems, the prevalence of which was seriously underestimated until recently. Sex therapy can be useful in many of these cases because psychological factors often interact with physiological factors in producing the dysfunction (Hawton et al., 1992). Nevertheless, as noted by Mohr and Beutler (1990), the only available recourse for these disorders may be the use of some sort of mechanical aid. Inflatable penile prostheses often prove preferable to implanted prostheses that maintain a constant rigidity, despite the potential disruption the need to inflate them may entail. The combination of a vacuum device (which draws blood into the spongy tissue of the penis) and constricting rubber or plastic ring at the base of the penis (which keeps it there under pressure) also shows considerable promise for some men whose erectile problems prove resistant to psychological or medical treatments.

UNRESOLVED ISSUES

on Long-Term Consequences of Childhood Sexual Abuse

Many studies during the past decade have linked recollections of childhood sexual abuse with adult psychopathology. Typically, the studies have compared the prevalence of abuse memories in patients (usually women) with and without a certain diagnosis. For example, a study might compare the prevalence of memories of childhood sexual abuse in women with borderline personality disorder to that in women with other personality disorders. The best-established associations between childhood sexual abuse and adult disorders are with borderline personality disorder (Chapter 9) and dissociative identity disorder (Chapter 7). Relevant studies are often interpreted as showing that childhood sexual abuse is a causal factor in the disorders (Anderson et al., 1993; Paris, Zweig-Frank, & Guzder, 1994; Sanders & Giolas, 1991; Waller, 1994; Glod, 1993; Whitman & Munkel, 1991); however, the available evidence is insufficient to establish a causal link. This is because establishing causation on the basis of retrospective studies is fraught with methodological perils, and furthermore, a number of other plausible interpretations of the findings have not been excluded.

First, consider the association between childhood sexual abuse and borderline personality disorder (discussed in Chapter 9). Although early sexual abuse may well cause the personality disorder, a number of other explanations of the association are also conceivable. For example, it may be family pathology generally, and not sexual abuse per se, that causes borderline personality disorder. In this case sexual abuse would merely be a noncausal correlate of the true causal factors, which might include, for example, hostility between parents or the lack of appropriate expressions of parental love.

Alternatively, relatives of individuals with borderline personality disorder may be genetically or environmentally predisposed to commit impulsive acts such as sexual abuse. There is evidence that borderline personality traits run in families, though it is currently unclear if this is due to genetic factors (Nigg & Goldsmith, 1994). Regardless, this suggests that the association between childhood sexual abuse and adult borderline personality disorder could reflect the familiality of borderline personality traits rather than a causal association.

Another possibility is that this association is with *reports* of childhood sexual abuse rather than its actual occurrence. Persons with borderline personality disorder are known to be highly manipulative. If they believe they could receive extra sympathy by claiming abuse, they may be inclined to do so whether or not it actually occurred. Finally, borderline personality disorder is often characterized by sexual impulsivity. It is conceivable that even during childhood, individuals who will later be diagnosed with borderline personality disorder behaved in ways that made them more vulnerable to sexual advances of exploitative adults.

The association between childhood sexual abuse and dissociative identity disorder (discussed in Chapter 7) raises an additional alternative hypothesis about causation. This is the possibility that both dissociative identity disorder and (false) memories of childhood sexual abuse can be *iatrogenic* (literally, doctor-produced) phenomena, unintentional by-products of therapy (McHugh, 1993; Spanos, 1994). Highly hypnotizable people are especially likely to produce, under suggestion, a number of responses that resemble symptoms of dissociative identity disorder, including amnesia and the enactment of multiple selves (Spanos, 1994). Indeed, Spanos (1994) has argued that both dissociative identity disorder and hypnotic responding are intentional behaviors aimed at meeting the expectations of experimenters, therapists, or hypnotists. Highly suggestible and hypnotizable people may also be especially likely to produce memories of childhood sexual abuse for therapists who suggest to patients that such abuse is a likely cause of dissociative identity disorder or other problems (McHugh, 1993; Spanos, 1994). The previously mentioned case of Paul Ingram, who came to believe in his own guilt in a number of fantastically lurid sex crimes despite evidence that they never occurred, supports this possibility. Thus, the combination of suggestible patients and overly zealous therapists who "find what they are looking for" may account for the association between memories of sexual abuse and dissociative identity disorder.

We are not asserting that any of these alternatives is more likely than the possibility that sexual abuse causes borderline personality disorder or dissociative identity disorder. Moreover, we do not wish to minimize the pain that true victims of childhood sexual abuse often feel. However, scientific hypotheses succeed by the elimination of plausible rivals. If we wish to understand the consequences of childhood sexual abuse, we shall have to ask, and answer, methodologically and emotionally challenging questions.

Several lines of research may be helpful. For example, prospective studies of sexually abused children could eliminate the possibility that either intentional or unconscious retrospective distortion produced the associations. Similarly, studies following young children could conceivably discern whether certain behavioral tendencies related to adult diagnoses sometimes preceded sexual abuse. Studies of borderline personality disorder patients who were adopted could falsify a genetic hypothesis. If sexual abuse was found to be as common among such patients as among those reared with their biological relatives, this would show that the association was not due to genes causing both borderline personality disorder and sexual abuse. It would also be desirable for theorists to specify more precisely the hypothesized causal mechanisms linking childhood sexual abuse to specific disorders. Why, for instance, should borderline personality disorder be an especially common psychopathological outcome of childhood sexual abuse? If theories become more explicit, they will be easier to test.

Researchers of other disorders have faced similar challenges. For example, depression researchers have had to consider several alternative explanations for the association between depression and memories of recent stress, and they have found that the association is not entirely a causal one (Monroe & Simons, 1991). Research on childhood sexual abuse is still in its infancy, and so it is not surprising that available studies are not yet definitive. Progress will require more sophisticated designs and more attention to alternative hypotheses.

SUMMARY

Defining boundaries between normality and psychopathology in the area of variant sexuality may be more difficult than for any other topic covered in this book. Sociocultural influences on what have been viewed as normal or aberrant sexual practices abound, giving us reason to pause when we reflect on our own views of what is aberrant. Degeneracy theory and abstinence theory were very influential for long periods of time in the United States and many other Western cultures and led to very conservative views on heterosexual sexuality. The hypothesis that masturbation can cause insanity was also in-

fluential for several centuries and appeared in some psychiatry textbooks until the 1940s. In contrast to Western culture, in Melanesia homosexuality is practiced by all adolescent males in the context of male sexual initiation rites. In young adulthood, they make a rather abrupt transition to heterosexuality, in most cases without apparent difficulty. Until rather recently, in many Western cultures homosexuality was viewed as either criminal behavior or as a form of mental illness. However, since 1972 homosexuality is no longer considered by mental health professionals to be abnormal and is considered a normal sexual variant. Currently much research attention is being directed toward understanding the causal factors that determine sexual orientation. The causal factors being explored include a probable genetic component as well as various environmental variables.

Sexual deviations in the form of paraphilias involve persistent patterns of sexual behavior and arousal in which unusual objects or rituals or situations are required for full sexual satisfaction. They almost always occur in males. The paraphilias include: (a) fetishes (in which sexual interest centers on some inanimate object or anatomical part), (b) transvestic fetishism (which involves sexual arousal occurring through cross-dressing behavior), (c) voyeurism (in which sexual pleasure occurs through clandestine peeping), (d) exhibitionism (in which sexual pleasure occurs when the man exposes his genitals to others without their consent), (e) sadism (in which sexual arousal occurs through inflicting cruelty on one's sexual partner), (f) masochism (in which sexual arousal occurs when pain is inflicted on oneself), and (g) pedophilia (in which sexual attraction occurs to prepubescent children). What causes paraphilias is not well understood. One theory is that males are vulnerable to problems in erotic target location. In this view men are not born with an automatic attraction to either women or men but instead must learn which stimuli constitute a female or male sexual partner. Perhaps some men have nervous systems more prone to errors in targeting; this might explain why so many men with paraphilias have more than one.

Gender identity disorders occur in children and adults. Childhood gender identity disorder occurs in children who have cross-gender identification and gender dysphoria. Most boys who have this disorder grow up to have a homosexual sexual orientation; a few become transsexuals. Prospective studies of girls who have this disorder have not yet been reported. Transsexualism is a very rare disorder in which the person believes that he or she is trapped in the body of the wrong sex. It is now recognized that there are two distinct types of transsexuals: homosexual transsexuals (who are attracted to the people of their same biological sex) and nonhomosexual transsexuals (who are attracted to people of the opposite biological sex). The only known effective treatment for transsexuals is a sex change operation. Although its use remains highly controversial, it does appear to have fairly high success rates when the people are carefully diagnosed as being true transsexuals.

There are three overlapping categories of sexual abuse: pedophilia (another form of paraphilia), incest, and rape. All three kinds of sexual abuse occur at alarming rates today, although it is difficult to estimate their true prevalence. There are also many controversies surrounding how perpetrators of any of these categories of sexual abuse are discovered. These include controversies about the accuracy of children's testimony and about the accuracy of recovered memories of sexual abuse that may often occur in psychotherapy. Pedophiles engage in sexual activity with prepubescent children, and quite commonly they are indifferent to the sex of the child. Incest involves sexual molestation of family members; it overlaps with pedophilia when the sexual molestation is of young children. Rape can occur among strangers or among people who know each other, and involves force or threat of force. All sexual abuse can have serious short-term and long-term consequences for its victims. What leads people to engage in sexual abuse is poorly understood at this time. Treatment of sex offenders has not as yet proven highly effective in most cases, although promising research in this area is being conducted.

Sexual dysfunction involves impairment either in the desire for sexual gratification or in the ability to achieve it. There are generally considered to be four phases of the human sexual response: the desire phase, the excitement phase, the orgasm phase, and the resolution phase. Dysfunctions can occur around any of the first three phases. Both men and women can experience hypoactive sexual desire disorder, in which they have little or no interest in sex. In more extreme cases, they may develop sexual aversion disorder, which involves a strong disinclination to sexual activity. Dysfunctions of the arousal phase include male erectile disorder and female arousal disorder. Male erectile disorder can occur for psychological or physiological reasons, or a combination of the two. Dysfunctions of orgasm for men include premature ejaculation and male orgasmic disorder (retarded ejaculation), and for women include female orgasmic disorder. There are also two sexual pain disorders: dyspareunia (painful coitus) which can occur in women and occasionally in men, and vaginismus, which occurs in women. In the past 25 years remarkable progress has been made in treatment of sexual dysfunctions and for some of these dysfunctions the success rates for treatment are quite high.

KEY TERMS

sexual abuse (p. 399)
paraphilias (p. 404)
fetishism (p. 407)
transvestic fetishism (p. 408)
voyeurism (p. 409)
exhibitionism (p. 410)
sadism (p. 411)
masochism (p. 412)
gender identity disorder (p. 414)
cross-gender identification (p. 414)
gender dysphoria (p. 414)
transsexualism (p. 415)
pedophilia (p. 422)
incest (p. 423)
rape (p. 424)
sexual dysfunction (p. 430)
desire phase (p. 430)
excitement phase (p. 430)
orgasm (p. 431)
resolution (p. 431)
hypoactive sexual desire disorder (p. 431)
sexual aversion disorder (p. 431)
male erectile disorder (p. 432)
female sexual arousal disorder (p. 432)
premature ejaculation (p. 433)
male orgasmic disorder (p. 433)
female orgasmic disorder (p. 434)
vaginismus (p. 434)
dyspareunia (p. 434)

THE SCHIZOPHRENIAS AND DELUSIONAL DISORDERS

Heinrich Hermann Mebes, Untitled. Mebes (b.1842) was a watch and clock maker until he developed schizophrenia, after which he was confined to a mental institution near Berlin. He did many detailed watercolors, usually featuring prominent symbolic elements and bits of poetry.

With the schizophrenias, we move into a realm of disorder that represents in many ways the ultimate in psychological breakdown. These disorders include some of the most extreme of human behaviors, the ultimate in **psychosis,** a term referring to pervasive loss of contact with reality. The hallmark of **the schizophrenias** is thus a more or less sharp break with the world in which most less disturbed people live, a world that is rooted in a basic consensus about what is true and real in our shared experience. The typical schizophrenic person is thus someone who has lost or become detached from a set of anchoring points fundamental to adequate integration and communication with the surrounding human environment. To those around the schizophrenic he or she appears incomprehensible, perhaps even frightening.

If we look more closely, trying to identify the component processes underlying this detachment from reality, we observe in schizophrenics many psychological abnormalities. These include peculiarities in action, thinking, perception, feeling, sense of self, and manner of relating to others, with the features displayed varying from one patient to another. As is implied here, the group is a heterogeneous one, and this heterogeneity extends well beyond differences in current behavior. As we shall see, it includes as well marked variations in associated background features, in the course of the disorder in different people, and in the variety of outcomes they experience.

In the face of this heterogeneity, many clinicians and researchers have concluded that "schizophrenia" will probably someday be recognized as consisting of several separate and distinct conditions. We share that expectation, which explains our choice of the plural form in the title of this chapter.

As that title also indicates, we will in addition consider in this chapter the condition the DSM-IV calls *delusional disorder,* whose main features were formerly included under the classic rubric *paranoia,* or *"true" paranoia* (to distinguish it from the paranoid subtype of schizophrenia, described below). Patients with delusional disorders, like many schizophrenics, nurture, give voice to, and sometimes take actions based on, beliefs that are considered completely false and absurd by those around them. Unlike schizophrenics, however, persons with delusional disorders may otherwise behave quite normally. Their behavior does not show the gross disorganization and fragmentation characteristic of schizophrenia, and general behavioral deterioration is rarely observed in this disorder even when it proves chronic.

THE SCHIZOPHRENIAS

The disorders now called schizophrenia were at one time attributed to a type of mental deterioration beginning early in life. In 1860 the Belgian psychiatrist Benedict Morel described the case of a 13-year-old boy who had formerly been the most brilliant pupil in his school but who gradually lost interest in his studies, became increasingly withdrawn, lethargic, seclusive, and quiet, and appeared to have forgotten everything he had learned. He talked frequently of killing his father. Morel thought the boy's intellectual, moral, and physical functions had deteriorated as a result of brain degeneration of hereditary origin, and hence were irrecoverable. He used the term *démence précoce* (mental deterioration at an early age) to describe the condition and to distinguish it from the dementing disorders associated with old age.

The Latin form of this term—*dementia praecox*—was subsequently adopted by the German psychiatrist Emil Kraepelin to refer to a group of conditions that all seemed to have the feature of mental deterioration beginning early in life. Actually, however, the term is somewhat misleading, because there is no persuasive evidence of progressive (i.e., worsening over time) brain degeneration in the natural course of most instances of the disorder (Bogerts, 1993; Heaton et al., 1994).

It remained for a Swiss psychiatrist, Eugen Bleuler, to introduce in 1911 a more acceptable descriptive term for this general class of disorders. He used *schizophrenia* (split mind) because he thought the condition was characterized primarily by disorganization of thought processes, a lack of coherence between thought and emotion, and an inward orientation away (split off) from reality. The "splitting" thus does *not* refer to multiple personalities, an entirely different form of disorder discussed in Chapter 7 (and now called "dissociative identity disorder"). Instead, in schizophrenia there is a split within the intellect, between the intellect and emotion, and between the intellect and external reality. The subtitle of Bleuler's monograph on the subject (Bleuler, 1911/1950) was *The Group of Schizophrenias,* indicating his own belief in multiple forms in which this basic psychic splitting might be manifested.

Schizophrenic disorders seem to occur in virtually all societies, from the aboriginal settlements in the western Australian desert to the remote interior jungles of Malaysia to the most technologically advanced societies. However, incidence/prevalence rates for the schizophrenias are difficult to pin down precisely because of variations over time and place in the criteria for defining cases. Overall lifetime prevalence estimates have ranged from approximately 0.2 to 2.0 percent (American Psychiatric Association, 1994). The one-year prevalence rate for schizophrenia in the United States among persons 18 or older is estimated at 1.1 percent, or approximately two million affected persons (Regier et al., 1993). Because these disorders are frequently chronic, their incidence (occurrence or onset rate) would be expected to be considerably lower and is estimated in the DSM-IV manual (APA, 1994) as 1 per 10,000 persons per year. Detailed analysis of Epidemiologic Catchment Area (described in Chapter 1) data suggest that the latter rate seriously underestimates occurrence in the United States. Tien and Eaton (1992) estimate the U.S. cumulative occurrence rate at 2 per 1000 persons per year.

In recent years schizophrenia has been the primary diagnosis for nearly 40 percent of all admissions to state and county mental hospitals, far outstripping all other diagnostic categories; it has been the second most frequent primary diagnosis (the first being either mood or alcohol-related disorders) for every other type of inpatient psychiatric admission, including private hospitals (Manderscheid et al., 1985). Forty-five percent of schizophrenic persons receiving hospital care during a given year receive that care in state and county mental hospitals, a proportion exceeded only by patients with severe cognitive impairment (e.g., Alzheimer's dementia). During any given recent year more than 1 million people in the United States received outpatient care for a primary diagnosis of schizophrenia (Narrow et al., 1993). Because schizophrenic persons often require prolonged or repeated hospitalization, they have historically occupied about half of all available mental hospital beds in this country.

Although schizophrenic disorders sometimes first occur during childhood or old age, about three-fourths of all initial onsets occur between the ages of 15 and 45, with a median age in the mid-20s. The incidence rate, overall, appears to be about the same for males and females, but males tend to have earlier onsets (early to mid-20s versus late 20s for females), and many researchers believe males develop more severe forms of these disorders (Iacono & Beiser, 1992; Marcus et al., 1993; Tien & Eaton, 1992). The schizophrenias, because of their complexity, their high rate of incidence (especially at the beginning of adult life), and their tendency to recur or become chronic, are considered the most serious of all mental disorders, as well as among the most baffling.

A Case Study

We depart somewhat from our usual format in discussing the clinical syndromes to present first a unique and uniquely well-documented case study of schizophrenia. The case involves a family of six—two biological parents and their four monozygotic, quadruplet daughters—in which all four daughters became schizophrenic before age 25. Some appreciation of just how remarkable this circumstance is can be derived from the combined improbability of viable quadruplet births, identical heredity, and perfect concordance for schizophrenia; a fairly liberal estimate is that it would occur once in every 1.5 billion births. We are indebted for the thorough knowledge we have of this family to David Rosenthal (1963) and his colleagues, working under the auspices of the National Institute of Mental Health. For obvious reasons, certain specific but nonessential data, such as names and dates, have been omitted or altered in the report.

Background and Early Years Some time in the early 1930s, quadruplet girls were born to Mr. and Mrs. Henry Genain, the product of a marriage occasioned by Mr. Genain's threatening to kill the reluctant Mrs. Genain unless she consented to it. Except for their low birth weights, ranging from Nora's 4 lb, 8 oz., to Hester's 3 lb, the girls appeared to be reasonably normal babies, albeit premature. Hester had to be fitted with a truss (an abdominal compression device) because of a hernia but was nevertheless discharged from the hospital with her sisters as basically healthy some six weeks after the birth.

From birth, the girls received a great deal of attention from the media and the public. Early on, in fact, their parents started charging public admission to visit the home and view the babies, an enterprise that ended when the parents became concerned about the possibility of kidnapping or the transmission of some disease to the children. In subsequent years the children were encouraged in dancing and singing as a team, and they performed often at various functions. Partly as a result of their celebrity status, the girls tended to stick closely together for mutual protection; they even rebuffed children their own age, with the result that they became social isolates. They were encouraged in this social isolation by their parents, who shared strong anxieties about the dangers of "the outside world."

Notwithstanding their genetic identity and physical similarity, the girls were sharply differentiated by their parents. They were treated as though they were two sets of twins—a superior and talented set consisting of Nora and Myra, and an inferior, problematic set consisting of Iris and Hester. Hester—the "runt of the litter"—was regarded from an early age as oversexed. (Possibly because of irritation from her truss, Hester began to masturbate regularly by the age of three, a habit she continued for many years to the dismay of her parents.) Complying with parental attributions, the girls did in fact pair up for purposes of mutual support and intimacy; when threatened from the outside, however, they became a true foursome.

Mr. Genain's job was not very demanding, and he spent most of his time drinking and expressing his various fears and obsessions to his family. Prominent among these were fears that break-ins would occur at the home unless he patrolled the premises constantly with a loaded gun, and, especially as the girls developed into adolescence, that they would get into sexual trouble or be raped unless he watched over them with total dedication.

He imposed extreme restrictions and surveillance on the girls until the time of their breakdowns. Beginning at an early age and persisting through early adulthood, Mr. Genain insisted on being present when his daughters dressed and undressed. He even insisted on watching them change their sanitary pads during menstruation. He was himself sexually promiscuous and was reported to have sexually molested at least two of his daughters; possibly Myra, who persistently distanced herself from him, was the only one of the girls not to be molested.

Mr. Genain's preoccupation with sexuality, while extreme, was matched by that of his wife. Mrs. Genain managed to see sexuality and sexual threats in the most innocuous circumstances and yet seemingly ignored real sexual activity occurring in the home. When the girls complained to her about Mr. Genain's sexual approaches, she rationalized that Mr. Genain was merely testing their virtue; if they objected to his advances, then clearly all was well. Not that she saw Mr. Genain as a paragon of virtue; on the contrary, she recited his many faults to anyone who would listen. Nevertheless, she stuck by him to the end (a typically alcoholic end) and largely confirmed and supported his bizarre constructions of reality. Hester, the chronic masturbator, was a particular thorn in her side—all the more so when she discovered that, at about age 12, Hester had apparently introduced Iris to the practice of mutual masturbation, which Iris found pleasing. Apparently unable to think of any more appropriate response to this dilemma, the parents—on the questionable advice of a physician—forced the two girls to submit to clitoral circumcisions, a drastic measure that failed to alter their behavior. In general, however, Mrs. Genain enjoyed the status accorded her as the mother of quadruplets, and she remained unfailingly and overwhelmingly involved in the girls' lives. Most of her affection was reserved for the "good" quads, Nora and Myra.

Adolescence, Young Adulthood, and Breakdown
Except for their social isolation, the girls had a relatively uneventful junior high school and high school experience. They were regarded by their teachers as conforming, hard-working, and "nice," except for some competition among them with respect to grades and adult approval. Hester lagged behind the others, and Iris could not quite keep up with the remaining two in academic performance. In the summer before the girls' senior year, Hester, whose behavior had become peculiar and who was suffering from some type of psychogenic gastrointestinal distress, finally became disturbed to the point that her parents could hardly manage her. She was temperamental, often confused, destroyed household furnishings, tore both her own and her sisters' clothing, and on one occasion struck Nora and knocked her unconscious. Hester had just turned 18; she never recovered effective mental functioning.

The other three girls completed their senior year of high school. Outwardly they appeared to be normal adolescents, although they were not permitted to have boyfriends and continued to have physical difficulties, including menstrual irregularities and persistent enuresis (bed-wetting). Following graduation, they obtained employment as office workers. They continued to be spied on by their father, however, lest they become involved in sexual liaisons. Of the three, Myra maintained the most independence, defying her father's edict that she not go out at night.

None of the three young women was comfortable in the world of work. Nora was the first to evidence unusual "nervousness," and at age 20 began to have a series of vague physical complaints. She eventually quit her job and took to her bed at home, gradually becoming more disturbed. She stood on her knees and elbows until they became irritated and bled, and began to walk and talk in her sleep. Her behavior continued to deteriorate until, at age 22, she was admitted to a hospital with the diagnosis of schizophrenia. In the meantime, Iris had also become increasingly disturbed, and resigned from her job. She was troubled by "spastic colon," vomiting, insomnia, and the belief that people were paying her undue attention. In fact it was later learned that Mr. Genain may have been molesting her at the time. Within several months after Nora's first admission, Iris "just went to pieces." She screamed, was markedly agitated, complained of hearing voices and of people fighting, and drooled at meals, being unable to swallow anything but liquids. She, too, was hospitalized toward the end of her twenty-second year. The diagnosis was schizophrenia.

Myra did not break down until age 24. The onset was similar to that of her sisters. Myra resisted hospitalization and was not hospitalized until the entire family was shortly thereafter moved to the Clinical Center of the National Institute of Mental Health (NIMH). There, as a unit, they underwent the lengthy and detailed study of which this history is one product. On arrival, Myra was autistic, disordered in thought, and impaired in judgment and reality testing. She was diagnosed as schizophrenic. It may be significant that in the cases of Nora, Iris, and Myra, deterioration began shortly after an incident in which a man had made rather insistent "improper advances."

Course and Outcome   By the time they arrived at the Clinical Center at age 24, Nora had undergone

In 1981 the Genains performed a rendition of "Alice Blue Gown" at a birthday party held in their honor at the National Institute of Mental Health.

three separate hospital admissions and Iris five. Hester had somehow escaped hospitalization, although she was often bizarre and psychotic at home.

Once at the NIMH, the sisters were offered varied forms of treatment and care, including the new antipsychotic medications that had recently become available. They remained at the NIMH for three years. At the end of their stay, Myra was the only one capable of attaining a sustainable discharge. The other three sisters were transferred to a state hospital. Mr. Genain had died of liver disease in the interim.

It is important to note that, though the earliest symptoms of the quads were similar in certain respects, the courses and outcomes of their disorders differed markedly and, to some extent, in ways that might have been predicted from manifestations that appeared quite early. The behavior of Hester and Iris, as described in hospital records, was persistently deteriorated. By contrast, Nora and Myra did not evidence the marked behavioral disorganization of their less functional sisters, although Myra's behavior was the more consistently appropriate over time. The quads' outcomes show a corresponding pattern. At the time of Rosenthal's 1963 report, Myra was working steadily, married, and doing well. Nora was making a marginal adjustment outside the hospital. Iris was still fluctuating between periods of severe disturbance and relative lucidity in which she could manage brief stays outside of the hospital. Hester remained continuously hospitalized in a condition of severe psychosis and was considered essentially a "hopeless case."

It is a tribute to the scientific diligence of the NIMH staff and to David Rosenthal, who maintained both a human and a scientific interest in this unfortunate family, that we had a follow-up report some 20 years after the original one (DeLisi et al., 1984; Mirsky et al., 1984; Sargent, 1982a). In general, the relative adjustment of the sisters, then in their 50s, remained in 1982 as it had been in the 1960s. Myra continued to do well and had had two children in the interim. The other three women were living at home with their mother, with Nora continuing to show a higher level of functioning than Iris or Hester. All of the quads were on continuous medication, and even the beleaguered Hester appeared to have overcome to an extent her originally dismal prognosis. It is of considerable interest that newer techniques of neurological assessment showed that Nora had impairments of the central nervous system similar to those of Hester, and yet her outcome seemed far better than that of Hester or even Iris. It is possible that the original pairing of Iris with Hester was inappropriate (at least in the limited sense implied here) and destructive of Iris's development. In any event, we see that the quads, despite their identical heredity, array themselves along a considerable range of the possible outcomes associated with schizophrenic breakdown.

Interpretive Comment We have here, then, four genetically identical women, all of whom experienced schizophrenic disorders. The disorders, however, have been different in severity, chronicity, and eventual outcome. Obviously these differences must be ascribed to differences in the environments the quads experienced, including their intrauterine environments, which presumably contributed to their modest variations detectable at birth. Clearly Hester, possibly most compromised biologically and in relative parental disfavor from the beginning, faced the harshest environmental conditions, followed closely by her "twin," Iris. The outcome for these women has been grim. Myra was the most favored youngster and the one who experienced the least objectionable parental attention, partly owing to a greater independence and assertiveness than her sisters displayed. Nora was a close second in this respect but had the misfortune of being her incestuous father's "favorite"; in recent tests, she was also shown to have a compromised central nervous system (specifically, an imbalance of metabolic rates in different brain areas) comparable to that of Hester. Though Nora has not done as well as Myra, she has emerged as clearly superior in functioning to the other two sisters. We see here the considerable power of environmental forces in determining personal destiny, even in schizophrenia.

But let us look again. We have four genetically identical women, all of whom became schizophrenic within a period of six years—three of them within a period of some two years. Is this not a compelling case for genetic determination? An independent genealogical history suggests that the quads' father may have harbored some pathogenic genes, which could have been passed on to his daughters. On the other hand, we also see a far less-than-ideal environmental context for the girls' development. As Rosenthal (1963) pointed out, their parents failed spectacularly in the most elementary tasks of parenthood. Assuming the quads were at a genetically enhanced risk for schizophrenia, might they have been spared this outcome had their development occurred in a more psychosocially favorable climate? Unfortunately, there is no way to answer this question.

A plausible conclusion is that both heredity and environment, operating in an as yet poorly understood interaction, probably determined the Genain sisters' psychotic outcomes. To put it another way, it appears we are confronted here with a striking example of the diathesis-stress model of etiology (see Zubin & Spring, 1977), outlined in Chapter 3. We will encounter this type of complicated causal scenario repeatedly in the pages to follow.

The Clinical Picture in Schizophrenia

Sometimes schizophrenic disorders develop slowly and insidiously. In such cases a person may become seclusive, gradually seem to lose interest in the surrounding world, to spend much time daydreaming, to lose emotional responsivity, and to behave socially in mildly inappropriate ways, such as grimacing peculiarly or failing to appreciate social proprieties. This pattern of symptoms has traditionally been referred to as **process schizophrenia**—that is, it develops gradually over a period of time, not in response to obvious discrete stressors, and tends to be long-lasting. The outcome for process schizophrenia is considered generally unfavorable, partly perhaps because the need for treatment is usually not recognized until the behavior pattern has become firmly entrenched. *Poor premorbid* (referring to personality features existing before the occurrence of actual disorder) or *chronic* schizophrenia are alternative terms referring to this pattern.

In other cases, the onset of schizophrenic symptoms is sudden and dramatic and is marked by intense emotional turmoil and a nightmarish sense of confusion. This pattern, which is often associated with identifiable precipitating stressors, is referred to as **reactive schizophrenia** (alternatively, *good premorbid* or *acute* schizophrenia). Here the symptoms may clear up in a matter of weeks, though in some cases an acute episode is the prelude to a more chronic pattern.

Today the terms **negative-symptom schizophrenia** and **positive-symptom schizophrenia** are used to refer to two symptom patterns that appear to overlap considerably with the older process and reactive designations, respectively (Andreasen, 1985). While there is not complete agreement about what types of symptoms should be considered "negative" (Andreasen, 1985; McGlashan & Fenton, 1992; Raskin et al., 1993), the term refers to an *absence* or *deficit* of behaviors normally present in a person's repertoire, such as emotional expression, communicative speech, or reactivity to the environment. *Positive* symptoms, by contrast, are those in which something has been *added* to a normal repertoire of behavior and experience, such as marked emotional turmoil, motor agitation, delusional interpretation of events, or hallucinations. Although most patients exhibit both positive and negative symptoms during the course of their disorders, a preponderance of negative symptoms has increasingly been shown to have relatively grave prognostic significance (e.g., Fenton & McGlashan, 1994; McGlashan & Fenton, 1993).

It is sometimes held that antipsychotic medication affects only positive symptoms. This appears to be an incorrect clinical observation, however, since it has been known for many years that negative symptoms, such as social withdrawal, may also respond to these medications (NIMH Psychopharmacology Service Center Collaborative Study Group, 1964). This finding was reconfirmed by Kay and Singh (1989) and by Breier and colleagues (1994) in more rigorously designed studies. Another widespread belief, already mentioned, is that positive schizophrenia has a better long-term prognosis than negative schizophrenia, but the 36-month follow-up of their patients by Kay and Singh surprisingly found the opposite. Since there is growing evidence (e.g., Fenton & McGlashan, 1994) indicating that the latter finding is anomalous, we suspect that the difficulty here relates to uncertainty in the identification of positive versus negative symptoms.

One source of this uncertainty is undoubtedly the tendency to consider the positivity/negativity distinction to be dichotomous. In fact, it is not a dichotomy, nor even necessarily a single dimension. Research evidence indicates that these polar terms would better be conceived as the end points of an uninterrupted continuum, or possibly two separate and largely independent continua. Instances of schizophrenic disorder can be seen as distributing themselves in the familiar bell-shaped curve, with relatively few falling at either the negative- or positive-symptom extremes and most falling somewhere in the middle. We thus expect a large percentage of schizophrenic patients to display both positive and negative symptoms, as seems to be the case (Breier et al., 1994; Guelfi, Faustman, & Csernansky, 1989). Everything considered, therefore, we remain somewhat doubtful that the distinction now designated by the positive/negative rubric will prove to be basic to the organization of schizophrenic psychopathology. Similar reservations have been expressed by Andreasen and colleagues (1990) following a more comprehensive review of the evidence.

Another distinction commonly emphasized by researchers is that between paranoid and nonparanoid symptom patterns in schizophrenia. The paranoid is

Odd behavior and active withdrawal from the social environment are frequently observed phenomena in schizophrenia.

one of the classical subtypes of schizophrenia, of which more is said below. In the paranoid pattern, delusions, particularly organized persecutory or grandiose ones, are a dominant feature; in the nonparanoid forms, delusions, if present at all, tend to be incidental to a generalized confusion and of inconsistent content. There is considerable evidence that important differences exist between those who exhibit a predominantly paranoid symptom pattern and those who exhibit few, or no, or inconsistent paranoid symptoms.

In general, paranoid schizophrenics tend to be more reactive than process in type and to have more benign courses and outcomes (Kendler et al., 1994b; Ritzler, 1981); they are less likely to show the striking kinds of cognitive or attentional deficits seen in other forms of the disorder (Rabin, Doneson, & Jentons, 1979). They may also be genetically less vulnerable to schizophrenia than nonparanoid types (Kendler & Davis, 1981). It has been found, however, that a substantial number of people originally diagnosed as having paranoid forms of schizophrenic disorder are later diagnosed as having nonparanoid ones (Kendler & Tsuang, 1981). Also, there appears to be a small subgroup of paranoid schizophrenic people whose disorders are extremely intractable and chronic.

Whether positive, negative, paranoid, or nonparanoid in the general sense of these terms, schizophrenia encompasses many specific symptoms that vary greatly over time in an individual's life and from one person to another, perhaps especially with respect to the emergence or progression of negative symptoms

(McGlashan & Fenton, 1993). The basic experience in schizophrenia, however, seems to be disorganization in perception, thought, and emotion to the extent that the affected person is no longer able to perform customary social roles in an adequate fashion. The DSM-IV specifies in concrete terms a list of criteria for the diagnosis, reproduced in HIGHLIGHT 12.1. What follows is a more elaborated version of the schizophrenia construct as it has evolved to this point.

Disturbance of Language and Communication
First described at length by Bleuler (1911/1950) and often referred to as *formal thought disorder,* communication disturbance is usually considered a prime indicator of a schizophrenic disorder. Basically, an affected person fails to make sense, despite seeming to conform to the semantic and syntactic rules governing verbal communication. The failure is not attributable to low intelligence, poor education, or cultural deprivation. Meehl (1962) aptly referred to the process as one of "cognitive slippage"; others have referred to it as "derailment" or "loosening" of associations. However labeled, the phenomenon is readily recognized by experienced clinicians: The patient seems to be using words in combinations that sound communicative, but the listener can understand little or nothing of what is said. As an example from the files of one of the authors, consider the following excerpt from a letter addressed to Queen Beatrix of the Netherlands by a highly intelligent schizophrenic man:

HIGHLIGHT | 12.1

DSM-IV Criteria for the Diagnosis of Schizophrenia

A. *Characteristic symptoms:* Two (or more) of the following, each present for a significant portion of time during a 1-month period (or less if successfully treated):

(1) delusions
(2) hallucinations
(3) disorganized speech (e.g., frequent derailment or incoherence)
(4) grossly disorganized or catatonic behavior
(5) negative symptoms, i.e., affective flattening, alogia [little speech, or little substance of ideas contained in speech], or avolition [deficient or absence of "will"]

Note: Only one Criterion A symptom is required if delusions are bizarre or hallucinations consist of a voice keeping up a running commentary on the person's behavior or thoughts, or two or more voices conversing with each other.

B. *Social/occupational dysfunction:* For a significant portion of

the time since the onset of the disturbance, one or more major areas of functioning such as work, interpersonal relations, or self-care are markedly below the level achieved prior to the onset (or when the onset is in childhood or adolescence, failure to achieve expected level of interpersonal, academic, or occupational achievement).

C. *Duration:* Continuous signs of the disturbance persist for at least 6 months. This 6-month period must include at least 1 month of symptoms (or less if successfully treated) that meet Criterion A (i.e., active-phase symptoms) and may include periods of prodromal or residual symptoms. During these prodomal or residual periods, the signs of the disturbance may be manifested by only negative symptoms or two or more symptoms listed in Criterion A present in an attenuated form (e.g., odd beliefs, unusual perceptual experiences).

D. *Schizoaffective and Mood Disorder exclusion:* Schizoaffective Disorder and Mood Disorder With

Psychotic Features have been ruled out because either (1) no Major Depressive, Manic, or Mixed Episodes have occurred concurrently with active-phase symptoms; or (2) if mood episodes have occurred during active-phase symptoms, their total duration has been brief relative to the duration of the active and residual periods.

E. *Substance/general medical condition exclusion:* The disturbance is not due to the direct physiologic effects of a substance (e.g., a drug of abuse, a medication) or a general medical condition.

F. *Relationship to a Pervasive Developmental Disorder:* If there is a history of Autistic Disorder or another Pervasive Developmental Disorder, the additional diagnosis of Schizophrenia is made only if prominent delusions or hallucinations are also present for at least a month (or less if successfully treated).

American Psychiatric Association, 1994, pp. 285–86.

I have also "killed" my ex-wife, [name], in a 2.5 to 3.0 hours sex bout in Devon Pennsylvania in 1976, while two Pitcairns were residing in my next room closet, hearing the event. Enclosed, please find my urology report, indicating that my male genitals, specifically my penis, are within normal size and that I'm capable of normal intercourse with any woman, signed by Dr. [name], a urologist and surgeon who performed a circumcision on me in 1982. *Conclusion:* I cannot be a nincompoop in a physical sense (unless Society would feed me chemicals for my picture in the nincompoop book).

Disturbance of Thought Content Disturbances in the content of thought typically involve certain stan-

dard types of **delusion** (false belief). Prominent among these are beliefs that one's thoughts, feelings, or actions are being controlled by external agents; that one's private thoughts are being broadcast indiscriminately to others; that thoughts are being inserted into one's brain by alien forces; that some mysterious agency has robbed one of one's thoughts; or that some neutral environmental event (such as a television program or a billboard) has an intended personal meaning, often termed an "idea of reference." Other absurd propositions, including delusions of grotesque bodily changes, are regularly observed.

Disruption of Perception Major perceptual disruption often accompanies the criteria already indicated. The patient seems unable to sort out and process the great mass of sensory information to which all of us are constantly exposed. As a result, stimuli overwhelm the meager resources the person has for information processing. This point is illustrated in the following statements of schizophrenic people: "I feel like I'm too alert . . . everything seems to come pouring in at once . . . I can't seem to keep anything out. . . ." "My nerves seem supersensitive . . . objects seem brighter . . . noises are louder . . . my feelings are so intense . . . things seem so vivid and they come at me like a flood from a broken dam." "It seems like nothing ever stops. Thoughts just keep coming in and racing round in my head . . . and getting broken up . . . sort of into pieces of thoughts and images . . . like tearing up a picture. And everything is out of control . . . I can't seem to stop it." It is estimated that approximately 50 percent of patients diagnosed as schizophrenic experience this breakdown of perceptual selectivity during the onset of their disorders (Freedman & Chapman, 1973). Other even more dramatic perceptual phenomena include **hallucinations**—false perceptions, such as "voices" that only the schizophrenic person can hear. Hallucinations in the schizophrenias are most often auditory, although they can also be visual and even olfactory. The typical hallucination is one in which a voice (or voices) keeps up a running commentary on the person's behaviors or thoughts.

Inappropriate Emotion   The schizophrenic syndromes are often said to include an element of clearly inappropriate emotion, or affect. In the more severe or chronic cases, the picture is usually one of apparent anhedonia (inability to experience joy or pleasure) and emotional shallowness or "blunting" (lack of intensity or clear definition). The person may appear virtually emotionless, so that even the most compelling and dramatic events produce at most an intellectual recognition of what is happening. We must be cautious in interpreting this sign, however, because evidence suggests that the deficit is only one of expressiveness, not of feeling per se (Berenbaum & Oltmanns, 1992; Kring et al., 1993). In other instances, particularly in the acute phases, the person may show strong affect, but the emotion clashes with the situation or with the content of his or her thoughts.

Confused Sense of Self   Schizophrenic persons may feel confused about their identity to the point of loss of a subjective sense of self or of personal agency. Delusional assumption of a new identity is not uncommon. In other instances the person may be perplexed about aspects of his or her own body, including its gender, or may be uncertain about the boundaries separating the self from the rest of the

world. The latter confusion is often associated with frightening "cosmic" or "oceanic" feelings of being somehow intimately tied up with universal powers, including the deity. These feelings appear to be related to ideas of external control and similar delusions.

Disrupted Volition   Goal-directed activity is almost universally disrupted in schizophrenic individuals. The impairment always occurs in areas of routine daily functioning, such as work, social relations, and self-care, such that observers note that the person is not himself or herself any more. The picture is thus one of deterioration from a previously mastered standard of performance in everyday affairs. For example, the person may no longer maintain minimal standards of personal hygiene, or may evidence a profound disregard of personal safety and health.

Retreat to an Inner World   Ties to the external world are almost by definition loosened in the schizophrenic disorders. In extreme instances the withdrawal from reality seems deliberate and involves active disengagement from the environment. This rejection of the external world may be accompanied by the elaboration of an inner world in which the person develops illogical and fantastic ideas, including the creation of strange beings who interact with the person in various self-directed dramas. Since the days of Bleuler, this process has generally been referred to as *autism*.

Disturbed Motor Behavior   Various peculiarities of movement are sometimes observed in the schizophrenias; indeed, this is the chief and defining characteristic of catatonic schizophrenia, of which more will be said later. These motor disturbances range from an excited sort of hyperactivity to a marked decrease in all movement or an apparent clumsiness. Also included here are various forms of rigid posturing, mutism, ritualistic mannerisms, and bizarre grimacing.

Problems in Defining Schizophrenia

Criteria for the diagnosis of schizophrenia have varied considerably over the past century (Hegarty et al., 1994). In an effort to provide for a clear-cut diagnosis of schizophrenia and to sharply distinguish it from mood or other disorders, diagnostic criteria since the DSM-III of 1980 have been far more exact and explicit than those in earlier DSM editions. Recalling our discussion of these matters in Chapter 1, such an approach almost necessarily enhances diagnostic reliability (that is, the agreement on what diagnosis should be assigned). Whether it does the same for validity (the conceptual and predictive meaningfulness of the diagnosis) depends on the adequacy with which the category, so defined, captures some essential truth about a distinctive psychopathological entity that is to be called *schizophrenia*. While no reasonable person doubts the reality of the behavioral phenomena described above, it has proven difficult to identify or to formulate in exact terms the central nature of this presumed entity.

Despite the dramatic quality of the associated clinical phenomena, therefore, it must be kept in mind that schizophrenia remains a *provisional construct* (Andreasen & Carpenter, 1993), one whose definition has evolved and changed over time—with substantial effects on incidence/prevalence rates relative to other disorders (Carson & Sanislow, 1993), and even on observed clinical outcomes for persons assigned the diagnosis (Hegarty et al., 1994). Criteria for applying the diagnosis may change with future changes in conceptualization, as they have in each of the three most recent editions of the DSM since 1980.

In pointing out the changing empirical foundations for the construct of schizophrenia, we are not suggesting that it should be abandoned—still less that we can offer a superior alternative solution to the continuing conceptual confusion attending this type of disorder. Consensus on the definition of a disorder, and hence reliability in diagnosing it, are after all essential to the conduct of relevant research. Our intent is to ensure that the student avoid the common error of attributing to the provisional construct of "schizophrenia" a substantive existence—a reification—that available evidence cannot support. There is clearly *something* decidedly wrong, quite apart from mere violation of convention, with the mental functioning of the persons who acquire this diagnosis (Keith, 1993). Unfortunately, however, accurate diagnosis in itself does not at present provide us with any confident understanding of what that underlying "something" may be.

Subtypes of Schizophrenia

Recent editions of the DSM have listed five subtypes of schizophrenia, based on the differing clinical pictures long recognized to be variants of a common theme of disorder; they are summarized in HIGHLIGHT 12.2. We will focus on four of these here: undifferentiated, catatonic, disorganized, and paranoid. Of these, the undifferentiated and paranoid types are the most common today.

Undifferentiated Type As the term implies, the diagnosis of **schizophrenia, undifferentiated type,** is something of a "wastebasket" category. A person so diagnosed meets the usual criteria for schizophrenia—including (in varying combinations) delusions, hallucinations, disordered thoughts, and bizarre behaviors—but does not clearly fit into one of the other types because of a mixed symptom picture. People in the acute, early phases of a schizophrenic breakdown frequently exhibit undifferentiated symptoms, as do those who are in transitional phases from one to another of the standard subtypes.

Probably most instances of acute, reactive schizophrenic breakdown occurring for the first time appear undifferentiated in type. However, current diagnostic criteria (that is, DSM-IV) preclude the diagnosis of schizophrenia unless there have been signs of the disorder for at least six months, by which time a stable pattern may develop, consistent with a more definite indication of type. Some schizophrenic patients, on the other hand, remain undifferentiated over long time periods. The case of Rick Wheeler is illustrative of the latter course:

Rick Wheeler, 26 years old, neatly groomed, and friendly and cheerful in disposition, was removed from an airplane by airport police because he was creating a disturbance—from his own account probably because he was "on another dimension." On arrest, he was oriented to the extent of knowing where he was, his name, and the current date, but his report of these facts was embedded in a peculiar and circumstantial context involving science fiction themes. Investigation revealed he had been discharged from a nearby state mental hospital three days earlier. He was brought to another hospital by police.

On admission, physical examination and laboratory studies were normal, but Rick claimed he was Jesus Christ and that he could move mountains. His speech was extremely difficult to follow because of incoherence and derailment. For example, he explained his wish to leave the city, "because things happen here I don't approve of. I approve of other things but I don't approve of the other things. And believe me it's worse for them in the end." He complained that the Devil wanted to kill him and that his food contained "ground-up corpses." He was born, he claimed, from his father's sexual organs.

Background investigation revealed that Rick's difficulties began, after a successful academic start, in elementary school: "I could compre-

Types of Schizophrenia

Type	Characteristics
Undifferentiated type	A pattern of symptoms in which there is a rapidly changing mixture of all or most of the primary indicators of schizophrenia. Commonly observed are indications of perplexity, confusion, emotional turmoil, delusions of reference, excitement, dreamlike autism, depression, and fear. Most often this picture is seen in patients who are in the process of breaking down and becoming schizophrenic. It is also seen, however, when major changes are occurring in the adjustive demands impinging on a person with an already-established schizophrenic psychosis. In such cases, it frequently foreshadows an impending change to another primary schizophrenic subtype.
Paranoid type	A symptom picture dominated by absurd, illogical, and changeable delusions, frequently accompanied by vivid hallucinations, with a resulting impairment of critical judgment and erratic, unpredictable, and occasionally dangerous behavior. In chronic cases, there is usually less disorganization of behavior than in other types of schizophrenia, and less extreme withdrawal from social interaction.
Catatonic type	Often characterized by alternating periods of extreme withdrawal and extreme excitement, although in some cases one or the other reaction predominates. In the withdrawal reaction there is a sudden loss of all animation and a tendency to remain motionless for hours or even days in a single position. The clinical picture may undergo an abrupt change, with excitement coming on suddenly, wherein an individual may talk or shout incoherently, pace rapidly, and engage in uninhibited, impulsive, and frenzied behavior. In this state, an individual may be dangerous.
Disorganized type	Usually occurs at an earlier age than most other types of schizophrenia, and represents a more severe disintegration of the personality. Emotional distortion and blunting typically are manifested in inappropriate laughter and silliness, peculiar mannerisms, and bizarre, often obscene, behavior.
Residual type	Mild indications of schizophrenia shown by individuals in remission following a schizophrenic episode.

hend but I couldn't store . . . it's like looking at something but being unable to take it in." He thereafter maintained a D average until he dropped out halfway through his junior year of high school. He had never held a full-time job, and his social adjustment had always been poor. He showed no interest in women until he married, at age 19, a patient he'd met during one of the earliest of some 20 of his hospitalizations, beginning at age 16. A daughter was born from this match, but Rick had lost track of both her and his wife; he had shown no further interest in women. Rick himself was the eldest of five children; there was no known mental disorder in any of his first-degree relatives (that is, siblings and parents).

Unable to maintain employment, Rick had been supported mainly on federal disability welfare—and by virtue of patienthood in public hospitals. His hospital admissions and discharges showed a substantial correlation with his varying financial status; that is, he tended to be released from the hospital around the first of the month, when his welfare check was due, and to be readmitted (or alternatively sent to jail) following some public altercation after his money had run out. Numerous attempts to commit Rick to the hospital indefinitely on an involuntary basis had failed because he was able to appear competent at court appearances. He had, however, been declared incompetent to receive his own checks, and various relatives had stepped forward to handle his finances. Now they are afraid to do so because Rick set his grandmother's house afire, having concluded (erroneously, as it turned out) that she was withholding some of his money. He had also threatened others and had been arrested several times for carrying concealed weapons.

In the latest hospitalization, two different antipsychotic medications were tried over a period of five weeks with no discernible improvement. Rick still claimed supernatural powers and special connections with several national governments; was still refusing food because of its contamination with ground corpses; and was still threatening bodily harm to people he found uncooperative. A further attempt was made to commit him and to place his affairs under legal guardianship. As Rick had rather boastfully predicted, this attempt failed because of his lucid defense of himself, and the court dismissed the action. He was discharged to a protected boarding house but disappeared four days later. (Adapted from Spitzer et al., 1983, pp. 153–155)

Fortunately, most patients who show this type of chaotic, undifferentiated pattern do not have the early and slowly developing, insidious onset seen in Rick's case. On the contrary, the breakdown erupts suddenly out of the context of a seemingly unremarkable life history, usually following a period of stress. The initial diagnosis in such cases is *schizophreniform disorder* (see below), and the episode usually clears up in a matter of weeks or, at most, months. Recurrent episodes, however, are not uncommon in schizophreniform disorder, especially in the absence of vigorous follow-up treatment, leading to the diagnosis of schizophrenia. In some few instances, treatment efforts are unsuccessful, and the mixed symptoms of the early undifferentiated disorder slide into a more chronic phase, typically developing both the more specific symptoms of other types and symptoms of increasing negativity.

Catatonic Type Though catatonic reactions may appear with dramatic suddenness, a patient usually has a background of eccentric behavior, often accompanied by some degree of withdrawal from reality. Though at one time common in Europe and North America, catatonic reactions have become less frequent in recent years.

The central feature of **schizophrenia, catatonic type,** is pronounced motor symptoms, either of an

This painting was made by a male patient diagnosed as suffering from undifferentiated schizophrenia. Over a period of about nine years, he did hundreds of paintings in which the tops of the heads of males were always missing, though the females were complete. Although the therapist tried several maneuvers to get him to paint a man's head, the patient never did.

excited or a stuporous type, which sometimes make for difficulty in differentiating this condition from a psychotic mood disorder. The clinical picture is often an early manifestation of a disorder that will become chronic and intractable unless the underlying process is somehow arrested.

Some catatonic patients alternate between periods of extreme stupor and extreme excitement, sometimes quite violent, but in most cases one reaction or the other is predominant. In a study of 250 people diagnosed as suffering from catatonic schizophrenia, Morrison (1973) found that 110 were predominantly withdrawn, 67 were predominantly excited, and 73 were considered "mixed." No significant differences were found between these groups with regard to age, sex, or education.

During a catatonic stupor, a person loses all animation and tends to remain motionless in a rigid, unchanging position—mute and staring into space—sometimes maintaining the same position for hours or even days, until the hands and feet become blue and swollen because of immobility. One patient felt that he had to hold his hand out flat because the forces of "good" and "evil" were waging a "war of the worlds" on his hand, and if he moved it, he might tilt the precarious balance in favor of the evil forces. Surprisingly, despite their seeming withdrawal and apparent lack of attention to their surroundings, catatonic individuals may later give detailed accounts of events that were going on around them.

Some of these patients are highly suggestible and will automatically obey commands or imitate the actions of others (echopraxia) or mimic their phrases (echolalia). If a patient's arm is raised to an awkward and uncomfortable position, he or she may keep it there for minutes or even hours. Ordinarily, patients in a catatonic stupor stubbornly resist any effort to change their position and may become mute, resist all attempts at feeding, and refuse to comply with even the slightest request. They pay no attention to bowel or bladder control and may drool. Their facial expression is typically vacant, and their skin appears waxy. Threats and painful stimuli have no effect, and they may have to be dressed and washed by nursing personnel.

Catatonic patients may pass suddenly from states of extreme stupor to great excitement, during which they seem to be under great "pressure of activity" and may become violent, being in these respects indistinguishable from some bipolar manic patients. They may talk or shout excitedly and incoherently, pace rapidly back and forth, openly indulge in sexual activities, attempt self-mutilation or even suicide, or impulsively attack and try to kill others. The suddenness and extreme frenzy of these attacks make such patients dangerous to both themselves and others. These excited states may last a few hours, days, or even weeks, if sedating medication is not administered. The following case illustrates some of the symptoms typical of catatonic reactions:

Todd Phillips, a 16-year-old high school student, was referred to a psychiatric hospital by his family physician. His family had been very upset by his increasingly strange behavior over the preceding eight months. They had consulted their family physician, who treated him with small doses of antipsychotic medication, without any improvement.

Although Todd has had many problems since he was a small child, there was a distinct change about eight months ago. He began spending more and more time in his room and seemed uninterested in doing many of his usual activities. His grades dropped. He started stuttering. He used to weigh about 215 pounds, but began to eat less, and lost 35 pounds. For no reason, he started drinking large quantities of water.

More recently, there was a change for the worse. A few months ago he began taking Tai Chi lessons and often stood for long periods in karatelike positions, oblivious to what was going on around him. He stopped doing his homework. He took an inordinately long time to get dressed, eat his meals, or bathe. Before getting dressed in the morning he would go through an elaborate ritual of arranging his clothes on the bed before putting them on. When his parents asked him a question, he repeated the question over and over and did not seem to hear or understand what was said.

At school he received demerits for the first time for being late to class. His family began to lose patience with him when he eventually refused to go to school. When his father tried to get him out of bed in the morning, he lay motionless, sometimes having wet the bed during the night. It was at this point that his parents, in desperation, consulted their family physician.

When first seen in the hospital, Todd was a disheveled looking, somewhat obese adolescent, standing motionless in the center of the room with his head flexed forward and his hands at his sides. He appeared perplexed, but was correctly oriented to time and place. He was able to do simple calculations, and his recent and remote memory were intact. He answered questions slowly and in a peculiar manner. An example of his speech follows:

Q: Why did you come to the hospital?

A: Why did I come? Why did I come to the hospital? I came to the hospital because of crazy things with my hands. Sometimes my hands jump up like that . . . wait a minute . . . I guess it's happening. . . . Well, yes, see it's been happening (making robotlike gestures with his hands).

Q: What thoughts go through your head?

A: What thoughts go through my head? What thoughts go through my head? Well, I think about things . . . like . . . yes, well . . . I think thoughts . . . I have thoughts. I think thoughts.

Q: What thoughts?

A: What thoughts? What kinds of thoughts? I think thoughts.

Q: Do you hear voices?

A: Do I hear voices? I hear voices. People talk. Do I hear voices? No. . . . People talk. I hear voices. I hear voices when people talk.

Q: Are you sick?

A: Am I sick? No I'm not sick . . . these fidgeting habits, these fidgeting habits. I have habits. I have fidgeting habits.

Throughout the examination he made repetitive chewing and biting motions. Occasionally, when questioned, he would smile enigmatically. He seemed unresponsive to much of what was

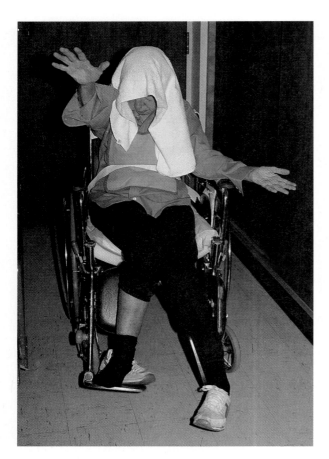

Peculiar posturing is a defining feature of the catatonic subtype of schizophrenia.

going on around him. His infrequent movements were slow and jerky, and he often assumed the karatelike postures that his parents described, in which he would remain frozen. If the examiner placed the patient's hands in an awkward position the patient remained frozen in that position for several minutes. (Spitzer et al., 1983, pp. 139–40)

Although the matter is far from settled, some clinicians interpret a catatonic patient's immobility as a way of coping with his or her reduced filtering ability and increased vulnerability to stimulation: It seems to provide a feeling of some control over external sources of stimulation, though not necessarily over inner ones. Freeman (1960) has cited the explanation advanced by one patient: "I did not want to move, because if I did everything changed around me and upset me horribly so I remained still to hold onto a sense of permanence" (p. 932).

Disorganized Type   Compared with the other subtypes of schizophrenia, **schizophrenia, disorganized type,** usually occurs at an earlier age and represents a more severe disintegration of the personality. Fortunately, it is considerably less common than the other forms. In pre-DSM-III classifications, this type was called *hebephrenic* schizophrenia.

Typically, an affected person has a history of oddness, overscrupulousness about trivial things, and preoccupation with obscure religious and philosophical issues. Frequently, he or she broods over the dire results of masturbation or minor infractions of social conventions. While schoolmates are enjoying normal play and social activities, this person gradually becomes more seclusive and more preoccupied with fantasies.

As the disorder progresses, the person becomes emotionally indifferent and infantile. A silly smile and inappropriate, shallow laughter after little or no provocation are common symptoms. If asked the reason for his or her laughter, the patient may state that he or she does not know or may volunteer some wholly irrelevant and unsatisfactory explanation. Speech becomes incoherent and may include considerable baby talk, childish giggling, a repetitious use of similar-sounding words, and a derailing of associated thoughts that may give a punlike quality to speech. In some instances, speech becomes completely incoherent, a "word salad."

Hallucinations, particularly auditory ones, are common. The voices heard by these patients may accuse them of immoral practices, "pour filth" into their minds, and call them vile names. Delusions are usually of a sexual, religious, hypochondriacal, or persecutory nature, and they are typically changeable, unsystematized, and fantastic. For example, one woman insisted not only that she was being followed by enemies but that she had already been killed a number of times. Another claimed that a long tube extended from the Kremlin directly to her uterus, through which she was being invaded by Russians.

In occasional cases, individuals become hostile and aggressive. They may exhibit peculiar mannerisms and other bizarre forms of behavior. These behaviors may take the form of word salad; facial grimaces; talking and gesturing to themselves; sudden, inexplicable laughter and weeping; and in some cases an abnormal interest in urine and feces, which they may smear on walls and even on themselves. Obscene behavior and the absence of any modesty or sense of shame are characteristic. Although they may exhibit outbursts of anger and temper tantrums in connection with fantasies, they are indifferent to real-life situations, no matter how horrifying or gruesome the latter may be. The clinical picture in disorganized schizophrenia is exemplified in the following interview:

> The patient was a divorcee, 32 years of age, who had come to the hospital with bizarre delusions, hallucinations, and severe personality disintegration. She had a record of alcoholism, promiscuity, and possible incestuous relations with a brother. The following conversation shows typical hebephrenic responses to questioning.
>
> Doctor: How do you feel today?
>
> Patient: Fine.
>
> Doctor: When did you come here?
>
> Patient: 1416, you remember, doctor (silly giggle).
>
> Doctor: Do you know why you are here?
>
> Patient: Well, in 1951 I changed into two men. President Truman was judge at my trial. I was convicted and hung (silly giggle). My brother and I were given back our normal bodies 5 years ago. I am a policewoman. I keep a dictaphone concealed on my person.
>
> Doctor: Can you tell me the name of this place?
>
> Patient: I have not been a drinker for 16 years. I am taking a mental rest after a "carter" assignment or "quill." You know, a "penwrap." I had contracts with Warner Brothers Studios and Eugene broke phonograph records but Mike protested. I have been with the police department for 35 years. I am made of flesh and blood—see doctor (pulling up her dress).
>
> Doctor: Are you married?
>
> Patient: No. I am not attracted to men (silly giggle). I have a companionship arrangement with my brother. I am a "looner". . . a bachelor.

The prognosis is generally poor if a person develops disorganized schizophrenia. To at least some extent, the disorganized variety of schizophrenia may be regarded as the "last stop" on a downward-coursing path of process schizophrenic psychosis. At this point, no form of treatment intervention yet discovered has a marked likelihood of effecting more than a modest recovery.

Paranoid Type Formerly about one-half of all schizophrenic first admissions to hospitals were diagnosed as **schizophrenia, paranoid type.** In recent years, however, the incidence of the paranoid type has shown a substantial decrease, while the undifferentiated type has shown a marked increase. The reasons for these changes are unknown.

Frequently, paranoid-type schizophrenic persons show histories of increasing suspiciousness and of severe difficulties in interpersonal relationships. The eventual symptom picture is dominated by absurd, illogical, and often changing delusions. Persecutory delusions are the most frequent and may involve a wide range of bizarre ideas and plots. An individual may become highly suspicious of relatives or associates and may complain of being watched, followed, poisoned, talked about, or influenced by various tormenting devices rigged up by "enemies."

In addition to persecutory themes, themes of grandeur are also common in paranoid-type delusions. Persons with such delusions may, for example, claim to be the world's greatest economist or philosopher, or some prominent person of the past, such as Napoleon, the Virgin Mary, or even Jesus Christ. These delusions are frequently accompanied by vivid auditory, visual, and other hallucinations. Patients may hear singing, or God speaking, or the voices of their enemies, or they may see angels or feel damaging rays piercing their bodies at various points.

An individual's thinking and behavior become centered on the themes of persecution, grandeur, or both in a pathological "paranoid construction" that—for all its distortion of reality—provides a sense of identity and importance perhaps not otherwise attainable for the person. There thus tends to be a higher level of adaptive coping and of cognitive integrative skills in a paranoid-type schizophrenic person than in other schizophrenic individuals. This relative preservation of intact cognitive functioning is undoubtedly one of the important bases for the paranoid-nonparanoid distinction noted earlier and regarded as important by many clinicians and researchers.

Despite this seeming relative "advantage" that paranoid-type schizophrenic individuals enjoy, such people are far from easy to deal with. The weaving of delusions and hallucinations into a paranoid construction results in a loss of critical judgment and in erratic, unpredictable behavior. In response to a command from a "voice," such a person may commit violent acts. Thus, paranoid schizophrenic patients can sometimes be dangerous, as when they attack people they are convinced have been persecuting them. Somewhat paradoxically, such problems are exacerbated by the fact that such people show less bizarre behavior and less extreme withdrawal from the out-

A patient diagnosed as a paranoid schizophrenic was unable to respond at all when asked by a therapist to make an original drawing. Therefore, with the therapist's help, a picture (top left) was selected from a magazine for the patient to copy. One of his first attempts (top right) was a pencil drawing on manila paper showing great visual distortion, as well as an inability to use colors and difficulty in using letters of the alphabet. The evident visual distortion was a diagnostic aid for the therapist, who was able to learn from it that the patient, who was extremely fearful, saw things in this distorted way, aggravating his fear. In the picture at bottom left, the patient has shown obvious improvement, although it was not until a year after therapy began that he was able to execute a painting with the realism of the picture at bottom right.

side world than individuals with other types of schizophrenia; as a consequence, they are less likely to be confined in protective environments.

The following conversation is between a clinician and a man diagnosed as a chronic paranoid schizophrenic. The case illustrates well the illogical, delusional symptom picture, together with continued attention to misinterpreted external data, that these individuals experience:

Doctor: What's your name?

Patient: Who are you?

Doctor: I'm a doctor. Who are you?

Patient: I can't tell you who I am.

Doctor: Why can't you tell me?

Patient: You wouldn't believe me.

Doctor: What are you doing here?

Patient: Well, I've been sent here to thwart the Russians. I'm the only one in the world who knows how to deal with them. They got their spies all around here though to get me, but I'm smarter than any of them.

Doctor: What are you going to do to thwart the Russians?

Patient: I'm organizing.

Doctor: Whom are you going to organize?

Patient: Everybody. I'm the only man in the world who can do that, but they're trying to get me. But I'm going to use my atomic bomb media to blow them up.

Doctor: You must be a terribly important person then.

Patient: Well, of course.

Doctor: What do you call yourself?

Patient: You used to know me as Franklin D. Roosevelt.

Doctor: Isn't he dead?

Patient: Sure he's dead, but I'm alive.

Doctor: But you're Franklin D. Roosevelt?

Patient: His spirit. He, God, and I figured this out. And now I'm going to make a race of healthy people. My agents are lining them up. Say, who are you?

Doctor: I'm a doctor here.

Patient: You don't look like a doctor. You look like a Russian to me.

Doctor: How can you tell a Russian from one of your agents?

Patient: I read eyes. I get all my signs from eyes. I look into your eyes and get all my signs from them.

Doctor: Do you sometimes hear voices telling you someone is a Russian?

Patient: No, I just look into eyes. I got a mirror here to look into my own eyes. I know everything that's going on. I can tell by the color, by the way it's shaped.

Doctor: Did you have any trouble with people before you came here?

Patient: Well, only the Russians. They were trying to surround me in my neighborhood. One day they tried to drop a bomb on me from the fire escape.

Doctor: How could you tell it was a bomb?

Patient: I just knew.

Although it is true, as we have seen, that many paranoid schizophrenic individuals have histories of gradual onset and long-lasting difficulties in interpersonal relationships and productive functioning, it is also true that few of them show the true process pattern of schizophrenia (Ritzler, 1981). Sometimes, indeed, onset is quite rapid and occurs in individuals with entirely adequate pasts.

Other Schizophrenic Patterns The remaining subcategories of schizophrenia contained in DSM-IV deserve brief mention. **Schizophrenia, residual type,** which is the fifth officially recognized type of schizophrenia, is a category used for people who

have experienced an episode of schizophrenia from which they have recovered sufficiently so as not to show prominent psychotic symptoms. They nevertheless still manifest some mild signs of their past disorder, such as odd beliefs, flat affect, or eccentric behavior.

As was noted in Chapter 6, the term **schizoaffective disorder** (bipolar or depressive subtype) is applied to individuals who show features of both schizophrenia and severe affective disorder. In the DSM-IV classification, this disorder is not listed as a formal subtype of schizophrenic disorder, although it is placed under that rubric.

Schizophreniform disorder, which shares an indistinct taxonomic status identical to that of schizoaffective, is a category reserved for schizophrenia-like psychoses of less than six months' duration. It may include any of the symptoms described in the preceding sections, but is probably most often seen in an undifferentiated form. Brief psychotic states of this sort may or may not be related to subsequent psychiatric disorder (Strakowski, 1994). At present, however, all recent-onset cases of true schizophrenia presumably must first receive a diagnosis of schizophreniform disorder. Because of the possibility of an early and lasting remission in a first episode of schizophrenic breakdown, prognosis for schizophreniform disorder (where it is a manifestation of recent-onset schizophrenic symptoms) is better than for established forms of schizophrenia, and it appears likely that by keeping it out of the formal category of schizophrenic disorder the potentially harmful effects of labeling may be reduced.

Causal Factors in Schizophrenia

Despite an enormous research investment going back many years and continuing to the present day, the causal factors underlying the schizophrenias remain unclear, particularly in their details. Primary responsibility has been attributed variously to (a) biological factors; (b) psychosocial factors, including pathogenic interpersonal and family patterns, and decompensation under excessive stress; and (c) sociocultural factors, especially as influences on the types and incidence of schizophrenic disorders. These three sets of factors are not mutually exclusive, of course, and it seems likely that each is involved in at least some cases. We will discuss biological factors first and in relatively greater detail because of the prominence they have attained in contemporary thinking about schizophrenia, and also because of the related high activity and ferment currently occurring in this area of research.

Biological Factors in Schizophrenia Research relating to biological factors implicated in the causal pattern leading to schizophrenia has been concentrated on heredity and on various biochemical, neurophysiological, and neuroanatomical processes. Each of these reseach foci will be discussed in what follows.

Heredity. In view of the disproportionate incidence of schizophrenia in the family backgrounds of index schizophrenic patients (that is, the diagnosed group of people who provide the starting point for inquiry), genetic factors are believed to play an important causal role in many instances of the disorder. Though the evidence is persuasive, it remains circumstantial in that it is difficult to disentangle from possibly detrimental environmental factors, making for problems in precisely quantifying the genetic contribution in the causal pattern leading to the disorder. In addition, researchers have largely been frustrated in their attempts to identify the mechanisms involved in the genetic factor's influence in the production of schizophrenic behavior.

The questions raised here are serious ones, in part because we remain dependent on essentially pedigree strategies for demonstrating the genetic effect. No specific gene or chromosomal gene locus has as yet been identified as being reliably implicated in schizophrenia (Kendler & Diehl, 1993), and many investigators believe this ongoing search will continue to prove frustrating based on an increasing likelihood of *polygenic* involvement. That is, current thinking emphasizes the notion of a multiplicity of genes operating in concert to enhance the schizophrenia risk (Gottesman, 1991). Therefore, the knowledge we have been able to glean thus far is based entirely on findings of higher-than-expected rates of schizophrenia among biological relatives of schizophrenic persons, where these rates are regularly observed to increase with increases in the closeness of the blood relationship (i.e., in gene-sharing or consanguinity). We begin our review with studies conducted on twins.

Twin Studies. The general strategy of twin studies was discussed in Chapter 3 and more specifically in relation to anxiety and mood disorders in Chapters 5 and 6. As in the mood disorders, schizophrenia concordance rates for identical twins are routinely, and over very many studies, found to be significantly higher than those for fraternal twins or ordinary siblings.

Although the incidence of schizophrenia among twins is no greater than for the general population, study after study has shown a higher concordance for schizophrenia among identical (monozygotic—MZ) twins over people related in any other way, including fraternal (dizygotic—DZ) twinship. Depending on a variety of factors, the degree of this difference varies substantially from one study to another. One source of potential confusion in this area is the investigators' choice of emphasizing the "pairwise" versus the "probandwise" method of calculating concordance rates. By the former method, each concordant pair is counted only once; in the probandwise method a given concordant pair may be counted twice, provided the inclusion in the study of each twin of a pair was determined independently of the other. For technical (and readily defended) reasons, geneticists favor the probandwise method. Most abnormal psychology students, in our experience, grasp more easily pairwise concordance figures, and for this reason we report pairwise figures in what follows. It should be understood that these may somewhat underestimate the magnitude of genetic influence.

We are fortunate in having available a review of the premier worldwide literature on twin studies in schizophrenia, recently published by Torrey and colleagues (1994). Considering only the eight most adequately conducted of such studies, the overall pairwise concordance rate for schizophrenia in MZ twins is 28 percent; that is, the likelihood of finding schizophrenia in a monozygotic co-twin of a schizophrenic proband is approximately 28 in 100 worldwide. The corresponding figure for DZ twinships is 6 percent. By adopting even more stringent standards and including the data of only the three most rigorous studies thus far conducted, these concordance figures become 26 and 8 percent, respectively. Although these rates appear not exceptionally high in absolute terms, they nevertheless convey a powerful message. Given one co-twin who is schizophrenic, a reduction in shared genes from 100 percent to (approximately) 50 percent is associated with a three- to fivefold decrease in the schizophrenia risk. Also, 50 percent gene-sharing with a schizophrenic proband is associated with a risk level some six to eight times greater than that of the general population.

If schizophrenia were exclusively a genetic disorder, the concordance rate for identical twins would, of course, be 100 percent. In fact, however, there are more discordant than concordant pairs, notwithstanding the remarkable example of the Genain sisters. On the other hand, concordance of significant magnitude clearly exists, and twin studies show us that predisposition for the disorder is associated with genetic variables. Interpretation of this finding, however, is not completely straightforward, in part because common environmental factors might also be implicated in the occurrence of concordant outcomes. The environments, both prenatal and postnatal, of identical twins will be more similar *on average* than the environments of individuals sharing any other type of relationship. There is evidence, for example, that the occurrence of challenging life events is significantly correlated in twin pairs, and more so in MZs than DZs (Kendler et al., 1993b); that is, MZs are more like each other not only genetically, but also in the amount of stress they experience.

Other factors also complicate the picture. A good example of these interpretive hazards is provided in studies of identical twins who are discordant for the diagnosis of schizophrenia. These are sets of twins in which one member of the pair meets diagnostic criteria for schizophrenia but the other does not over some period of time during which he or she may be considered still at risk. By rendering the genetic variable constant, such a strategy has the potential of revealing possible nongenetic factors critical in the development of schizophrenia. Unfortunately, this ideal turns out to be difficult, perhaps impossible, to realize. As pointed out by Torrey and colleagues (1994), we can be certain that "identical" twins are identical only at the moment of the original splitting of the zygote. From that point on, recent studies show, a host of influences may intervene that could differentially affect the development of the two embryos. These include chromosomal changes and gene mutations, differences in circulation and oxygenation, differential response on exposure to infectious agents and to drugs and chemicals, and congenital brain anomalies.

To be sure, these potentially disruptive conditions, when they occur, are more likely to be shared by MZ than by DZ twins, but there are ample instances of unshared effects in MZ pairs (see Pollin & Stabenau, 1968; Suddath et al., 1990). If any such effects were to make an *independent* (i.e., nongenetic) contribution to enhanced risk for schizophrenia, as seems conceivable, it compromises the clarity with which we can draw genetic etiologic conclusions from the classical twin study method. That is, the higher concordance rate for schizophrenia in MZ than in DZ twins might be a consequence, at least in part, of a higher rate of shared pathogenic factors *other than* tainted genes. Another possibility is that shared genes produce an anomalous condition, which then may or may not adversely affect the twins' development to the same degree. In short, the classical twin method of investigation, in schizophrenia at least, poses significant

These monozygotic (genetically identical) twin sisters are discordant for schizophrenia, which has affected only the twin on the right. Not uncommon, discordance affords an opportunity for certain types of research on the causes of schizophrenia.

problems as to the meaning of results obtained, especially in consideration of divergent outcomes with respect to MZ twins.

By far the most thorough and searching of available investigations of concordant and discordant psychopathological outcomes among MZ twins was the centerpiece of a recent report published by Torrey and colleagues (1994), to which reference has already been made. We can do no more here than selectively summarize the relevant major findings of this book-length work, concentrating our attention on 27 pairs of MZ twins who were discordant for schizophrenia. Below are listed the main statistically significant differences that differentiated the schizophrenic from the nonschizophrenic co-twins over the 27 pairs.

- Approximately 30 percent of the discordant affected twins were described as having been "different" during early childhood (e.g., shy and withdrawn, aggressive, or odd). Many of these differences were suggestive of early central nervous system dysfunction.

- Discordant affected twins showed widespread changes in brain structure, in particular bilateral decrements in size of the hippocampus-amygdala. However, changes in brain structure were uncorrelated with clinical aspects of the disorder.

- Discordant affected twins showed prominent alterations in brain function as assessed by cerebral blood flow, neuropsychological tests, neurological examination, and smooth pursuit eye movement (see p. 466). Reduced blood flow to the frontal lobes ("hypofrontality") was especially prominent and was associated with reduced size of the anterior hippocampus. Moderate or severe cognitive impairment in neuropsychological tests was observed in 14 of the 27 affected twins. The nonschizophrenic co-twins of discordant pairs, while less neurologically impaired than their disordered siblings, were more impaired than a set of normal control MZ twins.

- When schizophrenic persons from discordant and concordant pairs are compared, no significant differences in clinical or potential etiologic variables are found.

These results would seem to establish beyond reasonable doubt that genetically identical individuals can manifest widespread biological differences, particularly in neurological integrity, that are associated with relative risk for the development of schizophrenia. It should be noted, however, that none of the findings is of sufficient magnitude to predict outcomes for individual cases. Also, there were a few striking inconsistencies in the data, such that in these few cases the "well" twin appeared more biologically compromised than his or her schizophrenic co-twin. As the authors acknowledge, the results of this study, while intriguing, in themselves provide no clear resolution of basic questions concerning the ultimate source or sources of vulnerability to the development of schizophrenia. They do, of course, strongly implicate neurological anomalies as often playing a role in the causal pattern.

Returning to the specific issue of genetic influences, a seemingly "cleaner" investigative strategy employing discordant twins was pioneered by Fischer (1971, 1973). Reasoning that genetic influence, if present, would show up in the *offspring* of the *nonschizophrenic* twins of discordant pairs, she found exactly that outcome in a search of official records in Denmark. Gottesman and Bertelson (1989), in a follow-up of Fischer's subjects, have

reported an age-corrected schizophrenia incidence rate (that is, a rate taking into account predicted breakdowns for subjects not yet beyond the age of risk) of 17.4 percent for the offspring of the nonschizophrenic monozygotic twins. This rate, which far exceeds normal expectancy, was not significantly different from that for offspring of the schizophrenic members of discordant pairs, or from that for offspring of schizophrenic dizygotic twins. Assuming that exposure to schizophrenic aunts and uncles would have, at most, limited etiologic significance, these results give impressive support to the genetic hypothesis. They also, as the authors note, indicate that the implicated predisposition may remain "unexpressed" (as in the nonschizophrenic twins of discordant pairs) unless "released" by unknown environmental factors.

Adoption Studies. Several studies have attempted to overcome the shortcomings of the twin method in achieving a true separation of hereditary from environmental influences by using what is called the adoption strategy. In one version of this strategy, concordance rates of schizophrenia are compared for the biological and the adoptive relatives of persons who have been adopted out of their biological families at an early age (preferably at birth) and have subsequently become schizophrenic. If rates of schizophrenia are greater among the patients' biological than adoptive relatives, a hereditary influence is strongly suggested; the reverse pattern would of course argue for environmental causation.

Heston (1966) was apparently the first to use one of several variants of this basic method. In a follow-up study of 47 people who had been born to schizophrenic mothers in a state mental hospital and placed with relatives or in foster homes shortly after birth, Heston found that 16.6 percent of these subjects were later diagnosed as schizophrenic. In contrast, none of the 50 control subjects selected from among residents of the same foster homes—whose biological mothers were not schizophrenic—later became schizophrenic. In addition to the greater probability of being diagnosed schizophrenic, Heston found that the offspring of schizophrenic mothers were more likely to be diagnosed as mentally retarded, neurotic, and psychopathic (that is, antisocial). They also had been involved more frequently in criminal activities and had spent more time in penal institutions. These findings suggest that the genetic liability is not specific to schizophrenia but also includes a liability for other forms of psychopathology.

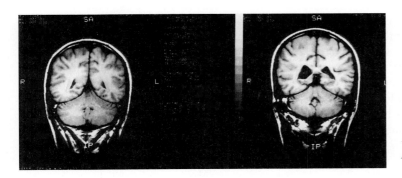

MRI scans of monozygotic twins. In the schizo-phrenic twin (right), the brain's ventricles are larger than in the normal twin's brain (left).

Independent of Heston's work, a large-scale and multifaceted adoption study was undertaken in Denmark with American investigators working in collaboration with Danish professionals (Kety, 1987; Kety et al., 1968, 1978, 1994; Rosenthal et al., 1968; Wender et al., 1974). The well-publicized results of these studies, arguing the case for a genetic contribution to schizophrenia, have had an enormous impact on the field. We concentrate here on the most recent follow-up report (Kety et al., 1994), in which certain anomalies noted earlier in the data of the study (see Carson & Sanislow, 1993) appear to have been overcome. Using a national sample of schizophrenic adoptees and their biological and adoptive relatives (together with suitable control cases), the data show a preponderance of schizophrenia in the *biological* relatives of schizophrenic adoptees. Specifically, the diagnosis of "chronic schizophrenia" was ten times more frequent in these relatives than in the biological relatives of nonschizophrenic control adoptees. By contrast, adoptive relatives of schizophrenic adoptees had an unremarkable incidence rate for schizophrenia.

The problems associated with the original reports of this study, which included use of vague, pre-DSM-III diagnostic criteria, had actually been resolved to an extent prior to Kety and colleagues' (1994) most recent update. Procedurally, the improvement involved an independent reanalysis of the study's primary data. This reanalysis, conducted by Kendler and Gruenberg (1984), included the rediagnosis of all cases using DSM-III criteria and the use of other more advanced techniques to improve precision. Kendler and Gruenberg found convincing evidence of a modest genetic contribution to a certain class of disorders having schizophrenia-like features. They included, in addition to schizophrenia, schizotypal, and paranoid personality disorders; the three together

were said to constitute a "schizophrenia spectrum," a group of disorders believed to share a common, genetically determined diathesis. Thus, as Heston's early work had suggested, the vulnerability conveyed by genetic influences appeared here not to be specific for schizophrenia per se but to involve a broader range of compromised functioning.

The Kendler and Gruenberg (1984) study has also recently been updated and expanded to the Danish population at large. In this later work (Kendler, Gruenberg, & Kinney, 1994a) the focus shifted to adoptees having DSM-III diagnoses of schizophrenia, schizotypal personality disorder, and schizoaffective (but mainly schizophrenic symptoms) disorder because these diagnoses were found to have maximum levels of (biological) family coherence. The notion of "schizophrenia spectrum" disorders was thus adjusted somewhat from the earlier study. The results again showed a concentration of spectrum diagnoses in the biological relatives of adoptees having these same diagnoses.

The Danish adoption studies did not include independent assessments of the child-rearing adequacy of the adoptive families into which index (those who became schizophrenic) and control (those who did not) youngsters had been placed. It remained for Tienari and colleagues (Tienari et al., 1985, 1987; Tienari, 1991) to add this feature to their research plan. This study, still in progress, involves a follow-up of the adopted-away children of all women in Finland hospitalized for schizophrenia, beginning in 1960. Of the 306 index (children whose mothers were schizophrenic) and control (comparable children whose mothers were normal) adoptees evaluated as of the latest (Tienari, 1991) available report, there were only five instances of psychosis or severe personality disorder (the report does not distinguish between these) among either

index ($n = 55$) or control ($n = 68$) children who
were raised in adoptive families independently rated
to be psychologically "healthy." Two of these five
cases were in fact controls, the offspring of normal
mothers. Of the adoptees raised in families considered disturbed, 38 of 83 (46 percent) index children and 24 of 100 (24 percent) controls had become either psychotic or severely personality
disordered.

Supporting earlier work, these results show a
moderate genetic effect—the differential "healthy"
and "severe disorder" rates of index versus control
adoptees irrespective of family context. The magnitude of that effect, however, is actually exceeded by
one associated with the variable of relative family
disorganization. Tienari (1991) interprets these results as indicating an interaction between genetic
vulnerability and an unfavorable family environment
in the causal pathway leading to schizophrenia, an
idea that seems plausible and not inconsistent with
the genetic evidence already reported. Unfortunately, however, we cannot be certain that the emergence of odd or psychotic behavior in adoptees did
not precede and cause, in whole or in part, the disorganization of their adoptive families. Analyses to
examine this possibility are reported to be in
progress.

Studies of High-Risk Children. The research
strategy of long-term monitoring of children
known to be at high risk for schizophrenia (by
virtue of having been born to a schizophrenic parent) is basically intended to identify the environmental factors that cause breakdown (or resistance
to it) in predisposed people. As we have seen in
Chapter 1, this strategy, pioneered by Mednick and
Schulsinger (1968) and followed up by numerous
additional research projects (for reviews see Cornblatt et al., 1992; Erlenmeyer-Kimling & Cornblatt, 1992; Garmezy, 1978a, 1978b; Neale & Oltmanns, 1980; Rieder, 1979; Watt et al., 1984), has
thus far not paid off very well in terms of isolating
specific environmental factors. In saying this, however, we must acknowledge both the enormous difficulties that attend long-term and complicated
projects of this sort and our own admiration for
those who undertake them.

The difficulties are well illustrated in the first
(and so far only) summary report of the Israeli-
NIMH High-Risk Study (see Schizophrenia Bulletin, Vol. 11, No. 1, 1985). This project, begun in
1967, compared the outcomes of an index group of
high-risk Israeli children who remained with their
biological families to those brought up in the surro-
gate-parent settlement communities known as kibbutzim, relative to closely matched control groups

of low-risk youngsters. "High risk" was defined as
having a schizophrenic mother.

Many behavioral differences were found between
index and control children, almost always favoring
the controls; few were found for the variable of kibbutz versus normal rearing. Especially impressive
was a high frequency of soft neurological signs (such
as poor coordination) observed in index children in
two separate examinations five years apart. On the
critical measure of psychopathological outcome at
15 years following the beginning of the project (the
average subject age was 25), rearing context proved
apparently significant, although only in index cases
and in an unexpected direction. Considering only
schizophrenia and schizophrenia "spectrum" diagnoses, 9 of 46 index cases and 0 of 44 control cases
had become disordered; 6 of the 9 casualties had
been kibbutz-reared and hence to a considerable degree isolated from exposure to a psychotic parent.
These trends are, if anything, strengthened when
other diagnoses are included. Mirsky and colleagues
(1985), who report these data, speculate that kibbutz living tends to evoke symptoms (although only
in predisposed individuals) because it precludes privacy and "escape."

It may be noted in passing that, once again in this
study, the children considered at risk on grounds
that were at least implicitly genetic (their mothers
being schizophrenic) were discovered as a group to
be mildly neurologically compromised in childhood.
In light of our earlier discussion and the related Torrey and colleagues (1994) findings on discordant
identical twins, we can by no means be certain that
such compromise, which might itself be a causal factor in schizophrenic outcomes, was mediated by the
inheritance of deficient genes. As in the discordant
twin study, the neurologic impairment may have
been caused by factors other than faulty inheritance.

Although the available results of high-risk studies
have generally proven difficult to interpret, they
have supported the observation that having a schizophrenic parent is a good predictor of psychological
disorder, including schizophrenia. It seems likely
that some of this predictability comes about as a result of the genetic transmission of vulnerability to
schizophrenia.

Summing up, the question of genetic transmissibil-
ity of a predisposition to schizophrenia is not as easily
answered as it may appear to be when first posed. We
are convinced that some genetic influence does make
certain individuals abnormally vulnerable to schizophrenia. The data indicate that no such genetic contribution to etiology is sufficient in itself to produce
schizophrenia, and they provide no basis for concluding that such a contribution is a necessary condition

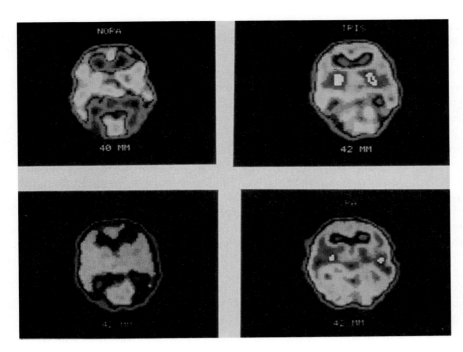

PET scans of the Genain quadruplets suggest a possible psychosocial impact resulting from the early matching of two pairs of cotwins. The scans indicate comparatively more severe brain impairment for Hester and Nora. The large areas of blue and yellow show that their brains consume lower levels of glucose, one indicator of lessened brain activity. The orange spots on the scan of Iris and Myra suggest more normal energy usage. Yet it is Iris, originally "matched" with Hester, who has had the poorer clinical outcome than either Nora or Myra.

for a schizophrenic outcome. Indeed, most people who develop schizophrenia have no close relatives who are also known to have had the disorder—although, as we shall see, some of these normal relatives may share biological anomalies statistically associated with a schizophrenia diagnosis. Based on the best available studies, the aggregate average risk of schizophrenia for *first-degree* (sharing 50 percent genes) relatives of index cases is 4.8 percent, approximately nine times the rate for control cases (Kendler & Diehl, 1993).

Biochemical Factors. The idea that serious mental disorders are due to "chemical imbalances" in the brain is now common. To be useful to clinicians and researchers, however, such an idea must be reformulated into hypotheses that are as explicit and specific as possible. We cannot effectively address the general question of possible biochemically based contributions to the onset or maintenance of schizophrenic behaviors in the absence of clues that tell us where to look and what to look for. At present, as in the case of the severe mood disorders, the search is governed largely by attempts to discover the site and nature of central nervous system effects induced by drugs that diminish the behavioral expression of the disorder. In general, drugs that do so are ones found to alter (by up- or down-regulation) the likelihood that a nerve impulse arriving at a synapse will cross the synapse and "fire" the next neuron in the chain.

In schizophrenia research, the most attractive of these specific ideas has been the **dopamine hypothesis** (Sacher et al., 1978; Snyder, 1978), based on

the observation that all of the early antischizophrenic drugs (called neuroleptics) had the common property of blocking dopamine-mediated neural transmission. Dopamine is a neurotransmitter like norepinephrine, of which it is a chemical precursor. It appears to be the main neurotransmitter for perhaps a half-dozen identified brain pathways. According to the dopamine hypothesis, then, schizophrenia is the product of an excess of dopamine activity at certain synaptic sites. Variants of this view include hypotheses that a schizophrenic person has too many postsynaptic dopamine receptors or that these receptors have for some reason become supersensitive. In recent years, however, the dopamine hypothesis has proved inadequate as a general formulation of etiology (Carlsson, 1988; Koreen et al., 1994; Lieberman & Koreen, 1993).

Dopamine-blocking drugs, for example, are therapeutically nonspecific for schizophrenia (that is, they are also used effectively to treat psychotic symptoms associated with various other disordered states, such as neuropsychological disorders, some manias, and even drug-induced "bad trips"). Additionally, the receptor-blocking effect is accomplished too quickly (within hours) to be consistent with the clinical picture of a gradual improvement (often over several weeks) following initiation of neuroleptic drug therapy in schizophrenia. In other words, if only excess dopamine activity were the cause of schizophrenia, these drugs should have ameliorative effects almost immediately; they do not. Moreover, their therapeutic activity depends not so much on curtailing excessive dopaminergic activity as on reducing it to *abnormally* low levels, which creates additional problems of an often serious nature (e.g., tardive dyskinesia; see Chapter 16, p. 610). In light of these and other observations, Davis (1978) has suggested that some other (unspecified) factor causes schizophrenia, the symptoms of which are then amplified by dopaminergic neural transmission.

More recent research has provided no serious challenge to this view, although it has shown the dopaminergic systems within the brain to be far more complicated than was originally thought. For example, we now know that more than one type of dopamine receptor site exists on the dendrites of postsynaptic neurons, and that these are involved in differing biochemical processes. The dopamine hypothesis has also been weakened by the emergence of the second-generation antipsychotic drug clozapine. The side effects of this drug have a profile that is very different from that of the dopamine blockers, suggesting that its antipsychotic mode of action significantly differs from that of the neuroleptics. Clozapine has a potent and early-appearing antipsychotic effect for approximately 30 percent of those schizophrenic patients showing little or no response to standard neuroleptic medication (Kane et al., 1988), and the proportion of patients responding positively continues to increase to a maximum of 50–75 percent for up to six months or more of continuing clozapine therapy (Lieberman et al., 1994; Meltzer, 1992).

Other biochemical theories of schizophrenia have been, and doubtless will continue to be, advanced, but to date no other such theory appears anywhere near as promising as had the dopamine theory through much of the past 25 years (Lieberman & Koreen, 1993). The fact is that the brain chemistry of schizophrenia remains very imperfectly understood. Ultimately, it seems likely that a complete understanding of the biochemistry of these disorders will have to include a sense of how other influences may interact with whatever biochemical abnormalities are discovered to accompany schizophrenic behavior.

Neurophysiological Factors. Much recent research has focused on the role of neurophysiological disturbances in schizophrenia, such as an imbalance in various neurophysiologic processes and inappropriate autonomic arousal. Such disordered physiology would disrupt normal attentional and information-processing capabilities, and there seems to be a growing consensus that disturbances of this type underlie the cognitive and perceptual distortions characteristic of schizophrenia.

A substantial proportion of schizophrenic persons are found to be deficient in their ability to track a moving target visually, a skill referred to as smooth pursuit eye movement, or SPEM (Levy et al., 1983, 1993; Lieberman et al., 1993a). The deficiency is sometimes attributed to a disorder of nonvoluntary attention. An impressive amount of evidence also indicates that many close relatives of schizophrenics share this SPEM deficit (e.g., Clementz et al., 1992; Iacono et al., 1992; Kuechenmeister et al., 1977; Levy et al., 1994)—far more in fact than share the diagnosis (Levy et al., 1993). This would suggest an inherited source for the difficulty while simultaneously ruling it out as a specific indicator for the disorder. Earlier research in this area has been well reviewed by Neale and Oltmanns (1980), and follow-up studies have continued to establish the reliability of the phenomenon (e.g., Holzman et al., 1988; Iacono et al., 1992). Many researchers (e.g., Braff, 1993; George & Neufeld, 1985; Neale & Oltmanns, 1980) believe that a deeper analysis of such deficits might enhance our understanding of hallucinations and other of the more dramatic phenomena of schizophrenia. Progress on this front, however, will require analysis of what is unique to schizophrenia in producing the SPEM deficit, since the gross deficit itself is also shared by psychotic mood-disordered subjects (Sweeney et al., 1994).

Some findings that may be related indicate that persons who are merely "at risk" for schizophrenia often experience difficulties in maintaining attention, in processing information, and in certain other indicators of cognitive functioning before a schizophrenic breakdown (Buchsbaum et al., 1978; Cornblatt & Keilp, 1994; Dworkin et al., 1993; Erlenmeyer-Kimling & Cornblatt, 1978; Fish et al., 1992; Marcus et al., 1985, 1993; Mednick, 1978; Silberman & Tassone, 1985; Spring & Zubin, 1978). Also possibly related are certain anomalies shown by many schizophrenic persons in electroencephalographic (brain wave) reactions to momentary sensory stimulation (Friedman & Squires-Wheeler, 1994; Pritchard, 1986), recently demonstrated in subjects merely at risk for the disorder by virtue of having somewhat peculiar thought processes (Stelmack, Houlihan, & McGarry-Roberts, 1993). Neurologic abnormalities, such as reflex hyperactivity and deficit performance in neuropsychological testing, have also been found in the close relatives of schizophrenic individuals (Kinney, Woods, & Yurgelun-Todd, 1986; Kremen et al., 1994).

Additional research literature, going back many decades, documents an enormous variety of other ways in which attentional and cognitive processes seemingly dependent on intact neurophysiologic functioning are disrupted among schizophrenic persons. As even our brief review shows, the disjointed array of findings reported remains baffling in the absence of a conceptual framework within which the "pieces" of the schizophrenia puzzle can be put together. Ideally, such an overarching conception would incorporate the correlative findings in close relatives and other nonschizophrenic "at risk" subjects. As yet, however, the role of these abnormalities in the development of schizophrenia remains unclear.

Abnormal neurophysiological processes in schizophrenia could be genetic in origin, but some at least could also be the product of biological deviations caused by other factors, as suggested in the discordant MZ twin data reviewed earlier. Problems of this sort could as likely arise from unknown intrauterine conditions or mechanical difficulties in the birth process as from faulty genes. Obstetrical complications in the histories of people who later become schizophrenic appear to be well above normative expectations (Cannon et al., 1993; Gureje, Bamidele, & Raji, 1994; Torrey et al., 1994), although it is possible that resultant early brain injury contributes to schizophrenic outcomes only among genetically predisposed persons (see Marcus et al., 1993). Such observations have led to a resurgence of interest in an old question—that of the anatomical intactness of the schizophrenic brain—to which we now turn.

Neuroanatomical Factors. Research on the structural properties of the brain in living subjects was difficult until the development of modern computer-dependent technologies, such as computerized axial tomography (CAT) and magnetic resonance imaging (MRI). The use of these techniques in the study of schizophrenic people's brains has developed at an accelerating pace in recent years, with interesting results.

Much evidence now indicates that in some cases of schizophrenia, particularly among those of chronic, negative-symptom course, there is an abnormal enlargement of the brain's ventricles—the hollow areas filled with cerebrospinal fluid lying deep within the core (Andreasen et al., 1982a, 1982b, 1986; Boronow et al., 1985; Carpenter et al., 1993; Goetz & Van Kammen, 1986; Gur & Pearlson, 1993; Gur et al., 1994; Pearlson et al., 1989; Raz, 1993). Several other associated anatomical anomalies, such as enlarged sulci (the fissures in the surface of the cerebral cortex), are often reported as well. In fact, the same anomalies are sometimes found in the "normal" family members of schizophrenic patients (Cannon & Marco, 1994; DeLisi et al., 1986b) and in the high-risk offspring of schizophrenic mothers (Cannon et al., 1993, 1994). In the latter instance, they appear to be associated with low birth weight and the possibility of fetal damage from some unknown agent, possibly infectious (Lyon et al., 1989; Silverton et al., 1985).

Because the brain normally occupies the rigid enclosure of the skull fully, enlarged ventricles imply a loss of brain tissue mass—possibly some type of atrophy or degeneration. Enlarged sulci have a similar significance. Some more direct evidence (e.g., Nestor et al., 1993) indicates deficient size of temporal lobe structures as well. Signs of what appears to be degeneration have been reported by Bernhardt, Meertz, and Schonfeldt-Bausch (1985) and Brown and colleagues (1986) in postmortem studies of the brains of individuals who had been schizophrenic. Bogerts (1993), however, in reviewing some 50 such studies going back many years, concludes that the findings are generally not consistent with the notion of progressive degeneration and favor the hypothesis of some type of anomaly in prenatal brain development.

The findings of an organic brain anomaly associated with some cases (overall about 50 percent exceeding the normal range, according to Cannon and Marco [1994]) is of enormous potential significance for at least the types of schizophrenia primarily implicated. Although it has been suggested that at least some of these brain abnormalities could be due to long-term use of antipsychotic medication (Breggin, 1990), examinations of the brains of schizophrenic people who have never taken therapeutic drugs show that this type of brain anomaly is not limited to patients having long histories of exposure to neuroleptic drugs (e.g., Lieberman et al., 1993b; Saykin et al., 1994; Weinberger et al., 1982). The observation of similar abnormalities among normal family members who have not taken drugs supports this finding.

The attention of brain researchers in schizophrenia has in recent years tended to focus on the frontal lobes, again with interesting results. These studies have mostly involved the positron emission tomography (PET) technique to measure metabolic activity at various sites in the brain while subjects are occupied with certain assigned tasks. Many recent studies have demonstrated abnormally low frontal lobe activation—called *hypofrontality*—among schizophrenic persons when they engage in tasks supposedly requiring substantial frontal lobe involvement, such as the Wisconsin Card Sorting Test (WCST). Evidence of such hypofrontality has been reported for only the schizophrenic co-twins of discordant monozygotic twin pairs (Berman et al., 1992), for never-medicated patients (Buchsbaum et al., 1992), and especially for patients having high levels of negative versus positive symptoms (Andreasen et al., 1992; Wolkin et al., 1992). It should be cautioned, however, that the levels of "hypofrontality" observed among schizophrenic persons are often only marginally, albeit statistically significantly, different from levels observed in normal control subjects, with much overlap between the groups (e.g., Buchsbaum et al., 1992). Also, unlike persons with proven frontal-lobe damage, it appears that schizophrenic individuals who have difficulty with the WCST can be trained to perform normally on the instrument (Metz et al., 1994).

In an overall review of neuroimaging studies in schizophrenia, Gur and Pearlson (1993) conclude that the evidence implicates primarily three brain regions: the frontal, the temporolimbic (i.e., the temporal lobes and the adjacent, interior limbic system structures), and the basal ganglia (subcortical neural centers chiefly involved in integrative functions). These authors also note, however, that few of the findings are specific for schizophrenia, being also observed (usually in lesser degree) in other conditions such as the mood disorders. In any event, the conclusion of temporolimbic involvement is consistent with the types of deficit functioning observed in an extensive neuropsychological investigation of unmedicated, first-episode schizophrenic patients reported by Saykin and colleagues (1994).

While daunting problems of interpretation persist, these largely quite recent discoveries of brain anomalies in substantial numbers of schizophrenic patients are important not only in their own right but also because they invite integration with certain other exciting research initiatives of recent years. In particular, they relate to research on impaired neuropsychological test performances of schizophrenic people (Blanchard & Neale, 1994; Heaton et al., 1994; Levin & Yurgelun-Todd, 1989; Saykin et al., 1994) and to the already-noted neurologic impairments of some children who are at risk for schizophrenia (e.g., Dworkin et al., 1993; Fish et al, 1992; Marcus et al., 1993; Torrey et al., 1994). As suggested earlier, however, these brain abnormalities do not appear to be progressively developing ones (Bogerts, 1993; Heaton et al., 1994). Rather, it seems that these defects, often beginning before birth, enhance the risk for schizophrenia and are then detectable in substantial numbers of adult schizophrenic persons.

We should also note in this connection the evidence that many persons diagnosed as having a schizotypal personality pattern show behavioral deficits (such as poor perceptual-motor coordination or distinctive anomalies in reaction-time performance) suggestive of subtle neurological impairment (Lenzenweger, 1994; Lenzenweger & Korfine, 1994; Rosenbaum, Shore, & Chapin, 1988; Siever, 1985). This schizotypal pattern is conceived as one manifestation of a general schizophrenia "spectrum" of disorder and to render the person at risk for the full syndrome (Lenzenweger, 1994; Meehl, 1990).

For a number of years researchers have noted that people who become schizophrenic are more likely than people in general to have been born in the winter and early spring months—about an 8 percent deviation from norms (DeLisi, Crow, & Hirsch, 1986a). This peculiar observation, which itself is now beyond dispute, has given rise to a variety of hypotheses involving what has come to be called "the season of birth effect" in the development of schizophrenia. Some of these hypotheses directly relate to the question of compromised brain integrity in schizophrenia, as will be seen. In part because of that implication, the seasonal effect has been a source of sharp controversy. Lewis (1989a, 1989b, 1990; Lewis & Griffin, 1981), for example, has dismissed the original observation itself as a mere artifact of time spent at risk for persons affected. Lewis's analysis has been attacked (see issue #1 of the *Schizophrenia Bulletin* of 1990, Vol. 16), in our judgment none too effectively. Earlier on, however, Bradbury and Miller (1985), in a thorough review of the evidence then available, concluded that after correcting for the possible distortion, the evidence still pointed to some type of prenatal or early postnatal pathogenic influence associated with season, one that would bias development in favor of a schizophrenic outcome. Their best guess was some type of infectious process or obstetrical complications (or both).

Accumulating evidence suggests that Bradbury and Miller may have been on the right track. Several studies have suggested that, historically, influenza epidemics are associated at a higher-than-chance level with the gestation periods of persons who later became schizophrenic. The latest of these studies as of this writing, reported by Takei and colleagues (1994), identifies the supposedly critical peak infectious period as five months before birth, but includes the extremely curious finding that the association exists only for females, not males. Seemingly important and possibly related findings, recently reported by Torrey and colleagues (1993), establish a strong timewise correlation between the occurrence of stillbirths and the live births of persons who become schizophrenic, both being elevated in winter months. The investigators suggest that there appears to be a common factor for both stillbirths and schizophrenia risk, presumably some infectious agent; in the one case, according to this hypothesis, it leads to death of the fetus, while in the other to brain changes that enhance vulnerability to schizophrenia.

Interpreting the Biological Evidence. We trust the reader is by now convinced that the case for the role of biological factors in the etiology of schizophrenia has been established. The evidence for some sort of causal contribution from this broad source is, in a word, overwhelming. Impressive as it is, however, we remain in the dark about precisely how biological factors, operating either singly or in combination, are implicated in producing schizophrenic outcomes. Nor do we know which factors are most important—either in the aggregate or in individual cases.

In summary, then, biologically oriented research, particularly in recent years, has given us a wealth of new insights regarding the nature of schizophrenia and some of the sources of vulnerability to it. Our best bet at present is that it will prove not to provide a complete answer to the riddle of schizophrenia—that is, biological findings will have to be supplemented by pertinent psychosocial and sociocultural research in order to provide a comprehensive understanding, and eventually control, of the problem. This is hardly an extraordinary conclusion; the diathesis-stress model, which is often involved in characterizations of schizophrenia (Zubin & Spring, 1977), envisages exactly that sort of scenario. We turn now to an examination of the evidence relating to psychosocial influences in schizophrenia.

Psychosocial Factors in Schizophrenia Some behavioral scientists (e.g., Whitaker, 1992) dispute the idea that schizophrenia is caused primarily by biological factors. Noting that genetic and other biological factors are only part of the diathesis-stress combination, they emphasize the role of psychosocial factors in contributing to the disorder. Some researchers have argued that the proximate origins of the disorder are psychosocial; others have shown that psychosocial stress is related to the decompensation shown in schizophrenic episodes, whatever the role of biological factors in the underlying etiology of the disorder.

When we consider psychosocial influences, however, we are unlikely to see huge effects that dramatically alter the probability of someone becoming schizophrenic. In light of the frequency of abuse, trauma, and other less-than-ideal conditions of developmental experience, it is likely that truly potent and readily detected influences of this kind—if they existed—would already be well known. More realistically, we might hope to discover causal factors of

small magnitude, ones that in combination with other pathogenic influences (including biological ones) might create added vulnerability to the point of exceeding some threshold beyond which any given person experiencing normal levels of stress may evidence psychosis.

It is, in our opinion, unfortunate and counterproductive that biological and psychosocial research are often conceived as mutually antagonistic, and that they rarely make contact with one another (Carson & Sanislow, 1993). One of us (Carson, 1991) has referred to this problem as one of widespread "tunnel vision" in the perspectives of scientists of both research camps. Although much lip service is paid to the evidence of interaction between biological and psychosocial variables in schizophrenia, studies that actually engage the interaction are rare.

One aspect of the imputed interaction is the often neglected fact that many of the biologically based deficits of the type reviewed in the preceding section would very likely influence the personality and social development of affected children in detrimental ways (see Zborowski & Garske, 1993). This idea has been a central element in the important contributions of psychologist Paul Meehl (1962, 1989, 1990a) in tracing the developmental course of schizophrenic outcomes. A recent ingenious series of studies reported by Walker and her colleagues (Grimes & Walker, 1994; Walker et al., 1993, 1994) illustrates how such interactions of the biological and the psychosocial might play themselves out.

These investigators gathered family home movies made during the childhoods of 32 persons who eventually succumbed to schizophrenia. Trained observers made "blind" (i.e., they were uninformed as to outcomes) ratings of certain dimensions of the emotional (Grimes & Walker, 1994) and facial expressions (Walker et al., 1993), motor skills, and neuromotor abnormalities (Walker et al., 1994) of these children and of their healthy-outcome siblings from the same movie clips. The facial and emotional expressions, and the motor competence, of the preschizophrenic and the healthy-outcome children were found by the raters to differ significantly and in ways apparently disadvantageous to the former group. The preschizophrenic children showed less—and less positive than negative—emotion, had poorer motor skills, and showed a higher rate of peculiar movements suggestive of neuromotor abnormalities. In other words, these children, in some instances before age two, were already showing behavioral abnormality not unlike that encountered in our earlier discussion of biological factors in schizophrenia. It is a reasonable hypothesis, therefore, that these preschizophrenic children as a group suffered from subtle neurological impairment of unknown origin.

Evidence already reviewed indicates that (a) these early-appearing subtle impairments are probably not progressive, and (b) they do not inevitably eventuate in a diagnosis of schizophrenia. It seems possible, however, that if persistent, they might affect transactions with the social environment in a disadvantageous manner and hence have negative effects on various aspects of personality development and functioning. The child who rarely manifests joy (even on celebratory family occasions such as birthdays), whose emotional expressiveness is prevailingly in the bland to negative range, who is motorically clumsy or awkward, and who may evidence peculiar involuntary movements, is likely to have a far less stress-free early life than the child endowed with the opposite characteristics. Minimally, such a scenario suggests that the occurrence of challenging life events ("stress") is not independent of a potentially pathogenic biological "diathesis."

Conceptual support for this admittedly speculative interpretation is provided in another recent study by Dworkin and colleagues (1993) involving interviews of normal children having a schizophrenic parent (and therefore being "at risk"). Compared with children of mood-disordered and normal parents, these youngsters were found to have more "affective deficits" and social incompetence, which were in turn associated, respectively, with observed neuromotor and attentional dysfunctions. Commenting on the increasing evidence of personality factors possibly mediating between biological liabilities and schizophrenic outcomes, Berenbaum and Fujita (1994) urge that researchers pay more attention to these likely psychosocially based contributions to the emergence of schizophrenic behavior, including findings of widespread personality deviations in relatives.

In making these comments, Berenbaum and Fujita (1994) address an issue that, in our judgment, is a serious one. We refer to the fact that research on psychosocial factors in the development of schizophrenia has been exceedingly sparse in recent years, especially compared with the research investment in biological correlates. As a result, much of the available psychosocially oriented research in schizophrenia is seriously dated. Much of it is also of poor quality, in part because it was planned and carried out in an era of less rigorous standards, and one in which less was in fact known about the proper design of research studies. It could also be argued that as a general rule research on psychosocial variables is inherently more complex and difficult than biologically oriented research. For these reasons, our discussion of psychosocial factors in schizophrenia will be relatively brief.

Pathogenic Parent-Child and Family Interactions. Studies of interactions in families having schizophrenic offspring have focused on such factors as (a) "schizophrenogenic" (schizophrenia-causing) parents; (b) destructive marital interactions; and (c) faulty communication. The focus of research has shifted in recent years from parent-child to total family interactions. Before we proceed, however, let us take a moment to gain some perspective on this sensitive topic.

In the early years of attention to family variables in schizophrenia, parents were routinely assumed to have caused their children's disorders through hostility, deliberate rejection, or gross parental ineptitude. Many professionals blamed parents, and their feedback to them was often angry and insensitive, if not brutal. We hope that nothing in the following discussion appears to condone such attitudes. Most of the parents we have known, whether or not they experienced the "bad luck" (Meehl, 1978, 1989) of schizophrenia in a child, have done the best that could reasonably be expected, within the limits of their own situations, to foster their children's happiness and success. Some parents are cruel and abusive, but there is no evidence that such a pattern is especially associated with schizophrenic outcomes. Apart from the fact that blaming parents does not help and may indeed worsen matters, blame could only be based on an oversimplified and erroneous notion of how people come to be schizophrenic.

"Schizophrenogenic" Parenting. Beginning in the 1940s, studies examined the parents of schizophrenic persons, particularly (and prejudicially) the mothers of male patients. Termed **schizophrenogenic,** these mothers were characterized on uncontrolled clinical observational grounds as rejecting, domineering, cold, overprotective, and impervious to the feelings and needs of others (e.g., Fromm-Reichmann, 1948). Such a mother was said to reject her child and at the same time to depend on the child for her emotional satisfaction. For this reason, it was suggested, she tended to dominate, possessively overprotect, and smother the child—encouraging dependence on her. The characteristics attributed to the "schizophrenogenic mother" have also been alleged on the same weak grounds to be causally involved in many other types of offspring outcome—such as anorexia in girls and male homosexuality—so much so that the concept of the "schizophrenogenic mother," never supported by robust research, was largely abandoned by the 1970s.

Studies have shown a high incidence of emotional disturbances on the part of both mothers and fathers of schizophrenic persons. Kaufman and colleagues (1960) reported that a large proportion of both the mothers and fathers of 80 schizophrenic children and adolescents studied were emotionally disturbed: The mothers almost uniformly used psychotic-like defense patterns, and the fathers likewise used seriously maladaptive coping patterns. Other studies concerned with the mental health of schizophrenics' parents, reviewed by Hirsch and Leff (1975), came to basically similar conclusions.

As was indicated in Chapter 3, however, we cannot reasonably assume that disturbance always passes from parent to offspring; it can work in the other direction as well. Whatever the original source of the difficulty, it appears that once it begins the members of a family may stimulate each other to increasingly pathological behavior. For example, studies by Mishler and Waxler (1968) and Liem (1974) both found that parents' attempts to deal with the disturbed behavior of schizophrenic sons and daughters had pathological effects on their own behavior and communication patterns. In fact, the bidirectionality of effects may be the single most robust finding we have gleaned from studying the families of schizophrenic people.

Destructive Family Interactions. Of particular interest here is the work of Theodore Lidz and his associates, which continued over some two decades. In an initial clinical study of 14 families with schizophrenic offspring, Lidz, Fleck, and Cornelison (1965) failed to find a single family that was reasonably well integrated. Eight of the 14 couples lived in a state of severe chronic discord in which continuation of the marriage was constantly threatened—a condition the investigators called **marital schism.** The other six couples in this study had achieved a state of equilibrium in which the relationship was maintained at the expense of a basic distortion in family relationships; in these cases, family members entered into a "collusion" in which the seriously disturbed behavior of one or the other parent was redefined as normal. This pattern was referred to as **marital skew.** Lidz (1978) proposed that a major effect of such severe family disturbance is the encouragement of "egocentric cognitive regression" in children subjected to it. We remind the reader again that family disturbance does not lead to schizophrenia for the large majority of persons experiencing it, and the investigations reported made no attempt to assess biologically based predispositions among the schizophrenia casualties.

As was by deliberate selection the case in the families studied by Lidz and colleagues, schizophrenic people often have psychologically healthy siblings who were raised with them in the same families. How have these siblings escaped the presumed pathology of the family context? A possible answer is that they were not biologically predisposed. But it is also probably true, as emphasized by the Lidz group, that the subculture of a family is not constant—that every child raised within a family experiences a family pattern in many ways unique to him or her. Stabenau and Pollin (1968; Stabenau et al., 1965), taking a direct approach to this issue, studied families in which nontwin siblings were discordant for schizophrenia and for juvenile delinquency. They found that 17 of their 19 "psychopathology siblings" (9 of 10 for schizophrenic siblings alone), compared with only 2 of 29 controls, had encountered periods of maximum family crisis during the presumably critical period of early childhood. These crises, which were identified by the families themselves, included financial disasters, major parental strife, and depressive episodes in one or another parent, among other things. We cannot, of course, be certain that these results are free of retrospective memory distortion.

Faulty Communication. Gregory Bateson (1959, 1960) was one of the first investigators to emphasize the conflicting and confusing nature of communications among members of schizophrenic families. He used the term **double-bind communication** to describe one such pattern. In this pattern the parent presents to the child ideas, feelings, and demands that are mutually incompatible. For example, a mother may be verbally loving and accepting but emotionally anxious and rejecting; or she may complain about her son's lack of affection but freeze up or punish him when he approaches her affectionately. The mother subtly but effectively prohibits comment on such paradoxes, and the father is too weak and ineffectual to intervene. In essence, according to Bateson's etiologic hypothesis, such a son is continually placed in situations where he cannot win, and he becomes increasingly anxious; presumably, such disorganized and contradictory communications in the family come to be reflected in his own thinking. Unfortunately, no solid confirmation of the pathogenicity of double-bind communications has ever been reported.

Singer and Wynne (1963, 1965a, 1965b) linked the thought disorders in schizophrenia to two styles of thinking and communication in the family— amorphous and fragmented. The amorphous pattern is characterized by a failure in differentiation; here, attention toward feelings, objects, or people is loosely organized, vague, and drifting. Fragmented thinking involves greater differentiation but lowered integration, with erratic and disruptive shifts in communication. In their later research, Singer and Wynne (Singer, Wynne, & Toohey, 1978; Wynne, Toohey, & Doane, 1979) referred generally to "communication deviance" (or "transactional style deviance") as being at the heart of the purported negative effects parents have on their preschizophrenic children.

Following up on this research, Goldstein and his colleagues (Doane et al., 1981; Goldstein, 1985; Goldstein et al., 1978; Lewis, Rodnick, & Goldstein, 1981), in a longitudinal study employing a variant of the "high-risk" strategy (that is, subjects who had been psychological clinic patients, but not schizophrenic, as adolescents were followed into adulthood), confirmed such an effect. Specifically, they found that high parental communication deviance, measured during their children's adolescence, did indeed predict the occurrence of adult schizophrenic spectrum disorders among these offspring. A family atmosphere of negative affect appears to increase the likelihood of such outcomes. These findings, reviewed by Goldstein and Strachan (1987), are intriguing in controlling for reverse (schizophrenic) child-to-parent influence in the creation of parental deviance. However, the study's design cannot rule out the possibility of a common genetic influence affecting both parents and offspring, one leading to odd communication in parents and (independently) to schizophrenia in offspring.

The point just made illustrates the unfortunate fact that the interpretation of findings relating to potential psychosocial influences in causing schizophrenia is at least as difficult and hazardous as we found characteristic of many findings in the biological domain. Perhaps, as was suggested earlier, clearer answers might be forthcoming if both groups joined forces.

Excessive Life Stress and Decompensation. Brown (1972) found a marked increase in the severity of life stress during the ten-week period prior to a person's schizophrenic breakdown. Problems typically centered on difficulties in intimate personal relationships. Similarly, Schwartz and Myers (1977) found interpersonal stressors to be significantly more common among schizophrenic people than among members of a matched control group. We remind the reader also that life stressors, like schizophrenia itself, have been shown to have a higher co-occurrence rate in monozygotic twins than in ordinary siblings (Kendler et al., 1993b), thus suggesting that some part of the elevated concordance for schizophrenia in MZ twins may be due as much to shared stress as shared genes.

While the primary etiology issue remains clouded, we do know that relapse into schizophrenia following remission is associated with a certain type of negative communication, called **expressed emotion (EE),** directed at the patient by family members (Hooley, 1985; Miklowitz, Goldstein, & Falloon, 1983; Vaughn & Leff, 1976, 1981). Originally observed in Great Britain, the effect has also been demonstrated in the United States (Hooley, 1985; Vaughn et al., 1984). Two components appear critical in the pathogenic effects of EE: emotional overinvolvement with the patient, and excessive criticalness. Expressed emotion may be especially intense where family members harbor the view that the disorder and its symptoms are under the voluntary control of the patient (Weisman et al., 1993).

Significantly, EE tends to be associated with familial communication deviance as previously described (Doane et al., 1985; Goldstein, 1985; Miklowitz et al., 1986). Parker, Johnston, and Hayward (1988) pointed out that EE is most likely to occur where a former patient is highly disturbed, a circumstance that might itself prompt rehospitalization. The force of this criticism is mitigated by findings that EE predicts schizophrenia before its initial onset (Goldstein, 1985). Finally, early results from intervention attempts to reduce EE and associated behaviors in family members have been very encouraging in terms of relapse prevention (Falloon et al., 1985; Hogarty et al., 1986).

As we noted, the course of decompensation (deterioration, disorganization of thought and personality) in reactive (primarily positive-symptom) schizophrenia tends to be sudden, while that in process (primarily negative-symptom) schizophrenia tends to be gradual. The actual degree of decompensation may vary markedly, depending on the severity of stress and the makeup of the individual. The course of recovery or recompensation may also be relatively rapid or slow. Similarly, the degree of recovery may be complete, even leading to a better-adjusted person than before; it may be partial but sufficient or insufficient for adequate adjustment; or it may be nonexistent, with the individual eventually developing an intractable, chronic, prevailingly negative-symptom schizophrenia (see Fenton & McGlashan, 1994).

Sociocultural Factors in Schizophrenia Despite occasional assertions that incidence/prevalence rates for schizophrenia are basically invariant throughout the world, there is in fact a 10- to 20-fold variation in occurrence of the disorder in the various social groupings and geographic regions for which such epidemiologic data are available (Stevens & Hallick, 1992). That is, large deviations away from the worldwide mean are observed to occur in both directions. No satisfactory biological explanation for this variation has as yet been identified (Kirch, 1993), and the possibility that the differences reflect intercultural social factors pertinent to the emergence of schizophrenic psychoses cannot at present be ruled out (Torrey, 1987). Alas, we also have no satisfactory explanation for why some cultural factors might enhance the risk for schizophrenia, while others would seem to diminish it. We appear to have here, then, another of those fascinating puzzles that are so common in the study of schizophrenia.

Systematic differences in the content and form of schizophrenia between cultures and even subcultures have been documented by various investigators over many years. Often, cases within a particular subculture tend to have a distinctive form. Among the aborigines of West Malaysia, Kinzie and Bolton (1973) found the acute type to be by far the most common manifestation; they also noted that symptom content often "had an obvious cultural overlay, for example, seeing a 'river ghost' or 'men-like spirits' or talking to one's 'soul'" (p. 773). However, the clinical picture seems to be changing as rural Africans and other people from developing nations are increasingly exposed to modern technology and social change (Copeland, 1968; Kinzie & Bolton, 1973; Torrey, 1973, 1979).

An important consideration in cross-cultural studies is that opinions concerning what is normal or abnormal by professionals from another culture may not always correspond with the opinions held by members of the community in question (Butcher, Narikiyo, & Vitousek, 1993). For example, in describing the schizophrenic disorders of members of Hawaiians of Japanese descent professional observers emphasized seclusiveness and shallow, blunted emotionality. Other members of their own group, on the other hand, were impressed by evidence of uncontrolled emotionality and distrust, behaviors that are strongly counter to the community's values (Katz et al., 1978).

Focusing on sociocultural factors within our own society, Murphy (1968) early on summarized the abundant evidence that the prevalence of schizophrenia in the United States is inversely related to socioeconomic status: The lower the status, the higher the prevalence of schizophrenia. Although the data on this point are perhaps not as clear as Murphy and others have indicated (Sanua, 1969), his conclusion would be accepted as basically accurate by most contemporary investigators. Interestingly, a reverse effect seems to exist in India; there, the upper classes (castes) experience higher rates of schizophrenia than the lower classes (Torrey, 1979).

Although it has been suggested (Kohn, 1973) that the conditions of lower-class existence are themselves stressful and in addition impair an individual's ability to deal resourcefully with stresss, there is also compelling evidence that lower-class membership can be a result of schizophrenia. Affected individuals often drift downward on the socioeconomic ladder because the disorder impedes effective coping with ordinary life demands; many such cases may be found among the homeless mentally disordered. We should also emphasize that alleged ethnic differences in the prevalence and clinical pictures of schizophrenia—for example, between African Americans and Caucasians—disappear when social class, education, and related socioeconomic conditions are equated (Lindsey & Paul, 1989; Snowden & Cheung, 1990).

In concluding our review of the causal factors in schizophrenia, it may be pointed out that research on the causation of human behavior is, as the late David Shakow (1969) expressed it, "fiendishly complex," even with normal subjects:

> Research with disturbed human beings is even more so, particularly with those with whom it is difficult to communicate, among them schizophrenics. The marked range of schizophrenia, the marked variance within the range and within the individual, the variety of shapes that the psychosis takes, and both the excessive and compensatory behaviors that characterize it, all reflect this special complexity. Recent years have seen the complication further enhanced by the use of a great variety of therapeutic devices, such as drugs, that alter both the physiological and psychological nature of the organism. Research with schizophrenics, therefore, calls for awareness not only of the factors creating variance in normal human beings, but also of the many additional sources of variance this form of psychosis introduces. (Shakow, 1969, p. 618)

In general, and as Shakow implies, there appears to be no one clinical entity or causal sequence in schizophrenia. Rather we seem to be dealing with several types of psychologically maladaptive processes resulting from an interaction of biological, psychosocial, and sociocultural factors; the role of these factors undoubtedly varies according to the given case and clinical picture. Often the interaction appears to involve a vicious spiral that, once initiated, propels the person into a process of decreasing availability of coping resources in the face of increasing demands for performance adequacy. Some people panic and undergo a sort of psychobiological collapse; others appear to become gradually apathetic and demoralized, retreating from the unmanageable and perhaps (to them) unintelligible real world both physically and psychologically. Whatever the initial picture, outcomes are not at first notably predictable (Strakowski, 1994; Vaillant, 1978) and typically become more so only after weeks, months, or, in some cases of rapidly altering clinical pictures, even years.

Treatments and Outcomes

For roughly a century before the 1950s the prognosis for schizophrenia was generally considered extremely unfavorable, even hopeless. Patients receiving the diagnosis, unless their families were wealthy and could afford the expense of private psychiatric hospitalization, were routinely shuttled to remote, forbidding, overcrowded, and environmentally bleak public hospitals. Once "safely" incarcerated they were treated—if at all—by poorly trained, overworked staff with ineffective techniques that were often, in addition, objectively cruel (e.g., straitjackets) or predictably terrifying (e.g., electroconvulsive "shock" therapy, as it was originally called). As often as not, perhaps after a brief trial at one of the pointless "therapies" offered, the patient was simply left to fashion a tolerable adjustment to an institution he or she was never expected to leave. Such an adjustment, long continued, would in most instances ensure the erosion of capacities and skills essential to self-maintenance outside of the institution. Thus, complying with the self-fulfilling prophecies of their dismal prognoses, most admitted patients, in fact, did not ever leave.

For most schizophrenic persons, the outlook today is not nearly so bleak. Improvement came with dramatic suddenness when the phenothiazine class of drugs—then referred to as "major tranquilizers"—were introduced in the mid-1950s. Pharmacotherapy (treatment by drugs), especially when combined with other modern treatment methods, permits most patients to be treated in outpatient clinics; a schizophrenic person who enters a mental hospital or other facility as an inpatient for the first time has an 80–90 percent chance of being discharged within a matter of weeks or, at most, months. The rate of readmission, however, is still extremely high, and many patients experience repeated discharges and readmissions in what is commonly referred to as the "revolving door" pattern. Exact figures on readmissions are difficult to calculate, however; the "careers" of individual patients are not readily tracked owing to general instability (Weinstein, 1983).

Overall, about 25 percent of schizophrenic patients in time recover permanently and without debilitating residual problems; only some 10 percent now show the classical pattern of inexorable deterioration and intractable, profound disability (M. Bleuler, 1978). The latter outcome, the most tragic and feared course a schizophrenic process may take, has thus not been completely eradicated with alterations in hospital practice and the availability of new treatment approaches. Here the downward spiral of increasing deficit, disorganization, preponderance of negative symptoms, and ultimately retreat from the human community still cannot be interrupted by any means known. In some instances the progression occurs remarkably rapidly, reaching a stable state of profound dilapidation in a year or less. More typically, the deteriorating course lasts for several years, normally stabilizing at a low functioning level within five years (M. Bleuler, 1978; Fenton & McGlashan, 1994; McGlashan & Fenton, 1993). Even in severe cases of maximally poor prognosis, however, the outlook may not be completely hopeless. Although the "course" may be as long as 40 years or more, recoveries may still occur, albeit rarely (M. Bleuler, 1978).

The rest of the people who experience a first schizophrenic episode—some 65 percent of the total—show varying degrees of personality impoverishment, oddities of thought and behavior, and episodic psychotic behavior. Obviously, this is the group most likely to show the "revolving door" pattern, with brief periods of hospitalization interspersed among more lengthy periods of sustainable but marginal living on the outside. Many of these persons become "street people," and some of them are too dysfunctional to take advantage of government social programs that may provide, for example, shelter, food, and minimal financial support. Abuse of "recreational" drugs may be a serious problem for this intermediate-outcome group, and such abuse is associated with increased likelihood of psychotic relapses (Linszen, Dingemans, & Lenior, 1994).

As we have done with respect to other disorders, we will postpone until later chapters a detailed discussion of the various kinds of treatment employed for schizophrenia. Here we note merely that, contrary to widespread belief, such treatment is—or should be—by no means limited to drugs. While antipsychotic medication has unquestionably been a boon in ameliorating some of the more disturbing symptoms of schizophrenia, the residual problems left unaffected can remain a very serious obstacle to full participation in society. Consider in this regard the remarks of the distinguished Harvard social psychologist Roger Brown, who attended a meeting of Schizophrenics Anonymous in order to familiarize himself with the problems of these people:

[The group leader] began with an optimistic testimony about how things were going with him, designed in part to buck up the others. Some of them also spoke hopefully; others were silent and stared at the floor throughout. I gradually felt hope draining out of the group as they began to talk of their inability to hold jobs, of living on welfare, of finding themselves overwhelmed by simple demands. Nothing bizarre was said or done; there was rather a pervasive sense of inadequacy, of lives in which each day was a dreadful trial. Doughnuts and coffee were served, and then each one, still alone, trailed off into the Cambridge night.

What I saw a little of at that meeting of Schizophrenics Anonymous is simply that there is something about schizophrenia that the antipsychotic drugs do not cure or even always remit on a long-term basis (Brown & Herrnstein, 1975, p. 641).

Unfortunately, Brown's assessment of the antipsychotic drugs is in our experience painfully accurate. The marked social deficits Brown so well describes are extremely common accompaniments of schizophrenic disorders and may indeed be more disabling in their continuously disruptive effects than an occasional eruption of psychotic symptoms. There is little evidence that long-term rates of *social* recovery from schizophrenia have been notably affected by the availability of these drugs (see Harding et al., 1987a, 1987b). HIGHLIGHT 12.3 summarizes a recent confirmatory review of overall treatment outcomes in schizophrenia during the past 100 years.

In light of available evidence of considerable psychosocial contribution to the etiology of schizophrenia, much of it reviewed in this chapter, we think it short-sighted to approach the treatment of this type of disorder from an exclusively biological perspective. In fact, a recent review of studies combining biological and psychological treatments for schizophrenia suggests that the combination of drugs plus psychosocial treatment measures is often superior to drugs alone (Klerman et al., 1994).

Several forms of psychosocial intervention in schizophrenia can claim at least modest empirical validation (Emmelkamp, 1994). These include a therapeutic community-based program having minimal professional oversight (Fairweather et al., 1969; Fairweather, 1980), a rigorous token economy program for chronic state hospital patients (Paul & Lentz, 1977), specialized individual psychotherapy provided by therapists highly experienced with this

group (Karon & Vandenbos, 1981), social-skills training (Halford & Haynes, 1991), and family interventions designed to reduce high levels of expressed emotion (Tarrier & Barrowclough, 1990). Perhaps it is time to take another look at what carefully designed and evaluated psychosocial interventions have to offer in coping with this most baffling of psychopathological conditions.

DELUSIONAL (PARANOID) DISORDER

The term **paranoia** has been in use a long time. The ancient Greeks and Romans used it to refer more or less indiscriminately to any mental disorder. Our present, more limited use of the term stems from the work of Kraepelin, who reserved it for cases showing delusions and impaired contact with reality but without the bizarreness, fragmentation, and severe personality disorganization characteristic of schizophrenia.

Currently two main types of psychoses are included under the DSM-IV headings relating to (nonschizophrenic) paranoid disorders: **delusional disorder,** formerly called paranoia or paranoid disorder, and **shared psychotic disorder,** in which two or more people develop persistent, interlocking delusional ideas. The latter condition, historically known as *folie à deux,* is described briefly in HIGHLIGHT 12.4. Brief episodes (i.e., lasting one month or less) of otherwise uncomplicated delusional thinking are included in the category "Brief Psychotic Disorder." Our focus in this section will be on delusional disorder. As there is little recent literature on this disorder, we will be forced to focus on a number of early studies. Because these studies used the traditional terminology *paranoia* and *paranoid disorder,* we will use those terms and the newer delusional disorder classification interchangeably.

DSM-IV requires that diagnoses of delusional disorder be specified by type, based on the predominant theme of the delusions present. These types are as follows:

Persecutory type. The predominant delusional theme is that one (or someone to whom one is closely related) is being subjected to some kind of malevolent treatment, such as spying, stalking, or the spreading of false rumors of illegal or immoral behavior. Legal actions of one sort or another are often instituted to redress the alleged injustice, and in extreme cases more direct and dangerous modes of counteraction are employed,

HIGHLIGHT 12.3

A Century of Treatments and Outcomes in Schizophrenia

Hegarty and colleagues (1994) have recently published an extraordinary study of worldwide clinical outcomes in treated schizophrenia on a decade-by-decade basis from 1895 through 1991. Using the technique of quantitative review on 320 studies (of a total of 821) meeting relatively stringent criteria of data quality, the clinical outcomes of 51,800 schizophrenic patients followed up for at least one year (311,400 person-years of follow-up in all) were assessed and reduced to common metric formats yielding overall "improved" versus "not improved" outcome status decisions. Placement in the "improved" category required the patient to have been described as "recovered, in remission, well without residual symptoms, minimally or mildly symptomatic, improved without significant deficit, socially recovered, or working or living independently" (p. 1410). For the most part, results are reported as weighted (for number) average percentages of patients declared "improved" for the various comparisons of interest.

The main results may be summarized as follows:

1. The overall proportion of patients considered improved over the entire century, independent of length of follow-up, was 40.2 percent.

2. There was a statistically significant variation in improvement rates over the decades examined (before 1916, 1916–25, 1926–35, 1936–45, 1946–55, 1956–65, 1966–75, 1976–85, and 1986–91).

3. The overall improvement rate in the period 1895–1915 was approximately 30 percent, falling to approximately 25 percent in the 1916–25 decade. Thereafter there was an increase to slightly under 40 percent, which was maintained over the three decades from 1926 to 1955. In the two decades comprising 1956–75 improvement rates increased again, remaining constant at about 50 percent. Improvement rates declined again in the 1976–85 decade, to approximately 46 percent. In the most recent and briefer period assessed, 1986–91 (six years), improvement rates declined again to about the level of the long 1926 to 1955 plateau—that is, about 38 percent.

4. These substantial variations in schizophrenia outcomes over the past century are not random. Strong inference indicates that they are determined by identifiable alterations over time in psychiatric practice. The abrupt and substantial two-decade elevation in im-

provement rates beginning in 1956 exactly coincides with the introduction and rapid adoption of the then-new antipsychotic drugs, such as chlorpromazine (Thorazine). The recent and continuing decline in improvement rates beginning with the 1976–85 decade may initially seem alarming, but it too has a straightforward explanation. Building through the 1970s, and culminating with the introduction of DSM-III in 1980, there was a pronounced trend toward the adoption of stricter criteria for the diagnosis of schizophrenia, such as requiring that the patient have exhibited psychotic symptoms over some minimal period prior to applying the diagnosis. These stricter criteria, sometimes called neo-Kraepelinian (as opposed to Bleulerian) and made progressively more stringent in DSM-III-R and DSM-IV, have the effect of limiting the diagnosis to more severely disturbed patients—such as those with increased levels of negative symptoms. Sicker patients are harder to treat effectively, and hence less likely to be improved on follow-up. In short, we have not lost therapeutic ground since 1976—only changed the rules of engagement, or more specifically the average severity of psychopathology in the patient group addressed.

such as attempted (and sometimes completed) murder.

Jealous type. The predominant theme is that one's sexual partner is being unfaithful.

Erotomanic type. The predominant theme is that some other person of higher status, frequently someone of considerable prominence, is in love with one and wants to start a sexual liaison.

Somatic type. The predominant theme is an unshakable belief in having some physical illness or disorder, often esoteric or exotic in nature.

Grandiose type. The predominant theme is that one is a person of extraordinary status, power, ability, talent, beauty, etc., or that one has a special relationship with someone having such attributes, usually someone of celebrity status.

Mixed. This diagnosis is used where there are combinations of the above but when no single theme predominates.

Of these types, the persecutory is by far the most common, and our discussion will focus on this form of the disorder.

Folie à Deux: Shared Psychotic Disorder

A relatively neglected phenomenon in the psychoses is that of *folie à deux*—a form of psychological "contagion" in which one person copies and incorporates into his or her own personality functioning the delusions and other psychotic patterns of another person. (*Folie à deux*, the traditional term, has been relabeled "Shared Psychotic Disorder" in DSM-IV.) Familial relationships between individuals in 103 cases studied by Gralnick (1942) fell within one of the following four categories:

sister ⇄ sister	40 cases
husband ⇄ wife	28 cases
mother ⇄ child	24 cases
brother ⇄ brother	11 cases

Among the explanatory factors, all environmental, emphasized by Gralnick were (a) length of association, (b) dominance-submission, (c) type of familial relationship, and (d) prepsychotic personality. The high incidence in the husband-wife category is particularly striking because common heredity plays no part as an etiological factor in these cases.

In another study, Soni and Rockley (1974) reported on eight cases of *folie à deux* seen at a European hospital. Their findings supported those of Gralnick and emphasized the role of pathological prepsychotic characteristics, such as increased suggestability and submissive roles, as well as the type of relationship in explaining why these patients acquired their partner's delusions.

Although the formal diagnosis of delusional disorder is rare in clinic and mental hospital populations, this observation provides a somewhat misleading picture of its actual occurrence. Many exploited inventors, fanatical reformers, self-styled prophets, morbidly jealous spouses, persecuted teachers, business executives, or other professionals fall into this category. Unless they become a serious nuisance, these people are usually able to maintain themselves in the community and do not recognize their paranoid condition nor seek help to alleviate it. In some instances, however, they are potentially dangerous, and in virtually all instances they are inveterate "injustice-detectors," inclined to undertake retributive actions of one sort or another against their supposed tormenters.

The Clinical Picture in Delusional Disorder

A paranoid, or delusional, individual feels singled out and taken advantage of, mistreated, plotted against, stolen from, spied on, ignored, or otherwise mistreated by "enemies." The delusional system usually centers on one major theme, such as financial matters, a job, an invention, an unfaithful spouse, or another life affair. For example, a woman who is failing on the job may insist that her fellow workers and superiors have it in for her because they are jealous of her great ability and efficiency. As a result, she may quit her job and go to work elsewhere, only to find friction developing again and her new job in jeopardy. Now she may become convinced that the first company has written to her present employer and has turned everyone against her so that she has not been given a fair chance. With time, more and more of the environment is integrated into her delusional system as each additional experience is misconstrued and interpreted in the light of her delusional ideas. See HIGHLIGHT 12.5 for a list of characteristics typical of paranoid thinking.

Although the evidence that paranoid people advance to justify their claims may be tenuous and inconclusive, they are unwilling to accept any other possible explanation and are impervious to reason. A husband may be convinced of his spouse's unfaithfulness because on two separate occasions when he answered the phone the party at the other end hung up. Argument and logic are futile. In fact, any questioning of his delusions only convinces him that his interrogator has sold out to his enemies. The following case illustrates the sometimes tragic results of paranoid delusions:

Milner cited the case of a paranoid man, aged 33, who murdered his wife by battering her head with a hammer. Prior to the murder, he had become convinced that his wife was suffering from some strange disease and that she had purposely infected him because she wished him to die. He believed that this disease was due to a "cancer-consumption" germ. He attributed his conclusion in part to his wife's alleged sexual

---

HIGHLIGHT | 12.5

Sequence of Events in a Paranoid Mode of Thinking

A number of investigators have concluded that the most useful perspective from which to view paranoia is in terms of a *mode of thinking*. The sequence of events that appears to characterize this mode of thinking may be summarized as follows:

1. *Suspiciousness*—the individual mistrusts the motives of others, fears he or she will be taken advantage of, and is constantly on the alert.

2. *Protective thinking*—the individual selectively perceives the actions of others to confirm suspicions and blames others for his or her failures.

3. *Hostility*—the individual responds to alleged injustices and mistreatment with anger and hostility and becomes increasingly suspicious.

4. *Paranoid illumination*—the moment when everything "falls into place"; the individual finally understands the strange feelings and events being experienced.

5. *Delusions*—the individual has delusions of influence and persecution that may be based on "some grain of truth," presented in a logical and convincing way; often, the later development of delusions of grandeur.

Over time, a paranoid individual may incorporate additional life areas, people, and events into the delusional system, creating a "pseudo-community" whose purpose is to carry out some action against him or her. Paranoid individuals who respond in this manner may come to feel that all the attention they are receiving from others is indicative of their unique abilities and importance, thus paving the way for delusions of grandeur.

Based in part on Meissner (1978) and Swanson, Bohnert, and Smith (1970).

---

perversion and also gave the following reasons for his belief:

1. His wife had insured him for a small sum immediately after marriage.
2. A young man who had been friendly with his wife before their marriage died suddenly.
3. A child who had lived in the same house as his wife's parents suffered from fits. (He also believed that his wife's parents were suffering from the same disease.)
4. For several months before the crime his food had had a queer taste, and for a few weeks before the crime he had suffered from a pain in the chest and an unpleasant taste in the mouth. (1949, p. 130)

Although ideas of persecution predominate, many paranoid individuals develop delusions of grandeur in which they endow themselves with superior or unique abilities. Such "exalted" ideas usually center on messianic missions, political or social reforms, or remarkable inventions. Paranoid people who are religious may consider themselves appointed by God to save the world and may spend most of their time "preaching" and "crusading." Threats of fire and brimstone, burning in hell, and similar persuasive devices are liberally employed.

Many paranoid people become attached to extremist political movements and are tireless and fanatical crusaders, although they often do their cause more harm than good by their self-righteousness and their highly strained condemnations of others.

Some paranoid individuals develop remarkable inventions that they have endless trouble in patenting or selling. Gradually they become convinced that a plot is afoot to steal their invention, or that enemies of the United States are working against them to prevent the country from receiving the benefits of their remarkable talents. Hoffman cited the case of a man who went to Washington to get presidential assistance in obtaining a patent for a flame thrower that, he claimed, could destroy all the enemies of the United States. He would patiently explain who he was: "There's God who is Number 1, and Jesus Christ who is Number 2, and me, I am Number 3" (1943, p. 574).

Aside from the delusional system, such an individual may appear perfectly normal in conversation, emotionality, and conduct. Hallucinations and the other obvious signs of psychopathology are rarely found. This normal appearance, together with the logical and coherent way in which the delusional ideas are presented, may make the individual most convincing, perhaps especially to persons awash in their own uncertainties. The following case is typical:

An engineer developed detailed plans for eliminating the fog in San Francisco and other large cities by means of a system of reflectors that would heat the air by solar radiation and cause the fog to lift. The company for which he worked examined the plans and found them unsound. This rejection upset him greatly and he resigned his position, stating that the other engineers in the company were not qualified to pass judgment on any complex and advanced engineering projects like his. Instead of attempting to obtain other employment, he then devoted full time trying to find some other engineering firm that would have the vision and technical proficiency to see the great potential of his idea. He would present his plans convincingly but become highly suspicious and hostile when questions concerning their feasibility were raised. Eventually, he became convinced that there was a conspiracy among a large number of engineering firms to steal his plans and use them for their own profit. He reported his suspicions to the police, threatening to do something about the situation himself unless they took action. As a consequence, he was hospitalized for observation and diagnosed as suffering from paranoia.

The diagnosis of delusional disorder may be rendered difficult at times because of the unclarity of the term *delusion*. It is not always possible to determine the truth or falsity of an idea, and some ideas that are patently false are held with sincerity and conviction by very many people. For this reason, formal definitions of "delusion" (as in DSM-IV) usually specify that an idea must be held as preposterous by the majority of a person's own community. As the example of Columbus's much ridiculed fifteenth-century belief that the earth was round shows, however, this qualification does not always solve the problem. These and other difficulties surrounding the notion of delusional thinking have received a thorough and much needed airing in a book edited by Oltmanns and Maher (1988). They suggest, incidentally, that delusional thinking is not so different from normal thinking as we would perhaps like to think. The problem also remains, of course, of differentiating delusional disorder from paranoid personality disorder (Chapter 9), which also involves a judgment call as to whether or not clearly eccentric and convoluted thinking merits the designation "delusional," that is, "psychotic." A clinician is well-advised in equivocal cases to be diligent in devising probes to test for magical elements

in the "evidence" underlying the patient's paranoid constructions.

A patient's delusional system is apt to be particularly convincing if one accepts the basic premise or premises on which it is based. For example, where the delusional system develops around some actual injustice, it may be difficult to distinguish between fact and fancy. As a result, the individual's family and friends, as well as well-meaning public officials, may be convinced of the truth of the claims. However, the individual's inability to see the facts in any other light, typical lack of solid evidence for far-reaching conclusions, and hostile, suspicious, and uncommunicative attitude when the delusional ideas are questioned usually provide clues that something is wrong.

Paranoid individuals are not always as dangerous as popular fiction and drama suggest, but the chance always exists that they will decide to take matters into their own hands and deal with their enemies in the only way that seems effective. In one instance, a paranoid school principal became convinced that the school board was discriminating against him and shot and killed most of the board members. In another case, a paranoid man shot and killed a group of seven people he thought had been following him.

The number of husbands and wives who have been killed or seriously injured by suspicious, paranoid mates is extremely large worldwide (DeKay & Buss, 1992). As Swanson, Bohnert, and Smith (1970) have pointed out, such murderous violence is commonly associated with jealousy and the loss of self-esteem; the spouse feels that he or she has been deceived, taken advantage of, and humiliated, often on observational grounds that could more readily be interpreted as benign. Interestingly, the types of situations likely to evoke these murderous spousal attacks may be different for husbands and wives, according to a review and analysis by DeKay and Buss (1992); husbands are more sensitive to issues involving sexual infidelity, whereas wives react more to suspicion that the mate may have an alternate emotional attachment. Paranoid people may also, of course, get involved in violent and subversive activities, terrorism, and political assassinations. In many such instances we believe the concept of group paranoia to have considerable explanatory merit.

Causal Factors in Delusional Disorder

Most of us on various occasions may wonder if we are not jinxed, when it seems as if everything we do goes wrong and the cards seem to be stacked against us. Many people go through life feeling underrated

The insistent way the owner of this car has chosen to broadcast his or her ideas and the ideas themselves, which are hostile, suspicious, and a distortion of factual evidence, indicate delusional thinking.

and frustrated, brooding over fancied and real injustices. Meissner (1978) regards such attitudes as a normal and essential phase of personality development, a necessary component in the achievement of personal identity and autonomy. Most people, according to this view, are able to grow beyond this phase, where a central feature is the need for an enemy. Some few are not, however, in which case they chronically entertain paranoid explanations of whatever problems they may have.

We have already noted that individuals with paranoid schizophrenia tend not to show the extensive cognitive disorganization seen in other forms of schizophrenia. Also, while the maintenance of a severely paranoid "fix" on the world does indeed require drastic contortions of a person's basic cognitive resources, it also requires that the person be relatively deft in dealing with the information the environment provides. If an individual were so impaired cognitively as to be unable to function on a day-by-day basis, the alertness and selectively efficient information processing essential to the effective maintenance of an organized delusional system would, of course, be unavailable. Implied in these observations is the idea that severe disruption of cognitive processes per se may not be implicated in the causal pattern leading to delusional, or paranoid, forms of psychosis, and might indeed be a factor that, if present, would discourage their development.

Most delusionally disordered persons seem as children to have been aloof, suspicious, seclusive, secretive, stubborn, and resentful of punishment. When crossed, they became sullen and morose.

Rarely do these pre-paranoid individuals show a history of normal play with other children or good socialization in terms of warm, affectionate relationships (Sarvis, 1962; Schwartz, 1963; Swanson et al., 1970). The seeds may thus be sown quite early for a stand-offish and relatively unfriendly interpersonal style. Such a child may understandably be unpopular with peers—in effect, an aversive stimulus. Thus, as Lemert (1962) has noted, an unduly suspicious or coldly rejecting person frequently becomes a target of actual discrimination and mistreatment. Ever alert to injustices, both imagined and real, such an individual finds abundant "proof" of persecution.

In this context, Grunebaum and Perlman (1973) have pointed to the naivete of a pre-paranoid person in assessing the interpersonal world—in terms of who can be trusted and who cannot—as a fertile source of hurtful interactions. As they express it, "The ability to trust others realistically requires that the individual be able to tolerate minor and major violations of trust that are part of normal human relationships" (p. 32). The pre-paranoid individual is unprepared for the "facts of life," however, tending to both trust and mistrust inappropriately and to overreact when others are perceived, accurately or not, as betraying the trust.

Where delusional disorder develops, it usually does so gradually, as mounting failures and seeming betrayals force these individuals to an elaboration of their defensive structures. To avoid self-devaluation, they search for "logical" reasons for their lack of success. Why were they denied a much-deserved recognition or promotion? Why was it given to someone obviously far less qualified? They become more vigilant, begin to scrutinize the environment, search for hidden meanings, and ask leading questions. They ponder like a detective over the "clues" they pick up, trying to fit them into some sort of meaningful picture.

Gradually the picture begins to crystallize—a process commonly referred to as "paranoid illumination." It becomes apparent that they are being singled out for some obscure reason, that other people are working against them, that they are being interfered with. In essence, they protect themselves against the intolerable assumption, "There is something wrong with me," with the defensive transformation, "They are doing something to me." They have failed not because of any inferiority or lack on their part, but because others are working against them. They are on the side of good and the progress of humankind, while their enemies are allied with the forces of evil. With this as their fundamental defensive premise, they proceed to distort and falsify the facts to fit it and gradually develop a logical, fixed, delusional system. Cameron (1959) has referred to this process as the building up of a paranoid "pseudo-community" in which an individual organizes surrounding people (both real and sometimes imaginary) into a structured group whose purpose is to carry out some despicable or violent action against him or her.

The role of highly selective information processing in the development of these delusional systems should be emphasized. Once these individuals begin to suspect that others are working against them, they start carefully noting the slightest signs pointing in the direction of their suspicions and ignore all evidence to the contrary (Swanson et al., 1970).

With this frame of reference, it is quite easy, in our highly competitive and sometimes ruthless world, for paranoid persons to find ample evidence that others are working against them. This attitude itself leads to a vicious circle, for their suspiciousness, distrust, and criticism of others drive their friends and well-wishers away and keep them in continual friction with other people, generating new incidents for them to magnify. Often others do in fact find that they must conspire behind their backs in order to keep peace and cope with their eccentricities, thus adding additional evidence of foul play and victimization. When this feedback process spins out of control, as it too often does, tragic consequences may ensue.

Treatments and Outcomes

We do not have established, empirically validated approaches for the treatment of delusional disorders. It is generally conceded that, once a delusional system is well established, it is extremely difficult to dismantle it by any of the treatment methods commonly employed by mental health professionals. It is usually impossible to communicate with such individuals in a rational way concerning their problems. In addition, they are not prone to seek treatment, which many would interpret as an admission of weakness, but are more likely to seek justice for all the wrong done to them.

An offer of medication—even if any genuinely promising ones were available—is very likely to be refused, and may indeed be woven into a delusional system involving conspiracy and intended harm. Nor is hospitalization likely to help, for delusionally disordered persons are likely to see it as a form of unjust incarceration and persecution. If forcibly hospitalized, they are apt to regard themselves as superior to hospital staff as well as other patients and will usually complain that their families and the staff

have conspired to have them "put away" illegally and for no valid reason. Not uncommonly, they seek legal redress, and sometimes they are successful in gaining a court-ordered release, particularly if they have not as yet been charged with any crime. Seeing nothing wrong with themselves, they refuse to cooperate or participate in anything resembling "treatment."

Eventually, however, many hospitalized delusional persons realize that their failure to curb their actions or expression of their delusional ideas will result in prolonged hospitalization. As a result, they may make a pretext of renouncing their delusions, admitting that they did hold such ideas but claiming that they now realize the ideas are absurd and are giving them up. After their release, they are often more reserved in expressing their ideas and in annoying other people, but they are usually far from recovered. Thus the prognosis for complete recovery from paranoia has traditionally been unfavorable.

UNRESOLVED ISSUES

on Schizophrenia

The unresolved issues concerning schizophrenia are so manifold that a truly adequate accounting of them would require the better part of an additional chapter. We will point out, therefore, only a few of the many problems we encounter in this realm of psychopathology. Issues of treatment, in particular, will be postponed to Chapters 16 and 17.

A major hurdle confronts us at the outset in trying to come to grips with the nature of this disorder where the conceptual boundaries are both murky and shifting. While we have had, since the advent of DSM-III in 1980, a set of explicit defining criteria that when properly applied will permit us to say who is and who is not schizophrenic with a high degree of reliability, these criteria have continued to change in successive revisions of the manual.

We do not intend to suggest in taking this critical stance that we have a better set of criteria to offer. Rather, we suspect that tinkering with the definitional criteria for "schizophrenia" without having solid research data to support the effort will never produce a satisfactory solution, and it is unclear that such data can be produced in the absence of fundamental redirections of approach. What is needed is some sort of reconceptualization that enables us to view the pertinent phenomena in a new and more productive light. We feel reasonably certain that any such major conceptual advance will entail not one but many "schizophrenias." That is, it is likely that the class of people who merit this diagnosis is heterogeneous not merely in terms of manifest behavior (which is obviously the case), but also in terms of the nature and development of the sources of their aberrant behavior. An important implication is that there probably exists no single "core" condition. Another implication is that efforts at identification and differentiation of basic subgroups should have a high research priority. Beyond that, the crystal ball is notably hazy—in large part because of the sheer magnitude and diversity of the seemingly reliable observations researchers continue to place before us.

In the aggregate, those findings point to the likely operation of a host of moderating variables, at varying levels of observation from the biomolecular to the sociocultural, that influence outcomes with respect to every risk factor for schizophrenia so far discovered. That being the case, it would seem that the organization of our scientific efforts at unraveling the mysteries leaves much to be desired, because it consists in the main of separate camps of relatively narrow scientific disciplines, ones moreover with a history of rarely looking at what might be happening in other camps. Since the evidence suggests that the schizophrenias result from interactions among variables that cross traditional disciplinary boundaries, interdisciplinary isolation would seem a dysfunctional state of affairs. To put it another way, few if any individual investigators are prepared to deal with more than limited portions of this complicated matrix. For the future, the situation would seem to call for widespread, intensive collaboration among many different kinds of scientists in seeking solutions to what Gottesman and Shields (1982) have aptly termed the "epigenetic puzzle" of the schizophrenias.

Schizophrenia confronts society with massive problems of how to take care of people who seem unable, or unmotivated, to take care of themselves (neither institutionalization nor deinstitutionalization has worked, granting that neither has been competently managed), but most of its manifestations do not involve violence or danger to others. The delusional (paranoid) disorders, on the other hand, are associated often enough with acts of violence that they confront us once again with difficult questions relating to jurisprudence, civil rights, and appropriate measures, if any, of containment and intervention. As in the case of suicide, discussed in the Chapter 6, the professional mental health community needs direction

from the larger society on what level of homicidal (or other violent) risk is tolerable in light of the uncertainty in predicting individual patients' behavior. Elimination or significant reduction of such uncertainty is not likely in the foreseeable future.

SUMMARY

The schizophrenic disorders, involving largely psychotic phenomena, include some of the most extreme deviations to be found in the domain of psychopathology. Markedly heterogeneous in their organization, they manifest a profile of disordered functioning in the areas of language and communication, content of thought, perception, emotional expression, identity confusion, disrupted volition, autistic retreat, and pecularities of motor behavior.

One extraordinary case—that of the Genain quadruplets—sheds light on the sources and the complexity of schizophrenic disorders. All four of the Genain sisters became schizophrenic prior to the age of 25. After carefully tracking the progress of the Genains through the years, researchers have concluded that both biological and psychosocial factors contributed to their vulnerability to schizophrenia.

Classical subtypes of schizophrenia include undifferentiated (mixed symptoms not fitting into other categories or moving rapidly among them), catatonic (involving chiefly motor symptoms), disorganized (incoherent, silly, or inappropriate affect and behavior), and paranoid (persistent ideas or hallucinations regarding persecution or grandiosity, or other themes). Modern research has tended to focus on positive-symptom (hallucinations and delusions) versus negative-symptom (emotional blunting) schizophrenia. Given these variations as well as other anomalies, some have questioned whether such a "thing" as schizophrenia exists. The credence of such questions is enhanced by the uncertain validity of the diagnostic criteria for schizophrenia.

Hardly anybody questions the existence of a cluster of behaviors, called schizophrenic, that are unintelligible to the average person. Such behaviors have been correlated with biological, psychosocial, and sociocultural variables. As yet, however, none of these broad sources of behavioral variation has been definitely established as encompassing *the* sole etiologic factor in schizophrenia. In fact, no such single factor is likely to be responsible. The evidence at all levels of observation suggests that complex interactions involving numerous influences, probably different in different patients, are involved.

The delusional (paranoid) disorders, in which schizophrenic disorganization seems not to be a significant factor, form a subgroup of psychoses that are even less well understood than the others. A paranoid individual harbors ideas of persecution, grandiosity, both, or more rarely of other patently false content. The person, however, is entirely functional—including, often, highly organized cognitive functioning—in areas that do not impinge on the delusional thought structure (the paranoid construction) in which the person is centrally involved. These people can often function at a marginal level in society. Some of them, however, become dangerous, exposing problems at the interface between mental health professionals and society at large that continue unresolved. Treatment of chronically paranoid persons is currently difficult, at best.

 KEY TERMS

psychosis (p. 443)
the schizophrenias (p. 443)
process schizophrenia (poor premorbid or chronic schizophrenia) (p. 448)
reactive schizophrenia (good premorbid or acute schizophrenia) (p. 448)
negative-symptom schizophrenia (p. 448)
positive-symptom schizophrenia (p. 448)
delusion (p. 450)
hallucination (p. 451)
schizophrenia, undifferentiated type (p. 452)
schizophrenia, catatonic type (p. 454)
schizophrenia, disorganized type (p. 456)
schizophrenia, paranoid type (p. 457)

schizophrenia, residual type (p. 459)
schizoaffective disorder (p. 459)
schizophreniform disorder (p. 459)
dopamine hypothesis (p. 465)
schizophrenogenic (p. 470)
marital schism (p. 471)
marital skew (p. 471)
double-bind communication (p. 471)
expressed emotion (EE) (p. 472)
paranoia (p. 475)
delusional disorder (p. 475)
shared psychotic disorder (p. 475)

CHAPTER

13

BRAIN DISORDERS AND OTHER COGNITIVE IMPAIRMENTS

Freddie Brice, Hole in the Head. *Brice (b. 1920), was born in Charleston, South Carolina. He was raised primarily by his mother, who worked in a cotton mill. After moving to New York to find work, primarily as a ship painter at the Brooklyn Navy Yard, Brice spent time in reform school, jail, and psychiatric hospitals. It was in a psychiatric day program that he learned to paint. He often sings and laughs while he works; "painting gives me joy," he says.*

In contrast to most kinds of abnormal behavior, some problems arise partly as a consequence of structural defects in the brain tissue—many of them due to damage of one sort or another. Such damage typically involves loss of nerve cells (neurons) and can impair the brain's normal physiological functioning. As the brain is the organ of behavior, damage to it may disrupt effective thought, feeling, and action. The relationship of deficits associated with organic brain defects to abnormal behavior is complicated and often unclear. Accordingly, it seems wise at this point to digress slightly from the main task of clinical description to get a better understanding of brain damage and brain dysfunction.

When structural defects in the brain are present before birth or occur at an early age, mental retardation may result, its severity depending to a large extent on the magnitude of the defect. In mental retardation, a child fails to develop sufficient skills to cope adequately and independently with environmental demands. As we shall see, most mentally retarded people do not suffer from gross brain damage, but virtually all those who can be described as severely retarded have some form of demonstrable organic pathology. Other people who sustain prenatal or perinatal (that is, during birth) brain damage may experience normal mental development in most aspects of behavior, but suffer from specific cognitive or motor deficits, such as learning disorders or spasticity (excessive muscle contraction that impairs motor performance).

Sometimes the intact brain sustains damage after it has completed normal biological development. A wide variety of injuries, diseases, and toxic substances may cause the functional impairment or death of neurons or their connections, which may lead to obvious deficits in psychological functioning. In some cases such damage is associated with behavior that is not only impaired but also highly maladaptive—even psychotic. People who sustain serious brain damage after they have mastered the basic tasks of life are in a very different situation from those who start life with a deficit of this kind. When brain injury occurs in an older child or adult, there is a loss in established functioning. This loss—this deprivation of already acquired and customary skills—can be painfully obvious to the victim, adding an often pronounced psychological burden to the organic one.

In other cases the impairment may extend to the capacity for realistic self-appraisal, leaving these patients relatively unaware of their losses and thus poorly motivated for rehabilitation. Many victims may also have to cope with the idea of little improvement or, worse, with a prognosis involving inevitable progressive decline. The psychological impact in such cases can be devastating.

In this chapter we will first discuss those disorders that occur when the normal adolescent or adult brain has suffered significant organic impairment or damage, following which we will move to a consideration of compromised brain functioning that is either congenital or arises in the earliest phases of psychological development.

BRAIN IMPAIRMENT AND ADULT DISORDER

Prior to the DSM-IV of 1994, most of the disorders to be considered in this section were called **organic mental disorders,** an outmoded term that failed to distinguish between the direct *neurological* consequences of brain injury, including various cognitive deficits, and the *psychopathological* problems sometimes accompanying such injury, such as depression or paranoid delusions. Since the latter types of abnormal "mental" phenomena are common in people with no demonstrable brain anomalies, the implication that they were in some other cases caused by brain damage was at best unproven and at worst possibly seriously misleading.

The destruction of brain tissue may involve only limited behavioral deficits or a wide range of psychological impairments, depending on (a) the nature, location, and extent of neural damage; (b) the premorbid (predisorder) personality of the individual; (c) the individual's total life situation; and (d) the amount of time since the first appearance of the condition. Although the degree of mental impairment is usually directly related to the extent of damage, in some cases involving relatively severe brain damage, mental change is astonishingly slight; in other cases of apparently mild and limited damage there may be profoundly altered functioning.

Adult Brain Damage and Disordered Mental Functioning

The fundamental disorders we shall be dealing with in this section are always in the strictest sense *neuropsychological* ones, although psychopathological problems may be associated with them. Some "mental" symptoms in organic mental disorders are therefore the more or less direct product of the physical interruption of established neural pathways in the brain. The bases of these symptoms are relatively

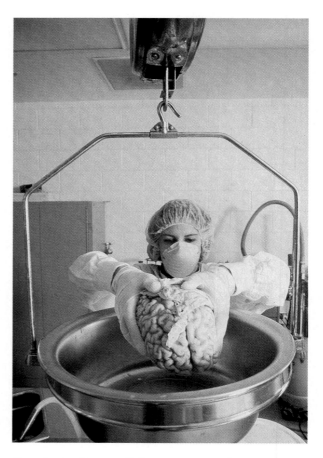

Some brain diseases, Alzheimer's among them, can be diagnosed with certainty only at autopsy. Clinicians must be conscientious in their diagnostic efforts with live patients because of the potentially serious consequences of error.

well understood, and the symptoms themselves have relatively constant features in people with comparable types of brain injury in terms of location and extent. For example, with mild to moderate *diffuse* (widespread) damage, such as might occur with moderate oxygen deprivation or the ingestion of toxic substances, attentional and self-monitoring impairments are quite common. Such a person, for example, may complain of memory problems due to an inability to sustain focused retrieval efforts, while showing an intact ability to store new information. Severe diffuse damage results in dementia, described later.

In contrast to diffuse damage, *focal brain lesions* are circumscribed areas of abnormal change in brain structure, such as might occur with traumatic injury to a part of the head. With progressive brain disease, such as Alzheimer's disease or expanding brain tumors, one may see a gradual spreading over more and more focal sites, leading to permanent damage that is both diffuse and severe. Some consequences of organic brain disorders that have mainly focal origins but commonly appear in the context of progressively diffuse damage are as follows:

1. *Impairment of memory*—the individual has notable trouble remembering recent events and less trouble remembering events of the remote past, with a tendency in some patients to confabulate; that is, to "invent" memories to fill in gaps. In severe instances no new experience can be retained for more than a few minutes. It either fails entirely to be stored in long-term memory or is stored in a way that provides no means for it to be readily retrieved at a later time.

2. *Impairment of orientation*—the individual is unable to locate himself or herself accurately, especially in time but also in space or in relation to the personal identities of self or others.

3. *Impairment of learning, comprehension, and judgment*—the individual displays ideation tending to be concrete and impoverished and is unable to think on higher conceptual levels or to plan with foresight.

4. *Impairment of emotional control or modulation*—the individual manifests emotional overreactivity and easy arousal to laughter, tears, rage, and other extreme emotions.

5. *Apathy or emotional blunting*—the individual shows little emotion, especially where deterioration is advanced.

6. *Impairment in the initiation of behavior*—the individual lacks "self-starting" capability and may have to be repeatedly reminded about what to do next, even where the behavior involved remains well within the person's range of competence.

7. *Impairment of controls over matters of propriety and ethical conduct*—the individual may manifest a marked lowering of personal standards in appearance, personal hygiene, sexuality, language, and so on.

8. *Impairment of receptive and expressive language*—the individual may be unable to comprehend written or spoken language, or may be unable to communicate thoughts orally or in writing.

9. *Impaired visuospatial ability*—the individual has difficulty in coordinating motor activity with the characteristics of the visual environment, affecting performance in graphomotor (handwriting and drawing), constructional (e.g., assembling things), and other tasks dependent on such skills.

The Neuropsychology/Psychopathology Interaction Most people who have a neuropsychological disorder do not develop psychopathological symptoms, such as panic attacks, dissociative episodes, or delusions, although many will show at least mild deficits in cognitive processing and self-regulation. The psychopathological symptoms that do sometimes accompany brain impairment are less predictable than those just listed and more likely to show individual nuances consistent with the prior personality and the total psychological situation confronting the patient. We consider it important for reasons of clarity to try to maintain a sharp distinction *conceptually* between neurological (or neuropsychological) and psychopathological types of "mental" symptoms.

In general, then, we are concerned here with people who have both neurological disease and psychopathological disorder. Though the distinction between these differing types of disorders is reasonably clear in the abstract, it becomes murky in many cases as psychopathology and neuropathology can become inextricably enmeshed with one another. We emphasize again that it is erroneous to assume that a psychological disorder, for example, a serious depression accompanying deficits produced by brain injury, is necessarily and completely explained by reference to the patient's brain damage; it might better be explained in terms of the psychological challenge presented by the patient's awareness of dramatically lessened competence.

The variable effects of significant impairment on individuals are explained by the fact that an individual is a functional unit and reacts as such to all stressors, whether they are organic or psychological. A well-integrated personality can usually withstand brain damage (or any other stress) better than a rigid, immature, or otherwise psychologically handicapped one—except where brain damage is so severe or its location so critical as to destroy the integrity of the personality. Similarly, an individual who has a favorable life situation is likely to have a better prognosis than one who does not. Because the brain is the center for the integration of behavior, however, there are limits to the amount of brain damage that anyone can tolerate or compensate for without exhibiting behavior that is decidedly abnormal.

Hardware and Software We believe that it is somewhat hazardous to employ computer analogies in discussions of the brain and mental processes. However, such an analogy seems to be useful in the context of the present discussion of the relationship of brain impairment to behavioral abnormalities.

When computers fail to do what we want and expect them to do for us, our troubleshooting speculations normally begin with two possibilities: (a) a hardware problem—perhaps a "sticky" chip, a deficient power supply, or a defective resistor or capacitator; or (b) a software problem, such as having a "bug" in our program of procedural instructions or an error in the data we load into a machine that is in perfect working order. Note that the software programs and data we load into computers have an essentially symbolic, informational status that is prior to and independent of the physical characteristics of the machine itself, although the physical state of the machine is transformed by the act of loading information into it. The information in a loaded machine could, in principle and with great difficulty, be completely and errorlessly reconstructed from a detailed description of the physical state of the machine. The two cannot for that reason be considered identical entities, however, nor is it reasonable to hold that the state of the machine is in any sense more "basic" than the information loaded into it.

We may thus consider the intact human brain to be a highly programmable system of hardware, and psychosocial experience in both its developmental and current aspects to be functionally equivalent to software. Using our analogy, neuropsychological disorders by definition have hardware defects as their primary cause. In other words, in such situations the brain cannot perform the physical operations called for by virtue of a breakdown in one or another (or several) of its components. The direct "symptoms" of such a breakdown should be, within reason, predictable from a knowledge of how these components "work."

A breakdown in the brain's hardware will necessarily have pervasive effects on the processing of software, or past and present experience. Indeed, in the case of extensive hardware damage, much or perhaps most previously loaded information may be lost because the structural components in which it had been encoded are no longer operative; new information for the same reason fails to be adequately loaded. Such a condition is known clinically as *dementia*. With less extensive hardware damage, we see effects that depend to a considerable extent on the particular characteristics of the software that constitutes the record of an individual's life experience, which is unique. We thus expect to see more variation in the "mental" symptoms manifested. To use an obvious example, the delusion that one is Napoleon, rather common in the nineteenth century, would not have been seen in an eighteenth-century demented patient who lived before Napoleon became famous. Such symptoms are at most only indirect manifestations of organic hardware breakdown; their content is obviously a product of life experience, and they sometimes occur in

the absence of any demonstrable hardware breakdown at all. In this case, we must consider the possibility that they are due entirely to serious flaws in the individual's personality, or (in our analogy) software.

It is obvious that people vary a great deal in the adequacy, complexity, and resourcefulness of the software programs their experiences have provided. Indeed, as we will see later in this chapter, such variations are to a certain extent what IQ tests attempt to measure. It is equally obvious that few people have programs ready to compensate for the loss of basic competencies and skills that have become so automatized that their flawless performance requires no deliberate attention or effort. Coping with such loss puts a premium on the adaptive flexibility of a person's existing software library. *Failure* to cope adequately, on the other hand, places an additional load of stress and frustration on an already limited system, one that may be further compromised by newly acquired hardware defects. Such a system, we suggest, is likely to develop indirect, secondary psychopathological symptoms, such as the delusional assumption of a new and more impressive personal identity.

General Clinical Features of Neuropsychological Disorders The regenerative capacities of the central nervous system are limited. Although recovery of function following brain injury is often quite rapid, much of this is due to the resolution of temporary conditions, such as edema (swelling), produced in tissue spared from actual damage. With possibly minor exceptions, cell bodies and neural pathways in the brain do not have the power of regeneration, which means that their destruction is permanent. Some functions lost as a result of actual brain damage may be relearned, typically at a compromised and less efficient level, or the injured person may develop techniques to compensate for what is missing. Recovery from disabilities following an irreversible brain lesion may be relatively complete or limited, and it may proceed rapidly or slowly. Because there are limits to both the plasticity and compensatory capacities of the brain, however, brain damage leads to more or less extensive permanent diminishment or loss of function over a wide range of physical and psychological abilities. In general, as already noted, the greater the amount of tissue damage, the greater the impairment of function.

The location of the damage may also play a significant role in determining a patient's ultimate neuropsychological status. The brain is highly specialized, each part—each cell in fact—making a unique contribution to the functional whole of an organ-

Implications of Brain Damage

It is difficult to predict the effects of focal injuries to the brain. Because there is some localization of function (as indicated in this drawing of the right cerebral hemisphere), damage to a particular area may cause impairment of the behavioral functioning mediated by the site of the damage. For example, a significant lesion of the occipital lobe is likely to result in some impairment of vision or visual perception. However, the awesome complexity of the brain's organization ensures that virtually all behavior is in fact the product of neuronal activity in many parts of the brain, some in all probability quite distant from the site of primary mediation. A lesion in one of the frontal lobes, for example, might influence neuronal activity at a site in the subcortical limbic system, thus producing some type of emotional dysregulation for the person affected. The result is that brain-behavior relationships are never as simple as graphic brain localization charts (such as this one) make them appear to be.

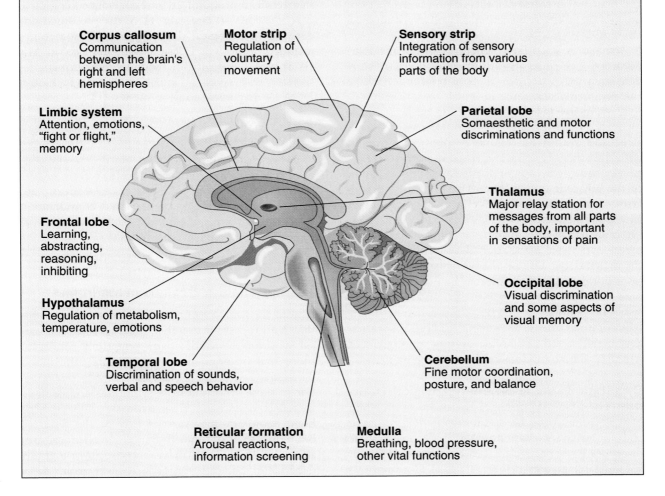

Corpus callosum
Communication between the brain's right and left hemispheres

Motor strip
Regulation of voluntary movement

Sensory strip
Integration of sensory information from various parts of the body

Limbic system
Attention, emotions, "fight or flight," memory

Parietal lobe
Somaesthetic and motor discriminations and functions

Frontal lobe
Learning, abstracting, reasoning, inhibiting

Thalamus
Major relay station for messages from all parts of the body, important in sensations of pain

Hypothalamus
Regulation of metabolism, temperature, emotions

Occipital lobe
Visual discrimination and some aspects of visual memory

Temporal lobe
Discrimination of sounds, verbal and speech behavior

Cerebellum
Fine motor coordination, posture, and balance

Reticular formation
Arousal reactions, information screening

Medulla
Breathing, blood pressure, other vital functions

ism's activity (see HIGHLIGHT 13.1). Thus the two hemispheres, while interacting intimately at many levels, are involved in somewhat different types of mental processing. For example, functions that are dependent on serial processing of familiar information, such as language, take place mostly in the left hemisphere for nearly everyone. The right hemisphere is generally specialized for configurational or *gestalt* processing, which is best suited for grasping overall meanings in novel situations, reasoning on a nonverbal, intuitive level, and appreciation of spatial relations. Even within hemispheres, the various lobes and areas within lobes mediate somewhat specialized functions.

Although none of these relationships between brain location and behavior can be considered constant or universal, it is possible to make broad generalizations about the likely effects of damage to particular parts of the brain. Damage to the frontal areas, for example, is associated with either of two contrasting clinical pictures: (a) behavioral inertia, passivity, apathy, and an inability to give up a given stream of associations or initiate a new one (perseverative thought); or (b) impulsiveness, distractibility, and insufficient ethical restraint. Damage to specific areas of the right parietal lobe may produce impairment of visual-motor coordination or distortions of body image, while damage to the left parietal may impair certain aspects of language function, including reading and writing, as well as arithmetical abilities.

Damage to identified structures within the temporal lobes disrupts an early stage of memory storage, such that extensive bilateral temporal damage can produce a syndrome in which remote memory remains relatively intact but nothing new can be effectively stored for later retrieval. Damage to other structures within the temporal lobes is associated with disturbances of eating, sexuality, and the emotions, probably by way of disrupting the functioning of the adjacent limbic lobe. The latter is a deeper center that mediates these "primitive" functions in extensive interaction with frontal-lobe structures. Occipital damage produces a variety of visual impairments and visual association deficits, the nature of the deficit depending on the particular site of the lesion. For example, a person may be unable to recognize familiar faces or to visualize and understand symbolic stimuli correctly. Unfortunately, many types of brain disease are general and diffuse in their destructive effects, thereby causing multiple and widespread interruptions of the brain's circuitry.

Diagnostic Issues in Neuropsychological Disorders The DSM-IV manages the diagnostic coding of various neuropsychological disorders in different and somewhat inconsistent ways. Traditionally, these disorders have been classified by disease entity or recognizable medical disorder, such as Huntington's disease, general paresis, and so on. That is, the principal etiologic factor, the underlying neurological disease process, was specified in the diagnostic term applied. As we have seen, however, such basically medical disorders that may have various kinds of associated mental symptoms are normally coded not on Axis I but on Axis III of the DSM-IV. The associated *mental* conditions are then typically coded on

Axis I, normally with the qualifying phrase, "Due to [a specified General Medical Condition]" (i.e., the disease process indicated on Axis III). Many of the common neuropsychological disorders are handled in this manner, but there are important exceptions, as noted below.

Some pathologic brain changes that may produce significant mental symptoms are related to the pathogenic effects of abusing certain substances, such as long-term, excessive alcohol consumption (see Chapter 10). In these cases a specific etiologic notation is included in the Axis I diagnosis, as in "Substance-Induced Persisting Amnestic Disorder" (referring to a circumscribed and characteristic type of memory impairment). DSM-IV also deals in a special way with certain conditions, often progressive, that result in pronounced and generalized cognitive deterioration, or *dementia*. Here the presumed underlying neurological disease process is sometimes included in the Axis I designation, and also on Axis III as well. Thus, notable cognitive impairment associated with cerebrovascular disease might have a DSM-IV diagnostic code as follows:

Axis I: Vascular Dementia
Axis III: Occlusion, cerebral artery

Bearing in mind these basic and potentially confusing issues concerning relationships between the brain, mental contents and processes, behavior, and formal diagnosis, we move now to a consideration of several of the more common and important neuropsychological clinical syndromes.

Neuropsychological Symptom Syndromes

As we have seen, a syndrome is a group of symptoms that tend to cluster together. The neuropsychological syndromes include many symptoms similar to those that occur in the schizophrenias, the mood disorders, and certain Axis II personality disorders, but in these syndromes the symptoms are assumed to reflect underlying brain pathology. The specific brain pathology may vary; it may be the result of brain disease or of the withdrawal of a chemical substance on which a person has become physiologically dependent. For our purposes, we will group these symptom syndromes into four categories: (a) delirium and dementia; (b) amnestic syndrome; (c) neuropsychological delusional and mood syndromes; and (d) neuropsychological personality syndromes.

We should note that more than one syndrome may be present at a time in a given patient and that syndromes and patterns of syndromes may change over a particular disorder's course of development.

As already noted, some syndromes mimic at the behavioral level the types of disorders we have described in previous chapters. Although we suspect these are often basically the same types of (primarily psychogenic) disorders as those discussed earlier, clinicians always need to be alert to the possibility that brain impairment may be responsible for the symptoms observed. Failure to do so could obviously result in serious diagnostic errors (Geschwind, 1975; Malamud, 1975; Weinberger, 1984).

Delirium and Dementia The syndrome called **delirium** is characterized by the relatively rapid onset of widespread disorganization of the higher mental processes; it is caused by a generalized disturbance in brain metabolism. Information-processing capacities are impaired, affecting such basic functions as attention, perception, memory, and thinking; and the patient may have frightening hallucinations. The syndrome often includes abnormal psychomotor activity, such as wild thrashing about, and disturbance of the sleep cycle. Delirium reflects a breakdown in the functional integrity of the brain. In this respect, it may be seen as only one step above coma and, in fact, it may lead to coma. A delirious person is essentially unable to carry out purposeful mental activity of any kind; current experience appears to make no contact with the person's previously acquired store of knowledge.

Delirious states tend to be acute conditions that rarely last more than a week, terminating in recovery or, less often, in death due to the underlying injury or disease. Delirium may result from several conditions, including head injury, toxic or metabolic disturbances, oxygen deprivation, insufficient delivery of blood to brain tissues, or precipitous withdrawal from alcohol or other drugs in an addicted person.

Dementia, already mentioned, has as its essential feature a normally progressive deterioration of brain functioning occurring after the completion of brain maturation (after, that is, about 15 years of age). Early in the course of the disease, an individual is alert and fairly well attuned to events in the environment. Episodic (memory for events), but not necessarily semantic (language and concept), memory functioning is typically affected in the early stages, especially memory for recent events. Patients with dementia also show increasingly marked deficits in abstract thinking, the acquisition of new knowledge or skills, visuospatial comprehension, motor control, problem solving, and judgment. Personality deterioration and loss of motivation accompany these other deficits. Normally, dementia is also accompanied by an impairment in emotional control and in moral and ethical sensibilities. It may be progressive or static; occasionally it is even reversible. Its course depends to a large extent on the nature of the etiology.

Etiologic factors in dementia are many and varied. They include degenerative processes that usually, but not always, affect older individuals. Other causes may be repeated cerebrovascular accidents (strokes); certain infectious diseases, such as syphilis,

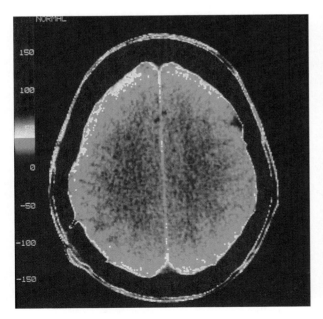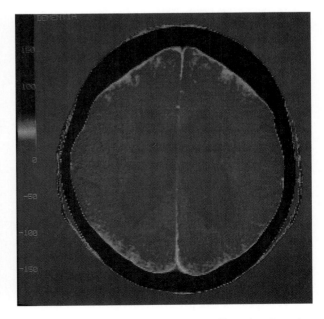

Dramatic differences show up in these CAT scans of a normal brain (left) and the brain of a person afflicted with probable Alzheimer's dementia (right). The dark blue areas in both hemispheres of the diseased brain indicate an enlargement of the ventricles (the large, hollow spaces deep within the brain) due to the degeneration of the brain tissue.

HIGHLIGHT 13.2

Dementia in 417 Patients Fully Evaluated for Dementia

Diagnosis	Number	Percent
Alzheimer's disease or dementia of unknown cause	199	47.7
Alcoholic dementia	42	10.0
Multi-infarct dementia [VAD]	39	9.4
Normal pressure hydrocephalus	25	6.0
Intracranial masses [tumors]	20	4.8
Huntington's disease	12	2.9
Drug toxicity	10	2.4
Posttraumatic	7	1.7
Other identified dementing diseases[a]	28	6.7
Pseudodementias[b]	28	6.7
Dementia uncertain	7	1.7

[a]Including epilepsy, subarachnoid hemorrhage, encephalitis, amyotropic lateral sclerosis, Parkinson's disease, hyperthyroidism, syphilis, liver disease, and cerebral anoxia episode, all less than 1 percent incidence.

[b]Including depression (16), schizophrenia (5), mania (2), "hysteria" (1), and not demented (4).

Based on Wells (1979).

meningitis, and AIDS; intracranial tumors and abscesses; certain dietary deficiencies; severe or repeated head injury; anoxia (lack of oxygen); and the ingestion or inhalation of toxic substances. As HIGHLIGHT 13.2 makes clear, the most common cause of dementia is degenerative brain disease, particularly Alzheimer's disease.

The Amnestic Syndrome The essential feature of the **amnestic syndrome** is a striking deficit in the ability to recall ongoing events more than a few minutes after they have taken place. Immediate memory and, to a lesser extent, memory for events that occurred before the disorder's development remain largely intact, as does memory for words and concepts. An amnestic individual, then, is constrained to live for the most part only in the present or the remote past; the recent past is for most practical purposes unavailable. We should add here that the question of whether the recent past is unavailable in some absolute sense is subject to differing interpretations. Some evidence suggests that these individuals may recognize or even recollect events of the recent past if given sufficient cues, which would

indicate that the information has been stored. Thus the difficulty may be in the retrieval mechanism (Hirst, 1982; Warrington & Weiskrantz, 1973).

In contrast to the dementia syndrome, overall cognitive functioning in the amnestic syndrome remains relatively intact. Theoretically, the disorder involves chiefly the relationship between the short-term and long-term memory systems; the contents of the former, always limited in scope and ephemeral in duration, are not stored in the latter in a way that permits ready accessibility or retrieval (Hirst, 1982).

In the most common forms of amnestic syndrome, those associated with alcohol or barbiturate addiction, the disorder may be irreversible. A wide range of other pathogenic factors may produce the amnestic syndrome. In these cases, depending on the nature and extent of damage to the affected neural structures and on the treatment undertaken, the syndrome may in time abate wholly, in part, or not at all.

Neuropsychological Delusional and Mood Syndromes In this type of delusional syndrome, false beliefs or belief systems arise in a setting of known or suspected brain impairment and are considered a principal clinical manifestation of this organic pathology. These delusions vary in content depending to some extent on the particular etiology. For example, a distinctly paranoid and suspicious delusional system is commonly seen with long-standing abuse of amphetamine drugs, whereas grandiose and expansive delusions are more characteristic of advanced neurosyphilis (general paresis). In addition to infectious processes and the abuse of certain drugs, etiological factors in the neuropsychological delusional syndrome include head injury and intracranial tumors.

Some cases of serious mood disturbance appear to be caused by disruptions in the normal physiology of cerebral function. Such conditions may closely resemble the symptoms seen in either depressive or manic mood disorders. Severe depressive syndromes, whether or not associated with organic pathology, may on superficial examination appear as dementias, in which case the term *pseudodementia* is often applied. The reaction may be minimal or severe, and the course of the disorder varies widely, depending on the nature of the organic pathology. Etiological factors include cerebrovascular accidents (strokes), Parkinson's disease, head injury, withdrawal of certain drugs, intracranial tumors or tumors of the hormone-secreting organs, and excessive use of steroid (adrenocortical hormone) drugs or certain other medications. Of course, an awareness of lost function or a hopeless outlook might itself make a person depressed, thus indicating a need for special care in the diagnostic process when there is reason to believe the patient harbors pessimistic thoughts about his or her clinical outcome (see Teri & Wagner, 1992).

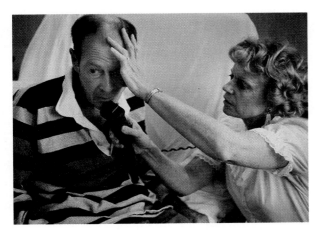

This man has Parkinson's disease, which may be associated with a neuropsychological mood syndrome, a cluster of symptoms that closely resembles those seen in either depressive or manic mood disorders.

Neuropsychological Personality Syndromes The essential feature of these syndromes is a change in an individual's general personality style or traits following brain impairment. Normally the change is in a socially negative direction; it may include impaired social judgment, lessened control of emotions and impulses, diminished concern about the consequences of one's behavior, and an inability to sustain goal-directed activity. Many different etiologies are associated with the neuropsychological personality syndromes, and the course of the disorder depends on its etiology. Occasionally, as when it is induced by medication, it may be transitory. Often, however, it is the first sign of impending deterioration, as when a kindly and gentle old man makes sexual advances toward a child or when a conservative executive suddenly begins to engage in unwise financial dealings. Some evidence indicates that a common feature in the organic personality syndrome may be damage to the frontal lobes (Crockett, Clark, & Klonoff, 1981; Sherwin & Geschwind, 1978; Stuss, Gow, & Heatherington, 1992), perhaps especially the *right* frontal (Borod, 1992).

The DSM-IV classification lists several different mental disorders in which brain impairment or other "general medical conditions" are believed to be contributory; many of these are related to drug abuse and involve only temporary physiological disruption (see Chapter 10). The disorders we will discuss in the following sections are longer-term disorders in which major, usually permanent, brain pathology occurs but in which an individual's emotional, motivational, and behavioral reactions to the loss of function also play an important role. Indeed, as was earlier suggested, it is often impossible to distinguish between maladaptive behavior that is directly caused by neuropsychological dysfunction and that which is basically part of an individual's psychological reaction to the deficits and disabilities experienced (Fabrega, 1981; Geschwind, 1975; Teri & Wagner, 1992).

The three types of neuropsychological mental disorder we will discuss in greater detail are HIV-1 infection of the brain, dementia of the Alzheimer's type, and disorders involving traumatic head injury. Vascular (formerly multi-infarct) dementia will be briefly addressed in the section on Alzheimer's, chiefly as a contrast to that disease.

Neuropsychological Disorder with HIV-1 Infection

Our discussion of mental disorder associated with the HIV-1 virus will necessarily be rather brief because these problems are relatively newly recognized ones. As we saw in Chapter 8, the devastating effects on the immune system produced by infection with the HIV Type 1 virus renders its victims "opportunistically" susceptible to a wide variety of other infectious agents. When neuropsychological syndromes were first observed among AIDS patients early in the last decade, it was assumed that they were due to secondary infections of this sort or to the brain tumors also associated with immune system incompetence. Then, in 1983, Snider and colleagues published the first systematic evidence that the presence of the HIV-1 virus (or a mutant form of it) could itself result in the destruction of brain cells. Since then, several different forms of such HIV-induced central nervous system pathology have been identified, some of which appear to be associated with the emergence of psychotic (e.g., delusional) phenomena (Sewell et al., 1994). To date, however, most attention has focused on the **AIDS dementia complex (ADC),** a generalized loss of cognitive functioning affecting a substantial proportion of AIDS patients.

The neuropathology of ADC involves various changes in the brain, among them generalized atrophy, edema, inflammatory cells, and patches of demyelination (loss of the myelin sheath surrounding nerve fibers), as described by various investigators (Gabuzda & Hirsch, 1987; Gray, Gherardi, & Scaravilli, 1988; Price et al. 1988a; Sewell et al., 1994). No brain area may be spared, but the damage appears concentrated in subcortical regions, notably the central white matter, the tissue surrounding the ventricles, and deeper gray matter structures such as the basal ganglia and thalamus.

Clinical features, which tend to appear as a late phase of HIV infection (although often before the full development of AIDS itself), usually begin with psychomotor slowing, diminished concentration, mild memory difficulties, and perhaps slight motor clumsiness. Progression is typically rapid after this point, with clear-cut dementia appearing in many cases within one year, although considerably longer periods have been reported. The later phases of ADC can be quite grim and include behavioral regression, confusion, psychotic thinking, apathy, and marked withdrawal, leading before death to an incontinent, bedridden state (Navia, Jordan, & Price, 1986; Price et al., 1988a, 1988b).

As many as 80 percent of patients with full-blown AIDS have neuropathological findings at autopsy (Petito, 1988). Thirty-eight percent of 121 living AIDS patients studied by Navia and colleagues (1986) met DSM criteria for dementia. Patients with **AIDS-related complex (ARC),** a pre-AIDS manifestation of HIV infection involving minor infections, various nonspecific symptoms (such as unexplained fever), and blood cell count abnormalities, may also experience cognitive difficulty, although it may be too subtle to be readily detected on clinical observation alone. In one study (Grant et al., 1987), 54 percent of ARC patients demonstrated definite impairment on a neuropsychological test battery. Other studies, reviewed by Grant and Heaton (1990), have shown inconsistent evidence of neuropsychological compromise in pre-ARC people who are merely infected with the HIV-1 virus. Significant numbers of infected persons were also found to be neuropsychologically compromised in a cross-national study recently reported by Maj and colleagues (1994), although these investigators emphasize the subtlety of the deficits detected and their lack of substantial impact on social functioning in otherwise asymptomatic persons. Depression, a frequent accompaniment of HIV infection, does not appear to account for the compromised neuropsychological test performance observed in these patients (Beason-Hazen, Nasrallah, & Bornstein, 1994).

The overall evidence is thus compelling that infection with the HIV-1 virus poses a substantial threat to the anatomical integrity of the brain, quite apart from its other frightening characteristics. As of this writing, it is not known what protects the minority of AIDS patients who show no central nervous system involvement during the entire course of their illnesses.

The question of treatment for ADC is of course intimately tied to that involving control or eradication of the HIV-1 infection itself. Until recently, it was impossible to feel confident about our prospects because of the enormous and unprecedented challenges presented by the complex structure and life cycle of this virus (McCutchan, 1990). This picture may be improving with advances in antiviral therapy. For example, Sidtis, Gatsonis, and Price (1993) have recently reported apparent arrest and in some instances even reversal of ADC progression among many persons treated with zidovudine (AZT); unfortunately, experience with AZT therapy in the more general AIDS context indicates that this effect will probably prove temporary because the virus adapts over time to the presence of AZT. It remains true therefore that prevention of infection is the only certain defensive strategy, a circumstance not unlike the problem posed by neurosyphilis, another sexually transmitted and potentially dementing disease, in an earlier era. In general, humankind has not done well in controlling the spread of sexually transmitted diseases through cautious sexual behavior, and, as was noted in Chapter 8, that pattern seems to be repeating itself with respect to the HIV-1 virus.

Dementia of the Alzheimer's Type

While the dementia complicating many cases of HIV-1 infection is a very serious concern, especially for the family and friends of victims, it is dwarfed in magnitude by the problems our society faces in coping with the dementias that are the most salient aspect of Alzheimer's disease, officially (as on Axis I of DSM-IV) termed **Dementia of the Alzheimer's Type (DAT).** DAT takes its name from Alois Alzheimer, a German neuropsychiatrist, who first described it in 1907.

It is a commonplace observation that the organs of the body deteriorate with aging. The cause or causes of this deterioration, however, remain largely obscure; science has not yet solved the riddle of aging. Of course, the brain—truly the master organ—is not spared in the aging process. Over time it too wears out, or degenerates. Mental disorders that sometimes accompany this brain degeneration and occur in old age have traditionally been called **senile dementias.** Unfortunately, a number of rare conditions result in degenerative changes in brain tissue earlier in life. Disorders associated with such earlier degeneration of the brain are known as **presenile dementias.**

Not only is the age of onset different in the presenile dementias, but they are also distinguished from the senile dementias by their different behavioral manifestations and brain tissue alterations (see HIGHLIGHT 13.3). One important exception is Alzheimer's disease, which is a typical and common senile disorder but which can, in some people, occur well before old age. Alzheimer's disease is associated with a characteristic dementia syndrome having an insidious onset and a usually slow but progressively deteriorating course, terminating in death.

The DAT diagnosis is normally rendered only after all other potential causes of dementia are ruled out by case history, physical examination, and laboratory tests. As earlier noted, the parallel *medical* diagnosis, Alzheimer's disease, is coded on Axis III, although it is usually not possible to establish definitely the presence of the distinctive Alzheimer neuropathology (described below) in living patients. Brain imaging techniques, such as that of magnetic resonance imaging (MRI), may provide supportive evidence in showing enlarged ventricles or widening in the folds (sulci) of the cerebral cortex, indicating brain atrophy. Nevertheless, the use of antemortem (before death) criteria for the diagnosis of DAT is

somewhat imprecise (Carlsson, 1986), with considerable possibility of overdiagnosing the condition (Hartford, 1986). In late 1994, a new and potentially quite accurate antemortem diagnostic test for Alzheimer's disease was announced (Scinto et al., reported by Pennisi, 1994), one involving an abnormal (excessive) response to a drug (tropicamide) that causes pupillary dilation when applied to the eye. This test may eventually enable accurate diagnosis in living patients.

When we picture a "typical" Alzheimer patient, we imagine a person of advanced age. Although most patients are older, for some, DAT is a presenile dementia that begins in their 40s or 50s; in such cases the progress of the disease and its associated dementia is often rapid. For example, in one study of early-onset DAT (Heyman et al., 1987) the five-year cumulative mortality rate was 2.5 times the expected rate, with the younger of these patients contributing disproportionately to the excess in deaths. Considerable evidence suggests an especially substantial genetic contribution in early-onset DAT (Davies, 1986), although different genes may well be involved in different families (Breitner et al., 1993). These early-onset cases, occurring in comparatively young and vigorous patients, portray the tragedy of Alzheimer's disease in an especially stark light.

In fact no way exists to portray the ravages of this disorder in other than an alarming fashion, even if we restrict attention to the more typical instance of onset after age 65. Survival to at least that point is becoming increasingly routine, and after the first decade of the twenty-first century, the first members of the enormous post–World War II baby boom generation will enter the age range of maximum risk. If we have not solved the problem of curing or preventing DAT by that time or shortly thereafter, the social and economic consequences will clearly be devastating (Fisher & Carstensen, 1990).

Nor is there any real assurance, despite our rapidly advancing knowledge about the disorder, that a solution will be found. Just as people do not die of old age per se but rather of failing organs, there is no cure or preventive measure for the aging of living organisms. Some investigators, for example, Selkoe (1986), suggest that Alzheimer's "disease" is merely the product of the aging process as manifested in a particular organ, the brain. Early onset is early brain aging, probably for the most part genetically determined. Prevention or cure, according to this view, would therefore approximate in its unlikelihood the discovery of the Fountain of Youth. Somewhat reassuringly, other researchers, Comfort (1984) and Glenner (1986), for example, reject this

Presenile Dementias

In addition to early-occurring Alzheimer's disease, two other forms of presenile dementia occur with sufficient frequency to deserve mention: Pick's disease and Huntington's disease.

Pick's Disease

Even rarer than early-onset Alzheimer's disease, Pick's disease (first described by Arnold Pick of Prague in 1892) is a degenerative disorder of the brain, usually having its onset in people between the ages of 45 and 50. Its cause is unknown. Women are apparently more subject to Pick's disease than men, at a ratio of about three to two. Onset is slow and insidious, involving difficulty in thinking, slight memory defects, easy fatiga-

bility, and, often, character changes with a lowering of many social inhibitions. At first there is a circumscribed atrophy of the frontal and temporal lobes; as the atrophy becomes more severe, the mental deterioration becomes progressively greater and includes apathy and disorientation as well as the impairment of judgment and other intellectual functions. The disease usually runs a fatal course within two to seven years.

Huntington's Disease

Huntington's disease is a genetically determined (autosomal dominant) degenerative disorder of the central nervous system. It was first described by the American neurologist George Huntington in 1872.

With an incidence rate of about 5 cases per 100,000 people, the disease usually occurs in individuals between 30 and 50 years of age. Behavior deterioration often becomes apparent several years before there are any detectable neurological manifestations (Lyle & Gottesman, 1977). The disease itself is characterized by a chronic, progressive chorea (involuntary and irregular twitching, jerking movements) with mental deterioration leading to dementia and death within 10 to 20 years. Although Huntington's disease cannot be cured or even arrested at the present time, it can be prevented, at least in theory, by genetic counseling, because its occurrence is a function of known genetic laws.

notion and hold that DAT is a specific disease process, hence in principle both preventable and curable.

Yet a third, and intermediate, view of the problem is offered by Gatz and colleagues (1994), who note that many eventually fatal organ system failures, Alzheimer's disease among them, seem to be the product not of a single or even a limited array of specific causal factors. Rather, they are the result of an accumulation of risk factors that ultimately exceed some clinical threshold and produce disease. Advancing age, of course, increases risk exposure. This view leaves open the possibility of reducing or delaying the occurrence of DAT through deliberately limiting exposure to risks, some of which are clearly environmental or otherwise potentially controllable. Gatz and her colleagues mention a variety of likely candidates, such as reduced alcohol consumption, for preventive interventions of this type.

The magnitude of the problem of DAT—often seriously underestimated—is already straining societal and family resources, both economic (Max, 1993) and emotional (see below). As shown in the table of HIGHLIGHT 13.2, the disorder accounts for nearly 50 percent of all cases of dementia of whatever cause. The ratio is doubtless considerably

higher for older people. It is estimated that one of every six people in the United States over age 65 is clinically demented, and that one of every ten people in this age range suffers from DAT (Evans et al., 1989). The prevalence rate of DAT may approach 50 percent by age 85 (Fisher & Carstensen, 1990), and a recent United Kingdom study indicates that, in each five-year interval from ages 75 to 89, there is an approximate doubling of the rate of new cases of DAT (Paykel et al., 1994). There are thus some 4 million living victims in the United States alone, and the number is increasing rapidly with the advancing age of the population. About 30 to 40 percent of nursing home residents are DAT patients (Kolata, 1981a). Some of these patients reside in mental hospitals or other types of institutional settings. Most, however, live in the community, typically with family members (Gurland & Cross, 1982), a circumstance that is often extremely stressful for caregivers (Brane, 1986; Fisher & Carstensen, 1990; Intrieri & Rapp, 1994).

The Clinical Picture in DAT As already noted, the onset of Alzheimer's disease in older people is usually gradual, involving slow mental deterioration. In some cases a physical ailment or some other stressful

Written reminders can help Alzheimer's victims lead relatively normal lives. In the early stages, they can remember how to do things once they are reminded to do them. Later on, they may lose the ability to do even simple tasks.

event is a dividing point, but usually an individual passes into a demented state almost imperceptibly, so that it is impossible to date the onset of the disorder precisely. The clinical picture may vary markedly from one person to another, depending on the nature and extent of brain degeneration, the premorbid personality of the individual, the particular stressors present, and the degree of environmental support.

Symptoms often begin with the person's gradual withdrawal from active engagement with life. There is a narrowing of social and other interests, a lessening of mental alertness and adaptability, and a lowering of tolerance to new ideas and changes in routine. Often thoughts and activities become self-centered and childlike, including a preoccupation with the bodily functions of eating, digestion, and excretion. As these changes—typical in a lesser degree of many older people—become more severe, additional symptoms, such as impaired memory for recent events, "empty" speech (in which grammar and syntax remain intact but vague expressions replace meaningful nouns and verbs), messiness, impaired judgment, agitation, and periods of confusion, make their appearance. Specific symptoms may vary considerably from patient to patient and from day to day for the same patient; thus the clinical picture is by no means uniform until the terminal stages, when the patient is reduced to a vegetative level. There is also, of course, individual variation in the rapidity of the disorder's progression. In rare instances the symptoms may reverse and partial function may return, but in true DAT this reversal will invariably prove temporary.

The end stages of Alzheimer's disease involve a depressingly similar pattern of reduction to a vegetative existence and ultimate death from some disease that overwhelms a person's limited defensive resources. Before this point, there is, as noted, some distinctiveness in patient behavior. Allowing for individual differences, a given victim is likely to show one of the several dominant behavioral manifestations described in the following paragraphs.

Approximately half of all DAT patients display a course of simple deterioration. That is, they gradually lose various mental capacities, typically beginning with memory for recent events and progressing to disorientation, poor judgment, neglect of personal hygiene, and loss of contact with reality to an extent precluding independent functioning as adults. Distinctly psychopathological symptoms (such as delusions), if they occur at all, are likely to be transitory and inconsistent over time. The following case—involving an engineer who had retired some seven years prior to his hospitalization—is typical of simple deterioration resulting from DAT:

During the past five years, he had shown a progressive loss of interest in his surroundings and during the last year had become increasingly "childish." His wife and eldest son had brought him to the hospital because they felt they could no longer care for him in their home, particularly because of the grandchildren. They stated that he had become careless in his eating and other personal habits and was restless and prone to wandering about at night. He could not seem to remember anything that had happened during the day but was garrulous concerning events of his childhood and middle years.

After admission to the hospital, the patient seemed to deteriorate rapidly. He could rarely remember what had happened a few minutes before, although his memory for remote events of his childhood remained good. When he was visited by his wife and children, he mistook them for old friends, nor could he recall anything about the visit a few minutes after they had departed. The following brief conversation with the patient, which took place after he had been in the hospital for nine months and about three months before his death, shows his disorientation for time and person:

Doctor: How are you today, Mr. ____?

Patient: Oh . . . hello (looks at doctor in rather puzzled way as if trying to make out who he is).

Doctor: Do you know where you are now?

Patient: Why yes . . . I am at home. I must paint the house this summer. It has needed painting for a long time but it seems like I just keep putting it off.

Doctor: Can you tell me the day today?

Patient: Isn't today Sunday . . . why, yes, the children are coming over for dinner today. We always have dinner for the whole family on Sunday. My wife was here just a minute ago but I guess she has gone back into the kitchen.

In a less frequent manifestation of Alzheimer's disease, a person develops a decidedly paranoid orientation to the environment, becoming markedly suspicious and often convinced that others are engaged in various injurious plots and schemes. Uncooperativeness and verbal abuse are common accompaniments, making the task of caregiving significantly more stressful. In the early phases of this reaction pattern, the cognitive deficits characteristic of Alzheimer's disease (memory loss, disorientation) may not be prominent, perhaps enabling the person to be quite observant and even logical in building the "case" for others' threatening activities. Though themes of victimization predominate in this form of the disorder, also common is the so-called jealousy delusion in which the person persistently accuses his or her partner or spouse—who is often of advanced age and physically debilitated—of being sexually unfaithful. Family members may be accused of various foul deeds, such as poisoning the patient's food or plotting to steal the patient's funds. Fortunately, punitive retribution in the form of physical attacks on the "evildoers" is rare, but a combative pattern does occasionally occur, complicating the patient's management. The following case is fairly typical of the paranoid reaction type:

A woman of 74 had been referred to a hospital after the death of her husband because she had become uncooperative and was convinced that her relatives were trying to steal the insurance money her husband had left her. In the hospital, she complained that the other patients had joined together against her and were trying to steal her belongings. She frequently refused to eat, on the grounds that the food tasted funny and had probably been poisoned. She grew in-

creasingly irritable and disoriented for time and person. She avidly scanned magazines in the ward reading room but could not remember anything she had looked at. The following conversation reveals some of her symptoms:

Doctor: Do you find that magazine interesting?

Patient: Why do you care? Can't you see I'm busy?

Doctor: Would you mind telling me something about what you are reading?

Patient: It's none of your business . . . I am reading about my relatives. They want me to die so that they can steal my money.

Doctor: Do you have any evidence of this?

Patient: Yes, plenty. They poison my food and they have turned the other women against me. They are all out to get my money. They even stole my sweater.

Doctor: Can you tell me what you had for breakfast?

Patient: . . . (Pause) I didn't eat breakfast . . . it was poisoned and I refused to eat it. They are all against me.

Paranoid orientations tend to develop in people who have been sensitive and suspicious. Existing personality tendencies are apparently intensified by degenerative brain changes and the stress accompanying advancing age.

Other patterns seen in Alzheimer patients are comparatively infrequent. Some patients are confused but amiable, usually showing marked memory impairment and a tendency to engage in seemingly pointless activities, such as hoarding useless objects or repetitively performing household tasks in a ritualized manner. Other patients become severely agitated, with or without an accompanying "hand-wringing" depression. Depressed Alzheimer patients tend to develop extremely morbid preoccupations and delusions, such as hypochondriacal ideas about having various horrible diseases, often seen as punishment for past sins. Suicide is a possibility in such cases should a patient be physically capable of carrying out the act.

In some cases, the progress of the disease is unusually rapid and a patient moves quickly into a state of incoherence verging on delirium. This mental clouding is frequently accompanied by marked agitation and unpredictable combativeness, severely trying the resources of caregivers. As we have seen, all Alzheimer patients who survive long enough eventually enter a stage of continuous delirium.

With appropriate treatment, which may include medication and the maintenance of a calm, reassuring, and unprovocative social milieu, many people with Alzheimer's disease show some symptom alleviation. In general, however, deterioration continues its downward course over a period of months or years. Eventually, patients become oblivious of their surroundings, bedridden, and reduced to a vegetative existence. Resistance to disease is lowered, and death usually results from pneumonia or some other infection.

Causal Factors in DAT The fundamental neuropathology of the Alzheimer's brain has been known for some time. Readily determined by microscopic examination of tissue specimens, it has three elements: (a) the widespread appearance of "senile plaques," small areas of dark-colored matter that are in part the debris of damaged nerve terminals; (b) the tangling of the normally regular patterning of neurofibrils (strandlike protein filaments) within neuronal cell bodies; and (c) the abnormal appearance of small holes in neuronal tissue, called granulovacuoles, which derive from cell degeneration. Absolute confirmation of the diagnosis of DAT at present rests on observation of these changes in tissue samples, which is why it can usually be accomplished only after a patient has died. When sufficiently numerous, these microscopic alterations of the brain's substance lead to generalized brain atrophy, which may be visualized in live patients by imaging techniques. Unfortunately from the diagnostic standpoint, such atrophy may occur with several other disease conditions as well, and even as a correlate of normal aging.

Another important alteration in DAT concerns the neurotransmitter acetylcholine (ACh), which is known to be important in the mediation of memory. While there is widespread destruction of neurons in DAT, particularly in a small area of the hippocampus (Adler, 1994), evidence suggests that among the earliest and most severely affected are a cluster of cell bodies located in the basal forebrain and involved in the release of ACh (Coyle, Price, & DeLong, 1983; Whitehouse et al., 1982). This observation and related ones (e.g., Wester et al., 1988) have given rise to the ACh depletion theory of DAT etiology. Although the evidence is not conclusive, the theory does integrate an impressive array of research data. For example, a temporary

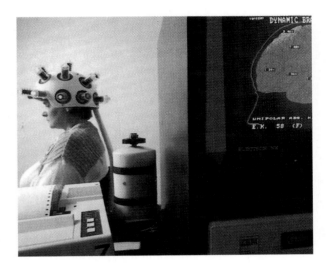

An electrode headset picks up signals from the brain of a 58-year-old woman, and a computer turns them into the brain map on the screen. Brain-mapping can detect the depletion of acetylcholine, which is thought to play a role in the production of Alzheimer's disease.

DAT-like syndrome may be produced in normal subjects who are given ACh-blocking drugs (Kopelman, 1986); the newly approved drug tacrine (Cognex), which increases available brain ACh, is temporarily helpful in improving cognitive function in some DAT patients (Whitehouse, 1993); and finally the promising new pupillary dilation diagnostic technique mentioned earlier appears to depend upon pharmacodynamic effects involving ACh (Scinto et al., reported in Pennisi, 1994).

If we make the reasonable assumption that ACh depletion plays at least some role in the production of DAT symptoms, there is still the question of what place it occupies in the presumed causal chain. What, for example, causes the degeneration of ACh-releasing cells? Several hypotheses purport to answer such questions, but none has so far gained a consensus acceptance.

Some investigators have taken the more direct approach of trying to discover the sources of the primary DAT lesions such as neurofibrillary tangles and senile plaques. The search has yielded a considerable amount of information concerning, in particular, the composition of the latter. These plaques contain cell debris, but their cores consist of a sticky protein substance, called beta amyloid, that also occurs in abnormal abundance in other parts of DAT patients' brains (see Gajdusek, 1986; Hardy et al., 1986; Kang et al., 1987). This finding may turn out to be extremely important in leading to an understanding of DAT, in part because it may serve as a bridge to certain exciting new discoveries relating to the genetics of DAT, as reported below.

We have already mentioned that early-onset DAT, in common with numerous other instances of early-onset disease, seems to have a prominent genetic component in its etiology. In one interesting study involving early onset, Nee (reported in Sargent, 1982b) traced the disease back eight generations in one family that immigrated to this continent in 1837. Of 531 family members, 53 were identified as suffering from the disease, even though those who lived to 65 without symptoms were considered free of it. Collateral findings of this NIMH project showed that the mean interval between the onset of symptoms and death was 6 years (although in one case it was 24), and that the age at onset ranged between 44 and 64 years. In fact, widespread evidence shows that a general vulnerability to the development of DAT, even in very late-onset cases, may be inherited (Breitner, 1986; Breitner et al., 1993; Davies, 1986; Mohs et al., 1987; Sturt, 1986).

Much of this evidence points to a genetic connection with Down syndrome (to be discussed later in the chapter), which is due to a trisomy (tripling) involving chromosome 21. Most people with Down syndrome who survive beyond about age 40 develop a DAT-like dementia (Bauer & Shea, 1986; Janicki & Dalton, 1993), with comparable neuropathological changes (Schapiro & Rapoport, 1987). Anomalies of chromosome 21 have also been implicated in DAT (e.g., Van Broeckhoven et al., 1987), although that is plainly not the only site of origin for genetic influences in the disorder (Breitner et al., 1993; Clark & Goate, 1993). Barnes (1987) reported evidence that the same regions of chromosome 21 are involved in both Down syndrome and DAT, and that one of the genes in this region contributes to the production of the amyloid protein figuring so prominently in the neuropathology of DAT. Hardy and colleagues (as reported by Marx, 1991) identified a gene mutation on chromosome 21 in a DAT-prone family, one that could be implicated in the release of beta amyloid.

Owing to this impressive record of gradually narrowing the field in the search for the primary etiology of DAT, conditions had become quite favorable by the early 1990s for the emergence of a major breakthrough that would tie together the strands of the etiologic picture. The beginnings of that breakthrough may have come with the discovery, largely by Duke University scientists, of the role of a blood protein, apolipoprotein-E (ApoE), in somehow enhancing the buildup of beta amyloid, which is asso-

ciated with cell death. The Duke team's theory minimizes the causal role of amyloid, considering its excess accumulation an effect of processes involved in cell death, which they believe is caused by ApoE-induced neurofibrillary tangling (*Wall Street Journal*, Nov. 8, 1993, pp. B1, B2). Other investigators (e.g., Potter et al., reported in Pennisi, 1994), while accepting the probable importance of ApoE, have continued, with considerable success, to focus on the potential of this protein to facilitate amyloid deposits directly. The genetic tie-in actually concerns three genetically distinct forms of ApoE; the risk of developing late-onset DAT varies quite markedly with the type of ApoE inherited (*Duke University Dialogue*, June 10, 1994, pp. 6, 11).

Exciting as they are, however, these recent discoveries still do not account for all cases of DAT. Many people inheriting the most "risky" ApoE gene do not succumb to DAT, and some who do succumb to the disease have no such gene. Many findings suggest that nongenetic variables are importantly involved in the etiology of DAT (Henderson, 1986), as is perhaps most clearly demonstrated in the occurrence of substantial numbers of monozygotic twins discordant for the disease (Breitner et al., 1993). For example, both Nee and colleagues (1987) and Renvoize and colleagues (1986) have described monozygotic twins discordant for DAT, a circumstance that is most readily explained by some sort of critical environmental influence. Unfortunately, we have little solid information about environmental risk factors; most hypotheses advanced in this area involve environmental toxins, but there are also suggestions that a past history of head trauma or of alcohol abuse may be implicated (Gatz et al., 1994).

Recent progress in understanding DAT is impressive. Although there are still many loose ends to be tied together, and some that may remain resistant to our best efforts, the progress of the last 15 years in coming to grips with DAT has been nothing less than astonishing. These investigations are truly science of the highest order effectively directed at a human problem of enormous and increasing scope.

Treatments and Outcomes in DAT There is as yet no known treatment for DAT—medical, psychosocial, retraining-based, or rehabilitative, including attempts at preserving or replenishing brain ACh—that produces a sustained reversal or interruption of the deteriorating course. Until some means of accomplishing such an effect appears, we will have to content ourselves with palliative measures that diminish patient and caregiver distress and relieve as far as possible those complications of the disorder, such as combativeness, that increase the difficulties of management.

Concerning the latter objectives, Fisher and Carstensen (1990) reviewed the literature on behavioral approaches used to control several of the common problematic behaviors that are associated with DAT (and with other dementing disorders as well), such as wandering off, incontinence, inappropriate sexual behavior, and inadequate self-care skills. Because behavioral approaches need not be dependent on complex cognitive and communicational abilities, which are apt to be lacking in these patients, they may be particularly appropriate for therapeutic intervention with this group. In general, reports of results are moderately encouraging in terms of reducing unnecessary frustration and embarrassment for the patient and difficulty for the caregiver.

There has also been active treatment research focused on the consistent findings of ACh depletion in DAT. The reasoning here is that it might be possible to improve functioning by administering drugs that enhance the availability of brain ACh. Currently, the most effective way of doing so is by inhibiting the production of the principal enzyme involved in the metabolic breakdown of ACh, acetylcholinesterase. This is the rationale for the newly available drug tacrine (Cognex). Roth (1993) describes this type of pharmacologic intervention as "promising," and we would hope this prediction to be confirmed in future research. The limited findings so far available, however, suggest effects that are mostly quite limited and inconsistent (Whitehouse, 1993). Several other types of potentially cognition-enhancing drugs are currently being studied (Cardenas, 1993).

Other medications may be of some help for patients who experience difficulty in modulating their emotions and impulses. Some depressed DAT patients respond reasonably well to antidepressant or stimulant medication. Where medications are used, however, dosages must be carefully monitored because unanticipated effects are common and because the frequently debilitated state of these patients makes them susceptible to an exaggerated response.

As we have seen, neuronal cells that have died with the advance of Alzheimer's neuropathology are permanently lost; hence, even if some treatment were found to terminate a patient's disease, he or she would still be left seriously impaired. The real key to effective intervention must therefore be seen as preventive, or at least as deployable at the first sign of Alzheimer's onset, sparing the bulk of the brain's neurons. Eventually, for example, we might be able to identify and reduce or eliminate the environmental hazards that play a role in stimulating the development of Alzheimer's (Gatz et al., 1994).

Clearly, however, the most promising development in regard to prevention possibilities relates to the apolipoprotein (ApoE) research described above. Conceivably, it will prove possible to fashion interventions—for example by administering targeted drugs—that counteract pathogenic processes associated with inheritance of the high-risk ApoE genes. That would truly be a momentous achievement.

In the meantime, any comprehensive approach to therapeutic intervention must consider the extremely difficult situation of caregivers. With advancing DAT, they are confronted not only with many difficult management problems but also with the "social death" of the patient as a person and their own "anticipatory grief" (Gilhooly et al., 1994). They are, as a group, at extraordinarily high risk for depression (Cohen & Eisdorfer, 1988). They tend to consume high quantities of psychotropic medication themselves and to report many stress symptoms (George, 1984; Hinrichsen & Niederehe, 1994). Because the basic problem usually seems to be one of high and sustained stress, any measures found successful in the reduction and management of stress and the enhancement of coping resources could be helpful in easing caregivers' burdens (Costa, Whitfield, & Stewart, 1989). Group support programs, for example, may produce measurable reductions in experienced stress and depression (e.g., Glosser & Wexler, 1985; Hebert et al., 1994; Kahan et al., 1985).

Whether or not, or at what point, to institutionalize a DAT patient whose requirements for care threaten to overwhelm his or her spouse or other family members can be a vexing and emotional decision (Cohen et al., 1993). It can also be one with significant financial implications because, on average, nursing home care is about twice as costly as home care (Hu, Huang, & Cartwright, 1986). As we have seen, most DAT patients are cared for at home, mostly for emotional reasons, such as continuing love, loyalty, and a sense of obligation to the stricken parent or partner. In one sense at least, the home care decision is a justifiable one; the move to an institution, particularly one lacking in social stimulation and support, may result in an abrupt worsening of symptoms and sometimes a markedly enhanced rate of deterioration—demonstrating once again the power of psychosocial influences even in the case of widespread brain destruction. On the other hand, the emergence of marked confusion, gross and argumentative demeanor, stuporous depression, inappropriate sexual behavior, and disorientation for time, place, and person, not to mention possible sudden eruption of combative violence, can put an intolerable strain on caregivers. Because in all likelihood such conditions will worsen over time, wisdom dictates an early rather than a late removal to an institution, which in any event is where most DAT patients will have to spend their final weeks or months.

A Note on Vascular Dementia Vascular (formerly multi-infarct) dementia (VAD), frequently confused with DAT because of its somewhat similar clinical picture and its increasing incidence and prevalence rates with advancing age, is actually an entirely different disease in terms of its underlying neuropathology. In this disorder, a series of cerebral infarcts—interruptions of the blood supply to parts of the brain because of arterial disease, commonly known as strokes—cumulatively destroy neurons over expanding brain regions. The affected regions become soft and may degenerate over time, leaving only cavities. Although this disorder tends to have a more heterogeneous early clinical picture (Wallin & Blennow, 1993), the progressive loss of cells leads to brain atrophy and behavioral impairments that ultimately mimic those of DAT. The decline, however, is less smooth in course because of (a) the discrete character of infarct events and the processes they initiate; (b) variations over time in the volume of blood delivered by a seriously clogged artery, producing variations in the functional adequacy of cells that have not yet succumbed to oxygen deprivation; and (c) a tendency to be associated with more severe behavioral complications (Sultzer et al., 1993). VAD is far less common than DAT, accounting for only some 10 percent of dementia cases. One reason for this is that VAD has a much shorter average course because of a patient's vulnerability to sudden death from a large infarct or one that affects vital centers. Occasionally, an unfortunate patient will be discovered to have both DAT and VAD.

The medical treatment of VAD, while hazardous and complicated, offers slightly more hope at this time than that of DAT. Unlike DAT, the basic problem of cerebral arteriosclerosis can be medically managed to some extent, perhaps decreasing the likelihood of further strokes.

The psychological and behavioral aspects of the dementia caused by DAT and VAD are similar in many respects, and any management measure found useful in one is likely to be applicable in the other. Likewise, the maintenance of any gains achieved cannot be taken for granted because of the generally progressive nature of the underlying brain pathology. The daunting problems facing caregivers are also much the same in the two conditions, indicating the appropriateness of support groups, stress reduction techniques, and the like.

Disorders Involving Head Injury

Since ancient times, traumatic brain injuries have provided a rich source of material for speculation about mental functions. Hippocrates pointed out that injuries to the head could cause sensory and motor disorders, and Galen included head injuries among the major causes of mental disorders. Head injuries occur frequently, particularly as a result of falls, blows, and accidents. It has been estimated that well over a million people in the United States suffer head injuries each year in automobile and industrial accidents; a sizable number of cases are the result of bullets or other objects actually penetrating the cranium. Significant brain damage is sustained in some 300,000 of these instances (Chance, 1986). Relatively few people with head injuries find their way into mental hospitals because many head injuries do not involve appreciable damage to the brain, and even where they do psychopathological complications are often not observed.

The Clinical Picture in Disorders with Head Injuries Clinicians distinguish three general types of traumatic head injury because the clinical pictures and residual problems vary somewhat among them: (a) closed head injury (CHI, in which the cranium remains intact); (b) penetrating head injury (PHI, in which the cranium, as well as the underlying brain, are penetrated by some object, such as a bullet) and (c) skull fracture, with or without compression of the brain by fragmented bone concavity. Posttrauma epilepsy, for example, is unusual in CHI but a rather common outcome of the other two forms of head injury. The damage to the brain in CHI is indirect, so to speak, produced by inertial forces that cause it to come into violent contact with the interior skull wall, or rotational forces that twist the brain mass relative to the brain stem.

Neuropsychologically significant head injuries usually give rise to immediate acute reactions, such as unconsciousness and disruption of circulatory, metabolic, and neurotransmitter regulation. Normally, if a head injury is sufficiently severe to result in unconsciousness, the person experiences *retrograde amnesia*, or inability to recall events immediately preceding the injury. Apparently, such trauma interferes with the brain's capacity to consolidate into long-term storage the events that were still being processed at the time of the trauma. *Anterograde amnesia*, which refers to an inability to effectively store in memory events happening during variable periods of time *after* the trauma, is also occasionally observed and is regarded by many as a negative prognostic sign.

A person rendered unconscious by a head injury usually passes through stages of stupor and confusion on the way to recovering clear consciousness. This recovery of consciousness may be complete in the course of minutes, or it may take hours or days. In rare cases an individual may live for extended periods of time without regaining consciousness, a condition known as coma. In such cases the prognosis for substantial improvement is poor. In some instances, significant cognitive or personality alterations following injury are observed even where a person experiences no loss of consciousness.

The persistence and severity of posttrauma disruptions of brain function depend on the degree and type of injury. They may lead to early death or may clear up entirely. Quite often they develop into chronic disorders in which the individual's future cognitive and behavioral functioning is compromised. In relatively severe but nonfatal brain injury, most of the recovery that will be experienced tends to occur in the earliest posttrauma phase, although sometimes return of function may still occur after several years. Individual courses of recovery are highly variable (Crepeau & Scherzer, 1993; Powell & Wilson, 1994). In DSM-IV, brain injuries having notable, long-standing effects on adaptive functioning are coded on Axis I using the appropriate syndromal descriptive phrase, with the qualifier "due to head trauma."

Following a severe cerebral injury, a person's pulse, temperature, blood pressure, and important aspects of brain metabolism are all affected, and survival may be uncertain. The duration of the coma is generally related to the severity of the injury. If the patient survives, coma may be followed by delirium, in which acute excitement is manifested, with disorientation, hallucinations, and generally agitated, restless, and confused activity. Often the patient talks incessantly in a disconnected fashion, with no insight into the disturbed condition. Gradually the confusion clears up and the individual regains contact with reality. Again, the severity and duration of residual symptoms depend primarily on the nature and extent of the cerebral damage, the premorbid personality of the patient, and the life situation to which he or she will return.

Fortunately, the brain is an extraordinarily well protected organ; but even so, a hard blow on the head may result in a skull fracture in which portions of bone press on or are driven into the brain tissue. Even without a fracture, the force of the blow may result in small, pinpoint hemorrhages throughout the brain or in the rupturing of larger blood vessels in the brain. Some degree of bleeding, or *intracranial hemorrhage,* can occur with even relatively low-

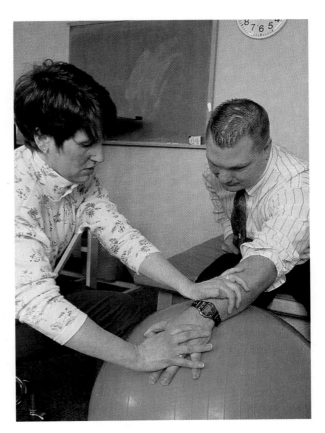

This police officer, who received a gunshot head wound in the line of duty, is receiving therapy to improve muscle tone and function in his left arm.

impact head injuries. In severe injuries, there may be gross bleeding or hemorrhaging at the site of the damage. Enough blood may accumulate within the rigid confines of the skull that disruptive pressure is exerted on neighboring regions of the brain; a common form of this problem is the *subdural hematoma,* which, if not relieved by aspiration of the excess blood, may endanger vital brain functions or produce permanent neuronal damage. When the hemorrhaging involves small spots of bleeding—often microscopic sleeves of red cells encircling tiny blood vessels—the condition is referred to as *petechial hemorrhages.* Some evidence shows tiny, scattered petechial hemorrhages in most brain injuries, but in fatal cases they are usually multiple or generalized throughout the brain. Serious levels of brain swelling, or *cerebral edema,* occur in many cases of severe damage, increasing the risk of significant mental impairment or death unless promptly treated.

Professional boxers are likely to suffer such petechial hemorrhaging from repeated blows to the head; they may develop a form of encephalopathy (characterized by an area or areas of permanently damaged brain tissue) from the accumulated damage of such injuries. Consequently, some former boxers suffer from impaired memory, slurred speech, inability to concentrate, involuntary movements, and other symptoms—a condition popularly referred to as being "punch-drunk." Johnson (1969) found abnormal electroencephalograms in 10 of 17 retired boxers; Earl (1966) noted that two former welterweight champions suffered so much brain damage in their professional fights that they were confined in mental institutions before they reached the age of 30.

Even where an injury seems relatively mild with good return of function, careful neuropsychological assessment may reveal subtle residual impairment. Large numbers of relatively mild closed-head brain *concussions* (violent shock to tissues) and *contusions* (bruises) occur every year as a result of auto collisions, athletic injuries, falls, and other mishaps. Temporary loss of consciousness and postimpact confusion are the most common and salient immediate symptoms. There is considerable controversy about whether these mild brain injuries produce significant long-standing symptoms or impairments of various abilities (Dikmen & Levin, 1993; Zasler, 1993). Brown, Fann, and Grant (1994), for example, have made a strong argument that "postconcussional disorder" should be included in the DSM as a separate diagnosis based on evidence of diffuse postinjury changes in cognitive ability, personality, brain anatomy and electrophysiology (EEG), and general life functioning. So far, at least, that argument has not prevailed, although the recommended diagnosis is included as one of a large number of provisional candidates said to need "further study" in a DSM-IV Appendix.

Perhaps the most famous historical example of traumatic brain injury is the celebrated American crowbar case reported by Dr. J. M. Harlow in 1868 (Dr. Harlow's original report was recently reprinted in *History of Psychiatry*, 1993, Vol. 4, pp. 271–81). Because it is of both historical and descriptive significance, it merits our attention:

The accident occurred in Cavendish, Vt., on the line of the Rutland and Burlington Railroad, at that time being built, on the 13th of September, 1848, and was occasioned by the premature explosion of a blast, when this iron, known to blasters as a tamping iron, and which I now show you, was shot through the face and head.

The subject of it was Phineas P. Gage, a perfectly healthy, strong and active young man, twenty-five years of age . . . Gage was foreman of a gang of men employed in excavating rock, for the road way. . . .

The missile entered by its pointed end, the left side of the face, immediately anterior to the angle of the lower jaw, and passing obliquely upwards, and obliquely backwards, emerged in the median line, at the back part of the frontal bone, near the coronal suture. . . .

The iron which thus traversed the head, is round and rendered comparatively smooth by use, and is three feet seven inches in length, one and one fourth inches in its largest diameter, and weighs thirteen and one fourth pounds. . . .

The patient was thrown upon his back by the explosion, and gave a few convulsive motions of the extremities, but spoke in a few minutes. His men (with whom he was a great favorite) took him in their arms and carried him to the road, only a few rods distant, and put him into an ox cart, in which he rode, supported in a sitting posture, fully three quarters of a mile to his hotel. He got out of the cart himself, with a little assistance from his men, and an hour afterwards (with what I could aid him by taking hold of his left arm) walked up a long flight of stairs, and got upon the bed in the room where he was dressed. He seemed perfectly conscious, but was becoming exhausted from the hemorrhage, which by this time, was quite profuse, the blood pouring from the lacerated sinus in the top of his head, and also finding its way into the stomach, which ejected it as often as every fifteen or twenty minutes. He bore his sufferings with firmness, and directed my attention to the hole in his cheek, saying, "the iron entered there and passed through my head."

Some time later Dr. Harlow made the following report:

His physical health is good, and I am inclined to say that he has recovered. Has no pain in head, but says it has a queer feeling which he is not able to describe. Applied for his situation as foreman, but is undecided whether to work or travel. His contractors, who regarded him as the

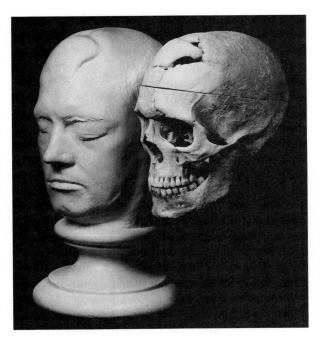

A cast of the head and the actual skull of Phineas Gage. Note the places in the skull pierced by the iron rod.

most efficient and capable foreman in their employ previous to his injury considered the change in his mind so marked that they could not give him his place again. The equilibrium or balance, so to speak, between his intellectual faculties and animal propensities, seems to have been destroyed. He is fitful, irreverent, indulging at times in the grossest profanity (which was not previously his custom), manifesting but little deference for his fellows, impatient of restraint or advice when it conflicts with his desires, at times pertinaciously obstinate, yet capricious and vacillating, devising many plans of future operations, which are no sooner arranged than they are abandoned in turn for others ... his mind is radically changed, so decidedly that his friends and acquaintances said he was "no longer Gage."

It is evident from the above account that Gage acquired a severe frontal brain wound as well as a neuropsychological personality syndrome from his encounter with the crowbar. As Stuss and colleagues (1992) have noted, Gage's persistent posttrauma difficulties are fairly characteristic for severe frontal-lobe damage; emotional dyscontrol and personality

alterations, including impairment of self-reflective awareness, are often prominent features of behavior change due to this type of injury. In general, however, personality disturbances secondary to traumatic brain injury are somewhat unpredictable owing to the varied structural pathology apt to be involved in such injuries (Prigatano, 1992).

Treatments and Outcomes Immediate treatment for brain damage due to head injury is primarily a medical matter. Prompt treatment may prevent further injury or damage—for example, when pooled blood under pressure must be removed from the skull. In moderate to severe cases, immediate medical treatment may have to be supplemented by a long-range program of reeducation and rehabilitation.

Although many head trauma patients show few residual effects from their injury, particularly if they have experienced only a brief loss of consciousness, other patients sustain definite and long-lasting impairment. Common aftereffects of moderate brain injury are chronic headaches, anxiety, irritability, dizziness, easy fatigability, and impaired memory and concentration. Where the brain damage is extensive, a patient's general intellectual level may be markedly reduced, especially if he or she has suffered severe temporal- or parietal-lobe lesions. Most victims have significant delays in returning to their occupations, and many are unable to return at all (Dikmen et al, 1994); other losses of adult social roles are also common (Hallett et al., 1994). In addition, various specific neurological and psychological defects may follow localized brain damage, as we have seen. Some 2–4 percent of head injury cases develop posttraumatic epilepsy, usually within two years of the head injury but sometimes much later.

In a minority of brain injury cases, notable personality changes occur, such as those described in the historic case of Phineas Gage. Other kinds of personality changes include passivity, loss of drive and spontaneity, agitation, anxiety, depression, and paranoid suspiciousness. Like cognitive changes, the kinds of personality changes that emerge in severely damaged people will depend, in large measure, on the site and extent of their injury (Prigatano, 1992).

The great majority of people suffering from mild concussions improve to a near normal status within a short time. With moderate brain injuries, it takes longer for patients to reach their maximum level of improvement, and many suffer from headaches and other symptoms for prolonged periods. A few develop chronic, incapacitating symptoms. In severe brain injury cases, the prognosis is less favorable

(Jennett et al., 1976; Powell & Wilson, 1994). Many of these patients have to adjust to lower levels of occupational and social functioning (Dikmen et al., 1994), while others are so impaired intellectually that they require continuing supervision and, sometimes, institutionalization. Even in cases where considerable amounts of brain tissue have been destroyed, however, some patients are able to become socially independent. In many cases there is improvement with time, due largely to reeducation and to intact brain areas taking over new functions (Powell & Wilson, 1994).

In general, the following factors indicate a favorable prognosis in cases of head injury: (a) a short period of unconsciousness or posttraumatic amnesia; (b) minimal or no cognitive impairment; (c) a well-integrated pre-injury personality; (d) higher educational attainment; (e) stable pre-injury work history; (f) motivation to recover or make the most of residual capacities; (g) a favorable life situation to which to return; (h) early intervention; and (i) an appropriate program of rehabilitation and retraining (Brooks, 1974; Dikmen et al., 1994; Diller & Gordon, 1981; Mackay, 1994).

The last-mentioned factor, crucial for the future functioning of many brain-injured individuals (Giles, 1994), and demonstrably effective when approached in a comprehensive way (e.g., Malec et al., 1993), is unfortunately far from generally available (Chance, 1986). Even where such specialized treatment centers are conveniently located, they may be too expensive for patients to take advantage of them. Encouraging in recent years is a trend toward community-wide organization to cope with the rehabilitation challenges of brain-injured persons (e.g., Huber & Edelberg, 1993; McLaughlin & Peters, 1993; Seaman et al., 1993).

Other factors may also have a direct bearing on the outcome of brain injuries. As we mentioned earlier, the results of brain damage in young childhood differ from those in adolescence and adulthood, although in both instances the results may range from death to any number of neurological disorders, including epilepsy and mental retardation. Moreover, the outlook for individuals who are also victims of alcoholism, drug dependence, or other organic conditions may be unfavorable. Alcoholics, in particular, are prone to head injuries and other accidents and do not have good improvement records, possibly because many of them also have brain deficits related to excessive drinking (Mearns & Lees-Haley, 1993). Severe emotional conflicts sometimes appear to predispose an individual to accidents and also may delay recovery. Although malingering is thought to be rare in brain injury cases, the hope of receiving monetary compensation—for example, from an insurance settlement—may influence individuals to exaggerate and maintain symptoms.

MENTAL RETARDATION

The American Psychiatric Association (1994) in DSM-IV defines **mental retardation** as "significantly subaverage general intellectual functioning . . . that is accompanied by significant limitations in adaptive functioning" (p. 39) in certain skill areas such as self-care, work, health, and safety. To qualify for the diagnosis, these problems must have begun before the age of 18. Mental retardation is thus defined in terms of level of behavioral performance. The definition says nothing about causal factors—which may be primarily biological, psychosocial, sociocultural, or a combination of these. By definition, any functional equivalent of mental retardation that has its onset after age 17 must be considered a dementia rather than mental retardation. The distinction is an important one, because, as was pointed out early in the chapter, the psychological situation of a person who acquires a pronounced impairment of intellectual functioning after attaining maturity is vastly different from that of a person whose intellectual resources were subnormal throughout all or most of his or her development.

In contrast to other developmental disorders, mental retardation is coded (with reference to a particular level as described below) on Axis II of DSM-IV, along with the personality disorders. The reason for this inconsistency is not explained in the DSM manual. In any event, mental retardation, like other DSM diagnostic categories, is treated as a specific type of disorder, although it may occur in combination with other disorders appearing on either Axis I or Axis II. In fact other psychiatric disorders, especially psychoses (Jacobson, 1990), occur at a markedly higher rate among retarded people than in the general population (Borthwick-Duffy, 1994; Sturmey & Sevin, 1993).

Mental retardation occurs among children throughout the world. In its most severe forms, it is a source of great hardship to parents as well as an economic and social burden on a community. The point prevalence rate of diagnosed mental retardation in the United States is estimated to be about 1 percent, which would indicate a population estimate of some 2.6 million people. This figure is considerably lower than the hypothetical estimate based on an IQ cutoff score of about 70, which is the dividing point used by DSM-IV. Thus many—probably a majority—of persons with IQs below 70 are not officially diagnosed as retarded, suggesting that they are "making it" in terms of meeting adaptational demands at a minimally acceptable level. Nevertheless, most states have laws providing that persons with IQs below 70 who show socially incompetent or persistently problematic behavior can be classified as mentally retarded, and if judged otherwise unmanageable may be placed in an institution. Informally, IQ scores between about 70 and 90 are often referred to as "borderline" or (in the upper part of the range) "dull-normal."

Initial diagnoses of mental retardation seem to increase markedly at ages 5 to 6, to peak at age 15, and to drop off sharply after that. For the most part, these age-related changes in time of first diagnosis reflect changes in life demands. During early childhood, individuals with only a mild degree of intellectual impairment, who constitute the vast majority of the mentally retarded, often appear to be normal. Their subaverage intellectual functioning becomes apparent only when difficulties with schoolwork lead to a diagnostic evaluation. When adequate facilities are available for their education, children in this group can usually master essential school skills and achieve a satisfactory level of socially adaptive behavior. Following the school years, they usually make a more or less acceptable adjustment in the community and thus lose the identity of being mentally retarded.

Levels of Mental Retardation

It is important to remind ourselves once again that any classification system in the behavioral field will have strong features of both arbitrariness and pragmatism. In mental retardation, attempts to define varying levels of impairment have tended to rely increasingly on measurement—largely by means of standardized intelligence (IQ) tests (Robinson & Robinson, 1976). In the previously quoted DSM-IV definition, for example, the phrase "significantly subaverage general intellectual functioning" translates directly and officially into an IQ test score that is more than two standard deviations below the population mean. That mean, which represents the average test performance for children of a given age, is 100. The standard deviation of most IQ tests is about 15 points, and approximately two-thirds of the population score between plus and minus one standard deviation unit from the mean—that is, between 85 and 115. Thus a score of two standard deviations below the mean would be an IQ of approximately 70. Under the assumption that IQ scores are

normally distributed in the familiar bell-shaped form, about 2.5 percent of the population would score in the range below IQ 70.

It is not necessarily improper to define mental retardation in this way, provided we keep in mind the implications of the definition. The original IQ tests were devised for the explicit purpose of predicting academic achievement among schoolchildren. Other IQ tests developed later were also validated largely on school performance and on the basis of how well they could predict scores on the original tests. Generally, then, what IQ tests measure is an individual's likely level of success in dealing with conventional academic materials, and in fact they do this very well when properly utilized. Thus when we speak of varying levels of mental retardation, we are to a great extent speaking of levels of ability to succeed at schoolwork.

Of course, this reliance on IQ scores is tempered somewhat by the other main part of the definition—the presence of concurrent "significant limitations in adaptive functioning." The same dual criteria are involved in the officially recognized "levels" of retardation, although the IQ score often tends in practice to be the dominant consideration. This emphasis on the IQ score is reasonable at the lower end of the scale, because a person with an IQ of 50 or below will inevitably exhibit gross deficiencies in overall adaptive behavior as well. At the higher ranges of "retarded" IQ scores, however, behavioral adaptiveness and IQ score seem to be at least partially independent of one another. It should also be noted that differing social environments, such as rural versus urban, are differentially challenging both intellectually and behaviorally.

The DSM-IV recognizes four degrees of severity of mental retardation. These are indicated in the table below, together with their corresponding IQ ranges:

Diagnosed Level of Mental Retardation	Corresponding IQ Range
Mild retardation	50–55 to approximately 70
Moderate retardation	35–40 to 50–55
Severe retardation	20–25 to 35–40
Profound retardation	below 20–25

In former times the American Psychiatric Association (publisher of DSM-IV) and the American Association on Mental Retardation (AAMR) generally agreed on definitions of mental retardation and specifications of levels or degrees of it. In 1992 the AAMR broke away from this tradition (Luckasson et al., 1992), adopting IQ 75 as the cutoff point for the diagnosis of mental retardation (thus expanding the pool of eligibles). In addition, the AAMR proposal substitutes "patterns and intensity of supports needed" (intermittent, limited, extensive, and pervasive) for the levels of severity indicated above; the "steps" of the two systems for characterizing severity are not directly comparable. Several more technical revisions of standard diagnostic procedure are also called for in the AAMR approach. Many professionals have voiced criticism of the new AAMR-proposed guidelines and view this divergence of approaches as unfortunate and as increasing the potential for disagreement and confusion in rendering the mental retardation diagnosis (see MacMillan, Gresham, & Siperstein, 1993). It seems clear, however, that the AAMR intent was to advance its agenda to provide increased services for retarded persons.

The various levels of mental retardation, as defined in DSM-IV, are described in greater detail in the following sections:

1. *Mild mental retardation.* Mildly retarded individuals constitute by far the largest number of those diagnosed as mentally retarded. Within the educational context people in this group are considered "educable," and their intellectual levels as adults are comparable with those of average 8- to 11-year-old children. Statements such as the latter, however, should not be taken too literally. A mildly retarded adult with a "mental age" of, say, 10 (that is, intelligence test performance is at the level of the average 10-year-old) may not in fact be comparable to the normal 10-year-old in information-processing ability (Weiss, Weisz, & Bromfield, 1986).

The social adjustment of mildly retarded people often approximates that of adolescents, although they tend to lack normal adolescents' imagination, inventiveness, and judgment. Ordinarily, they do not show signs of brain pathology or other physical anomalies, but often they require some measure of supervision because of their limited abilities to foresee the consequences of their actions. Individuals at a somewhat higher, "borderline" IQ level (about 71–84) may also need special services to maximize their potentials (Zetlin & Murtaugh, 1990). With early diagnosis, parental assistance, and special educational programs, the great majority of borderline and mildly retarded individuals can adjust socially, master simple academic and occupational skills, and become self-supporting citizens (Schalock, Harper, & Carver, 1981).

2. *Moderate mental retardation.* Moderately retarded individuals are likely to fall in the educational category of "trainable," which means that they are presumed able to master certain routine skills, such

Mildly retarded individuals constitute the largest number of those labeled mentally retarded. With help, a great majority of these individuals can adjust socially, master simple academic and occupational skills, and become self-supporting citizens.

as cooking or minor janitorial work, if provided specialized instruction in these activities. In adult life, individuals classified as moderately retarded attain intellectual levels similar to those of average four- to seven-year-old children. Although some can be taught to read and write a little and may manage to achieve a fair command of spoken language, their rate of learning is slow, and their level of conceptualizing extremely limited. Physically, they usually appear clumsy and ungainly, and they suffer from bodily deformities and poor motor coordination. Some of these moderately retarded people are hostile and aggressive; more typically they present an affable, unthreatening personality picture. Very rarely, extraordinary specialized skills, such as outstanding musical ability (see Hill, 1975), are found in moderately retarded individuals; well documented empirically, these phenomena have never been adequately explained. In general, with early diagnosis, parental help, and adequate opportunities for training, most moderately retarded individuals can achieve partial independence in daily self-care, acceptable behavior, and economic usefulness in a family or other sheltered environment.

3. *Severe mental retardation.* Severely retarded individuals are sometimes referred to as dependent retarded. In these individuals, motor and speech development are severely retarded, and sensory defects and motor handicaps are common. They can develop limited levels of personal hygiene and self-help

skills, which somewhat lessen their dependence, but they are always dependent on others for care. However, many profit to some extent from training and can perform simple occupational tasks under supervision.

4. *Profound mental retardation.* The term *life-support retarded* is sometimes used to refer to profoundly retarded individuals. Most of these people are severely deficient in adaptive behavior and unable to master any but the simplest tasks. Useful speech, if it develops at all, is rudimentary. Severe physical deformities, central nervous system pathology, and retarded growth are typical; convulsive seizures, mutism, deafness, and other physical anomalies are also common. These individuals must remain in custodial care all their lives. They tend, however, to have poor health and low resistance to disease and thus a short life expectancy.

Severe and profound cases of mental retardation can usually be readily diagnosed in infancy because of the presence of obvious physical malformations, grossly delayed habit training (e.g., taking solid food), and other obvious symptoms of abnormality. Although these individuals show a marked impairment of overall intellectual functioning, they may have considerably more ability in some areas than in others.

Contrary to common understanding, the distribution of IQ scores does not precisely fit "normal curve" expectations, especially in the lower IQ or mental retardation range. This range shows a substantial frequency bulge, disrupting the normal taper of the bell curve in its descent toward a theoretical zero occurrence of cases at its leftmost (lowest IQ) extreme. This finding suggests the operation of an intruding factor that tends to inflate beyond normal-curve expectancy the numbers of cases at lower IQ ranges—specifically the presence of major congenital abnormalities, brain injuries, or both that are not characteristic of normally distributed phenomena. The bulge is frequently called the "bump of pathology." The next section addresses these pathological anomalies.

Brain Defects in Mental Retardation

Some cases of mental retardation—something on the order of 25 percent—occur in association with known organic brain pathology. In these cases, retardation is virtually always at least moderate, and it is often severe. Profound retardation, fortunately rare, always includes obvious organic impairment. Organically caused retardation is in essential respects

similar to dementia as earlier described, except for a different history of prior functioning. In fact, in the past, a young person with organically caused retardation was referred to as *amented,* as distinct from a demented person. In this section we will consider five biological conditions that may lead to mental retardation, noting some of the possible interrelations between them. Then we will review some of the major clinical types of mental retardation associated with these organic causes.

Genetic-Chromosomal Factors   Mental retardation tends to run in families. This tendency is particularly true of mild retardation. Poverty and sociocultural deprivation, however, also tend to run in families, and with early and continued exposure to such conditions, even the inheritance of average intellectual potential may not prevent subaverage intellectual functioning.

Genetic and chromosomal factors play a much clearer role in the etiology of relatively infrequent but more severe types of mental retardation, such as Down syndrome (discussed below) or an inheritable condition known as *fragile X,* a constriction or breaking off of the end portion of the long arm of the X sex chromosome that appears determined by a specific gene defect (de Vries et al., 1994). In such conditions genetic aberrations are responsible for metabolic alterations that adversely affect the brain's development. Genetic defects leading to metabolic alterations may, of course, involve many other developmental anomalies besides mental retardation. In general, mental retardation associated with known genetic-chromosomal defects is moderate to severe in degree.

Infections and Toxic Agents   Mental retardation may be associated with a wide range of conditions due to infection. If a pregnant woman is infected with syphilis or HIV-1, or if she gets German measles, her child may suffer brain damage. Brain damage may also result from infections occurring after birth, such as viral encephalitis.

A number of toxic agents, such as carbon monoxide and lead, may cause brain damage during fetal development or after birth. In some instances, immunological agents, such as antitetanus serum or typhoid vaccine, may lead to brain damage. Similarly, certain drugs, including an excess of alcohol, taken by a pregnant woman may lead to congenital malformations; an overdose of drugs administered to an infant may result in toxicity and brain damage. In rare cases, brain damage results from incompatibility in blood types between mother and fetus—conditions known as Rh, or ABO, system incompatibility.

Fortunately, early diagnosis and blood transfusions can now minimize the effects of such incompatibility.

Prematurity and Trauma (Physical Injury) Follow-up studies of children born prematurely and weighing less than about 5.5 pounds at birth have revealed a high incidence of neurological disorders and often mental retardation. In fact, small premature babies are many times more likely to be mentally retarded than normal-sized infants.

Physical injury at birth can also result in retardation. Isaacson (1970) has estimated that in 1 birth out of 1000 brain damage occurs that will prevent the child from reaching the intelligence level of an average 12-year-old. Although the fetus is normally well protected by its fluid-filled bag during gestation, and its skull appears designed to resist delivery stressors, accidents do happen during delivery and after birth. Difficulties in labor due to malposition of the fetus or other complications may irreparably damage the infant's brain. Bleeding within the brain is probably the most common result of such birth trauma. *Hypoxia*—lack of sufficient oxygen to the brain stemming from delayed breathing or other causes—is another type of birth trauma that may damage the brain.

Ionizing Radiation In recent decades a good deal of scientific attention has been focused on the damaging effects of ionizing radiation on sex cells and other bodily cells and tissues. Radiation may act directly on the fertilized ovum or may produce gene mutations in the sex cells of either or both parents, which, in turn, may lead to defective offspring. Sources of harmful radiation were once limited primarily to high-energy X rays used in medicine for diagnosis and therapy, but the list has grown to include nuclear weapons testing and leakages at nuclear power plants, among others.

Malnutrition and Other Biological Factors It has long been believed that dietary deficiencies in protein and other essential nutrients during early development can result in irreversible physical and mental damage. However, current thinking on the association between malnutrition and mental retardation outcomes suggests that the direct causal link originally posited may be oversimplified. In a recent review of the problem, Ricciuti (1993) cites growing evidence that the negative impact of malnutrition on mental development may be more indirect by altering a child's responsiveness, curiosity, and motivation to learn. These losses would then lead, according to this hypothesis, to a relative retardation of

intellectual facility. If Ricciuti is right, at least some malnutrition-induced intellectual deficit may be viewed as a special case of psychosocial deprivation, also believed to be implicated in retardation outcomes, as described below.

A limited number of cases of mental retardation are clearly associated with organic brain pathology. In some instances—particularly of the severe and profound types—the specific causes are uncertain or unknown, although extensive brain pathology is evident. In the following sections we will deal with three relatively well-understood types of organically caused mental retardation.

Organic Retardation Syndromes

Mental retardation stemming primarily from biological causes can be classified into several recognizable clinical types, of which Down syndrome, phenylketonuria, and cranial anomalies will be discussed here. HIGHLIGHT 13.4 presents information on several other well-known forms.

Down Syndrome First described by Langdon Down in 1866, **Down syndrome** is the best known of the clinical conditions associated with moderate and severe mental retardation. About 1 in every 600 babies born in the United States is diagnosed as having Down syndrome, a condition that "has life-long implications for physical appearance, intellectual achievement and general functioning" (Golden & Davis, 1974, p. 7). The availability of *amniocentesis* and increasingly of *chorionic villus sampling* has made it possible to detect in utero the extra chromosome (47 rather than the normal 46) that is the hallmark of Down pathology. The possibility of elective abortion should the fetus prove chromosomally defective, while helpful for individual families, appears not to have affected substantially the overall incidence of the disorder. Because of demographic shifts, most Down syndrome infants in recent decades have been born to mothers under 35 years of age, not a group for whom chromosomal assessment is routinely recommended (Evans & Hamerton, 1985).

A number of physical features are often found among children with Down syndrome, but few of these children have all of the characteristics commonly thought of as typifying this group. In such children, the eyes appear almond-shaped, and the skin of the eyelids tends to be abnormally thick. The face and nose are often flat and broad, as is the back of the head. The tongue, which seems too large for the mouth, may show deep fissures. The iris of the

HIGHLIGHT 13.4

Other Disorders Sometimes Associated with Mental Retardation

Clinical Type	Symptoms	Causes
No. 18 trisomy syndrome	Peculiar pattern of multiple congenital anomalies, the most common being low-set malformed ears, flexion of fingers, small jaw, and heart defects	Autosomal anomaly of chromosome 18
Tay-Sachs disease	Hypertonicity, listlessness, blindness, progressive spastic paralysis, and convulsions (death by the third year)	Disorder of lipoid metabolism, carried by a single recessive gene
Turner's syndrome	In females only; webbing of neck, increased carrying angle of forearm, and sexual infantilism	Sex chromosome anomaly (XO); mental retardation may occur but is infrequent
Klinefelter's syndrome	In males only; features vary from case to case, the only constant finding being the presence of small testes after puberty	Sex chromosome anomaly (XXY)
Niemann-Pick's disease	Onset usually in infancy, with loss of weight, dehydration, and progressive paralysis	Disorder of lipoid metabolism
Bilirubin encephalopathy	Abnormal levels of bilirubin (a toxic substance released by red cell destruction) in the blood; motor incoordination frequent	Often, Rh (ABO) blood group incompatibility between mother and fetus
Rubella, congenital	Visual difficulties most common, with cataracts and retinal problems often occurring together and with deafness and anomalies in the valves and septa of the heart	The mother's contraction of rubella (German measles) during the first few months of her pregnancy

Based on American Psychiatric Association (1968, 1972); Clarke, Clarke, and Berg (1985); Holvey and Talbott (1972); Robinson and Robinson (1976).

eye is frequently speckled. The neck is often short and broad, as are the hands. The fingers are stubby, and the little finger is often more noticeably curved than the other fingers. Although facial surgery is sometimes tried to correct the more stigmatizing features, its success is often limited (Dodd & Leahy, 1989; Katz & Kravetz, 1989).

Interestingly, there appears to be little, if any, correlation between the extent of physical anomalies and the degree of mental retardation in individuals with Down syndrome. Death rates for children with Down syndrome have decreased dramatically in the past half century. In 1919, the life expectancy at birth for such children was about nine years; most of

the deaths were due to gross physical problems, and a large proportion occurred in the first year. Thanks to antibiotics, surgical correction of lethal anatomical defects, and better general medical care, many more of these children now live to adulthood (Smith & Berg, 1976).

Despite their problems, children with Down syndrome are usually able to learn self-help skills, acceptable social behavior, and routine manual skills that enable them to be of assistance in a family or institutional setting. The traditional view has been that Down syndrome youngsters are unusually placid and affectionate. Research has questioned the validity of this generalization. These children may

Today many more Down syndrome children are living to adulthood than in the past and are able to learn self-help, social, and manual skills. It is not unusual for Down syndrome children to be mainstreamed to some extent with unimpaired children, such as this girl in a ballet class. Down syndrome children tend to remain relatively unimpaired in their appreciation of spatial relationships and visual-motor coordination; they show their greatest deficits in verbal and language-related skills.

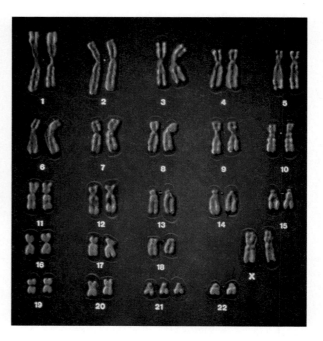

This is a reproduction (karyotype) of the chromosomes of a female patient with Down syndrome. Note the triple (rather than the normal paired) representation at chromosome 21.

indeed be very docile, but probably in no greater proportion than normal youngsters; they may also be equally (or more) difficult in various areas (Bridges & Cicchetti, 1982). In general, the adequacy of a child's social relationships is positively correlated with both IQ level and a supportive home environment (Sloper et al., 1990).

Research has also suggested that the intellectual defect in Down syndrome may not be consistent across various abilities. Down syndrome children tend to remain relatively unimpaired in their appreciation of spatial relationships and in visual-motor coordination, although some recent evidence disputes this conclusion (Uecker et al., 1993); research data are quite consistent in showing that they have their greatest deficits in verbal and language-related skills (Azari et al., 1994; Mahoney, Glover, & Finger, 1981; Silverstein et al., 1982). Since spatial functions are known to be partially localized in the right cerebral hemisphere, and language-related functions in the left cerebral hemisphere, some investigators speculate that the syndrome is especially crippling to the left hemisphere.

Traditionally, the cause of Down syndrome was assumed to be faulty heredity. A number of early studies demonstrated, however, that more than a single case of Down syndrome in a family was unlikely, occurring in less than 1 family in 100 of those already affected. As a consequence of this finding, investigators turned to the study of metabolic factors and concluded that Down syndrome was proba-

bly due to some sort of glandular imbalance. Then, in 1959, the French scientists Lejeune, Turpin, and Gauthier found 47 chromosomes, instead of the usual 46, in several Down syndrome subjects. A trisomy of chromosome 21 (an error of reproductive cell division in which chromosome 21 is present in triplicate rather than the normal pair) has now been identified as a characteristic of Down syndrome children, being present in at least 94 percent of cases meeting strict Down syndrome criteria. As was noted earlier, it may be significant that this is the same chromosome that has been implicated in recent research on Alzheimer's disease, especially since persons with Down syndrome are at extremely high risk for Alzheimer's as they get into and beyond their late 30s (Bauer & Shea, 1986; Cole et al., 1994; Prasher & Kirshnan, 1993; Reid, 1985; Schapiro, Haxby, & Grady, 1992).

Researchers have long believed that the "extra" chromosome in Down syndrome is contributed by the mother. In 1973, however, it was learned that in some cases it is contributed by the father (Sasaki & Hara, 1973; Uchida, 1973). The reason for the trisomy of chromosome 21 is not clear, but the defect seems definitely related to parental age at conception. It has been known for many years that the incidence of Down syndrome increases on an accelerating slope (from the 20s on) with increasing age of the mother. A woman in her 20s has about 1 chance in 2000 of conceiving a Down syndrome baby, whereas the risk for a woman in her 40s is 1 in 50 (Holvey & Talbot, 1972). As in the case of all birth defects, the risk of having a Down syndrome baby is also high for very young mothers whose reproductive systems have not yet fully matured. The advanced maternal age correlation led naturally to the inference that an older woman's capacity to produce a chromosomally normal fetus was somehow impaired by the aging process. This observed effect obscured for many years a potential male contribution, since older men tend to have older women partners.

More recent research has strongly indicated that the father's age at conception is also implicated in Down syndrome, particularly at higher ages (Hook, 1980; Stene et al., 1981). In one study involving 1279 cases of Down syndrome in Japan, Matsunaga and associates (1978) demonstrated an overall increase in incidence with advancing paternal age when maternal age was controlled. The risk for fathers aged 55 years and over was more than twice that for fathers in their early 20s. Curiously, these investigators noted that, in their sample, fathers in their early 40s had a lower risk factor than slightly younger as well as older men.

Thus it seems that advancing age in either parent increases the risk of the trisomy 21 anomaly, although the maternal age effect is the larger one. As yet we do not understand how aging produces this effect. A reasonable guess is that aging is related to cumulative exposure to varied environmental hazards, such as radiation, that might have adverse effects on the processes involved in zygote formation or development.

Phenylketonuria (PKU) In **phenylketonuria (PKU),** a baby appears normal at birth but lacks a liver enzyme needed to break down phenylalanine, an amino acid found in many foods. The genetic error results in retardation only when significant quantities of phenylalanine are ingested, something that is virtually certain to occur if the child's condition remains undiagnosed. If the condition is undetected, the amount of phenylalanine in the blood increases and eventually produces brain damage.

The disorder usually becomes apparent between 6 and 12 months after birth, although such symptoms as vomiting, a peculiar odor, infantile eczema, and seizures may occur during the early weeks of life. Often the first symptoms noticed are signs of mental retardation, which may be moderate to severe depending on the degree to which the disease has progressed. Lack of motor coordination and other neurological problems caused by the brain damage are also common, and often the eyes, skin, and hair of untreated PKU patients are very pale. PKU was unidentified until 1934, when a Norwegian mother sought to learn the reason for her child's mental retardation and peculiar musty odor. She consulted with many physicians to no avail until Dr. Asbjorn Folling found phenylpyruvic acid in the child's urine and concluded that the child had a disorder of phenylalanine metabolism (Centerwall & Centerwall, 1961).

Most older PKU patients show severe to profound mental retardation, with the median IQ of untreated phenylketonuric adults being about 20. Curiously, however, a number of seriously retarded PKU patients have PKU relatives with less severely affected intelligence. In addition, Perry (1970) reported the cases of two untreated PKU patients with superior intelligence. These findings have made PKU something of an enigma. It results from a liver enzyme deficiency involving one or more recessive genes, and 1 person in 70 is thought to be a carrier. There may be varying degrees of PKU, however, or another (unknown) genetic factor may lessen the destructive potential of the enzyme defect (Burns, 1972).

The early detection of PKU by examining urine for the presence of phenylpyruvic acid is now routine in developed countries, and dietary treatment (such as the elimination of phenylalanine-containing foods) and related procedures can be used to prevent the disorder. With early detection and treatment—preferably before an infant is six months old—the deterioration process can usually be arrested so that levels of intellectual functioning may range from borderline to normal. A few children suffer mental retardation despite restricted phenylalanine intake and other measures, however. Dietary restriction in late-diagnosed PKU may improve the clinical picture somewhat, but there is no real substitute for early detection and prompt intervention (Pavone et al., 1993).

For a baby to inherit PKU, it appears that both parents must carry the recessive genes. Thus when one child in a family is discovered to have PKU, it is especially critical that other children in the family be screened as well. Also, a pregnant PKU mother whose risk status has been successfully addressed by early dietary intervention may damage her at-risk fetus unless she maintains rigorous control of phenylalanine intake.

Cranial Anomalies Mental retardation is associated with a number of conditions that involve alterations in head size and shape and for which the causal factors have not been definitely established (Robinson

& Robinson, 1976). In the rare condition known as **macrocephaly** (large-headedness), for example, there is an increase in the size and weight of the brain, an enlargement of the skull, visual impairment, convulsions, and other neurological symptoms, resulting from the abnormal growth of glia cells that form the supporting structure for brain tissue. Other more common cranial anomalies include *microcephaly* and *hydrocephalus,* which we will discuss in more detail.

Microcephaly. The term **microcephaly** means "small-headedness." It refers to a type of mental retardation resulting from impaired development of the brain and a consequent failure of the cranium to attain normal size. In an early study of postmortem examinations of microcephalic individuals' brains, Greenfield and Wolfson (1935) reported that practically all cases examined showed development to have been arrested at the fourth or fifth month of fetal life.

The most obvious characteristic of microcephaly is the small head, the circumference of which rarely exceeds 17 inches, as compared with the normal size of approximately 22 inches. Penrose (1963) also described microcephalic youngsters as being invariably short in stature but having relatively normal musculature and sex organs. Beyond these characteristics, they differ considerably from one another in appearance, although there is a tendency for the skull to be cone-shaped, with a receding chin and forehead. Microcephalic children fall within the moderate, severe, and profound categories of mental retardation, but most show little language development and are extremely limited in mental capacity.

Microcephaly may result from a wide range of factors that impair brain development, including intrauterine infections and pelvic irradiation during the mother's early months of pregnancy (Koch, 1967). Miller (1970) noted a number of cases of microcephaly in Hiroshima and Nagasaki that apparently resulted from the atomic bomb explosions during World War II. The role of genetic factors is not clear, although there is speculation that a single recessive gene is involved in a primary, inherited form of the disorder (Robinson & Robinson, 1976). Treatment is ineffective once faulty development has occurred; at present, preventive measures focus on the avoidance of infection and radiation during pregnancy.

Hydrocephalus. **Hydrocephalus** is a relatively rare condition in which the accumulation of an abnormal amount of cerebrospinal fluid within the cranium causes damage to the brain tissues and enlargement of the skull. In congenital cases, the head is either already enlarged at birth or begins to enlarge soon thereafter, presumably as a result of a disturbance in the formation, absorption, or circulation of the cerebrospinal fluid (Robinson & Robinson, 1976). The disorder can also develop in infancy or early childhood, following the development of a brain tumor, subdural hematoma, meningitis, or other conditions. In these cases the condition appears to result from a blockage of the cerebrospinal pathways and an accumulation of fluid in certain brain areas.

The clinical picture in hydrocephalus depends on the extent of neural damage, which, in turn, depends on the age at onset and the duration and severity of the disorder. In chronic cases, the chief symptom is the gradual enlargement of the upper part of the head out of proportion to the face and the rest of the body. While the expansion of the skull helps minimize destructive pressure on the brain, serious brain damage occurs nonetheless. This damage leads to intellectual impairment and such other effects as convulsions and impairment or loss of sight and hearing. The degree of intellectual impairment varies, being severe or profound in advanced cases.

A good deal of attention has been directed to the surgical treatment of hydrocephalus, in which shunting devices are inserted to drain cerebrospinal fluid. With early diagnosis and treatment, this condition can usually be arrested before severe brain damage has occurred (Geisz & Steinhausen, 1974). Even with significant brain damage, carefully planned interventions that take into account both strengths and weaknesses in intellectual functioning show much promise (Baron & Goldberger, 1993).

Cultural-Familial Mental Retardation

Investigators formerly believed that all mental retardation was the result of faulty genes or of other causes of brain impairment. In recent decades, however, it has become apparent that adverse sociocultural conditions, particularly those involving a deprivation of normal environmental stimulation, may play a primary role in the etiology of mental retardation. Two subtypes of mental retardation fall in this general category: (a) mental retardation associated with extreme sensory and social deprivation, such as prolonged isolation during the developmental years, as is occasionally inflicted on children by disturbed parents; and (b) **cultural-familial retardation,** in which a child is not subjected to extreme isolation but rather suffers from an inferior quality of interaction with the cultural environment and with other people. Because such sociocultural impoverishment

Table 13.1   *Average IQs of 586 Milwaukee Children*

Maternal IQ	Age of Children in Months						
	13–35	36–59	60–83	84–107	108–131	132–167	168+
80+ (*n* = 48)	95	93	90	94	87.5	94	90
< 80 (*n* = 40)	95	76	84	80	75	70	67.5

From Garber (1988, p. 23)

may be associated with genetic deficiency in some cases, a child born to a family in such circumstances may be doubly jeopardized. In any event, it has proven all but impossible to assess the differential influences of nature and nurture in these cases.

Because most mental retardation is of the cultural-familial type, our discussion will focus on it. Consider Table 13.1 that depicts the average IQs of 586 Milwaukee children in differing age ranges. The children were separated according to whether or not the IQs of their mothers, all of whom dwelt in slum areas under deprived circumstances, fell below 80. Note that the two groups of children did not differ in IQ at ages 1 through 2 and that both scored within the normal range. The children whose mothers had IQs of 80 or above continued to manifest average IQs in the normal range through age 14. However, children of mothers of IQ less than 80 showed, on average, a progressive (and, after age 5, nonreversing) decline with advancing age that approached the upper limits of the mental retardation range by age 14. Such a progressive loss is not easy to reconcile with a hereditary interpretation; it suggests, rather, the cumulative effects of a deficient environment, one well indexed by the mothers' IQ levels.

Garber (1988) contends that the effect is due to the inadequacy of low IQ mothers in stimulating intellectual growth. Specifically, he maintains that the mothering person is normally responsible for creating the "microenvironment" determining a child's rate of cognitive development, and that a low maternal IQ—which is associated with verbal and other skill deficits—tends to foster an environment that is deficient in cognitively enriching experience. Although this conclusion is consistent with most available evidence, it would be tragic to convert such evidence to an assignment of blame against low-IQ women. They need help, not blame, and when they get this help, the IQs of their children may be substantially elevated (Garber, 1988; Ramey & Haskins, 1981; Turkheimer, 1991; Zigler & Muenchow, 1992; Zigler & Styfco, 1994).

Whatever the specific etiology, children whose retardation is cultural-familial in origin are usually only mildly retarded. They show no identifiable brain pathology and are usually not diagnosed as mentally retarded until they enter school and have difficulties with their studies. As many investigators have pointed out, most of these children come from economically deprived, unstable, and often disrupted family backgrounds characterized by a lack of intellectual stimulation, an inferior quality of interaction with others, and general environmental deprivation (e.g., Birns & Bridger, 1977; Braginsky & Braginsky, 1974; Feuerstein, 1977):

> They are raised in homes with absent fathers and with physically or emotionally unavailable mothers. During infancy they are not exposed to the same quality and quantity of tactile and kinesthetic stimulations as other children. Often they are left unattended in a crib or on the floor of the dwelling. Although there are noises, odors, and colors in the environment, the stimuli are not as organized as those found in middle-class and upper-class environments. For example, the number of words they hear is limited, with sentences brief and most commands carrying a negative connotation. (Tarjan & Eisenberg, 1972, p. 16)

Since a child's current level of intellectual functioning is based largely on previous learning—and since schoolwork requires complex skills, such as being able to control one's attention, follow instructions, and recognize the meaning of a considerable range of words—these children are at a disadvantage from the beginning because they have not had an opportunity to learn requisite background skills or to be motivated toward learning. Thus with each succeeding year, unless remedial measures are undertaken, they tend to fall further behind in school performance. They also fall further behind in relative ratings on intelligence tests, which, as we have seen, are measures of ability for schoolwork. A report by the American Psychological Association (1970) noted the following: "Mental retardation is primarily a psychosocial and psychoeducational problem—a deficit in adaptation to the demands and expectations of society evidenced by the individual's relative difficulty in learning, problem solving, adapting to new situations, and abstract thinking" (p. 267).

The causal pattern in cultural-familial mental retardation is believed to include an impoverished and intellectually deprived developmental history.

This statement was not intended to minimize the possible role of adverse biological factors, including genetic deficiencies, in the total causal pattern. Certainly many of these children reveal histories of prematurity, inadequate diet, and little or no medical care. In the great majority of cases of cultural-familial mental retardation, however, no neurological or physical dysfunction has been demonstrated. Thus, efforts to understand mild mental retardation have focused increasingly on the role of environmental factors in impeding intellectual growth. The likelihood that many of these factors will prove preventable or reversible has given rise to as yet incompletely realized hopes for effective, widespread intervention, as will be seen.

The Problem of Assessment

Because mental retardation is defined in terms of both intellectual (academic) and social competence, it is essential to assess both of these characteristics before labeling a person mentally retarded. Unfortunately, neither of the preceding tasks is easy. Errors in IQ assessment can stem from a variety of sources, including (a) errors in administering and scoring tests; (b) the personal characteristics of a child, such as a language problem or lack of motivation to do well on tests; (c) temporary disrupting circumstances in the child's life, such as illness or family stress, and (d) limitations in the tests themselves.

Although the assessment of social competence may seem less complicated, especially if it is based on clinical observations and ratings, it is subject to many of the same errors as the measurement of IQ. In the elaborated version of adaptive skills assessment recently proposed by the AAMR (Luckasson et al., 1992), noted above, many of the skills included cannot be reliably measured with existing techniques (MacMillan et al., 1993). Also, the criteria used by the person or persons doing the assessing are of particular importance. For example, if children are well adapted socially to life in an urban ghetto but not to the demands of a formal school setting, should they be evaluated as having a high, intermediate, or low level of social competence? Competence for what? It is doubtful that judgments of this kind can be made objectively, that is, without reference to particular value orientations.

To label a child mentally retarded is likely to have profound effects on both the child's self-concept and the reactions of others, and thus on his or her entire future life. Most immediately, it may lead to a disadvantaged upbringing by discouraged, demoralized parents (Richardson, Koller, & Katz, 1985), to say nothing of the likely effects on overburdened schoolteachers. Over the long term, such a label may become a self-fulfilling prophecy fueled by the tendency to behave in ways consistent with one's self-concept and others' expectations. Obviously it is a label that has profound ethical and social implications; it should never be affixed to anyone without the most careful and considered judgment.

Treatments, Outcomes, and Prevention

A number of programs have demonstrated that significant changes in adaptive capacity are possible through special education and other rehabilitative measures. The degree of change that can be expected is related, of course, to an individual's particular situation and level of mental retardation.

Treatment Facilities and Methods One problem that causes anxiety for the parents of a mentally retarded child is whether to put the child in an institution. In general, children who are institutionalized fall into two groups: (a) those who, in infancy and childhood, manifest severe mental retardation and associated physical impairment, and who enter an institution at an early age; and (b) those who have no physical impairments but show relatively mild mental retardation and a failure to adjust socially in adolescence, eventually being institutionalized chiefly because of delinquency or other problem behavior (see Stattin & Klackenberg-Larsson, 1993). In these cases, social incompetence is the main factor in the decision. The families of those in the first group come from all socioeconomic levels, whereas a significantly higher percentage of the families of those in the second group come from lower educational and occupational strata.

The effect of being institutionalized in adolescence depends heavily, of course, on an institution's facilities as well as on individual factors. For the many retarded teenagers who do not have families in a position to take care of them, community-oriented residential care seems particularly promising (Alexander, Huganir, & Zigler, 1985; Landesman-Dwyer, 1981; Seidl, 1974; Thacher, 1978), although for maximum effectiveness great care must be taken in adequately assessing needs and in the recruitment of staff personnel (Petronko, Harris, & Kormann, 1994).

For the mentally retarded who do not require institutionalization, educational and training facilities have historically been woefully inadequate. It still appears that a very substantial proportion of mentally retarded people in the United States are never reached by services appropriate to their specific needs (Luckasson et al., 1992; Tyor & Bell, 1984).

This neglect is especially tragic in view of what we now know about helping these people. For example, classes for the mildly retarded, which usually emphasize reading and other basic school subjects, budgeting and money matters, and the development of occupational skills, have succeeded in helping many people become independent, productive community members. Classes for the moderately and severely retarded usually have more limited objectives, but they emphasize the development of self-care and other skills that enable individuals to function adequately and to be of assistance in either a family or institutional setting. Just mastering toilet training and learning to eat and dress properly may mean the difference between remaining at home and being placed elsewhere.

Today there are only some 80,000 individuals still in institutions for the retarded, roughly half the number that were residents a mere 25 years ago. Even many of these more seriously affected persons are being helped to be partly self-supporting in community programs (Brown, 1977; Landesman-

Dwyer, 1981; McDonnell et al., 1993; Robinson & Robinson, 1976; Thacher, 1978). These developments reflect both the new optimism that has come to prevail and also, in many instances, new laws and judicial decisions favorable to the rights of retarded people and their families. A notable example is Public Law 94-142, passed by Congress in 1975. This statute, termed the Education for All Handicapped Children Act, asserts the right of mentally retarded people to be educated at public expense in "the least restrictive environment" possible.

During the 1970s, there was a rapid increase in alternate forms of care for the mentally retarded (Tyor & Bell, 1984). These included, but were not limited to, the use of decentralized regional facilities for short-term evaluation and training; small private hospitals specializing in rehabilitative techniques; group homes or "halfway houses" integrated into the local community; nursing homes for the elderly retarded; the placement of severely retarded children in more "enriched" foster-home environments; and varied forms of support to the family for own-home care. The last quarter century, in short, has seen a marked enhancement of alternative modes of dealing with retarded citizens, rendering obsolete many public institutions formerly devoted exclusively to this type of care.

Although much remains to be learned about the most effective educational and training procedures to use with the mentally retarded—particularly the moderate and severe types—new techniques, materials, and specially trained teachers have produced encouraging results. For example, computer-assisted instruction has been found to be more efficient as well as less expensive than traditional tutor-guided instruction (Brebner, Hallworth, & Brown, 1977; Hallworth, 1977). New uses for the computer in this field are developing at a rapid rate (Lovett, 1985). Operant-conditioning methods are being used increasingly to teach a wide variety of skills (Kiernan, 1985). Specifically targeted independence training in various everyday functions (Matson, 1981) obviously has great promise. A technique for teaching improved thinking skills, developed by Reuven Feuerstein in Israel, has been extensively evaluated and produces substantial, though not spectacular, improvements in cognitive functioning (e.g., Arbitman-Smith, Haywood, & Bransford, 1984).

Typically, educational and training procedures involve mapping out target areas of improvement, such as personal grooming, social behavior, basic academic skills, and (for retarded adults) simple occupational skills (see Forness & Kavale, 1993). Within each area, specific skills are divided into simple components that can be learned and reinforced before more complex behaviors are required. Training that builds on step-by-step progression can bring retarded individuals repeated experiences of success and lead to substantial progress even by those previously regarded as uneducable (see McDonnell et al., 1993).

For mildly retarded youngsters, the question of what schooling is best is likely to challenge both parents and school officials. For many years, organized parents' groups have fought an uphill battle to ensure the availability of special education classes for retarded children in the public schools, having learned that isolation from peers tends to compound the problem. Too often, however, success in getting a retarded child into a public school has meant that the child is treated as very special indeed and—along with other retarded students—becomes isolated within the school. We have now learned that this type of "special" education may have serious limitations in terms of a child's social and educational development, and that many such children fare better by attending regular classes for at least much of the day. Of course, this type of approach—called **mainstreaming**—does require careful planning, a high level of teacher skill, and facilitative teacher attitudes (Birns & Bridger, 1977; Borg & Ascione, 1982; Budoff, 1977; Hanrahan, Goodman, & Rapagna, 1990; Kozleski & Jackson, 1993; Stafford & Green, 1993).

Substantial research has led to the conclusion that mainstreaming is not the hoped-for panacea for retarded children (Gottlieb, 1981). Such programs are difficult to launch and to maintain (Lieberman, 1982); their success (or lack of it) seems to depend largely on such change-resistant influences as teacher attitudes and overall classroom climate (Haywood, Meyers, & Switsky, 1982; Miller, 1989; Schumm & Vaughn, 1992). Moreover, any educational gains may come at the expense of deficits in self-esteem suffered by handicapped children as they interact intensively with more cognitively advantaged peers (Haywood et al., 1982). Gresham (1982) argues that such dangers may be decreased or eliminated if retarded children are given social skills training before they enter a mainstream classroom. Also, when the situation is sensitively managed, the normal classmates of mainstreamed children may themselves derive benefits from the experience (Lincoln et al., 1992). A variant of mainstreaming called the Parallel Alternate Curriculum program, which emphasizes specialized instruction in a regular classroom setting, has shown much promise. Even here, however, much attention must be given to teaching-staff development (Chandler, 1985; Smith & Smith, 1985).

A reasonable conclusion at this time is that school systems should not attempt mainstreaming without

The mainstreaming of mildly retarded children into regular classes for much of the day requires careful planning and a high level of teacher skill and facilitative teacher attitudes.

a great deal of advance planning and preparation. In other words, mere window dressing to achieve an appearance of progressive educational practice is not enough; the system's leadership must be thoroughly committed to overcoming deeply entrenched attitudes and procedures within the education bureaucracy to ensure the success of the effort.

Frontiers in Prevention More than three decades ago, President John F. Kennedy had the following to say about mental retardation:

> Studies have demonstrated that large numbers of children in urban and rural slums, including preschool children, lack the stimulus necessary for proper development in their intelligence. Even when there is no organic impairment, prolonged neglect and a lack of stimulus and opportunity for learning can result in the failure of young minds to develop. Other studies have shown that, if proper opportunities for learning are provided early enough, many of these deprived children can and will learn and achieve as much as children from more favored neighborhoods. The self-perpetuating intellectual blight should not be allowed to continue. (1963, p. 286)

President Kennedy's remarks are as valid and relevant today as they were when first issued. He may, however, have underestimated the difficulties of the task. In addition, much change in the body politic has occurred in the interim, not all of it supportive of the widespread social changes he advocated.

Perhaps the most important surviving element of that 1960s era in the area of mental retardation has involved efforts to reach high-risk children early with the intensive cognitive stimulation believed to underlie the sound development of mental ability. Project Head Start is a well-known example operating at the local community level, one whose effectiveness is difficult to measure and therefore subject to controversy (Gamble & Zigler, 1989). In fact, however, local Head Start programs have varied widely in their organizational and management expertise and in their commitment to making a difference in the lives of their child clientele. Perhaps inevitably, too, politics and bureaucratic bumbling have often served to dull the cutting edge Head Start was fashioned to provide (Zigler & Muenchow, 1992). In the end, no program of early intervention can guarantee a successful outcome. Nevertheless, the available outcome data are clear in showing that well-managed Head Start programs have amassed a very creditable record in launching children on the path to educational and occupational accomplishment; considering the stakes in failed and socially costly lives, they appear to be an excellent community investment (Zigler & Styfco, 1994).

At the national level, a similar intention has inspired specialized television programming for children, such as *Sesame Street* and *Reading Rainbow*. Rigorous assessment of the effectiveness of such efforts has never been satisfactorily completed, but they do appear to have positive effects on many children. Ironically, the children who seem to benefit most from these efforts are the children least in need of them—the children of relatively affluent families in which education is strongly valued and in which the parents are likely to encourage their children to watch enriching television programming.

Also somewhat sobering is the possibility that the educational performance of many Head Start children increases primarily because of temporarily enhanced motivation rather than higher rates of cognitive development (Zigler et al., 1982). Where the environment continues to be harmful over time, the gain for many youngsters exposed to short-term enrichment programs may be lost (Garber, 1988; Gray & Ramsey, 1982). Obviously, much remains to be learned and done in the area of maintaining early gains. Where notable and sustainable gains have not been unequivocally demonstrated, the necessary financial investment may attract the kind of short-

sighted political opposition commonly directed at expensive "social" programs (see Chafel, 1992). The irony is that the money is spent anyway, usually at compounded rates of increase, on such things as ADC (welfare-based aid to dependent children), chronic institutionalization, correctional facilities, and the "war on drugs."

The federal initiatives begun by the Kennedy administration have eroded over the years. Demands on the federal budget for programs seen as having greater national priority have increased, and the funds committed for helping the retarded have suffered devaluation through inflation. Beginning with the Nixon administration of the early 1970s, serious cutbacks were made in training and research in all of the mental health disciplines. The trend has become worse since that time as the national debt has increased to unprecedented levels and as many states have likewise experienced severe fiscal problems. As a result, we have not been able to capitalize fully on our increased understanding of how to reverse or prevent the deficits experienced by mentally retarded youngsters and adults.

SPECIFIC LEARNING DISORDERS

In contrast to generalized developmental disorders such as mental retardation and autism (addressed in Chapter 14), **specific learning disorders** have a circumscribed character and may occur in children who are otherwise normal or even gifted in their overall functioning. The inadequate development may be manifested in academic, language, speech, or motor-skills areas, and it is not due to any demonstrable physical or neurological defect. The diagnosis is restricted to those cases in which there is clear impairment in school performance or (if the person is not a student) in daily living activities, not due to mental retardation or a "pervasive developmental disorder," such as autism. Skill deficits due to attention-deficit hyperactivity disorder, described in Chapter 14, are coded under that diagnosis. This coding presents another diagnostic dilemma because some investigators hold that an attentional deficit is basic to many learning disorders; evidence for the latter view is equivocal (see Faraone et al., 1993). We will focus in this section on specific developmental disorders involving academic skills, also known as specific learning disabilities, or—in DSM-IV terms—simply learning disorders (formerly academic skills disorders). Children with these disorders are more generally said to be *learning disabled* (LD). Significantly more boys than girls are diagnosed as learning disabled, but proportional estimates of this gender discrepancy have varied widely from study to study.

The Clinical Picture in Learning Disorders

Learning disabled children are identified as such because of a disparity between their expected academic achievement level and their actual academic performance in one or more school subjects, such as math, spelling, writing, or reading. (Reading problems are commonly known as *dyslexia*.) Typically, these children have IQs, family backgrounds, and exposure to cultural norms and symbols that are consistent with at least average achievement in school. They do not have obvious crippling emotional problems, nor do they seem to be lacking in motivation, cooperativeness, or eagerness to please their teachers and parents—at least not at the outset of their formal education. Nevertheless, they fail, often abysmally and usually with a stubborn, puzzling persistence. Why? As we will see, satisfactory answers are hard to come by.

Frustration for teachers, school officials, parents, professional helpers, and perhaps most notably for the victims themselves (although the last may go unnoticed in the general turmoil) is virtually guaranteed in this scenario, and it is likely to complicate efforts to find a solution. Wenar (1990) poignantly depicts the problem:

> You are a child clinical psychologist. It has been a rough day. The climax was a phone call to the principal of Wykwyre Junior High School. It is the kind of suburban school in which children from two-swimming-pool families do not speak to children from one-swimming-pool families. The call had been about Jon Hastings, a 16-year-old with a long history of school failures. The intelligence test showed him to be bright enough to do college work, and yet he is only in the eighth grade. He is articulate, has a talent for making miniature rockets and speedboats, and a real flair for drawing cartoons. Yet the written word is Jon's nemesis. He reads laboriously one word at a time, while his writing is even more painfully slow. Because of repeated failures and because he is now a social misfit with peers, he has begun cutting up in class and talking back to the teacher.
>
> You had phoned the principal to suggest ways of bypassing Jon's reading disability. Since he is sufficiently bright to absorb most of the lecture material, could he be given oral examinations every now and then? If he were taught to type, could he type in-

stead of writing his examinations? Would the principal consider introducing special classes for all the learning-disabled children?

> The principal was suave and ingratiating and a compendium of the resistances you have run up against in the past. He "understood your concern" but asked that you "look at the situation from my point of view." The school had "tried everything possible to no avail," "the boy is incorrigible," "you can't help a child unless the child wants help," and finally—you could feel this one coming, since you had heard it so often—"I can't give one student a favor without giving a favor to all of them. I'd have half the mothers in my office next day demanding something extra to pull their child's grades up." (p. 197)

It is unfortunately the case that LD, despite its having been recognized as a distinct and rather common type of disorder for more than 35 years, and despite its having generated a voluminous research literature, still fails to be given the status it deserves in many school jurisdictions. Instead, as in the preceding example, the familiar diversion of blaming the victim and of attributing the affected child's problems to various character deficiencies is still routinely employed by many classroom teachers and school administrators, whether in public or private settings (see Fischer, 1993; Moats & Lyon, 1993). Where lockstep uniformity is the rule, as it is in most public and many "alternative" educational systems, a youngster who learns academic skills slowly or in a different way is treated as a troublemaker, as a threat to the prevailing theory of education. The consequences of these encounters between LD children and rigidly doctrinaire or regimented school systems can be disastrous to a child's self-esteem and general psychological well-being, and research indicates that these effects do not necessarily dissipate after secondary schooling ends (Brinckerhoff, 1993; Bruck, 1987; Saracoglu, Minden, & Wilchesky, 1989; Walters & Croen, 1993; Wilczenski, 1993). Thus even where LD difficulties are no longer a significant impediment, an individual may bear the scars of many painful school-related episodes of failure into maturity and beyond.

Causal Factors in Learning Disorders

Probably the most generally held view of the cause of specific learning disabilities is that they are the products of subtle central nervous system impairments. In particular, these disabilities are thought to result from some sort of immaturity, defect, or dysregulation limited to those brain areas supposedly mediating, for normal children, the cognitive skills and/or behaviors that LD children cannot efficiently acquire. A few years back the term *minimal brain dysfunction* (MBD) was in popular use to refer to such presumed organic malfunction—until it was generally recognized that nobody had the slightest idea what the term really meant. While some LD children show definite or highly suggestive evidence of brain disease, such as cerebral palsy, epilepsy, or a history of severe head trauma (e.g., Yule & Rutter, 1985), the large majority do not. In others, there may be subtle indications, "soft signs," of neurological compromise, but again such findings are by no means routine. Overall, there is no convincing evidence of a specific central nervous system dysfunction among LD children generally (Durrant, 1994; Schwartz & Johnson, 1985). The search for such factors has lessened in recent years, possibly because investigators have become discouraged by the meager findings thus far.

A variant of the central nervous system dysfunction hypothesis proposes some type of defect or imbalance in the brain's normal laterality—that is, in the tendency for specific functions to be localized to a large extent in either the right or the left side of the brain. Studies in this area, mainly concerned with dyslexia, have failed to produce a consistent or coherent set of findings (Kessler, 1988). They have also been plagued with many methodological shortcomings (Durrant, 1994; Hynd & Semrud-Clikeman, 1989).

Some investigators believe that the various forms of LD, or vulnerability to develop them, may be genetically transmitted. This issue seems not to have been studied with the same intensity or methodologic rigor as in other disorders. Two family pedigree studies, those of Hallgren (1950) and Finucci and colleagues (1976), showed evidence of familial concordance for "reading disorders" (dyslexia), and Owen (1978) cites a twin study in which monozygocity was associated with 100 percent concordance for reading disorders. Very recently, identification of a gene region for dyslexia on chromosome 6 has been reported, although the specific gene implicated has not yet been determined (*Science News*, October 22, 1994, p. 271). Although it would be somewhat surprising if a single gene were to be identified as the causal factor in all cases of reading disorder, the hypothesis of a genetic contribution to at least the dyslexic form of LD appears increasingly promising.

Summing up, biological or organic hypotheses concerning the etiology of LD, though widely held, tend to be vague on mechanisms and—excepting dyslexia—do not have an exceptionally strong record of evidence supporting them. They continue

Dyslexia is a learning disability that interferes with the ability to read and write. This dyslexic student is transposing letters and writing other letters backward. Learning disabled children, frustrated by their academic failures, may become social failures as well. If undiagnosed, these children may be seen by school authorities as troublesome and intractable, thus compounding their problems and further damaging their self-esteem. The long-term academic, social, and personal adjustment for those who grew up with undiagnosed dyslexia is generally discouraging, but there are important exceptions.

to have a sort of intuitive appeal that is at least as great as alternative psychosocial theories of causation.

Psychosocially based hypotheses about the origins of LD generally derive from psychodynamic, learning, or cognitive perspectives, or a combination of them. To date, none of them has sufficient empirical support to warrant extended discussion. The apparent complexity of the psychological processes involved in LD (see Ceci & Baker, 1987) evidently makes it difficult to do definitive studies on potential causal factors. Thus the research that is available, most of it again directed to the problem of dyslexia, tends to be riddled with problems of subject selection, inappropriate controls, and other serious methodological flaws (Durrant, 1994; Vellutino, 1987).

Despite what appears to be a multitude of seemingly differing factors involved in LD, there may yet be some common elements. This is the position taken by Worden (1986), who argues that we should study what characterizes the approaches taken by good learners to be able to identify the areas of significant weakness from which LD children suffer. He offers the following list as a beginning in this direction:

1. What memory strategies are used by normal or good learners, and in what manner do these differ from those employed by LD children?

2. How do normal or good learners monitor their ongoing performances? For example, how do good learners use performance information to gauge where they are being successful and where not, and to introduce corrective action as needed?

3. What metastrategy information is used by good learners and not by LD children? For example, do LD children understand the advantage of having a strategy at all, as in dealing with the time constraints of many school tasks?

4. What motivates good learners, and how does this differ from the motivation of poor learners? Is a learner's orientation one of seeking success or of avoiding failure? To what is success or failure attributed: oneself, task difficulty, chance, or some other factor?

Worden's approach to analyzing the complex issues involved in academic skill acquisition strikes us as a potentially useful beginning. However, even precise information on the manner in which LD children's learning approaches differ from those of normal children would still leave us with unanswered questions about the sources of these differences. Nevertheless, pursuit of this idea might produce a set of rational, fine-tuned strategies for intervening to correct LD children's inefficient modes of learning. We are not aware of any follow-up studies along this line.

Treatments and Outcomes

Because we do not yet have a confident grasp on what is "wrong" with the average LD child, we have had limited success in treating these children. While many informal and single-case reports claim success for various treatment approaches, there are few well-designed and well-executed outcome studies on specific treatments for LD problems. Focusing on reading disorders, where most of the effort has been concentrated, Gittelman's (1983) review contains little evidence of impressive results. Moreover, any short-term gains that are made tend in many cases to diminish or even disappear over time (Yule & Rutter, 1985).

Recently, Ellis (1993) has offered a comprehensive intervention model to facilitate learning in LD, called Integrative Strategy Instruction (ISI), that has inspired considerable interest among professionals in the field (see Houck, 1993; Hutchinson, 1993; Parker, 1993; Walsh, 1993). Organized according to particular content areas, it envisions a variety of teacher-directed instructional strategies directed at key aspects of the learning process: orienting, fram-

ing, applying, and extending. Although the model is too new to have been tested empirically for efficacy, its knowledge-based and systematic character is a welcome addition to the analysis of the educational problems presented by LD children. Its application would seem to demand, however, high levels of administrative flexibility and teacher skill, neither of which can be taken for granted in the average school environment (see Hutchinson, 1993; Parker, 1993).

It is encouraging that increasing efforts are being made to identify and provide services for LD students in higher education settings. Many of these students are sufficiently bright and resourceful to circumvent lower-level educational barriers to find themselves confronted with challenges requiring skills they simply do not have. Walters and Croen (1993), for example, describe such efforts in a medical school environment; they stress the need for early identification, provision of appropriate support, and arranging minimal accommodations for medical students having LD problems. Yanok (1993) describes an apparently successful "developmental education program" for LD college students, thus providing for these individuals an "equal educational opportunity."

We have only limited data on the long-term, adult adjustments of people who grew up with the personal, academic, and social problems LD generally entails. Two studies of college students with LD (Gregg & Hoy, 1989; Saracoglu et al., 1989) suggested that as a group they continue to have problems—academic, personal, and social—into the postsecondary education years. Cato and Rice (1982) extracted from the available literature a lengthy list of somewhat discouraging problems experienced by the typical LD adult. These include—in addition to expected difficulties with self-confidence—continuing problems with deficits in the ordinary skills, such as math, that these people originally encountered as children. The authors did note, however, that there are considerable individual differences in these outcomes, thus reminding us that some adults with LD are able to manage very well.

UNRESOLVED ISSUES

on Cultural-Familial Retardation

The problem of cultural-familial mental retardation continues to be a baffling and frustrating one—complicated in no small measure by sensitive issues of race relations and imputed ethnic differences in native abilities. No scientifically respectable evidence suggests that the quality of brain tissue is in any degree correlated with race or ethnicity. A great deal of evidence, on the other hand, shows that different ethnic groups, on average, vary considerably in performance on standardized tests designed to predict academic achievement. The very controversial book *The Bell Curve* (Herrnstein & Murray, 1994) contains the most recent comprehensive discussion of such intergroup differences in average IQ test scores. Unfortunately, we have long been encouraged to regard such tests as more or less directly measuring "intelligence," which they do not—unless one is willing to accept school grades as the primary defining element of that construct. IQ tests are and have always been validated primarily on their ability to predict school performance.

Schools may reasonably be viewed as having the principal function of transmitting a culture's approved products from earlier to later generations; approved products are those deemed valuable by a cultural elite. So-called intelligence tests, then, are designed to measure the facility with which a child may be expected to acquire and adequately process what the school offers. It does not seem farfetched to suggest that a child's performance in school will be determined to a considerable extent by the amount of prior and continuing extracurricular exposure he or she has to the products of the dominant culture that the school represents. Indeed, we have a fair amount of empirical evidence showing that this is so. We also have a fair amount of empirical evidence suggesting that a person's IQ ("intelligence" quotient) rises significantly with enhanced exposure to these cultural products. It is therefore more than a mere possibility that what IQ tests mostly measure is prior exposure to approved cultural products. Considered from this perspective, the notion of a "culture-free" IQ test that would also do well at predicting school grades is a practical impossibility.

The fact that African Americans in the United States are disproportionately represented among those labeled "retarded" is clearly related to the prominence of the IQ measure in the definition of retardation. African Americans have a persistent 15-point deficit, on average, relative to whites on this type of test. However interpreted—whether in terms of "test bias" or in terms of a "real" difference (and from the preceding argument we suggest that these are the same things)—one implication seems clear. Namely, African Americans as a group are seriously disadvantaged in engagements with the standard educational system. Relative success in such engagements, as already noted, is mostly what IQ tests are designed to predict, and for the most part they do so effectively. If, as is often said (we have our own small doubts), conventional academic success leads to such happiness and riches as are attainable in our larger culture, then enormously disproportionate numbers of African Americans will continue to be excluded from the good life unless some remedy for this problem can be found.

As we have seen, serious and broad-based efforts to find a remedy were begun in the 1960s, Project Head Start being a notable example. Much was learned in the programs that were launched during that era, one of the most important lessons being that genuine and sustained advance was costly and difficult. For example, we learned that the gains in academic skill acquired in an enriched preschool experience, as in Head Start, were not lasting without a more general environmental enrichment. However, subsequent changes in national priorities and in the political atmosphere, particularly at the federal level, precluded a vigorous follow-up of these initiatives. We have not regained momentum in this area, nor does it appear likely, as of this writing, that we soon will. If progress in laying to rest the cold war and in the achievement of "the new world order" were happily to continue, however, sufficient funds and energies might be liberated to contemplate seriously a new national order, one in which all of our children might truly be granted equal opportunity. It is a cruel deception, in our judgment, to suggest that they have it now.

SUMMARY

The neuropsychological mental disorders are those in which mental symptoms of a neurologic or psychopathologic sort (such as cognitive deterioration and delusions, respectively) are presumed to appear as a result of malfunction of the brain's "hardware," typically involving the destruction of brain tissue. Generally, these disorders are in some primary sense physical diseases and are accordingly coded on Axis III of DSM-IV, in addition to a descriptive Axis I coding that pertains to the nature of the mental symptoms manifested. The current DSM recognizes certain characteristic neuropsychological syndromes that form a basis for an Axis I psychiatric diagnosis where the precise organic etiology is unknown or is implied in an accompanying Axis III disease; those discussed here are delirium, dementia, amnestic syndrome, and neuropsychological delusional, mood, and personality syndromes. These syndromes are conceived as the primary behavioral indicators for organic brain disease. Some of them mimic disorders in which no gross brain pathology can be demonstrated, which may present problems in diagnosis.

Neuropsychological disorders may be acute and transitory; in this case, brain functioning is only temporarily compromised. Chronic neuropsychological disorders, on which we have focused, involve the permanent loss of neural cells. Psychosocial interventions are often helpful in minimizing psychopathologic reactions in the chronically disordered, although these people will remain neurologically disabled.

The primary causes of brain tissue destruction are many and varied; common ones include certain infectious diseases (such as the HIV-1 virus), brain tumors, physical trauma, degenerative processes (as in Alzheimer's disease), and cerebrovascular arteriosclerosis, often manifested as vascular dementia. The correlation between neurologic brain impairment and psychiatric disorder, however, is not an especially strong one: Some people who have severe damage develop no severe mental symptoms, while others with slight damage have extreme reactions. Although such inconsistencies are not completely understood, it appears that an individual's premorbid personality and life situation are also important in determining his or her reactions to brain damage.

Elderly people are at particular risk for the development of chronic organic mental disorders, especially those related to brain degeneration caused by Alzheimer's disease. As at younger ages, the reaction to brain damage is determined by many nonbiological factors. With disproportionate increases in the numbers of elderly people in the population, and the upcoming wave of baby boomers who will become at risk beginning early in the twenty-first century, we face staggering social, emotional, and economic problems unless some way can be found to prevent or effectively treat Alzheimer's disease.

When serious organic brain impairment occurs before the age of 18, and especially where it is congenital or is acquired shortly after birth, the cognitive and behavioral deficits experienced are referred to as mental retardation. Relatively common forms of such mental retardation, which in these cases is normally at least moderate in severity, include Down syndrome, phenylketonuria (PKU), and certain cranial anomalies. This organic type of mental deficit accounts for only some 25 percent of all cases of mental retardation. Mental retardation diagnoses, regardless of the underlying origins of the deficit condition, are always coded on Axis II of DSM-IV.

The large majority—some 75 percent—of mental retardation cases are unrelated to obvious physical defects and are considered cultural-familial in origin, a term that acknowledges our inability to disentangle genetic and environmental influences in the disorder. Caution is warranted in applying the label "mentally retarded," in part because of the heavy reliance on IQ test scores in its definition. The IQ test is—and always has been—a measure of academic skill, not of ability to survive and perhaps even prosper in other areas of life. A variety of evidence points to the conclusion that cultural-familial retardation may be treatable and even preventable, provided we can find the means of providing the necessary cognitive stimulation to socially and economically deprived children.

Specific learning disorders are those in which failure of mastery is limited to circumscribed areas, chiefly involving academic skills such as reading; general cognitive ability may be normal or superior. Affected children are commonly described as learning disabled (LD). Here again some localized defect in brain development is usually considered the primary cause, although independent corroboration of an organic cause is the exception rather than the rule. These disorders create great turmoil and frustration in victims, their families, schools, and professional helpers. Various remedies, most involving training regimens of one sort or another, are tried and apparently are sometimes successful. However, solid outcome research in the area of intervention techniques is seriously lacking. The long-term prognosis for LD, overall, is not particularly encouraging.

KEY TERMS

organic mental disorders (p. 486)
delirium (p. 491)
dementia (p. 491)
amnestic syndrome (p. 492)
AIDS dementia complex (ADC) (p. 494)
AIDS-related complex (ARC) (p. 494)
dementia of the Alzheimer's type (DAT) (p. 495)
senile dementias (p. 495)
presenile dementias (p. 495)

mental retardation (p. 506)
Down syndrome (p. 510)
phenylketonuria (PKU) (p. 513)
macrocephaly (p. 514)
microcephaly (p. 514)
hydrocephalus (p. 514)
cultural-familial retardation (p. 514)
mainstreaming (p. 518)
specific learning disorders (p. 519)

CHAPTER

14

DISORDERS OF CHILDHOOD AND ADOLESCENCE

Dwight Mackintosh, My Mother Baking Bread. *Mackintosh (b. 1906),*
a native of California, was admitted into a mental institution at the
age of 16 after having become "unmanageable at home." He remained
in state mental hospitals until the deinstitutionalization movement in-
spired his release in 1978. His brother, Earl, remembered that Dwight
had been interested in art as a boy and took him to the Creative Growth
Art Center in Oakland, California, where he began to draw and paint
earnestly. People are the primary subject of his art, and drawing his
only way of expressing his interest in them; otherwise, he is deeply with-
drawn.

During the nineteenth century, little account was taken of the special characteristics of psychopathology in children; maladaptive patterns that are considered relatively specific to childhood, such as autism, received virtually no attention at all. Since the turn of the twentieth century, with the advent of the mental health movement and the availability of child guidance facilities, marked strides have been made in assessing, treating, and understanding the maladaptive behavior patterns of children and adolescents. This progress has, however, lagged behind efforts to deal with adult psychopathology. In fact, as we will see, early efforts at classifying problems of childhood were simply downward extensions of adult-oriented diagnostic systems.

These early conceptualizations seemed to reflect a prevailing view of children as "miniature adults" and failed to take into account special problems, such as those associated with the developmental changes that normally take place in a child or adolescent. Only recently have we come to realize that we cannot fully understand childhood disorders without taking into account these developmental processes; in fact, the field is often referred to as **developmental psychopathology.** Today, even though great progress has been made in providing treatment for disturbed children, our facilities are woefully inadequate in relation to the magnitude of the task, and most problem children do not receive psychological attention (Links, Boyle, & Offord, 1989). The numbers of children affected by psychological problems are considerable. For example, recent studies (Brandenberg et al., 1990; and the Office of Technology Assessment, 1986) suggest that as many as 12–15 percent of American children have psychological disorders.

Recent multisite studies in several countries have provided estimates of childhood disorder that range from 17 to 22 percent (Costello, 1989; Institute of Medicine, 1989; Verhulst & Koot, 1992; and Zill & Schoenborn, 1990). In most studies, maladjustment is found more commonly among boys than among girls. In one survey of psychological disorder in children, Anderson and colleagues (1987) found that 17.6 percent of 11-year-old children studied had one or more disorders. Boys were diagnosed more frequently than girls at 1.7 to 1. The most prevalent disorders were attention-deficit hyperactivity disorder and separation anxiety disorders. More recently, Zill and Schoenborn (1990) reported that rates of childhood disorders varied by gender with boys having higher rates of emotional problems over the childhood and adolescent years. However, for some diagnostic problems rates for girls are higher than for boys.

In the first section of this chapter we will note some general characteristics of maladaptive behavior in children compared with adult disorders. Next we will examine the issues surrounding the diagnostic classification of children's disorders. Then we will look at a number of important disorders of childhood and adolescence. In the final section we will give detailed consideration to some of the special factors involved in both the treatment and prevention of children's problems.

MALADAPTIVE BEHAVIOR IN DIFFERENT LIFE PERIODS

Because personality differentiation, developmental tasks, and typical stressors differ in childhood, adolescence, and adulthood, we would expect to find some differences in maladaptive behavior in these periods. The special characteristics of childhood disorders are discussed here.

Varying Clinical Pictures

The clinical picture in childhood disorders tends to be distinct from those of other life periods. Some of the emotional disturbances of childhood may be relatively short-lived, undifferentiated, and changeable compared with those of later life (Lewis et al., 1988). It should be kept in mind, however, that some childhood disorders severely affect future development. One study found that individuals who had been hospitalized as child psychiatric patients (between the ages of 5 and 17) showed excess mortality in unnatural deaths (about twice the rate of the general population) when followed up from 4 to 15 years later (Kuperman, Black, & Burns, 1988). Suicide accounted for most of these deaths, and the suicide rate was significantly greater than in the general population.

Special Vulnerabilities of Young Children

Young children do not have as complex and realistic a view of themselves and their world as they will have at a later age. They have less self-understanding and have not yet developed a stable sense of identity and an adequate frame of reference regarding reality, possibility, and value. Immediately perceived threats are tempered less by considerations of the past or future and thus tend to be seen as disproportionately important. As a result, children often have more difficulty in coping with stressful events than do adults (Compas & Epping, 1993; Kepel-Benson & Ollendick, 1993). A follow-up study of young victims of the Buffalo Creek flood, for example, found that children

are at risk of posttraumatic stress disorder after a disaster, especially if the family atmosphere is troubled (Green et al., 1991) (see HIGHLIGHT 14.1).

Children's limited perspectives, as might be expected, lead them to use unrealistic concepts to explain events. For example, a child who commits suicide may be trying to rejoin a dead parent, sibling, or pet. For young children, suicide—or violence against another person—may be undertaken without any real understanding that death is final.

Children also are more dependent on other people than are adults. Though in some ways this dependency serves as a buffer against other dangers, it also makes them highly vulnerable to experiences of rejection, disappointment, and failure. On the other hand, although their inexperience and lack of self-sufficiency make them easily upset by problems that seem minor to the average adult, children typically recover more quickly from their hurts. Moreover, many problematic behaviors and threats to adjustment emerge over the course of *normal* development (Kazdin, 1992). Indeed, several behaviors that characterize maladjustment or emotional disturbance are relatively common in childhood. It is imperative that we view a child's behavior in reference to normal childhood development. We cannot understand or consider as "abnormal" a child's behavior without considering whether the behavior in question is appropriate for the child's age. Behavior such as temper tantrums or eating inedible objects might be viewed as symptoms of abnormal behavior at age ten but not at age two. Despite the somewhat distinctive characteristics of childhood disturbances at different ages, there is no sharp line of demarcation between the maladaptive behavior patterns of childhood and those of adolescence, nor between those of adolescence and those of adulthood. Thus, although our focus in this chapter will be on the behavior disorders of children and adolescents, we will find some inevitable overlap with those of later life periods. In this context, it is useful to emphasize the basic continuity of a person's behavior over time.

THE CLASSIFICATION OF CHILDHOOD AND ADOLESCENT DISORDERS

Diagnosis of the psychological disorders of childhood has traditionally been a rather confused practice, and until the 1950s no formal, specific system was available for classifying the emotional problems of children and adolescents. Kraepelin's (1883) classic textbook on the classification of mental disorders did not include childhood disorders. Not until

HIGHLIGHT 14.1

Psychological Adjustment Problems of Children in Disasters

Children are particularly vulnerable to highly stressful situations following in the wake of a disaster such as a hurricane, automobile accident, or the loss of an immediate family member. In the aftermath of a disaster, many children show increased specific disaster-related fears, increased dependence on adults, problems with separating from adults in their environment, sleeping difficulties, irritability, and often regressed behavior such as bedwetting or soiling (Saylor, 1993; Vogel & Vogel, 1993). As described in Chapter 4, the symptoms of posttraumatic stress disorder in children often persist months after the disaster has occurred (Swenson et al., 1991).

Some disaster situations are likely to be more upsetting to children than others. For example, children are more likely to become distressed in situations that involve life-threatening events or those in which a close family member dies or is seriously injured. Additionally, some children are more vulnerable to psychological problems following a disaster than others. For example, younger children appear to be more vulnerable to experiencing posttraumatic stress

than older children, and girls tend to report more overall posttraumatic symptoms such as anxiety and depression than do boys.

The special problems that children face in disasters require thoughtful preparation and timely intervention if long-term problems are going to be averted. An effective program for dealing with children's problems in disasters was described by Vogel and Venberg (1993). This four-phase model describes strategies for managing children's adjustment difficulties in a disaster through several strategies:

1. *Predisaster preparation is important to organize services to the community for effective response to potential disaster.* Predisaster preparation includes the development of a disaster response network to respond to children's needs in the event of a disaster, particularly if one is imminent.

2. *Intervention close to the disaster impact is crucial* (Joyner & Swenson, 1993). Initial interventions after a disaster involve mounting efforts to help children during the period of confusion by providing

crisis intervention counseling and identifying those with unusually severe reactions (see Chapter 18).

3. *Short-term adaptation interventions are aimed at helping children resume their normal lives.* During this phase of disaster recovery, the goal is to help children make the transition back into normal activity. For example, the school-based social support program provided after Hurricane Hugo (see Chapter 4) greatly assisted children in their reentry to school (Stewart et al., 1992). Classroom activities are often arranged to promote a greater understanding of the circumstances surrounding the disaster and to promote reentry into normal routine. Family therapy and crisis intervention therapy would be provided for those children most adversely affected by the disaster.

4. Finally, *long-term adaptation services may be needed for children experiencing severe trauma.* Children experiencing severe reactions to the disaster might need to be seen on a longer-term basis in individual psychological treatment or family therapy.

1952, when the first formal psychiatric nomenclature (DSM-I) was published, was a classification system for childhood disorders made available. The DSM-I system, however, was quite limited and included only two childhood emotional disorders: childhood schizophrenia and adjustment reaction of childhood. In 1966, the Group for the Advancement of Psychiatry provided a classification system for children that was detailed and comprehensive. In the 1968 revision of the DSM (DSM-II) several additional categories were included. A growing concern remained, however, both among clinicians attempting to diagnose and treat childhood problems and among researchers attempting to broaden our understanding of childhood psychopathology, that the then-current ways of viewing psychological dis-

orders in children and adolescents were inappropriate and inaccurate for several reasons. The greatest problem stemmed from the fact that the same classification system that had been developed for adults was used for childhood problems. Many disorders such as autism, learning disabilities, and school phobias have no counterpart in adult psychopathology. Second, the early systems ignored the fact that in childhood disorders, environmental factors play an important part in the expression of symptoms; that is, symptoms are highly influenced by a family's acceptance or rejection of the behavior. For example, either extreme tolerance of deviant behavior or total rejection and neglect could lead a child's extreme behavior to be viewed as "normal." Third, symptoms were not considered with respect to a child's

It's easy to spot the one child in this group who seems especially vulnerable to the stress of classroom competition. While others have their hands raised or otherwise look alert, her demeanor is withdrawn. Children's inexperience and lack of self-sufficiency make them easily upset by problems that may seem minor to the average adult, and they often have more difficulty in coping with stressful events than they will have when they are older.

developmental level. Some of the problem behaviors might be considered age-appropriate, and troubling behaviors might simply be ones the child will eventually outgrow.

Over the years, discontent with the classification system for childhood behavior problems has led to considerable rethinking, discussion, and empirical investigation of the issues related to diagnosis. You may recall that in Chapter 1 we discussed various methods of classification. In the classification of childhood disorders, two of these methods—the categorical and the dimensional—have both been prominent. The first approach, a *categorical strategy,* is typically used by clinicians and has evolved from previous diagnostic classification systems. DSM-IV is an example of a categorical strategy. In this strategy, a clinician—or, in the case of DSM-IV, a panel of clinicians—arrives at a descriptive class or category by reviewing the diagnostic literature on the behaviors that appear to define that class of children. For example, the similar behaviors that appear in children who are judged to fit the diagnostic class *attention-deficit hyperactivity disorder* are used as the defining criteria of that class. The second approach—which is rarely used by clinicians but which is favored by many empirical researchers in psychopathology—is a *dimensional strategy.* This approach involves the application of sophisticated statistical methods to provide clear behavior clusters or "dimensions" for the widely observed symptoms manifested by children. A researcher gathers his or her symptomatic information through teachers', parents', or clinicians' observations or through a child's presenting symptoms—that is, the behaviors

characteristic of the clinical picture at the time the child is first seen by professional personnel. The researcher then allows the statistical method—for example, factor analysis—to determine the various behavior dimensions evidenced by an individual child. For example, the Child Behavior Checklist (CBCL) is the most widely researched and used dimensional strategy for assessing childhood behavior problems. Achenbach (1985) and colleagues (Achenbach & Edelbrock, 1983; Achenbach & McConaughy, 1985; Achenbach & Weisz, 1975) rated the symptoms of problem children based on two broad dimensions: internalizing and externalizing, which describe the differing tendencies to deal with problems through internal suffering or through external actions against the environment. "Internalizing" symptoms might include depression, social withdrawal, and anxiety, while "externalizing" symptoms might include hyperactivity, aggression, and delinquent behavior.

Both systems are based on observation of a child's behavior, and both result in classifying the child according to the presence or absence of symptoms or problem behaviors. There are marked differences between the systems, however. The categorical approach can require the presence of relatively few symptoms to arrive at a diagnosis. The dimensional approach, on the other hand, usually requires the presence of a number of related symptoms before an individual is considered to have a problem, that is, it usually takes a number of related symptoms on a particular dimension to be considered "extreme." As a result, a categorical system will tend to have many categories defined by few, sometimes quite rare, behaviors, while dimensional approaches typically involve a small number of general classes covering numerous related behaviors.

Broadly, the categorical approach follows the disease model of psychopathology and attempts to classify problem behavior in children into meaningful classes of mental disorders to provide useful prognoses and treatments. The dimensional approach is based on the idea that these behaviors are continuous and are found even among many normal children; it attempts to provide an objective classification scheme for assessing the relative frequency of these behavioral problems in an individual or group. It is possible to see benefits and problems in both these approaches to classification. Because this textbook focuses on the clinical manifestation of disorders, including infrequent symptoms that would be minimized in a dimensional approach, we will, for practical purposes, follow the DSM-IV classification system of childhood and adolescent disorders. Keep in mind, however, that the approach taken here is only one possible way of viewing disorders.

DISORDERS OF CHILDHOOD

In this section we will discuss several disorders of childhood with a focus on describing the clinical picture of each syndrome, surveying the possible causal factors, and outlining treatment approaches that have proved effective. A broader discussion of treatment methods can be found in Chapters 16 and 17.

The disorders that will be covered are attention-deficit hyperactivity disorder, conduct disorder (including juvenile delinquency), anxiety disorders of childhood, depressive disorders, several other special symptom disorders, and autism. Some of these disorders are less stable than most of the abnormal behavior patterns discussed in earlier chapters and are also perhaps more amenable to treatment. If treatment is not received, childhood developmental problems sometimes merge almost imperceptibly into more serious and chronic disorders as the child passes into adulthood, or they manifest themselves later as different disorders (Gelfand, Jenson, & Drew, 1988).

Attention-Deficit Hyperactivity Disorder

Attention-deficit hyperactivity disorder (ADHD), often referred to as **hyperactivity,** is characterized by difficulties that interfere with effective task-oriented behavior in children, particularly impulsivity, excessive motor activity, and difficulties in sustaining attention. The symptoms of attention-deficit hyperactivity disorder are relatively common among children seen at child guidance centers. In fact, hyperactive children are the most frequent psychological referrals to mental health and pediatric facilities, and it is estimated that between 3 and 5 percent of elementary school–aged children manifest the symptoms (Ross & Pelham, 1981). Attention-deficit hyperactivity disorder is the most frequent disorder among preadolescent boys, with a 6.7 percent prevalence (Anderson et al., 1987). The disorder, which is six to nine times more prevalent among boys than girls (DSM-IV), occurs with the greatest frequency before age eight and tends to become less frequent and with briefer episodes thereafter. As we will see, some residual effects, such as attention difficulties, may persist into adolescence or adulthood.

The Clinical Picture in Attention-Deficit Hyperactivity Disorder As the term implies, attention-deficit hyperactive children show excessive or exaggerated muscular activity—for example, aimless or haphazard running or fidgeting. Difficulty in sustaining attention is another central feature of the

disorder. Hyperactive children are highly distractible and often fail to follow instructions or respond to demands placed on them. Impulsive behavior and a low frustration tolerance are also characteristic. Perhaps as a result of their behavioral problems, hyperactive children are often lower in intelligence, usually about 7 to 15 IQ points below average. Hyperactive children tend to talk incessantly and to be socially uninhibited and immature. Barkley (1990) pointed out that hyperactive children usually have great difficulties in getting along with their parents because they do not obey rules. Their behavior problems also result in their being viewed negatively by their peers. In general, however, hyperactive children do not appear to be anxious, although their overactivity, restlessness, and distractibility are often interpreted as indications of anxiety. Usually they do poorly in school, commonly showing specific learning disabilities, such as difficulties in reading or in learning other basic school subjects. Hyperactive children also pose behavior problems in the elementary grades. The following case, involving an eight-year-old girl, reveals a typical clinical picture:

The subject was referred to a community clinic because of overactive, inattentive, and disruptive behavior. She was a problem to her teacher and to other students because of her hyperactivity and her uninhibited behavior. She would impulsively hit other children, knock things off their desks, erase material on the blackboard, and damage books and other school property. She seemed to be in perpetual motion—talking, moving about, and darting from one area of the classroom to another. She demanded an inordinate amount of attention from her parents and her teacher, and she was intensely jealous of other children, including her own brother and sister. Despite her hyperactive behavior, inferior school performance, and other problems, she was considerably above average in intelligence. Nevertheless, she felt "stupid" and had a seriously devaluated self-image. Neurological tests revealed no significant organic brain disorder.

Causal Factors in Attention-Deficit Hyperactivity Disorder The lack of clarity in diagnosing hyperactivity results, in part, from the lack of reliable assessment instruments. This unclear differentiation makes it difficult for researchers to evaluate whether biological conditions are involved in causing the disorder.

Children with ADHD are described as overactive, impulsive, and having a low tolerance for frustration and an inability to delay gratification. Incessant talkers, they tend not to obey rules and often run the risk of a multitude of problems with schoolwork, teachers, and other students.

The extent to which the problem occurring in ADHD children results from environmental or biological factors is unclear. In a recent comprehensive review of the relationship between externalizing behavior and underachievement, Hinshaw (1992) suggests that low intellectual capacity may be causally linked to both underachievement and externalizing behavior—placing biological factors as likely important precursors in the process. The potential genetic basis for ADHD has not, however, been established. Although by no means overwhelming, there is some support for the idea that ADHD is a familial disorder (Farone, Biederman, & Milberger, 1994). For example, one study reported that siblings of ADHD children were more likely to have had academic tutoring and to have been placed in special classes than controls (Farone et al., 1993). Moreover, brothers of identified ADHD children were more likely to have lower scores on reading tests than controls.

One early viewpoint that received a great deal of public attention suggested that hyperactivity in children may be produced by dietary factors—particularly food coloring (Feingold, 1977). However, the food-additive theory of hyperactivity has generally been discredited (Mattes & Gittelman, 1981; Stare, Whelan, & Sheridan, 1980). Firm conclusions as to the potential biological basis for ADHD must await further research.

The search for psychological causes of hyperactivity has had similarly inconclusive results. Investigators have not clearly established any psychological causes for the disorder, although they have emphasized both temperament and learning factors. Some evidence shows that the home environment is influential in the development of the disorder (Paternite

& Loney, 1980). One study suggested that family pathology, particularly parental personality problems, leads to hyperactivity in children. Morrison (1980) found that many parents of hyperactive children had psychological problems; for example, a large number were found to have clinical diagnoses of personality disorder or hysteria. Currently, ADHD is considered to have multiple causes and effects (Barker, 1990; Hinshaw, 1992).

Treatments and Outcomes Although the hyperactive syndrome was first described more than 100 years ago, disagreement remains over the most effective methods of treatment, especially regarding the use of drugs to calm a hyperactive child. As with other problem behaviors, variations in treatment procedures may be required to meet the needs of individual children.

Interestingly, research has shown that cerebral stimulants, such as amphetamines, have a quieting effect on hyperactive children—just the opposite of what we would expect from their effects on adults (Green & Warshauer, 1981; Pelham et al., 1992). Such medication decreases hyperactive children's overactivity and distractibility and at the same time increases their attention and ability to concentrate. As a result they are often able to function much better at school (Klorman et al., 1994). Some authorities (Pliszka, 1991) consider stimulants the first drug of choice for treating ADHD. In fact, many hyperactive children who have not been acceptable in regular classes can function and progress in a relatively normal manner when they use such drugs. The medication does not appear to affect their intelligence, but rather seems to help them use their basic capacities more effectively (National Institute of Mental Health, 1971). Although the drugs do not "cure" hyperactivity, they have reduced the behavioral symptoms in about half to two-thirds of the cases in which medication appears warranted. For example, it has been found that medication reduced the problems of inattention but not the impulsivity in hyperactive children (Matier et al., 1992).

While the short-term pharmacologic effect of stimulants on the symptoms of hyperactive children is apparently well established, their long-term effects are not well known. Carlson and Bunner (1993) reported that studies of achievement over long periods of time failed to show that medication has beneficial effects. Some concern has been expressed about the effects of the drugs, particularly when used in heavy dosages over time. Some questions that have been raised concerning the use of these drugs are discussed in HIGHLIGHT 14.2. The use of drug therapy with children will be taken up again in Chapter 16.

Another effective approach to treating hyperactive children involves behavior therapy techniques featuring positive reinforcement and the structuring of learning materials and tasks in a way that minimizes error and maximizes immediate feedback and success (Abramowitz et al., 1992). The use of behavioral treatment methods (see Chapter 17) for hyperactivity has reportedly been quite successful, at least for short-term gains.

The continued use of psychological therapy with medication in a total treatment program has reportedly shown good success. Pelham and colleagues (1980) found that the combination of behavioral intervention and psychostimulant medication was more effective than either treatment alone in modifying the behavior of hyperactive children. Satterfield, Satterfield, and Cantwell (1981) reported that individualized treatment of various types in conjunction with the use of medication resulted in favorable treatment outcomes in a three-year follow-up. In a more recent study, Pelham and colleagues (1993) found that both behavior modification and medication therapy significantly reduced ADHD. Medication, however, appeared to be the more effective element in the treatment.

It should be kept in mind that even though behavioral interventions and medication have reportedly enjoyed short-term successes, there has been insufficient critical evaluation of the long-term effects of either treatment method. One follow-up study of the drug treatment of 75 children over a 10- to 12-year period reported that young adults who had been hyperactive children had less education than control subjects and had a history of more auto accidents and more geographical moves. The authors found, however, that only a minority of the formerly hyperactive subjects continued their antisocial behavior into adulthood or developed severe psychopathology (Weiss et al., 1979).

It is clear from an evaluation of research on the treatment of hyperactivity that, in addition to a general disagreement about the nature of hyperactivity, an equal degree of controversy exists about the most effective treatment approach.

Even without treatment, hyperactive behavior tends to diminish by the time some of the children reach their middle teens. Research has demonstrated, however, that many hyperactive children retain ADHD into early adulthood (Lie, 1992) or go on to have other psychological problems in their late teens and early adulthood. Hechtman, Weiss, and Perlman (1980), for example, found that hyperactive children had significantly more problems than control subjects when they reached young adulthood. Carroll and Rounsaville (1993) found that 34.6 percent of treatment-seeking cocaine abusers in their study met the criteria for ADHD when they were children. In a 16-year follow-up study of ADHD children, about 25 percent never completed high school compared with 2 percent for controls (Mannuzza et al., 1993). Another longitudinal study of ADHD was conducted by Gittleman and colleagues (1985). These investigators evaluated and followed up a group of 101 boys aged 6 through 12 who showed hyperactivity, contrasting their later adjustment, at 16 to 23 years of age, with a control sample of 100 nonhyperactive boys. They found that most boys who had been diagnosed as hyperactive showed diminished symptom patterns in later adolescence and early adulthood. However, the full attention-deficit disorder persisted in 31 percent of the hyperactive boys, while only 3 percent of the control sample showed hyperactive symptoms at follow-up. The authors also found that the hyperactive boys showed a greater likelihood of developing psychiatric problems than the control boys. Their "most striking finding is the degree to which the syndrome consisting of impulsivity, inattention, and hyperactivity persisted" (p. 943), and boys in which the hyperactivity persisted had a greater likelihood of developing conduct disorders. Hyperactive boys who did not receive a clinical diagnosis at follow-up showed no differences from the control boys (Mannuzza et al., 1988).

Conduct Disorders

The next group of disorders emphasizes a child's or an adolescent's relationship to social norms and

HIGHLIGHT 14.2

Drug Therapy with Children Diagnosed as ADHD

One of the most widely used treatments for attention deficit hyperactivity disorder (ADHD) is psychostimulant medication (Horn et al., 1991). It is estimated that as many as 750,000 children receive medication, such as Ritalin, for overactive behavior every day (Safer & Krager, 1988), even though these medications are only found to be effective in about 75 percent of hyperactive children (DuPaul & Barkley, 1990).

The use of psychostimulant drugs with hyperactive children frequently meets with enthusiasm on the part of parents, school administrators, and clinicians because of their demonstrated effectiveness in controlling disruptive behavior, at least over short periods (Gittelman-Klein, 1987). The reduction in negative behavior, it is assumed, promotes more effective learning and enables the child to adapt better to the school environment and to get along better with peers. However, a number of questions have been raised concerning the increasing use of drugs in the treatment of hyperactive children. The principal questions include:

1. *Who is being selected for treatment?* It is important that an accurate diagnosis be obtained before drug treatment is initiated. However, many question the adequacy of the assessment procedures used

in identifying children who actually need medication. For example, a clear-cut distinction is not always made between children who appear to need drug therapy because of hyperactivity and children whose inattention and restlessness may be the result of hunger, crowded classrooms, irrelevant curriculum content, or anxiety and depression stemming from problems at home.

2. *Are drugs sometimes being used simply to control the child's behavior for the convenience of adults, for example, "to keep peace in the classroom"?* Those who raise this question point to the possibility that children who manifest bewilderment, anger, restlessness, or lethargy at school may only be showing a normal reaction to educational procedures that fail to spark their interest or meet their needs. These investigators maintain that to label such children as "sick"—as evidencing hyperactivity or some other behavior disorder—and to treat them through medication is to sidestep the difficult and expensive alternative of providing better educational programs.

3. *Are the effects of medication worth the side effects that accompany its use?* Drugs like Ritalin sometimes have undesirable side effects, such as severe insomnia, decreased appetite, dysphoria, dizziness, and headaches. Recently

these drugs have also been suspected as a cause of growth retardation. Appropriate therapeutic dosages are often difficult to assure and higher-than-therapeutic dosages are not uncommon. Excessive dosages have been found to produce brief paranoid psychoses in some individuals (Greenhill, 1992). Even with drugs that seem to produce minimal side effects, the possibility of adverse long-range effects resulting from sustained use during early growth and development is still being assessed.

Drug therapy for children should be used with extreme caution, and only with those children for whom other alternatives simply do not work. It is also important that drug therapy be undertaken only with the informed consent of the parent, as well as that of the child if he or she is old enough, and that the child not be given the sole responsibility for taking the medication—a procedure that can lead to misuse of the drug. At the same time, it is important to recognize that the drugs do help some children. Finally, children who do benefit from drug therapy also need other therapeutic measures for dealing with coexisting problems, such as learning deficiencies and psychological, interpersonal, and family difficulties (DuPaul & Barkley, 1990; Greenhill, 1992).

rules of conduct. In **conduct disorders,** aggressive or antisocial behavior is the focus. With these disorders, it is important to distinguish between persistent antisocial acts, in which the rights of others are violated, and the less serious pranks often carried out by "normal" children and adolescents. We should point out, too, that conduct disorders involve misdeeds that may or may not be against the

law; *juvenile delinquency*—to be discussed in the next section—is the legal term used to refer to violations of the law committed by minors.

The behavior to be described in the following sections may appear to be similar to the early stages in the development of personality disorders, discussed in Chapter 9. Indeed, the personality characteristics and causal considerations are much the same. It is difficult, if not impossible, to distinguish among a conduct disorder, a "predelinquent" pattern of behavior, and the early stages in the development of an antisocial personality. Behaviorally, the patterns are alike and may simply represent three ways of describing or accounting for the same behavior. As described in Chapter 9, adult antisocial personalities, as children, showed the aggressive behavior and rule violations that often are labeled conduct disorders, and many came into contact with the authorities as a result of this delinquent behavior. There is substantial evidence that in some children disruptive behavior problems "gradually emerge from childhood onward in an orderly fashion" (Loeber et al., 1992). Fortunately, however, not all children who are described as having conduct disorders or who engage in delinquent behavior grow up to become antisocial personalities or commit themselves to lives of crime. As we will see, although the conduct disorders are quite serious and complex to treat, there are effective ways of working with disordered children.

The Clinical Picture in Conduct Disorders The essential symptomatic behavior in the conduct disorders involves a persistent, repetitive violation of rules and a disregard for the rights of others. The following case is typical of children with conduct disorder and illustrates many of the features commonly found:

> Craig, an 8-year-old boy, had already established himself as a social outcast by the time he entered first grade. Previously, he had been expelled from kindergarten two times in two years for being unmanageable. His mother brought him to a mental health center at the insistence of the school when she attempted to enroll him in the first grade. Within the first week of school, Craig's quarrelsome and defiant behavior had tried the special education teacher, who was reputedly "excellent" with problem children like him, to the point where she recommended his suspension from school. His classmates likewise were completely unsympathetic to Craig, whom they viewed as a bully. At even the slightest sign of movement on his part, the other children would tell the teacher that Craig was "being bad again."
>
> At home, Craig was uncontrollable. His mother and six other children lived with his domineering grandmother. Craig's mother was ineffective at disciplining or managing her children. She worked long hours as a domestic maid and "did not feel like hassling with those kids" when she got home. Her present husband, the father of the three youngest children (including Craig), had deserted the family.

In general, children who are seen as conduct-disordered manifest such characteristics as overt or covert hostility, disobedience, physical and verbal aggressiveness, quarrelsomeness, vengefulness, and destructiveness. Lying, solitary stealing, and temper tantrums are common. Such children tend to be sexually uninhibited and inclined toward sexual aggressiveness. Some may engage in firesetting (Forehand et al., 1991), vandalism, robbery, and even homicidal acts.

Causal Factors in Conduct Disorders Our understanding of what factors are associated with the development of conduct problems in childhood has increased tremendously in the past 15 years. An important precursor of the antisocial behavior seen in children with conduct disorder is often what is now called *oppositional defiant disorder,* the essential feature of which "is a recurrent pattern of negativistic, defiant, disobedient and hostile behavior toward authority figures that persists for at least 6 months" (DSM-IV, p. 91). This disorder usually begins by the age of six years, whereas full-blown conduct disorder does not typically begin until the age of nine. Prospective studies have found a developmental sequence from oppositional defiant disorder to conduct disorder, with common risk factors for both conditions (Hinshaw, 1994). That is, virtually all cases of conduct disorder were preceded developmentally by oppositional defiant disorder, although only about 25 percent of children with oppositional defiant disorder go on to develop conduct disorder within a three-year period (Lahey et al., 1992). The risk factors for both include family discord, socioeconomic disadvantage, and antisocial behavior in the parents (Hinshaw, 1994).

Evidence has accumulated that a genetic predisposition leading to low verbal intelligence, mild neuropsychological problems, and difficult temperament sets the stage for this early-onset conduct disorder through a set of self-perpetuating mechanisms (Caspi, Elder, & Herbener, 1990; Hinshaw, 1994; Moffitt & Lynam, 1994). The child's difficult temperament may lead to an insecure attachment because parents find it hard to engage in the good parenting that would lead to a secure attachment. In addition, low verbal intelligence and/or mild neuropsychological deficits (some of which may involve deficiencies in self-control functions such as sustaining attention, planning, self-monitoring, inhibiting unsuccessful or impulsive behaviors) which have been documented in many of these children, may help set the stage for a lifelong course of difficulties. In attempting to explain why the relatively mild neuropsychological deficits typically seen can have such pervasive effects, Moffitt and Lynam hypothesize:

> Perhaps the effects of early neuropsychological vulnerabilities are amplified over time as children interact with their environments, to later culminate in conduct disorder. For example, a preschooler who has difficulty understanding language may resist his mother's efforts to read to him, which delays his school readiness. When he enters school, the modal curriculum may not allow for teaching that is tailored to his readiness level, especially if the school is crowded and the resources are poor. After a few years of school failure, he will be chronologically older than his class mates, and thus be socially rejected. He may be tracked into a remedial class, containing pupils who have behavioral disorders as well as learning disabilities. Daily association with conduct-disordered peers brings familiarity with delinquent behaviors, and he adopts delinquent ways to gain acceptance by peers. In this way, a relatively mild neuropsychological deficit might initiate an invidious sequence of interactions between individual characteristics and social contexts, culminating in an antisocial personality style. (1994, pp. 243–44)

Children who develop conduct disorder early are much more likely to develop psychopathy or antisocial personality disorder as adults than are adolescents who develop conduct disorder suddenly in adolescence (Hinshaw, 1994; Moffitt, 1993b). Thus, it is the pervasiveness of the problems first associated with oppositional defiant disorder, and then with early-onset conduct disorder, which is the pattern associated with an adult diagnosis of psychopathy or antisocial personality. Although only about 25–40 percent of cases of early-onset conduct disorder go on to develop adult antisocial personality disorder, over 80 percent of boys with early-onset conduct disorder do continue to have multiple problems of social dysfunction (in friendships, intimate relationships, and vocational activities) even if they do not meet full criteria for antisocial personality disorder (Hinshaw, 1994; Zoccolillo et al., 1992). By contrast, most adolescents who develop conduct disorder in adolescence do not go on to become adult

Hostility and aggressive behavior have been found to play a role in the development of conduct disorder. Children who develop this disorder early in childhood are at special risk for problems later in life.

psychopaths or antisocial personalities but instead have problems limited to the adolescent years. These adolescent-onset cases also do not share the same set of risk factors that the child-onset cases have, including low verbal intelligence, neuropsychological deficits, and impulsive and attentional problems (Hinshaw, 1994; Moffitt & Lynam, 1994).

In addition to these genetic or constitutional liabilities that may predispose to conduct disorder and adult psychopathy and antisocial personality, a host of environmental factors also may contribute. For example, Coie and Lenox (1994) have summarized evidence showing that children who are aggressive and socially unskilled are often rejected by their peers and that such rejection can lead to "a spiraling sequence of social interactions with peers that exacerbates the tendency toward antisocial behavior (Dodge, 1980)" (Coie & Lenox, 1994). They have also shown that it is the socially rejected subgroup of aggressive children who are at the highest risk for adolescent delinquency and probably for adult antisocial personality. In addition, parents and teachers may react with strong negative affect, such as anger, to aggressive children (Capaldi & Patterson, 1994), and parents and teachers may in turn also reject these aggressive children. The combination of rejection by parents, peers, and teachers leads these children to become isolated and alienated. Not surprisingly, they often turn to deviant peer groups for companionship (Coie & Lenox, 1994), at which point a good deal of imitation of the antisocial behavior of their deviant peer models may occur.

Investigators generally seem to agree that the family setting of a conduct-disordered child is typically characterized by ineffective parenting, rejection, harsh and inconsistent discipline, and often parental neglect (Frick et al., 1992; Patterson, De-Barsyshe, & Ramsey, 1989; Patterson, Reid, & Dishion, 1992). Frequently, the parents have an unstable marital relationship (Osborn, 1992), are emotionally disturbed or sociopathic, and do not provide the child with consistent guidance, acceptance, or affection. Family discord, such as the conflict and disharmony accompanying divorce, is instrumental in the development of conduct disorders (Chess & Thomas, 1984; Robins, 1991). In a disproportionate number of cases, the child may have a single parent, a stepparent, or a series of stepparents. Regardless of whether the family is intact, a child in a conflict-charged home feels overtly rejected. Rutter and Quinton (1984b), for example, concluded that family discord and hostility were "the chief mediating variables" in the association between disturbed parents and disturbed children, particularly with regard to the development of conduct disorders in children and adolescents. These parental factors are conceptualized as contributing to poor and ineffective parenting skills—especially ineffective discipline and supervision. "These children are trained by the family directly in antisocial behavior by coercive interchanges and indirectly by lack of monitoring and consistent discipline" (Capaldi & Patterson, 1994, p. 169). This in turn all too often leads to association with deviant peers and the opportunity for further learning of antisocial behavior.

In addition to the familial factors, a number of other psychosocial and sociocultural contextual variables probably contribute to the probability that a child will develop conduct disorder, and later adult psychopathy or antisocial personality disorder. As summarized by Capaldi and Patterson (1994), these include low socioeconomic status, poor neighborhoods, parental stress, and depression.

Treatments and Outcomes Therapy for a conduct-disordered child is likely to be ineffective unless some means can be found for modifying the child's environment. One interesting and often effective treatment strategy with conduct disorder in children is the *cohesive family model* (Patterson et al., 1992; Webster-Stratton, 1991). In this approach, parents of conduct-disordered children are viewed as lacking in parenting skills and fail to socialize the children by behaving in inconsistent ways, thereby reinforcing inappropriate behavior. Patterson and his colleagues have developed a "coercive hypothesis" which holds that children learn to escape or avoid parental criticism by escalating their negative behavior. This tactic in turn increases their parents' aversive interactions and criticism. The child observes the increased anger in his or her parents and models this aggressive pattern. The parental attention to the child's negative behaviors actually serves to reinforce the negative, aggressive behavior instead of suppressing it. Viewing the genesis of conduct problems as emerging from the parent-child interaction places the treatment focus on the interaction between the child and the parents (Patterson et al., 1992).

Obtaining treatment cooperation from parents who are themselves in conflict with each other is often a very difficult process. Often an overburdened parent who is separated or divorced and working simply does not have the time or inclination to learn and practice a more adequate parental role. In some cases, the circumstances may call for a child to be removed from the home and placed in a foster home or institution, with the expectation of a later return to the home if intervening therapy with the parents appears to justify it. Unfortunately, children who are removed to new environments often interpret this removal as further rejection—not only by their parents but by society as well. Unless the changed environment offers a warm, kindly, and accepting—yet consistent and firm—setting, such children are likely to make little progress. Even then, treatment may have only a temporary effect. Faretra (1981) followed up 66 aggressive and disturbed adolescents who had been admitted to an inpatient unit. She found that antisocial and criminal behavior persisted into adulthood with a lessening of psychiatric involvement. Many conduct-disordered children go on to have personality disorders as adults (Rutter, 1988; Zeitlin, 1986).

Aggressiveness at an early age has been found to be related to adult personality disorder (Zoccolillo et al., 1992) or criminal behavior. Stattin and Magnusson (1989) conducted a study of 1027 boys and girls between late childhood and early adolescence using teacher ratings made at ages 10 and 13. An evaluation of the recorded behavior problems of the boys through age 26 found that high ratings of childhood aggressiveness were characteristic of subjects who later committed violent crimes and damage to public property. The relationship between early aggressiveness and later crime was not found for girls.

By and large, our society tends to take a punitive, rather than rehabilitative, attitude toward an antisocial, aggressive youth. Thus, the emphasis is on punishment and on "teaching the child a lesson." Such "treatment," however, appears to intensify rather than correct the behavior. Where treatment is unsuccessful, the end product is likely to be an antisocial personality with aggressive behavior.

The advent of behavior therapy techniques has, however, made the outlook brighter for children who manifest conduct disorders (Kazdin, 1988). Teaching control techniques to the parents of such children is particularly important, so that they function as therapists in reinforcing desirable behavior and modifying the environmental conditions that have been reinforcing maladaptive behavior. The changes brought about when they consistently accept and reward their child's positive behavior and stop focusing attention on the negative behavior may finally change their perception of and feelings toward the child, leading to the basic acceptance that the child has so badly needed.

Though effective techniques for behavioral management can be taught to parents, often they have difficulty carrying out treatment plans. If this is the case, other techniques, such as family therapy or parental counseling, can be employed to ensure that the parent or person responsible for the child's discipline is sufficiently assertive to follow through on the program.

Delinquent Behavior

In this section we will examine one of the most troublesome and extensive problems in childhood and adolescence: delinquent behavior. This behavior includes such acts as destruction of property, violence against other people, and various behaviors contrary to the needs and rights of others and in violation of society's laws (Henggeler, 1989). As noted earlier, the term **juvenile delinquency** is a legal one; it refers to illegal acts committed by individuals under the age of 16, 17, or 18 (depending on state law). Children under eight who commit such acts are not considered delinquents, because it is assumed that they are too immature to understand the significance and consequences of their actions. Delinquency is generally regarded as calling for some punishment or corrective action.

The Incidence and Severity of Delinquent Acts

The actual incidence of juvenile delinquency is difficult to determine because many delinquent acts are not reported. Of the 2 million young people who go through the juvenile courts each year in the United States, about half are there for actions, such as running away, that are not considered crimes for adults. These actions are referred to as status offenses (see HIGHLIGHT 14.3). In 1988, arrests of people under 18 years of age accounted for 28 percent of all crime (Uniform Crime Reports, 1992). Juveniles accounted for over one out of every three arrests for robbery, one out of three arrests for crimes against property, one out of six arrests for rape, and one out

of eleven arrests for murder. Although most of the juvenile crime was committed by males, the rate has also risen for females. About 1 teenager out of every 15 in the nation was arrested. Well over half of the juveniles who are arrested each year have prior police records (Uniform Crime Reports, 1992). Female delinquents are commonly apprehended for drug use, sexual offenses, running away from home, and "incorrigibility," but crimes against property, such as stealing, have markedly increased among this group. Male delinquents are commonly arrested for drug usage and crimes against property; to a lesser extent, they are arrested for armed robbery, aggravated assault, and other crimes against people.

Fear of violent juvenile crime has created in many people the idea that juvenile criminals as a group are uncontrollable and antisocial personalities. Indeed, a high percentage of violent crimes (17.5 percent) are committed by persons under 18 years of age or younger (Uniform Crime Reports, 1992).

Both the incidence and the severity of delinquent behavior are disproportionately high for lower-class adolescents (Zimring, 1979). It may also be noted that the delinquency rate for socially disadvantaged youths appears about equal for whites and non-whites (Uniform Crime Reports, 1992). Although much juvenile crime is committed by lower-class youth, some problems have been noted in all social strata (Elliott, Dunford, & Huizinga, 1987).

Causal Factors in Delinquency In an interesting theoretical analysis of delinquency, Moffitt (1993) points out that most contemporary views of delinquency have failed to recognize the heterogeneity of delinquency and calls for a more refined view of its origins. She notes that a small group of adolescents show continuous delinquency over time whereas most delinquent adolescents engage in delinquent acts and discontinue this behavior soon afterward. Moffitt suggests that the small group of "continuous" delinquents actually evolve from oppositional defiant behavior to conduct disorder then to adult antisocial personality while most people who engage in delinquent acts as adolescents do not follow this trend. The individuals who show adolescence-limited delinquency are thought to do so as a result of social mimicry—they mimic their more antisocial peers but discontinue this behavior when they ultimately respond to changing contingencies. That is, they lose their motivation for delinquency as they mature and respond to other contingencies in their environment.

Various conditions, singly and in combination, may be involved in the development of delinquent behavior. Several key variables seem to play a part in

Problems That Lead Children to Run Away

Of serious concern in the United States is the problem of youngsters who run away from home—an estimated 1 million or more each year. Although the average age is about 15, an increasing number are in the 11- to 14-year-old age bracket. Many of these runaways are from the suburbs, and at least half are girls. The following case illustrates this problem:

Joan, an attractive girl who looked older than her 12 years, came to the attention of juvenile authorities when her parents reported her as a runaway. Twice before she had run away from home, but no report had been filed. In the first instance, she had gone to the home of a girlfriend and returned two days later; in the second, she had hitchhiked to another city with an older boy and returned home about a week later. Investigation revealed that the girl was having difficulty in school and was living in a family situation torn by bickering and dissension. In explaining why she ran away from home, she stated simply that she "just couldn't take it anymore—all that quarreling and criticism, and no one really cared anyway."

Why do children and adolescents run away? English (1973) concluded that reasons for running away from home tend to fall into three categories: (a) getting out of a destructive family situation, as in the case of a girl who runs away to avoid sexual advances by her father or stepfather; (b) running away in an effort to better the family situation; and (c) having a secret, unsharable problem, such as, for girls, being pregnant.

In a study of runaway girls, Homer (1974) distinguished between "run from's," who had usually fought with their parents and run away because they were unable to resolve the situation or their anger, and "run to's," who were seeking something outside the home. The "run to's" were typically seeking pleasure—sex, drugs, liquor, escape from school, or a peer group with similar interests. Usually they stayed with friends or at other "peer-established" facilities. The "run from's" usually ran away from home only once, while the "run to's" were more likely to be repetitive runaways.

An increasing number of children are "run from's" who are trying to get away from intolerable home situations. Several recent studies have pointed to the possibility that children who run away have been physically or sexually abused (Famularo, et al., 1990; Feitel et al., 1992; Powers, Ecken-

rode, & Jaklitsch, 1990). In some instances, for economic or other reasons, they are actually encouraged to leave—and their parents do not want them back. Most do not feel that they can return to their parents but instead want a foster home where they will be treated well and respected.

The majority of runaways are not reported. Of those who are, about 90 percent or more are located by law enforcement officers and, when feasible, returned home. Beginning in 1974, a toll-free hotline was established that informs runaways where the nearest temporary shelter is located and enables them to send messages to their parents if they wish. Treatment for runaways is similar to that for individuals who manifest other emotional problems during childhood and adolescence. Often family therapy is an essential part of the treatment program. In some instances—as in those involving parental abuse, unconcern, or lack of cooperation—juvenile authorities may place a child in a foster home. Parents, however, are by no means always the primary reason for their child's running away, and a "what-have-we-done-wrong" attitude may lead to unnecessary feelings of guilt. One of the toll-free numbers is 1-800-621-4000. This hotline does not operate in either Alaska or Hawaii.

---

the genesis of delinquency: personal pathology, pathogenic family patterns, undesirable peer relationships, general sociocultural factors, and special stress.

Personal Pathology. A number of investigators have attempted to understand delinquents in terms of pervasive patterns and sources of personal pathology:

1. *Genetic determinants.* Although the research on genetic determinants of antisocial behavior is far from conclusive, some evidence indicates possible hereditary contributions to criminality. Schulsinger (1980) identified 57 sociopathic adoptees from psychiatric and police files in Denmark and matched them with 57 nonsociopathic control adoptees on the basis of age, sex, social class, geographic region, and age at adoption. He found that natural parents

of the adopted sociopaths, particularly fathers, were more likely to have sociopathic characteristics than the natural parents of the controls. Because these natural parents had little contact with their offspring, thus reducing the possibility of environmental influence, the results are interpreted as reflecting the possibility of some genetic transmission of a predisposition to antisocial behavior.

2. *Brain damage and learning disability.* In a distinct minority of delinquency cases—an estimated 1 percent or less—brain pathology results in lowered inhibitory controls and a tendency toward episodes of violent behavior. Such adolescents are often hyperactive, impulsive, emotionally unstable, and unable to inhibit themselves when strongly stimulated. Fortunately, their inner controls appear to improve during later adolescence and young adulthood. The actual role intellectual factors, particularly learning disabilities, play in causing juvenile delinquency is still being debated. In a recent review of the evidence, Lombardo and Lombardo (1991) concluded that there is no empirical evidence linking learning disabilities with delinquency. However, Lynam, Moffitt, and Stouthamer-Loeber (1993) found a clear relationship between low intelligence and delinquency.

3. *Psychological disorders.* A small percentage of delinquent acts appear to be directly associated with behavior disorders, such as hyperactivity (Loeber et al., 1992). Delinquent acts associated with psychotic behavior often involve a pattern of prolonged emotional hurt and turmoil, culminating, after long frustration, in an outburst of violent behavior (Bandura, 1973). In the case of psychologically disturbed delinquents, the delinquent act is a by-product of severe personality maladjustment rather than a reflection of antisocial attitudes.

4. *Antisocial traits.* Many habitual delinquents appear to share the traits typical of antisocial personalities—they are impulsive, defiant, resentful, devoid of feelings of remorse or guilt, incapable of establishing and maintaining close interpersonal ties, and seemingly unable to profit from experience. Because they lack needed reality and ethical controls, they often engage in seemingly senseless acts that are not planned but occur on the spur of the moment. They may steal a small sum of money they do not need, or they may steal a car, drive it a few blocks, and abandon it. In some instances, they engage in impulsive acts of violence that are not committed for personal gain but rather reflect underlying resentment and hostility toward the world. In essence, these individuals are "unsocialized."

5. *Drug abuse.* Many delinquent acts—particularly theft, prostitution, and assault—are directly as-

Teen prostitution is often directly associated with alcohol or drug use. For female addicts, prostitution is a means of obtaining money.

sociated with alcohol or drug use. Most adolescents who abuse hard drugs, such as heroin, are forced to steal to maintain their habit, which can be very expensive. In the case of female addicts, theft may be combined with or replaced by prostitution as a means of obtaining money.

Pathogenic Family Patterns. In evaluating the role of pathogenic family patterns in delinquency, it should be emphasized that a given pattern is only one of many interacting factors. Of the various patterns that have been emphasized in the research on juvenile delinquency, the following appear to be the most important:

1. *Parental absence or family conflict.* Parents may be missing because of desertion, separation, death, or imprisonment. Several investigators have pointed to the high incidence of multiple or missing parental figures in the backgrounds of delinquent youths (Lefkowitz et al., 1977). In general, delinquency appears to be much more common among youths coming from homes in which parents have separated or divorced than from homes in which a parent has died, suggesting that parental conflict may be a key element in causing delinquency. As we have seen, the effects of parental absence vary. Parental separation or divorce may be less serious for children than parental conflict and dissension. It is parental disharmony and conflict in lieu of a stable home life that appears to be an important causal variable.

2. *Parental rejection and faulty discipline.* In many cases, one or both parents reject a child. When the father is the rejecting parent, it is difficult for a boy to identify with him and use him as a model for his own development. In an early study of 26 aggressively delinquent boys, Bandura and Walters

(1963) delineated a pattern in which rejection by the father was combined with inconsistent handling of the boy by both parents. To complicate the pathogenic picture, the father typically used physically punitive methods of discipline, thus modeling aggressive behavior and augmenting the hostility that the boy already felt toward him. The end result of such a pattern was a hostile, defiant, inadequately socialized youth who lacked normal inner controls and tended to act out his aggressive impulses in antisocial behavior.

The detrimental effects of parental rejection and inconsistent discipline are by no means attributable only to fathers. Researchers have found that such behavior by either parent is associated with aggression, lying, stealing, running away from home, and a wide range of other difficulties (Lefkowitz et al., 1977). Often, too, inconsistent discipline may involve more complex family interactions, as when a mother imposes severe restrictions on a youth's behavior and then leaves "policing" to a timid or uncaring father who fails to follow through. In general, parental supervision has been found to be inversely related to delinquency—higher rates of delinquency are found in families that provide less supervision for their children (Morton & Ewald, 1987).

3. *Antisocial parental models.* Several investigators have found a high incidence of antisocial traits in the parents of delinquents—particularly but not exclusively in the father (Bandura, 1973). These traits included alcoholism, brutality, antisocial attitudes, failure to provide, frequent unnecessary absences from home, and other characteristics that made the father an inadequate and unacceptable model. Elkind (1967), for example, cited the case of a

> father who encouraged his 17-year-old son to drink, frequent prostitutes, and generally "raise hell." This particular father was awakened late one night by the police who had caught his son in a raid on a so-called "massage" parlor. The father's reaction was, "Why aren't you guys out catching crooks?" This same father would boast to his coworkers that his son was "all boy" and "a chip off the old block." (p. 313)

Psychopathic fathers—and mothers—may contribute in various ways to the delinquent behavior of girls as well. Covert encouragement of sexual promiscuity is fairly common, and in some instances there is actual incest with the daughter. In a study of 30 delinquent girls, Scharfman and Clark (1967) found evidence of serious psychopathology in one or both parents of 22 of the girls, including three cases of incest and many other types of early sexual experience. These investigators also reported a high

Youth gangs offer acceptance and affection that are often absent in the adolescent's home and school environment.

incidence of parental absence (only 11 of the 30 girls lived with both parents) and harsh, irrational, and inconsistent discipline:

> Any form of consistent discipline or rational setting of limits was unknown to the girls in their homes. Rather, there was an almost regular pattern of indifference to the activities or whereabouts of these girls, often with the mother overtly or indirectly suggesting delinquent behavior by her own actions. This would alternate with unpredictable, irrational, and violent punishment. (p. 443)

4. *Limited parental relationships outside the family.* Some research suggests that the parents' interpersonal relationships outside the family may contribute to their children's delinquency (Griest & Wells, 1983). Wahler (1980) found that the children's acting-out behavior was inversely related to the amount of friendly contacts that parents had outside the home. Wahler, Hughey, and Gordon (1981) reported that mothers who are isolated or who have negative community interactions are less likely to "track" or control their children's behavior in the community than parents who have friendly relationships outside the family.

Undesirable Peer Relationships. Delinquency tends to be a shared experience. In their study of delinquents in the Flint, Michigan, area, Haney and Gold (1973) found that about two-thirds of delinquent acts were committed in association with one or two other people, and most of the remainder involved three or four other people. Usually the offender and the companion or companions were of the same sex. Interestingly, girls were more likely than boys to have a constant friend or companion in delinquency. The role of gang membership in delinquency is discussed in the next section.

General Sociocultural Factors. Broad social conditions may also tend to produce or support delinquency. Interrelated factors that appear to be of key importance include alienation and rebellion, social rejection, and the psychological support afforded by membership in a delinquent gang.

Feelings of alienation and rebellion are common to many teenagers from all socioeconomic levels. Alienated teenagers may outwardly submit passively to their elders' demands, or they may openly disobey parental and other adult authority and create no end of problems for themselves and their families. In either event, alienation from family and from the broader society exposes them to becoming captives of their peers, to whom they may turn for guidance and approval.

Our society has become increasingly aware of young people who lack the motivation or ability to do well in school and who drop out as soon as they can (Schwartz & Johnson, 1985). With increasing automation and the demand for occupational skills, there are few jobs for which they can qualify. There are also many students who graduate from high school but whose training does not qualify them for available jobs. Whether these young people come from upper-, middle-, or lower-income homes, and whether they drop out or continue through high school, they have one crucial problem in common—they discover that they are not needed in our society. They are victims of social progress—"social rejects." While some are able to obtain training in specific job areas, others appear unable to find or hold jobs, and still others drift aimlessly from one unsatisfactory job to another.

Among adolescents who join gangs, we are dealing not so much with personal psychopathology as with organized group pathology involving rebellion against the norms of society. As Jenkins (1969) has expressed it:

> The socialized delinquent represents not a failure of socialization but a limitation of loyalty to a more or less predatory peer group. The basic capacity for so-

cial relations has been achieved. What is lacking is an effective integration with the larger society as a contributing member. (p. 73)

Although the problem of delinquent gangs is most prevalent in lower-socioeconomic areas, it is by no means restricted to them. Further, delinquent gangs are not a male province—in recent years, females have also formed gangs. Nor does the problem of juvenile delinquent gangs occur only in particular racial, ethnic, or social groups. It is pervasive, most particularly in inner-city areas. Though there are many reasons for joining gangs, most members appear to feel inadequate in and rejected by the larger society. Gang membership gives members a sense of belonging and a means of gaining some measure of status and approval. It may also represent a means of committing robberies and other illegal acts for financial gain—acts that an individual could not successfully perform alone (Feldman & Weisfeld, 1973).

We should emphasize that the most delinquents do not belong to delinquent gangs, though gang membership may be increasing because young people appear to be joining groups for protection. Not all delinquent gangs are highly organized, cohesive groups. Recently, however, there seems to be an increase in both the organization and cohesiveness of delinquent gangs and in the violence of their activities.

Dealing with Delinquency If they have adequate facilities and personnel, juvenile institutions and training schools can be of great help to youths who need to be removed from aversive environments. These institutions can give youths a chance to learn about themselves and their world, to further their education and develop needed skills, and to find purpose and meaning in their lives. In such settings, young people may have the opportunity to receive psychological counseling and group therapy. In these situations it is of key importance that peer group pressures be channeled in the direction of resocialization, rather than toward repetitive delinquent behavior. Behavior therapy techniques based on the assumption that delinquent behavior is learned, maintained, and changed according to the same principles as other learned behavior have shown promise in the rehabilitation of juvenile offenders who require institutionalization. Counseling with parents and related environmental changes are generally of vital importance in a total rehabilitation program.

Probation is widely used with juvenile offenders and may be granted either in lieu of or after a period of institutionalization. Many delinquents can be guided into constructive behavior without being removed from their family or community.

The recidivism rate for delinquents—the most commonly used measure for assessing rehabilitation programs—depends heavily on the type of offenders being dealt with and on the particular facility or procedures used. The overall recidivism rate for delinquents sent to training schools has been estimated to be high (Uniform Crime Reports, 1989). Because many crimes are committed by juveniles who have been recently released from custody or who were not incarcerated after being arrested, a number of state officials have become advocates of stiffer penalties for some types of juvenile crime. Individuals who commit crimes of violence or armed assault, or who have a long history of arrests, are often being given harsher penalties than they once would have been (Fersch, 1980).

Anxiety Disorders of Childhood and Adolescence

In modern society, no one is totally insulated from anxiety-producing events or situations. Most children are vulnerable to fears and uncertainties as a part of growing up, and most children encounter many normal developmental steps and environmental demands that challenge their adaptation skills. Anxiety disorders are apparently quite common in the general population. Kashani and Orvaschel (1988) reported that 8.7 percent of their community-based school sample clearly met diagnostic criteria for an anxiety diagnosis based on a diagnostic interview.

Children with anxiety disorders are more extreme in their behavior than those experiencing "normal" anxiety. These children appear to share many of the following characteristics: oversensitivity, unrealistic fears, shyness and timidity, pervasive feelings of inadequacy, sleep disturbances, and fear of school. Children diagnosed as suffering from an anxiety disorder typically attempt to cope with their fears by becoming overly dependent on others for support and help.

In DSM-IV, anxiety disorders of childhood and adolescence are covered in two subclassifications: separation anxiety disorder and overanxious disorder. Both syndromes are more common among boys than among girls. We will briefly describe the clinical picture in each of these syndromes, then deal with causal factors and treatment considerations.

Separation Anxiety Disorder Separation anxiety disorder is the most common of the childhood anxi-

ety disorders (Bernstein & Borchardt, 1991), reportedly occurring with a prevalence of 2.4 percent of children in a population health study (Bowen, Offord, & Boyle, 1990). Children with **separation anxiety disorder** are characterized by unrealistic fears, oversensitivity, self-consciousness, nightmares, and chronic anxiety. They lack self-confidence, are apprehensive in new situations, and tend to be immature for their age. Such children are described by their parents as shy, sensitive, nervous, submissive, easily discouraged, worried, and frequently moved to tears. Typically, they are overly dependent, particularly on their parents. The essential feature in the clinical picture of this disorder is excessive anxiety about separation from major attachment figures, such as mother, and from familiar home surroundings. In many cases a clear psychosocial stressor can be identified, such as the death of a relative or a pet. The following case illustrates the clinical picture in this disorder:

Johnny was a highly sensitive six-year-old boy who suffered from numerous fears, nightmares, and chronic anxiety. He was terrified of being separated from his mother, even for a brief period. When his mother tried to enroll him in kindergarten, he became so upset when she left the room that the principal arranged for her to remain in the classroom. After two weeks, however, this arrangement had to be discontinued, and Johnny had to be withdrawn from kindergarten because his mother could not leave him even for a few minutes. Later, when his mother attempted to enroll him in the first grade, Johnny manifested the same intense anxiety and unwillingness to be separated from her. At the suggestion of the school counselor, Johnny's mother brought him to a community clinic for assistance with the problem. The therapist who initially saw Johnny and his mother was wearing a white clinic jacket, which led to a severe panic reaction on Johnny's part. His mother had to hold him to keep him from running away, and he did not settle down until the therapist removed his jacket. Johnny's mother explained that "he is terrified of doctors, and it is almost impossible to get him to a physician even when he is sick."

When children with separation anxiety disorder are actually separated from their attachment figures, they typically become preoccupied with morbid fears, such as the worry that their parents are going to become ill or die. They cling helplessly to adults, have difficulty sleeping, and become intensely demanding.

Overanxious Disorder Children with **overanxious disorder** are characterized by excessive worry and persistent fear; however, their fears are usually not specific and are not due to a recent stressful event. Such a child appears generally anxious and may worry a great deal about future events. He or she is preoccupied with trivial problems. His or her anxiety may also be expressed in somatic ways—stomach distress, shortness of breath, dizziness, headaches, and the like. Sleeping problems, especially difficulty in falling asleep, are common. Many children showing overanxious disorder appear to have personality characteristics such as perfectionistic ideas and obsessional self-doubt. One study (Bowen et al., 1990) found overanxious disorder in 3.6 percent of a sample of children in a large epidemiological study in Canada. The disorder is illustrated in the following case:

Cindy, an overweight eleven-year-old girl, was taken to the emergency room following an "attack" of dizziness, faintness, and shortness of breath. She believed she was having a heart attack because of the discomfort she was experiencing in her chest. Cindy had a long history of health problems and concerns and was a frequent visitor to doctors. She had missed, on the average, three days of school a week since school had begun four months before.

Cindy was viewed by her mother as a "very good girl" but "sickly." Cindy was good about helping around the house and with her two younger sisters. She seemed conscientious and concerned about doing things right but seemed to lack self-confidence. She always checked out things with her mother, sometimes several times. She was particularly concerned about safety and would, for example, ask her mother frequently if the kitchen stove was turned off correctly.

Cindy would become extremely fearful at times, often for no external reason. For example, on one clear summer day a few months before, she had become panicked over the possibility that a tornado might strike and had insisted that her family take shelter for several hours in the basement.

Causal Factors in Anxiety Disorders A number of causal factors have been emphasized in explanations of the childhood anxiety disorders. The more important appear to be the following:

1. An unusual constitutional sensitivity, an easy conditionability by aversive stimuli, and a buildup and generalization of "surplus fear reactions."

2. The undermining of feelings of adequacy and security by early illnesses, accidents, or losses that involved pain and discomfort. The traumatic effect of such experiences is often due partly to such children finding themselves in unfamiliar situations, as during hospitalization. The traumatic nature of certain life changes, such as moving away from friends and into a new situation, can have an intensely negative effect on a child's adjustment. Kashani and colleagues (1981a) found that the most common recent life event for children receiving psychiatric care was moving to a new school district.

3. The "modeling" effect of an overanxious and protective parent who sensitizes a child to the dangers and threats of the outside world. Often the parent's overprotectiveness communicates a lack of confidence in the child's ability to cope, thus reinforcing the child's feelings of inadequacy.

4. The failure of an indifferent or detached parent to provide adequate guidance for a child's development. Although the child is not necessarily rejected, neither is he or she adequately supported in mastering essential competencies and in gaining a positive self-concept. Repeated experiences of failure, stemming from poor learning skills, may lead to subsequent patterns of anxiety or withdrawal in the face of "threatening" situations. Other children may perform adequately but are overcritical of themselves and feel intensely anxious and devaluated when they perceive themselves as failing to do well enough to earn their parents' love and respect.

5. Finally, the role that social-environmental factors might play in the development of anxiety-based disorders, though important, is not clearly understood. One recent study (Last & Perrin, 1993) reported that there were clear differences between African American and white children with respect to types of anxiety disorders. White children were more likely to present with school refusal than African American children who showed more PTSD symptoms. This difference might result from differing patterns of referral in African American or white families or might reflect differing environmental stressors placed on the children. Further research is needed to determine the implications of these findings.

The various causal factors we have been discussing in relation to childhood anxiety disorders can obviously occur in differing degrees and combinations. All of them, however, are consistent with the view that these disorders essentially result from maladaptive learning.

Treatments and Outcomes The anxiety disorders of childhood may continue into adolescence and young adulthood—first leading to maladaptive avoidance behavior and later to increasingly idiosyncratic thinking and behavior. Typically, however, this is not the case. As affected children grow and have wider interactions in school and in peer-group activities, they often benefit from such corrective experiences as making friends and succeeding at given tasks. Teachers who are aware of the needs of both overanxious and shy, withdrawn children are often able to ensure successful experiences for them.

Psychopharmacological treatment of anxiety disorders in children and adolescents is becoming more common today (Kutcher et al., 1992) although the effectiveness of drugs such as imipramine with problems such as overanxious disorder have questionable efficacy. Moreover, one factor contributing to caution in using medications in these disorders is the diagnostic uncertainty involved. Anxiety is often found to coexist with other conditions, particularly depression (Gittelman, 1988) and ADHD (Andreason et al., 1987). Often there is not the diagnostic clarity required for cautious use of antianxiety medication.

Behavior therapy procedures, sometimes used in school settings, often help anxious children. Such procedures include assertiveness training, help with mastering essential competencies, and desensitization. Recently, one researcher reported the successful use of cognitive-behavioral treatment with 9- to 13-year-old children with anxiety disorders (Kendall, 1994). With children, behavioral treatment approaches such as desensitization must be explicitly tailored to a particular problem, and in vivo methods (using graded real-life situations) may be more effective than the use of imagined situations. Although behavior therapy has been demonstrated to be effective with anxious children, some investigators have questioned whether it is superior to other approaches (Barrios & Hartman, 1988). For a look at two other therapies that are often successful with children experiencing anxiety, see HIGHLIGHT 14.4.

Childhood Depression

Clinicians working with children in mental health settings have long noted a pattern of symptoms that seemed indicative of depression. Spitz (1946) first described the problem, which he called *anaclitic depression,* as a behavior pattern, similar to adult depression,

that occurred in children experiencing prolonged separation from their mothers. This specific childhood depression syndrome included slowed development and such symptomatic behavior as weepiness, sadness, immobility, and apathy. Recent research has confirmed that depression in children and adolescents occurs with alarming frequency. Estimates of the frequency of depressive symptoms in children have ranged from 13 percent (Kashani et al., 1982) to 23 percent (Kashani, Venzke, & Millar, 1981). Lefkowitz and Tesiny (1985), in a large-scale study of "normal" children in an elementary school system, found the overall prevalence rate of depressive symptoms to be 5.2 percent. A marked rise in depressive symptoms occurs during teenage years (Fleming, Offord, & Boyle, 1989; Peterson et al., 1993). Lewinsohn and colleagues (1993) surveyed 1710 high school students and reported that point prevalence (the rate at the time of the assessment) was 2.9 percent and that lifetime prevalence was 20.4 percent. Depression occurs at about twice the rate for adolescent girls as for adolescent boys. Lewinsohn and colleagues (1993) also reported that 7.1 percent of the adolescents surveyed reported having attempted suicide in the past and, in a more recent epidemiological study, Lewinsohn, Rohde, and Seeley (1994) pointed out that 1.7 percent of adolescents between 14 and 18 had made a suicide attempt.

The Clinical Picture in Childhood Depression Childhood depression has been recognized as a diagnostic problem by a number of investigators (Herzog & Rathbun, 1982; Kashani et al., 1981b; Ryan et al., 1987). It includes behaviors such as withdrawal, crying, avoidance of eye contact, physical complaints, poor appetite, even aggressive behavior, and in some cases suicide (Rao et al., 1993).

Currently, childhood depression is classified using the mood disorder categories in the DSM-IV adult diagnostic system. This use of adult diagnostic depressive categories with children is considered to be appropriate by many. Lobovits and Handel (1985), for example, found that adult diagnostic categories could reliably be used with children. They conclude that the use of adult diagnostic criteria with children "offers a useful starting point for untangling the confusion surrounding the diagnosis and prevalence rate of childhood disorder" (p. 52).

Causal Factors in Childhood Depression The causal factors described in the childhood anxiety disorders are pertinent to the depressive disorders as well.

Biological Factors. Research on affective disorders has focused attention upon a possible genetic component in child and adolescent depression. Clearly,

Family Therapy and Play Therapy with Children

For a number of reasons, therapeutic intervention with children experiencing psychological problems is often a more complicated process than providing psychotherapy for adults. First, the source of a child's problem and the means for changing are often not within the child's power but instead are imbedded in the context of complex family interaction patterns. To remedy the child's problems, it is often necessary to alter those pathological family interaction patterns that produce or maintain the child's behavior. Second, even if the child's problems are viewed as primary and in need of specific therapeutic intervention, he or she may not be motivated for therapy or sufficiently verbal to gain understanding through psychotherapeutic methods that work with adults. Consequently, effective psychological treatment with children may involve using more indirect methods, such as treating an entire family in family therapy or providing individual psychological therapy for children in a less intrusive and more familiar way—through play in play therapy. We will examine these two approaches in more detail.

Family Therapy

Several family therapy approaches have been developed (Minuchin, 1974; Patterson et al., 1992). These differ in some important ways, for example, in terms of how the family is defined (whether to include extended family members); what the treatment process will focus on (for example, whether communications between the family members or the "aberrant behavior" of the problem family members is the focus); what procedures are used in treatment (for example, analyzing and interpreting hidden messages in the family communications or altering the reward and punishment contingencies through behavioral assessment and reinforcement). Regardless of their differences, all family therapies view a child's problems, at least in part, as an outgrowth of pathological interaction patterns within the family, and they attempt to bring about positive change in family

members through analysis and modification of the deviant family patterns.

How effective is family therapy at improving disruptive family relationships and promoting a more positive atmosphere for children? Hazelrigg, Cooper, and Borduin (1987), after comparing the research to date on family therapy, concluded that family therapy had positive effects when contrasted with no-treatment control samples or with alternative treatment approaches, such as individual therapy. In a recent meta-analytic study that included the results of 163 treatment trials, Shadish and colleagues (1993) found that the average therapy client was better off at termination than 70 percent of the clients in nontreatment conditions. They concluded that treatment outcome research strongly supported the effectiveness of family therapy.

Play Therapy

As a treatment technique, play therapy emerged out of efforts to apply psychodynamic therapy to children. A number of factors limit the application of traditional psychodynamic therapy methods to children. Children do not voluntarily seek treatment and their motivation for self-change is different than for many troubled adults. They tend to be oriented to the present and lack the capability for insight and self-scrutiny that therapy requires. Their perceptions of their therapist differ from those of adult patients, and they may have an unrealistic view that the therapist can magically change their environment (Wenar, 1990).

Through their play, children often express their feelings, fears, and emotions in a direct and uncensored fashion, providing a clinician with a considerable means of understanding a child's problems and feelings. The activity of play has become a valuable source of obtaining personality and problem information about children. Psychodynamic techniques have been adapted for children by using play activity (in lieu of free association, used with adults) to enable a therapist to in-

fer emotional conflicts, inappropriate affects, and excessive emotions a child might be experiencing. Play therapy sessions are usually centered on doll or puppet play to give a child a vehicle for expressing feelings. Other activities, particularly construction with different materials, such as play dough, crayons, and paper, are also used to encourage free expression.

In a play therapy session, the therapist usually needs to provide some structure or to guide play activities so that the child can express pertinent feelings. This might mean that the therapist asks direct questions of the child during the play session, such as: "Is the doll happy now?" or "What makes the doll cry?"

In addition to using play activity as a means of understanding a troubled child's problems, it also provides a medium for bringing about change in the child's behavior. A central process in play therapy is that the therapist, through interpretation, providing emotional support, and clarification of feelings (often by labeling them for the child), provides the child with a corrective emotional experience. That is, the therapist provides the child with an accepting and trusting relationship that promotes healthier personality and relationship development. The play therapy situation enables the child to reexperience conflict or problems in the safety of the therapy room, thereby providing a chance to conquer fears, to acclimate to necessary life changes, or to gain a feeling of security to replace the anxiety and uncertainty that had troubled him or her.

How effective is play therapy in reducing a child's problems and promoting better adjustment? When compared with adult treatment studies, play therapy compares quite favorably. Casey and Berman (1985) conducted a careful study of treatment research with children and concluded that such treatment "appears to match the efficacy of psychotherapy with adults" (p. 395). Play therapy was found to be as effective as other types of treatment, such as behavior therapy.

there appears to be an association between parental depression and behavioral and mood problems in children. Mufson, Weissman, and Warner (1992) found that children of parents with major depression were more impaired, received more psychological treatment, and had more psychological diagnoses than children of parents with no psychological disorders. The suicide attempt rate is higher for children of depressed parents (7.8 percent) than for the offspring of control parents (Weissman et al., 1992).

Learning Factors. Maladaptive learning appears to be important in childhood depressive disorders (Kaslow, Deering, & Racusin, 1994). Children who are exposed to negative parental behavior or negative emotional states may develop depressed affect themselves.

One important area of recent research is focusing on the mother-child interaction in the transmission of depressed affect. Specifically, investigators have been evaluating the possibility that mothers who are depressed, through their interactions with their infants, transfer their low mood to them. Depression among mothers is not uncommon and can result from several sources. Of course, many women who are clinically depressed have children. Some women, however, become depressed during pregnancy or following the delivery of their child. Several investigators have reported that marital distress, delivery complications, and difficulties with the infant are associated with depression in the mothers (Campbell et al., 1990; Sameroff, Seifer, & Zax, 1982).

Extensive research supports the view that the patterns of mother-infant behavior are critical to the development of attachment in a child (Egeland & Farber, 1984). Negative (depressed) affect and constricted mood on the part of a mother, manifested in unresponsive facial expressions and irritable behavior, can produce similar responses in her infant (Cohn & Tronick, 1983; Tronick & Cohn, 1989). Cohn and Campbell (in press) have shown that "infants respond in specific and characteristic ways to depressed maternal affect, and that these effects carry over to situations in which mothers no longer behave in a depressed way."

Cohn and colleagues (Cohn & Campbell, in press) have shown that when mothers interact with their depressed infants the children respond by turning away from them. Even nondepressed mothers, when trained to simulate a constricted-depressed interaction with their child, produce similar learned coping responses. Moreover, these infant coping responses persist even after the mother has stopped interacting with a "depressive" interaction style (Cohn & Tronick, 1983).

The extent to which an infant's negative response to a mother's depressed, constricted mood results in later childhood depression has not been fully determined. This research is highly suggestive, however, and may eventually lead to a fuller understanding of the possible link between a mother's mood and her child's behavior.

Another important line of research in childhood depression involves the cognitive-behavioral perspective. Considerable evidence has accumulated that "depressive symptoms are positively correlated with the tendency to attribute positive events to external, specific, and unstable causes and negative events to internal, global, and stable causes" (Garber & Hilsman, 1992; Hinshaw, 1992). For example, the child may learn to attribute peer rejection or teasing to a mistaken belief that he or she has some internal flaw. Hinshaw (1993) considers the tendency to develop distorted "mental representations" an important cause of disorders such as depression and conduct disorder.

Treatments and Outcomes The view that childhood and adolescent depression is like in kind to adult depression (Ryan et al., 1987) has prompted researchers to treat these mood disorders with medications such as imipramine and desimpramine that have worked with adult depression (Puig-Antich et al., 1985). The results, however, have not been very encouraging (Peterson et al., 1993; Ryan, 1992) in that some studies have failed to show antidepressant medication to be more effective than a placebo (Puig-Antich et al., 1985). Ambrosini and colleagues (1993), in their extensive evaluation of antidepressant medication treatment for children and adolescents, concluded that clinicians should not assume that children and adolescents will respond as adults to antidepressants.

More troublesome, however, are the undesirable side effects (i.e., nausea, headaches, nervousness, insomnia, and even seizures) that have been found to accompany use of antidepressant drugs with children and adolescents. Several accidental deaths have been reported for antidepressant medication; for example, the Medical Letter (1990) recently reported three deaths in children treated with normal dosages of desimpramine.

When depressed children and adolescents receive psychotherapy, treatment generally follows the model used with children suffering from anxiety disorders. An important facet of psychological therapy with children is providing a supportive emotional environment for them to learn more adaptive coping strategies and effective emotional expression. Older children and adolescents can often benefit from a positive therapeutic relationship in which they can discuss their feelings openly. Younger children or those with less developed verbal skills may benefit from play therapy. Controlled studies of psychological treatment with depressed adolescents have shown significantly reduced symptoms with psychological therapy (Kahn et al., 1990; Lewinsohn et al., 1990). Rawson and Tabb (1993) showed that short-term residential treatment was effective with depressed children ages 8–14 years of age.

An important aspect in the treatment of depression in young people is the necessity of a suicide appraisal (Berman & Jobes, 1991), as illustrated by the following case:

Jack was admitted to a child psychiatric hospital unit after he attempted to stab himself in the stomach with a medium sized kitchen knife. The suicide attempt was foiled by his mother, who pulled the knife away from her son. This suicide attempt occurred immediately after Jack had an argument with his father. Jack felt that his "father hates me" and that "I would be better off dead." A variety of factors made Jack vulnerable to suicidal tendencies. Jack grew up in an atmosphere in which there was intense disagreement between his parents. His father drank heavily and when drunk would physically assault his mother. Jack's mother was chronically depressed and often said that "life is not worth living." However, she loved her son and felt that because he needed her, she must continue to work and manage the home. Jack has a serious learning disability, and he struggled to maintain his school grades. He had a private tutor who helped him overcome his sad feelings and shame. Often, when teased by his classmates, he thought about ending his life. (Pfeffer, 1985, pp. 218–19)

Depressed mood has come to be viewed as an important risk factor in suicide among children and adolescents (Posener, Le Haye, & Cheifetz, 1989; Rubenstein et al., 1989; Slap et al., 1989; Velez & Cohen, 1987). In fact, over 5000 American adolescents kill themselves each year (Youth Suicide in the United States, 1986), and suicide has tripled for individuals between the ages of 15 and 24 during the 1980s (Blumenthal, 1990). Children who attempt suicide are at greater risk for subsequent suicidal

episodes than nonattempters, particularly within the first two years after their initial attempt (Pfeffer et al., 1994).

Other Symptom Disorders

The behavior disorders we will deal with in this section—elimination disorders (enuresis and encopresis), sleepwalking, and tics—typically involve a single outstanding symptom rather than a pervasive maladaptive pattern.

Functional Enuresis The term **enuresis** refers to the habitual involuntary discharge of urine, usually at night, after the age of expected continence (age five). In DSM-IV, functional enuresis refers to bedwetting that is not organically caused. Children who have primary functional enuresis have never been continent; children who have secondary functional enuresis have been continent for at least a year, but have regressed.

Enuresis may vary in frequency, from nightly occurrence to occasional instances when a child is under considerable stress or is unduly tired. It has been estimated that some 4–5 million children and adolescents in the United States suffer from the inconvenience and embarrassment of this disorder. Estimates of the prevalence of enuresis reported in DSM-IV are 7 percent for boys and 3 percent for girls at age five; 3 percent for boys and 2 percent for girls at age ten; and 1 percent for boys and almost nonexistent for girls at age eighteen. Research has shown that there are clear sex differences in enuresis as well as age differences. In one extensive epidemiological study of enuresis in Holland, Verhulst and colleagues (1985) determined that between the ages of five and eight, enuresis is about two to three times more common among boys than among girls. The percentages for boys also diminish at a slower rate; the decline for girls between ages four and six is about 71 percent, while the decline for boys is only 16 percent. The authors recommend that the age criteria for boys' enuresis be extended to age eight because it is at about age nine that approximately the same percentage of boys as girls reach "dryness," that is, wetting the bed less than once a month.

Enuresis may result from a variety of organic conditions, such as disturbed cerebral control of the bladder (Kaada & Retvedt, 1981), neurological dysfunction (Lunsing et al., 1991), or other medical factors such as small functional bladder capacity and weak urethral spinchter (Dahl, 1992). One group of researchers reported that 11 percent of their enuretic patients had disorders of the urinary tract (Watanabe et al., 1994). However, most investigators have pointed to a number of other possible causal factors: (a) faulty learning, resulting in the failure to acquire a needed adaptive response—that is, inhibition of reflex bladder emptying; (b) personal immaturity, associated with or stemming from emotional problems; (c) disturbed family interactions, particularly those that lead to sustained anxiety, hostility, or both; and (d) stressful events (Haug Schnabel, 1992). For example, a child may regress to bedwetting when a new baby enters the family and becomes the center of attention. In adolescence, enuresis is often associated with other psychological problems. Research evidence supports a multiplicity of possible causes for enuresis, with many cases being explained by either environmental factors or maturational lags (Christie, 1981; Houts, 1991).

Medical treatment of enuresis typically centers on using medications, such as imipramine, in which the mechanism underlying the action of the drug is unclear but it may simply decrease the deepest stages of sleep to light sleep enabling the child to recognize bodily needs more effectively (Dahl, 1992). More recently, an intranasal desmopressin (DDAVP) has been used to help children "manage" urine more effectively. DDAVP, a hormone replacement, apparently "increases urine concentration, decreases urine volume, and decreases enuretic events" (Dahl, 1992). The use of medication to treat enuretic children is no panacea—the drugs appear to be effective only with a subset of enuretic children and then only temporarily. Dahl (1992) cautions that medications by themselves do not cure enuresis and that there is frequent relapse when the drug is discontinued or the child habituates to the medication.

Conditioning procedures have proved to be the most effective treatment of enuresis (Frimen & Warzak, 1990). Mowrer and Mowrer (1938) introduced a procedure in which a child may sleep on a pad that is wired to a battery-operated bell. At the first few drops of urine, the bell is set off, thus awakening the child. Through conditioning, the child comes to associate bladder tension with awakening. Fortunately, with or without treatment, the incidence of enuresis tends to decrease significantly with age. Nevertheless, many experts believe that enuresis should be treated in childhood because no way currently exists to identify which children will remain enuretic into adulthood. In a recent comparison and evaluation of research on the treatment of bedwetting, Houts, Berman, and Abramson (1994) concluded that treated children were more improved at follow-up than nontreated children. They also found that psychological treatment was more effective in reducing bedwetting than were physical treatments.

Functional Encopresis The term **encopresis** describes children who have not learned appropriate toileting for bowel movements after age four. This condition is less common than enuresis. However, about 2.3 percent of eight-year-old boys and 0.7 percent of eight-year-old girls are encopretic (Bellman, 1966). The following list of characteristics was provided by Levine (1976) from a study of 102 cases of encopretic children: The average age was seven, with a range from ages four to thirteen; about one-third of encopretic children were also enuretic; and a large sex difference was found, with about six times more boys than girls in the sample. Many of the children soiled their clothing when they were under stress. A common time was in the late afternoon after school; few children actually had this problem at school. Most of the children reported that they did not know when they needed to have a bowel movement.

Many encopretic children suffer from constipation; thus an important element in the diagnosis of the disorder involves a physical examination to determine whether physiological factors are contributing to the disorder. The treatment of encopresis usually involves both medical and psychological aspects (Dawson, Griffith, & Boeke, 1990). Levine and Bakow (1975) found that, of the encopretic children they studied who were treated by medical and behavioral procedures, more than half were cured—that is, no additional incidents occurred within six months following treatment. An additional 25 percent were improved.

Sleepwalking (Somnambulism) Though the onset of sleepwalking disorder is usually between the ages of 6 and 12, the disorder is classified broadly under sleep disorders in DSM-IV rather than under disorders of infancy, childhood, and adolescence. The symptoms of **sleepwalking disorder** involve repeated episodes in which a person leaves his or her bed and walks around without being conscious of the experience or remembering it later.

Statistics are meager, but one epidemiological study in Sweden reported that 40 percent of a random sample of children experienced sleepwalking episodes (Klackenberg, 1987). Children subject to this problem usually go to sleep in a normal manner but arise during the second or third hour of sleep. They may walk to another room of the house or even outside, and they may engage in complex activities. Finally they return to bed and in the morning remember nothing that has taken place.

While moving about, sleepwalkers' eyes are partially or fully open; they avoid obstacles, listen when spoken to, and ordinarily respond to commands, such as to return to bed. Shaking them will usually awaken sleepwalkers, and they will be surprised and perplexed at finding themselves in an unexpected place. Sleepwalking episodes usually last from 15 to 30 minutes. The risk of injury during sleepwalking is illustrated by the following case study:

14-year-old Donald Elliot got up from his bunk in his sleep, looked in the refrigerator, then, still asleep, walked out the back door. It would have been just another sleepwalking episode except that Donald was in a camper-pickup truck traveling 50 miles an hour on the San Diego freeway. Miraculously, he escaped with cuts and bruises. But his experience, and that of many other sleepwalkers, disproves one of the myths about somnambulism: that people who walk in their sleep don't hurt themselves. (Taves, 1969, p. 41)

The causes of sleepwalking are not fully understood. Kales and associates (1966) have shown that sleepwalking takes place during NREM (non–rapid eye movement) sleep. It appears to be related to some anxiety-arousing situation that has just occurred or is expected to occur in the near future (Klackenberg, 1987).

Little attention has been given to the treatment of sleepwalking. Clement (1970), however, has reported on the treatment of a seven-year-old boy through behavior therapy, as described in HIGHLIGHT 14.5. Nagaraja (1974) has reported the successful treatment of an eight-year-old boy and a nine-year-old girl with a combination of tranquilizers and psychotherapy. Nevertheless, a good deal of additional research is needed before we can deter-

---

HIGHLIGHT 14.5

The Treatment of Sleepwalking Utilizing Conditioning Procedures

Bobby, a 7-year-old boy, walked in his sleep an average of four times a week. His mother kept a record indicating that Bobby's sleepwalking episodes were associated with nightmares, perspiring, and talking in his sleep. During the actual sleepwalking, Bobby usually was glassy-eyed and unsteady on his feet. On one occasion, he started out the front door. The sleepwalking had commenced about six weeks before the boy was brought for therapy. Usually an episode would begin about 45 to 90 minutes after he had gone to bed.

During treatment, the therapist learned that just before each sleepwalking episode Bobby usually had a nightmare about being chased by "a big black bug." In his dream, Bobby thought "the bug would eat off his legs if it caught him" (Clement, 1970, p.

23). Bobby's sleepwalking episodes usually showed the following sequence: After his nightmare began, he perspired freely, moaned and talked in his sleep, tossed and turned, and finally got up and walked through the house. He did not remember the sleepwalking episode when he awoke the next morning.

Assessment data revealed no neurological or other medical problems and indicated that Bobby was of normal intelligence. He was, however, found to be "a very anxious, guilt-ridden little boy who avoided performing assertive and aggressive behaviors appropriate to his age and sex" (p. 23). Assertiveness training and related measures were used but were not effective. The therapist then focused treatment on having Bobby's mother awaken the boy

each time he showed signs of an impending episode. After washing Bobby's face with cold water and making sure he was fully awake, the mother would return him to bed, where he was "to hit and tear up a picture of the big black bug." (At the start of the treatment program, Bobby had made up several of these drawings.)

Eventually, the nightmare was associated with awakening, and Bobby learned to wake up on most occasions when he was having a bad dream. Clement considered the basic behavior therapy model in this case to follow that used in the conditioning treatment for enuresis, where a waking response is elicited by an intense stimulus just as urination is beginning and becomes associated with, and eventually prevents, nocturnal bedwetting.

mine the most effective treatment procedures for sleepwalking.

Tics A **tic** is a persistent, intermittent muscle twitch or spasm, usually limited to a localized muscle group. The term is used broadly to include blinking the eye, twitching the mouth, licking the lips, shrugging the shoulders, twisting the neck, clearing the throat, blowing the nose, and grimacing, among other actions. Tics occur most frequently between the ages of 6 and 14 (Schowalter, 1980). In some instances, as in clearing the throat, an individual may be aware of the tic when it occurs; but usually he or she performs the act habitually and does not notice it. In fact, many individuals do not even realize they have a tic unless someone brings it to their attention. The psychological impact tics can have on an adolescent is exemplified in the following case:

> An adolescent who had wanted very much to be a teacher told the school counselor that he was thinking of giving up his plans. When asked the reason, he explained that several friends had told him that he had a persistent twitching of the mouth muscles when he answered questions in class. He had been unaware of this muscle twitch and even after being told about it could not tell when it took place. However, he became acutely self-conscious and was reluctant to answer questions or enter into class discussions. As a result, his general level of tension increased, and so did the frequency of the tic, which now became apparent even when he was talking to his friends. Thus a vicious circle had been established. Fortunately, it proved amenable to treatment by conditioning and assertiveness training.

An extreme tic disorder involving multiple motor and vocal patterns is **Tourette's syndrome.** This disorder typically involves uncontrollable head movements with accompanying sounds, such as grunts, clicks, yelps, sniffs, or words. About one-third of individuals with Tourette's syndrome manifest *coprolalia,* which is a complex vocal tic involving the uttering of obscenities. The average age of onset for Tourette's syndrome is age 7, and most cases have an onset before age 14. The disorder is about three times more frequent among males. Although the exact cause of Tourette's syndrome is undeter-

mined, evidence suggests an organic basis for the syndrome.

Most tics, however, do not have an organic basis but usually stem from psychological causes, such as self-consciousness or tension in social situations. As in the case of the adolescent boy previously described, an individual's awareness of the tic often increases the tension—and the tic. Tics have been successfully treated by means of drugs, psychotherapy, and conditioning techniques. Ollendick (1981) reported success in treating tics by using behavioral techniques of self-monitoring and overcorrection.

PERVASIVE DEVELOPMENTAL DISORDER: AUTISM

We next turn our attention to one of the most puzzling and disabling disorders of childhood—**autism,** a developmental disorder that involves a wide range of problematic behaviors, including deficits in language, perceptual, and motor development; defective reality testing; and an inability to function in social situations. The following case illustrates some of the behaviors that may be seen in an autistic child:

> The boy is five years old. When spoken to, he turns his head away. Sometimes he mumbles unintelligibly. He is neither toilet trained nor able to feed himself. He actively resists being touched. He dislikes sounds and is uncommunicative. He cannot relate to others and avoids looking anyone in the eye. He often engages in routine manipulative activities, such as dropping an object, picking it up, and dropping it again. He shows a pathological need for sameness. While seated, he often rocks back and forth in a rhythmic motion for hours. Any change in routine is highly upsetting to him.

Autism in infancy and childhood was first described by Kanner (1943). It afflicts some 80,000 American children—about 4 children in 10,000—and occurs about four or five times more frequently among boys than girls (Ritvo et al., 1989; Schreibman & Koegel, 1975; Steffenburg & Gillberg, 1986; Werry, 1979). A recent epidemiological study of four regions of France reported similar rates, 4.9

per 10,000, with boys about two to one (Fombonne & du Mazaubrun, 1992). It is usually identified before a child is 30 months of age and may be suspected in the early weeks of life. Autistic children come from all socioeconomic levels, ethnic backgrounds, and family patterns. It was once believed that autism was more prevalent among families in upper-socioeconomic levels; however, this finding may have been due to the particular sampling methods used in earlier studies (Wing, 1980). A recent epidemiological survey (Ritvo et al., 1989) has supported the view that autism is not associated with parental education, occupation, racial origin, or religion.

The Clinical Picture in Autistic Disorder

Autistic children form a heterogeneous population, with varying degrees of impairments and capabilities. In this section we will discuss some of the behaviors that may be evident in autism. A cardinal and typical sign is that a child seems apart or aloof from others, even in the earliest stages of life (Adrien et al., 1992). Mothers often remember such babies as never being "cuddly," never reaching out when being picked up, never smiling or looking at them while being fed, and never appearing to notice the comings and goings of other people. Typically, autistic children do not show any need for affection or contact with anyone, usually not even seeming to know or care who their parents are. Several recent studies, however, have questioned this view that autistic children are emotionally "flat." These studies (Capps et al., 1993; Sigman et al., 1992) have shown that autistic children do express emotions and should not be considered as having an apparent lack of emotional reaction as noted in traditional descriptions of the disorder.

The absence or severely restricted use of speech is characteristic of autistic children. Autistic children have been considered to have an "imitative deficit" and do not effectively learn by imitation (Smith & Bryson, 1994). This dysfunction might explain the characteristic absence or limited use of speech by autistic children. If speech is present, it is almost never used to communicate except in the most rudimentary fashion, as by saying "yes" in answer to a question or by the use of **echolalia** (parrot-like repetition of a few words). Although the echoing of parents' verbal behavior is found to a small degree in normal children as they experiment with their ability to produce articulate speech, persistent echolalia is found in about 75 percent of autistic children (Prizant, 1983). Some research has focused on try-

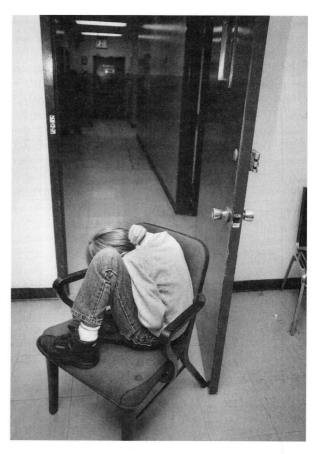

Extreme withdrawal from others is typical of autistic children.

ing to understand if echolalia in autistic children is functional. Prizant and Duchan (1981) analyzed echolalic verbalizations—previously believed to be meaningless—according to tone, latency, and other speech characteristics. They concluded that, far from being meaningless, these verbalizations could help clinicians or researchers understand the communicative and cognitive functioning of autistic children. Nevertheless, these utterances remain highly cryptic and are, of course, an inadequate substitute for true language functioning.

The usual picture of an autistic child as lacking in language ability and being wholly withdrawn is probably oversimplified. Researchers have found that autistic children vary considerably in language skill and at least some autistic children do comprehend language, even though they may not use it to express themselves as other children do (Wetherby & Prizant, 1992).

Autistic children seem to actively arrange the environment on their own terms in an effort to exclude or limit variety and intervention from other people, preferring instead a limited and solitary routine. Autistic children often show an active aversion to auditory stimuli, crying even at the sound of a parent's voice. The pattern is not always consistent, however; autistic children "may at one moment be severely agitated or panicked by a very soft sound and at another time be totally oblivious to loud noise" (Ritvo & Ornitz, 1970, p. 6).

Self-stimulation is often characteristic of these children, usually taking the form of such repetitive movements as head banging, spinning, and rocking, which may continue by the hour. Other bizarre as well as repetitive behaviors are typical. Such behavior is well described by Gajzago and Prior (1974) in the case of a young autistic boy:

> A was described as a screaming, severely disturbed child who ran around in circles making high-pitched sounds for hours. He also liked to sit in boxes, under mats, and [under] blankets. He habitually piled up all furniture and bedding in the center of the room. At times he was thought deaf—though he also showed extreme fear of loud noises. He refused all food except in a bottle, refused to wear clothes, chewed stones and paper, whirled himself, and spun objects. . . . He played repetitively with the same toys for months, lining things in rows, collected objects such as bottle tops, and insisted on having two of everything, one in each hand. He became extremely upset if interrupted and if the order or arrangement of things were altered. (p. 264)

In contrast to the behavior just described, some autistic children are skilled at fitting objects together. Thus their performance on puzzles or form boards may be average or above. Even in the manipulation of objects, however, difficulty with meaning is apparent. For example, when pictures are to be arranged in an order that tells a story, autistic children show a marked deficiency in performance.

Although some have regarded autistic children as potentially of normal intelligence, this view has been challenged by a number of investigators who consider most of these children to be mentally retarded (American Psychological Association, 1994). Prior and Wherry (1986) reported that about three-fourths of autistic children were mentally retarded. Some autistic children, however, show markedly discrepant abilities, such as astounding memory capabilities, as Dustin Hoffman depicted in the movie *Rain*

Man. In this context, Goodman (1972) described the case of an "autistic-savant" who showed unusual ability at an early age in calendar calculating (rapidly determining the day of any calendar date in history) as well as in other areas, such as naming the capitals of most states and countries and rapid calculation that allowed him to win a lot of money in Las Vegas. Nevertheless, his language development was severely retarded, and he showed the indifference to others and related symptoms characteristic of autistic children.

Much has been learned recently about the cognitive deficits of autistic children (Wenar, 1990). Compared with other groups of children on cognitive or intellectual tasks, autistic children often show impairment (James & Barry, 1981; Ritvo & Freeman, 1978; Schopler, 1983). Boucher (1981), for example, found autistic children significantly impaired on memory tasks when compared with both normal and retarded children. Whether this cognitive impairment is the result of actual organic brain damage or of motivational deficits has not been established. Koegel and Mentis (1985) have raised the possibility that the deficits result from motivational differences; they found that autistic children can learn and perform tasks at a higher level if motivation for a task is found and appropriate reinforcement is provided.

Many autistic children become preoccupied with and form strong attachments to unusual objects, such as rocks, light switches, film negatives, or keys. In some instances the object is so large or bizarre that merely carrying it around interferes with other activities. When their preoccupation with the object is disturbed—for example, by its removal or by attempts to substitute something in its place—or when anything familiar in their environment is altered even slightly, they may have a violent temper tantrum or a crying spell that continues until the familiar situation is restored. Thus autistic children are often said to be "obsessed with the maintenance of sameness." Furthermore, autistic children have been referred to as "negativistic" because they seemingly do not comply with requests. However, this observation has been questioned in a study by Volkmar, Hoder, and Cohen (1985). They found that, under the carefully structured and reinforcing conditions in a clinic setting, autistic children were not negativistic and generally complied with requests made by staff.

In summary, autistic children typically show difficulties in relationships to other people, in perceptual-cognitive functioning, in language development, and in the development of a sense of identity (L. K. Wing, 1976). They also engage in bizarre and repetitive activities, demonstrate a fascination with unusual objects, and show an obsessive need to maintain environmental sameness. This is indeed a heavy set of handicaps.

Causal Factors in Autism

The precise cause or causes of autism are unknown. However, evidence has accumulated that defective genes or damage from radiation or other conditions during prenatal development may play a significant role in the etiologic picture (Abramson et al., 1992; Rutter, 1991b; Smalley, 1991). Evidence for a genetic contribution to autism comes from examining the risk for autism in the siblings of autistic children. The best estimates are that families with one autistic child show a 3–5 percent risk of a sibling being autistic as well. Although this figure may seem low in an absolute sense, it is in fact extremely high given that the population frequency of autism is approximately 5 in 10,000 (Smalley, 1991). Twin studies have also consistently shown higher concordance rates among monozygotic than among dizygotic twins, although all such studies are limited by small sample sizes given the extreme rarity of the disorder. Nevertheless, the conclusion from family and twin studies is that 80–90 percent of the variance in risk for autism is based on genetic factors, making it probably the most heritable of the various forms of psychopathology discussed in this text (Rutter, 1991b; Smalley, 1991). Nevertheless, the exact mode of genetic transmission is not yet understood, and it seems likely that relatives may also show an increased risk for other cognitive and social deficits that are milder in form than true autism (Smalley, 1991). In other words, there may be a spectrum of disorders related to autism.

It seems likely at this point that the disorder we call autism involves both multiple kinds of deficit (Goodman, 1989) and multiple etiologic pathways (Gillberg, 1990). Thus we should perhaps not expect to find large risk factors accounting for all autistic outcomes, nor even exceptional levels of consistency from one study to another where differing samples of autistic youngsters have been evaluated. Some investigators have pointed to the existence of a possible genetic defect—a fragile site on the X chromosome, referred to as the "fragile X syndrome" (Brown et al., 1986; Tsai & Ghaziuddin, 1992) that may occur in about 8 percent of autistic males (Smalley, 1991). In addition, 15–20 percent of males with the fragile X syndrome are also diagnosed with autism, further suggesting a link between the two syndromes. Nevertheless, there also appear to be differences between autism and the

fragile X syndrome, suggesting that there are some qualitative differences between the two syndromes (Smalley, 1991). Even subtler constitutional defects may also exist in autism. Most investigators believe that autism begins with some type of inborn defect that impairs an infant's perceptual-cognitive functioning—the ability to process incoming stimuli and to relate to the world.

Sociocultural factors have also been postulated as causal elements in autism. In his early studies of childhood autism, Kanner (1943) concluded that an innate disorder in a child is exacerbated by a cold and unresponsive mother, the first factor resulting in social withdrawal and the second tending to maintain this isolation. Most investigators, however, have failed to find the parents of autistic children to be "emotional refrigerators" (Schreibman & Koegel, 1975; Wolff & Morris, 1971).

Clearly, much remains to be learned about the etiology of childhood autism. It appears most reasonable to suppose, however, that this disorder normally begins with an inborn defect or defects in brain functioning, regardless of what other causal factors may subsequently become involved.

Treatments and Outcomes

Medical treatment of autistic children has often been tried but has not proven effective (Rutter, 1985). The drug most often used in the treatment of autism is haloperidol (Haldol) (Campbell, 1987), but the data on its effectiveness do not warrant use unless a child's behavior is unmanageable by other means (Sloman, 1991). Recently, the drug clonidine, an antihypertensive medication, has been used with reportedly moderate effects at reducing the severity of the symptoms (Fankhauser et al., 1992). However, no currently available medication reduces the symptoms of autism enough to encourage general use. We will thus direct our attention to a variety of psychological procedures that have been more successful in treating autistic children.

In an extensive study of autistic children who were mentally retarded, socially unresponsive, and behaviorally disturbed, Bartak and colleagues at the Maudsley Hospital in England obtained significant results with educational procedures. Children who were assigned to a structured treatment unit focusing on formal schooling showed greater progress than those placed in units stressing play therapy, either free or structured (Bartak & Rutter, 1973; Russell, 1975). As a result of this work, Bartak (1978) suggested a "qualified optimism" for the educational progress of autistic children. The best predictor of a positive outcome in the treatment of autism, according to Bartak and Rutter (1976), is intelligence.

Behavior therapy in an institutional setting has been used successfully in the elimination of self-injurious behavior, the mastery of the fundamentals of social behavior, and the development of some language skills (Lovaas, 1977; Powers, 1992; Williams, Koegel, & Egel, 1981). Lovaas (1987) reported highly positive results from a long-term experimental treatment program of autistic children. Of the treated children, 47 percent achieved normal intellectual functioning and another 40 percent attained the mildly retarded level. In comparison, only 2 percent of the untreated, control children achieved normal functioning and 45 percent attained mildly retarded functioning. These remarkable results did, however, require a considerable staffing effort, with well-qualified therapists working each child at least 40 hours per week for two years. Interestingly, studies on the effectiveness of behavior therapy with institutionalized children have found that children who were discharged to their parents continued to improve, whereas those who remained in an institution tended to lose much of what they had gained (Lovaas, 1977). Recently, Kamps and colleagues (1992) and Koegel and colleagues (1992) reported positive effects in programs designed to teach autistic children to imitate social interactions.

Some of the most impressive results with autistic children have been obtained in projects that involve parents, with treatment in the home preferable to hospital-based therapy (Rutter, 1985; Schopler, Mesibov, & Baker, 1982). Treatment "contracts" with parents specify the desired behavior changes in their child and spell out the explicit techniques for bringing about these changes. Such contracting acknowledges the value of the parents as potential change agents—in contrast with the previously held belief that the parents were somehow to blame for their child's disorder (Schopler, 1978). Perhaps the most favorable results are those of Schreibman and Koegel (1975), who reported successful outcomes in the treatment of 10 of 16 autistic children. These investigators relied heavily on the use of parents as therapists to reinforce normal behavior in their children. They concluded that autism is potentially a "defeatable horror."

It is too early to evaluate the long-term effectiveness of these newer treatment methods or the degree of improvement they actually bring about. The prognosis for autistic children, particularly for children showing symptoms before the age of two, is poor (Hoshino et al., 1980). Commonly, the long-term results of autism treatments have been unfavorable. A great deal of attention has been given recently to high-functioning autistic children (children who meet the criteria for autism yet develop functional speech). Ritvo and colleagues (1988) studied 11 parents whom they believed met diagnostic criteria for autism (they were identified through having had children who were autistic). These individuals had been able to make modest adjustments to life, hold down jobs, and get married. The outcome in autism is often problematic, however. Clarke and colleagues (1989) followed up five high-functioning autistic children and found that four of them later developed symptoms of psychosis.

One important factor limiting treatment success is the problems autistic children experience in generalizing behavior outside the treatment context (Handleman, Gill, & Alessandri, 1988). Children with severe developmental disabilities do not transfer skills across situations very well. Consequently, learned behavior in one situation does not appear to help them meet challenges in others. This important component needs to be addressed if training or treatment programs are to be successful. Changes in the law in 1990 with respect to providing services for disabled children (Public Law 101-476) assure equal access to an appropriate education in the least restrictive environment for all children. It is likely that more focus will be placed on integrating school-age children with autism into traditional learning environments.

At our present state of knowledge the long-term prognosis for many autistic children is still guarded. Even with intensive long-term care in a clinical facility, where gratifying improvements may be brought about in specific behaviors, children are a long way from becoming "normal." Gillberg and Schaumann (1981) have noted that some autistic children make substantial improvement during childhood, only to deteriorate, showing symptom aggravation, at the onset of puberty. In spite of a few remarkable cases of dramatic success, the overall prognosis for autistic children remains guarded. Less than one-fourth of the autistic children who receive treatment appear to attain even marginal adjustment in later life.

PLANNING BETTER PROGRAMS TO HELP CHILDREN AND YOUTH

In our discussion of several problems of childhood and adolescence, we have noted the wide range of treatment procedures available, as well as the marked differences in outcomes. In concluding the chapter, we will discuss certain special factors associated with the treatment of children, the problem of child abuse, and the need for child advocacy and the rights of children, to prevent the occurrence of negative conditions that inhibit their optimal development.

Special Factors Associated with Treatment for Children and Adolescents

Mental health treatment, psychotherapy, and behavior therapy have been found to be as effective with children and adolescents as with adults (Casey & Berman, 1985; Kazdin et al., 1990; Weisz et al., 1987; and Weisz, Weiss, & Donenberg, 1992). A number of special factors must be considered in relation to treatment for children and adolescents:

1. *The child's inability to seek assistance.* Most emotionally disturbed children who need assistance are not in a position to ask for it themselves or to transport themselves to and from child treatment clinics. Thus, unlike an adult, who can usually seek help, a child is dependent, primarily on his or her parents. Adults should realize when a child needs professional help and take the initiative in obtaining it. Sometimes, however, adults neglect this responsibility. Plotkin (1981) has pointed out: "Parents have traditionally had the right to consent to health services for their children. In situations where the interest of the parents and children differ the rule has

had unfortunate consequences and has left treatment professionals in a quandary" (p. 121).

The law identifies four areas in which treatment without parental consent is permitted: (a) in the case of mature minors (those considered to be capable of making decisions about themselves); (b) in the case of emancipated minors (those living independently—away from their parents); (c) in emergency situations; and (d) in situations in which a court orders treatment. Many children, of course, come to the attention of treatment agencies as a consequence of school referrals, delinquent acts, or parental abuse.

2. *The need to recognize special vulnerabilities that children and youth might experience that place them at great risk for developing emotional problems.* Many families provide an undesirable environment for their growing children. Studies have shown that up to a fourth of American children may be living in inadequate homes. Disruptive childhood experiences have been found to be a risk factor for adult problems. For example, a recent epidemiological study (Susser, Moore, & Link, 1993) reported that 23 percent of newly homeless men in New York city reported a history of out-of-home care as children, and another study by Caudill and colleagues (1994) reported that clients with a parental history of substance abuse were at over twice the risk for antisocial personality disorders.

Children growing up in pathogenic homes are at a double disadvantage. Not only are they deprived from the standpoint of environmental influence on

Family discord is often an important causal element in childhood psychopathology.

their personality development (Crouch & Milner, 1993), but they also lack parents who will perceive their need for help and actively seek and participate in treatment programs. Inadequate or inattentive parenting can result in a failure to recognize serious signs of developing emotional problems.

High-risk behaviors or conditions need to be recognized and taken into consideration (Kazdin, 1992). For example, there are a number of behaviors such as engaging in sexual acts, using alcohol or drugs, or delinquent behavior, that young people might engage in that place them at great risk for developing later emotional problems. Moreover, there are situations that can "happen" to young people, such as physical or sexual abuse, parental divorce, family turbulence, and homelessness, that place young people at great risk for emotional distress and subsequent maladaptive behavior.

3. *The need for treatment of the parents as well as the child.* Because many of the behavior disorders specific to childhood appear to grow out of pathogenic family interactions, it is often essential for the parents, as well as their child, to receive treatment. In some instances, in fact, the treatment program may focus on the parents entirely, as in the case of child abuse.

Increasingly, then, the treatment of children has come to mean family therapy, in which one or both parents, along with the child and siblings, may participate in all phases of the program. Many therapists discover that fathers are particularly difficult to engage in the treatment process. For working parents and for parents who basically reject the affected child, such treatment may be difficult to arrange (Gaudin, 1993), especially in the case of poorer families who lack transportation and money. Thus, both parental and economic factors help determine which emotionally disturbed children will receive assistance.

4. *The possibility of using parents as change agents.* In essence, the parents are trained in techniques that enable them to help their child. Typically, such training focuses on helping the parents understand the child's behavior disorder and learn to reinforce adaptive behavior while withholding reinforcement for undesirable behavior. Encouraging results have been obtained with parents who care about their children and want to help (Atkeson & Forehand, 1978; Forehand, 1993; Lexow & Aronson, 1975; Mash et al., 1976; O'Dell, 1974; Webster-Stratton, 1991).

5. *The problem of placing the child outside the family.* Most communities have juvenile facilities

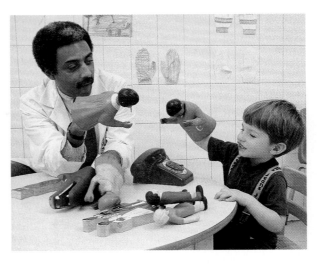

Children can often express their feelings more directly through play than in words, as shown in this play therapy session.

that, day or night, will provide protective care and custody for young victims of unfit homes, abandonment, abuse, neglect, and related conditions. Depending on the home situation and the special needs of the child, he or she will later either be returned to his or her parents or placed elsewhere. In the latter instance, four types of facilities are commonly relied on: foster homes, private institutions for the care of children, county or state institutions, or the homes of relatives. At any one time, over half a million children are living in foster-care facilities.

The quality of a child's new home, of course, is a crucial determinant of whether the child's problems will be alleviated or made worse. Although efforts are made to screen the placement facilities and maintain contact with the situation through follow-up visits, there have been too many reported cases of mistreatment in the new home.

In cases of child abuse, child abandonment, or a serious childhood behavior problem that parents cannot control, it has often been assumed that the only feasible action was to take the child out of the home and find a temporary substitute. With such a child's own home so obviously inadequate, the hope has been that a more stable outside placement would be better. But when children are taken from their homes and placed in an institution (which promptly tries to change them) or in a series of foster homes (where they obviously do not really belong), they are likely to feel rejected by their own parents, unwanted by their new caretakers, rootless, constantly insecure—and lonely and bitter.

Accordingly, the trend today is toward permanent planning. First, every effort is made to hold a family together and to give the parents the support and guidance they need for adequate childrearing. If this is impossible, then efforts are made to free the child legally for adoption and to find an adoptive home as soon as possible. This, of course, means that the public agencies need specially trained staffs with reasonable caseloads and access to resources that they and their clients may need.

6. *The importance of intervening early, before problems become acute.* Over the last 20 years, a primary concern of many researchers and clinicians has been to identify and provide early help for children who are at special risk. Rather than wait until these children develop acute psychological problems that may require therapy or major changes in living arrangements, psychologists are attempting to identify conditions in such children's lives that seem likely to bring about or maintain behavior problems and, where such conditions exist, to intervene before a child's development has been seriously distorted. An example of this approach is provided in the work of Wallerstein and Kelly (1980):

These researchers identified children who were at risk for psychological disturbance as a result of their parents going through a divorce. Each of the 66 participating families was seen by a clinician, and the children were seen separately for several sessions. The goals of the counseling sessions were to provide the children with a means of expressing their worries and frustrations and to strengthen their resources for dealing with them.

In addition to the counseling sessions, there were several follow-up sessions after the divorce to examine the psychological changes in the children and the changes in the family structure over time. The interventions were judged to be successful in lowering the tension levels in the family situations and in enhancing the children's adjustment to their new living arrangements.

Another type of early intervention has been developed in response to the special vulnerability children experience in the wake of disaster such as a hurricane, accident, or trauma such as a hostage-tak-

ing or shooting. Children and adolescents often require considerable support and attention to deal with traumatic events, a circumstance that is all too frequent in today's world. Individual and small-group psychological therapy might be implemented for victims of trauma (Gillis, 1993), support programs might operate thorough school-based interventions (Klingman, 1993), or community-based programs might be implemented, as in the period following the Hurricane Hugo disaster in Charleston, South Carolina (Joyner & Swenson, 1993). All of these efforts are aimed at providing immediate emotional support and problem resolution to reduce the posttraumatic symptoms and prevent the occurrence of long-term maladjustment problems (see the discussion on crisis intervention techniques in Chapter 18).

Such early intervention has the double goal of reducing the stressors in a child's life and strengthening the child's coping mechanisms. If successful, it can effectively reduce the number and intensity of later problems, thus averting problems for both the individuals concerned and the broader society. It is apparent that children's needs can be met only if adequate preventive and treatment facilities for children exist and are available to the children who need assistance. In the next section, we will look at the specific issue of child abuse, which is of growing concern to researchers and practitioners who want to know what causes it and how it can be prevented. In our final section, we will look at the leadership that government agencies have been providing in identifying the special needs of children and youth, and we will also discuss our society's responsibility to meet those needs.

Child Abuse

The human species has a pretty dismal record when it comes to caring for its offspring. As DeMause (1990) pointed out:

The history of humanity is founded upon child assault. All families once practiced infanticide. All states trace their origin to child sacrifice. All religions began with the mutilation and murder of children. All nations sanction the killing, maiming, and starving of children in wars and depressions.... Child assault is, in fact, humanity's most powerful and successful historical group-fantasy. Using children as scapegoats to relieve personal internal conflict has proved an extremely effective way to maintain our collective psychological homeostasis. Those who dare disturb this central group-fantasy run the risk of being declared guilty of impiety and considered disturbers of the world peace. . . . Historically, all cultures that have left records probably practiced widespread infanticide (p. 1–2)

In contemporary society, we deplore the idea that children were commonly mistreated in the past. Society's goals today encompass the ideals of kind and gentle treatment of our children and we collectively believe that the future of our society depends upon the proper care of our young. However, this lofty ideal is clearly not realized, as a growing and troublesome number of cases of child maltreatment makes clear. Child abuse is an increasing concern in the United States (Gelles & Cornell, 1990). A Department of Health and Human Services Report (House of Representatives, 1990) indicated that the numbers of children reported as abused and neglected rose 64 percent from 1980 to 1988, for an astounding total of 2.2 million cases of childhood maltreatment reported in 1988. Some evidence suggests that boys are more often physically abused than girls. It is usually clear that many children brought to the attention of legal agencies for abuse have been abused before (Kempe & Kempe, 1979; President's Commission on Mental Health, 1978).

In a survey of family violence, Gelles (1978) reported that violence well beyond ordinary physical punishment is widespread in parent-child relationships. Milder forms of punishment, Gelles found, were common among respondents; for example, 71 percent of parents reported having slapped or spanked their children, 46 percent reported pushing and shoving incidents, and around 10 percent reported having thrown something at their children. Gelles extrapolated estimates of serious violence from his survey to the general population and concluded that 46 percent of American children had suffered serious abuse, such as being kicked, bitten, or punched by parents.

The seriousness of the child abuse problem in our society was not realized until the 1960s, when researchers began to report case after case like the following two:

The mother of a 29-month-old boy claimed he was a behavior problem, beat him with a stick and screwdriver handle, dropped him on the floor, beat his head on the wall or threw him against it, choked him to force his mouth open to eat, and burned him on the face and hands.

After she had severely beaten him, the mother found the child dead.

Because her 2½-year-old daughter did not respond readily enough to toilet training the mother became indignant and in a fit of temper over the child's inability to control a bowel movement gave her an enema with near scalding water. To save the child's life a doctor was forced to perform a colostomy (Earl, 1965).

Many abused children show impaired cognitive ability and memory when compared with control children (Friedrich, Einbender, & Luecke, 1983). In addition, abused children are likely to show problems in social adjustment and are particularly likely to feel that the outcomes of events are determined by external factors beyond their own control (Kinzl & Biebl, 1992; Toth, Manly, & Cicchetti, 1992). They are also more likely to experience depressive symptoms (Bushnell, Wells, & Oakley-Browne, 1992; Sternberg et al., 1992; Toth et al., 1992). Abused children are dramatically less likely to assume personal responsibility for themselves, and they generally demonstrate less interpersonal sensitivity than control children. Abused children also tend to show more self-destructive behavior than nonabused control subjects (Green, 1978), and physically abused children may be more likely to abuse their own children when they become parents (Malinosky-Rummel & Hansen, 1993). Childhood victimization was also found to be significantly related to the number of lifetime symptoms of antisocial personality disorder and predictive of a diagnosis of antisocial disorder in a recent study by Luntz and Widom (1994).

When the abuse involves a sexual component, such as incest or rape, the long-range consequences can be very marked (Kendall-Tackett et al., 1993). Individuals who have been sexually abused are more likely to develop substance abuse problems (Hernandez, 1992). Watkins and Bentovim (1992) reported that approximately 2–5 percent of men in the adult population have been sexually abused, often resulting in lifelong negative consequences such as sexual problems (e.g., exhibitionism, homophobic behavior, depression, anxiety) and even a tendency to recapitulate this experience as an adult. Jackson and colleagues (1990) found that women who had experienced intrafamily sexual abuse had significantly poorer social adjustment, especially in dating relationships. The women also reported significantly lower sexual satisfaction, more sexual dysfunctions, and lower self-esteem than control women. Adults who have been sexually abused as children often show serious psychological symptoms such as a tendency to use dissociative defense mechanisms to excess, excessive preoccupation with bodily functions, and lowered self-esteem (Nash et al., 1993).

The role of sexual abuse in causing psychological problems has recently been the subject of several longitudinal studies. A number of investigators have followed up sexually abused children to study the long-term effects of abuse on a victim's behavior. A large percentage of sexually abused children experience intense psychological symptoms following the incident (for example, 74 percent reported by Bentovim, Boston, & Van Elburg, 1987). At follow-up, however, the improvement often seems dramatic. Similarly, several other studies have reported substantial improvement of sexually abused victims at follow-up (Bentovim et al., 1987; Conte, Berliner, & Schuerman, 1986). One study found that 55 percent of victims had substantially improved at follow-up 18 months later, particularly in terms of sleeping problems, fears of the offender, and anxiety. However, 28 percent of the victims showed worsening behavior, such as family conflict and inappropriate attention seeking (Gomes-Schwartz, Horowitz, & Cardarelli, 1990).

Several investigators have conceptualized the residual symptoms of sexual abuse as a type of post-traumatic stress disorder (PTSD) because the symptoms experienced are similar; for example, nightmares, flashbacks, sleep problems, and feelings of estrangement (Donaldson & Gardner, 1985; Frederick, 1986). However, other investigators (e.g., Finkelhor, 1990) object to this explanation on grounds that viewing these symptoms as an example of PTSD will "lead us to miss some of [the] most serious effects" of the sexual abuse experience such as prolonged depression or anxiety (p. 329).

Causal Factors in Child Abuse Since the 1960s, a great deal of research has been aimed at finding out which parents abuse their children and why, in the hope that ultimately these parents can be stopped, or better yet, prevented, from abusing their children. It is important to realize that in most cases it is not possible to find a single cause of child abuse. As Jay Belsky (1993) has pointed out, "There is no one pathway to these disturbances in parenting; rather, maltreatment seems to arise when stressors outweigh supports and risks are greater than protective factors" (p. 427). We now know that parents who physically abuse their children tend to be

young, with most under 30. In most reported cases, they come from the lower-socioeconomic levels (Egeland & Erickson, 1990; Peterson & Brown, 1994). An important common factor among families with abusing parents is a higher-than-average degree of frustration; many stressors are present in their lives, including marital discord, high unemployment, and alcohol abuse (Egeland, Cicchetti, & Taraldson, 1976). Recent evidence suggests that levels of caregiver stress plays an important part in child abuse and neglect (Hillson & Kuiper, 1994). Many incidents of physical abuse occur as parental reactions to a child's misbehavior in areas such as fighting, sexual behavior, aggression, and so on (Herrenkohl, Herrenkohl, & Egolf, 1983). Although no clear and consistent personality pattern emerges as typical of child-abusing parents, they seem to show a higher-than-average rate of psychological disturbance (Serrano et al., 1979). Some evidence from personality testing shows that they tend to be aggressive, nonconforming, selfish, and lacking in appropriate impulse control (Lund, 1975).

The Prevention of Child Abuse Practitioners and child protection agencies have begun an extensive effort to reduce the amount and impact of child abuse. Their efforts include the following:

- Community education programs have been developed to increase public awareness of the problem. Television advertisements have been especially effective at sensitizing parents and children to potential abuse.

- Child protection teams have been organized by many state and county welfare departments to investigate and intervene in reported cases of child abuse.

- Teams of mental health specialists in many community mental health centers are working to evaluate and provide psychological treatment for both abused children and their parents.

- Parent support groups, often made up of former child abusers, are forming that can offer abusing parents or those at risk for child abuse alternative ways of behaving toward their children. All states require physicians and other professionals to report cases of child abuse that come to their attention.

One of the most effective treatment strategies for eliminating or reducing child abuse involves parent-focused interventions that include teaching parents clearly defined child training strategies

Community education programs to increase public awareness of the problem of child abuse are but one of the current efforts to reduce the amount and impact of child abuse.

aimed at improving child-rearing skills (Wolfe & Wekerle, 1993). Research aimed at enabling early intervention with parents identified as likely to abuse their children has been promising. Wolfe and colleagues (1988) identified women who were at high risk for maltreatment of their children. They randomly assigned mothers to either a treatment or a control group. The treatment consisted of behaviorally oriented parent training that provided child management skills, instruction in child care, modeling, rehearsal instructions to give clear, concise demands, and the use of "time out" as a punishment. The study showed that this early intervention reduced the risk for child abuse among the mothers provided the treatment. Through such efforts on many levels it is hoped that children will be spared abuse and that abusive or potentially abusive parents will be helped to be more effective and nurturant.

Unfortunately, child abuse all too frequently produces maladaptive social behavior in its victims. The treatment of abused children needs to address the problems of social adjustment, depression, and poor interpersonal skills that these children exhibit. An interesting treatment approach to reducing the negative consequences of child abuse is the use of peers to help modify abused children's tendency to withdraw and their poor social skills. Fantuzzo and colleagues (1988) trained peer confederates to make play overtures to abused children. They found that peer-initiated efforts were more effective at increasing the social interaction of withdrawn children than adult-initiated treatment efforts. Further work on rehabilitative efforts is

needed to assist these unfortunate children in overcoming the psychologically disabling effects of being abused.

Child Advocacy Programs

Today there are nearly 68 million people under age 18 in the United States (Spencer, 1989). Unfortunately both treatment and preventive programs for our society's children have been—and remain—inadequate. In 1970 the National Institute of Mental Health pointed out that fewer than 1 percent of the disturbed children in our society were receiving any kind of treatment, and less than half of those children were getting adequate help. In the same year, in its final report, *Crisis in Child Mental Health: Challenge for the 1970s,* the Joint Commission on the Mental Health of Children (1970) referred to our lack of commitment to our children and youth as a "national tragedy."

Unfortunately, eight years later, the President's Commission on Mental Health (1978) was still calling attention to the fact that children and adolescents were not receiving mental health services commensurate with their needs. The commission's report recommended again that greater efforts and financial resources be expended to serve the mental health needs of children and youth. It appears, however, that the needed financial support and redirected program focuses have not materialized in the years since the report was issued.

In 1989, the United Nations General Assembly adopted the UN Convention on the Rights of the

Child, which provides a detailed definition of the rights of children in political, economic, social and cultural areas. This international recognition of the rights of children can potentially have a great impact on promoting humane treatment of children (Wilcox & Naimark, 1991).

One approach in the United States that has been designed to meet mental health needs, mental health child advocacy, has been prominent in recent years. Advocacy programs attempt to help children or others receive services that they need but often are unable to obtain for themselves. In some cases, advocacy seeks to better conditions for underserved populations by changing the system (Meyers & Parsons, 1987; Roberts & Peterson, 1984).

Twice in recent years the federal government has established a National Center for Child Advocacy to coordinate the many kinds of work for children's welfare performed by different government agencies. Both times the new agency proved ineffective and was given up after a year or so. Currently, the fragmentation in children's services means that different agencies serve different needs; no government agency is charged with considering the whole child and planning comprehensively for children who need help.

Outside the federal government, until recently, advocacy efforts for children have been supported largely by legal and special-interest citizens' groups, such as the Children's Defense Fund, a public-interest organization based in Washington, D.C. Mental health professionals have typically not been involved. Today, however, there is greater interdisciplinary involvement in attempts to provide effective advocacy programs for children (Gentry & Eron, 1993; Hermalin & Morell, 1986).

Unfortunately, although such programs have made important local gains toward bettering conditions for mentally disabled children, a great deal of confusion, inconsistency, and uncertainty still persist in the advocacy movement as a whole (Levine & Perkins, 1987), and the need for improving the accountability of mental health services for children still exists (Burchard & Schafer, 1992). In addition, the mood at both federal and state levels has for some time been to cut back on funds for social services.

Clearly, the challenge issued in 1970 by the Joint Commission on the Mental Health of Children has not been adequately answered (Cohen et al., 1992) although some important beginning steps have been taken in the work toward child advocacy and new efforts to identify and help high-risk children have been made (National Advisory Mental Health

Council, 1990). If the direction and momentum of these efforts can be maintained and if sufficient financial support for them can be procured, the psychological environment for children could substantially improve.

UNRESOLVED ISSUES

On Parental Pathology and Childhood and Adolescent Disorders

Do parents who are experiencing emotional problems transmit their problems to their children in some way? The evidence seems to be clear that children of disturbed parents are more vulnerable to developing psychological problems themselves than children of parents without emotional problems. For example, children of parents who were clinically depressed have been found to show poorer psychological functioning and more psychological disorders, including major depression, substance abuse, and internalization problems (Forehand, 1993; Gotlib & Colby, 1987; Weissman et al., 1987). Other emotional disorders in parents have also been found to be associated with emotional problems in children. For example, children of parents diagnosed with an anxiety disorder have been found to show more fears and more mood disturbance than children of control (community) parents (Turner, Beidel, & Costello, 1987). Parental pathology has also been found to be related to more conduct disorders in children (Dumas, Gibson, & Albin, 1989).

The actual mechanisms for the transmission of pathology from parent to child remain unclear. Researchers have noted, however, that it is not specific diagnoses among parents that result in specific disorders in children (Hammen et al., 1987), but the stress and symptoms that parents experience that influence children's behavior. Some research suggests that the mechanisms for causing behavior problems in children are to be found in learning processes. For example, maternal depression has been found to be associated with undesirable parenting practices, such as unresponsiveness, inattention, intrusiveness, inept discipline, and negative perceptions of children (Gelfand & Teti, 1990). Other researchers have pointed to family problems that create unfavorable emotional states; for example, tensions evolving from such incidents as parental divorce (Kornberg & Caplan, 1980) may produce psychological problems and achievement problems in youngsters (Bisnaire, Firestone, & Rynard, 1990).

Although emotionally upsetting events, such as divorce, are thought to cause childhood disorders, relationships between these and specific childhood psychopathology have not been documented. Some research has indicated that children suffer negative short-term and long-term effects of parental divorce (Amato & Keith, 1991; Wallerstein, 1991). Short-term effects include adjustment difficulties, low self-esteem, and higher rates of conduct disorders; long-term effects include shattered views of the world as a safe and reliable place, anger, and sexual promiscuity.

Recent evidence suggests that it is not divorce per se that produces disorder in a child—it is parental pathology. Lahey and colleagues (1988) found that parental divorce alone did not account for increased conduct disorder among boys. Rather, antisocial personality characteristics among parents were associated with conduct problems, suggesting that parental identification may be involved.

One extensive effort to understand the relationships between parental pathology and problems in children has been the Rochester longitudinal risk study (Sameroff et al., 1987). These investigators have followed up a sample of chronically ill schizophrenic women and their offspring to determine what, if any, impact their psychological problems and other possible risk factors (such as socioeconomic status, race, and family size) have on the development of behavior problems in their children. The women were initially assessed during their pregnancy and followed periodically since then. Their children have been evaluated over several periods since their birth. Sameroff and colleagues found that specific maternal diagnoses had the least impact on the development of behavior problems in the children. They reported that both socioeconomic status and the severity of the mother's illness had a greater impact on the child's developing problems. Children with multiple risk factors had much worse outcomes than children with fewer risk factors. The Rochester Adaptive Behavior Inventory (RABI) was used to obtain objective ratings of social-emotional competence on the children at the four-year follow-up. The risk variables studied were chronicity of illness, anxiety, parental education and occupation, interaction skill, minority status, family support, family size, and the presence of stressful life events. Children who received the lowest ratings on social and emotional competency tended to have the greatest risk for developing emotional problems (Sameroff et al., 1987). Generally, the more risk factors, the lower the children's ratings. The investigators also reported that although children of schizophrenic mothers are indeed at high risk for developing emotional problems, so too were children of severely ill

mothers and those from poor and minority backgrounds.

Whether the transmission of psychopathology from parent to child is due to faulty learning processes, genetic transmission, or some combination of these and other factors, it seems clear that at least some childhood and adolescent disorders are related to parental psychopathology. The precise mechanism or mechanisms for the transmission itself remains for future research to untangle.

SUMMARY

Traditionally, diagnosing behavior problems of children and adolescents has been a rather confused practice, in part because children have sometimes been viewed as "miniature" adults. It was not until the second half of the twentieth century that a diagnostic classification system focused clearly on the special problems of children.

Two broad approaches to the classification of childhood and adolescent behavior problems have been undertaken: a categorical approach, reflected most extensively in the DSM-IV, and a dimensional approach. Both classification approaches involve organized classes of observed behaviors. In the categorical approach, symptoms of behavior problems are grouped together as syndromes based on clinical observations. In the dimensional approach, a broad range of observed behaviors are submitted to multivariate statistical techniques; the symptoms that group together make up the diagnostic classes referred to as "dimensions."

In this chapter, the DSM-IV classification system is followed in order to provide clinical descriptions of a wide range of childhood behavior problems. Attention-deficit hyperactivity disorder is one of the more frequent behavior problems of childhood. In this disorder, the child shows impulsive, overactive behavior that interferes with his or her ability to accomplish tasks. There is some controversy over the explicit criteria used to distinguish hyperactive children from "normal" children or from children who exhibit other behavior disorders, such as conduct disorders. This lack of clarity in defining hyperactivity increases the difficulty of determining causal factors for the disorder. The major approaches to treating hyperactive children have been medication and behavior therapy. Using medications, such as amphetamines, with children is somewhat controversial. Behavior therapy, particularly cognitive-behavioral methods, has shown a great deal of promise in modifying the behavior of hyperactive children.

Another common behavior problem among children is that of conduct disorder. In this disorder, a child engages in persistent aggressive or antisocial acts. In cases where the child's misdeeds involve illegal activities, the terms *delinquent* or *juvenile delinquent* may be applied. A number of potential causes of conduct disorder or delinquent behavior have been determined, ranging from biological factors to personal pathology to social conditions. Treatment of conduct disorders and delinquent behavior is often frustrating and difficult; treatment is likely to be ineffective unless some means can be found for modifying a child's environment.

Another group of disorders, the childhood anxiety disorders, are quite different from the conduct disorders. Children who suffer from these disorders typically do not cause difficulty for others through their aggressive conduct. Rather they are fearful, shy, withdrawn, insecure, and have difficulty adapting to outside demands. The anxiety disorders may be characterized by extreme anxiety, withdrawal, or avoidance behavior. A likely cause for these disorders is early family relationships that generate anxiety and prevent the child from developing more adaptive coping skills. Behavior therapy approaches—such as assertiveness training and desensitization—may be helpful in treating this kind of disorder.

Several other disorders of childhood involve behavior problems centering on a single outstanding symptom rather than pervasive maladaptive patterns. The symptoms may involve enuresis, encopresis, sleepwalking, or tics. In these disorders, treatment is generally more successful than in the other disorders just described.

Finally, this chapter addressed one of the most severe and inexplicable childhood disorders—autism. In this disorder, extreme maladaptive behavior occurs during the early years and prevents affected children from developing psychologically. Autistic children, for example, seem to remain aloof from others, never responding to or seemingly not caring about what goes on around them. Many never learn to speak. These disorders likely have a biological basis, although definite proof of such a basis has proven elusive. Neither medical nor psychological treatment has been notably successful in fully normalizing the behavior of autistic children, but newer instructional and behavior-modification techniques have sometimes scored significant gains in improving their ability to function. In general, at present the long-term prognosis in autism appears discouraging.

A number of potential causal factors were considered for the disorders of childhood and adolescence. Although genetic predisposition appears to be important in several disorders, parental psychopathology, family disruption, and stressful circumstances, such as parental death or desertion and child abuse, can have an important causal influence. Recent research has underscored the importance of multiple risk factors in the development of psychopathology.

There are special problems, and special opportunities, involved in treating childhood disorders. The need for preventive and treatment programs for children is always growing, and in recent years the concept of child advocacy has become a reality in some states. Child abuse is a serious problem that has and continues to foster both research and clinical efforts into finding causes and devising preventive measures and treatment. Unfortunately, financial and other resources necessary for such services are not always readily available, and the future of programs for improving psychological environments for children remains uncertain.

KEY TERMS

developmental psycho-
   pathology (p. 527)
attention-deficit hyperactivity
   disorder (ADHD) (p. 531)
hyperactivity (p. 531)
conduct disorders (p. 534)
juvenile delinquency (p. 538)
oppositional defiant
   disorder (p. 535)
separation anxiety disorder
   (p. 543)

overanxious disorder (p. 544)
enuresis (p. 548)
encopresis (p. 549)
sleepwalking disorder
   (p. 549)
tic (p. 551)
Tourette's syndrome (p. 551)
autism (p. 551)
echolalia (p. 552)

CUTTING EDGE *1*

UNPREDICTABLE AND UNCONTROLLABLE STRESS AND PTSD

What features do the stressors known to cause PTSD have in common? Why do only some people who experience these stressors develop PTSD? Researchers in this area are looking increasingly at studies of stress in animals to answer these questions. For the past 30 years, extensive research in animals has shown that two of the most important determinants of how an organism responds to stress are whether the stressors are unpredictable or uncontrollable or both. An unpredictable stressor occurs without warning and its nature may be unforeseen. With an uncontrollable stressor, there is no way to respond to reduce its impact, such as by escape or avoidance. In general, both people and animals are more stressed by unpredictable and uncontrollable stressors than by stressors that are of equal physical magnitude but that are either predictable or controllable or both (e.g., Mineka & Hendersen, 1985).

These findings have not gone unnoticed by theorists and researchers interested in PTSD. Several investigators have noted many parallels in the symptoms of PTSD and the behavioral and physiological consequences of unpredictable and uncontrollable stress in animals (e.g., Basoglu & Mineka, 1992; Foa, Zinbarg, & Olasov-Rothbaum, 1992; Friedman, Charney, & Deutch, 1995; Mineka & Zinbarg, 1996, 1997). It is known, for example, that uncontrollable stress stimulates some noradrenergic brain systems and increases levels of central and peripheral norepinephrine (Friedman et al., 1995; Southwick, Yehuda, & Morgan, 1995). This led PTSD researchers to hypothesize that administration of a drug called *yohimbine* to persons with PTSD might increase their symptoms, because yohimbine is known to activate noradrenergic neurons. Consistent with this hypothesis, Southwick and colleagues (1993, 1995) found that 40 percent of a group of 20 veterans of the Vietnam War with PTSD experienced flashbacks when they took yohimbine; no control subjects without PTSD experienced flashbacks. In addition, the veterans with PTSD showed increases in other symptoms, such as intrusive traumatic thoughts, emotional numbing, and grief.

Uncontrollable stress in animals is also known to cause stress-induced analgesia (SIA), or diminished sensitivity to pain. Formerly neutral conditioned stimuli that are paired with uncontrollable stress can also become conditioned to elicit this analgesia. This SIA is known to work through the production of endogenous, or internally produced, opiate-like substances in the brain (Southwick et al., 1995; van der Kolk & Saporta, 1993). It can be reversed by the administration of a drug called *naloxone,* which is a biological antagonist of these opiate-like substances. PTSD researchers now believe that many of the symptoms of emotional numbing seen in people with PTSD may be caused by this same kind of SIA, rather than being a psychological defensive reaction against remembering the trauma (as previously thought by psychodynamic theorists). Consistent with this are results from a study by Pitman and his colleagues (1990) in which veterans with and without PTSD who watched a film depicting combat in Vietnam (certainly a conditioned stimulus for trauma) were later given a pain sensitivity test. Those with PTSD showed reduced pain sensitivity relative to those without PTSD. Those with PTSD also showed a relative blunting of emotional responses to the film. These effects were reversed when naloxone was administered. This and other studies support the idea that the symptoms of emotional numbing in PTSD stem from the opioid-mediated SIA that has developed because of the experience of uncontrollable stress.

If unpredictable and uncontrollable stressors are most likely to produce PTSD, what factors might influence which of the people who experience those stressors will be most likely to develop PTSD? Again, researchers have turned to the animal literature for answers (e.g., Mineka & Zinbarg, 1996, 1997). For example, it is known that prior experience with uncontrollable stressors can *sensitize* the organism, that is, make it more susceptible to the negative consequences of later experiences with uncontrollable trauma. Several studies of PTSD have confirmed that this is indeed the case, with victims of childhood abuse being more susceptible to PTSD in response to both sexual and nonsexual assault in adulthood (see Foa et al., 1992; Mineka & Zinbarg, 1996, 1997). In addition, soldiers who had been physically abused in childhood were more likely to develop PTSD during the Vietnam war (Bremner et al., 1993; Post, Weiss, & Smith, 1995).

By contrast, the animal literature also illustrates that the effects of uncontrollable stress can sometimes be *prevented* or minimized by prior experience with controllable stressors (see Mineka & Zinbarg, 1996, 1997). It is thought that experience with controllable stressors produces a sense of mastery that then allows the organism to cope better with subsequent uncontrollable stressors. This led Basoglu, Mineka and colleagues (in press) to hypothesize that the torture survivors in Turkey described on page 149 may not have shown very high rates of PTSD or other psychopathology because they were all political activists in Turkey during the time of a very repressive political regime. As political activists they had a greater sense of predictability and probably a greater sense of control regarding their torture experience than other people would have. This came from prior experience with similar stressors, stoicism training, knowledge about torture methods, and commitment to a cause. This may be why only 33% of

these survivors had ever qualified for a diagnosis of PTSD in spite of the fact that these 55 people had experienced an average of 23 different forms of torture and an average of 291 total exposures to torture.

Recently a new sample of 34 torture survivors who were *not* political activists (but who were also not criminals) were interviewed and assessed using the same methods as in the study by Basoglu and coworkers (1994). These survivors of torture experienced significantly fewer different forms of torture, and over a much shorter period, than had the political activists. Yet they showed significantly more symptoms of PTSD and general psychopathology. Basoglu and colleagues (in press) hypothesized that this was because the nonactivist sample had a diminished sense of psychological predictability or immunization because their torture experience came "out of the blue," without any prior training in stoicism, any knowledge of torture methods, or commitment to a cause. The researchers developed a measure of "psychological preparedness for trauma" that assessed how well the survivors had been prepared and psychologically immunized before their torture experience. Not surprisingly, the political activist sample scored much higher on this measure of psychological preparedness than did the nonactivist sample. Of greatest interest, however, was the finding that, across the two studies, the single best predictor of the number of PTSD or general psychopathology symptoms the torture survivors exhibited was their degree of psychological preparedness; those who were more prepared showed fewer symptoms of PTSD and general psychopathology. In other words, psychological preparedness predicted symptoms better than did

nine other variables, such as the number of torture events experienced, duration of detention, or time since last torture.

Increasing attention is being paid by PTSD researchers to studies of unpredictable and uncontrollable stress in animals. Considerable research now supports the hypothesis that perceptions of uncontrollability and unpredictability play an important role in the development and maintenance of PTSD symptoms. Moreover, the animal literature showing that prior experiences with uncontrollable stressors may sensitize an organism to the negative effects of subsequent experience with other uncontrollable stressors has led to important new findings regarding which individuals may be most susceptible to PTSD. Finally, the animal literature on predictability and immunization may help to explain why some people, such as the political activists who experienced extreme levels of torture, may show relatively low rates of PTSD.

REFERENCES

Basoglu, M., Mineka, S., Paker, M., Aker, T., Gok. S., & Livanou, M. (in press). Psychological preparedness for trauma as a protective factor in survivors of torture. *Psychol. Med.*

Bremner, J., Southwick, S., Johnson, D., Yehuda, R., & Charney, D. (1993). Childhood physical abuse and combat-related posttraumatic stress disorder in Vietnam veterans. *Amer. J. Psychiat., 150*, 235–239.

Foa, E., Zinbarg, R., & Olasov-Rothbaum, B. (1992). Uncontrollability and unpredictability in post-traumatic stress disorder: An animal model. *Psychol. Bull., 112*, 218–238.

Friedman, M., Charney, D., & Deutch, A. (1995). Key questions and a research agenda for the future. In M. J. Friedman, D. Charney, and A. Deutch (Eds.), *Neurobiological and clinical consequences of stress: From normal adaptation to PTSD* (pp. 527–533). Philadelphia: Lippincott-Raven Publishers.

Mineka, S., & Zinbarg, R. (1996). Conditioning and ethological models of anxiety disorders: Stress-in-dynamic-context anxiety models. In D. Hope (Ed.), *Perspectives on anxiety, panic, and fear.* 43rd Annual Nebraska Symposium on Motivation. Lincoln, NE: University of Nebraska Press. pp. 135–211.

Mineka, S., & Zinbarg, R. (1997). Experimental approaches to understanding the mood and anxiety disorders. In J. Adair (Ed.), *Advances in psychological research,* Vol. 2. Psychology Press.

Pitman, R., van der Kolk, V., Orr, S., & Greenberg, M. (1990). Naloxone reversible stress-induced analgesia in posttraumatic stress disorder. *Arch. Gen. Psychiat., 47,* 970–976.

Post, R., Weiss, S., & Smith, M. (1995). Sensitization and kindling: Implications for the evolving neural substrates of post-traumatic stress disorder. In M. J. Friedman, D. Charney, and A. Deutch (Eds.), *Neurobiological and clinical consequences of stress: From normal adaptation to PTSD* (pp. 203–224). Philadelphia: Lippincott-Raven Publishers.

Southwick, S., Krystal, J., Morgan, C. et al. (1993). Abnormal noradrenergic function in posttrau-matic stress disorder. *Arch. Gen. Psychiat., 50,* 266–274.

Southwick, S., Yehuda, R., & Morgan, C. (1995). Clinical studies of neurotransmitter alterations in post-traumatic stress disorder. In M. J. Friedman, D. Charney, and A. Deutch (Eds.), *Neurobiological and clinical consequences of stress: From normal adaptation to PTSD* (pp. 335–349). Lippincott-Raven Publishers: Philadelphia.

Van der Kolk, B., & Saporta, J. (1993). Biological response to psychic trauma. In J. Wilson and B. Raphael (Eds.), *International handbook of traumatic stress syndromes* (pp. 25–33). London: Plenum Press.

CUTTING EDGE 2

NEW FINDINGS ON AN "ANXIETY GENE" AND ON ANXIETY SENSITIVITY

In late 1996 scientists reported having identified a specific gene related to anxiety and neuroticism. This gene affects the brain's ability to use the neurotransmitter 5-hydroxytryptamine or serotonin, which has long been known to be involved in emotions as well as thinking processes. Indeed, many drugs now used to treat anxiety and depression are thought to work primarily through the effects they exert on the brain's serotonin system.

This is one of the first times that a specific gene has been identified that affects an important human personality trait—specifically, who is prone to anxiety and other negative moods and who is prone to a more stable, "laid-back" attitude. The gene affects what is called the *serotonin transporter*—molecules separate from serotonin itself that allow nerve cells to transport serotonin from the synaptic cleft into the nerve cell—usually "re-uptake" into the presynaptic neuron for storage and reuse (see Highlight 3.1, page 70). Researchers discovered that there are two important varieties of the gene—called 5-HTT (for 5HT transporter). The so-called long subtype has some extra DNA in it that the so-called short subtype lacks. Evidence indicates that the shorter version of the gene produces fewer serotonin transporter molecules, resulting in lower levels of serotonin uptake in certain key areas of the brain than occurs in people who have the longer version of the gene. Of greatest interest,

however, is that people with the shorter version of the gene score significantly higher on scales measuring neuroticism or proneness to negative moods, such as anxiety, tension, sadness, and so on (Lesch et al., 1996).

The scientists emphasized that the size of the relationship between this transporter gene and neuroticism is quite small, accounting for only about 4 percent of the variance in people's neuroticism levels. Thus, many other, as yet unidentified, genes as well as experiential factors combine with this 5-HTT gene to determine a person's level of neuroticism (Goldman, 1996). Nevertheless, these findings are considered very important because neuroticism is one of the three or four most basic human personality dimensions (Watson, Clark, & Harkness, 1994) and because people with high levels of neuroticism are known to be at increased risk for both anxiety and depressive disorders (Clark, Watson, & Mineka, 1994). It is also of interest that about 70 percent of the 500 people studied had the short subtype of the gene. In other words, most of us have the more anxiety-prone gene. The search for specific genes related to other major psychiatric disorders, such as schizophrenia and bipolar disorder, has not yet been successful.

At about the same time that these findings on the anxiety gene were released, two other important new studies provided the best

evidence to date that anxiety sensitivity (see pages 175–176) does indeed seem to serve as a vulnerability factor for panic attacks. Schmidt, Lerew, and Jackson (in press) followed over 1400 young adults undergoing basic military training for five weeks. The study design was excellent for the purpose of testing a diathesis-stress model for the onset of panic disorder, because people with varying levels of the diathesis were all followed and studied during a period of high levels of unpredictable and uncontrollable stress; it is fairly well known that panic attacks often begin during highly stressful times (e.g., Pollard, Pollard, & Corn, 1989). Schmidt and colleagues (in press) found that high levels of anxiety sensitivity (the extent to which a person believes that autonomic arousal and other symptoms of anxiety can have harmful consequences) predicted the development of spontaneous panic attacks during this highly stressful period. For example, of those scoring in the top 10 percent on the Anxiety Sensitivity Index (Peterson & Reiss, 1987), 20 percent experienced at least one panic attack during the five weeks of basic training; only 6 percent of the remaining study participants had a panic attack in the same period. Of those scoring in the top 25 percent on this index, 13 percent had at least one panic attack during this period, whereas of those scoring in the bottom 25 percent, only 3 percent panicked.

The high rates of panic attacks in those scoring high on anxiety sensitivity are particularly remarkable, because overall this sample of military cadets had very low levels of anxiety sensitivity compared with the general population (one could well imagine that most people high on anxiety sensitivity would be likely to avoid the military because of its unique demands and risks). It was also noteworthy that anxiety itself did not significantly predict who would panic—only *anxiety sensitivity* was a predictor. Moreover, anxiety sensitivity, but not anxiety, also served as a risk factor for functional impairment with peer and supervisory relationships, for poor physical health, and for poor overall performance.

In a second important study Telch and his colleagues (1997) followed over 500 college students for one year, half of whom were high in anxiety sensitivity (but had never yet had a panic attack) and half of whom were low in anxiety sensitivity. At the end of the year, the students were interviewed to determine if they had experienced panic attacks during the year. Although these students were not undergoing the degree of stress that the military cadets were in the Schmidt et al. study (in press), the results were nonetheless quite simi-

lar. Nearly 10 percent of those in the high anxiety-sensitivity group had experienced at least one unexpected panic attack during the one-year follow-up period, whereas less than 4 percent of those in the low anxiety-sensitivity group had experienced an unexpected panic attack.

These studies provide by far the strongest evidence to date that anxiety sensitivity does seem to serve as a risk factor or diathesis for the development of panic and functional impairment from anxiety symptoms. Given this evidence that anxiety sensitivity serves as a diathesis for the development of panic attacks, prevention programs designed to reduce anxiety sensitivity in those at risk now become possible. It is known that cognitive-behavioral treatment for panic disorder itself reduces anxiety sensitivity (Mineka, Rozensky, & Martinovich, 1997; Telch et al., 1993), and so one would expect that similar procedures could be used to reduce anxiety sensitivity before people at risk ever develop panic attacks. One such ongoing prevention project is currently being conducted in Texas (Telch et al., 1997), so we should soon know not only whether a brief cognitive-behavioral intervention program given to those high in anxiety sensitivity can reduce anxiety sensitivity (Harrington et al., 1995) but also whether this translates into reduced vulnerability to panic attacks.

REFERENCES

Goldman, D. (1996). High anxiety. *Science, 274,* 1483–1484.

Harrington, P. J., Telch, M. J., Abplanalp, B., & Hamilton, A. C. (November 1995). *Lowering anxiety sensitivity in nonclinical subjects: Preliminary evidence for a panic prevention program.* Poster presented at the meeting of the Association for the Advancement of Behavior Therapy. Washington DC.

Lesch, K.-P., Bengel, D., Heils, A., Sabol, S., Greenberg, B., Petri, S., Benjamin, J., Müller, C., Hamer, D., & Murphy, D. (1996). Association of anxiety-related traits with a polymorphism in the serotonin transporter gene regulatory region. *Science, 274,* 1527–1531.

Mineka, S., Rozensky, R., & Martinovich, Z. (1997). *Cognitive-behavior therapy for panic disorder with carefully supervised novice therapists can produce similar outcomes to those seen with more experienced therapists.* Unpublished manuscript.

Peterson, R. A., & Reiss, S. (1987). *Test manual for the anxiety sensitivity index.* Orland Park, IL: International Diagnostic Systems.

Schmidt, N. B., Lerew, D. R., & Jackson, R. J. (in press). The role of anxiety sensitivity in the pathogenesis of panic: Prospective evaluation of spontaneous panic attacks during acute stress. *J. Abnorm. Psychol.*

Telch, M. J., Alpbanalp, B., Harrington, P., Owen, C., & Hattiengadi, N. (1997). *Can reduction in anxiety sensitivity reduce vulnerability to panic attacks?* Unpublished manuscript.

Telch, M. J., Lucas, J. A., Schmidt, N. B., Hanna, H. H., Jaimez, T. L., & Lucas, R. (1993). Group cognitive-behavioral treatment of panic disorder. *Behav. Res. Ther., 31,* 279–287.

See Chapter 6, page 230

CUTTING EDGE 3

DEPRESSION AND DOMESTIC VIOLENCE

A strong concordance exists between distressed adult relationships and the presence of a mood disorder in one or both partners (Fruzzetti, 1996; Gotlib & Hammen, 1992; O'Leary, Christian, & Mendell, 1994). These forms of relationship distress may include the occurrence of violent abuse.

It has long been known that mood-disordered persons have an enhanced risk for engaging in violence, including family violence. Until fairly recently, however, virtually all of that enhanced risk was thought to be related to the lack of control and disinhibition associated with manic or hypomanic episodes. Continuing research developments, beginning in the 1980s (e.g., Maiuro et al., 1988), increasingly call that view into question and implicate depressive disorders in the occurrence of much violence, specifically domestic violence.

Men who attack their partners violently—some women also attack men, but usually less violently (Jacobson et al., 1994; O'Leary, 1995)—commonly do so as a means of attempting, by inspiring fear in the partner, to control a situation they perceive as threatening their "proprietary" assumptions about the partnership (e.g., Maiuro et al., 1988; Murphy, Meyer, & O'Leary, 1994; Wilson & Daly, 1996). Such men tend to be highly emotionally dependent on their partners, despite appearances to the contrary, and they tolerate poorly signs of a partner's autonomy. Their underlying sense of inadequacy fuels their desperate attempts to maintain control over the partnership. Too often, the result is a violent attack (Murphy, Meyer, & O'Leary, 1994).

A compelling example is provided in the notoriety attending the recent trials of former football superstar O. J. Simpson for the murder of his former wife, Nicole, and her friend Ron Goldman. Although the identity of the murderer may never be known "beyond a reasonable doubt," much evidence implicates Simpson. In any event, there is essentially no doubt that he was violently abusive toward his wife during and after their marriage, as described in a recent summary of the evidence by Meyer and Osborne (1996). These authors also make a convincing case that Mr. Simpson was in fact a prime example of the syndrome under discussion here, which includes a substantial component of painfully depressive symptoms.

Although it appears not to have been a factor in the Simpson case, many partnered men who experience marital distress and become depressed tend to be "unsuccessful," either chronically or in response to recent reversals of fortune. Self-perceived "failure," in terms of conventional male values such as providing for the economic needs of the family, is thus often a complicating factor (Pan, Neidig, & O'Leary, 1994; Vinokur, Price, & Caplan, 1996). Although these men frequently show evidence of high levels of "rejection sensitivity," their behavior in fact invites rejection, which increases the likelihood of heightened relationship friction (Downey & Feldman, 1996) and thus the further development of depressive symptoms (Fruzzetti, 1996). In this process of escalating dysphoria, many men turn to alcohol or other disinhibiting drugs as a type of "self-medication" to reduce stress and relieve depression, thus making it even more likely that they will impulsively attempt a violent solution to end their acute despair (Leonard & Senchak, 1996; Pan, Neidig, & O'Leary, 1994). Like other dysfunctional reactions to a deteriorating relationship, this one, too, almost always makes matters worse.

The causal relationships among depression, marital distress, and familial violence thus appear to be mutually reinforcing and multidirectional in nature. In fact, the victims of physical abuse are themselves likely to become clinically depressed (O'Leary, 1995), thus diminishing their abilities to take effective action. Once these behaviors are established as a pattern, it becomes extremely difficult, even with professional help, to disentangle cause from effect and to restore mutual understanding, respect, trust, and effective nonviolent functioning. Unfortunately, as pointed out by Fruzzetti (1996), the DSM, which recognizes disorders as exclusively "within" individuals, provides no adequate diagnostic recognition of this common scenario.

Despite the difficulties of establishing primacy within the entangled causal pattern in abusive relationships, contemporary research suggests that there is often evidence of problematic early attachment processes among the people involved. Deriving from the work of Bowlby (1980) in England, psychologists have in recent years developed apparently reliable and valid means of measuring adults' attachment propensities (Griffin & Bartholomew, 1994), usually differentiating among three "levels" having significant implications for adult relationships. A person with a *secure* attachment pattern comfortably "connects with" and engages others at optimal levels of intimacy and mutual autonomy. *Insecure* attachment patterns include the *anxious-ambivalent*, involving high intimacy needs mixed with anxiety and conflictful, unstable attachments, and the *avoidant*, which involves an active distancing of the self from others. The general hypothesis advanced here is that partners with insecure attachment patterns, particularly the anxious-ambivalent variety, are at significantly increased risk for marital distress, depression, and domestic violence.

In support of this hypothesis, Woike, Osier, and Candela (1996) recently demonstrated a significantly high level of violent relationship imagery (male perpetrators, female victims) among anxious-attachment male college students. Anxious-attachment women in this study had more violent imagery specifically involving female victims than did secure or avoidant-attachment women. The import of such findings, however, may go beyond mere violent imagery. Maiuro and colleagues (1988) found evidence of

disturbed attachment patterns in their sample of domestically violent men. Moreover, relationship difficulties associated with insecure attachment patterns may surface early in romantic pairing, as demonstrated by Simpson, Rholes, & Phillips (1996) in a study of college-age dating couples. In addition, Roberts, Gotlib, and Kassell (1996) have recently demonstrated what appears to be a causal relationship between attachment insecurity and the emergence of depressive symptoms, as mediated by self-esteem deficits. As already noted, depressive symptoms in the marital context are associated with a substantially enhanced risk of domestic violence, which sometimes proves deadly.

REFERENCES

Downey, G., & Feldman, S. I. (1996). Implications of rejection sensitivity for intimate relationships. *J. Pers. Soc. Psychol.*, 70, 1327–1343.

Fruzzetti, A. E. (1996). Causes and consequences: Individual distress in the context of couple interactions. *J. Consult. Clin. Psychol.*, 64, 1192–1201.

Griffin, D., & Bartholomew, K. (1994). Models of the self and other: Fundamental dimensions underlying measures of adult attachment. *J. Pers. Soc. Psychol.*, 67, 430–445.

Jacobson, N. S., Gottman, J. M., Waltz, J., Rushe, R., Babcock, J., & Holtzworth-Munroe, A. (1994). Affect, verbal content, and psychophysiology in the arguments of couples with a violent husband. *J. Consult. Clin. Psychol.*, 62, 982–988.

Leonard, K. E., & Senchak, M. (1996). Prospective prediction of husband marital aggression within newlywed couples. *J. Abnorm. Psychol.*, 105, 369–380.

Maiuro, R. D., Cahn, T. S., Vitaliano, P. P., Wagner, B. C., & Zegree, J. B. (1988). Anger, hostil-

ity, and depression in domestically violent versus generally assaultive men and nonviolent control subjects. *J. Consult. Clin. Psychol.*, 56, 17–23.

Meyer, R. G., & Osborne, Y. H. (1996). *Case studies in abnormal behavior* (3rd ed.). Boston: Allyn and Bacon.

Murphy, C. M., Meyer, S-L, & O'Leary, K. D. (1994). Dependency characteristics of partner assaultive men. *J. Abnorm. Psychol.*, 103, 729–735.

O'Leary, K. D. (1995). Assessment and treatment of partner abuse. *Clin. Res. Dig. Suppl. Bull. 12*, 13, 1–2.

O'Leary, K. D., Christian, J. L., & Mendell, N. R. (1994). A closer look at the link between marital discord and depressive symptomatology. *J. Soc. Clin. Psychol.* 13, 33–41.

Pan, H. S., Neidig, P. H., & O'Leary, K. D. (1994). Predicting mild and severe husband-to-wife physical aggression. *J. Consult. Clin. Psychol.* 62, 975–981.

Roberts, J. E., Gotlib, I. H., & Kassel, J. D. (1996). Adult attachment security and symptoms of depression: The mediating roles of dysfunctional attitudes and low self-esteem. *J. Pers. Soc. Psychol.*, 70, 310–320.

Simpson, J. A., Rholes, W. S., & Phillips, D. (1996). Conflict in close relationships: An attachment perspective. *J. Pers. Soc. Psychol.*, 71, 899–914.

Vinokur, A. D., Price, R. H., & Caplan, R. D. (1996). Hard times and hurtful partners: How financial strain affects depression and relationship satisfaction of unemployed persons and their spouses. *J. Pers. Soc. Psychol.*, 71, 166–179.

Wilson, M. I., & Daly, M. (1996). Male sexual proprietariness and violence against wives. *Curr. Dir. Psychol. Sci.*, 5, 2–7.

Woike, B. A., Osier, T. J., & Candela, K. (1996). Attachment styles and violent imagery in thematic stories about relationships. *Pers. Soc. Psychol. Bull.*, 22, 1030–1034.

See Chapter 7, page 274

CUTTING EDGE 4

RECOVERED MEMORIES OF ABUSE AND DISSOCIATIVE DISORDERS: CONTINUING CONTROVERSY

Since the relevant chapter (7) was written the conflict between "believers" and "nonbelievers" has intensified regarding the clinical reality of Dissociative Identity Disorder (DID) and related phenomena, and the association of the latter with childhood experiences of abuse, particularly sexual abuse. To simplify, the major opponents in this conflict are the clinicians who try to "treat" these conditions and the more scientifically oriented mental health professionals who as a group doubt the validity of both the diagnosis and its alleged source in childhood abuse. With rare exceptions, evidence for the causal connection between DID and childhood abuse is restricted to "recovered memories" of adults being treated for dissociative experiences, thus inviting the criticism that false memories of abuse are implanted in the process of biased and erroneously conducted treatment.

Attempting to mediate on the issue of the validity of treatment-recovered memories, the American Psychological Association (APA) in 1994 convened a "balanced" panel of experts, the Working Group on the Investigation of Memories of Childhood Abuse. As one measure of the amount of dissent and controversy raging in this field, indications are strong that this group was unable over the many months of its existence to reach any consensus. Although some working group re-

ports have been issued and more APA-sponsored documents are promised, there remains, in our judgment, little hope of achieving consensus on this issue at any time in the foreseeable future. As reported by the APA's Chief Executive Officer, Raymond Fowler (personal communication, February 27, 1997), "the working group agreed on almost nothing." The upshot is that the public remains entirely divided and confused as to what to believe about the validity of recovered memories of childhood abuse. This in turn means that the role such abuse might play in causing adult disorders, particularly those involving dissociative phenomena, is also extremely unclear.

The controversy has been sharpened by the recent posthumous publication of a notably provocative work, *Multiple identities and false memories,* by Nicholas Spanos (1996). In this book, Spanos, picking up on a theme of his own and of Krippner's (1994) already introduced in Chapter 7 reviews impressive evidence indicating that the occurrence of dissociative phenomena over time and place is markedly correlated with cultural and professional acceptance of these phenomena. He buttresses this argument by noting a bizarre distribution (significantly greater than chance would indicate) of cases of DID treated by various mental health clinicians. Most clinicians claim never or

rarely to have encountered such clinical phenomena; the many cases now appearing in the professional literature are contributed by a few clinicians who strongly support the current notion of widespread dissociative disorder resulting from childhood abuse. Spanos argues that these observations are more consistent with a "sociocognitive" than with a medical or mental-disorder perspective on "dissociative" behavior. That is, the disordered behavior is largely the product of a suggestive social context, including, too often, the context of treatment for it.

Spanos (1996) also contests the idea that there is anything unique or even surprising about contemporary clinical observations concerning dissociative disorders. He regards them as intimately related to a variety of other phenomena, both historical and contemporary. Among these he includes glossolalia (involuntary "speaking in tongues," practiced among several contemporary religious groups in the United States) and certain classical demonstrations of "hysterical" disorder.

According to Spanos (1996), in short, DID is a type of self-absorbed role-playing inspired by popular culture and inadvertently reinforced and taught to vulnerable patients by well-meaning but misguided therapists specializing in the treatment of these conditions. Thus, patients who develop DID are unflatteringly described by Spanos as, typically,

> chronically disturbed, unhappy, polysymptomatic (usually female) people who are emotionally needy and who use displays of physical and psychological symptoms as a means of conveying their distress and gaining and maintaining the attention of their therapists and others (p. 259). . . . [DID is] a pattern of self-construal and interpersonal responding used by some . . . troubled women to express dissatisfactions, "make sense" of their troubled lives, and attain some succor by adopting a variant of the sick role (p. 293).

We regard it as likely that Spanos's work will be passionately attacked by those committed to the view that DID and related phenomena are in every sense "real" mental disorders, and ones moreover that are for the most part the outcome of severe childhood sexual abuse. Unfortunately, passion—and the Spanos book is far from lacking in that quality—will not help in resolving the outstanding questions surrounding this field of inquiry, ones that have serious and widespread social implications. Although we find some of the phenomena often reported in recovered memories, such as lengthy, enforced participation in murderous satanic cults, as being almost without exception beyond belief, we are decidedly less certain about some of the more central issues that Spanos raises. These include, for example, the "reality" of DID as well as the purported role

of early sexual abuse in causing pathological dissociation.

Lacking clear, unimpeachable evidence that would compel a consensus among responsible members of both the clinical and the scientific communities, our only reasonable recourse is to insist strongly that clinicians caring for persons suspected of having these conditions be held to the highest of professional standards of practice. There is widespread evidence of deviance from those standards, which is undoubtedly an important source of the impatience, irritation, and anger emanating from the more scientifically inclined in the mental health professions. To the extent that poor practice has resulted from ignorance and confusion, there is hope that the present unsatisfactory situation may be alleviated by a more informed and cautious approach.

A significant step forward in this regard is the recent appearance of still another book addressing this extremely complex clinical problem—*Recovered memories of abuse: Assessment, therapy, forensics,* by Kenneth Pope and Laura Brown (1996). The work is basically a "survival manual" for practitioners who are undaunted by the challenges this group of patients present and who venture to treat them. Unlike Spanos's (1996) offering, this book acknowledges the possibly "real" occurrence of DID and related clinical syndromes, as well as the possibility of a causal link between DID and childhood sexual abuse. It is also completely frank in confronting the contentious issues pervading the field and in recommending procedures that, if generally adopted, would lessen the likelihood of error on the part of overzealous practitioners.

The recommended approach of Pope and Brown (1996) emphasizes the importance of profes-

sional competence in three areas: intellectual, emotional, and procedural. The last of these refers to skill in "doing," in actually carrying out with expertise the elements of a carefully formulated assessment and treatment plan.

Intellectual competence, as the term implies, refers to the adequacy of the practitioner's knowledge of the basic psychological processes likely to be involved where possible abuse becomes an issue—such as memory functioning, developmental theory, and the nature and consequences of psychic trauma. Included here would be sophistication about the common pitfalls involved in developing inferences from observations, thus encouraging the practitioner to be self-critical in case formulation. Emotional competence refers to the practitioner's resilience in coping with the frequently dramatic clinical material that may come to light in working with patients who have recovered memories of abuse. The therapist who "loses it" in this regard is likely to make serious mistakes in case management. Pope and Brown recommend frequent consultation with professional colleagues, or in more serious instances perhaps even personal therapy, for practitioners who may themselves become at risk for engaging in aberrant professional behavior in working with this challenging clinical population.

REFERENCES

Pope, K. S., & Brown, L. S. (1996). *Recovered memories of abuse: Assessment, therapy, forensics.* Washington, DC: American Psychological Association.

Spanos, N. P. (1996). *Multiple identities and false memories: A sociocognitive perspective.* Washington, DC: American Psychological Association.

CUTTING EDGE 5

DEPRESSION AND CORONARY HEART DISEASE

Until the past few years the primary psychological variable recognized as affecting coronary heart disease (CHD) was Type A behavior—particularly the hostility component (see pages 288–292). Now, however, we are learning that depression also dramatically affects risk for CHD and has a negative effect on the progression of CHD once it has been diagnosed (Shapiro, 1996). At first it was noticed that people with heart disease were more likely to be depressed than were healthy people. Several studies have shown that 15 to 20 percent of people who have a heart attack are clinically depressed—a much higher figure than would be expected in the general population (Chesney, 1996; Shapiro, 1996). Such findings led investigators to examine the effects of depression on the course of CHD. Several studies now indicate that heart attack patients who are depressed at the time of their heart attack or shortly afterward show a greatly increased risk for future coronary events and cardiac death (Chesney, 1996; Shapiro, 1996). In their initial study, for example, Frasure-Smith, Lesperance, and Talajic (1993) followed 222 patients for six months who had had a heart attack. These investigators found that the clinically depressed patients were five times more likely to die in the next six months than were their nondepressed counterparts. Moreover, depression was as good a predictor of death from heart disease as were such medical variables as prior heart attacks or poor heart

functioning. After adjusting for these other variables, they estimated that the relative risk of death associated with depression was still four times greater. Frasure-Smith and colleagues (1995) assessed these patients again 18 months after their initial heart attack and found that depression as assessed within 10 days of the initial heart attack was associated with a nearly eightfold increase in mortality (Shapiro, 1996). Ladwig, Roll, and Breithardt (1994) reached similar conclusions.

Other studies have shown that clinical depression is a *risk factor* for later developing CHD. For example, Pratt and her colleagues (1996) followed over 1500 men and women with no prior history of heart disease for 14 years. They found that 8 percent of those who had suffered major depression and 6 percent of those who had suffered mild depression at some point had a heart attack during the 14-year follow-up interval. By contrast, only 3 percent of those without a history of depression suffered heart attacks. When medical history and other variables were taken into account, those who had suffered major depression were found to be four times more likely to have had a heart attack. Similar findings had also been reported in several earlier studies (Chesney, 1996; Scheier & Bridges, 1995; Shapiro, 1996).

Two mechanisms have been proposed to explain the association between depression and CHD. The first is that depressed people may engage in more be-

haviors known to put people at risk for CHD. For example, depressed people are less likely to eat well or exercise, are more likely to smoke, and are perhaps less likely to take medications for such conditions as high blood pressure (Chesney, 1996; Kolata, 1997). Depressed people are also known to lack social support, which has also been linked to CHD (Eriksen, 1994).

Second, it may be that depression is linked to CHD through biochemical mechanisms. As discussed in Chapter 6, many depressed people have elevated levels of the stress hormone cortisol. They also have elevated rates of norepinephrine in their blood, which can increase blood pressure and heart rate (Kolata, 1997). So although depressed people may appear lethargic, their elevated stress hormones may damage their hearts. It is also known that depressed persons show lower heart rate variability in response to behavioral changes (e.g., walking versus sitting down when heart rate *should* change). High heart rates and low heart rate variability are also known to be associated with changes in sympathetic–parasympathetic balance, which may increase cardiac arrhythmias that often precede sudden death (Chesney, 1996; Frasure-Smith et al., 1993).

Given the high levels of comorbidity between anxiety and mood disorders discussed in Chapter 6, it is not surprising that a similar link might also be found between anxiety and CHD. Several studies suggest such a relationship. For example, De Silva (1993) found that patients with established CHD (e.g., coronary artery disease, angina, or prior heart attack) were at increased risk for sudden death when exposed to anxiety-provoking stressors. A recent study by Leor, Poole, and Kloner (1996) found a transient fivefold increase in sudden cardiac death in the days immediately following a 1994 California earthquake. The deaths were associated primarily with the emotional stress caused by the earthquake (Shapiro, 1996). Another study has documented a relationship between phobic anxiety and increased risk for sudden cardiac death. Kawachi and colleagues (1994a) followed nearly 34,000 male professionals for two years who had been assessed for panic disorder, agoraphobia, and generalized anxiety. Men with the highest levels of phobic anxiety were three times more likely to have a fatal heart attack than were men with the lowest levels of phobic anxiety. Sudden cardiac death was six times higher in the men with the highest levels of anxiety. However, there was *no* association found between anxiety and *nonfatal* attacks. The findings were replicated in a second study of nearly 2300 men who were participating in a normative aging study (Kawachi et al., 1994b, 1995).

Given these strong associations between depression (and anxiety) and risk for CHD, increasing attention is being paid to the need

for treatment interventions. Most people with clinical depression are untreated, unnecessarily increasing their risk for CHD. Of those with major depression at the time of a heart attack, approximately one-half remain depressed or have relapsed one year later without treatment (Hance et al., 1996). Yet there is promising evidence that various treatments can help heart attack patients who are depressed. Linden, Stossel, and Maurice's (1996) review of the literature on psychosocial interventions for depression in CHD patients found good evidence that psychosocial interventions can decrease depression, systolic blood pressure, heart rate, and cholesterol levels. Moreover, patients who did not receive psychosocial treatment were 1.7 times more likely to die from their CHD, and 1.8 times more likely to have another heart attack in a two-year follow-up period than were patients who were treated for their depression and anxiety. Drug treatments are also considered more promising than in the past because the new class of antidepressants—the SSRIs (see Chapters 6 and 16)—are not contraindicated for patients with CHD as older tricyclic antidepressants often were (Chesney, 1996; Shapiro, 1996). Finally, at least one study has shown that cardiac rehabilitation and exercise programs that are frequently suggested to patients who have had a heart attack to improve their physical condition also significantly improves depression (Milani, Lavie, & Cassidy, 1996).

Fortunately, the findings reviewed here have not gone unnoticed by researchers at the National Heart, Lung, and Blood Institute of the National Institutes of Health. A very large study is now being conducted of 3000 heart attack patients at eight clinical sites across the

United States to investigate whether interventions directed at decreasing depression immediately after a heart attack actually reduce the risk of future heart attacks and cardiac death. This is one more indication of the influence that behavioral medicine is having on drawing attention to the importance of psychological rather than purely medical variables in prevention of the leading cause of death in the United States today.

REFERENCES

Chesney, M. (1996). New behavioral risk factors for coronary heart disease: Implications for intervention. In K. Orth-Gomer & N. Schneiderman (Eds.), *Behavioral medicine approaches to cardiovascular disease prevention* (pp. 169–182). Mahwah, NJ: Lawrence Erlbaum.

De Silva, R. A. (1993). Cardiac arrhythmias and sudden cardiac death. In A. Stoudemire, B. Fogel (Eds.), *Medical-psychiatric practice* (vol 2, p. 199). Washington, DC: American Psychiatric Press.

Eriksen, W. (1994). The role of social support in the pathogenesis of coronary heart disease. A literature review. *Fam. Pract., 11,* 201–209.

Frasure-Smith, N., Lesperance, F., & Talajic, M. (1993). Depression following myocardial infarction: Impact on 6-month survival. *JAMA., 270,* 1819–1825.

Frasure-Smith, N., Lesperance, F., & Talajic, M. (1995). Depression and 18-month prognosis following myocardial infarction. *Circulation, 91,* 999.

Hance, M., Carney, R., Freedland, K., & Skala, J. (1996). Depression in patients with coronary heart disease: A 12 month follow-up. *Gen. Hosp. Psychiat., 18,* 61–65.

Kawachi, I., Colditz, G., Ascherio, A., et al. (1994a). Prospective study of phobic anxiety and risk of coronary heart disease in men. *Circulation, 89,* 1992.

Kawachi, I., Sparrow, D., Vokonas, P., et al. (1994b). Symptoms of anxiety and risk of coronary heart disease: The normative aging study. *Circulation, 90,* 2225.

Kawachi, I., Sparrow, D., Vokonas, P., et al. (1995). Decreased heart rate variability in men with phobic anxiety (data from the normative aging study.) *Amer. J. Cardiol., 75,* 882.

Kolata, G. (1997). Does depression or heart disease come first? *New York Times,* January 14, 1997.

Ladwig, K., Roll, G., Breithardt, G., et al. (1994). Post-infarction depression and incomplete recovery 6 months after acute myocardial infarction. *Lancet, 343,* 20–23.

Leor, W., Poole, W., & Kloner, R. (1996). Sudden cardiac death triggered by an earthquake. *New Engl. J. Med., 334,* 413.

Linden, W., Stossel, C., & Maurice, J. (1996). Psychosocial interventions for patients with coronary artery disease. *Arch. Intern. Med., 157,* 745–752.

Milani, R., Lavie, C., & Cassidy, M. (1996). Effects of cardiac rehabilitation and exercise training programs on depression in patients after major coronary events. *Amer. Heart J., 132,* 726–732.

Pratt, L., Ford, D., Crum, R. Armenian, H., Galb, J., & Eaton, W. (1996). Depression, psychotropic medication, and risk of myocardial infarction. *Circulation, 94,* 3123–3129.

Scheier, M., & Bridges, M. (1995). Person variables and health: Personality predispositions and acute psychological states as shared determinants for disease. *Psychosom. Med. 57,* 255–268.

Shapiro, P. A. (1996). Psychiatric aspects of cardiovascular disease. *Psychiat. Clin. N. Amer., 19,* 613–629.

ASSESSMENT, TREATMENT, AND PREVENTION

CHAPTER

15

CLINICAL
ASSESSMENT

Adolf Wölffli, Irren-Anstalt Band-Hain. Wölffli (1864–1930), born in Bern, Switzerland, was abandoned by his father in early childhood and at the age of eight was removed from the care of his mother—occurrences that marked the beginning of violent, erratic behaviors that finally culminated in a schizophrenic breakdown. Wölffli created an imaginary world in much of his artwork, one in which elements and symbols are arranged according to his paranoid thinking.

A patient's "presenting complaint" to a clinician usually initiates a process of assessment, whereby the clinician attempts to understand the nature and extent of the problem for which help is being sought. At times this process of inquiry is convoluted and challenging, reminiscent of a Sherlock Holmes exercise in inductive and deductive logic. On other occasions assessment is a relatively straightforward matter in which the clinician may, with a high probability of being correct, come to a rapid conclusion about the basis for the complaint and the proper disposition of the case. Pediatricians whose practices tend to be confined to a local clientele, for example, know what childhood infections are "going around" at a given time. A child who has complaints that mimic the characteristic symptom profile for a common infection will likely be found to have that disease. Even so, the conscientious pediatrician will usually want to confirm an initial diagnostic impression with lab studies that identify the infectious organism involved before initiating specifically targeted treatment.

Confirming diagnostic impressions is thus a matter of good practice even in the most routine clinical situations. For the mental health practitioner, few clinical situations are as routine as our pediatric example, and adequate techniques for confirming initial impressions may prove far more elusive. With rare exceptions, the "lab work" essential to much medical assessment is irrelevant in this domain. Psychological disorders usually lack identifying biological characteristics. Furthermore, they are always interlaced with the personalities of the individuals suffering them and usually with the entire surrounding social fabric. Every instance is likely to be the product of a complex organization of contributing factors, many of which may not be apparent either immediately or after many months of intense scrutiny in the course of psychotherapy. As this last statement implies, psychological assessment or diagnosis can be an ongoing process that proceeds along with, rather than only preceding, treatment efforts.

In addition, as we have seen in earlier chapters, even where a specific diagnosis may be confidently determined, it will normally provide little of direct clinical significance beyond a descriptive summary of the behavioral observations the clinician has been able to make. It will not reveal, as do most medical diagnoses, the underlying pathologic processes producing the condition (for example, fever) that is observed. For these reasons the assessment of mental disorders is usually more difficult, more uncertain, and more protracted than it is for physical diseases.

It is no less critically important, however. No rational, specific treatment plan can be instituted without at least some general notion of what problems need to be addressed. As treatment proceeds, it is guided by the clinician's continuing assessment of the client's problems.

We will focus in this chapter on procedures especially appropriate to an initial clinical assessment, where an attempt is made to identify the main dimensions of a client's problem and to predict the likely course of events under various conditions. It is at this initial stage that crucial decisions have to be made—such as what if any treatment approach is to be offered, whether the problem will require hospitalization, to what extent family members will need to be included as co-clients, and so on. Sometimes these decisions must be made quickly, as in emergency conditions, and without recourse to critical information that would probably (but not necessarily) become available with extended client contact. As will be seen, various psychological measurement instruments are employed to maximize assessment efficiency in this type of pretreatment examination process (Gaw & Beutler, 1995).

A less obvious but equally important function of pretreatment assessment is that of establishing baselines for various psychological functions so that the effects produced by treatment can be measured. Criteria based on these measurements may be established as part of the treatment plan, such that the therapy is considered successful and is terminated only when the client's behavior meets these predetermined criteria. Also, as will be seen in Chapters 16 and 17, comparison of posttreatment with pretreatment assessment results is an essential feature of many research projects designed to evaluate the efficacy of various therapies.

Two other relatively common applications of psychological assessments will also be described in this chapter. The first application, involving determining whether an individual is experiencing psychological adjustment problems, centers on the use of psychological tests in court testimony. The second variant of this pretreatment assessment is the use of psychological assessment instruments in screening candidates for various roles and occupations. Here the effort is basically one of identifying persons who appear to be psychologically unfit (or, alternatively, highly suited) for the type of assignment or work sought. For example, a police recruit who appears to have uncertain control of anger and aggressive impulses may need to be counseled about possibly adopting another occupational goal, or about seeking therapy to remedy a lack of con-

trol that could be dangerous in an occupation involving both great stress and constant access to lethal weapons.

In this chapter, we will review some of the more commonly used assessment procedures and show how the data obtained can be integrated into a coherent clinical picture for use in making decisions about referral and treatment. Our survey will include a discussion of neuropsychological assessment, the clinical interview, behavioral observation, and personality assessment through the use of projective and objective psychological tests.

Let us look first at what, exactly, a clinician is trying to learn during the psychological assessment of a client.

THE INFORMATION SOUGHT IN ASSESSMENT

What does a clinician need to know? First, of course, *the problem must be identified*. Is it a situational problem precipitated by some environmental stressor, a manifestation of a more pervasive and long-term disorder, or is it perhaps some combination of the two? Is there any evidence of recent deterioration in cognitive functioning? What is the duration of the current complaint and how is the person dealing with the problem? What, if any, prior help has been sought? Are there indications of self-defeating behavior and personality deterioration, or is the individual using available personal and environmental resources in a good effort to cope? How pervasively has the problem affected the person's performance of important social roles? Does the individual's symptomatic behavior fit any of the diagnostic patterns in the DSM-IV?

As we have seen, there has been a trend against overdependence on diagnostic labeling, particularly since a diagnosis provides only a limited perspective on a patient's problems. On the other hand, it is often important to have an adequate classification of the presenting problem for a number of reasons. In many cases, a formal diagnosis is necessary before insurance claims can be filed. Clinically, knowledge of a person's type of disorder can help in planning and managing the appropriate treatment. Administratively, it is essential to know the range of diagnostic problems that are represented among the patient or client population and for which treatment facilities need to be available. If most patients at a facility have been diagnosed as having personality disorders, for example, then the staffing, physical environment, and treatment facilities should be arranged accordingly. Thus, the nature of the difficulty needs to be understood as clearly as possible, including a categorization if appropriate.

For most clinical purposes, a formal diagnostic classification per se is much less important than having *a basic understanding of the individual's history, intellectual functioning, personality characteristics, and environmental pressures and resources.* That is, an adequate assessment includes much more than the diagnostic label. For example, it should include an objective description of the person's behavior. How does the person characteristically respond to other people? Are there excesses in behavior, such as eating or drinking too much? Are there notable deficits, as, for example, in social skills? How appropriate is the person's behavior? Is the person manifesting behavior that would be acceptable in some contexts but is often displayed where it is plainly unresponsive to the situation or to reasonable social expectations? Excesses, deficits, and appropriateness are key dimensions to be noted if the clinician is to understand the particular disorder that has brought the individual to the clinic or hospital.

In addition, assessment needs to include *a description of any relevant long-term personality characteristics.* Has the person typically responded in deviant ways to particular kinds of situations, for example, ones requiring submission to legitimate authority? Do there seem to be personality traits or behavior patterns that predispose the individual to behave in maladaptive ways across a broad range of circumstances? Does the person tend to become enmeshed with others to the point of losing his or her identity, or is he or she so self-contained that intimate exchange is routinely aborted? Is the person able to accept help from others? Is the person capable of genuine affection, or of accepting appropriate responsibility for others' welfare? Such questions are necessarily at the heart of many assessment efforts.

It is also important to assess *the social context in which the individual operates.* What kinds of environmental demands are typically placed on the person, and what supports or special stressors exist in his or her life situation? For example, being the primary caretaker for a spouse suffering from Alzheimer's disease is sufficiently challenging that relatively few can manage the task without significant psychological impairment, especially where outside supports are lacking. As we have seen, the DSM-IV classification includes guidelines for rating both the severity of the stressors in a person's current environment and the level of a person's overall adjustment in meeting the demands of a complex social environment.

The diverse and often conflicting bits of information about the individual's personality traits, behavior patterns, environmental demands, and so on must then be integrated into a consistent and meaningful picture. Some clinicians refer to this picture as a **dynamic formulation,** because it not only describes the current situation but includes hypotheses about what is driving the person to behave in maladaptive ways. At this point in the assessment, the clinician should have a plausible explanation, for example, for why a normally passive and mild-mannered man suddenly flew into a rage and started breaking up furniture.

The formulation should *allow the clinician to develop hypotheses about the client's future behavior* as well. What is the likelihood of improvement or deterioration if the person's problems are left untreated? Which behaviors should be the initial focus of change, and what treatment methods are likely to be most efficient in producing this change? How much change might reasonably be expected from a particular type of treatment?

Where feasible, decisions about treatment are made collaboratively with the consent and approval of the individual. In cases of severe disorder, however, they may have to be made without the patient's participation or in rare instances even without consulting responsible kin. As has already been indicated, a knowledge of the patient's strengths and resources is important; in short, what qualities does the patient bring to treatment that can enhance the chances of improvement?

VARYING TYPES OF ASSESSMENT DATA

Because a wide range of factors can play important roles in causing and maintaining maladaptive behavior, assessment may involve the coordinated use of physical, psychological, and environmental assessment procedures. As we have indicated, however, the nature and comprehensiveness of clinical assessments vary depending on the problem and the treatment agency's facilities. Assessment by phone in a suicide prevention center (Stelmachers, 1995), for example, is quite different from assessment aimed at determining whether a hospitalized patient is sufficiently intelligent, verbal, and psychologically minded to be likely to profit significantly from individual psychotherapy.

Furthermore, exactly how a clinician goes about the assessment process often depends on his or her basic orientation. For example, a biologically oriented clinician, typically a psychiatrist or other medical practitioner, will likely focus on biological assessment methods aimed at determining any underlying organic malfunctioning that may be causing the maladaptive behavior. A psychoanalytically oriented clinician may choose unstructured personality assessment techniques, such as the Rorschach inkblots or the Thematic Apperception Test (TAT), to identify latent intrapsychic conflicts. A behaviorally oriented clinician, in an effort to determine the functional relationships between environmental events or reinforcements and the abnormal behavior, will rely on such techniques as behavioral observation and systematic self-monitoring to identify maladaptive learned patterns; for a cognitively oriented behaviorist, the focus would shift to the dysfunctional thoughts supposedly mediating those patterns. A humanistically oriented clinician might use interview techniques to uncover blocked or distorted personal growth, and an interpersonally oriented clinician might use such techniques as personal confrontations and behavioral observations to pinpoint difficulties in interpersonal relationships.

The preceding examples represent general trends and are in no way meant to imply that clinicians of a particular orientation limit themselves to a particular assessment method or that each assessment technique is limited to a particular theoretical orientation. Such trends are instead a matter of emphasis and point up the fact that certain types of assessments are more conducive than others to uncovering particular causal factors, or for eliciting information about symptomatic behavior central to understanding and treating the disorder within a given conceptual framework.

In what follows, we will discuss the way in which both physical and psychosocial data are collected. Then we will examine an actual psychological study that has drawn on a variety of assessment data.

IMPORTANCE OF RAPPORT BETWEEN THE CLINICIAN AND THE CLIENT

Before psychological assessment can proceed effectively to provide a clear understanding of the patient's behavior and symptoms, good rapport needs to be established between the clinician and the person being evaluated. Important components of a good relationship in a clinical assessment situation include the following:

- Clients need to be feel that the testing will help the practitioner gain a clear understanding of their problems. Clients need to understand how the tests will be used and how the psychologist will incorporate them in the clinical evaluation.

- Individuals being assessed in mental health settings are asked to provide a great deal of personal information. They need to be assured that the feelings, beliefs, attitudes, and personal history that they are disclosing will be appropriately used and will be kept in strict confidence and made available only to therapists or others involved in the case. An important aspect of confidentiality is that the test results are released to a third party only if the client signs an appropriate release form. In cases in which the person is being tested for a third party, such as the court system, the client in effect becomes the referring source—the judge ordering the evaluation—not the individual being tested. In these cases the testing relationship is likely to be strained and rapport is likely to be difficult. Of course, in a court-ordered evaluation the person's test-taking behavior is likely to be very different from what it would be otherwise, and the test interpretation needs to reflect this different motivational set.

- Clients being tested in a clinical situation are usually highly motivated to be evaluated and usually like to know the results of the testing. Moreover, providing test feedback in a clinical setting can be an important element in the treatment process (Beutler, 1995). Interestingly, when patients are given appropriate feedback on the test results they tend to improve—just from gaining a perspective on their problems from the testing. Finn and Tonsager (1992) recently showed that the test feedback process itself can be a powerful clinical intervention. They conducted a clinical study in which one group of patients from a therapy waiting list was provided MMPI-2 test feedback. The second group of patients from the waiting list was administered the MMPI-2 but not given test feedback. The results of the study were informative: They found that persons who were provided feedback on their MMPI-2, compared with the control group, showed a significant decline in reported symptoms and an increase in measured self-esteem.

ASSESSMENT OF THE PHYSICAL ORGANISM

In some situations or with certain psychological problems, a medical evaluation is necessary to rule out physical abnormalities that may be causing or contributing to the problem. The medical evaluation may include both general physical and special examinations aimed at assessing the structural (anatomical) and functional (physiological) integrity of the brain as a behaviorally significant physical system.

The General Physical Examination

A physical examination consists of the kinds of procedures most of us have experienced in getting a "medical checkup." Typically, a medical history is obtained and the major systems of the body are checked. This part of the assessment procedure is of obvious import for disorders that entail physical problems, such as psychogenically induced disease, and somatoform, addictive, and organic brain syndromes. In addition, a variety of organic conditions, including various hormonal irregularities, can produce in some people behavioral symptoms that closely mimic those of mental disorders usually considered to have predominantly psychosocial origins. A case in point is the problem of chronic back pain in which psychological factors might play an important part. A diagnostic error in this type of situation resulting in surgery that proves ineffective could prove costly; hence, in equivocal cases most clinicians insist on a medical clearance before initiating psychosocially based interventions.

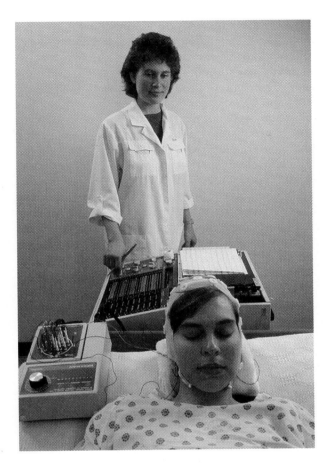

An electroencephalogram (EEG), a graphic record of the brain's electrical activity, is obtained by placing electrodes on the scalp that pick up brain impulses.

The Neurological Examination

Because brain pathology is involved in some mental disorders, a specialized neurological examination is frequently given in addition to the general medical examination. This may involve getting an **electroencephalogram (EEG)** to assess brain-wave patterns in awake and sleeping states. An EEG is a graphic record of the brain's electrical activity. It is obtained by placing electrodes on the scalp and amplifying the minute brain-wave impulses from various brain areas; these amplified impulses drive oscillating pens whose deviations are traced on a strip of paper moving at a constant speed. Much is known about the normal pattern of brain impulses in waking and sleeping states and under various conditions of sensory stimulation. Significant divergences from the normal pattern can thus reflect abnormalities of brain function, such as might be caused by a brain tumor or other lesion. When an EEG reveals a **dysrhythmia** in the brain's electrical activity, other specialized techniques may be used in an attempt to arrive at a more precise diagnosis of the problem.

Radiological technology, such as **computerized axial tomography**, known in brief as the **CAT scan**, is one of these specialized techniques. Through the use of X rays, a CAT scan reveals images of parts of the brain that might be diseased. This procedure has revolutionized neurological study in recent years by providing rapid access, without surgery, to accurate information about the localization and extent of anomalies in the brain's structural characteristics. The procedure involves the use of computer analysis applied to X-ray beams across sections of a patient's brain to produce images that a neurologist can then interpret.

A newer scanning technique is **positron emission tomography,** the **PET scan.** Though a CAT scan is limited to distinguishing anatomical features, such as the shape of a particular internal structure, a PET scan allows for an appraisal of how an organ is functioning by measuring metabolic processes. The PET scan provides metabolic portraits through tracking natural compounds, like glucose, as they are metabolized by the brain or other organs. By revealing areas of differential metabolic activity, the PET scan enables a medical specialist to obtain more clear-cut diagnoses of brain pathology by, for example, pinpointing sites responsible for epileptic seizures, trauma from head injury or stroke, and brain tumors. Thus the PET scan may be able to reveal problems that are not immediately apparent anatomically. Moreover, the use of PET scans in research on brain pathology occurring in abnormal conditions, such as schizophrenia, depression, and alcoholism has the potential of leading to important discoveries about the organic processes underlying these disorders, thus providing clues to more effective treatment. To date, unfortunately, progress on this front has not, in our judgment, proved very illuminating.

The newest of these internal scanning techniques is **nuclear magnetic resonance imaging (MRI).** Like a CAT scan, this procedure allows visualization of the anatomical features of internal organs, including the brain. Unlike a CAT scan, protracted X-ray of the site of interest is not required, and yet the images obtained are often decidedly clearer. Essentially, MRI involves the precise measurement of variations in magnetic fields that are caused by the varying amounts of water content of various organs and parts of organs. In this manner the anatomical structure of a cross section at any given plane through an organ such as the brain can be computed and graphically depicted with astonishing structural differentiation and clarity. MRI thus makes possible, by noninvasive means, visualization of all but the most minute abnormalities of brain structure. It has been particularly useful in confirming degenerative brain processes, as manifested, for example, in enlarged cerebrospinal fluid spaces within the brain. Therefore, MRI studies have considerable potential to illuminate the contribution of brain anomalies to "nonorganic" psychoses, such as schizophrenia, and some progress in this area has in fact been made, as noted in Chapter 12.

The Neuropsychological Examination

The techniques so far described are fairly accurate in identifying abnormalities in the brain's physical properties. Usually, although by no means always, such abnormalities are accompanied by gross impairments in behavior and varied psychological deficits, although the nature of the latter may not be accurately predicted even after precisely localizing these physical abnormalities. Also, behavioral and psychological impairments due to organic brain abnormalities may become manifest before any organic

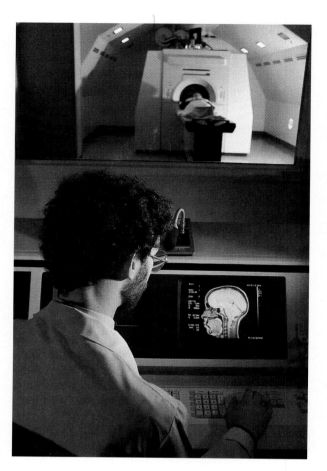

Nuclear magnetic resonance imaging (MRI) allows visualization of the anatomical features of the brain without protracted X-raying, as in CAT scans. In MRI an anatomical structure can be computed and graphically depicted with astonishing differentiation and clarity.

brain lesion is detectable by scanning or other means. In these instances reliable techniques are needed to measure any alteration in behavioral or psychological functioning that has occurred because of the organic brain pathology. This need is met by a growing cadre of psychologists specializing in **neuropsychological assessment,** which involves the use of an expanding array of testing devices to measure a person's cognitive, perceptual, and motor performance as clues to the extent and location of brain damage.

In many instances of known or suspected organic brain involvement, a clinical neuropsychologist will administer a test battery to a patient. The person's performance on standardized tasks, particularly perceptual-motor ones, can give valuable clues about any cognitive and intellectual impairment following brain damage (Filskov & Locklear, 1982; Miller, 1992; Reitan & Wolfson, 1985). Such testing can even provide clues as to the probable location of the brain damage, though PET scans, MRIs, and other

HIGHLIGHT | 15.1

Neuropsychological Examinations: Determining Brain-Behavior Relationships

The Halstead-Reitan battery is a neuropsychological examination composed of several tests and variables from which an "index of impairment" can be computed (Reitan & Wolfson, 1985). In addition, it provides specific information about a subject's functioning in several skill areas. Though it typically takes 4–6 hours to complete and requires substantial administrative time, it is being used increasingly in neurological evaluations because it yields a great deal of useful information about an individual's cognitive and motor processes (Filskov & Boll, 1986; Filskov & Goldstein, 1974; Filskov & Locklear, 1982). The Halstead-Reitan battery for adults is made up of the following tests:

1. *The Halstead Category Test* measures a subject's ability to learn and remember material and can provide clues as to his or her judgment and impulsivity. The subject is presented with a stimulus (on a screen) that suggests a number between 1 and 4. The subject presses a button indicating which number is "correct." A cor-

rect choice is followed by the sound of a pleasant doorbell and an incorrect choice by a loud buzzer. The person is required to determine from the pattern of buzzers and bells what the underlying principle of the correct choice is.

2. *The Tactual Performance Test* measures a subject's motor speed, response to the unfamiliar, and ability to learn and use tactile and kinesthetic cues. The test consists of a board that has spaces for ten blocks of varied shapes. The subject is blindfolded (never actually seeing the board) and asked to place the blocks into the correct grooves in the board. Later, the subject is asked to draw the blocks and the board from tactile memory.

3. *The Rhythm Test* is an auditory perception task used to measure attention and sustained concentration. It is a subtest of Seashore's Test of musical talent and includes 30 pairs of rhythmic beats that are presented on a tape recorder. On this test, a subject is required to determine if the pairs are the same or different.

4. *The Speech Sounds Perception Test* is a test to determine if an individual can identify spoken words. Nonsense words are presented on a tape recorder, and the subject is asked to identify the presented word from a list of four printed words. This task measures the subject's concentration, attention, and comprehension.

5. *The Finger Oscillation Task* measures the speed at which an individual can depress a lever with the index finger. Several trials are given with each hand.

In addition to the Halstead-Reitan battery, other tests, referred to as allied procedures, may be used in a neuropsychology laboratory. For example, Boll (1980) recommends the use of the modified Halstead-Wepman Aphasia Screening Test for obtaining information about a subject's language ability and about his or her abilities to identify numbers and body parts, to follow directions, to spell, and to pantomime simple actions.

physical tests are more effective in determining the exact location of the injury.

Many neuropsychologists prefer to select a highly individualized array of tests to administer, depending on a patient's case history and other available information. Others opt for a battery consisting of a standard set of tests that have been preselected so as to sample in a systematic and comprehensive manner a broad range of psychological competencies known to be adversely affected by various types of brain injury. The use of a constant set of tests has many research and clinical advantages, although it may compromise flexibility. One such standard battery, widely used, is the Halstead-Reitan, whose components are described in HIGHLIGHT 15.1.

Typically taking about six hours to administer, the Halstead-Reitan can be a problem in some clini-

cal settings where time and funding are limited. Understandably, examinee fatigue may also be a limiting factor, particularly where a patient is not well. Another neuropsychological battery, the Luria-Nebraska (Golden, 1978), which takes only about two and a half hours to administer, has received much attention as an alternative to the Halstead-Reitan. Both these batteries, as well as others of similar purpose and construction, provide their information without the risks attendant to more invasive neurological examination procedures (Filskov & Goldstein, 1974). Still, however, the Halstead-Reitan battery continues to grow in use because it yields a great deal of useful information—more than the Luria-Nebraska—about a patient's cognitive and motor processes (Boll, 1980; Filskov & Locklear, 1982; Hartlage, Asken, & Hornsby, 1987).

In summary, the medical and neuropsychological sciences are developing many new procedures to assess brain functioning and behavioral manifestations of organic disorder. Medical procedures to assess organic brain damage include EEGs and CAT, PET, and MRI scans. The new technology holds a great deal of promise for detecting and evaluating organic brain dysfunction and for providing increased understanding of brain functioning through graphic mapping of the brain. Neuropsychological testing provides a clinician with important behavioral information on how organic brain damage is affecting a person's present functioning.

PSYCHOSOCIAL ASSESSMENT

Psychosocial assessment attempts to provide a realistic picture of an individual in interaction with the environment. This picture includes relevant information concerning the individual's personality makeup and present level of functioning, as well as information about the stressors and resources in his or her life situation. For example, early in the process, clinicians may act like puzzle solvers, absorbing as much information about the client as possible—present feelings, attitudes, memories, demographic facts, and so on—and trying to fit the pieces together into a meaningful pattern. They typically formulate hypotheses and discard or confirm them as they proceed. Starting with a global technique, such as a clinical interview, clinicians may later select more specific assessment tasks or tests. The following are some of the psychosocial procedures that may be used.

Assessment Interviews

An assessment interview, often considered the central element of the assessment process, usually involves a face-to-face interaction in which a clinician obtains information about various aspects of a patient's situation, behavior, and personality makeup. The interview may vary from a simple set of questions or prompts, as in the *mental status exam* used chiefly by psychiatrists and other physicians, to a more extended and detailed format. It may be relatively open in character, with an interviewer making moment-to-moment decisions about his or her next question based on responses to prior ones, or it may be more tightly controlled and structured so as to ensure that a particular set of questions is introduced. In the latter case, the interviewer may choose

from a number of highly structured, standardized interview formats whose reliability has been established in prior research. As used here, *reliability* means simply that two interviewers assessing the same client will generate highly similar conclusions about the client, a type of consensus that research shows can by no means be taken for granted.

Although we know of few clinicians who express enthusiasm for the more controlled and structured type of assessment interview, the research data are clear in showing it to yield far more reliable results, in general, than the more flexible format. There appears to be widespread overconfidence among clinicians in the accuracy of their own methods and judgments (Garb, 1989; Kleinmuntz, 1990). On the other hand, every rule has its exceptions, and we have seen brilliantly conducted assessment interviews where each question was fashioned on the spur of the moment. In most instances, however, an assessor would be wise to conduct an interview that is carefully structured in terms of goals, comprehensive symptom review, other content to be explored, and the type of relationship the interviewer attempts to establish with the subject. Such an approach is likely to minimize error over the long term, although we acknowledge that a more creative and spontaneous interview format may be more productive in particular clinical situations.

The reliability of the assessment interview may also be enhanced by the use of rating scales that help focus inquiry and quantify the interview data. For example, a subject may be rated on a three-, five-, or seven-point scale with respect to self-esteem, anxiety, and various other characteristics. Such a structured and preselected format is particularly effective in giving a comprehensive impression or "profile" of the subject and his or her life situation, and in revealing specific problems or crises—such as marital difficulties, drug dependence, or suicidal fantasies—that may require immediate therapeutic intervention.

As already suggested, clinical interviews are subject to error and have been criticized as an unreliable source of information on which to base important clinical decisions. Evidence of this unreliability includes the fact that different clinicians have often arrived at different formal diagnoses based on interview data they elicit for a particular patient. It is chiefly for this reason that recent versions of the DSM (that is, III, III-R, and IV) have emphasized an "operational" assessment approach, one that specifies observable criteria for diagnosis and provides specific guidelines for making diagnostic judgments. A clinician who is seeking to render a formal diagnosis thus must incorporate at least minimal structure into the interview or risk missing data essential to such a diagnosis. "Winging it" has limited use in this type of assessment process. Although the available data on the improved reliability of psychiatric diagnoses have shown the operational approach to have decided advantages, there has also doubtless been some cost in reducing interviewer flexibility and in encouraging undue preoccupation with observable "signs" at the expense of overall understanding of patient functioning (Simons, 1987).

As was suggested in Chapter 1, the developments just described can be characterized as favoring the removal of the diagnostician, as a subjective judge, from the diagnostic process; to the degree possible, diagnosis is rendered "automatic." But if a human judge is unnecessary—perhaps even a troublesome source of error—then why not take the further step of computerizing the diagnostic process? Computers, after all, are superb at remembering and following explicitly stated rules for decision making. Where clinically feasible, they can even be used online to ask the same sorts of questions, and elicit the same sorts of answers, as would a human interviewer; that is, a patient can be "interviewed" by a computer terminal or console.

In fact, efforts of this sort have already been developed (Erdman, Klein, & Greist, 1985). Computer programs with highly sophisticated branching subroutines are available to "tailor-make" a diagnostic interview for a patient. Stein (1987), for example, described a program called the Computerized Diagnostic Interview for Children that can conduct a standard psychiatric interview. Several more specific clinical assessment tasks have been adapted for computer administration. For example, Fowler and colleagues (1987) have designed a Clinical Problem Checklist that can provide a therapist with an overview of a client's presenting symptoms. Allen and Skinner (1987) have designed a computer program that takes down a client's alcohol- and drug-abuse history, and Giannetti (1987) has a computer program that records a client's social history. All these programs are fairly easy to administer and can provide a clinician with a wealth of reliable and useful data. A computer-based diagnostic interview program for DSM-IV that can be quite valuable to the clinician conducting a diagnostic evaluation has been published. (see HIGHLIGHT 15.2).

Despite the progress made in reducing subjective factors by computerizing or otherwise making various aspects of the assessment process relatively automatic, it is important to understand that excessive reliance on such techniques can introduce error. The complexity of human behavior is bound to produce many exceptions to any rule. In the final analysis, therefore, there is probably no adequate substitute for expert clinical judgment (Carson, 1990b). Where such judgment is available when needed, these techniques can substantially improve assessment efficiency.

The Clinical Observation of Behavior

Direct observation of an individual's characteristic behavior has long been considered important for adequate psychosocial assessment. The main purpose of direct observation is to learn more about the person's psychological functioning through the objective description of appearance and behavior in various contexts. Though such observations would ideally occur within the person's natural environment, they are typically confined to clinic or hospital settings. For example, a brief description is usually made of a subject's behavior on hospital admission, and more detailed observations are made periodically on the ward. These descriptions include information about the subject's personal hygiene, emotional behavior, delusions or hallucinations, anxiety, sexual behavior, aggressive or suicidal tendencies, and so on.

In addition to making their own observations, many clinicians enlist their patients' help by providing instruction in self-observation and objective reporting of behavior, thoughts, and feelings as they occur in various natural settings. Such **self-monitoring** can be a valuable aid in determining the kinds of situations, possibly previously unrecognized, in which maladaptive behavior is likely to be evoked, and numerous studies also show it to have therapeutic benefits in its own right. Alternatively, a patient may be asked to fill out a more or less formal self-report or a checklist concerning problematic reactions experienced in various situations. Many instruments have been published in the professional literature and are commercially available to clinicians. These approaches recognize that people are excellent sources of information about themselves. Assuming that the right questions are asked and that people are willing to disclose information about themselves, the results can have a crucial bearing on treatment planning—for example, by providing essential information for structuring a behavioral treatment intervention.

As in the case of interviews, the use of **rating scales** in clinical observation and in self-reports helps not only to organize information but also to encourage reliability and objectivity. That is, the formal structure of a scale is likely to keep unwarranted observer inferences to a minimum. Rating scales

Clinical Diagnosis by Electronic Computer: The D-Tree

The process of clinical diagnosis can be a complicated and difficult one at times. The current clinical diagnosis system, DSM-IV, contains a number of explicit rules for each diagnostic category that define the symptoms and behavior that the patient must show to meet the particular diagnosis. The diagnostic system was developed in such a way that if the diagnostic criteria are explicitly followed the appropriate diagnostic "match" will be reliably made. One difficulty, of course, is that there are many different diagnostic categories with similar exclusion and inclusion rules. Therefore, the clinician needs to approach the classification task in a highly systematic manner, for example, following a branching strategy until the appropriate diagnostic classification is reached. The recommended diagnostic process follows a "decision tree" approach. Such an approach allows the practitioner to follow the hierarchial structure of DSM-IV and ask the appropriate questions for each diagnostic question until the most appropriate category is reached.

A decision tree begins with a set of particular clinical features. "When one of these features is a prominent part of the presenting clinical picture, the clinician can follow the series of questions to rule in or out various disorders" (American Psychiatric Association, 1994). Sev-

eral standard decision trees are provided in DSM-IV, for example, a decision tree to develop a differential diagnosis of mental disorders due to a general medical condition and a decision tree to differentially diagnose psychotic disorders. The decision tree approach to classification is illustrated below. The clinician follows the logical flow chart and determines the presence or absence of the criteria for the patient in question. The following decision tree for somatoform disorders from DSM-IV illustrates this approach on the next page.

The branching strategy for the decision tree presents the clinician with a sequence of specific diagnostic questions such as "are hallucinations present," to which "yes" or "no" responses determine the appropriate next question until a particular diagnosis is confirmed. Given the fact that a clinician can be presented with all of the appropriate questions in a systematic manner, this decision sequence could be asked and recorded in a very automatic, systematic way by a computer. The diagnostic process, in terms of the appropriate sequence of questions to address, has been demonstrated to be effectively accomplished by computer. Michael First, a noted psychiatrist who has a substantial background and education in computer programming, wrote a diagnostic program for DSM-III-

R that came to be widely used by psychiatrists for both clinical assessment and training. He has recently revised this computer program, the D-Tree (Multi Health Systems, 1995) to provide DSM-IV diagnoses.

The D-Tree computer software is designed to guide the practitioner through the diagnostic process by presenting appropriate questions to the clinician. When all relevant information is provided, the computer gives the most likely DSM-IV diagnosis. If the clinician fails to provide the needed information in response to a question, the program halts and an instruction urges the clinician to seek the needed information. If, for example, the D-Tree program requests information about whether the patient has had auditory hallucinations and the practitioner has failed to assess this area, then he or she might reinterview the patient to obtain the needed data.

The D-Tree program has been a highly successful means of providing reliable clinical diagnoses as well as serving as a training guide for DSM-IV. Practitioners who use this computer aid soon become aware of the explicit rules to follow in developing DSM-IV diagnoses and the need to obtain clear verification of all the elements of a diagnosis before conclusions are reached about the patient.

commonly used are those that enable a rater to indicate not only the presence or absence of a trait or behavior but also its prominence. The following is an example of such a rating-scale item; the observer would check the most appropriate alternative.

Sexual behavior:

_____1. Sexually assaultive: aggressively approaches males or females with sexual intent.

_____2. Sexually soliciting: exposes genitals with sexual intent, makes overt sexual advances to other patients or staff, masturbates openly.

_____3. No overt sexual behavior: not preoccupied with discussion or sexual matters.

_____4. Avoids sex topics: made uneasy by discussion of sex, becomes disturbed if approached sexually by others.

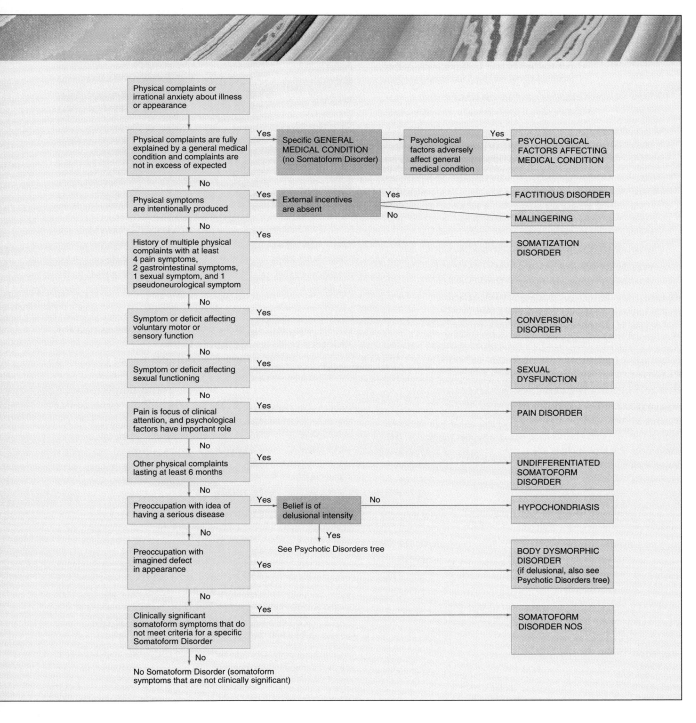

_____5. Excessive prudishness about sex: considers sex filthy, condemns sexual behavior in others, becomes panic-stricken if approached sexually.

Ratings like these may be made not only as part of an initial evaluation but also to check on the course or outcome of treatment.

One of the rating scales most widely used for recording observations in clinical practice and in psychiatric research is the *Brief Psychiatric Rating Scale (BPRS)*. The BPRS provides a structured and quantifiable format for rating clinical symptoms, such as somatic concern, anxiety, emotional withdrawal, guilt feelings, hostility, suspiciousness, and unusual thought patterns. It contains 18 scales that are scored from ratings made by a clinician following an interview with a patient. The distinct patterns of behavior reflected in the BPRS ratings enable clinicians to make a standardized comparison of their patients' symptoms with the behavior of other psychiatric patients (Overall & Hollister, 1982). The BPRS has been found to be an extremely useful instrument in clinical research, especially for the purpose of assigning patients to treatment groups on the basis of similarity in symptoms. A similar but more specifically targeted instrument, the *Hamilton Rating Scale for Depression (HRSD)*, has become almost the standard in this respect for selecting clinically depressed research subjects, and also for assessing the response of such subjects to various treatments.

Observations made in clinical settings by trained observers can provide behavioral data useful in ongoing clinical management. Paul and colleagues (Mariotto, Paul, & Licht, 1995; Paul & Lentz, 1977; Rich, Paul, & Mariotto, 1988), for example, have developed a comprehensive behavioral assessment program that they have implemented experimentally in a number of hospitals. The program includes evaluating the behavior of chronic patients and monitoring the activities of staff members working with them. Through the use of observational rating systems, they have been able to measure staff behavior in the daily management of patients and ongoing patient behavior on the ward. The behavioral ratings can be used to pinpoint specific behaviors to be changed on the part of members of either group.

Recently, a good deal of attention has focused on observing a subject's behavior in his or her natural surroundings (Leichtman, 1995). For example, children with behavior problems may be observed at home, at school, and in their peer groups. Here the purpose is to obtain a sampling of their behavior in ordinary situations to understand the problems they are facing, the coping patterns they are using, and the environmental conditions that may be reinforcing their maladaptive behavior.

The procedures described above focus on a subject's overt behavior, omitting the often equally important consideration of concurrent mental events—that is, the individual's ongoing thoughts. In an attempt to sample naturally occurring thoughts, psychologists are experimenting with having individuals carry small electronic beepers that produce a signal, such as a soft tone, at unexpected intervals. At each signal, the person is to write down or electronically record whatever thoughts the signal interrupted. These "thought reports" can then be analyzed in various ways, and can be used for some kinds of personality assessment and diagnosis as well

It can be helpful to both a practitioner and a client to observe and assess the client's behavior in an everyday setting, such as his or her home, where there is the opportunity to talk with family members and to discern the stressors and resources in the client's life situation.

as for monitoring progress in psychological therapy (Klinger & Kroll-Mensing, 1995).

In situations where it is not feasible to observe a subject's behavior in everyday settings—as when he or she is institutionalized—an entire family may be asked to meet together in the clinic or hospital where their interactions and difficulties can be observed and studied. In other cases, a social worker may obtain relevant data by visiting a subject's home, talking with family members and others, and observing the stressors and resources in the subject's life situation. In addition to providing important assessment data, this procedure incorporates the "observers" into the therapy program, thereby enhancing the therapy.

Where the object of study is a child, Jones, Reid, and Patterson (1975) have developed a method for coding and quantifying the observations of the child's behavior at school and at home. Concrete instances of behavior and interaction can be observed, recorded, and coded, either by trained observers or by the parents themselves. This method provides the clinician with information about the stimuli that are controlling the child's interactions, which in turn makes it possible for the clinician to evaluate the quality of the child's interactions and to identify the situations that result in behavior problems.

In still other situations where observation in a natural setting is not possible, a clinician may construct or contrive observational opportunities that can provide information about a person's response to particular circumstances. For example, a person who has a phobia for snakes might be placed in a situation where snakelike objects and pictures are presented.

An often-used procedure that enables a clinician to observe a client's behavior directly is **role playing**. The client is instructed to play a part—for example, someone standing up for his or her rights. Role playing a situation like this not only can provide assessment information for the clinician but also can serve as a vehicle for new learning for the client.

Psychological Tests

Interviews and behavioral observation are relatively direct attempts to determine a person's beliefs, attitudes, and problems. Psychological tests, on the other hand, are a more indirect means of assessing psychological characteristics. Scientifically developed psychological tests (as opposed to the recreational ones sometimes appearing in newspapers and magazines) are standardized sets of procedures or tasks for obtaining samples of behavior; a subject's responses to the standardized stimuli are compared with those of other people having comparable demographic characteristics, usually through established test norms or test score distributions. From these comparisons, a clinician can then draw inferences about how much the person's psychological qualities differ from those of a reference group, typically a psychologically normal one. Among the characteristics these tests can measure are coping patterns, motive patterns, personality characteristics, role behaviors, values, levels of depression or anxiety, and intellectual functioning. Impressive advances in the technology of test development have in fact made it possible to develop instruments of acceptable reliability and validity to measure almost any conceivable psychological characteristic in which people vary.

Though more precise and often more reliable than interviews or less standardized observational techniques, psychological tests are far from perfect tools. Their value often depends on the competence of the clinician who interprets them (Carson, 1990b). In general, they are useful diagnostic tools for psychologists in much the same way that blood tests, X-ray films, or MRI scans are useful to physicians. In all these cases, pathology may be revealed in people who appear to be normal, or a general impression of "something wrong" can be checked against more precise information.

Two general categories of psychological tests for use in clinical practice are *intelligence tests* and *personality tests*. We discuss each in the following sections.

Intelligence Tests A clinician can choose from a wide range of intelligence tests. The Wechsler Intelligence Scale for Children-Revised (WISC-R) and the current edition of the Stanford-Binet Intelligence Scale are widely used in clinical settings for measuring the intellectual abilities of children. Probably the most commonly used test for measuring adult intelligence is the Wechsler Adult Intelligence Scale-Revised (WAIS-R). It includes both verbal and performance material and consists of 11 subtests. A brief description of two of the subtests—one verbal and one performance—will serve to illustrate the type of functions the WAIS-R measures:

General information (verbal). This subtest consists of questions designed to evaluate the individual's range of information on material that is ordinarily encountered. For example, the individual is asked to do such things as tell how many weeks there are in a year, name the colors of the American flag, and tell who Martin Luther King was.

Picture completion (performance). This subtest consists of 20 cards showing pictures, each with a part missing; the subject's task is to indicate what is missing. This test is designed to measure the individual's ability to discriminate between essential and nonessential elements in a situation. (Wechsler, 1981)

Individually administered intelligence tests—such as the WISC-R, WAIS-R, and the Stanford-Binet—typically require 2–3 hours to administer, score, and interpret. In many clinical situations, there is not sufficient time or funding to use these tests in every assessment situation. In cases where intellectual impairment or organic brain damage is thought to be central to a patient's problem, intelligence testing may be the most crucial diagnostic procedure to include in the test battery. Moreover, information about the cognitive functioning of patients can provide valuable clues as to the person's intellectual resources in dealing with problems (Zetzer & Beutler, 1995). Yet in many clinical settings and for many clinical cases, gaining a thorough understanding of a client's problems and initiating a treatment program do not require knowing the kind of detailed information about intellectual functioning these instruments provide. In these cases, intelligence testing would not be recommended.

Personality Tests There are a great many tests designed to measure personal characteristics other than intellectual facility. It is customary to group

A psychologist administering the WISC, an intelligence test that provides information about how well a child performs on a variety of cognitive challenges. An individually administered test such as this can require considerable time—often 2–3 hours—to give, score, and interpret; as such, it is appropriate to use these types of tests primarily when intelligence testing is considered critical to the diagnosis.

these personality tests into *projective* and *objective* tests.

Projective Tests. **Projective tests** are unstructured in that they rely on various ambiguous stimuli, such as inkblots or pictures, rather than explicit verbal questions, and subjects' responses are not limited to the "true," "false," or "cannot say" variety. Through their interpretations of these ambiguous materials, subjects reveal a good deal about their personal preoccupations, conflicts, motives, coping techniques, and other personality characteristics. An assumption underlying the use of projective techniques is that in trying to make sense out of vague, unstructured stimuli, individuals "project" their own problems, motives, and wishes into the situation, inasmuch as they have little else on which to rely in formulating their responses to these materials (Lerner, 1995).

Such responses are akin to the childhood pastime of detecting familiar scenes in cloud formations, with the important exception that the stimuli are in this case fixed and largely the same for all subjects. It is the latter circumstance that permits determination of the normative range of responses to the test materials, which in turn can be used to identify objectively deviant responding. Thus projective tests are aimed at discovering the ways in which an individual's past learning and personality structure may lead him or her to organize and perceive ambiguous information from the environment. Prominent among the several projective tests in common use are the Rorschach Test, the Thematic Apperception Test (TAT), and sentence-completion tests.

The **Rorschach Test** is named after the Swiss psychiatrist Hermann Rorschach, who initiated experimental use of inkblots in personality assessment in 1911. The test uses ten inkblot pictures to which a subject responds in succession after being instructed somewhat as follows (Exner, 1993):

> People may see many different things in these inkblot pictures; now tell me what you see, what it makes you think of, what it means to you.

The following excerpts are taken from the responses of a subject to one of the actual blots:

> "This looks like two men with genital organs exposed. They have had a terrible fight and blood has splashed up against the wall. They have knives or sharp instruments in their hands and have just cut up a body. They have already taken out the lungs and other organs. The body is dismembered . . . nothing remains but a shell . . . the pelvic region. They were fighting as to who will complete the final dismemberment . . . like two vultures swooping down. . . ."

The extremely gory, violent content of this response was not common for the particular blot, nor for any other blot in the series. While no responsible examiner would base conclusions on a single instance, such content was consistent with other data from this subject, who was diagnosed as an antisocial personality with strong hostility.

Use of the Rorschach in clinical assessment is complicated and requires considerable training (Exner, 1991; Exner & Weiner, 1994). Methods of administering the test vary, and some approaches can take several hours and hence must compete for time with other essential clinical services. Furthermore, the results of the Rorschach can be unreliable

The Rorschach Inkblot Test, which uses blots similar to those illustrated here, is a well-known projective test.

because of the subjective nature of test data interpretations. In addition, the types of clinical treatments used in most of today's mental health facilities generally require specific behavioral descriptions rather than descriptions of deep-seated personality dynamics, such as those that typically result from Rorschach Test interpretation.

The Rorschach has been criticized, to some extent unfairly, as an instrument with low or negligible validity. In the hands of a skilled interpreter, the Rorschach has been shown to be useful in uncovering certain psychodynamic issues, such as the impact of unconscious motivations on current perceptions of others. Furthermore, there have been attempts to move beyond the original discursive and free-wheeling approaches and to objectify Rorschach interpretations by clearly specifying test variables and empirically exploring their relationship to external criteria, such as clinical diagnosis (Exner, 1995).

The Rorschach, although generally considered an open-ended, subjective instrument aimed at studying a person's personality as a uniquely organized system ("idiographically"), has recently been adapted for computer interpretation. Exner (1987) has developed a computer-based interpretation system for the Rorschach that, after scored responses are input, provides scoring summaries and a listing of likely personality descriptions and references about a person's

adjustment. The Exner Comprehensive Rorschach System (an example of which can be found in the case study of Esteban in HIGHLIGHT 15.4 on pages 586–588) may answer the criticism that Rorschach interpretation is unreliable, because the computer output provides a reliable and invariant set of descriptors for any given set of Rorschach scores. Assuming that clinicians agree on the scoring of particular responses, the computer outputs, that is, the interpretations, will be the same. Butcher and Rouse (in press) recently reviewed the clinical assessment research literature over the past 20 years including the major clinical assessment methods and found that the Rorschach was the second most frequently researched clinical instrument, the MMPI/MMPI-2 being first. Research studies involving the Rorschach have been fairly steady over the past 20 years with roughly about 80 to 100 articles per year.

The **Thematic Apperception Test (TAT)** was introduced in 1935 by its coauthors, Morgan and Murray of the Harvard Psychological Clinic. It uses a series of simple pictures, some highly representational and others quite abstract, about which a subject is instructed to make up stories. The content of the pictures, much of it depicting people in various contexts, is highly ambiguous as to actions and motives, so that subjects tend to project their own conflicts and worries into it (Bellak & Abrams, 1993).

Several scoring and interpretation systems have been developed to focus on different aspects of a subject's stories, such as expressions of needs (Atkinson, 1992), the person's perception of reality (Arnold, 1962), and the person's fantasies (Klinger, 1979). Generally these systems are time-consuming, and little evidence shows that they make a clinically significant contribution. Hence, most often a clinician simply makes a qualitative and subjective determination of how the story content reflects the person's underlying traits, motives, and preoccupations. Such interpretations often depend as much on "art" as on "science," and there is much room for error in such an informal procedure.

An example of the way a subject's problems may be reflected in TAT stories is shown in the following story based on Card 1 (a picture of a boy staring at a violin on a table in front of him). The client, David, was a 15-year-old boy who had been referred to the clinic by his parents because of their concern about his withdrawal and poor work at school:

David was generally cooperative during the testing although he remained rather unemotional and unenthusiastic throughout. When he was

The Thematic Apperception Test, or TAT, asks a patient to develop stories about the people depicted in a series of drawings. The patient's stories about the people shown in the cards are thought to reflect personality characteristics, motives, beliefs, attitudes, problems, and symptoms of the person taking the test.

given Card 1 of the TAT, he paused for over a minute, carefully scrutinizing the card.

"I think this is a . . . uh . . . machine gun . . . yeah, it's a machine gun. The guy is staring at it. Maybe he got it for his birthday or stole it or something." (Pause. The examiner reminded him that he was to make up a story about the picture.)

"OK. This boy, I'll call him Karl, found this machine gun . . . a Browning automatic rifle . . . in his garage. He kept it in his room for protection. One day he decided to take it to school to quiet down the jocks that lord it over everyone. When he walked into the locker hall, he cut loose on the top jock, Amos, and wasted him. Nobody bothered him after that because they knew he kept the BAR in his locker."

It was inferred from this story that David was experiencing a high level of frustration and anger in his life. The extent of this anger was reflected in his perception of the violin in the picture as a machine gun—a potential instrument of violence. The clinician concluded that David was feeling threatened not only by people at school but even in his own home where he needed "protection." This example shows how stories based on TAT cards may provide a clinician with information about a person's conflicts and worries as well as clues as to how the person is handling these problems.

The TAT has been criticized on several grounds in recent years. There is a "dated" quality to the test stimuli: the pictures, developed in the 1930s, appear quaint to many contemporary subjects who have difficulty identifying with the characters in the pictures. Subjects will often preface their stories with, "This is something from a movie I saw on the Late Show." Additionally, the TAT can require a great deal of time to administer and interpret. Interpretation of responses to the TAT is generally subjective and limits the reliability and validity of the test. Again, however, we must note that some examiners, notably those who have long experience in the instrument's use, are capable of astonishingly accurate interpretations with TAT stories. Typically, they have difficulty in teaching these skills to others. On reflection, such an observation should not be unduly surprising, but it does point up the essentially "artistic" element involved at this skill level.

Another projective procedure that has proven useful in personality assessment is the **sentence-completion test.** There are a number of such tests designed for children, adolescents, and adults. Such tests consist of the beginnings of sentences that a subject is asked to complete, as in these examples:

1. I wish_____
2. My mother _____
3. Sex _____
4. I hate _____
5. People _____

Sentence-completion tests are somewhat more structured than the Rorschach and most other projective tests. They help examiners pinpoint important clues to an individual's problems, attitudes, and symptoms through the content of his or her responses. Interpretation of the item responses, however, is generally subjective and unreliable. Despite the fact that the test stimuli (the sentence stems) are standard, interpretation is usually done in an ad hoc manner and without benefit of norms.

In sum, projective tests have an important place in many clinical settings, particularly those that attempt to obtain a comprehensive picture of a person's psychodynamic functioning and have the necessary trained staff to conduct extensive individual psychological evaluations. The great strengths of projective techniques—their unstructured nature and their focus on the unique aspects of personality—are at the same time their weaknesses because they make interpretation subjective, unreliable, and difficult to validate. Moreover, projective tests typically require a great deal of time to administer and advanced skill to interpret—both scarce quantities in many clinical settings.

Objective Tests. **Objective tests** are structured—that is, they typically use questionnaires, self-inventories, or rating scales in which questions or items are carefully phrased and alternative responses are specified as choices. They therefore involve a far more controlled format than projective devices and thus are more amenable to objectively based quantification. One virtue of such quantification is that of precision, which in turn enhances the reliability of test outcomes.

One of the major structured inventories for personality assessment is the **Minnesota Multiphasic Personality Inventory (MMPI),** now the **MMPI-2** after a recent revision. We focus on it here because in many ways it is the prototype and the standard of this class of instruments.

Several years in development, the MMPI was introduced for general use in 1943 by Hathaway and McKinley; it is today the most widely used personality test for both clinical assessment and psychopathologic research in the United States (Lubin et al., 1984, 1985; Piotrowski & Keller, 1992) and is the assessment instrument most frequently taught in graduate clinical psychology programs (Piotrowski & Zalewski, 1993). Moreover, translated versions of the inventory are widely used internationally. In all, the MMPI has been translated into more than 115 languages, and it is used in over 46 countries (Butcher, 1984). International use of the revised inventory is increasing at a fast rate. Since it was published in 1989, there have been over 25 translations of the MMPI-2 (Butcher, in press).

The original MMPI, a kind of self-report technique, consisted of 550 items covering topics ranging from physical condition and psychological states to moral and social attitudes. Normally, subjects are encouraged to answer all of the items either *true* or *false*. Some sample items follow:

I sometimes keep on at a thing until others lose their patience with me. T F

Bad words, often terrible words, come into my mind and I cannot get rid of them. T F

I often feel as if things were not real. T F

Someone has it in for me. T F

(Hathaway & McKinley, 1951, p. 28)

The pool of items for the MMPI was originally administered to a large group of normal individuals (affectionately called the "Minnesota normals") and several quite homogeneous groups of patients having particular psychiatric diagnoses. Answers to all the items were then item-analyzed to see which ones differentiated the various groups. On the basis of the findings, ten clinical scales were constructed, each consisting of the items that were answered by one of the patient groups in the direction opposite to the predominant response of the normal group. This rather ingenious method of scorable item selection, known as *empirical keying,* was original to the MMPI and doubtless accounts for much of the instrument's power. Note that it involves no subjective prejudgment about the "meaning" of a true or false answer to any item; that meaning resides entirely in whether or not the answer is the same as that deviantly given by patients of varying diagnoses. Most examiners do not even review the actual responses made because doing so encourages speculative hypotheses that have a likelihood of being wrong. Should an examinee's pattern of true/false responses closely approximate that of a particular pathological group, it is a reasonable inference that he or she shares other psychiatrically significant characteristics with that group—and may in fact "psychologically" be a member of that group.

Each of these ten "clinical" scales, then, measures tendencies to respond in psychologically deviant ways. Raw scores on these scales are compared with the corresponding scores of the normal population, many of whom did (and do) answer a few items in the critical direction, and the results are plotted on the standard MMPI profile form. By drawing a line connecting the scores for the different scales, a clinician can construct a profile that shows how far from normal a patient's performance is on each of the scales. The *Schizophrenia scale,* for example (and to reiterate the basic strategy), is made up of the items that schizophrenic patients consistently answered in a way that differentiated them from normal individuals. People who score high (relative to norms) on this scale, though not necessarily schizophrenic, often show propensities typical of the schizophrenic population. For instance, high scorers on this scale may be socially inept, withdrawn, and have peculiar thought processes; they may have diminished contact with reality and in severe cases may have delusions and hallucinations.

The MMPI also includes a number of validity scales to detect whether a patient has answered the questions in a straightforward, honest manner. Extreme endorsement of the items on any of these scales may invalidate the test, while lesser endorsements frequently contribute important interpretive insights. In addition to the validity scales and the ten clinical scales, hundreds of "special" scales have been devised, four of which have become so widely used for both clinical and research purposes that they are now listed on the MMPI profile form. There is in principle no limit to the number of additional scales that could be generated from the MMPI item pool and available item norms.

Clinically, the MMPI is used in several ways to evaluate a patient's personality characteristics and clinical problems. Perhaps the most typical use of the MMPI is as a *diagnostic standard.* As we have seen, the individual's profile pattern is compared with profiles of known patient groups. If the profile matches a group, information about patients in this group can suggest a broad *descriptive diagnosis* for the patient under study. Another approach to MMPI interpretation, *content interpretation,* is used to supplement the empirical correlates provided in the just-described approach. Here, a clinician focuses on the content themes in a person's response to the inventory. For example, if an individual endorses an unusually large number of items about fears, a clinician might well conclude that the subject is preoccupied with fear.

The original MMPI, in spite of being the most widely used personality measure, has not been without its critics. Some psychodynamically oriented clinicians felt that the MMPI (like other structured, objective tests) was superficial and did not adequately reflect the complexities of an individual taking the test. Some behaviorally oriented critics, on the other hand, criticized the MMPI, and in fact the entire genre of personality tests, as being too oriented toward measuring unobservable "mentalistic" constructs, such as traits. A more specific criticism was leveled at the datedness of the MMPI, including in particular its anachronistic item pool and narrow, out-of-date norms. The original MMPI dated from the early 1940s, and even though much of the MMPI interpretive research is much more recent, the item pool and the basic scaling of raw response data had remained unchanged. In response to these criticisms, the publisher of the MMPI contracted to underwrite a revision of the instrument. This revised MMPI, designated MMPI-2 for adults, became available for general professional use in mid-1989 (Butcher et al., 1989) and the MMPI-A, for adolescents (Butcher et al., 1992) was published in 1992. Perhaps inevitably, in light of the distinction of its forebear and the strong loyalties to it, some early reservations were expressed. However, the MMPI-2 has now effectively replaced the original instrument and most users now use the revised versions.

We will provide a brief discussion of the changes that have been made to the original instrument. The scales listed on the standard original MMPI-2 profile form are given in HIGHLIGHT 15.3. The most important changes introduced with MMPI-2 were directed at overcoming the deficiencies already noted—namely (a) the outmoded idioms and sometimes prejudicial language of some of the items in the pool; and (b) the outdated and demographically unrepresentative character of the normal standardization sample, most of whose members came from rural parts of Minnesota in the 1930s. A third major alteration, too technical for detailed discussion here, involves the scaling method used to convert raw scale scores to standardized ones having common parameters (that is, means and standard deviations).

Changes made in the original MMPI item pool can be summarized as follows:

- The original item pool was edited and modernized to eliminate expressions that were out of date and to delete objectionable items (about 14 percent of the items required alteration). Additional items were written to address additional problem areas, such as treatment compliance, Type A behavior, suicide, and personality problems. Two separate item pools were established: an adult form and an adolescent form, designated MMPI-A.

- The new adult normative sample for MMPI-2—2600 subjects randomly sampled from seven communities across the United States—is considerably more representative of the American population than was that for the original MMPI. Efforts were made to include representative groups from different racial and ethnic backgrounds, age groups, and social classes.

- The adolescent form of the MMPI (MMPI-A) was standardized on 815 girls and 805 boys who were students in public and private schools in seven regions of the United States. Designed for use with youngsters aged 14 through 18, it contains a number of new scales. Its basic clinical scales, as in the case of MMPI-2, are the same as for the original MMPI.

The MMPI-2 has been validated in several clinical studies to date (Butcher & Graham, 1994). The clinical scales, which have been retained in their original form apart from minimal item deletion or rewording, seem, as expected, to measure the same properties of personality organization and functioning as they always have. A comparable stability of meaning is observed for the standard validity scales (also essentially unchanged), which have been reinforced with three additional scales to detect tendencies to respond untruthfully to some items. The essential psychometric comparability of the main scales of the two adult versions has been empirically demonstrated by Ben-Porath and Butcher (1989). The basic MMPI-2 profile form is reproduced in HIGHLIGHT 15.4 in the case study of Esteban.

Overall, then, the authors of MMPI-2 have retained the central elements of the original instru-

HIGHLIGHT | 15.3

The Scales of the MMPI-2

Validity Scales

Cannot say scale (?)	Measures the total number of unanswered items
Lie scale (L)	Measures the tendency to claim excessive virtue or to try to present an overall favorable image
Infrequency scale (F)	Measures the tendency to falsely claim or exaggerate psychological problems in the first part of the booklet; alternatively, detects random responding
Infrequency scale (Fb)	Measures the tendency to falsely claim or exaggerate psychological problems on items toward the end of the booklet
Defensiveness scale (K)	Measures the tendency to see oneself in an unrealistically positive way
Response Inconsistency scale (VRIN)	Measures the tendency to endorse items in an inconsistent or random manner
Response Inconsistency scale (TRIN)	Measures the tendency to endorse items in an inconsistent true or false manner

Clinical Scales

Scale 1	Hypochondriasis (Hs)	Measures excessive somatic concern and physical complaints
Scale 2	Depression (D)	Measures symptomatic depression
Scale 3	Hysteria (Hy)	Measures hysteroid personality features such as a "rose-colored glasses" view of the world and the tendency to develop physical problems under stress
Scale 4	Psychopathic deviate (Pd)	Measures antisocial tendencies
Scale 5	Masculinity-femininity (Mf)	Measures gender-role reversal
Scale 6	Paranoia (Pa)	Measures suspicious, paranoid ideation
Scale 7	Psychasthenia (Pt)	Measures anxiety and obsessive, worrying behavior
Scale 8	Schizophrenia (Sc)	Measures peculiarities in thinking, feeling, and social behavior
Scale 9	Hypomania (Ma)	Measures elated mood state and tendencies to yield to impulses
Scale 0	Social introversion (Si)	Measures social anxiety, withdrawal, and overcontrol

Special Scales

Scale *A*	Anxiety	A factor analytic scale measuring general maladjustment and anxiety
Scale *R*	Repression	A factor analytic scale measuring overcontrol and neurotic defensiveness
Scale *Es*	Ego strength	An empirical scale measuring potential response to short-term psychotherapy
Scale *Mac*	MacAndrew Revised Addiction Scale (MAC-R)	An empirical scale measuring proneness to become addicted to various substances

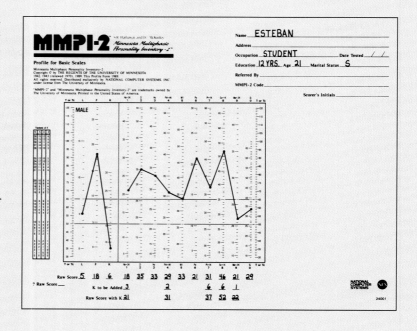

HIGHLIGHT | 15.4

Esteban's MMPI-2 Profile and MMPI-2 Computer-Based Report

Esteban was originally tested with the original MMPI. His responses from that testing were converted to the MMPI-2 format by J. N. Butcher. The computer-based report for the MMPI-2 norms is provided. The validity scales are shown in the column at left (the column in which the word "MALE" appears). The clinical scales are to the right. The special scales are not included in this version of the profile. (HIGHLIGHT 15.3 on page 585 describes each of these scales.) Based on the scores originally obtained and those you see displayed in the chart, a computer produced the narrative descriptions given here. On page 588 are hypotheses about the psychological functioning of Esteban from a computer-generated report of his Rorschach protocol performed by the Exner Comprehensive Rorschach System.

Computer-Based Report: The MMPI-2

Profile Validity

This MMPI-2 profile should be interpreted with caution. There is some possibility that the clinical report is an exaggerated picture of his present situation. He presented an unusual number of psychological problems and symptoms. His test-taking attitudes should be evaluated to determine if his response pattern is a valid approach to the testing. This extreme response set could result from poor reading ability, confusion, disori-

entation, stress, or a need to seek attention for his problems. Clinical patients with this profile are often confused, distractible, and show memory problems. Evidence of delusions and thought disorder may be present.

Symptomatic Pattern

His MMPI-2 profile reflects a high degree of psychological distress at this time. The client is presenting with a mixed pattern of psychological symptoms. He appears to be tense, apathetic, and withdrawn, and is experiencing some personality deterioration. He seems to be quite confused and disorganized, and probably secretly broods

about unusual beliefs and suspicions. Autistic behavior and inappropriate affect are characteristic features of individuals with this profile. Some evidence of an active psychotic process is apparent. He may have delusions and occult preoccupations, and may feel that others are against him because of his beliefs. In interviews, he is likely to be vague, circumstantial, and tangential, and may be quite preoccupied with abstract ideas.

He is having problems concentrating, feels agitated, and is functioning at a very low level of psychological efficiency. He feels apathetic, indifferent, and like a passive participant in life. He also

ment but have added a number of features and refinements to it, including provision for systematic "content" profile analysis. As was the authors' intent, the scales of MMPI-2 correlate highly with those of the original MMPI. Some interpretive adjustments need to be made with respect to relative scale elevations, however, because the new norma-

tive base may have slightly altered the meaning to be assigned to interscale relationships. Experience with the new version to date indicates that practitioners are able, with little change in their interpretive approaches, to use it in the same way they did the original instrument. Recent research (Hargrave et al., 1994; Morrison, Edwards, & Weissman, 1994; and

feels that he has little energy left over from mere survival to expend on any pleasure in life. He may be showing signs of serious psychopathology such as delusions, problems in thinking, and inappropriate affect. His long-standing lack of achievement and his work behavior have caused him many problems.

Many individuals with this profile consider committing suicide and he may actually have serious plans for self-destruction.

He experiences some conflicts concerning his sex-role identity, appearing somewhat passive and effeminate in his orientation toward life. He may appear somewhat insecure in the masculine role and may be uncomfortable in his relationships with women.

His response content indicates that he is preoccupied with feeling guilty and unworthy, and feels that he deserves to be punished for wrongs he has committed. He feels regretful and unhappy about life, complains about having no zest for life, and seems plagued by anxiety and worry about the future. According to his response content there is a strong possibility that he has contemplated suicide. A careful evaluation of this possibility is suggested. He views his physical health as failing and reports numerous somatic complaints. He feels that life is no longer worthwhile and that he is losing control of his thought processes. He reports in his response content that he feels things

more, or more intensely, than others do.

Interpersonal Relations

Disturbed interpersonal relationships are characteristic of individuals with this profile type. He feels vulnerable to interpersonal hurt, lacks trust, and may never form close, satisfying interpersonal ties. He feels very insecure in relationships and may be preoccupied with guilt and self-defeating behavior. Many individuals with this profile are so self-preoccupied and unskilled in sex-role behavior that they never develop rewarding heterosexual relationships. Some never marry.

Behavioral Stability

Individuals with this profile type often lead chronically stormy, chaotic lives.

Diagnostic Considerations

The most likely diagnosis for individuals with this MMPI-2 profile type is Schizophrenia, possibly Paranoid type, or Paranoid Disorder. Similar clients tend to also have features of an affective disorder. In addition, there seems to be a long-standing pattern of maladjustment that is characteristic of people with severe personality disorders.

Because this behavioral pattern may also be associated with Organic Brain Syndrome or Substance-Induced Organic Mental Disorder, these possibilities should be evaluated.

Treatment Considerations

Individuals with this profile may be experiencing considerable personality deterioration, which may require hospitalization if they are considered dangerous to themselves or others.

Psychotropic medication may reduce their thinking disturbance and mood disorder. Outpatient treatment may be complicated by their regressed or disorganized behavior. Multiple-problem life situations and difficulties forming interpersonal relationships make patients with this profile poor candidates for relationship-based psychotherapy. Day treatment programs or other such structured settings may be helpful in providing a stabilizing treatment environment. Long-term adjustment is a problem. Frequent, brief "management" therapy contacts may be helpful in structuring his activities. Insight-oriented or relationship therapies tend not to be helpful for individuals with these severe problems and may actually exacerbate the symptoms. He probably would have difficulty establishing a trusting working relationship with a therapist.

Minnesota Multiphasic Personality Inventory-2. Copyright The University of Minnesota 1943 (renewed 1970), 1989. This form 1989. Reprinted by permission.

Tellegen & Ben-Porath, 1992) has shown that the two versions produce essentially comparable results.

Another kind of objective self-report personality inventory uses the statistical procedure of **factor analysis,** a method for reducing a large array of intercorrelated measures to the minimum number of "factors" necessary to account for the observed overlap or associations among them. Because their scales are a product of such a refinement process, tests of this type are considered to measure purportedly basic and relatively independent personality traits. The goal is to measure one trait at a time with maximum precision and selectivity; a personality profile can then be drawn showing the degree to

```
SUBJECT NAME:ESTEBAN.MMPI          AGE:21  SEX:M  RACE:W  MS:Sin  ED:14


        SEMANTIC INTERPRETATION OF THE RORSCHACH
        PROTOCOL UTILIZING THE COMPREHENSIVE SYSTEM
        (COPYRIGHT 1976, 1985 BY JOHN E. EXNER, JR.)

    THE FOLLOWING COMPUTER-BASED INTERPRETATION IS DERIVED ** EXCLUSIVELY **
FROM THE STRUCTURAL DATA OF THE RECORD AND DOES NOT INCLUDE CONSIDERATION OF
THE SEQUENCE OF SCORES OR THE VERBAL MATERIAL. IT IS INTENDED AS A GUIDE FROM
WHICH THE INTERPRETER OF THE TOTAL PROTOCOL CAN PROCEED TO STUDY AND REFINE
THE HYPOTHESES GENERATED FROM THESE ACTUARIAL FINDINGS.


                        * * * * *

1.  THE RECORD APPEARS TO BE VALID AND INTERPRETIVELY USEFUL.

2.  THIS IS THE TYPE OF PERSON WHO IS PRONE TO TRY TO OVERSIMPLIFY STIMULI
    IN ORDER TO MAKE THE WORLD LESS THREATENING AND/OR DEMANDING.  THIS
    BASIC COPING STYLE TENDS TO BE PERVASIVE WHEN NEW SITUATIONS AND/OR
    STRESSES OCCUR. WHEN DONE TO EXCESS, AS APPEARS TO BE THE CASE HERE,
    THE SUBJECT IS LIKELY TO EXPERIENCE FREQUENT SOCIAL DIFFICULTIES
    BECAUSE THE STYLE PROMOTES A NEGLECT OF THE DEMANDS AND/OR
    EXPECTATIONS OF THE ENVIRONMENT.

3.  THIS SUBJECT USUALLY HAS ENOUGH RESOURCE ACCESSABLE TO PARTICIPATE
    MEANINGFULLY IN THE FORMULATION AND DIRECTION OF RESPONSES.  TOLERANCE
    FOR STRESS IS LIKE THAT OF MOST PEOPLE, THAT IS, CONTROLS USUALLY WILL
    NOT FALTER UNLESS THE STRESS IS UNEXPECTED AND INTENSE OR PROLONGED
    UNREASONABLY.

4.  THERE IS EVIDENCE INDICATING THE PRESENCE OF CONSIDERABLE SUBJECTIVELY
    FELT DISTRESS.

5.  THIS SUBJECT TENDS TO INTERNALIZE FEELINGS MUCH MORE THAN IS CUSTOMARY
    AND THIS OFTEN RESULTS IN SUBSTANTIAL DISCOMFORT THAT CAN TAKE THE
    FORM OF TENSION AND/OR ANXIETY.

6.  THIS IS THE TYPE OF PERSON WHO PREFERS TO DELAY MAKING RESPONSES IN
    COPING SITUATIONS UNTIL TIME HAS BEEN ALLOWED TO CONSIDER RESPONSE
    POSSIBILITIES AND THEIR POTENTIAL CONSEQUENCES.  SUCH PEOPLE LIKE TO
    KEEP THEIR EMOTIONS ASIDE UNDER THESE CONDITIONS.

7.  THIS PERSON TENDS TO USE DELIBERATE THINKING MORE FOR THE PURPOSE OF
    CREATING FANTASY THROUGH WHICH TO IGNORE THE WORLD THAN TO CONFRONT
    PROBLEMS DIRECTLY. THIS IS A SERIOUS PROBLEM BECAUSE THE BASIC COPING
    STYLE IS BEING USED MORE FOR FLIGHT THAN TO ADAPT TO THE EXTERNAL
    WORLD.

8.  THIS TYPE OF PERSON IS NOT VERY FLEXIBLE IN THINKING, VALUES, OR
    ATTITUDES.  IN EFFECT, PEOPLE SUCH AS THIS HAVE SOME DIFFICULTY IN
    SHIFTING PERSPECTIVES OR VIEWPOINTS.
=====================================================================
(c)1976, 1985 by John E. Exner, Jr.
```

```
SUBJECT NAME:ESTEBAN.MMPI          AGE:21  SEX:M  RACE:W  MS:Sin  ED:14
    PAGE -2-
=====================================================================
9.  THERE IS A STRONG POSSIBILITY THAT THIS IS A PERSON WHO PREFERS TO
    AVOID INITIATING BEHAVIORS, AND INSTEAD, TENDS TOWARDS A MORE PASSIVE
    ROLE IN PROBLEM SOLVING AND INTERPERSONAL RELATIONSHIPS.

10. THIS SUBJECT DOES NOT MODULATE EMOTIONAL DISPLAYS AS MUCH AS MOST
    ADULTS AND, BECAUSE OF THIS, IS PRONE TO BECOME VERY INFLUENCED BY
    FEELINGS IN MOST THINKING, DECISIONS, AND BEHAVIORS.

11. THIS IS A PERSON WHO IS VERY ATTRACTED TO BEING AROUND EMOTIONAL
    STIMULI. THIS MAY POSE A SIGNIFICANT PROBLEM IN ADAPTATION BECAUSE OF
    PROBLEMS IN CONTROL. THAT IS, THE MORE EMOTIONAL STIMULI BEING
    PROCESSED, THE GREATER THE DEMAND FOR EMOTIONAL EXCHANGE. IF THAT
    EXCHANGE IS NOT WELL CONTROLLED, PROBLEMS CAN EASILY OCCUR.

12. THIS IS AN INDIVIDUAL WHO DOES NOT EXPERIENCE NEEDS FOR CLOSENESS IN
    WAYS THAT ARE COMMON TO MOST PEOPLE.  AS A RESULT, THEY ARE TYPICALLY
    LESS COMFORTABLE IN INTERPERSONAL SITUATIONS, HAVE SOME DIFFICULTIES
    IN CREATING AND SUSTAINING DEEP RELATIONSHIPS, ARE MORE CONCERNED WITH
    ISSUES OF PERSONAL SPACE, AND MAY APPEAR MUCH MORE GUARDED AND/OR
    DISTANT TO OTHERS.

13. THIS SUBJECT HAS AS MUCH INTEREST IN OTHERS AS DO MOST ADULTS AND
    CHILDREN. HOWEVER, THE SUBJECT DOES NOT APPEAR TO HAVE A VERY
    REALISTIC UNDERSTANDING OF PEOPLE.  INSTEAD, CONCEPTIONS OF OTHERS
    TEND TO BE DERIVED MORE FROM IMAGINATION THAN FROM REAL EXPERIENCE.

14. THIS SUBJECT APPEARS TO HAVE AN UNUSUAL BODY PREOCCUPATION.

15. THIS SUBJECT APPEARS TO HAVE A MARKED SEXUAL PREOCCUPATION.

16. THIS SUBJECT IS VERY PRONE TO INTERPRET STIMULUS CUES IN A UNIQUE AND
    OVERPERSONALIZED MANNER. PEOPLE SUCH AS THIS OFTEN VIEW THEIR WORLD
    WITH THEIR OWN SPECIAL SET OF BIASES AND ARE LESS CONCERNED WITH BEING
    CONVENTIONAL AND/OR ACCEPTABLE TO OTHERS.

17. IN SPITE OF THE ABOVE MENTIONED TENDENCY TO MISINTERPRET OR OVERPERSON-
    ALIZE THE INTERPRETATION OF STIMULUS CUES, THE SUBJECT DOES TEND TO
    RESPOND IN CONVENTIONAL WAYS TO SITUATIONS IN WHICH CONVENTIONAL OR
    EXPECTED RESPONSES ARE OBVIOUS AND EASILY IDENTIFIED.

18. MUCH OF THE COGNITIVE ACTIVITY OF THIS SUBJECT IS LESS SOPHISTICATED
    OR LESS MATURE THAN MOST. THIS MAY BE A FUNCTION OF A
    DEVELOPMENTAL LAG, DISORGANIZATION, OR MAY SIMPLY REFLECT A RELUCTANCE
    TO COMMIT RESOURCES TO A TASK.

19. THIS SUBJECT TENDS TO SCAN A STIMULUS FIELD HASTILY AND NOT
    METHODICALLY.  THESE KINDS OF PEOPLE OFTEN COME TO DECISIONS
    PREMATURELY AND ERRONEOUSLY SIMPLY BECAUSE THEY HAVE NOT PROCESSED ALL
    AVAILABLE INFORMATION ADEQUATELY.  THIS SHOULD NOT BE CONFUSED WITH
=====================================================================
(c)1976, 1985 by John E. Exner, Jr.
```

which several such methodologically rarefied traits are characteristic of an individual, as well as the overall pattern of the traits.

Self-report inventories, such as the MMPI, have a number of advantages over other types of personality tests. They are cost-effective, highly reliable, and objective; they also can be scored and interpreted, or if desired even administered, by computer. A number of general criticisms, however, have been leveled against the use of self-report inventories. As we have seen, some clinicians consider them to be too mechanistic to accurately portray the complexity of human beings and their problems. Also, because these tests require a subject to read, comprehend, and answer verbal material, patients who are illiterate or confused cannot take the test. Furthermore, the individual's cooperation is required in self-report inventories, and it is possible that the subject may distort his or her answers to create a particular impression. The validity scales of the MMPI-2 are a direct attempt to deal with this last criticism.

Computer Interpretation of Objective Personality Tests. Scientifically constructed objective personality inventories, because of their scoring formats and emphasis on test validation, lend themselves particularly well to computer scoring and interpretation. The earliest practical applications of computer technology to test scoring and interpretation involved the MMPI. Over 35 years ago, psychologists at the Mayo Clinic programmed a computer to score and interpret clinical profiles. A number of other highly sophisticated MMPI and MMPI-2 interpretation systems have subsequently been developed (Butcher, 1995; Fowler, 1987).

Computer-based MMPI interpretation systems typically employ powerful **actuarial procedures.** In such systems, descriptions of the actual behavior or other established characteristics of many subjects with particular patterns of test scores have been stored in the computer. Whenever a person turns up with one of these test score patterns, the appropriate description is printed out in the computer's evaluation. Such descriptions have been written and stored for a number of different test score patterns, most of them based on MMPI-2 scores.

The accumulation of precise actuarial data for an instrument like the MMPI-2 is difficult, time-consuming, and expensive. This is in part because of the complexity of the instrument itself, since the potential number of significantly different MMPI-2 profile patterns is legion. The profiles of many subjects therefore do not "fit" the profile types for which actuarial data are available. Problems of actuarial data acquisition also arise at the other end, the events or conditions detected or predicted by the instrument. Many conditions that are of vital clinical importance are relatively rare (for example, suicide) or are psychologically complex (for example, possible psychogenic components in a patient's physical illness), thus making it difficult to accumulate a sufficient number of cases to serve as an adequate actuarial

```
SUBJECT NAME:ESTEBAN.MMPI          AGE:21  SEX:M  RACE:W  MS:Sin  ED:14

    PAGE -3-

==========================================================================
    IMPULSIVENESS ALTHOUGH SOME DECISIONS AND BEHAVIORS THAT RESULT MAY
    HAVE THAT FEATURE.  IT IS A CONSEQUENCE OF NEGLECT IN SCANNING AND
    ORGANIZING TACTICS WHICH MAY BE THE PRODUCT OF A PERCEPTUAL DEFICIT,
    PSYCHOLOGICAL HABITS DEVELOPED EARLY IN LIFE, OR CAN BE A FUNCTION OF
    COGNITIVE DISARRAY PROVOKED BY NEUROLOGICALLY RELATED OR
    PSYCHPATHOLOGICAL PROBLEMS.  IT SHOULD ALSO BE NOTED FOR THIS SUBJECT
    THAT THE COMPOSITE OF HASTY SCANNING OF STIMULUS FIELDS PLUS LIMITED
    EMOTIONAL CONTROLS IS ONE IMPORTANT FACTOR THAT LEADS TO IMPULSIVE
    LIKE BEHAVIORS.

20. THIS PERSON USUALLY SEEKS AN ECONOMICAL APPROACH TO PROBLEM SOLVING OR
    COPING BY FOCUSING MORE ON THE EASILY MANAGED ASPECTS OF A SITUATION
    AND TENDING TO NEGLECT BROADER ISSUES THAT MAY BE PRESENT.  THIS IS
    TYPICAL OF MANY PEOPLE AND CAN BE AN ASSET.  HOWEVER, IT CAN ALSO
    BECOME A LIABILITY IN MORE COMPLEX AND DEMANDING SITUATIONS THAT
    REQUIRE HIGHER LEVELS OF MOTIVATION AND EFFORT TO ACHIEVE EFFECTIVE
    RESULTS.

21. THIS PERSON IS SOMEWHAT CONSERVATIVE IN SETTING GOALS.  USUALLY PEOPLE
    LIKE THIS WANT TO COMMIT THEMSELVES ONLY TO OBJECTIVES WHICH OFFER A
    SIGNIFICANT PROBABILITY OF SUCCESS.

22. THIS PERSON TENDS TO USE INTELLECTUALIZATION AS A BASIC TACTIC TO
    CONTEND WITH EMOTIONAL THREATS AND STRESSES. PEOPLE LIKE THIS ARE
    OFTEN VERY RESISTIVE DURING EARLY PHASES OF INTERVENTION AS THIS
    TENDENCY TOWARD DENIAL CAUSES THEM TO AVOID ANY AFFECTIVE
    CONFRONTATIONS.

              * * *  END OF REPORT  * * *




==========================================================================
(c)1976, 1985 by John E. Exner, Jr.
```

Semantic interpretation of the Rorschach protocol utilizing the comprehensive system.

data base. In these situations, the interpretive program writer is forced to fall back on general clinical lore and wisdom to formulate clinical descriptions appropriate to the types of profiles actually obtained. Hence, the best programs are written by expert clinicians who have long experience with the instrument and keep up with its continuously developing research base (Carson, 1990b).

Examples of computer-generated descriptions appear in the evaluations reprinted in HIGHLIGHT 15.4 (pages 586–588). Sometimes the different paragraphs generated by the computer will have elements that seem inconsistent. These inconsistencies result from the fact that different parts of a subject's test pattern call up different paragraphs from the computer. The computer simply prints out blindly what has been found to be typical for people making similar scores on the various clinical scales. The computer cannot integrate the descriptions it picks up, however. At this point the human element comes in: In the clinical use of computers, it is always essential that a trained professional further interpret and monitor the assessment data (American Psychological Association, 1986).

Computerized personality assessment is no longer a novelty, but an important, dependable adjunct to clinical assessment. Computerized psychological evaluations are a quick and efficient means of providing a clinician with needed information early in the decision-making process. Some lingering controversies surrounding computerized psychological

assessment are discussed in the "Unresolved Issues" section at the end of this chapter.

Psychological Assessment in Forensic or Legal Cases

One of the most extensive and fastest-growing applications of psychological tests involves their use in court cases. Applications range from assessments to provide information about the mental state of felons on trial, to assess the psychological adjustment of litigants in civil court cases, and to aid in the determination of child custody in divorce cases.

Many different psychological tests have been employed to evaluate defendants or litigants. If there is a question of cognitive impairment, the WAIS-R or a Halstead-Reitan Neuropsychological Battery might be used. When an individual's psychological adjustment is an issue, the MMPI-2 is the most frequently employed psychological test (Pope, Butcher, & Seelen, 1993) because of its objectivity (less reliant upon interpreter's judgment) and extensive validity base. Due in large part to their scientific acceptability, well-known psychological tests, such as the WAIS-R and MMPI-2, are widely accepted by courts as appropriate assessment instruments. In order for a test to be allowed into testimony, it must be deemed to be an accepted standard. The primary means of assuring that tests are appropriate for court testimony is that they are standardized and are not experimental procedures (Ogloff, 1995; Pope et al., 1993).

The three situations in which psychological tests are most often used in court settings will be illustrated:

Mr. A., a thirty-four-year-old man, on trial for serial rapes, alleged that he was not guilty of the crimes for which he was charged due to insanity. His counsel pleaded that he suffered from multiple personality disorder and that the alleged crimes were committed under the influence of "another personality"; the man was not aware that he was committing a crime. The prosecution employed a team of experts (a psychiatrist and two psychologists) to evaluate the defendant for multiple personality disorder [DID]. The evaluation included a psychiatric interview, personal history, and a battery of psychological tests, including the MMPI, TAT, and Rorschach. The results of the evaluation were not consistent with a diagnosis of multiple personality disorder [DID] but instead suggested malingering.

In a civil law suit, Ms. B., age 29, sought damages from her employer following an incident in which she complained that she had been sexually harassed by the manager of her department. She alleged that on a number of occasions his blatant sexual advances had caused her great anguish and difficulty in her marriage. She claimed that her psychological adjustment during and after the harassment incidents had been extremely difficult and had prevented her from effectively pursing her work. Her therapist supported a diagnosis of post-traumatic stress disorder in her case. (The manager involved in the incident was fired from the company.) Defense attorneys sought a psychological evaluation of Ms. B.

A psychiatric interview and psychological tests were administered, including the Beck Depression Inventory, MMPI-2, TAT, and Rorschach. The conclusions were that she was probably experiencing some post-traumatic symptoms at the time of the evaluation, but that there was evidence that she was exaggerating her symptoms and her disability. Before the trial, the case was settled out of court for a small portion of the original amount claimed.

In a family court case, Mr. & Ms. T. were both seeking custody of their three year old daughter following an acrimonious divorce. During the proceedings, Mr. T., a successful contractor, ac-

cused (wrongly as it turned out) Ms. T. of sexually abusing their daughter and sought the termination of her parental rights. A court-appointed psychological evaluation was conducted to assess the emotional stability of Ms. T. and to appraise her suitability as a parent. The court-appointed psychologist did not find that Ms. T. suffered from emotional problems that would make her an unfit mother. Following the trial, the court ruled in favor of full custody for Ms. T. with supervised visits for Mr. T. In addition, the court awarded her $1,000,000 in damages as a result of the false accusation of abuse.

Psychological tests, though for the most part developed for other than court applications, have been found to provide valuable information for court cases—particularly if they contain a means of assessing the person's test-taking attitudes. The MMPI-2, for example, contains several measures that provide an appraisal of the person's cooperativeness or frankness in responding to the test items (Berry et al., 1993). Because many litigants or defendants in criminal cases, when tested, attempt to present themselves in a particular way (for example, to appear disturbed in the case of an insanity plea or impeccably virtuous when trying to present a false or exaggerated physical injury), their motivations to "fake good" or "fake bad" tend to result in noncredible test patterns.

Although psychological tests may be considered very useful in some forensic circumstances, their use has clear limitations (Faust, Ziskin, & Hiers, 1991; Faust, 1994; Heilbrun, 1992). The use of psychological assessment in court is nevertheless widespread and likely to increase in the future, given the increasing number of situations in which mental health adjustment is becoming an issue for courts to evaluate.

The Use of Psychological Tests in Personnel Screening

Many people who are experiencing personal problems or extreme psychological distress are able to function well enough in their job to get by. Some occupations, however, including those of airline flight crews, police officers, fire fighters, air-traffic controllers, nuclear power plant workers, and certain military specialties require a consistently higher level of psychological performance or greater emotional stability than others; these jobs allow for less personal variation in performance. Emotional problems in such employees can be extremely dangerous to other employees and to society as a whole. For example, someone who holds a key position in a nuclear power plant control room and is experiencing symptoms of severe depression may be significantly impaired, possibly resulting in a failure to recognize problems requiring prompt and decisive action.

The potential impact that mistakes in some occupations can have on the lives and safety of others makes the selection of employees and the monitoring of their mental health particularly critical. The psychological disorders that prompted several Los Angeles police officers to repeatedly strike with their nightsticks a prone and helpless motorist in March 1991, as recorded on videotape, are not simply an internal police matter; they are also a significant issue of concern for all of us. The potential for job failure or for psychological maladjustment under stress is so great in some high-stress occupations that measures need to be taken in the hiring process to evaluate applicants for emotional adjustment.

Psychological Screening for Emotional Problems
The use of personality tests in personnel screening has a long tradition. In fact, the first formal use of a standardized personality scale, the Woodworth Personal Data Sheet, was implemented to screen out World War I draftees who were psychologically unfit for military service (Woodworth, 1920). Today, psychological tests are widely used for personnel screening in occupations that require a high degree of emotional stability or great public trust. A recent controversial extension of this work is the attempt by some private corporations to assess potential employees for "honesty."

An important distinction needs to be made between personnel selection and personnel screening or, phrased differently, between "screening in" versus "screening out" job candidates. In situations where certain personality characteristics are desired for a particular job, a psychologist would choose instruments that directly assess those qualities, such as the 16 Personality Factor Inventory, which measures "normal" personality characteristics, such as dominance or sociability.

Personnel screening for emotional stability, on the other hand, requires a somewhat different set of assumptions. One assumption is that personality or emotional problems, such as poor reality contact, impulsivity, or low self-esteem, would adversely affect the way in which a person would function in a critical job. In this situation, a psychologist could choose an instrument to assess the presence of psy-

chopathology or maladjustment, such as the MMPI-2. To extend an earlier example, in police officer selection, an applicant with an MMPI-2 profile pattern reflecting tendencies toward extreme aggressiveness, making hasty generalizations about others, and impulsivity would be eliminated from consideration or would undergo further evaluation to determine if these personality factors had resulted in negative job behaviors in the past.

Issues in Personality Test Job Screening Before implementing psychological assessment for preemployment screening, an ethically responsible psychologist needs to consider a number of issues to determine both the relevance and appropriateness of the procedures to be used. The following questions need to be addressed:

1. How should the preemployment test be used, or how much weight should be given to a particular test in preemployment decisions? Psychological tests should not be the sole means of determining whether a person is hired. Instruments like the MMPI-2 should be used in conjunction with an employment interview, a background check, an evaluation of previous work record, and so on.

2. Is the use of a psychological test an unwarranted invasion of privacy? Undeniably, many (and perhaps in a certain sense all) psychological tests, especially clinical tests like the MMPI, invade an individual's privacy by asking many personal questions concerning symptoms, attitudes, and lifestyles. Concerns over invasion of privacy have long been expressed, and the question of the appropriateness of these tests in employment selection has been the subject of congressional hearings (see Brayfield et al., 1965). The appropriateness of personality testing in employment decisions has also been tested in court (*McKenna* v. *Fargo*, 1978; *Soroka* v. *Dayton-Hudson*, 1991). In the *McKenna* v. *Fargo* case, the use of the MMPI in screening for some occupations was found to be appropriate while in the *Soroka* v. *Dayton-Hudson* case some of the item content of the original MMPI was considered an invasion of privacy (these items were dropped in the MMPI-2). Therefore, the question becomes one of determining whether a particular test used is a warranted invasion of privacy—that is, determining whether the particular placement decisions being made are consistent with the greater interests of society. For some occupations, such decisions are deemed justifiable; it is considered within the criterion of "public good" that people being placed in positions of high responsibility are emotionally stable according to the best information available.

3. Are the procedures fair to all candidates, including members of ethnic minorities? The question of the fairness of psychological tests in personnel screening is an important one. In order for a psychological test to be considered appropriate (both ethically and legally) for use in personnel selection situations, it must be demonstrated that the test does not unfairly portray or discriminate against ethnic minorities. This question needs to be addressed for each psychological test or personnel procedure used. The tests used must also have a demonstrated validity for the particular test application. In the case of the MMPI, which is the most widely used clinical test in personnel screening, minority group performance has been widely studied (Butcher, 1979; Dahlstrom, Lachar, & Dahlstrom, 1986; King, Carroll, & Fuller, 1977; Wennerholm & Lopez-Roig, 1983). If a person can read the items (if his or her reading level is adequate or a foreign language version is administered, if necessary), the MMPI-2 does not portray or discriminate against various ethnic minority subjects in an unfair manner. Given the more representative normative sample for MMPI-2, it is even less likely than its predecessor to present a problem in this respect.

A Psychological Case Study: Esteban

In this section, we will illustrate psychological assessment through a diagnostic case study of a young man who presented a complicated clinical picture that was substantially clarified through psychological and neuropsychological assessment. This is an unusual case in several respects: The young man's problems were quite severe and involved both psychological and organic elements; the case involved cross-cultural considerations—the young man was from South America and assessment was done in both English and Spanish (the latter only as necessary); and a number of psychological specialists participated in the assessment study, including a neuropsychologist, a behaviorally oriented clinical psychologist, a Hispanic clinical psychologist, and a psychiatrist.

Esteban, a 21-year-old student from Colombia, South America, had been enrolled in an English language program at a small college in the United States. He had become disruptive in school, evidencing loud, obnoxious behavior in class and quarreling with his roommates (whom he accused of stealing his wallet). After a period of time during which his behavior did not improve, he was expelled from the program. The director of the program indicated that he felt Esteban needed psychological

help for his problems, which included not only the behavioral problems but also, reportedly, severe headaches and confused thinking. The director added that Esteban would be considered for readmission only if he showed significant improvement in therapy.

On hearing of his expulsion, Esteban's parents, who were well-to-do international banking entrepreneurs, flew in from South America and arranged for a complete physical examination for him at a well-known medical center in New York. After an extensive medical and neurological examination to determine the source of his headaches and confusion, Esteban was diagnosed as having some "diffuse" brain impairment, but he was found to be otherwise in good health. His parents then sought a further, more definitive neurological examination. The neurologist at the second hospital recommended a psychological and neuropsychological examination because he suspected that Esteban's mild neurological condition would not account for his extreme psychological and behavioral symptoms. He referred the family to a psychologist for assessment and treatment. Because Esteban was experiencing a number of pressing situational problems—for example, his behavior problems continued, he appeared anxious to find a new English program, and, as we will see, he had some hard issues to face about his career aspirations to become a physician—the psychologist decided to begin with therapy immediately, concurrent with the additional assessment evaluation.

Interviews and Behavior Observations Esteban was seen in the initial session with his parents. The interview was conducted in English with some translation into Spanish (mostly by Esteban) because the parents knew little English. Throughout the session, Esteban was disorganized and distractible. He had difficulty keeping to the topic being discussed and periodically interrupted his own conversation with seemingly random impulses to show the interviewer papers, books, pamphlets, and the like from his knapsack. He talked incessantly, often loudly. He was not at all defensive about his problems but talked freely about his symptoms and attitudes. His behavior resembled that of a hyperactive child—he was excitable, impulsive, and immature. He did not appear to be psychotic; he reported no hallucinations or delusions and was in contact with reality. He related well with the interviewer, seemed to enjoy the session, and expressed an interest in having additional sessions.

During subsequent interviews, Esteban expressed frequent physical complaints, such as headaches, tension, and sleeping problems. He reported that he had a great deal of difficulty concentrating on his studies. He could not study because he always found other things to do—particularly talking about religion. He was seemingly outgoing and sociable and had no difficulty initiating conversations with other people. He tended, however, to say socially inappropriate things or become frustrated and lose his temper easily. For example, during one family interview, he became enraged and kicked his mother.

Family History Esteban's father was a Spanish-Colombian banker in his mid-sixties. He was well-dressed, somewhat passive, though visibly quite warm toward his son. He had his share of difficulties in recent years; severe business problems coupled with two heart attacks had brought on a depressive episode that had left him ineffective in dealing with his business. His wife and her brother, an attorney from Madrid, had to straighten out the business problems. She reported that her husband had had several depressive episodes in the past and that Esteban's moods resembled her husband's in his earlier years.

Esteban's mother was a tense, worried, and somewhat hypochondriacal woman who appeared to be rather domineering. Before the first and second interviews, she handed the therapist, in secret, written "explanations" of her son's problems. Her own history revealed that she was unhappy in her marriage and that she lived only for her children, on whom she doted.

Esteban's brother, Juan, was an engineering student at an American university and apparently was doing well academically and socially. He was one year older than Esteban.

Esteban's childhood had been marked with problems. His mother reported that although he had been a good baby—noting that he had been pretty and happy as a small child—he had changed after age 2½. At about that time, he had fallen on his head and was unconscious for a while; he was not hospitalized. Beginning in the preschool years, he exhibited behavioral problems, including temper tantrums, negativism, and an inability to get along with peers. These problems continued when he began school. He frequently refused to go to school, had periods of aggressive behavior, and appeared in general to be "hyperactive." It appeared that he was probably overprotected and "infantilized" by his mother.

Esteban was quite close to his brother Juan, with whom he reported having had extensive homosexual relations when they were growing up. The "darkest day" in Esteban's life was reportedly when Juan broke off the homosexual relationship with him at age 16 and told him to "go and find men." Although he later carried on a platonic relationship with a woman in Colombia, it was never a serious one. Esteban had strong homosexual urges of which he was consciously aware and attempted to control through a growing preoccupation with religion.

Esteban had been in psychotherapy on several occasions since he was 11 years old. After he graduated from high school, he attended law school in Colombia for a quarter, but dropped out because he "wanted to become a doctor instead." (In Colombia, professional schools are combined with college.) He left school, according to his parents' report, because he could not adapt. He worked for a time in the family business but had difficulty getting along with other employees and was encouraged to try other work. When that failed, his parents sent him to the United States to study English, rationalizing that Colombia was not as good an environment for him as the United States.

Intelligence Testing Esteban underwent psychological testing to evaluate further the possibility of neurological deficits and to determine if he had the intellectual capabilities to proceed with a demanding academic career. He scored in the borderline to average range of intelligence on the WAIS-R (English version) and on the WAIS (Spanish version). He was particularly deficient in tasks involving practical judgment, common sense, concentration, visual-motor coordination, and concept formation. In addition, on memory tests, he showed a below average memory ability, such as a poor immediate recall of ideas from paragraphs read aloud (in both English and Spanish). Under most circumstances, people with similar deficits are able to live comfortable, fulfilling lives in careers whose formal intellectual demands are relatively modest. It was clear from the test data and Esteban's behavior during testing that his stated career aspirations—seemingly nurtured by his parents—exceeded his abilities and might well be a factor in much of his frustration.

Personality Testing Esteban was given both the Rorschach Test and the MMPI. Both tests have been used extensively with Hispanic subjects. The Rorschach is believed by some to be particularly well-suited for cases like Esteban's because the test stimuli are relatively unstructured and not culture-bound. Esteban's performance on the Rorschach revealed tension, anxiety, and a preoccupation with morbid topics. He appeared to be overly concerned about his health, prone to depression, indecisive and yet at other times impulsive and careless. His responses were often immature and he showed a strong and persistent ambivalence toward females. In some responses, he viewed females in highly aggressive ways—often a fusion of sexual and aggressive images was evident. In general, he demonstrated aloofness and an inability to relate well to other people. Although his Rorschach responses suggested that he could view the world in conventional ways and was probably not psychotic, at times he had difficulty controlling his impulses. Esteban's Rorschach protocol was computer analyzed using the Exner Comprehensive Rorschach System.

Esteban took the original version of the MMPI in both English and Spanish. His MMPI profile was virtually identical in both languages. It has been converted to MMPI-2 format and is reproduced in HIGHLIGHT 15.4 (pages 586–588) along with the MMPI-2-based computer interpretation of his test scores.

Summary of the Psychological Assessment Esteban showed mild neurological deficits on neuropsychological testing and borderline intellectual ability. He clearly did not have the academic ability to pursue a medical career. Demanding intellectual tasks placed a great deal of stress on him and resulted in frustration. Furthermore, his poor memory made learning complex material very difficult.

The MMPI-2 interpretation indicated that Esteban's disorganized behavior and symptomatic patterns reflected a serious psychological disorder. Although he was not currently psychotic, both his past behavior and his test performance suggested that he was functioning marginally and that he showed the potential for personality deterioration in some situations.

Esteban's most salient psychological problems concerned his tendency to become frustrated and his ready loss of impulse control. He was volatile and became upset easily. Additionally, it appeared that Esteban's relative isolation during his early years (due in part to his overprotective mother) did not prepare him to function adequately in many social situations. Another important problem area for Esteban was in psychosexual adjustment. The psychological test results and his personal history clearly indicated a gender-identity confusion.

Within the parameters of DSM-IV, Esteban would receive an Axis I diagnosis of organic personality syndrome and an Axis II diagnosis of borderline personality disorder. Furthermore, it was recommended that he undertake social-skills training and that—rather than a career in medicine—he be encouraged to pursue occupational goals more in keeping with his abilities. Psychotropic medication (Lithium and Mellaril) were prescribed for his emotional control problems.

A Follow-up Note. Esteban was seen in psychological therapy twice a week and was kept on medication. He was also seen in a social-skills training program for ten sessions. Through the help of his therapist, he was admitted to a less-demanding English program, which seemed more appropriate for his abilities.

For the first six months, Esteban made considerable progress, especially after his behavior became somewhat stabilized, largely, it appeared, as a result of the medications. He became less impulsive and more in control of his anger. He successfully completed the English classes in which he was enrolled. During this period, he lived with his mother, who had taken up a temporary residence near the college. She then returned to Colombia, and Esteban moved into an apartment with a roommate, with whom, however, he had increasing difficulty.

Several weeks after his mother left, Esteban quit going to therapy and quit taking his medication. He began to frequent local gay bars, at first out of curiosity but later to seek male lovers. At the same time, his preoccupation with religion increased and he moved into a house near campus that was operated by a fundamentalist religious cult. His parents, quite concerned by his overt homosexual behavior (which he described in detail over the phone, adding the suggestion that they visit the gay bar with him), returned to the United States. Realizing that they could not stay permanently to supervise Esteban, they then sought a residential treatment program that would provide him with a more structured living arrangement. All assessment and therapy records were forwarded to those in charge of the residential program.

THE INTEGRATION OF ASSESSMENT DATA

As assessment data are collected, their significance must be interpreted so that they can be integrated into a coherent working model for use in planning or changing treatment. Clinicians in individual private practice normally assume this often arduous task on their own.

In a clinic or hospital setting, assessment data are usually evaluated in a staff conference attended by members of an interdisciplinary team (perhaps a clinical psychologist, a psychiatrist, a social worker, and other mental health personnel) who are concerned with the decisions to be made regarding treatment. By putting together all the information they have gathered, they can see whether the find-

In a clinic or hospital setting, assessment data are usually evaluated in a staff conference attended by members of an interdisciplinary team, including, for example, a clinical psychologist, a psychiatrist, a social worker, and a psychiatric nurse. Sharing findings may lead to a diagnostic classification for a patient and a course of treatment. Staff decisions can have far-reaching consequences for patients; as such, it is important that clinicians be aware of the limitations of assessment.

ings complement each other and form a definitive clinical picture or whether gaps or discrepancies exist that necessitate further investigation.

At the time of an original assessment, integration of all the data may lead to agreement on a tentative diagnostic classification for a patient. In any case, the findings of each member of the team, as well as the recommendations for treatment, are entered in the case record, so that it will always be possible to check back and see why a certain course of therapy was undertaken, how accurate the clinical assessment was, and how valid the treatment decision turned out to be.

New assessment data collected during the course of therapy provide feedback on its effectiveness and serve as a basis for making needed modifications in an ongoing treatment program. As we have noted, clinical assessment data are also commonly used in evaluating the final outcome of therapy and in comparing the effectiveness of different therapeutic and preventive approaches. Summers (1979), among others, has pointed out the importance of assessing a patient's level of functioning prior to hospital discharge. Too often, individuals who cannot function well outside a mental hospital are released into the community with little or no provision for continuing mental health care.

The decisions made on the basis of assessment data may have far-reaching implications for the people under study. A staff decision may determine whether a depressed person will be hospitalized or remain with his or her family; whether divorce will be accepted as a solution to an unhappy marriage or a further attempt will be made to salvage the relationship; or whether an accused person will be declared competent to stand trial. Thus a valid deci-

sion, based on accurate assessment data, is of far more than theoretical importance. Because of the impact that assessment can have on the lives of others, it is important that those involved keep several possible factors in mind in evaluating test results:

1. *Potential cultural bias of the instrument or the clinician.* There is the possibility that psychological tests may not elicit valid information from a patient from a minority group (Gray-Little, 1995). A clinician from one sociocultural background may have trouble assessing objectively the behavior of someone from another background, such as a Southeast Asian refugee. It is important to assure, as Timbrook and Graham (1994) have done with the MMPI-2, that the instrument can be confidently used with persons from minority groups.

2. *Theoretical orientation of the clinician.* Assessment is inevitably influenced by a clinician's assumptions, perceptions, and theoretical orientation. For example, a psychoanalyst and a behaviorist might assess the same behaviors quite differently. If the differing assessments should lead to treatment recommendations of significantly differing efficacy for a client's problems, these biases could have serious repercussions.

3. *Overemphasis on internal traits.* Many clinicians overemphasize personality traits as the cause of patients' problems without due attention to the possible role of stressors or other circumstances in their life situations. An undue focus on a patient's personality, which may be encouraged by some assessment techniques, can divert attention from potentially critical environmental factors.

4. *Insufficient validation.* Many psychological assessment procedures have not been sufficiently

validated. For example, unlike many of the personality scales, widely used procedures for behavioral observation and behavioral self-report have not been subjected to strict psychometric validation. The tendency on the part of clinicians to accept the results of these procedures at face value has recently been giving way to a broader recognition of the need for more explicit validation.

5. *Inaccurate data or premature evaluation.* There is always the possibility that some assessment data—and any diagnostic label or treatment based on them—may be inaccurate. Some risk is always involved in making predictions for an individual on the basis of group data or averages; although "schizophrenic" symptoms normatively imply a difficult treatment course, for example, some people who have them recover quickly even without treatment and never experience another episode. Inaccurate data or premature conclusions not only may lead to a misunderstanding of a patient's problem but may close off attempts to get further information, with possibly grave consequences for the patient.

UNRESOLVED ISSUES

on the Use of Computerized Assessment

Perhaps the most dramatic innovation in clinical assessment during the last 35 years has been the increasing sophistication and use of computers in individual assessment. As we have seen, computers are effectively used in assessment both to gather information directly from an individual and to put together and evaluate all the information that has been gathered previously through interviews, tests, and other assessment procedures (Bloom, 1992). By comparing the incoming information with data previously stored in its memory banks, a computer can perform a wide range of assessment tasks. It can supply a probable diagnosis, indicate the likelihood of certain kinds of behavior, suggest the most appropriate form of treatment, predict the outcome, and print out a summary report concerning the subject. In many of these functions, a computer is actually superior to a clinician because it is more efficient and accurate in recalling stored material.

With the increased efficiency and reliability accompanying the use of computers in clinical practice, one might expect a near unanimous welcoming of computers into the clinic. This is not the case, however. There is controversy over computerized

assessment and a reluctance on the part of some practitioners to use computer-based tests in their practice. We will discuss these general issues in turn.

Concerns have been raised by some psychologists that the widespread use of computer-based assessment procedures is not sufficiently supported by pertinent research (Matarazzo, 1986). In addition, some believe that unvalidated measures have been "oversold" to the point that external professional sanctions or even laws might be required to ensure compliance with standards of good practice (Lanyon, 1984; Matarazzo, 1986). Matarazzo, particularly, feels that reliance on present-day computer-based assessment procedures is problematic because it will increase the cost of health care—with the ready availability of such procedures, clinicians will be tempted to "overtest."

In a rejoinder to Matarazzo's critique, Fowler and Butcher (1986) questioned Matarazzo's position that there are such serious problems with computerized psychological assessment that external controls or legislation are required. Although acknowledging that some largely unvalidated software programs and weak test measures are commercially available, and that practitioners need to exercise care in using computer-based tests, they considered the substantial progress in computer-based psychological testing over the past 35 years to justify further development. According to Fowler and Butcher, many of the problems addressed by Matarazzo have already been resolved and are reflected in the APA guidelines for computer-based assessment (American Psychological Association, 1986). Matarazzo's concern that professionals would "overtest" and increase health care costs was considered by Fowler and Butcher to be overstated. Research has shown that the use of computers in psychological testing can actually reduce the cost of services.

Another of Matarazzo's concerns, in which he called for viewing computerized psychological reports as tools rather than ends in themselves, is an important but not a new concern. The recommendation that computerized tests be considered as working hypotheses and not as final recommendations has been a policy since the earliest days of computer assessment and is a central assumption of the American Psychological Association's (1986) most recent guidelines on computer-based assessment. Practitioners should not employ computer-based interpretations as the ultimate criterion. The final responsibility in a diagnostic study rests with a human clinician—it is she or he who must decide the relevance and utility to the particular case of the various and sometimes contradictory elements of a computer narrative printout.

The second issue raised here is the reluctance of some clinicians to use computer-based test interpretations in spite of their demonstrated utility and low cost. Even though many clinics and independent practitioners acquire microcomputers for record-keeping and billing purposes, a smaller number incorporate computer-based clinical assessment procedures into their practice. Possible reasons for the underutilization of computer-based assessment procedures include the following:

- Practitioners trained before the computer age may feel uncomfortable with computers or may not have time to become acquainted with them.

- Many practitioners limit their practice to psychological treatment and do not do extensive pretreatment assessments of their cases. Many also have little interest in, or time for, the systematic evaluation of treatment efficacy that periodic formal assessments would facilitate.

- To some clinicians the impersonal and mechanized look of the booklets and answer sheets common to much computerized assessment is contrary to the image and style of warm and personal engagement they hope to convey to clients.

- Some clinicians view computer-based assessment as a threat to their own functioning. Some are concerned, as suggested in Matarazzo's (1986) critique, that computer-assessment specialists seek to replace human diagnostic functioning with automated reports. Others are concerned that unqualified practitioners may gain access to such reports and "set up shop" as competitors.

Some of these concerns are not unlike those expressed by many craftspersons or production personnel in industry when computers and robots come to the workplace. Are human practitioners in danger of being replaced by computers? Not at all. Computers in psychological assessment have intrinsic limitations consigning them to an accessory role in the process; they would not be useful, in fact quite the contrary, if employed as the sole means of evaluation. It is the clinician who must assume the major organizing role and accept the responsibility for an assessment. An unqualified person wholly dependent on computerized reports for carrying on a practice would quickly be identified as incompetent by discerning referral sources, and probably by most self-referred clients; a thriving practice would not be a likely outcome. On the other hand, judicious use of computerized assessment can free up much time

for doing those things that can only be accomplished by the personal application of high levels of clinical skill and wisdom (Carson, 1990b).

 ## SUMMARY

Clinical assessment is one of the most important and complex activities facing mental health professionals. The extent to which a person's problems are understood and appropriately treated depend largely on the adequacy of the psychological assessment. The goals of psychological assessment include identifying and describing the individual's symptoms; determining the chronicity and severity of the problem; evaluating the potential causal factors in the person's background; and exploring the individual's personal resources, which might be assets in his or her treatment program.

Interdisciplinary sources of assessment data include both physical evaluation methods and psychosocial assessment techniques. Because many psychological problems have physical components, either as underlying causal factors or as symptom patterns, it is often important to include a medical examination in the psychological assessment. In cases where organic brain damage is suspected, it is important to have neurological tests—such as an EEG or a CAT, PET, or MRI scan—to aid in determining the site and extent of organic brain disorder. In addition, it may be important to have the person take a battery of neuropsychological tests to determine if or in what manner the underlying brain disorder is affecting his or her mental and behavioral capabilities.

Psychosocial assessment methods are techniques for gathering relevant psychological information for clinical decisions about patients. The most widely used and most flexible psychosocial assessment methods are the clinical interview and behavior observation. These methods provide a wealth of clinical information. They may be subject, however, to extraneous influences that make them somewhat unreliable, and structured interview formats and objective behavior rating scales have been developed to improve their reliability.

Whereas interviews and behavior observations attempt to assess an individual's beliefs, attitudes, and symptoms directly, psychological tests attempt to measure these aspects of personality indirectly. Psychological tests include standardized stimuli for collecting behavior samples that can be compared with other individuals through test norms. Two different personality testing approaches have been developed:

(a) projective tests, such as the Rorschach, in which unstructured stimuli are presented to a subject, who then "projects" meaning or structure on to the stimulus, thereby revealing "hidden" motives, feelings, and so on; and (b) objective tests, or personality inventories, in which a subject is required to read and respond to itemized statements or questions. Objective personality tests provide a cost-effective means of collecting a great deal of personality information rapidly. The MMPI, the most widely used and validated objective personality inventory, and MMPI-2 and MMPI-A, its recently revised offspring, provide a number of clinically relevant scales for describing abnormal behavior.

Psychological tests are widely used in settings other than clinical assessment situations. For example, tests like the MMPI-2, because of their objectivity in describing personality, are widely used in courts for assessing questions such as whether an individual is competent to stand trial or whether a personal injury claimant is suffering from stress following an alleged injury. Another nonclinical setting in which personality assessment is widely used is for personnel screening for positions that require emotionally stable people such as airline pilots, police officers, and nuclear power plant workers.

Possibly the most dramatic recent innovation in clinical assessment involves the widespread use of computers in the administration, scoring, and interpretation of psychological tests. It is now possible to obtain immediate interpretation of psychological test results, either through a direct computer interactive approach or through a modem to a mainframe computer that interprets tests. In the past few years, rapid developments have been taking place in the computer assessment area. It is conceivable that, within the next few years, most clinical assessments will involve computers in some capacity, either for administration, scoring, and interpretation or for completing an entire test battery. Of course, mental health professionals will still play a major role in determining the appropriateness and adequacy of the computer's diagnostic output.

KEY TERMS

dynamic formulation (p. 569)
electroencephalogram
   (EEG) (p. 571)
dysrhythmia (p. 571)
computerized axial tomo-
   graphy (CAT scan)
   (p. 571)
positron emission tomo-
   graphy (PET scan)
   (p. 571)
nuclear magnetic resonance
   imaging (MRI) (p. 572)
neuropsychological
   assessment (p. 572)
self-monitoring (p. 575)

rating scales (p. 575)
role playing (p. 579)
projective tests (p. 580)
Rorschach Test (p. 580)
Thematic Apperception Test
   (TAT) (p. 581)
sentence-completion test
   (p. 582)
objective tests (p. 582)
Minnesota Multiphasic
   Personality Inventory
   (MMPI/MMPI-2/
   MMPI-A) (p. 583)
factor analysis (p. 588)
actuarial procedures (p. 589)

BIOLOGICALLY
BASED THERAPIES

Johann Knüpfer, Glory of My Savior. *Knüpfer (1866–1910) lived at home and worked at a variety of manual jobs until he was nearly 30. Thereafter he married, unhappily, and left his wife, eventually becoming a vagrant. He attempted suicide in 1902 and was committed to a mental hospital near Heidelberg. Once there, Knüpfer began to draw. His art is detailed and orderly, and often illustrates religious preoccupations.*

Therapy is directed toward modifying maladaptive behavior and fostering adaptive behavior. The concept of therapy is not new. Throughout recorded history, human beings have tried to help each other with life's problems—including mental disorders—in both informal and formal ways. In Chapter 2 we noted the wide range of procedures that have, throughout history, been advocated for helping the mentally disturbed—from exorcism to incarceration and torture, from understanding and kindness to the most extreme cruelty.

Today both biological and psychological procedures are used in attempts to help individuals overcome psychopathology. In this chapter we will focus on biological methods that have evolved for the treatment of mental disorders, such as the schizophrenias, mood disorders, and disorders in which severe anxiety is central. In the next chapter we will focus on psychological approaches.

EARLY ATTEMPTS AT BIOLOGICAL INTERVENTION

The idea that a disordered mind might be set straight by treatment directed at the body goes back, as we have seen, to ancient times. From Hippocrates in ancient Greece to Paracelsus in medieval Europe to Kraepelin in Europe at the turn of this century, and on to modern psychiatrists, there have always been those who believed that, ultimately, the cure of mental aberration would be through alteration of an organism's biological state. Today we still have no reliable knowledge of point-to-point correspondence between certain behaviors and particular events in the brain at cellular or subcellular levels. Nonetheless, the dictum "no twisted thought without a twisted molecule," while philosophically and scientifically naive in certain respects, has been deeply internalized by many workers in the mental health field. For them, it is but a small step to conclude that the search for treatment methods should concentrate on finding effective means of rearranging or reconstituting aberrant molecules—of changing the presumed physical substrate of abnormal behavior.

The history of psychiatry reflects interesting, though by today's standards often extreme and primitive, methods of treating mental illness by altering bodily processes. Some have been widely used in several periods of history. For example, ridding the body of unwanted substances by purging (with laxatives and emetics) was a typical treatment in ancient Rome, during the medieval period, and during

Some of the stranger instruments used for treatment of the mentally ill in the eighteenth and nineteenth centuries are shown here: at left, glass cups and scarificators—which make cuts in the skin—that were used for bleeding patients; at right, an electrostatic generator that was used to shock patients.

the eighteenth century (Agnew, 1985). In fact, purging was so widespread during some periods, particularly the eighteenth century, that it was a common practice in medicine and among people in general. Other seemingly more barbaric techniques, such as bleeding, have been widely used as treatments of the mentally disordered just as they have been used for a broad range of physical diseases. The use of bleeding was apparently consistent and acceptable to the views of medical science in the eighteenth century. Interestingly, many medical procedures were derived from or paralleled research and development in other sciences. For example, after the discovery of electricity, many efforts to use electrical stimulation to alter mental states ensued. Early electrical devices were used to stimulate patients' nerves, muscles, and organs as a treatment for a variety of illnesses. The rationale behind early somatic efforts to "treat" mental patients was often unclear, although frightening patients out of their madness or punishing the demons within may have been as much a reason as was any belief that an individual's bodily processes were being restored.

In general, as more has been learned in the various subfields of medicine, treatment measures have become more benign and less risky. As researchers come to understand scientifically the nature of a disorder, they typically are then able to develop biological treatments that are more precisely designed to meet the specific problem. The specificity of these new treatments typically means that they have fewer potentially damaging side effects.

The human brain and mind have yielded their secrets grudgingly. As a result, relative to other medical subdisciplines, psychiatry has had a slow and often uncertain development. It should not be surprising, therefore, to find that it has contributed its own array of dubious treatment techniques in the comparatively short history of its recognition as a medical subspecialty. By 1917, with the discovery of Wagner-Jauregg that general paresis, or neurosyphilis, could be curbed by intentionally infecting a patient with malaria (the consequent fevers were lethal to the spirochete), the stage was set for the development of extraordinarily bold and often hazardous new treatments. Wagner-Jauregg later received the Nobel Prize for his discovery. We will look now at two treatments that emerged during this period: the convulsive therapies and psychosurgery.

Coma and Convulsive Therapies

The first acknowledged medical use of inducing convulsions to treat individuals with mental disorders has been attributed to the Swiss physician-alchemist Paracelsus (1493–1591). He reported a case in which he induced a patient to drink camphor until he experienced convulsions (Mowbray, 1959) in order to cure him of his "lunacy." During the eighteenth century camphor-induced convulsions were used by several physicians to treat mania—in 1764 by Leopold von Aurenbrugger, in 1785 by Oliver, and in 1798 by Weickhardt (see Sandford,

1966). The cure seems to have been forgotten or was not widely adopted, and no use of it was reported during the nineteenth century.

The modern originator of convulsion therapy was Von Meduna, a Hungarian physician, who was apparently unaware of these early efforts to use camphor in the induction of convulsions to treat mania when he published his own observations on inducing epileptic seizures to treat schizophrenia in 1934. Von Meduna speculated—erroneously, as it turned out—that schizophrenia rarely occurred in people with epilepsy. This observation led to the inference that schizophrenia and epilepsy were somehow incompatible, and that one might be able to cure schizophrenia by inducing convulsions. Von Meduna conducted his first experiments on rats and then used camphor to induce convulsions in a schizophrenic patient who relatively quickly regained lucidity after the convulsive therapy. Shortly afterward, Von Meduna began to use a drug called Metrazol rather than camphor to induce convulsions because it operated more rapidly. Von Meduna's work, though not without its critics, provided a great deal of hope that some mental disorders that were previously unresponsive to treatment might now be treatable.

Insulin Coma Therapy Rarely used today, **insulin coma therapy** was introduced by Sakel in 1932 as a physiological treatment for schizophrenia and was also used as a treatment for morphine withdrawal. The technique involves administration of increasing amounts of insulin (a hormone that regulates sugar metabolism in the body) daily until a patient goes into "shock"—actually a hypoglycemic coma caused by an acute deficiency of glucose (sugar) in the blood. Coma-inducing doses of insulin are administered daily thereafter until the patient has experienced approximately 50 comas, each an hour or more in duration. The comas are terminated by administering glucose. This treatment causes profound biological and physiological stress, especially to the cardiovascular and nervous systems. The patient must be closely monitored both during and after the comatose state because of a variety of medical complications that may ensue, including some that are fatal.

The results of insulin coma therapy have been generally disappointing. Where patients have shown improvement, it has been difficult to determine whether it was due to the experience of the comas or to some other aspect of the treatment, such as the markedly increased attention of the medical staff. Moreover, patients who do improve tend to be those who would improve readily under other treatment regimens as well; severe, chronic schizophrenic patients remain for the most part unimproved. Finally, the relapse rate for those who improve has been high. With such a record—and in the face of marked medical risks—it is hardly surprising that the use of this therapeutic method has largely disappeared (Kalinowski & Hippius, 1969).

Electroconvulsive Shock Therapy Shortly after the discovery of electricity, mild electrical stimulation was used in the treatment of mental disorders. As early as 1849 the physician John Charles Bucknill, working with asylum patients, used electrical stimulation of the skin and potassium oxide to successfully treat patients with melancholic depression (Beveridge & Renvoize, 1988). During the latter part of the nineteenth century, the therapeutic use of electrical stimulation was fairly widespread. Toward the end of the century, however, concern over its safe use resulted in a diminished application of electricity for treatment.

The potential value of electrostimulation therapy was reconsidered after Von Meduna's encouraging work on Metrazol-induced seizures in the treatment of mental disorders. In 1938 two Italian physicians, U. Cerletti and L. Bini, after visiting a slaughterhouse and seeing animals rendered unconscious by electric shock, tried the simplest method of all—that of passing an electric current through a patient's head. The method, which became known as **electroconvulsive therapy (ECT),** is much more widely used today than insulin therapy, mostly because of its effectiveness in alleviating depressive episodes. Although ECT is known to be effective, the mechanism by which it works has never been adequately explained. Some researchers believe that the therapeutic effect is brought about by changes in the levels of certain neurotransmitters or by changes in receptor sensitivity (Fink, 1992).

There are two types of ECT—bilateral and unilateral. The latter is a more recent introduction and is considered, by some, less intrusive. We will review both here. The technique of administering ECT has changed considerably since it was developed by Cerletti and Bini (Khan et al., 1993) although the basic procedure remains similar: An electric current of approximately 150 volts is passed from one side of a patient's head to the other for up to about 1½ seconds. The patient immediately loses consciousness and undergoes marked muscle contractions. Today, anesthetics and muscle-relaxant premedication are usually used to prevent violent contractions and careful, continuous monitoring during the procedure lowers side effects and risk. In the days before such medication was available, the initial seizure was sometimes so violent as to fracture vertebrae, one of several potential complications of this therapy.

After awakening several minutes later, the patient has amnesia for the period immediately preceding the therapy, and is usually somewhat confused for the next hour or so. Normally, a treatment series consists of less than a dozen sessions, although in times past there was widespread overuse of the technique as a means of controlling excited or violent behavior. With repeated treatments, usually administered three times weekly, the patient gradually becomes disoriented, a state that usually clears after termination of the treatments.

Some years ago, a modification in the standard method of administering ECT was introduced. Instead of placing the electrodes on each side of the head in the temple region, thereby causing a transverse flow of current through both cerebral hemispheres, the new procedure involves limiting current flow through only one side of the brain, typically the nondominant (right side, for most people). This procedure is called *unilateral ECT,* and strong evidence shows that it lessens distressing side effects (such as memory impairment) without decreasing therapeutic effectiveness (Daniel & Crovitz, 1983b; Squire, 1977; Squire & Slater, 1978). However, other studies suggest that it may not be as effective as bilateral ECT, and so many suggest reserving the unilateral form for those who have especially prominent memory problems with bilateral ECT (Fink, 1992; Weiner & Krystal, 1994). Evidence gathered in the early 1980s (Daniel & Crovitz, 1983a) also suggested that the use of a lower-energy, pulsating electrical stimulus may produce less mental impairment than the standard treatment, and this is now often used (Fink, 1992; Weiner & Krystal, 1994).

The results of ECT in alleviating some cases of depression are generally acknowledged. A dramatic early example of successful ECT treatments is provided in the autobiographical account of Lenore McCall (1947/1961), who suffered a severe depressive disorder in her middle years.

Ms. McCall, a well-educated woman of affluent circumstances and the mother of three children, noticed a feeling of persistent fatigue as the first sign of her impending descent into depression. Too fearful to seek help, she at first attempted to fight off her increasingly profound apathy by engaging in excessive activity, a defensive strategy that accomplished little but the depletion of her remaining strength and emotional reserves.

In due course, she noticed that her mental processes seemed to be deteriorating—her memory appeared impaired and she could concentrate only with great difficulty. Emotionally, she felt an enormous loneliness, bleakness of experience, and increasingly intense fear about what was happening to her mind. She came to view her past small errors of commission and omission as the most heinous of crimes and increasingly withdrew from contact with her husband and children. Eventually, at her husband's and her physician's insistence, she was hospitalized despite her own vigorous resistance. She felt betrayed, and shortly thereafter attempted suicide by shattering a drinking glass and ingesting its fragments; to her great disappointment, she survived.

Ms. McCall thereafter spent nearly four years continuously in two separate mental hospitals, during which time she deteriorated further. She was silent and withdrawn, behaved in a mechanical fashion, lost an alarming amount of weight, and underwent a seemingly premature aging process. She felt that she emitted an offensive odor. At this time, ECT was introduced into the therapeutic procedures in use at her hospital.

A series of ECT treatments was given to Ms. McCall over about a three-month period. Then, one day, she woke up in the morning with a totally changed outlook: "I sat up suddenly, my heart pounding. I looked around the room and a sweep of wonder surged over me. God in heaven, I'm well. I'm myself. . . ." After a brief period of convalescence, she went home to her husband and children to try to pick up the threads of their painfully severed lives. She did so, and then wrote the engrossing and informative book from which this history is taken.

At present, the use of ECT is still considered controversial. Public concerns about the treatment as portrayed in novels such as Kesey's *One Flew Over the Cuckoo's Nest* have created negative feelings about its use. Responding to these concerns, the residents of Berkeley, California, voted in November 1982 to ban the use of ECT treatment within that city (*Science News,* November 13, 1982), an action that was later judicially overturned. Though the wisdom of holding public elections on such issues may be questioned, the event demonstrates citizen awareness and concern about the treatment mental patients receive. Moreover, there have been a number of malpractice lawsuits brought against psychia-

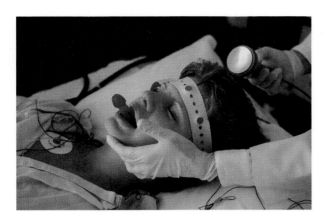

A patient administered electroconvulsive therapy (ECT) today is given sedative and muscle-relaxant premedication to prevent violent contractions. In the days before such medication was available, the initial seizure was sometimes so violent as to fracture vertebrae.

trists who use ECT, primarily over the failure to obtain appropriate patient consent (Leong & Eth, 1991).

However, some authorities support the use of ECT as the only effective way of dealing with some severely depressed and suicidal patients. Moreover, Mukherjee, Sackeim, and Schnur (1994), evaluating the research on ECT over the past 50 years, concluded that ECT is also an effective treatment for patients with manic disorders who have not responded to pharmacotherapy (80 percent effective overall with difficult to treat patients). For example, Husain and colleagues (1993) reported on the use of a long-term (two-year) treatment of an elderly woman with recurring mania. The authors pointed out that the ECT (81 sessions in all) was the only effective means of controlling her manic episodes and proved to be both safe and cost-effective.

Others within the profession deplore what they consider to be a lack of objective appraisals of ECT. These contrary views would have been easier to dismiss in the 1940s, because little else of proven efficacy was then available. Today there are effective alternative approaches—such as antidepressant medication—in abundance. Moreover, memory impairment resulting from the ECT can remain for some months (Squire, Slater, & Chase, 1975), or, as some attest, even years (Breggin, 1979, 1991). The damage created by electroshock is difficult to estimate in precise terms, but some critics think it could be substantial (Breggin, 1979, Palmer, 1981). It is possible that electroconvulsive treatment destroys a varying number of central nervous system neurons causing such side effects as memory loss or impairment. The extent and permanence of brain damage

from ECT has been extensively debated within the field. Weiner (1984) disputes claims of extensive brain damage resulting from ECT, particularly if the ECT is administered unilaterally with "brief pulse" stimulation of the nondominant hemisphere (Weiner et al., 1986). Recent and very carefully done studies using brain imaging techniques have made a compelling case that there is no relationship between ECT (at least properly administered) and brain damage (e.g., Coffey et al., 1991).

In 1985 the National Institute of Mental Health sponsored a Consensus Development Conference on electroconvulsive therapy to evaluate the issues surrounding the use of ECT (National Institute of Mental Health, 1985a). A panel of experts in psychiatry, psychology, neurology, psychopharmacology, epidemiology, and law, along with several laypersons, considered evidence as to (a) the effectiveness of ECT for patients with various disorders; (b) the risks of ECT; (c) the indications for administration of ECT; and (d) the best ways to implement ECT with patients.

The panel recognized a number of potential risks associated with the use of ECT and concluded that these risks have been virtually eliminated. Mortality following ECT, a significant problem in the early days of the treatment, has also been significantly reduced to about 2.9 deaths per 10,000 patients. The injury and mortality rates are considered comparable to other somatic treatments, such as barbiturate anesthetics. The panel reached a number of conclusions as to which disorders responded best to ECT. They agreed that the effect of ECT was well established for some types of depression, particularly delusional depression and "endogenous" depression. They also concluded that ECT can be effectively used with some types of manic disorders, particularly acute mania. On the other hand, they found that ECT was not particularly effective with some depressions, such as dysthymic disorder. Although ECT is sometimes used with certain types of schizophrenia, the evidence for effectiveness is not convincing. The NIMH consensus panel concluded that relapse rates following ECT were high unless the treatment was followed by maintenance doses of antidepressant medication.

More recently, the American Psychiatric Association (1992) and the Canadian Psychiatric Association (Enns & Reiss, 1992) have established clearer guidelines and standards for using ECT, training staff who conduct ECT, and policies for obtaining informed consent from patients.

Despite all the questions and controversy, the therapeutic efficacy of ECT, at least for some depressions and acute mania, is well established in the research literature (Abrams, 1988, 1994; Fink,

1979; Scovern & Kilman, 1980) and in personal testimonials from those who have been helped by it (Endler, 1990).

Psychosurgery

Brain surgery used in the treatment of functional or central nervous system disorders has been called **psychosurgery.** Mindus and colleagues (1993), however, object to this term because the "psyche" is not being operated upon. They prefer to use the term *neurosurgery* instead. We will use both terms in this text to refer to brain surgery for emotional disorders.

Although brain surgery was used occasionally in the nineteenth century to treat mental disorders by relieving pressure in the brain (Berrios, 1990), it was not considered a treatment for psychological problems until this century. In 1935 in Portugal, Antonio Moniz introduced a psychosurgical procedure in which the frontal lobes of the brain were severed from the deeper centers underlying them. This technique eventually evolved into an operation known as **prefrontal lobotomy.** This operation stands as a dubious tribute to the extremes to which professionals have sometimes been driven in their search for effective treatments for the psychoses. In retrospect, it is ironic that this procedure—which results in permanent structural changes in the brain of the patient and has been highly criticized by many within the profession—won Moniz the 1949 Nobel Prize in Medicine.

In the two decades between 1935 and 1955 (after which the new antipsychotic drugs became widely available), tens of thousands of mental patients in this country and abroad were subjected to prefrontal lobotomy and related neurosurgical procedures. In fact, in some settings, as many as 50 patients were treated in a single day (Freeman, 1959). As is often the case with newly developed therapeutic techniques, initial reports of results tended to be enthusiastic, downplaying complications (including a 1–4 percent death rate) and undesirable side effects. It was eventually recognized, however, that the "side effects" of psychosurgery could be very undesirable indeed. In some instances they included a permanent inability to inhibit impulses; in others, an unnatural "tranquility," with undesirable shallowness or absence of feeling. By 1951 the Soviet Union had banned all such operations; though rarely performed today, they are still permitted by law in the United States and in many other countries and, as we will see, have been making a comeback in modified form as a psychiatric treatment today for some difficult-to-treat disorders. See

HIGHLIGHT 16.1 for an illustration of the sometimes tragic outcome of lobotomy.

The advent of the major antipsychotic drugs caused an immediate decrease in the widespread use of psychosurgery, especially prefrontal lobotomy. Such operations are rare today and are used only as a last resort for the intractable psychoses, severely and chronically debilitating obsessive-compulsive disorders, and occasionally for the control of severe pain in cases of terminal illness.

Despite the evolution of more precise techniques, continuing concern has been voiced about such operations. In the mid-1970s the Congress of the United States called a special national commission to evaluate their effects. The commission's report indicated some surprisingly beneficial effects that had been achieved with modern psychosurgery—for example, the alleviation of chronic depression—but it also warned that such benefits were often achieved at the expense of the loss of certain cognitive capacities. The commission recommended that cautious exploration of these techniques be continued with selected patients (Culliton, 1976).

The debate about the benefits and potential damage resulting from psychosurgery received a thorough airing in two fascinating books by Elliot Valenstein (1980, 1986). Valenstein scrutinized the procedures of psychosurgery—and by implication other "brain-disabling" therapies—in relation to the psychiatric, ethical, legal, and social issues they raise. In the 1986 book *Great and Desperate Cures,* Valenstein examined the historical basis of psychosurgery and explained how an unproven and potentially life-threatening treatment could emerge in a field devoted to scientific explanation and become an accepted treatment method with little empirical justification. Factors underlying this premature and "desperate" acceptance of psychosurgery included psychiatry's need to "gain respectability" as a medical science by having an organic-surgical treatment method; the professional rivalry between psychiatry, neurology, and neurosurgery; and the need to provide a cost-effective treatment and maintain control over mental hospitals.

When psychosurgery is employed today it is a far more circumspect procedure than in the heyday of lobotomies. Patients are more carefully screened and given more careful postoperative monitoring. Moreover, today the permanent damage to the brain has been substantially minimized and fewer detrimental side effects follow. Modern surgical techniques involve the selective destruction of minute areas of the brain; for example, in the "cingulotomy" procedure—which seems to relieve the subjective experience of pain, including "psychic" pain—a small bun-

HIGHLIGHT 16.1

The Accomplishments and Subsequent Tragedy of Rosemary Kennedy

One of the tragic victims of the zeal to perform prefrontal lobotomies to alleviate behavior problems was Rosemary Kennedy, the sister of President John F. Kennedy and Senators Robert and Edward Kennedy. Rosemary was the third child of Joseph and Rose Kennedy, born during the height of the flu epidemic of 1918. She was a beautiful baby, with a sweet temperament, but as she grew, her mother became more and more concerned about her developmental delays compared to her brothers and sisters. When the family finally concluded that Rosemary likely was retarded since birth from unknown causes, the best experts in the country at the time could offer no guidance: "We went from doctor to doctor. From all, we heard the same answer: 'I'm sorry, but we can do nothing.' For my husband and me it was nerve-racking and incomprehensible" (Goodwin, 1988, p. 416).

Rose Kennedy and the family rebelled against the suggestion that Rosemary be institutionalized. Instead, she was kept at home with the benefit of a special governess and many private tutors. She participated fully in the Kennedy's family activities, and she made considerable progress. Doris Kearns Goodwin (1988), a biographer of

the Fitzgerald and Kennedy families, described an arithmetic paper that the 9-year-old Rosemary completed on February 21, 1927. She correctly answered several multiplication (428 times 32) and division (3924 divided by 6) problems. By the age of 18 years, Rosemary had obtained a fifth-grade level in English and remained at the fourth-grade level in math that she had obtained by age 9.

Because of the considerable stigma associated with mental retardation at the time, Rosemary's parents kept her condition hidden from those outside the family, a major task given the scrutiny of the family by the press. Although her parents and siblings were always nearby to protect her, Rosemary developed the social skills needed to be presented successfully as a debutante and later to the King and Queen of England at Buckingham Palace. The British press complimented Rose Kennedy for her beautiful daughters, never even noticing Rosemary's mental retardation.

Unfortunately, Rosemary's behavior deteriorated around the beginning of World War II when the family returned to the United States from England, where Joseph Kennedy had been ambassador. There are several possible

explanations for this deterioration, including her increasing frustration about not being able to do all the things her siblings were able to do and having to leave the school in England where she had felt successful. The 21-year-old Rosemary became quite violent and frequently ran away from home or her convent school. There was considerable concern for her safety, and Joseph Kennedy—without Rose's knowledge—turned to the medical experts of the time, searching for a solution.

These experts convinced Joe that the miracle treatment lay in prefrontal lobotomy. Rosemary Kennedy became one of the thousands submitted to that "desperate" cure. In Rosemary's case, the surgery was a tragic failure—all her previous accomplishments were wiped out, leaving little of her former personality and adaptive ability intact: "They knew right away that it wasn't successful. You could see by looking at her that something was wrong, for her head was tilted and her capacity to speak was almost entirely gone. There was no question now that she could no longer take care of herself and that the only answer was an institution." (Ann Gargan King, a cousin, as reported by Goodwin, 1988, p. 744)

---

dle of nerve fibers connecting the frontal lobes with a deeper structure known as the limbic system is interrupted with virtually pinpoint precision (Jenike et al., 1991). Another type of neurosurgery—the "capsulotomy" procedure, originally developed in Sweden—is a surgical operation that involves drilling very small holes in the patient's skull (employing careful measurement) and inserting tiny thermal electrodes in the brain. The electrodes are caused to heat up, which destroys the adjacent cellular structures. Reportedly, patients do not experience subjec-

tive distress from the procedures (Meyerson & Mindus, 1988; Sweet & Meyerson, 1990). Contemporary use of neurosurgery in the treatment of severe mental disorders is recommended only for patients who have not responded to all other forms of treatment considered standard for the disorder for a period of five years, and who are experiencing extreme disabling symptoms. Patients are accepted for neurosurgical treatment only if they are rationally capable of understanding the procedure and provide informed consent.

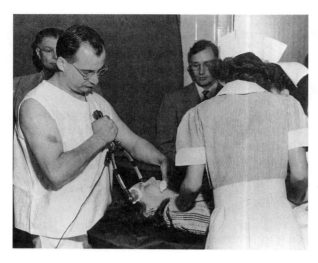
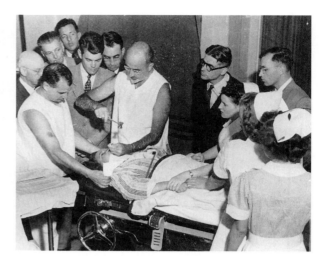

Shown here is a demonstration of a transorbital lobotomy, which was used extensively in this country from the 1940s until the late 1950s. First, a doctor administers ECT to anesthetize the patient (left). Immediately following ECT, another doctor performs the actual lobotomy (right). It is estimated that tens of thousands of patients were subjected to such procedures, resulting in permanent brain damage (which was, after all, the actual intent of the procedure) and sometimes death.

Although there have not yet been enough controlled studies of these new psychosurgery techniques published at this time to warrant firm conclusions, research has been encouraging. For example, Mindus and colleagues (1993) described an overall satisfactory result of psychosurgery in 253 severe obsessive-compulsive patients. About two-thirds of these patients were found to be symptom-free or much improved over their previous symptom levels after the surgery. Also, important to the acceptability of an experimental procedure is the relative absence of negative side effects. In this respect, Mindus and colleagues (1993) reported that no deaths occurred as a result of the psychosurgery and that the risk of suicide (often reported as a frequent outcome of psychosurgery in the past) was not found to be increased in patients undergoing the procedure.

THE EMERGENCE OF PHARMACOLOGICAL METHODS OF TREATMENT

A long-term goal of medicine has been to discover drugs that can effectively combat the ravages of mental disorder. This goal, one of the pursuits of **pharmacology,** the science of drugs, has until the last few decades remained elusive. Early efforts in this direction were limited largely to a search for drugs that would have soothing, calming, or sleep-inducing effects—drugs that would make it easier to manage distraught, excited, and sometimes violent patients. Little thought was given to the possibility that the status and course of the disorder itself might actually be brought under control by appropriate medication; the focus was on rendering a patient's overt behavior more manageable and thereby making restraints, such as straitjackets, unnecessary.

As the field of psychopharmacology developed, many such compounds were introduced and tried in the mental hospital setting. Almost without exception, however, those that produced the desired calming effects proved to have serious shortcomings. At effective dosage levels, they often produced severe drowsiness if not outright sleep, and many of them were dangerously addicting. On the whole, little real progress was made in this field until the mid-1950s, at which point, as we will see, a genuine revolution in the treatment of the more severe disorders occurred. This breakthrough was followed shortly by the discovery of drugs helpful in the treatment of the less severe anxiety-based disorders, and also by recognition of the therapeutic benefits of antidepressants and lithium salts for the mood disorders.

Types of Drugs Used in Therapy

In this section we will trace the discovery of the four types of chemical agents now commonly used in therapy for mental disorders—antipsychotic drugs, antidepressant drugs, antianxiety drugs (minor tranquilizers), and lithium. These drugs are sometimes

Straitjackets and other forms of restraint were used on out-of-control patients before the advent of antipsychotic drugs.

referred to as *psychotropic* (literally mind-turning or mind-altering) *drugs,* in that their main effect is on an individual's mental life. As we examine drugs used in therapy, it is important to remember that people differ in how rapidly they metabolize drugs—that is, in how quickly their bodies break down the drugs once ingested. What this means is that people differ, too, in what dosage of a drug they may need to experience the desired therapeutic effect. Determining correct dosage is a critical factor of drug therapy because too much or too little of a drug can be ineffective and (in the case of too much) even life-threatening, depending on the individual.

Antipsychotic Drugs The **antipsychotic drugs** as a group are sometimes called *major tranquilizers,* but this term is somewhat misleading. They are used with the major disorders, such as the schizophrenias, but they do more than tranquilize. Though they do indeed produce a calming effect on many patients, their unique quality is that of somehow alleviating or reducing the intensity of psychotic symptoms, such as delusions and hallucinations. In some cases, in fact, a patient who is already excessively "tranquil" (for example, withdrawn or immobile) becomes active and responsive to the environment under treatment by these drugs. In contrast, the antianxiety drugs, to be described shortly, are effec-

tive in reducing tension without in any way affecting psychotic symptoms.

Although the benefits of the antipsychotic drugs have often been exaggerated, it is difficult to convey the truly enormous influence they have had in altering the environment of the typical mental hospital. One of the authors, as part of his training, worked several months in the maximum security ward of one such hospital just before the introduction of this type of medication in 1955. The ward patients fulfilled the common stereotypes of individuals "gone mad." Bizarreness, nudity, wild screaming, and an ever-present threat of violence pervaded the atmosphere. Fearfulness and a nearly total preoccupation with the maintenance of control characterized the staff's attitude. Such an attitude was not unrealistic in terms of the frequency of serious physical assaults by patients, but it was hardly conducive to the development or maintenance of an effective therapeutic program.

Then, quite suddenly—within a period of perhaps a month—all of this dramatically changed. The patients began receiving the new antipsychotic medication. The ward became a place in which one could get to know one's patients on a personal level and perhaps even initiate programs of "milieu therapy," a form of psychosocial therapy in which the entire facility is regarded as a therapeutic community, and the emphasis is on developing a meaningful and constructive environment in which the patients participate in the regulation of their own activities. Promising reports of changes in hospital environments began to appear in the professional literature. A new era in hospital treatment had arrived, aided enormously and in many instances actually made possible by the development of these extraordinary drugs.

The beginnings of this development were quite commonplace. For centuries, the root of the plant *rauwolfia* (snakeroot) had been used in India for the treatment of mental disorders. In 1943 the *Indian Medical Gazette* reported improvements in manic reactions, schizophrenia, and other types of psychopathology following the use of *reserpine,* a drug derived from rauwolfia. Early enthusiasm for the drug was tempered, however, by the finding that it also might produce low blood pressure, nasal congestion, and, perhaps most seriously, severe depression. Reanalysis of this latter finding suggested that the danger of serious depression was mainly for patients with a prior history of depression (Mendels & Frazer, 1974). Reserpine is now used mainly for the control of hypertension.

Meanwhile, the first of the phenothiazine family of drugs, *chlorpromazine* (Thorazine), was being synthesized in the early 1950s by one of the major pharmaceutical houses. It was first marketed at about the same time that reserpine was introduced, and it quickly proved to have virtually the same benefits but fewer undesirable side effects. Chlorpromazine soon became the treatment of choice for schizophrenia.

The remarkable early successes reported with chlorpromazine led quickly to a bandwagon effect among other pharmaceutical companies, who began to manufacture and market their own variants of the basic phenothiazine compound. Some of the best known variants are trifluoperazine (Stelazine), promazine (Sparine), prochlorperazine (Compazine), thioridazine (Mellaril), perphenazine (Trilafon), and fluphenazine (Prolixin). Currently, too, there are at least six classes of nonphenothiazine antipsychotic drugs available in the United States, of which the best known is haloperidol (Haldol). This diversity becomes less bewildering when it is remembered that virtually all of the antipsychotics accomplish a common biochemical effect, namely the blocking of dopamine receptors, as was noted in Chapter 12.

With persistent use or at high dosage, however, all of these preparations have varying degrees of troublesome side effects, such as dryness of the mouth and throat, muscular stiffness, jaundice, and a Parkinson-like syndrome involving tremors of the extremities and immobility of the facial muscles. Which side effects develop appears to depend on the particular compound used in relation to the particular vulnerabilities of the treated patient. Many of these side effects are temporary and may be relieved by substituting another drug of the same class, by switching to a different class of drug, or by reducing the dosage. We should also note that some schizophrenic individuals, particularly those with negative symptoms or chronic schizophrenia, do not respond to antipsychotic drug therapy and may indeed be made worse by it (Buckley, 1982).

For certain patients, a particularly troublesome side effect of long-term antipsychotic drug treatment is the development of a disfiguring disturbance of motor control, particularly of the facial muscles, known as **tardive dyskinesia.** Symptoms of tardive dyskinesia, which often seem to disappear when a patient is asleep, are both dramatic to an observer and disabling to the patient. The symptoms involve involuntary movements of the tongue, lips, jaw, and extremities. An individual with tardive dyskinesia may show involuntary limb movement and usually shows characteristic chewing movements, lip smacking, and sucking of the mouth. The disturbance is believed to be due to an imbal-

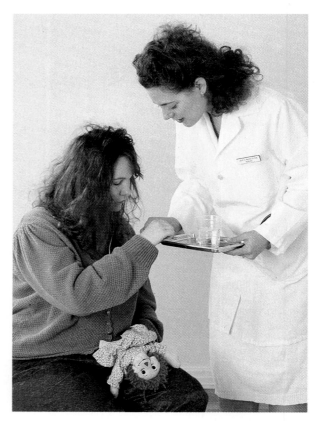

The introduction of antipsychotic drugs in hospital treatment of the mentally ill was a major breakthrough in altering the environment of the typical mental hospital.

ance in dopamine and acetylcholine activity in the brain, secondary to alterations in receptor sensitivity by antipsychotics and other drugs commonly used in combination to control their side effects. Side effects of tardive dyskinesia can occur months to years after the antipsychotic drug treatment is initiated and after the treatment has been stopped or the drug reduced in dosage.

Recent efforts have been undertaken to study possible characteristics of schizophrenic persons who might develop medication side effects such as tardive dyskinesia (Leonard et al., 1992). Crow (1980) proposed a distinction (noted in Chapter 12) between positive symptoms such as hallucinations, delusions, and thinking disturbance and negative symptoms such as poverty of speech and flat affect. Crow and colleagues (1983) reported that abnormal involuntary movements are associated with the presence of negative symptoms, a finding that has been supported by more recent research (Liddle et al., 1993). Moreover, there is some indication that abnormal movements are associated with aging (Kane & Smith, 1982). These studies suggest that different pathological factors might contribute to the development of schizophrenia and the manifestation of symptoms.

Tardive dyskinesia develops in approximately 10–20 percent of people who take phenothiazines for long periods of time (Kane et al., 1986; Torrey, 1983). It may occur in an even higher percentage of alcohol-abusing schizophrenics (Dixon et al., 1992; Olivera, Kiefer, & Manley, 1990) and is especially likely in people over 55. The manifestation of the disturbance appears to fluctuate in patients over time (Bergen et al., 1989). The use of antipsychotic medications in treatment is usually discontinued if a patient shows symptoms of tardive dyskinesia. Although there are medications that control the symptoms of tardive dyskinesia, drug therapy is generally not recommended (American Medical Association, 1986). In some cases where the patient continues to display psychotic symptoms, the use of antipsychotic medication treatment may be resumed; however, discontinuation of the treatment is recommended if any symptoms of tardive dyskinesia reappear. To reduce the chances of this disturbance during the drug treatment of chronic schizophrenics, clinicians are more frequently using what is called "target dosing" (Rosen, 1986), which entails administering a drug when symptoms appear or are likely to appear rather than giving continuous dosages, as commonly practiced in the past.

Another trend in the treatment of schizophrenia involves the application of lower doses of standard drugs to reduce negative side effects. Hogarty and colleagues (1988) have shown that lower-dose-treated schizophrenics actually showed more improvement than normal-dose-treated patients in terms of many observable behaviors. Moreover, relapse rates were found to be comparable to patients treated with normal doses.

The range of effects achieved by the antipsychotic drugs may be illustrated by two brief case histories of patients who served as subjects in a clinical research project designed to evaluate differing treatment approaches to the schizophrenias (Grinspoon, Ewalt, & Shader, 1972):

Ms. W. was a 19-year-old, white, married woman who was admitted to the treatment unit as a result of gradually increasing agitation and hallucinations over a three-month period. At the outset of her hospitalization, Ms. W. continued to have auditory and visual hallucinations and appeared frightened, angry, and confused. She believed that she had a unique relationship with God or the devil. Her thought content displayed loosening of associations, and her affect was inappropriate to this content. Her condition continued to deteriorate for more than two weeks, at which point medication was begun.

Ms. W. was assigned to a treatment group in which the patients were receiving thioridazine (Mellaril). She responded dramatically during the first week of treatment. Her behavior became, for the most part, quiet and appropriate, and she made some attempts at socialization. She continued to improve, but by the fourth week of treatment began to show signs of mild depression. Her medication was increased, and she resumed her favorable course. By the sixth week she was dealing with various reality issues in her life in a reasonably effective manner, and by the ninth week she was spending considerable time at home, returning to the hospital in a pleasant and cheerful mood. She was discharged exactly 100 days after her admission, being then completely free of symptoms.

Mr. S., the eldest of three sons in a fairly religious Jewish family, was admitted to the hospital after developing marked paranoid ideation and hallucinations during his first weeks of college. He had looked forward to going to college, an elite New England school, but his insecurity once on campus caused him to become unduly boastful about his prowess with drinking and women. He stayed up late at night to engage in "bull sessions" and neglected his studies and other responsibilities. Within ten days he panicked about his ability to keep up and tried frantically to rearrange his course schedule and his life, to no avail.

His sense of incompetence was transformed over time into the idea that others—including all the students in his dormitory—were against him, and that fellow male students were perhaps flirting homosexually with him. By the time of his referral to the college infirmary, he was convinced that the college was a fraud he would have to expose, that the CIA was plotting against him, and that someone was going to kill him. He heard voices and smelled strange odors. He also showed a marked loosening of associations and flat, inappropriate affect. At the time of his transfer to the hospital, he was diagnosed as an acute paranoid schizophrenic.

Mr. S. was assigned to a treatment group receiving haloperidol (Haldol). His initial response to treatment was rapid and favorable, but observers noted that his behavior remained immature. Then suddenly during the fifth week of treatment, he became tense, negativistic, and hostile. Thereafter, he gradually became less defiant and angry, and he responded well to a daycare program prescribed by his therapist, although he was nervous and apprehensive about being outside the hospital. He was discharged as improved ten weeks after the initiation of his drug therapy.

Three months later Mr. S. was readmitted to the hospital. Although he had done well at first, he had begun to deteriorate concurrently with his doctor-monitored withdrawal from haloperidol. His behavior showed increasing signs of a lack of effective control. He began to set random fires and was described by the investigators as "sociopathic." Two days after his readmission, he signed himself out of the hospital "against medical advice." His parents immediately arranged for his confinement in another hospital, and the investigators subsequently lost contact with him.

Recent research with treatment-resistant schizophrenics has focused on possible alternative drugs. One such compound that differs from the phenothiazines, clozapine (a dibenzodiazepine), has produced very promising results (Breier et al., 1994; Marder et al., 1993). Kane and colleagues (1988) studied the therapeutic effects of clozapine with a large group of treatment-resistant schizophrenics and found the treatment effects modestly encouraging. Thirty percent of the treatment-resistant patients improved under the regimen and no negative side effects were noted. More recent research (Meltzer, 1992) has suggested that up to 60 percent of phenothiazine-resistant patients may benefit from clozapine if it is continued for several months. Further research on the side effects of this drug is indicated, however, because some studies have found that about 1–2 percent of the patients taking the drug develop an immune deficiency that is life-threatening and that has resulted in the death of several patients.

Even though clozapine has been heralded as the most effective treatment for schizophrenia, its use requires considerable caution and careful monitoring (Marder et al., 1993). The potentially lethal characteristic of the drug requires a highly structured blood-monitoring system along with the medication to guard against its misuse. Unfortunately, the cost of the drug in combination with this moni-

toring system makes the treatment expensive and has threatened to drastically limit its availability for many patients needing the drug (Winslow, 1990). Such economic considerations may be shortsighted. Meltzer and colleagues (1993) have shown that clozapine can be very cost-effective by reducing the need for rehospitalization. Two newer antipsychotic drugs awaiting release from the Food and Drug Administration at this time are risperidone and remosipride. These drugs, similar to clozapine, suppress psychotic thinking without many of the negative side effects associated with antipsychotic medications such as the phenothiazines, particularly tardive dyskinesia (Meltzer, 1993).

Antidepressant Drugs The **antidepressant drugs** made their appearance shortly after the introduction of reserpine and chlorpromazine. Although many of these drugs were initially introduced as antidepressants they have also been found to be effective with other disorders. There are several basic classes of antidepressant compounds:

The first group, the *monoamine oxidase (MAO) inhibitors,* include isocarboxazid (Marplan), phenelzine (Nardil), and tranylcypromine (Parnate) (see Chapter 6). These drugs inhibit the activity of *monoamine oxidase,* an enzyme present in the synaptic cleft that helps break down the monoamine neurotransmitters (such as serotonin and norepinephrine) that have been released into the cleft. As discussed in Chapter 6, the early monoamine hypothesis of depression proposed that these drugs work through increasing the availability of the monoamines by working against their breakdown. Today we know that their effects are much more complex than this, but we still don't know exactly how they operate to reduce depression.

Another group of antidepressants, the *tricyclics or TCAs,* operate to inhibit the re-uptake of serotonin and norepinephrine once they have been released into the synapse. As discussed in Chapter 6, the theory that these drugs work by increasing norepinephrine activity is now known to be oversimplified. In particular, although the immediate short-term effects of tricyclics are to increase the availability of norepinephrine and serotonin in the synapses, the long-term effects of these drugs (when they begin to have their clinical effects after two to four weeks) are to produce functional decreases in available norepinephrine and serotonin (Goodwin & Jamison, 1990; Prior & Sulser, 1991; Shelton et al., 1991; Siever & Davis, 1985; Thase et al., 1985). It is also known that when the tricyclics are taken for several weeks they act to decrease the number and sensitivity of certain types of receptors and to increase the responsiveness of others (Goodwin & Jamison, 1990; McNeal & Cimbolic, 1986; Shelton et al., 1991).

Of the main classes of antidepressants, the tricyclics and their variants have been most often used. This is largely because other available medications such as the MAO inhibitors are more toxic and require troublesome dietary restrictions; in addition, they are widely believed to have less potent therapeutic effects. Nevertheless, some patients who do not respond favorably to tricyclics will subsequently do well on an MAO inhibitor. Although the MAO inhibitors are more toxic than the tricyclics, the tricyclics also have unpleasant side effects such as dry mouth, tiredness, dizziness, blurred vision, constipation, and occasional erectile dysfunction in men. Therefore, some patients do not continue taking the drug long enough for it to have its antidepressant effect. In addition, because these drugs are highly toxic when taken in large doses, there is some risk in prescribing them for suicidal patients who might use them for an overdose. Commonly used tricyclics are imipramine (Tofranil), amitriptyline (Elavil), and nortriptyline (Aventyl).

Tricyclic antidepressant drugs continue to be developed, tested, and marketed at a high rate. Among the more recent entrants to the field are amoxapine (Asendin) and maprotiline (Ludiomil). Amoxapine is a tricyclic related to certain of the antipsychotic drugs and thus may prove to have a special role in the treatment of schizoaffective disorder.

A "second generation" antidepressant, chemically unrelated to other antidepressant medications, are the *serotonin selective re-uptake inhibitors or SSRIs*, such as fluoxetine (Prozac), and the *aminoketones* (Bupropion). As their name implies, the SSRIs serve to inhibit the re-uptake of serotonin following its release into the synapse. Unlike the tricyclics, they *selectively* inhibit the re-uptake of serotonin rather than inhibiting the re-uptake of both serotonin and norepinephrine. One SSRI, fluoxetine—better known by the trade name Prozac—has become the preferred antidepressant drug in the 1990s (see the "Unresolved Issues" section). Prozac is thought to be a relatively "safe" drug in that it is not considered physiologically addicting and is not found to be fatal in overdose as the tricyclics can be. Clinical trials with fluoxetine have reported that patients tend to improve after about three weeks of treatment with the drug. Several adverse side effects of Prozac were reported, particularly nausea, nervousness, and insomnia (Cole & Bodkin, 1990; Tacke, 1990). In addition, after a few weeks on the drug, some patients have experienced increased blood pressure and others have reported suicidal urges and agitation (Cole & Bodkin, 1990; Papp & Gorman, 1990). However, more recent studies have found fluoxetine to be no more associated with suicide than other antidepressants (Fava & Rosenbaum, 1991; Mann & Kapur, 1991).

The *triazolopyridines,* such as trazodone (Desyrel), are technically not tricyclics at all, but rather tetracyclics; they have mixed effects on serotonin (Preskorn & Burke, 1992). The chemical addition of an extra carbon ring is in each case claimed to reduce problematic side effects. Trazodone appeared on introduction to be a very promising drug (Moore, 1982). One study reported, however, that permanent erectile dysfunction can result from prolonged use (Lansky & Selzer, 1984).

The use of antidepressant medication has increased substantially in the United States over the past ten years. Olfson (1993) surveyed over 6000 office-based psychiatrists and found that prescriptions for antidepressant medication increased from 17.9 percent of all prescriptions in 1980 to 24.2 percent in 1985, and 30.4 percent in 1989. Most patients receiving antidepressants were women, but the rate for men was increasing, particularly for older men.

Pharmacological treatment for depression often produces dramatic results. Improvement in response to antidepressant medication is in sharp contrast to the effects of antipsychotic medications, which apparently only suppress schizophrenic symptoms. This statement, however, must be tempered with the observation that persons suffering from severe depression, unlike people with severe schizophrenia, often respond to any treatment or even no treatment at all. However, depression is often a recurrent disorder, and so drugs have to be administered over long periods. If the drugs are discontinued when symptoms have just remitted, there is a high probability of relapse, probably because the underlying depressive episode is still present and only its symptomatic expression has been suppressed (Frank et al., 1990). Long-term administration of these drugs is often effective in prevention as well as in treatment of patients subject to recurrent episodes (Montgomery, 1994).

Over the past ten years, a great deal of research has been undertaken to determine how drugs operate to alleviate depression (McNeal & Cimbolic, 1986), and which treatment or combination of treatments is appropriate for patients who are depressed (Hollon & Beck, 1986, 1994; Klerman et al., 1994). Hollon and Beck (1994) conclude that at present evidence suggests only a very modest superiority of combined treatment over cognitive or drug treatment alone. Moreover, little progress has been made in identifying patient characteristics or other clinical factors that relate to success by a given treatment method. In one nationwide study on psychological and pharmacological treatment for depression, Keller and colleagues (1986) found that there were no consistent patient characteristics related to whether a person received psychotherapy or medications for depression. More recently, Hollon and Beck (1994) also concluded that there are still no clear indications that patients with particular characteristics respond better to medication as opposed to cognitive therapy.

Overall, the use of antidepressant medication in the treatment of depressive episodes has shown considerable short-term effectiveness in spite of our lack of specific understanding of how it works and with what type of patient particular treatments are best suited. Nevertheless, a minority of severely depressed patients respond to neither type of antidepressant compound, in which case alternative modes of intervention, such as ECT, may be tried.

In addition to their usefulness in treating depression, the antidepressant drugs are also widely used in the treatment of various other disorders. For example, as discussed in Chapter 5, some of the tricyclic antidepressants (especially imipramine and clomipramine) are useful in the treatment of panic disorder (McNally, 1994; Wolfe & Maser, 1994). However, some people with panic disorder are greatly bothered by the side effects of these drugs (which create some of the symptoms panic patients are hypersensitive to) and so they quickly discontinue the medication. In the past five years a number of studies have suggested fluvoxamine, a unicyclic rather than tricyclic antidepressant, is highly promising in the treatment of panic disorder (McNally, 1994).

In addition, several antidepressant drugs are used in the treatment of obsessive-compulsive disorder (see Chapter 5). Clomipramine (a tricyclic antidepressant that has greater effects on serotonin activity than do other tricyclics) has generally been considered to be the drug treatment of choice for obsessive-compulsive disorder. However, drugs from the SSRI category (such as Prozac) also show considerable promise and have fewer troublesome side effects than does clomipramine (DeVeaugh-Geiss, 1991; Riggs & Foa, 1993).

Antidepressants have also been used effectively in the treatment of generalized anxiety disorder (Barlow, 1988; Rickels et al., 1993). Moreover, the monoamine oxidase inhibitors have been shown to be effective in the treatment of social phobia (Liebowitz et al., 1992).

Finally, antidepressant drugs are also widely used in the treatment of bulimia. Many, but not all, studies have shown that the tricyclics are useful in reducing binge-eating, relative to placebo (Mitchell & Zwann, 1993). In addition, Prozac has recently shown promising results in the treatment of bulimia, although more studies need to be done before a clear picture of its usefulness emerges.

Antianxiety Drugs   If it is true, as some have observed, that ours is the age of anxiety, it is certainly no less true that ours is also the age of the search for anxiety reducers. Millions of prescription medications alleged to contain anxiety- and tension-relieving substances are consumed daily by the American public. In addition, Americans use other methods to reduce their anxiety—ranging from biofeedback to the practice of ancient Eastern religious rituals—that promise to relieve "uptight" feelings. The nonprescription drug market, which includes alcoholic beverages, marijuana, and decidedly more problematic substances, has had an unprecedented growth rate since the 1960s—much of it presumably due to the same widespread wish for anxiety relief.

Besides the barbiturates (see Chapter 10), which are seldom used in treatment today because they have high addictive potential and a low margin of dosage safety, two additional classes of prescription **antianxiety drugs** (minor tranquilizers) have gained widespread acceptance in recent years. One of these, the propanediols (mostly meprobamate compounds), seems to operate mainly through the reduction of muscular tension, which in turn is experienced by a patient as calming and emotionally soothing. Meprobamate drugs are marketed under the trade names Miltown and Equanil.

The other class of antianxiety drugs is the benzodiazepines. Until recently, their use in this country was increasing at an alarming rate; however, thanks to effective public warnings about the addictive potential of these drugs, this trend is now leveling off (see HIGHLIGHT 16.2). Under this rubric are included chlordiazepoxide (Librium), diazepam (Valium), oxazepam (Serax), clorazepate (Tranxene), flurazepam (Dalmane), and alprazolam (Xanax). In experimental studies on animals, the most striking effect of these drugs has been the recurrence of behavior previously inhibited by conditioned fears, without serious impairment in overall behavioral efficiency. Benzodiazepines, in other words, somehow selectively diminish generalized anxiety yet leave adaptive behaviors largely intact. They are thus far superior to many other types of anxiety-reducing drugs, which tend to produce widespread negative effects on adaptive functioning.

Nevertheless, all of the antianxiety drugs have a basically sedative effect on an organism, and many patients treated with them complain of drowsiness

HIGHLIGHT 16.2

Chemically Induced Sleep: Is It Worth the Risks?

Each year about 4 percent of the population of the United States obtain a prescription for medication to help them sleep (Mendelson, 1987). Prescriptions for the benzodiazepine class of antianxiety drugs, the most widely used sleep medications, have been estimated to exceed 70 million per year in the United States. The most common benzodiazepine prescribed specifically for this purpose is flurazepam (Dalmane). Some 8 million individuals use this general class of drug sometime during any one year, and up to 2 million people take these pills nightly for more than two months at a time. It is prescribed for many patients hospitalized for physical disease.

Reacting to this overuse of anxiety medication, the Institute of Medicine (IOM) of the National Academy of Sciences issued a report outlining the hazards of this remedy for sleeping difficulties—difficulties that in any case they found to be severely overestimated on a routine basis by the people allegedly suffering from them. Noting that the barbiturates justly deserve their reputation as dangerous drugs, the IOM report indicated that the benzodiazepines may be just as risky, and in some cases more so. For example, flurazepam, while not quite as addicting as the barbiturates, remains in the body in the form of metabolites far longer than do the barbiturates, resulting in a buildup of toxic substances in the body that may reach a critical level within a week of regular ingestion. Although flurazepam overdose is usually not in itself lethal, it may interact with other drugs, such as alcohol, to produce lethal effects. Because of these readily misunderstood characteristics, the IOM concluded that, overall, flurazepam does not diminish the number of deaths attributable to sleeping pill medication, relative to earlier types of "hypnotic" drugs, such as the barbiturates.

A particularly worrisome aspect of this problem is the fact that a certain amount of benign "insomnia" naturally accompanies advancing age. Nevertheless, elderly people receive some 39 percent of all sleeping pill prescriptions. For these individuals there is a real danger that the side effects of these drugs, such as daytime lethargy and clouding of consciousness, may be considered indicators of senile deterioration by family members and even by professional caretakers. Considering the risks involved in taking these drugs, it seems appropriate to keep in mind an observation of one of the IOM members: Losing some sleep now and then is not a life-threatening problem (Smith, 1979).

---

and lethargy (Kutcher et al., 1992). This has been a particular problem among schoolchildren treated with these drugs. We must also emphasize that all of these drugs have the serious potential of inducing dependence when used unwisely or in excess (Bassuk, Schoonover, & Gelenberg, 1983; Levenson, 1981). Because of their potential for producing dependence, withdrawal from these drugs can be extremely difficult and must generally be accomplished slowly over a matter of weeks or months. This is especially true of the high-potency benzodiazapine Xanax, which is widely used in the treatment of panic disorder (see Chapter 5). Moreover, relapse rates following discontinuation of these drugs is extremely high. For example, as many as 60–80 percent of panic patients relapse following discontinuation of Xanax (McNally, 1994).

Anxiety drugs' range of application is quite broad. They are used in all manner of conditions in which tension and anxiety may be significant components, including anxiety-based and psychophysiologic disorders. They are also used as supplementary treatment in certain neurological disorders to control such symptoms as convulsive seizures, but they have little place in the treatment of the psychoses. They are among the most widely prescribed drugs available to physicians, a fact that has caused concern among some leaders in the medical and psychiatric fields.

Continuing research on benzodiazepines and related compounds is turning up promising leads that will almost certainly result in important future advances in the treatment of anxiety and other conditions. It is now known that the benzodiazapines probably exert their effects through stimulating the action of GABA (*gamma aminobutyric acid*), a neurotransmitter now thought to be functionally deficient in people with generalized anxiety (Redmond, 1985). GABA ordinarily plays an important role in the way our brain inhibits anxiety in stressful situations; the benzodiazapines appear to increase GABA activity in certain parts of the brain known to be implicated in anxiety, such as the limbic system, and thereby reduce anxiety. Additionally, because these compounds also have sedative, muscle-relaxant, and anticonvulsive properties, it might be possible to differentiate specific receptors for each, and to discover variant compounds that will selectively bind to them. In fact, researchers at one large pharmaceutical company have already discovered a chemical that appears to counteract anxiety and convulsions without being a muscle relaxant or sedative. Research in this area has important implications for our basic understanding of brain processes, in addition to its obvious clinical import.

Lithium for the Bipolar Mood Disorders

Lithium is the lightest of the metals. Its simple salts, such as lithium carbonate, were discovered—as early as 1949 by John Cade in Australia—to be effective in treating manic disorders. One of Cade's (1949) own cases will serve well as an illustration of the effects of lithium treatment:

> Mr. W. B. was a 51-year-old man who had been in a state of chronic manic excitement for five years. So obnoxious and destructive was his behavior that he had long been regarded as the most difficult patient on his ward in the hospital.
>
> He was started on treatment with a lithium compound, and within three weeks his behavior had improved to the point that transfer to the convalescent ward was deemed appropriate. He remained in the hospital for another two months, during which his behavior continued to be essentially normal. Prior to discharge, he was switched to another form of lithium salts because the one he had been taking had caused stomach upset.
>
> He was soon back at his job and living a happy and productive life. In fact, he felt so well that, contrary to instructions, he stopped taking his lithium. Thereafter he steadily became more irritable and erratic; some six months following his discharge, he had to cease work. In another five weeks he was back at the hospital in an acute manic state.
>
> Lithium therapy was immediately reestablished, with prompt positive results. In another month Mr. W. B. was pronounced ready to return to home and work, provided he would continue taking a prescribed dosage of lithium.

Some 20 years passed before lithium treatment was introduced in the United States. This delay may have been, in part, for two reasons. First, if not used at the proper dosage, lithium can be toxic, causing numerous side effects, such as delirium, convulsions, and even death. At the same time, if lithium is to have any notable therapeutic effect, it must be used in quantities within the range of potential dangerousness, which varies among different individuals. Thus, at the outset of lithium treatment, a patient's blood levels of lithium must be monitored carefully in relation to observable behavioral effects so that the minimum effective dosage can be established. For each individual, there is a relatively narrow range of effectiveness for the drug. Too little of the drug and the therapeutic effect will be negligible; too much of the drug and the effect could be lethal. In addition to these potentially dangerous side effects, lithium has some other unpleasant side effects in some patients, such as lethargy, decreased motor coordination, and gastrointestinal difficulties. Moreover, many bipolar patients seem to miss the highs and the abundance of energy associated with their hypomanic episodes, so when faced with unpleasant side effects and the loss of these highs, they may stop taking the drug.

A second possible reason for the delay in widespread lithium usage in the United States may have been the simple fact that researchers were skeptical that it was the lithium itself that was producing the beneficial results; the lithium compounds used in treatment are simple inorganic salts that have no known physiological function (Berger, 1978). Lithium, then, is a somewhat peculiar drug.

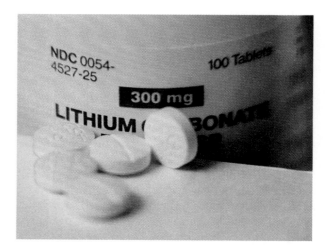

Lithium treatment requires careful monitoring of the dosage—too much can be lethal and too little is ineffective. There is no doubt, however, that the drug has been a boon to those people who have experienced repeated bouts with mania, depression, or both throughout their adult lives.

Its curious qualities notwithstanding, there can be no doubt at this point concerning lithium's remarkable effectiveness in promptly resolving about 70–80 percent of clearly defined manic states (Hughes & Pierattini, 1992), particularly cases in which other psychiatric disorders are not also present (Black et al., 1988). In addition, as we saw in Chapter 6, lithium is sometimes successful in relieving depression, although possibly only in those patients who are subject to both manic and depressive episodes—that is, who are bipolar in type (Bassuk et al., 1983; Berger, 1978; Segal, Yager, & Sullivan, 1976). Other research, however, suggests that there may be a subclass of unipolar depressive patients who benefit from lithium treatment (Abou-Saleh, 1992; Goodwin & Jamison, 1990).

The drug has been a boon, especially to those people who heretofore have experienced repeated bouts with mania, depression, or both throughout their adult lives. For many, these cycles can now be modulated or even prevented by regular maintenance doses of lithium—for example, by taking a single tablet each morning and evening. Psychiatry may thus have achieved its first essentially preventive treatment method—although, for some patients maintained on the drug for lengthy periods, there may be serious complications, including kidney damage (Bassuk et al., 1983) and memory and motor-speed problems (Shaw et al., 1987). There is also some recent evidence that the prevention of further attacks of mania by lithium maintenance treatment may be less reliable than was once thought. In one study, 40 percent of such patients relapsed within 1.7 years following hospital discharge (Harrow et al., 1990).

The biochemical basis of lithium's therapeutic effect is unknown. One hypothesis is that lithium, being a mineral salt, may have an effect on electrolyte balances, which may alter the properties of neurotransmission within the brain. So far, however, this connection remains largely speculative. Clearly, the riddle of exactly what occurs will be solved only by more and better research.

Recently another drug has been used with considerable success to treat bipolar disorders. The drug carbamazepine (Tegretol), used extensively as an anticonvulsant agent to control epileptic seizures, has been found effective in controlling rapidly cycling mood and reducing aggressivity in bipolar disorders (Ballenger, 1988; Gerner, 1993). On the other hand, in one study its use was somewhat disappointing for the treatment of acute mania (Lusznat, Murphy, & Nunn, 1988), which suggests that carbamazepine may be more useful in preventive treatment. Carbamazepine has been associated with significant side effects, especially neurological problems, such as an awkward gait and increased or distorted reflexes (Birkhimer, Curtis, & Jann, 1985). As such, careful monitoring of carbamezipine treatment, as with lithium use, is required.

Drug Therapy for Children

Our discussion of the use of drugs in treating maladaptive behavior would be incomplete without some reiteration of their role in the management of childhood disturbances and disorders. We have already addressed this matter to some extent in Chapter 14. Although our society has often been too quick to label as deviant (and thus to "treat") various annoying or inconvenient behaviors in which children sometimes indulge, it is nevertheless true that some children do evidence more or less serious behavior disorders. It is also true that some of them may be helped by the judicious use of medication.

Antianxiety, antipsychotic, and antidepressant medications have all been used effectively with children who are, respectively, excessively anxious or "nervous," psychotic, or depressed (Ryan, 1992). Considerable caution must be exercised in the use of these powerful drugs with children, however, to be certain that dosage levels are within tolerable limits for a small and as yet biologically immature organism. Not only are excessive blood levels of these drugs physically dangerous, but in some instances they may produce paradoxical reversal effects—that is, a child's problem may become more severe (Bassuk et al., 1983).

Though the diagnostic terms *hyperactivity, hyperkinesis,* and *specific learning disability* have been used somewhat inconsistently in recent years, there appears to be a subset of highly distractable youngsters of normal but unevenly developed cognitive ability who benefit dramatically, and paradoxically, from drugs that stimulate the central nervous system (Greenhill, 1992). As we saw in Chapter 14, the most widely used of these stimulants are the amphetamines; a closely related compound known as methylphenidate (Ritalin) is also used. Recently, Whalen and colleagues (1989) found that hyperactive children treated with Ritalin were viewed more positively by other children. In certain instances, these drugs promptly terminate hyperactivity, which typically results in an increased attention span and an ability to do schoolwork (Weiss & Hechtman, 1979; Wender, Reimherr, & Wood, 1981). Normally, a child thus helped is kept on the drug until he or she reaches adolescence, when hyperactivity is thought to diminish by an as yet unknown natural process (Bassuk et al., 1983).

A Biopsychosocial Perspective on Pharmacological Therapy

Modern psychopharmacology has brought a reduction in the severity and chronicity of many types of psychopathology, particularly the psychoses. It has helped many individuals who would otherwise require hospitalization to function in their family and community settings; it has led to the earlier discharge of those who do require hospitalization and to the greater effectiveness of after-care programs; and it has made restraints and locked wards largely obsolete. All in all, pharmacological therapy not only has outmoded more drastic forms of treatment but has led to a much more favorable hospital climate for patients and staff alike (see HIGHLIGHT 16.3 for a summary of the drugs used in psychopharmacological therapy).

Nevertheless, a number of complications and limitations arise in the use of psychotropic drugs. Aside from possible undesirable side effects, the problem of matching drug and dosage to the needs of a given individual is often a difficult one, and it is sometimes necessary to change medication in the course of treatment. In addition, the use of medications in isolation from other treatment methods is usually inappropriate and ineffective because drugs themselves do not cure disorders. As many investigators have pointed out, drugs tend to alleviate symptoms by inducing biochemical changes rather than bring an individual to grips with personal or situational factors that may be reinforcing maladaptive behaviors. Although the reduction in anxiety, depression, disturbed thinking, and other symptoms may tempt therapists to regard a patient as "recovered," it seems important to include psychotherapy in the total program if such gains are to be maintained or improved on (Beitman & Klerman, 1991). This point is underscored by the observations of relatively high relapse rates when drugs are discontinued for a variety of disorders.

On the other hand, the failure to incorporate medication into a psychotherapeutic treatment program can lead to serious problems. A recent court case, *Osherhoff* v. *Chestnut Lodge,* raised a number of issues concerning the importance of clinical diagnosis, the effectiveness of medication, and appropriate treatment intervention (Klerman, 1990). Osherhoff, a physician, was severely depressed and functioning so ineffectively that his

family hospitalized him at Chestnut Lodge, an exclusively psychoanalytic treatment facility. He was treated with intensive psychoanalytic treatment, without medication, four times a week. After several months, his family became concerned over his lack of progress; he had lost 40 pounds, was experiencing severe sleep disturbance, had marked psychomotor agitation to the point that his pacing caused his feet to become swollen and blistered. The family sought a reevaluation of his case. The staff, in a case conference, decided to continue the treatment program that had been initiated. Dr. Osherhoff's condition worsened and his family had him discharged and admitted into another facility where he was treated with a combination of phenothiazines and tricyclic antidepressants. He improved markedly and was discharged in three months. Later he filed a suit claiming that Chestnut Lodge had not administered the proper treatment—drug therapy—which had caused him to lose a year of employment in his medical practice. Preliminary court arbitration indicated an initial award of damages to Dr. Osherhoff; however, the case was settled out of court before a final judgment was rendered. A number of complicated issues were involved in the case, but the finding that therapists may be liable for failing to provide medication to patients is an important and potentially disruptive new development in the field.

Thus the combination of chemical and psychological forms of therapy is fast becoming the major thrust of current research and treatment for severe psychopathology (Goldstein, 1991; Richelson, 1993). This integrative approach involves the use of psychotropic medication and psychosocial approaches, such as behavior therapy or psychoanalysis (Carpenter & Keith, 1986). It has been shown to be valuable with both adults (Ward, 1991) and children (McClellan & Wherry, 1992). The combined therapeutic approach appears to be especially useful with treatment-resistant disorders in which major mental disorders and persistent personality disorders are involved. The use of drugs can facilitate the patient's accessibility to psychotherapy and can serve to reduce noncompliant behavior in therapy. Marcus and Bradley (1990), for example, found this approach to be effective in about two-thirds of such treatment-resistant cases. The most effective uses of drugs in the treatment of psychological disorders involve drug administrations that are embedded in the context of other treatment approaches (Klerman, 1991); for example, the use of antidepressant medication along with cognitive-behavioral treatment for depression (Rush & Hollon, 1991). Overall, there is some

HIGHLIGHT | 16.3

Frequently Used Drugs in the Treatment of Mental and Behavioral Disorders

Class	Generic Name	Trade Name	Used to Treat	Effects
Antipsychotic				
(a) phenothiazines	chlorpromazine	Thorazine	Psychotic (especially	Somewhat variable
	thioridazine	Mellaril	schizophrenia)	in achieving
	promazine	Sparine	symptoms, such as	intended purpose of
	trifluoperazine	Stelazine	extreme agitation,	suppression of
	prochlorperazine	Compazine	delusions, and	psychotic symptoms.
	perphenazine	Trilafon	hallucinations;	Side effects, such as
	fluphenazine	Prolixin	aggressive or violent	dry mouth, are often
	triflupromazine	Temaril	behavior	uncomfortable. In
				long-term use may
(b) butyrophenone	haloperidol	Haldol		produce motor
				disturbances, such as
(c) thioxanthenes	thiothixine	Navane		Parkinsonism and
	chlorprothixene	Taractan		tardive dyskinesia.
(d) dibenzodiazepine	clozapine	Clozaril	Schizophrenia	Suppresses psychotic thinking. Side effects include sedation, seizure, hypotension, fever, vomiting.
	risperidone	Risperdal	Psychotic	Like clozapine, they
	remoxipride		(schizophrenic	suppress psychotic thinking,
			symptoms)	but appear to produce fewer negative side effects and tardive dyskinesia.
Antidepressant				
(a) tricyclics	imipramine	Tofranil	Relatively severe	Somewhat variable in
	amitriptyline	Elavil	depressive	alleviating symptoms, and
	nortriptyline	Aventyl	symptoms,	noticeable effects may be
	protriptyline	Vivactil	especially of	delayed up to three weeks.
	doxepin	Sinequan	psychotic severity	Side effects may cause
	trimipramine maleate	Surmontil	and unipolar in type; also used in	discomfort.
	clomipramine	Anafranil	treatment of panic disorder & OCD	
(b) monoamine oxidase (MAO) inhibitors	isocarboxazid	Marplan	Depression,	Multiple side effects—some
	phenelzine	Nardil	panic disorder	of them dangerous. Use of
	tranylcypromine	Parnate		MAO inhibitors requires dietary restrictions.
(c) SSRIs norepinephrine/ serotonin reuptake inhibitor	fluoxetine	Prozac	Depressive symptoms, obsessive-compulsive disorder, panic disorder	Fluoxetine is effective in reducing symptoms. Effects take about 3 weeks. Safety is considered high; overdose unlikely. Side effect profile is favorable, though some nausea and insomnia have been reported.
	sertralin	Zoloft	Depression	Reduces depression, not considered addicting.
	paroxetine	Paxil	Depression	Minimal side effects.

HIGHLIGHT | 16.3

Continued from page 620

Class	Generic Name	Trade Name	Used to Treat	Effects
(d) triazolopyridinese		Trazodone	Depression	Less likelihood of response than TCAs. Not much used today. Minimal risk of overdose. Side effects include cognitive slowing.
(e) aminoketones		Bupropion	Depression	Used with patients who have not not responded to TCAs or SSRIs.
Antimanic (bipolar)	lithium carbonate	Eskalith Lithane Lithonate Lithotabs Phi-Lithium	Manic episodes and some severe depressions, particularly recurrent ones or those alternating with mania	Usually effective in resolving manic episodes, but highly variable in effects on depression, probably because the latter is a less homogeneous grouping. Multiple side effects unless carefully monitored; high toxicity potential.
	carbamazepine	Tegretol	Manic episodes	Effective in treating bipolar disorders. Neurotoxic side effects have been noted, including unsteady gait, tremor, ataxia, and increased restlessness.
	valproate	Depakote	Bipolar disorder	Fewer side effects than lithium. Often used with bipolar patients who cannot take lithium.
Antianxiety (minor tranquilizers) (a) propanediols	meprobamate	Equanil Miltown	Nonpsychotic personality problems in which anxiety, tension, or panic attacks are prominent features; also used as anticonvulsants and as sleep-inducers (especially flurazepam)	Somewhat variable in achieving intended purpose of tension reduction. Used often to treat alcohol withdrawal symptoms. Side effects include drowsiness and lethargy.
(b) benzodiazepines	diazepam chlordiazepoxide flurazepam oxazepam clorazepate alprazolam prazepam	Valium Librium Dalmane Serax Tranxene Xanax Centrax		
Stimulant	dextroamphetamine amphetamine methylphenidate	Dexedrine Benzedrine Ritalin	Hyperactivity, distractability, specific learning disabilities, and, occasionally, extreme hypoactivity	Rather unpredictable. When maximally effective, can enable otherwise uneducable children to attend regular schools. Side effects often troublesome, including recently discovered retardation of growth.

Based on data from Bohn (1993); Dunner (1993); Goodman et al. (1985); Preskorn & Burke (1992); Tacke (1989).

reason to be optimistic about the combined use of drugs and psychosocial approaches, especially in the more severe disorders, such as schizophrenia and the major mood disorders (Beckham & Leber, 1985a; Klerman et al., 1994; Smith, Glass, & Miller, 1980).

UNRESOLVED ISSUES

Has Pharmacology Opened the Door to Personality Change?

The drug Prozac (fluoxetine) and others pharmacologically similar to it in primarily inhibiting the reuptake mechanism for the neurotransmitter serotonin, such as Paxil (paroxetine) and Zoloft (sertraline), are now among the drugs most prescribed by physicians. Originally considered antidepressants for use in the specific *psychiatric* treatment of relatively severe mood disorders, they are now also widely employed by many physicians, even nonpsychiatrists, to ease patients' often vague complaints of feeling unhappy. In this respect they have come to occupy a role in general medical practice not unlike that of the benzodiazepines (antianxiety agents such as Valium) during the 1970s and 1980s. The pharmacologic message appears to be that many people feel "better" when they have lots of serotonin available in the neuronal synapses of their brains.

What is the nature of this "feeling better"? Can we account for it in terms of more specific psychoactive properties of these drugs? These questions have been addressed in a thoughtful and scholarly manner by psychiatrist Peter Kramer (1993) in his popular and in certain respects startling book *Listening to Prozac*. Kramer's thesis is that Prozac does more than merely ameliorate depressive states—it actually in many instances transforms personality, usually in a very positive, self-esteem–enhancing way. He reports cases in which people claim to be functioning far better than they were before becoming depressed—literally "better than well"—or to have discovered, while on the drug, a "true" self different from and more satisfying than their previous self. In light of such remarkable effects on subjective well-being, patients are often understandably reluctant to give up the drug. That aspect, too, is reminiscent of the serious problems the overuse of benzodiazepines eventually produced.

Kramer examines several hypotheses concerning the basic psychological processes affected by

Prozac, but he essentially suggests that the person on the drug experiences a diminished sensitivity to disapproval, criticism, or rejection by others. Obviously, such an effect would be of considerable benefit to those inhibited persons, not rare in the human species, who are overly dependent on maintaining uninterrupted signs of affection and approval from others, and who are miserable when they receive negative feedback. But just as obviously, there is a limit to the adaptiveness of any such imperviousness and self-containment, one that can be observed in situations where the person may appear almost entirely oblivious of others' opinions of his or her behavior. It is a bit disconcerting to contemplate living in a world in which that level of subjective social invulnerability and insensitivity toward others would be shared by everyone.

To his considerable credit, Kramer addresses forthrightly the disturbing questions raised by the availability of a prescription drug that seems not only to ameliorate disorder but in addition, for many persons, to alter their personalities, albeit mostly in ways they find pleasing. Recovery from disorder may in this context be superseded by other and quite different goals, ones with which psychiatrists or other professionals may be unprepared to deal. And Kramer is undoubtedly correct in his prediction that Prozac will prove to be only among the first of a large number of "legitimate" drugs having comparable personality-altering properties that will eventually become available. To put it another way, it seems likely that we are about to enter an era of "cosmetic psychopharmacology," conceivably one in which persons may even get to choose major aspects of their personalities, just as some now do the shapes of their noses. Such considerations give rise to the bizarre and somewhat ghastly conjecture that one day many social groups may be composed of pharmacologically synthetic personalities.

Kramer, in the authors' judgment, has performed a valuable service in alerting us to the profound problems as well as to the promise of anticipated developments in the field of psychopharmacology. Nevertheless, we think a caveat is in order. Kramer may be unduly swayed by the power of the biological model to explain and modify human personality. Time will tell whether pharmacology will have these powerful effects on human development and interpersonal behavior. We expect, however, that future research will likely demonstrate that there is far more complexity to human behavior than can be altered by the medications at hand.

SUMMARY

Except for the development of electroconvulsive therapy (ECT) beginning in 1938, the biological approach to the treatment of mental disorders, at least on this continent and in Europe, had made little headway until about 1955. Indeed, some of the early biological treatments, such as insulin coma therapy and lobotomy, may have done more harm than good, as did many early medical treatments for purely physical diseases.

The mode of therapeutic action of ECT, which continues to be widely used, is not yet understood. There is little doubt, however, of its efficacy for certain patients, especially those suffering from severe depression. Appropriate premedication together with other modifications in technique (for example, unilateral placement of electrodes) have made this treatment relatively safe and, for the most part, have checked the serious or long-term side effects. Nevertheless, controversy about this method of treatment persists. Obviously, ECT should be used with caution and circumspection, and preferably only after less dramatic methods have been tried and have failed.

The antipsychotic compound chlorpromazine (Thorazine) became widely available in the mid-1950s. It was followed shortly by numerous other related (that is, phenothiazine class) and nonrelated antipsychotic drugs of proven effectiveness in diminishing psychotic (especially schizophrenic) symptoms. Thus was initiated a true revolution in the treatment of severe mental disorders—one that, among other things, permanently altered the environment and the function of mental hospitals. Within a short period, too, the antidepressant medications became available to help patients with severe depression. They are also widely used in the treatment of several anxiety disorders and show some promise in the treatment of bulimia. Finally, in the late 1960s (after an unaccountable delay in its introduction in this country), the antimanic drug lithium was recognized as having major therapeutic significance. With the availability of these three types of drugs, the major psychoses—for the first time in history—now came to be seen as generally and effectively treatable.

Meanwhile, antianxiety drugs (mild tranquilizers) had been developed that circumvented many of the problems of the barbiturates used earlier in combating excessive tension and anxiety. This development extended the benefit of effective drug treatment to many people who were struggling with neurotic problems or with high-stress life circumstances. The meprobamates (for example, Equanil) were the first of these new antianxiety drugs but were largely superseded by the more potent benzodiazepines (such as Valium and Xanax) for general use.

New biological treatments for mental disorders will doubtless continue to be proposed, but, as in the case of insulin therapy, many will prove undeserving of a high degree of confidence. A measure of caution is recommended concerning claims made by the proponents of newly introduced therapies.

Finally, the admittedly impressive gains in biological treatment methods may cause us to lose sight of important psychological processes that may be intrinsic to any mental disorder. In fact, some evidence shows that combinations of biologically and psychologically based approaches may be more successful than either alone, at least with some of the more severe disorders.

KEY TERMS

insulin coma therapy (p. 603)
electroconvulsive therapy (ECT) (p. 603)
psychosurgery (p. 606)
prefrontal lobotomy (p. 606)
pharmacology (p. 608)
antipsychotic drugs (p. 609)
tardive dyskinesia (p. 610)
antidepressant drugs (p. 612)
antianxiety drugs (p. 614)

CHAPTER

17

PSYCHOLOGICALLY BASED THERAPIES

P. M. Wentworth, Untitled. Wentworth, a mysterious figure, lived in California, where he worked as a night watchman. His paintings date primarily from the 1950s, and he died sometime in the early 1960s. His artwork—about 40 drawings—was discovered by a psychologist at Sacramento State College. Wentworth was said to have been inspired to draw by staring at the night sky before confronting a blank sheet of paper.

Most of us have experienced a time or situation when we were dramatically helped by "talking things over" with a relative or friend. Or perhaps we made a drastic change in our customary behavior after a particular event led to new understanding. As the noted psychoanalyst Franz Alexander (1946) pointed out long ago, formal psychotherapy as practiced by a mental health professional shares many aspects in common with this type of familiar experience. Most therapists, like all good listeners, rely on a common repertoire of receptiveness, warmth, empathy, and a nonjudgmental approach to the problems their clients present. Most, however, also introduce into the relationship psychological interventions that are designed to promote new understandings, behaviors, or both on the client's part. The fact that these interventions are deliberately planned and systematically guided by certain theoretical preconceptions (of the kind discussed in Chapter 3) is what distinguishes professional **psychotherapy,** the treatment of mental disorders by psychological methods, from more informal helping relationships. As we will see, it is the varying nature of these theoretical concepts that largely distinguishes a given type of psychotherapy from the others available.

Psychotherapy is based on the assumption that, even in cases where physical pathology is present, an individual's perceptions, evaluations, expectations, and coping strategies also play a role in the development of the disorder and will probably need to be changed if maximum benefit is to be realized. The belief that people with psychological problems can change—can learn more adaptive ways of perceiving, evaluating, and behaving—is the conviction underlying all psychotherapy.

To achieve constructive change, a psychotherapist may attempt to (a) change maladaptive behavior patterns; (b) minimize or eliminate environmental conditions that may be causing or maintaining such behavior; (c) improve interpersonal and other competencies; (d) resolve handicapping or disabling conflicts among motives; (e) modify individuals' cognitions, their dysfunctional beliefs about themselves and their world; (f) reduce or remove distressing or disabling emotional reactions; and (g) foster a clear-cut sense of identity. All these strategies can open pathways to a more meaningful and fulfilling existence.

Achieving these changes is by no means easy. Sometimes a person's distorted view of the world and unhealthy self-concept are the end products of faulty parent-child relationships reinforced by many years of life experiences. In other instances, inadequate occupational, marital, or social adjustment requires major changes in a person's life situation, in addition to psychotherapy. Magnifying such difficulties is the fact that it is often easier to hold to one's present problematic but familiar course than to risk change and the unpredictability it entails. It would be too much to expect that a psychotherapist, even a highly skilled and experienced one, could in a short time undo an individual's entire past history and prepare him or her to cope with a difficult life situation in a fully adequate manner. Psychotherapists can offer no magical transformations of either selfhood or the realities in which people live their lives. Nevertheless, psychotherapy holds promise in even the most severe mental disorders, and indeed for certain of them may provide the only realistic hope for significant and lasting change.

It has been estimated that several hundred "therapeutic approaches" exist, ranging from psychoanalysis to Zen meditation. Indeed, the last few decades have witnessed a stream of "new therapies"—each winning avid proponents and followers for a time. The faddism in the popular literature on self-change might give the casual reader the idea that the entire field of psychotherapy is in constant flux. In reality, professional psychotherapy has shown both considerable stability over time and coherence around a few basic orientations, albeit ones that vary appreciably in the "visions" they embody of the world and of human nature (Andrews, 1989a). This chapter will explore the most widely used and accepted of these formal psychological treatment approaches.

AN OVERVIEW OF PSYCHOLOGICAL TREATMENT

Before we turn our attention to specific psychological intervention techniques, we will attempt to gain perspective by considering more closely the individuals involved in therapy and their relationship.

Who Receives Psychotherapy?

People who receive psychotherapy vary widely in their problems and their motivations to solve them. Perhaps the most obvious candidates for psychological treatment are individuals experiencing sudden and highly stressful situations, people who feel so overwhelmed by the crisis conditions in which they find themselves that they cannot manage on their own. These people typically feel quite vulnerable and tend to be open to psychological treatment because they are motivated to alter their present intolerable mental states. They often respond well to short-term, directive, crisis-oriented treatment (to be discussed in Chapter 18). In such situations, clients may gain considerably, in a brief time, from the outside perspective provided by their therapist.

Some people enter psychological therapy somewhat as a surprise to themselves. Perhaps they had consulted a physician for their headache or stomach pain, only to be told that there was nothing physically wrong with them. Such individuals, referred to a therapist, may at first resist the idea that their physical symptoms are emotionally based, especially if the referring physician has been brusque or unclear as to the rationale for his or her judgment. The resistant attitudes often encountered following this type of referral underscore the fact that motivation to enter treatment differs widely among psychotherapy clients. Reluctant clients may come from many sources—for example, an alcoholic whose spouse threatens "either therapy or divorce," or a suspected felon whose attorney advises that things will go better at trial if it can be announced that the suspect has "entered therapy." A substantial number of angry parents bring their children to therapists with demands that their "uncontrollable" behavior, viewed as independent of the family context, be "fixed."

Many people entering therapy have experienced long-term psychological distress and have had lengthy histories of maladjustment. They may have had interpersonal problems for some time or may have felt susceptible to low moods that are difficult for them to dispel. Chronic unhappiness and inability to feel confident and secure may finally prompt them to seek outside help. These individuals seek psychological assistance out of dissatisfaction and despair. They may enter treatment with a high degree of motivation, but, as therapy proceeds, their persistent patterns of maladaptive behavior may become resistant forces with which a therapist must contend. For example, a narcissistic client who anticipates therapist praise and admiration may become disenchanted and hostile when these are not forthcoming.

Some people who enter therapy have problems that would be considered relatively normal. That is, they appear to have achieved success, have financial stability, have generally accepting and loving families, and have accomplished many of their life goals. They enter therapy not out of personal despair or impossible interpersonal involvements, but out of a sense that they have not lived up to their own expectations and realized their own potential. These people, partly because their problems are more manage-able than the problems of others, may make sub-stantial gains in personal growth. Much of these therapeutic gains can be attributed to their high de-gree of motivation and personal resources. Individu-als who seem to have the best prognosis for person-ality change, according to repeated research outcomes, have been described in terms of the so-called YAVIS pattern (Schofield, 1964)—they are Young, Attractive, Verbal, Intelligent, and Success-ful. Ironically, those who tend to do best in psy-chotherapy are those who seem objectively to need it least.

Psychotherapy, however, is not just for people who have clearly defined problems, high levels of motivation, and an ability to gain ready insight into their behavior. Psychotherapeutic interventions have been applied to a wide variety of chronic problems. Even a severely disturbed psychotic client may profit from a therapeutic relationship that takes into ac-count his or her level of functioning and maintains therapeutic subgoals that are within the client's pre-sent capabilities.

It should be clear from this brief description of individuals in psychological therapy that there is in-deed no "typical" client, nor, as we will see, is there a "model" therapy. No currently used form of ther-apy is applicable to all types of clients, and all of the standard therapies can document some successes. Most authorities agree that client variables, such as motivation and the seriousness of the problem, are exceedingly important to the outcome of therapy (Garfield, 1994; Lambert & Bergin, 1994; Roun-saville, Weissman, & Prusoff, 1981). As we will see, the various therapies have relatively greater success when a therapist takes the characteristics of a partic-ular client into account in determining the treat-ment of choice.

Who Provides Psychotherapeutic Services?

Members of many different professions have tradi-tionally provided advice and counsel to individuals in emotional distress. Physicians, in addition to car-ing for their clients' physical problems, often be-come trusted advisers in emotional matters as well. In past eras, before the advent of health mainte-nance organizations and highly differentiated med-ical specialties, the family physician was called on for virtually all health questions. Even today, the med-ical practitioner—although he or she may have little psychological background and limited time to spend with individual clients—may be asked to give con-sultation in psychological matters. Many physicians

are trained to recognize psychological problems that are beyond their expertise and to refer patients to psychological specialists.

Another professional group that deals extensively with people's emotional problems is the clergy. Members of the clergy are usually in intimate con-tact with the emotional needs and problems of their congregations. A minister, priest, or rabbi may be the first professional to encounter a person experi-encing an emotional crisis. Although some clergy are trained counselors, most limit their counseling to religious matters and spiritual support and do not attempt to provide psychotherapy. Rather, like gen-eral-practice physicians, they are trained to recog-nize problems that require professional management and refer troubled people to mental health special-ists.

The three types of mental health professionals found most often in mental health settings are clini-cal psychologists, psychiatrists, and psychiatric social workers (see HIGHLIGHT 17.1). The **clinical psy-chologist** typically has training at the undergradu-ate level in psychology and has a Ph.D. or Psy.D. degree in clinical psychology, with specialization in person-ality theory, abnormal psychology, psychological as-sessment, and psychotherapy. Most clinical psychol-ogists receive broad clinical experience in assessment and psychotherapy in addition to their mental health research training. The **psychiatrist** is an M.D. who has had further training—minimally a three-year res-idency—in dealing with clients in a mental health setting. The medical training of psychiatrists quali-fies them for administering somatic therapies, such as electroconvulsive therapy and psychotropic med-ication. In addition, during residency, psychiatric residents receive supervision in psychotherapy. **Psy-chiatric social workers** are usually trained in social science at the bachelor's level and may hold an M.S.W. or Ph.D. from a school of social work. Their graduate training usually involves courses in family evaluation, psychotherapy, and supervised field ex-periences.

In a clinic or hospital, as opposed to an individual practice setting, a wide range of medical, psycholog-ical, and social work procedures may be used. These range from the use of drugs to individual or group psychotherapy and to home, school, or job visits aimed at modifying adverse conditions in a client's life. Often the latter—as in helping a teacher be-come more understanding and supportive of a child client's needs—is as important as treatment directed toward modifying the client's personality makeup, behavior, or both.

This willingness to use a variety of procedures is reflected in the frequent use of a team approach to

Personnel in Psychotherapy

Professional

Clinical Psychologist

Ph.D. in psychology with both research and clinical skill specialization. One-year internship in a psychiatric hospital or mental health center. Or, Psy.D. in psychology (a professional degree with more clinical than research specialization) plus one-year internship in a psychiatric hospital or mental health center.

Counseling Psychologist

Ph.D. in psychology plus internship in a marital- or student-counseling setting; normally, a counseling psychologist deals with adjustment problems not involving mental disorder.

School Psychologist

Ideally a person having doctoral training in child-clinical psychology, with additional training and experience in academic and learning problems. At present, many school systems lack the resources to maintain an adequate school psychology program.

Psychiatrist

M.D. degree with residency training (usually three years) in a psychiatric hospital or mental health facility.

Psychoanalyst

M.D. or Ph.D. degree plus intensive training in the theory and practice of psychoanalysis.

Psychiatric Social Worker

B.A., M.S.W., or Ph.D. degree with specialized clinical training in mental health settings.

Psychiatric Nurse

R.N. degree plus specialized training in the care and treatment of psychiatric clients. Nurses can attain M.A. and Ph.D. degrees in psychiatric nursing.

Occupational Therapist

B.S. in occupational therapy plus internship training with physically or psychologically handicapped individuals, helping them make the most of their resources.

Pastoral Counselor

Ministerial background plus training in psychology. Internship in mental health facility as a chaplain.

Paraprofessional

Community Mental Health Worker

Capable person with limited professional training who works under professional direction (especially crisis intervention).

Alcohol- or Drug-Abuse Counselor

Limited professional training but trained in the evaluation and management of alcohol- and drug-addicted people.

In both mental health clinics and hospitals, personnel from several fields may function as an interdisciplinary team—for example, a psychiatrist, a clinical psychologist, a social worker, a psychiatric nurse, and an occupational therapist may work together.

---

assessment and treatment, particularly in group practice and institutional settings. This approach ideally involves the coordinated efforts of medical, psychological, social work, and other mental health personnel working together as the needs of each case warrant. Also of key importance is the current practice of providing treatment facilities in the community. Instead of considering maladjustment as an individual's private misery, which in the past often required confinement in a distant mental hospital, this approach integrates family and community resources in the treatment.

The Therapeutic Relationship

The therapeutic relationship is formed out of what both a careseeker and a caregiver bring to the thera-

peutic situation. The client's major contribution is his or her motivation. The humanistic tenet—that all humans are at base far more like each other than different and possess an inner drive toward mental and physical health—makes effective psychotherapy possible. Just as physical medicine, properly used, essentially frees and cooperates with the body's own healing mechanisms, an important ally for a psychotherapist is the client's own drive toward wholeness and toward the development of unrealized potentialities. Although this inner drive is often obscured in severely disturbed clients, most anxious and confused people are sufficiently discouraged with their situation to be eager to cooperate in any program that holds hope for improvement.

Motivation to change is probably the most crucial element in determining the success or failure of psychotherapy, and a wise therapist is appropriately cautious about accepting an unmotivated client. Not all prospective clients, regardless of their need for treatment, are ready for the discomfort that effective therapy may entail. Even the motivation of self-referred clients may dissipate in the face of the painful confrontations good therapy may require.

Almost as important is a client's expectation of receiving help. This expectancy is often sufficient in itself to bring about some improvement (Frank, 1978). Just as a placebo pill often lessens pain for someone who believes it will do so, a person who expects to be helped by psychotherapy is likely to be helped, almost regardless of the particular methods used by a therapist. The downside of this fact is that a therapist who appears inept, bumbling, or unconfident may compromise potential benefits even where the treatment plan is entirely appropriate for the presenting problem. Therapists are usually the first to admit that their "art" is inexact and dependent on what a client and therapist bring to the experience of treatment.

To the art of therapy, a therapist brings a variety of professional skills and methods intended to help individuals see themselves and their situations more objectively—that is, to gain a different perspective. Insight and new perspective, however, are only a start and not usually enough alone to bring about the necessary changes in behavior. Besides helping provide a new perspective, most therapy situations also offer a client a protected setting in which he or she is helped to practice new ways of feeling and acting, gradually developing both the courage and the ability to take responsibility for acting in more effective and satisfying ways.

To bring about such changes, an effective psychotherapist must interact with a client in such a manner as to discourage old and dysfunctional behavior patterns and induce new and more functional ones in their place. Because clients will present varying challenges in this regard, the therapist must be flexible enough to deploy a variety of interactive styles. For example, a therapist who inadvertently but unfailingly takes charge in finding solutions for clients' problems will have considerable difficulty in working with people presenting serious difficulties in the area of inhibited autonomy, as in dependent personality disorder. To at least some extent, effective therapy depends on a good match between client and therapist (Talley, Strupp, & Morey, 1990). Hence, a therapist's own personality is necessarily a factor of some importance in determining therapeutic outcomes, quite aside from his or her background and training or the particular formal treatment plan adopted (Beutler, Machado, & Neufeldt, 1994; Lambert, 1989).

Despite general agreement among psychotherapists on these aspects of the client-therapist relationship, professionals can and do differ in their diagnoses and treatments of psychological disorders. This statement should not be surprising, of course. Even in the treatment of physical disorders, we sometimes find that physicians disagree. In psychopathology, such disagreements are even more common. The differing viewpoints on human motivation and behavior

Effective psychotherapy is a "working alliance," requiring a good therapeutic relationship.

outlined in Chapter 3 lead to quite different appraisals of exactly what "the problem" is and how a person should be helped to overcome it. The next section provides a brief perspective on the several types of therapy available and on how they are able to coexist and complement one another, despite their evident differences.

A Perspective on Therapeutic Pluralism

Mastering the sometimes bewildering array of available therapeutic techniques is difficult at best. One way of attempting to do so is to reduce the domain to five general types or classes of therapy interventions according to the principal client subsystem targeted for therapeutic attention: Cognition, Affect, Physiology, Environment, and Behavioral Response (CAPER). The CAPER framework (which is illustrated in HIGHLIGHT 17.2) is our own attempt to summarize this complex domain; we hope it will be of value to you by providing a convenient orienting framework.

According to this scheme, biological therapies, reviewed in the preceding chapter, would be considered Type P therapies because they involve direct at-

HIGHLIGHT   17.2

CAPER: Classes of Therapeutic Strategies According to the Primary Target for Change

The accompanying figure depicts in schematic fashion the situation of a typical psychotherapy client, who is conceived here as a conglomerate of mutually influencing cognitions, affects, and physiologic states. A principal output of this system is overt behavioral responding, some of which is maladaptive or abnormal. The impact of this abnormal behavior on the environment (chiefly the social or interpersonal environment) generates information-laden reactions that are in turn registered by the client's cognition-affect-physiologic system. (The reverse direction arrow from behavior to client acknowledges the scattered evidence that this type of influence also occurs.) In the case of persisting behavioral abnormality, we assume that much of the information gleaned from the reacting environment is such as to "confirm," or at least not disconfirm, client cognitions, affects, and associated physiologic states; were it otherwise, we would anticipate a restructuring of the system and, typically, a termination of the abnormal behavior. Therapy is thus a matter of interrupting the self-sustaining loop supporting the behavioral abnormality. Seen in this

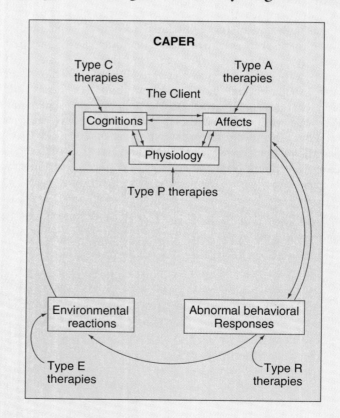

light, therapy might conceivably be effective by inducing positive change in any one of the component nodes of the loop. Differing types of therapy, here organized into Types C (cognitive), A (affec-

tive), P (physiologic), E (environmental), and R (behavioral response), do in fact tend to focus efforts at therapeutic change on one or another of these nodes, as further described in the text.

tempts to alter a client's Physiology in the hope that such change will result in beneficial alteration in other systems as well. Operant conditioning therapies, on the other hand, would practically always be of Type R because of their focus on bringing about direct changes in maladaptive behavioral Responding through the manipulation of reinforcement contingencies. Type C, A, and E therapies involve, in turn, interventions focused respectively on maladaptive client Cognitions and Affects, and on pathology-sustaining reactions in the client's Environment. Therapists have at least these choices in deciding where their efforts should primarily be directed.

As we will see, and indeed as might be anticipated, not all therapies fit neatly into one or another of the types. Usually, however, a dominant therapeutic target is discernible that makes such classification feasible. Of course, such a classification scheme becomes irrelevant for truly comprehensive programs of therapy, such as the so-called multimodal, but these seem (unfortunately, we think) the exception rather than the rule in clinical practice. Although most therapists describe themselves as "eclectic" in orientation, most favor particular approaches, and some commentators (e.g., Patterson, 1989) doubt even the possibility of "integration." We will point out in the following sections what seem to be the dominant types (C, A, P, E, or R) of the several kinds of psychotherapy to be described.

Before proceeding, one other aspect of HIGHLIGHT 17.2 deserves mention—namely, its form as a continuous loop. We think this form reflects the reality of the relationships among (a) the client, conceived as a system of integrated cognitions, affects, and physiologic reactions or states; (b) his or her abnormal behavioral response output, assumed to be a product of (a); and (c) the reactions of the person's environment to that output, in turn "feeding back" to the person's cognition-affect-physiologic system information that tends to support or confirm the "contents" of the system. This aspect of our model is neither idiosyncratic nor new, and developments of certain of its facets now commonly appear in the professional literature (e.g., Andrews, 1989b; Safran, 1990a, 1990b; Strupp, 1993; Wachtel, 1993).

The model has two important and related implications for therapy. First, the question of causal primacy, of how the abnormal behavior got started, is not especially relevant; once in operation, the loop, theoretically, is self-sustaining. Second, it should be possible to effect a positive overall outcome by fostering adaptive change in any pertinent component

of the loop, whether physiology, cognitions, affects, overt responses, or even the reacting environment. That is, effective therapy consists of interrupting this pathology-sustaining loop. In our view, then, most competing types of therapy can realistically claim their share of successes (Smith et al., 1980) precisely because they induce adaptive change in one or another of these critical system components, thereby (perhaps unwittingly) positively affecting the whole (see Stiles, Shapiro, & Elliott, 1986).

Maintaining this overview as a backdrop, we now will consider several forms of psychotherapy that have evolved over the century since Sigmund Freud's first such effort. In fact, we will begin with that tradition.

PSYCHODYNAMIC THERAPY

Psychodynamic therapy is a psychological treatment approach that focuses on individual personality dynamics from a psychoanalytic perspective (see Chapter 3). It is practiced in two basic forms: (a) classical psychoanalysis, and (b) psychoanalytically oriented psychotherapy. Therapists who practice either form are often referred to as psychoanalysts or, simply, analysts. As developed by Freud and his immediate followers, classical psychoanalysis is an intensive, long-term procedure for uncovering repressed memories, thoughts, fears, and conflicts presumably stemming from problems in early psychosexual development—and helping individuals come to terms with them in light of the realities of adult life. It is thought that gaining insight into such repressed material frees individuals from the need to keep squandering their energies on repression and other defense mechanisms. Instead, they can bring their personality resources to bear on consciously resolving the anxieties that prompted the repression in the first place. Freed from this load of threatening material and from the effort of keeping it out of consciousness (so the theory states), they can turn their energies to better personality integration and more effective living.

In psychoanalytically oriented psychotherapy the treatment and the ideas guiding it may depart substantially from the principles and procedures laid out by orthodox Freudian theory, yet the therapy is still based on psychoanalytic concepts. For example, many psychoanalytically oriented therapists schedule less frequent sessions and use techniques such as active challenging of defenses in an effort to shorten total treatment time. We will examine first Freud's original treatment methods, in part because of their historical significance and enormous influence; then we will look briefly at some of the contemporary modifications of psychoanalytic therapy.

Freudian Psychoanalysis

Psychoanalysis is a system of therapy that evolved over a period of years during Freud's long career. It is not an easy system of therapy to describe, and the problem is complicated by the fact that many people have inaccurate conceptions of it based on cartoons and other forms of caricature. The best way to begin our discussion is to describe the four basic techniques of this form of therapy: free association, analysis of dreams, analysis of resistance, and analysis of transference. Then we will note some of the most important changes that have taken place in psychoanalytic therapy since Freud's time.

Free Association As we saw in Chapter 2, Freud used hypnosis in his early work to free repressed thoughts from his clients' unconscious (see HIGHLIGHT 17.3). Later, he stopped using hypnosis in favor of a more direct method of gaining access to a person's hidden thoughts and fears—**free association.**

The basic rule of free association is that an individual must say whatever comes into his or her mind, regardless of how personal, painful, or seemingly irrelevant it may be. Usually a client sits comfortably in a chair or lies in a relaxed position on a couch and gives a running account of all the thoughts, feelings, and desires that come to mind as one idea leads to another. The therapist usually takes a position behind the client so as not to in any way distract or disrupt the free flow of associations.

Although such a running account of whatever comes into one's head may seem random, Freud did not view it as such; rather, he believed that associations are determined like other events. As we have seen, he also thought that the conscious represents a relatively small part of the mind, while the preconscious and unconscious are the much larger portions. The purpose of free association is to explore thoroughly the contents of the preconscious, that part of mind considered subject to conscious attention but largely ignored. The preconscious contents, it is thought, contain derivatives of repressed unconscious material, which if properly "interpreted" can lead to an uncovering of the latter. Analytic interpretation involves a therapist's tying together a client's often disconnected ideas, beliefs, actions, and so forth into a meaningful explanation to help the client gain insight into the relationship between his or her maladaptive behavior and the repressed (unconscious) events and fantasies that drive it.

Analysis of Dreams Another important, related procedure for uncovering unconscious material is dream analysis. When a person is asleep, repressive defenses are said to be lowered and forbidden desires and feelings may find an outlet in dreams. For this reason, dreams have been referred to as the "royal road to the unconscious." Some motives, however, are so unacceptable to an individual that even in dreams they are not revealed openly but are expressed in disguised or symbolic form. Thus a dream has two kinds of content: **manifest content,** which is the dream as it appears to the dreamer, and **latent content,** composed of the actual motives that are seeking expression but are so painful or unacceptable that they are disguised.

It is a therapist's task to uncover these disguised meanings by studying the images that appear in the manifest content of a client's dream and his or her preconscious associations to them. For example, a client's dream of being engulfed in a tidal wave may be interpreted by a therapist as indicating that the client feels in danger of being overwhelmed by inadequately repressed fears and hostilities.

Analysis of Resistance During the process of free association or of associating to dreams, an individual may evidence **resistance**—an unwillingness or inability to talk about certain thoughts, motives, or experiences (Strean, 1985). For example, a client may be talking about an important childhood experience and then suddenly switch topics, perhaps stating, "It really isn't that important," or "It is too absurd to discuss." Resistance may also be evidenced by the client's giving a too-glib interpretation of some association, or coming late to an appointment, or even "forgetting" an appointment altogether. Because resistance prevents painful and threatening material from entering awareness, its sources must be sought if an individual is to face the problem and learn to deal with it in a realistic manner.

Analysis of Transference As client and therapist interact, the relationship between them may become complex and emotionally involved. Often people carry over and apply to their therapist attitudes and feelings that they had in their relations with a parent or other person close to them in the past, a process known as **transference.** Thus clients may react to their analyst as they did to that earlier person and feel the same love, hostility, or rejection that they felt long ago. If the analyst is operating according to the prescribed role of maintaining an impersonal stance of detached attention, the often affect-laden reactions of the client can be interpreted, it is held, as a type of projection—inappropriate to the present

The Use of Hypnosis in Therapy

Hypnosis was known among the ancient Egyptians and other early peoples, but its modern use in psychotherapy dates only from the time of Mesmer, as we saw in Chapter 2. Since that time, there have been periodic fluctuations in the popularity of hypnosis in psychotherapy, and differing viewpoints have arisen concerning the exact nature of hypnotic phenomena. In general, hypnosis may be defined as an altered state of consciousness involving extreme suggestibility. Hypnotic induction procedures are designed to bring about a heightened state of selective attention in which a subject "tunes out" irrelevant stimuli and concentrates solely on the hypnotist's suggestions. The induction of hypnosis and its therapeutic uses are briefly outlined here:

1. *Induction of hypnosis.* Hypnosis may be induced by a variety of techniques, most of which involve the following factors: (a) enlisting a subject's cooperation and allaying any fears of hypnosis; (b) having the subject assume a comfortable position and relax completely; (c) narrowing and focusing the subject's attention, perhaps by having him or her gaze on some bright object; and (d) directing the subject's activities by means of suggestions. The latter often involves establishing the assumption that normal bodily reactions have in fact come about at the direction of the hypnotist. For example, a subject may be directed to gaze upward toward an object and then be told, "Your eyelids are starting to feel heavy." This is a normal reaction to the strain of looking upward, but the subject thinks it is caused by the hypnotist; thus the way is paved to accept further suggestions.

2. *Recall of buried memories.* Traumatic experiences that have been repressed from consciousness may be recovered under hypnosis. This technique was used in treating combat-exhaustion cases during World War II. Under hypnosis, an amnesic soldier could relive his battle experience, thus discharging the emotional tensions associated with it and permitting the experience to be assimilated into his self-structure. Civilian reactions involving amnesia may be similarly handled. As was noted in Chapter 7, the use of hypnosis to recover memories of alleged childhood abuse has come under fire in recent years as evidence has mounted that some overzealous hypnotist-therapists have encouraged the "recall" of false memories.

3. *Age regression.* Closely related to memory recall is hypnotic age regression. A hypnotized woman, for example, may be told that she is now a six-year-old child again and will subsequently act, talk, and think much as she did at the age of six. Regression to the age just preceding the onset of phobias often brings to light the traumatic experiences that precipitated them. Here again, reliving the traumatic experience may desensitize a subject to it. Age regression below the point at which an individual acquired verbally mediated memory is not possible. Contrary to what some claim, age regression to "past lives" is also not possible.

4. *Dream induction.* Dreams can be induced through hypnosis, although some investigators consider hypnotic dreams to more nearly resemble fantasies than nocturnal dreams. In any event, hypnotic dreams may be used to explore intrapsychic conflicts along the lines of dream analysis worked out by Freud. Perhaps the particular value of such dreams is that a therapist can suggest the theme about which the hypnotic dream should center, using it much like a projective technique in exploring an individual's inner conflicts.

5. *Posthypnotic suggestion.* One of the hypnotic phenomena most widely used in psychotherapy is posthypnotic suggestion. In this technique, a therapist makes suggestions to a subject during the hypnotic state for behavior to be carried out later in the waking state, with the subject remaining unaware of the source of the behavior. For example, a subject may be told that he or she will no longer have a desire to smoke upon coming out of the hypnotic state. Although such suggestions do carry over into the waking state, their duration is usually short. That is, the individual may again experience a desire to smoke in a few hours or a few days. This time factor can be partially compensated for, however, by regular reinforcement of the posthypnotic suggestion in booster sessions.

Some investigators attribute the altered state of consciousness in hypnosis to the subject's strong motivation to meet the demand characteristics of the situation. Barber (1969), for example, has shown that many of the behaviors induced under hypnosis can be replicated in nonhypnotized subjects simply by giving instructions which they are strongly motivated to follow. The preponderance of research evidence, however, indicates that behavior induced in hypnotized subjects does differ significantly from that evidenced during simulated hypnosis or role enactment (Diamond, 1974; Fromm & Shor, 1972; Hilgard, 1973, 1974; Miller & Springer, 1974; Nace, Orne, & Hammer, 1974; Rhue, Lynn, & Kirsch, 1993). For example, a number of investigators have offered dramatic evidence that the pain response can be brought almost completely under hypnotic control in many subjects, permitting a degree of pain reduction well beyond that produced in nonhypnotized subjects.

Such drugs as sodium pentothal can be used to produce phenomena similar to those manifested in a hypnotic trance. This form of biological therapy is referred to as narcoanalysis or narcosynthesis. Sodium pentothal has been used to treat severe cases of combat exhaustion involving amnesia.

Freud's office. Freud had his patients use the couch during psychoanalysis, both to enhance relaxation and to avoid distracting eye contact.

situation, yet highly revealing of central issues in the client's life.

By recognizing the transference relationship, a therapist may provide the client with insight as to the meaning of his or her reactions in the present context, and may also introduce a corrective emotional experience by refusing as it were to engage the person on the basis of his or her unwarranted assumptions about the nature of the therapeutic relationship. If the client expects rejection and criticism, for example, the therapist is careful to maintain a neutral manner. In this way it may be possible for the individual to "work through" the conflict in feelings about the real parent or perhaps to overcome feelings of hostility and self-devaluation that stemmed from the earlier parental rejection. In essence, the pathogenic effects of an undesirable early relationship are counteracted by working through a similar emotional conflict in a therapeutic setting. Because a person's reliving of a pathogenic past relationship in a sense recreates the neurosis in real life, this experience is often referred to as a *transference neurosis.*

It is not possible here to consider at length the complexities of transference relationships, but we can stress that a client's attitudes toward his or her therapist usually do not follow such simple patterns as our example suggests. Often the client is ambivalent—distrusting the therapist and feeling hostile toward him or her as a symbol of authority, but at the same time seeking acceptance and love. In addition, the problems of transference are not confined to the client, for the therapist may also have a mixture of feelings toward the client. This phenomenon is known as **counter-transference** and must be recog-

nized and handled properly by the therapist. For this reason, it is considered important that therapists have a thorough understanding of their own motives, conflicts, and "weak spots"; in fact, all psychoanalysts themselves undergo psychoanalysis before they begin independent practice.

The resolution of the transference neurosis is said to be the key element in effecting a psychoanalytic "cure." Such resolution can only occur if an analyst successfully avoids the pitfalls of counter-transference. That is, the analyst must focus on control of the "environmental" (i.e., his or her own) reaction to a client's behavior. Accordingly, we consider psychoanalysis and psychoanalytically oriented therapy to be primarily Type E in character.

Psychodynamic Therapy Since Freud

The original version of psychoanalysis is practiced only rarely today. Arduous and expensive in time, money, and emotional commitment, it normally entails three to five one-hour sessions per week, and it may take several years until both analyst and client are satisfied that all major issues in the client's life have been satisfactorily resolved. In light of these heavy demands, most psychoanalytic/psychodynamic therapists have worked out modifications in procedure designed to shorten the time and expense required. Mann (1973), for example, has described an approach that follows psychodynamic methods but is confined to a 12-session treatment course aimed at symptom relief. Other psychoanalytically oriented approaches have recently been reviewed by Henry and colleagues (1994).

Probably the most extensive program of short-term psychodynamic therapy, one involving a strong research/evaluation component, is that of Strupp and colleagues at Vanderbilt University (Strupp, 1981, 1993; Strupp & Binder, 1984). This therapy, known as time-limited dynamic psychotherapy, goes beyond symptom relief and aims for lasting modification of an individual's personality by applying modified psychodynamic principles in therapy that lasts for 25–30 sessions. The modifications introduced here have a substantial interpersonal focus, in keeping with a clear trend of contemporary psychodynamic thinking.

The interpersonal focus of much modern psychodynamic therapy, including approaches deriving from the object-relations focus of contemporary psychoanalysis (Cashdan, 1988), has roots in England as well as the United States. (As was seen in Chapter 3, a major American figure in this development was Harry Stack Sullivan.) Most generally these procedures make central and build on one of Freud's most brilliant insights—that a person's current relationship to the social environment is determined significantly by persistent, unconscious memory traces, or schemas, laid down in his or her earliest relationships with significant others. While the classical analysts have tended to see these script-like recreations of the past as played out mainly under the special circumstances of transference in psychoanalytic treatment, interpersonal therapists hold that these precedents are always operative in a person's relationship to all others, not just to his or her therapist.

Often a client's schemas about what people are like and what one may expect from them are not only erroneous in terms of present circumstances but also quite destructive in their effects on current interpersonal functioning. Sometimes they lead to repeating the same mistakes and the same poor choices in relationships time and time again, and to the maintenance of highly dysfunctional self-fulfilling prophecies (Carson, 1982; Wachtel, 1993). Interpersonal and object-relations therapists tend to ignore the sorts of libidinal drives and psychic structures Freudians emphasize and tend instead to focus their efforts on correcting their clients' distorted views of the interpersonal environment. In this respect the approach is indistinguishable from certain aspects of cognitive therapy, although interpersonalists tend more to use their own relationship to clients as the laboratory for the latter's acquisition of new and more functional cognitive schemas.

An important variant of interpersonally based psychotherapy, interpersonal psychotherapy (IPT) for depression, has been developed in recent years by a group of therapist-researchers from Harvard and Yale. As will be seen below, it was featured prominently in a national study comparing various treatments for depression, one we will consider in greater detail in discussing outcome research.

Other differences in contemporary psychodynamic treatment have also evolved. For example, today's analytic therapists tend to place more emphasis on current ego functioning and see the ego as a developing and controlling agent in an individual's life, not merely an uncertain regulator of uncompromising drives. Thus an individual is seen as more capable of being in control and less dominated by early repressed sexuality than in traditional analysis. Although childhood events are still viewed as important formative experiences, most modern psychodynamic therapists also place more emphasis on clients' current life situations and less on their childhood experiences. Many important contemporary situations are, of course, ones involving other people, thus making for a certain rapprochement with other trends already noted.

Evaluation of Psychodynamic Therapy

Despite such modifications, psychodynamic therapy is still commonly criticized for being relatively time-consuming and expensive; for being based on a questionable, stultified, and sometimes cultlike approach to human nature; for neglecting a client's immediate problems in the search for unconscious conflicts in the remote past; and for inadequate proof of general effectiveness. Concerning the last of these, we actually have relatively little solid research data on the efficacy of either the classical or the newer variants of psychodynamic therapy. With notable exceptions, such as the Vanderbilt psychotherapy project previously noted (see Strupp & Binder, 1984; Strupp, 1993), rigorous research on outcomes has not been a strength of the psychodynamic therapies.

The criticisms noted above have been mostly directed at classical psychoanalysis, and in our judgment are merited to a degree. With a few exceptions, analysts have been less than eager to subject their treatment outcomes to rigorous scrutiny, and when they have done so (see Smith et al., 1980; Wallerstein, 1989) the results have not been especially impressive, at least when considered in relation to the usually optimistic goals and considerable investments involved. Because it expects a person to achieve insight and major personality change, psychoanalysis is also limited in its applicability. For example, it appears best suited for people who are average or above in intelligence and economically well off, and who do not suffer from severe psychopathology. In the present era of concern for "cost-effectiveness" and "accountability" in the mental therapy field, classical psychoanalysis appears increasingly to be a therapy for the elite.

Nevertheless, many people do feel that they have profited from psychoanalytic therapy—particularly in terms of greater self-understanding, relief from inner conflict and anxiety, and improved interpersonal relationships. Psychoanalytically oriented psychotherapy remains the treatment of choice for many individuals who are seeking extensive self-evaluation or insight into themselves. Even some behavior therapists, when seeking treatment for themselves, have selected this approach over behavioral methods (Gochman, Allgood, & Geer, 1982), which surely says something about the value they place on it.

BEHAVIOR THERAPY

Although the use of conditioning techniques in therapy has a long history, it was not until the 1960s that **behavior therapy,** the use of therapeutic procedures based (as originally formulated) on the principles of classical and operant conditioning, really came into its own. The major reason for the long delay was the dominant position of psychoanalysis in the field. In recent years, however, the therapeutic potential of behavior therapy techniques has been strikingly demonstrated in dealing with a wide variety of maladaptive behaviors, and literally thousands of research publications have dealt with the systematic application of behavior-change principles to modify maladaptive behavior.

In the behavioral perspective, as we saw in Chapter 3, a maladjusted person (unless suffering from brain pathology) is seen as differing from other people only in (a) having failed to acquire competencies needed for coping with the problems of living, (b) having learned faulty reactions or coping patterns that are being maintained by some kind of reinforcement, or (c) both. Thus a behavior therapist specifies in advance the precise maladaptive behaviors to be modified and the adaptive behaviors to be achieved, as well as the specific learning principles or procedures to be used in producing the desired results.

Instead of exploring past traumatic events or inner conflicts, behavior therapists attempt to modify problem behaviors directly by extinguishing or counter-conditioning maladaptive reactions, such as anxiety, or by manipulating environmental contingencies—that is, by the use of reward, suspension of reward, or, occasionally, punishment to shape overt actions. Indeed, for the strict behaviorist, "personality" does not exist except in the form of a collection of modifiable habits. Behavior therapy techniques seem especially effective in altering maladaptive behavior when a reinforcement is administered contiguous with a desired response, and when a person knows what is expected and why the reinforcement is given. The ultimate goal, of course, is not only to achieve the desired responses but to bring them under the control and self-monitoring of the individual.

We have cited many examples of the application of behavior therapy in earlier chapters. In this section, we will elaborate briefly on the key techniques of behavior therapy.

Extinction

Because learned behavior patterns tend to weaken and disappear over time if they are not reinforced, often the simplest way to eliminate a maladaptive pattern is to remove the reinforcement for it. This is especially true in situations where maladaptive behavior has been reinforced unknowingly by others, an extremely common occurrence as illustrated by this case:

Billy, a 6-year-old first grader, was brought to a psychological clinic by his parents because he "hated school" and his teacher had told them that his showing-off behavior was disrupting the class and making him unpopular. It became apparent in observing Billy and his parents during the initial interview that both his mother and father were noncritical and approving of everything he did. After further assessment, a three-phase program of therapy was undertaken: (a) the parents were helped to discriminate between showing-off behavior and appropriate behavior on Billy's part; (b) the parents were instructed to show a loss of interest and attention when Billy engaged in showing-off behavior while continuing to show their approval of appropriate behavior; and (c) Billy's teacher was instructed to ignore Billy, insofar as it was feasible, when he engaged in showing-off behavior, and to devote her attention at those times to children who were behaving more appropriately.

Although Billy's showing-off behavior in class increased during the first few days of this behavior therapy program, it diminished markedly thereafter when it was no longer reinforced by his parents and teacher. As his maladaptive behavior diminished, he was better accepted by his classmates, which, in turn, helped reinforce more appropriate behavior patterns and changed his negative attitude toward school.

Billy's therapy, thus, was basically of the Type R sort (direct modification of maladaptive responses), as mediated by a Type E strategy—changing the environmental reaction (of his parents and teacher) to the behavior.

Two techniques that rely on the principle of extinction are *implosive therapy* and *flooding.* Both focus on extinguishing the conditioned fear and accompanying avoidance behavior induced by anxiety-arousing stimuli and can thus be used to treat anxiety disorders. Accordingly, they are primarily Type A therapies in focusing on the modification of the affect of anxiety. The techniques are roughly similar, except that **implosive therapy,** as that term is now generally used, involves having a client imagine (in vitro) anxiety-arousing situations, usually with much coaching and modeling provided by a therapist; **flooding,** on the other hand, involves inducing a client to undergo repeated exposures to his or her real-life (in vivo) anxiety-arousing situations, usually again with the therapist in an active coaching role.

In implosion, clients are asked to imagine and relive aversive scenes associated with their anxiety. However, instead of trying to banish anxiety from the treatment sessions, as in the older technique of systematic desensitization, a therapist deliberately attempts to elicit a massive "implosion" of anxiety. This is somewhat reminiscent of psychodynamic approaches because it often deals with past trauma and conceptualizes anxiety as a response to internal threat, though most traditional analysts would doubtless strongly disapprove of the procedure. With repeated exposure in a "safe" setting, the stimulus loses its power to elicit anxiety (classical extinction), and the derivative avoidance behavior thus becomes nonfunctional and hence unreinforced by anxiety reduction (operant extinction). Hypnosis or drugs may be used to enhance vivid imagery under implosive therapy.

In a report of an actual case, Stampfl (1975) described a young woman who could not swim and was terrified of water—particularly of sinking under the water. Although she knew it was irrational, she was so terrified of water "that she wore a life preserver when she took a bath" (p. 66). She was in-

Flooding is a technique that involves placing an individual in a real-life, anxiety-arousing situation with the goal of extinguishing the conditioned avoidance of an anxiety-provoking stimulus. For example, a client with a fear of heights may be taken to the top of a tall building to demonstrate that the feared consequences do not occur.

structed by the therapist to imagine in minute detail taking a bath without a life preserver in a "bottomless" tub, and slipping under the water. Initially, the client showed intense anxiety, and the scene was repeated over and over. In addition, she was given a "homework" assignment in which she was asked to imagine herself drowning. Eventually, after imagining the worst and finding that nothing happened, her anxiety diminished. After the fourteenth therapy session, she was able to take baths without feelings of anxiety; the maladaptive behavior had been effectively extinguished.

Imaginal procedures have some limitations, an obvious one being that not all persons are capable of vividly imagining the required scenes. In a study of clients with agoraphobia, Emmelkamp and Wessels (1975) concluded that prolonged exposure in vivo plainly proved superior to simple reliance on the imagination, and in recent years the flooding procedure seems to have gained a definite ascendancy over that of in vitro imagining wherever it is possible to identify in concrete terms those situations evoking anxiety, and to induce the client to confront them directly (Barlow, 1988, 1993). On the other hand, some anxiety-inducing situations are not readily or judiciously reproducible in real life, as where they refer to memories of unique past events such as natural disasters, or where in vivo exposure to them might be objectively dangerous. For example, it is desirable for the traumatized rape victim to confront the circumstances surrounding the attack (Calhoun & Resick, 1993), but it would obviously be fool-hardy to recommend that she patrol crime-infested neighborhoods at night. Imaginal procedures remain, therefore, a vital part of the therapeutic extinction armamentarium.

Reports on the effectiveness of implosive therapy and flooding have generally been very favorable (Emmelkamp, 1994); they may be considered the treatments of choice for simple phobias (Foa & Kozak, 1985) and perhaps an essential part of effective treatment for several other anxiety disorders, for instance, panic disorder with or without agoraphobia (Craske & Barlow, 1993), social phobia (Hope & Heimberg, 1993), and obsessive-compulsive disorder (Riggs & Foa, 1993). They have been used effectively in treating anxiety disorders in children (Kendall, 1994). Some investigators, however, have reported unfavorable as well as favorable results (Emmelkamp & Wessels, 1975; Mealiea, 1967; Wolpe, 1969b).

These mixed results appear to be particularly true of flooding in vivo. For example, Emmelkamp and Wessels (1975) found that flooding in vivo was terrifying for some clients. In one case, the agoraphobic client "hid in a cellar out of fear of being sent into the street for 90 minutes by the therapist" (p. 14). On the other hand, the flooding procedure can be made relatively bearable without diminished effectiveness for even a severely fearful client by increasing therapist support and active guidance during exposure, as was demonstrated by Williams and Zane (1989) in a study also involving the treatment of agoraphobia. In general, it appears that while many clients respond favorably to implosion or flooding, some do not respond, and a few suffer an exacerbation of their phobias. This finding suggests a need for caution in the use of these techniques, particularly because they involve experiences that may be traumatic.

A modified form of flooding that involves repeated exposure to the somatic cues usually preceding panic (for example, heart palpitations experienced at the beginning of a "false alarm"), rather than to traumatizing situations themselves, may provide a key to circumventing undesirable reactions to exposure treatment. Accumulating evidence shows that it is these sorts of cues that trigger full-blown anxiety attacks, and Barlow and associates (e.g., Barlow et al., 1989; Craske & Barlow, 1993) have developed effective procedures for extinguishing this type of chain reaction, for example, by teaching clients to self-induce their false alarm symptoms repeatedly ("interoceptive exposure"). In an important study in which the exposure to anticipatory cues procedure was a centerpiece in a treatment package for panic disorder, this treatment was demonstrated to be far superior to drug treatment with alprazolam (Xanax), a benzodiazepine compound touted as having strong antipanic properties, but one also noted for its addictive potential (Klosko et al., 1990).

Systematic Desensitization

The process of extinction can be applied to behavior that is positively reinforced or negatively reinforced. Of the two, behavior that is negatively reinforced—reinforced by the successful avoidance of a painful situation—is harder to deal with. Because someone with negatively reinforced maladaptive behavior becomes anxious and withdraws at the first sign of the painful situation, he or she never gets a chance to find out whether the expected aversive consequences do in fact come about. In addition, the avoidance is anxiety-reducing and hence is itself reinforced.

One technique that has proven especially useful in extinguishing negatively reinforced behavior involves eliciting an antagonistic or competing response. Because it is difficult if not impossible to feel both pleasant and anxious at the same time, the method of **systematic desensitization** is aimed at teaching a person to relax or behave in some other way that is inconsistent with anxiety while in the presence (real or imagined) of the anxiety-producing stimulus. It may therefore be considered a type of counter-conditioning procedure. The term *systematic* refers to the carefully graduated manner in which the person is exposed to the feared stimulus, the procedural opposite of implosion and flooding. Systematic desensitization is not used exclusively to deal with avoidance behaviors brought about by negative reinforcement—that is, by successfully avoiding aversive experience. It can be used for other kinds of behavioral problems as well. In general, however, it is a Type A therapeutic procedure aimed at anxiety reduction.

The prototype of this approach is the classic experiment of Jones (1924), in which she successfully eliminated a small boy's conditioned fears of a white rabbit and other furry animals. First she brought the rabbit just inside the door at the far end of the room while the boy, Peter, was eating. On successive days, the rabbit was gradually brought closer until Peter could pat it with one hand while eating with the other.

Wolpe (1958; Rachman & Hodgson, 1980) elaborated on the procedure developed by Jones and devised the term *systematic desensitization* to refer to it. On the assumption that most anxiety-based patterns are, fundamentally, conditioned responses, Wolpe worked out a way to train a client to remain calm and relaxed in situations that formerly produced anxiety. Wolpe's approach is elegant in its simplicity, and his method is equally straightforward.

A client is taught to enter a state of relaxation, typically by progressive concentration on relaxing various muscle groups. Meanwhile, in collaboration with the therapist, an "anxiety hierarchy" is constructed consisting of imagined scenes graded as to their capacity to elicit anxiety. For example, were the problem one of disabling sexual anxiety, a low-anxiety scene might be a candlelight dinner with the prospective partner, while a high-anxiety scene might be imagining the penis actually entering the vagina.

Active therapy sessions consist of repeatedly imagining the scenes in the hierarchy under conditions of deep relaxation, beginning with the minimum anxiety items and gradually working toward those rated in the more extreme ranges. A session is terminated at any point where the client reports experiencing significant anxiety, the next session resuming at a lower point in the hierarchy. Treatment continues until all items in the hierarchy can be imagined without notable discomfort, by which point the client's real-life difficulties will typically have shown substantial improvement. The usual duration of a desensitization session is about 30 minutes, and the sessions are often given two to three times per week. The overall therapy program may, of course, take a number of weeks or even months. Kennedy and Kimura (1974) have shown, however, that even clients who have progressed only 25–50 percent of the way through their anxiety hierarchy show significant therapeutic gains.

Several variants of systematic desensitization have been devised. One variation involves the use of a tape recorder to enable a client to carry out the desensitization process at home. Another utilizes group desensitization procedures—as in "marathon" desensitization groups, in which the entire program is compressed into a few days of intensive treatment. One of the present authors routinely em-

Joseph Wolpe is shown here conducting systematic desensitization therapy to reduce a client's anxiety. The client, in a relaxed state, is told to imagine the weakest anxiety on her list of anxiety-producing stimuli. If she feels anxious, she is instructed to stop imagining and relax again.

ploys hypnosis to induce relaxation (the standard relaxation training can be quite tedious) and to achieve vividness in the imagining of hierarchy scenes. Perhaps the most important variation is in vivo desensitization, which is essentially similar to flooding but typically involves graduated exposure to the feared situations after a state of relaxation has been attained.

You will probably have concluded by this point that the truly essential element in the behavioral treatment of anxiety is repeated *exposure* of a client to the stimuli, even if only imaginally, that elicit the fear response, regardless of the methods employed in achieving that end. Despite some continued wrangling among proponents of one or another specific procedure, that conclusion appears to be fair and accurate. Where a therapist has a choice—that is, depending on the nature of the problem and on client cooperation and tolerance—in vivo procedures seem to have an edge in efficiency and possibly in ultimate efficacy over those employing imagery as the mode of confrontation (Emmelkamp, 1994). Overall, the outcome record for exposure treatments is impressive (Clum et al., 1993; Emmelkamp, 1994).

Aversion Therapy

Aversion therapy involves modifying undesirable behavior by the old-fashioned method of punishment. Punishment may involve either the removal of desired reinforcers or the use of aversive stimuli, but the basic idea is to reduce the "temptation value" of stimuli that elicit undesirable behavior. The most commonly used aversive stimulus is electric shock, although drugs may also be used. As we will see, however, punishment is rarely employed as the sole method of treatment.

Apparently the first formal use of aversion therapy was made by Kantorovich (1930), who administered electric shocks to alcoholics in association with the sight, smell, and taste of alcohol, an early version of the Antabuse drug treatment in use today (Antabuse produces nausea when a person drinks alcohol—see Chapter 10). Since that time, aversion therapy has been used in the treatment of a wide range of maladaptive behaviors, including smoking, drinking, overeating, drug dependence, gambling, sexual deviance, and bizarre psychotic behavior. As normally employed, it is a Type R therapeutic procedure, targeted at suppression of problematic responses. Because we have described the use of aversion therapy earlier in the course of our discussion of certain abnormal behavior patterns, we will restrict ourselves here to a review of a few brief examples and principles.

Lovaas (1977) found punishment by electric shock to be effective in extreme cases of severely disturbed autistic children. In one case, a seven-year-old autistic boy, diagnosed as severely retarded, had to be kept in restraints 24 hours a day because he would continually beat his head with his fists or bang it against the walls of his crib, inflicting serious injuries. Though it may seem paradoxical to employ punishment to reduce the frequency of self-destructive behavior, electric shock following this behavior was nevertheless effective, bringing about complete inhibition of the maladaptive behavior pattern in a relatively short time (Bucher & Lovaas, 1967).

The use of electric shock as an aversive stimulus, however, has generally diminished in recent years because of the ethical and "image" problems involved in its use and because the new behaviors induced by it do not automatically generalize to other settings (Harris & Ersner-Hershfield, 1978). Also, less dangerous and more effective procedures have been found. The method of choice today is probably differential reinforcement of other responses (DOR), in which behaviors incompatible with the undesired behavior are positively reinforced. For example, for a child who indulges in antisocial, destructive behavior, positive reinforcement might be used for every sign of constructive play. At the same time, any reinforcement that has been maintaining maladaptive behavior is removed. Lovaas and colleagues, who first reported the successful use of electric shock with autistic children, now recommend the use of nonpunitive treatment for self-injurious behavior (Russo, Carr, & Lovaas, 1980).

Aversion therapy is primarily a way—often quite an effective one—of stopping maladaptive responses for a brief period of time. With this interruption, an opportunity exists for substituting new behavior or for changing a lifestyle by encouraging more adaptive alternative patterns that will prove reinforcing in themselves. This point is particularly important because otherwise a client may simply refrain from maladaptive responses in "unsafe" therapy situations, where such behavior leads to immediate aversive results, but keep making them in "safe" real-life situations, where there is no fear of immediate discomfort. Also, there is little likelihood that a previously gratifying but maladaptive behavior pattern will be permanently relinquished unless alternative forms of gratification are learned during the aversion therapy. A therapist who believes it possible to "take away" something without "giving something back" is likely to be disappointed. This is an important point in regard to the treatment of addictions and paraphilias, one often not appreciated in otherwise well-designed treatment programs.

Modeling

As Bandura (1977b) has pointed out,

> Learning would be exceedingly laborious, not to mention hazardous, if people had to rely solely on the effects of their own actions to inform them what to do. Fortunately, most human behavior is learned observationally through modeling: from observing others one forms an idea of how new behaviors are performed, and on later occasions this coded information serves as a guide for action. Because people can learn from example what to do, at least in approximate form, before performing any behavior, they are spared needless error. (p. 22)

Although reinforcement of modeled behavior can influence whether an observer-learner attends to a model's actions and strengthens the response imitated, observational learning does not seem to require extrinsic reinforcement. Rather, according to Bandura, reinforcement functions as a facilitative condition to learning. Anticipation of a reinforcement may also make a person more likely to perform a behavior.

As the name implies, **modeling** involves the learning of skills through imitating another person, such as a parent or therapist, who performs the behavior; as such, it is a Type R procedure. A client may be exposed to behaviors or roles in peers or therapists and encouraged to imitate the desired new responses. For example, modeling may be used to promote the learning of simple skills, such as self-feeding in a profoundly mentally retarded child, or more complex ones, such as being more effective in social situations for a shy, withdrawn adolescent.

As we have noted, modeling and imitation are used in various forms of behavior therapy. Bandura (1964) found that live modeling of fearlessness combined with instruction and guided participation is the most effective desensitization treatment, resulting in the elimination of snake phobias in over 90 percent of the cases treated.

Systematic Use of Reinforcement

Often referred to as *contingency management,* systematic programs involving the use of reinforcement to elicit and maintain effective behavior (Type R therapy) have achieved notable success, particularly in institutional settings. Response shaping, token economies, and behavioral contracting are among the most widely used of such techniques.

Response Shaping Positive reinforcement is often used in **response shaping,** that is, in establishing by gradual approximation a response that is not initially in an individual's behavior repertoire. This technique has been used extensively in working with children's behavior problems. The following case reported by Wolf, Risley, and Mees (1964) is illustrative:

Positive reinforcement is an effective technique for managing behavior problems, with food or other treats or privileges often used as reinforcers. This autistic child is being reinforced for some positive behavior by being stroked with a feather tickler.

> A 3-year-old autistic boy lacked nominal verbal and social behavior. He did not eat properly, engaged in self-destructive behavior, such as banging his head and scratching his face, and manifested ungovernable tantrums. He had recently had a cataract operation, and required glasses for the development of normal vision. He refused to wear his glasses, however, and broke pair after pair.
>
> The technique of shaping was decided on to counteract the problem with his glasses. Initially, the boy was trained to expect a bit of candy or fruit at the sound of a toy noisemaker. Then training was begun with empty eyeglass frames. First the boy was reinforced with the candy or fruit for picking them up, then for holding them, then for carrying them around, then for bringing the frames closer to the eyes, and then for putting the empty frames on his head at any angle. Through successive approximations, the boy finally learned to wear his glasses up to twelve hours a day.

Token Economies Approval and other intangible reinforcers may be ineffective in behavior modification programs, especially those dealing with severely maladaptive behavior. In such instances, appropriate behaviors may be rewarded with tangible reinforcers in the form of tokens that can later be exchanged for desired objects or privileges (Kazdin, 1980). In working with hospitalized schizophrenic clients, for example, Ayllon and Azrin (1968) found that using the commissary, listening to records, and going to movies were considered highly desirable activities by most clients. Consequently, these activities were chosen as reinforcers for socially appropriate behavior. To participate in any of them, a client had to earn a number of tokens by demonstrating appropriate ward behavior. In Chapter 18, we will describe another token economy program, an extraordinarily successful one, with chronic hospitalized clients who had been considered resistant to treatment (Paul, 1982; Paul & Lentz, 1977).

Token economies have been used to establish adaptive behaviors ranging from elementary responses, such as eating and making one's bed, to the daily performance of responsible hospital jobs. In the latter instance, the token economy resembles the outside world where an individual is paid for his or her work in tokens (money) that can later be exchanged for desired objects and activities. The use of tokens as reinforcers for appropriate behavior has a number of distinct advantages: (a) the number of tokens earned depends directly on the amount of desirable behavior shown; (b) tokens, like money in the outside world, may be made a general medium of currency in terms of what they will "purchase"; hence they are not readily subject to satiation and tend to maintain their incentive value; (c) tokens can reduce the delay that often occurs between appropriate performance and reinforcement; (d) the number of tokens earned and the way in which they are "spent" are largely up to the client; and (e) tokens tend to bridge the gap between the institutional environment and the demands and system of payment that will be encountered in the outside world.

The ultimate goal in token economies, as in other programs of extrinsic reinforcement, is not only to achieve desired responses but to bring such responses to a level where their adaptive consequences will be reinforcing in their own right—thus enabling natural rather than artificial rewards to maintain the desired behavior. For example, extrinsic reinforcers may be used initially to help children overcome reading difficulties, but once a child becomes proficient in reading, this skill will presumably provide intrinsic reinforcement as the child comes to enjoy reading for its own sake.

Although their effectiveness has been clearly demonstrated with chronic schizophrenic clients, mentally retarded residents in institutional settings, and children, the use of token economies has not been extensive in recent years (Paul & Menditto, 1992). In part, this neglect is a result of budget-inspired reductions in trained hospital treatment staffs, which are required for the effective management of such programs. Token economies are also poorly understood by lay persons, many of whom see them as inhumane or crassly manipulative. If these people are "sick," so the thought goes, they should have medicine and not be expected to "perform" for simple amenities. Unfortunately, such thinking makes for chronic social disability.

Behavioral Contracting A technique called **behavioral contracting** is used in some types of psychotherapy and behavior therapy to identify the behaviors that are to be changed and to maximize the probability that these changes will occur and be maintained (Nelson & Mowry, 1976). By definition, a contract is an agreement between two or more parties—such as a therapist and a client, a parent and a teenager, or a husband and a wife—that governs the nature of an exchange. The agreement, often in writing, specifies a client's obligations to change as well as the responsibilities of the other party to provide something the client wants in re-

turn, such as tangible rewards, privileges, or therapeutic attention. Behavior therapists frequently make behavioral contracting an explicit focus of treatment, thus helping establish the treatment as a joint enterprise for which both parties have responsibility.

Behavioral contracting can facilitate therapy in several ways: (a) the structuring of the treatment relationship can be explicitly stated, giving the client a clear idea of each person's role in the treatment; (b) the actual responsibilities of the client are outlined and a system of rewards is built in for changed behavior; (c) the limitations of the treatment, in terms of the length and focus of the sessions, are specified; (d) by agreement, some behaviors (for example, the client's sexual orientation) may be eliminated from the treatment focus, thereby establishing the "appropriate content" of the treatment sessions; (e) clear treatment goals can be defined; and (f) criteria for determining success or failure in achieving these goals can be built into the program.

Sometimes a contract is negotiated between a disruptive child and a teacher, according to which the child will maintain or receive certain privileges as long as he or she behaves in accordance with the contract. Usually the school principal is also a party to such a contract to ensure the enforcement of certain conditions that the teacher may not be in a position to enforce, such as removing the child from the classroom for engaging in certain types of misbehavior. Another common application of contracting is in behavioral couples therapy, where the principles governing the exchange of "reinforcements" between the distressed parties is formally negotiated and sometimes even committed to writing (e.g., Cordova & Jacobson, 1993). These techniques have a good record in outcome studies (Shadish et al., 1993).

We know of no therapist who seriously believes in the long-term feasibility of such formal therapeutic contracts as a means of regulating interpersonal behavior. Rather, as in the case of aversion therapy, contracts provide an opportunity to interrupt for a time self-sustaining dysfunctional behavior, thus permitting the emergence of new responses that may prove more adaptive and satisfying.

Assertiveness Therapy

Assertiveness therapy or training has been used as an alternative to relaxation in the desensitization procedure and as a means of developing more effective coping techniques. It appears particularly useful in helping people who have difficulties in interpersonal interactions because of anxiety responses that may prevent them from speaking up, claiming their rights, or even from showing appropriate affection. Such inhibition may lead to continual inner turmoil, particularly if a person feels strongly about a situation. Assertiveness therapy may also be indicated in cases where individuals consistently allow others to take advantage of them or maneuver them into uncomfortable situations.

Assertiveness is viewed as the open and appropriate expression of thoughts and feelings, with due regard to the rights of others (Lange & Jakubowski, 1976). Assertiveness training programs typically follow stages in which the desired assertive behaviors are first practiced in a therapy setting. Then, guided by the therapist, the client is encouraged to practice the new, more appropriately assertive behaviors in real-life situations. Often attention is focused on developing more effective interpersonal skills. For example, a client may learn to ask the other person such questions as "Is anything wrong? You don't seem to be your usual self today." Such questions put the focus on the other person without suggesting an aggressive or hostile intent on the part of the speaker. Each act of intentional assertion is believed to inhibit the anxiety associated with the situation and therefore to weaken the maladaptive anxiety-response pattern. At the same time, it tends to foster more adaptive interpersonal behaviors. Assertiveness therapy is a Type R procedure.

Although assertiveness therapy is a highly useful procedure in certain types of situations, it does have limitations. For example, Wolpe (1969b) has pointed out that it is largely irrelevant for phobias involving nonpersonal stimuli. It may also be of little use in some types of interpersonal situations; for instance, if a person has been rejected by someone, assertive behavior may tend to aggravate rather than resolve the problem. However, in interpersonal situations where maladaptive anxiety can be traced to lack of self-assertiveness, this type of therapy appears particularly effective.

Biofeedback Treatment

Historically it was generally believed that voluntary control over physiological processes, such as heart rate, galvanic skin response, and blood pressure, was not possible. In the early 1960s, however, this view began to change. A number of investigators, aided by the development of sensitive electronic instruments that could accurately measure physiological responses, demonstrated that many of the processes formerly thought to be "involuntary" were modifiable by learning procedures—operant learning and classical conditioning. Kimmel (1974) demon-

strated, for example, that the galvanic skin response could be conditioned by operant learning techniques.

The importance of the autonomic nervous system in the development of abnormal behavior has long been recognized. For example, autonomic arousal is an important factor in anxiety states. Thus many researchers have applied techniques developed in the autonomic conditioning studies in an attempt to modify the internal environment of troubled persons to bring about more adaptive behavior—for instance, to modify heart rates in clients with irregular heartbeats (Weiss & Engel, 1971), to treat stuttering by feeding back information on the electric potential of muscles in the speech apparatus (Lanyon, Barrington, & Newman, 1976), and to reduce lower-back pain (Wolf, Nacht, & Kelly, 1982) and chronic headaches (Blanchard et al., 1983).

This Type P treatment approach—in which a person is taught to influence his or her own physiological processes—is referred to as **biofeedback.** Several steps are typical in the process of biofeedback treatment: (a) monitoring the physiological response that is to be modified (perhaps blood pressure or skin temperature); (b) converting the information to a visual or auditory signal; and (c) providing a means of prompt feedback—indicating to a subject as rapidly as possible when the desired change is taking place (Blanchard & Epstein, 1978). Given this feedback, the subject may then seek to reduce his or her emotionality, as by lowering the skin temperature. For the most part, biofeedback is oriented to reducing the reactivity of some organ system innervated by the autonomic nervous system—very often a physiological component of the anxiety response.

Although there is general agreement that many physiological processes can be regulated to some extent by learning, the application of biofeedback procedures to alter abnormal behavior has produced equivocal results. Demonstrations of clinical biofeedback applications abound, but carefully controlled research has often not supported earlier impressions of widespread clinically significant improvement.

Blanchard and Young (1973, 1974) pointed out that the effects of biofeedback procedures are generally small and often do not generalize to situations outside the laboratory, where the biofeedback devices are not present. Two well-controlled studies failed to show a significant treatment effect for biofeedback in persons with migraine (Kewman & Roberts, 1979) or Raynaud's disease (Gugliemi, 1979). On the other hand, tension headache victims may respond more favorably to biofeedback (Blanchard, 1994). Also, Flor and Birbaumer (1993) demonstrated in a well-controlled recent study a rather impressive effect of electromyographic (muscle tension) biofeedback in the control of musculoskeletal pain of the back and jaw, one that survived a 24-month follow-up.

Unfortunately, this study did not include a relaxation training comparison group. Where that comparison has been made, biofeedback usually has not been shown to be any more effective than relaxation training, leading to the suggestion that biofeedback may simply be a more elaborate (and usually more costly) means of teaching clients relaxation (Blanchard & Epstein, 1978; Blanchard et al., 1980; Tarler-Beniolo, 1978). Relaxation training, in itself, continues to amass a very creditable record in the treatment of various medical conditions, as shown in a recent quantitative review by Carlson and Hoyle (1993). Although no final judgment on this matter can as yet be made, we would note that—as with almost any treatment procedure—a small percentage of clients may be expected to show an unusually good response to biofeedback treatment.

Evaluation of Behavior Therapy

Compared with psychoanalytic and other psychotherapies, behavior therapy appears to have three distinct advantages. First, the treatment approach is precise. The target behaviors to be modified are specified, the methods to be used are clearly delineated, and the results can be readily evaluated (Marks, 1982). Second, the use of explicit learning principles is a sound basis for effective interventions as a result of their demonstrated scientific validity (Kazdin & Wilson, 1978). Third, the economy of time and costs is quite good. Not surprisingly, then, the overall outcomes achieved with behavior therapy compare very favorably with those of other approaches (Smith et al., 1980). Behavior therapy usually achieves results in a short period of time because it is generally directed to specific symptoms, leading to faster relief of a client's distress and to lower costs.

As with other approaches, the range of effectiveness of behavior therapy is not unlimited, and it works better with certain kinds of problems than with others. Generally, the more pervasive and vaguely defined the client's problem, the less likely that behavior therapy will be useful. For example, it appears to be only rarely employed to treat Axis II personality disorders, where specific symptoms are rare. On the other hand, behavioral techniques are the backbone of modern approaches to treating sexual dysfunctions, as discussed in Chapter 11. Quantitative reviews of therapeutic outcomes confirms the expectation that behavior therapy has a particu-

lar place in the treatment of anxiety disorders, where the powerful Type A exposure techniques of behavior therapy can be brought to bear (Andrews & Harvey, 1981; Clum et al., 1993; Smith et al., 1980). Smith and colleagues' (1980) quantitative review in fact reveals the less expected finding of a relatively good outcome record with the psychoses. Thus, although behavior therapy is not a cure-all, it has earned in a relatively brief period a highly respected place among the available psychosocial treatment approaches.

COGNITIVE-BEHAVIOR THERAPY

As we have seen, early behavior therapists focused on observable behavior. They regarded the inner thoughts of their clients as not really part of the causal chain, and in their zeal to be objective they focused on the relationship between observable behaviors and observable reinforcing conditions. Thus they were often viewed as mechanistic technicians who simply manipulated their clients without considering them as people. Other behavior therapists such as Wolpe did not attend exclusively to overt behavior given that he did use systematic exposure to imagined frightening scenes as a therapeutic technique. Nevertheless, his focus was not on the role of cognitive processes per se in psychopathology, and clearly his therapeutic techniques did not try to manipulate cognitive processes directly.

Starting in the 1970s, however, a number of behavior therapists began to reappraise the importance of "private events"—thoughts, perceptions, evaluations, and self-statements—seeing them as processes that mediate the effects of objective stimulus conditions and thus help determine behavior and emotions (Borkovec, 1985; Mahoney & Arnkoff, 1978). If they help to determine behavior and emotions, including maladaptive behavior and emotions, then perhaps they can be changed so as to correct maladaptive behaviors and emotions.

Homme (1965), a student of Skinner, began this exodus from strict behaviorism in a paper arguing that these private events were behaviors that could be objectively analyzed. He proposed, as had Dollard and Miller (1950) earlier, that thoughts be regarded as emitted internal events comparable to emitted external behaviors, and that a technology be developed for modifying thoughts by using the same learning principles that were proving so effective in changing outer behavior. These internal, private events he called *coverants,* considering them to be operants of the mind. Following Homme's "coverant behaviorism," many investigators began to study the role of covert events, such as thoughts and assumptions, in psychopathology and began to develop methods to manipulate them.

As the term suggests, **cognitive-behavior therapy** stems from both cognitive psychology, with its emphasis on the effects of thoughts on behavior and on the study of the very nature of our cognitive processes, and behaviorism, with its rigorous methodology and performance-oriented focus. At the present time, there is no single set of techniques that define cognitive-behavior therapy: Numerous methods are being developed with varying emphases. Two main themes seem to characterize them all, however: (a) the conviction that cognitive processes influence affect, motivation, and behavior; and (b) the use of cognitive and behavior-change techniques in a pragmatic (hypothesis-testing) manner. That is, much of the content of the therapy sessions and homework assignments is analogous to experiments in which a therapist and a client apply learning principles to alter the client's cognitions, continuously evaluating the effects that the changes in cognitions have on subsequent thoughts, feelings, and overt behavior.

The exact nature of the relationship between emotion, cognition, and behavior, a venerable problem whose philosophical roots are in the distant past, is far from clear even today. Can it be, for example, that thoughts, by some accounts ephemeral and immaterial in nature, cause emotions and behavior? Any serious discussion of such an issue would take us far afield, but it is important to understand that the intellectual status of cognitive therapy fuels some controversy. Aaron Beck (Beck & Weishaar, 1989), an important leader in the field, acknowledges that disordered cognitions are not a cause of abnormal behavior or emotions, but rather are an intrinsic (yet alterable) element of such behavior and emotions. If the critical cognitive components can be changed, according to this view, then the behavior and maladaptive emotions will change. Because altering cognitions is central in these therapies, we consider them to be Type C approaches. In our discussion, we will focus on three approaches to cognitive-behavior therapy: the rational-emotive therapy of Albert Ellis, the stress-inoculation training of Donald Meichenbaum, and the cognitive-behavior therapies of Beck.

Rational-Emotive Therapy

One of the earliest behaviorally oriented cognitive therapies (developed considerably before Homme's influential paper) was the **rational-emotive therapy (RET)** of Albert Ellis (1958, 1973, 1975, 1989). RET attempts to change a client's basic maladaptive thought processes, on which maladaptive emotional responses and thus behavior are presumed to depend. In its infancy, RET was viewed skeptically by many professionals who doubted its effectiveness, but it has now become one of the most widely used therapeutic approaches (Ellis, 1989).

Ellis posited that a well-functioning individual behaves rationally and in tune with empirical reality. For Ellis, thoughts do have causal primacy in behavior, notably emotional behavior. Unfortunately, many of us have learned unrealistic beliefs and perfectionistic values that cause us to expect too much of ourselves, leading us to behave irrationally and then to feel unnecessarily that we are worthless failures. For example, a person may continually think, "I should be able to win everyone's love and approval" or "I should be thoroughly adequate and competent in everything I do." Such unrealistic assumptions and self-demands inevitably lead to ineffective and self-defeating behavior in the real world, which reacts accordingly, and then to the recognition of failure and the emotional response of self-devaluation. This emotional response is thus the necessary consequence not of "reality," but of an individual's faulty expectations, interpretations, and self-demands.

As a more specific example, consider a man who has an intense emotional reaction of despair with deep feelings of worthlessness, unlovability, and self-devaluation when he is jilted by his fiancée. With a stronger self-concept and a more realistic picture of both himself and his fiancée, as well as of their actual relationship, his emotional reaction might have been one of relief. It is his interpretation of the situation and of himself, rather than the objective situation, that has led to his intense emotional reaction.

Ellis (1970) believed that one or more of the following core irrational beliefs are at the root of most psychological maladjustment:

- One should be loved by everyone for everything one does.
- Certain acts are awful or wicked, and people who perform them should be severely punished.
- It is horrible when things are not the way we would like them to be.
- If something may be dangerous or fearsome, one should be terribly upset about it.
- It is better to avoid life problems if possible than to face them.

- One needs something stronger or more powerful than oneself to rely on.

- One should be thoroughly competent, intelligent, and achieving in all respects.

- Because something once affected one's life, it will indefinitely affect it.

- One must have certain and perfect self-control.

- Happiness can be achieved by inertia and inaction.

- We have virtually no control over our emotions and cannot help having certain feelings.

Irrationality can, however, be viewed in different ways. Arnkoff and Glass (1982) cautioned against an overly simplistic view of irrational behavior as the mere holding of irrational beliefs. Rather, they contended that irrationality may also involve faulty thought processes reflecting a "close-mindedness" that is more resistant to change than Ellis's view suggests. Moreover, it is also a mistake to think that people without any kind of psychopathology always think and behave in a rational manner. Instead, most of us have a variety of positive illusions that contribute to our not being anxious or depressed (e.g., Bandura, 1986; Taylor & Brown, 1988).

The task of rational-emotive therapy is to restructure an individual's belief system and self-evaluation, especially with respect to the irrational "shoulds," "oughts," and "musts" that are preventing a more positive sense of self-worth and a creative, emotionally satisfying, and fulfilling life. Several methods are used. One method is to dispute a person's false beliefs through rational confrontation. For example, an RET therapist dealing with the jilted young man previously discussed might ask, "Why should your fiancée's changing her mind mean that you are worthless?" Here the therapist would teach the client to identify and dispute the beliefs that were producing the negative emotional consequences.

A rational-emotive therapist also uses behaviorally oriented techniques, usually to help clients practice living in accord with their new beliefs and philosophy. Sometimes, for example, homework assignments are given to encourage clients to have new experiences and break negative chains of behavior. For example, clients might be instructed to reward themselves by an external reinforcer, such as a food treat, after working 15 minutes at disputing their beliefs. Another method of self-reinforcement might be through covert self-statements such as "You are doing a really good job."

Although the techniques vary dramatically, in some ways the philosophy underlying rational-emo-

tive therapy can be viewed as somewhat similar to that underlying humanistic therapy (to be discussed in a later section) because both take a clear stand on personal worth and human values. Rational-emotive therapy aims at increasing an individual's feelings of self-worth and clearing the way for self-actualization by removing the false beliefs that have been stumbling blocks to personal growth.

Stress-Inoculation Therapy

A second cognitive-behavioral approach to treatment is **stress-inoculation therapy**—a type of self-instructional training focused on altering self-statements an individual routinely makes in stress-producing situations. Here the approach is to restructure these statements so as to improve functioning under stressful conditions (Meichenbaum & Cameron, 1982). Like other cognitive-behavior therapies, stress-inoculation therapy assumes that a person's problems result from maladaptive beliefs that are leading to negative emotional states and maladaptive behavior, familiar elements in the causal chain cognitive theorists have posited.

Stress-inoculation therapy usually involves three stages. In the initial phase, cognitive preparation, client and therapist together explore the client's beliefs and attitudes about the problem situation and the self-statements to which they are leading. The focus is on how the person's self-talk can influence later performance and behavior. Together, the therapist and the client agree on new self-statements that would be more adaptive. Then the second phase of the stress inoculation, skill acquisition and rehearsal, is begun. In this phase, more adaptive self-statements are learned and practiced. For example, a person undergoing stress-inoculation therapy for coping with the "feeling of being overwhelmed" would rehearse self-statements such as,

- When fear comes, just pause.

- Keep the focus on the present; what is it you have to do?

- Label your fear from 0 to 10 and watch it change.

- You should expect your fear to rise.

- Don't try to eliminate fear totally; just keep it manageable.

- You can convince yourself to do it. You can reason fear away.

- It will be over shortly.

- It's not the worst thing that can happen.

- Just think about something else.

- Do something that will prevent you from thinking about fear.

- Describe what is around you. That way you won't think about worrying. (Meichenbaum, 1974, p. 16)

The third phase of stress-inoculation therapy, application and practice, involves applying the new coping strategies in actual situations. This practice is graduated in such a way that the client attempts easier situations first and only gradually enters more stressful situations as he or she feels confident of mastering them.

Beck's Cognitive-Behavior Therapies

Beck's cognitive-behavior approach was originally developed for the treatment of depression (Beck et al., 1979; Hollon & Beck, 1978) and was later extended to anxiety disorders, eating disorders and obesity, conduct disorder in children, personality disorders, and substance abuse (Beck, 1985; Beck & Emery, 1985; Beck et al., 1990, 1993; Hollon & Beck, 1994). One basic assumption underlying this approach is that problems like depression result from clients' illogical thinking about themselves, the world they live in, and the future.

In the initial phases clients are taught the connection between their patterns of thinking and their emotional responses. They are taught to identify their own automatic thoughts and to keep records of their thought content and their emotional reactions. By then learning, with the therapist's help, about the logical errors in their thinking, they learn to challenge the validity of these automatic thoughts. The logical errors in their thinking lead them to (a) selectively perceive the world as harmful while ignoring evidence to the contrary; (b) overgeneralize on the basis of limited examples—for example, seeing themselves as totally worthless because they were laid off at work; (c) magnify the significance of undesirable events—for example, seeing the job loss as the end of the world for them; and (d) engage in absolutistic thinking—for example, exaggerating the importance of someone's mildly critical comment and perceiving it as proof of their instant descent from goodness to worthlessness.

In Beck's cognitive-behavior therapy, clients are not persuaded to change their beliefs by debate and persuasion as in rational-emotive therapy; rather, they are encouraged to gather information about themselves through unbiased experiments that allow them to disconfirm their false beliefs. Together, a therapist and a client identify the client's beliefs and expectations and formulate them as hypotheses to be tested. They then design ways in which the client can check out these hypotheses in the real world. These disconfirmation experiments are planned to give the individual successful experiences, thereby interrupting the destructive sequence previously described. They are arranged according to difficulty, so that the least difficult (or risky) tasks will be accomplished successfully before the more difficult ones are attempted (see HIGHLIGHT 17.4).

In the treatment of depression, sometimes a client and a therapist schedule the client's daily activities on an hour-by-hour basis. Such activity scheduling is an important part of therapy with depressed individuals because by reducing such clients' inactivity, it interrupts their tendencies to ruminate about themselves. An important part of the arrangement is the scheduling of pleasurable events, because many depressed clients have lost the capacity for gaining pleasure from their own activities. Both the scheduled pleasurable activities and the rewarding experiences that derive from carrying out the behavioral experiments tend to increase an individual's satisfaction and positive mood.

Besides planning the behavioral assignments, evaluating the results in subsequent sessions, and planning further disconfirmation experiments, such therapy sessions for depression include several other cognitive emphases. For example, the client is encouraged to discover underlying dysfunctional assumptions or depressogenic schemas that may be leading to self-defeating tendencies. These generally become evident over the course of therapy as the client and the therapist examine the themes of the client's automatic thoughts. Because these depressogenic schemas are seen as creating the person's vulnerability to depression, this phase of treatment is considered essential in ensuring resistance to relapse when the client faces stressful life events in the future. That is, without changing the underlying cognitive vulnerability factors, the client may show short-term improvement but will still be subject to recurrent depression.

The general approach is similar for disorders other than depression, although the exact focus of the treatment, of course, differs if one is treating a client with panic disorder, generalized anxiety, bulimia, or substance abuse. For example, as was seen in Chapter 5, in panic disorder the focus is on identifying the automatic thoughts about feared bodily sensations and on teaching the client to correct logical errors in those automatic thoughts—basically to decatastrophize the experience of panic (Clark, 1988). For

Cognitive-Behavioral Therapy for a Case of Depression

Rush, Khatami, and Beck (1975) have reported several cases of successful treatment using cognitive clarification and behavioral assignments for clients with recurring chronic depression. The following case illustrates their approach:

A 53-year-old white male engineer's initial depressive episode 15 years ago necessitated several months' absence from work. Following medication and psychotherapy, he was asymptomatic up to four years ago. At that time, sadness, pessimism, loss of appetite and weight, and heavy use of alcohol returned.

Two years later, he was hospitalized for six weeks and treated with lithium and imipramine. He had three subsequent hospitalizations with adequate trials of several different tricyclics [antidepressant drugs]. During his last hospitalization, two weeks prior to initiating cognitive-behavioral therapy, he was treated with 10 sessions of ECT [electroconvulsive therapy]. His symptoms were only partially relieved with these various treatments.

When the client started cognitive-behavioral therapy, he showed moderate psychomotor retardation. He was anxious, sad, tearful, and pessimistic. He was self-depreciating and self-reproachful without any interest in life. He reported decreased appetite, early morning awakening, lack of sexual interest, and worries about his physical health. Initially he was treated with weekly sessions for 3 months, then biweekly for 2 months. Treatment, terminated after 5 months, consisted of 20 sessions. He was evaluated 12 months after the conclusion of therapy.

Therapist and client set an initial goal of his becoming physically active (i.e., doing more things no matter how small or trivial). The client and his wife kept a separate list of his activities. The list included raking leaves, having dinner, and assisting his wife in apartment sales, etc. His cognitive distortions were identified by comparing his assessment of each activity with that of his wife. Alternative ways of interpreting his experiences were then considered.

In comparing his wife's resume of his past experiences, he became aware that he had (1) undervalued his past by failing to mention many previous accomplishments, (2) regarded himself as far more responsible for his "failures" than she did, and (3) concluded that he was worthless since he had not succeeded in attaining certain goals in the past. When the two accounts were contrasted he could discern many of his cognitive distortions. In subsequent sessions, his wife continued to serve as an "objectifier." In midtherapy, the client compiled a list of new attitudes that he had acquired since initiating therapy.

These included:

(1) I am starting at a lower level of functioning at my job, but it will improve if I persist.
(2) I know that once I get going in the morning, everything will run all right for the rest of the day.
(3) I can't achieve everything at once.
(4) I have my periods of ups and downs, but in the long run I feel better.
(5) My expectations from my job and life should be scaled down to a realistic level.
(6) Giving in to avoidance never helps and only leads to further avoidance.

He was instructed to reread this list daily for several weeks even though he already knew the content. The log was continued, and subsequent assumptions reflected in the log were compared to the assumptions listed above.

As the client became gradually less depressed, he returned to his job for the first time in 2 years. He undertook new activities (e.g., camping, going out of town) as he continued his log. (pp. 400–401)

The focus of the therapy was on encouraging the client to restructure his thought content—to reduce the negative self-judgments and to evaluate his actual achievements more realistically. Making and reviewing the list of new attitudes gave the client more perspective on his life situation, which resulted in an improved mood, less self-blame, and more willingness to risk alternative behavior.

The negative emotional impact of situations and events such as rejection and isolation can lead to "catastrophizing," which may increase performance deficits. Cognitive therapy is "decatastrophizing."

generalized anxiety disorder, the client is taught to correct the tendencies to overestimate the presence and likelihood of danger and to underestimate his or her ability to cope in a variety of situations (Beck & Emery, 1985). In bulimia, the cognitive approach proposes that the person has overvalued ideas about body weight and shape, which are often fueled by low self-esteem and fears of being unattractive. These beliefs are thought to lead to a tendency to diet excessively, which in turn increases the probability of losing control by bingeing and purging. The cognitive part of the treatment involves getting these clients to identify and change their maladaptive beliefs regarding weight and body image, as well as about what foods are "safe" or "dangerous" (Agras, 1993; Fairburn et al., 1993).

Evaluation of Cognitive-Behavior Therapies

In spite of the widespread attention and popularity that Ellis's rational-emotive therapy has enjoyed, surprisingly little research has been conducted to document its efficacy—especially for carefully diagnosed clinical populations (Hollon & Beck, 1986). It has been shown to be useful in reducing test anxiety and speech anxiety, but it is inferior to exposure-based therapies in the treatment of more severe anxiety disorders such as agoraphobia and social phobia (Haaga & Davison, 1989, 1992). It hasn't yet been compared with cognitive or interpersonal therapy for the treatment of depression (discussed in Chapter 6), so we don't know whether it is as effective as these two proven treatments. In general, it may be most useful in helping generally healthy people to cope better with everyday stress and perhaps prevent them from developing full-blown anxiety or depressive disorders (Haaga & Davison, 1989, 1992).

Stress-inoculation therapy has been successfully used with a number of clinical problems, especially anger (Novaco, 1977, 1979), pain (Turk, Meichenbaum, & Genest, 1983; see Masters et al., 1986, for a review), Type A behavior (Jenni & Wollersheim, 1979), and mild forms of anxiety (Meichenbaum, 1975). (See also Denicola & Sandler, 1980; Holcomb, 1979; Klepac et al., 1981.) This approach is particularly suited to increasing the adaptive capabilities of individuals who have shown a vulnerability to developing problems in certain stressful situations. In addition to its value as a therapeutic technique for identified problems, stress-inoculation therapy may be a useful method for preventing behavior disorders. Although the preventive value of this and other cognitive-behavioral therapy procedures has not been demonstrated by empirical study, many believe that the incidence of maladjustment might be reduced if more individuals' general coping skills were improved (Meichenbaum & Jaremko, 1983).

A review of research evaluating Beck's type of cognitive-behavioral treatment methods suggests that these approaches to intervention are extremely effective in alleviating many different types of disorders (see Hollon & Beck, 1994, for a comprehensive review). In the case of depression, considerable evidence, reviewed in Chapter 6, suggests that cognitive-behavior therapy is at least comparable to drug treatment in all but perhaps the most severe cases (e.g., psychotic depression). Moreover, it has superior long-term advantages; several studies have shown that relapse in the one to two years of posttreatment was less likely if a client had been treated with cognitive therapy, whether or not there was also treatment with antidepressant drugs (Evans et al., 1992; Simons et al., 1986).

Although clinical depression was the first disorder for which there was good documented efficacy, many empirical studies in the past decade have compared cognitive-behavioral methods with other treatment approaches for a variety of other clinical disorders. The most dramatic recent results have been in the treatment of panic disorder and generalized anxiety disorder, but cognitive-behavior therapy is also now seen as the treatment of choice for bulimia and conduct disorder in children (Hollon & Beck, 1994). There are also promising results in the treatment of substance abuse (Beck et al., 1993) and of certain personality disorders (Beck et al., 1990; Linehan, 1993).

The combined use of cognitive and behavior therapy approaches is growing rapidly. There remains disagreement about whether the effects of cognitive-behavioral treatments are actually mediated by cognitive change, as the cognitive theorists propose (Hollon & Beck, 1994; Hollon, DeRubeis, & Evans, 1987). But at least for depression and panic disorder it does appear that cognitive change is the best predictor of long-term outcome, as would be predicted by cognitive theory (Clark et al., 1993; Hollon, Evans, & DeRubeis, 1990). We anticipate that in the next few years more attention will be devoted to these important questions about how cognitive-behavior therapy works. Indeed, these questions have assumed increased importance in light of the striking and widely documented success of this mode of therapy.

HUMANISTIC-EXPERIENTIAL THERAPIES

The **humanistic-experiential therapies** emerged as significant treatment approaches during the post–World War II era. To a large extent, they developed in reaction to the psychodynamic and behavioral perspectives, which many feel do not accurately take into account either the existential problems or the full potentialities of human beings. In a society dominated by self-interest, mechanization, computerization, mass deception, and "mindless" bureaucracy, proponents of the humanistic-experiential therapies see psychopathology as stemming in many cases from problems of alienation, depersonalization, loneliness, and a failure to find meaning and genuine fulfillment. Problems of this sort, it is held, are not likely to be solved either by delving into forgotten memories or by correcting specific responses.

The humanistic-experiential therapies follow some variant of the general humanistic and existential perspectives outlined in Chapter 3. They are based on the assumption that we have both the freedom and the responsibility to control our own behavior—that we can reflect on our problems, make choices, and take positive action. Whereas some behavior therapists see themselves as "behavior engineers," responsible for changing specific behaviors they deem problematic by appropriate modifications in a person's environment, humanistic-experiential therapists feel that a client must take most of the responsibility for the direction and success of therapy, with a therapist merely serving as counselor, guide, and facilitator. These therapies may be carried out with individual clients or with groups of clients (see HIGHLIGHT 17.5). Although differing among themselves in details, the central focus of humanistic-experiential therapies is always that of expanding

a client's "awareness"; accordingly, we consider them Type C (cognition-oriented) approaches.

Client-Centered Therapy

The **client-centered (person-centered) therapy** of Carl Rogers (1951, 1961, 1966) actually antedated the strong movement toward behavior therapy that began in the 1950s and the "humanistic revolution" of the 1960s. It was developed in the 1940s as a truly innovative alternative to psychoanalysis, the only major psychotherapy of the time.

Rogers rejected both Freud's view of the primacy of irrational instinct and of the therapist's role as prober, interpreter, and director of the therapeutic process. Instead, believing in the natural power of an organism to heal itself, he saw psychotherapy as a process of removing the constraints and hobbling restrictions that often prevent this process from operating. These constraints, he believed, grow out of unrealistic demands that people tend to place on themselves when they believe, as a condition of self-worth, that they should not have certain kinds of feelings, such as hostility. By denying that they do in fact have such feelings, they become unaware of their actual "gut" reactions. As they lose touch with their own genuine experience, the result is lowered integration, impaired personal relationships, and various forms of maladjustment.

The primary objective of Rogerian therapy is to resolve this incongruence—to help clients become able to accept and be themselves. To this end, client-centered therapists establish a psychological climate in which clients can feel unconditionally accepted, understood, and valued as people. In this climate they can begin to feel free for perhaps the first time to explore their real feelings and thoughts and to accept hates and angers and "ugly feelings" as parts of themselves. As their self-concept becomes more congruent with their actual experiencing, they become more self-accepting and more open to new experience and new perspectives; in short, they become better-integrated people.

In client-centered therapy, also called *nondirective therapy,* it is not the therapist's task to direct the course of therapy. Thus a therapist does not give answers or interpret what a client says or probe for unconscious conflicts or even steer the client onto certain topics. Rather he or she simply listens attentively and acceptingly to what the client wants to talk about, interrupting only to restate in other words what the client is saying. Such restatements, without any judgment or interpretation by the therapist, help the client clarify further the feelings and ideas that he or she is exploring—really to look at

HIGHLIGHT   17.5

Group Therapy

The treatment of clients in groups first received impetus in the military during World War II, when psychotherapists were in short supply. Group therapy was found to be effective in dealing with a variety of problems, and it rapidly became an important therapeutic approach in civilian life. In fact, all the major systematic approaches to psychotherapy that we have discussed—psychoanalysis, behavior therapy, and so on—have been applied in group as well as individual settings.

Group therapy has traditionally involved a relatively small group of clients in a clinic or hospital setting, using a variety of procedures depending on the age, needs, and potentialities of the clients and the orientation of the therapists. The degree of structure and of client participation in the group process varies in different types of groups. Most often, groups are informal, and many follow the format of en-counter groups. Occasionally, however, more or less formal lectures and visual materials are presented to clients as a group. For example, a group of alcoholic clients may be shown a film depicting the detrimental effects of excessive drinking on the human body, with a group discussion afterward. Although this approach by itself has not proven effective in combating alcoholism, it is often a useful adjunct to other forms of group therapy.

An interesting form of group therapy is psychodrama, based on role-playing techniques. A client, assisted by staff members or other clients, is encouraged to act out problem situations in a theater-like setting. This technique frees the individual to express anxieties and hostilities or relive traumatic experiences in a situation that simulates real life but is more sheltered. The goal is to help the client achieve emotional catharsis, increased un-derstanding, and improved interpersonal competencies. This form of therapy, developed initially by Moreno (1959), has proved beneficial for the clients who make up the "audience" as well as for those who participate on the "stage" (Sundberg & Tyler, 1962; Yablonsky, 1975).

Group therapy may also be almost completely unstructured, as in activity groups where children with emotional problems are allowed to act out their aggressions in the safety and control of the group setting.

In a recent review of group therapy research, Bednar and Kaul (1994) concluded that the field is in need of more penetrating observations regarding the processes central to group treatment, which might in turn lead to more productive conceptualizations about what, uniquely, group therapies might offer in the domain of mental health treatment.

them and acknowledge them. The following excerpt from a counselor's second interview with a young woman will serve to illustrate these techniques of reflection and clarification:

Alice: I was thinking about this business of standards. I somehow developed a sort of a knack, I guess, of—well—habit—of trying to make people feel at ease around me, or to make things go along smoothly. . . .

Counselor: In other words, what you did was always in the direction of trying to keep things smooth and to make other people feel better and to smooth the situation.

Alice: Yes. I think that's what it was. Now the reason why I did it probably was—I mean, not that I was a good little Samaritan going around making other people happy, but that was probably the role that felt easiest for me to play. I'd been doing it around home so much. I just didn't stand up for my own convictions, until I don't know whether I have any convictions to stand up for.

Counselor: You feel that for a long time you've been playing the role of kind of smoothing out the frictions or differences or what not.

Alice: M-hm.

Counselor: Rather than having any opinion or reaction of your own in the situation. Is that it?

Alice: That's it. Or that I haven't been really honestly being myself, or actually knowing what my real self is, and that I've been just playing a sort of a false role. Whatever role no one else was playing, and that needed to be played at the time, I'd try to fill it in. (Rogers, 1951, pp. 152–53)

In a survey of trends in psychotherapy and counseling, Rogers was rated one of the most influential psychotherapists among clinical practitioners (Smith, 1982). In addition to his influence in clinical settings, Rogers was a pioneer in attempting to carry out empirical research on psychotherapy. Using recordings of therapy sessions, he was later able to make objective analyses of what was said, of the client-counselor relationships, and of the ongoing processes in these therapy sessions. He was also able to compare a client's behavior and attitudes at different stages of therapy. These comparisons revealed a typical sequence: Early sessions were dominated by negative feelings and discouragement. Then, after a time, tentative statements of hope and greater self-acceptance began to appear. Eventually, positive feelings, a reaching out toward others, greater self-confidence, and interest in future plans appeared. This characteristic sequence gave support to Rogers's hypothesis that, once freed to do so, individuals have the capacity to lead themselves to psychological health.

Pure client-centered psychotherapy, as originally practiced, is rarely used today. It did, however, open the way for a variety of humanistically oriented therapies in which the focus is a client's present conscious problems and in which it is assumed that the client is the primary actor in the curative process, with the therapist essentially being a facilitator. The newer humanistic therapies thus accept Rogers's concept of an active self, capable of sound value choices; they also emphasize the importance of a high degree of empathy, warmth, and unconditional positive regard from the therapist. They differ from original client-centered therapy in having found various shortcuts by which the therapist, going beyond simple reflection and clarification, can hasten and help focus the client's search for wholeness. Such a therapist might, for example, directly confront a client's deceitful mode of self-presentation. It is still the client's search and the client's insights that are seen as central in therapy, however.

Existential Therapy

Several important concepts underlie **existential psychotherapy.** The existentialist perspective, like the client-centered, emphasizes the importance of the human situation *as perceived by an individual.* The focus is thus on the person's own phenomenologic experience rather than on any notion of objective reality, being in this respect a forerunner of so-called postmodern thought. Existentialists are

deeply concerned about the predicament of humankind, the breakdown of traditional faith, the alienation and depersonalization of individuals in contemporary society, and the lack of meaning in people's lives. They see people, however, as having a high degree of freedom and thus as capable both of doing something about their predicament and of being responsible for doing the best they can. The unique ability of human beings to be aware of their mortality and to reflect on and question their existence confronts them with the responsibility for *being*—for deciding what kind of person to become within the constraint of a single lifetime, for establishing their own values, and for actualizing their potentialities.

Existential therapists do not follow any rigidly prescribed procedures, but emphasize the uniqueness of each individual and his or her "way of being in the world." They stress the importance of being aware of one's own existence—challenging an individual directly with questions concerning the meaning and purpose of existence—and of the therapeutic encounter—the complex relationship established between two interacting human beings in the therapeutic situation as they both try to be open and "authentic." In contrast to both psychoanalysis and behavior therapy, existential therapy calls for therapists to share themselves—their feelings, their values, and their own existence.

Besides being authentic themselves, it is the task of existential therapists to keep a client responding authentically to the inescapable intersubjectivity of relations with others (Havens, 1974; May, 1969). For example, if a client says, "I hate you just like I hated my father," a therapist might respond by saying, "I am not your father, I am me, and you have to deal with me as Dr. S., not as your father." The focus is on the here and now—on what a person is choosing to do, and therefore to be, at this moment. This sense of immediacy, of the urgency of experience, is the touchstone of existential therapy and sets the stage for the individual to clarify and choose between alternative ways of being.

With what types of clients and which clinical problems does existential therapy work best? Like classical psychoanalytic therapy, existential psychotherapy is directed primarily toward intelligent and verbal people who appear to be having existential crises. The existential treatment approach is believed to work best with individuals who have anxiety-based disorders or personality disorders rather than psychoses. The following case illustrates the type of problem situation that would lend itself to treatment in the existential framework:

A 42-year-old business executive seeks therapy because he feels that life has lost its meaning—he no longer feels that family matters are important to him (his wife is busy starting her career and his only child recently got married and moved to Alaska). Additionally, his work, at which he has had extraordinary success—earning him both financial security and respect—no longer holds meaning for him. He views his days as "wasted and worthless"—he feels both "bored and panicked"—and he goes through the motions of the business day feeling "numb," as though he isn't even there. At times, he feels fearful and overwhelmed with a sense of dread that this is all that life has left for him.

Gestalt Therapy

The term *gestalt* means "whole," and **gestalt therapy** emphasizes the unity of mind and body—placing strong emphasis on the need to integrate thought, feeling, and action. Gestalt therapy was developed by Frederick (Fritz) Perls (1967, 1969) as a means of teaching clients to recognize the bodily processes and emotions they had been blocking off from awareness. As with the client-centered and existential approaches, the main goal of gestalt therapy is to increase an individual's self-awareness and self-acceptance.

Although gestalt therapy is commonly used in a group setting, the emphasis is on one person at a time with whom a therapist works intensively, attempting to help identify aspects of the individual's self or world that are not being acknowledged in awareness. The individual may be asked to act out fantasies concerning feelings and conflicts, or to "be" one part of a conflict while sitting in one chair and then switch chairs to take the part of the "adversary." Often the therapist or other group members will ask questions like, "What are you aware of in your body now?" or "What does it feel like in your gut when you think of that?"

In Perls's approach to therapy, a good deal of emphasis is also placed on dreams, but with an emphasis very different from that of classical psychoanalysis. In gestalt theory, every element of a dream, including seemingly inconsequential, impersonal objects, are considered to be representations of unacknowledged aspects of the dreamer's self. The therapist urges the client to suspend normal critical judgment and to "be" the object in the dream, reporting then on the experience. For example, Perls

asked a middle-aged woman who had dreamed of a lake to "be" the lake, with the following result:

"I'm a lake . . . I'm drying up, and disappearing, soaking into the earth . . . (with a touch of surprise) dying. . . . But when I soak into the earth, I become a part of the earth—so maybe I water the surrounding area, so . . . even in the lake, even in my bed, flowers can grow (sighs). . . . New life can grow . . . from me (cries). . . . (sadly, but with conviction) I can paint—I can create—I can create beauty. I can no longer reproduce. . . . but I . . . I'm . . . I . . . keep wanting to say I'm food . . . I . . . as water becomes . . . I water the earth, and give life-growing things, the water—they need both the earth and water, and the . . . and the air and the sun, but as the water from the lake, I can play a part in something, and producing—feeding." (Perls, 1969, pp. 81–82)

In gestalt therapy sessions, the focus is on the more obvious elements of a person's behavior. Such sessions are often called "gestalt awareness training" because the therapeutic results of the experience stem from the process of becoming more aware of one's total self and environment. The technique of working through unresolved conflicts is called "taking care of unfinished business." We all go through life, according to Perls, with unfinished or unresolved traumas and conflicts. We carry the excess baggage of these unfinished situations into new relationships and tend to reenact them in our relations with other people. If we are able to complete our past unfinished business, we then have less psychological tension to cope with and can be more realistically aware of ourselves and our world.

Expressing themselves in front of the group, perhaps taking the part of first one and then another fragment of a scene, and denied the use of their usual techniques for avoiding self-awareness, clients are brought to an "impasse," at which point they must confront their feelings and conflicts. According to Perls, "In the safe emergency of the therapeutic situation, the neurotic discovers that the world does not fall to pieces if he or she gets angry, sexy, joyous, mournful" (1967, p. 331). Thus clients find that they can, after all, get beyond impasses on their own.

Evaluation of the Humanistic-Experiential Therapies

The humanistic-experiential therapies have been criticized for their lack of highly systematized models of human behavior and its specific aberrations, their lack of agreed-upon therapeutic procedures, and their vagueness about what is supposed to happen between client and therapist. These very features, however, are seen by many proponents of this general approach as contributing to its strength and vitality. Systematized theories can reduce individuals to abstractions, which can diminish their perceived worth and deny their uniqueness. Because people are so different, we should expect that different techniques are appropriate for different cases. Rigorous research on the outcomes produced by the humanistic-existential therapies is rare, but some has been carried out on the gestalt variety. This technique has a respectable, though unspectacular, record (Smith et al., 1980).

In any event, many of the humanistic-experiential concepts—the uniqueness of each individual, the satisfaction that comes from developing and using one's potentials, the importance of the search for meaning and fulfillment, and the human power for choice and self-direction—have had a major impact on our contemporary views of both human nature and psychotherapy.

THERAPY FOR INTERPERSONAL RELATIONSHIPS

In Chapter 3, we noted the interpersonal perspective's emphasis on the role of faulty communications, interactions, and relationships in maladaptive behavior. This viewpoint has had an important impact on approaches to therapy—particularly, as we have seen, on contemporary psychodynamic therapy (e.g., Horowitz, Rosenberg, & Bartholomew, 1993; Strupp, 1993) but also in the behavioral, humanistic, and existential therapies. For example, in behavior and cognitive-behavior therapy we have seen a notable rise in concern with the client-therapist relationship and a growing emphasis on modifying social reinforcements that may be maintaining maladaptive responses; in humanistic and existential therapies we have seen the focus on such problems as lack of acceptance, relatedness, and love in a person's life. Important new therapies for the Axis II personality disorders, such as those of Benjamin (1993) and of Linehan (1993), strongly emphasize the client-therapist interpersonal relationship as a dominant vehicle for bringing about constructive change.

Although the interpersonal perspective is increasingly seen as essential to fully understanding many types of "individual" disorder, many problems brought to practitioners are explicitly relationship problems. That is, the presenting complaint is not so much one of dissatisfaction with self or one's own behavior as one of inability to achieve satisfactory accords with others. A common example is couples' or marital distress. The maladaptive behavior is in these instances shared between the members of the relationship; it is, to use the contemporary term, "systemic" (Gurman, Kniskern, & Pinsof, 1986). Such problems require therapeutic techniques that focus on relationships as much as or more than on individuals. As was seen in Chapter 11, many problems presenting as individual sexual dysfunctions turn out to be systemic in character. In this section, we will explore the growing fields of couples and family therapy as examples of this type of multiple-client intervention. In general, these therapies, when placed in the context of helping individuals to change, focus on altering the reactions of the interpersonal environment to the behavior of each involved person. To this extent, they may be considered chiefly Type E approaches.

It is important to note that couples and family therapies can be and are conducted from any of the perspectives discussed in this chapter and in Chapter 3 (see Alexander, Holtzworth-Munroe, & Jameson's [1994] review for examples). Thus behavioral marital therapy, often utilizing a contracting approach, is one of several widely available variations on the theme.

Couples Counseling (Marital Therapy)

The large numbers of couples seeking assistance with relationship problems have made couples counseling a growing field of therapy. Typically the partners are seen together, and therapy focuses on clarifying and improving their interactions and relationships. Therapy for only one of the partners has proved less effective for resolving such problems (Gurman & Kniskern, 1978), although it is quite routine at the start of couples therapy for each partner secretly to harbor the wish that only the other will have to do the changing (e.g., Cordova & Jacobson, 1993). It is almost always necessary, however, that both partners alter their reactions to the other.

Couples counseling, or **marital therapy,** includes a wide range of concepts and procedures.

Treatment of the entire family may be desirable where abnormal behavior patterns in individuals are maintained by family dynamics.

Most therapists emphasize mutual need gratification, social role expectations, communication patterns, and similar interpersonal factors. Not surprisingly, happily married couples tend to differ from unhappily married couples in that they remain good friends, talk more to each other, keep channels of communication open, make more use of nonverbal communication, and show more sensitivity to each other's feelings and needs. For example, in a study comparing distressed versus nondistressed couples, Margolin and Wampold (1981) found that nondistressed couples showed more problem-solving behavior than distressed couples, a result found often in studies of this sort. The extremely common scenario, "He never talks to me, he withdraws" versus "All she ever does is bitch and complain, so who needs to talk," is one whose resolution obviously calls for considerable problem-solving skill, not to mention a degree of maturity and patience in employing it.

Faulty role expectations often play havoc with marital adjustment. For example, Paul (1971) cited the case of a couple who came for marital therapy when the 39-year-old husband was about to divorce his wife to marry a much younger woman. During therapy, he broke into sobs of grief as he recalled the death of his Aunt Anna, who had always accepted him as he was and created an atmosphere of peace and contentment. In reviewing this incident, the husband realized that his girlfriend represented his lifelong search for another Aunt Anna. This led to a reconciliation with his wife, who was now more understanding of his needs, feelings, and role expectations and thus altered her behavior toward her husband accordingly.

One of the difficulties in couples therapy is the intense emotional involvement of the partners, which makes it difficult for them to perceive and accept the realities of their relationship. Often wives can see clearly what is "wrong" with their husbands but not what attitudes and behaviors of their own are contributing to the relationship, while husbands tend to have remarkable "insight" into their wives' flaws but not their own. To help correct this problem, videotape recordings have been used increasingly to recapture crucial moments of intense interaction between the partners. By watching playbacks of these tapes after immediate tensions have diminished, the partners can gain a fuller awareness of the nature of their interactions. Thus a husband may realize for the first time that he tries to dominate rather than listen to his wife and consider her needs and expectations, or a wife may realize that she is continually undermining her husband's feelings of worth and esteem. The following statement was made by a young wife after viewing a videotape playback of the couple's first therapy session:

"See! There it is—loud and clear! As usual you didn't let me express my feelings or opinions, you just interrupted me with your own. You're always telling me what I think without asking me what I think. And I can see what I have been doing in response—withdrawing into silence. I feel like, what's the use of talking." In achieving this shared insight about a dominant pattern in their interactions, the couple was able to work out a much more satisfactory marital relationship within a few months.

Other relatively new and innovative approaches to couples therapy include training the partners to use Rogerian nondirective techniques in listening to each other and helping each other clarify and verbalize their feelings and reactions. A mutual readiness to really listen and try to understand what the other is experiencing—and an acceptance of whatever comes out in this process—can be both therapeutic for the individuals and productive of a more open and honest relationship in the future.

Behavioral therapy has also been used to bring about desired changes in marital relationships. The partners, for example, may be taught to reinforce instances of desired behavior while withdrawing reinforcement for undesired behavior. In a study comparing behavioral with insight-oriented psychodynamic marital therapy, neither proved superior to the other, but both significantly outperformed a waiting-list control condition (Snyder & Wills, 1989).

How effective in general are couples therapies at resolving relationship crises and promoting more effective marriages or intimate partnerships? One study involved a five-year follow-up of 320 former marital therapy clients and compared their divorce rates with those of the general population (Cookerly, 1980). In cases in which both partners underwent therapy together, 56.4 percent had remained married for the five-year period; in cases in which other types of therapy were used, 29 percent had remained married. All forms of therapy were associated with significantly better results in resolving marital crises and keeping marriages together than was the use of no therapy at all. This conclusion is also supported in Gurman and colleagues' (1986) more recent review of numerous outcome studies. Finally, couples therapy has been successfully used as an adjunct in the treatment of individual problems, such as depression, phobias, and alcohol abuse (Alexander et al., 1994; Jacobson, Holtzworth-Munroe, & Schmaling, 1989; Shadish et al., 1993).

Of course, a motivational factor in outcome assessments of this sort makes interpretation somewhat difficult. People strongly motivated to stay in their relationships are more likely to give couples therapy a serious try than their less motivated counterparts. Such motivation may itself, irrespective of therapy, make for partnership longevity or, perhaps, tolerance of partner abnormality. On the other hand, as we have seen, strong motivation is a key element in the likely success of any psychological therapy, so the research on outcomes of couples therapy has a certain face validity even acknowledging some unclarity about the role of motivational variations.

Family Therapy

Therapy for a family group overlaps with couples and marital therapy but has somewhat different roots. Whereas marital therapy developed in response to the large number of clients who came for assistance with couples' problems, family therapy began with the finding that many people who had shown marked improvement in individual therapy—often in institutional settings—had a relapse on their return home. It soon became apparent that many of these people came from disturbed family settings that required modification if they were to maintain their gains. A pioneer in the field of family therapy has described the problem as follows:

> Psychopathology in the individual is a product of the way he deals with his intimate relations, the way they deal with him, and the way other family members involve him in their relations with each other. Further, the appearance of symptomatic behavior in an individual is necessary for the continued function of a particular family system. Therefore, changes in the individual can occur only if the family system changes. . . . (Haley, 1962, p. 70)

This viewpoint led to an important concept in the field of psychotherapy, namely, that the problem or disorder shown by an "identified client" is often only a symptom of a larger family problem. A careful study of the family of a disturbed child, for example, may reveal that the child is merely reflecting the pathology of the family unit. As a result, most family therapists share the view that the family—not simply the designated "client"—must be directly involved in therapy if lasting improvement is to be achieved. This is a conclusion also implied in our pathogenic loop model described earlier. Its application is increasingly seen in attempts to understand relapse after recovery from even severe disorder, as in the work on expressed emotion (EE) in mood disorders and schizophrenia (see Chapters 6 and 12).

Perhaps the most widely used approach to family therapy is the "conjoint family therapy" of Satir (1967). Her emphasis is on improving faulty communications, interactions, and relationships among family members and on fostering a family system that better meets the needs of each member. The following example shows Satir's emphasis on the problem of faulty communication:

> Husband: She never comes up to me and kisses me. I am always the one to make the overtures.
>
> Therapist: Is this the way you see yourself behaving with your husband?
>
> Wife: Yes, I would say he is the demonstrative one. I didn't know he wanted me to make the overtures.
>
> Th: Have you told your wife that you would like this from her—more open demonstration of affection?
>
> H: Well, no you'd think she'd know.
>
> W: No, how would I know? You always said you didn't like aggressive women.
>
> H: I don't, I don't like dominating women.
>
> W: Well, I thought you meant women who make the overtures. How am I to know what you want?
>
> Th: You'd have a better idea if he had been able to tell you. (Satir, 1967, pp. 72–73)

Another encouraging approach to resolving family disturbances is called **structural family therapy** (Minuchin, 1974). This approach, based on "systems theory," assumes that a family system itself is more influential than individual personality or intrapsychic conflicts in producing abnormal behavior. It assumes that the family system has contributed to the characteristic behaviors that individual family members have developed; if the family context changes, then the individual members will have altered experiences in the family and will behave differently in accordance with the changed requirements of the new family context. Thus an important goal of structural family therapy is to change the organization of the family in such a way that the family members will behave more positively and supportively toward each other.

Structural family therapy is focused on present interactions and requires an active but not directive approach on the part of a therapist. Initially, the therapist gathers information about the family—a "structural map" of the typical family interaction patterns—by acting like one of the family and participating in the family interactions as an insider. In this way, the therapist discovers whether the family system has rigid or flexible boundaries, who dominates

Both partners typically participate in couples counseling or marital therapy.

the power structure, who gets blamed when things go wrong, and so on.

Armed with this understanding, the therapist then uses himself or herself as a change medium for altering the interaction among the members. For example, Aponte and Hoffman (1973) reported the successful use of structural family therapy in treating an anorexic 14-year-old girl:

> Analyzing the communications in the family, the therapists saw a competitive struggle for the father's attention and observed that the girl, Laura, was able to succeed in this competition and get "cuddly" attention from her father by not eating. To bring the hidden dynamics out into the open, they worked at getting the family members to express their desires more directly—in words instead of through cryptic behavioral messages. In time, Laura became much more able to verbalize her wishes for affection and gave up the unacceptable and dangerous method of not eating.

Structural family therapy has also been used successfully in the treatment of bulimia (Schwartz, Barrett, & Saba, 1983), childhood psychosomatic disorders (Minuchin et al., 1975), and narcotic addiction (Stanton & Todd, 1976).

As with couples problems, maladaptive family relationships have also been successfully overcome by behaviorally oriented therapies. With this type of therapy, Huff (1969) has suggested that the therapist's task is to reduce the aversive value of the family for the identified client as well as that of the client for other family members. "The therapist does this by actively manipulating the relationship between members so that the relationship changes to a more positively reinforcing and reciprocal one" (p. 26).

After reviewing family therapy approaches, Gurman and Kniskern (1978) concluded that structural family therapy had had more impressive results than most other experientially and analytically oriented approaches they had reviewed. By the time of their subsequent review eight years later (Gurman et al., 1986), the conclusion had shifted somewhat to favor behavioral intervention. A recent quantitative review by Shadish and colleagues (1993) supports the latter conclusion.

THE INTEGRATION OF THERAPY APPROACHES

Although an integration of psychoanalysis and learning theory was attempted as early as 1950 by Dollard and Miller in their *Personality and Psychotherapy,* the two treatment approaches diverged significantly in the 1960s and 1970s as the learning-based behavioral therapies began to assert themselves. Recently, a great deal has been written about the possibility of gaining a rapprochement between behavior therapy and other schools of therapy, particularly psychodynamic therapy (Arkowitz & Messer, 1984; Goldfried, Greenberg, & Marmar, 1990; Marmor & Woods, 1980; Norcross & Goldfried, 1992; Wachtel, 1977, 1982). At first, this trend may seem surprising, given the generally competitive atmosphere and the critical struggles that have traditionally existed between psychoanalysts and behavior therapists. Early behaviorists were adamant in their criticism of psychoanalysis as inefficient and mystical. The analysts reacted with strong counterarguments, partly in their own defense but also in keeping with their belief that behavioral therapies were superficial and treated only symptoms, while psychoanalytic treatments sought "deeper" and more permanent cures.

Over the years, however, behavioral and psychoanalytic proponents have had time to become accustomed (or perhaps "desensitized") to each other's criticisms. With the wide dissemination and practice of behavioral methods, it has become apparent to

some psychodynamically oriented therapists that behavioral methods are quite effective in the treatment of many disorders. Similarly, many behaviorally oriented therapists have concluded that it is not simply the application of a *technique* that brings about change in a client. They acknowledge that "relationship" factors are exceedingly important even when rigorous behavior modification procedures are being used (Lazarus, 1981, 1985). In addition, research comparing both treatment methods has generally shown that neither approach has been demonstrated invariably to be superior to the other (Sloane et al., 1975), although, overall, there seems to be a small but consistent advantage for behavioral and cognitive-behavioral methods (Dobson, 1989; Engels et al., 1993; Lambert & Bergin, 1994; Miller & Berman, 1983; Shadish et al., 1993; Smith et al., 1980).

Kendall (1982b) has concisely summarized the reasons for the current interest in integrating behavior therapy with other methods. He noted that (a) some behaviorists have concluded that the human organism is multifaceted and that focusing only on "behavior" is not sufficient as a treatment goal; (b) the "less than perfect" success of available therapy methods justifies combining the most successful treatment strategies from all approaches; (c) integrating diverse therapies might inspire a new enthusiasm and promote novel applications of varied treatment methods and perhaps promote new formulations of old problems; and (d) integrating diverse therapy schools would require members of a given school to begin to question the assumptions underlying their treatment approaches and would promote a broad reappraisal from different perspectives. A similar argument has been made more recently by Robins and Hayes (1993) in regard to the need for cognitive therapies to remain open to contributions from other approaches. Our own "loop" model is, of course, completely in accord with this perspective.

According to Kendall, however, inherent problems face the integrationist position. First, no common language unites the various therapy schools. Second, it is much easier for a trainee to learn a single therapeutic approach than to learn elements of various approaches. Finally, basic conceptual differences exist that would preclude a fully satisfactory merger between behavior therapy and psychodynamic therapy, such as their different emphases on etiological factors, treatment goals, and methods.

Further examination of therapeutic methods from the vantage point of alternative views may, in time, lead to interestingly amalgamated psychosocial therapies. It does not appear at this point, however, that many of the advocates of the various positions will be able to put aside their long identification with particular schools and easily assimilate alien notions and practices, notwithstanding a common self-description among therapists as "eclectic."

Meanwhile, an equally if not more vexing problem concerns the integration of psychosocial and biological forms of treatment. As shown in earlier chapters, combined treatment of this sort, where it has been tried, has often proved to be more effective than either alone. In this area we confront not only philosophical differences but interdisciplinary political and economic ones as well. Although there is a developing movement among a segment of clinical psychologists, endorsed to a degree by the American Psychological Association, to seek prescription-writing privileges that would permit them to administer psychoactive drugs (strongly opposed by organized medicine and psychiatry), as of this writing the overwhelming majority of nonmedical therapists may not legally do so. Even among clinical psychologists, many are opposed to this trend, mostly out of concern that easy access to drug treatment will corrupt the further and much needed development of even more powerful forms of psychosocial intervention.

In our judgment, the latter concern has merit; too frequently, we have seen the clinical process distorted by hasty and exclusive recourse to what is usually, at best, palliative medication. Still, judicious combined treatment surely has much to recommend it for certain types of disorder (Klerman et al., 1994), and it is inconvenient, typically more costly, and potentially involves enhanced risks for pharmacologic and psychosocial treatment of the same client to be managed by different practitioners. It will be interesting to see how this issue is played out by the mental health professions in the coming years.

THE EVALUATION OF SUCCESS IN PSYCHOTHERAPY

Competition between the various "brands" of therapies has tended to obscure the actual successes of psychosocial treatment. Four and a half decades ago, Hans Eysenck (1952), a well-known British psychologist, shook the field by concluding in his review of evidence on treatment outcomes that people who were untreated or simply placed on a waiting list for psychotherapy improved about as much as those who received therapy. This pronouncement prompted a flurry of research activity and a thorough reanalysis of the existing data. Reevaluation of

therapy-outcome research accomplished before Eysenck's review, as well as a great deal done since, has painted a different and far more positive picture of the overall effectiveness of psychotherapy (Lambert & Bergin, 1994).

Problems of Evaluation

Evaluating the effectiveness of psychological treatment is a difficult enterprise for several reasons. At best, it is an inexact process, dependent on imperfect measurement and outcome data. For example, attempts at evaluation generally depend on one or more of the following sources of information: (a) a therapist's impression of changes that have occurred, (b) a client's reports of change, (c) reports from the client's family or friends, (d) comparison of pretreatment and posttreatment personality test scores, and (e) measures of change in selected overt behaviors.

Unfortunately, each of these sources has serious limitations. A therapist may not be the best judge of a client's progress, since any therapist is likely to be biased in favor of seeing himself or herself as competent and successful. Furthermore, therapists can inflate improvement averages by consciously or unconsciously encouraging difficult clients to discontinue therapy. The problem of how to manage "dropouts" complicates most therapy-outcome studies (for example, are they to be counted as "failures" when in fact they receive little or none of the therapy being evaluated?). It has also been somewhat facetiously remarked that a therapist often thinks a client is getting better because he or she is getting accustomed to the client's symptoms.

A client, also, is an unreliable source concerning the outcomes of therapy. Clients may not only want to think that they are getting better for personal reasons, but they may report that they are being helped in an attempt to please the therapist. In addition, because therapy often requires a considerable investment of time, money, and sometimes emotional distress, the idea that it is useless is a dissonant one. Family and relatives may also be inclined to "see" the improvement they had hoped for, although they often seem to be more realistic than either the therapist or the client in their long-term evaluations.

Outside clinical ratings by an independent observer are sometimes used in psychotherapy-outcome research to evaluate the progress of a client; these may be more objective than ratings by those directly involved in the therapy. Another widely used objective measure of client change is performance on psychological tests. A client evaluated in this way takes a battery of tests before and after therapy and the differences in scores are assumed to reflect progress or deterioration. Although such tests may indeed show changes, these may sometimes be artifactual, as with *regression to the mean* phenomena (Speer, 1992), where very high (or low) scores tend on repeated measurement to drift toward the average of their own distributions—yielding a false impression that some real change has been documented. Also, the particular tests chosen are likely to focus on the theoretical predictions of the therapist or researcher. They are not necessarily valid predictors of how the client will behave in real life, nor can they give any indication of whether the changes that have occurred are likely to be enduring. Concerning the latter point, however, there is now abundant evidence from long-term follow-up that the effects of psychotherapy in general, as variously measured, are decidedly not ephemeral or temporary (e.g., Lambert & Bergin, 1994; Nicholson & Berman, 1983).

Changes in preselected and specifically denoted behaviors appear to be the safest measures of outcome, especially where the occurrence of these outside the therapy situation itself is systematically monitored. Such techniques, including client self-monitoring, have been widely and effectively used, especially by behavior therapists. Generalized terms such as *recovery, marked improvement,* and *moderate improvement,* as applied to initially problematic behavior and often used in outcome research, are open to considerable differences in interpretation. In addition, even under the best of circumstances there is always the possibility that improvement will be attributed to the particular form of treatment used, when it is in fact a product of other events in a client's life or even of "spontaneous" change.

In spite of these difficulties, however, it is to at least some extent possible to study the effectiveness of various treatment approaches separately—determining what procedures work best with various types of individuals (Kendall & Norton-Ford, 1982; Smith et al., 1980). In the course of our discussion of abnormal behavior patterns, we have mentioned a number of such studies, most of which have demonstrated positive outcomes from psychotherapy.

In this context, it is pertinent to ask what happens to people who do not obtain formal treatment. In view of the many ways that people can help each other, it is not surprising that often considerable improvement occurs without professional therapeutic intervention. Relevant here is the observation that treatment offered by professional therapists has not, in general, been clearly demonstrated to be superior

in outcome to nonprofessionally administered therapies (Christensen & Jacobson, 1994). Also, some forms of psychopathology, such as manic and depressive episodes and some instances of schizophrenia, appear to run a fairly brief course with or without treatment, and there are many other instances in which disturbed people improve over time for reasons that are not apparent.

Nevertheless, even if many emotionally disturbed persons tend to improve over time without psychotherapy, it seems clear that psychotherapy can often accelerate improvement or ensure desired behavior change that might not otherwise occur (Lambert & Bergin, 1994; Telch, 1981). Most researchers today would agree that psychotherapy is more effective than no treatment, and indeed the pertinent evidence, widely cited throughout this chapter and the entire text, is strongly confirmatory. The chances of an "average" client benefiting significantly from psychological treatment are, overall, impressive (Lambert & Bergin, 1994).

Furthermore, improvement seems a function of the number of therapy sessions undertaken—with the largest gains achieved early (that is, within six months) in the therapeutic relationship (Howard et al., 1986). Very long-term psychotherapy is actually quite rare, but such cases tend to create the impression, even among professionals, that disordered behavior is more intractable than for the most part it actually is. In one study of this problem (Howard et al., 1989), 56 percent of the total therapy sessions offered by a clinic were "consumed" by only 16 percent of the clients.

Nonetheless, the issue of treatment evaluation remains vital—both ethically and practically—if psychologists and other mental health personnel are to be justified in intervening in other people's lives. The issue becomes especially vital in light of evidence that some clients are *harmed* in their encounters with psychotherapists (Lambert & Bergin, 1994; Mays & Franks, 1985; Strupp, Hadley, & Gomes-Schwartz, 1977). This problem of negative effects, which many therapists acknowledge when directly queried (see Appendix C, pp. 223–343, of the Strupp et al. [1977] volume for interesting first-person accounts), is addressed further in the "Unresolved Issues" section.

Finally, we must note some problems in the growing trend for varied psychological treatments to be directly compared, within the same study, with the outcomes of biological treatments, usually drug therapies. Although such studies have frequently reported the "superiority" of one or the other of these therapy types in the treatment of various disorders, we remain skeptical that a truly definitive comparison of the outcomes of the two forms of therapy is ultimately possible. In fact, it is not clear that a completely valid outcome study can be done with psychosocial treatment when the design of the study adheres to established modes of evaluating the efficacy of drugs, as most by custom do. As Stiles and Shapiro (1989) have pointed out in a detailed examination of the issues involved, psychotherapy and drug therapy differ on many dimensions of critical importance in deciding on, and in interpreting, issues both of study design and the outcome measures used.

Take, for example, a therapist himself or herself as a variable, including such attributes as experience in treating the particular disorder, interpersonal skill, familiarity with the subcultural background of a client, faith in the treatment, and perhaps even personal attractiveness or charisma as experienced by the client. We have solid reason, based on available research findings, to believe that such things may be of crucial significance in determining the outcome of any psychosocial treatment effort (see Beutler et al., 1994; Lambert & Bergin, 1994). Now contrast this with the typical situation for drug treatment. Here, the "active ingredient" of the treatment is pretty much the same no matter who writes the prescription, and a therapist's personal attributes or his or her experience in treating the disorder (with the possible exception of a nonspecific placebo component) are largely irrelevant. With such important differences that vary in uncontrolled (and probably uncontrollable) ways in psychotherapy versus drug-comparison studies, it is not easy to see how any general and unequivocal conclusions regarding differential effectiveness could be made, almost regardless of the quantitative results obtained.

Precisely this sort of difficulty attends perhaps the best-known and most widely cited study of this sort, the NIMH-sponsored multisite "model" study of the treatment of depression (Elkin et al., 1989). In this study, two psychosocial treatments, cognitive-behavior therapy (CBT) and interpersonal therapy (IPT), were compared with antidepressant drug treatment (imipramine) plus general clinical management (IMIP-CM) and placebo pills plus clinical management (PLA-CM). We note in passing that the supposed "blinding" (with respect to who gets active drug and who gets placebo) for the latter two conditions is rarely successfully achieved (Greenberg et al., 1992). The immediate posttreatment results, in brief, were that the IMIP-CM treatment was slightly superior to CBT and IPT, especially for more severely depressed patients, with the PLA-CM group coming in last but nevertheless significantly benefiting. However, because

of a very common design defect (admittedly a difficult one) treatments were confounded with treating personnel, who were in turn confounded with treatment sites. The upshot was a statistically significant interaction of treatments-by-sites (i.e., therapists) in determining patients' clinical outcomes. In other words, the relative outcomes of the several treatments substantially depended on the characteristics of the therapists administering them, a result we would *routinely* predict to the extent that psychosocial therapeutic influence is involved. And, incidentally, the not inconsiderable improvement of PLA-CM patients in the study (recovery rates of 15–40 percent, depending on initial severity) can *only* be attributed to psychosocial or some other unknown influence.

Taking the reported results of this study at face value, then, would entail the *erroneous* conclusion that, in cases of severe depression, antidepressant drugs are the treatment of choice. In fact, the modest reported IMIP-CM overall treatment superiority is on careful examination shown to be true of only one of the three study sites employed, as recently pointed out by Hollon, Shelton, and Davis (1993). The original report (Elkin et al., 1989) notes that CBT therapists at one of the sites, and IPT therapists at another, produced results entirely comparable to those of the overall IMIP-CM treatment condition. We know from another source (O'Malley et al., 1988), indeed, that the IPT therapists used in this study showed widely varying aptitudes for conducting this type of treatment even before the study began. A reasonable conclusion from this study would seem to be that the characteristics of the *therapist*, in relation to the therapy to be employed, are of crucial significance in determining outcomes, perhaps (and somewhat surprisingly) even with respect to drug treatment.

We have examined the above study in some detail only because it illustrates certain problems in psychotherapy outcome research, not because it sheds a great deal of light on the therapy of depression. In fact, a report of an 18-month follow-up of the patients in this study (Shea et al., 1992) is also remarkable for what it does *not* communicate (e.g., gross numbers and percentages and only minimal inferential probability statistics are reported), rather weakly concluding that *none* of the four treatment conditions was sufficiently potent "for most patients to achieve full recovery and lasting remission" (p. 782). We question whether this statement accurately captures the meaning of the results as reported, which are relatively unfavorable to the drug treatment and positive for CBT. However, outcomes in the various available treatments for depression as an issue in itself has been discussed earlier, so we shall dispense with any attempt to address that specific topic here.

Social Values and Psychotherapy

The criticism has been raised—from both inside and outside the mental health professions—that psychotherapy can be viewed as an attempt to get people adjusted to a "sick" society rather than to encourage them to work toward its improvement. As a consequence, psychotherapy has often been considered the guardian of the status quo. This issue is perhaps easier for us to place in perspective by looking at other cultures. For example, there have been frequent allegations that psychiatry was until recently used as a means of political control in the Soviet Union, an abuse that has now been officially acknowledged (see *Schizophrenia Bulletin,* 1990, v. 16, no. 4). It is encouraging to note that these practices had been all but universally condemned by the international mental health community. Although few people make the claim that psychiatry in the Western world is used to gain control over social critics, there is nevertheless the possibility that therapists are, in some ways, placed in the roles of "gatekeepers" of social values. Such charges, of course, bring us back to the question we raised in Chapter 1: What do we mean by abnormal? Our answer to that question can only be made in the light of our values.

In a broader perspective, of course, we are concerned with the complex and controversial issue of the role of values in science. Psychotherapy is not, or at least should not be, a system of ethics; it is a set of tools to be used at the discretion of a therapist in pursuit of a client's welfare. Thus mental health professionals are confronted with the same kinds of questions that confront scientists in general. Should a physical scientist who helps develop thermonuclear weapons be morally concerned about how they are used? Similarly, should a psychologist or behavioral scientist who develops powerful techniques of behavior control be concerned about how they are used?

Many psychologists and other scientists try to sidestep this issue by insisting that science is value-free—that it is concerned only with gathering "facts," not with how they are applied. Each time therapists decide that one behavior should be eliminated or substituted for another, however, they are making a value choice. The increasing social awareness of today's mental health professionals has brought into sharp focus ethical questions concerning their roles as therapists and value models, as well as their roles as agents for maintaining the status quo or fostering social change. For example, is a therapist to assume the depression of a young homemaker-mother who is abused by a drunken husband to be an internally based disorder requiring "treatment," as once would have been routine? Or does the therapist perhaps not have a larger responsibility to look beyond this individual-pathology viewpoint and confront the abnormality of the marital relationship? Therapy takes place in a context that involves the values of the therapist, the client, and the society in which they live. There are strong pressures on a therapist—from parents, schools, courts, and other social institutions—to help people adjust to "the world as it is." At the same time, there are many counterpressures, particularly from young people who are seeking support in their attempts to become authentic people rather than blind conformists.

The dilemma in which contemporary therapists may find themselves is illustrated by the following case:

> A 15-year-old high school sophomore is sent to a therapist because her parents have discovered that she has been having sexual intercourse with her boyfriend. The girl tells the therapist that she thoroughly enjoys such relations and feels no guilt or remorse over her behavior, even though her parents strongly disapprove. In addition, she reports that she is quite aware of the danger of becoming pregnant and is careful to take contraceptive measures.

What is the role of the therapist in such a case? Should the girl be encouraged to conform to her parents' mores and postpone sexual activity until she is older and more mature? Or should the parents be helped to adjust to the pattern of sexual behavior she has chosen? What should be the therapist's goal? As was noted earlier, it is not unusual to find some individuals being referred for psychological treatment because their behavior, not particularly destructive or disturbing, has caused concern among family members who wish the therapist to "fix" them.

It is apparent that there are diametrically opposed ways of dealing with problems in therapy. Society must enforce conformity to certain norms if it is to maintain its organization and survive. But how does one distinguish between norms that are vital for the common good and those that are irrelevant, outmoded, or arbitrarily imposed by thoughtless devotion to a particular subgroup's notion of revealed truth? It is often up to individual therapists to decide what path to take, and this requires value decisions on their part concerning what is best for an individual and for the larger society. Thus a mental health professional is confronted with the problem of "who (or what) controls the controller"; that is, of developing ethical standards and societal safeguards to prevent misuse of the techniques they have developed for modifying individual and group behavior (Lakin, 1991).

 ## UNRESOLVED ISSUES

on Psychotherapy

Probably no treatment procedure in medicine or surgery is without risk in the sense of potentially harmful or even fatal effects on a client. Generally speaking, moreover, the more potent the treatment in terms of potential dramatic benefit, the more risky the procedure. The situation appears to be no different with respect to psychotherapy. As we have noted, the outcomes of psychotherapy do not range from neutral (no effect) to positive, but rather seem to encompass a significant negative or deteriorative effect. The extreme is client suicide, although we certainly do not suggest that all such outcomes could be avoided with more skillful psychotherapy. In any event, some client-psychotherapist relationships, approaching perhaps 10 percent (Lambert & Bergin, 1994), apparently result in the client's being worse off than if psychotherapy had never been undertaken.

Our judgment about the gravity of this situation would be less severe if it were taken more seriously among professional psychotherapists than our experience suggests, and if we knew more about how to prevent it. We do have some guidelines about factors that should be considered, based in part on reviews of the issue in books by Mays and Franks (1985) and Strupp and colleagues (1977). We know that clients with certain types of disorders that are notoriously difficult to treat (such as borderline personality disorder) are more likely than others to deteriorate in treatment. We have also known for some time that an overly aggressive, intrusive, abruptly defense-challenging therapeutic style can be dangerous to client functioning, particularly where it is un-

modulated by therapist warmth and empathy. Similarly, the concurrent occurrence of uncontrollable negative events (such as divorce) in a client's life outside therapy can obviously interfere with therapeutic progress.

Obvious therapeutic impasses account for only a portion of the failures. In other instances a bewildering network of interactive factors operate together and idiosyncratically in an individual case (for example, the "match" of therapist and client characteristics) to produce deteriorating outcomes. Our impression, supported by some evidence reviewed by Lambert (1989) and Lambert and Bergin (1994), is that certain therapists, probably for reasons of personality, just do not do well with certain types of client problems. In light of these intangible factors, we take it as every therapist's responsibility to monitor his or her work with various types of clients to discover any such deficiencies, and to refer promptly to other therapists those persons with whom one may be ill-equipped to work.

A special case of therapeutic harm is the problem of therapist-client sexual entanglements, typically seduction of a client (or "former" client) by a therapist, which is considered unethical conduct. Given the frequently intense and intimate quality of therapeutic relationships, we should perhaps not be surprised that the issue of sexual attraction arises. In fact, Pope, Sonne, and Holroyd (1993) have recently published a searching, book-length analysis of the problem, together with suggested solutions for dealing with it in an effective and ethical manner. What is astonishing is the apparent frequency with which it is manifested in exploitive and unprofessional behavior on the part of therapists—all the more so in light of the fact that virtually all authorities agree that such liaisons are nearly always destructive of client functioning in the long run.

A variety of evidence, including anonymous admissions of therapists in various surveys over the years, suggests that this source of client abuse and likely negative outcome is by no means rare. A substantial proportion of the complaints received and processed by state licensing boards and by ethics boards of professional mental health associations involve this type of alleged misconduct. In a national survey of psychologists (Pope & Vetter, 1991), half the respondents reported assessing or treating at least one client who had been sexually intimate with a prior therapist, a total of 958 separate instances; 90 percent of these encounters were judged to have been of harm to the client, with an 11 percent subsequent hospitalization rate and a 14 percent rate of attempted suicide. Most of the victims (87 percent) were female, and three of them were children.

Even these chilling statistics, however, do not do justice to the magnitude of the problem in terms of already vulnerable lives being further undermined, nor do they speak to the difficulties victims often have in seeking redress for their psychic injury. That gap has been partially filled with the publication of a remarkable and courageous book by Bates and Brodsky (1989) that deals informatively with these subjects. In it, Bates renders a compelling account of her own sexual victimization by a therapist, one who, incredibly, has given a prominent address on "the problem" before a national professional audience. Her "second victimization," involving painful and humiliating experiences, occurred when she instituted legal means to discourage this man from further violations of professional trust. The book, thoroughly researched, offers little encouragement that an offender in this area can be reliably rehabilitated, and yet it has proven extremely difficult to achieve prevention through license revocation or other professional or legal sanction.

Even allowing for the likelihood of occasional fraudulent or frivolous client complaints in this area—the Pope and Vetter data suggest a frequency of 4 percent—the well-established occurrence of this type of event indicates an appalling level of misconduct, and probable client injury, among people holding themselves out to be "psychotherapists," which incidentally is not in most jurisdictions a legally regulated self-description. A prospective client seeking therapy needs to be sufficiently wary to determine that the therapist chosen is one of the large majority committed to high ethical and professional standards.

Unfortunately, there are otherwise few guidelines a prospective client can reliably employ in choosing a therapist. Reputation in the community and among professional colleagues and quality of background training and experience are obvious things to consider. We think that a "trial" interview or brief series of them is a good idea as a means of assessing one's "fit" and comfort with a given therapist's style. In the end, however, we do not have the data to predict with even reasonable assurance the outcome or likely benefit of any particular therapist-client relationship. This is a knowledge gap on which research is badly needed.

Finally, we should comment briefly on the seeming disarray of the field of therapy with its many competing variations. One aspect of the competition, already noted, involves a currently intense struggle, fueled by interprofessional rivalries, concerning the place of biological therapies in the mental health field. In this chapter we focus on the several varieties of psychosocial approach. We have already indicated our judgment that probably most

of these are "right," at least in the limited sense that they have fashioned intervention techniques having a high probability, when sensitively applied, of helping people overcome their problems. The obvious question, then, is this: Why doesn't the typical therapist employ a multifaceted, multitargeted approach to every client with whom treatment is undertaken, instead of doing his or her "own thing," be it psychoanalysis, behavioral, gestalt, or some other therapy? Wouldn't this approach maximize treatment efficiency? We suspect so, and we have no entirely satisfactory answer to the first part of our query. Ideological commitment has historically been very strong in this field—in large part because virtually nobody had solid research data with which to back their claims. That situation is changing rapidly, but the commitment tends to remain despite the change and despite sincere efforts (e.g., Goldfried et al., 1990; Goldfried & Safran, 1986; Norcross & Goldfried, 1992) to enhance communication across the many intersecting barriers. As every therapist knows, dysfunctional habits are often hard to break.

 ## SUMMARY

Psychotherapy is aimed at the reduction of abnormal behavior in individuals through psychological means. The goals of psychotherapy include changing maladaptive behavior, minimizing or eliminating stressful environmental conditions, reducing negative affect, improving interpersonal competencies, resolving personal conflicts, modifying a person's inaccurate assumptions about himself or herself, and fostering a more positive self-image. Although these goals are by no means easy to achieve, psychological treatment methods have been shown to be generally effective in promoting adaptive psychological functioning in many troubled people.

Many approaches to psychological treatment ("schools of psychotherapy") have been developed to treat individuals with psychological disorders. We have organized these approaches into a scheme that focuses attention on the primary target selected for intervention, employing the acronym CAPER. Type C therapies are directed at a client's maladaptive Cognitions; Type A at dysregulated Affects or emotions; Type P at pathogenic Physiologic reactions or states; Type E at the reactive Environment; and Type R at the aberrant behavioral Responses themselves. We argued that, because these elements are organized in an unending loop, positive change in any one of them will produce a good therapeutic effect overall.

Nevertheless, this chapter is developed in accord with the traditional breakdown of "schools" of therapy. One of the oldest approaches to psychological treatment, psychoanalysis, was originated nearly a century ago by Sigmund Freud. Although complicated systems of psychodynamic therapy have evolved since Freud's time, many features of "orthodox" psychoanalysis today closely resemble Freud's original system. Several other schools of therapy have developed out of the psychoanalytic tradition. These approaches accept some elements of Freudian theory but diverge on key points, such as the length of time to be devoted to therapy or the role of the ego in personality dynamics. By and large, we consider them Type E therapies because of the attention they give to the management of "transference."

A second major approach to psychological intervention is behavior therapy. Originating over 50 years ago, behavior therapy has come to be used extensively in treating clinical problems. Behavior therapy approaches make use of a number of techniques, such as systematic desensitization and biofeedback (which are Type A and Type P therapies, respectively). Other behavior therapy techniques include aversion therapy, modeling, reinforcement approaches, and assertiveness therapy (all Type R therapies). Recently, behavior therapy methods have been applied to internal processes—that is, thought or cognitions (Type C)—with a great deal of success. Known as cognitive-behavioral therapy, this approach attempts to modify a person's self-statements to change his or her behavior. Cognitive-behavioral methods have been used for a wide variety of clinical problems—from depression to anger control—and with a range of clinical populations.

Several other psychological treatment methods have been referred to as humanistic-experiential therapies (which we regard as primarily Type C, owing to their focus on "awareness"). One of the earliest of these approaches is the client-centered, or person-centered, therapy of Carl Rogers. This treatment approach, originating in the 1940s, has received broad acceptance and has provided a valuable conceptualization of the client-therapist interaction as well as specific techniques for generating personal change or personal growth in motivated clients.

In addition to individual treatment approaches, some psychological treatment methods are applied in group settings, such as group therapy and marital or family therapy. These approaches typically assume that a person's problems lie partly in his or her interactions with others. Consequently, the focus of treatment is to change ways of interacting among individuals in the social or family context (a Type E approach).

In recent years an attempt has been made to integrate behavior therapy methods with other psychological treatment approaches, particularly psychodynamic therapy. This effort is a result of the recognition that elements from both approaches can be used to increase our understanding of troubled clients and to bring about desired behavior changes. These integration issues are actually part of a broader problem of therapists largely doing their "own thing," addressed in the chapter's "Unresolved Issues" section.

Evaluation of the success of psychotherapy in producing desired changes in clients is difficult. Research in psychotherapy, however, has shown that most treatment approaches are more effective than no treatment at all. Beyond the question of evaluating the success of psychotherapy lie other, larger questions involving the ethical dilemmas posed by therapy. Does psychotherapy encourage conformity to the status quo? Should it do this? These constitute some of the difficult moral and social issues that daily confront mental health professionals.

Other unresolved issues include the often perplexing occurrence of negative or deteriorative outcomes in psychotherapy. One likely source of such outcomes, by no means the only or necessarily most common, is sexual misconduct on the part of a therapist.

KEY TERMS

psychotherapy (p. 625)
clinical psychologist (p. 627)
psychiatrist (p. 627)
psychiatric social workers (p. 627)
psychodynamic therapy (p. 631)
free association (p. 632)
manifest content (p. 632)
latent content (p. 632)
resistance (p. 632)
transference (p. 632)
counter-transference (p. 634)
behavior therapy (p. 636)
implosive therapy (p. 637)
flooding (p. 637)
systematic desensitization (p. 638)
aversion therapy (p. 639)
modeling (p. 640)
response shaping (p. 641)

token economies (p. 641)
behavioral contracting (p. 642)
assertiveness therapy (p. 642)
biofeedback (p. 643)
cognitive-behavior therapy (p. 645)
rational-emotive therapy (RET) (p. 645)
stress-inoculation therapy (p. 646)
humanistic-experiential therapies (p. 650)
client-centered (person-centered) therapy (p. 650)
existential psychotherapy (p. 652)
gestalt therapy (p. 653)
couples counseling (marital therapy) (p. 654)
structural family therapy (p. 657)

CONTEMPORARY ISSUES IN ABNORMAL PSYCHOLOGY

Lee Godie, Three Female Heads. *Godie (b. 1908) lived for many years on the streets of Chicago, often in front of the Chicago Art Institute, where she would work on her paintings. After many years of separation from her family, Godie was reunited with her adult daughter after the daughter read an article about her in* The Wall Street Journal *in 1989. Since 1991 Godie's daughter has been her mother's legal guardian.*

Over the years, most efforts toward mental health have been largely restorative, geared toward helping people only after they have already developed serious problems. Before the 1960s, mental health professionals typically did not become involved until after an individual had suffered a breakdown; then they often sent such persons for treatment far away from their home communities, often compounding their distress and disrupting their lives.

Seemingly, a more effective strategy would be to try to catch problems before they become severe, or better yet, to establish conditions in which psychological disorders will not occur. The causes of many mental disorders, however, are not sufficiently understood to enable practitioners to initiate explicit preventive programs. Efforts toward prevention in the mental health field are still based largely on hypotheses about what works rather than on substantial empirical research. Nonetheless, many professionals believe that preventive mental health efforts are worthwhile.

Of course, preventive efforts, like treatment programs, cost money. During periods of economic decline, federal, state, and local governments typically reduce their support for such programs. Unfortunately, programs aimed at prevention, because of their long-range scope and their often indirect focus, are considered to be relatively unattractive because they appear less cost-effective than other programs with more obvious outcome criteria. The irony, of course, is that prevention can be in the long run far less costly than the treatment of mental disorders and their effects (Lorion, 1990).

Where preventive efforts fail and a serious mental health problem develops, today's professionals emphasize the importance of prompt treatment. It is considered preferable, too, that the treatment be in the individual's own community so that clinicians can use available family and other familiar supports and minimize the disruption to the person's life. If hospitalization becomes necessary, every effort is made to prevent the disorder from becoming chronic and to return the person to the community as soon as possible, with whatever aftercare and continued support may be needed. On occasion, as is obvious to even the casual urban observer, such efforts fail, and a person is sent back into the community without adequate support and well before he or she is capable of independent functioning.

In this last chapter, we will examine the kinds of measures that are being taken to prevent maladaptive behavior or limit its seriousness. Our discussion will begin with a review of preventive strategies.

Next, we will explore some factors related to the care and hospitalization of people with severe psychological problems: commitment, deinstitutionalization, and assessment of dangerousness. Closely related to these factors are the matters of (a) a therapist's duty to warn others if a client threatens violence and (b) the use—and some think abuse—of the insanity defense as a plea in capital crimes. Next, we will briefly survey the scope of organized efforts for mental health both in the United States and throughout the world. Finally, we will conclude the chapter by considering what each of us can do to foster mental health.

PERSPECTIVES ON PREVENTION

In our present discussion we will use the concepts of primary, secondary, and tertiary prevention, which are widely used in public health efforts to describe general strategies of disease prevention. **Primary prevention** is aimed at reducing the possibility of disease or disorder and fostering positive health. **Secondary prevention** is typically emergency or crisis intervention, and involves efforts to reduce the impact, duration, or spread of a problem that has already developed—if possible, catching it before it has become serious. **Tertiary prevention** seeks to reduce the long-term consequences of disorders or serious problems. These preventive strategies, although primarily devised for understanding and controlling infectious physical diseases, provide a useful perspective in the mental health field as well. As we hope to show, all three types of intervention are of critical importance in reducing the enormous toll of mentally disordered functioning in our society.

Primary Prevention

We begin our discussion of primary prevention with the recently published report of a panel of experts in the field appointed to advise a conference on prevention sponsored by the National Institute of Mental Health (Coie et al., 1993). The panel identified as a recognizable area of inquiry the field of "prevention science," outlined a conceptual framework defining the boundaries of this discipline, and recommended certain directions for a proposed national research program that would capitalize on the knowledge already amassed by investigators working in this and closely related areas. They focused their discussion on those influences considered to be likely or potential "precursors of dysfunction or health, called *risk factors* and *protective factors,* respectively" (p. 1013).

The panel summarized its findings in a set of basic observations, which may be paraphrased as follows:

1. *Risk factors have complex relations to clinical disorders.* That is, it is rare for either particular risk factors or particular disorders to be related to one another in specific and exclusive ways. Rather, particular disorders (e.g., schizophrenia) are usually found to be associated not with single risk factors but with a host of differing ones; similarly, particular risk factors (e.g., physical abuse) are only rarely found to have a range of effect limited to only one or a very few types of disorder, presumably because they tend to disrupt adaptive developmental processes in many different ways at different developmental stages. Also, personal characteristics may interact with environmental risk factors in ways that may enhance or mitigate their pathogenic effects.

2. *The salience of risk factors may fluctuate developmentally.* In other words, certain risk factors are associated with deleterious effects only if they occur during a limited span of the developmental years, while others seem to operate over a much longer developmental span. For example, association with deviant peers may be predictive of antisocial behavior only in adolescence, whereas parental neglect appears to be a risk factor from childhood through adolescence.

3. *Exposure to many risk factors has cumulative effects.* That is, multiple risk factors have additive effects with respect to a person's overall vulnerability to mental disorder. The probability of a disordered outcome increases with increases in the number, duration, and potency ("toxicity") of the risk factors to which the person has been exposed.

4. *Diverse disorders share fundamental risk factors in common.* There appear to be certain "generic" risk factors whose effects are very widespread in terms of the variety of pathologic outcomes with which they are associated. The panel provided a list of 30 such factors, assorted into various categories and reproduced in Table 18.1, that are known to be associated with many types of adult disorder.

5. *Promoting protective factors against dysfunction.* As was noted in Chapter 3, risk exposure, even at extreme levels, does not invariably predict disorder. The effects of risk factors can be reduced by a variety of protective elements either within the person or the surrounding social environment. For ex-

Table 18.1   *Risk Factors Known to be Associated with Psychological Disorder*

Family Circumstances
Low social class
Family conflict
Mental illness in the family
Large family size
Poor bonding to parents
Family disorganization
Communication deviance

Emotional Difficulties
Child abuse
Apathy or emotional blunting
Emotional immaturity
Stressful life events
Low self-esteem
Emotional dyscontrol

School Problems
Academic failure
Scholastic demoralization

Ecological Context
Neighborhood disorganization
Racial injustice
Unemployment
Extreme poverty

Constitutional Handicaps
Perinatal complications
Sensory disabilities
Organic handicaps
Neurochemical imbalance

Interpersonal Problems
Peer rejection
Alienation and isolation

Skill Development Delays
Subnormal intelligence
Social incompetence
Attentional deficits
Reading disabilities
Poor work skills and habits

(Coie et al., 1993, p. 1022)

ample, the occurrence of childhood disorders appears to be mitigated by certain individual characteristics pertaining to temperament, personality dispositions, and skills, and also by a protective environment that provides parental warmth, social support, appropriate monitoring and supervision, and opportunity for bonding with prosocial models. Where risk factors are difficult to identify or to eliminate, the most effective preventive strategy may involve attempts to enhance protective factors.

In short, we are concerned in primary prevention with two key tasks: altering conditions that can cause or contribute to mental disorders (risk factors) and establishing conditions that foster positive mental health (protective factors). Epidemiological studies are particularly important in this area because they help investigators obtain information about the incidence and distribution of various maladaptive behaviors needing prevention efforts (Dohrenwend & Dohrenwend, 1982). These findings can then be used to suggest what preventive efforts might be most appropriate. For example, various epidemiological studies and reviews have shown that certain groups are at high risk for mental disorders, including recently divorced people (Bloom et al., 1978), the physically disabled (Freemen, Malkin, & Hastings, 1975), elderly people living alone (Neugarten, 1977), physically abused children (Malinosky-Rummel & Hansen, 1993), and people who have been uprooted from their homes (Westermeyer et al., 1991). Although findings such as these may be the

basis for immediate secondary prevention, they may also aid later in primary prevention by telling us what to look for and where to look—in essence by focusing our efforts in the right direction. Primary prevention includes biological, psychosocial, and sociocultural efforts. As Kessler and Albee (1975) have noted, "Everything aimed at improving the human condition, at making life more fulfilling and meaningful, may be considered to be part of primary prevention of mental or emotional disturbance" (p. 557).

Biological Measures Biologically based primary prevention begins with help in family planning and includes both prenatal and postnatal care. A good deal of current emphasis is being placed on guidance in family planning—how many children to have, when to have them in relation to marital and other family conditions, and even whether to have children at all. Such guidance may include genetic counseling, in which tests for genetic defects may be given to potential parents to assess their risk of having children with birth defects that can result in mental disorders.

Breakthroughs in genetic research have also made it possible to detect and sometimes alleviate genetic defects before a baby is born; when in utero treatment is not feasible, such information provides the parents with the choice of having an abortion rather than going on to bear a baby with serious defects. Continued progress in genetic research may make it possible to identify genetic disorders early or even to correct faulty genes, thus providing humankind with fantastic new power to prevent hereditary pathology.

Many of the goals of health psychology can also be viewed as primary prevention. Efforts geared toward improving one's diet, establishing a routine of physical exercise, and developing overall good health habits can do much to improve one's physical well-being. To the extent that physical illness always produces some sort of psychological stress that can result in such problems as depression, good health is primary prevention with respect to good mental health.

Psychosocial Measures In regarding normality as optimal development and functioning rather than as the mere absence of pathology, we imply that people need opportunities to learn physical, intellectual, emotional, and social competencies. The first requirement of psychosocial "health" is that a person develop the skills needed for effective problem solving, for expressing emotions constructively, and for satisfying relationships with others; failure to develop these "protective" skills places the individual at a serious disadvantage in coping with stresses and often unavoidable mental disorder risk factors.

The second requirement for psychosocial health is that a person acquire an accurate frame of reference on which to build his or her identity. We have seen repeatedly that when people's assumptions about themselves or their world are inaccurate, their behavior is likely to be maladaptive. Likewise, an inability to find satisfying values that foster a meaningful and fulfilling life constitutes a fertile source of maladjustment and mental disorders.

Third, psychosocial well-being also requires preparation for the types of problems a person is likely to encounter during given life stages. For example, pregnancy and childbirth usually have a great deal of emotional significance for both parents; in addition, the arrival of a new infant in the home places an enormously increased demand on the resources of caregivers and may disturb family equilibrium or exacerbate an already disturbed marital situation. Young people who want to marry and have children must be prepared for the tasks of building a mutually satisfying relationship and helping children develop their abilities. The latter is a particularly formidable responsibility for teenage parents, who are themselves still struggling to become independent adults. Similarly, a person needs to be prepared adequately for other developmental tasks characteristic of given life periods, including retirement and old age.

In recent years, psychosocial measures aimed at primary prevention have received a great deal of attention. The field of behavioral medicine has had substantial influence here. As we saw in Chapter 8, efforts are being made to change the psychological factors underlying unhealthful habits, such as smoking, excessive drinking, and poor eating, that may be contributing to the development of both physical and psychological problems.

Sociocultural Measures The relationship between an individual and his or her community is a reciprocal one, a fact Americans sometimes forget in a culture that has historically placed an unusually high value on individualism. We need autonomy and freedom to be ourselves, but we also need to belong

Parenting education is one of several early-intervention, primary prevention strategies.

and contribute to a community. Without a supportive community, individual development is stifled.

At the same time, without responsible, psychologically healthy individuals, the community will not thrive and, in turn, cannot be supportive. When a community begins to fail, therefore, there is considerable danger that the failure will become self-sustaining; the psychosocially impaired victims of disorganized communities lack the wherewithal to create better communities to protect and sustain the psychological health of those who come after them, thus ensuring a persistently unprotective environment. Sociocultural efforts toward primary prevention are focused on making the community as nourishing as possible for the individuals within it.

With our growing realization of the importance of pathological social conditions in producing maladaptive behavior, increased attention must be devoted to creating social conditions that will foster healthy development and functioning in individuals. Efforts to create these conditions are seen in a broad spectrum of social measures ranging from public education and Social Security to economic planning and social legislation directed at ensuring adequate health care for all citizens.

Primary prevention through social change in the community is difficult. Although the whole psychological climate can ultimately be changed by a social movement, such as the civil rights movement of the 1960s, the payoff of such efforts is generally far in the future and may be difficult or impossible to predict or measure. Efforts at psychologically desirable social change are also likely to involve ideological and political issues that may inspire powerful opposition, including opposition from government itself. According to an analysis by Humphreys and Rappaport (1993), for example, the Reagan and Bush administrations during the 1980s severely undercut Community Mental Health Center social programs in favor of agencies involved in the "war on drugs." This effort, in redirecting attention to purported defects of individual character, was said to be more in keeping with a conservative political philosophy; that is, the basic problem, according to this view, is one of personal moral weakness ("How should kids deal with a drug-saturated environment? Just say no."), *not* social disorganization. Although drug abuse *is* a matter of individual behavior, it does not follow that countermeasures must be individually directed. Some examples of more broad-based programs are given in what follows.

An Illustration of Primary Prevention Strategies

Though difficult to formulate and even more difficult to mobilize and carry out, primary prevention efforts can bring about major improvements if successful. We will look in this section at the mobilization of primary prevention resources aimed at curtailing or reducing the problem of teenage alcohol and drug abuse.

Although drug use among most adolescent groups has declined in recent times (Oetting & Beauvais, 1990), teenage drug and alcohol use is still viewed as one of today's most significant psychological and community problems. Mental health professionals and political figures alike have called for a more concerted effort to deal with this enormous social problem. It is clear that traditional health or psychological intervention models, aimed at individual remediation only after a youngster has become addicted to narcotics or alcohol, have not significantly reduced the problem of drug and alcohol abuse among teenagers. Moreover, these treatment approaches are typically implemented only after the child has seriously compromised his or her life opportunities through drug or alcohol use.

Many contemporary researchers and theorists have taken a more proactive position. They have attempted to establish programs that prevent the development of abuse disorders before young people become so involved with drugs or alcohol that their lives are altered to the point that future adjustment becomes difficult, if not impossible. These recent prevention strategies have taken several diverse and hopeful directions, addressing somewhat different aspects of teenagers' lives. We will examine several that show promise and then discuss the limitations of these prevention approaches.

Education Programs. Drug and alcohol education programs represent a prevention strategy aimed at providing information about the damaging effects of these substances. Many are school-based and are usually premised on the idea that if children are made aware of the dangers of drugs and alcohol, they will choose not to begin using them. Englander-Golden and colleagues (1986), for example, provided "Say it straight" training to sixth through eighth graders in which they taught them both the dangers of drug and alcohol abuse and how to be assertive enough to resist drugs and alcohol in spite of peer pressure. In a follow-up evaluation, these investigators reported that youngsters who were trained in the program had a lower rate of drug- and alcohol-related suspensions from school than did children who received no training.

A similar program, Project Northland, geared to the prevention of alcohol abuse, targets junior high school students in northeastern Minnesota, but involves a much broader community-wide intervention effort (Perry et al., 1993). One of its facets, for

Efforts to teach school children about the dangers of drugs before they reach the age of maximum risk have become common.

example, is home-based and recruits parents to participate with their children in exercises designed to enhance awareness of the risks of alcohol abuse; preliminary findings are encouraging (Williams et al., in press).

Intervention Programs for High-Risk Teens. Intervention programs involve identifying high-risk teenagers and providing special approaches to circumvent their further use of alcohol or potentially dangerous drugs. Programs such as these are often school-based efforts and are not strictly prevention programs; rather, they are treatment programs that provide early intervention for high-risk teens who are vulnerable to drug or alcohol use, in order to reduce the likelihood of their becoming further involved with these substances. Newman and colleagues (1988–1989) described a procedure for the early identification of young people who are having difficulties in school because of drug and alcohol use. The developers of this program train teachers and administrators to identify and manage alcohol- and drug-use problems. Critical to this intervention is a fair and consistently enforced drug and alcohol policy in the schools.

Parent Education and Family-Based Intervention Programs. Because parents typically underestimate their own children's drug and alcohol use (Silverman & Silverman, 1987), several programs have been aimed at increasing parents' awareness of the extent of the problem and at teaching them ways to deal with drug and alcohol use in the family context. These programs teach parents how to recognize

drug- or alcohol-abuse problems so that youngsters can be diverted away from negative and self-destructive behaviors. One such program by Grady, Gersick, and Boratynski (1985) worked with parents whose children were about to become teenagers. They first assessed parents' skill in dealing with drug-related issues; then they trained parents to understand and respond empathically to youngsters who might be exposed to drugs during their adolescent years. Parents were then taught to respond to their children's questions and concerns and to help them consider alternative, more adaptive behavior.

Other family-oriented programs have aimed at strengthening family bonds and providing more positive family relationships to insulate a child from external negative influences. For example, DeMarsh and Kumpfer (1985) developed a program that focused on involving parents or a family in the positive socialization of a child by increasing communications within the family and enhancing parents' child-management skills.

When there is a drug or alcohol problem, assuring family cooperation in the treatment program can be problematic, and many programs have reported low rates of participation. In an effort to increase the participation rate, Szapocznik and colleagues (1988) used family-systems therapeutic techniques to reduce the resistance of families to drug treatment. They reported that 77 percent of the families completed the treatment program compared with only 25 percent in a control condition.

Peer Group Influence Programs. Clearly, peers exert a powerful influence on teenagers in every aspect of their lives, including drug and alcohol abuse. Programs designed to help youngsters overcome negative pressures from peers focus on teaching social skills and assertiveness. Of course, peer pressure can be positive as well—in this case, influencing a teen not to use drugs or alcohol—and many programs focus on the positive aspects of peer pressure. Swadi and Zeitlin (1988) advocated the positive use of peer influence because for teenagers such influence seems much more powerful than the influence of others, including teachers and parents.

Programs to Increase Self-Esteem. Programs designed to increase a sense of self-worth attempt to ensure that young people will be able to fend for themselves more assuredly and not fall into dependent, negative relationships with stronger and more dominant peers. Pentz (1983) designed one such program by providing teenagers with social-skills training and the modeling of appropriate behaviors to reduce drug use and other related negative behaviors, such as truancy. In another program, Botvin (1983) relied on cognitive-behavioral intervention techniques to enhance teenagers' feelings of competency in basic life skills and improve their problem-solving skills. This approach was thought to be effective in reducing the impact of tobacco, alcohol, and marijuana use (Botvin et al., 1990).

Mass Media and Modeling Programs. Recognizing the huge "market" potential of teenagers, advertisers have been adept in exploiting the tremendous value the appearance of sophistication has for this age group. Most youngsters are bombarded with drug- or alcohol-related stimuli in TV commercials, movies, and other visual blitzes. Airing such TV commercials or programs at times that children may view them serves to glamorize alcohol or drug use. Several recent efforts have been aimed at deglamorizing or counteracting these messages by showing commercials that graphically depict the negative aspects of alcohol and drug use (Coombs, Paulson, & Palley, 1988; Schilling & McAlister, 1990).

The various prevention strategies discussed here are by no means mutually exclusive. Most programs do not rely on a single intervention strategy but incorporate two or more (Forman & Linney, 1988; Perry & Murray, 1985). For example, Botvin and Tortu (1988) described a five-stage program involving both didactic and peer interaction interventions designed to enhance youngsters' self-esteem and enable them to function effectively in social contexts to resist negative peer influences. In the first component of this program, several sessions are devoted to biofeedback demonstrations of the effects of cigarettes, marijuana, and alcohol on heart rate. In the second component, several sessions are aimed at teaching participants how to make effective decisions. In the third component, sessions focus on aiding the youngsters in understanding their self-image and improving their self-esteem. In the fourth component, teenagers are taught to deal with anxiety, particularly social anxiety. Finally, the fifth component of the program involves training the teens in both social communication and assertiveness, thus ensuring a more effective peer group interaction.

How successful are primary prevention programs at reducing the overall impact of adolescent drug and alcohol use? It is difficult to say. Some researchers have concluded that drug and alcohol education programs have only limited success (Tobler, 1986). Conducting rigorous research in primary prevention is often problematic because the interventions may be only remotely connected to the behavior being targeted for change. Moreover, it is typically impossible to monitor and control in a single study all of the relevant variables influencing drug and alcohol use. Clearly, too, it is difficult to provide a powerful enough intervention to offset the motivation to use or sell drugs many youngsters experience. For many young people living in extreme poverty, the only way they can tolerate or possibly get out of the ghetto is through using or selling drugs. The recent decline in drug use among teenagers does not include minorities living in ghettos, barrios, or American Indian reservations, where drug use continues to grow at record levels (Oetting & Beauvais, 1990).

Some critics of drug and alcohol prevention programs consider drug and alcohol problems in adolescence to be the result of early socialization processes—and not amenable to superficial reeducation efforts occurring so late in a youngster's life. Shedler and Block (1990), in a well-controlled longitudinal study in which subjects were carefully studied from about age 5 to age 18, found clear precursors to frequent drug use in the youngsters' early personality development. They found that teenagers developing drug-abuse patterns in their late teens had clear psychological maladjustment in early childhood, well before they were exposed to drugs; these psychological problems predisposed the adolescents to drug abuse. As such, Shedler and Block considered the "peer-centered" or recent environmental influence explanations to be flawed and inadequate to explain the behavior. They thus argued that many of the drug education program efforts are inadequate to address the true source of the problem: the personality syndrome that appears to underlie drug abuse.

We must be careful in assessing this conclusion, however, in part because it might be viewed as implying that intervention efforts are doomed to failure in the face of behavioral propensities that are predetermined and unalterable, thus justifying public inaction and an attitude of helplessness. Few investigators have ever doubted that relatively enduring personality risk factors make certain children more vulnerable than their less-troubled peers to the attractions of drug and alcohol abuse. On the other side of the coin is the example of some unusually resourceful youngsters who have emerged drug-free from deplorably high-risk environments. The point is that acknowledging the significant contribution early-appearing personal dispositions may make to outcomes does not imply that attempts to modify negative environmental influences are irrelevant. It would appear that we need to intensify efforts at early identification of those children whose personality development is veering toward a high-risk status and to apply intervention techniques to divert this trend.

Unfortunately, many of the recent programs that have been initiated in response to the drug crisis are of the "too little, too late" variety. The lackluster performance or outright failure of some drug prevention efforts may hinder future research. Because of the lack of clear research findings and the uncertain effectiveness of prevention programs, it is difficult to convince lawmakers or funding agencies that more support for such programs is needed or worth the effort. Policy makers may take such unproductive results as an indication that primary prevention efforts are not effective in reducing the problem behavior being addressed. Thus more substantial, better-designed, and longer-range programs that might be powerful enough to bring about major changes may not be supported.

Secondary Prevention

Secondary prevention emphasizes the early detection and prompt treatment of maladaptive behavior in a person's family and community setting. In some cases—for example, in a crisis or after a disaster—secondary prevention involves immediate and relatively brief intervention to prevent any long-term behavioral consequences. In other cases, secondary prevention is aimed at longer-term consulting and educational services to reduce the consequences of some identified maladaptive behavior or problem. We will look briefly at both types of secondary prevention and then follow with an in-depth examination of secondary prevention efforts after an airplane crash.

Crisis Intervention   Crisis intervention has emerged in response to a widespread need for immediate help for individuals and families confronted with especially stressful situations—be they disasters or family situations that have become intolerable (Auerbach & Stolberg, 1986; Butcher & Dunn, 1989; Butcher, Stelmachers, & Maudal, 1983; Gist & Lubin, 1989; Mitchell & Resnik, 1981; Taylor, 1989). Often, people in crisis are in a state of acute turmoil and feel overwhelmed and incapable of dealing with the stress by themselves. They do not have time to wait for the customary initial therapy appointment, nor are they usually in a position to continue therapy over a sustained period of time. They need immediate assistance.

To meet this need, two modes of therapeutic intervention have been developed: (a) short-term crisis therapy involving face-to-face discussion; and (b) the telephone hot line. These forms of crisis intervention are usually handled either by professional mental health personnel or by paraprofessionals—lay people who have been trained for this work.

Short-Term Crisis Therapy.   **Short-term crisis therapy,** as the name implies, is of brief duration and focuses on the immediate problem with which an individual or family is having difficulty. Although medical problems may also require emergency treatment, we are concerned here with personal or family problems of an emotional nature. In such crisis situations, a therapist is usually very active, helping to clarify the problem, suggesting plans of action, providing reassurance, and otherwise giving needed information and support. In essence, the therapist tries to provide as much help as the individual or family will accept.

If the problem involves psychological disturbance in one of the family members, emphasis is usually placed on mobilizing the support of other family members. Often this enables the person to avoid hospitalization and a disruption of family life. Crisis intervention may also involve bringing other mental health or medical personnel into the treatment picture. Most individuals and families who come for short-term crisis therapy do not continue in treatment for more than one to six sessions. An example of crisis intervention as a secondary preventive effort is given in HIGHLIGHT 18.1.

The Telephone Hot Line.   As we noted in Chapter 6, recent years have seen a new approach to dealing with people undergoing crises—the telephone hot line. Today all major cities in the United States and most smaller ones have developed some form of telephone hot line to help people undergoing peri-

Crisis Intervention in Troubled Families

Family crises can result from many sources; for example, a family may lose its home through economic emergency, or a family member may die or become severely ill, or one of the family members may become psychotic, or, as in the following case, one of the family members may attempt suicide:

> A 17-year-old girl, Leah, was brought into the emergency department of a general hospital by her mother, father, and maternal grandmother. She had walked into her parents' bedroom earlier in the morning and announced that she had swallowed all her mother's pills. The parents had brought their daughter for emergency medical treatment and were enraged when a psychiatrist was called. The history was obtained from mother, since Leah said little, and mother answered every question. During the interview, father paced in and out of the room, repeatedly declaring that he was taking his daughter home. He aggressively asked each person who entered the room "What do you want?" but each time left before a response was possible. Grandmother sat in the room, announcing from time to time, "That girl always makes trouble."
>
> Leah was the oldest of three children. None of them attended school. According to mother, she tutored them at home. Mother also worked outside of the home and complained about how much she had to do. Leah "won't even go to the store alone, so I must accompany her every-

where." Mother said that her husband had told her not to bother with Leah, who would only get married and leave them anyway. But she (mother) had to "bother" because Leah could not go out alone in their neighborhood.
>
> When asked about the suicide attempt, Leah said she would "do it again" if she went home. She wanted to talk to someone about the fights with mother that made her so angry she wanted to die. Mother said it was father's fault. He worked erratically, drank heavily, and made them live in a bad house in a poor neighborhood. They had terrible neighbors who were "nosey" and bothered them.
>
> Since Leah had indicated she still had suicidal intentions and the family conflict continued unabated, hospitalization was recommended. In response, Leah immediately announced she was better and would go home. She said she would not stay in the hospital. Her mother said she could never persuade her to stay and the family gathered itself up to leave (Kress, 1984, p. 419–420).

The family crisis in this case brought to light several difficult problems due, in part, to the psychopathology of the individuals in the family—adjustment problems that threatened the integrity of the family organization. While Leah appeared to be the most disturbed, other family members seemed to have significant psychological problems that directly affected the family strife as well. The suicide attempt, like many other crises a

family is unprepared to resolve, required outside intervention. Not only was an immediate solution needed for the present emergency, but psychological intervention for the longer-term problem of the family's inability to resolve conflict was recommended. However, the closed, almost reclusive, nature of the family suggested that treatment for the individuals involved and for the disturbed family relationships, though needed, was not likely to be accepted at that point. Neither Leah nor her father appeared open to examining their problems or to changing their behavior. Unfortunately, we have no follow-up on the case of Leah. This is often the situation in crisis therapy, where the intervention efforts are limited to what can be accomplished only during the immediate crisis; that is, many such clients never return for more therapy, no matter how adamant the crisis worker's recommendation that they do so.

As is by now obvious, crisis intervention therapy with families is usually different and more limited in scope than family therapy as described in Chapter 17. The goals of family crisis intervention do not involve changing the basic family functioning, as in family therapy, but are usually limited to returning a disrupted family to precrisis functioning (Umana, Gross, & McConville, 1980). For example, the mental health practitioner's task in the case of Leah involved resolving the immediate emergency and helping ease her life-threatening state of mind while, hopefully, engaging her family in future family or individual treatment to resolve the pressing problems that appeared to have caused the immediate crisis, but this didn't happen.

ods of severe stress. Although the threat of suicide is the most dramatic example, the range of problems that people call about is virtually unlimited—from breaking up with someone to being on a bad drug trip. In addition, there are specific hot lines in various communities for rape victims and for runaways who need assistance.

As with other crisis intervention, a person handling hot-line calls is confronted with the problem of rapidly assessing what is wrong and how bad it is. Even if an accurate assessment is possible and the hot-line worker does everything within his or her power to help the caller, a distraught person may hang up without leaving any name, telephone number, or address. This can be a deeply disturbing experience for the hot-line counselor—particularly if, for example, the caller has announced that he or she has just swallowed a lethal dose of sleeping pills. Even in less severe cases, of course, the hot-line worker may never learn whether the caller's problem has been solved. In other instances, however, the caller may be induced to come in for counseling, making more personal contact possible.

For a therapist or volunteer counselor, crisis intervention is probably the most discouraging of any treatment approach that we have discussed. The urgency of the intervention and the frequent inability to provide any therapeutic closure or follow-up are probably key factors in this discouragement. Free clinics and crisis centers have reported that their counselors—many of whom are volunteers—tend to burn out after a short period of time. Despite the high frustration level of this work, however, crisis intervention counselors fill a crucial need in the mental health field, particularly for the young people who make up most of their clients. This need is recognized by the many community mental health centers and general hospitals that provide emergency psychological services, either through hot lines or walk-in services. For thousands of people in desperate trouble, an invaluable social support is provided by the fact that there is somewhere they can go for immediate help or someone they can call who will listen to their problems and try to help them. Thus the continuing need for crisis intervention services and telephone hot lines is evident.

Consultation and Education of Intermediaries
Often, community mental health professionals, such as psychologists and psychiatrists, are able to reach a larger group of people in need of secondary prevention efforts by working through primary care professionals, such as teachers, social workers, and police personnel (Iscoe, Bloom, & Spielberger, 1977; Levine & Perkins, 1987; Mann, 1978). For such

programs, mental health professionals identify a population at risk for the development of psychological disorder and then work with the personnel in community institutions who have frequent contact with members of this population. For example, police officers might be trained to direct persons involved in domestic quarrels to seek mental health services rather than to settle their differences through violence.

Mental health professionals had originally intended that *consultation and education* (C & E) be included among the services offered by all community mental health centers. According to this plan, the impact of these centers, while more indirect, could be much more widely distributed—helping people experiencing problems by increasing the skill and sensitivity of those who routinely come into contact with them in the community and are in a position to make their lives either more stressful or less so. Currently, however, most community mental health centers provide little such indirect care, having become deluged with the problems of providing direct service, including dispensing and monitoring the effects of psychoactive drugs, to overwhelming numbers of mental hospital patients discharged into the community by deinstitutionalization. Many centers have managed to maintain a C & E relationship with schools or other juvenile services, but for the most part the widespread outreach function originally envisaged for community mental health centers has been abandoned, very often because of a low priority in funding. Thus has another good idea in prevention come essentially to naught in encounters with governmental bureaucracies preoccupied with the achievement of immediate and highly visible results.

An Illustration of Secondary Prevention The immediate consequences of an air crash are devastating. Survivors typically have traumatic responses to the accident that impair their immediate functioning and place great demands on their psychological adjustment for weeks after the disaster. Family members of victims often experience extensive psychological trauma after the accident; they may need to make extensive changes during their loved one's lengthy recovery period or, more likely, they will need to make major life changes to adjust to their loved one's death. Even rescue personnel caught up in dealing with the aftermath of an airline disaster may suffer from posttraumatic stress disorder.

In many respects the emotional responses of and adjustive demands placed on air crash victims are similar to those of victims of natural disasters, such as hurricanes, floods, earthquakes, and volcanic eruptions (Manglesdorff, 1985). A number of special considerations, however, influence the intensity of the problems seen following airplane crashes: Typically airplane crashes are sudden and unexpected; they are usually quite chaotic in terms of their destruction; and air disasters usually occur away from one's familiar settings and with people who are strangers. Consequently, the sense of community that characterizes response to many disasters is lacking. In addition, the impact of an air disaster has a strong emotional irradiation effect; that is, it affects a larger number of people than those immediately involved in the accident itself.

Air disasters differ from natural disasters in another important respect—they usually involve considerable blame and anger that can aggravate or intensify the emotional reactions of survivors even months after the crash. Most airports are required to have a disaster plan that includes rescue and evacuation procedures to deal with an airplane crash. Some airport disaster plans have incorporated a psychological support program to provide emergency mental health services to survivors and the family members of crash victims as well as to rescue workers (Butcher, 1980; Butcher & Dunn, 1989).

These programs are viewed as secondary prevention efforts in that they are aimed at providing emergency psychological services to prevent the development of psychological disorders or to reduce the severity of such problems if they occur. Three types of secondary prevention services have been shown to be effective in dealing with the psychological problems related to air disasters: immediate crisis intervention services to crash survivors and surviving family members; crisis telephone hot-line services to provide information and referrals to victims who lack crisis intervention services; and postdisaster debriefing sessions for secondary victims, such as rescue personnel, affected by the disaster. We will look at each of these services briefly.

Postdisaster Crisis Therapy. Timing is critical to crisis intervention, which, when supplied in the immediate aftermath of a disaster, can reduce the emotional distress experienced and can result in a more effective future psychological adjustment (Butcher & Hatcher, 1988; Williams, Solomon, & Bartone, 1988). Crisis intervention treatment involves providing a victim with a supportive, understanding crisis-intervention specialist to enable the victim to express his or her intense feelings about the incident.

Few situations are more intimidating for a mental health professional than to be suddenly asked to treat previously unknown, acutely aggrieved persons—especially those who have just suffered a sud-

The provision of counseling during the aftermath of a disaster—in this case, the Los Angeles earthquake—has been shown to reduce long-term maladaptive reactions.

den loss, such as in a disaster. At these times human beings, regardless of their previous level of adjustment, need a great deal more emotional support than traditional mental health professionals normally provide. How do trained crisis counselors help disaster victims manage their emotional distress in the aftermath of a disaster?

First of all, a crisis counselor provides objective emotional support. The mental health professional must maintain an objective perspective when faced with the intense grief and confusion that accompanies tragedy. It is human for people working with trauma victims to be affected by traumatic events as much as others are. Even hardened rescue personnel such as police officers and fire fighters may become immediately engrossed in and severely affected by the intense loss in an air disaster. The traditionally distant roles of mental health providers are swept away in situations involving loss through disaster. The crisis worker must strive to maintain a balanced perspective to help those involved in the disaster who will be more intensely affected and will have a more diminished perspective. The mental health professional tries to provide a long-term perspective—to allow victims to see that there is hope of surviving psychologically.

A crisis counselor also serves as a source of information and a buffer against misinformation coming from rumor. Disasters are always followed by periods of confusion, misinformation, and negative emotional states. One important role of the mental health professional in disaster response efforts is to obtain, decipher, and clearly communicate to victims the most accurate picture of the situation obtainable at the moment; unfortunately, this may include information of traumatic import to those counseled, such as news that a loved one has been declared dead. The crisis intervention specialist must be knowledgeable about disaster victims' options to provide the information they need for personal decisions.

Finally, a crisis counselor provides practical suggestions to promote adaptation. An important facet of the mental health professional's role in dealing with disaster victims is to guide them through the difficult times by providing a perspective on the problems being faced and by offering valuable guidance for alleviating those problems.

Crisis Telephone Hot-Line Counseling Services. After an air disaster, confusion prevails. Airplane disasters always involve considerable psychological turmoil and may produce psychological problems among passengers and crew members. Inaccurate information and anxiety-producing doubts can create a state of tension that results in demoralization and negative behavior, such as absenteeism from work, excessive drinking, and morale problems.

An effective way to deal with this psychological uncertainty and reduce the negative atmosphere following an air disaster is to provide telephone counseling services—an informational hot line of sorts—for all those who feel the need to discuss their concerns, be they airline employees or passenger families. For example, a 24-hour crisis telephone hot-line counseling service was established shortly after the crash of an airliner in Detroit, Michigan, in 1987 in which 156 people died; it continued in operation for four weeks. This service was staffed by qualified psychologists in crisis counseling who provided counseling, information, and referral services.

Postdisaster Debriefing Sessions. One goal of a disaster response program is to provide aftercare psychological services to passenger-victims, surviving family members, and rescue personnel. Those who appear to function well at the disaster site may experience difficulties after the immediate crisis has subsided and they have returned to family and normal duties. Even experienced disaster workers who are well trained and effective at the site can be affected later by the pressures and problems experienced during the disaster.

The desire to "unwind" in a psychologically safe environment and to share one's experience of the disaster are universal needs of people following a traumatic situation. Debriefing sessions are designed to provide those who might be directly affected by the accident an opportunity to relate their experiences and to express their feelings and concerns about the disaster. Mitchell (1985) and Keating (1987), for example, have explored the use of de-

briefing sessions in dealing with emergency workers and found this approach to be effective in reducing the emotional reactions of emergency workers to traumatic events.

Immediate crisis intervention, telephone hot-line counseling, and debriefing programs have become standard efforts following major disasters to help victims and emergency workers return more quickly and effectively to normal functioning. By reducing the impact of a tragedy, these programs attempt to prevent the development of more severe psychological disorders.

Tertiary Prevention

Tertiary prevention involves efforts aimed at reducing the impact of a disorder and restoring a person to functioning once a mental health problem has been identified. Mental health rehabilitative efforts are important aspects of tertiary prevention and will be discussed in the following sections.

The Mental Hospital as a Therapeutic Community Most of the traditional forms of therapy that we discussed in Chapters 16 and 17 may, of course, be used in a hospital setting to promote tertiary prevention. In addition, in many mental hospitals these techniques are being supplemented by efforts to make the hospital environment itself a "therapeutic community" (Gunderson, 1980; Jones, 1953; Paul & Lentz, 1977). That is, all the ongoing activities of the hospital are brought into the total treatment program, and the environment, or milieu, is a crucial aspect of the therapy. This approach is thus often referred to as **milieu therapy.** Three general therapeutic principles guide the milieu approach to treatment:

1. Staff expectations are clearly communicated to patients. Both positive and negative feedback are used to encourage appropriate verbalizations and actions by patients.

2. Patients are encouraged to become involved in all decisions made and all actions taken concerning them. A self-care, do-it-yourself attitude prevails.

3. All patients belong to social groups on the ward. The experience of group cohesiveness gives the patients support and encouragement, and the related process of group pressure helps exert control over their behavior.

In a therapeutic community, as few restraints as possible are placed on patients' freedom, and the orientation is toward encouraging patients to take responsibility for their behavior and to participate actively in their treatment programs. Open wards permit patients to use the grounds and premises. Self-government programs give patients responsibility for managing their own affairs and those of the ward. All hospital personnel are expected to treat the patients as human beings who merit consideration and courtesy. Research has shown that intensive milieu programs significantly benefit even relatively briefly hospitalized patients (Gunderson, 1980).

The interaction among patients—whether in group therapy sessions, social events, or other activities—is planned in such a way as to be of therapeutic benefit. In fact, it is becoming apparent that often the most beneficial aspect of a therapeutic community is the interaction among the patients themselves. Differences in social roles and backgrounds may make empathy between staff and patients difficult, but fellow patients have been there—they have had similar problems and breakdowns and have experienced the anxiety and humiliation of being labeled mentally ill and hospitalized. Thus, constructive relationships frequently develop among patients in a supportive, encouraging milieu.

Another highly successful method for helping patients take increased responsibility for their own behavior is the use of **social-learning programs.** Such programs normally make use of learning principles and techniques, such as token economies, to shape more socially acceptable behavior (Paul, 1979; Paul & Lentz, 1977; Paul & Menditto, 1992; Rhoades, 1981).

A persistent concern with hospitalization is that the mental hospital may become a permanent refuge from the world, either because it offers total escape from the demands of everyday living or because it encourages patients to settle into a chronic sick role with a permanent excuse for letting other people take care of them. The original rationale for the deinstitutionalization policy of recent years was that it would tend to forestall these negative adaptations to hospital confinement. To keep the focus on returning patients to the community and on preventing a return to the institution, contemporary hospital staffs try to establish close ties with patients' families and communities and to maintain a recovery-expectant attitude.

Between 70 and 90 percent of patients labeled as psychotic and admitted to mental hospitals can now be discharged within a few weeks, or at most a few months. Current estimates suggest that there are about 2 to 3 million chronically mentally ill individuals in America, of whom about half reside in mental hospitals and the other half live in nursing homes or in the community (Narrow et al., 1993; Regier et al., 1993; Talbott, 1985; Tien & Eaton, 1992).

Even where disorders have become chronic, effective treatment methods have been developed. In one of the most extensive and well-controlled studies of chronic hospitalized patients, Paul and Lentz (1977) compared the relative effectiveness of three treatment approaches:

1. Milieu therapy, focused on structuring a patient's environment to provide clear communications of expectations, and to get the patient involved in the treatment and participating in the therapeutic community through the group process.

2. A social-learning treatment program, organized around learning principles and using a rigorously programmed token economy system, with ward staff as reinforcing agents. Undesirable behavior was not reinforced, whereas the accumulation of many tokens through effective functioning could result in attractive lifestyle amenities not normally available in public mental hospitals.

3. Traditional mental hospital treatments, including pharmacotherapy, occupational therapy, recreational therapy, activity therapy, and individual or group therapy. No systematic application of milieu therapy or the social-learning program was given to this group.

The treatment project covered a period of six years, with an initial phase of staff training, patient assessment, and baseline recording; a treatment phase; an aftercare phase; and a long (year and a half) follow-up. The changes targeted included resocialization, the learning of new roles, and the reduction or elimination of bizarre behavior. There were 28 chronic schizophrenic patients in each treatment group, matched for age, sex, socioeconomic level, symptoms, and duration of hospitalization. The results of the study were impressive. Both milieu therapy and the social-learning program produced significant improvement in overall functioning and resulted in more successful hospital releases than the traditional hospital care. The behaviorally based social-learning program, however, was clearly superior to the more diffuse program of milieu therapy, as evidenced by the fact that over 90 percent of the released patients from the social-learning program remained continuously in the community, compared with 70 percent of the released patients who had had milieu therapy. The figure for the traditional treatment program was less than 50 percent.

Despite the promise of the token economy approach, emulating as it does certain "real world" principles of exchange the patient will face outside the institution, it has not fared particularly well in terms of public acceptance (Paul & Menditto, 1992). Many feel that it is cruel and inhumane to expect mental patients to govern their behavior in accordance with a prescribed schedule of reinforcements. One might ask in this connection, however, whether it is more humane to consign the patient to the status of a passive and helpless recipient of whatever the environment may somewhat unpredictably have to offer, which in many institutional settings is not very much. Is that truly the message we would wish to convey about the patient's relationship to his or her environment? Probably not, especially in light of the considerable evidence (e.g., Braginsky, Braginsky, & Ring, 1969) that chronic mental patients are as a group surprisingly adept, in fact, at managing outcomes that are within their range of control.

Aftercare Programs Even where hospitalization has successfully modified maladaptive behavior and a patient has learned needed occupational and interpersonal skills, readjustment in the community following release may still be difficult. Many studies have shown that in the past up to 45 percent of schizophrenic patients have been readmitted within the first year after their discharge. This is where tertiary prevention can play a major role, especially in terms of providing former clients and patients with supportive services that will help them toward long-term psychological well-being (Paul & Lentz, 1977). Aftercare programs can help smooth the transition from institutional to community life and reduce the number of relapses. Glasscote (1978) found that only 16 percent of patients who received adequate aftercare were readmitted within the first six months compared with 37 percent for patients not receiving aftercare. By the end of five years, more of both groups had been readmitted, but 47 percent of the aftercare group were still in the community, compared with only 30 percent of the group who had not received aftercare.

Aftercare is the responsibility of community mental health facilities and personnel, the community as a whole, and, of course, the person's family. Its goal is to ensure that released patients will be helped to make an adequate readjustment and return to full participation in their home and community with a minimum of delay and difficulty. Sometimes aftercare includes a "halfway" period in which a released patient has a gradual return to the outside world in what were formerly termed halfway houses. Community-based treatment programs, now referred to as aftercare programs, are live-in facilities that serve as a home base for former patients as they make the transition back to adequate functioning in the community. Typically, community-based facilities are run not by professional mental health personnel but by the residents themselves.

There is even some evidence that community-based living is preferable to hospital confinement for patients who are still actively psychotic. In a note-

In addition to providing prompt and intense inpatient therapy for patients who need it, tertiary prevention also involves provisions for aftercare, such as this halfway house, to smooth the transition from institutional to community life.

worthy program with a group of seriously disturbed mental patients, Fairweather and colleagues (1969, 1980; Fairweather & Fergus, 1993) demonstrated that these patients could function in the community, living in a patient-run facility, even to the extent of responsibly (and profitably) operating a service business. Initially, a member of the research staff coordinated the daily operations of the "Lodge," but he was shortly replaced by a layperson. The patients were given full responsibility for operating the Lodge, for regulating each other's behavior, for earning money, and for purchasing and preparing food. Forty months after their discharge, a comparison was made of these former patients and a comparable group of 75 patients who had been discharged at the same time but had not had the Lodge experience. Whereas most members of the Lodge facility were able to hold income-producing jobs, to manage their daily lives, and to adjust in the outside world, the majority of those who had not had the community group-living experience were unable to adjust to life on the outside and required rehospitalization.

Day hospital facilities within or sponsored by community mental health centers may also be used as alternatives to hospitalization. For example, Penk, Charles, and Van Hoose (1978) showed that partial hospitalization in a day treatment setting resulted in as much improvement (at a lower cost) as full inpatient psychiatric treatment in a group of patients they studied. It would seem, however, that considerable care must be taken in the selection of patients for this less restrictive approach. The risk of untoward consequences, including involvement with the police, may be increased where other social supports are minimal and where patients are prone to substance abuse (Caton et al., 1993).

Similar community-based treatment facilities have been established for alcoholics, drug addicts, and other people attempting to make an adjustment into the community after institutionalization. Such facilities may be said to be specialized in the sense that all residents share similar backgrounds and problems, and this seems to contribute to the facilities' effectiveness.

One of the chief problems of community-based treatment facilities is that of gaining the acceptance and support of community residents (Fairweather, 1994). As Dennes (1974) pointed out in the early years of the growth of community-based treatment, this requires educational and other social measures directed toward increasing community understanding, acceptance, and tolerance of troubled people who may differ somewhat from community norms. The viability of such an approach, however, is demonstrated in the example of Geel, Belgium—"the town that cares"—which we discussed in Chapter 2.

CONTROVERSIAL ISSUES AND THE MENTALLY DISORDERED

A number of important issues arise related to the legal status of the mentally ill. These issues are the subject matter of **forensic psychology,** or **forensic psychiatry,** and they center on the rights of mental patients and the rights of members of society to be protected from disturbed individuals. For a survey of some of the legal rights that have been gained for the mentally ill over the years, see HIGHLIGHT 18.2.

The issues we will cover in this section are those that have been the center of controversy for many years. We will first review the procedures involved in involuntarily committing disturbed and dangerous individuals to psychiatric institutions. Next, we will turn to the assessment of dangerousness in disturbed persons; we will also discuss a related issue, which has become of key concern to psychotherapists—the court decision that psychotherapists have a duty to protect potential victims of any threatened violence by their patients. In addition, we will examine the controversial insanity defense for capital crimes as well as the issue of deinstitutionalization, or what some have called the premature "dumping" of mental patients into the community. Finally, in the "Unresolved Issues" section we will discuss certain continuing problems that exist at the broad interface where mental health and legal issues come together, problems that are due in part at least to failures of communication and collaboration between the two with respect to challenges they share.

The Commitment Process

Persons with psychological problems or behaviors that are so extreme and severe as to pose a threat to themselves or others may require protective confinement. Those who commit crimes, whether or not they have a psychological disorder, are dealt with primarily through the judicial system—arrest, court trial, and, if convicted, possible confinement in a penal institution. Persons who are judged to be potentially dangerous because of their psychological state may, after civil commitment procedures, be confined in a mental institution. The steps in the commitment process vary slightly depending on state law (we will here use Minnesota as our model), the locally available community mental health resources, and the nature of the problem—for example, commitment procedures for a mentally retarded person will be different from those for a person with an alcohol-abuse problem.

A distinction should be made here between voluntary hospitalization and involuntary commitment. In most cases, people enter mental institutions without a court order; that is, they accept voluntary commitment or hospitalization. In these cases, they can, with sufficient notice, leave the hospital if they wish. In cases in which a person is believed to be dangerous or unable to provide for his or her own care, the need for involuntary commitment may arise.

Being mentally ill is not sufficient grounds for placing a person in a mental institution against his or her will. Although procedures vary somewhat from state to state, several conditions beyond mental illness usually must be met before formal commitment can occur (Schwitzgebel & Schwitzgebel, 1980). In brief, the person must be judged to be:

Patient Advocacy: Important Court Decisions Regarding Patient Rights

Several important court decisions in recent years have helped establish certain basic rights for individuals suffering from mental disorders, but have also curtailed these rights with continuing controversy:

Right to treatment. In 1972, a U.S. District Court in Alabama made a landmark decision in the case of *Wyatt* v. *Stickney.* The ruling held that a mentally ill or mentally retarded person had a right to receive treatment. Since the decision, the state of Alabama has increased its budget for the treatment of mental health and mental retardation by 300 percent.

Freedom from custodial confinement. In 1975, the U.S. Supreme Court upheld the principle that patients have a right to freedom from custodial confinement if they are not dangerous to themselves or others and if they can safely survive outside of custody. In the *Donaldson* v. *O'Connor* decision, the defendants were required to pay Donaldson $10,000 for having kept him in custody without providing treatment.

Right to compensation for work. In 1973, a U.S. District Court ruled in the case of *Souder* v.

Brennan (the secretary of labor) that a patient in a nonfederal mental institution who performed work must be paid according to the Fair Labor Standards Act. Although a 1978 Supreme Court ruling nullified the part of the lower court's decision dealing with state hospitals, the ruling still applied to mentally ill and mentally retarded patients in private facilities.

Right to live in a community. In 1974, the U.S. District Court decided, in the case of *Staff* v. *Miller,* that released state mental hospital patients had a right to live in "adult homes" in the community.

Right to less restrictive treatment. In 1975, a U.S. District Court issued a landmark decision in the case of *Dixon* v. *Weinberger.* The ruling established the right of individuals to receive treatment in less restrictive facilities than mental institutions.

Right to legal counsel at commitment hearings. The State Supreme Court of Wisconsin decided in 1976, in the case of *Memmel* v. *Mundy,* that an individual had the right to legal counsel during the commitment process.

Right to refuse treatment. Several court decisions have provided rulings and some states have enacted legislation permitting patients to refuse certain treatments, such as electroconvulsive therapy and psychosurgery.

The need for confinement must be shown by clear, convincing evidence. In 1979, the U.S. Supreme Court ruled, in the case of *Addington* v. *Texas,* that a person's need to be kept in an institution must be based on demonstrable evidence.

Limitation on patients' rights to refuse psychotropic medication. In 1990 the U.S. Supreme Court ruled, in *Washington* v. *Harper,* that a Washington state prison could override a disturbed prisoner's refusal of psychotropic medications, based on a finding that the prison's review process adequately protected the patient's rights. We see in this instance that changes in the national political climate can reverse prior trends appearing to favor patients' rights.

Based on Bernard (1979); Hermann (1990); National Association for Mental Health (1979); and Mental Health Law Project (1987).

- Dangerous to himself or herself, or to others
- Incapable of providing for his or her basic physical needs
- Unable to make responsible decisions about hospitalization
- And/or in need of treatment or care in a hospital

The use of the "dangerousness" complaint as grounds for civil commitment has apparently increased in recent years (McNeil & Binder, 1986). Typically, filing a petition for a commitment hearing is the first step in the process of committing a person involuntarily. This petition is usually filed by a concerned person, such as a relative, physician, or mental health professional. When a petition is filed, a judge appoints two examiners to evaluate the "proposed patient." In Minnesota, for example, one examiner must be a physician (not necessarily a psychiatrist); the other can be a psychiatrist or a psychologist. The patient is asked to appear voluntarily for psychiatric examination before the commitment hearing. The hearing must be held within 14 days, which can be extended for 30 more days if good cause for the extension can be shown. The law requires that the court-appointed examiners interview the patient before the hearing.

If a person is committed to a mental hospital for treatment, the hospital must report to the court within 60 days as to whether the person needs to be confined even longer. If no report is given by the hospital, the patient must be released. If the hospital indicates that the person needs further treatment, then the commitment period becomes indeterminate, subject to periodic reevaluations.

Because the decision to commit a person is based on the conclusions of others about the person's capabilities and his or her potential for dangerous behavior, the civil commitment process leaves open the possibility of the unwarranted violation of a person's civil rights. As a consequence, most states have stringent safeguards in the procedures to assure that any person who is the subject of a petition for commitment is granted due process, including rights to formal hearings with representation by legal counsel. If there is not time to get a court order for commitment or if there is imminent danger, however, the law allows emergency hospitalization without a formal commitment hearing. In such cases, a physician must sign a statement saying that an imminent danger exists. The patient can then be picked up (usually by the police) and detained under a "hold order," usually not to exceed 72 hours, unless a petition for commitment is filed within that period.

Involuntary commitment in a psychiatric facility is, in large part, contingent on a determination that a person is dangerous and needs to be confined out of a need to protect himself or herself or society. We will now turn to the important question of evaluating patients in terms of their potential dangerousness.

The Assessment of "Dangerousness"

As we have seen, though most psychiatric patients are not considered dangerous and need no special safety precautions, some are violent and require close supervision—perhaps confinement until their dangerousness is no longer a problem. Few psychiatric patients are assaultive at or prior to their admission to psychiatric facilities. Rates of assaultiveness vary from setting to setting, though in all reported studies the number of assaultive patients is relatively low. Nevertheless, the issue, involving as it does life

and death considerations, deserves the most careful scrutiny as to *any* enhanced risk of violence mental disorders may entail. Fortunately, the question of the overall relationship between violence and mental disorder, one that is far more complex than may appear, has been competently and thoroughly addressed in a recent review by Monahan (1992). He summarizes his findings as follows:

> Whether the measure is the prevalence of violence among the disordered or the prevalence of disorder among the violent, whether the sample is people who are selected for treatment as inmates or people randomly chosen from the open community, and no matter how many social and demographic factors are statistically taken into account, there appears to be a relationship between mental disorder and violent behavior. Mental disorder may be a robust and significant factor for the occurrence of violence, as an increasing number of clinical researchers in recent years have averred. . . ." (p. 519)

Monahan (1992) goes on to note, however, that policy implications and implications pertaining to the social image of former mental patients and the manner in which these are managed in the media must be tempered by two additional and well-established findings: (a) the increased risk of violence appears limited to persons who are *currently experiencing* psychotic symptoms, and (b) *approximately 90 percent of all currently disordered persons show no propensity toward violence.*

The determination that a patient is potentially dangerous is a difficult one to make (Litwack & Schlesinger, 1987). A 43-year-old homeless Cuban refugee, for example, who had only a few days earlier undergone a psychiatric evaluation and been released, stabbed two tourists to death on the Staten Island Ferry because "God told him to kill" (*Time*, July 21, 1986). Westley Allan Dodd, condemned molester, mutilator, and murderer of numerous children, by his own admission continued undetected in his violent crimes during the several periods of therapy he underwent by court order (*Time*, January 11, 1993). Obviously, determining potential dangerousness is a crucial judgment for mental health professionals to make—not only from a therapeutic standpoint, to assure that the most appropriate treatment is conducted, but also from the legal point of view of responsibility to the larger society. A clinician has a clear responsibility to attempt to protect the public from potential violence or other uncontrolled behavior of dangerous patients. A dramatic incident of a failure to assess the extent of a patient's dangerousness was reported by Gorin (1980, 1982) on the television news program *60 Minutes:*

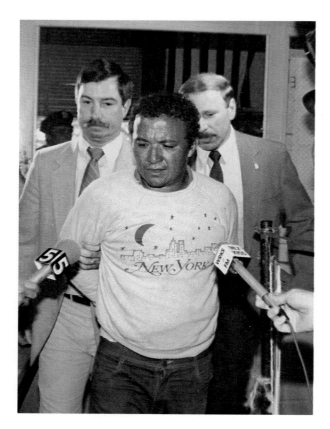

Juan Gonzalez stabbed and killed two people and injured nine others on the Staten Island Ferry. A few days before the incident, Gonzalez had undergone psychiatric evaluation after making wild death threats on the street. Though doctors concluded that he had a psychotic paranoid disorder, Gonzalez was released after two days because there was not enough space at the facility and he could not be involuntarily committed to a mental institution.

In December, 1979, Mrs. Eva B. was brutally stabbed to death by her former husband while a police dispatcher listened to her terrified screams over the telephone. Only hours before the stabbing incident occurred, Mr. B., who had attacked Mrs. B. eight times in the past, had been judged by two staff psychiatrists not to be dangerous. He had then been released, as part of his treatment, on a temporary pass from the Pilgrim State Hospital in New York. The hospital staff had released Mr. B. from confinement at this time despite the fact that both the judge and the prosecuting attorney who had been involved in his trial (for attempting to kill his wife) had independently written the New York State Department of Mental Health recommending that Mr. B. be held in the strictest confinement because of his persistent threats against Mrs. B. (Indeed,

on two previous occasions, Mr. B. had escaped from the hospital and attempted to kill her.) The judge and attorney had also recommended that Mrs. B. should be warned if Mr. B. was released. Ironically, six hours after she had been murdered, a telegram from the hospital was delivered to Mrs. B.'s home warning her that her husband had not returned from his pass.

Looking beyond what appears to be some failure to follow through on the court's recommendations, this case illustrates a number of difficult yet critical dilemmas involved in trying to identify or predict dangerousness in psychiatric patients. First, it emphasizes the fact that some people are capable of uncontrolled violent behavior and hence are potentially dangerous if left unsupervised in the community. It also reflects the dilemma faced by mental health professionals who, attempting to rehabilitate disturbed patients by gradually easing them back into society, must exhibit some degree of trust in these individuals. Finally, and critically, it illustrates the fact that it is very difficult—for professionals and laypersons alike—to accurately appraise "dangerousness" in some individuals.

Attempts to Predict Dangerousness It is usually an easy matter to determine, after the fact, that a person has committed a violent act or acts and has demonstrated "dangerous behavior." The difficulty comes when one attempts to determine in advance if the person is going to commit some particular violent act. Assessing a general state of "dangerousness" is not the same thing as the far more formidable task of predicting whether a designated violent act will occur. How well do mental health professionals do in predicting the occurrence of dangerous acts? A general answer to this question would have to be "not very well," but there are several problems to be considered in coming to an adequate appreciation of the difficulties of the task. Perhaps the foremost is that the definition of what is "dangerous" is itself unclear. It turns out to depend, to a large extent, on who is asked. Some people have a limited or restrictive definition of what behaviors are dangerous and are willing to tolerate more aggressive behavior than others, who in turn view a broader range of behaviors as potentially dangerous. There is of course a consensus about the dangerousness of extreme behaviors such as murder and assault with a deadly weapon, but as we move away from such obvious cases public consensus tends to fade rather rapidly. Rape, for example, has only recently attained the serious criminal status it is now usually accorded, but even here there are local pockets of resistance in which rape is still (erroneously) considered to be an inconsequential and excusable infraction having little or no predictiveness as to "real" violence (see Segal & Stermac, 1990).

Violent acts are particularly difficult to predict because they are apparently determined as much by situational circumstances as they are by an individual's personality traits or violent predispositions. It is, of course, impossible to predict with any great certainty what environmental circumstances are going to occur or what particular circumstances will provoke or instigate aggression for any given violently disposed person. One obvious and significantly predictive risk factor is a past history of violence (Megargee, 1993; Noble & Rodger, 1989), but clinicians are not always able to unearth this type of background information.

As already noted, some types of patients, particularly actively schizophrenic and manic individuals (Binder & McNiel, 1988) or patients with well-entrenched delusions (de Pauw & Szulecka, 1988), are far more likely to commit violent acts than the average for the mental patient group as a whole. Martell and Dietz (1992) have recently reported a study of persons convicted of pushing or attempting to push unsuspecting victims, about half of whom were killed or seriously injured, into the paths of trains approaching subway stations in New York City. Most of the perpetrators of this gruesome crime, whose incidence has risen in recent years, were both psychotic and homeless at the time of the act.

Mental health professionals typically err on the conservative side when assessing "violence proneness" in a patient; that is, they overpredict violence. They consider some individuals more dangerous than they actually are and, in general, predict a greater percentage of clients to be dangerous, requiring protective confinement, than actually become involved in violent acts (Megargee, 1995; Monahan, 1981). Such a trend is of course quite understandable from the standpoint of the practitioner, considering the potentially serious consequences of a "false negative" judgment. It is likely, however, that many innocent patients thereby sustain a violation of their civil rights. Given a certain irreducible level of uncertainty in the prediction of violence, it is not obvious how this dilemma can be completely resolved.

Methods for Assessing Potential for Dangerousness Evaluating a person's potential for committing violent acts is difficult because only part of the equation is available for study:

$$\frac{\text{predisposing personality} + \text{environmental instigation}}{= \text{aggressive act}}$$

As we have noted, psychologists and psychiatrists usually do not know enough about the environmental circumstances the person will encounter to evaluate what the instigation to aggression will be. Predictions of dangerousness focus, then, primarily on aspects of the individual's personality.

The two major sources of personality information are data from personality tests and the individual's previous history. Personality testing can reveal whether the individual shows personality traits of hostility, aggressiveness, impulsiveness, poor judgment, and so on. Notwithstanding the already noted readiness of practitioners to predict the likelihood of violence based on such factors, many individuals having these characteristics never do act on them. The use of previous history—such as having committed prior aggression, having verbalized threats of aggression, having an available means of committing violence (such as possession of a gun), and so on—are useful predictors (Monahan, 1981). Like personality testing, however, these data only focus on the individual factors and do not account for the situational forces that impinge on the person, which may include notably provocative behavior on the part of the victim (Megargee, 1993).

The prediction of violence is even more difficult in the case of an overcontrolled offender, one of whose more salient characteristics is a subaverage level of manifestly aggressive behavior prior to the commission of an aggressive act, very often an extremely violent one. Megargee (1970) studied extensively the "overcontrolled hostile" person who is the epitome of well-controlled behavior but who, typically on only one occasion, loses control and murderously attacks another person. Examples of this type of killer are dramatic: the high school honor student, reportedly civic-minded and fond of helping sick and old people, who is arrested for torturing and killing a three-year-old girl in his neighborhood; or the mild, passive father of four who loses his temper over being cheated by a car dealer and beats the man to death with a tire iron. These examples illustrate the most difficult type of aggressive behavior to predict—the sudden, violent, impulsive act of a seemingly well-controlled and "normal" individual.

A general pessimism has prevailed in recent years about our ability to predict dangerousness. Several studies in violence prediction, however, have attempted to improve prediction by identifying persons at risk for violence. Using demographic data on family background, history of violence, friendships, and substance use, Klassen and O'Connor (1988) were able to identify 76 percent of the people who later became violent. They concluded that predictive assessments could be improved even more if the context in which violence occurs is taken into consideration.

The Duty to Protect: Implications of the Tarasoff Decision What should a therapist do on learning that one of his or her patients is planning to harm one or more other persons? Can the therapist violate the legally sanctioned confidence of the therapy contract and take action to prevent the patient from committing the act? Today in probably most of the states the therapist not only can violate confidentiality with impunity but may be required by law to do so—that is, to take action to protect persons from the threat of imminent violence against them. In its original form, this requirement was conceived as a duty to warn the prospective victim. The duty-to-warn legal doctrine was given a great deal of impetus in a California court ruling in the case of *Tarasoff v. The Regents of the University of California et al.* (Mills, Sullivan, & Eth, 1987).

In this case, Prosenjit Poddar was being seen in outpatient psychotherapy by a psychologist at the university mental health facility. During his treatment, Mr. Poddar indicated that he intended to kill his former girlfriend, Tatiana Tarasoff, when she returned from vacation. The psychologist, concerned about the threat, discussed the case with his supervisors, and they agreed that Mr. Poddar was dangerous and should be committed for further observation and treatment. They informed the campus police, who picked up Mr. Poddar for questioning. The police judged Mr. Poddar to be rational and released him after he promised to leave Ms. Tarasoff alone. Mr. Poddar then terminated treatment with the psychologist. About two months later, he stabbed Ms. Tarasoff to death. Her parents later sued the University of California and its staff involved in the case for their failure to hospitalize Mr. Poddar and their failure to warn Ms. Tarasoff about the threat to her life. In due course the California Supreme Court in 1974 ruled that the defendants were not liable for failing to hospitalize Mr. Poddar; it did, however, find them liable for their failure to warn the victim. Ironically, Prosenjit Poddar, the criminal, was released on a trial technicality and returned home to India. In a later analysis of the case, Knapp (1980) said that the court

> ruled that difficulty in determining dangerousness does not exempt a psychotherapist from attempting to protect others when a determination of dangerousness exists. The court acknowledged that confidentiality was important to the psychotherapeutic

relationship but stated that the protective privilege ends where the public peril begins. (p. 610)

The duty-to-warn ruling in the **Tarasoff decision,** while spelling out a therapist's responsibility in situations where there has been an explicit threat on a specific person's life, left other areas of application unclear. For example, does this ruling apply in cases where a patient threatens to commit suicide, and how might the therapist's responsibility be met in such a case? What if anything should a therapist do when the object of violence is not clearly named, such as when global threats are made? Would the duty-to-warn ruling hold up in other states? Or might deleterious effects on patient-therapist relationships outweigh any public benefit to be derived from the duty to warn? Responding to mounting pressures for clarification, chiefly from mental health professional organizations, the California Supreme Court issued a revised opinion in 1976, called *Tarasoff II*. In this decision the Court ruled that the duty was to *protect*, rather than specifically to warn, the prospective victim, but it left vague the question of how this duty might be discharged—presumably in order to provide practitioners with enhanced latitude in dealing with danger to third parties. However, the granting of such latitude would seem to carry with it the possibility of being held liable for providing inadequate protection based on rules not yet formulated at the time intervention is contemplated, as was the problem for the original *Tarasoff* defendants. Meanwhile, numerous other lawsuits in other jurisdictions had been filed and had been adjudicated in inconsistent and confusing ways (Mills et al., 1987).

The many perplexing issues for practitioners left in the wake of *Tarasoff* were partly resolved, at least in California, by the legislature's adoption in 1985 of a new state law essentially establishing that the duty to protect is discharged if the therapist makes "reasonable efforts" to inform potential victims *and* an appropriate law enforcement agency of the pending threat. In other jurisdictions, however, the inconsistent judicial fallout from *Tarasoff* has continued and has been a source of much anxiety and confusion among mental health professionals, many of whom continue to believe on ethical and clinical grounds that strict confidentiality is an absolute and inviolable trust. A small minority of states, for example, Maryland and Pennsylvania, has explicitly affirmed the latter position, repudiating *Tarasoff* altogether (Mills et al., 1987). Official professional ethics codes, such as that of the American Psychological Association (1992), normally compel compliance with relevant law regardless of personal predilections to the contrary. Where the law is itself vague or equivocal, however, as it often is in this area, there is of course much room for idiosyncratic and biased interpretation.

No uniformly applicable, national resolution of the problem is evident as of this writing. Until one becomes available, clinicians would be well advised to follow closely systematic and preferably written protocols for staged responses to the varying levels of explicitness and imminence contained in client threats of violence, and to carefully document and justify, again in writing, their decisions for actions taken (Gross et al., 1987). An analysis of adjudicated court cases undertaken by Mills (1984) suggests that the judgment of practitioner liability as a practical matter usually turns on the degree of *foreseeability* of the violence directed at explicitly designated victims.

The Insanity Defense

> The picture in the February 13, 1992, issue of *Time* said it all. The largest frame offered Jeffrey Dahmer, on trial for the murder, dismemberment, and cannibalization of 15 men in Milwaukee. The top right-hand frame pictured David Berkowitz, the "Son of Sam," who terrorized New York City for 13 months in 1976–1977 while killing six people and wounding seven others. The bottom right-hand frame showed John Hinckley, the would-be assassin of President Ronald Reagan in 1981. (Steadman et al., 1993, p. 1)

What linked the three infamous persons named here, apart from their murderous exploits, was their shared claim that they were in fact not legally responsible for their criminal acts—that is, each attempted to use the so-called **insanity defense** ("not guilty by reason of insanity") as a means of avoiding the legally prescribed consequences of their crimes. In technical legal terms, in other words, these men were invoking the ancient doctrine that their acts, while guilty ones (*actus rea*), lacked moral blameworthiness because they were unaccompanied by the corresponding (and, for a guilty judgment, legally mandated) intentional state of mind (*mens rea*)—the underlying assumption being that "insanity" somehow precludes or absolves the harboring of a guilty intent. Whatever the operational and conceptual conundrums involved in this doctrine—and these on the face of it would appear to be legion—they were rendered moot in the Dahmer and Berkowitz cases because the planned insanity defenses proved unsuccessful, as is the usual outcome (Steadman et al., 1993).

The outcome of the Hinckley case was different in a number of important respects, at base because in this instance the insanity defense was successful. Hinckley pleaded "not guilty by reason of insanity" (NGRI) at trial, and in June of 1982 was acquitted on those grounds. His acquittal immediately unleashed a storm of public protest and of widespread, often unduly hasty attempts to reform the law pertaining to the NGRI defense so as to make it a less-attractive option to capital case defendants and their attorneys. Hinckley himself was committed to the care of a federally operated high-security mental hospital, ostensibly to be involuntarily retained there until such time as his disorder remits sufficiently that his release would not constitute a danger to himself or others. He remains incarcerated at this writing, and it seems doubtful that he will be declared sufficiently "well" to be "discharged" any time in the foreseeable future. His release would almost certainly bring forth another public outcry demanding abolition or limitation of the insanity defense. In our judgment, there is in all of this arrangement a certain unsatisfactorily indirect and disingenuous quality, one perhaps encouraged by a persistent failure of legal scholars to examine critically and rigorously the guilt-absolving insanity construct and the *mens rea* doctrine from which it derives.

In any event, in recent years the use of the NGRI defense in capital crime trials has been surrounded by controversy, largely owing to the uproar created by the outcome of the Hinckley trial (Steadman et al., 1993). Public concern, especially in cases of high

The use of the insanity defense in highly publicized cases, such as John Hinckley's assassination attempt on President Reagan in 1981, has led to controversy over whether it legitimately protects a mentally ill offender's rights or is a contrivance to avoid criminal responsibility.

visibility, that guilty (in the *actus rea* sense) defendants may feign mental disorder and fraudulently profit from this plea in avoiding criminal responsibility is evidently never far beneath the surface. Good defense attorneys are of course aware of this public cynicism, which is likely to be shared by juries, and attempt to counteract it in various ways, often by portraying their purportedly "insane at the time of the act" clients to have been themselves at an earlier time victims of extraordinarily heinous and traumatic acts. Some of them undoubtedly were, but the strategy of creating sympathy while offering a plausible reason for the "insane" act would have a compelling attraction in any case.

Despite some features that make it an appealing option to consider, especially where the undisputed facts are strongly aligned against the defendant, the NGRI defense has actually been employed quite rarely—in less than 2 percent of capital cases in the United States over time (Fersch, 1980; Steadman et al., 1993). Studies have confirmed the fact, however, that persons acquitted of crimes by reason of insanity spend less time, on the whole, in a psychiatric hospital than persons who are convicted of crimes spend in prison (Kahn & Raifman, 1981; Pasewark, Pantle, & Steadman, 1982).

To this point in the discussion, we have used the term "insanity defense" loosely, which is anathema to actual legal practice; we must now become more attentive to the many more precise legal nuances involved. Established precedents defining the insanity defense are as follows:

1. *The M'Naughten Rule (1843).* Under this ruling, people are believed to be sane unless it can be proved that, at the time of committing the act, they were laboring under such a defect of reason (from a disease of the mind) that they did not know the nature and quality of the act they were doing—or, if they did know they were committing the act, they did not know that what they were doing was wrong.

2. *The irresistible impulse rule (1887).* A second precedent in the insanity defense is the doctrine of the "irresistible impulse." This view holds that accused persons might not be responsible for their acts, even if they knew that what they were doing was wrong (according to the M'Naughten Rule), if they had lost the power to choose between right and wrong. That is, they could not avoid doing the act in question because they were compelled beyond their will to commit the act (Fersch, 1980).

3. *The Durham Rule.* In 1954, Judge David Bazelon, in a decision of the U. S. Court of Appeals, broadened the insanity defense further. Bazelon did not believe that the previous precedents allowed for a sufficient application of established scientific knowledge of mental illness and proposed a test that would be based on this knowledge. Under this rule, the accused is "not criminally responsible if his or her unlawful act was the product of mental disease or mental defect." New Hampshire, where this standard originated, is presently the only state subscribing to it.

4. *The American Law Institute (ALI) standard (1962).* This test combines the cognitive aspect of M'Naughten with the volitional focus of irresistible impulse in holding that the perpetrator is not legally responsible if at the time of the act he or she, owing to mental disease or defect, lacked "substantial capacity" either to appreciate its criminal character or to conform his or her behavior to the law's requirements.

5. *The Federal Insanity Defense Reform Act (IDRA).* Adopted by Congress in 1984 as the standard regarding the insanity defense to be applied in all federal jurisdictions, this act abolished the volitional element of the ALI standard and modified the cognitive one to read "unable to appreciate," thus bringing the definition quite close to M'Naughten. IDRA also specified that the mental disorder involved must be a severe one, and shifted the burden of proof from the prosecution to the defense; that is, the defense must clearly and convincingly establish the defendant's insanity, as opposed to the prior requirement that the prosecution clearly and convincingly demonstrate the defendant to have been sane when the prohibited act was committed.

This shifting of the burden of proof for the insanity defense, by the way, was an extremely common reform instituted by the states in the wake of protests of excessive laxity provoked by the Hinckley acquittal. Like the many other types of reform proposed at that time, the intent was to discourage use of the insanity defense and to make its success improbable if it *were* used. Unlike the average reform instituted, this one proved quite effective in altering litigation practices in the intended direction, according to the extensive data gathered by Steadman and colleagues (1993).

At the present time, nearly all of the 50 states and the District of Columbia subscribe to a version of either the ALI or the more restrictive M'Naughten standard. Three states—Idaho, Montana, and Utah—have entirely abolished the attribution of insanity as an acceptable defense for wrongdoing, a somewhat draconian solution that compensates in clarity for what some feel it lacks in compassion.

New York is a special case. While it uses a version of M'Naughten to define insanity, with the burden of proof on the defense, an elaborate procedural code has been enacted whose effect is to promote fairness in outcomes while ensuring lengthy and restrictive hospital commitment for defendants judged to be dangerous; it appears to have worked well (Steadman et al., 1993).

As we have seen, with the expansion of the diagnostic classification of mental disorder, a broad range of behaviors can be defined as mental disease or defect. Which mental diseases serve to excuse a defendant from criminal responsibility? Generally, under M'Naughten, psychotic disorders were the basis of the insanity defense, although that would appear an arguable proposition; but under the Durham or ALI Rules other conditions (such as personality disorder or dissociative disorder) might also apply. How, then, is guilt or innocence determined? Many authorities believe that the insanity defense requires of the courts an impossible task—to determine guilt or innocence by reason of insanity on the basis of psychiatric testimony. In many cases, this has involved conflicting testimony because both the prosecution and the defense have "their" panel of expert psychiatric witnesses, who typically are in complete disagreement (Fersch, 1980; Marvit, 1981). From a certain point of view, of course, the question such experts are asked to resolve is fundamentally unanswerable; it may even be meaningless in the sense that no conceivable empirical observation could unequivocally decide, after the fact, whether the defendant's mental state at the time of the crime was exculpatory by any rule of law so far proposed, or indeed imaginable.

It may well be, therefore, that the notion of exculpation by reason of insanity, while defensible and humane in some abstract sense, is so basically flawed conceptually and procedurally that we are in need of a serious rethinking of the entire matter. Meanwhile, it would seem wise to employ stringent standards for the insanity defense, such as the federal IDRA rules or the relevant and carefully considered statutory procedures enacted in New York State (see Steadman et al., 1993, for details).

Finally, it should be noted that several states have adopted the optional plea/verdict of "guilty but mentally ill" (GBMI). In these cases, a defendant may be sentenced but placed in a treatment facility rather than in a prison. This two-part judgment serves to prevent the type of situation in which a person commits a murder, is found not guilty by reason of insanity, is turned over to a mental health facility, is found to be rational and in no further need of treatment by the hospital staff, and is unconditionally released to the community after only a minimal period of confinement. Under the two-part decision, such a person would remain in the custody of the correctional department until the full sentence is served. Marvit (1981) has suggested that this approach might "realistically balance the interest of the mentally ill offender's rights and the community's need to control criminal behavior" (p. 23). However, in Georgia, one of the states adopting this option, GBMI defendants received longer sentences and longer periods of confinement than those pleading NGRI and losing. Overall, outcomes from use of the GBMI standard, often employed in a plea-bargaining strategy, have been disappointing (Steadman et al., 1993).

Deinstitutionalization

As we learned in Chapter 2, public asylums or mental hospitals were originally viewed as the most humane settings for dealing with chronic patients; many of these institutions were originally operated according to the benign and gentle principles of "moral therapy." The people who founded the institutions and the society that supported them saw these facilities as havens for retarded or disturbed individuals who could not survive in the world on their own. Ironically, though, and coincident with huge and successive waves of immigrants arriving on our shores beginning in the later nineteenth century, hospitals gradually became overcrowded, hospital staffs overworked, and taxpayers increasingly restive about escalating costs; over time patient care deteriorated to a point that probably had never before been seen in America.

Mental hospitals, founded out of a concern for human welfare, came to be viewed as horrid places where humane care was far more a proclaimed philosophy than a practical reality. Bassuk and Gerson (1978) noted that, "the reform movement [of the late nineteenth and early twentieth centuries], having seen its original objectives apparently accomplished, had ceased to be a significant influence" (p. 47).

By the 1940s the network of state mental hospitals, once proudly hailed as a superb example of humanitarianism toward the helpless and "hopelessly insane" (so it was conceived) creatures incarcerated within their high walls, had become "The Shame of the States" (Deutsch, 1948). On average, they were dreadfully neglected, demoralized places, bureaucratically administered by nonpsychiatrist physicians, many of them so lacking in personal and professional skills that they could not otherwise maintain gainful employment. Physical abuse of patients was common, sometimes under the guise of cruel "treatments" such as "regressive" ECT (multiple electrically induced convulsions per day), straitjackets, and various forms of "hydrotherapy" (e.g., "wet packs" and lengthy, restrained immersion in laced-canvas-covered tubs). Psychological abuse, needless to say, was routine (Goffman, 1961).

Coincident with the introduction of the phenothiazine class of antipsychotic drugs in the mid-1950s and with the newer and more optimistic attitudes prevailing among mental health professionals trained after World War II, this sorry state of affairs had begun to change. By then, however, mental hospitals and mental hospitalization had acquired very unsavory reputations, reinforced by an abysmal performance record in terms of discharge rates (Bockhoven, 1972). An increasingly intense and widespread disenchantment with the by now often very large and growing state mental hospitals became, by the 1960s, impossible for governmental officials to ignore. Many authorities, not without ample corroborating evidence, concluded that these institutions were serving primarily as substandard human "warehouses" for the mentally impaired, and that they dehumanized individuals rather than helped them resolve their problems and return to society.

Mental hospital reformers saw this growing movement as an opportunity to rid society of an unwelcome evil; hospital administrators and staff members initially viewed it as a way of lowering the patient census to manageable numbers; and state governments viewed the movement with favor because it allowed legislatures (ever concerned about budgets) to reduce state spending. Many reformers recommended that some state mental hospitals be permanently closed and their residents either placed in more humane facilities or returned to their families and communities (Bachrach, 1976). In fact, in a number of cases, the courts summarily ordered closure of some particularly offensive institutions.

Paralleling these developments was the effort, on the part of the federal government and many concerned people, to develop expanded community resources to provide chronic patients with continued psychiatric care in their local communities. Supporters of this effort believed then—and many do now—that society should be able to integrate these people back into the community and treat those who must remain with the least restrictive alternative. This movement, referred to in the aggregate as **deinstitutionalization,** has become today the source of yet

another raging controversy in the mental health field. Some authorities consider the emptying of the mental hospitals to be a positive expression of society's desire to free previously confined persons, while others speak of the "abandonment" of chronic patients to a cruel and harsh existence, which for many includes homelessness. Many citizens, too, complain of being harassed, intimidated, and frightened by obviously disturbed persons wandering the streets of their neighborhoods. The problems are real enough, but they have come about to a large extent because the planned community efforts to fill the gaps in service never really materialized at effective levels (Grob, 1994).

There has indeed been a significant reduction in state and county mental hospital populations, from over a half million in 1950 (Lerman, 1981) to about 100,000 in recent years (Narrow et al., 1993); these figures are all the more impressive in proportional terms, inasmuch as the U.S. population grew by nearly 100 million in the intervening years. A number of factors have interacted to alter the pattern of mental hospital admissions and discharges over the past 40 years. As has been noted in previous chapters, the introduction of the antipsychotic drugs made it possible for many patients who would formerly have required confinement to be released into the community. The availability of these drugs led many to believe (falsely) that all mental health problems could be managed with medication. In addition, the changing treatment philosophy and the desire to eliminate mental institutions was accompanied by the belief that society wanted and could financially afford to provide better community-based care for chronic patients outside of large mental hospitals.

In theory, the movement to close the public mental hospitals seemed workable. According to plan, many community-based mental health centers would be opened and would provide continuing care to the residents of hospitals after discharge. Residents would be given welfare funds (supposedly costing the government less than it takes to maintain large mental hospitals) and would be administered medication to keep them stabilized until they could obtain continuing care. Many patients would be discharged to home and family, while others would be placed in smaller, homelike board-and-care facilities or nursing homes.

Many unforeseen problems arose, however. Many residents of mental institutions had no families or homes to go to; board-and-care facilities were often substandard; the community mental health centers were ill-prepared and insufficiently funded to provide needed services for chronic patients, particu-

Some homeless people, casualties of indiscriminate deinstitutionalization, are seriously mentally disordered.

larly as national funding priorities shifted during the 1980s (Humphreys & Rappaport, 1993); many patients had not been carefully selected for discharge and were not ready for community living; and many of those who were discharged were not followed up sufficiently or with enough regularity to ensure their successful adaptation outside the hospital. Indeed, countless patients were discharged to fates that were even more dehumanizing than the conditions in any of the hospitals (Westermeyer, 1987). The following case illustrates the situation:

> Dave B., age 49, had been hospitalized for 25 years in a state mental hospital. When the hospital was scheduled for phaseout, many of the patients, particularly those who were regressed or aggressive, were transferred to another state hospital. Dave was a borderline mentally retarded man who had periodic episodes of psychosis. At the time of hospital closing, however, he was not hallucinating and was "reasonably intact." Dave

was considered to be one of the "less disturbed" residents because his psychotic behavior was less pronounced and he presented no dangerous problems.

> He was discharged to a board-and-care facility (actually an old hotel whose clientele consisted mostly of former inpatients). At first, Dave seemed to fit in well at the facility; mostly he sat in his room or in the outside hallway, and he caused no trouble for the caretakers. Two weeks after he arrived, he wandered off the hotel grounds and was missing for several days. The police eventually found him living in the city dump. He had apparently quit taking his medication and when he was discovered he was regressed and catatonic. He was readmitted to a state hospital.

By the early 1980s cases like Dave's had become commonplace in large cities throughout the nation. Vagrants and "bag ladies" appeared in abundance on city streets, and in transport terminals, flophouses, and the virtually always overwhelmed shelters for homeless persons hastily expanded in futile efforts to contain the tide of recently discharged patients. Street crime soared, as did the death rate among these hapless persons who were for the most part wholly lacking in survival resources for the harsh urban environment. As Westermeyer (1982a) noted:

> Patients are returned to the community, armed with drugs to control their illness. The worst aspects of their illnesses may be under control. But many of the patients are not ready to function in society. They need a gradual reintroduction—facilities where someone else can see that they take their drugs, see their psychiatrists, get food, clothing and shelter. Such care is too often more than families can provide and such services are not generally available in a community. As a result, the numbers of bag ladies and men, vagrants and mentally disabled people, living in lonely hotels and dangerous streets, have burgeoned. (p. 2)

The full extent of problems created by deinstitutionalization is not precisely known. The ambiguity comes, in part, from the scarcity of rigorous followup data on patients who have been discharged from mental hospitals. There have not been a sufficient number of adequate research studies in this area. Moreover, such research investigations have tended to be difficult to conduct because the patients are transient and are hard to keep track of over time.

Certainly not all homeless people are former mental patients, but evidence suggests that deinstitutionalization has contributed substantially to the number of homeless people (Jones, 1983; Lamb, 1984). Researchers have also demonstrated that a greater percentage of homeless people have significant psychopathology, as reflected in higher rates of hospitalization and felony convictions, than people who have homes (see Fischer et al., 1986). More recently, Rossi (1990) estimated that 33 percent of homeless individuals suffer from chronic mental disorder and about 33 percent have severe addiction problems.

In spite of the problems just described, some data on patient discharge and outcome status support the deinstitutionalization process. Braun and colleagues (1981), for example, concluded:

> The most satisfactory studies allow the qualified conclusion that selected patients managed outside the hospital in experimental programs do no worse and by some criteria have psychiatric outcomes superior to those of hospitalized control patients. (p. 747)

These same researchers, however, also concluded that deinstitutionalization is likely to be unsuccessful if continuing care in the community is not available or if it is inadequate.

The various approaches that have been implemented to circumvent patient failures to readjust to the community have not been particularly successful at reducing hospital readmissions and therefore at further reducing the average daily census in state hospitals. Nevertheless, advocates for deinstitutionalization continue to maintain that this is the most desirable approach to treating the chronically mental ill. The controversy over deinstitutionalization is likely to continue over some time, with advocates on both sides of the issue, until more definitive research is conducted.

Meanwhile, the extent to which private (as opposed to publicly supported) mental health care, particularly private hospitalization, has expanded to fill at least part of the gap left by deinstitutionalization and inadequate funding for community mental health centers is not generally recognized. Deinstitutionalization notwithstanding, some 70 percent of all the dollars spent on mental health care are spent for hospitalization, much of it of the acute, short-term variety. These data, gathered by Kiesler and Simpkins (1993; Kiesler, 1993), indicate that the national investment in this relatively very costly type of approach is a huge one—in fact constituting an "unnoticed majority" of the total mental health in-

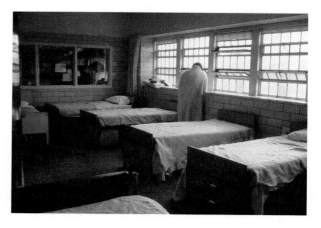

The extent of problems created by deinstitutionalization is not fully known, but some evidence suggests that the emptying of mental hospitals has contributed to the number of homeless people. Deinstitutionalization is not likely to be successful unless continuing care is available and adequate in the community, and unless it allows for readmission to the hospital for short periods if necessary.

tervention effort of the nation. Many of these inpatient stays, moreover, occur in nonspecialized (i.e., nonpsychiatric) units of general hospitals, a setting whose overall effectiveness in dealing with mental patients is questionable.

Care in specialized, private mental hospitals or in specialized psychiatric units of private medical centers has long been an option for those families able to afford it—usually, until relatively recently, only wealthy ones. However, the mental health system appears to have undergone considerable evolution over time, due in large part to changes in funding for mental health care, with the result already noted. This phenomenon, referred to as the "privatization" of the mental health system (Dorwart et al., 1989), has developed primarily because private insurance companies have been persuaded to cover the cost of inpatient mental health services. Several large private hospital corporations have filled the treatment void left by the public mental hospital cutbacks and are providing inpatient psychiatric care for a substantial proportion of those patients currently receiving any type of formal treatment.

The result is that there has been *no* notable overall reduction in mental hospitalization in recent times (Kiesler, 1993). Rather, the demographics of the inpatient population has shifted in favor of a more socioeconomically advantaged group—that is, those who have medical insurance that contains provisions for psychiatric hospitalization. Because mental disorders are often chronic, this type of insurance tends to be very expensive (and hence aversive to employers), excluding many persons and families in less than affluent circumstances. With the continuing downsizing of public facilities, where do these people go? Some of them, as we have seen, go into the streets.

Another related development in the care of chronic mental patients is the growth and expansion of private nursing home facilities, particularly for the elderly mentally disordered. Since the deinstitutionalization movement spurred the discharge of psychiatric patients into the community, alternative care facilities have expanded to fill the need for continued care (Morlock, 1989). This expansion of facilities has been made possible through financial incentives provided by Medicare to fund treatment. Nursing homes have become the largest single setting to care for the chronic mentally ill. Mentally ill persons make up over 51 percent of the nursing home population at present (Goldman, Feder, & Scanlon, 1986).

As this is being written, the federal government is struggling with the problem of how to cope with the enormous costs involved in attempting to provide adequate and universal medical insurance coverage for all citizens. A huge part of the problem of needed health care reform is related to the escalating costs of hospitalization, felt by many to be out of control. It remains to be seen at this point whether the mental health sector will receive due consideration in whatever arrangements are finally enacted by the Congress. A factor of considerable importance here is the possibility that private hospitalization has come to be overutilized, relative to other less expensive but at least equally effective forms of intervention, in the mental health and substance abuse arenas (Kiesler, 1993; Kiesler & Simpkins, 1993; VandenBos, 1993). Plausible alternatives that do not involve inpatient care include enhanced preventive intervention and rehabilitative psychotherapy (VandenBos, 1993).

ORGANIZED EFFORTS FOR MENTAL HEALTH

Public awareness of the magnitude and severity of our contemporary mental health problem and the interest of government, professional, and lay organizations have prompted programs directed at better understanding, more effective treatment, and long-range prevention. Efforts to improve mental health are apparent not only in our society, but also in many other countries; and international as well as national and local organizations and approaches are involved.

U.S. Efforts for Mental Health

In the United States, the primary responsibility for dealing with mental disorders fell initially to state and local agencies. During World War II, however, the extent of mental disorders in the United States was brought to public attention when a large number of young men—two out of every seven recruits—were rejected for military service for psychiatric reasons. This discovery led to a variety of organized measures for coping with the nation's mental health problem.

The Federal Government and Mental Health In 1946, aware of the need for more research, training, and services in the field of mental health, Congress passed its first comprehensive mental health bill, the National Mental Health Act, which laid the basis for the federal government's programs in the 1950s and 1960s.

The 1946 bill provided for the establishment of a National Institute of Mental Health (NIMH) in or near Washington, D.C., to serve as a central research and training center and as headquarters for the administration of a grant-in-aid program. The grant-in-aid feature was designed to foster research and training elsewhere in the nation and to help state and local communities expand and improve their own mental health services. New powers were conferred on the NIMH in 1956, when Congress, under Title V of the Health Amendments Act, authorized the institute to provide "mental health project grants" for experimental studies, pilot projects, surveys, and general research having to do with the understanding, assessment, treatment, and aftercare of mental disorders. The present status of NIMH is that of a separate Institute under the National Institutes of Health, Public Health Service, U.S. Department of Health and Human Services.

The NIMH (a) conducts and supports research on the biological, psychosocial, and sociocultural aspects of mental disorders; (b) supports the training of professional and paraprofessional personnel in the mental health field; (c) assists communities in planning, establishing, and maintaining more effective mental health programs; and (d) provides information on mental health to the public and to the scientific community. Two companion institutes—the National Institute on Alcohol Abuse and Alcoholism (NIAAA) and the National Institute on

Drug Abuse (NIDA)—perform comparable functions in these more specialized fields.

Although the federal government provides leadership and financial aid, the states and localities actually plan and run most NIMH programs. In addition, the states establish, maintain, and supervise their own mental hospitals and clinics, leading to considerable variation among the states in the adequacy with which these responsibilities are met. A number of states have also pioneered, through their legislation, in the development of community mental health centers; rehabilitation services in the community for former patients; and facilities for dealing with alcoholism, drug abuse, and other special mental health problems. In the 1980s, federal support for mental health programs diminished considerably. Most state and local governments, which were expected to assume much of the support of mental health activities, have not been able to fund programs and facilities at 1960s and 1970s levels. As a result, many programs devoted to mental health training, research, and service have been greatly reduced or even abandoned. As to the future, there is, as already noted, considerable uncertainty about the extent to which problems of mental health will be included in forthcoming revisions of national health care policy, and about what forms any such inclusion might take.

Professional Organizations and Mental Health
A number of national professional organizations exist in the mental health field. These include the American Psychological Association (APA), the American Psychological Society (APS), the American Psychiatric Association (APA), the American Medical Association (AMA), and the Association for the Advancement of Behavior Therapy (AABT).

One of the most important functions of these organizations is to set and maintain high professional and ethical standards within their special areas. This function may include (a) establishing and reviewing training qualifications for professional and paraprofessional personnel; (b) setting standards and procedures for the accreditation of undergraduate and graduate training programs; (c) setting standards for the accreditation of clinics, hospitals, or other service operations and carrying out inspections to see that the standards are followed; and (d) investigating reported cases of unethical or unprofessional conduct and taking disciplinary action when necessary.

A second key function of these professional organizations involves communication and information exchange within their areas via meetings, symposia, workshops, refresher courses, the publication of

professional and scientific journals, and related activities. In addition, all such organizations sponsor programs of public education as a means of advancing the interests of their professions, drawing attention to mental health needs, and attracting students to careers in their areas.

A third key function of professional organizations, one that is receiving increasing attention, is the application of insights and methods to contemporary social problems—for example, in lobbying national and local government agencies to provide more services for homeless people. Professional mental health organizations are in a unique position to serve as consultants on mental health problems and programs.

The Role of Voluntary Mental Health Organizations and Agencies Although professional mental health personnel and organizations can give expert technical advice with regard to mental health needs and programs, real progress in helping plan and implement these programs must come from an informed and concerned citizenry. In fact, it has been repeatedly, and quite rightly, stated that it has been primarily concerned nonprofessionals who have blazed the trails in the mental health field.

Prominent among the many voluntary mental health agencies is the National Association for Mental Health (NAMH). This organization was founded in 1950 by the merger of the National Committee for Mental Hygiene, the National Mental Health Foundation, and the Psychiatric Foundation; it was further expanded in 1962 by merging with the National Organization for Mentally Ill Children. Through its national governing body and some 1000 local affiliates, the NAMH works for the improvement of services in community clinics and mental hospitals; it helps recruit, train, and place volunteers for service in treatment and aftercare programs; and it works for enlightened mental health legislation and for the provision of needed facilities and personnel. It also carries on special educational programs aimed at fostering positive mental health and helping people understand mental disorders. In addition, the National Association for Mental Health has been actively involved in many court decisions affecting patient rights (NAMH, 1979). In several cases the NAMH has sponsored litigation or served as *amicus curiae* (friend of the court) in efforts to establish the rights of mental patients to treatment, to freedom from custodial confinement, to freedom to live in the community, and to protection of their confidentiality.

With a program and organization similar to that of the NAMH, the National Association for Retarded Citizens (NARC) works to reduce the incidence of mental retardation, to seek community and residential treatment centers and services for the retarded, and to carry on a program of education aimed at better public understanding of retarded individuals and greater support for legislation on their behalf. The NARC also fosters scientific research into mental retardation, the recruitment and training of volunteer workers, and programs of community action.

These and other voluntary health organizations, such as Alcoholics Anonymous, need the backing of a wide constituency of knowledgeable and involved citizens in order to succeed.

Mental Health Resources in Private Industry

Personal problems—such as marital distress or other family problems, alcohol or drug abuse, financial difficulties, or job-related stress—can adversely affect employee morale and performance. Psychological difficulties among employees may result in numerous problems, such as absenteeism, accident proneness, poor productivity, and high job turnover. The National Institute for Occupational Safety and Health (NIOSH) recognizes psychological disorders as one of the ten leading work-related health problems (Millar, 1990), and work-related mental health risk factors may be increasing with changes in the economy, in technology, and in demographic factors in the work force (Sauter, Murphy, & Hurrell, 1990).

While a great deal more research is needed in the identification of specific mental health risk factors in work situations, available knowledge (e.g., Sauter et al., 1990) suggests that serious unrecognized problems may exist in the following areas of job design and conditions of work.

1. *Work load and work pace.* The critical factor here appears to be the degree of *control* the worker may have over the pace of work rather than output demand per se. Machine-paced assembly work may be particularly hazardous to mental health.

2. *Work schedule.* Rotating "shifts" and night work have been associated with elevated risk for psychological difficulties.

3. *Role stressors.* Role ambiguity (e.g., who has responsibility for what?), said to be common in many work situations, has a negative impact on mental and physical health, as does role conflict (incompatible role demands).

4. *Career security factors.* Feelings of insecurity relating to issues such as job future or obsolescence, career development, and encouragement of early retirement adversely affect mental and physical health.

5. *Interpersonal relations.* Poor or unsupportive relationships among work colleagues significantly increase the risk for untoward psychological reactions.

6. *Job content.* Job dissatisfaction and poor mental health have been associated with work assignments involving fragmented, narrow, invariant tasks that allow for little creativity or sense of meaning with respect to contribution to the ultimate product.

Many corporations have long recognized the importance of worker mental health and of enhancing mental health–promoting factors in the workplace, and yet it has been a relatively recent phenomenon to see them act on this knowledge. Today many companies have expanded their "obligations" to employees to include numerous psychological services. Often referred to as employee-assistance programs (EAPs), these are the means through which larger corporations can actively provide mental health services to employees and their family members. In general, employers have been slower to deal with issues of job design and work environment as additional means of maximizing worker mental health. The latter would appear to be an area of expanding possibilities for the future (see Keita & Jones, 1990).

International Efforts for Mental Health

Mental health is a major problem not only in the United States but of course in the rest of the world

Employee-assistance programs are a relatively recent phenomenon that recognizes the link between psychological difficulties and job problems. Corporations are increasingly providing personal counseling and referral programs for employees having legal, financial, marital, and substance-abuse problems. Shown here is one such employee program that provides drug-rehabilitation telephone counseling.

as well. Indeed, many of the unfavorable conditions in this country with regard to the causes and treatment of mental disorders are greatly magnified in poorer countries and countries with repressive governments. The severity of the world mental health problem is shown in the World Health Organization's estimates that mental disorders affect more than 200 million people worldwide. The recognition of this great problem served to bring about the formation of several international organizations at the end of World War II. We will briefly discuss here the World Health Organization (WHO) and the World Federation for Mental Health.

The World Health Organization The World Health Organization (WHO) has always been keenly aware of the close interrelationships between physical, psychosocial, and sociocultural factors—such as the influence of rapid change and social disruption on both physical and mental health; the impossibility of major progress toward mental health in societies where a large proportion of the population suffer from malnutrition, parasites, and disease; and the frequent psychological and cultural barriers to successful programs in family planning and public health.

Formed after World War II as part of the UN system, WHO's earliest focus was on physical diseases; through its efforts dramatic progress has been made toward the conquest of ancient scourges like smallpox and malaria. Over the years, mental health, too, became an increasing concern among the member countries. In response, WHO's present program now integrates mental health concerns with the broad problems of overall health and socioeconomic development that must be faced by member countries (WHO, 1978a).

WHO has headquarters in Geneva and regional offices for Africa, the Americas, Southeast Asia, Europe, the Eastern Mediterranean, and the Western Pacific. Hence its activities extend into areas with diverse physical environments, types of social organization, and mental health facilities. It enters a country only on invitation, helping identify the basic health needs of each country and working with the local authorities to plan and carry out the most useful and appropriate programs. Where possible, it strives to make its services available over a period of several years to ensure continuity and success for the programs that are undertaken.

Another important contribution of WHO has been its International Classification of Diseases, which enables clinicians and researchers in different countries to use a uniform set of diagnostic categories (WHO, 1978b). As we have seen, the American Psychiatric Association's DSM-IV classification has been coordinated with the WHO ICD-10 classification (Sartorius et al., 1993).

The World Federation for Mental Health The World Federation for Mental Health was established in 1948 as an international congress of nongovernmental organizations and individuals concerned with mental health. Its purpose is to promote international cooperation between governmental and nongovernmental mental health agencies, and its membership now extends to more than 50 countries. The federation has been granted consultative status by WHO and it assists the UN agencies by collecting information on mental health conditions all over the world.

We have now seen something of the maze of local, national, and international measures that are being undertaken in the mental health field. We can expect these efforts to continue. Furthermore, we can expect to see more and more mental health problems unraveled to reveal discoverable causes and to respond to treatment and prevention by scientific means. The 1990s have already witnessed an amazing openness and a diminishing of previously impassable borders. Along with this increased interchange of ideas and cooperation, we expect to see a broader interchange of mental health collaboration. Reductions in international tension and a greater international cooperation in the sciences and health planning will likely promote more sharing of information and views on mental health.

CHALLENGES FOR THE FUTURE

The media confront us daily with the stark truth that we have a long way to go before our dreams of a better world are realized. Many question whether the United States or any other technologically advanced nation can achieve mental health for the majority of its citizens in our time. Racism, poverty, youth violence, the uprooting of third-world populations, and other social problems that contribute to mental disorder sometimes seem insurmountable.

Events in the rest of the world affect us also, both directly and indirectly. Worldwide economic instability and shortages and the possibility of the destruction of our planet's life support system breed widespread anxiety about the future. The vast resources we have spent on military programs over the past half-century to protect against perceived threats have absorbed funds and energy that otherwise might have been turned to meeting human and social needs here and elsewhere in the world. The limited resources we are now willing to apply to solving mental health problems prevent the solution of major problems resulting from drug and alcohol abuse, homelessness, broken families, and squalid living conditions for many.

The Need for Planning

It seems imperative that more effective planning be done at community, national, and international levels if mental health problems are going to be reduced or eliminated. Many challenges must be met if we are to create a better world for ourselves and future generations. Without slackening our efforts to meet needs at home, we will probably find it increasingly essential to participate more broadly in international measures toward reducing group tensions and promoting mental health and a better world for people everywhere. At the same time, we can expect that measures undertaken to reduce international conflict and improve the general condition of humankind will make their contribution to our own nation's social progress and mental health. Both kinds of measures will require understanding and moral commitment from concerned citizens.

Within our own country, as well as the rest of the industrialized world, progress in lengthening the life span has brought with it burgeoning problems in the prevalence of disorders associated with advanced age, particularly in the area of dementing conditions such as Alzheimer's disease. As was noted in Chapter 13, there can be no assurance at this time that we will find the means of eradicating or arresting this threat before it has overwhelmed us in terms of the numbers of already living people affected. Planning and preparation would seem our only rational hope of forestalling a potential disaster of unprecedented yet predictable magnitude; we need to make a beginning.

The Individual's Contribution

Each man can make a difference, and each man should try.

—John F. Kennedy

The history of abnormal psychology provides clear examples of individuals whose efforts were instrumental in changing thinking about problems. Recall that Pinel took off the chains, Dorothea Dix initiated a movement to improve the conditions of asylums, and Clifford Beers inspired the modern mental health movement with his autobiographical account of his own experience with mental illness.

Who may lead the next revolution in mental health is anyone's guess. What is clear is that a great deal can be accomplished by individual effort.

When students become aware of the tremendous scope of the mental health problem both nationally and internationally and the woefully inadequate facilities for coping with it, they often ask, "What can I do?" Thus it seems appropriate to suggest a few of the lines of action interested students can profitably take.

Many opportunities in mental health work are open to trained personnel, both professional and paraprofessional. Social work, clinical psychology, psychiatry, and other mental health occupations are rewarding in terms of personal fulfillment. In addition, many occupations, ranging from law enforcement to teaching and the ministry, can and do play key roles in the mental health and well-being of many people. Training in all these fields usually offers individuals opportunities to work in community clinics and related facilities, to gain experience in understanding the needs and problems of people in distress, and to become familiar with community resources.

Citizens can find many ways to be of direct service if they are familiar with national and international resources and programs, and if they invest the effort necessary to learn about their community's special needs and problems. Whatever their roles in life—student, teacher, police officer, lawyer, homemaker, business executive, or trade unionist—their interests are directly at stake. For although the mental health of a nation may be manifested in many ways—in its purposes, courage, moral responsibility, scientific and cultural achievements, and quality of daily life—its health and resources derive ultimately from the individuals within it. In a participatory democracy, it is they who plan and implement the nation's goals.

Besides accepting some measure of responsibility for the mental health of others through the quality of one's own interpersonal relationships, there are several other constructive courses of action open to each citizen, including (a) serving as a volunteer in a mental hospital, community mental health center, or service organization; (b) supporting realistic measures for ensuring comprehensive health services for all age groups; and (c) working toward improved public education, responsible government, the alleviation of group prejudice, and the establishment of a more sane and harmonious world.

All of us are concerned with mental health for personal as well as altruistic reasons, for we want to overcome the harassing problems of contemporary living and find our share of happiness in a meaningful and fulfilling life. To do so, we may sometimes need the courage to admit that our problems are too much for us. When existence seems futile or the going becomes too difficult, it may help to remind ourselves of the following basic facts, which have been emphasized throughout this text: From time to time, each of us has serious difficulties in coping with the problems of living. During such crisis periods, we may need psychological and related assistance. Such difficulties are not a disgrace; they can happen to anyone if the stress is sufficiently severe. The early detection and correction of maladaptive behavior is of great importance in preventing the development of more severe or chronic conditions. Preventive measures—primary, secondary, and tertiary—are the most effective long-range approach to the solution of both individual and group mental health problems.

Recognizing these facts is essential because statistics show that almost all of us will at some time in our lives have to deal with severely maladaptive behavior or mental disorder either in ourselves or in someone close to us. Our interdependence and the loss to us all, individually and collectively, when any one of us fails to achieve his or her potential are eloquently expressed in the famous lines of John Donne (1624):

> No man is an island, entire of itself; every man is a piece of the continent, a part of the main. If a clod be washed away by the sea, Europe is less, as well as if a promontory were, as well as if a manor of thy friends or of thine own were: any man's death diminishes mé, because I am involved in mankind, and therefore never send to know for whom the bell tolls; it tolls for thee.

UNRESOLVED ISSUES

on The Law–Mental Health Interface

In its "Introduction" the DSM-IV contains a "Cautionary Statement" that reads, in part:

> The purpose of DSM-IV is to provide clear descriptions of diagnostic categories in order to enable clinicians and investigators to diagnose, communicate about, study, and treat people with various mental disorders. It is to be understood that inclusion here, for clinical and research purposes, of a diagnostic category such as Pathological Gambling or Pedophilia does not imply that the condition meets legal or other nonmedical criteria for what constitutes mental disease, mental disorder, or mental disability. The clinical and scientific considerations involved in categorization of these conditions as mental disorders may not be wholly relevant to legal judgments, for example, that take into account such issues as individual re-

sponsibility, disability determination, and competency. (American Psychiatric Association, 1994, p. xxvii)

One might wish that such a statement, asserting (as we read it) the essential independence of professional diagnoses of mental disorder and questions that often go to the heart of issues in jurisprudence, would put an end to the endless and frequently baffling courtroom dramas in which (respectively competent and noncolluding) mental health expert witnesses and attorneys try—rarely with any great success—to achieve a common framework for communicating clearly between themselves and with judges and juries. Based on the problem's refractory history and on considerable collective experience as participants in such encounters, the authors doubt that the statement will have the intended effect—any more than did similar statements in DSM-IV's predecessors. If a disorder is "on the books," attorneys are very likely to attempt to make use of it, where feasible, in pursuit of their clients' interests; indeed, they may be ethically obliged to do so (see also the related "Unresolved Issues" section of Chapter 4, pp. 153–154).

As we see perhaps most clearly in the case of the insanity defense, the law tends to frame its issues relating to the mental states of parties to a trial in ways not ultimately resolvable by any scientifically reliable assessment methods known or available to mental health professionals. However, since no other definable group of potential experts has more, or even as much, likelihood of casting light into this darkness, the task usually defaults to psychiatrists and clinical psychologists. Since, unlike ordinary witnesses at trial, persons qualifying as experts are permitted to render "opinions," the way is open for the frequent and professionally embarrassing contradictions of expert testimony mentioned earlier in the chapter.

Though the insanity defense remains a major and relatively familiar unresolved issue at the law-mental health interface, it is by no means the only one. A large number of such problems hinge on questions of *malingering,* deceitfully behaving in such a manner as to claim a mental or physical disorder or disability that one in fact does not have, normally in order to gain some legal advantage. The assessment of a defendant's competency to stand trial sometimes involves this issue, as indeed does the assessment of a convict's competency to be executed (some jurisdictions requiring that condemned persons be able to understand why they are being put to death). Again in this case, the mental health professional often becomes a principal witness, more or less by default.

Issues of this sort are also common in civil proceedings in which a person allegedly injured by the negligent behavior of another seeks financial compensation. The injury claimed by the plaintiff in such a suit is often one that proves difficult to document objectively and/or to be a readily understandable consequence of the causal event, for instance, a minor traffic "fender bender." Often complicating such cases is the question of *unconscious* malingering, sometimes referred to as "secondary gain," thought to be an element in many genuine instances of conversion disorder, a mental disorder recognized as such in the DSM (see Chapter 7). While certain observations and assessment procedures available to trained mental health practitioners may well tilt the probabilities in one direction or the other, findings approaching reasonable certainty (in the scientific, rather than the legal, meaning of this term) about malingering or its absence are normally unattainable in situations of this sort. Training and experience in a mental health discipline does not confer the ability to read minds.

Possibly the most bizarrely fascinating of the unresolved issues at the law–mental health interface are those raised by the phenomenon of multiple personality disorder, now called *dissociative identity disorder* (DID), which as we saw in Chapter 7 has become a somewhat common diagnosis in recent years. Although some professionals dispute even the existence of such a condition, its controversial nature is not a compelling consideration in the legal context. It appears in the DSM-IV (as it did in all of DSM-IV's predecessors), and despite the disclaimer quoted at the beginning of this discussion, that makes it a genuine clinical entity within the legal community, as already noted.

The general nature of the problem can be stated quite succinctly: Within a legal system strongly oriented to the precise identification of *individual* responsibility for acts, what if any are the limits of the assignment of responsibility and sanctions for infractions of the law where the same physical space and body are occupied at different times by more than one distinct and legally recognizable person? The magnitude of the potential legal havoc involved here might best be captured in a listing of only *some* of the problems already encountered or certain to be encountered in due course:

- Who, among various co-personalities, is empowered to sign for withdrawals from a bank account?
- Are the provisions and obligations of a contract entered into by one constituent personality binding to all others, regardless of their particular desires in the matter?
- Does the swearing of an oath, as in court, apply to the entire collection of personalities, or must each be sworn individually if he or she is to testify?

- In the case of a guilty verdict for the criminal act of a given personality, where other personalities did not acquiesce in the crime, how should punishment be fairly meted out?
- If no constituent personality meets a test of insanity, is it reasonable and lawful to declare DID itself an instance of insanity?
- Has rape occurred where the co-personalities of a 26-year-old woman who had acquiesced to intercourse vehemently objected to its occurrence (as in a case that was actually prosecuted in Wisconsin in 1990)?
- And, of course, the most common real-life legal dilemma: Should an individual, as the primary personality, be held legally accountable for, say, a capital crime that evidence suggests may have actually been committed surreptitiously, so to speak, by an alter personality?

The scenario just mentioned has rather often been the contention underlying a plea of "not guilty by reason of insanity" (NGRI). Usually, as in the case of the Hillside Strangler Kenneth Bianchi (convicted of 12 rapes and murders in California and Washington State), it has failed. On a very few occasions, however, the NGRI plea in association with a claim that the actual criminal was a DID alter has worked, as in the well-publicized 1978 case of Ohio resident Billy Milligan, claiming to be host to ten personalities and accused of raping four women (*New York Times,* May 9, 1994).

The legal conundrums inspired by the DID construct admittedly have a quality of whimsy about them, perhaps especially for persons not trained in the sometimes arcane ways of the law. It would be well to remind ourselves, therefore, that the problems encountered here are often serious ones—sometimes, indeed, *deadly* serious.

A fundamental function of the law is that of providing an instrument for the unbiased, just, and peaceful resolution of disputable conflicts of interest among human beings and between human beings and their societies. As such, the law functions as a kind of final arbiter in situations that are commonly among the most convoluted and perplexing in human experience, and it is often called upon to render its judgments in the absence of pertinent but unobtainable knowledge. As we have seen, many of the issues it deems critical are concerned with the private states of mind of its subjects, a difficult challenge that is shared by the scientists and professionals of the mental health disciplines. This common challenge would seem to call for high levels of collaboration and mutual inquiry between scholars in the two domains, but such cooperative ventures have in fact been historically rare. Perhaps it is time to seek means of overcoming that traditional isolation.

SUMMARY

Increasingly today, professionals are trying not only to cure mental health problems but also to prevent them, or at least reduce their effects. Prevention can be viewed as focusing on three levels. Primary prevention is aimed at reducing the possibility of disorder and fostering positive mental health efforts. Secondary prevention attempts to reduce the impact or duration of a problem that has already occurred. Tertiary prevention attempts to reduce the long-term consequences of having had a disorder.

In recent years, several legal issues concerning the treatment of mental patients have surfaced. The commitment process and procedures for committing individuals for inpatient care have been reconsidered. Being "mentally ill" is not considered sufficient grounds for commitment. There must be, in addition, evidence that the individual is either dangerous to himself or herself or represents a danger to society. It is not an easy matter, even for trained professionals, to determine in advance if a person is "dangerous" and likely to cause harm to others. Nevertheless, professionals must, at times, make such judgments. Recent court rulings have found professionals liable when patients they were treating caused harm to others. The *Tarasoff II* decision held that a therapist has a duty to protect potential victims if his or her patient has threatened to kill them.

Another important issue of forensic psychology involves the insanity plea for capital crimes. Many mental health and legal professionals, journalists, and laypersons have questioned the present use of the "not guilty by reason of insanity" (NGRI) defense. The original legal precedent, the M'Naughten Rule, held that, at the time of committing the act, the accused must have been laboring under such a defect of reason as to not know the nature and quality of the act or to not know that what he or she was doing was wrong. More recent broadenings of the insanity plea, as in the American Law Institute standard, leave open the possibility of valid NGRI pleas by persons who are not diagnosed to be psychotic. This broadening of the insanity plea led to its use in more and more cases, and decisions have often involved conflicting psychiatric testimony. The successful use of the NGRI defense by John Hinckley, attempted assassin of President Reagan, set off a storm of protest, resulting ultimately in widespread tightening of insanity defense laws. One effective

and widely adopted reform was to shift the burden of proof to the defense in such cases.

There has been a great deal of legal controversy recently over the release of patients from public mental hospitals, called deinstitutionalization, and the failure to provide adequate follow-up of these patients in the community. In their zeal to close large psychiatric institutions, many administrators underestimated the amount of care that would be needed after discharge, and overestimated communities' abilities to deal with patients with chronic problems. The result was that some chronic patients were placed in circumstances that required more adaptive abilities than they possessed. Recent work in the area of aftercare for former mental patients has provided clearer guidelines for discharge and therapeutic follow-up. Meanwhile, there has been a burgeoning use of private hospitalization in psychiatric care, an expensive alternative not normally available to the less than affluent.

A large number of organizations are concerned and involved with establishing organized efforts for mental health. Several government agencies have mental health as their primary mission. For example, federal agencies such as the National Institute of Mental Health (NIMH), the National Institute on Drug Abuse (NIDA), and the National Institute on Alcohol Abuse and Alcoholism (NIAAA) are devoted to promoting varied research, training, and service. State and county government agencies may focus their efforts on the delivery of mental health services to residents on an inpatient or outpatient basis.

Mental health programming in the United States is also the concern of several professional and mental health organizations, many corporations, and a number of voluntary mental health organizations. In addition, international organizations, such as the World Health Organization (WHO) and the World Federation for Mental Health, have contributed to mental health programs worldwide.

Multiple unresolved issues continue to exist at the interface of the legal and mental health professions, indicating the desirability of increased collaboration between them.

KEY TERMS

primary prevention (p. 668)
secondary prevention (p. 668)
tertiary prevention (p. 668)
short-term crisis therapy (p. 674)
milieu therapy (p. 678)

social-learning programs (p. 679)
forensic psychology (forensic psychiatry) (p. 681)
Tarasoff decision (p. 686)
the insanity defense (p. 687)
deinstitutionalization (p. 690)

See Chapter 15, page 572

CUTTING EDGE 6

FUNCTIONAL MAGNETIC RESONANCE IMAGING

Magnetic resonance imaging (MRI) has increasingly replaced computerized axial tomography (CAT) as the technique of choice in detecting structural (anatomical) anomalies in the central nervous system, particularly the brain. The images of the interior of the brain are frequently sharper with MRI than with CAT because of the former's superior ability to differentiate subtle variations in soft tissue. In addition, the MRI procedure is normally far less complicated to administer, and it does not (like CAT) subject the patient to ionizing radiation. In fact, the major problem encountered with MRI is that some patients have a claustrophobic reaction to being placed into the narrow cylinder of the MRI machine, necessitated for containing the magnetic field and blocking out external radio signals.

When Chapter 15 was written, the technique known as *functional MRI* (fMRI) had only recently been developed and had not yet been applied in the study of psychopathology. The main purpose of this addendum is to update rapidly progressing developments in this area.

As originally developed and employed, MRI could reveal brain *structure* but not brain *activity*. For the latter, clinicians and investigators remained dependent on positron emission tomography (PET) scans, whose principal shortcoming is the very expensive requirement of having a cyclotron nearby to produce the short-lived radioactive atoms needed to carry out the procedure. Because of this expense, the number of available centers in the United States equipped to do PET scans is estimated to be fewer than 100. The required introduction of radioactive substances, albeit short-lived ones, into the patient's body is also worrisome to many clinicians. It was apparent by the mid-1980s that adapting the MRI technique would be of tremendous advantage in revealing the workings of the brain as well as its anatomy, hence functional MRI. This breakthrough, considered by many to be the most revolutionary of all the imaging techniques, was accomplished in the early 1990s (*Harvard Mental Health Letter, 13*(7), January, 1997).

The specific mechanisms underlying fMRI assessment (not to mention those involved in MRI itself) are too technical to be reviewed in detail here. Simply put, in its most common form fMRI measures changes in local oxygenation (i.e., blood flow) of specific areas of brain tissue that in turn depend on neuronal activity in those specific regions. Ongoing psychological activity, such as sensations, images, and thoughts, can thus be "mapped," at least in principle, revealing the specific areas of the brain that appear to be involved in their neurophysiological mediation. Because the measurement of change in this context is critically time dependent, the emergence of fMRI required the development of high-speed devices for enhancing the recording process as well as the computerized analysis of incoming data. These improvements are now widely available and will doubtless lead to a marked increase in studies of disordered persons using functional imaging.

To date, however, little has been published in the area of mental disorder, most of the work thus far having concentrated on mapping the visual area of the cerebral cortex. A transitional study was recently presented at a national meeting by Paula Tallal and associates (as reported by Travis, 1996a). In this work, involving small samples, a group of reading-disordered (dyslexic) children was shown to be deficient in activation of a grape-sized brain region called V5 when challenged with fast-moving visual stimuli. This region is in fact believed to be involved in the processing (as reading entails) of rapidly moving visual stimuli, thus providing a potentially important clue concerning the origins of reading disorders. For another interesting technique, see the photograph and caption on the next page.

In another recently published study, also involving small samples, Breiter and colleagues (1996) reported abnormally high activation in several brain regions

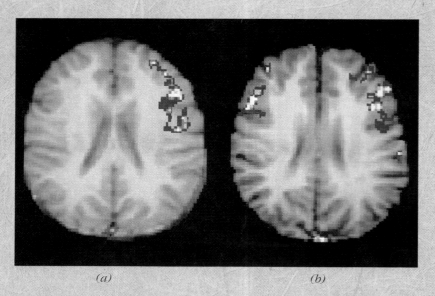

(a)   *(b)*

In a study of 19 men and 19 women, researchers recently reported the first direct evidence that male and female brains tend to function differently during a specific task (Shaywitz et al., 1995). In these fMRIs, the orientation is as if from below the brain, so the left hemisphere is on the right and vice versa. During the first step in the process of sounding out words, Broca's area, the small left-hemisphere area associated with speech, was active in the men's brains (a). Eight women also had this pattern, but the brains of the other 11 showed activity on both sides (b). The two sexes performed equally well on the task, leading the researchers to conclude that nature has efficiently provided the brain with different routes to the same ability. However, the results might help explain why left-hemisphere damage is less likely to cause language problems in women than men following a stroke.

among obsessive–compulsive subjects when they were challenged with simulated "provocative" stimuli, for example, for a patient preoccupied with contamination, holding a towel "dipped in toilet water." Unfortunately, a good deal of data were rendered unusable because of subject movement while in the MRI apparatus, a condition that may indicate a problem with the use of the technique in psychiatric populations. Even minimal head movement during critical phases of the examination precludes obtaining an adequate fMRI (or MRI) recording. Many mentally disordered patients are highly tense and agitated, particularly when challenged with stressors. In addition, many of the tasks mental health researchers might wish to employ in such assessments (e.g., approach to or avoidance of phobic stimuli) are not physically possible if the patient cannot move his or her head. This last problem, at least, may at times be circumvented with the use of yet another marvel of contemporary technology, that is, virtual reality. Geoffrey Aguirre and his associates at the University of Pennsylvania (as reported by Travis, 1996b) have begun experimenting, apparently successfully, with the creation of virtual environments that allow immobilized fMRI subjects to engage a simulated but compelling environment.

Several investigators have recently become involved in the use of fMRI to try to pinpoint areas of aberrant brain functioning in schiz-ophrenia, as reported by McCarley, Hsiao, Freedman, Pfefferbaum, and Donchin (1996). Cohen and Green (1995), for example, have reported an association between the occurrence of auditory hallucinations among persons diagnosed as schizophrenic and activation of brain centers believed to be involved in the reception of speech.

Given the unique advantages of fMRI brain imaging, mental health researchers will continue to find ways to cope with the relatively minor problems it poses for often distraught psychiatric patients. The scientific future of the approach thus appears ensured.

REFERENCES

Breiter, H. C., Rauch, S. L., Kwong, K. K., Baker, J. R., Weisskopf, R. M., Kennedy, D. N., Kendrick, A. D., Davis T. L., Jiang, A., Cohen, M. S., Stern, C. E., Belliveau, J. W., Baer, L., O'Sullivan, R. L., Savage, C. R., Jernike, M. A., & Rosen, B. R. (1996). Functional magnetic resonance imaging of symptom provocation in obsessive-compulsive disorder. *Arch. Gen. Psychiat., 53,* 595–606.

Cohen, M. S., & Green, M. (1995). Where the voices come from: Imaging the schizophrenic auditory hallucinations. Presented at Society for Neuroscience, Abstracts, San Diego, CA, October 1995.

McCarley, R. W. Hsiao, J. K., Freedman, R., Pfefferbaum, A., & Donchin, E. (1996). Neuroimaging and the cognitive neuroscience of schizophrenia. *Schizo. Bull., 22,* 703–725.

Shaywitz, Bennet A., Shaywitz, Sally E., Pugh, Kenneth R. et al. (1995). Sex differences in the functional organization of the brain for language. *Nature, 373,* 607–609.

Travis, J. (1996a). Visualizing vision in dyslexic brains. *Sci. News, 149,* 105.

Travis, J. (1996b). Brains in space: Virtual reality helps explain how the brain finds its way. *Sci. News, 149,* 28–29.

CUTTING EDGE 7
NEW DEVELOPMENTS IN THE TREATMENT OF DEPRESSION

Pharmacological researchers continue to develop medications for the treatment of mental disorders, thus serving to expand the range of clinical treatment options. Much effort is currently focused on developing safer medications with less troublesome side effects. The federal agency responsible for monitoring the safety of medication, the Food and Drug Administration, has recently approved several new treatments for depression. Two new drugs, nefazodone and venlafaxine, which have shown early promise at reducing depression effectively with fewer problematic side effects, are likely to be used widely in pharmacological therapy in the future.

NEFAZODONE (SERZONE)

Nefazodone is an orally administered antidepressant with a chemical structure related to that of phenylpiperazine (Desyrel) and is rather dissimilar in chemical structure and operation to the SSRIs, which are widely used antidepressants (*Medical Letter,* 1995; *Physician's Desk Reference,* 1997a). Nefazodone is believed to work by blocking postsynaptic serotonin absorption, in contrast to the SSRIs which operate to block serotonin reuptake into the presynaptic neuron. Nefazodone has been found to differ from other antidepressants in producing fewer unwanted side effects, such as sexual dysfunction and sleeping disorders.

A period of clinical trials with nefazodone has been successfully completed, and the drug has been found to be effective in treating a broad range of depressive disorders, including dysthymia, major depres-

sion, and even some cases of bipolar disorder. Nefazodone has been shown to be as effective as imipramine in reducing major depression (Rickels et al., 1994). Some caution has been recommended, however, when the drug is given to bipolar patients who are not currently being treated with a mood-regulating medication such as lithium. This medication, like many antidepressants, can trigger manic episodes in bipolar patients. An additional consideration for prescribing nefazodone is that it can interact negatively with other medications. For example, the use of nefazodone with antianxiety compounds such as alprazolam (Xanax) or triazolam (Halcion) or with antihistamine medication such as terfenadine (Seldane) could prove life-threatening. Caution has also been suggested in prescribing nefazodone to persons who have liver disease. The clinical trials indicated that such persons should receive reduced dosages of nefazodone.

The antidepressant effect associated with nefazodone is usually experienced within two to three weeks after the patient begins to take the medication, somewhat earlier than other medications, such as amitriptyline (Elavil). One important finding from the preliminary trials is that nefazodone appears to work in a similar manner in elderly patients and younger patients, although at a lower dosage. This medication therefore might prove to be an effective alternative treatment for older patients for whom biochemical therapy for depression is often problematic.

Although nefazodone is considered to be a relatively problem-free

drug, some side effects have been reported: dry mouth, lethargy, nausea, and dizziness. Overall, however, the reported side effects of nefazodone have compared very favorably with those of other antidepressants. The drug has been found to be relatively safe and is not likely to be fatal if taken in excess. Several cases of overdose have been reported for patients taking nefazodone, but none of these incidents resulted in a fatality.

VENLAFAXINE (EFFEXOR)

Another antidepressant medication, venlafaxine, which has recently been approved for use by the Food and Drug Administration, has been available in other countries for some time. This drug is one of a new class of antidepressants, referred to as phenethylamines. In several recent drug trials Venlafaxine has been demonstrated to be an effective antidepressant for treating major depressive episodes. Venlafaxine is chemically unrelated to other commonly used antidepressant compounds such as tricyclic or tetracyclic drugs, and it is chemically different from nefazodone (*Physician's Desk Reference,* 1997b). One clear advantage of this new drug is that it begins to operate much faster than other antidepressants—in about two weeks—and may provide earlier relief for depressed patients.

The clinical effectiveness of venlafaxine has been established through controlled clinical trials. The drug appears to work best on major depressive disorder, reducing the affective disorder symptoms as effectively as other antidepressants. There are clear contraindications for using venlafaxine, however. First, patients who are taking monoamine oxidase inhibitors (MAOI) should not take venlafaxine because the combination of these medications is life-threatening. Thus, when an antidepressant medication is changed, a period of 14 days is required for the effects of the initial medication to wear off before the new drug is initiated. Second, insufficient information exists on the use of venlafaxine in patients with heart disease. Several potential side effects also have been found with venlafaxine, including increases in blood pressure. Therefore, one important contraindication to the use of venlafaxine is hypertension. Some patients also reported experiencing an increase in symptoms of anxiety when they used the drug. These unwanted psychological concomitants might be problematic for some patients.

Another potentially troublesome problem connected with venlafaxine is possible changes in appetite and weight. Anorexia and weight loss were reported in a significant percentage of patients in the clinical trials. In cases in which weight loss could be problematic for the patient, venlafaxine may not be the drug of choice.

The two newly approved antidepressants, nefazodone and venlafaxine, show a great deal of promise for reducing symptoms of depression in a broad range of patients. Moreover, early trials suggest that they are both relatively safe medications, that is, drug overdose (a frequent problem in pharmacological therapy with depressed patients) is a less threatening consequence than with other medications. Finally, both drugs have been shown to have fewer adverse side effects than other antidepressant medications.

In spite of all this attention and interest in developing new and safer medications for depression, recent evidence questions whether medications are actually the preferred treatment—especially as the medical community has claimed them to be for severe depression. As discussed more extensively in Chapter 17, one very large NIMH collaborative study (Elkin et al., 1989) for the treatment of depression concluded that medications were superior to cognitive therapy in the treatment of severe depression, and recent medical guidelines have been based on the results of that one study. DeRubeis (1997), however, has challenged this conclusion in a quantitative review of the literature. Collapsing the results of four very similar studies, DeRubeis finds that cognitive therapy is as effective as medication in the treatment of severe depression. He notes that only one study (the NIMH collaborative study), which accounts for only a third of the relevant results, found medications to be superior to cognitive therapy.

Moreover, this was not because medications did more poorly in the other three studies, but rather because cognitive therapy did more poorly in the NIMH study—and then only at two of the three study sites. Finally, the other three studies actually showed a slight advantage to cognitive therapy over medication (DeRubeis, 1997)!

That the effectiveness of cognitive therapy may differ more across studies than does the effectiveness of medications is not surprising given that administration of medications is fairly standard across sites, whereas the administration of cognitive therapy requires specialized training in its techniques and not every cognitive therapist may show comparable expertise (DeRubeis, 1997). Although one could use this as an argument for medications being more practical, there are good reasons not to draw this conclusion. Specifically, there are strong suggestions from several of these studies that cognitive therapy provides protection against relapse (a big problem in the treatment of depression discussed in Chapter 6) that is not provided by medication. At a minimum medical treatment guidelines should be more careful to note the advantages and disadvantages of pharmacotherapy so that consumers (depressed patients and their relatives) can make more informed choices about which type of treatment to try. Persons, Thase, and Crits-Cristoph (1996) reached a very similar conclusion in a more qualitative review of the research literature in which they criticized current medical guidelines on very similar grounds.

REFERENCES

DeRubeis, R. (1997). *Cognitive therapy IS as effective as medications for severe depression: A mega-analysis.* Paper presented at the meeting of the American Psychological Society, Washington, DC. May 1997.

The Medical Letter (1995). Nefazodone for depression. 37 (946) 33–35.

Persons, J., Thase, M., & Crits-Christoph, P. (1996). The role of psychotherapy in the treatment of depression. *Arch. Gen. Psychiat.* 53, 283–290.

Physician's Desk Reference (1997a). Serzone (pp. 776–779). (51st ed.) Montvale, NJ: Medical Economics Company.

Physician's Desk Reference (1997b). Effexor (pp. 2825–2829). (51st ed.) Montvale, NJ: Medical Economics Company.

Rickels, K., Schweizer, E., Clary, C., Fox, I., & Weise, C. (1994). Nefazodone and imipramine in major depression: A placebo-controlled trial. *Br. J. Psychiat.* 164, 802–805.

CUTTING EDGE 8

A RAY OF HOPE IN PREVENTING ALCOHOL AND OTHER DRUG PROBLEMS

Prominent social forces such as attractive advertising, the influence of peer groups, negative parental role models, and the ready availability of many drugs are instrumental in promoting the early use of alcohol, tobacco, and illegal drugs in young people. Because these factors influence adolescents to begin using alcohol and drugs, it might appear reasonable to think that if these forces could be counterbalanced with equally powerful alternative influences, substance use might be delayed or even blocked altogether. This is easier said than done, and social efforts to alleviate the substance abuse problem have proved insufficient. Recent years have witnessed a sharp increase in marijuana, alcohol, and tobacco use among adolescents (Johnston, O'Mally, & Bachman, 1995). The extent and often dramatic impact of alcohol and drug use among adolescents are alarming, particularly that for binge drinking (National Institute on Drug Abuse, 1996). A recent survey found that 55% of 8th graders, 71% of 10th graders, 81% of 12th graders, and 90% of college students have tried alcohol. Heavy drinking, defined as five or more drinks in a row, has shown an alarming rate of incidence (15% for 8th graders, 24% for 10th graders, 30% for 12th graders, and 40% for college students). Heavy alcohol use among young people can lead to tragic consequences such as motor vehicle accidents involving emergency room admissions (National Clear-

inghouse for Alcohol and Drug Information, 1996) or in which several young people die as a result of drinking and driving (National Highway Traffic Safety Administration, 1990).

The federal government has approached the drug abuse problem with three broad strategies:

1. *Interfering with and reducing the supply of drugs available.* Policing our borders to intercept shipments of drugs has had little impact on their availability. The supply of illegal drugs seems to be endless. Even when drug agents know a shipment of illegal drugs is bound for the United States from suppliers in South America, they are often unable to stop it. Moreover, drug interception programs do little to affect the supply of alcohol and tobacco—the two drugs most abused by adolescents. These drugs are, of course, available in corner stores and even in the adolescent's home. Reducing the supply of these drugs to adolescents is extremely difficult.
2. *Providing treatment services for those who develop drug problems.* Although much money is spent each year on amelioration efforts, the treatment of substance abuse is perhaps the least effective avenue to reducing the problem. Addictive disorders are very intractable, and treatment failures are the rule rather than the exception. Therapeutic

programs for those addicted to drugs or alcohol, though necessary, are not the answer to eliminating or even reducing the problems in our society.
3. *Encouraging prevention.* By far the most desirable and potentially most powerful means of reducing the drug problem in our country is through prevention methods aimed at alerting citizens to the problems of drugs and teaching young people ways to avoid using them (Botvin & Botvin, 1992; Botvin et al., 1995). Several past efforts have had limited success in resolving the adolescent drug abuse crisis. As noted in the text, the lackluster performance of prevention programs has provided little reason for optimism. Initially promising prevention efforts have often failed to show the desired reduction in substance use for a number of reasons. The intervention typically has not been conducted long enough to show the desired effect; the intervention efforts have not

been powerful enough to make a sufficient impact on the participants; or the intervention may not have been well implemented.

Two recent publications developed through comprehensive longitudinal prevention programs provide reason for optimism. Project Northland, developed by Perry and colleagues (1996) is a broad-based, action-oriented prevention program that involves many facets of the community to delay the onset of drinking in young teenagers. The community intervention approach followed by Project Northland researchers incorporates a number of elements to support a strong "no use" message during early adolescence. This project was initiated with great care to eliminate past methodological woes and provide a sound, comprehensive intervention philosophy.

The goals of Project Northland are to prevent or reduce alcohol use among adolescents by using a multilevel, community-based approach. The investigators conducted their program in 24 school districts in communities in northern Minnesota, an area that has been notorious for high rates of alcohol abuse in the past. The intervention included implementing a social-behavioral curriculum in the schools (beginning at the sixth grade), incorporating parent education programs, enlisting and involving peer leadership, and developing community-wide activities to alter the messages that young people typically receive about alcohol. Assessments were made annually to measure the use of alcohol among both the identified target population and the control samples. The program encompasses a set of four activity booklets for students to complete as homework assignments with

their parents over a period of four weeks. Each booklet has activities that contain explicit behavioral objectives (e.g., how to establish family rules about drinking). Elected peer leaders provide activity tasks each week, with the assistance of their teachers. These sessions are conducted in small groups. Intensive teacher training sessions are provided before the intervention program begins, as well as peer-leader training. During the intervention phase of the program each child is asked to return score cards (signed by parents to record participation) on a prominently displayed scoreboard. Students receive prizes for completion of the first two booklets (e.g., a pen) and a T-shirt at the end of the program. The program ends with an event at each school that brings fifth-graders and their parents together for an evening event. During the week before the event, students work together in pairs on poster projects with alcohol-related messages that are presented to parents during the evening event.

Project Northland staff have been able to maintain broad participation in the program over three years and have shown that multilevel, targeted prevention programs for young adolescents are effective in reducing their alcohol use. Significantly lower rates (21% less) of alcohol use, cigarette smoking, and marijuana use were reported by adolescents in the intervention schools than by those in the reference schools, most of whom reserved the DARE program.

Another extensive and comprehensive drug prevention program with even more impressive results was recently completed by Botvin and his colleagues (Botvin et al., 1995). This five-year program involved 3597 adolescents in 56 public schools, who were followed up for five years begin-

ning in the seventh grade. The initial intervention consisted of 15 classes, ten booster sessions in the eighth grade, and five booster sessions in the ninth grade. The adolescents were taught specific drug-resistance skills and general life skills in a classroom-based program. Like the Northland Project, this study found that drug abuse prevention programs conducted during junior high school "can produce meaningful and durable reductions" in tobacco, alcohol, and marijuana use if they teach social resistance skills and general life skills. Significant reductions in substance use were reported for the experimental schools compared with the control schools. There were 44% fewer drug users and 66% fewer polydrug users (tobacco, marijuana, and alcohol) in the prevention group. It was found, however, that "booster" sessions were necessary for the effect to be maintained.

These projects have clearly shown an effective path toward reducing the extent of substance abuse in young people. Carefully implemented educational programs along with teaching young people the skills needed to resist demands to begin using alcohol and drugs are powerful interventions. Armed with appropriate information and having practice at resisting others around them, adolescents can be successful in avoiding alcohol or drug use. The visible success of these programs has come to the attention of educators in other school districts, and a number of efforts are under way to "export" these laboratory programs for broader use elsewhere in America.

REFERENCES

Botvin, G. J., Baker, E., Dusenbury, L., Botvin, E. M., and Diaz, T. (1995). Long-term follow-up results of a randomized drug abuse prevention trial in a white middle-class population. *JAMA. 273*, 1106–1112.

Botvin, G. J. & Botvin, E. M. (1992). School-based and community based prevention approaches. In J. H. Lowinson, P. Ruiz, R. B. Millman (eds.) *Substance abuse: A comprehensive textbook* (pp. 910–927). Baltimore: Williams & Wilkins.

Johnston, L. D., O'Malley, P. M., & Bachman, J. G. (1995). *National survey results on drug use from the Monitoring the Future Study,*

1975–1995. Washington, DC: U.S. Dept. of Health and Human Services. NIH Publication.

National Institute on Drug Abuse (1996). *National survey results on drug use from the Monitoring the Future Study, 1975–1995.* Washington, DC: U.S. Dept. of Health and Human Services. NIH Publication 96-4139.

National Highway Traffic Safety Administration (1990). *Alcohol and highway safety 1989: A review of the state of knowledge.* Washington, DC: U.S. Dept. of Transportation.

National Clearinghouse for Alcohol and Drug Information (1996). *DAWN Survey.* Drug Awareness Network, Washington, D.C.

Perry, C. L., Williams, C. L., Veblen-Mortenson, S., Toomey, T., Komro, K. A., Anstine, P. S., McGovern, P. G., Finnegan, J. R., Forster, J. L., Wagenaar, A., and Wolfson, M. (1996). Project Northland: Outcomes of a Communitywide alcohol use prevention program during early adolescence. *American Journal of Public Health, 86,* 956–965.

CUTTING EDGE 9

THE CRISIS IN MENTAL HEALTH CARE

Health care costs are reportedly rising more rapidly than any other aspect of the American economy (Resnick & DeLeon, 1995). O'Conner (1996) pointed out that some businesses spent as much on health care as their employees earned. Over the past decade, health care costs have skyrocketed as the number of people receiving services has increased over 30% per year (Giles, 1993). About one out of every three Americans experience psychological problems that could qualify them for a psychiatric diagnosis (Regier et. al., 1988), and about one in five of these receives mental health treatment (Castro, 1993). It has recently been estimated that psychiatric treatment accounts for about one-quarter of all hospital days in America (Kiesler & Sibulkin, 1987).

In response to these needs, health care administrators have created a diverse array of programs in an attempt to provide services at a cost that society can afford. *Managed health care* refers to a system of corporations that secure services from hospitals, physicians, and other health care providers for a designated population (Resnick et al., 1994). Managed health care providers attempt to offer services at lower costs by limiting traditional services, using stringent review procedures, and using lower-cost brief treatment options (Glazer & Gray, 1996). These systems operate by marketing health care plans to employers or individuals. For a fixed prepaid fee, employers and individuals subscribe to a health service company or an HMO (health maintenance organization), which entitles them to the services provided by that health plan (Resnick et al., 1994). These programs establish a treatment staff through a system of professionals, referred to as "panels," who are considered to be effective and efficient in providing a wide range of services (Cummings, 1995). Some HMOs (referred to as open-panel systems) allow patients some choice of health providers and allow any qualified professional in the community to participate. Most systems, however, are of the close-panel type, which limit the selection of available providers. Benefits vary from plan to plan and usually include limits on the problems covered or the maximum amount of care provided or services available. To keep costs low, some HMOs operate according to a system of "capitation," a method of payment in which a health provider contracts to deliver all the health care services required by a population for a fixed cost or flat fee per enrolled member or employee (Richardson & Austad, 1994). The HMOs assume some risk, but capitation allows for great profit if the subscriber's fees can be set higher than the cost of providing health services.

In one common approach to reducing health care costs, the managed care agency negotiates a reduced price directly with the provider. The provider then bills the health service organization for the time spent, and the HMO can obtain "low bid" services from the health professional (Richardson & Austad, 1994). This approach poses little financial risk to the provider. As might be apparent to the casual observer of managed care systems, the procedures for determining the amount of money paid to providers have frequently been a problem for mental health professionals— psychologists and psychiatrists (Resnick et al., 1994). The HMO representative, or "gate keeper" to reimbursement, often a medical generalist who is untrained in psychiatric disorders or psychosocial interventions, controls access to therapy and sometimes the type of treatment to be provided (Resnick et al., 1994). In some systems of managed care, the gate keeper might be a business professional who is viewed by the health service provider as blocking adequate treatment by demanding that the psychologist periodically justify treatment decisions to someone who has little or no background in mental health. In such situations conflicts frequently develop, and patients may be deprived of appropriate and necessary care (Resnick et al., 1994).

Managed care programs differ widely in the modes and quality of mental health services provided. Although their stated intention is to provide the most effective treatments available, decisions about what treatments to provide are often based more on business factors than on treatment considerations. HMOs that are overly cost conscious have come to be viewed by many in the field as simply tending to business to the neglect of the patient's needs (Karon, 1995; Hoyt & Austad, 1992; Schreter, Sharfstein, & Schreter, 1994).

The mental health services typically covered by HMOs include less expensive and less labor-intensive approaches. As might be expected, pharmacotherapy is the most frequent mental health treatment provided by HMOs. Some managed health care systems have advocated the use of somatic therapies in an attempt to contain costs. Gibson (1994) pointed out, for example, that Federal Employees Blue Cross reviewers once followed a set of guidelines promoting the use of radical medical procedures (psychosurgery, insulin therapy, high-dosage drug therapy, and ECT) over psychosocial interventions and low-dosage pharmacotherapy. Psychosocial interventions such as individual psychotherapy are discouraged or limited to relatively few sessions. Lazarus (1996) pointed out that long-term psychotherapy has been virtually eliminated for all but a small number of wealthy private clients. On the other hand, group psychotherapy is often promoted and encouraged because it gives the appearance of being cost effective.

Most managed care corporations have adopted the model of providing focused, brief, intermittent mental health treatment (Cummings, 1995; Hoyt & Austad, 1992) for most problems. Patients who require longer treatments or need inpatient hospitalization are typically not well served in managed care organizations (Gabbard, 1994). In fact, long-term mental health treatment is typically discouraged by managed health care organizations. For example, most managed care groups approve only short inpatient stays (less than ten days) and four to six sessions of outpatient mental health treatment at a time.

Although a great deal of energy has been invested in resolving society's health care delivery problems, there is little evidence that these efforts have either served to slow the increasing costs of mental health care or have enabled professionals to better meet mental health treatment needs.

The ultimate success of managed mental health care programs depends on their ability to control both access to treatment and quality of services. Interestingly, few if any of the decisions regarding the amount and type of services provided are guided directly by empirical criteria. Decisions of whether to cover 8 versus 20 sessions of psychotherapy, for example, are arbitrary and often seem capricious both to the practitioner and to the patient (Harwood et al., in press). Harwood and colleagues have pointed out that service decisions often rest on uncertain assumptions. They concluded that there are no consistently accepted criteria for selecting among psychosocial interventions, or for that matter, for determining when to provide various combinations of psychosocial and medical treatments.

A clear rift has developed between service providers and managers. Available services are often governed more by financial concerns than by a mental health professional's judgment. Practitioners, as a result, are expressing outrage over the situation. O'Conner (1996) referred to this reaction by the mental health profession as "mourning the loss of autonomy." Lazarus (1996) pointed out that psychiatrists have actively resisted managed care and the resulting reduction of mental health services in several ways. "Examples of resistance include verbally abusing utilization reviewers, involving patients and families in insurance disputes, referring medically unstable patients into provider networks, failing to comply with managed care procedures, and targeting managed care firms for litigation" (p. 101). Lawsuits have been directed at health maintenance organizations for failing to provide appropriate and needed service. Sleek (1997) recently described a lawsuit in which seven psychologists were suing a managed care corporation for circumventing the psychologist's judgment, reducing necessary treatment sessions, and dropping them from the managed care panel. The extent to which such clashes will adversely affect the provision of mental health services is uncertain. It appears likely, however, that conflict will be prominent over the next few years as managed care systems assume more control over the mental health system.

A number of observers have criticized the quality of mental health services offered by HMOs (Karon, 1995), citing a number of deleterious effects within the caregiving professions. Many HMOs have solved some "cost" problems by employing individuals to provide therapy who are not trained at the doctoral level. Less trained people (holders of bachelor's and master's degrees) are increasingly asked to provide therapy. Consequently, some independent psychologists and psychiatrists have left the field because of the lack of a livable income from conducting psychotherapy. We are aware of many devoted mental health practitioners who have altered their careers and moved into occupations that are not connected with health care.

Critics of managed care argue that there is no convincing evidence that current efforts are actually controlling costs (Gabbard, 1994; Harwood et al., in press) and that there is no scientific support for the limited benefit options being exercised (England, 1994). Some have pointed out that the administrative costs for managed care centers (including high salaries for HMO executives) are exorbitant. Gabbard (1994), for example, estimated that about one-fourth of the health care expenditures in the United States goes for managed care administration.

The revolution in health care has clearly created controversy in the field of psychotherapy. The mental health field is being drastically altered by economic considerations. These growing pains are likely to continue as our society attempts to come to terms with the cost of health care and the need to provide care for citizens who desperately need help. One thing appears to be certain: The nature of the mental health professions is changing. Whether these changes are for better or worse is yet to be determined.

REFERENCES

Brody, D. S. (1996). What is the role of the primary care physician in managed mental health care? In A. Lazarus (Ed.). *Controversies in managed mental health care* (pp. 29–40). Washington, DC: American Psychiatric Press.**Castro, J.** (1993). What price mental health? *Time,* May 31, 59–60.

Cummings, N. A. (1995). Impact of managed care on employment and training: A primer for survival. *Prof. Psychol. Res. Pract., 26,* 10–15.

England, M. J. (1994). From fee-for-service to accountable health plans. In R. K. Schreter, S. S. Sharfstein, & C. A. Schreter

(Eds.). *Allies and adversaries* (pp. 3–8). Washington, DC: American Psychiatric Press.

Gabbard, G. O. (1994). Inpatient services: The clinician's view. In R. K. Schreter, S. S. Sharfstein, & C. A. Schreter (Eds.). *Allies and adversaries* (pp. 22–30). Washington, DC: American Psychiatric Press.

Gibson, R. W. (1994). Quality of care guidelines: The clinician's view. In R. K. Schreter, S. S. Sharfstein, & C. A. Schreter (Eds.), *Allies and adversaries* (pp. 169–186). Washington, DC: American Psychiatric Press.

Giles, T. R. (1993). *Managed mental health care: A guide to practitioners, employers, and hospital administrators.* Boston: Allyn & Bacon.

Glazer, W. M. & Gray, G. V. (1996). How effective is utilization review? In A. Lazarus (Ed.). *Controversies in managed mental health care* (pp. 179–196). Washington, DC: American Psychiatric Press.

Harwood, T. M., Beutler, L. E., Fisher, D., Monica Sandowicz, M., Albanese, A. L., & Baker, M. (In press). Clinical decision making in managed health care. In J. N. Butcher (Ed.). *Personality assessment in managed health care* (pp. 13–41). New York: Oxford University Press.

Hoyt, M. F., & Austad, C. S. (1992). Psychotherapy in a staff model health maintenance organization: Providing and assuring quality care in the future. *Psychotherapy, 29,* 119–129.

Karon, B. P. (1995). Provision of psychotherapy under managed health care: A growing crisis and national nightmare. *Prof. Psychol. Res. Pract., 26,* 5–9.

Kielser, C. & Sibulkin, A. (1987). *Mental hospitalization: Myths and facts about a national crisis.* Newbury Park, CA: Sage Publications.

Klerman, G. L., Weissman, M. M., Markowitz, J., Glick, I., Wilner, P. J., Mason, B., & Shear, M. K. (1994). Medication and psychotherapy. In A. E. Bergin & S. L. Garfield (Eds.). *Handbook of psychotherapy and behavior change* (4th ed.) (pp. 734–782). New York: Wiley.

Lazarus, A. (1996). Can psychiatrists become efficient case managers? In A. Lazarus (1996). *Controversies in managed mental health care* (pp. 319–336). Washington, DC: American Psychiatric Press.

O'Conner, S. J. (1996). Who will manage the managers? In A. Lazarus (Ed.). *Controversies in managed mental health care* (pp. 383–403). Washington, DC: American Psychiatric Press.

Pomerantz, J. M., Liptzin, B., Carter, A., & Perlman, M. S. (1996). Is private practice compatible with managed care? In A. Lazarus (Ed.). *Controversies in managed mental health care* (pp. 17–29). Washington, DC: American Psychiatric Press.

Regier, D. A., Boyd, J. H., Burke, J. D., Rae, D. S., Myers, J. K., Kramer, M., Robins, C. N., George, L. K., Karno, M., & Locke, B. Z. (1988). One month prevalence of mental disorders in the U.S. *Arch. Gen. Psychol., 45,* 977–986.

Resnick, R. J., Bottinelli, R. W., Puder-York, M., Harris, B., & O'Keefe, B. E. (1994). Basic issues in managed mental health services. In R. L. Lowman & R. J. Resnick (Eds.). *The mental health professional's guide to managed care* (pp. 41–62). Washington, DC: American Psychological Association.

Resnick, R. J., & DeLeon, P. H. (1995). News from Washington, DC. *Prof. Psychol. Res. Pract., 26,* 3–4.

Richardson, L. M., & Austad, C. S. (1994). Realities of mental health practice in managed-care settings. In R. L. Lowman & R. J. Resnick (Eds.). *The mental health professional's guide to managed care* (151–167). Washington, DC: American Psychological Association.

Schreter, R. K., Sharfstein, S. S., & Schreter, C. A. (Eds.). (1994). *Allies and adversaries.* Washington, DC: American Psychiatric Press.

Sleek, S. (1997). Lawsuit seeks to return clinical control to providers. *Monitor,* January, p. 36.

GLOSSARY

Many of the key terms listed in the glossary appear in bold-face when first introduced in the text discussion. A number of other terms commonly encountered in this or other psychology texts are also included; you are encouraged to make use of this glossary both as a general reference tool and as a study aid for the course in abnormal psychology.

Abnormal behavior. Maladaptive behavior detrimental to an individual and/or a group.

Abnormal psychology. Field of psychology concerned with the study, assessment, treatment, and prevention of abnormal behavior.

Abstinence. Refraining altogether from the use of a particular addictive substance or from a particular behavior.

Accommodation. Cognitive process whereby new information causes a reorganization of previously existing cognitive frameworks.

Activation (arousal). Energy mobilization required for an organism to pursue its goals and meet its needs.

Actuarial approach. Application of probability statistics to human behavior.

Actuarial procedures. Methods whereby data about many subjects' behavior is stored and analyzed by computer.

Acute (disorder). Term used to describe a disorder of sudden onset and relatively short duration, usually with intense symptoms.

Acute stress disorder. Disorder following a traumatic event that occurs within four weeks of the event and lasts for a minimum of two days and a maximum of four weeks.

Acute schizophrenia. See **Reactive schizophrenia.**

Addictive behavior. Behavior based on the pathological need for a substance or activity; it may involve the abuse of substances, such as alcohol or cocaine, or excessive indulgence in food or gambling.

Adjustment. Outcome of a person's efforts to deal with stress and meet his or her needs.

Adjustment disorder. A disorder in which a person has difficulty behaving adaptively when faced with a common stressor.

Adjustment disorder with depressed mood. Moderately severe mood disorder similar to dysthymic disorder but having an identifiable, though not severe, psychosocial stressor occurring within three months before the onset of depression, and not exceeding six months in duration.

Adrenal cortex. Outer layer of the adrenal glands; secretes the adrenal steroids and other hormones.

Adrenal glands. Endocrine glands located at the upper end of the kidneys; consist of inner adrenal medulla and outer adrenal cortex.

Adrenaline. Hormone secreted by the adrenal medulla during strong emotion; causes such bodily changes as an increase in blood sugar and a rise in blood pressure. Also called *epinephrine.*

Advocacy. Approach to meeting mental health needs in which advocates, often an interested group of volunteers, attempt to help children or others receive services that they need but often are unable to obtain for themselves.

Advocacy programs. Programs aimed at helping people in underserved populations to obtain aid with which to improve their situations.

Affect. Emotion or feeling.

Aftercare. Follow-up therapy after release from a hospital.

Aggression. Behavior aimed at hurting or destroying someone or something.

Agitation. Marked restlessness and psychomotor excitement.

Agoraphobia. Fear of being in places or situations from which escape would be physically difficult or psychologically embarrassing, or in which help would be unavailable, should a panic attack occur.

AIDS-dementia complex (ADC). Generalized loss of cognitive functioning as a result of HIV-1 infection.

AIDS-related complex (ARC). Pre-AIDS manifestation of HIV infection involving minor infections, various nonspecific symptoms (such as unexplained fever), blood cell count abnormalities, and sometimes cognitive difficulties.

Alarm and mobilization reaction. First state of the general adaptation syndrome, characterized by the mobilization of defenses to cope with a stressful situation.

Alcoholic. Person with a serious drinking problem, whose drinking impairs life adjustment in terms of health, personal relationships, and occupational functioning.

Alcoholism. Dependence on alcohol that seriously interferes with life adjustment.

Alexithymia. Term used to denote a personality pattern in which a person is unable to communicate distress in other than somatic language.

Alienation. Lack or loss of relationships to others.

Alter personalities. In a person with dissociative identity disorder, personalities other than the host personality.

Alzheimer's disease. See **Dementia of the Alzheimer's type.**

Amnesia. Total or partial loss of memory.

Amnestic syndrome. Inability to remember events more than a few minutes after they have occurred or the inability to recall the recent and remote past.

Amniocentesis. Technique that involves drawing fluid from the amniotic sac of a pregnant woman so that the sloughed-off fetal cells can be examined for chromosomal irregularities, including that of Down syndrome.

Amphetamine. Drug that produces a psychologically stimulating and energizing effect.

Analogue studies. Studies in which a researcher attempts to simulate the conditions under investigation.

Anal stage. In psychoanalytic theory, stage of psychosexual development in which behavior is presumably focused on anal pleasure and activities.

Androgen. Hormone associated with the development and maintenance of male characteristics.

Anesthesia. Loss or impairment of sensitivity (usually to touch but often applied to sensitivity to pain and other senses as well).

Anhedonia. Inability to experience pleasure or joy.

Anorexia nervosa. Disorder involving severe loss of body weight, accompanied by an intense fear of gaining weight or becoming "fat."

Anoxia. Lack of sufficient oxygen.

Antabuse. Drug used in the treatment of alcoholism.

Anterograde amnesia. Loss of memory for events that occur *following* trauma or shock.

Antianxiety drugs. Drugs that are used primarily for alleviating anxiety.

Antibody. Circulating blood substance coded for detection of and binding to a particular antigen.

Antidepressant drugs. Drugs that are used primarily to elevate mood and relieve depression.

Antigen. Substance detected as "foreign" by the body's immune defenses, giving rise to the immune reaction.

Antipsychotic drugs. Group of drugs that produce a calming effect on many patients as well as alleviate or reduce the intensity of psychotic symptoms, such as delusions and hallucinations and sometimes negative symptoms.

Antisocial personality disorder. Personality disorder involving disregard for the rights of others, impulsivity, and aggressive and irresponsible behavior.

Anxiety. A generalized feeling of apprehension about possible danger.

Anxiety disorder. A disorder involving an unrealistic, irrational fear or anxiety of disabling intensity. DSM-IV lists seven types of anxiety disorder: phobia (specific or social), panic disorder (with or without agoraphobia), generalized anxiety disorder, obsessive-compulsive disorder, and posttraumatic stress disorder.

Aphasia. Loss or impairment of ability to communicate and understand language symbols—involving loss of power of expression by speech, writing, or signs, or loss of ability to comprehend written or spoken language—resulting from brain injury or disease.

Apraxia. Loss of ability to perform purposeful movements.

Arousal. See **Activation.**

Arteriosclerosis. Degenerative thickening and hardening of the walls of the arteries, occurring usually in old age.

Assertiveness therapy. Behavior therapy technique for helping people become more self-assertive in interpersonal relationships.

Assimilation. Cognitive process whereby new information is fitted into previously existing cognitive frameworks.

Asylums. Institutions established solely for the care of the mentally ill.

At risk. Condition of being considered vulnerable to the development of certain abnormal behaviors.

Atrophy. Wasting away or shrinking of a bodily organ, particularly muscle tissue.

Attention-deficit hyperactivity disorder (ADHD). Disorder of childhood characterized by difficulties that interfere with task-oriented behavior, such as impulsivity, excessive motor activity, and an inability to focus attention for appropriate periods of time. Also known as hyperactivity.

Attributions. Causes assigned to things that happen.

Autism. Pervasive developmental disorder beginning in infancy involving a wide range of abnormalities, including deficits in language, perceptual, and motor development; defective reality testing; and social withdrawal.

Autonomic nervous system. Section of the nervous system that regulates the internal organs; consists primarily of ganglia connected with the brain stem and spinal cord; may be subdivided into the sympathetic and parasympathetic systems.

Autonomic reactivity. Individual's characteristic degree of emotional reactivity to stress.

Autonomy. Self-reliance; the sense of being an independent person.

Autosome. Any chromosome other than those determining sex.

Aversion therapy. Form of behavior therapy in which punishment or aversive stimulation is used to eliminate undesired responses.

Aversive conditioning. Use of noxious stimuli to suppress unwanted behavior.

Aversive stimulus. Stimulus that elicits psychic or physical pain.

Avoidance conditioning. Form of conditioning in which a subject learns to behave in a certain way in order to avoid an unpleasant stimulus.

Avoidant personality disorder. Personality disorder characterized by hypersensitivity to rejection, limited social relationships, and low self-esteem.

Barbiturate. Type of synthetic sedative drug.

Baseline. The initial level of responses emitted by an organism.

Behavioral contracting. Positive reinforcement technique using a contract, often between family members, stipulating privileges and responsibilities.

Behavioral medicine. Broad interdisciplinary approach to the treatment of physical disorders thought to have psychological factors as major aspects of their causal patterns.

Behavioral perspective. A theoretical viewpoint organized around the theme that learning is central in determining human behavior.

Behavioral sciences. Various interrelated disciplines, including psychology, sociology, and anthropology, that focus on human behavior.

Behavior disorder. Synonym for psychological problem.

Behaviorism. School of psychology that formerly restricted itself primarily to study of overt behavior.

Behavior modification. Change of specific behaviors by learning techniques.

Behavior therapy. Therapeutic procedures based primarily on principles of classical and operant conditioning.

Benign. Of a mild, self-limiting nature; not malignant.

Biofeedback. Treatment technique in which a person is taught to influence physiological processes formerly thought to be involuntary.

Biogenic amines. Chemicals that serve as neurotransmitters or modulators.

Biological clocks. Regular biological cycles of sleep, activity, and metabolism characteristic of each species.

Biological viewpoint. Approach to mental disorders emphasizing biological causation.

Bipolar disorder. Mood disorder in which a person experiences both manic and depressive episodes.

Bipolar disorder with a seasonal pattern. Bipolar disorder with recurrences in particular seasons of the year.

Bisexuality. Sexual attraction to both females and males.

Blocking. Involuntary inhibition of recall, ideation, or communication (including sudden stoppage of speech).

Blood-injury phobia. Persistent and disproportionate fear of the sight of blood or injury.

Borderline personality disorder. Personality disorder characterized by instability in interpersonal relationships, self-image, and moods.

Brain pathology. Diseased or disordered condition of the brain.

Brain waves. Minute oscillations of electrical potential given off by neurons in the cerebral cortex and measured by the electroencephalograph.

Brief Psychiatric Rating Scale (BPRS). Objective method of rating clinical symptoms that provides scores on 18 variables (e.g., somatic concern, anxiety, withdrawal, hostility, and bizarre thinking).

Brief psychotherapy. Short-term therapy, usually 8 to 10 sessions, focused on restoring an individual's functioning and offering emotional support.

Bulimia nervosa. Recurring episodes of seemingly uncontrollable binge-eating, often accompanied by extreme efforts to purge in order to prevent weight gain.

Caffeine. Chemical compound found in many commonly available drinks and foods, whose negative effects can include intoxication, restlessness, nervousness, excitement, insomnia, muscle twitching, and gastrointestinal complaints.

Cardiovascular. Pertaining to the heart and blood vessels.

Case study. An in-depth examination of an individual or family.

Castrating. Refers to any source of injury to or deprivation of the genitals, or more broadly, to a threat to the masculinity or femininity of an individual.

Castration anxiety. As postulated by Freud, the anxiety a young boy experiences when he desires his mother while at the same time viewing his father as a rival and fearing that his father may harm him by removing his penis; this anxiety forces the boy to repress his sexual desire for his mother and his hostility toward his father.

Catalepsy. Condition in which the muscles are waxy and semirigid, tending to maintain the limbs in any position in which they are placed.

Catecholamine. Class of amines sharing a similar chemical structure and involved chiefly in neural transmission.

Categorical approach. Approach to classifying abnormal behavior that assumes that (a) all human behavior can be sharply divided into the categories normal and abnormal, and (b) there exist discrete, nonoverlapping classes or types of abnormal behavior, often referred to as mental illnesses or diseases.

Catharsis. Discharge of emotional tension associated with something, such as by talking about past traumas.

CAT scan. See **Computerized axial tomography.**

Causal pattern. In a cause-and-effect relationship, a situation in which more than one causal factor is involved.

Causation. Relationship in which the preceding variable causes the other(s).

Central nervous system (CNS). The brain and spinal cord.

Cerebral arteriosclerosis. Hardening of the arteries in the brain.

Cerebral cortex. Surface layers of the cerebrum.

Cerebral hemorrhage. Bleeding into brain tissue from a ruptured blood vessel.

Cerebral laceration. Tearing of brain tissue associated with severe head injury.

Cerebral syphilis. Syphilitic infection of the brain.

Cerebral thrombosis. Formation of a clot or thrombus in the vascular system of the brain.

Cerebrovascular accident (CVA). Blockage or rupture of large blood vessel in brain leading to both focal and generalized impairment of brain function. Also called *stroke.*

Cerebrum. Main part of brain; divided into left and right hemispheres.

Chemotherapy. Use of drugs to treat mental disorders.

Child abuse. Infliction of physical or psychological damage on a child by parents or other adults.

Child advocacy. Movement concerned with protecting rights and ensuring well-being of children.

Chorea. Pathological condition characterized by jerky, irregular, involuntary movements. See also **Huntington's disease.**

Chromosomal anomalies. Inherited defects or vulnerabilities caused by irregularities in chromosomes.

Chromosomes. Chainlike structures within cell nucleus that contain genes.

Chronic. Term used to describe a disorder that is a relatively permanent maladaptive pattern or condition.

Chronic schizophrenia. See **Process schizophrenia.**

Circadian rhythms. The 24-hour rhythmic fluctuations in sleep, activity, and metabolic processes of plants and animals. See also **Biological clocks.**

Civil commitment. Procedure whereby a person certified as mentally disordered can be hospitalized, either voluntarily or against his or her will.

Classical (respondent) conditioning. Basic form of learning in which a previously neutral stimulus comes to elicit a response that was previously only elicited by a stimulus that automatically elicited that response.

Claustrophobia. Irrational fear of small enclosed places.

Client-centered (person-centered) psychotherapy. Nondirective approach to psychotherapy developed chiefly by Carl Rogers and based on his personality theory.

Clinical picture. Diagnostic picture formed by observation of patient's behavior or by all available assessment data.

Clinical problem checklist. Computer-administered psychological assessment procedure for surveying the range of psychological problems a patient is experiencing.

Clinical psychologist. Mental health professional with Ph.D. degree or Psy.D. degree in clinical psychology and clinical experience in assessment and psychotherapy.

Clinical psychology. Field of psychology concerned with the understanding, assessment, treatment, and prevention of maladaptive behavior.

Cocaine. Stimulating and pain-reducing psychoactive drug.

Cognition. Act, process, or product of knowing or perceiving.

Cognitive-behavioral perspective. A theory of abnormal behavior that focuses on how thoughts and information processing can become distorted and lead to maladaptive emotions and behavior.

Cognitive-behavior therapy. Therapy based on altering dysfunctional thoughts and cognitive distortions.

Cognitive dissonance. Condition of tension existing when several of one's beliefs and attitudes are inconsistent with one another.

Cognitive map. Network of assumptions that form a person's "frame of reference" for interpreting and coping with his or her world.

Cognitive processes (cognition). Mental processes, including perception, memory, and reasoning, by which one acquires knowledge, solves problems, and makes plans.

Cognitive restructuring. Cognitive-behavioral therapy that aims to change a person's false or maladaptive frame of reference.

Collective unconscious. Term used by Carl Jung to refer to that portion of the unconscious that he considered common to all humanity.

Coma. Profound stupor with unconsciousness.

Community mental health. Application of psychosocial and sociocultural principles to the improvement of given environments.

Community psychology. Use of community resources in dealing with maladaptive behavior; tends to be more concerned with community intervention rather than with personal or individual change.

Compulsions. Repetitive behaviors or mental acts such as cleaning or checking that a person feels driven to perform in response to an obsession.

Compulsive gambling. See **Pathological gambling.**

Computer assessment. Use of computers to obtain or interpret assessment data.

Computerized axial tomography (CAT scan). Radiological technique used to locate and assess the extent of organic damage without surgery.

Concordance rates. The percentage of twins who share a diagnosis or trait.

Conditioning. Simple form of learning involving stimulus and response. See also **Classical conditioning** and **Operant conditioning.**

Conduct disorders. Childhood disorders marked by persistent acts of aggressive or antisocial behavior that may or may not be against the law.

Confabulation. Filling in of memory gaps with false and often irrelevant details.

Confidentiality. Commitment on part of a professional person to keep information he or she obtains from a client confidential.

Conflict. Simultaneous arousal of opposing impulses, desires, or motives.

Congenital. Existing at birth or before birth but not necessarily hereditary.

Congenital defect. Genetic defect or environmental condition occurring before birth and causing a child to develop a physical or psychological anomaly.

Consciousness. Awareness of inner and/or outer environment.

Constitution. Relatively constant biological makeup of an individual, resulting from the interaction of heredity and environment.

Constitutional liability. Any detrimental characteristic that is either innate or acquired so early and in such strength that it is functionally similar to a genetic characteristic.

Consultation. Community intervention approach that aims at helping individuals at risk for disorder by working indirectly through caretaker institutions (e.g., police and teachers).

Contingency. Relationship, usually causal, between two events in which one is usually followed by the other.

Continuous reinforcement. Reward or reinforcement given regularly after each correct response.

Control group. Group of subjects compared with an experimental group in assessing the effects of independent variables.

Contributory cause. A condition that increases the probability of developing a disorder but that is neither necessary nor sufficient for it to occur.

Conversion disorder. Type of somatoform disorder in which pseudoneurological symptoms of some physical malfunction or loss of control appear without any underlying organic pathology; previously called *hysteria*.

Convulsion. Pathological, involuntary muscular contractions.

Coping strategies. Efforts used to deal with stress.

Coprolalia. Verbal tic in which an individual utters obscenities aloud.

Coronary heart disease (CHD). Potentially lethal blockage of the arteries supplying blood to the heart muscle, or myocardium.

Corpus callosum. Nerve fibers that connect the two hemispheres of the brain.

Correlation. The tendency of two variables to covary. With positive correlation, as one variable goes up, so does the other; with negative correlation as one variable goes up the other goes down.

Corticovisceral control mechanisms. Brain mechanisms that regulate autonomic and other bodily functions.

Counseling psychology. Field of psychology that focuses on helping people with problems pertaining to education, marriage, or occupation.

Counter-transference. In psychodynamic therapy, inappropriate feelings of transference on the part of the therapist toward the client.

Couples counseling (marital therapy). Treatment for disordered interpersonal relationships involving sessions with both members of the relationship present.

Coverants. Internal, private events, such as thoughts and assumptions, to which conditioning principles are applied in cognitive-behavioral therapy.

Covert. Concealed, disguised, not directly observable.

Covert sensitization. Behavioral treatment method for extinguishing undesirable behavior by associating noxious mental images with that behavior.

Criminal responsibility. Legal question of whether a person should be permitted to use insanity as a defense after having committed a crime.

Crisis. Stress situation that approaches or exceeds adaptive capacities of an individual or group.

Crisis intervention. Various methods for rendering therapeutic assistance to an individual or group during a period of crisis.

Criterion group. Group of subjects who exhibit the variable or disorder under study.

Cross-gender identification. The desire to be, or the insistence that one is, of the opposite sex.

Cultural-familial retardation. Mental retardation as a result of an inferior quality of interaction with the cultural environment and with other people, with no evidence of brain pathology.

Cultural relativism. Position that one cannot apply universal standards of normality or abnormality to all societies.

Cyclothymia. Mild mood disorder characterized by cyclical periods of hypomanic and depressive symptoms.

Day hospital. Community-based mental hospital where patients are treated during the day, returning to their homes at night.

Decompensation. Loss of adaptive functioning under excessive stress.

Defense mechanism. See **Ego-defense mechanism.**

Defense-oriented response. Behavior directed primarily at protecting the self from hurt and disorganization rather than at coping with the demands of a stressor.

Deinstitutionalization. Movement to provide chronic patients with continued psychiatric care in the local community rather than committing them to institutions.

Delinquency. Antisocial or illegal behavior by a minor.

Delirium. State of mental confusion characterized by relatively rapid onset of widespread disorganization of the higher mental processes, caused by a generalized disturbance in brain metabolism. May include impaired perception, memory, and thinking and abnormal psychomotor activity.

Delirium tremens. Acute delirium associated with prolonged alcoholism; characterized by intense anxiety, tremors, and hallucinations.

Delusion. Firm belief opposed to reality but maintained in spite of strong evidence to the contrary.

Delusional disorder. Type of psychosis characterized by a systematized delusional system; formerly called *paranoia* and *paranoid disorder.*

Delusional system. Internally coherent, systematized pattern of delusions.

Delusion of grandeur. False belief that one is a noted or famous person, such as Napoleon or the Virgin Mary.

Delusion of persecution. False belief that one is being mistreated or interfered with by one's enemies.

Dementia. Progressive deterioration of brain functioning occurring after the completion of brain maturation in adolescence. Characterized by deficits in memory, thinking, and behavior.

Dementia of the Alzheimer's type (DAT). Disorder associated with a progressive dementia syndrome ultimately terminating in death. Onset may be in middle or old age, and symptoms include memory loss, withdrawal, confusion, and impaired judgment.

Dementia praecox. Older term for schizophrenia.

Demonology. Viewpoint emphasizing supernatural causation of mental disorder, especially "possession" by evil spirits or forces.

Denial of reality. Ego-defense mechanism by means of which a person protects himself or herself from unpleasant aspects of reality by refusing to acknowledge them.

Dependency. Tendency to rely overly on others.

Dependent personality disorder. Personality disorder marked by clinging and submissive behavior and feelings of panic or discomfort at having to be alone.

Dependent variable. In an experiment, the factor that the hypothesis predicts will change with changes in the independent variable.

Depersonalization. Loss of sense of personal identity, often with a feeling of being something or someone else.

Depersonalization disorder. Dissociative disorder in which there is a loss of the sense of self.

Depression. Emotional state characterized by extreme sadness and dejection.

Depressive personality disorder. Provisional personality disorder in DSM-IV that involves a pattern of depressive cognitions that begins in early childhood and is pervasive in nature.

Derealization. Experience in which the external world is perceived as distorted and as lacking a stable and palpable existence.

Desensitization. Therapeutic process by means of which reactions to traumatic experiences are reduced in intensity by repeatedly exposing a person to them in mild form, either in reality or in fantasy, while remaining in a state of relaxation.

Desire phase. First phase of the human sexual response, consisting of fantasies about sexual activity or a sense of desire to have sexual activity.

Deterrence. Premise that punishment for criminal offenses will deter that criminal and others from future criminal acts.

Detox. Center or facility for receiving and detoxifying alcohol- or drug-intoxicated individuals.

Detoxification. Treatment directed toward ridding the body of alcohol or other drugs.

Developmental disorder. Problem that is rooted in deviations in the development process itself, thus disrupting the acquisition of skills and adaptive behavior and often interfering with the transition to well-functioning adulthood.

Developmental psychopathology. Field of psychology that studies disorders of childhood within the context of developmental processes.

Deviant behavior. Behavior that deviates markedly from the average or norm.

Diagnosis. Determination of the nature and extent of a specific disorder.

Diathesis. Predisposition or vulnerability toward developing a given disorder.

Diathesis-stress model. View of abnormal behavior as the result of stress operating on an individual with a biological, psychosocial, or sociocultural predisposition toward developing a specific disorder.

Dimensional approach. Approach to classifying abnormal behavior that assumes that a person's typical behavior is the product of differing strengths or intensities of behavior along several definable dimensions, such as mood, emotional stability, aggressiveness, gender, identity, anxiousness, interpersonal trust, clarity of thinking and communication, social introversion, and so on.

Directive therapy. Type of therapeutic approach in which a therapist supplies direct answers to problems and takes much of the responsibility for the progress of therapy.

Disaster syndrome. Response pattern that appears to characterize the initial and long-lasting reactions of many victims of catastrophes.

Discordant marriage. Family in which one or both of the parents is not gaining satisfaction from the relationship and one spouse may express frustration and disillusionment in hostile ways, such as nagging, belittling, and purposely doing things to annoy the other person.

Discrimination. Learning to interpret and respond differently to two or more similar stimuli.

Disintegration. Loss of organization or integration in any organized system.

Disorganization. Severely impaired integration.

Disorientation. Mental confusion with respect to time, place, or person.

Displacement. Ego-defense mechanism in which an emotional attitude or symbolic meaning is transferred from one object or concept to another.

Disrupted family. Family that is incomplete as a result of death, divorce, separation, or some other circumstance.

Dissociation. The human mind's capacity to mediate complex mental activity in channels split off from or independent of conscious awareness.

Dissociative amnesia. Psychogenically caused memory failure.

Dissociative disorders. Conditions involving a disruption in the sense of a coherent and stable personal identity.

Dissociative identity disorder. Condition in which a person manifests two or more complete systems of personality. Formerly called *multiple personality disorder.*

Distress. Negative stress, leading to sorrow, anguish, or sense of misfortune.

Disturbed family. Family in which one or both parents behave in grossly eccentric or abnormal ways and may keep the home in constant emotional turmoil.

Dizygotic (fraternal) twins. Twins that develop from two separate eggs.

DNA. Deoxyribonucleic acid, principal component of genes.

Dominant gene. A gene whose hereditary characteristics prevail in the offspring.

Dopamine. Catecholamine neurotransmitter substance.

Dopamine hypothesis. Hypothesis that schizophrenia is the result of an excess of dopamine activity at certain synaptic sites.

Double-bind. Situation in which a person will be disapproved for performing a given act and equally disapproved if he or she does not perform it.

Double-bind communication. Type of faulty communication in which the one person (e.g., a parent) presents to another (e.g., a child) ideas, feelings, and demands that are mutually incompatible.

Down syndrome. Form of moderate to severe mental retardation associated with chromosomal abnormality and typically accompanied by characteristic physical features.

Dream analysis. Psychotherapeutic technique involving the interpretation of a patient's dreams.

Drive. Internal conditions directing an organism toward a specific goal, usually involving biological rather than psychological motives.

Drug abuse. Use of a drug to the extent that it interferes with health and/or occupational or social adjustment.

Drug addiction (dependence). Physiological and/or psychological dependence on a drug.

Drug therapy. See **Chemotherapy** and **Pharmacotherapy.**

DSM-IV. Current diagnostic manual of the American Psychiatric Association.

Dwarfism. Condition of arrested growth and very short stature.

Dyad. Two-person group.

Dynamic formulation. Integrated evaluation of a client's traits, attitudes, conflicts, and symptoms that attempts to explain his or her problem.

Dysfunction. Impairment or disturbance in the functioning of an organ or in behavior.

Dysfunctional beliefs. Negative beliefs that are rigid, extreme, and counterproductive.

Dyslexia. Impairment of the ability to read.

Dyspareunia. Painful coitus in a male or a female.

Dysrhythmia. Abnormal brain-wave pattern.

Dysthymia. Moderately severe mood disorder characterized by extended periods of nonpsychotic depression and brief periods of normal moods.

Echolalia. Meaningless repetition of words by an individual, usually of whatever has been said to that person.

Edema. Swelling of tissues.

EEG. See **Electroencephalogram.**

Ego. In psychoanalytic theory, the rational subsystem of the personality that mediates between id and superego demands and reality. More generally, a person's self-concept.

Egocentric. Preoccupied with one's own concerns and relatively insensitive to the concerns of others.

Ego-defense mechanism. Psychic mechanism that acts to maintain a person's feelings of adequacy and worth rather than to cope directly with an anxiety-provoking situation; usually unconscious and reality-distorting. Also called *defense mechanism.*

Electra complex. In psychoanalytic theory, an excessive emotional attachment (love) of a daughter for her father.

Electroconvulsive therapy (ECT). Use of electricity to produce convulsions and unconsciousness; a treatment used primarily for severe depression. Also known as *electroshock therapy.*

Electroencephalogram (EEG). Graphic record of the brain's electrical activity, obtained by placing electrodes on the scalp and measuring the brain-wave impulses from various brain areas.

Embolism. Lodgment of a blood clot in a blood vessel too small to permit its passage.

Emotion. Strong feeling accompanied by physiological changes.

Emotional disturbance. Psychological disorder.

Emotional insulation. Ego-defense mechanism in which a person reduces anxiety by withdrawing into a shell of passivity.

Empathy. Ability to understand and to some extent share the state of mind of another person.

Encephalitis. Inflammation of the brain.

Encopresis. Disorder defined by having bowel movements in one's clothing after the age of four.

Encounter group. Small group designed to provide an intensive interpersonal experience focusing on feelings and group interactions; used in therapy or to promote personal growth.

Endocrine glands. Ductless glands that secrete hormones directly into the lymph or bloodstream.

Endogenous factors. Factors originating within an organism that affect behavior.

Endorphins. Opiate-like substances produced in the brain and pituitary gland in response to stimulation; thought to play a role in an organism's reaction to pain.

Enuresis. Bed wetting; involuntary discharge of urine after the age of expected continence (age five).

Environmental psychology. Field of psychology focusing on the effects of an environmental setting on an individual's feelings and behavior.

Epidemiology. Study of the distribution of diseases, disorders, or health-related behaviors in a given population. Mental health epidemiology is the study of the distribution of mental disorders.

Epilepsy. Group of disorders varying from momentary lapses of consciousness to generalized convulsions.

Epinephrine. Hormone secreted by the adrenal medulla; also called *adrenaline*.

Episodic (disorder). Term to describe a disorder that tends to abate and to recur.

Equilibrium. Steady state; balance.

Erectile insufficiency. Inability of a male to achieve erection.

Erotic. Pertaining to sexual stimulation and gratification.

Escape learning. Conditioned response in which a subject learns to terminate or escape an aversive stimulus.

Essential hypertension. High blood pressure with no known physical cause.

Estrogens. Female hormones produced by the ovaries.

Ethnic group. Group of people who are treated as distinctive in terms of culture and group patterns.

Etiology. Causation; the systematic study of the causes of disorders.

Euphoria. Exaggerated feeling of well-being and contentment.

Eustress. Positive stress.

Exacerbate. Intensify.

Excitement phase. Phase of the human sexual response in which there is a subjective sense of sexual pleasure and physiological changes, including penile erection in the male and vaginal lubrication and enlargement in the female.

Exhaustion and disintegration. Third and final stage in the general adaptation syndrome, in which an organism is no longer able to resist continuing stress; at the biological level may result in death.

Exhibitionism. Public display or exposure of genitals to others in inappropriate circumstances and without their consent.

Existential anxiety. Anxiety concerning one's ability to find a satisfying and fulfilling way of life.

Existentialism. View of human beings that emphasizes an individual's responsibility for becoming the kind of person he or she should be.

Existential neurosis. Disorder characterized by feelings of alienation, meaninglessness, and apathy.

Existential psychotherapy. Type of therapy that is based on existential thought and focuses on individual uniqueness and authenticity on the part of both client and therapist.

Exogenous. Originating from or due to external causes.

Exorcism. Religiously inspired treatment procedure designed to drive out evil spirits or forces from a "possessed" person.

Experimental group. Group of subjects used to assess the effects of independent variables.

Experimental method. Rigorous scientific procedure by which hypotheses are tested.

Expressed emotion (EE). Type of negative communication involving excessive criticism and emotional over-involvement directed at a patient by family members.

Extinction. Gradual disappearance of a conditioned response when it is no longer reinforced.

Extraversion. Personality type oriented toward the outer world of people and things rather than concepts and intellectual concerns.

Factitious disorders. Conditions in which symptoms are feigned in order to satisfy the psychological need to assume and maintain a sick role.

Factor analysis. Statistical technique used for reducing a large array of intercorrelated measures to the minimum number of factors necessary to account for the observed overlap among them.

Fading. Technique whereby a stimulus causing some reaction is gradually replaced by a previously neutral stimulus, such that the latter acquires the property of producing the reaction in question.

False memories. "Memories" of events that did not actually happen, often produced by highly leading and suggestive techniques.

Familial. Pertaining to characteristics that tend to run in families and have a higher incidence in certain families than in the general population.

Family therapy. Form of interpersonal therapy focusing on relationships within a family.

Fantasy. Daydream; also, an ego-defense mechanism by means of which a person escapes from the world of reality and gratifies his or her desires in fantasy achievements.

Fear. A basic emotion that involves activation of the "fight or flight" response.

Feedback. Explicit information pertaining to internal physiological processes or to the social consequences of one's overt behavior.

Female orgasmic disorder. Persistent or recurrent delay in or absence of orgasm following a normal sexual excitement phase.

Female sexual arousal disorder. Sexual dysfunction involving an absence of sexual arousal feelings and unresponsiveness to most or all forms of erotic stimulation.

Fetal alcohol syndrome. Observed pattern in infants of alcoholic mothers in which there is a characteristic facial or limb irregularity, low body weight, and behavioral abnormality.

Fetishism. Sexual variant in which sexual interest centers on some inanimate object or nonsexual part of the body.

Fetus. Embryo after the sixth week following conception.

Fixation. In psychoanalytic theory, unreasonable or exaggerated attachment to some person or arresting of emotional development on a childhood or adolescent level.

Fixed-interval schedule. Schedule of reinforcement based on fixed period of time after previous reinforced response.

Fixed-ratio schedule. Schedule of reinforcement based on reinforcement after fixed number of nonreinforced responses.

Flashback. Involuntary recurrence of perceptual distortions or hallucinations weeks or months after taking a drug; in post-traumatic stress disorder, a dissociative state in which the person briefly relives the traumatic experience.

Flooding. Anxiety-eliciting technique involving placing a client in a real-life, anxiety-arousing situation.

Folie à deux. See **Shared psychotic disorder.**

Follow-up study. Research procedure in which people are studied over a period of time or are recontacted at a later time after initial study.

Forensic psychology and psychiatry. Branches of psychology and psychiatry dealing with legal problems relating to mental disorders.

Fraternal twins. Dizygotic twins; fertilized by separate germ cells, thus not having same genetic inheritance. May be of the same or opposite sex.

Free association. Psychoanalytic procedure for probing the unconscious in which a person gives a running account of every thought and feeling.

Free-floating anxiety. Anxiety not referable to any specific situation or cause.

Frontal lobe. Portion of the brain active in reasoning and other higher thought processes.

Frustration. Thwarting of a need or desire.

Frustration tolerance. See **Stress tolerance.**

Fugue. Dissociative disorder that entails loss of memory accompanied by actual physical flight from one's present life situation to a new environment or less threatening former one.

Functional psychoses. Severe mental disorders for which a specific organic pathology has not been demonstrated.

Gambling. Wagering on games or events in which chance largely determines the outcome.

Gender dysphoria. Persistent discomfort about one's biological sex or the sense that the gender role of that sex is inappropriate.

Gender identity. Individual's identification as being male or female.

Gender identity disorder. Identification with members of the opposite sex, and persistent discomfort with one's anatomical sexual identity.

General adaptation syndrome (GAS). A model of a person's reaction to excessive stress; consists of the alarm reaction, the stage of resistance, and exhaustion.

Generalization. Tendency of a response that has been conditioned to one stimulus to be elicited by other, similar stimuli.

Generalized anxiety disorder. Anxiety disorder characterized by chronic excessive worry about a number of events or activities, with no obvious threat present, as well as by a variety of symptoms of tension, irritability, or restlessness.

Generalized reinforcer. Reinforcer, such as money, that may influence a wide range of stimuli and behaviors.

General paresis. Mental disorder associated with syphilis of the brain.

Genes. Ultramicroscopic areas of DNA that are responsible for the transmission of hereditary traits.

Genetic code. Means by which DNA controls the sequence and structure of proteins manufactured within each cell and also makes exact duplicates of itself.

Genetic counseling. Counseling prospective parents concerning the probability of their having defective offspring as a result of genetic defects.

Genetic inheritance. Potential for development and behavior determined at conception by egg and sperm cells.

Genetics. Science of the inheritance of traits and the mechanisms of this inheritance.

Genitalia. Organs of reproduction, especially the external organs.

Genital stage. In psychoanalytic theory, the final stage of psychosexual development involving shift from auto-eroticism to heterosexual interest.

Genotype. Genetic characteristics inherited by an individual.

Geriatrics. Science of the diseases and treatment of the aged.

Germ cells. Reproductive cells (female ovum and male sperm) that unite to produce a new individual.

Gerontology. Science dealing with the study of old age.

Gestalt psychology. School of psychology that emphasizes patterns rather than elements or connections, taking the view that the whole is more than the sum of its parts.

Gestalt therapy. Type of psychotherapy emphasizing wholeness of the person and integration of thought, feeling, and action.

Gigantism. Abnormally tall stature resulting from hyperfunctioning of the pituitary.

Glucocorticoids. Adrenocortical hormones involved in sugar metabolism but also having widespread effects on injury-repair mechanisms and resistance to disease; they include hydrocortisone, corticosterone, and cortisone.

Gonads. Sex glands.

Good premorbid schizophrenia. See **Reactive schizophrenia.**

Group therapy. Psychotherapy with two or more people at the same time.

Guilt. Feelings of culpability arising from behavior or desires contrary to one's ethical principles. Involves both self-devaluation and apprehension growing out of fears of punishment.

Habit. Any product of learning, whether it is a customary or transitory mode of response.

Habituation. Process whereby a person's response to the same stimulus lessens with repeated presentations.

Halfway house. Facility that provides aftercare following institutionalization, seeking to ease a person's adjustment to the community.

Hallucination. A perception in which things are seen or heard that are not real or present.

Hallucinogens. Drugs or chemicals capable of producing hallucinations.

Hallucinosis. Persistent hallucinations in the presence of known or suspected organic brain pathology.

Hashish. Strongest drug derived from the hemp plant; a relative of marijuana that is usually smoked.

Health psychology. Subspecialty within behavioral medicine that deals with psychology's contributions to diagnosis, treatment, and prevention of these psychological components of physical illnesses.

Hebephrenic schizophrenia. See **Schizophrenia, disorganized type.**

Hemiplegia. Paralysis of one lateral half of the body.

Heredity. Genetic transmission of characteristics from parents to their children.

Hermaphroditism. Anatomical sexual abnormality in which a person has sex organs of both sexes.

Heroin. Powerful psychoactive drug, chemically derived from morphine, that relieves pain but is even more intense and addictive than morphine.

Heterosexuality. Sexual interest in a member of the opposite sex.

Hierarchy of needs. Concept that needs arrange themselves in a hierarchy in terms of importance, from the most basic biological needs to those psychological needs concerned with self-actualization.

High-risk. Term applied to persons showing great vulnerability to physical or mental disorders.

Histrionic personality disorder. A personality disorder characterized by excessive attention-seeking, emotional instability, and self-dramatization.

Homeostasis. Tendency of organisms to maintain conditions making possible a constant level of physiological functioning.

Homosexuality. Sexual preference for a member of one's own sex.

Hormones. Chemicals released by the endocrine glands that regulate development of and activity in various bodily organs.

Hostility. Emotional reaction or drive toward the destruction or damage of an object interpreted as a source of frustration or threat.

Host personality. The principal personality in a person with dissociative identity disorder.

Humanistic-experiential therapies. Psychotherapies emphasizing personal growth and self-direction.

Humanistic perspective. Approach to understanding abnormal behavior that views basic human nature as "good" and emphasizes people's inherent capacity for growth and self-actualization.

Huntington's disease. Incurable disease of hereditary origin, which is manifested in jerking, twitching movements and mental deterioration. Formerly called *Huntington's chorea.*

Hydrocephalus. Relatively rare condition in which the accumulation of an abnormal amount of cerebrospinal fluid within the cranium causes damage to the brain tissues and enlargement of the skull.

Hydrotherapy. Use of hot or cold baths, ice packs, etc., in treatment.

Hyper-. Prefix meaning increased or excessive.

Hyperactivity. See **Attention-deficit hyperactivity disorder.**

Hyperobesity. Extreme overweight; more than 100 pounds over ideal body weight.

Hypertension. High blood pressure.

Hyperthymic temperament. Personality type involving lifelong hypomanic adjustment.

Hyperventilation. Rapid breathing associated with intense anxiety.

Hypesthesia. Partial loss of sensitivity.

Hypnosis. Trancelike mental state induced in a cooperative subject by suggestion.

Hypnotherapy. Use of hypnosis in psychotherapy.

Hypo-. Prefix meaning decreased or insufficient.

Hypoactive sexual desire disorder. Sexual dysfunction in which either a man or a woman shows little or no sexual drive or interest.

Hypochondriacal delusions. Delusions concerning various horrible disease conditions, such as the belief that one's brain is turning to dust.

Hypochondriasis. Condition dominated by preoccupation with bodily processes and fear of presumed diseases.

Hypomania. Mild form of mania.

Hypothalamus. Key structure at the base of the brain; important in emotion and motivation.

Hypothesis. Statement or proposition, usually based on observation, which is tested in an experiment; may be denied or supported by experimental results but never conclusively proved.

Hypoxia. Insufficient delivery of oxygen to an organ, especially the brain.

Hysteria. Older term used for conversion disorders; involves the appearance of symptoms of organic illness in the absence of any related organic pathology.

ICD-10. See **International Classification of Diseases.**

Id. In psychoanalytic terminology, the reservoir of instinctual drives; the most inaccessible and primitive stratum of the mind.

Identical twins. Monozygotic twins; developed from a single fertilized egg.

Identification. Ego-defense mechanism in which a person identifies himself or herself with some person or institution, usually of an illustrious nature.

Ideology. System of beliefs.

Illusion. Misinterpretation of sensory data; false perception.

Immaturity. Pattern of childhood maladaptive behaviors suggesting lack of adaptive skills.

Immune reaction. Complex defensive reaction initiated on detection of an antigen invading the body.

Immune system. The body's principal means of defending itself against the intrusion of foreign substances.

Implicit memory. Memory that occurs wthout awareness.

Implicit perception. Perception that occurs below the conscious level.

Implosion. Therapeutic technique in which clients are asked to imagine and relive aversive scenes associated with the anxiety; the assumption here is that, with repeated exposure in a "safe" setting, the aversive stimulus will lose its power to elicit anxiety.

Implosive therapy. Type of behavior therapy in which extinction of anxiety is achieved by eliciting, through the imagination, a massive implosion of anxiety.

Incentive. External inducement to behave in a certain way.

Incest. Culturally prohibited sexual relations between family members, such as a brother and sister or a parent and child.

Incidence. Occurrence rate of a given disorder in a given population.

Independent variable. Factor whose effects are being examined in an experiment; it is manipulated in some way while the other variables are held constant.

Index case. In a genetic study, an individual who evidences the trait in which the investigator is interested. Same as **proband.**

Infantile autism. See **Autism.**

Inhibition. Restraint of impulse or desire.

Innate. Inborn.

Inpatient. Hospitalized patient.

Insanity. Legal term for mental disorder, implying lack of responsibility for one's acts and inability to manage one's affairs.

Insanity defense. "Not guilty by reason of insanity" plea used as a legal defense in criminal trials.

Insight. Clinically, a person's understanding of his or her illness or of the motivations underlying a behavior pattern; in general psychology, the sudden grasp or understanding of meaningful relationships in a situation.

Insight therapy. Type of psychotherapy focusing on helping a client achieve greater self-understanding with respect to his or her motives, values, coping patterns, and so on.

Insomnia. Difficulty in sleeping.

Instinct. Inborn tendency to particular behavior patterns under certain conditions in the absence of learning.

Instrumental (operant) conditioning. Type of conditioning in which a subject is reinforced for making a predetermined response, such as pressing a lever.

Insulin coma therapy. Biological treatment that involves administration of increasing amounts of insulin until a patient goes into shock; the treatment is extremely dangerous and rarely used today.

Intellectualization. Ego-defense mechanism by which a person achieves some measure of insulation from emotional hurt by cutting off or distorting the emotional charge that normally accompanies hurtful situations.

Intelligence. The ability to learn, reason, and adapt.

Intelligence quotient (IQ). Measurement of "intelligence" expressed as a number or position on a scale.

Intelligence test. Test used in establishing a subject's level of intellectual capability.

Interdisciplinary (multidisciplinary) approach. Integration of various scientific disciplines in understanding, assessing, treating, and preventing mental disorders.

Intermittent reinforcement. Reinforcement given intermittently rather than after every response.

International Classification of Diseases (ICD-10). System of classification of disorders published by the World Health Organization.

Interoceptive fears. Fears of various internal bodily sensations.

Interpersonal accommodation. Reciprocal process of give and take meant to promote satisfactory interpersonal relationships.

Interpersonal perspective. Approach to understanding abnormal behavior that views much of psychopathology as rooted in maladaptive behavior we have learned while dealing with our interpersonal environments; it thus focuses on our relationships, past and present, with other people.

Intrapsychic conflict. Psychoanalytic concept referring to conflict between the id, ego, and superego.

Introjection. Internal process by which a child incorporates symbolically, through images and memories, some person viewed with strong emotion.

Intromission. Insertion of the penis into the vagina or anus.

Introspection. Observing (and often reporting on) one's inner experiences.

Introversion. Direction of interest toward one's inner world of experience and toward concepts rather than external events and objects.

In vivo. Taking place in a real-life situation as opposed to the therapeutic or laboratory setting.

Ionizing radiation. Form of radiation; major cause of gene mutations.

Isolation. Ego-defense mechanism by means of which contradictory attitudes or feelings that normally accompany particular attitudes are kept apart, thus preventing conflict or hurt.

Juvenile delinquency. Legal term used to refer to illegal acts committed by individuals under the age of 16, 17, or 18 (depending on state law).

Juvenile paresis. General paresis in children, usually of congenital origin.

Klinefelter's syndrome. Type of mental retardation associated with sex chromosome anomaly.

La belle indifférence. Unconcern about serious illness or disability that is characteristic of conversion disorder.

Labeling. Assigning a person to a particular diagnostic category, such as schizophrenia.

Lability. Instability, particularly with regard to affect.

Latency stage. In psychoanalytic theory, a stage of psychosexual development during which sexual motivations recede in importance and a child is preoccupied with developing skills and other activities.

Latent. Inactive or dormant.

Latent content. In psychoanalytic theory, repressed motives indirectly expressed in the manifest content of dreams.

Law of effect. Principle that responses that have rewarding consequences are strengthened and those that have aversive consequences are weakened or eliminated.

Learned helplessness theory of depression. A cognitive theory of depression that suggests that an organism that learns that it has no control over aversive events will show motivational, cognitive, and emotional deficits that are similar to those shown by depressed persons.

Learning. Modification of behavior as a consequence of experience.

Learning disabled (LD). Term used to describe children who exhibit deficits in academic skills.

Lesbian. Female homosexual.

Lesion. Anatomically localized area of tissue pathology in an organ.

Lethality scale. Criteria used to assess the likelihood of a person's committing suicide.

Libido. In general psychoanalytic terminology, the instinctual drives of the id, the basic energy of life. In a narrow sense, the drive for sexual gratification.

Life crisis. Stress situation that approaches or exceeds a person's adjustive capacity.

Life history method. Technique of psychological observation in which the development of particular forms of behavior is traced by means of records of a subject's past or present behavior.

Lifestyle. General pattern of assumptions, motives, cognitive styles, and coping techniques that characterize a person's behavior and give it consistency.

Lifetime prevalence. The proportion of persons in a population who have ever had a disorder.

Lobotomy. See **Prefrontal lobotomy.**

Locomotor ataxia. Muscular incoordination usually resulting from syphilitic damage to the spinal-cord pathways.

LSD (lysergic acid diethylamide). Potent chemically synthesized hallucinogen that is odorless, colorless, and tasteless and that can produce intoxication with an amount smaller than a grain of salt.

Lunacy. Old term roughly synonymous with insanity.

Lycanthropy. Delusion of being a wolf.

Lymphocyte. Generalized term for white blood cells involved in immune protection.

Macrocephaly. Type of mental retardation characterized by an increase in the size and weight of the brain as a result of abnormal growth of glial cells in the brain.

Macrophage. Literally, "big eater." A white blood cell that destroys antigens by engulfment.

Madness. Nontechnical synonym for severe mental disorder.

Mainstreaming. Placement of mentally retarded children in regular school classrooms for all or part of the day.

Major depressive disorder. Severe mood disorder in which only depressive episodes occur. Besides depression, the disorder involves other symptoms such as fatigue, sleep disturbance, loss of appetite and weight, psychomotor slowing, difficulty concentrating, self-denunciation, and guilt.

Major tranquilizers. Antipsychotic drugs, such as the phenothiazines.

Maladaptive (abnormal) behavior. Behavior that is detrimental to the well-being of an individual and/or group.

Maladjustment. More or less enduring failure of adjustment; lack of harmony with self or environment.

Male erectile disorder. Sexual dysfunction in which a male is unable to achieve or maintain an erection sufficient for successful sexual intercourse.

Male orgasmic disorder. Retarded ejaculation or the inability to ejaculate during intercourse.

Malingering. Faking illness or disability symptoms consciously in order to gain some specific objective.

Mania. Emotional state characterized by intense and unrealistic feelings of excitement and euphoria.

Manic-depressive psychoses. Older term denoting a group of psychotic disorders characterized by prolonged periods of excitement and overactivity (mania) or by periods of depression and underactivity (depression) or by alternation of the two. Now known as *bipolar disorders.*

Manifest content. In psychoanalytic theory, the apparent meaning of a dream; masks the latent content.

Marijuana. Mild hallucinogenic drug derived from the hemp plant, often smoked in cigarettes called reefers or joints.

Marital schism. Marriage characterized by severe chronic discord that threatens continuation of the marital relationship.

Marital skew. Marriage maintained at the expense of a distorted relationship.

Marital therapy. See **Couples counseling.**

Masked disorder. "Masking" of underlying depression or other emotional disturbance by delinquent behavior or other patterns seemingly unrelated to the basic disturbance.

Masochism. Sexual variant in which a person obtains sexual pleasure from experiencing pain or humiliation.

Mass hysteria. Group outbreak of hysterical reactions.

Masturbation. Self-stimulation of genitals for sexual gratification.

Maternal deprivation. Lack of adequate care and stimulation by the mother or mother surrogate.

Maturation. Process of development and body change resulting from heredity rather than learning.

Medical model. View of disordered behavior as a symptom of a disease process, rather than a pattern representing faulty learning or cognition.

Melancholic type. Subtype of major depression that involves loss of interest or pleasure in almost all activities, and other symptoms, including early morning awakenings, worse depression in the morning, psychomotor agitation or retardation, loss of appetite or weight, and excessive guilt.

Meninges. Membranes that envelop the brain and spinal cord.

Mental age (MA). Scale unit indicating level of intelligence in relation to chronological age.

Mental disorder. Entire range of abnormal behavior patterns.

Mental hygiene movement. Movement that, as a method of treatment for the mentally ill, focused almost exclusively on the physical well-being of hospitalized mental patients.

Mental illness. Serious mental disorder.

Mental retardation. Significantly subaverage general intellectual functioning accompanied by significant limitations in adaptive functioning that is obvious during the developmental period.

Mescaline. Hallucinogenic drug derived from the peyote cactus.

Mesmerism. Theories of "animal magnetism" (hypnosis) formulated by Anton Mesmer.

Methadone. Synthetic narcotic related to heroin; used in treatment of heroin addiction because it replaces the craving for heroin and weans a person from heroin addiction.

Microcephaly. Form of mental retardation characterized by an abnormally small cranium and retarded development of the brain.

Migraine. Intensely painful, recurrent headache that typically involves only one side of the head and may be accompanied by nausea and other disturbances.

Mild (disorder). Disorder of a low order of severity.

Milieu. Immediate environment, physical or social or both.

Milieu therapy. General approach to therapy for hospitalized patients that focuses on making the hospital environment itself a part of the treatment program.

Minnesota Multiphasic Personality Inventory (MMPI/MMPI-2/MMPI-A). Widely used and empirically validated personality scales.

Minor tranquilizers. Antianxiety drugs, such as the benzodiazepines.

Model. Analogy that helps a scientist order findings and see important relationships among them.

Modeling. Form of learning in which a person learns by watching someone else (a model) perform a desired response.

Moderate (disorder). Disorder of an intermediate order of severity.

Monozygotic twins. Identical twins, developed from one fertilized egg.

Mood-congruent. Consistent with a person's mood.

Mood disorders. Disorders that have as their most prominent features disturbances of mood that are intense and persistent enough to be clearly maladaptive.

Mood-incongruent. Inconsistent with a person's mood.

Moral management. Wide-ranging method of treatment for the mentally ill that focuses on a patient's social, individual, and occupational needs.

Moral therapy. Therapy based on provision of kindness, understanding, and favorable environment; prevalent during early part of the nineteenth century.

Morbid. Unhealthy, pathological.

Morphine. Addictive drug derived from opium.

Motivation. Often used as a synonym for drive or activation; implies that an organism's actions are partly determined in direction and strength by its own inner nature.

Motive. Internal condition that directs action toward some goal; term usually used to include both the drive and the goal to which it is directed.

Multi-infarct dementia. See **Vascular dementia.**

Multiple personality disorder. See **Dissociative identity disorder.**

Mutant gene. Gene that has undergone some change in structure.

Mutation. Change in the composition of a gene, usually causing harmful or abnormal characteristics to appear in the offspring.

Mutism. Refusal or inability to speak.

Nancy School, The. Group of physicians in nineteenth-century Europe who accepted the view that hysteria was a sort of self-hypnosis.

Narcissism. Self-love.

Narcissistic personality disorder. Personality disorder characterized by grandiosity, an exaggerated sense of self-importance, preoccupation with being admired, and exploitation of others.

Narcolepsy. Disorder characterized by transient, compulsive states of sleepiness.

Narcotic drugs. Drugs, such as morphine, that lead to physiological dependence and increased tolerance.

Natural killer cell. White blood cell that destroys antigens by chemical dissolution.

Necessary cause. A condition that must exist for a disorder to occur.

Need. Biological or psychological condition whose gratification is necessary for the maintenance of homeostasis or for self-actualization.

Negative automatic thoughts. Thoughts that are just below the surface of awareness and that involve unpleasant pessimistic predictions.

Negative cognitive triad. Negative thoughts about the self, the world, and the future.

Negative-symptom schizophrenia. Schizophrenia characterized by an absence or deficit of normal or desirable behaviors, such as communicative speech and emotional reactivity.

Negativism. Form of aggressive withdrawal that involves refusing to cooperate or obey commands, or doing the exact opposite of what has been requested.

Neologism. New word; feature of language disturbance in schizophrenia.

Neonate. Newborn infant.

Neoplasm. Tumor.

Nervous breakdown. General term used to refer broadly to lowered integration and inability to deal adequately with one's life situation.

Neurological examination. Examination to determine the presence and extent of organic damage to the nervous system.

Neurology. Field concerned with the study of the brain and nervous system and disorders thereof.

Neuron. Individual nerve cell.

Neurophysiology. Branch of biology concerned with the functioning of nervous tissue and the nervous system.

Neuropsychological assessment. Use of psychological tests that measure a subject's cognitive, perceptual, and motor performance to determine the extent and locus of brain damage.

Neuropsychological disorders. Disorders that occur when there has been significant organic impairment or damage to a normal adolescent or adult brain.

Neurosis. Term historically used to characterize maladaptive behavior resulting from intrapsychic conflict and marked by prominent use of defense mechanisms.

Neurosyphilis. Syphilis affecting the central nervous system.

Neurotic behavior. Anxiety-driven, exaggerated use of avoidance behaviors and defense mechanisms.

Neuroticism. Personality pattern including anxiety, angry hostility, depression, self-consciousness, impulsiveness, and vulnerability.

Neurotransmitters. Chemical substances that transmit nerve impulses from one neuron to another.

Nicotine. Addictive akaloid that is the chief active ingredient in tobacco.

Night hospital. Mental hospital in which an individual may receive treatment during all or part of the night while carrying on his or her usual occupation in the daytime.

Nihilistic delusion. Fixed belief that everything is unreal.

Nondirective therapy. Approach to psychotherapy in which a therapist refrains from advice or direction of the therapy. See also **Client-centered psychotherapy.**

Norepinephrine. Catecholamine neurotransmitter substance.

Norm. Standard based on the measurement of a large group of people; used for comparing the scores of an individual with those of others in a defined group.

Normal. Conforming to the usual or norm; healthy.

Normal distribution. Tendency for most members of a population to cluster around a central point or average with respect to a given trait, with the rest spreading out to the two extremes.

NREM sleep. Stages of sleep not characterized by the rapid eye movements that accompany dreaming.

Nuclear magnetic resonance imaging (MRI). Internal scanning technique involving measurement of variations in magnetic fields that allows visualization of the anatomical features of internal organs, including the brain.

Objective tests. Structured tests, such as a questionnaires, self-inventories, or rating scales, used in psychological assessment.

Object-relations. In psychoanalytic theory, a viewpoint that emphasizes interpersonal relationships by focusing on internalized "objects" that can have varying conflicting properties.

Observational method. Systematic technique by which observers are trained to watch and record behavior without bias.

Obsessions. Recurrent and persistent thoughts, impulses, or images that a person experiences as intrusive and inappropriate but has difficulty suppressing.

Obsessive-compulsive disorder. Anxiety disorder characterized by the persistent intrusion of unwanted and intrusive thoughts or distressing images; these are usually accompanied by compulsive behaviors designed to neutralize the obsessive thoughts or images.

Obsessive-compulsive personality disorder. Personality disorder characterized by excessive concern with maintaining order, control, and adherence to rules.

Occipital lobe. Portion of cerebrum concerned chiefly with visual function.

Oedipus complex. Desire for sexual relations with parent of opposite sex, specifically that of a boy for his mother.

Olfactory hallucinations. Hallucinations involving the sense of smell.

Operant conditioning. Form of learning in which a particular response is reinforced and becomes more likely to occur.

Operational definition. Defining a concept on the basis of a set of operations that can be observed and measured.

Opium. Narcotic drug that leads to physiological dependence and the development of tolerance; derivatives are morphine, heroin, and codeine.

Oral stage. First stage of psychosexual development in Freudian theory, in which mouth or oral activities are the primary source of pleasure.

Organic mental disorders. Mental disorders associated with organic brain pathology. Called *brain disorders* in DSM-IV.

Organic viewpoint. Concept that all mental disorders have an organic basis. See also **Biological viewpoint**.

Orgasm. Phase of the human sexual response during which there is a release of sexual tension and a peaking of sexual pleasure.

Outcome research. Studies of effectiveness of treatment.

Outpatient. Ambulatory client who visits a hospital or clinic for examination and treatment, as distinct from a hospitalized client.

Ovaries. Female gonads.

Overanxious disorder. Disorder of childhood characterized by excessive worry and persistent fears unrelated to any specific event; often includes somatic and sleeping problems.

Overcompensation. Type of ego-defense mechanism in which an undesirable trait is covered up by exaggerating a desirable trait.

Overloading. Subjecting an organism to excessive stress, e.g., forcing the organism to handle or "process" an excessive amount of information.

Overprotection. Shielding a child to the extent that he or she becomes too dependent on the parent.

Overt behavior. Activities that can be observed by an outsider.

Ovum. Female gamete or germ cell.

Pain disorder. A somatoform condition characterized by the report of pain of sufficient duration and severity to cause significant life disruption in the absence of medical pathology that would explain it.

Panic. A basic emotion involving the activation of the "fight or flight" response.

Panic disorder. Type of anxiety disorder involving recurring and unexpected panic attacks.

Paradigm. Model or pattern; in research, a basic design specifying concepts considered legitimate and procedures to be used in the collection and interpretation of data.

Paranoia. Symptoms of delusions and impaired contact with reality but without the severe personality disorganization characteristic of schizophrenia.

Paranoid personality disorder. Personality disorder characterized by pervasive suspiciousness and distrust of others.

Paraphilias. Sexual behavior patterns in which unusual objects, rituals, or situations are required for full sexual satisfaction.

Paraprofessional. Person who has been trained in mental health services, but not at the professional level.

Parasympathetic nervous system. Division of the autonomic nervous system that controls most of the basic metabolic functions essential for life.

Paresis. See **General paresis**.

Paresthesia. Exceptional sensations, such as tingling.

Parkinson's disease. Progressive disease characterized by a masklike, expressionless face and various neurological symptoms, such as tremors.

Passive-aggressive personality disorder. Provisional personality disorder in DSM-IV characterized by a pattern of passive resistance to demands in social or occupational situations, which may take such forms as procrastinating, "forgetting," or sulking.

Pathogenic. Pertaining to conditions that lead to pathology.

Pathological gambling. Addictive disorder in which gambling disrupts a person's life.

Pathology. Abnormal physical or mental condition.

PCP. Phencyclidine; developed as a tranquilizer but not marketed because of its unpredictability. Known on the street as "angel dust," this drug produces stuporous conditions and, at times, prolonged comas or psychoses.

Pedophilia. Sexual variant in which an adult's preferred or exclusive sexual partner is a prepubertal child.

Perception. Interpretation of sensory input.

Perceptual filtering. Processes involved in selective attention to aspects of the great mass of incoming stimuli that continually impinge on an organism.

Performance test. Test in which perceptual-motor rather than verbal content is emphasized.

Peripheral nervous system. Nerve fibers passing between the central nervous system and the sense organs, muscles, and glands.

Perseveration. Persistent continuation of a line of thought or activity once it is under way. Clinically inappropriate repetition.

Personality. Unique pattern of traits that characterizes an individual.

Personality disorders. Conditions involving long-standing patterns of inflexible and maladaptive behavior serious enough to interfere with social and/or occupational functioning.

Personality profile. Graphic summary from several tests or subtests of the same test battery or scale that shows the personality configuration of an individual or group of individuals.

Person-centered therapy. See **Client-centered therapy**.

Pervasive developmental disorder. Severe disorder of childhood marked by deficits in language, perceptual, and motor development; defective reality testing; and inability to function in social situations.

Pessimistic attributional style. Cognitive style involving a tendency to make internal, stable, and global attributions for negative life events.

PET scan. See **Positron emission tomography.**

Phagocyte. Circulating white blood cell that binds to antigens and partially destroys them by engulfment.

Phallic stage. In psychoanalytic theory, the stage of psychosexual development during which genital exploration and manipulation occur.

Pharmacology. The science of drugs.

Pharmacotherapy. Treatment by means of drugs.

Phenomenological. Referring to the immediate perceiving and experiencing of an individual.

Phenotype. The observed structural and functional characteristics of an individual that result from an interaction between the genotype and the environment.

Phenylketonuria (PKU). Type of mental retardation resulting from a metabolic deficiency.

Phobia. Persistent and disproportionate fear of some specific object or situation that presents little or no actual danger to a person.

Physiological dependence. Type of drug dependence involving withdrawal symptoms when drug is discontinued.

Pick's disease. Form of presenile dementia.

Pineal gland. Small gland at the base of the brain that helps regulate the body's biological clock and may also pace sexual development.

Pituitary gland. Endocrine gland associated with many regulatory functions.

Placebo effect. Positive effect experienced after an inactive treatment is administered in such a way that a person thinks he or she is receiving an active treatment.

Play therapy. Use of play activities in psychotherapy with children.

Pleasure principle. In psychoanalysis, the demand that an instinctual need be immediately gratified, regardless of reality.

Polygenic. Caused by the action of many genes together in an additive or interactive fashion.

Poor premorbid schizophrenia. See **Process schizophrenia.**

Positive reinforcer. Reinforcer that increases the probability of recurrence of a given response.

Positive-symptom schizophrenia. Schizophrenic disorders characterized by elements added to normal behavior, such as delusions and hallucinations.

Positron emission tomography (PET scan). Scanning technique that measures the level of metabolic activity in particular regions of the body.

Posthypnotic amnesia. Subject's lack of memory for the period during which he or she was hypnotized.

Posthypnotic suggestion. Suggestion given during hypnosis to be carried out by a subject after he or she is brought out of hypnosis.

Postpartum depression. Depression occurring after childbirth.

Posttraumatic stress disorder (PTSD). Disorder that occurs following an extreme traumatic stress or in which a person shows symptoms of reexperiencing the event of avoiding reminders of the trauma, and of persistent symptoms of increased arousal.

Predisposition. Increased likelihood that a person will develop certain symptoms under given stress conditions.

Prefrontal lobotomy. Surgical procedure used before the advent of antipsychotic drugs in which frontal lobes of the brain were severed from the deeper centers underlying them, resulting in permanent brain damage.

Prejudice. Emotionally toned conception favorable or unfavorable to some person, group, or idea—typically in the absence of sound evidence.

Premature ejaculation. Persistent and recurrent onset of orgasm and ejaculation with minimal sexual stimulation.

Prematurity. Birth of an infant before the end of a normal period of pregnancy.

Premorbid. Existing before the onset of mental disorder.

Prenatal. Before birth.

Presenile dementia. Senile brain deterioration before old age.

Prevalence. Term that refers to the rate of active cases of something under study (in this case, a disorder) that can be identified at a given period in time.

Primary prevention. Preventive efforts aimed at reducing the possibility of disease or disorder and fostering positive health.

Primary process thinking. Gratification of an id demand by means of imagery or fantasy; a psychoanalytic concept.

Primary reaction tendencies. Constitutional tendencies apparent in infancy, such as sensitivity and activity level.

Proband. In a genetic study, the original individual who evidences the trait in which the investigator is interested. Same as **index case.**

Problem checklist. Inventory used in behavioral assessment to determine an individual's fears, moods, and other problems.

Problem drinker. Behavioral term referring to one who has serious problems associated with drinking.

Process schizophrenia. Schizophrenic pattern—marked by seclusiveness, gradual lack of interest in the surrounding world, diminished emotional responsivity, and mildly inappropriate responses—that develops gradually and tends to be long-lasting; alternatively known as *poor premorbid schizophrenia* and *chronic schizophrenia.*

Prognosis. Prediction as to the probable course and outcome of a disorder.

Projection. Ego-defense mechanism in which a person attributes unacceptable desires and impulses to others.

Projective tests. Techniques that use neutral or ambiguous stimuli that a subject is encouraged to interpret and from which the subject's personality characteristics can be analyzed.

Prospective research. Research that focuses, before the fact, on people who have a higher-than-average likelihood of becoming psychologically disordered, following them over time.

Protective factors. Influences that modify a person's response to an environmental stressor, making it less likely that the person will experience the adverse effects of the stressor.

Prototypal approach. Approach to classifying abnormal behavior that assumes the existence of prototypes of behavior disorders that, rather than being mutually exclusive, may blend into others with which they share many characteristics.

Psilocybin. Hallucinogenic drug derived from a mushroom.

Psychedelic drugs. Drugs such as LSD that often produce hallucinations.

Psychiatric nursing. Field of nursing primarily concerned with mental disorders.

Psychiatric social worker. Professional having graduate training in social work with psychiatric specialization, typically involving a master's degree.

Psychiatrist. Medical doctor who specializes in the diagnosis and treatment of mental disorders.

Psychiatry. Field of medicine concerned with understanding, assessing, treating, and preventing mental disorders.

Psychic trauma. Any aversive experience that inflicts serious psychological damage on a person.

Psychoactive drugs. Drugs that affect mental functioning.

Psychoactive substance abuse. Pathological use of a substance resulting in potentially hazardous behavior or in continued use despite a persistent social, psychological, occupational, or health problem.

Psychoactive substance dependence. Use of a psychoactive substance to the point that one has a physiological need for it.

Psychoanalysis. Theoretical model and therapeutic approach developed by Freud.

Psychoanalytic perspective. Theory of psychopathology, initially developed by Freud, that emphasizes the inner dynamics of unconscious motives.

Psychodrama. Psychotherapeutic technique in which the acting of various roles is a cardinal part.

Psychodynamic perspectives. Theories of psychopathology based on Freud's theories but modified and revised.

Psychodynamic therapy. Treatment focusing on individual personality dynamics from a psychodynamic perspective.

Psychogenic. Of psychological origin: originating in the psychological functioning of an individual.

Psychogenic amnesia. Amnesia of psychological origin, common in initial reactions to intolerable traumatic experiences.

Psychohistory. A field of study analyzing history according to psychoanalytic principles.

Psychological autopsy. Analytical procedure used to determine whether or not death was self-inflicted.

Psychological need. Need emerging out of environmental interactions, e.g., the need for social approval.

Psychological screening. Use of psychological procedures or tests to detect psychological problems among applicants in preemployment evaluations.

Psychological test. Standardized procedure designed to measure a subject's performance on a specified task.

Psychomotor. Involving both psychological and physical activity.

Psychomotor retardation. Slowing down of psychological and motor functions.

Psychoneuroimmunology. Field whose focus is understanding the psychological influences on the nervous system's control of immune responsiveness.

Psychopathology. Abnormal behavior.

Psychopathy. A condition involving the features of antisocial personality disorder plus the traits of lack of empathy, inflated self-appraisal, and glib and superficial charm.

Psychopharmacological drugs. Drugs used in treatment of mental disorders.

Psychophysiologic (psychosomatic) disorders. Physical disorders in which psychological factors are believed to play a major causative role.

Psychosexual development. Freudian view of development as involving a succession of stages, each characterized by a dominant mode of achieving libidinal pleasure.

Psychosexual stages of development. According to Freudian theory, there are five stages of psychosexual development, each characterized by a dominant mode of achieving sexual pleasure: the oral stage, the anal stage, the phallic stage, the latency stage, and the genital stage.

Psychosis. Serious mental disorder involving a loss of contact with reality, as when hallucinations or delusions are present.

Psychosocial deprivation. Lack of needed stimulation and interaction during early life.

Psychosocial viewpoints. Approaches to understanding behavior disorders that emphasize the importance of early experience and an awareness of social influences and psychological processes within an individual.

Psychosurgery. Brain surgery used in the treatment of functional mental disorders.

Psychotherapy. Treatment of mental disorders by psychological methods.

Psychotropic drugs. Drugs whose main effects are mental or behavioral in nature.

Q-sort. Personality inventory in which a subject, or a clinician, sorts a number of statements into piles according to their applicability to the subject.

Racism. Prejudice and discrimination directed toward individuals or groups because of their racial background.

Random sample. Sample drawn in such a way that each member of a population has an equal chance of being selected; hopefully representative of the population from which it is drawn.

Rape. Sexual activity that occurs under actual or threatened forcible coercion of one person by another.

Rapid cycling. A pattern of bipolar disorder involving at least four manic or depressive episodes per year.

Rapport. Interpersonal relationship characterized by a spirit of cooperation, confidence, and harmony.

Rating scales. Devices for evaluating oneself or someone else with regard to specific traits.

Rational-emotive therapy. Form of psychotherapy focusing on cognitive and emotional restructuring to foster adaptive behavior.

Rationalization. Ego-defense mechanism in which a person devises "good" reasons to justify his or her actions.

Reaction formation. Ego-defense mechanism in which a person's conscious attitudes and overt behavior are opposite to repressed unconscious wishes.

Reactive schizophrenia. Schizophrenia pattern—marked by confusion and intense emotional turmoil—that normally develops suddenly and has identifiable precipitating stressors; alternatively known as *good premorbid schizophrenia* and *acute schizophrenia*.

Reality principle. Awareness of the demands of the environment and adjustment of behavior to meet these demands.

Reality testing. Behavior aimed at testing or exploring the nature of a person's social and physical environment; often used more specifically to refer to the testing of the limits of permissiveness of the social environment.

Recessive gene. Gene that is effective only when paired with an identical gene.

Recidivism. Shift back to one's original behavior (often delinquent or criminal) after a period of treatment or rehabilitation.

Recompensation. Increase in integration or inner organization. Opposite of *decompensation*.

Recurrence. A new occurrence of a disorder after a significant period of time.

Recurrent. Used to describe a disorder pattern that tends to come and go.

Referral. Sending or recommending an individual and/or family for psychological assessment and/or treatment.

Regression. Ego-defense mechanism in which a person retreats to the use of less mature responses in attempting to cope with stress and maintain ego integrity.

Rehabilitation. Use of reeducation rather than punishment to overcome behavioral deficits.

Reinforcement. In classical conditioning, the process of following the conditioned stimulus with the unconditioned stimulus; in operant conditioning, the rewarding of desired responses.

Relapse. The return of the symptoms of a disorder after a fairly short period of time.

Reliability. Degree to which a test or measuring device produces the same result each time it is used to measure the same thing.

Remission. Marked improvement or recovery appearing in the course of a mental illness; may or may not be permanent.

REM sleep. Stage of sleep involving rapid eye movements (REM), associated with dreaming.

Representative sample. Small group selected in such a way as to be representative of the larger group from which it is drawn.

Repression. Ego-defense mechanism by means of which dangerous desires and intolerable memories are kept out of consciousness.

Resilience. The ability to overcome challenging or threatening circumstances.

Resistance. In psychodynamic treatment, the client's avoidance of certain topics as a means of preventing threatening material from entering awareness.

Resistance to extinction. Tendency of a conditioned response to persist despite lack of reinforcement.

Resolution. Final phase of the human sexual response, during which a person has a sense of relaxation and well-being.

Response shaping. Positive reinforcement technique used in therapy to establish a response not initially in a person's behavioral repertoire.

Reticular activating system (RAS). Fibers going from the reticular formation to higher brain centers and presumably functioning as a general arousal system.

Reticular formation. Neural nuclei and fibers in the brain stem that apparently play an important role in arousing and alerting an organism and in controlling attention.

Retrograde amnesia. Loss of memory for events during a circumscribed period prior to brain injury or damage.

Retrospective research. Research that looks backward from the present.

Retrospective study. Research approach that attempts to retrace earlier events in the life of a subject.

Rigidity. Tendency to follow established coping patterns, with failure to see alternatives or extreme difficulty in changing one's established patterns.

Ritalin. Central nervous system stimulant often used to treat attention-deficit hyperactivity disorder in children.

Role playing. Form of assessment or psychotherapy in which a person acts out a social role other than his or her own or tries out a new role.

Rorschach test. Series of inkblots to which a subject responds with associations that come to mind. Analysis of these responses enables a clinician to infer personality characteristics.

Sadism. Sexual variant in which sexual gratification is obtained by inflicting pain or humiliation on a sexual partner.

Sample. Group on which measurements are taken; should normally be representative of the population about which an inference is to be made.

Sampling. The process of selecting a representative subgroup from a defined population of interest.

Scapegoating. Displacement of aggression onto some object, person, or group other than the source of frustration.

Schedule of reinforcement. Program of rewards for requisite behavior.

Schema. An organized representation of prior knowledge about a concept or about some stimulus that helps guide a person's processing of current information.

Schizoaffective disorder. Major mood disorder in which a person also has at least two major symptoms of schizophrenia, such as hallucinations and delusions.

Schizoid personality disorder. Personality disorder characterized by an inability to form social relationships or express feelings, a lack of social skills, and indifference.

Schizophrenia. Psychosis characterized by the breakdown of integrated personality functioning, withdrawal from reality, emotional blunting and distortion, and disturbances in thought and behavior.

Schizophrenia, catatonic type. Type of schizophrenia in which the central feature is pronounced motor symptoms, either of an excited or stuporous type, which sometimes make it difficult to differentiate this condition from a psychotic mood disorder.

Schizophrenia, disorganized type. Type of schizophrenia that usually begins at an earlier age and represents a more severe disintegration of the personality than in the other types of schizophrenia.

Schizophrenia, paranoid type. Type of schizophrenia in which a person is increasingly suspicious, has severe difficulties in interpersonal relationships, and experiences absurd, illogical, and often changing delusions.

Schizophrenia, residual type. Diagnostic category used for people regarded as having recovered from a schizophrenic episode but still manifesting some signs of their past disorder.

Schizophrenia, undifferentiated type. Type of schizophrenia in which a person meets the usual criteria for being schizophrenic—including (in varying combinations) delusions, hallucinations, thought disorder, and bizarre behavior—but does not clearly fit into one of the other types because of a mixed symptom picture.

Schizophreniform disorder. Category of schizophrenic disorder, usually in an undifferentiated form, of less than six months duration.

Schizophrenogenic. Schizophrenia-causing.

Schizotypal personality disorder. Personality disorder in which social withdrawal, cognitive distortions, and eccentricity of thought and perception are distinguishing traits.

Seasonal affective disorder. Mood disorder involving at least two episodes of depression in the past two years occuring at the same time of year (most commonly fall or winter), with remission also occurring at the same time of year (most commonly spring).

Secondary gain. Indirect benefit from psychopathological symptoms.

Secondary prevention. Prevention techniques that typically involve emergency or crisis intervention, with efforts focused on reducing the impact, duration, or spread of a problem.

Secondary process thinking. Reality-oriented rational processes of the ego.

Secondary reinforcer. Reinforcement provided by a stimulus that has gained reward value by being associated with a primary reinforcing stimulus.

Sedative. Drug used to reduce tension and induce relaxation and sleep.

Selective vigilance. Tuning of attentional and perceptual processes toward stimuli relevant or central to goal-directed behavior, with decreased sensitivity to stimuli irrelevant or peripheral to this purpose.

Self (ego). Integrating core of a personality that mediates between needs and reality.

Self-acceptance. Being satisfied with one's attributes and qualities while remaining aware of one's limitations.

Self-actualizing. Achieving one's full potentialities as a human being.

Self-concept. A person's sense of his or her own identity, worth, capabilities, and limitations.

Self-esteem. Feeling of personal worth.

Self-evaluation. Way in which an individual views the self, in terms of worth, adequacy, etc.

Self-ideal (ego-ideal). Person or "self" a person thinks he or she could and should be.

Self-identity. Individual's delineation and awareness of his or her continuing identity as a person.

Self-instructional training. Cognitive-behavioral method aimed at teaching a person to alter his or her covert behavior.

Self-monitoring. Observing and recording one's own behavior, thoughts, and feelings.

Self-reinforcement. Reward of self for desired or appropriate behavior.

Self-report inventory. Procedure in which a subject is asked to respond to statements in terms of their applicability to him or her.

Self-schema. Our concept of what we are, what we might become, and what is important to us.

Self-statements. A person's implicit verbalizations of what he or she is experiencing.

Self-system. According to Sullivan's interpersonal theory, a system that protects a person from anxiety by controlling awareness—the person simply does not attend to elements of experience that cause anxiety and may even block out of consciousness especially severe anxiety-arousing experiences.

Senile. Pertaining to old age.

Senile dementia. Deteriorative brain changes due to aging.

Sensate focus learning. Training to derive pleasure from touching one's partner and being touched by him or her; used in sexual therapy to enhance sexual feelings and help overcome sexual dysfunction.

Sensory deprivation. Restriction of sensory stimulation below the level required for normal functioning of the central nervous system.

Sentence-completion test. Projective technique utilizing incomplete sentences that a subject is to complete, analysis of which enables a clinician to infer personality dynamics.

Separation anxiety disorder. Childhood disorder characterized by unrealistic fears, oversensitivity, self-consciousness, nightmares, and chronic anxiety.

Separation-individuation. According to Mahler, a developmental phase in which a child gains an internal representation of self as distinct from representations of other objects.

Sequelae. Symptoms remaining as the aftermath of a disorder.

Severe (disorder). Disorder of a high degree of seriousness.

Severe major depressive episode with psychotic features. Major depression involving loss of contact with reality, often in the form of delusions or hallucinations.

Sex chromosomes. Pair of chromosomes inherited by an individual that determine sex and certain other characteristics.

Sexual abuse. Sexual contact that involves pressured or forced sexual contact.

Sexual aversion disorder. Sexual dysfunction in which a person shows extreme aversion to, and avoidance of, all genital sexual contact with a partner.

Sexual dysfunction. Impairment either in the desire for sexual gratification or in the ability to achieve it.

Shaping. Form of instrumental conditioning; at first, all responses resembling the desired one are reinforced, then only the closest approximations, until finally the desired response is attained.

Shared psychotic disorder. Psychosis in which two or more people develop persistent, interlocking delusional ideas. Also known as *folie à deux*.

Sheltered workshops. Workshops where mentally retarded or otherwise handicapped persons can engage in constructive work in the community.

Short-term crisis therapy. Brief therapy that focuses on the immediate problem—personal or family problems of an emotional nature—with which an individual or family is having difficulty.

Siblings. Offspring of the same parents.

Sick role. Protected role provided by society via the medical model for a person suffering from severe physical or mental disorder.

Sign. Observable manifestation of a physical or mental disorder.

Significant others. In interpersonal theory, parents or others on whom an infant is dependent for meeting all physical and psychological needs.

Simple phobia. See **Specific phobia.**

Simple tension headaches. Commonplace headaches in which stress leads to contraction of the muscles surrounding the skull; these contractions, in turn, result in vascular constrictions that cause headache pain.

Situational test. Test that measures performance in a simulated life situation.

Sleepwalking disorder. Disorder of childhood that involves repeated episodes in which a child leaves his or her bed and walks around without being conscious of the experience or remembering it later. Also known as *somnambulism*.

Social exchange view. Model of interpersonal relationships based on the premise that such relationships are formed for mutual need gratification.

Social introversion. Trait characterized by shy, withdrawn, and inhibited behavior.

Socialization. Process by which a child acquires the values and impulse controls deemed appropriate by his or her culture.

Social-learning programs. Behavioral programs using learning techniques, especially token economies, to help patients assume more responsibility for their own behavior.

Social norms. Group standards concerning behaviors viewed as acceptable or unacceptable.

Social pathology. Abnormal patterns of social organization, attitudes, or behavior; undesirable social conditions that tend to produce individual pathology.

Social phobia. Persistent and disproportionate fear of one or more situations in which one is exposed to focused scrutiny by others and the corollary fear that one may do something embarrassing or humiliating.

Social role. Behavior expected of a person occupying a given position in a group.

"Social" self. Facade a person displays to others as contrasted with the private self.

Social work. Applied offshoot of sociology concerned with the analysis of social environments and providing services that assist the adjustment of a client in both family and community settings.

Social worker. Person in a mental health field with a master's degree in social work (MSW) plus supervised training in clinical or social service agencies.

Sociocultural viewpoint. Pertaining to broad social conditions that influence the development and/or behavior of individuals and groups.

Socioeconomic status. Position on social and economic scale in community; determined largely by income and occupational level.

Sociogenic. Having its roots in sociocultural conditions.

Sociopathic personality. See **Psychopathy**.

Sodium pentothal. Barbiturate drug sometimes used in psychotherapy to produce a state of relaxation and suggestibility.

Somatic. Pertaining to the body.

Somatic weakness. Special vulnerability of given organ systems to stress.

Somatization disorder. Somatoform disorder beginning before age 30 and continuing for many years, characterized by multiple complaints of physical ailments that are inadequately explained by findings of physical illness or injury.

Somatoform disorders. Conditions involving physical complaints or disabilities occurring in the absence of any physical pathology that could account for them.

Somnambulism. See **Sleepwalking disorder**.

Spasm. Intense, involuntary, usually painful contraction of a muscle or group of muscles.

Spasticity. Marked hypertonicity or continual overcontraction of muscles, causing stiffness, awkwardness, and motor incoordination.

Specific learning disorders. Developmental disorders involving deficits in specific academic skills.

Specific phobia. A persistent and disproportionate fear of something, such as an animal (snakes, insects) or some aspect of the environment (high places, water).

Sperm. Male gamete or germ cell.

Split-brain research. Research associated with split-brain surgery, which cuts off the transmission of information from one cerebral hemisphere to the other, through severing the corpus callosum.

Spontaneous recovery. The return of a learned response at some time after extinction has occurred.

Stage of exhaustion. Third and final stage in the general adaptation syndrome, in which an organism is no longer able to resist continuing stress; may result in death.

Stage of resistance. Second stage of the general adaptation syndrome.

Standardization. Procedure for establishing the expected performance range on a test.

Stanford-Binet. Standardized intelligence test for children.

Startle reaction. Sudden involuntary motor reaction to intense unexpected stimuli; may result from mild stimuli if a person is hypersensitive.

Statutory rape. Sexual intercourse with a minor.

Steady states (homeostasis). Tendency of an organism to maintain conditions making possible a constant level of physiological functioning.

Stereotype. Generalized notion of how people of a given race, religion, or other group will appear, think, feel, or act.

Stereotypy. Persistent and inappropriate repetition of phrases, gestures, or acts.

Stimulants. Drugs that tend to increase feelings of alertness, reduce feelings of fatigue, and enable a person to stay awake over sustained periods of time.

Stimulus generalization. Spread of a conditioned response to some stimulus similar to, but not identical with, the conditioned stimulus.

Stress. Internal responses caused by the application of a stressor.

Stress-inoculation therapy. Type of self-instructional training focused on altering self-statements that a person habitually makes in order to restructure his or her characteristic approach to stress-producing situations.

Stress-inoculation training. Cognitive-behavioral technique that prepares people to tolerate an anticipated threat by the use of positive self-statements.

Stressor. Any adjustive demand that requires coping behavior on the part of an individual or group.

Stress tolerance. Nature, degree, and duration of stress that a person can tolerate without undergoing serious personality decompensation.

Stroke. See **Cerebrovascular accident**.

Structural family therapy. Treatment of an entire family by analysis of interaction among family members.

Stupor. Condition of lethargy and unresponsiveness, with partial or complete unconsciousness.

St. Vitus's dance. Hysterical chorea of common occurrence during the Middle Ages.

Sublimation. Ego-defense mechanism by means of which frustrated sexual energy is partially channeled into substitutive activities.

Substance abuse. Maladaptive pattern of substance use manifested by recurrent and significant adverse consequences related to the use of the substance.

Substance dependence. Severe form of substance use disorder involving physiological dependence on the substance, tolerance, withdrawal, and compulsive drug taking.

Substance-related disorders. Patterns of maladaptive behavior centered on the regular use of a substance, such as drugs or alcohol.

Substitution. Acceptance of substitute goals or satisfactions in place of those originally sought after or desired.

Successive approximation. See **Shaping.**

Sufficient cause. A condition that guarantees the occurence of a disorder.

Suicide. Taking one's own life.

Suicidology. Study of the causes and prevention of suicide.

Superego. Conscience; ethical or moral dimensions (attitudes) of personality.

Suppression. Conscious forcing of desires or thoughts out of consciousness; conscious inhibition of desires or impulses.

Surrogate. Substitute for another person, as parent or mate.

Symbol. Image, word, object, or activity that is used to represent something else.

Symbolism. Representation of one idea or object by another.

Sympathetic division. Division of the autonomic nervous system that is active in emergency conditions of extreme cold, violent effort, and emotions.

Symptom. Manifestation of a physical or mental disorder as experienced or reported by the patient.

Syndrome. Group or pattern of symptoms that occur together in a disorder and represent the typical picture of the disorder.

System. Assemblage of interdependent parts, living or nonliving.

Systematic desensitization. Behavior therapy technique for eliminating maladaptive anxiety responses by teaching a person to relax or behave in some other way that is inconsistent with anxiety while in the presence of the anxiety-producing stimulus.

Tachycardia. Rapid heartbeat.

Tactual hallucinations. Hallucinations involving the sense of touch.

Tarantism. Dancing mania that occurred in Italy and later spread to Germany and the rest of Europe, where it was known as St. Vitus's dance.

Tarasoff decision. Ruling by a California court (1974) that a therapist has a duty to warn a prospective victim threatened by a client in therapy.

Tardive dyskinesia. Neurological disorder resulting from excessive use of phenothiazines. The drug side effects can occur months to years after treatment has been initiated or has stopped. The symptoms involve involuntary movements of the tongue, lips, jaw, and extremities.

Task-oriented response. Behavior directed primarily at dealing with the requirements of a stressor rather than at defending the self.

Tay-Sachs disease. Genetic disorder of lipoid metabolism usually resulting in death by age three.

T-cell. Generic type of lymphocyte crucial in immune functioning and having several subtypes that support and regulate the entire immune reaction.

Telepathy. Communication from one person to another without use of any known sense organs.

Temperament. Pattern of emotional and arousal responses that are considered to be primarily hereditary or constitutional.

Temporal lobe. Portion of cerebrum located in front of the occipital lobe and separated from frontal and parietal lobes by the fissure of Sylvius.

Tension. Condition arising from the mobilization of psychobiological resources to meet a threat; physically, involves an increase in muscle tone and other emergency changes; psychologically, is characterized by feelings of strain, uneasiness, and anxiety.

Tertiary prevention. Preventive techniques focusing on reducing long-term consequences of disorders or serious problems.

Testes. Male reproductive glands or gonads.

Testosterone. Male sex hormone.

Test reliability. Consistency with which a test measures a given trait on repeated administrations of the test to given subjects.

Test validity. Degree to which a test actually measures what it was designed to measure.

Thematic Apperception Test (TAT). Psychological test composed of a series of pictures about which a subject makes up a story. Analysis of the story gives a clinician clues about the person's conflicts, traits, personality dynamics, etc.

Therapeutic. Pertaining to treatment or healing.

Therapeutic community. Hospital environment used for therapeutic purposes.

Therapy. Treatment; application of various treatment techniques.

Thyroid. Endocrine gland located in the neck that influences body metabolism, rate of physical growth, and development of intelligence.

Thyroxin. Hormone secreted by the thyroid glands.

Tic. Persistent, intermittent muscle twitch or spasm, often of the facial muscles.

Token economy. Reinforcement technique often used in hospital or institutional settings in which patients are rewarded for socially constructive behavior with tokens that can then be exchanged for desired objects or activities.

Tolerance. Physiological condition in which an increased dosage of an addictive drug is needed to obtain effects previously produced by a smaller dose.

Tourette's syndrome. Extreme tic disorder in which an affected person has extensive uncontrollable motor and verbal mannerisms.

Toxic. Poisonous.

Toxicity. Poisonous nature of a substance.

Trait. Characteristic of a person that can be observed or measured.

Trance. Sleeplike state in which the range of consciousness is limited and voluntary activities are suspended; a deep hypnotic state.

Tranquilizers. Drugs used for reduction of psychotic symptoms and/or reduction of anxiety and tension. See also **Major tranquilizers** and **Minor tranquilizers.**

Transference. In psychodynamic therapy, process whereby a client projects attitudes and emotions applicable to another significant person onto the therapist.

Transsexualism. Identification of oneself with members of the opposite sex, as opposed to acceptance of one's anatomical sexual identity. Gender identity disorder in adults.

Transvestic fetishism. Achievement of sexual arousal and satisfaction by dressing as a member of the opposite sex.

Trauma. Severe psychological or physiological stressor.

Traumatic. Pertaining to a wound or injury, or to psychic shock.

Traumatic childhood abuse. Mistreatment in childhood severe enough to cause psychological damage.

Treatment contract. Explicit arrangement between a therapist and a client designed to bring about specific behavioral changes.

Tremor. Repeated fine spastic movement.

Type A behavior pattern. Complex set of behaviors—involving excessive competitive drive in the absence of well-defined goals, impatience or time urgency, and hostility—that may be observed in some people under stressful or challenging circumstances.

Unconscious. As used by Freud, psychological material that has been repressed. Also, loss of consciousness; lack of awareness.

Underarousal. Inadequate physiological response to a given stimulus.

Undoing. Ego-defense mechanism by means of which a person performs activities designed to atone for his or her misdeeds, thereby, in a sense, "undoing" them.

Unipolar disorder. Severe mood disorder in which only depressive episodes occur, as opposed to bipolar disorder, in which both manic and depressive episodes occur.

Vaginismus. Involuntary spasm of the muscles at the entrance to the vagina that prevents penetration and sexual intercourse.

Validity. Extent to which a measuring instrument actually measures what it purports to measure.

Variable. Characteristic or property that may assume any one of a set of different qualities or quantities.

Vascular dementia (VAD). A brain disorder in which a series of cerebral infarcts (strokes) destroy neurons, leading to brain atrophy and behavioral impairments.

Vasomotor. Pertaining to the walls of the blood vessels.

Vegetative. Withdrawn or deteriorated to the point of leading a passive, vegetable-like existence.

Verbal test. Test in which a subject's ability to understand and use words and concepts is important in making the required responses.

Vertigo. Dizziness.

Virilism. Accentuation of masculine secondary sex characteristsics, especially in a woman or young boy, caused by hormonal imbalance.

Viscera. Internal organs.

Voyeurism. Achievement of sexual pleasure through clandestine "peeping," usually watching other people disrobe and/or engage in sexual activities.

Vulnerabilities. Factors rendering a person susceptible to behaving abnormally.

Wechsler Intelligence Scale for Children (WISC). Standardized intelligence test for children.

Withdrawal. Intellectual, emotional, or physical retreat.

Withdrawal symptoms. Physical symptoms such as sweating, tremors, and tension that accompany abstinence from an addictive drug.

Word salad. Jumbled or incoherent use of words by psychotic or disoriented individuals.

X chromosome. Sex-determining chromosome: all female gametes contain X chromosomes, and if the fertilized ovum has also received an X chromosome from its father it will be female.

XYY syndrome. Chromosomal anomaly in males (presence of an extra Y chromosome) possibly related to impulsive behavior.

Y chromosome. Sex-determining chromosome found in half of the total number of male gametes; uniting with X chromosome provided by a female produces a male offspring.

Zygote. Fertilized egg cell formed by the union of male and female gametes.

REFERENCES

JOURNAL ABBREVIATIONS

Acta Neurol. Scandin.—*Acta Neurologica Scandinavica*
Acta Psychiatr. Scandin.—*Acta Psychiatrica Scandinavica*
Alcoholism: Clin. Exper. Res.—*Alcoholism: Clinical and Experimental Research*
Am. J. Community Psychol.—*American Journal of Community Psychology*
Amer. J. Clin. Nutri.—*American Journal of Clinical Nutrition*
Amer. J. Drug Alcoh. Abuse—*American Journal of Drug and Alcohol Abuse*
Amer. J. Epidemiol.—*American Journal of Epidemiology*
Amer. J. Med. Genet.—*American Journal of Medical Genetics*
Amer. J. Med. Sci.—*American Journal of the Medical Sciences*
Amer. J. Ment. Def.—*American Journal of Mental Deficiency*
Amer. J. Ment. Retard—*American Journal of Mental Retardation*
Amer. J. Nurs.—*American Journal of Nursing*
Amer. J. Occup. Ther.—*American Journal of Occupational Therapy*
Amer. J. Orthopsychiat.—*American Journal of Orthopsychiatry*
Amer. J. Psychiat.—*American Journal of Psychiatry*
Amer. J. Psychoanal.—*American Journal of Psychoanalysis*
Amer. J. Psychother.—*American Journal of Psychotherapy*
Amer. J. Pub. Hlth.—*American Journal of Public Health*
Amer. Psychol.—*American Psychologist*
Ann. Int. Med.—*Annals of Internal Medicine*
Ann. Neurol.—*Annuls of Neurology*
Ann. NY Acad. Sci.—*Annals of the New York Academy of Science*
Annu. Rev. Med.—*Annual Review of Medicine*
Annu. Rev. Psychol.—*Annual Review of Psychology*
Arch. Gen. Psychiat.—*Archives of General Psychiatry*
Arch. Gerontol. Geriatr.—*Archives of Gerontology and Geriatrics*
Arch. Int. Med.—*Archives of Internal Medicine*
Arch. Neurol.—*Archives of Neurology*
Arch. Sex. Behav.—*Archives of Sexual Behavior*
Behav. Mod.—*Behavior Modification*
Behav. Res. Ther.—*Behavior Research and Therapy*
Behav. Ther.—*Behavior Therapy*
Behav. Today—*Behavior Today*
Biol. Psychiat.—*Biological Psychiatry*
Br. J. Ophthalmol.—*British Journal of Ophthalmology*
Brit. J. Addict.—*British Journal of Addiction*
Brit. J. Psychiat.—*British Journal of Psychiatry*
Brit. Med. J.—*British Medical Journal*
Canad. J. Behav. Sci.—*Canadian Journal of Behavioural Science*
Canad. J. Psychiat.—*Canadian Journal of Psychiatry*
Child Ab. Negl.—*Child Abuse and Neglect*
Child Develop.—*Child Development*
Child Psychiat. Human Devel.—*Child Psychiatry and Human Development*
Clin. Pediat.—*Clinical Pediatrics*
Clin. Pharm.—*Clinical Pharmacy*
Clin. Psychol. Rev.—*Clinical Psychology Review*
Clin. Psychol.—*The Clinical Psychologist*
Cog. Ther. Res.—*Cognitive Therapy and Research*
Coll. Stud. J.—*College Student Journal*
Comm. Ment. Hlth. J.—*Community Mental Health Journal*
Compr. Psychiat.—*Comprehensive Psychiatry*
Contemp. Psychol.—*Contemporary Psychology*
Crim. Just. Behav.—*Criminal Justice and Behavior*

Curr. Dir. Psychol. Sci.—*Current Directions in Psychological Science*
Develop. Med. Child Neurol.—*Developmental Medicine & Child Neurology*
Develop. Psychol.—*Developmental Psychology*
Develop. Psychopath.—*Development and Psychopathology*
Dis. Nerv. Sys.—*Diseases of the Nervous System*
Except.—*Exceptionality*
Fam. Hlth.—*Family Health*
Fam. Plann. Perspect.—*Family Planning Perspectives*
Fam. Process—*Family Process*
Fed. Proc.—*Federal Proceedings*
Hlth. Psychol.—*Health Psychology*
Hosp. Comm. Psychiat.—*Hospital and Community Psychiatry*
Human Behav.—*Human Behavior*
Human Develop.—*Human Development*
Human Genet.—*Human Genetics*
Int. J. Clin. Exp. Hypn.—*International Journal of Clinical and Experimental Hypnosis*
Int. Rev. Psychiat.—*International Reveiw of Psychiatry*
Integr. Psychiat.—*Integrative Psychiatry*
Inter. J. Addictions—*International Journal of Addictions*
Inter. J. Ment. Hlth.—*International Journal of Mental Health*
Inter. J. Psychiat.—*International Journal of Psychiatry*
Inter. J. Psychoanal.—*International Journal of Psychoanalysis*
Inter. J. Soc. Psychiat.—*International Journal of Social Psychiatry*
J. Abnorm. Child Psychol.—*Journal of Abnormal Child Psychology*
J. Abnorm. Psychol.—*Journal of Abnormal Psychology*
J. Abnorm. Soc. Psychol.—*Journal of Abnormal and Social Psychology*
J. Affect. Dis.—*Journal of Affective Disorders*
J. Amer. Acad. Adoles. Psychiat.—*Journal of the American Academy of Adolescent Psychiatry*
J. Amer. Acad. Child Adoles. Psychiat.—*Journal of the American Academy of Child and Adolescent Psychiatry*
J. Amer. Acad. Child Psychiat.—*Journal of the American Academy of Child Psychiatry*
J. Amer. Geriat. Soc.—*Journal of the American Geriatrics Society*
J. Anxiety Dis.—*Journal of Anxiety Disorders*
J. Appl. Beh. Anal.—*Journal of Applied Behavior Analysis*
J. Autism Devel. Dis.—*Journal of Autism and Developmental Disorders*
J. Behav. Assess.—*Journal of Behavioral Assessment*
J. Behav. Med.—*Journal of Behavioral Medicine*
J. Chem. Depen. Treat.—*Journal of Chemical Dependency Treatment*
J. Child Psychol. Psychiat.—*Journal of Child Psychology and Psychiatry.*
J. Clin. Child Psychol.—*Journal of Clinical Child Psychology*
J. Clin. Psychiat.—*Journal of Clinical Psychiatry*
J. Clin. Psychol.—*Journal of Clinical Psychology*
J. Clin. Psychopharm.—*Journal of Clinical Psychopharmacology*
J. Cog. Rehab.—*Journal of Cognitive Rehabilitation*
J. Comm. Psychol.—*Journal of Community Psychology*
J. Cons. Clin. Psychol.—*Journal of Consulting and Clinical Psychology*
J. Couns. Psychol.—*Journal of Counseling Psychology*
J. Edu. Psychol.—*Journal of Educational Psychology*
J. Exper. Psychol.—*Journal of Experimental Psychology*
J. Fam. Pract.—*Journal of Family Practice*

J. Gen. Psychol.—*Journal of General Psychology*
J. Gerontol.—*Journal of Gerontology*
J. Head Trauma Rehab.—*Journal of Head Trauma Rehabilitation*
J. His. Behav. Sci.—*Journal of the History of the Behaviorial Sciences*
J. Intell. Dis. Res.—*Journal of Intellectual Disability Research*
J. Interpers. Violen.—*Journal of Interpersonal Violence*
J. Learn. Dis.—*Journal of Learning Disabilities*
J. Ment. Sci.—*Journal of Mental Science*
J. Nerv. Ment. Dis.—*Journal of Nervous and Mental Diseases*
J. Neurol. Neurosurg. Psychiatry—*Journal of Neurology, Neurosurgery, & Psychiatry*
J. Neuropsychiat. Clin. Neurosci.—*Journal of Neuropsychiatry and Clinical Neurosciences*
J. Pediat. Psychol.—*Journal of Pediatric Psychology*
J. Pers. Assess.—*Journal of Personality Assessment*
J. Pers. Soc. Psychol.—*Journal of Personality and Social Psychology*
J. Personal. Dis.—*Journal of Personality Disorders*
J. Personal.—*Journal of Personality*
J. Prim. Prevent.—*Journal of Primary Prevention*
J. Psychiat. Res.—*Journal of Psychiatric Research*
J. Psychoact. Drugs—*Journal of Psychoactive Drugs*
J. Psychohist.—*Journal of Psychohistory*
J. Psychol.—*Journal of Psychology*
J. Psychopath. Behav. Assess.—*Journal of Psychopathology and Behavioral Assessment*
J. Psychopharm.—*Journal of Psychopharmacology*
J. Psychosom. Res.—*Journal of Psychosomatic Research*
J. Sex Marit. Ther.—*Journal of Sex and Marital Therapy*
J. Sex. Res.—*Journal of Sex Research*
J. Speech Hear. Dis.—*Journal of Speech and Hearing Disorders*
J. Stud. Alcoh.—*Journal of Studies on Alcohol*
J. Subst. Abuse—*Journal of Substance Abuse*
J. Trauma. Stress—*Journal of Traumatic Stress*
JAMA—*Journal of the American Medical Association*
Monogr. Soc. Res. Child Develop.—*Monographs of the Society for Research in Child Development*
Neurobiol. Aging—*Neurobiology of Aging*
New Engl. J. Med.—*New England Journal of Medicine*
Personal. Indiv. Diff.—*Personality and Individual Differences*
Profess. Psychol.—*Professional Psychology*
Prog. Neuropsychopharmacol. Biol. Psychiatry—*Progress in Neuropsychopharmacology & Biological Psychiatry*
Psych. Today—*Psychology Today*
Psychiat. Ann.—*Psychiatric Annals*
Psychiat. Clin. N. Amer.—*Psychiatric Clinics of North America*
Psychiat. News—*Psychiatric News*
Psychiat. Res.—*Psychiatric Research*
Psychol. Aging—*Psychology and Aging*
Psychol. Assess.—*Psychological Assessment*
Psychol. Bull.—*Psychological Bulletin*
Psychol. Inq.—*Psychological Inquiry*
Psychol. Med.—*Psychological Medicine*
Psychol. Rep.—*Psychological Reports*
Psychol. Rev.—*Psychological Review*
Psychol. Sci.—*Psychological Science*
Psychopharm. Bull.—*Psychopharmacology Bulletin*
Psychosom. Med.—*Psychosomatic Medicine*
Q. J. Exp. Psych. [A]—*Quarterly Journal of Experimental Psychology: [A] Human Experimental Psychology*
Schizo. Bull.—*Schizophrenia Bulletin*
School Psychol. Rev.—*School Psychology Review*
Sci. News—*Science News*
Scientif. Amer.—*Scientific American*
Soc. Psychiat.—*Social Psychiatry*
Soc. Psychiat. Psychiatr. Epidemiol.—*Social Psychiatry and Psychiatric Epidemiology*
Soc. Sci. Med.—*Social Science and Medicine*

Abel, E. L. (1988). Fetal alcohol syndrome in families. *Neurotoxicology and Teratology, 10,* 1–2.
Abel, E. L. (1990). *Fetal alcohol syndrome.* New York: Plenum.

Abel, E. L., Martier, Kruger, M., Ager, J., & Sokol, R. J. (1993). Ratings of fetal alcohol syndrome facial features by medical providers and biomedical scientists. *Alcoholism: Clin. Exper. Res., 17*(3), 717–721.
Abel, G. G., & Rouleau, J. (1990). The nature and extent of sexual assault. W. L. Marshall, D. R. Laws, & H. E. Barbaree (Eds.), *Handbook of sexual assault: Issues, theories, and treatment of the offender* (pp. 9–22). New York: Plenum.
Abel, G. G., Barlow, D. H., Blanchard, E. B., & Guild, D. (1977). The components of rapists' sexual arousal. *Arch. Gen. Psychiat., 34,* 895–903.
Abel, G. G., Blanchard, E. B., Becker, J. V., & Djenderejian, A. (1978). Differentiating sexual aggressives with penile measures. *Crim. Just. Behav., 5,* 315–32.
Abou-Saleh, M. T. (1992). Lithium. In E. S. Paykel (Ed.), *Handbook of affective disorders* (2nd ed.). New York: Guilford.
Abraham, H. D., & Wolf, E. (1988). Visual function in past users of LSD: Psychophysical findings. *J. Abnorm. Psychol., 97,* 443–47.
Abraham, K. (1960a). Notes on the psychoanalytic treatment of manic depressive insanity and allied conditions. In *Selected papers on psychoanalysis.* New York: Basic Books. (Original work published 1911.)
Abraham, K. (1960b). The first pregenital stage of libido. In *Selected papers on psychoanalysis.* New York: Basic Books. (Original work published 1916.)
Abrahamson, D. J., Barlow, D. H., & Abrahamson, L. S. (1989). Differential effects of performance demand and distraction on sexually functional and dysfunctional males. *J. Abnorm. Psychol., 98,* 241–47.
Abrahamson, D. J., Barlow, D. H., Sakheim, D. K., Beck, J. G., & Athanasiou, R. (1985). Effects of distraction on sexual responding in functional and dysfunctional men. *Behav. Ther., 16,* 503–15.
Abramowitz, A. J., Eckstrand, D., O'Leary, S. G., & Dulcan, M. K. (1992). Children's responses to stimulant medication and two intensities of a behavioral intervention. Special issue: Treatment of children with attention deficit hyperactivity disorder (ADHD). *Behav. Mod., 16,* 193–202.
Abrams, R. (1988). *Electroconvulsive treatment: It apparently works, but how and at what risks are not yet clear.* New York: Oxford University Press.
Abrams, R. (1992). *Electroconvulsive therapy.* Oxford: Oxford University Press.
Abrams, R. (1994). The treatment that will not die. *Psychiat. Clin. N. Amer., 17,* 525–30.
Abramson, L. Y., Metalsky, G. I., & Alloy, L. B. (1989). Hopelessness depression: A theory-based subtype of depression. *Psychol. Rev., 96,* 358–372.
Abramson, L. Y., Seligman, M. E. P. (1977) Modeling psychopathology in the laboratory: History and rationale. In M. Maser & M. E. P. Seligman (Eds.), *Psychopathology: Experimental Models.* San Francisco: Freeman.
Abramson, L. Y., Seligman, M. E. P., & Teasdale, J. D. (1978). Learned helplessness in humans: Critique and reformulation. *J. Abnorm. Psychol., 87,* 49–74.
Abramson, R. K., Wright, H. H., Cuccaro, M. L., & Lawrence, L. G. (1992). Biological liability in families with autism. *J. Amer. Acad. Child Adoles. Psychiat., 31,* 370–71.
Achenbach, T. M. (1985). *Assessment and taxonomy of child and adolescent psychopathology.* Beverly Hills, CA: Sage.
Achenbach, T. M., & Edelbrock, C. S. (1983). *Manual for the child behavior checklist and revised child behavior profile.* Burlington, VT: University of Vermont.
Achenbach, T. M., & McConaughy, S. H. (1985). *Child interview checklist self-report form; Child interview checklist-observation form.* Burlington, VT: University of Vermont.
Achenbach, T. M., & Weisz, J. R. (1975). Impulsivity-reflectivity and cognitive development in preschoolers: A longitudinal analysis of developmental and trait variance. *Develop. Psychol., 11,* 413–14.
ACSF Investigators. (1992). AIDS and sexual behaviour in France. *Nature, 360,* 407–9.

Adam, B. S., Everett, B. L., & O'Neal, E. (1992). PTSD in physically and sexually abused psychiatrically hospitalized children. *Child Psychiat. Human Develop., 23,* 3–8.

Adams, D. M., & Overholser, J. C. (1992). Suicidal behavior and history of substance abuse. *Amer. J. Drug Alcoh. Abuse, 18,* 343–54.

Adams, H. E., & McAnulty, R. D. (1993). Sexual disorders: The paraphilias. In P. Sutker & H. Adams (Eds.), *Comprehensive handbook of psychopathology.* (2nd ed.) (pp. 563–79). New York: Plenum.

Adams, M. S., & Neel, J. V. (1967). Children of incest. *Pediatrics, 40,* 55–62.

Ader, R., & Cohen, N. (1984). Behavior and the immune system. In W. D. Gentry (Ed.), *Handbook of behavioral medicine* (pp. 117–73). New York: Guilford.

Adler, A. (1943). Neuropsychiatric complications in victims of Boston's Coconut Grove disaster. *JAMA, 123,* 1098–1101.

Adler, T. (1994). Alzheimer's causes unique cell death. *Sci. News, 146*(13), 198.

Adrien, J. L., Perrot, A., Sauvage, D., & Leddet, I. (1992). Early symptoms in autism from family home movies: Evaluation and comparison between 1st and 2nd year of life using I.B.S.E. scale. *Acta Paedopsychiatrica International Journal of Child and Adolescent Psychiatry, 55,* 71–75.

Affleck, G., Tennen, H., Urrows, S., & Higgins, P. (1994). Person and contextual features of daily stress reactivity: Individual differences in relations of undesirable daily events with mood disturbance and chronic pain intensity. *J. of Pers. Soc. Psychol., 66*(2), 329–40.

Agnew, J. (1985). Man's purgative passion. *Amer. J. Psychother., 39*(2), 236–46.

Agras, W. S. (1982). Behavioral medicine in the 1980's: Non-random connections. *J. Cons. Clin. Psychol., 50*(6), 820–40.

Agras, W. S. (1993). Short term psychological treatments for binge eating. In C. Fairburn & G. T. Wilson (Eds.), *Binge eating: Nature, assessment, and treatment.* New York: Guilford.

Agras, W. S., Schneider, J. A., Arnow, B., Raeburn, S. D., & Telch, C. F. (1989). Cognitive-behavioral and response-prevention treatments for bulimia nervosa. *J. Cons. Clin. Psychol., 57,* 215–21.

Aiken, L. R. (1994). *Dying, death, and bereavement* (3rd ed.). Boston: Allyn & Bacon.

Akhtar, S., Wig, N. N., Varma, V. K., Pershad, D., & Verma, S. K. (1975). Phenomenological analysis of symptoms in obsessive-compulsive neurosis. *Brit. J. Psychiat., 127,* 342–8.

Akiskal, H. S. (1979). A biobehavioral approach to depression. In R. A. Depue (Ed.), *The psychobiology of depressive disorders: Implications for the effects of stress.* New York: Academic Press.

Akiskal, H. S. (1989). Validating affective personality types. In L. N. Robins & J. E. Barrett (Eds.), *The validity of psychiatric diagnosis.* New York: Raven Press.

Akiskal, H. S., & Simmons, R. C. (1985). Chronic and refractory depressions: Evaluation and management. In E. E. Becham & W. R. Leber (Eds.), *Handbook of depression: Treatment, assessment, and research* (pp. 587–605). Homewood, IL: Dorsey Press.

Akiskal, H.S., Chen, S., Davis, G., Puzantian, V., Kashgarian, M., & Bolinger, J. (1985) Borderline: An adjective in search of a noun. *Clinical Psychiatry, 46,* 41–48.

Akiskal, H. S., Khani, M. K., & Scott-Strauss, A. (1979). Cyclothymic temperamental disorders. *Psychiat. Clin. N. Amer., 2,* 527–54.

Alander, R., & Campbell, T. (1975, Spring). An evaluation of an alcohol and drug recovery program: A case study of the Oldsmobile experience. *Human Resource Management,* 14–18.

Albertson's Inc. v. Worker's Compensation Board of the State of California, 131, Cal App 3d, 182 Cal Reptr 304, 1982.

Alcoholics Anonymous (1989). *Comments on AA's triennial surveys.* New York: AA World Service.

Alden, L., & Capp, R. (1988). Characteristics predicting social functioning and treatment response in clients impaired by extreme shyness: Age of onset and the public/private shyness distinction. *Canad. J. Behav. Sci., 20,* 40–49.

Alexander, A. B. (1977). Chronic asthma. In R. B. Williams, Jr., & W. D. Gentry (Eds.), *Behavioral approaches to medical treatment* (pp. 7–24). Cambridge, MA: Ballinger.

Alexander, A. B. (1981). Behavioral approaches to the treatment of bronchial asthma. In C. K. Prokop & L. A. Bradley (Eds.), *Medical psychology: Contributions to behavioral medicine.* New York: Academic Press.

Alexander, F. (1946). Individual psychotherapy. *Psychosom. Med., 8,* 110–15.

Alexander, F. (1948). *Fundamentals of psychoanalysis.* New York: Norton.

Alexander, F. (1950). *Psychosomatic medicine.* New York: Norton.

Alexander, J. F., Holtzworth-Munroe, A., & Jameson, P. B. (1994). The process and outcome of marital and family therapy: Research review and evaluation. In A. E. Bergin & S. L. Garfield (Eds.), *Handbook of psychotherapy and behavior change* (4th ed., pp. 595–630). New York: Wiley.

Alexander, K., Huganir, L. S., & Zigler, E. (1985). Effects of different living settings on the performance of mentally retarded individuals. *Amer. J. Ment. Def., 90,* 9–17.

Alison, N. G. (1994). Fetal alcohol syndrome: Implications for psychologists. *Clin. Psychol. Rev., 14,* 91–111.

Al-Issa, I. (1982). Does culture make a difference in psychopathology? In I. Al-Issa (Ed.), *Culture and psychopathology.* Baltimore: University Park Press.

Allen, B., & Skinner, H. (1987). Lifestyle assessment using microcomputers. In J. N. Butcher (Ed.), *Computerized psychological assessment: A practitioner's guide.* New York: Basic Books.

Allerton, W. S. (1970). Psychiatric casualties in Vietnam. *Roche Medical Image and Commentary, 12*(8), 27.

Allodi, F. A. (1994). Post-traumatic stress disorder in hostages and victims of torture. *Psychiat. Clin. of N. Amer., 17,* 279–88.

Alloy, L. B., Kelly, K. A., Mineka, S., & Clements, C. M. (1990). Comorbidity in anxiety and depressive disorders: A helplessness/hopelessness perspective. In J. D. Maser & C. R. Cloninger (Eds.), *Comorbidity in anxiety and mood disorders* (pp. 499–543). Washington, DC: American Psychiatric Press.

Alloy, L. B., & Tabachnick, N. (1984). Assessment of covariation by humans and animals: The joint influence of prior expectations and current situational information. *Psychol. Rev., 91,* 112–149.

Alterman, A. I. (1988). Patterns of familial alcoholism, alcoholism severity, and psychopathology. *J. Nerv. Ment. Dis., 176,* 167–75.

Alterman, A. I., Searles, J. S., & Hall, J. G. (1989). Failure to find differences in drinking behavior as a function of familial risk for alcoholism: A replication. *J. Cons. Clin. Psychol., 98,* 50–53.

Amato, P. R. (1988). Long-term implications of parental divorce for adult self concept. *Journal of Family Issues, 9,* 201–213.

Amato, P. R., & Keith, B. (1991). Parental divorce and the well-being of children: A meta-analysis. *Psychol. Bull., 110,* 26–46.

Ambrosini, P. J., Bianchi, M. D., Rabinovich, H., & Elia, J. (1993). Antidepressant treatments in children and adolescents: II Anxiety, physical, and behavioral disorders. *J. Amer. Acad. Child Adoles. Psychiat., 32,* 483–93.

Amcoff, S. (1980). The impact of malnutrition on the learning situation. In H. M. Sinclair & G. R. Howat (Eds.), *World nutrition and nutrition education.* New York: Oxford University Press.

American Medical Association Committee on Human Sexuality. (1972). *Human Sexuality.* (p. 40). Chicago: American Medical Association.

American Medical Association, Department of Mental Health. (1968). The crutch that cripples: Drug dependence, Part 1. *Today's Health, 46*(9), 11–12, 70–72.

American Psychiatric Association. (1968). *Diagnostic and statistical manual of mental disorders* (2nd ed.). Washington, DC: Author.

American Psychiatric Association. (1972). Classification of mental retardation. *Supplement to the Amer. J. Psychiat.*, *128*(11), 1–45.

American Psychiatric Association. (1980). *Diagnostic and statistical manual of mental disorders* (3rd ed.). Washington, DC: Author.

American Psychiatric Association. (1987). *Diagnostic and statistical manual of mental disorders* (3rd ed.—rev.). Washington, DC: Author.

American Psychiatric Association. (1990). *The practice of ECT: Recommendations for treatment, training, privileging.* Washington, D.C.: Author.

American Psychiatric Association. (1994). *Diagnostic and statistical manual of mental disorders (DSM-IV)* (4th ed.). Washington, DC: Author.

American Psychological Association. (1970). Psychology and mental retardation. *Amer. Psychol.*, *25*, 267–68.

American Psychological Association. (1986). *Guidelines for computer-based tests and interpretations.* Washington, DC: Author.

American Psychological Association. (1992). Ethical principles of psychologists and code of conduct. *Amer. Psychol.*, *47*(12), 1597–611.

Anand, K. J. S., & Arnold, J. H. (1994). Opioid tolerance and dependence in infants and children. *Critical Care Medicine*, *22*, 334–42.

Andersen, B. L. (1983). Primary orgasmic dysfunction: Diagnostic considerations and review of treatment. *Psychol. Bull.*, *93*, 105–36.

Anderson, B. L., Kiecolt-Glaser, J. K., & Glaser, R. (1994). A biobehavioral model of cancer stress and disease course. *Amer. Psychol.*, *49*(5), 389–404.

Anderson, G., Yasenik, L., & Ross, C. A. (1993). Dissociative experiences and disorders among women who identify themselves as sexual abuse survivors. *Child Ab. Negl.*, *17*, 677–86.

Anderson, J. C., Williams, S., McGee, R., & Silva, P. A. (1987). DSM III disorders in preadolescent children. *Arch. Gen. Psychiat.*, *44*, 69–80.

Anderson, N. B., & Jackson, J. S. (1987). Race, ethnicity, and health psychology: The example of essential hypertension. In G. C. Stone (Ed.), *Health psychology: A discipline and a profession* (pp. 265–84). Chicago: University of Chicago Press.

Andrasik, F., Blanchard, E. B., Arena, J. G., Teders, S. J., Teevan, R. C., & Rodichok, L. D. (1982). Psychological functioning in headache sufferers. *Psychosom. Med.*, *44*, 171–82.

Andrasik, F., Holroyd, K. A., & Abell, T. (1979). Prevalence of headache within a college student population: A preliminary analysis. *Headache*, *20*, 384–87.

Andreasen, N. C. (1982). Concepts, diagnosis and classification. In E. S. Paykel (Ed.), *Handbook of affective disorders.* New York: Guilford.

Andreasen, N. C. (1984). *The broken brain: The biological revolution in psychiatry.* New York: Harper & Row.

Andreasen, N. C. (1985). Positive vs. negative schizophrenia: A critical evaluation. *Schizo. Bull.*, *11*, 380–89.

Andreasen, N. C., & Carpenter, W. T., Jr. (1993). Diagnosis and classification of schizophrenia. *Schizo. Bull.*, *19*(2), 199–214.

Andreasen, N. C., Flaum, M., Swayze, V. W., Tyrrell, G., & Arndt, S. (1990). Positive and negative symptoms in schizophrenia: A critical reappraisal. *Arch. Gen. Psychiat.*, *47*, 615–21.

Andreasen, N. C., Nasrallah, H. A., Dunn, V., Olson, S. C., & Grove, W. M. (1986). Structural abnormalities in the frontal system in schizophrenia: A magnetic resonance imaging study. *Arch. Gen. Psychiat.* *43*, 136–44.

Andreasen, N. C., Olsen, S. A., Dennert, J. W., & Smith, M. R. (1982a). Ventricular enlargement in schizophrenia: Definition and prevalence. *Amer. J. Psychiat.*, *139*, 292–96.

Andreasen, N. C., Olsen, S. A., Dennert, J. W., & Smith, M. R. (1982b). Ventricular enlargement in schizophrenia: Relationship to positive and negative symptoms. *Amer. J. Psychiat.*, *139*, 297–302.

Andreasen, N. C., Rezai, K., Alliger, R., Swayze, V. W., Flaum, M., Kirchner, P., Cohen, G., & O'Leary, D. S. (1992). Hypofrontality in neuroleptic-naive patients and in patients with chronic schizophrenia. *Arch. Gen. Psychiat.*, *49*(12), 959–65.

Andrews, G., & Harvey, R. (1981). Does psychotherapy benefit neurotic patients? A reanalysis of the Smith, Glass, and Miller data. *Arch. Gen. Psychiat.*, *38*, 1203–8.

Andrews, J. D. W. (1989a). Integrating visions of reality: Interpersonal diagnosis and the existential vision. *Amer. Psychol.*, *44*, 803–17.

Andrews, J. D. W. (1989b). Psychotherapy of depression: A self-confirmation model. *Psychol. Rev.*, *96*, 576–607.

Anthony, J. C., & Petronis, K. R. (1991). Panic attacks and suicide attempts. *Arch. Gen. Psychiat.*, *48*, 1114.

Antoni, M. H., Schneiderman, N., Fletcher, M. A., & Goldstein, D. A. (1990). Psychoneuroimmunology and HIV-1. *J. Cons. Clin. Psychol.*, *58*, 38–49.

Apfelbaum, B. (1989). Retarded ejaculation: A much-misunderstood syndrome. In S. R. Leiblum & R. C. Rosen (Eds.), *Principles and practice of sex therapy* (2nd ed., pp. 168–206). New York: Guilford.

Aponte, H., & Hoffman, L. (1973). The open door. A structural approach to a family with an anorectic child. *Fam. Process*, *12*, 144.

Appelbaum, P. S., Jick, R. Z., Grisso, T., Givelber, D., Silver, E., & Steadman, H. J. (1993). Use of posttraumatic stress disorder to support an insanity defense. *Amer. J. Psychiat.*, *150*, 229–34.

Arana, G. W., Baldessarini, R. J., & Ornsteen, M. (1985). The dexamethasone suppression test for diagnosis and prognosis in psychiatry: Commentary and review. *Arch. Gen. Psychiat.*, *42*, 1193–1204.

Arbitman-Smith, R., Haywood, H. C., & Bransford, J. D. (1984). Assessing cognitive change. In P. Brooks, C. M. Sperber, & R. McCauley (Eds.), *Learning and cognition in the mentally retarded* (pp. 433–72). Hillsdale, NJ: Erlbaum.

Aring, C. D. (1974). The Gheel experience: Eternal spirit of the chainless mind! *JAMA*, *230*(7), 998–1001.

Aring, C. D. (1975a). Gheel: The town that cares. *Fam. Hlth.*, *7*(4), 54–55, 58, 60.

Aring, C. D. (1975b). Science and the citizen. *Scientif. Amer.*, *232*(1), 48–49; 52–53.

Arkowitz, H., & Messer, S. B. (Eds.). (1984). *Psychoanalytic and behavior therapy. Is integration possible?* New York: Plenum.

Arndt, I. O. McLellan, A. T., Dorozynsky, L., Woody, G. E., & O'Brien, C. P. (1994). Desipramine treatment for cocaine dependence: Role of antisocial personality disorder. *J. Nerv. Ment. Dis.*, *182*, 151–56.

Arnkoff, D. B., & Glass, C. R. (1982). Clinical cognitive constructs: Examination, evaluation, and elaboration. In P. C. Kendall (Ed.), *Advances in cognitive-behavioral research and therapy* (Vol. 1, pp. 2–30). New York: Academic Press.

Arnold, M. B. (1962). *Story sequence analysis: A new method of measuring motivation and predicting achievement.* New York: Columbia University Press.

Aronoff, B. (1987). *Needs assessments: What have we learned? Experiences from Refugee Assistance Programs in Hawaii.* Paper given at the Refugee Assistance Program: Mental Health Workgroup Meeting, UCLA, February 12–13.

Asarnow, J. R. (1992). Suicidal ideation and attempts during middle childhood: Associations with perceived family stress and depression among child psychiatric inpatients. *J. Child Clinical Psychol.*, *21*, 35–40.

Atkeson, B. M., & Forehand, R. (1978). Parent behavior training for problem children: An examination of studies using multiple outcome measures. *J. Abnorm. Child Psychol.*, *6*, 449–60.

Atkeson, B. M., Calhoun, K. S., Resick, P. A., & Ellis, E. M. (1982). Victims of rape: Repeated assessment of depressive symptoms. *J. Cons. Clin. Psychol., 50,* 96–102.

Atkinson, J. W. (1992). Motivational determinants of thematic apperception. In C. P. Smith, J. W. Atkinson, & J. Veroff (Eds.). *Motivation and personality: Handbook of thematic content analysis* (pp. 21–48). New York: Cambridge University Press.

Auerbach, S. M., & Stolberg, A. L. (1986). *Crisis intervention with children and families.* New York: Hemisphere Press.

Averill, J. R. (1973). Personal control over aversive stimuli and its relationship to stress. *Psychol. Bull., 80*(4), 286–303.

Ayllon, T., & Azrin, N. H. (1968). *The token economy: A motivational system for therapy and rehabilitation.* New York: Appleton-Century-Crofts.

Azari, N. P., Horwitz, B., Pettigrew, K. D., & Grady, C. L. (1994). Abnormal pattern of glucose metabolic rates involving language areas in young adults with Down syndrome. *Brain & Language, 46*(1), 1–20.

Bachrach, L. L. (1976). *Deinstitutionalization: An analytic review and sociological perspective.* U.S. Department of Health, Education, and Welfare. National Institute of Mental Health, Washington, DC: U.S. Government Printing Office.

Baer, L., Jenike, M. A., Black, D. W., Treece, C., et al. (1992). Effect of Axis II diagnosis on treatment outcome with clomipramine in 55 patients with obsessive-compulsive disorder. *Arch. Gen. Psychiat., 49*(11), 862–6.

Baer, L., Jenike, M. A., Ricciardi, J. N., Holland, A. D., et al. (1990). Standardized assessment of personality disorders in obsessive-compulsive disorder. *Arch. Gen. Psychiat., 47*(9), 826–30.

Bailey, J. M. & Pillard, R. C. (1991). A genetic study of male sexual orientation. *Arch. Gen. Psychiat., 48,* 1089–96.

Bailey, J. M., & Zucker, K. J. (1995). Childhood sex-typed behavior and sexual orientation: A conceptual analysis and quantitative review. *Develop. Psychol., 31,* 43–55.

Bailey, J. M., Gaulin, S., Agyei, Y., & Gladue, B. A. (1994). Effects of gender and sexual orientation on evolutionarily relevant aspects of human mating psychology. *J. Pers. Soc. Psychol. 66,* 1081–93.

Bailey, J. M., Pillard, R. C., Neale, M. C., & Agyei, Y. (1993). Heritable factors influence female sexual orientation. *Arch. Gen. Psychiat., 50,* 217–23.

Baker, L. A., & Daniels, D. (1990). Nonshared environmental influences and personality differences in adult twins. *J. Pers. Soc. Psychol., 58,* 103–10.

Baldwin, A. L., Baldwin, C., & Cole, R. E. (1990). Stress-resistant families and stress-resistant children. In J. Rolf, A. S. Masten, D. Cicchetti, K. H. Nuechterlein, & S. Weintraub (Eds.), *Risk and protective factors in the development of psychopathology.* New York: Cambridge University Press.

Bales, R. F. (1946). Cultural differences in rates of alcoholism. *Quarterly Journal of Studies in Alcoholism, 6,* 480–99.

Ballenger, J. C. (1988). The clinical use of carbamazepine in affective disorders. *J. Clin. Psychiat., 49,* 13–19.

Balshem, M., Oxman, G., Van Rooyen, D., & Girod, K. (1992). Syphilis, sex and crack cocaine: Images of risk and morality. *Soc. Sci. and Med., 35,* 147–60.

Bandura, A. (1964). *Principles of behavior modification.* New York: Holt, Rinehart & Winston.

Bandura, A. (1969). *Principles of behavior modification.* New York: Holt, Rinehart & Winston.

Bandura, A. (1973). *Aggression: A social learning analysis.* Englewood Cliffs, NJ: Prentice-Hall.

Bandura, A. (1974). Behavior theory and the models of man. *Amer. Psychol., 29*(12), 859–69.

Bandura, A. (1977a). Self-efficacy: Toward a unifying theory of behavioral change. *Psychol. Rev., 84*(2), 191–215.

Bandura, A. (1977b). *Social learning theory.* Englewood Cliffs, NJ: Prentice-Hall.

Bandura, A. (1986). *Social foundations of thought and action: A social cognitive theory.* Englewood Cliffs, NJ: Prentice-Hall.

Bandura, A., & Walters, R. H. (1963). *Social learning and personality development.* New York: Holt, Rinehart & Winston.

Bannister, G., Jr. (1975). Cognitive and behavior therapy in a case of compulsive gambling. *Cog. Ther. Res., 1,* 223–27.

Barbach, L. G., & Levine, L. (1980). *Shared intimacies.* Garden City, NY: Anchor Press/Doubleday.

Barbaree, H. E. (1990). Stimulus control of sexual arousal: Its role in sexual assault. In W. L. Marshall, D. R. Laws, & H. E. Barbaree (Eds.), *Handbook of sexual assault* (pp. 115–42). New York: Plenum.

Barbaree, H. E., Seto, M., Serin, R., Amos, N., & Preston, D. (1994). Comparisons between sexual and nonsexual rapist subtypes: Sexual arousal to rape, offense precursors, and offense characteristics. *Crim. Just. Behav., 21,* 95–114.

Barber, T. X. (1969). *Hypnosis: A scientific approach.* New York: Van Nostrand Reinhold.

Barchas, J., Akil, H., Elliott, G., Holman, R., & Watson, S. (1978, May 26). Behavioral neurochemistry: Neuroregulators and behavioral states. *Science, 200,* 964–73.

Barlow, D. H. (1974). The treatment of sexual deviation: Toward a comprehensive behavioral approach. In K. S. Calhoun, H. E. Adams, & K. M. Mitchell (Eds.), *Innovative treatment methods in psychopathology.* New York: Wiley Interscience.

Barlow, D. H. (1986). Causes of sexual dysfunction: The role of anxiety and cognitive interference. *J. Cons. Clin. Psychol., 54,* 140–48.

Barlow, D. H. (1988). *Anxiety and its disorders: The nature and treatment of anxiety and panic.* New York: Guilford.

Barlow, D. H. (1991a). Disorders of emotion. *Psychological Inquiry, 2,* 58–71.

Barlow, D. H. (1991b). The nature of anxiety: Anxiety, depression, and emotional disorders. In R. M. Rapee & D. H. Barlow (Eds.), *Chronic anxiety: Generalized anxiety disorder and mixed anxiety-depression* (pp. 1–28). New York: Guilford.

Barlow, D. H. (Ed.). (1993). *Clinical handbook of psychological disorders* (2nd ed.). New York: Guilford.

Barlow, D. H., & Cerny, J. A. (1988). *Psychological treatment of panic.* New York: Guilford.

Barlow, D. H., Craske, M. G., Cerny, J. A., & Klosko, J. S. (1989). Behavioral treatment of panic disorder. *Behav. Ther., 20,* 261–82.

Barlow, D. H., Sakheim, D. K., & Beck, J. G. (1983). Anxiety increases sexual arousal. *J. Abnorm. Psychol., 92,* 49–54.

Barnard, K., Morisset, C., & Spieker, S. (1993). Preventative interventions: Enhancing parent-infant relationships. In C. H. Zeanah, Jr. (Ed.), *Handbook of infant development.* New York: Guilford.

Barnes, G. E., & Prosen, H. (1985). Parental death and depression. *J. Abnorm. Psychol., 94,* 64–69.

Barnett, P. A., & Gotlib, I. H. (1988a). Dysfunctional attitudes and psychosocial stress: The differential prediction of subsequent depression and general psychological distress. *Motivation and Emotion, 12,* 251–70.

Barnett, P. A., & Gotlib, I. H. (1988b). Psychosocial functioning and depression: Distinguishing among antecedents, concomitants, and consequences. *Psychol. Bull., 104,* 97–126.

Baroff, G. S. (1986). *Mental retardation: Nature, cause, and management.* Washington: Hemisphere.

Baron, I. S., & Goldberger, E. (1993). Neuropsychological disturbances of hydrocephalic children with implications for special education and rehabilitation. *Neuropsychological Rehabilitation, 3*(4), 389–410.

Barry, H., III. (1982). Cultural variations in alcohol abuse. In I. Al-Issa (Ed.), *Culture and psychopathology.* Baltimore: University Park Press.

Barsky, A. J., Wool, C., Barnett, M. C., & Cleary, P. D. (1994). Histories of childhood trauma in adult hypochondriacal patients. *Amer. J. Psychiat., 151*(3), 397–401.

Barsky, A. J., Wyshak, G., & Klerman, G. L. (1992). Psychiatric comorbidity in DSM-III-R hypochondriasis. *Arch. Gen. Psychiat., 49*(2), 101–8.

Bartak, L. (1978). Educational approaches. In M. Rutter & E. Schopler (Eds.), *Autism: A reappraisal of concepts and treatment*. New York: Plenum.

Bartak, L., & Rutter, M. (1973). Special education treatment of autistic children: A comparative study, I. *J. Child Psychol. Psychiat., 14*, 161–79.

Bartak, L., & Rutter, M. (1976). Differences between mentally retarded and normally intelligent autistic children. *Journal of Autism and Childhood Schizophrenia, 6*, 109–20.

Başoğlu, M., & Mineka, S. (1992). The role of uncontrollable and unpredictable stress in post-traumatic stress responses in torture survivors. In M. Başoğlu (Ed.), *Torture and its consequences: Current treatment approaches* (pp. 182–225). Cambridge: Cambridge University Press.

Başoğlu, M., Paker, M., Paker, O., Ozmen, E., Marks, I., Sahin, D., & Sarimurat, N. (1994). Psychological effects of torture: A comparison of tortured with nontortured political activists in Turkey. *Amer. J. Psychiat., 151*, 76–81.

Bass, E., & Davis, L. (1988). *The courage to heal*. New York: Harper & Row.

Bassuk, E. L., & Gerson, S. (1978). Deinstitutionalization and mental health services. *Scientif. Amer., 238*(2), 46–53.

Bassuk, E. L., Schoonover, S. C., & Gelenberg, A. J. (1983). *The practitioner's guide to psychiatric drugs* (2nd ed.). New York: Plenum.

Bates, C. M., & Brodsky, A. M. (1989). *Sex in the therapy hour: A case of professional incest*. New York: Guilford.

Bateson, G. (1959). Cultural problems posed by a study of schizophrenic process. In A. Auerbach (Ed.), *Schizophrenia: An integrated approach*. New York: Ronald Press.

Bateson, G. (1960). Minimal requirements for a theory of schizophrenia. *Arch. Gen. Psychiat., 2*, 477–91.

Baucom, D. H. (1983). Sex role identity and the decision to regain control among women: A learned helplessness investigation. *J. Pers. Soc. Psychol., 44*, 334–43.

Bauer, A. M., & Shea, T. M. (1986). Alzheimer's disease and Down syndrome: A review and implications for adult services. *Education and Training of the Mentally Retarded, 21*, 144–50.

Baum, A., Gatchel, R. J., & Schaeffer, M. A. (1983). Emotional, behavioral, and physiological effects of chronic stress at Three Mile Island. *J. Cons. Clin. Psychol., 51*, 565–72.

Baumeister, R. F. (1990). Suicide as escape from self. *Psychol. Rev., 97*, 90–113.

Baumrind, D. (1967). Child care practices anteceding three patterns of preschool behavior. *Genetic Psychology Monographs, 75*, 43–88.

Baumrind, D. (1971). Current patterns of parental authority. *Develop. Psychol., 4*(1), 1–103.

Baumrind, D. (1975). *Early socialization and the discipline controversy*. Morristown, NJ: General Learning Press.

Baumrind, D. (1982). An explanatory study of socialization effects on black children: Some black-white comparisons. *Child Develop., 43*, 261–267.

Baumrind, D. (1991). Effective parenting during the early adolescent transition. In P. A. Cowan & E. M. Hetherington (Eds.), *Family transitions* (pp. 111–164). Hillsdale, NJ: Erlbaum.

Baumrind, D. (1993). The average expectable environment is not good enough: A response to Scarr. *Child Develop., 64*, 1299–1317.

Baxter, L. R., Jr., Phelps, M. E., Mazziotta, J. C., Schwartz, J. M., & Gerner, R. H. (1985). Cerebral metabolic rates for glucose in mood disorders: Studies with positron emission tomography and fluorodeoxyglucose F18. *Arch. Gen. Psychiat., 42*, 441–47.

Baxter, L. R., Schwartz, J. M., Bergman, K. S., Szuba, M. P., Guze, B. H., Mazziota, J. C., Alazraki, A., Selin, C., Ferng, H.-K., Munford, P. & Phelps, M. (1992). Caudate glucose metabolic rate changes with both drug and behavior therapy for obsessive-compulsive disorder. *Arch. Gen. Psychiat., 49*, 681–9.

Baxter, L. R., Jr., Schwartz, J. M., & Guze, B. H. (1991). Brain imaging: Toward a neuroanatomy of OCD. In J. Zohar, T. Insel, & S. Rasmussen (Eds.), *The psychobiology of obsessive-compulsive disorder*. New York: Springer.

Bayer, R. (1981). *Homosexuality and American psychiatry*. New York: Basic Books.

Beach, S. R. H., & O'Leary, K. D. (1992). Treating depression in the context of marital discord: Outcome and predictors of response of marital therapy versus cognitive therapy. *Behav. Ther., 23*, 507–28.

Beardslee, W. R., Bemporad, J., Keller, M. B., & Klerman, G. L. (1983). Children of parents with major affective disorder: A review. *Amer. J. Psychiat., 140*, 825–32.

Beason-Hazen, S., Nasrallah, H. A., & Bornstein, R. A. (1994). Self-report of symptoms and neuropsychological performance in asymptomatic HIV-positive individuals. *J. Neuropsychiat. Clin. Neurosci., 6*(1), 43–49.

Bebbington, P., Brugha, T., McCarthy, B., Potter, J., Sturt, E., Wykes, T., Katz, R., & McGuffin, P. (1988). The Camberwell collaborative depression study I. Depressed probands: Adversity and the form of depression. *Brit. J. Psychiat., 152*, 754–65.

Beck, A. T. (1967). *Depression: Clinical, experimental and theoretical aspects*. New York: Harper & Row.

Beck, A. T. (1976). *Cognitive therapy and the emotional disorders*. New York: International Universities Press.

Beck, A. T. (1983). Cognitive therapy of depression: New perspectives. In P. J. Clayton & J. E. Barrett (Eds.), *Treatment of depression: Old controversies and new approaches* (pp. 265–90). New York: Raven Press.

Beck, A. T. (1985). Theoretical perspectives on clinical anxiety. In A. H. Tuma & J. D. Maser (Eds.), *Anxiety and the anxiety disorders* (pp. 183–98). Hillsdale, NJ: Erlbaum.

Beck, A. T., & Emery, G., (with) Greenberg, R. L. (1985). *Anxiety disorders and phobias: A cognitive perspective*. New York: Basic Books.

Beck, A. T., & Ward, C. H. (1961). Dreams of depressed patients: Characteristic themes in manifest content. *Arch. Gen. Psychiat. (Chicago), 5*, 462–67.

Beck, A. T., & Weishaar, M. (1989). Cognitive therapy. In A. Freeman, K. M. Simon, L. E. Beutler, & H. Arkowitz (Eds.), *Comprehensive handbook of cognitive therapy* (pp. 21–36). New York: Plenum.

Beck, A. T., Beck, R., & Kovacs, M. (1975). Classification of suicidal behaviors: I. Qualifying intent and medical lethality. *Amer. J. Psychiat., 132*(3), 285–87.

Beck, A. T., Brown, G., & Steer, R. A. (1989). Prediction of eventual suicide in psychiatric inpatients by clinical ratings of hopelessness. *J. Cons. Clin. Psychol., 57*, 309–10.

Beck, A. T., Freeman, A., and Associates (1990). *Cognitive therapy of personality disorders*. New York: Guilford.

Beck, A. T., Hollon, S. D., Young, J. E., Bedrosian, R. C., & Budenz, D. (1985). Treatment of depression with cognitive therapy and amitriptyline. *Arch. Gen. Psychiat., 42*, 142–48.

Beck, A. T., Rush, A. J., Shaw, B., & Emery, G. (1979). *Cognitive therapy of depression: A treatment manual*. New York: Guilford.

Beck, A. T., Steer, R., Kovacs, M., & Garrison, B. (1985) Hopelessness and eventual suicide: A 10-year prospective study of patients hospitalized with suicidal ideation. *Amer. J. Psychiat., 142*, 559–563.

Beck, A. T., Steer, R. A., Sanderson, W. C., & Skeie, T. M. (1991). Panic disorder and suicidal ideation and behavior: Discrepant findings in psychiatric outpatients. *Amer. J. Psychiat., 148*, 1195–9.

Beck, A. T., Wright, F., Newman, C., & Liese, B. (1993). *Cognitive therapy of substance abuse*. New York: Guilford.

Beck, J. G. (1992) Behavioral approaches to sexual dysfunction. In S. Turner, K. Calhoun, & H. Adams (Eds.), *Handbook of clinical behavior therapy* (2nd ed.). New York: Wiley.

Becker, E., Rinck, M., & Margraf, J. (1994). Memory bias in panic disorder. *J. Abnorm. Psychol., 103*, 396–9.

Becker, J. V., & Kaplan, M. S. (1991). Rape victims: Issues, theories, and treatment. *Ann. Rev. Sex Res., 2,* 267–92.

Beckham, E. E., & Leber, W. R. (1985a). The comparative efficacy of psychotherapy and pharmacotherapy for depression. In E. E. Beckham & W. R. Leber (Eds.), *Handbook of depression: Treatment, assessment, and research* (pp. 316–42). Homewood, IL: Dorsey Press.

Beckham, E. E., & Leber, W. R. (Eds.). (1985b). *Handbook of depression: Treatment, assessment, and research.* Homewood, IL: Dorsey Press.

Bednar, R. L., & Kaul, T. (1994). Experiential group research. In A. E. Bergin & S. L. Garfield (Eds.), *Handbook of psychotherapy and behavior change* (4th ed., pp. 631–63). New York: Wiley.

Beech, H. R., Burns, L. E., & Sheffield, B. F. (1982). *A behavioral approach to the management of stress.* New York: Wiley.

Beers, C. (1970). *A mind that found itself* (rev. ed.). New York: Doubleday. (Originally published in 1908.)

Beitman, B. D., & Klerman, G. L. (Eds), (1991). *Integrating pharmacotherapy and psychotherapy.* Washington, DC: American Psychiatric Press.

Bell, A. P., & Weinberg, M. S. (1978). *Homosexualities: A study of diversity among men and women.* New York: Simon & Schuster.

Bell, A. P., Weinberg, M. S., & Hammersmith, S. K. (1981). *Sexual preference: Its development in men and women.* Bloomington, IN: Indiana University Press.

Bell, E., Jr. (1958). The basis of effective military psychiatry. *Dis. Nerv. Sys., 19,* 283–88.

Bellak, L. & Abrams, D. M. (1993). *The Thematic Apperception Test, the Children's Apperception Test, and the Senior Apperception Technique in clinical use.* Boston: Allyn & Bacon.

Bellman, M. (1966). Studies on encopresis. *Acta Paediatr. Scandin.* Suppl., *170,* 121.

Belsher, G. & Costello, C. G. (1988). Relapse after recovery from unipolar depression: A critical review. *Psychol. Bull., 104,* 84–96.

Belsky, J. (1993). Etiology of child maltreatment: A developmental-ecological analysis. *Psychol. Bull., 114,* 413–34.

Belter, R. W., & Shannon, M. P. (1993). Impact of natural disasters on children and families. In C. F. Saylor (Ed.), *Children and disasters* (pp. 85–104). New York: Plenum.

Bem, D. J. (1972). Self-perception theory. In L. Berkowitz (Ed.), *Advances in experimental social psychology* (Vol. 6). New York: Academic Press.

Bemis, K. M. (1978). Current approaches to the etiology and treatment of anorexia nervosa. *Psychol. Bull., 85,* 593–617.

Ben-Porath, Y. S., & Butcher, J. N. (1989). The comparability of MMPI and MMPI-2 scales and profiles. *Psychol. Assess., 1,* 345–47.

Benedict, R. (1934). Anthropology and the abnormal. *J. Gen. Psychol., 10,* 59–82.

Bengelsdorf, I. S. (1970, Mar. 5). Alcohol, morphine addictions believed chemically similar. *Los Angeles Times,* II, 7.

Benjamin, L. S. (1974). Structural analysis of social behavior. *Psychol. Rev., 81,* 392–425.

Benjamin, L. S. (1982). Use of structural analysis of social behavior (SASB) to guide intervention in psychotherapy. In J. C. Anchin & D. L. Kiesler (Eds.), *Handbook of interpersonal psychotherapy.* New York: Pergamon.

Benjamin, L. S. (1993). *Interpersonal diagnosis and treatment of personality disorders.* New York: Guilford.

Benjamin, L. S. (1994). SASB: A bridge between personality theory and clinical psychology. *Psychol. Inq., 5,* 273–316.

Bennett, A. E. (1947). Mad doctors. *J. Nerv. Ment. Dis., 106,* 11–18.

Bentler, P. M., & Prince, C. (1969). Personality characteristics of male transvestites. III. *J. Abnorm. Psychol., 74*(2), 140–43.

Bentler, P. M., & Prince, C. (1970). Psychiatric symptomology in transvestites. *J. Clin. Psychol., 26*(4), 434–35.

Bentler, P. M., Shearman, R. W., & Prince, C. (1970). Personality characteristics of male transvestites. *J. Clin. Psychol., 126*(3), 287–91.

Bentovim, A., Boston, P., & Van Elburg, A. (1987). Child sexual abuse—children and families referred to a treatment project and the effects of intervention. *Brit. Med. J., 295,* 1453–57.

Berenbaum, H., & Fujita, F. (1994). Schizophrenia and personality: Exploring the boundaries and connections between vulnerability and outcome. *J. Abnorm. Psychol., 103*(1), 148–58.

Berenbaum, H., & Garske, J. P. (1993). The effect of stress on hedonic capacity. *J. Abnorm. Psychol., 102,* 474–81.

Berenbaum, S. A., & Hines, M. (1992). Early androgens are related to childhood sex-typed toy preferences. *Psychol. Sci., 3,* 203–206.

Berg, A. (1954). *The sadist* (O. Illner & G. Godwin, Trans.). New York: Medical Press of New York.

Bergen, J. A., Eyland, E. A., Campbell, J. A., Jenkins, P., Kellehear, K., Richards, A., & Beumont, P. J. V. (1989). The course of tardive dyskinesia in patients on long-term neuroleptics. *Brit. J. Psychiat., 154,* 523–28.

Berger, P. A. (1978). Medical treatment of mental illness. *Science, 200,* 974–81.

Bergin, A. E., & Lambert, M. J. (1978). The evaluation of therapeutic outcomes. In S. L. Garfield & A. E. Bergin (Eds.), *Handbook of psychotherapy and behavior change* (2nd ed.). New York: Wiley.

Berlin, F. S. (1994, May). The case for castration, part 2. *Washington Monthly, 26,* 28–29.

Berlin, F. S., & Malin, H. M. (1991). Media distortion of the public's perception of recidivism and psychiatric rehabilitation. *Amer. J. Psychiat., 148,* 1572–76.

Berman, A. L., & Jobes, D. A. (1991). *Adolescent suicide.* Washington, DC: American Psychological Association.

Berman, A. L., & Jobes, D. A. (1992). Suicidal behavior of adolescents. In B. Bongar (Ed.), *Suicide: Guidelines for assessment, management and treatment.* New York: Oxford University Press.

Berman, K. F., Torrey, E. F., Daniel, D. G., & Weinberger, D. R. (1992). Regional cerebral blood flow in monozygotic twins discordant and concordant for schizophrenia. *Arch. Gen. Psychiat., 49*(12), 927–34.

Bernhardt, B., Meertz, E., & Schonfeldt-Bausch, P. (1985). Basal ganglia and limbic system pathology in schizophrenia: A morphometric study of brain volume and shrinkage. *Arch. Gen. Psychiat., 42,* 784–91.

Bernstein, E. M., & Putnam, F. W. (1986). Development, reliability, and validity of a dissociation scale. *J. Nerv. Ment. Dis., 174,* 727–35.

Bernstein, G. A., & Borchardt, C. M. (1991). Anxiety disorders of childhood and adolescence: A critical review. *J. Amer. Acad. Adoles. Psychiat., 30,* 519–32.

Berrios, G. (1990). A British contribution to the history of functional brain surgery. Special Issue: History of psychopharmacology. *J. Psychopharm., 4,* 140–44.

Bertelsen, A., Harvald, B., & Hauge, M. (1977). A Danish twin study of manic depressive disorders. *Brit. J. Psychiat., 130,* 330–51.

Besharov, D. J. (1992, July). Yes: Consider chemical treatment. *ABA Journal, 78,* 42.

Beutler, L. E., Machado, P. P., & Neufeldt, S. A. (1994). Therapist variables. In A. E. Bergin & S. L. Garfield (Eds.), *Handbook of psychotherapy and behavior change* (4th ed., pp. 229–69). New York: Wiley.

Beveridge, A. W., & Renvoize, E. B. (1988). Electricity: A history of its use in the treatment of mental illness in Britain during the second half of the 19th century. *Brit. J. Psychiat., 153,* 157–62.

Bibring, E. (1953). The mechanism of depression. In P. Greenacre (Ed.), *Affective disorders* (pp. 13–48). New York: International University Press.

Bieber, I., Dain, H. J., Dince, P. R., Drellich, M. G., Grand, H. G., Gundlach, R. H., Kremer, M. W., Rifkin, A. H., Wilbur, C. B. & Bieber, T. B. (1962). *Homosexuality: A psychoanalytic study of male homosexuals.* New York: Basic Books.

Biederman, J., Rosenbaum, J. F., Hirschfeld, D. R., Faraone, S., Bolduc, E., Gersten, M., Meminger, S., Kagan, J., Snidman, N. & Reznick, J. S. (1990). Psychiatric correlates of behavioral inhibition in young children of parents with and without psychiatric disorders. *Arch. Gen. Psychiat., 47,* 21–26.

Bifulco, A. T., Brown, G. W., & Harris, T. O. (1987). Childhood loss of parent, lack of adequate parental care and adult depression: A replication. *J. Affect. Dis., 12,* 115–28.

Billings, A. G., Cronkite, R. C., & Moos, R. H. (1983). Social-environmental factors in unipolar depression: Comparisons of depressed patients and nondepressed controls. *J. Abnorm. Psychol., 92,* 119–33.

Billy, J. O. G., Tanfer, K., Grady, W. R., & Klepinger, D. H. (1993). The sexual behavior of men in the United States. *Fam. Plann. Perspect., 25,* 52–60.

Binder, R. L., & McNiel, D. E. (1988). Effects of diagnosis and context of dangerousness. *Amer. J. Psychiat., 145,* 788–92.

Birkhimer, L. J., Curtis, J. L., & Jann, M. W. (1985). Use of carbamazepine in psychiatric disorders. *Clin. Pharm., 4,* 425–34.

Birns, B., & Bridger, W. (1977). Cognitive development and social class. In J. Wortis (Ed.), *Mental retardation and developmental disabilities* (Vol. 9, pp. 203–33). New York: Brunner/Mazel.

Bishop, E. R., Mobley, M. C., & Farr, W. F., Jr. (1978). Lateralization of conversion symptoms. *Compr. Psychiat., 19,* 393–96.

Bisnaire, L. M., Firestone, P., & Rynard, D. (1990). Factors associated with academic achievement in children following parental separation. *Amer. J. Orthopsychiat., 60,* 67–76.

Black, A. (1974). The natural history of obsessional neurosis. In H. R. Beech (Ed.), *Obsessional states.* London: Methuen.

Black, D. W., Noyes, R., Goldstein, R. B., & Blum, N. (1992) A family study of obsessive-compulsive disorder. *Arch. Gen. Psychiat., 49,* 362–368.

Black, D. W., Winoker, G., Bell, S., Nasrallah, A., & Hulbert, J. (1988). Complicated mania: Comorbidity and immediate outcome in the treatment of mania. *Arch. Gen. Psychiat., 45,* 232–36.

Black, D. W., Yates, W., Petty, F., Noyes, R., & Brown, K. (1986). Suicidal behavior in alcoholic males. *Compr. Psychiat., 273*(3), 227–33.

Blackburn, I. M., Bishop, S., Glen, A. I. M., Whalley, L. J., & Christie, J. E. (1981). The efficacy of cognitive therapy in depression: A treatment trial using cognitive therapy and pharmacotherapy, each alone and in combination. *Brit. J. Psychiat., 139,* 181–89.

Blaine, J. D. (1992). Introduction. In J.D. Blaine (Ed.), *Buprenorphine: An alternative treatment for opioid dependence* (pp. 1–4). Washington, DC: U.S. Department of Health and Human Services.

Blanchard, E. B. (1992). Psychological treatment of benign headache disorders. *J. Cons. Clin. Psychol., 60*(4), 537–51.

Blanchard, E. B. (1994). Behavioral medicine and health psycholgy. In A. E. Bergin & S. L. Garfield (Eds.), *Handbook of psychotherapy and behavior change* (pp. 701–33). New York: Wiley.

Blanchard, E. B., & Andrasik, F. (1982). Psychological assessment and treatment of headache: Recent developments and emerging issues. *J. Cons. Clin. Psychol., 50*(6), 859–79.

Blanchard, E. B., & Epstein, L. H. (1978). *A biofeedback primer.* Reading, MA: Addison-Wesley.

Blanchard, E. B., & Young, L. D. (1973). Self-control of cardiac functioning: A promise as yet unfulfilled. *Psychol. Bull., 79,* 145–63.

Blanchard, E. B., & Young, L. D. (1974). Clinical applications of biofeedback training: A review of evidence. *Arch. Gen. Psychiat., 30,* 573–89.

Blanchard, E. B., Andrasik, F., Ahles, T. A., Teders, S. J., & O'Keefe, D. (1980). Migraine and tension headache: A meta-analytic review. *Behav. Ther., 11,* 613–31.

Blanchard, E. B., Andrasik, F., Neff, D. F., Saunders, N. L., Arena, J. G., Pallmeyer, T. P., Teders, S. J., & Jurish, S. G. (1983). Four process studies in the behavioral treatment of chronic headache. *Behav. Res. Ther., 21,* 209–20.

Blanchard, E. B., Appelbaum, K. A., Radnitz, C. L., Michultka, D., Morrill, B., Kirsch, C., Hillhouse, J., Evans, D. D., Guarnieri, P., Attanasio, V., Andrasik, F., Jaccard J., & Dentinger, M. P. (1990a). Placebo-controlled evaluation of abbreviated progressive muscle relaxation and of relaxation combined with cognitive therapy in the treatment of tension headache. *J. Cons. Clin. Psychol., 58,* 210–15.

Blanchard, E. B., Appelbaum, K. A., Radnitz, C. L., Merrill, B., Michultka, D., Kirsch, C., Guarinieri, P., Millhouse, J., Evans, D. D., Jaccard, J., & Barron, K. D. (1990b). A controlled evaluation of thermal biofeedback and thermal biofeedback combined with cognitive therapy in the treatment of vascular headache. *J. Cons. Clin. Psychol., 58,* 216–24.

Blanchard, E. B., Miller, S. T., Abel G. G., Haynes, M. R., & Wicker, R. (1979). Evaluation of biofeedback in treatment of borderline essential hypertension. *J. Appl. Beh. Anal., 12,* 99–109.

Blanchard, J. J., & Neale, J. M. (1994). The neuropsychological signature of schizophrenia: Generalized or differential deficit. *Amer. J. Psychiat., 151*(1), 40–48.

Blanchard, R., (1985). Typology of male-to-female transsexualism. *Arch. Sex. Behav., 14,* 247–61.

Blanchard, R. (1989). The classification and labeling of nonhomosexual gender dysphorias. *Arch. Sex. Behav., 18,* 315–34.

Blanchard, R. (1991). Clinical observations and systematic study of autogynephilia. *J. Sex Marit. Ther., 17,* 235–51.

Blanchard, R. (1992). Nonmonotonic relation of autogynephilia and heterosexual attraction. *J. Abnorm. Psych., 101,* 271–76.

Blanchard, R. (1994). A structural equation model for age at clinical presentation in nonhomosexual male gender dysphorics. *Arch. Sex. Behav., 23,* 311–32.

Blanchard, R., & Hucker S. J. (1991). Age, transvestitism, bondage, and concurrent paraphilic activities in 117 fatal cases of autoerotic asphyxia. *Brit. J. Psychiat., 159,* 371–77.

Bland, R., Orn, H., & Newman, S. (1988). Lifetime prevalence of psychiatric disorders in Edmonton. *Acta Psychiatr. Scandin., 77* (Suppl. 338), 24–32.

Blashfield, R. K., & Breen, M. J. (1989). Face validity of the DSM-III-R personality disorders. *Amer. J. Psychiat., 146,* 1575–79.

Blaszczynski, A., McConaghy, N., & Frankova, A. (1989). Crime, antisocial personality and pathological gambling. *Journal of Gambling Behavior, 5,* 137–52.

Blatt, S. (1974). Levels of object representation in anaclitic and introjective depression. *The Psychoanalytic Study of the Child, 24,* 107–57.

Blatt, S., & Zuroff, D. (1992). Interpersonal relatedness and self definition: Two prototypes for depression. *Clin. Psychol. Rev., 12,* 527–62.

Blatt, S. J., D'Afflitti, J. P., & Quinlan, D. M. (1976). Experiences of depression in normal young adults. *J. Abnorm. Psychol., 85,* 383–89.

Blazer, D., George, L. K., Landerman, R., Pennybacker, M., & Melville, M. L. (1985). Psychiatric disorders: A rural/urban comparison. *Arch. Gen. Psychiat., 42,* 651–56.

Bleeker, E. (1968). Many asthma attacks psychological. *Sci. News, 93*(17), 406.

Blehar, M. C., & Rosenthal, N. E. (1989). Seasonal affective disorders and phototherapy: Report of a National Institute of Mental Health-sponsored workshop. *Arch. Gen. Psychiat., 46,* 469–74.

Bleuler, E. (1950). *Dementia praecox or the group of schizophrenias.* New York: International Universities Press. (Originally published in 1911.)

Bleuler, M. (1978). The long-term course of schizophrenic psychoses. In L. C. Wynne, R. L. Cromwell, & S. Matthysse (Eds.), *The nature of schizophrenia: New approaches to research and treatment* (pp. 631–36). New York: Wiley.

Bloch, H. S. (1969). Army clinical psychiatry in the combat zone—1967–1968. *Amer. J. Psychiat., 126,* 289.

Block, J. H., Block, J., & Gjerde, P. F. (1986) The personality of children prior to divorce: A prospective study. *Child Develop., 57,* 827–840.

Block, J., & Gjerde, P. F. (1990) Depressive symptoms in late adolescence: A longitudinal perspective on personality antecedents. In J. Rolf, A. S. Masten, D. Cicchetti, K. H. Nuechterlein, & S. Weintraub (Eds), *Risk and protective factors in the development of psychopathology.* New York: Cambridge University Press.

Bloom, B. L. (1992). Computer-assisted psychological intervention: A review and commentary. *Clin. Psychol. Rev., 12,* 169–197.

Bloom, B. L., Asher, S. J., & White, S. W. (1978). Marital disruption as a stressor: A review and analysis. *Psychol. Bull., 85,* 867–94.

Blount, R. L., Dahlquist, L. M., Baer, R. A., & Wuori, D. (1984). A brief, effective method for teaching children to swallow pills. *Behav. Ther., 15,* 381–87.

Blum, R. (1969). *Society and drugs* (Vol. 1). San Francisco: Jossey-Bass.

Blume, E. S. (1990). *Secret survivors: Uncovering incest and its aftereffects.* New York: Ballantine.

Blumenthal, S. J. (1990). Youth suicide: Risk factors, assessment, and treatment of adolescent and young adult suicidal patients. *Psychiat. Clin. N. Amer., 13,* 511–56.

Bockhoven, J. S. (1972). *Moral treatment in community mental health.* New York: Springer.

Boehm, G. (1968). At last—a nonaddicting substitute for morphine? *Today's Health, 46*(4), 69–72.

Bogerts, B. (1993). Recent advances in the neuropathology of schizophrenia. *Schizo. Bull., 19*(2), 431–45.

Bohn, M. J. (1993). Alcoholism. *Psychiat. Clin. N. Amer., 16,* 679–92.

Bolen, D. W., & Boyd, W. H. (1968). Gambling and the gambler. *Arch. Gen. Psychiatr., 18*(5), 617–30.

Bolen, D. W., Caldwell, A. B., & Boyd, W. H. (1975, June). *Personality traits of pathological gamblers.* Paper presented at the Second Annual Conference on Gambling, Lake Tahoe, NV.

Bolger, N. (1990). Coping as a personality process: A prospective study. *J. Pers. Soc. Psychol., 59,* 525–37.

Boll, T. J. (1980). The Halstead-Reitan neuropsychological battery. In S. B. Filskov & T. J. Boll (Eds.), *Handbook of neurophysiology.* New York: Wiley Interscience.

Bolles, R. C., & Fanselow, M. S. (1982). Endorphins and behavior. *Annu. Rev. Psychol., 33,* 87–101.

Booth, B. M., Cook, C. L., & Blow, F. C. (1992a). Comorbid mental disorders in patients with AMA discharges from alcoholism treatment. *Hosp. Comm. Psychiat., 43,* 730–31.

Booth, B. M., Russel, D. W., Soucek, S., & Laughlin, P. R. (1992b). Social support and outcome of alcoholism treatment: An exploratory analysis. *Amer. J. Drug Alcoh. Abuse, 18,* 87–101.

Booth, B. M., Russell, D. W., Yates, W. R., & Laughlin, P. R. (1992c). Social support and depression in men during alcoholism treatment. *J. Subst. Abuse, 4,* 57–67.

Booth-Kewley, S., & Friedman, H. S. (1987). Psychological predictors of heart disease: A quantitative review. *Psychol. Bull., 101,* 343–62.

Borg, W. R., & Ascione, F. R. (1982). Classroom management in elementary mainstreaming classrooms. *J. Educ. Psychol., 74,* 84–95.

Borkovec, T. D. (1970). Autonomic reactivity to sensory stimulation in psychopathic, neurotic, and normal juvenile delinquents. *J. Cons. Clin. Psychol., 35,* 217–22.

Borkovec, T. D. (1985). The role of cognitive and somatic cues in anxiety and anxiety disorders: Worry and relation-induced anxiety. In A. H. Tuma & J. D. Maser (Eds.), *Anxiety and the anxiety disorders* (pp. 463–78). Hillsdale, NJ: Erlbaum.

Borkovec, T. D. (1988). Worry: Physiological and cognitive processes. In P. Eelen (Ed.), *Anxiety and the anxiety disorders.* Hillsdale, NJ: Erlbaum.

Borkovec, T. D., Shadick, R. N., & Hopkins, M. (1991). The nature of normal and pathological worry. In R. M. Rapee & D. H. Barlow (Eds.), *Chronic Anxiety.* New York: Guilford.

Borod, J. C. (1992). Interhemispheric and intrahemispheric control of emotion: A focus on unilateral brain damage. *J. Cons. Clin. Psychol., 60*(3), 339–48.

Boronow, J., Pickar, D., Ninan, P. T., Roy, A., & Hommer, D. (1985). Atrophy limited to the third ventricle in chronic schizophrenic patients: Report of a controlled series. *Arch. Gen. Psychiat., 42,* 266–71.

Borthwick-Duffy, S. A. (1994). Epidemiology and prevalence of psychopathology in people with mental retardation. *J. Cons. Clin. Psychol., 62*(1), 17–27.

Borus, J. F. (1974). Incidence maladjustment in Vietnam returnees. *Arch. Gen. Psychiat., 30*(4), 554–57.

Boskind-White, M., & White, W. C. (1983). *Bulimarexia: The binge-purge cycle.* New York: Norton.

Boskind-White, M., & White, W. C. (1986). Bulimarexia: A historical-sociocultural perspective. In K. D. Brownell & J. P. Foreyt (Eds.), *Handbook of eating disorders* (pp. 353–66). New York: Basic Books.

Botvin, G. J. (1983). Prevention of adolescent substance abuse through the development of personal and social competence. *National Institute on Drug Abuse Research Monograph Series, 47,* 115–40.

Botvin, G. J., & Tortu, S. (1988). Preventing substance abuse through life skills training. In R. H. Price, E. L. Cowen, R. P. Lorion, & J. Ramos-McKay (Eds.), *14 ounces of prevention.* Washington, DC: American Psychological Association.

Botvin, G. J., Baker, E., Dusenbury, L., Tortu, S., & Botvin, E. M. (1990). Preventing adolescent drug abuse through a multimodal cognitive-behavioral approach: Results of a 3 year study. *J. Cons. Clin. Psychol., 58,* 437–57.

Boucher, J. (1981). Memory for recent events in autistic children. *J. Autism Devel. Dis., 11*(3), 293–301.

Bourdon, K. H., Boyd, J. H., Rae, D. S., Burns, B. J., Thompson, J. W., & Locke, B. Z. (1988). Gender differences in phobias: Results of the ECA community survey. *Journal of Anxiety Disorders, 2,* 227–41.

Bourne, P. G. (1970). Military psychiatry and the Vietnam experience. *Amer. J. Psychiat., 127*(4), 481–88.

Bouton, M. E. (1994). Conditioning, remembering, and forgetting. *J. Exper. Psychol.: Animal Behavior Processes, 20,* 219–231.

Bowen, R. C., Offord, D. R., & Boyle, M. H. (1990). The prevalence of overanxious disorder and separation anxiety disorder: Results from the Ontario Child Health Study. *J. Amer. Acad. Child Adoles. Psychiat., 29,* 753–58.

Bowlby, J. (1960). Separation anxiety. *Inter. J. Psychoanal., 41,* 89–93.

Bowlby, J. (1973). *Separation: Anxiety and anger. Psychology of attachment and loss series* (Vol. 2). New York: Basic Books.

Bowlby, J. (1980). *Attachment and loss, III: Loss, sadness, and depression.* New York: Basic Books.

Boyd, J. H., & Weissman, M. M. (1985). Epidemiology of major affective disorders. In R. Michels, J. O. Cavenar, H. K. H. Brodie, A. M. Cooper, S. B. Guze, L. L. Judd, G. L. Klerman, & A. J. Solnit (Eds.), *Psychiatry* (Vol. 3). Philadelphia: Lippincott.

Boyd, J. H., Burke, J. D., Gruenberg, E., Holzer, C. E., Rae, D. S., George, L. K., Karno, M., Stoltzman, R., McEvoy, L., & Nestadt, G. (1984). Exclusion criteria of DSM-III: A study of co-occurrence of hierarchy-free syndromes. *Arch. of Gen. Psychiat., 41,* 983–89.

Boyd, W. H., & Bolen, D. W. (1970). The compulsive gambler and spouse in group psychotherapy. *International Journal of Group Psychotherapy, 20,* 77–90.

Bradbury, T. N., & Miller, G. A. (1985). Season of birth in schizophrenia: A review of evidence, methodology, and etiology. *Psychol. Bull., 98,* 569–94.

Bradford, J. M. (1990) The antiandrogen and hormonal treatment of sex offenders. In W. L. Marshall, D. R. Laws, & H. E. Barbaree (Eds.), *Handbook of sexual assault: Issues, theories, and treatment of the offender* (pp. 363–85). New York: Plenum.

Bradley, L. A., & Prokop, C. K. (1981). The relationship between medical psychology and behavioral medicine. In C. K. Prokop & L. A. Bradley (Eds.), *Medical psychology: Contributions to behavioral medicine.* New York: Academic Press.

Bradley, L. A., & Prokop, C. K. (1982). Research methods in contemporary medical psychology. In P. C. Kendall & J. N. Butcher (Eds.), *Handbook of research methods in clinical psychology.* New York: Wiley Interscience.

Braff, D. L. (1993). Information processing and attention dysfunctions in schizophrenia. *Schizo. Bull., 19*(2), 233–59.

Braginsky, B. M., & Braginsky, D. D. (1974). The mentally retarded: Society's Hansels and Gretels. *Psych. Today, 7*(10), 18, 20–21, 24, 26, 28–30.

Braginsky, B. M., Braginsky, D. D., & Ring, K. (1969). *Methods of madness: The mental hospital as a last resort.* New York: Holt, Rinehart & Winston.

Brandsma, J. M., Maultsby, M. C., & Welsh, R. J. (1980). *Outpatient treatment of alcoholism: A review and comparative study.* Baltimore: University Park Press.

Brane, G. (1986). Normal aging and dementia disorders: Coping and crisis in the family. *Prog. in Neuropsychopharmacol. Biol. Psychiatry, 10,* 287–95.

Braun, B. G., & Sachs, R. G. (1985). The development of multiple personality disorder: Predisposing, precipitating, and perpetuating factors. In R. P. Kluft (Eds.), *Childhood antecedents of multiple personality disorder* (pp. 37–64). Washington, DC: American Psychiatric Press.

Braun, P., Kochansky, G., Shapiro, R., Greenberg, S., Gudeman, J. E., Johnson, S., & Shore, M. (1981). Overview: Deinstitutionalization of psychiatric patients, a critical review of outcome studies. *Amer. J. Psychiat., 138*(6), 736–49.

Brayfield, A. H., et al. (1965). Special Issue: Testing and public policy. *Amer. Psychol., 20,* 857–1005.

Brebner, A., Hallworth, H. J., & Brown, R. I. (1977). Computer-assisted instruction programs and terminals for the mentally retarded. In P. Mittler (Ed.), *Research to practice in mental retardation* (Vol. 2, pp. 421–26). Baltimore: University Park Press.

Brecksville V. A. Medical Center. (1981). *Annual report for 1981: Gambling treatment program.* Cleveland, OH.

Breggin, P. R. (1979). *Electroshock: Its brain-disabling effects.* New York: Springer.

Breggin, P. R. (1990). Brain damage, dementia, and persistent cognitive dysfunction associated with neuroleptic drugs: Evidence, etiology, implications. *Journal of Mind and Behavior, 11*(3–4), 425–63.

Breggin, P. R. (1991). *Toxic psychiatry.* New York: St. Martin's Press.

Breier, A., Buchanan, R. W., Kirkpatrick, B., Davis, O. R., Irish, D., Summerfelt, A., & Carpenter, W. T. (1994). Effects of clozapine on positive and negative symptoms in outpatients with schizophrenia. *Amer. J. Psychiat., 151*(1), 20–26.

Breier, A., Charney, D. S., & Heninger, G. R. (1984). Major depression in patients with agoraphobia and panic disorder. *Arch. Gen. Psychiat., 41,* 1129–35.

Breitner, J. C. S., (1986). On methodology and appropriate inference regarding possible genetic factors in typical, late-onset AD. *Neurobiol. Aging, 7,* 476–77.

Breitner, J. C. S., Gatz, M., Bergem, A. L. M., Christian, J. C., Mortimer, J. A., McClearn, G. E., Heston, L. L., Welsh, K. A., Anthony, J. C., Folstein, M. F., & Radebaugh, T. S. (1993). Use of twin cohorts for research in Alzheimer's disease. *Neurology, 43,* 261–67.

Bremner, J. D., Southwick, S. M., & Charney, D. S. (1995). Etiological factors in the development of posttraumatic stress disorder. In C. M. Mazure (Ed.). *Does stress cause psychiatric illness?* Washington, DC: American Psychiatric Association.

Breslau, N. (1990). Does brain dysfunction increase children's vulnerability to environmental stress? *Arch. Gen. Psychiat., 47,* 15–20.

Breslau, N., Davis, G.C., Andreski, P., & Peterson, E. (1991). Traumatic events and posttraumatic stress disorder in an urban population of young adults. *Arch. Gen. Psychiat., 48,* 218–22.

Breton, J. J., Valla, J. P., & Lambert, J. (1993). Industrial disaster and mental health of children and their parents. *J. Amer. Acad. Child Adoles. Psychiat., 32,* 438–45.

Bretschneider, J. G., & McCoy, N. L. (1988). Sexual interest and behavior in healthy 80- to 102-year-olds. *Arch. Sex. Behav., 17,* 109–29.

Brewin, C. R., Andrews, B., & Gotlib, I. H. (1993). Psychopathology and early experience: A reappraisal of retrospective reports. *Psychol. Bull., 113,* 82–98.

Bridges, F. A., & Cicchetti, D. (1982). Mothers' ratings of the temperament characteristics of Down's Syndrome infants. *Develop. Psychol., 18,* 238–44.

Brinckerhoff, L. C. (1993). Self-advocacy: A critical skill for college students with learning disabilities. *Family & Community Health, 16*(3), 23–33.

Brom, D., Kleber, R. J., & Defares, P. B. (1989). Brief psychotherapy for posttraumatic stress disorders. *J. Cons. Clin. Psychol., 57,* 607–12.

Brom, D., Kleber, R. J., & Hofman, M. C. (1993). Victims of traffic accidents: Incidence and prevention of post-traumatic stress disorder. *J. Clin. Psychol., 49,* 131–40.

Brookoff, D., Cook, C. S., Williams, C., & Mann, C. S. (1994). Testing reckless drivers for cocaine and marijuana. *New Engl. J. Med., 331,* 518–22.

Brooks, D. N. (1974). Recognition, memory, and head injury. *J. Neurol. Neurosurg. Psychiatry, 37*(7), 794–801.

Broun, H. & Leech, M. (1927). *Anthony Comstock: Roundsman of the Lord* (pp. 55–56, 80–81). New York: Literary Guild of America.

Brown, G. W. (1972). Life-events and psychiatric illness: Some thoughts on methodology and causality. *J. Psychosom. Res., 16,* 311–20.

Brown, G. W., & Harris, T. O. (1978). *Social origins of depression.* London: Tavistock.

Brown, G. W., & Harris, T. O. (1989). *Life events and illness.* New York: Guilford.

Brown, G. W., Harris, T., O. & Bifulco, A. T. (1985). Long-term effects of early loss of parent. In M. Rutter, C. E. Izard, & P. B. Read (Eds.), *Depression in childhood: Clinical and developmental perspectives* (pp. 251–96). New York: Guilford.

Brown, J. D., & McGill, K. L. (1989). The cost of good fortune: When positive life events produce negative health consequences. *J. Pers. Soc. Psychol., 57,* 1103–10.

Brown, J. F., & Menninger, K. A. (1940). *Psychodynamics of abnormal behavior.* New York: McGraw-Hill.

Brown, P. (1994). Toward a psychobiological model of dissociation and posttraumatic stress disorder. In S. J. Lynn & J. W. Rhue (Eds.), *Dissociation: Clinical and theoretical perspectives* (pp. 94–122). New York: Guilford.

Brown, R. I. (1977). An integrated program for the mentally handicapped. In P. Mittler (Ed.), *Research to practice in mental retardation* (Vol. 2, pp. 387–88). Baltimore: University Park Press.

Brown, R., Colter, N., Corsellis, J. A. N., Crow, T. J., & Frith, C. D. (1986). Postmortem evidence of structural brain changes in schizophrenia: Differences in brain weight, temporal horn area, and parahippocampal gyrus compared with average data. *Arch. Gen. Psychiat., 43,* 36–42.

Brown, S. J., Fann, J. R., & Grant, I. (1994). Postconcussional disorder: Time to acknowledge a common source of neurobehavioral morbidity. *J. Neuropsychiat. & Clin. Neurosci., 6*(1), 15–22.

Brown, T. A., O'Leary, T. A., & Barlow, D. H. (1993). Generalized anxiety disorder. In D. H. Barlow (Ed.), *Clinical handbook of psychological disorders.* New York: Guilford.

Brown, W. T., Jenkins, E. C., Cohen, I. L., Fisch, G. S., Wolf-Schein, E. G., Gross, A., Fein, D., Mason-Brothers, A., Ritvo, E., Ruttenberg, B. A., Bentley, W., & Castell, S. (1986). Fragile x and autism: A multicenter survey. *Amer. J. Med. Genet., 23,* 341–52.

Browne, A., & Finkelhor, D. (1986). Impact of child sexual abuse: A review of the research. *Psychol. Bull. 99,* 66–77.

Browne, E. G. (1921). *Arabian Medicine.* New York: Macmillan.

Brownell, K. D., & Rodin, J. (1994). The dieting maelstrom: Is it possible and advisable to lose weight? *Amer. Psychol., 39,* 781–91.

Brownell, K. D., & Wadden, T. A. (1992). Etiology and treatment of obesity: Understanding a serious, prevalent, and refractory disorder. *J. Cons. Clin. Psychol., 60,* 505–17.

Brownmiller, S. (1975). *Against our will: Men, women, and rape.* New York: Simon & Schuster.

Brozek, J., & Schurch, B. (1984). *Malnutrition and behavior: Critical assessment of key issues.* Lausanne, Switzerland: Nestle Foundation.

Bruch, H. (1973). *Eating disorders: Obesity, anorexia nervosa and the person within.* New York: Basic Books.

Bruch, H. (1986). Anorexia nervosa: The therapeutic task. In K. D. Brownell & J. P. Foreyt (Eds.), *Handbook of eating disorders* (pp. 328–32). New York: Basic Books.

Bruch, H. (1988). *Conversations with anorexics.* New York: Basic Books.

Bruck, M. (1987). Social and emotional adjustments of learning-disabled children. In S. J. Ceci (Ed.), *Handbook of cognitive, social, and neuropsychological aspects of learning disabilities* (Vol. 1, pp. 361–80). Hillsdale, NJ: Erlbaum.

Bruck, M., Ceci., S.J., Francouer, E., & Renick, A. (1995) Anatomically detailed dolls do not facilitate preschoolers' reports of a pediatric examination involving genital touch. *J. Exper. Psychol. Applied, 1,* 95–109.

Bry, B. H., McKeon, P., & Pandina, R. J. (1982). The extent of drug use as a function of number of risk factors. *J. Abnorm. Psychol., 91*(4), 273–79.

Bucher, B., & Lovaas, O. I. (1967). Use of aversive stimulation in behavior modification. In M. R. Jones (Ed.), *Miami symposium on the prediction of behavior 1967: Aversive stimulation* (pp. 77–145). Coral Gables, FL: University of Miami Press.

Buchsbaum, M. S., Haier, R. J., Potkin, S. G., Nuechterlein, K., Bracha, H. S., Katz, M., Lohr, J., Wu, J., Lottenberg, S., Jerabek, P. A., Trenary, M., Tafalla, R., Reynolds, C., & Bunney, W. E., Jr. (1992). Frontostriatal disorder of cerebral metabolism in never-medicated schizophrenics. *Arch. Gen. Psychiat., 49*(12), 935–41.

Buchsbaum, M. S., Murphy, D. L., Coursey, R. D., Lake, C. R., & Zeigler, M. G. (1978). Platelet monoamine oxidase, plasma dopamine betahydroxylase and attention in a "biochemical high-risk" sample. In L. C. Wynne, R. L. Cromwell, & S. Matthysse (Eds.), *The nature of schizophrenia: New approaches to research and treatment* (pp. 387–96). New York: Wiley.

Buckley, P. (1982). Identifying schizophrenic patients who should not receive medication. *Schizo. Bull., 8,* 429–32.

Buckley, P., Thompson, P., Way, L., & Meltzer, H. Y. (1994). Substance abuse among patients with treatment-resistant schizophrenia: Characteristics and implications for clozapine therapy. *Amer. J. Psychiat., 151,* 385–89.

Buckner, H. T. (1970). The transvestic career path. *Psychiatry, 3*(3), 381–89.

Budoff, M. (1977). The mentally retarded child in the mainstream of the public school: His relation to the school administration, his teachers, and his age-mates. In P. Mittler (Ed.), *Research to practice in mental retardation* (Vol. 2, pp. 307–13). Baltimore: University Park Press.

Bullard, D. M., Glaser, H. H., Heagarty, M. C., & Pivcheck, E. C. (1967). Failure to thrive in the neglected child. *Amer. J. Orthopsychiat., 37,* 680–90.

Bumbalo, J. H., & Young, D. E. (1973). The self-help phenomenon. *Amer. J. Nurs., 73,* 1588–91.

Bumpass, L. (1984). Some characteristics of children's second families. *American Journal of Sociology, 90,* 608–623.

Bunn, J. V., Booth, B. M., Cook, C. A. L., Blow, F. C., & Fortney, J. C. (1994). The relationship between mortality and intensity of inpatient alcoholism treatment. *Amer. J. Pub. Hlth., 84,* 211–14.

Burchard, J. D., & Schafer, M. (1992). Improving accountability in a service delivery system in children's mental health. *Clin. Psychol. Rev., 12,* 867–82.

Burgess, A. W., & Holmstrom, L. (1974). Rape trauma syndrome. *Amer. J. Psychiat., 131,* 981–86.

Burgess, A. W., & Holmstrom, L. (1976). Coping behavior of the rape victim. *Amer. J. Psychiat., 133,* 413–18.

Burke, K. C., Burke, J. D., Regier, D. A., & Rae, D. S. (1990). Age at onset of selected mental disorders in five community populations. *Arch. Gen. Psychiat., 47,* 511–18.

Burns, G. W. (1972). *The science of genetics.* New York: Macmillan.

Burros, W. M. (1974). The growing burden of impotence. *Fam. Hlth., 6*(5), 18–21.

Burstein, A. (1985). How common is delayed posttraumatic stress disorder? *Amer. J. Psychiat., 142*(7), 887.

Bushnell, J. A., Wells, J. E., & Oakley-Browne, M. A. (1992). Long-term effects of intrafamilial sexual abuse in childhood. *Acta Psychiatr. Scandin., 85,* 136–42.

Buss, D. M. (1989). Sex differences in human mate preferences: Evolutionary hypotheses tested in 37 cultures. *Behavioral and Brain Sciences, 12,* 1–49.

Buss, D. M. (1994). *The evolution of desire* (pp. 144–48). New York: Basic Books.

Butcher, J. N. (1979). Use of the MMPI in industry. In J. N. Butcher (Ed.), *New developments in the use of the MMPI.* Minneapolis: University of Minnesota Press.

Butcher, J. N. (1980, Nov.). The role of crisis intervention in an airport disaster plan. *Aviation, Space and Environmental Medicine,* 1260–62.

Butcher, J. N. (1984). Current developments in MMPI use: An international perspective. In J. N. Butcher & C. D. Spielberger (Eds.), *Advances in personality assessment* (Vol. 4). Hillsdale, NJ: Erlbaum.

Butcher, J. N. (1995). How to use computer-based reports. In J.N. Butcher (Ed.), *Clinical personality assessment: Practical considerations* (pp. 78–94). New York: Oxford University Press.

Butcher, J. N. (Ed.). (in press). *International applications of the MMPI-2: A handbook of research and clinical applications.* Minneapolis, MN: University of Minnesota Press.

Butcher, J. N., & Dunn, L. (1989). Human responses and treatment needs in airline disasters. In R. Gist and B. Lubin (Eds.), *Psychosocial aspects of disaster.* New York: Wiley.

Butcher, J. N., & Graham, J. R. (1994). The MMPI-2: A new standard for personality assessment and research in counseling settings. *Measurement and Evaluation in Counseling and Development, 27,* 131–50.

Butcher, J. N., & Hatcher, C. (1988). The neglected entity in air disaster planning: Psychological services. *Amer. Psychol., 43,* 724–29.

Butcher, J. N., & Pancheri, P. (1976). *Handbook of international MMPI research.* Minneapolis: University of Minnesota Press.

Butcher, J. N., & Rouse, S. (in press). Personality assessment. *Ann. Rev. Psychol.* (in press).

Butcher, J. N., Dahlstrom, W. G., Graham, J. R., Tellegen, A., & Kaemmer, B. (1989). *Minnesota Multiphasic Personality Inventory: MMPI-2: Manual for administration and scoring.* Minneapolis: University of Minnesota Press.

Butcher, J. N., Narikiyo, T., & Vitousek, K. B. (1993). Understanding abnormal behavior in cultural context. In P. B. Sutker & H. E. Adams (Eds.), *Comprehensive handbook of psychopathology* (pp. 83–105). New York: Plenum.

Butcher, J. N., Stelmachers, Z. T., & Maudal, G. R. (1983). Crisis intervention and emergency psychotherapy. In I. Weiner (Ed.), *Handbook of clinical methods* (2nd ed.). New York: Wiley.

Butcher, J. N., Williams, C. L., Graham, J. R., Archer, R., Tellegen, A., Ben-Porath, Y. S., & Kaemmer, B. (1992). *MMPI-A: Manual for administration, scoring, and interpretation.* Minneapolis: University of Minnesota Press.

Butler, G. (1989). Issues in the application of cognitive and behavioral strategies to the treatment of social phobia. *Clin. Psychol. Rev., 9,* 91–186.

Button, E. (1993). *Eating disorders: Personal construct theory and change.* New York: Wiley.

Byassee, J. E. (1977). Essential hypertension. In R. B. Williams, Jr. & W. D. Gentry (Eds.), *Behavioral approaches to medical treatment* (pp. 113–37). Cambridge, MA: Ballinger.

Bychowski, G. (1950). On neurotic obesity. *Psychoanal. Rev., 37,* 301–19.

Cade, J. F. J. (1949). Lithium salts in the treatment of psychotic excitement. *Medical Journal of Australia, 36* (part II): 349–52.

Cadoret, R. J., O'Gorman, T. W., Troughton, E., & Heywood, E. (1985). Alcoholism and antisocial personality: Interrelationships and environmental factors. *Arch. Gen. Psychiat., 42,* 161–67.

Cadoret, R. J., Troughton, E., & O'Gorman, T. W. (1987). Genetic and environmental factors in alcohol abuse and antisocial personality. *J. Stud. Alcoh., 48,* 1–8.

Calhoun, K. S., & Resick, P. A. (1993). Post-traumatic stress disorder. In D. H. Barlow (Eds.), *Clinical handbook of psychological disorders* (pp. 48–98). New York: Guilford.

Cameron, N. (1959). Paranoid conditions and paranoia. In S. Arieti (Ed.), *American handbook of psychiatry*. New York: Basic Books.

Campbell, D. (1926). *Arabian medicine and its influence on the Middle Ages*. New York: Dutton.

Campbell, M. (1987). Drug treatment of infantile autism: The past decade. In H. Meltzer (Ed.), *Psychopharmacology: The third generation of progress* (pp. 1225–31). New York: Raven Press.

Campbell, S. B., Cohn, J. F., Ross, S., Elmore, M., & Popper, S. (1990, April). *Postpartum adaptation and postpartum depression in primiparous women*. International Conference of Infant Studies, Montreal.

Cannon, T. D., & Marco, E. (1994). Structural brain abnormalities as indicators of vulnerability to schizophrenia. *Schizo. Bull., 20*(1), 89–102.

Cannon, T. D., Mednick, S. A., Parnas, J., Schulsinger, F., Praestholm, J., & Vestergaard, A. (1993). Developmental brain abnormalities in the offspring of schizophrenic mothers: I. Contributions of genetic and perinatal factors. *Arch. Gen. Psychiat., 50*(7), 551–64.

Cannon, T. D., Mednick, S. A., Parnas, J., Schulsinger, F., Praestholm, J., & Vestergaard, A. (1994). Developmental brain abnormalities in the offspring of schizophrenic mothers: II. Structural brain characteristics of schizophrenia and schizotypal personality disorder. *Arch. Gen. Psychiat., 51*(12), 955–62.

Cannon, W. B. (1929). *Bodily changes in pain, hunger, fear and rage*. New York: Appleton.

Cantor, N., Smith, E., French, R. D. S., & Mezzich, J. (1980). Psychiatric diagnosis as prototype categorization. *J. Abnorm. Psychol., 89,* 181–93.

Capaldi, D. M., & Patterson, G. R. (1994). Interrelated influences of contextual factors on antisocial behavior in childhood and adolescence for males. In D. C. Fowles, P. Sutker, & S. H. Goodman (Eds.), *Progress in experimental personality and psychopathology research*. New York: Springer.

Capron, C. & Duyme, M. (1989). Assessment of effects of socio-economic status on IQ in a full cross-fostering study. *Nature, 340,* 552–554.

Capps, L., Kasari, C., Yirmiya, N., & Sigman, M. (1993). Parental perception of emotional expressiveness in children with autism. *J. Cons. Clin. Psychol., 61,* 475–84.

Cardenas, D. D. (1993). Cognition-enhancing drugs. *J. Head Trauma Rehab., 8*(4), 112–14.

Carey, G. (1992). Twin imitation for antisocial behavior: Implications for genetic and family environment research. *J. Abnorm. Psychol., 101*(1), 18–25.

Carey, G. (1993). Genetics and violence. In A. J. Reiss & J. A. Roth (Eds.), *Understanding and preventing violence*. Washington, DC: National Academy Press.

Carey, G., & DiLalla, D. L. (1994). Personality and psychopathology: Genetic perspectives. *J. Abnorm. Psychol., 103,* 32–43.

Carey, G., & Gottesman, I. I. (1981). Twin and family studies of anxiety, phobia and obsessive disorders. In D. F. Klien & J. Rabkin (Eds.), *Anxiety: New research and changing concepts* (pp. 117–36). New York: Raven Press.

Carlson, C. L., & Bunner, M. R. (1993). Effects of methylphenidate on the academic performance of children with Attention Deficit Hyperactivity Disorder and learning disabilities. *School Psychol. Rev., 22,* 184–98.

Carlson, C. R., & Hoyle, R. H. (1993). Efficacy of abbreviated progressive muscle relaxation training: A quantitative review of behavioral medicine research. *J. Cons. Clin. Psychol., 61*(6), 1059–67.

Carlson, E. B., & Armstrong, J. (1994). The diagnosis and assessment of dissociative disorders. In S. J. Lynn & J. W. Rhue (Eds.), *Dissociation: Clinical and theoretical perspectives* (pp. 159–74). New York: Guilford.

Carlson, E. B., & Rosser-Hogan, R. (1993). Mental health status of Cambodian refugees ten years after leaving their homes. *Amer. J. Orthopsychiat., 63,* 223–31.

Carlson, M. (1990, Jan. 29). Six years of torture. *Time, 135,* 26–27.

Carlsson, A. (1986). Searching for antemortem markers premature. *Neurobiol. Aging, 7,* 400–1.

Carlsson, A. (1988). The current status of the dopamine hypothesis of schizophrenia. *Neuropsychopharmacology, 1,* 179–86.

Carothers, J. C. (1947). A study of mental derangement in Africans, and an attempt to explain its peculiarities more especially in relation to the African attitude of life. *J. Ment. Sci., 93,* 548–97.

Carothers, J. C. (1951). Frontal lobe function and the African. *J. Ment. Sci., 97,* 12–48.

Carothers, J. C. (1959). Culture, psychiatry, and the written word. *Psychiatry, 22,* 307–20.

Carpenter, W. T., & Keith, S. J. (1986). Integrative treatments in schizophrenia. *Psychiat. Clin. N. Amer., 9,* 153–64.

Carpenter, W. T., & Strauss, J. S. (1979). Diagnostic issues in schizophrenia. In L. Bellak (Ed.), *Disorders of the schizophrenic syndrome*. New York: Basic Books.

Carpenter, W. T., Buchanan, R. W., Kirkpatrick, B., Tamminga, C., & Wood, F. (1993). Strong inference, theory testing, and the neuroanatomy of schizophrenia. *Arch. of Gen. Psychiat., 50*(10), 825–31.

Carr, A. T. (1971). Compulsive neurosis: Two psychophysiological studies. *Bull. Brit. Psychol. Soc., 24,* 256–57.

Carroll, B. J. (1982). The dexamethasone suppression test for melancholia. *Brit. J. Psychiat., 140,* 292–304.

Carroll, K. M. (1993). A comparison of alternate systems for diagnosing antisocial personality disorder in cocaine abusers. *Compr. Psychiat., 181,* 436–43.

Carroll, K. M., & Rounsaville, B. J. (1993). History and significance and childhood attention deficit disorder in treatment-seeking cocaine abusers. *Compr. Psychiat., 34,* 75–82.

Carroll, K. M., Ball, S. A., & Rounsaville, B. J. (1993). A comparison of alternate systems for diagnosing antisocial personality disorder in cocaine abusers. *J. Nerv. Ment. Dis., 181,* 436–43.

Carroll, K. M., Power, M. E., Bryant, K. J., & Rounsaville, B. J. (1992). One-year follow-up status of treatment-seeking cocaine abusers: Psychopathology and dependence severity as predictors of outcome. *J. Nerv. Ment. Dis., 181,* 71–79.

Carroll, K. M., Rounsaville, B. J., Gordon, L. T., Nich, C., Jatlow, P., Bisighini, R. M., & Gawin, F. H. (1994). Psychotherapy and pharmacotherapy for ambulatory cocaine abusers. *Arch. Gen. Psychiat., 51,* 177–87.

Carruthers, M., (1980). Hazardous occupations and the heart. In C. L. Cooper & R. Payne (Eds.), *Current concerns in occupational stress*. New York: Wiley.

Carskadon, M. A. (1990). Patterns of sleep and sleepiness in adolescents. *Pediatrician, 17,* 5–12.

Carson, R. C. (1979). Personality and exchange in developing relationships. In R. L. Burgess & T. L. Huston (Eds.), *Social exchange in developing relationships*. New York: Academic Press.

Carson, R. C. (1982). Self-fulfilling prophecy, maladaptive behavior, and psychotherapy. In J. C. Anchin & D. J. Kiesler (Eds.), *Handbook of interpersonal psychotherapy* (pp. 64–77). New York: Pergamon.

Carson, R. C. (1989). Personality. *Ann. Rev. Psychol.* (Vol. 40, pp. 227–48). Palo Alto, CA: Annual Reviews.

Carson, R. C. (1990a). Needed: A new beginning. *Contemp. Psychol., 35,* 11–12.

Carson, R. C. (1990b). Assessment: What role the assessor? *J. Pers. Assess., 54,* 435–45.

Carson, R. C. (1991). Tunnel vision and schizophrenia. In W. F. Flack, D.R. Miller & M. Wiener (Eds.), *What is schizophrenia?* (pp. 245–49). New York: Springer-Verlag.

Carson, R. C. (1993). Can the Big Five help salvage the DSM? *Psychol. Inq., 4,* 98–100.

Carson, R. C. (1994a). Reflections on SASB and the assessment enterprise. *Psychol. Inq., 5,* 317–19.

Carson, R. C. (1994b, Aug.). Continuity in personality and its derangements. In S. Strack (Chair), *Circumplex models of personality: Timothy Leary's legacy.* Symposium conducted at the meeting of the American Psychological Association, Los Angeles.

Carson, R. C., & Sanislow, C. A. (1993). The schizophrenias. In P. B. Sutker & H. E. Adams (Eds.), *Comprehensive handbook of psychopathology* (2d ed. pp. 295–333). New York: Plenum.

Carson, T. P., & Carson, R. C. (1984). The affective disorders. In H. E. Adams & P. B. Sutker (Eds.), *Comprehensive handbook of psychopathology.* New York: Plenum.

Carstairs, G. M., & Kapur, R. L. (1976). *The great universe of Kota: Stress, change and mental disorder in an Indian village.* Berkeley, CA: University of California Press.

Casey, R. J., & Berman, J. S. (1985). The outcome of psychotherapy with children. *Psychol. Bull., 98,* 388–400.

Cashdan, S. (1988). *Object relations therapy: Using the relationship.* New York: Norton.

Caspi, A., & Moffitt, T. E. (in press). The continuity of maladaptive behavior: From description to understanding in the study of antisocial behavior. In D. Cicchetti & C. Cohen (Eds.), *Manual of developmental psychopathology.* New York: Wiley.

Caspi, A., Elder, G. H., & Herbener, E. S. (1990). Childhood personality and the prediction of life-course patterns. In L. N. Robins & M. Rutter (Eds.), *Straight and devious pathways from childhood to adulthood.* Cambridge, UK: Cambridge University Press.

Cassano, G. B., Akiskal, H. S., Savino, M., Musetti, L., & Perugi, G. (1992). Proposed subtypes of bipolar II and related disorders: With hypomanic episodes (or cyclothymia) and with hyperthymic temperament. *J. Affect. Dis., 26,* 127–40.

Cassano, G. B., Musetti, L., Perugi, G., Mignani, V., Soriani, A., McNair, D.M., & Akiskal, H. S. (1987). *Major depression subcategories: Their potentiality for clinical research. In: Diagnosis and treatment of depression. "Quo Vadis?"* Symposium, Sanofi Group, May 11–12, Montpellier, France.

Castiglioni, A. (1946). *Adventures of the mind.* New York: Knopf.

Cate, R. M., & Lloyd, S. A. (1992). *Courtship.* Newbury Park, CA: Sage.

Cato, C., & Rice, B. D. (1982). *Report from the study group on rehabilitation of clients with specific learning disabilities.* St. Louis: National Institute of Handicapped Research.

Caton, C. L. M., Wyatt, R. J., Felix, A., Grunberg, J., & Dominguez, B. (1993). Follow-up of chronically homeless mentally ill men. *Amer. J. Psychiat., 150*(11), 1639–42.

Caudill, B. D., Hoffman, J. A., Hubbard, R. L., Flynn, P. M., & Luckey, J. W. (1994). Parental history of substance abuse as a risk factor in predicting crack smokers' substance use, illegal activities, and psychiatric status. *Amer. J. Drug Alcoh. Abuse, 20,* 341–54.

Ceci, S. J. (in press). False beliefs: Some developmental and clinical considerations. In D. Schacter, J. Coyle, L. Sullivan, M. Mesulam, & G. Fischbach (Eds.), *Memory distortions: Interdisciplinary perspectives.* New York: Harvard University Press.

Ceci, S. J., & Baker, J. C. (1987). How shall we conceptualize the language problems of learning-disabled children? In S. J. Ceci (Ed.), *Handbook of cognitive, social, and neuropsychological aspects of learning disabilities* (Vol. 2, pp. 103–14). Hillsdale, NJ: Erlbaum.

Centerwall, W. R., & Centerwall, S. A. (1961). Phenylketonuria (Folling's disease): The story of its discovery. *Journal of the History of Medicine, 16,* 292–96.

Chafel, J. A. (1992). Funding Head Start: What are the issues? *Amer. J. Orthopsychiat., 62*(1), 9–21.

Chambers, R. E. (1952). Discussion of "Survival factors . . . " *Amer. J. Psychiat., 109,* 247–48.

Chambless, D. L., & Mason, J. (1986). Sex, sex role stereotyping, and agoraphobia. *Behav. Res. Ther., 24,* 231–5.

Chance, P. (1986, Oct.). Life after head injury. *Psych. Today, 20,* 62–69.

Chandler, H. N. (1985). The kids-in-between: Some solutions. *J. Learn. Dis. 18,* 368.

Chappel, J. N. (1993). Long-term recovery from alcoholism. *Psychiat. Clin. N. Amer., 16,* 177–87.

Charney, F. L. (1979). Inpatient treatment programs. In W. H. Reid (Ed.), *The psychopath: A comprehensive study of antisocial disorders and behaviors.* New York: Brunner/Mazel.

Charney, D. S., Woods, S. W., Goodman, W. K., & Heninger, G. R. (1987) Neurobiological mechanisms of panic anxiety: Biochemical and behavioral correlates of yohombine-induced panic attacks. *Amer. J. Psychiat., 144,* 1030–1036.

Chase, T., The Troops for (1990). *When rabbit howls.* New York: Jove.

Chassin, L., Pillow, D. R., Curran, P. J., Molina, B. S., & Barrera, M. (1993). Relation of parental alcoholism in early adolescent substance use: A test of three mediating mechanisms. *J. Abnorm. Psychol., 102,* 3–19.

Chassin, L., Rogosch, F., & Barrera, M. (1991). Substance use and symptomatology among adolescent children of alcoholics. *J. Abnorm. Psychol., 100,* 449–463.

Checkley, S. (1992). Neuroendocrinology. In E.S. Paykel (Ed.), *Handbook of affective disorders* (2nd ed.). New York: Guilford.

Chemtob, C. M., Hamada, R. S., Roitblat, H. L., & Muraoka, M. Y. (1994). Anger, impulsivity, and anger control in combat-related post-traumatic stress disorder. *J. Cons. Clin. Psychol., 62,* 827–32.

Chess, S., & Thomas, A. (1984). *Origins and evolution of behavior disorders: From infancy to early adult life.* New York: Brunner/Mazel.

Chesser, E. (1971). *Strange loves: The human aspects of sexual deviation.* New York: William Morrow.

Cheung, F. M., & Song, W. Z. (1989). A review of clinical applications of the MMPI in China. *Psychol. Assess., 1,* 230–37.

Chic, J., Gough, K., Falkowski, W., & Kershaw, P. (1992). Disulfiram treatment of alcoholism. *Brit. J. Psychiat., 161,* 84–89.

Christensen, A., & Jacobson, N. S. (1994). Who (or what) can do psychotherapy: The status and challenge of nonprofessional therapies. *Psychol. Sci., 5*(1), 8–14.

Christiansen, B. A., Smith, G. T., Roehling, P. V., & Goldman, M. S. (1989). Using alcohol expectancies to predict adolescent drinking behavior after one year. *J. Cons. Clin. Psychol., 57,* 93–99.

Christie, B. L. (1981). Childhood enuresis: Current thoughts on causes and cures. *Social Work Health Care, 6*(3), 77–90.

Chrousos, G. B. & Gold, P. W. (1992). The concepts of stress and stress system disorders: Overview of physical and behavioral homeostasis. *JAMA, 267,* 1244–52.

Chu, J. A., & Dill, D. L. (1990). Dissociative symptoms in relation to childhood physical and sexual abuse. *Amer. J. Psychiat., 147,* 887–92.

Cicchetti, D. (1990). A historical perspective on the discipline of developmental psychopathology. In J. Rolf, A. S. Masten, D. Cicchetti, K. H. Nuechterlein, & S. Weintraub (Eds.), *Risk and protective factors in the development of psychopathology.* New York: Cambridge University Press.

Clark, C. R. (1987). Specific intent and diminished capacity. In A. Hess and I. Weiner (Eds.), *Handbook of forensic psychology.* New York: Wiley.

Clark, D. A., Beck, A. T., & Beck, J. S. (1994a). Symptom difference in major depression, dysthymia, panic disorder, and generalized anxiety disorder. *Amer. J. Psychiat., 151,* 205–9.

Clark, D. A., Beck, A. T., & Stewart, B. (1990). Cognitive specificity and positive-negative affectivity: Complementary or contradictory views on anxiety and depression. *J. Abnorm. Psychol., 99,* 148–55.

Clark, D. A., Steer, R. A., & Beck, A. T. (1994b). Common and specific dimensions of self-reported anxiety and depression: Implications for the cognitive and tripartite models. *J. Abnorm. Psychol., 103,* 645–54.

Clark, D. C., & Fawcett, J. (1992). Review of empirical risk factors for evaluation of the suicidal patient. In B. Bongar (Ed.), *Suicide: Guidelines for assessment, management and treatment.* New York: Oxford University Press.

Clark, D. M. (1986). A cognitive approach to panic. *Behav. Res. Ther., 24,* 461–70.

Clark, D. M. (1988). A cognitive model of panic attacks. In S. Rachman, & J. D. Maser (Eds.), *Panic: Psychological perspectives.* Hillsdale, NJ: Erlbaum.

Clark, D. M., & Wells, A. (in press). A cognitive model of social phobia. To appear in R. G. Heimberg, M. Liebowitz, D. Hope, & F. Schneier (Eds.), *Social phobia: Diagnosis, assessment, and treatment.* New York: Guilford.

Clark, D. M., Salkovskis, P. M., & Anastasiades, P. (1990). Cognitive mediation of lactate induced panic. In R. M. Rapee (Chair) Experimental investigations of panic disorder. Symposium conducted at the meeting of the Association for Advancement of Behavior Therapy. San Francisco.

Clark, D. M., Salkovskis, P. M., Hackmann, A., Middleton, H., Anastasiades, P., & Gelder, M. (1994). A comparison of cognitive therapy, applied relaxation, and imipramine in the treatment of panic disorder. *Brit. J. Psychiat., 164,* 759–69.

Clark, L. A. (1992). Resolving taxonomic issues in personality disorders: The value of large-scale analyses of symptom data. *J. Pers. Dis., 6,* 360–76.

Clark, L. A., & Livesley, W. J. (1994). Two approaches to identifying dimensions of personality disorder. Convergence on the five-factor model. In P. T. Costa, Jr., & T. A. Widiger (Eds.), *Personality disorders and the five-factor model of personality.* Washington, DC: American Psychological Association.

Clark, L. A., & Watson, D. (1991a). "Theoretical and empirical issues in differentiating depression from anxiety." In J. Becker & A. Kleinman (Eds.), *Psychosocial aspects of depression.* Hillsdale, NJ: Erlbaum.

Clark, L. A., & Watson, D. (1991b). Tripartite model of anxiety and depression: Psychometric evidence and taxonomic implications. *J. Abnor. Psychol., 100,* 316–36.

Clark, L. A., Watson, D., & Mineka, S. (1994). Temperament, personality, and the mood and anxiety disorders. *J. Abnorm. Psychol., 103,* 103–16.

Clark, R. F., & Goate, A. M. (1993). Molecular genetics of Alzheimer's disease. *Arch. Neurol., 50*(11), 1164–72.

Clarke, A. M., Clarke, A. D. B., & Berg, J. M. (Eds.). (1985). *Mental deficiency: The changing outlook* (4th ed.). London: Methuen.

Clarke, D. J., Littlejohns, C. S., Corbett, J. A., & Joseph, S. (1989). Pervasive developmental disorders and psychoses in adult life. *Brit. J. Psychiat., 155,* 692–99.

Clarke, G. N., Sack, W. H., & Goff, B. (1993). Three forms of stress in Cambodian adolescent refugees. *J. Abnor. Child Psychol., 21,* 65–77.

Clayton, P. J. (1982). Bereavement. In E. S. Paykel (Ed.), *Handbook of affective disorders.* New York: Guilford.

Cleckley, H. M. (1941). *The mask of sanity* (1st ed.). St. Louis, MO: Mosby.

Cleckley, H.M. (1982). *The mask of sanity* (rev. ed.). New York: Plume.

Clement, P. (1970). Elimination of sleepwalking in a seven-year-old boy. *J. Cons. Clin. Psychol., 34*(1), 22–26.

Clementz, B. A., Grove, W. M., Iacono, W. G., & Sweeney, J. A. (1992). Smooth-pursuit eye movement dysfunction and liability for schizophrenia: Implications for genetic modeling. *J. Abnorm. Psychol., 101*(1), 117–29.

Cloitre, M., Heimberg, R. G., Liebowitz, M. R., & Gitow, A. (1992). Perceptions of control in panic disorder and social phobia. *Cog. Ther. Res., 16*(5), 569–77.

Cloninger, C. R. (1986). Somatoform and dissociative disorders. In G. Winokur & P. Clayton (Eds.), *The medical basis of psychiatry* (pp. 123–51). Philadelphia: Saunders.

Cloninger, C. R. (1987). A systematic method for clinical description and classification of personality invariants. *Arch. Gen. Psychiat., 44,* 161–67.

Cloninger, C. R., & Guze, S. B (1970). Psychiatric illness and female criminality: The role of sociopathy and hysteria in the antisocial woman. *Amer. J. Psychiat., 127*(3), 303–11.

Cloninger, C. R., Christiansen, K. O., Reich, T., & Gottesman, I. I. (1978). Implications of sex differences in the prevalences of antisocial personality, alcoholism, and criminality for familial transmission. *Arch. Gen. Psychiat., 35,* 941–51.

Cloninger, C. R., Reich, T., Sigvardsson, S., von Knorring, A. L., & Bohman, M. (1986). The effects of changes in alcohol use between generations on the inheritance of alcohol abuse. In *Alcoholism: A medical disorder.* Proceedings of the 76th Annual Meeting of the American Psychopathological Association.

Cloninger, C. R., Sigvardsson, S., Von Knorring, A. L., & Bohman, M. (1984). An adoption study of somatoform disorders: II. Identification of two discrete somatoform disorders. *Arch. Gen. Psychiat., 41,* 863–71.

Clum, G. A., Clum, G. A., & Surls, R. (1993). A meta-analysis of treatments for panic disorder. *J. Con. Clin. Psychol., 61*(2), 317–26.

Coates, T. J., Perry, C., Killen, J., & Slinkard, L. A. (1981). Primary prevention of cardiovascular disease in children and adolescents. In C. K. Prokop & L. A. Bradley (Eds.), *Medical psychology: Contributions to behavioral medicine.* New York: Academic Press.

Cockayne, T. O. (1864–1866). Leechdoms, wort cunning, and star craft of early England. London: Longman, Green, Longman, Roberts & Green.

Cockerham, W. (1981). *Sociology of mental disorder.* Englewood Cliffs, NJ: Prentice-Hall.

Coffey, C. E., Weiner, R. D., Djang, W. T., Figiel, G. S., Soady, S. A. R., Patterson, L. J., Holt, P. D., Spritzer, C. E., & Wilkinson, W. E. (1991). Brain anatomic effects of electroconvulsive therapy. *Arch. Gen. Psychiat., 48,* 1013–21.

Cohen, C. A., Gold, D. P., Shulman, K. I., & Wortley, J. T. (1993). Factors determining the decision to institutionalize dementing individuals: A prospective study. *Gerontologist, 33*(6), 714–20.

Cohen, D., & Eisdorfer, C. (1988). Depression in family members caring for a relative with Alzheimer's disease. *J. Amer. Geriat. Soc., 36,* 885–89.

Cohen, J., & Hansel, M. (1956). *Risk and gambling: A study of subjective probability.* New York: Philosophical Library.

Cohen, M. L., Seghorn, T., & Calmas, W. (1969). Sociometric study of the sex offender. *J. Abnorm. Psychol., 74,* 249–55.

Cohen, R., Singh, N. N., Hosick, J., & Tremaine, L. (1992). Implementing a responsive system of mental health services for children. *Clin. Psychol. Rev., 12,* 819–28.

Cohen, S. L., & Fiedler, J. E. (1974). Content analysis of multiple messages in suicide notes. *Life-Threatening Behavior, 4*(2), 75–95.

Cohen, S., Tyrrell, D. A. J., & Smith, A. P. (1993). Negative life events, perceived stress, negative affect, and susceptibility to the common cold. *J. Pers. Soc. Psychol., 64*(1), 131–40.

Cohn, J. F., & Tronick, E. Z. (1983). Three months infant's reaction to simulated maternal depression. *Child Develop. 54,* 185–93.

Coie, J. D. (1990). Toward a theory of peer rejection. In S. R. Asher & J. D. Coie (Eds.), *Peer rejection in childhood* (pp. 365–402). New York: Cambridge University Press.

Coie, J.D., & Cillessen, A.H.N. (1993). Peer rejection: Origins and effects on children's development. *Curr. Dir. Psychol. Sci.,* 2, 89-92.

Coie, J. D., & Dodge, K. A. (1983). Continuity and changes in children's sociometric status: A five-year longitudinal study. *Merrill-Palmer Quarterly, 29,* 261–82.

Coie, J. D., & Dodge, K. A. (1988). Multiple sources of data on social behavior and social status in school: A cross-age comparison. *Child Develop., 57,* 815–829.

Coie, J. D., Dodge, K. A., & Kupersmidt, J. B. (1990). Peer group behavior and social status. In S. R. Asher & J. D. Coie (Eds.), *Peer rejection in childhood.* New York: Cambridge University Press.

Coie, J.D., Dodge, K.A., Terry, R., & Wright, V. (1991). The role of aggression in peer relations: An analysis of aggression episodes in boys' play groups. *Child Develop., 62,* 812-826.

Coie, J. D., & Kupersmidt, J. B. (1983). A behavioral analysis of emerging social status in boys' groups. *Child Develop., 54,* 1400–16.

Coie, J.D., Lochman, J.E., Terry, R., & Hyman, C. (1992). Predicting adolescent disorder from childhood aggression and peer rejection. *J. Cons. Clin. Psychol., 60*(5), 783-792.

Coie, J. D., & Lenox, K. F. (1994). The development of antisocial individuals. In D. C. Fowles, P. Sutker, & S. H. Goodman (Eds.), *Progress in experimental personality and psychopathology research.* New York: Springer.

Coie, J. D., Watt, N. F., West, S. G., Hawkins, J. D., Asarnow, J. R., Markman, H. J., Ramey, S. L., Shure, M. B., & Long, B. (1993). The science of prevention: A conceptual framework and some directions for a national research program. *Amer. Psychol., 48*(10), 1013–22.

Cole, D. A. (1989). Psychopathology of adolescent suicide: Hopelessness, coping beliefs, and depression. *J. Abnorm. Psychol., 98,* 248–55.

Cole, G., Neal, J. W., Fraser, W. I., & Cowie, V. A. (1994). Autopsy findings in patients with mental handicap. *J. Intell. Dis. Res., 38*(1), 9–26.

Cole, J. O., & Bodkin, J. A. (1990). Antidepressant drug side effects. *J. Clin. Psychiat., 51,* 21–26.

Collins, G. B. (1993). Contemporary issues in the treatment of alcohol dependency. *Psychiat. Clin. N. Amer., 16,* 33–48.

Comfort, A. (1984). Alzheimer's disease or Alzheimerism? *Psychiat. Ann., 14,* 130–32.

Compas, B. E., & Epping, J. E. (1993). Stress and coping in children and families: Implications for children coping with disaster. In C. F. Saylor (Ed.), *Children and disasters* (pp. 11–28). New York: Plenum.

Comstock, B. S. (1992). Decision to hospitalize and alternatives to hospitalization. In B. Bongar (Ed.), *Suicide: Guidelines for assessment, management and treatment.* New York: Oxford University Press.

Connors, G. J., Maisto, S. A., & Derman, K. H. (1994). Alcohol-related expectancies and their applications to treatment. In R. R. Watson (Ed.), *Drug and alcohol abuse reviews: Vol. 3. Alcohol abuse treatment* (pp. 203–31). Totowa, NJ: Humana Press.

Conquest, R. (1986). *The harvest of sorrow: Soviet collectivization and the terror-famine.* New York: Oxford University Press.

Conte, H. R., & Karasu, T. B. (1992). A review of treatment studies of minor depression: 1980–1991. *Amer. J. Psychother., 46,* 58–74.

Conte, J., Berliner, L., & Schuerman, J. (1986). *The impact of sexual abuse on children* (Final Report No. MH 37133). Rockville, MD: National Institute of Mental Health.

Cook, M., & Mineka, S. (1987). Second-order conditioning and overshadowing in the observational conditioning of snake fear in monkeys. *Behav. Res. Ther., 25,* 349–64.

Cook, M., & Mineka, S. (1989). Observational conditioning of fear to fear-relevant versus fear-irrelevant stimuli in rhesus monkeys. *J. Abnorm. Psychol., 98,* 448–59.

Cook, M., & Mineka, S. (1990). Selective associations in the observational conditioning of fear in monkeys. *J. Exper. Psychol.: Animal Behavior Processes, 16,* 372–89.

Cook, M., & Mineka, S. (1991). Selective associations in the origins of phobic fears and their implications for behavior therapy. In P. Martin (Ed.), *Handbook of behavior therapy and psychological science: An integrative approach* (pp. 413–34). New York: Pergamon.

Cookerly, J. R. (1980). Does marital therapy do any lasting good? *Journal of Marital and Family Therapy, 6*(4), 393–97.

Coombs, R. H., Paulson, M. J., & Palley, R. (1988). The institutionalization of drug use in America: Hazardous adolescence, challenging parenthood. *J. Chem. Depen. Treat., 1*(2), 9–37.

Coons, P. (1986). The prevalence of multiple personality disorder. *Newsletter of the International Society for the Study of Multiple Personality and Dissociation, 4,* 6–8.

Coons, P. M. (1986). Treatment progress in 20 patients with multiple personality disorder. *J. Nerv. Ment. Dis., 174,* 715–21.

Cooper, A. J. (1969). A clinical study of "coital anxiety" in male potency disorders. *J. Psychosom. Res., 13*(2), 143–47.

Cooper, J. E., Kendell, R. E., Gurland, B. J., Sharpe, L., Copeland, J. R. M., & Simon, R. (1972). *Psychiatric diagnosis in New York and London.* London: Oxford University Press.

Cooper, M. L. (1994). Motivations for alcohol use among adolescents: Development and validation of a four-factor model. *Psychol. Assess., 6,* 117–28.

Coovert, D. L., Kinder, B. N., & Thompson, J. K. (1989). The psychosexual aspects of anorexia nervosa and bulimia: A review of the literature. *Clin. Psychol. Rev., 9,* 169–80.

Copeland, J. (1968). Aspects of mental illness in West African students. *Soc. Psychiat., 3*(1), 7–13.

Cordova, J. V., & Jacobson, N. S. (1993). Couple distress. In D. H. Barlow (Ed.), *Clinical handbook of psychological disorders* (2nd ed., pp. 481–512). New York: Guilford.

Cornblatt, B. A., & Keilp, J. G. (1994). Impaired attention, genetics, and the pathophysiology of schizophrenia. *Schizo. Bull., 20*(1), 31–46.

Cornblatt, B. A., Lenzenweger, M. F., Dworkin, R. H., & Erlenmeyer-Kimling, L. (1992). Childhood attentional dysfunctions predict social deficits in unaffected adults at risk for schizophrenia. *Brit. J. Psychiat., 16* (suppl. 18), 59–64.

Coryell, W., & Winokur, G. (1982). Course and outcome. In E. S. Paykel (Ed.), *Handbook of affective disorders.* New York: Guilford.

Coryell, W., & Winokur, G. (1992). Course and outcome. In E. S. Paykel (Ed.), *Handbook of affective disorders* (2nd ed.). New York: Guilford.

Coryell, W., Endicott, J., & Keller, M. (1987). The importance of psychotic features to major depression: Course and outcome during a 2-year follow-up. *Acta Psychiatr. Scandin., 75,* 78–85.

Coryell, W., Endicott, J., Keller, M., Andreasen, N., Grove, W., Hirschfeld, R. M. A., & Scheftner, W. (1989). Bipolar affective disorder and high achievement: A familial association. *Amer. J. Psychiat., 146,* 983–88.

Coryell, W., Keller, M., Lavori, P., & Endicott, J. (1990a). Affective syndromes, psychotic features, and prognosis: I. Depression. *Arch. Gen. Psychiat., 47,* 651–57.

Coryell, W., Keller, M., Lavori, P., & Endicott, J. (1990b). Affective syndromes, psychotic features, and prognosis: II. Mania. *Arch. Gen. Psychiat., 47,* 658–62.

Coryell, W., Winokur, G., Keller, M. B., & Scheftner, W. (1992). Alcoholism and primary major depression: A family study approach to co-existing disorders. *J. Affect. Dis., 24,* 93–99.

Costa, P. T., Jr., & McCrae, R. R. (1987). Neuroticism, somatic complaints, and disease: Is the bark worse than the bite? *J. Personal., 55,* 299–316.

Costa, P. T., Jr., & Widiger, T. A. (Ed.). (1994). *Personality disorders and the five-factor model of personality.* Washington, DC: American Psychological Association.

Costa, P. T., Jr., Whitfield, J. R., & Stewart, D. (Eds.). (1989). *Alzheimer's disease: Abstracts of the psychological and behavioral literature.* Washington, DC: American Psychological Association.

Costello, E. J. (1989). Developments in child psychiatric epidemiology. *J. Amer. Acad. Child Adoles. Psychiat., 28,* 836–41.

Cotler, S. B. (1971). The use of different behavioral techniques in treating a case of compulsive gambling. *Behav. Ther., 2,* 579–81.

Cotton, N. S. (1979). The familial incidence of alcoholism. *J. Stud. Alcoh., 40,* 89–116.

Cox, D. J. (1988). Incidence and nature of male genital exposure behavior as reported by college women. *J. Sex Res., 24,* 227–34.

Cox, D. J., Freundlich, A., & Meyer, R. G. (1975). Differential effectiveness of electromyographic feedback, verbal relaxation instructions, and medication placebo with tension headaches. *J. Cons. Clin. Psychol., 43,* 892–98.

Cox, W. M., & Klinger, E. (1988). A motivational model of alcohol use. *J. Abnorm. Psychol., 97,* 168–80.

Coyne, J. C. (1976). Depression and the response of others. *J. Abnorm. Psychol., 55*(2), 186–93.

Coyne, J. C., Kessler, R. C., Tal, M., Turnbull, J., Wortman, C., & Greden, J. (1987). Living with a depressed person: Burden and psychological distress. *J. Cons. Clin. Psychol., 55,* 347–52.

Craske, M. G., & Barlow, D. H. (1993). Panic disorder and agoraphobia. In D. H. Barlow (Eds.), *Clinical handbook of psychological disorders* (pp. 1–47). New York: Guilford.

Crepeau, F., & Scherzer, P. (1993). Predictors and indicators of work status after traumatic brain injury: A meta-analysis. *Neuropsychological Rehabilitation, 3*(1), 5–35.

Crino, R. D. (1991). Obsessive compulsive disorder. *Inter. Rev. Psychiat., 3,* 189–201.

Crisp, A. H., Douglas, J. W. B., Ross, J. M., & Stonehill, E. (1970). Some developmental aspects of disorders of weight. *J. Psychosom. Res., 14,* 313–20.

Crittenden, P. M. (1985). Maltreated infants: Vulnerability and resilience. *J. Child Psychol. Psychiat., 26,* 85–96.

Crittenden, P.M., & Ainsworth, M.D.S. (1989). Child maltreatment and attachment theory. In D. Cicchetti & V. Carlson (Eds.), *Child maltreatment: Theory and research on the causes and consequences of child abuse and neglect* (pp. 432-463). Cambridge: Cambridge University Press.

Crook, T., & Eliot, J. (1980). Parental death during childhood and adult depression: A critical review of the literature. *Psychol. Bull., 87,* 252–59.

Crouch, J. L., & Milner, J. S. (1993). Effective intervention with neglected families. *Crim. Just. Behav., 20,* 49–65.

Crowe, R. R., Noyes, R., Pauls, D. L., & Slymen, D. (1983). A family study of panic disorder. *Arch. Gen. Psychiat., 40,* 1065–9.

Culliton, B. J. (1970, Jan. 24). Pot facing stringent scientific examination. *Sci. News, 97*(4), 102–5.

Culliton, B. J. (1976). Psychosurgery: National Commission issues surprisingly favorable report. *Science, 194,* 299–301.

Cummings, E.M. (1987). Coping with background anger in early childhood. *Child Develop., 58,* 976–984.

Curry, S. J. (1993). Self-help interventions for smoking cessation. *J. Cons. Clin. Psychol., 61,* 790–803.

Custer, R. L. (1982). An overview of compulsive gambling. In P. A. Carone, S. F. Yolies, S. N. Kieffer, & L. W. Krinsky (Eds.), *Addictive disorders update.* New York: Human Sciences.

Dahl, R. E. (1992). The pharmacologic treatment of sleep disorders. *Psychiat. Clin. N. Amer., 15,* 161–78.

Dahl, R.E., Pelham, W.E., Wierson, M. (1991). The role of sleep disturbances in attention deficit disorder symptoms: A case study. *J. Pediat. Psychol., 16,* 229-239.

Dahlstrom, W. G., Lachar, D., & Dahlstrom, L. E. (1986). *MMPI patterns of American minorities.* Minneapolis: University of Minnesota Press.

Dain, N. (1964). *Concepts of insanity in the United States: 1789–1865.* New Brunswick, NJ: Rutgers University Press.

Daly, M., & Wilson, M. (1988) *Homicide.* New York: Aldine de Gruyter.

Daniel W. F., & Crovitz, H. F. (1983a). Acute memory impairment following electroconvulsive therapy: 1. Effects of electrical stimulus and number of treatments. *Acta Psychiatr. Scandin., 67,* 1–7.

Daniel, W. F., & Crovitz, H. F. (1983b). Acute memory impairment following electroconvulsive therapy: 2. Effects of electrode placement. *Acta Psychiatr. Scandin., 67,* 57–68.

Darbonne, A. R. (1969). Suicide and age: A suicide note analysis. *J. Cons. Clin. Psychol., 33,* 46–50.

Darke, J. L. (1990). Sexual aggression: Achieving power through humiliation. In W. L. Marshall, D. R. Laws, & H. E. Barbaree (Eds.), *Handbook of sexual assault* (pp. 55–72). New York: Plenum.

Davidson, A. D. (1979a, Spring). Coping with stress reactions in rescue workers: A program that worked. *Police Stress.*

Davidson, A. D. (1979b). Personal communication.

Davidson, J. R., Hughes, D. I., Blazer, D. C., et al., (1991). Post-traumatic stress disorder in the community: An epidemiological study. *Psychol. Med., 21,* 713–21.

Davidson, L. M., & Baum, A. (1986). Chronic stress and post-traumatic stress disorders. *J. Cons. Clin. Psychol., 54,* 303–8.

Davies, P. (1986). The genetics of Alzheimer's disease: A review and discussion of the implications. *Neurobiol. Aging, 7,* 459–66.

Davis, J. M. (1978). Dopamine theory of schizophrenia: A two-factor theory. In L. C. Wynne, R. L. Cromwell, & S. Matthysse (Eds.), *The nature of schizophrenia: New approaches to research and treatment* (pp. 105–15). New York: Wiley.

Dawson, D.A ., Harford, T. C., & Grant, B. F. (1992). Family history as a predictor of alcohol dependence. *Alcoholism: Clin. Exper. Res., 16,* 572–75.

Dawson, P. M., Griffith, K., & Boeke, K. M. (1990). Combined medical and psychological treatment of hospitalized children with encopresis. *Child Psychiat. Human Devel., 20,* 181–290.

de Pauw, K. W., & Szulecka, T. K. (1988). Dangerous delusions: Violence and misidentification syndromes. *Brit. J. Psychiat., 152,* 91–96.

De Silva, P., Rachman, S. J., & Seligman, M. E. P. (1977). Prepared phobias and obsessions: Therapeutic outcomes. *Behav. Res. Ther., 15,* 65–78.

de Vries, L. B. A., Halley, D. J. J., Oostra, B. A., & Niermeijer, M. F. (1994). The fragile-X syndrome: A growing gene causing familial intellectual disability. *J. Intellect. Dis. Res., 38*(1), 1–8.

Debuono, B. A., Zinner, S. H., Daamen, M., & McCormack, W. M. (1990). Sexual behavior of college women in 1975, 1986 and 1989. *New Eng. J. Med., 322,* 821–25.

DeFazio, V. J., Rustin, S., & Diamond, A. (1975). Symptom development in Vietnam era veterans. *Amer. J. Orthopsychiat., 45*(1), 158–63.

DeKay, W. T., & Buss, D. M. (1992). Human nature, individual differences, and the importance of context: Perspectives from evolutionary psychology. *Curr. Dir. Psychol. Sci., 1*(6), 184–189.

DeLisi, L. E., Crow, T. J., & Hirsch, S. R. (1986a). The third biannual winter workshops on schizophrenia. *Arch. Gen. Psychiat., 43,* 706–11.

DeLisi, L. E., Goldin, L. R., Hamovit, J. R., Maxwell, E., & Kuritz, D. (1986b). A family study of the association of increased ventricular size with schizophrenia. *Arch. Gen. Psychiat., 43,* 148–53.

DeLisi, L. E., Mirsky, A. F., Buchsbaum, M. S., van Kammen, D. P., Berman, K. F., Phelps, B. H., Karoum, F., Ko, G. N., Korpi, E. R., et al. (1984). The Genain quadruplets 25 years later: A diagnostic and biochemical followup. *Psychiat. Res., 13,* 59–76.

Deltito, J. A., & Stam, M. (1989). Psychopharmacological treatment of avoidant personality disorder. *Compr. Psychiat., 30,* 498–504.

DeMarsh, J., & Kumpfer, K. L. (1985). Family-oriented interventions for the prevention of chemical dependency in children and adolescents. Special Issue: Childhood and Chemical Abuse: Prevention and Intervention. *J. Child. Contem. Soc., 18*(1–2), 117–51.

DeMause, L. (1990). The history of child assault. *J. Psychohist., 18,* 1–29.

Denicola, J., & Sandler, J. (1980). Training abusive parents in child management and self-control skills. *Behav. Ther., 11,* 263–70.

Dennes, B. (1974). Returning madness to an accepting community. *Comm. Ment. Hlth. J., 10*(2), 163–72.

Department of Labor. (1991, Feb.). *Employment and earnings.* Bureau of Labor Statistics. Washington, DC: U.S. Government Printing Office.

Depue, R. A., & Iacono, W. G. (1989). Neurobehavioral aspects of affective disorders. *Ann. Rev. Psychol., 40,* 457–92.

Depue, R. A., & Monroe, S. M. (1986). Conceptualization and measurement of human disorder in life stress research: The problem of chronic disturbance. *Psychol. Bull., 99*(1), 36–51.

Depue, R. A., Slater, J. F., Wolfstetter-Kausch, H., Klein, D., Goplerud, E., & Farr, D. (1981). A behavioral paradigm for identifying persons at risk for bipolar disorder: A conceptual framework. *J. Abnorm. Psychol., 90,* 381–437.

Derr, R. F., & Gutmann, H. R. (1994). Alcoholic liver disease may be prevented with adequate nutrients. *Medical Hypotheses, 42,* 1–4.

Detera-Wadleigh, S. D., Berrettini, W. H., Goldin, L. R., Boorman, D., Anderson, S., & Gershon, E. S. (1987). Close linkage of c-harvey-ras-1 and the insulin gene to affective disorders is ruled out in three North American pedigrees. *Nature, 325,* 806–8.

Deutsch, A. (1948). *The shame of the states.* New York: Harcourt, Brace.

DeVeaugh-Geiss, J. (1991). Pharmacologic treatment of obsessive-compulsive disorder. In J. Zohar, T. Insel, & S. Rasmussen (Eds.), *The psychobiology of obsessive-compulsive disorder.* New York: Springer.

Dew, M.A., Bromet, E.J., & Schulberg, H.C. (1987). A comparative analysis of two community stressors' long-term mental health effects. *Am. J. Community Psychol., 15,* 167–184.

Dew, M.A., Penkower, L., & Bromet, E.J. (1991). Effects of unemployment on mental health in the contemporary family. *Behav. Mod., 15,* 501–544.

Diamond, M. C. (1988). *Enriching heredity: The impact of the environment on the anatomy of the brain.* New York: Free Press.

Diamond, M. J. (1974). Modification of hypnotizability: A review. *Psychol. Bull., 81*(3), 180–98.

DiClemente, C. C. (1993). Changing addictive behaviors: A process perspective. *Curr. Dir. Psychol. Sci., 2,* 101–6.

Dikmen, S. S., & Levin, H. S. (1993). Methodological issues in the study of mild head injury. *J. Head Trauma Rehab., 8*(3), 30–37.

Dikmen, S. S., Temkin, N. R., Machamer, J. E., & Holubkov, A. L. (1994). Employment following traumatic head injuries. *Arch. Neurol., 51*(2), 177–86.

Diller, L., & Gordon, W. A. (1981). Interventions for cognitive deficits in brain-injured adults. *J. Cons. Clin. Psychol., 49,* 822–34.

Dimberg, U., & Öhman, A. (1983). The effect of directional facial cues on electrodermal conditioning to facial stimuli. *Psychophysiology, 20,* 160–7.

Dinwiddie, S. H. (1992). Patterns of alcoholism inheritance. *J. Subst. Abuse, 4,* 155–63.

Diokno, A. C., Brown, M. B., & Herzog, A. R. (1990). Sexual function in the elderly. *Arch. Int. Med., 150,* 197–200.

DiPietro, L., Mossberg, H.-O., & Stunkard, A. J. (1994). A 40-year history of overweight children in Stockholm: Lifetime overweight, morbidity, and mortality. *International Journal of Obesity, 18,* 585–90.

Dishion, T. (1994). The peer context of troublesome child and adolescent behavior. In P.E. Leone (Ed.), *Understanding troubled and troubling youth: Multidisciplinary perspectives.* Newbury Park, CA: Sage.

Dixon, L., Weiden, P. J., Haas, G., & Sweeney, J. (1992). Increased tardive dyskinesia in alcohol-abusing schizophrenic patients. *Compr. Psychiat., 33,* 121–22.

Doane, J. A., Falloon, I. R. H., Goldstein, M. J., & Mintz, J. (1985). Parental affective style and the treatment of schizophrenia: Predicting course of illness and social functioning. *Arch. Gen. Psychiat., 42,* 34–42.

Doane, J. A., West, K., Goldstein, M. J., Rodnick, E., & Jones, J. (1981). Parental communication deviance and affective style as predictors of subsequent schizophrenia spectrum disorders in vulnerable adolescents. *Arch. Gen. Psychiat., 38,* 679–85.

Dobson, K. S. (1989). A meta-analysis of the efficacy of cognitive therapy for depression. *J. Cons. Clin. Psychol., 57,* 414–19.

Dodd, B., & Leahy, J. (1989). Facial prejudice. *Amer. J. Ment. Retard., 94,* 111.

Dodge, K. A. (1980). Social cognition and children's aggressive behavior. *Child Develop., 51,* 162–70.

Dodge, K. A. (1993). Social cognitive mechanisms in the development of conduct disorder and depression. *Ann. Rev. Psychol., 44,* 559–84.

Dodge, K.A., Bates, J.E., & Pettit, G.S. (1990). Mechanisms in the cycle of violence. *Science, 250,* 1678–1683.

Dodge, K. A., & Frame, C. L. (1982). Social cognition biases and deficits in aggressive boys. *Child Develop., 53,* 620–35.

Dodge, K. A., & Newman, J. P. (1981). Biased decision-making processes in aggressive boys. *J. Abnorm. Psychol., 90,* 375–79.

Dodge, K. A., Coie, J. D., & Brakke, N. P. (1982). Behavioral patterns of socially rejected and neglected preadolescents: The roles of social approach and aggression. *J. Abnorm. Child. Psychol. 10,* 389–410.

Dodge, K. A., Murphy, R. R., & Buchsbaum, K. (1984). The assessment of intention-cue detection skills in children: Implications for developmental psychopathology. *Child Develop., 55,* 163–73.

Dohrenwend, B. P., & Dohrenwend, B. S. (1982). Perspectives on the past and future of psychiatric epidemiology: The 1981 Rena Lapouse Lecture. *Amer. J. Pub. Hlth., 72*(1), 1271–79.

Dohrenwend, B. P., Dohrenwend, B. S., Gould, M. S., Link, B., Neugebauer, R., & Wunsch-Hitzig, R. (1980). *Mental illness in the United States: Epidemiological estimates.* New York: Praeger.

Dohrenwend, B. P., Shrout, P. E., Link, B. G., Skodol, A. E., & Martin, J. L. (1986). Overview and initial results from a risk factor study of depression and schizophrenia. In J.E. Barrett (Ed.), *Mental disorders in the community: Progress and challenge.* New York: Guilford.

Dohrenwend, B. P., Shrout, P. E., Link, B. G., Skodol, A. E., & Stueve, A. (1995). A case-control study of life events and other possible psychosocial risk factors for episodes of schizophrenia and major depression. In C. M. Mazure (Ed.), *Does stress cause psychiatric illness?* Washington, DC: American Psychiatric Press.

Dole, V. P., & Nyswander, M. (1967). The miracle of methadone in the narcotics jungle. *Roche Report, 4*(11), 1–2, 8, 11.

Dollard, J., & Miller, N. E. (1950). *Personality and psychotherapy.* New York: McGraw-Hill.

Donaldson, M. A., & Gardner, R., Jr. (1985). Diagnosis and treatment of traumatic stress among women after childhood incest. In C. R. Filley (Ed.), *Trauma and its wake: The study and treatment of post-traumatic stress disorder* (pp. 356–77). Newbury Park, CA: Sage.

Donne, J. (1624). Meditation XVII. *Devotions upon emergent occasions*. London.

Dooley, D., & Catalano, R. (1980). Economic change as a cause of behavioral disorder. *Psychol. Bull., 87*, 450–68.

Dorwart, R. A., Schlesinger, M., Horgan, C., & Davidson, H. (1989). The privatization of mental health care and directions for mental health services research. In C. A. Taube, D. Mechanic, & A. A. Hohmann (Eds.), *The future of mental health services research* (pp. 139–54). Washington, DC: U.S. Department of Health and Human Services.

Downey, G., & Coyne, J. C. (1990). Children of depressed parents: An integrative review. *Psychol. Bull., 108*, 50–76.

Draguns, J. G. (1979). Culture and personality. In A. J. Marsella, R. Tharp, & T. Cibowrowski (Eds.), *Perspectives in cross-cultural psychology*. New York: Academic Press.

Drotar, D. (Ed.). (1985). *New directions in failure to thrive: Implications for research and practice*. New York: Plenum Press.

Drug Enforcement Administration, Department of Justice. (1979). *Controlled Substance Inventory List*. Washington, DC.

Dryfoos, J. G. (1990). *Adolescents at risk: Prevalence and prevention*. New York: Oxford University Press.

Dumas, J. E., Gibson, J. A., & Albin, J. B. (1989). Behavioral correlates of maternal depressive symptomatology in conduct-disorder children. *J. Cons. Clin. Psychol., 57*, 516–21.

Dunbar, F., (1943). *Psychosomatic diagnosis*. New York: Harper & Row.

Dunbar, P. (1954). *Emotions and bodily changes* (4th ed.). New York: Columbia University Press.

Dunne, E. J. (1992). Following a suicide: Postvention. In B. Bongar (Ed.), *Suicide: Guidelines for assessment, management and treatment*. New York: Oxford University Press.

Dunner, D. L. (1993). *Psychiatric clinics of North America*. Philadelphia: Saunders.

DuPaul, G. I., & Barkley, R. A. (1990). Medication therapy. In R. A. Barkley (Ed.), *Attention deficit hyperactivity disorder: A handbook for diagnosis and treatment* (pp. 573–612). New York: Guilford.

Dura, J. R., & Bornstein, R. A. (1989). Differences between IQ and school achievement in anorexia nervosa. *J. Clin. Psychol., 45*, 433–35.

Durkheim, E. (1951). *Suicide: A study in sociology* (J. A. Spaulding & G. Simpson, Trans., G. Simpson, Ed.). New York: Free Press. (Originally published 1897.)

Durrant, J. E. (1994). A decade of research on learning disabilities: A report card on the state of the literature. *J. Learn. Dis., 27*(1), 25–33.

Dworkin, R. H., Cornblatt, B. A., Friedman, R., Kaplansky, L. M., Lewis, J. A., Rinaldi, A., Shilliday, C., & Erlenmeyer—Kimling, L. (1993). Childhood precursors of affective vs. social deficits in adolescents at risk for schizophrenia. *Schizo. Bull., 19*(3), 563–77.

Eagly, A.H., & Steffen, V.J. (1986). Gender and aggressive behavior: A meta-analytic review of the social psychological literature. *Psychol. Bull., 100*, 309–330.

Earl, H. G. (1965). 10,000 children battered and starved: Hundreds die. *Today's Health, 43*(9), 24–31.

Earl, H. G. (1966). Head injury: The big killer. *Today's Health, 44*(12), 19–21.

Earlywine, M., & Finn, P. R. (1990, March). Personality, drinking habits, and responses to cues for alcohol. Paper presented at the 5th Congress of the International Society for Biomedical Research on Alcoholism and the Research Society on Alcoholism, Toronto, Canada.

East, W. N. (1946). Sexual offenders. *J. Nerv. Ment. Dis., 103*, 626–46.

Eaton, W. W., & Keyl, P. M. (1990). Risk factors for the onset of Diagnostic Interview Schedule /DSM-III agoraphobia in a prospective, population based study. *Arch. Gen. Psychiat., 47*, 819–24.

Eaton, W. W., Dryman, A., & Weissman, M. M. (1991). Panic and phobia. In L. N. Robins & D. A. Regier (Eds.), *Psychiatric disorders in America* (pp. 155–79). New York: Free Press.

Ebigo, P. O. (1982). Development of a culture specific (Nigeria) screening scale of somatic complaints indicating psychiatric disturbance. *Culture, Medicine and Psychiatry, 6*, 29–43.

Edwards, C. C. (1973). What you can do to combat high blood pressure. *Fam. Hlth., 5*(11), 24–26.

Egbert, L., Battit, G., Welch, C., & Bartlett, M. (1964). Reduction of postoperative pain by encouragement and instruction of patients. *New Engl. J. Med., 270*, 825–27.

Egeland v. City of Minneapolis, 344 N.W. 2nd 597. (1984).

Egeland, B., & Erickson, M. F. (1990). Rising above the past: Strategies for helping new mothers to break the cycle of abuse and neglect. *Zero to Three, 11*, 29–35.

Egeland, B., & Farber, E. A. (1984). Infant-mother attachment: Factors related to its development and change over time. *Child Develop., 55*, 753–71.

Egeland, B. & Sroufe, L.A. (1981). Attachment and early maltreatment. *Child Develop., 52*, 44–52.

Egeland, B., Cicchetti, D., & Taraldson, B. (1976, Apr. 26). Child abuse: A family affair. *Proceedings of the N. P. Masse Research Seminar on Child Abuse*, 28–52. Paper presented Paris, France.

Egeland, J. A., Gerhard, D. S., Pauls, D. L., Sussex, J. N., Kidd, K. K., Allen, C. R., Hostetter, A. M., & Housman, D. E. (1987). Bipolar affective disorders linked to DNA markers on chromosome 11. *Nature, 325*, 783–87.

Egendorf, A. (1986). *Healing from the war*. Boston: Houghton Mifflin.

Ehlers, A. (1995). A 1-year prospective study of panic attacks: Clinical course and factors associated with maintenance. *J. Abnorm. Psychol., 104*.

Ehlers, A., Taylor, B., Margraf, J., Roth, W., & Birbaumer, R. (1988). Anxiety induced by false heart rate feedback in patients with panic disorder. *Behav. Res. Ther., 26*, 2–11.

Ehrhardt, A. A., & Meyer-Bahlburg, H. F. L. (1981). Effects of prenatal sex hormones on gender-related behavior. *Science, 211*, 1312–18.

Eisenberg, H. M. (1990). Behavioral changes after closed head injury in children. *J. Cons. Clin. Psychol., 58*, 93–98.

Eisenberg, P. & Lazarsfeld, P.F. (1938). The psychological effects of unemployment. *Psychol. Bull., 35*, 358–390.

El Guebaly, N., Staley, D., Leckie, A., & Koensgen, S. (1992). Adult children of alcoholics in treatment programs for anxiety disorders and substance abuse. *Canad. J. Psychiat., 37*, 544–48.

Elder, G. H., Shanahan, M. J., & Clipp, E. C. (1994). When war comes to men's lives: Life course patterns in family, work, and health. *Psychol. Aging, 9*, 3–17.

Elkin, I., Shea, M. T., Watkins, J. T., Imber, S. D., Sotsky, S. M., Collins, J. F., Glass, D. R., Pilkonis, P. A., Leber, W. R., Docherty, J. P., Fiester, S. J., & Parloff, M. B. (1989). National Institute of Mental Health Treatment of Depression Collaborative Research Program: General effectiveness of treatments. *Arch. Gen. Psychiat., 46*, 971–82.

Elkind, D. (1967). Middle-class delinquency. *Mental Hygiene, 51*, 80–84.

Ellicott, A., Hammen, C., Gitlin, M., Brown, G., & Jamison, K. (1990). Life events and the course of bipolar disorder. *Amer. J. Psychiat., 147*, 1194–98.

Elliott, D. S., Dunford, F. W., & Huizinga, D. (1987). The identification and prediction of career offenders utilizing self-reported and official data. In J. D. Burchard & S. N. Burchard (Eds.), *Prevention of delinquent behavior* (pp. 90–121). Newbury Park, CA: Sage.

Elliott, G. (1989). Stress and illness. In S. Cheren (Ed.), *Psychosomatic medicine: Theory, physiology, and practice* (Vol. 1, pp. 45–90). Madison, CT: International Universities Press.

Ellis, A. (1958). Rational psychotherapy. *J. Gen. Psychol., 59*, 35–49.

Ellis, A. (1970). *Reason and emotion in psychotherapy*. New York: Lyle Stuart.

Ellis, A. (1973). Rational-emotive therapy. In R. J. Corsini (Ed.), *Current psychotherapies*. Itasca, IL: Peacock Publishers.

Ellis, A. (1975). Creative job and happiness: The humanistic way. *The Humanist, 35*(1), 11–13.

Ellis, A. (1989). The history of cognition in psychotherapy. In A. Freeman, K. M. Simon, L. E. Beutler, & H. Arkowitz (Eds.), *Comprehensive handbook of cognitive therapy* (pp. 5–19). New York: Plenum.

Ellis, E. M., Atkeson, B. M., & Calhoun, K. S. (1982). An examination of differences between multiple- and single-incident victims of sexual assault. *J. Abnorm. Psychol., 91*, 221–24.

Ellis, E. S. (1993). Integrative Strategy Instruction: A potential model for teaching content area subjects to adolescents with learning disabilities. *J. Learn. Dis., 26*(6), 358–83.

Ellison, K. (1977). Personal communication.

Emmelkamp, P. M. G. (1994). Behavior therapy with adults. In A. E. Bergin & S. L. Garfield (Eds.), *Handbook of psychotherapy and behavior change* (4th ed., pp. 379–427). New York: Wiley

Emmelkamp, P. M. G., & Wessels, H. (1975). Flooding in imagination vs. flooding in vivo: A comparison with agoraphobics. *Behav. Res. Ther., 13*(1), 7–15.

Emery, R.E. (1982). Interparental conflict and the children of discord and divorce. *Psychol. Bull., 92*, 310–330.

Emery, R.E. (1989). Family violence. Special issue: Children and their development: Knowledge base, research agenda, and social policy application. *Amer. Psychol., 44*, 321–328.

Endicott, N. A. (1989). Psychosocial and behavioral factors in myocardial infarction and sudden cardiac death. In S. Cheren (Ed.), *Psychosomatic medicine: Theory, physiology, and practice* (Vol. 2, pp. 611–60). Madison, CT: International Universities Press.

Endler, N. (1990). *Holiday of darkness: A psychologist's journey out of his depression* (rev. ed.). Toronto: Wall & Thompson.

Engdahl, B. E., Harkness, A. R., Eberly, R. E., & Bielinski, J.2 (1993). Structural models of captivity trauma, resilence, and trauma response among former prisoners of war 20 and 40 years after release. *Soc. Psychiat. Psychiat. Epidemiol., 28*, 109–15.

Engel, G. L. (1977). The need for a new medical model: A challenge for biomedicine. *Science, 196*, 129–36.

Engels, G. I., Garnefski, N., & Diekstra, R. F. W. (1993). Efficacy of rational-emotive therapy: A quantitative analysis. *J. Cons. Clin. Psychol., 61*(6), 1083–90.

Englander-Golden, P., Elconin, J., Miller, K. J., & Schwarzkopf, A. B., (1986). Brief SAY IT STRAIGHT training and follow-up in adolescent substance abuse prevention. *J. Prim. Preven., 6*(4), 219–30.

English, C. J. (1973). Leaving home: A typology of runaways. *Society, 10*(5), 22–24.

Enns, M. W. & Reiss, J. P. (1992). Position paper: Electroconvulsive therapy. *Canad. J. Psychiat., 37*, 671–78.

Epstein, H. (1979). *Children of the holocaust: Conversations with sons and daughters of survivors*. New York: Putnam.

Epstein, L. H. (1992). Role of behavior theory in behavioral medicine. *J. Cons. Clin. Psychol., 60*(4), 493–98.

Epstein, S. (1994). Integration of the cognitive and the psychodynamic unconscious. *Amer. Psychol., 49*(8), 709–24.

Epstein, S., & Fenz, W. D. (1962). Theory and experiment on the measurement of approach-avoidance conflict. *J. Abnorm. Soc. Psychol., 64*(1), 97–112.

Epstein, S., & Fenz, W. D. (1965). Steepness of approach and avoidance gradients in humans as a function of experience: Theory and experiment. *J. Exper. Psychol., 70*(1), 1–12.

Erdman, H. P., Klein, M., & Greist, J. H. (1985). Direct patient computer interviewing. *J. Cons. Clin. Psychol., 53*(6), 760–73.

Erlenmeyer-Kimling, L., & Cornblatt, B. A. (1978). Attentional measures in a study of children at high risk for schizophrenia. In L. C. Wynne, R. L. Cromwell, & S. Matthysse (Eds.), *The nature of schizophrenia: New approaches to research and treatment* (pp. 359–65). New York: Wiley.

Erlenmeyer-Kimling, L., & Cornblatt, B. A. (1992). A summary of attentional findings in the New York high-risk project. *J. Psychiat. Res., 26*, 405–26.

Ernst, N. D., & Harlan, W. R. (1991). Obesity and cardiovascular disease in minority populations: Executive summary. Conference highlights, conclusions, and recommendations. *Amer. J. Clin. Nutri., 53*, 1507S–11S.

Eron, L. D., & Peterson, R. A. (1982). Abnormal behavior: Social approaches. In M. R. Rosenzweig & L. W. Porter (Eds.), *Annu. Rev. Psychol., 33*, 231–65.

Eron, L. D., Huesmann, L. R., Lefkowitz, M. M., & Walder, L. O. (1974). How learning conditions in early childhood—including mass media—relate to aggression in late adolescence. *Amer. J. Orthopsychiat., 44*(3), 412–23.

Esler, M., Julius, S., Zweifler, A., Randall, O., Harburgh, E., Gardiner, H., & DeQuattro, V. (1977). Mild high-renin essential hypertension: Neurogenic human hypertension? *New Engl. J. Med., 296*, 405–11.

Esquirol, E. (1845). *Mental maladies: Treatise on insanity*. Philadelphia: Lea & Blanchard.

Evans, D. A., Funkerstein, H., Albert, M. S., Scherr, P. A., Cook, N. R., Chown, M. J., Hebert, L. E., Hennekens, C. H., & Taylor, J. O. (1989). Prevalence of Alzheimer's disease in a community population of older persons. *JAMA, 262*, 2551–56.

Evans, J. A., & Hamerton, J. L. (1985). Chromosomal anomalies. In A. M. Clarke, A. D. B. Clarke, & J. M. Berg (Eds.). *Mental deficiency: The changing outlook* (4th ed., pp. 213–66). London: Methuen.

Evans, M. D., Hollon, S. D., DeRubeis, R. J., Piasecki, J. M., Grove, W. M., Garvey, M. J., & Tuason, V. B. (1992). Differential relapse following cognitive therapy and pharmacotherapy for depression. *Arch. Gen. Psychiat., 49*(10), 802–8.

Ewing, C. P. (1994, July). Plaintiff awarded $500,000 in landmark "recovered memories" lawsuit. *APA Monitor*, p. 22.

Exner, J. E. (1987). Computer assistance in Rorschach interpretation. In J. N. Butcher (Ed.), *Computerized psychological assessment: A practitioner's guide*. New York: Basic Books.

Exner, J. E. (1991). *The Rorschach: A comprehensive system. Vol. 2: Interpretation*. New York: Wiley.

Exner, J.E. (1993). *The Rorschach: A comprehensive system. Vol. 1: Basic Foundations*. New York: Wiley.

Exner, J. E. (1995). Why use personality tests? A brief historical view. In J. N. Butcher (Ed.), *Clinical personality assessment: Practical considerations* (10th ed., pp. 10–18). New York: Oxford University Press.

Exner, J. E. & Weiner, I. B. (1994). *The Rorschach: A comprehensive system. Vol. 3: Assessment of children and adolescents*. New York: Wiley.

Eyman, J. R., & Eyman, S. K. (1992). Psychological testing for potentially suicidal individuals. In B. Bongar (Ed.), *Suicide: Guidelines for assessment, management and treatment*. New York: Oxford University Press.

Eysenck, H. J. (1952). The effects of psychotherapy: An evaluation. *J. Cons. Psychol., 16*, 319–24.

Eysenck, H. J. (1960). *Behaviour therapy and the neuroses*. London: Pergamon.

Eysenck, H. J. (1965). Extroversion and the acquisition of eyeblink and GSR conditioned responses. *Psychol. Bull., 63*, 258–70.

Eysenck, M. W., Mogg, K., May, J., Richards, A., & Mathews, A. (1991). Bias in interpretation of ambiguous sentences related to threat in anxiety. *J. Abnorm. Psychol., 100*, 144–50.

Fabrega, H. (1981). Cultural programming of brain-behavior relationships. In J. R. Merikangas (Ed.), *Brain-behavior relationships*. Lexington, MA: Heath.

Fairbank, J. A., Schlenger, W. E., Caddell, J. M., & Woods, M. G. (1993). Post-traumatic stress disorder. In P. Sutker & H. E. Adams (Eds.), *Comprehensive handbook of psychopathology* (2nd ed., pp. 145–65). New York: Plenum

Fairburn, C. G., Jones, R., Peveler, R. C., Hope, R. A., & O'Connor, M. (1993). Psychotherapy and bulimia nervosa: Long-term effects of interpersonal psychotherapy, behavior therapy, and cognitive behavior therapy. *Arch. Gen. Psychiat., 50*(6), 419–28.

Fairburn, C.G., Peveler, R.C., Jones, R., Hope, R.A., & Doll, H.A. (in press). Predictors of 12-month outcome in bulimia nervosa and the influence of attitudes to shape and weight. *J. Cons.Clin. Psychol.*

Fairweather, G. W. (1994). *Keeping the balance: A psychologist's story.* Austin, TX: Fairweather Publishing.

Fairweather, G. W. (Ed.). (1980). *The Fairweather Lodge: A twenty-five year retrospective.* San Francisco: Jossey Bass.

Fairweather, G. W., & Fergus, E. O. (1993). *Empowering the mentally ill.* Austin, TX: Fairweather Publishing.

Fairweather, G. W., Sanders, D. H., Maynard, H., & Cressler, D. L. (1969). *Community life for the mentally ill: An alternative to institutional care.* Chicago: Aldine.

Fallon, A. E., & Rozin, P. (1985). Sex differences in perceptions of desirable body shape. *J. Abnorm. Psychol., 94,* 102–5.

Falloon, I. R. H., Boyd, J. L., McGill, C. W., Williamson, M., & Razani, J. (1985). Family management in the prevention of morbidity of schizophrenia: Clinical outcome of a two-year longitudinal study. *Arch. Gen. Psychiat., 42,* 887–96.

Falsetti, S. A., Resnick, H. S., Dansky, B. S., Lydiard, R. B., & Kilpatrick, D. G. (1995). Relationship of stress to panic disorder: Cause or effect? In C.M. Mazure (Ed.), *Does stress cause psychiatric illness?* Washington, DC: American Psychiatric Association.

Famularo, R., Kinscherff, R., Fenton, T., & Bolduc, S. M. (1990). Child maltreatment histories among runaway and delinquent children. *Clin. Pediat., 29,* 713–18.

Fankhauser, M. P., Karumanchi, V. C., German, M. L., & Yates, A. (1992). A double-blind, placebo-controlled study of the efficacy of transdermal clonidine in autism. *J. Clin. Psychiat., 53,* 77–82.

Fantuzzo, J. W., Jurecic, L., Stovall, A., Hightower, A. D., Goins, C., & Schachtel, D. (1988). Effects of adult and peer social initiations on the social behavior of withdrawn, maltreated, preschool children. *J. Cons. Clin. Psychol., 56,* 40–47.

Faraone, S. V., Biederman, J., Lehman, B. K., & Keenan, K. (1993a). Evidence for the independent familial transmission of attention deficit hyperactivity disorder and learning disabilities: Results from a family genetic study. *Amer. J. Psychiat. 150(6),* 891–95.

Faraone, S. V., Biederman, J., Lehman, B. F., Spencer, T., Norman, T., Seidman, L. J., Kraus, I., Perrin, J., Chen, W. J., & Tsuang, M. T. (1993b). Intellectual performance and school failure in children with Attention Deficit Hyperactivity Disorder and in their siblings. *J. Abnorm. Psychol., 102,* 616–23.

Faraone, S. V., Biederman, J., & Milberger, S. (1994). An exploratory study of ADHD among second-degree relatives of ADHD children. *Biol. Psychiat., 35,* 398–402.

Faraone, S. V., Kremen, W. S., & Tsuang, M. T. (1990). Genetic transmission of major affective disorders: Quantitative models and linkage analysis. *Psychol. Bull., 108,* 109–27.

Farber, E.A., & Egeland, B. (1987). Invulnerability among abused and neglected children. In E.J. Anthony & B. Cohler (Eds.), *The invulnerable child* (pp. 253–288). New York: Guilford.

Farberow, N. L. (1974). *Suicide.* Morristown, NJ: General Learning Press.

Farberow, N. L., & Litman, R. E. (1970). *A comprehensive suicide prevention program.* Suicide Prevention Center of Los Angeles, 1958–1969. Unpublished final report DHEW NIMH Grants No. MH 14946 & MH 00128. Los Angeles.

Farberow, N. L., Shneidman, E. S., & Leonard, C. (1963). Suicide among general medical and surgical hospital patients with malignant neoplasms. Veterans Administration, Dept. of Medicine and Surgery. *Medical Bulletin* MB-9, Feb. 25, 1963, 1–11.

Faretra, G. (1981). A profile of aggression from adolescence to adulthood: An 18-year follow-up of psychiatrically disturbed and violent adolescents. *Amer. J. Orthopsychiat., 51,* 439–53.

Farley, F. H., & Farley, S. V. (1972). Stimulus seeking motivation and delinquent motivation among institutionalized delinquent girls. *J. Cons. Clin. Psychol., 39,* 94–97.

Faust, D. (1994). Comment on Putnam, Adams, and Schneider, "One-day test-retest reliability of neuropsychological tests in a personal injury case." *Psychol. Assess., 6,* 3–4.

Fawcett, J., Scheftner, W., Clark, D., Hedeker, D., Gibbons, R., & Coryell, W. (1987). Clinical predictors of suicide in patients with major affective disorders: A controlled prospective study. *Amer. J. Psychiat., 144,* 35–40.

Fawzy, F. I., Fawzy, N. W., Hyun, C. S., Elashoff, R., Guthrie, D., Fahey, J. L., & Morton, D. L. (1993). Malignant melanoma: Effects of an early structured psychiatric intervention, coping, and affective state on recurrence and survival 6 years later. *Arch. Gen. Psychiat., 50(9),* 681–89.

Federal Bureau of Investigation. (1991). *Sourcebook of criminal justice statistics.* Washington, DC: U.S. Government Printing Office.

Feingold, B. F. (1977). Behavioral disturbances linked to the ingestion of food additives. *Delaware Medical Journal, 49,* 89–94.

Feitel, B., Margetson, N., Chamas, J., & Lipman, C. (1992). Psychosocial background and behavioral and emotional disorders of homeless and runaway youth. *Hosp. Comm. Psychiat., 43,* 155–59.

Feldman, R., & Weisfeld, G. (1973). An interdisciplinary study of crime. *Crime and Delinquency, 19(2),* 150–62.

Feldman, W., Feldman, E., Goodman, J. T., McGrath, P. J. Pless, R. P., Corsini, L., & Bennett, S. (1991). Is childhood sexual abuse really increasing in prevalence? An analysis of the evidence. *Pediatrics, 88,* 29–33.

Felsman, J.K., & Valliant, G.E. (1987). Resilient children as adults: A 40-year study. In E.J. Anthony & B.J. Cohler (Eds.), *The invulnerable child* (pp. 289–314). New York: Guilford.

Fenna, D., et. al. (1971). Ethanol metabolism in various racial groups. *Canadian Medical Association Journal, 105,* 472–75.

Fennell, M. J. V. (1989). Depression. In K. Hawton, P. M. Salkovskis, J. Kirk, & D. M. Clark (Eds.), *Cognitive behaviour therapy for psychiatric problems: A practical guide.* Oxford, UK: Oxford University Press.

Fenton, W. S., & McGlashan, T. H. (1994). Antecedents, symptom progression, and long-term outcome of the deficit syndrome in schizophrenia. *Amer. J. Psychiat., 151(3),* 351–56.

Fenz, W. D. (1971). Heart rate responses to a stressor: A comparison between primary and secondary psychopaths and normal controls. *Journal of Experimental Research in Personality, 5(1),* 7–13.

Ferholt, J.B., Rotnem, D.L., Genel, M., Leonard, M., Carey, M., & Hunter, D.E.K. (1985). A psychodynamic study of psychosomatic dwarfism. *J. Amer. Acad. Child Adol. Psychiat., 24,* 49–57.

Fersch, E. A., Jr. (1980). *Psychology and psychiatry in courts and corrections.* New York: Wiley.

Ferster, C. B. (1973). A functional analysis of depression. *Amer. Psychol., 28(10),* 857–70.

Ferster, C. B. (1974). Behavioral approaches to depression. In R. J. Friedman & M. M. Katz (Eds.), *The psychology of depression: Contemporary theory and research.* Washington DC: Hemisphere.

Feuerstein, R. (1977). Mediated learning experience: A theoretical basis for cognitive modifiability during adolescence. In P. Mittler (Ed.), *Research to practice in mental retardation* (Vol. 2, pp. 105–16). Baltimore: University Park Press.

Field, T., Healy, B. T., Goldstein, S., Guthertz, M. (1990). Behavior-state matching and synchrony in mother-infant interactions of nondepressed versus depressed dyads. *Devel. Psychol., 26,* 7–14.

Fields, J. Z., Turk, A., Durkin, M., Ravi, N. V., & Keshavarzian, A. (1994). Increased gastrointestinal symptoms in chronic alcoholics. *American Journal of Gastroenterology, 89,* 382–86.

Fierman, E. J., Hung, M. F., Pratt, L. A., Warshaw, M. G., Yonkers, K. A., Peterson, L. G., Epstein-Kaye, T. M., & Norton, H. S. (1993). Trauma and posttraumatic stress disorder in subjects with anxiety disorders. *Amer. J. Psychiat., 150,* 1872–74.

Fillmore, K. M., Golding, J. M., Leino, E. V., Ager, C. R., & Ferrer, H. P. (1994). Societal-level predictors of groups' drinking patterns: A research synthesis from the Collaborative Alcohol-Related Longitudinal Project. *Amer. J. Pub. Hlth., 84,* 247–53.

Filskov, S. B., & Boll, T. J. (1986). *Handbook of clinical neuropsychology* (2nd ed.). New York: Wiley.

Filskov, S. B., & Goldstein, S. G. (1974). Diagnostic validity of the Halstead-Reitan Neuropsychology battery. *J. Cons. Clin. Psychol., 42,* 383–88.

Filskov, S. B., & Locklear, E. (1982). A multidimensional perspective on clinical neuropsychology research. In P. C. Kendall & J. M. Butcher (Eds.), *Handbook of research methods in clinical psychology.* New York: Wiley.

Fincham, F. D., Beach, S. R. H., Moore, T., & Diener, C. (1994). The professional response to child sexual abuse: Whose interests are served? *Family Relations, 43,* 244–54.

Fine, M. A., & Sansone, R. A. (1990). Dilemmas in the management of suicidal behavior in individuals with borderline disorder. *Amer. J. Psychother., 44,* 160–71.

Fine, R. (1979). *A history of psychoanalysis.* New York: Columbia University Press.

Fink, M. (1979). *Convulsive therapy: Theory and practice.* New York: Raven Press.

Fink, M. (1992). Electroconvulsive therapy. In E. S. Paykel (Ed.), *Handbook of affective disorders* (2nd ed.). New York: Guilford.

Finkelhor, D. (1979). *Sexually victimized children.* New York: Free Press.

Finkelhor, D. (1984). *Child sexual abuse.* New York: Free Press.

Finkelhor, D. (1990). Early and long term effects of child sexual abuse: An update. *Profess. Psychol.: Research and Practice, 21,* 325–30.

Finkelhor, D., Hotaling, G., Lewis, I. A., & Smith, C. (1990). Sexual abuse in a national survey of adult men and women: Prevalence, characteristics, and risk factors. *Child Ab. Neg., 14,* 19–28.

Finkelstein, N. (1993). Treatment programming for alcohol and drug-dependent pregnant women. *Inter. J. Addictions, 28,* 1275–1309.

Finlay-Jones, R. A., & Brown, G. W. (1981). Types of stressful life events and the onset of anxiety and depressive disorders. *Psychol. Med., 11,* 803–15.

Finn, P. R. (1990, Mar.). *Dysfunction in stimulus-response modulation in men at high risk for alcoholism.* Paper presented at a symposium on the Genetics of Alcoholism: Recent Advances. Satellite Symposium of the Annual Meeting of the Research Society on Alcoholism, Montreal, Canada.

Finn, P. R., & Pihl, R. O. (1987). Men at high risk for alcoholism: The effect of alcohol on cardiovascular response to unavoidable shock. *J. Abnorm. Psychol., 96,* 230–36.

Finn, P. R., Earleywine, M., & Pihl, R. O. (1992). Sensation seeking, stress reactivity, and alcohol dampening discriminate the density of a family history of alcoholism. *Alcholism: Clin. Exper. Res., 16,* 585–90.

Finn, P. R., Zeitouni, N., & Pihl, R. (1990). Effects of alcohol on psychophysiological hyperactivity to nonaversive and aversive stimuli in men at high risk for alcoholism. *J. Abnorm. Psychol., 99,* 79–85.

Finn, S. E. & Tonsager, M. E. (1992). Therapeutic effects of providing MMPI-2 test feedback to college students awaiting therapy. *Psychol. Assess., 4,* 278–87.

Finucci, J. M., Guthrie, T., Childs, A. L., Abbey, H., & Childs, B. (1976). The genetics of specific reading disability. *Ann. Human Genet., 40,* 1–23.

Fischer, J. M. (1993). People with learning disabilities: Moral and ethical rights to equal opportunities. *Journal of Applied Rehabilitation Counseling, 24*(1), 3–7.

Fischer, M. (1971). Psychoses in the offspring of schizophrenic monozygotic twins and their normal co-twins. *Brit. J. Psychiat., 118,* 43–52.

Fischer, M. (1973). Genetic and environmental factors in schizophrenia: A study of schizophrenic twins and their families. *Acta Psychiatr. Scandin.,* Suppl. No. 238.

Fischer, P. J., Shapiro, S., Breakey, W. R., Anthony, J. C., & Kramer, M. (1986). Mental health and social characteristics of the homeless: A survey of mission users. *Amer. J. Pub. Hlth., 76*(5), 519–24.

Fischman, J. (1987, Feb.). Type A on trial. *Psych. Today, 21,* 42–50.

Fischman, M. W., & Schuster, C. R. (1982). Cocaine self-administration in humans. *Federal Proc., 41,* 241–46.

Fish, B., Marcus, J., Hans, S. L., Auerbach, J. G., & Perdue, S. (1992). Infants at risk for schizophrenia: Sequelae of a genetic neurointegrative defect: A review and replication analysis of pandysmaturation in the Jerusalem Infant Development Study. *Arch. Gen. Psychiat., 49*(3), 221–35.

Fisher, J. D., & Fisher, W. A. (1992). Changing AIDS-risk behavior. *Psychol. Bull., 111*(3), 455–74.

Fisher, J. E., & Carstensen, L. L. (1990). Behavior management for the dementias. *Clin. Psychol. Rev., 10,* 611–30.

Fiske, S. & Taylor, S. (1991). *Social Cognition,* 2nd ed. New York: McGraw Hill.

Flaum, M., & Andreasen, N. C. (1991). Diagnostic criteria for schizophrenia and related disorders: Options for DSM-IV. *Schizo. Bull., 17*(1), 133–56.

Fleming, J. E., Offord, D. R., & Boyle, M. H. (1989). Prevalence of childhood and adolescent depression in the community: Ontario Health Study. *Brit. J. Psychiat., 155,* 647–54.

Flor, H., & Birbaumer, N. (1993). Comparison of the efficacy of electromyographic biofeedback, cognitive-behavior therapy, and conservative medical interventions in the treatment of chronic musculoskeletal pain. *J. Cons. Clin. Psychol., 61*(4), 653–58.

Fluoxetine Bulimia Nervosa Collaborative Study Group. (1992). Fluoxetine in the treatment of bulimia nervosa. *Arch. Gen. Psychiat., 49*(2), 139–47.

Flynn, C. F., Sturges, M. S., Swarsen, R. J., & Kohn, G. M. (1993, Apr.). Alcoholism and treatment in airline aviators: One company's results. *Aviation, Space, and Environmental Medicine,* 314–18.

Foa, E. B., & Kozak, M. J. (1985). Treatment of anxiety disorders: Implications for psychopathology. In A. H. Tuma & J. D. Maser (Eds.), *Anxiety and the anxiety disorders* (pp. 421–52). Hillsdale, NJ: Erlbaum.

Foa, E., & Kozak, M. J. (1986). Emotional processing of fear: Exposure to corrective information. *Psychol. Bull., 99,* 20–35.

Foa, E. B., Steketee, G., & Young, M. C. (1984). Agoraphobia: Phenomenological aspects, associated characteristics, and theoretical considerations. *Clin. Psychol. Rev., 4,* 431–57.

Foley, M. A. Santini, C., & Sopasakis, M. (in press) Discriminating between memories: Evidence for children's spontaneous elaboration. *Journal of Experimental Child Psychology.*

Fombonne, E., & du Mazaubrun, C. (1992). Prevalence of infantile autism in four French regions. *Soc. Psychiat. Psychiat. Epidemiol., 27,* 203–10.

Fontana, A., & Rosenheck, R. (1994). Traumatic war stressors and psychiatric symptoms among World War II, Korean, and Vietnam War veterans. *Psychol. Aging, 9,* 27–33.

Forehand, R. (1993). Twenty years of research on parenting: Does it have practical implications for clinicians working with parents and children? *Clin. Psychol., 46,* 169–76.

Forehand, R., Wierson, M., Frame, C. L., & Kempton, T. (1991). Juvenile firesetting: A unique syndrome or an advanced level of antisocial behavior? *Behav. Res. Ther., 29,* 125–28.

Foreyt, J. P. (1986). Treating the diseases of the 1980s: Eating disorders. *Contemp. Psychol., 31,* 658–60.

Forgac, G. E., & Michaels, E. J. (1982). Personality characteristics of two types of male exhibitionists. *J. Abnorm. Psychol., 91,* 287–93.

Forman, S. G., & Linney, J. A. (1988). School-based prevention of adolescent substance abuse: Programs, implementation and future directions. *School Psychol. Rev., 17*(4), 550–58.

Forness, S. R., & Kavale, K. A. (1993). Strategies to improve basic learning and memory deficits in mental retardation: A meta-analysis of experimental studies. *Education and Training in Mental Retardation, 28*(2), 99–110.

Fowler, R. C., Rich, C. L., & Young, D. (1986) San Diego suicide study: Substance abuse in young cases. *Archiv. Gen. Psychiat., 43,* 962–965.

Fowler, R. D. (1987). Developing a computer based test interpretation system. In J. N. Butcher (Ed.), *Computerized psychological assessment: A practitioner's guide.* New York: Basic Books.

Fowler, R. D., & Butcher, J. N. (1986). Critique of Matarazzo's view of computerized testing: All sigma and no meaning. *Amer. Psychol., 41,* 94–96.

Fowler, R. D., Finkelstein, A., Penk, W., Bell, W., & Itzig, B. (1987). An automated problem-rating interview: The DPRI. In J. N. Butcher (Ed.), *Computerized psychological assessment: A practitioner's guide.* New York: Basic Books.

Fowles, D. C. (1980). The three arousal model: Implications of Gray's two-factor learning theory for heart rate, electrodermal activity, and psychopathy. *Psychophysiology, 17,* 87–104.

Fowles, D. C. (1993). Electrodermal activity and antisocial behavior: Empirical findings and theoretical issues. In J.-C. Roy, W. Boucsein, D. Fowles, & J. Gruzelier (Eds.), *Progress in electrodermal research.* London: Plenum

Fowles, D. C., & Missel, K. A. (1994). Electrodermal hyperactivity, motivation, and psychopathy: Theoretical issues. In D. C. Fowles, P. Sutker, & S. H. Goodman (Eds.), *Progress in experimental personality and psychopathology research.* New York: Springer.

Fowles, D. C., Sutker, P., & Goodman, S. H. (1994). *Progress in experimental personality and psychopathology research.* New York: Springer.

Frances, A. (1993). Dimensional diagnosis of personality: Not whether, but when and which. *Psychol. Inq., 4,* 110–11.

Frances, A., Widiger, T., & Fyer, M. R. (1990). The influence of classification methods on comorbidity. In J. D. Maser & C. R. Cloninger (Eds.), *Comorbidity of mood and anxiety disorders* (pp. 42–59). Washington, DC: American Psychiatric Press.

Frank, E., Anderson, C., & Rubenstein, D. (1978) Frequency of sexual dysfunction in normal couples. *New Engl. J. Med., 299,* 111–115.

Frank, E., Kupfer, D. J., Perel, J. M., Cornes, C., Jarett, D. B., Mallinger, A. G., Thase, M. E., McEachran, A. B., & Grochocinski, V. J. (1990). Three-year outcomes for maintenance therapies in recurrent depression. *Arch. Gen. Psychiat., 47,* 1093–99.

Frank, E., Prien, R. F., Jarrett, R. B., Keller, M. B., Kupfer, D. J., Lavori, P. W., Rush, A. J., & Weissman, M. M. (1991). Conceptualization and rationale for consensus definitions of terms in major depressive disorder: Remission, recovery, relapse, and recurrence. *Arch. Gen. Psychiat., 48,* 851–55.

Frank, J. D. (1978). *Persuasion and Healing* (2nd ed.). Baltimore: Johns Hopkins University Press.

Frankel, F. H. (1994). Dissociation in hysteria and hypnosis: A concept aggrandized. In S. J. Lynn & J. W. Rhue (Eds.), *Dissociation: Clinical and theoretical perspectives* (pp. 80–93). New York: Guilford.

Frayser, S. G. (1985). *Varieties of sexual experience: An anthropological perspective on human sexuality.* New Haven, CT: HRAF Press.

Frazier, P., & Burnett, J. (1994). Immediate coping strategies among rape victims. *J. Couns. Devel. 72,* 633–39.

Frazier, P., & Schauben, L. (1994). Causal attributions and recovery from rape and other stressful life events. *J. Soc. Clin. Psychol., 14,* 1–14.

Frederick, C. J. (1985). An introduction and overview of youth suicide. In M. L. Peck, N. L. Farberow, & R. E. Litman (Eds.), *Youth Suicide* (pp. 1–16). New York: Springer.

Frederick, C. J. (1986). Post-traumatic stress disorder and child-molestation. In A. Burgess & C. Hartman (Eds.), *Sexual exploitation of parents by health professionals* (pp. 133–42). New York: Praeger.

Freedman, B., & Chapman, L. J. (1973). Early subjective experience in schizophrenic episodes. *J. Abnorm. Psychol., 82*(1), 46–54.

Freeman, R. D., Malkin, S. F., & Hastings, J. O. (1975). Psychosocial problems of deaf children and their families: A comparative study. *Amer. Ann. Deaf, 120,* 391–405.

Freeman, T. (1960). On the psychopathology of schizophrenia. *J. Ment. Sci., 106,* 925–37.

Freeman, W. (1959). Psychosurgery. In S. Arieti (Ed.), *American handbook of psychiatry* (Vol. 2, pp. 1521–40). New York: Basic Books.

Fremouw, W. J., de Perczel, M., & Ellis, T. E. (1990). *Suicide risk: Assessment and response guidelines.* Elmsford, NY: Pergamon.

French, S. A., & Jeffery, R. W. (1994). Consequences of dieting to lose weight: Effects on physical and mental health. *Hlth. Psychol., 13,* 195–212.

Freud, A. (1946). *Ego and the mechanisms of defense.* New York: International Universities Press.

Freud, S. (1911). Mourning and melancholia. In W. Gaylin (Ed.), *The meaning of despair: Psychoanalytic contributions to the understanding of depression.* New York: Science House.

Freud, S. (1917). Mourning and melancholia. In W. Gaylin (Ed.), *The meaning of despair: Psychoanalytic contributions to the understanding of depression.* New York: Science House.

Freud, S. (1935). Letter to an American mother. Reprinted in Paul Friedman (1959), Sexual deviations. In S. Arieti (Ed.), *American Handbook of Psychiatry* (Vol. 1., pp. 606–7). New York: Basic Books.

Freund, K., & Blanchard, R. (1993). Erotic target location errors in male gender dysphorics, paedophiles, and fetishists. *Brit. J. Psychiat., 162,* 558–63.

Freund, K., & Kuban, M. (1993). Deficient erotic gender differentiation in pedophilia: A follow-up. *Arch. Sex. Behav., 22,* 619–28.

Freund, K., Langevin, R., Zajac, Y., Steiner, B., & Zajac, A. (1974). The transsexual syndrome in homosexual males. *J. Nerv. Ment. Dis., 158,* 145–53.

Freund, K., Watson, R. J., & Rienzo, D. (1989). Heterosexuality, homosexuality, and erotic age preference. *J. Sex Res., 26,* 107–17.

Frick, P. J., Lahey, B. B., Loeber, R., & Stouthamer-Loeber, M. (1992). Familial risk factors to opposition defiant disorder and conduct disorder: Parental psychopathology and maternal parenting. *J. Cons. Clin. Psychol., 60,* 49–55.

Friedman, D., & Squires-Wheeler, E. (1994). Event-related potentials (ERPs) as indicators of risk for schizophrenia. *Schizo. Bull., 20*(1), 63–74.

Friedman, H. S., & Booth-Kewley, S. (1987a). Personality, Type A behavior, and coronary heart disease: The role of emotional expression. *J. Pers. Soc. Psychol., 53,* 783–92.

Friedman, H. S., & Booth-Kewley, S. (1987b). The "disease-prone" personality: A meta-analytic view of the construct. *Amer. Psychol., 42,* 539–55.

Friedman, H. S., Hawley, P. H., & Tucker, J. S. (1994). Personality, health, and longevity. *Curr. Dir. Psychol. Sci., 3*(2), 37–41.

Friedman, H. S., Tucker, J. S., Tomlinson-Keasey, C., Schwartz, J. E., Wingard, D. L., & Criqui, M. H. (1993). Does childhood personality predict longevity? *J. Pers. Soc. Psychol., 65*(1), 176–85.

Friedman, J. H. (1974). Woman's role in male impotence. *Med. Asp. Human Sex., 8*(6), 8–23.

Friedman, M., & Rosenman, R. H. (1959). Association of specific overt behavior pattern with blood and cardiovascular findings. *JAMA, 169,* 1286.

Friedman, M., & Ulmer, D. (1984). *Treating Type A behavior and your heart.* New York: Knopf.

Friedman, M., Manwaring, J. H., Rosenman, R. H., Don-lon, G., & Ortega, P. (1973). Instantaneous and sudden death: Clinical and pathological differentiation in coronary artery disease. *JAMA, 225,* 1319–28.

Friedman, R., & Iwai, J. (1976). Genetic predisposition and stress-induced hypertension. *Science, 193,* 161–92.

Friedrich, W., Einbender, A. J., & Luecke, W. J. (1983). Cognitive and behavioral characteristics of physically abused children. *J. Cons. Clin. Psychol., 51*(2), 313–14.

Friman, P. C., & Warzak, W. J. (1990). Nocturnal enuresis: A prevalent, persistent, yet curable parasomnia. *Pediatrician, 17,* 38–45.

Fromm, E., & Shor, R. E. (1972). *Hypnosis: Research developments and perspectives.* Chicago: Aldine.

Fromm-Reichmann, F. (1948). Notes on the development of treatment of schizophrenics by psychoanalytic psychotherapy. *Psychiatry, 11,* 263–73.

Fulmer, R. H., & Lapidus, L. B. (1980). A study of professed reasons for beginning and continuing heroin use. *Inter. J. Addictions, 15,* 631–45.

Furby, L., Weinrott, M. R., & Blackshaw, L. (1989). Sex offender recidivism: A review. *Psychol. Bull., 105,* 3–30.

Furlong, W. B. (1971). How "speed" kills athletic careers. *Today's Health, 49*(2), 30–33, 62, 64, 66.

Furst, M. (1995). The D-Tree. *Multi-Health Systems,* Toronto, Canada: in press.

Fyer, A. J., Mannuzza, S., Chapman, T. F., Liebowitz, M. R., & Klein, D. F. (1993). A direct interview family study of social phobia. *Arch. Gen. Psychiat., 50,* 286–3.

Gabuzda, D. H., & Hirsch, M. S. (1987). Neurologic manifestations of infection with human immunodeficiency virus: Clinical features and pathogenesis. *Ann. Int. Med., 107,* 383–91.

Gager, N., & Schurr, C. (1976). *Sexual assault: Confronting rape in America.* New York: Grosset & Dunlap.

Gagnon, J., & Simon, W. (1973). *Sexual conduct: The social origins of human sexuality.* Chicago: Aldine.

Gajdusek, D. C. (1986). On the uniform source of amyloid in plaques, tangles, and vascular deposits. *Neurobiol. Aging, 7,* 453–54.

Gajzago, C., & Prior, M. (1974). Two cases of "recovery" in Kanner syndrome. *Arch. Gen. Psychiat., 31*(2), 264–68.

Galin, D., Diamond, R., & Braff, D. (1977). Lateralization of conversion symptoms: More frequent on the left. *Amer. J. Psychiat., 134,* 578–80.

Galler, J.R. (Ed.) (1984). *Human nutrition: A comprehensive treatise: Vol. 5. Nutrition and Behavior.* New York: Plenum Press.

Gamble, T. J., & Zigler, E. (1989). The head start synthesis project: A critique. *J. App. Devel. Psychol., 10,* 267–74.

Ganju, V., & Quan, H. (1987). *Mental health service needs of refugees in Texas.* Paper given at the Refugee Assistance Program: Mental Health Workgroup Meeting, UCLA, February 12–13.

Garb, H. N. (1989). Clinical judgment, clinical training, and professional experience. *Psychol. Bull., 105,* 387–96.

Garber, H. L. (1988). *The Milwaukee Project: Preventing mental retardation in children at risk.* Washington, DC: American Association on Mental Retardation.

Garber, J., Quiggle, N. L., Panak, W., & Dodge, K. A. (1994). Aggression and depression in children: Comorbidity, specificity, and cognitive processing. In D. Cicchetti & S. Toth (Eds.), *Rochester symposium on Developmental Psychopathology: Internalizing and externalizing expressions of dysfunctions* (pp. 225–264). Hillsdale, NJ: Erlbaum.

Gardner, M. (1993, Summer). The false memory syndrome. *Skeptical Inquirer, 17,* 370–75.

Garfield, S. L. (1986). Research on client variables in psychotherapy. In S. L. Garfield & A. E. Bergin (Eds.), *Handbook of psychotherapy and behavior change* (3rd ed., pp. 213–56). New York: Wiley.

Garfield, S. L. (1994). Research on client variables in psychotherapy. In A. E. Bergin & S. L. Garfield (Eds.), *Handbook of psychotherapy and behavior change* (4th ed., pp. 190–228). New York: Wiley.

Garmezy, N. (1978a). Current status of other high-risk research programs. In L. C. Wynne, R. L. Cromwell, & S. Matthysse (Eds.), *The nature of schizophrenia: New approaches to research and treatment.* New York: Wiley.

Garmezy, N. (1978b). Observations of high-risk research and premorbid development in schizophrenia. In L. C. Wynne, R. L. Cromwell, & S. Matthysse (Eds.), *The nature of schizophrenia: New approaches to research and treatment.* New York: Wiley.

Garner, D. M. (1986a). Cognitive-behavioral therapy for eating disorders. *Clin. Psychol., 39*(2), 36–39.

Garner, D. M. (1986b). Cognitive therapy for anorexia nervosa. In K. D. Brownell & J. P. Foreyt (Eds.), *Handbook of eating disorders* (pp. 301–27). New York: Basic Books.

Garner, D.M., & Wooley, S.C. (1991). Confronting the failure of behavioral and dietary treatments for obesity. *Clin. Psychol. Rev., 11,* 729–80.

Garrison, C. Z., Weinrich, M. W., Hardin, S. B., Weinrich, S., & Wang, L. (1993). Post-traumatic stress disorder in adolescents after a hurricane. *Amer. J. Epidemiol., 138,* 522–30.

Gatz, M., Lowe, B., Berg, S., Mortimer, J., & Pedersen, N. (1994). Dementia: Not just a search for the gene. *The Gerontologist, 34,* 251–255.

Gaudin, J.M., Jr. (1993). Effective intervention with neglectful families. *Crim. Just. Behav., 20,* 66–89.

Gawin, F. H., & Kleber, H. D. (1986). Abstinence symptomatology and psychiatric diagnosis in cocaine abusers. *Arch. Gen. Psychiat., 43,* 107–13.

Gebhard, P. H., Gagnon, J. H., Pomeroy, W. B., & Christenson, C. V. (1965). *Sex offenders: An analysis of types.* New York: Harper & Row.

Geis, G. (1977). Forcible rape: An introduction. In D. Chappell, R. Geis, & G. Geis (Eds.), *Forcible rape, the crime, the victim, and the offender* (pp. 1–37). New York: Columbia University Press.

Geiser, D. S. (1989). Psychosocial influences on human immunity. *Clin. Psychol. Rev., 9,* 689–715.

Geisz, D., & Steinhausen, H. (1974). On the "psychological development of children with hydrocephalus." (German) *Praxis der Kinderpsychologie und Kinderpsychiatrie, 23*(4), 113–18.

Gelfand, D. M., & Teti, D. M. (1990). The effects of maternal depression on children. *Clin. Psychol. Rev., 10,* 329–53.

Gelfand, D. M., Jenson, W. R., & Drew, C. J. (1988). *Understanding child behavior disorders* (2nd ed.). New York: Holt, Rinehart & Winston.

Gelles, R. J. (1978). Violence toward children in the United States. *Amer. J. Orthopsychiat., 48,* 580–90.

Gelles, R. J., & Cornell, C. P. (1990). *Intimate violence in families.* Newbury Park, CA: Sage.

Gentil, V., Lotufo-Neto, P., Andrade, L., Cordas, T., Bernik, M., Ramos, R., Maciel, L., Miyakawa, E., & Gorenstein, C. (1993). Clomipramine, a better reference drug for panic/agoraphobia. *J. Psychopharm., 7,* 316–24.

Gentry, J., & Eron, L. D. (1993). American Psychological Association Commission on violence and youth. *Amer. Psychol., 48,* 89.

Gentry, W. D. (1984). Behavioral medicine: A new research paradigm. In W. D. Gentry (Ed.), *Handbook of behavioral medicine* (pp. 1–12). New York: Guilford.

Gentry, W. D., Chesney, A. P., Gary, H. G., Hall, R. P., & Harburg, E. (1982). Habitual anger-coping styles: I. Effect of mean blood pressure and risk for essential hypertension. *Psychosom. Med., 44,* 195–202.

George, L., & Neufeld, R. W. J. (1985). Cognition and symptomatology in schizophrenia. *Schizo. Bull., 11,* 264–85.

George, L. K. (1984). *The burden of caregiving.* Center Reports of Advances in Research. Durham, NC: Duke University Center for the Study of Aging and Human Development.

Gerner, R. H. (1993). Treatment of acute mania. *Psychiat. Clin. N. Amer., 16,* 443–60.

Gershon, E. S. (1990). In F. K. Goodwin & K. R. Jamison (Eds.), *Genetics in manic-depressive illness* (pp. 373–401). New York: Oxford University Press.

Geschwind, N. (1975). The borderland of neurology and psychiatry: Some common misconceptions. In D. F. Benson & D. Blumer (Eds.), *Psychiatric aspects of neurological disease* (pp. 1–9). New York: Grune & Stratton.

Giannetti, R. A. (1987). The GOLPH Psychosocial History: Response contingent data acquisition and reporting. In J. N. Butcher (Ed.), *Computerized psychological assessment: A practitioners guide.* New York: Basic Books.

Gibbons, H. L. (1988). Alcohol, aviation, and safety revisited: a historical review and a suggestion. *Aviation, Space, and Environmental Medicine, 59,* 657–60.

Gilbert, J. G., & Lombardi, D. N. (1967). Personality characteristics of young male narcotic addicts. *J. Couns. Psychol., 31,* 536–38.

Gilbert, N. (1991, Spring). The phantom epidemic of sexual assault. *Public Interest,* 54–65 (12 pages).

Gilbert, N. (1992, May). Realities and mythologies of rape. *Society,* 4–11.

Giles, G. M. (1994). The status of brain injury rehabilitation. *Amer. J. Occup. Ther., 48*(3), 199–205.

Gilhooly, M. L. M., Sweeting, H. N., Whittick, J. E., & McKee, K. (1994). Family care of the dementing elderly. *Inter. Rev. Psychiat., 6*(1), 29–40.

Gillberg, C. U. (1990). Autism and pervasive developmental disorders. *J. Child Psychol. Psychiatry, 31,* 99–119.

Gillberg, C. U., & Schaumann, H. (1981). Infantile autism and puberty. *J. Autism Develop. Dis., 11*(4), 365–71.

Gillis, H. M. (1993). Individual and small-group psychotherapy for children involved in trauma and disaster. In C.F. Saylor (Ed.). *Children and disasters* (pp. 165–86). New York: Plenum

Gist, R., & Lubin, B. (Eds.). (1989). *Psychosocial aspects of disaster.* New York: Wiley.

Gitlin, M. J. (1993). Pharmacotherapy of personality disorders: Conceptual framework and clinical strategies. *J. Clin. Psychopharm., 13,* 343–53.

Gittelman, R. (1983). Treatment of reading disorders. In M. Rutter (Ed.), *Developmental neuropsychiatry* (pp. 520–39). New York: Guilford.

Gittelman, R (Ed.). (1986). *Anxiety disorders in childhood.* New York: Guilford.

Gittelman, R., Mannuzza, S., Shenker, R., & Bonagura, N. (1985). Hyperactive boys almost grown up. *Arch. Gen. Psychiat., 42,* 937–47.

Gittelman-Klein, R. (1980). Diagnosis and drug treatment of childhood disorders: Atention deficit disorder with hyperacctivity. In D. F. Klein, R. Gittelman-Klein, F. Quitkin, & A. Rifkin (Eds.), *Diagnosis and drug treatment of psychiatric disorders: Adults and children* (2nd ed., pp. 590–695). Baltimore, MD: Williams & Wilkins.

Glaser, R., Kiecolt-Glaser, J. K., Speicher, C. E., & Holliday, J. E. (1985). Stress, loneliness, and changes in herpes virus latency. *J. Behav. Med., 8,* 249–60.

Glaser, R., Rice, J., Sheridan, J., Fertel, R., Stout, J., Speicher, C., Pinsky, R., Kotur, M., Post, A., Beck, M., & Kiecolt-Glaser, J. (1987). Stress-related immune suppression: Health implications. *Brain, Behavior, and Immunity, 1,* 7–20.

Glasscote, R. (1978). What programs work and what programs do not work for chronic mental patients? In J. A. Talbott (Ed.), *The chronic mental patient: Problems, solutions and recommendations for a public policy.* Washington, DC: American Psychiatric Association.

Gleaves, D. L., & Eberenz, K. (1993). The psychopathology of anorexia nervosa: A factor analytic investigation. *J. Psychopath. Behav. Assess., 15*(2), 141–52.

Glenner, G. C. (1986). Marching backwards into the future. *Neurobiol. of Aging, 7,* 439–41.

Gleser, G., & Sacks, M. (1973). Ego defenses and reaction to stress: A validation study of the Defense Mechanisms Inventory. *J. Cons. Clin. Psychol., 40*(2), 181–87.

Glod, C. A. (1993). Long-term consequences of childhood physical and sexual abuse. *Archives of Psychiatric Nursing, 7,* 163–73.

Glosser, G., & Wexler, D. (1985). Participants' evaluation of education/support groups for families of patients with Alzheimer's disease and other dementias. *Gerontologist, 25,* 232–36.

Gochman, S. I., Allgood, B. A., & Geer, C. R. (1982). A look at today's behavior therapists. *Profess. Psychol., 13*(5), 605–9.

Goetz, K. L., & Van Kammen, D. P. (1986). Computerized axial tomography scans and subtypes of schizophrenia: A review of the literature. *J. Nerv. Ment. Dis., 174,* 31–41.

Goffman, E. (1961). *Asylums.* New York: Doubleday.

Gold, E. R. (1986). Long-term effects of sexual victimization in childhood: An attributional approach. *J. Cons. Clin. Psychol., 54,* 471–75.

Gold, M. S., & Rea, W. S. (1983). The role of endorphins in opiate addiction, withdrawal, and recovery. *Psychiat. Clin. N. Amer., 6,* 489–520.

Goldberg, D. P., & Bridges, K. (1988). Somatic presentations of psychiatric illness in primary care settings. *J. Psychoso. Res., 32,* 137–44.

Goldberg, J., True, W. R., Eisen, S. A., & Henderson, W. G. (1990). A twin study of the effects of the Vietnam War on posttraumatic stress disorder. *JAMA, 263,* 1227–32.

Goldberg, S., Schultz, C., Schultz, P., et al. (1986). Borderline and schizotypal personality disorders treated with low-dose thiothixene vs. placebo. *Arch. Gen. Psychiat., 43,* 680–86.

Golden, C. J. (1978). *Diagnosis and rehabilitation in clinical neuropsychology.* Springfield, IL: Charles C. Thomas.

Golden, D. A., & Davis, J. G. (1974). Counseling parents after the birth of an infant with Down's syndrome. *Children Today, 3*(2), 7–11.

Goldfeld, A. E., Mollica, R. R., Pesavento, B. H., & Faraone, S. V. (1988). The physical and psychological sequelae of torture—symptomatology and diagnosis. *JAMA, 259,* 2725–29.

Goldfried, M. R. (1980). Toward the delineation of therapeutic change principles. *Amer. Psychol., 35*(11), 991–99.

Goldfried, M. R., & Merbaum, M. (Eds.). (1973). *Behavior change through self control.* New York: Holt, Rinehart & Winston.

Goldfried, M. R., & Safran, J. D. (1986). Future directions in psychotherapy integration. In J. C. Norcross (Ed.), *Handbook of eclectic psychotherapy* (pp. 463–83). New York: Brunner/Mazel.

Goldfried, M. R., Greenberg, L. S., & Marmar, C. (1990). Individual psychotherapy: Process and outcome. *Annu. Rev. Psychol.* (Vol. 41, pp. 659–88). Palo Alto, CA: Annual Reviews.

Goldfried, M. R., Linehan, M. M., & Smith, J. L. (1978). Reduction of test anxiety through cognitive restructuring. *J. Cons. Clin. Psychol., 46*(1), 32–39.

Golding, J. M. (1994). Sexual assault history and physical health in randomly selected Los Angeles women. *Hlth. Psychol., 13*(2), 130–38.

Goldman, H. H., Feder, J., & Scanlon, W. (1986). Chronic mental patients in nursing homes: Reexamining data from the national nursing home survey. *Hosp. Comm. Psychiat., 37,* 269–72.

Goldsmith, S. J., Anger Friedfeld, K., Beren, S., & Rudolph, D. (1992). Psychiatric illness in patients presenting for obesity treatment. *International Journal of Eating Disorders, 12,* 63–71.

Goldsmith, W., & Cretekos, C. (1969). Unhappy odysseys: Psychiatric hospitalization among Vietnam returnees. *Amer. J. Psychiat., 20,* 78–83.

Goldstein, A. J., & Chambless, D. L. (1978). A reanalysis of agoraphobia. *Behav. Ther., 9,* 47–59.

Goldstein, A., et al. (1974, Mar. 4). Researchers isolate opiate receptor. *Behav. Today, 5*(9), 1.

Goldstein, M. J. (1985). Family factors that antedate the onset of schizophrenia and related disorders: The results of a fifteen year prospective longitudinal study. *Acta Psychiatr. Scandin.* (Suppl. No. 319), *71,* 7–18.

Goldstein, M. J. (1991). Schizophrenia and family therapy. In B. D. Beitman & G. L. Klerman (Eds.), *Integrating pharmacotherapy and psychotherapy* (pp. 291–310). Washington, DC: American Psychiatric Press.

Goldstein, M. J., & Strachan, A. M. (1987). The family and schizophrenia. In T. Jacob (Ed.), *Family interaction and psychopathology: Theories, methods, and findings* (pp. 481–508). New York: Plenum.

Goldstein, M. J., Rodnick, E. H., Jones, J. E., McPherson, S. R., & West, K. L. (1978). Family precursors of schizophrenia spectrum disorders. In L. C. Wynne, R. L. Cromwell, & S. Matthysse (Eds.), *The nature of schizophrenia: New approaches to research and treatment.* New York: Wiley.

Golub, A., & Johnson, B. D. (1994). A recent decline in cocaine use among youthful arrestees in Manhattan, 1987 through 1993. *Amer. J. Pub. Hlth., 84,* 1250–54.

Gomberg, E. S. (1989). Suicide rates among women with alcohol problems. *Amer. J. Pub. Hlth., 79,* 1363–65.

Gomes-Schwartz, B., Horowitz, J., & Cardarelli, A. (1990). *Child sexual abuse: The initial effects.* Newbury Park, CA: Sage.

Gonsiorek, J. C. (1982). The use of diagnostic concepts in working with gay and lesbian populations. In J. C. Gonsiorek (Ed.), *Homosexuality and psychotherapy.* New York: Hayworth Press.

Good, B. J., & Kleinman, A. M. (1985). Culture and anxiety: Cross-cultural evidence for the patterning of anxiety disorders. In A. H. Tuma & J.D. Master (Eds.), *Anxiety and the anxiety disorders.* Hillsdale, NJ: Erlbaum.

Goode, E. (1994, Sept. 19). Battling deviant behavior. *U.S. News and World Report,* 74–75.

Goodman, G., & Aman, C. (1990). Children's use of anatomically detailed dolls to recount an event. *Child Develop., 61,* 1859–71.

Goodman, R. (1989). Infantile autism: A syndrome of multiple primary deficits? *J. Autism Devel. Dis., 19,* 409–24.

Goodman, W. K., Price, L. H., Woods, S. W., & Charney, D. S. (1991). Pharmacological challenges in obsessive-compulsive disorder. In J. Zohar, T. Insel, & S. Rasmussen (Eds.), *The psychobiology of obsessive-compulsive disorder.* New York: Springer.

Goodwin, D. K. (1988). *The Fitzgeralds and the Kennedys: An American saga.* New York: St. Martin's Press.

Goodwin, D. W., Schulsinger, F., Hermansen, L., Guze, S. B., & Winokur, G. (1973). Alcohol problems in adoptees raised apart from alcoholic biological parents. *Arch. Gen. Psychiat., 28*(2), 238–43.

Goodwin, D. W., Schulsinger, F., Moller, N., Hermansen, L., Winokur, G., & Guze, S. B. (1974). Drinking problems in adopted and nonadopted sons of alcoholics. *Arch. Gen. Psychiat., 31*(2), 164–69.

Goodwin, F. K., & Jamison, K. R. (1990). *Manic-depressive illness.* New York: Oxford University Press.

Goodwin, G. M. (1992). Tricyclic and newer antidepressants. In E. S. Paykel (Ed.), *Handbook of affective disorders* (2nd ed.). New York: Guilford.

Goplerud, E., & Depue, R. A. (1985). Behavioral response to naturally occurring stress in cyclothymia and dysthymia. *J. Abnorm. Psychol., 94,* 128–39.

Gordon, M. (1992). The female fear. *Media Studies Journal, 6,* 130–136.

Gorenstein, E. E. (1982). Frontal lobe functions in psychopaths. *J. Abnorm. Psychol., 91,* 368–79.

Gorenstein, E. E. (1992). *The science of mental illness.* San Diego: Academic Press.

Gorin, N. (1980). Looking out for Mrs. Berwid. *Sixty Minutes.* (Narrated by Morley Safer.) New York: CBS Television News.

Gorin, N. (1982). It didn't have to happen. *Sixty Minutes.* (Narrated by Morley Safer.) New York: CBS Television News.

Gorlick, D. A. (1993). Overview of pharmacologic treatment approaches for alcohol and other drug addiction. *Psychiat. Clin. N. Amer., 16,* 141–56.

Gorman, J. M., Battista, D., Goetz, R. R., Dillon, D. J., Liebowitz, M. R., Fyer, A. J., Kahn, J. P., Sandberg, D., & Klein, D. F. (1989). A comparison of sodium bicarbonate and sodium lactate infusion in the induction of panic attacks. *Arch. Gen. Psychiat., 46,* 145–50.

Gorton, G., & Akhtar, S. (1990). The literature on personality disorders, 1985–1988: Trends, issues, and controversies. *Hosp. Comm. Psychiat., 41,* 39–51.

Gosslin, C. C., & Eysenck, S. B. G. (1980). The transvestite "double image": A preliminary report. *Personal. Indiv. Diff., 1,* 172–73.

Gotlib, I. H. & Avison, W. (1993) Children at risk for psychopathology. In C. Costello (Ed.), *Basic issues in psychopathology.* (pp. 271–319). New York: Guilford.

Gotlib, I. H., & Colby, C. A. (1987). *Treatment of depression: An interpersonal systems approach.* New York: Pergamon.

Gotlib, I. H., & Hammen, C. L. (1992). *Psychological aspects of depression: Toward a cognitive-interpersonal integration.* Chichester, UK: Wiley.

Gotlib, I. H., Whiffen, V., Mount, J., Milne, K., & Cordy, N. (1989). Prevalence rates and demographic characteristics associated with depression in pregnancy and the postpartum. *J. Cons. Clin. Psychol., 57,* 269–74.

Gotlib, I. H., Whiffen, V., Wallace, P., & Mount, J. (1991). A prospective investigation of postpartum depression: Factors involved in onset and recovery. *J. Abnorm. Psychol., 100,* 122–132.

Gottesman, I. I. (1991). *Schizophrenia genesis: The origins of madness.* New York: Freeman.

Gottesman, I. I., & Bertelsen, A. (1989). Confirming unexpressed genotypes for schizophrenia: Risks in the offspring of Fischer's Danish identical and fraternal discordant twins. *Arch. Gen. Psychiat., 46,* 867–72.

Gottesman, I. I., & Goldsmith, H. H. (in press). Developmental psychopathology of antisocial behavior: Inserting genes into its ontogenesis and epigenesis. In C. Nelson (Ed.), *Threats to optimal development: Integrating biological, social, and psychological risk factors* (Vol. 27). Hillsdale, NJ: Erlbaum.

Gottesman, I. I., & Shields, J. (1982). *Schizophrenia: The epigenetic puzzle.* Cambridge, UK: Cambridge University Press.

Gottheil, E., Thornton, C. C., Skoloda, T. E., & Alterman, A. I. (1982). Follow-up of abstinent and non-abstinent alcoholics. *Amer. J. Psychiat., 139*(5), 560–65.

Gottlieb, J. (1981). Mainstreaming: Fulfilling the promise? *Amer. J. Ment. Def., 86,* 115–26.

Gottschalk, L. A., Haer, J. L., & Bates, D. E. (1972). Effect of sensory overload on psychological state: Changes in social alienation—personal disorganization and cognitive-intellectual impairment. *Arch. Gen. Psychiat., 27*(4), 451–56.

Goy, R. W., & McEwen, B. S. (1980). *Sexual differentiation of the brain.* Cambridge: MIT Press.

Grady, K., Gersick, K. E., & Boratynski, M. (1985). Preparing parents for teenagers: A step in the prevention of adolescent substance abuse. *Family Relations: Journal of Applied Family and Child Studies, 34*(4), 541–49.

Graham, J. R. (1978a). *MMPI characteristics of alcoholics, drug abusers and pathological gamblers.* Paper presented at the 13th Annual Symposium on Recent Developments in the Use of the MMPI. Puebla, Mexico, March, 1978.

Graham, J. R. (1978b). The Minnesota Multiphasic Personality Inventory. In B. B. Wolman (Ed.), *Clinical diagnosis of mental disorders: A handbook.* New York: Plenum.

Gralnick, A. (1942). Folie a deux—The psychosis of association: A review of 103 cases and the entire English literature, with case presentations. *Psychiatric Quarterly, 14,* 230–63.

Grant, I., & Heaton, R. K. (1990). Human immunodeficiency virus-Type 1 (HIV-1) and the brain. *J. Cons. Clin. Psychol., 58,* 22–30.

Grant, I., Atkinson, J. H., Hesselink, J. R., Kennedy, C. J., Richman, D. D., Spector, S. A., & McCutchan, J. A. (1987). Evidence for early central nervous system involvement in the acquired immunodeficiency syndrome (AIDS) and other human immunodeficiency virus (HIV) infections. *Ann. Int. Med., 107,* 828–36.

Grant, S. J., & Sonti, G. (1994). Buprenorphine and morphine produce equivalent increases in extracellular single unit activity of dopamine neurons in the ventral tegmental area in vivo. *Synapse, 16*, 181–87.

Grant, V. W. (1953). A case study of fetishism. *J. Abnorm. Soc. Psychol., 48*, 142–49.

Gray, F., Gherardi, R., & Scaravilli, F. (1988). The neuropathology of the acquired immune deficiency syndrome (AIDS). *Brain, 111*, 245–66.

Gray, J. A. (1975). *Elements of a two-process theory of learning.* New York: Academic Press.

Gray, J. A. (1982). *The neuropsychology of anxiety.* New York: Oxford University Press.

Gray, J. A. (1987). *The psychology of fear and stress* (2d edition). New York: Cambridge University Press.

Gray, J. A. (1991). Fear, panic, and anxiety: What's in a name? *Psycho. Inq., 2*, 77–78.

Gray, W. W., & Ramsey, B. K. (1982). The early training project: A life-span view. *Human Develop., 25*, 48–57.

Gray-Little, B. (1995). The assessment of psychopathology in racial and ethnic minorities. In J. N. Butcher (Ed.), *Clinical personality assessment: Practical considerations* (pp. 141–157). New York: Oxford University Press.

Greeley, A. M. (1993, Mar. 20). How serious is the problem of sexual abuse by clergy? *America, 168*, 6–10.

Green, A. (1978). Self-destructive behavior in battered children. *Amer. J. Psychiat., 135*, 579–82.

Green, B. L., & Lindy, J. D. (1994). Post traumatic stress disorder in victims of disasters. *Psychiat. Clin. N. Amer., 17*, 301–10.

Green, B. L., Korol, M., Grace, M. C., Vary, M. G., Leonard, A. C., Gleser, G. C., & Smitson Cohen, S. (1991). Children and disaster: Age, gender, and parental effects on PTSD symptoms. *J. Amer. Acad. Child Adoles. Psychiat., 30*, 945–51.

Green, B. L., Lindy, J. D., Grace, M. C., & Leonard, A. C. (1992). Chronic posttraumatic stress disorder and diagnostic comorbidity in a disaster sample. *J. Nerv. Ment. Dis., 180*, 760–66.

Green, L., & Warshauer, D. (1981). Note on the "paradoxical" effect of stimulant drugs on hyperactivity with reference to the rate-dependency effect. *J. Nerv. Ment. Dis., 169*(3), 196–98.

Green, R. (1987). *The "sissy boy syndrome" and the development of homosexuality.* New Haven: Yale University Press.

Green, R. (1992). *Sexual science and the law.* Cambridge: Harvard University Press.

Green, R., & Fleming, D. (1990). Transsexual surgery follow-up: Status in the 1990's. In J. Bancroft, C. Davis, & H. Ruppel (Eds.), *Annual review of sex research.* Mt. Vernon, IA: Society for the Scientific Study of Sex.

Greenberg, R. P., Bornstein, R. F., Greenberg, M. D., & Fisher, S. (1992). A meta-analysis of antidepressant outcome under "blinder" conditions. *J. Cons. Clin. Psychol., 60*(5), 664–69.

Greene, S. M. (1989). The relationship between depression and hopelessness: Implications for current theories of depression. *Brit. J. Psychiat., 154*, 650–59.

Greenfield, J. C., & Wolfson, J. M. (1935). Microcephalia vera. *Archives of Neurology and Psychiatry, 33*, 1296–1316.

Greenhill, L. L. (1992). Pharmacologic treatment of attention deficit hyperactivity disorder. *Psychiat. Clin. N. Amer., 15*, 1–28.

Greer, S. (1964). Study of parental loss in neurotics and sociopaths. *Arch. Gen. Psychiat., 11*(2), 177–80.

Gregg, C., & Hoy, C. (1989). Coherence: The comprehension and production abilities of college writers who are normally achieving, learning disabled, and underprepared. *J. Learn. Dis., 22*, 370–72.

Greist, J. H. (1990). Treatment of obsessive-compulsive disorder: Psychotherapies, drugs, and other somatic treatments. *J. Clin. Psychiat., 51*, 44–50.

Gresham, F. M. (1982). Misguided mainstreaming: The case for social skills training with handicapped children. *Exceptional Children, 48*, 422–33.

Griest, D. L., & Wells, K. C. (1983). Behavioral family therapy with conduct disorders in children. *Behav. Ther., 14*, 37–53.

Grimes, K., & Walker, E. F. (1994). Childhood emotional expressions, educational attainment, and age at onset of illness in schizophrenia. *J. Abnorm. Psychol., 103*(4), 784–90.

Grinker, R. R. (1969). An essay on schizophrenia and science. *Arch. Gen. Psychiat., 20*, 1–24.

Grinspoon, L., Ewalt, J. R., & Shader, R. I. (1972). *Schizophrenia: Pharmacotherapy and psychotherapy.* Baltimore: Williams & Wilkins.

Grob, G. N. (1994). Mad, homeless, and unwanted: A history of the care of the chronically mentally ill in America. *Psychiat. Clin. N. Amer., 17*(3), 541–58.

Gross, B. H., Southard, M. J., Lamb, H. R., & Weinberger, L. (1987). Assessing dangerousness and responding appropriately: Hedland expands the clinician's liability established by Tarasoff. *J. Clin. Psychiat., 48*, 9–12.

Groth, A. N., Hobson, W. F., & Gary, T. (1982). Heterosexuality, homosexuality, and pedophilia: Sexual offenses against children. In A. Scacco (Ed.), *Male rape: A casebook of sexual aggression.* New York: AMS Press.

Groth, N. A. (1979). *Men who rape.* New York: Plenum.

Group for the Advancement of Psychiatry. (1966). *Psychopathological disorders in childhood. Theoretical considerations and a proposed classification system.* Washington, DC: GAP Report # 2.

Gruder, C. L., Mermelstein, R. J., Kirkendol, S., Hedeker, D., Wong, S. C., Schreckengost, J., Warnecke, R. B., Burzette, R., & Miller, T. Q. (1993). Effects of social support and relapse prevention training as adjuncts to a televised smoking cessation intervention. *J. Cons. Clin. Psychol., 61*, 113–20.

Grunebaum, H., & Perlman, M. S. (1973). Paranoia and naivete. *Arch. Gen. Psychiat., 28*(1), 30–32.

Guelfi, G. P., Faustman, W. O., & Csernansky, J. G. (1989). Independence of positive and negative symptoms in a population of schizophrenic patients. *J. Nerv. Ment. Dis., 177*, 285–90.

Guerra, F. (1971). *The pre-Columbian mind.* New York: Seminar Press.

Gugliemi, R. S. (1979). *A double-blind study of the effectiveness of skin temperature biofeedback as a treatment for Raynaud's disease.* Unpublished doctoral dissertation, University of Minnesota.

Gunderson, J. G. (1980). A reevaluation of milieu therapy for nonchronic schizophrenic patients. *Schizo. Bull., 6*(1), 64–69.

Gunderson, J. G., & Philips, K. A. (1991). A current view of the interface between borderline personality disorder and depression. *Amer. J. Psychiat., 148*, 967–75.

Gunderson, J. G., & Singer, M. T. (1986). Defining borderline patients: An overview. In M. H. Stone (Ed.), *Essential papers on borderline disorders* (pp. 453–74). New York: New York University Press.

Gunn, J. (1993). Castration is not the answer. *Brit. Med. J., 307*, 790–91.

Gur, R. E., & Pearlson, G. D. (1993). Neuroimaging in schizophrenia research. *Schizo. Bull., 19*(2), 337–53.

Gur, R. E., Mozley, P. D., Shtasel, D. L., Cannon, T. D., Gallacher, F., Turetsky, B., Grossman, R., & Gur, R. C. (1994). Clinical subtypes of schizophrenia: Differences in brain and CFS volume. *Amer. J. Psychiat., 151*(3), 343–50.

Gureje, O., Bamidele, R., & Raji, O. (1994). Early brain trauma and schizophrenia in Nigerian patients. *Amer. J. Psychiat., 151*(3), 368–71.

Gurland, B. J., & Cross, P. S. (1982). Epidemiology of psychopathology in old age. In L. F. Jarvik & G. W. Small (Eds.), *Psychiatric clinics of North America.* Philadelphia: Saunders.

Gurman, A. S., & Kniskern, D. P. (1978). Research on marital and family therapy: Progress, perspective and prospect. In S. L. Garfield & A. E. Bergin (Eds.), *Handbook of psychotherapy and behavior change.* New York: Wiley.

Gurman, A. S., Kniskern, D. P., & Pinsof, W. M. (1986). Research on marital and family therapies. In S. L. Garfield & A. E. Bergin (Eds.), *Handbook of psychotherapy and behavior change* (3d ed. pp. 565–626). New York: Wiley.

Gurtman, M. B. (1986). Depression and the response of others: Reevaluating the reevaluation. *J. Abnorm. Psychol., 95,* 99–101.

Guze, S. B., Cloninger, C. R., Martin, R. L., & Clayton, P. J. (1986). A follow-up and family study of Briquet's Syndrome. *Brit. J. Psychiat., 149,* 17–23.

Haaga, D. A., & Davison, G. C. (1989). Outcome studies of rational-emotive therapy. In M. Bernard & R. DeGiuseppe (Eds.), *Inside rational-emotive therapy.* New York: Academic Press.

Haaga, D. A., & Davison, G. C. (1992). Disappearing differences do not always reflect healthy integration: An analysis of cognitive therapy and rational-emotive therapy. *Journal of Psychotherapy Integration, 1,* 287–303.

Haaga, D. A., Dyck, M. J., & Ernst, D. (1991). Empirical status of cognitive theory of depression. *Psychol. Bull., 110* (2), 215–36.

Halberstam, M. (1972). Can you make yourself sick? A doctor's report on psychosomatic illness. *Today's Health, 50*(12), 24–29.

Haley, J. (1962). Whither family therapy. *Family Process, 1,* 69–100.

Haley, S. A. (1978). Treatment implications of post-combat stress response syndromes for mental health professionals. In C. R. Figley (Ed.), *Stress disorders among Vietnam veterans.* New York: Brunner/Mazel.

Halford, W. K., & Haynes, R. (1991) Psychosocial rehabilitation of chronic schizophrenic patients: Recent findings on social skills training and family psychoeducation. *Clin. Psychol. Rev., 11,* 23–44.

Hallett, J. D., Zasler, N. D., Maurer, P., & Cash, S. (1994). Role change after traumatic brain injury in adults. *Amer. J. Occup. Ther., 48*(3), 241–46.

Hallgren, B. (1950). Specific dyslexia ("congenital word-blindness"). *Acta Neurol. Scandin.,* Suppl., *65,* 1–287.

Hallworth, H. J. (1977). Computer-assisted instruction for the mentally retarded. In P. Milder (Ed.), *Research to practice in mental retardation* (Vol. 2, pp. 419–20). Baltimore: University Park Press.

Halmi, K. A., Falk, J. R., & Schwartz, E. (1981). Binge-eating and vomiting: A survey of a college population. *Psychol. Med., 11,* 697–706.

Hamer, D. H., Hu, S., Magnuson, V. L., Hu, N., & Pattatucci, A. M. L. (1993). A linkage between DNA markers on the X chromosome and male sexual orientation. *Science, 261,* 321–27.

Hammen, C. L. (1991) Generation of stress in the course of unipolar depression. *J. Abnorm. Psychol., 100,* 555–561.

Hammen, C. L. (1995). Stress and the course of unipolar disorders. In C.M. Mazure (Ed.), *Does stress cause psychiatric illness?* Washington, DC: American Psychiatric Press.

Hammen, C. L., & Peters, S. D. (1977). Differential responses to male and female depressive reactions. *J. Cons. Clin. Psychol., 45,* 994–1001.

Hammen, C. L., & Peters, S. D. (1978). Interpersonal consequences of depression: Responses to men and women enacting a depressed role. *J. Abnorm. Psychol., 87*(3), 322–32.

Hammen, C. L., Adrian, C., Gordon, D., Burge, D., Jaenicke, C., & Hiroto, D. (1987). Children of depressed mothers: Maternal strain and symptom predictors of dysfunction. *J. Abnorm. Psychol., 96,* 190–98.

Handleman, J. S., Gill, M. J., & Alessandri, M. (1988). Generalization by severely developmentally disabled children: Issues, advances, and future directions. *The Behavior Therapist, 11,* 221–23.

Haney, B., & Gold, M. (1973). The juvenile delinquent nobody knows. *Psych. Today, 7*(4), 48–52, 55.

Hanrahan, J., Goodman, W., & Rapagna, S. (1990). Preparing mentally retarded students for mainstreaming: Priorities of regular class and special school teachers. *Amer. J. Ment. Retard., 94,* 470–74.

Harburgh, E., Erfurt, J. C., Hauenstein, L. S., Chape, C., Schull, W. J., & Schork, M. A. (1973). Socioecological stress, suppressed hostility, skin color, and black-white male blood pressure: Detroit. *Psychosom. Med., 35,* 276–96.

Harder, D. W., Strauss, J. S., Greenwald, D. F., Kokes, R. F., et al. (1989). Life events and psychopathology severity: Comparisons between psychiatric inpatients and outpatients. *J. Clin. Psychol., 45,* 202–9.

Harding, C. M., Brooks, G. W., Ashikaga, T., Strauss, J. S., & Breier, A. (1987a). The Vermont longitudinal study of persons with severe mental illness, I: Methodology, study sample, and overall status 32 years later. *Amer. J. Psychiat., 144,* 718–26.

Harding, C. M., Brooks, G. W., Ashikaga, T., Strauss, J. S., & Breier, A. (1987b). The Vermont longitudinal study of persons with severe mental illness, II: Long-term outcome of subjects who retrospectively met DSM-III criteria for schizophrenia. *Amer. J. Psychiat., 144,* 727–35.

Hardy, J. A., Mann, D. M., Wester, P., & Winblad, B. (1986). An integrative hypothesis concerning the pathogenesis and progression of Alzheimer's disease. *Neurobiol. of Aging, 7,* 489–502.

Hare, E. H. (1962). Masturbatory insanity: The history of an idea. *J. Ment. Sci., 108,* 1–25.

Hare, R. D. (1968). Psychopathy, autonomic functioning and the orienting response. *J. Abnorm. Psychol., 73* (Monograph Suppl. 3, part 2), 1–24.

Hare, R. D. (1970). *Psychopathy: Theory and research.* New York: Wiley.

Hare, R. D. (1978a). Electrodermal and cardiovascular correlates of psychopathy. In R. D. Hare & D. Schalling (Eds.), *Psychopathic behavior: Approaches to research* (pp. 107–43). Chichester, UK: Wiley.

Hare, R. D. (1978b). Psychopathy and electrodermal responses to nonsignal stimulation. *Biol. Psych., 6,* 237–46.

Hare, R. D. (1980). A research scale for the assessment of psychopathy in criminal populations. *Personal. Indiv. Diff., 1,* 111–119.

Hare, R. D. (1984). Performance of psychopaths on cognitive tasks related to frontal lobe function. *J. Abnorm. Psychol., 93*(2), 133–40.

Hare, R. D. (1985a). Comparison of the procedures for the assessment of psychopathy. *J. Cons. Clin. Psychol., 53,* 7–16.

Hare, R. D. (1985b). *The psychopathy checklist.* Unpublished manuscript, University of British Columbia, Vancouver, Canada.

Hare, R. D. (1991). *The Hare psychopathy checklist—Revised.* Toronto: Multi-Health Systems.

Hare, R. D., & Hart, S. D. (1993). Psychopathy, mental disorder, and crime. In S. Hodgins (Ed.), *Mental disorder and crime.* Newbury Park, CA: Sage.

Hare, R. D., Hart, S. D., & Harpur, T. J.(1991). Psychopathy and DSM-IV criteria for antisocial personality disorder. *J. Abnorm. Psychol., 100,* 391–98.

Hare, R. D., McPherson, L. M., & Forth, A. E. (1988). Male psychopaths and their criminal careers. *J. Cons. Clin. Psychology, 56,* 710–14.

Harford, T. C., & Parker, D. A. (1994). Antisocial behavior, family history, and alcohol dependence symptoms. *Alcoholism (NY), 18,* 265–68.

Hargrave, G. E., Hiatt, D., Ogard, E. M., & Karr, C. (1994). Comparison of MMPI and MMPI-2 for a sample of Peace Officers. *Psychol. Assess., 6,* 27–32.

Harlow, J. M. (1868). Recovery from the passage of an iron bar through the head. *Publication of the Massachusetts Medical Society, 2,* 327.

Harlow, J. M. (1993). Recovery from the passage of an iron bar through the head. *History of Psychiatry, 4,* 271–81.

Harpur, T. J., & Hare, R. D. (1994). Assessment of psychopathy as a function of age. *J. Abnorm. Psychol., 103,* 604–9.

Harpur, T. J., Hare, R. D., & Hakstian, A. R. (1989). Two-factor conceptualization of psychopathy: Construct validity and assessment implications. *Psychol. Assess., 1* (1), 6–17.

Harpur, T.J., Hart, S.D., & Hare, R.D. (1993). The personality of the psychopath.

Harris, G. T., Rice, M. E., & Cormier, C. A. (1991). Psychopathy and violent recidivism. *Law and Human Behavior, 15,* 625–37.

Harris, S. L., & Ersner-Hershfield, R. (1978). Behavioral suppression of seriously disruptive behavior in psychotic and retarded patients: A review of punishment and its alternatives. *Psychol. Bull., 85,* 1352–75.

Harris, T. O., Brown, G. W., & Bifulco, A. (1986). Loss of parent in childhood and adult psychiatric disorder: The role of lack of adequate parental care. *Psychol. Med., 16,* 641–59.

Harrow, M., Goldberg, J. F., Grossman, L. S., & Meltzer, H. Y. (1990). Outcome in manic disorders: A naturalistic follow-up study. *Arch. Gen. Psychiat., 47,* 665–71.

Hartford, J. T. (1986). A review of antemortem markers of Alzheimer's disease. *Neurobiol. of Aging, 7,* 401–2.

Hartlage, L., Asken, M., & Hornsby, J. (1987). *Essentials of neuropsychological assessment.* New York: Springer.

Hartmann, E., Milofsky, E., Vaillant, G., Oldfield, M., & Falke, R. (1984). Vulnerability to schizophrenia: Predormation. *Arch. Gen. Psychiat., 41,* 1050–56.

Hartup, W. W. (1983). Peer relations. In P. H. Mussen (Ed.), *Handbook of child psychology* (Vol. 4, pp. 274–385). New York: Wiley.

Hathaway, S. R., & McKinley, J. C. (1951). *The Minnesota multiphasic personality inventory* (rev. ed.). New York: Psychological Corporation.

Hauff, E., & Vaglum, P. (1994). Chronic posttraumatic stress disorder in Vietnamese refugees. *J. Nerv. Ment.Dis., 182,* 85–90.

Haug Schnabel, G. (1992). Daytime and nighttime enuresis: A functional disorder and its ethological decoding. *Behaviour, 120,* 232–61.

Havens, L. L. (1974). The existential use of the self. *Amer. J. Psychiat., 131*(1), 1–10.

Hawton, K. (1992). Suicide and attempted suicide. In E. S. Paykel (Ed.), *Handbook of affective disorders* (2nd ed.). New York: Guilford.

Hawton, K., Catalan, J., & Fagg, J. (1992). Sex therapy for erectile dysfunction: Characteristics of couples, treatment outcome, and prognostic factors. *Arch. Sex. Behav., 21,* 161–75.

Haynes, S. G., Feinleib, M., & Kannel, W. B. (1980). The relationship of psychosocial factors to coronary heart disease in the Framingham study: III. Eight-year incidence of coronary heart disease. *Amer. J. Epidemiol., 111,* 37–58.

Haywood, H. C., Meyers, C. E., & Switsky, H. N. (1982). *Ann. Rev. Psychol., 33.*

Hazelrigg, M., Cooper, H., & Borduin, C. (1987). Evaluating the effectiveness of family therapies: An integrative review and analysis. *Psychol. Bull., 101,* 428–42.

Healy, D., & Williams, J. M. G. (1988). Dysrhythmia, dysphoria, and depression: The interaction of learned helplessness and circadian dysrhythmia in the pathogenesis of depression. *Psychol. Bull., 103,* 163–78.

Hearn, M. D., Murray, D. M., & Luepker, R. V. (1989). Hostility, coronary heart disease, and total mortality: A 33-year follow-up study of university students. *J. Behav. Med., 12,* 105–21.

Heaton, R., Paulsen, J. S., McAdams, L. A., Kuck, J., Zisook, S., Braff, D., Harris, M. J., & Jesta, D. V. (1994). Neuropsychological deficits in schizophrenics: Relationship to age, chronicity, and dementia. *Arch. Gen. Psychiat., 51*(6), 469–76.

Hebert, R., Leclerc, G., Bravo, G., & Girouard, D. (1994). Efficacy of a support group programme for caregivers of demented patients in the community: A randomized control trial. *Arch. Gerontol. Geriatr., 18,* 1–14.

Hechtman, L., Weiss, G., & Perlman, T. (1980). Hyperactives as young adults: Self-esteem and social skills. *Canad. J. Psychiat., 25*(6), 478–83.

Hefez, A. (1985). The role of the press and the medical community in the epidemic of "mysterious gas poisoning" in the Jordan West Bank. *Amer. J. Psychiat., 142,* 833–37.

Hegarty, J. D., Baldessarini, R. J., Tohen, M., Waternaux, C., & Oepen, G. (1994). One hundred years of schizophrenia: A meta-analysis of the outcome literature. *Amer. J. Psychiat., 151*(10), 1409–16.

Heider, F. (1958). *The psychology of interpersonal relations.* New York: Wiley.

Heilbrun, K. (1992). The role of psychological testing in forensic assessment. *Law and Human Behavior, 16,* 257–72.

Heiman, J. R., & Grafton-Becker, V. (1989). Orgasmic disorders in women. In S. R. Leiblum & R. C. Rosen (Eds.), *Principles and practice of sex therapy* (2nd ed., pp. 51–88). New York: Guilford.

Heller, K., Sher, K. J., & Benson, C. S. (1982). Problems associated with risk of overprediction in studies of offspring of alcoholics: Implications for prevention. *Clin. Psychol. Rev., 2,* 183–200.

Hellman, R., Green, R., Gray, J., & Williams, K. (1981). Childhood sexual identity, childhood religiosity, and homophobia as influences in the development of transsexualism, homosexuality and heterosexuality. *Arch. Gen. Psychiat., 38,* 910–15.

Helzer, J. E., Robins, L. N., & McEvoy, L. (1987). Post-traumatic stress disorder in the general population: Findings from the Epidemiological Catchment Area Survey. *New Engl. J. Med., 317,* 1630–34.

Henderson, V. W. (1986). Non-genetic factors in Alzheimer's disease pathogenesis. *Neurobiol. of Aging, 7,* 585–87.

Hendin, H. (1975). Student suicide: Death as a life-style. *J. Nerv. Ment. Dis., 160*(3), 204–19.

Henggeler, S. W. (1989). Delinquency in adolescence. Newbury Park, CA: Sage.

Henriques, J. B., & Davidson, R. J. (1990). Regional brain electrical asymmetries discriminate between previously depressed and healthy control subjects. *J. Abnorm. Psychol., 99,* 22–31.

Henriques, J. B., & Davidson, R. J. (1991). Left frontal hypoactivation in depression. *J. Abnorm. Psychol., 100,* 535–45.

Henry, W. P., Strupp, H. H., Schacht, T. E., & Gaston, L. (1994). Psychodynamic approaches. In A. E. Bergin & S. L. Garfield (Eds.), *Handbook of psychotherapy and behavior change* (4th ed., pp. 467–508). New York: Wiley.

Herbert, J. D., Hope, D. A., & Bellack, A. S. (1992). Validity of the distinction between generalized social phobia and avoidant personality disorder. *J. Abnorm. Psychol., 101,* 332–39.

Herbert, T. B., & Cohen, S. (1993). Depression and immunity: A meta-analytic review. *Psychol. Bull., 113*(3), 472–86.

Herd, J. A. (1984). Cardiovascular disease and hypertension. In W. D. Gentry (Ed.), *Handbook of behavioral medicine* (pp. 222–81). New York: Guilford.

Herdt, G., & Stoller, R. G. (1990). *Intimate communications: Erotics and the study of a culture.* New York: Columbia University Press.

Herek, G. (1989, Aug. 1). The tyranny of 10%. *The Advocate,* 46–49.

Hermalin, J., & Morell, J. A. (Eds.). (1986). *Prevention planning in mental health.* Beverly Hills, CA: Sage.

Herman, J. L. (1993, March/April). The abuses of memory. *Mother Jones, 18,* 3–4.

Herman, J. L. (1994, Spring). Presuming to know the truth. *Nieman Reports, 48,* 43–46.

Herman, J. L. (1990). Sex offenders: A feminist perspective. In W. L. Marshall, D. R. Laws, & H. E. Barbaree (Eds.), *Handbook of sexual assault* (pp. 177–94). New York: Plenum.

Herman, J. L., Perry, J. C., & van der Kolk, B. A. (1989). Childhood trauma in borderline personality disorder. *Amer. J. Psychiat., 146,* 490–95.

Hermann, D. H. J. (1990). Autonomy, self determination, the right of involuntarily committed persons to refuse treatment, and the use of substituted judgment in medication decisions involving incompetent persons. *International Journal of Law and Psychiatry, 13,* 361–85.

Hernandez, J. T. (1992). Substance abuse among sexually abused adolescents. *Journal of Adolescent Health, 13,* 658–62.

Herrenkohl, R. C., Herrenkohl, E. C., & Egolf, B. P. (1983). Circumstances surrounding the occurrence of child maltreatment. *J. Cons. Clin. Psychol., 51*(3), 424–31.

Herrnstein, R., & Murray, C. (1994). *The bell curve.* New York: Free Press.

Herzog, D. B., & Rathbun, J. M. (1982). Childhood depression: Developmental considerations. *American Journal of Disorders in Children, 136*(2), 15–20.

Heston, L. (1966). Psychiatric disorders in foster home reared children of schizophrenic mothers. *Brit. J. Psychiat., 112,* 819–25.

Hetherington, E. M. (1991) The role of individual differences and family relationships in children's coping with divorce and remarriage. In P.S. Cowan & E.M. Hetherington (Eds.), *Family transitions* (pp. 165–194). Hillsdale, NJ: Erlbaum.

Hetherington, E.M., Stanley-Hagan, M., & Anderson, E.R. (1989). Marital transitions: A child's perspective. *Amer. Psychol., 44,* 303–312.

Hetherington, E.M. & Parke, R.D. (1993). *Child psychology: A contemporary viewpoint,* 4th ed. New York: McGraw Hill.

Heyman, A., Wilkinson, W. E., Hurwitz, B. J., Helms, M. J., et al. (1987). Early-onset Alzheimer's disease: Clinical predictors of institutionalization and death. *Neurology, 37,* 980–84.

Hibbert, G. A. (1984). Ideational components of anxiety: Their origin and content. *Brit. J. Psychiat., 144,* 618–24.

Hilgard, E. R. (1973). The domain of hypnosis: With some comments on alternative paradigms. *Amer. Psychol., 28*(11), 972–82.

Hilgard, E. R. (1974). Weapon against pain: Hypnosis is no mirage. *Psych. Today, 8*(6), 120–22, 126, 128.

Hilgard, E. R. (1977). *Divided consciousness: Multiple controls in human thought and action.* New York: Wiley.

Hilgard, E. R. (1994). Neodissociation theory. In S. J. Lynn & J. W. Rhue (Eds.), *Dissociation: Clinical and theoretical perspectives* (pp. 32–51). New York: Guilford.

Hill, A. L. (1975). Investigation of calendar calculating by an idiot savant. *Amer. J. Psychiat., 132*(5), 557–59.

Hillson, J. M., & Kuiper, N. A. (1994). A stress and coping model of child treatment. *Clin. Psychol. Rev, 14,* 261–85.

Himle, J. A., & Hill, E. M. (1991). Alcohol abuse and anxiety disorders: Evidence from the Epidemiologic Catchment Area Survey. *J. Anxiety Dis., 5,* 237–45.

Hinrichsen, G. A., & Niederehe, G. (1994). Dementia management strategies and adjustment of family members of older patients. *Gerontologist, 34*(1), 95–102.

Hinshaw, S. P. (1992). Externalizing behavior problems and academic underachievement in childhood and adolescence: Causal relationships and underlying mechanisms. *Psychol. Bull., 111,* 127–55.

Hinshaw, S. P. (1994). Conduct disorder in childhood: Conceptualization, diagnosis, comorbidity, and risk status for antisocial functioning in adulthood. In D. C. Fowles, P. Sutker, & S. H. Goodman (Eds.), *Progress in experimental personality and psychopathology research.* New York: Springer.

Hiroto, D. S., & Seligman, M. E. P. (1975). Generality of learned helplessness in man. *J. Pers. Soc. Psychol., 31*(2), 311–27.

Hirsch, S. R., & Leff, J. P. (1975). *Abnormalities in parents of schizophrenics.* London: Oxford University Press.

Hirschfeld, M. (1948). *Sexual anomalies* (p. 167). New York: Emerson.

Hirschfeld, R. M. A., & Cross, C. K. (1982). Epidemiology of affective categories. *Arch. Gen. Psychiat., 39,* 35–46.

Hirschfeld, R. M. A., Klerman, G. L., Andreasen, N. C., Clayton, P. J., & Keller, M. B. (1985). Situational major depressive disorder. *Arch. Gen. Psychiat., 42,* 1109–14.

Hirschfeld, R. M. A., Klerman, G. L., Clayton, P. J., Keller, M. B., McDonald-Scott, P., & Larkin, B. H. (1983). Assessing personality: Effects of the depressive state on trait measurement. *Amer. J. Psychiat., 140,* 695–99.

Hirschfeld, R. M. A., Klerman, G. L., Lavori, P., Keller, M. B., Griffith, P., & Coryell, W. (1989). Premorbid personality assessments of first onset of major depression. *Arch. Gen. Psychiat., 46,* 345–50.

Hirshfeld, D.R., Rosenbaum, J.F., Biederman, J., Bolduc, E.A., Faraone, S.V., Snidman, N., Reznick, J.S., Kagan, J. (1992). Stable behavioral inhibition and its association with anxiety disorder. *J. Amer. Acad. Child Adoles. Psychiat., 31,* 103–111.

Hirst, W. (1982). The amnesic syndrome: Descriptions and explanations. *Psychol. Bull., 91,* 435–60.

Hobfoll, S. E., Johnson, R., Eyle, N., & Tzemach, M. (1994). A nation's response to attack: Israeli's depressive reactions to the Gulf War. *J. Trauma. Stress, 7,* 59–73.

Hodkinson, S., Sherrington, R., Gurling, H., Marchbanks, R., Reeders, S., Mallet, J., McInnis, M., Petursson, H., & Brynjolfsson, J. (1987). Molecular evidence for heterogeneity in manic depression. *Nature, 325,* 805–6.

Hoffman, A. (1971). LSD discoverer disputes "chance" factor in finding. *Psychiat. News, 6*(8), 23–26.

Hoffman, J. L. (1943). Psychotic visitors to government offices in the national capital. *Amer. J. Psychiat., 99,* 571–75.

Hogarty, G. E., Anderson, C. M., Reiss, D. J., Kornblith, S. J., & Greenwald, D. P. (1986). Family psychoeducation, social skills training, and maintenance chemotherapy in the aftercare treatment of schizophrenia: 1. One-year effects of a controlled study. *Arch. Gen. Psychiat., 43,* 633–42.

Hogarty, G. E., McEvoy, J. P., Munetz, M., DiBarry, L., Bartone, P., Cather, R., Cooley, S. J., Ulrich, R. F., Carter, M., & Madonia, M. J. (1988). Dose of Fluphenazine, familial expressed emotion, and outcome in schizophrenia. *Arch. Gen. Psychiat., 45,* 797–805.

Hokanson, J. E., & Burgess, M. (1962). The effects of three types of aggression on vascular process. *J. Abnorm. Soc. Psychol., 64,* 446–49.

Hokanson, J. E., Hummer, J. T., & Butler, A. C. (1991). Interpersonal perceptions by depressed college students. *Cog. Ther. Res., 15,* 443–57.

Hokanson, J. E., Lowenstein, D. A., Hedeen, C., Howes, M. J. (1986). Dysphoric college students and roommates: A study of social behaviors over a three-month period. *Personality and Social Psychology Bulletin, 12,* 311–24.

Hokanson, J. E., Rubert, M. P., Welker, R. A., Hollander, G. R., & Hedeen, C. (1989). Interpersonal concomitants and antecedents of depression among college students. *J. Abnorm. Psychol., 98,* 209–17.

Holcomb, W. (1979). *Coping with severe stress: A clinical application of stress-inoculation therapy.* Unpublished doctoral dissertation, University of Missouri-Columbia.

Holden, R. R., Medonca, J. D., & Serin, R. C. (1989). Suicide, hopelessness, and social desirability: A test of an interactive model. *J. Cons. Clin. Psychol., 57,* 500–4.

Holder, H. D., Longabaugh, R., Miller, W. R., & Rubonis, A. V. (1991). The cost effectiveness of treatment for alcohol problems: A first approximation. *J. Stud. Alcoh., 52,* 517–540.

Holland, H. C. (1974). Displacement activity as a form of abnormal behavior in animals. In H. R. Beech (Ed.), *Obsessional states* (pp. 161–73). London: Methuen.

Hollander, E., DeCaria, C. M., Nitescu, A., Gully, R., Suckow, R. F., et al. (1992). Serotonergic function in obsessive-compulsive disorder: Behavioral and neuroendocrine responses to oral m-chlorophenylpiperazine and fenfluramine in patients and healthy volunteers. *Arch. Gen. Psychiat., 49,* 21–28.

Hollander, E., Liebowitz, M. R., Gorman, J. M., Cohen, B., Fyer, A., & Klein, D. F. (1989). Cortisol and sodium lactate-induced panic. *Arch. Gen. Psychiat., 46,* 135–40.

Hollon, S. D., & Beck, A. T. (1978). Psychotherapy and drug therapy: Comparisons and combinations. In S. L. Garfield & A. E. Bergin (Eds.), *Handbook of psychotherapy and behavior change* (pp. 437–90). New York: Wiley. (2nd edition, pp. 437–90).

Hollon, S. D. & Beck, A. T. (1994). Research on cognitive therapies. In A.E. Bergin & S. C. Garfield (Eds.), *Handbook of psychotherapy and behavior change* (4th ed., pp. 428–66). New York: Wiley.

Hollon, S. D. & Beck, A.T. (1994). Research on cognitive therapies. In A.E. Bergin & S.C. Garfield (Eds.), *Handbook of psychotherapy and behavior change* (4th ed.). New York: Wiley.

Hollon, S. D., Evans, M., & DeRubeis, R. (1990). Cognitive mediation of relapse prevention following treatment for depression: Implications of differential risk. In R. Ingram (Ed.), *Psychological aspects of depression*. New York: Plenum.

Hollon, S. D., & Beck, A. T. (1994). Cognitive and cognitive-behavioral therapies. In A. E. Bergin & S. L. Garfield (Eds.), *Handbook of psychotherapy and behavior change* (4th ed., pp. 428–66). New York: Wiley.

Hollon, S. D., DeRubeis, R. J., & Evans, M. D. (1987). Causal mediation of change in treatment for depression: Discriminating between nonspecificity and noncausality. *Psychol. Bull., 102*, 139–49.

Hollon, S. D., DeRubeis, R. J., Evans, M. D., Wiemer, M. J., Garvey, M. J., Grove, W. M., & Tuason, V. B. (1992). Cognitive therapy and pharmacotherapy for depression: Singly and in combination. *Arch. Gen. Psychiat., 49*(10), 774–81.

Hollon, S. D., Shelton, R. C., & Davis, D. D. (1993). Cognitive therapy for depression: Conceptual issues and clinical efficacy. *J. Cons. Clin. Psychol., 61*(2), 270–75.

Hollon, S. D., Shelton, R. C., & Loosen, P. T. (1991). Cognitive therapy and pharmacotherapy for depression. *J. Cons. Clin. Psychol., 59*, 88–99.

Holmes, T. H., & Rahe, R. H. (1967). The social readjustment rating scale. *J. Psychosom. Res., 11*(2), 213–18.

Holohan, C. J., & Moos, R. H. (1991). Life stressors, personal and social resources, and depression: A 4-year structural model. *J. Abnorm. Psychol. 100*, 31–38.

Holroyd, K. A., & Andrasik, F. (1978). Coping and the self-control of chronic tension headache. *J. Cons. Clin. Psychol., 46*, 1036–45.

Holroyd, K. A., Andrasik, F., & Westbrook, T. (1977). Cognitive control of tension headache. *Cog. Ther. Res., 1*, 121–33.

Holsboer, F. (1992). The hypothalmic-pituitary-adrenocortical system. In E. S. Paykel (Ed.), *Handbook of affective disorders* (2nd ed.). New York: Guilford.

Holt, C. S., Heimberg, R. G., & Hope, D. A. (1992). Avoidant personality disorder and the generalized subtype of social phobia. *J. Abnorm. Psychol., 101*, 318–25.

Holvey, D. N., & Talbott, J. H. (Eds.). (1972). *The Merck manual of diagnosis and therapy* (12th ed.). Rahway, NJ: Merck, Sharp, & Dohme Research Laboratories.

Holzman, P. S., Kringlen, E., Matthysse, S., Flanagan, S. D., Lipton, R. B., Cramer, G., Levin, S., Lange, K., & Levy, D. L. (1988). A single dominant gene can account for eye tracking dysfunctions and schizophrenia in offspring of discordant twins. *Arch. Gen. Psychiat., 45*, 641–47.

Homans, G. C. (1961). *Social behavior: Its elementary forms*. New York: Harcourt Brace Jovanovich.

Homer, L. E. (1974). The anatomy of a runaway. *Human Behav., 3*(4), 37.

Homme, L. E. (1965). Perspectives in psychology: Control of coverants, the operants of the mind (Vol. 24). *Psychol. Rec., 15*, 501–11.

Hook, E. B. (1980). Genetic counseling dilemmas: Down's syndrome, paternal age, and recurrence risk after remarriage. *Amer. J. Med. Genet., 5*, 145–51.

Hooker, E. (1957). The adjustment of the male overt homosexual. *Journal of Projective Techniques, 21*, 18–30.

Hooley, J. M. (1985). Expressed emotion: A review of the critical literature. *Clin. Psychol. Rev., 5*, 119–39.

Hooley, J. M. (1986). Expressed emotion and depression: Interactions between patients and high- versus low-expressed-emotion spouses. *J. Abnorm. Psychol., 95*, 237–46.

Hooley, J. M., & Teasdale, J. D. (1989). Predictors of relapse in unipolar depressives: Expressed emotion, marital distress, and perceived criticism. *J. Abnorm. Psychol., 98*, 229–35.

Hooley, J. M., Orley, J., & Teasdale, J. D. (1986). Levels of expressed emotion and relapse in depressed patients. *Brit. J. Psychiat., 148*, 642–47.

Hoon, P. W., Wincze, J. P., & Hoon, E. F. (1977). A test of reciprocal inhibition: Are anxiety and sexual arousal in women mutually inhibitory? *J. Abnorm. Psychol. 86*, 65–74.

Hope, D. A., & Heimberg, R. G. (1993). Social phobia and social anxiety. In D. H. Barlow (Eds.), *Clinical handbook of psychological disorders* (pp. 99–136). New York: Guilford.

Hope, D. A., Rapee, R. M., Heimberg, R. G., & Dombeck, M. J. (1990). Representations of the self in social phobia: Vulnerability to social threat. *Cog. Ther. Res., 14*, 177–89.

Horevitz, R. (1994). Dissociation and multiple personality: Conflicts and controversies. In S. J. Lynn & J. W. Rhue (Eds.), *Dissociation: Clinical and theoretical perspectives* (pp. 434–62). New York: Guilford.

Horevitz, R., & Loewenstein, R. J. (1994). The rational treatment of multiple personality disorder. In S. J. Lynn & J. W. Rhue (Eds.), *Dissociation: Clinical and theoretical perspectives* (pp. 289–316). New York: Guilford.

Horn, W. F., Islongo, N. S., Pascoe, J. M., & et al. (1991). Additive effects of psychostimulants, parent training, and self-control therapy with ADHD children. *J. Amer. Acad. Child Adoles. Psychiat., 30*, 233–40.

Hornig, C. D., & McNally, R. J. (1995). Panic disorder and suicide attempt: A reanalysis of data from the Epidemiologic Catchment Area study. *Brit. J. Psychiat., 67*, 76–79.

Horowitz, L. M., Rosenberg, S. E., & Bartholomew, K. (1993). Interpersonal problems, attachment styles, and outcome in brief dynamic psychotherapy. *J. Cons. Clin. Psychol., 61*(4), 549–60.

Horowitz, M. J., & Solomon, G. F. (1978). Delayed stress response syndromes in Vietnam veterans. In C. R. Figley (Ed.), *Stress disorders among Vietnam veterans: Theory, research, and treatment*. New York: Brunner/Mazel.

Horowitz, M. J., Wilner, N., & Alvarez, W. (1979). Impact of Events Scale: A measure of subjective stress. *Psychosom. Med., 41*, 209–18.

Horton, P. C., Louy, J. W., & Coppolillo, H. P. (1974). Personality disorder and transitional relatedness. *Arch. Gen. Psychiat., 30*(5), 618–22.

Hoshino, Y., et al. (1980). Early symptoms of autism in children and their diagnostic significance, *Japanese Journal of Child and Adolescent Psychiatry, 21*(5), 284–99.

Houck, C. K. (1993). Ellis's "potential" Integrative Strategy Instruction model: An appealing extension of previous efforts. *J. Learn. Dis., 26*(6), 399–403.

House of Representatives. (1990). *No place to call home: Discarded children in America*. A report of the Select Committee on Children, Youth, and Families. Washington, DC: U.S. Government Printing Office.

Houts, A. C. (1991). Nocturnal enuresis as a biobehavioral problem. *Behav. Ther., 22*, 133–51.

Houts, A. C., Berman, J. S., & Abramson, H. (1994). Effectiveness of psychological and pharmacological treatments for nocturnal enuresis. *J. Cons. Clin. Psychol., 62*, 737–45.

Howard, K. I., Davidson, C. V., O'Mahoney, M. T., & Orlinsky, D. E. (1989). Patterns of psychotherapy utilization. *Amer. J. Psychiat., 146*, 775–78.

Howard, K. I., Kopta, S. M., Krause, M. S., & Orlinsky, D. E. (1986). The dose-effect relationship in psychotherapy. *Amer. Psychol., 41*, 159–64.

Howes, M. J., Hokanson, J. E., & Loewenstein, D. A. (1985). Induction of depressive affect after prolonged exposure to a mildly depressed individual. *J. Pers. Soc. Psychol., 49*, 1110–13.

Hser, Y. I., Anglin, M. D., & Powers, K. (1993). A 24 year follow-up of California narcotics addicts. *Arch. Gen. Psychiat., 50*, 577–584.

Hsu, L. K. G. (1989). The gender gap in eating disorders: Why are the eating disorders more common among women? *Clin. Psychol. Rev., 9*, 393–407.

Hu, T. -W., Huang, L. -F., & Cartwright, W. (1986). Evaluation of the costs of caring for the senile demented elderly: A pilot study. *Gerontologist, 26*, 158–63.

Huber, L., & Edelberg, R. (1993). A community integration model of head injury rehabilitation. *J. Cogn. Rehab., 11*(2), 22–26.

Huff, F. W. (1969). A learning theory approach to family therapy. *The Family Coordinator, 18*(1), 22–26.

Hughes, A. L. (1992). The prevalence of illicit drug use in six metropolitan areas in the United States: Results from the 1991 National Household Survey on Drug Abuse. *Brit. J. Addict., 87*, 1481–85.

Hughes, J. R., & Pierattini, R. A. (1992). An introduction to pharmacotherapy for mental disorders. In J. Grabowski & G. R. VandenBos (Eds.), *Psychopharmabology: Basic mechanisms and applied interventions.* Washington, DC: American Psychological Association.

Hughes, J. R., Higgins, S. T., & Hatsukami, D. K. (1990). Effects of abstinence from tobacco: A critical review. In L. T. Kozlowski, H. Annis, & H. D. Cappell, et al. (Eds.), *Recent advances in alcohol and drug problems* (Vol. 10, pp. 317–97).

Hughes, P. L., Wells, L. A., Cunningham, C. J., & Ilstrup, D. M. (1986). Treating bulimia with desipramine: A double-blind, placebo-controlled study. *Arch. Gen. Psychiat., 43*, 182–86.

Humphrey, L. L. (1989). Observed family interactions among subtypes of eating disorders using Structural Analysis of Social Behavior. *J. Cons. Clin. Psychol., 57*, 206–14.

Humphreys, K., & Rappaport, J. (1993). From community mental health movement to the war on drugs: A study of the definition of social problems. *Amer. Psychol., 48*(8), 892–901.

Humphry, D., & Wickett, A. (1986). *The right to die: Understanding euthanasia.* New York: Harper & Row.

Hunt, M. (1975). *Sexual behavior in the 1970's.* New York: Dell.

Hunt, W. A. (1993). Are binge drinkers more at risk of developing brain damage? *Alcohol, 10*, 559–61.

Hunter, E. J. (1976). The prisoner of war: Coping with the stress of isolation. In R. H. Moos (Ed.), *Human adaptation: Coping with life crises.* Lexington, MA: Heath.

Hunter, E. J. (1978). The Vietnam POW veteran: Immediate and long-term effects. In C. R. Figley (Ed.), *Stress disorders among Vietnam veterans.* New York: Brunner/Mazel.

Hunter, E. J. (1981). Wartime stress: Family adjustment to loss (USIU Report No. TR-USIU-81-07). San Diego, CA: United States International University.

Husain, M. M., Meyer, D. E., Muttakin, M. H., & Weiner, M. F. (1993). Maintenance ECT for treatment of recurrent mania. *Amer. J. Psychiat., 150*, 985.

Hutchinson, N. L. (1993). Integrative Strategy Instruction: An elusive ideal for teaching adolescents with learning disabilities. *J. Learn. Dis., 26*(7), 428–32.

Huxley, A. (1965). Human potentialities. In R. E. Farson (Ed.), *Science and human affairs.* Palo Alto, CA: Science and Behavior Books.

Hyde, J. (1984) How large are gender differences in aggression? A developmental meta-analysis. *Develop. Psychol., 20*, 722–736.

Hymel, S., & Rubin, K. H. (1985). Children with peer relationships and social skills problems: Conceptual, methodological, and developmental issues. *Annals of child development* (Vol. 2). Greenwich, CT: JAI Press.

Hynd, G. W., & Semrud-Clikeman, M. (1989). Dyslexia and brain morphology. *Psychol. Bull., 106*, 447–82.

Iacono, W. G., & Beiser, M. (1992). Where are the women in first-episode studies of schzophrenia? *Schizo. Bull., 18*(3), 471–80.

Iacono, W. G., Moreau, M., Beiser, M., Fleming, J. A. E., & Tsung-Yi, L. (1992). Smooth-pursuit eye tracking in first-episode psychotic patients and their relatives. *J. Abnorm. Psychol., 101*(1), 104–16.

Iezzi, A., & Adams, H. E. (1993). Somatoform and factitious disorders. In P. B. Sutker & H. E. Adams (Eds.), *Comprehensive handbook of psychopathology* (pp. 167–202). New York: Plenum.

Ikemi, Y., Ago, Y., Nakagawa, S., Mori S., Takahashi, N., Suematsu, H., Sugita, M., & Matsubara, H. (1974). Psychosomatic mechanism under social changes in Japan. *J. Psychosom. Res., 18*(1), 15–24.

Imber, S. D., Glanz, L. M., Elkin, I., Sotsky, S. M., & Boyer, J. L. (1986). Ethical issues in psychotherapy research: Problems in a collaborative clinical trials study. *Amer. Psychol., 41*, 137–46.

Innala, S. M., & Ernulf, K. E. (1989). Asphyxiophilia in Scandinavia. *Arch. Sex. Behav., 18*, 181–90.

Insel, T. R. (1992). Toward a neuroanatomy of obsessive-compulsive disorder. *Arch. Gen. Psychiat., 49*, 739–44.

Institute of Medicine. (1989). *Research on children and adolescents with mental, behavioral, and developmental disorders.* Washington, DC: National Academy Press.

Intrieri, R. C., & Rapp, S. R. (1994). Self-control skillfulness and caregiver burden among help-seeking elders. *J. Gerontol., 49*(1), P19–P23.

Ironside, R., & Batchelor, I. R. C. (1945). The ocular manifestations of hysteria in relation to flying. *Br. J. Ophthalmol., 29*, 88–98.

Irwin, M., Daniels, M., Smith, T. L., Bloom, E., & Weiner, H. (1987). Impaired natural killer cell activity during bereavement. *Brain, Behavior, and Immunity, 1*, 98–104.

Isaacson, R. L. (1970). When brains are damaged. *Psych. Today, 3*(4), 38–42.

Iscoe, I., Bloom, B. L., & Spielberger, C. D. (Eds.). (1977). *Community psychology in transition.* Washington, DC: Hemisphere.

Isometsä, E. T., Henriksson, M. M., Aro, H. M., Heikkinen, M. E., Kuoppasalmi, K. I., Lonnqvist, J. K. (1994). Suicide in major depression. *Amer. J. Psychiat., 151*, 530–36.

Jackson, J. L., Calhoun, K., Amick, A. E., Maddever, H. M., & Habif, V. (1990). Young adult women who experienced childhood intrafamilial sexual abuse: Subsequent adjustment. *Arch. Sex. Behav., 19*, 211–21.

Jacobson, E. (1971). *Depression: Comparative studies of normal, neurotic, and psychotic conditions.* New York: International Universities Press.

Jacobson, J. W. (1990). Do some mental disorders occur less frequently among persons with mental retardation? *Amer. J. Ment. Retard., 94*, 596–602.

Jacobson, N. S., Dobson, K., Fruzzetti, A. E., Schmaling, K. B., Salusky, S. (1991). Marital therapy as a treatment for depression. *J. Cons. Clin. Psychol., 59*, 547–57.

Jacobson, N. S., Holtzworth-Munroe, A., & Schmaling, K. B. (1989). Marital therapy and spouse involvement in the treatment of depression, agoraphobia, and alcoholism. *J. Cons. Clin. Psychol., 57*, 5–10.

Jaffe, A. (1992). Cognitive factors associated with cocaine abuse and its treatment. In T. R. Kosten & H. D. Kleber (Eds.), *Cocaine: A clinician's guide.* New York: Guilford.

James, W. (1890). *Principles of psychology.* New York: Holt.

James, A. L., & Barry, R. J. (1981). General maturational lag as an essential correlate of early onset psychosis. *J. Autism Devel. Dis., 11*(3), 271–83.

Janicki, M. P., & Dalton, A. J. (1993). Alzheimer disease in a select population of older adults with mental retardation. *Irish Journal of Psychology: Special Issue, Psychological aspects of aging, 14*(1), 38–47.

Janis, I. L. (1958). *Psychological stress: Psychoanalytic and behavioral studies of surgical patients.* New York: Wiley.

Janis, I. L., & Leventhal H. (1965). Psychological aspects of physical illness and hospital care. In B. B. Wolman (Ed.), *Handbook of clinical psychology* (pp. 1360–77). New York: McGraw-Hill.

Janis, I. L., Mahl, G. F., Kagan, J., & Holt, R. R. (1969). *From personality: Dynamics, development, and assessment.* New York: Harcourt Brace Jovanovich.

Jarvik, M. E. (1967). The psychopharmacological revolution. *Psych. Today, 1*(1), 51–58.

Jeffrey, R. W., Wing, R. R., & Stunkard, A. J. (1978). Behavioral treatment of obesity: The state of the art, 1976. *Behav. Ther., 9*, 189–99.

Jemmott, J. B., III, & Locke, S. E. (1984). Psychosocial factors, immunologic mediation, and human susceptibility to infectious diseases: How much do we know? *Psychol. Bull., 95*, 78–108.

Jenike, M., Baer, L., Minichiello, W., Schwarts, C., & Carey, R. (1986). Concomitant obsessive-compulsive disorder and schizotypal personality disorder. *Amer. J. Psychiat., 143*, 530–2.

Jenkins, C. D., Zyzansky, S. J., & Rosenman, R. H. (1971). Progress toward validation of a computer-scored test for the Type A coronary-prone behavior pattern. *Psychosom. Med., 33*, 193–202.

Jenkins, C. D., Zyzanski, S. J., & Rosenman, R. H. (1976). Risk of new myocardial infarction in middle-age men with manifest coronary heart disease. *Circulation, 53*, 342–47.

Jenkins, R. L. (1969). Classification of behavior problems of children. *Amer. J. Psychiat., 125*(8), 68–75.

Jennet, B., et al. (1976). Predicting outcome in individual patients after severe head injury. *Lancet, 1*, 1031.

Jenni, M. A., & Wollersheim, J. P. (1979). Cognitive therapy, stress-management training and the type A behavior pattern. *Cog. Ther. Res., 3*(1), 61–73.

Jernigan, T. L., Schafer, K., Butters, N., & Cermak, L. S. (1991). Magnetic resonance imaging of alcoholic Korsakoff patients. *Neuropsychopharmacology, 4*, 175–86.

Joffe, R. T., & Offord, D. R. (1990). Epidemiology. In G. MacLean (Ed.), *Suicide in children and adolescents*. Toronto: Hogrefe & Huber.

Johnson, A. M., Wadsworth, J., Wellings, K., Bradshaw, S., & Field, J. (1992). Sexual lifestyles and HIV risk. *Nature, 360*, 410–12.

Johnson, J. (1969). The EEG in the traumatic encephalography of boxers. *Psychiatrica Clinica, 2*(4), 204–11.

Johnson, J. L., & McCown, W. G. (1993). Addictive behaviors and substance abuse. In P. B. Sutker & H. E. Adams (Eds.), *Comprehensive handbook of psychopathology* (2nd ed., pp. 437–49). New York: Plenum.

Johnson, J., Weissman, M. M., & Klerman, G. L. (1990). Panic disorder, comorbidity, and suicide attempts. *Arch. Gen. Psychiat., 47*, 805–4.

Johnson, S. L., & Roberts, J. E. (1995). Life events and bipolar disorder: Implications from biological theories. *Psychol. Bull., 117*, 434–449.

Joint Commission on the Mental Health of Children. (1970). *Crisis in child mental health: Challenge for the 1970's.* New York: Harper & Row.

Jones, E. E., Farina, A., Hastorf, A. H., Markus, H., & Miller, D. T. (1984). *Social stigma: The psychology of marked relationships.* New York: Freeman.

Jones, K. L., & Smith, B. W. (1975). The fetal alcohol syndrome. *Teratology, 12*, 1–10.

Jones, K. L., Smith, B. W., & Hansen, J. W. (1976). Fetal alcohol syndrome: A clinical delineation. *Ann. NY Acad. Sci., 273*, 130–37.

Jones, L. (1992) Specifying the temporal relationship between job loss and consequences: Implication for service delivery. *The Journal of Applied Social Sciences, 16*, 37–62.

Jones, M. (1953). *The therapeutic community.* New York: Basic Books.

Jones, M. C. (1924). A laboratory study of fear: The case of Peter. *Pedagogical Seminary, 31*, 308–15.

Jones, R. (1984). The pharmacology of cocaine. *National Institute on Drug Abuse Research Monograph Series 50.* Washington, DC: National Institute on Drug Abuse.

Jones, R. A. (1977). *Self-fulfilling prophecies: Social, psychological, and physiological effects of expectancies.* Hillsdale, NJ: Erlbaum.

Jones, R. E. (1983). Street people and psychiatry: An introduction. *Hosp. Comm. Psychiat., 34*, 807–11.

Jones, R. R., Reid, J. B., & Patterson, G. R. (1975). Naturalistic observation in clinical assessment. In P. M. Reynolds (Ed.), *Advances in psychological assessment* (Vol. 3). San Francisco: Jossey-Bass.

Joyce, E. M., & Robbins, T. W. (1991). Frontal lobe function in Korsakoff and non-Korsakoff alcoholics: Planning and spatial working memory. *Neuropsychologia, 29*, 709–23.

Joyner, C. D., & Swenson, C. C. (1993). Community-level intervention after a disaster. In C. F. Saylor (Ed.), *Children and disaster* (pp. 211–32). New York: Plenum.

Kaada, B., & Retvedt, A. (1981). Enuresis and hyperventilation response in the EEG. *Develop. Med. Child Neurol., 23*(5), 591–99.

Kagan, J., Gibbons, J.L., Johnson, M.O., Reznick, J.S., & Snidman, N. (1990). A temperamental disposition to the state of uncertainty. In J. Rolf, A.S. Masten, D. Cicchetti, K.H. Nuechterlein, & S. Weintraub (Eds.), *Risk and protective factors in the development of psychopathology.* New York: Cambridge University Press.

Kagan, J., Reznick, J. S., & Snidman, N. (1988). Biological bases of childhood shyness. *Science, 240*, 167–71.

Kagan, J., Reznick, R. J., Clarke, C., Snidman, N., & Garcia-Coll, C. (1984). Behavioral inhibition and the unfamiliar. *Child Develop., 55*, 2212–25.

Kahan, J., Kemp, B., Staples, F. R., & Brummel-Smith, K. (1985). Decreasing the burden in families caring for a relative with a dementing illness: A controlled study. *J. Amer. Geriat. Soc., 33*, 664–70.

Kahana, B., Harel, Z., & Kahana, E. (1988). Predictors of psychological well-being among survivors of the Holocaust. In J. P. Wilson, Z. Harel, & B. Kahana (Eds.), *Human adaptation to extreme stress: From the Holocaust to Vietnam* (pp. 171–92). New York: Plenum.

Kahn, J. S., Kehle, T. J., Jenson, W. R., & Clark, E. (1990). Comparison of cognitive-behavioral, relaxation, and self-modeling interventions for derprssion among middle-school students. *School Psychol. Rev. 19*, 196–211.

Kahn, M. W., & Raifman, L. (1981). Hospitalization versus imprisonment and the insanity plea. *Crim. Just. Behav., 8*(4), 483–90.

Kales, A., Paulson, M. J., Jacobson, A., & Kales, J. (1966). Somnambulism: Psychophysiological correlates. *Arch. Gen. Psychiat., 14*(6), 595–604.

Kalichman, S. C., Hunter, T. L., & Kelly, J. A. (1993). Perceptions of AIDS susceptibility among minority and nonminority women at risk for HIV infection. *J. Cons. Clin. Psychol., 60*(5), 725–32.

Kalin, N. H., Risch, S. C., Janowsky, D. S., & Murphy, D. L. (1981). Use of the dexamethasone suppression test in clinical psychiatry. *J. Clin. Psychopharm., 1*, 64–69.

Kalinowski, L. B., & Hippius, H. (1969). *Pharmacological, convulsive and other somatic treatments in psychiatry.* New York: Grune & Stratton.

Kalint, H. (1989). The nature of addiction: An analysis of the problem. In A. Goldstein (Ed.), *Molecullar and cellular aspects of the drug addictions* (pp. 1–28). New York: Springer-Verlag.

Kallmann, F. J. (1958). The use of genetics in psychiatry. *J. Ment. Sci., 104*, 542–49.

Kamps, D. M., Leonard, B. R., Vernon, S., & Dugan, E. P. (1992). Teaching social skills to students with autism to increase peer interactions in an integrated first-grade classroom. *J. Appl. Beh. Anal., 25*, 281–88.

Kandel, D. B., Davies, M., Karus, D., & Yamaguchi, K. (1986). The consequences in young adulthood of adolescent drug involvement. *Arch. Gen. Psychiat., 43*, 746–54.

Kandel, E., & Fried, D. (1989) Frontal-lobe dysfunction and antisocial behavior: A review. *J. Clin. Psychol., 45*, 404–13.

Kandel, E., Mednick, S. A., Kirkegaard-Sorensen, L., Hutchings, B., Knop, J., Rosenberg, R., & Schulsinger, F. (1988). IQ as a protective factor for subjects at high risk for antisocial behavior. *J. Cons. Clin. Psychol., 56*, 224–26.

Kane, J. M., & Smith, J. M. (1982). Tardive dyskinesia: Prevalence and risk factors, 1959–79. *Arch. Gen. Psychiat., 39,* 473–81.

Kane, J., Honigfeld, G., Singer, J., Meltzer, H., & Clozapine Collaborative Study Group. (1988). Clozapine for the treatment-resistant schizophrenic: A double-blind comparison with chlorpromazine. *Arch. Gen. Psychiat., 45,* 789–96.

Kang, J., Lemaire, H.-G., Unterbeck, A., Salbaum, J. M., et al. (1987). The precursor of Alzheimer's disease amyloid A4 protein resembles a cell surface receptor. *Nature, 325,* 733–36.

Kanin, E. J. (1985). Date rapists: Differential sexual socialization and relative deprivation. *Arch. Sex. Behav., 14,* 219–31.

Kanner, L., (1943). Autistic disturbances of effective content. *Nervous Child, 2,* 217–40.

Kantorovich, F. (1930). An attempt at associative reflex therapy in alcoholism. *Psychological Abstracts,* 4282.

Kaplan, H. S. (1974). *The new sex therapy.* New York: Brunner/Mazel.

Kaplan, H. S. (1987). *The illustrated manual of sex therapy* (2nd ed.). New York: Brunner/Mazel.

Karnesh, L. J. (with collaboration of Zucker, E. M.). (1945). *Handbook of psychiatry.* St. Louis: Mosby.

Karno, M., Golding, J. M., Sorenson, S. B., & Burnam, M. A. (1988). The epidemiology of obsessive-compulsive disorder in five U.S. communities. *Arch. Gen. Psychiat., 45,* 1094–99.

Karon, B. P., & Vandenbos, G. R. (1981) *Psychotherapy of schizophrenia: Treatment of choice.* New York: Jason Aronson.

Kashani, J. H., & Orvaschel, H. (1988). Anxiety disorders in mid-adolescence: A community sample. *Amer. J. Psychiat., 145,* 960–64.

Kashani, J. H., Hodges, K. K., Simonds, J. F., & Hilderbrand, E. (1981a). Life events and hospitalization in children: A comparison with a general population. *Brit. J. Psychiat., 139,* 221–25.

Kashani, J. H., Husain, A., Shekim, W. O., Hodges, K. K., Cytryn, L., & McKnew, D. H. (1981b). Current perspectives on childhood depression: An overview. *Amer. J. Psychiat., 138*(2), 143–53.

Kaslow, N. J., Deering, C. G., & Racusin, G. R. (1994). Depressed children and their families. *Clin. Psychol. Rev., 14,* 39–59.

Katerndahl, D. A., & Realini, J. P. (1993). Lifetime prevalence of panic states. *Amer. J. Psychiat., 150,* 246–9.

Katon, W., Egan, K., & Miller, D. (1985). Chronic pain: Lifetime psychiatric diagnoses and family history. *Amer. J. Psychiat., 142,* 1156–60.

Katon, W., Kleinman, A., & Rosen, G. (1982). Depression and somatization: A review. Part I. *Amer. J. Med., 72,* 127–35.

Katz, M. M., Sanborn, K. O., Lowery, H. A., & Ching, J. (1978). Ethnic studies in Hawaii: On psychopathology and social deviance. In L. C. Wynne, R. L. Cromwell, & S. Matthysse (Eds.), *The nature of schizophrenia: New approaches to research and treatment* (pp. 572–85). New York: Wiley.

Katz, R., & McGuffin, P. (1993). The genetics of affective disorders. In L. J. Chapman, J. P. Chapman, & D. C. Fowles (Eds.), *Progress in experimental personality and psychopathology research* (Vol. 16). New York: Springer.

Katz, R. C., Frazer, N., & Wilson, L. (1993). Sexual fears are increasing. *Psychol. Rep., 73,* 476–78.

Katz, S., & Kravetz, S. (1989). Facial plastic surgery for persons with Down syndrome: Research findings and their professional and social implications. *Amer. J. Ment. Retard., 94,* 101–10.

Kaufman, I., Frank, T., Heims, L., Herrick, J., Reiser, D., & Willer, L. (1960). Treatment implications of a new classification of parents of schizophrenic children. *Amer. J. Psychiat., 116,* 920–24.

Kaufman, J., & Zigler, E. (1989). The intergenerational transmission of child abuse. In D. Cicchetti, & V. Carlson (Eds.), *Child maltreatment: Theory and research on the causes and consequences of child abuse and neglect* (pp. 129–150). Cambridge: Cambridge University Press.

Kay, S. R., & Singh, M. M. (1989). The positive-negative distinction in drug-free schizophrenic patients. *Arch. Gen. Psychiat., 46,* 711–18.

Kazdin, A. E. (1980). *Behavior modification in applied settings* (2nd ed.). Homewood, IL: Dorsey Press.

Kazdin, A. E. (1992). Child and adolescent dysfunction and paths toward maladjustment: Targets for intervention. *Clin. Psychol. Rev., 12,* 795–818.

Kazdin, A. E. (1994). *Conduct disorders in childhood and adolescence.* Newbury Park, CA: Sage.

Kazdin, A. E., & Wilson, G. T. (1978). *Evaluation of behavior therapy: Issues, evidence and research strategies.* Cambridge, MA: Ballinger.

Kazdin, A. E., Bass, D., Ayers, W.A., & Rodgers, A. (1990). Empirical and clinical focus of child and adolescent psychotherapy research. *J. Cons. Clin. Psychol., 58,* 729–40.

Kazdin, A. E., Bass, D., Siegel, T., & Thomas, C. (1989). Cognitive behavioral therapy and relationship therapy in the treatment of children referred for antisocial behavior. *J. Cons. Clin. Psychol., 57,* 522–35.

Keating, J. P. (1987, Aug.). *An overview of research on human response during disasters: Major fires, earthquakes, tornadoes, and airplane accidents since 1980.* Paper presented at the American Psychological Association, New York.

Keefe, F. J., & Williams, D. A. (1989). New directions in pain assessment and treatment. *Clin. Psychol. Rev., 9,* 549–68.

Keefe, F. J., Dunsmore, J., & Burnett, R. (1992). Behavioral and cognitive-behavioral approaches to chronic pain: Recent advances and future directions. *J. Cons. Clin. Psychol., 60*(4), 528–36.

Keita, G. P., & Jones, J. M. (1990). Reducing adverse reactions to stress in the workplace: Psychology's expanding role. *Amer. Psychol., 45*(10), 1137–41.

Keith, S. J. (1993). Understanding the experience of schizophrenia (Editorial). *Amer. J. Psychiat., 150*(11), 1616–17.

Keller, M. B. (1985). Chronic and recurrent affective disorders: Incidence, course, and influencing factors. *Advances in Biochemical Psychopharmacology, 40,* 11–120.

Keller, M. B., & Shapiro, R. W. (1982). "Double depression": Superimposition of acute depressive episodes on chronic depressive disorders. *Amer. J. Psychiat., 139,* 438–42.

Keller, M. B., Lavori, P. W., Endicott, J., Coryell, W., & Flerman, G. (1983). "Double Depression": Two-year follow-up. *Amer. J. Psychiat., 140,* 689–94.

Keller, M. B., Lavori, P. W., Rice, J., Coryell, W., & Hirschfeld, R.M.A (1986). The persistant risk of chronicity in recurrent episodes of nonbipolar major depressive disorder: A prospective follow-up. *Amer. J. Psychiat., 143,* 24–28.

Keller, M. B., Shapiro, R. W., Lavori, P. W., & Wolfe, N. (1982). Recovery in major depressive disorder: Analysis with the life table and regression models. *Arch. Gen. Psychiat., 39,* 905–910.

Kellner, R. (1982). Disorders of impulse control (not elsewhere classified). In J. H. Griest, J. W. Jefferson, & R. L. Spitzer (Eds.), *Treatment of mental disorders.* New York: Oxford University Press.

Kellner, R. (1985). Functional somatic symptoms and hypochondriasis: A survey of empirical studies. *Arch. Gen. Psychiat., 42,* 821–33.

Kellner, R. (1990). Somatization: Theories and research. *J. Nerv. Ment. Dis., 178,* 150–60.

Kelly, J. A., & Murphy, D. A. (1992). Psychological interventions with AIDS and HIV: Prevention and treatment. *J. Cons. Clin. Psychol., 60*(4), 576–85.

Kemeny, M. E., Weiner, H., Taylor, S. E., Schneider, S., Visscher, B., & Fahey, J. L. (1994). Repeated bereavement, depressed mood, and immune parameters in HIV seropositive and seronegative gay men. *Hlth. Psychol., 13*(1), 14–24.

Kempe, R., & Kempe, H. (1979). *Child Abuse.* London: Fontana/Open Books.

Kendall, P. C. (1982a). Cognitive processes and procedures in behavior therapy. In C. M. Franks, G. T. Wilson, P. C. Kendall, & K. D. Brownell, (Eds.), *Annual Review of Behavior Therapy* (Vol. 8). New York: Guilford.

Kendall, P. C. (1982b). Integration: Behavior therapy and other schools of thought. *Behav. Ther., 13*, 559–71.

Kendall, P. C. (1994). Treating anxiety disorders in children: Results of a randomized clinical trial. *J. Cons. Clin. Psychol., 62*(1), 100–10.

Kendall, P. C., & Norton-Ford, J. D. (1982). Therapy outcome research methods. In P. C. Kendall & J. N. Butcher (Eds.), *Handbook of research methods in clinical psychology.* New York: Wiley.

Kendall-Tackett, K. A., Williams, L. M., & Finkelhor, D. (1993). Impact of sexual abuse on children: a review and synthesis of recent empirical studies. *Psychol. Bull., 113*, 164–80.

Kendler, K.S. (1993). Twin studies of psychiatric illness: Current status and future directions. *Arch. Gen. Psychiat., 50*, 905–915.

Kendler, K. S., & Davis, K. L. (1981). The genetics and biochemistry of paranoid schizophrenia and other paranoid psychoses. *Schizo. Bull., 7*, 689–709.

Kendler, K. S., & Diehl, S. R. (1993). The genetics of schizophrenia: A current, genetic-epidemiologic perspective. *Schizo. Bull., 19*(2), 261–85.

Kendler, K. S., & Gruenberg, A. M. (1982). Genetic relationship between paranoid personality disorder and the "schizophrenic" spectrum disorders. *Amer. J. Psychiat., 139*(9), 1185–86.

Kendler, K. S., & Gruenberg, A. M. (1984). An independent analysis of the Danish adoption study of schizophrenia: VI. The relationship between psychiatric disorders as defined by DSM-III in the relatives and adoptees. *Arch. Gen. Psychiat., 41*, 555–64.

Kendler, K. S., & Tsuang, M. T. (1981). Nosology of paranoid schizophrenia and other paranoid psychoses. *Schizo. Bull., 7*, 594–610.

Kendler, K. S., Gruenberg, A. M., & Kinney, D. K. (1994a). Independent diagnoses of adoptees and relatives as defined by DSM-III in the provincial and national samples of the Danish adoption study of schizophrenia. *Arch. Gen. Psychiat., 51*(6), 456–68.

Kendler, K. S., McGuire, M., Gruenberg, A. M., & Walsh, D. (1994b). Outcome and family study of the subtypes of schizophrenia in the west of Ireland. *Amer. J. Psychiat., 151*(6), 849–56.

Kendler, K. S., Neale, M. C., Kessler, R. C., Heath, A. C., & Eaves, L. J. (1992a). Generalized anxiety disorder in women: A population based twin study. *Arch. Gen. Psychiat., 49*, 267–72.

Kendler, K. S., Neale, M. C., Kessler, R. C., Heath, A. C., & Eaves, L. J. (1992b). The genetic epidemiology of phobias in women: The interrelationship of agoraphobia, social phobia, situational phobia, and simple phobia. *Arch. Gen. Psychiat., 49*, 273–81.

Kendler, K. S., Neale, M., Kessler, R. C., Heath, A. C., & Eaves, L. J. (1992c). A population-based twin study of major depression in women: The impact of varying definitions of illness. *Arch. Gen. Psychiat., 49*, 257–66.

Kendler, K. S., Neale, M. C., Kessler, R. C., Heath, A. C., & Eaves, L. J. (1992d). Major depression and generalized anxiety disorder. Same genes, (partly) different environments? *Arch. Gen. Psychiat., 49*, 716–22.

Kendler, K. S., Neale, M. C., Kessler, R. C., Heath, A. C., & Eaves, L. J. (1993a). Panic disorder in women: A population based twin study. *Psychological Medicine, 23*, 397–406.

Kendler, K. S., Neale, M., Kessler, R., Heath, A., & Eaves, L. (1993b). A twin study of recent life events and difficulties. *Arch. Gen. Psychiat., 50*(10), 789–96.

Kendler, K. S., Ochs, A. L., Gorman, A. M., Hewitt, J. K., Ross D. E., & Mirsky, A. F. (1991). The structure of schizotypy: A pilot multitrait twin study. *Psychiat. Res., 36*, 19–36.

Kennedy, J. F. (1963). Message from the President of the United States relative to mental illness and mental retardation. *Amer. Psychol., 18*, 280–89.

Kennedy, T. D., & Kimura, H. K. (1974). Transfer, behavioral improvement, and anxiety reduction in systematic desensitization. *J. Cons. Clin. Psychol., 42*(5), 720–28.

Keppel-Benson, J. M.. & Ollendick, T. H. (1993). Posttraumatic stress disorder in children and adolescents. In C.F. Saylor (Ed.)., *Children and disasters* (pp. 29–44). New York: Plenum.

Kern, P. A., Trozzolino, L., Wolfe, G., & Purdy, L. (1994). Combined use of behavior modification and very low-calorie diet in weight loss and weight maintenance. *Amer. J. Med. Sci., 307*, 325–28.

Kernberg, O. F. (1984). *Severe personality disorders.* New Haven, CT: Yale University Press.

Kernberg, O. F. (1985). *Borderline conditions and pathological narcissism.* Northvale, NJ: Jason Aronson.

Kesey, K. (1962). *One flew over the cuckoo's nest.* New York: Signet.

Kessler, J. W. (1988). *Psychopathology of childhood* (2nd ed.). Englewood Cliffs, NJ: Prentice-Hall.

Kessler, M., & Albee, G. W. (1975). Primary prevention. *Annu. Rev. Psychol., 26*, 557–91.

Kessler, R. C., McGonagle, K. A., Zhao, S., Nelson, C. B., Hughes, M., Eshleman, S., Wittchen, H.-U., & Kendler, K. S. (1994). Lifetime and 12-month prevalence of DSM-III-R psychiatric disorders in the United States: Results from the national comorbidity survey. *Arch. Gen. Psychiat., 51*, 8–19.

Kety, S.S. (1974). From rationalization to reason. *Amer. J. Psychiat., 131*, 957–963.

Kety, S. S. (1987). The significance of genetic factors in the etiology of schizophrenia. *J. Psychiat. Res., 21*, 423–29.

Kety, S. S., Rosenthal, D., Wender, P. H., & Schulsinger, F. (1968). The types and prevalence of mental illness in the biological and adoptive families of adopted schizophrenics. In D. Rosenthal & S. S. Kety (Eds.), *The transmission of schizophrenia.* Elmsford, NY: Pergamon.

Kety, S. S., Rosenthal, D., Wender, P. H., Schulsinger, F., & Jacobsen, B. (1975). Mental illness in the biological and adoptive families of adopted individuals who have become schizophrenics: A preliminary report based on psychiatric interviews. In R. Fieve, P. Rosenthal, & H. Brill (Eds.), *Genetic research in psychiatry.* Baltimore: Johns Hopkins University Press.

Kety, S. S., Rosenthal, D., Wender, P. H., Schulsinger, F., & Jacobsen, B. (1978). The biologic and adoptive families of adopted individuals who became schizophrenic: Prevalence of mental illness and other characteristics. In L. C. Wynne, R. L. Cromwell, & S. Matthyse (Eds.), *The nature of schizophrenia: New approaches to research and treatment* (pp. 25–37). New York: Wiley.

Kety, S. S., Wender, P. H., Jacobsen, B., Ingraham, L. J., Jansson, L., Faber, B., & Kinney, D. K. (1994). Mental illness in the biological and adoptive relatives of schizophrenic adoptees: Replication of the Copenhagen study in the rest of Denmark. *Arch. Gen. Psychiat., 51*(6), 442–55.

Kewman, D., & Roberts, A. H. (1979). *Skin temperature biofeedback and migraine headaches.* Paper presented at the Annual Conference of the Biofeedback Society of America, San Diego.

Keys, A., Brozek, J., Henschel, A., Mickelson, O., & Taylor, H. L. (1950). *The biology of human starvation.* Minneapolis: University of Minnesota Press.

Khan, A. E., Mirolo, H., Hughes, D., & Bierut, L. (1993). Electroconvulsive therapy. *Psychiat. Clin. N. Amer., 16*, 497–514.

Kidd, K. K., & Morton, L. A. (1989). The genetics of psychosomatic disorders. In S. Cheren (Ed.), *Psychosomatic medicine: Theory, physiology, and practice* (Vol. 1, pp. 385–424). Madison, CT: International Universities Press.

Kidson, M., & Jones, I. (1968). Psychiatric disorders among aborigines of the Australian Western Desert. *Arch. Gen. Psychiat., 19*, 413–22.

Kidson, M. A. (1973). Personality and hypertension. *J. Psychosom. Res., 17*(1), 35–41.

Kiecolt-Glaser, J., & Glaser, R. (1988). Psychological influences in immunity: Implications for AIDS. *Amer. Psychol., 43,* 892–98.

Kiecolt-Glaser, J. K., & Glaser, R. (1992). Psychoneuroimmunology: Can psychological interventions modulate immunity? *J. Cons. Clin. Psychol., 60*(4), 569–75.

Kiecolt-Glaser, J. K., Kennedy, S., Malkoff, S., Fisher, L., Speicher, D. E., & Glaser, R. (1988). Marital discord and immunity in males. *Psychosom. Med., 50,* 213–29.

Kiernan, C. (1985). Behaviour modification. In A. M. Clarke, A. D. B. Clarke, & J. M. Berg (Eds.), *Mental deficiency: The changing outlook* (4th ed., pp. 465–511). London: Methuen.

Kiersch, T. A. (1962). Amnesia: A clinical study of ninety-eight cases. *Amer. J. Psychiat., 119,* 57–60.

Kiesler, C. A. (1983). Social psychologic issues in studying consumer satisfaction with behavior therapy. *Behav. Ther., 14,* 226–36.

Kiesler, C. A. (1993). Mental Health Policy and Mental Hospitalization. *Curr. Dir. Psychol. Sci., 2*(3), 93–95.

Kiesler, C. A., & Simpkins, C. G. (1993). *The unnoticed majority in inpatient psychiatric care.* New York: Plenum.

Kiev, A. (1972). *Transcultural psychiatry.* New York: Free Press.

Kihlstrom, J. F. (1990). The psychological unconscious. In L. Pervin (Eds.), *Handbook of personality: Theory and research* (pp. 445–64). New York: Guilford.

Kihlstrom, J. F. (1994). One hundred years of hysteria. In S. J. Lynn & J. W. Rhue (Eds.), *Dissociation: Clinical and theoretical perspectives* (pp. 365–94). New York: Guilford.

Kihlstrom, J. F., Glisky, M. L., & Angiulo, M. J. (1994). Dissociative tendencies and dissociative disorders. *J. Abnorm. Psychol., 103*(1), 117–24.

Kihlstrom, J. F., Tataryn, D. J., & Hoyt, I. P. (1993). Dissociative disorders. In P. B. Sutker & H. E. Adams (Eds.), *Comprehensive handbook of psychopathology* (pp. 203–34). New York: Plenum.

Kilpatrick, D. G., Sutker, P. B., Roitch, J. C., & Miller, W. C. (1976). Personality correlates of polydrug users. *Psychol. Rep., 38,* 311–17.

Kim, A., Galanter, M., Castaneda, R., & Lifshutz, H. (1992). Crack cocaine use and sexual behavior among psychiatric inpatients. *Amer. J. Drug Alcoh. Abuse, 18,* 235–46.

Kim, K., & Jacobs, S. (1995). Stress bereavement and consequent psychiatric illness. In C. M. Mazure (Ed.)., *Does stress cause psychiatric illness?* Washington, DC: American Psychiatric Association.

Kimerling, R., & Calhoun, K. S. (1994). Somatic symptoms, social support, and treatment seeking among sexual assault victims. *J. Cons. Clin. Psychol., 62,* 333–40.

Kimmel, H. D. (1974). Instrumental conditioning of autonomically mediated responses. *Amer. Psychol., 29,* 325–35.

King, H. F., Carroll, J. L., & Fuller, G. B. (1977). Comparison of nonpsychiatric blacks and whites on the MMPI. *J. Clin. Psychol., 33,* 725–28.

Kinney, D. K., Woods, B. T., & Yurgelun-Todd, D. (1986). Neurologic abnormalities in schizophrenic patients and their families: II. Neurologic and psychiatric findings in relatives. *Arch. Gen. Psychiat., 43,* 665–68.

Kinsey, A. C., Pomeroy, W. B., & Martin, C. E. (1948). *Sexual behavior in the human male.* Philadelphia: Sanders.

Kinsey, A. C., Pomeroy, W. B., Martin, C. E., & Gebhard, P. H. (1953). *Sexual behavior in the human female.* Philadelphia: Saunders.

Kinzie, J. D., & Bolton, J. M. (1973). Psychiatry with the aborigines of West Malaysia. *Amer. J. Psychiat., 130*(7), 769–73.

Kinzl, J., & Biebl, W. (1992). Long–term effects of incest: Life events triggering mental disorders in female patients with sexual abuse in childhood. *Child Ab. Negl., 16,* 567–73.

Kirch, D. G. (1993). Infection and autoimmunity as etiologic factors in schizophrenia: A review and reappraisal. *Schizo. Bull., 19*(2), 355–70.

Kirmayer, L. J. (1984). Culture, affect, and somatization: Part I. *Transcultural Psychiatric Research Review, 21,* 159–88.

Kirmayer, L. J. (1991). The place of culture in psychiatric nosology: Taijin Kyofusho and DSM III-R. *J. Nerv. Ment. Dis., 179,* 19–28.

Kirmayer, L. J., Robbins, J. M., & Paris, J. (1994). Somatoform disorders: Personality and the social matrix of somatic distress. *J. Abnorm. Psychol., 103*(1), 125–36.

Kirsch, I., Lynn, S. J., & Rhue, J. W. (1993). Introduction to clinical hypnosis. In J. W. Rhue, S. J. Lynn, & I. Kirsch (Eds.), *Handbook of clinical hypnosis* (pp. 3–22). Washington, DC: American Psychological Association.

Kirstein, L., Prusoff, B., Weissman, M., & Dressler, D. M. (1975). Utilization review of treatment for suicide attempters. *Amer. J. Psychiat., 132*(1), 22–27.

Klackenberg, G. (1987). Incidence of parasomnias in children in a general population. In C. Guilleminault (Ed.), *Sleep and its disorders in children* (pp. 99–113). New York: Raven Press.

Klassen, D., & O'Connor, W. A. (1988). A prospective study of predictors of violence in adult male mental health admissions. *Law and Human Behavior, 12,* 143–58.

Klein, D. F. (1981). Anxiety reconceptualized. In D. F. Klein & J. Rabkin (Eds.), *Anxiety: New research and changing concepts.* New York: Raven Press.

Klein, D. N. (1990). Depressive personality: Reliability, validity, and relation to dysthymia. *J. Abnorm. Psychol., 99,* 412–21.

Klein, D. N., & Depue, R. A. (1984). Continued impairment in persons at risk for bipolar affective disorder: Results of a 19-month follow-up study. *J. Abnorm. Psychol., 93,* 345–47.

Klein, D. N., & Depue, R. A. (1985). Obsessional personality traits and risk for bipolar affective disorder: An offspring study. *J. Abnorm. Psychol., 94,* 291–397.

Klein, D. N., Depue, R. A., & Slater, J. F. (1985). Cyclothymia in the adolescent offspring of parents with bipolar affective disorder. *J. Abnorm. Psychol., 94,* 115–27.

Klein, D. N., Depue, R. A., & Slater, J. F. (1986). Inventory identification of cyclothymia: IX. Validations in offspring of bipolar I patients. *Arch. Gen. Psychiat., 43,* 441–46.

Klein, D. N., Riso, L. P., & Anderson, R. L. (1993). DSM-III-R dysthymia: Antecedents and underlying assumptions. In L.J. Chapman, J.P. Chapman, & D.C. Fowles (Eds.), *Experimental personality and psychopathology research* (Vol. 16). New York: Springer.

Klein, M. (1934). A contribution to the psychogenesis of manic-depressive states. In *Contributions to psychoanalysis, 1921–1945* (pp. 282–310). London: Hogarth Press.

Klein, R. G., Koplewicz, H. S., & Kanner, A. (1992). Imipramine treatment of children with separation anxiety disorder. *J. Amer. Acad. Child Adoles. Psychiat., 31,* 21–28.

Kleinman, A. M. (1986). *Social origins of distress and disease: Depression, neurasthenia and pain in modern China.* New Haven, CT: Yale University Press.

Kleinman, A. M., & Good, B. J. (1985). *Culture and depression.* Berkeley, CA: University of California Press.

Kleinman, P. H., Kang, S., Lipton, D. S., & Woody, G. E. (1992). Retention of cocaine abusers in outpatient psychytherapy. *Amer. J. Drug Alcoh. Abuse, 18,* 29–43.

Kleinmuntz, B. (1990). Why we still use our heads instead of formulas: Toward an integrative approach. *Psychol. Bull., 107,* 296–310.

Klepac, R. K., Hauge, G., Dowling, J., & McDonald, M. (1981). Direct and generalized effects of three components of stress-inoculation for increased pain tolerance. *Behav. Ther., 12,* 417–24.

Klerman, G. L. (1982). Practical issues in the treatment of depression and mania. In E. S. Paykel (Ed.), *Handbook of affective disorders.* New York: Guilford.

Klerman, G. L. (1990). The psychiatric patient's right to effective treatment: Implications of *Osheroff v. Chestnut Lodge. Amer. J. Psychiat., 147,* 409–18.

Klerman, G. L. (1991). Ideological conflicts in integrating pharmacotherapy and psychotherapy. In B. D. Beitman & G. L. Klerman (Eds.), *Integrating pharmacotherapy and psychotherapy* (pp. 3–20). Washington, DC: American Psychiatric Press.

Klerman, G.L. (1994). Drugs and psychotherapy. In A. Bergin & S. Garfield (Eds.), *Handbook of psychotherapy and behavior change* (4th ed.). New York: Wiley.

Klerman, G. L., Weissman, M. M., Markowitz, J. C., Glick, I., Wilner, P. J., Mason, B., & Shear, M. K. (1994). Medication and psychotherapy. In A. E. Bergin & S. L. Garfield (Eds.), *Handbook of psychotherapy and behavior change* (4th ed., pp. 734–82). New York: Wiley.

Klerman, G. L., Weissman, M. M., Rounsaville, B. J., & Chevron, E. S. (1984). *Interpersonal psychotherapy of depression.* New York: Basic Books.

Klinger, E. (1979). Modes of normal conscious flow. In K. S. Pope & J. L. Singer (Eds.), *The stream of consciousness: Scientific investigations into the flow of human experience.* New York: Plenum.

Klinger, E., & Kroll-Mensing, D. (1995). Idiothetic assessment. In J. N. Butcher (Ed.), *Clinical personality assessment: Practical considerations* (pp. 267–77). New York: Oxford University Press.

Klingman, A. (1993). School-based intervention following a disaster. In C. F. Saylor (Ed.), *Children and disasters* (pp. 187–210). New York: Plenum.

Klorman, R., Brumaghim, J. T., Fitzpatrick, P. A., Borgstedt, A. D., & Strauss, J. (1994). Clinical and cognitive effects of Methylphenidate on children with attention deficit disorders as a function of aggression, opporitionality and age. *J. Abnorm. Psychol., 103*, 206–21.

Klosko, J. S., Barlow, D. H., Tassinari, R., & Cerny, J. A. (1990). A comparison of alprazolam and behavior therapy in the treatment of panic disorder. *J. Cons. Clin. Psychol., 58*, 77–84.

Kluft, R. P. (1993). Basic principles in conducting the treatment of multiple personality disorder. In R. P. Kluft & C. G. Fine (Eds.), *Clinical perspectives on multiple personality disorder* (pp. 53–73). Washington: American Psychiatric Press.

Knapp, P. H. (1989). Psychosomatic aspects of bronchial asthma: A review. In S. Cheren (Ed.), *Psychosomatic medicine: Theory, physiology, and practice* (Vol. 2, pp. 503–64). Madison, CT: International Universities Press.

Knapp, S. (1980). A primer on malpractice for psychologists. *Profess. Psychol., 11*(4), 606–12.

Knight, R., & Prentky, R. (1990) Classifying sexual offenders: The development and corroboration of taxonomic models. In W. L. Marshall, D. R. Laws, & H. E. Barbaree (Eds.), *Handbook of sexual assault: Issues, theories, and treatment of the offender* (pp. 23–52). New York: Plenum.

Knight, R., Prentky, R., & Cerce, D. (1994) The development, reliability, and validity of an inventory for the multidimensional assessment of sex and aggression. *Crim. Just. Behav., 21*, 72–94.

Knowles, J. H. (1977). Editorial. *Science, 198*, 1103–4.

Kobasa, S. C. O. (1979). Stressful life events, personality, and health: An inquiry into hardiness. *J. Pers. Soc. Psychol., 37*(1), 1–11.

Kobasa, S. C. O. (1985). Personality and health: Specifying and strengthening the conceptual fit. In P. Shaver (Ed.), *Self situations and social behavior* (pp. 291–311). Beverly Hills, CA: Sage.

Koch, R. (1967). The multidisciplinary approach to mental retardation. In A. A. Baumeister (Ed.), *Mental retardation: Appraisal, education, and rehabilitation.* Chicago: Aldine.

Koegel, L. K., Koegel, R. L., Hurley, C., & Frea, W. D. (1992). Improving social skills and disruptive behavior in children with autism through self-management. *J. Appl. Behav. Anal., 25*, 341–53.

Koegel, R. L., & Mentis, M. (1985). Motivation in childhood autism: Can they or won't they? *J. Child Psychol. Psychiat., 26*(2), 185–91.

Kog, E., & Vandereycken, W. (1985). Family characteristics of anorexia nervosa and bulimia: A review of the research literature. *Clin. Psychol. Rev., 5*, 159–80.

Kohn, M. L. (1973). Social class and schizophrenia: A critical review and a reformulation. *Schizo. Bull., 7*, 60–79.

Kohut, H. (1977). *The restoration of the self.* New York: International Universities Press.

Kohut, H., & Wolff, E. (1978). The disorders of the self and their treatment: An outline. *Inter. J. Psychoanal., 59*, 413–26.

Kolata, G. B. (1981a). Clues to the cause of senile dementia: Patients with Alzheimer's disease seem to be deficient in a brain neurotransmitter. *Science, 211*, 1032–33.

Kolata, G. B. (1981b). Fetal alcohol advisory debated. *Science, 214*, 642–46.

Kolko, D. J., & Kazdin, A. E. (1991). Aggression and psychopathology in matchplaying and firesetting children. *J. Clin. Child Psychol., 20*, 191–201.

Kopelman, M. D. (1986). The cholinergic neurotransmitter system in human memory and dementia: A review. *Q. J. Exp. Psychol. [A], 38*, 535–73.

Kopelman, M. D. (1991). Non-verbal, short-term forgetting in the alcoholic Korsakoff syndrome and Alzheimer-type dementia. *Neuropsychologia, 29*, 737–47.

Kopp, C.B., & Kaler, S.R. (1989). Risk in infancy: Origins and implications. Special issue: Children and their development: Knowledge base, research agenda, and social policy application. *Amer. Psychol., 44*, 224–230.

Koranyi, E. K. (1989). Physiology of stress reviewed. In S. Cheren (Ed.), *Psychosomatic medicine: Theory, physiology, and practice* (Vol. 1, pp. 241–78). Madison, CT: International Universities Press.

Koreen, A. R., Lieberman, J., Alvir, J., Mayerhoff, D., Loebel, A., Chakos, M., Farooq, A., & Cooper, T. (1994). Plasma homovanillic acid levels in first-episode schizophrenia: Psychopathology and treatment response. *Arch. Gen. Psychiat., 51*(2), 132–38.

Kornberg, M. S., & Caplan, G. (1980). Risk factors and preventive intervention in child psychopathology: A review. *Journal of Prevention, 1*, 71–133.

Koscheyev, V. S. (1990, Oct.). *Psychological functioning of Chernobyl workers in the period after the nuclear accident.* Invited address. University of Minnesota.

Koscheyev, V. S., Martens, V. K., Kosenkov, A. A., Lartzev, M. A., & Leon, G. R. (1993). Psychological status of Chernobyl Nuclear Power Plant operators after the nuclear disaster. *J. Trauma. Stress, 6*, 561–68.

Koslow, S. H., Maas, J. W., Bowden, C. L., Davis, J. M., Hanin, I., & Javaid, J. (1983). CSF and urinary biogenic amines and metabolites in depression and mania: A controlled, univariate analysis. *Arch. Gen. Psychiat., 40*, 999–1010.

Koss, M. P. (1983). The scope of rape: Implications for the clinical treatment of victims. *Clin. Psychol., 36*, 88–91.

Koss, M. P. (1993). Detecting the scope of rape: A review of prevalence research methods. *J. Interpers. Violen., 8*, 198–222.

Koss, M. P., & Dinero, T. E. (1989). Discriminant analysis of risk factors for sexual victimization among a national sample of college women. *J. Cons. Clin. Psychol., 57*, 242–50.

Koss, M. P., & Oros, C. J. (1982). Sexual experiences survey: A research instrument investigating sexual aggression and victimization. *J. Cons. Clin. Psychol., 50*, 455–57.

Koss, M. P., Dinero, T. E., Seibel, C. A., & Cox, S. L. (1988). Stranger and acquaintance rape: Are there differences in the victim's experience? *Psychology of Women Quarterly, 12*, 1–23.

Koss, M. P., Gidycz, C. A., & Wisniewski, N. (1987). The scope of rape: Incidence and prevalence of sexual aggression and victimization in a national sample of higher education students. *J. Cons. Clin. Psychol., 55*, 162–70.

Kosten, T. R. (1989). Pharmacotherapeutic interventions for cocaine abuse. Matching patients to treatments. *J. Nerv. Ment. Dis., 177*, 379–89.

Kosten, T. R., & Rounsaville, B. J. (1986). Psychopathology in opioid addicts. *Psychiat. Clin. N. Amer., 9*, 515–32.

Kosten, T. R., Rounsaville, B. J., & Kleber, H. D. (1988). Antecedents and consequences of cocaine abuse among opioid addicts. A 2.5 year follow-up. *J. Nerv. Ment. Dis., 176*, 176–81.

Kosten, T. R., Silverman, D. G., Fleming, J., & Kosten, T. A. (1992). Intraveneous cocaine challenges during naltrexone maintenance: A preliminary study. *Biol. Psychiat., 32,* 543–48.

Kozleski, E. B., & Jackson, L. (1993). Taylor's story: Full inclusion in her neighborhood elementary school. *Except., 4*(3), 153–75.

Kraepelin, E. (1883). *Compendium der psychiatrie.* Leipzig: Abel.

Kraepelin, E. (1899). *Psychiatrie. Ein lehrbuch fur studierende und aerzte* (6th ed.). Leipzig: Barth.

Kraepelin, E. (1922). *Manic depressive insanity of paranoia* (trans. R. M. Barclay). Edinburgh: E. & S. Livingstone.

Krafft-Ebing, R. V. (1950). *Psychopathica sexualis.* New York: Pioneer Publications.

Kraines, S. H. (1948). *The therapy of the neuroses and psychoses* (3rd ed.). Philadelphia: Lea & Febiger.

Kramer, P. D. (1993). *Listening to Prozac: A psychiatrist explores antidepressant drugs and the remaking of the self.* New York: Viking Penguin.

Krantz, D. S., & Glass, D. C. (1984). Personality, behavior patterns, and physical illness: Conceptual and methodological issues. In W. D. Gentry (Ed.), *Handbook of behavioral medicine* (pp. 38–86). New York: Guilford.

Kreitman, N., Sainsbury, P., Pearce, K., & Costain, W. R. (1965). Hypochondriasis and depression in out-patients at a general hospital. *Brit. J. Psychiat., 3,* 607–15.

Kremen, W. S., Seidman, L. J., Pepple, J. R., Lyons, M. J., Tsuang, M. T., & Faraone, S. V. (1994). Neuropsychological risk indicators for schizophrenia: A review of family studies. *Schizo. Bull., 20*(1), 103–19.

Kress, H. W. (1984). Role of family and networks in emergency psychotherapy. In E. L. Bassuk & A. Birk (Eds.), *Emergency Psychiatry.* New York: Plenum.

Kriechman, A. M. (1987). Siblings with somatoform disorders in childhood and adolescence. *J. Amer. Acad. Child Adoles. Psychiat., 26,* 226–31.

Kring, A. M., Kerr, S. L., Smith, D. A., & Neale, J. M. (1993). Flat affect in schizophrenia does not reflect diminished subjective experience of emotion. *J. Abnorm. Psychol., 102*(4), 507–17.

Krippner, S. (1994). Cross-cultural treatment perspectives on dissociative disorders. In S. J. Lynn & J. W. Rhue (Eds.), *Dissociation: Clinical and theoretical perspectives* (pp. 338–64). New York: Guilford.

Kroll, J., & Bachrach, B. (1984). Sin and mental illness in the Middle Ages. *Psychol. Med., 14,* 507–14.

Krystal, H. (1968). *Massive psychic trauma.* New York: International Universities Press.

Kuczmarski, R. J. (1992). Prevalence of overweight and weight gain in the United States. *Amer. J. Clin. Nutri., 55* (Suppl), 495S–502S.

Kuechenmeister, C. A., Linton, P. H., Mueller, T. V., & White, H. B. (1977). Eye tracking in relation to age, sex, and illness. *Arch. Gen. Psychiat., 34,* 578–79.

Kuhn, T. S. (1962). *The structure of scientific revolutions.* Chicago: University of Chicago Press.

Kulka, R.A., Schlenger, W.E., Fairbank, J.A., Hough, R.L., Jordan, B.K., Marmar, C.R., & Weiss, D.S. (1990). *Trauma and the Vietnam War generation: Report of findings from the National Vietnam Veterans Readjustment Study.* Brunner/Mazel, Inc.: New York, NY.

Kuperman, S., Black, D. W., & Burns, T.L. (1988). Excess mortality among formerly hospitalized child psychiatric patients. *Arch. Gen. Psychiat., 45,* 277–82.

Kupersmidt, J.B., & Coie, J.D. (1990). Preadolescent peer status, aggression, and school adjustment as predictors of externalizing problems in adolescence. *Child Develop., 61,* 1350–1362.

Kupersmidt, J. B., Coie, J. D., & Dodge, K. A. (1990). The role of poor peer relationships in the development of disorder. In S. R. Asher & J. D. Coie (Eds.), *Peer rejection in childhood* (pp. 274–308). New York: Cambridge University Press.

Kushner, M. (1968). The operant control of intractable sneezing. In C. D. Spielberger (Ed.), *Contributions to general psychology: Selected readings for introductory psychology.* New York: Ronald Press.

Kutcher, S. & Mackenzie, S. (1988). Successful clonazepam treatment of adolescents with panic disorder. *J. Clin. Psychopharm., 8,* 299–301.

Kutcher, S. P., Reiter, S., Gardner, D. M., & Klein, R. G. (1992). The pharmacologic treatment of anxiety disorders in children and adolescents. *Psychiat. Clin. N. Amer., 15,* 41–68.

Ladd, G. W. (1983). Social networks of popular, average, and rejected children in school settings. *Merrill-Palmer Quarterly, 29,* 283–308.

Lahey, B. B., Hartdagen, S. E., Frick, P.J., McBurnett, K., Connor, R., & Hynd, G. W. (1988). Conduct disorder: Parsing the confounded relation to parental divorce and antisocial personality. *J. Abnorm. Psychol., 97,* 334–37.

Lahey, B. B., Loeber, R., Quay, H. C., Frick, P. J., & Grimm, S. (1992). Oppositional defiant and conduct disorders: Issues to be resolved for DSM-IV. *J. Amer. Acad. Child Adoles. Psychiat., 29,* 620–26.

Lake, C. R., Pickar, D., Ziegler, M. G., Lipper, S., Slater, S., & Murphy, D. L. (1982). High plasma norepinephrine levels in patients with major affective disorder. *Amer. J. Psychiat., 139,* 1315–18.

Lakin, M. (1991). *Coping with ethical dilemmas in psychotherapy.* Elmsford, NY: Pergamon.

Lamb, H. R. (1984). Deinstitutionalization and the homeless mentally ill. *Hosp. Comm. Psychiat., 35,* 899–907.

Lambert, M. J. (1989). The individual therapist's contribution to psychotherapy process and outcome. *Clin. Psychol. Rev., 9,* 469–85.

Lambert, M. J., & Bergin, A. E. (1994). The effectiveness of psychotherapy. In A. E. Bergin & S. L. Garfield (Eds.), *Handbook of psychotherapy and behavior change* (4th ed., pp. 143–89). New York: Wiley.

Lambert, M.C., Weisz, J.R., & Knight, F. (1989). Over and undercontrolled clinic referral problems of Jamaican and American children and adolescents: The culture general and culture specific. *J. Cons. Clin. Psychol., 57,* 467–472.

Landesman-Dwyer, S. (1981). Living in the community. *Amer. J. Ment. Def., 86,* 223–34.

Lang, A. R., & Kidorf, M. (1990). Problem drinking: Cognitive behavioral strategies for self control. In M. E. Thase, B. A. Edelstein, & M. Hersen (Eds.), *Handbook of outpatient treatment of adults* (pp. 413–42). New York: Plenum.

Lang, A. R., & Marlatt, G. A. (1983). Problem drinking: A social learning perspective. In R. J. Gatchel, A. Baum, & J. E. Singer (Eds.), *Handbook of psychology and health* (Vol. 1, pp. 121–69). Hillsdale, NJ: Erlbaum.

Lang, P. J. (1970). Autonomic control. *Psych. Today, 4*(5), 37–41.

Lang, P. J. (1968). Fear reduction and fear behavior: Problems in treating a construct. In J.M. Shlien (Ed.), *Research in psychotherapy* (Vol. 3). Washington DC: American Psychological Association.

Lang, P. J. (1971). Application of psychophysiological methods to the study of psychotherapy and behavior modification. In A. E. Bergin & S. L. Garfield (Eds.), *Handbook of psychotherapy and behavior change.* New York: Wiley.

Lang, P. J. (1985). The cognitive psychophysiology of emotion: Fear and anxiety. In A. H. Tuma & J. D. Maser (Eds.), *Anxiety and the anxiety disorders.* Hillsdale, NJ: Erlbaum.

Lange, W. R., Cabanilla, B. R., Moler, G., Bernacki, E. J., & Frankenfield, D. (1994). Preemployment drug screening at the Johns Hopkins Hospital, 1989 and 1991. *Amer. J. Drug Alcoh. Abuse, 20,* 35–46.

Langevin, R., Handy, L., Day, D., & Russon, A. (1985). Are incestuous fathers pedophilic, aggressive, and alcoholic? In R. Langevin (Ed.), *Erotic preference, gender identity, and aggression* (pp. 161–80). Hillsdale, NJ: Erlbaum.

Lansky, M. R., & Selzer, J. (1984). Priapism associated with trazodone therapy: Case report. *J. Clin. Psychiat., 45,* 232–33.

Lanyon, R. (1984). Personality assessment. *Annu. Rev. Psychol.* *35*, 689–701.

Lanyon, R. I., Barrington, C. C., & Newman, A. C. (1976). Modification of stuttering through EMG biofeedback: A preliminary study. *Behav. Ther., 7,* 96–103.

Last, C. G., & Perrin, S. (1993). Anxiety disorders in African-American and white children. *J. Abnorm. Child Psychol., 21,* 153–64.

Laufer, R. S., Brett, E., & Gallops, M. S. (1985). Dimensions of posttraumatic stress disorder among Vietnam veterans. *J. Nerv. Ment. Dis., 173*(9), 538–45.

Lawton, H. (1990). The field of psychohistory. *J. Psychohist., 17,* 353–64.

Lazarus, A. A. (1981). *The practice of multimodal therapy.* New York: McGraw-Hill.

Lazarus, A. A. (1989). Dyspareunia: A multimodal psychotherapeutic perspective. In S. R. Leiblum & R. C. Rosen (Eds.), *Principles and practice of sex therapy* (2nd ed., pp. 89–112). New York: Guilford.

Lazarus, A. A. (Ed.). (1985). *Casebook of multimodal therapy.* New York: Guilford.

Lazarus, R.S., & Folkman, S. (1984). *Stress appraisal and coping.* New York: Springer.

Leal, J., Ziedonis, D., & Kosten, T. (1994). Antisocial personality disorder as a prognostic factor for pharmacotherapy of cocaine dependence. *Drug and Alcohol Dependence, 35,* 31–35.

Leary, T. (1957). *Interpersonal diagnosis.* New York: Ronald.

Lease, C.A., & Ollendick, T.H. (1993). Development and psychopathology. In A.S. Bellack, & M. Hersen (Eds.), *Psychopathology in adulthood.* Needham, MA: Allyn and Bacon.

Lebedev, B. A. (1967). Corticovisceral psychosomatics. *Inter. J. Psychiat., 4*(3), 241–46.

Lebergott, S. (1964). *Manpower in economic growth: The American record since 1800.* New York: McGraw-Hill.

Lebra, W. (Ed.). (1976). Culture-bound syndromes, ethnopsychiatry and alternate therapies. In *Mental health research in Asia and the Pacific* (Vol. 4). Honolulu: University Press of Hawaii.

Lee, J. R., & Goodwin, M. E. (1987). Deinstitutionalization: A new scenario. *Journal of Mental Health Administration, 14,* 40–45.

Lefkowitz, M. M., & Tesiny, E. P. (1985). Depression in children: Prevalence and correlates. *J. Cons. Clin. Psychol., 53,* 647–56.

Lefkowitz, M. M., Eron, L. D., Walder, L. O., & Huesmann, L. R. (1977). *Growing up to be violent: A longitudinal study of the development of aggression.* New York: Pergamon.

Lehmann, H. E. (1967). Psychiatric disorders not in standard nomenclature. In A. M. Freedman, H. I. Kaplan, & H. S. Kaplan (Eds.), *Comprehensive textbook of psychiatry.* Baltimore: Williams & Wilkins.

Lehmann, L. (1985). The relationship of depression to other DSM-III Axis I disorders. In E. E. Beckham & W. R. Leber (Eds.), *Handbook of depression: Treatment, assessment, and research* (pp. 669–99). Homewood, IL: Dorsey Press.

Lehrer, P. M., & Murphy, A. I. (1991). Stress reactivity and perception of pain among tension headache sufferers. *Behav. Res. Ther., 29,* 61–69.

Lehrer, P. M., Sargunaraj, D., & Hochron, S. (1992). Psychological approaches to the treatment of asthma. *J. Cons. Clin. Psychol., 60*(4), 639–643.

Leiblum, S. R., & Pervin, L. A. (1980). *Principles and practice of sex therapy.* New York: Guilford.

Leiblum, S. R., & Rosen, R. C. (Eds.). (1989a). *Principles and practice of sex therapy* (2nd ed.). New York: Guilford.

Leiblum, S. R., & Rosen, R. C. (1989b). Introduction: Sex therapy in the age of AIDS. In S. R. Leiblum & R. C. Rosen (Eds.), *Principles and practice of sex therapy,* (2nd ed., pp. 1–18). New York: Guilford.

Leiblum, S. R., Pervin, L. A., & Campbell, E. H. (1989). The treatment of vaginismus: Success and failure. In S. R. Leiblum & R. C. Rosen (Eds.), *Principles and practice of sex therapy* (2nd ed., pp. 113–40). New York: Guilford.

Leichtman, M. (1995). Behavioral observations. In J. N. Butcher (Ed.). *Clinical personality assessment: Practical considerations* (pp. 251–66). New York: Oxford University Press.

Leichtman, M. D., & Ceci, S. J. (1995). The effect of stereotypes and suggestions on preschoolers' reports. *Develop. Psychol., 31* (June).

Lelliott, P., Marks, I., McNamee, G., & Tobena, A. (1989). Onset of panic disorder with agoraphobia. *Arch. Gen. Psychiat., 46,* 1000–4.

Lemert, E. M. (1962). Paranoia and the dynamics of exclusion. *Sociometry, 25,* 2–25.

Lencz, T., Raine, A., Scerbo, A., Redmon, M., Brodish, S., Holt, L., & Bird, L. (1993). Impaired eye tracking in undergraduates with schizotypal personality disorder. *Amer. J. Psychiat., 150,* 152–54.

Lenzenweger, M. F. (1994). Psychometric high-risk paradigm, perceptual aberrations, and schizotypy: An update. *Schizo. Bull., 20*(1), 121–35.

Lenzenweger, M. F., & Korfine, L. (1994). Perceptual aberrations, schizotypy, and the Wisconsin Card Sorting Test. *Schizo. Bull., 20*(2), 345–56.

Leon, G. L., Butcher, J. N., Kleinman, M., Goldberg, A., & Almagor, M. (1981). Survivors of the holocaust and their children: Current status and adjustment. *J. Pers. Soc. Psychol., 41*(3), 503–16.

Leon, G. R., & Chamberlain, K. (1973). Emotional arousal, eating patterns, and body image as differential factors associated with varying success in maintaining a weight loss. *J. Cons. Clin. Psychol., 40,* 474–80.

Leon, G. R., Eckert, E. D., Teed, D., & Buckwald, H. (1978). Changes in body image and other psychological factors after intestinal bypass surgery for massive obesity. *J. Behav. Med., 2,* 39–59.

Leon, G. R., Fulkerson, J. A., Perry, C. L., & Cudeck, R. (1993). Personality and behavioral vulnerabilities associated with risk status for eating disorders in adolescent girls. *J. Abnorm. Psychol., 102*(3), 438–44.

Leonard, B. E. (1990). *Fundamentals of psychopharmacology.* New York: Wiley.

Leong, G. B., & Eth, S. (1991). Legal and ethical issues in electroconvulsive therapy. *Psychiat. Clin. N. Amer., 14,* 1007–16.

Lepine, J. P., Chignon, J. M., & Teherani, M. (1993). Suicide attempts in patients with panic disorder. *Arch. Gen. Psychiat., 50* (2), 144–9.

Lerman, P. (1981). *Deinstitutionalization: A cross-problem analysis.* Rockville, MD: U.S. Department of Health and Human Services.

Lerner, P. M. (1995). Assessing adaptive capacities by means of the Rorschach. In J. N. Butcher (Ed.), *Clinical personality assessment: Practical considerations* (pp. 317–25). New York: Oxford University Press.

Lester, D. (1988). Youth suicide: A cross-cultural perspective. *Adolescence, 23,* 955–58.

LeVay, S. (1991). A difference in hypothalamic structure between heterosexual and homosexual men. *Science, 253,* 1034–37.

LeVay, S. (1993). *The sexual brain.* Cambridge, MA: MIT Press.

Levenson, A. J. (1981). *Basic psychopharmacology.* New York: Springer.

Levin, S., & Yurgelun-Todd, D. (1989). Contributions of clinical neuropsychology to the study of schizophrenia. *J. Abnorm. Psychol., 98,* 341–56.

Levine, M., & Perkins, D. V. (1987). *Principles of community psychology: Perspectives and applications.* New York: Oxford University Press.

Levine, M. D. (1976). Children with encopresis: A descriptive analysis. *Pediatrics, 56,* 412.

Levine, M. D., & Bakow, H. (1975). Children with encopresis: A study of treatment outcomes. *Pediatrics, 58,* 845.

Levitan, H. (1989). Onset situation in three psychosomatic illnesses. In S. Cheren (Ed.), *Psychosomatic medicine: Theory, physiology, and practice* (Vol 1., pp. 119–34). Madison, CT: International Universities Press.

Levor, R. M., Cohen, M. J., Naliboff, B. D., & McArthur, D. (1986). Psychosocial precursors and correlates of migraine headache. *J. Cons. Clin. Psychol., 54,* 347–53.

Levy, D. L., Holzman, P. S., Matthysse, S., & Mendell, N. R. (1993). Eye tracking dysfunction and schizophrenia: A critical perspective. *Schizo. Bull., 19*(3), 461–536.

Levy, D. L., Holzman, P. S., Matthysse, S., & Mendell, N. R. (1994). Eye tracking and schizophrenia: A selective review. *Schizo. Bull., 20*(1), 47–62.

Levy, D. L., Yasillo, N. J., Dorcus, E., Shaughnessy, R. Gibbons, R. D., Peterson, J., Janicak, P.G., Gaviria, M., & Davis, J. M. (1983). Relatives of unipolar and bipolar patients have normal pursuit. *Psychiat. Res., 10,* 285–93.

Lewinsohn, P. M. (1974). A behavioral approach to depression. In R. J. Friedman & M. M. Katz (Eds.), *The psychology of depression: Contemporary theory and research.* New York: Halstead Press.

Lewinsohn, P. M., & Rohde, P. (1993). The cognitive-behavioral treatment of depression in adolescents: Research and suggestions. *Clin. Psychol., 46,* 177–83.

Lewinsohn, P. M., Clarke, G. N., Hops, H., & Andrews, J. (1990). Cognitive-behavioral treatment for depressed adolescents. *Behav. Ther., 21,* 385–401.

Lewinsohn, P. M., Hoberman, H. M., & Rosenbaum, M. (1988). A prospective study of risk factors for unipolar depression. *J. Abnorm. Psychol., 97,* 251–64.

Lewinsohn, P. M., Hoberman, H. M., Teri, L., & Hautzinger, M. (1985). An integrative theory of depression. In S. Reiss & R. Bootzin (Eds.), *Theoretical issues in behavior therapy* (pp. 331–59). San Diego: Academic Press.

Lewinsohn, P. M., Hops, H., Roberts, R. E., Seeley, J. R., & Andrews, J. A. (1993). Adolescent psychopathology: I. Prevalence and incidence of depression and other DSM-III-R disorders in high school students. *J. Abnorm. Psychol., 102,* 133–44.

Lewinsohn, P. M., Rohde, P., & Seeley, J. R. (1994). Psychosocial risk factors for future adolescent suicide attempts. *J. Cons. Clin. Psychol., 62,* 297–305.

Lewinsohn, P. M., Zeiss, A. M., & Duncan, E. M. (1989). Probability of relapse after recovery from an episode of depression. *J. Abnorm. Psychol., 98,* 107–16.

Lewis, C. E., Cloninger, C. R., & Pais, J. (1983). Alcoholism, anti-social personality, and drug use in a criminal population. *Alcohol and Alcoholism, 18,* 53–60.

Lewis, C. E., Robins, L., & Rice, J. (1985). Association of alcoholism with antisocial personality in urban men. *J. Nerv. Ment. Dis., 173*(3), 166–74.

Lewis, J. M., Rodnick, E. H., & Goldstein, M. J. (1981). Intrafamilial interactive behavior, communication deviance, and risk for schizophrenia. *J. Abnorm. Psychol., 90,* 448–57.

Lewis, J. W., & Walter, D. (1992). Buprenorphine: Background to its development as a treatment for opiate dependence. In J. D. Blaine (Ed.), *Buprenorphine: An alternative treatment for opioid dependence* (pp. 5–11). Washington, DC: U.S. Department of Health and Human Services.

Lewis, M. S. (1989a). Age incidence and schizophrenia: Part I. The season of birth controversy. *Schizo. Bull., 15,* 59–73.

Lewis, M. S. (1989b). Age incidence and schizophrenia: Part II. Beyond age incidence. *Schizo. Bull., 15,* 75–80.

Lewis, M. S. (1990). *Res ipsa loquitur:* The author replies. *Schizo. Bull., 16,* 17–28.

Lewis, M. S., & Griffin, P. A. (1981). An explanation for the season of birth effect in schizophrenia and certain other diseases. *Psychol. Bull., 89,* 589–96.

Lewis, N. D. C. (1941). *A short history of psychiatric achievement.* New York: Norton.

Lewis, R. J., Dlugokinski, E. L., Caputo, L. M., & Griffin, R. B. (1988). Children at risk for emotional disorders: Risk and resource dimensions. *Clin. Psychol. Rev., 8,* 417–40.

Lewis, W. C. (1974). Hysteria: The consultant's dilemma. *Arch. Gen. Psychiat., 30*(2), 145–51.

Lexow, G. A., & Aronson, S. S. (1975). Health advocacy: A need, a concept, a model. *Children Today, 4*(1), 2–6, 36.

Liberman, R. P., & Raskin, D. E. (1971). Depression: A behavioral formulation. *Arch. Gen. Psychiat., 24*(6), 515–23.

Liberman, R. P., Mueser, K. T., & DeRisi, W. J. (1989). *Social skills training for psychiatric patients.* Elmsford, NY: Pergamon.

Liddle, P. F., Barnes, T. R. E., Speller, J., & Kibel, D. (1993). Negative symptoms as a risk factor for tardive dyskinesia in schizophrenia. *Brit. J. Psychiat., 163,* 776–80.

Lidz, T. (1978). Egocentric cognitive regression and the family setting of schizophrenic disorders. In L. C. Wynne, R. L. Cromwell, & S. Matthysse (Eds.), *The nature of schizophrenia: New approaches to research and treatment* (pp. 526–33). New York: Wiley.

Lidz, T. (1994). To the Editor. *Amer. J. Psychiat., 151,* 458–59.

Lidz, T., Fleck, S., & Cornelison, A. R. (1965). *Schizophrenia and the family.* New York: International Universities Press.

Lie, N. (1992). Follow-ups of children with attention deficit hyperactivity disorder (ADHD): Review of literature. *Acta Psychiatr. Scandin., 85,* 40–80.

Lieberman, J. A., & Koreen, A. R. (1993). Neurochemistry and neuroendocrinology of schizophrenia: A selective review. *Schizo. Bull., 19*(2), 371–429.

Lieberman, J. A., Jody, D., Alvir, J. M. J., Ashtari, M., Levy, D. L., Bogerts, B., Degreef, G., Mayerhoff, D. I., & Cooper, T. (1993a). Brain morphology, dopamine, and eye-tracking abnormalities in first-episode schizophrenia: Prevalence and clinical correlates. *Arch. Gen. Psychiat., 50*(5), 357–68.

Lieberman, J. A., Jody, D., Geisler, S., Alvir, J., Loebel, A., Szymanski, S., Woerner, M., & Borenstein, M. (1993b). Time course and biologic correlates of treatment response in first-episode schizophrenia. *Arch. Gen. Psychiat., 50*(5), 369–76.

Lieberman, J. A., Safferman, A. Z., Pollack, S., Szymanski, S., Johns, C., Howard, A., Kronig, M., Bookstein, P., & Kane, J. M. (1994). Clinical effects of clozapine in chronic schizophrenia: Response to treatment and predictors of outcome. *Amer. J. Psychiat., 151*(12), 1744–52.

Lieberman, L. M. (1982). The nightmare of scheduling. *J. Learn. Dis., 15,* 57–58.

Liebman, J. M., & Cooper, S. J. (1989). *The neuropharmacological basis of reward.* New York: Claredon Press.

Liebowitz, M. R., & Hollander, E. (1991). Obsessive-compulsive disorder: Psychobiological integration. In J. Zohar, T. Insel, & S. Rasmussen (Eds.), *The psychobiology of obsessive-compulsive disorder.* New York: Springer.

Liebowitz, M. R., Fyer, A. J., Gorman, J. M., Dillon, D., Appleby, I. L., Levy, G., Anderson, S., Palij, M., Davies, S. O., & Klein, D. F. (1984). Lactate provocation of panic. *Arch. Gen. Psychiat., 41,* 764–70.

Liebowitz, M. R., Gorman, J. M., Fyer, A. J., Levitt, M., Dillon, D., Levy, P., Appleby, I. L., Anderson, S., Palij, M., Davis, S. O., & Klein, D. F. (1985). Lactate provocation of panic attacks: II. Biochemical and physiological findings. *Arch. Gen. Psychiat., 42,* 709–19.

Liebowitz, M. R., Schneier, F. R., Campeas, R., Hollander, E., Hatterer, J., Fryer, A., Gorman, J., Papp, L., Davies, S., Gully, R., & Klein, D. R. (1992). Phenelzine vs. atenolol in social phobia: A placebo controlled comparison. *Arch. Gen. Psychiat., 49,* 290–300.

Liem, J. H. (1974). Effects of verbal communications of parents and children: A comparison of normal and schizophrenic families. *J. Cons. Clin. Psychol., 42,* 438–50.

Lifton, R. J. (1972). The "Gook syndrome" and "numbed warfare." *Saturday Review, 55*(47), 66–72.

Liljefors, I., & Rahe, R. H. (1970). An identical twin study of psychosocial factors in coronary heart disease in Sweden. *Psychosom. Med., 32*(5), 523–42.

Lima, B. R., & Pai, S. (1993). Response to the psychological consequences of disasters in Latin America. *Inter. J. Ment. Hlth., 21,* 59–71.

Lincoln, J., Batty, J., Townsend, R., & Collins, M. (1992). Working for greater inclusion of children with severe learning difficulties in mainstream secondary schools. *Educational & Child Psychology, 9*(4), 46–51.

Lindman, R. E., & Lang, A. R. (1994). The alcohol-aggression stereotype: A cross-cultural comparison of beliefs. *Inter. J. Addict., 29,* 1–13.

Lindsay D. S., Johnson, M. K., Kwon, P. (1991) Developmental changes in memory source monitoring. *Develop. Psychol., 52,* 297–318.

Lindsey, K. P., & Paul, G. L. (1989). Involuntary commitments to public mental institutions: Issues involving the over-representation of blacks and the assessment of relevant functioning. *Psychol. Bull., 106,* 171–83.

Linehan, M. M. (1987). Dialectical behavioral therapy: A cognitive behavioral approach to parasuicide. *J. Personal. Dis., 1,* 328–33.

Linehan, M. M. (1993). *Cognitive-behavioral treatment of borderline personality disorder: The dialectics of effective treatment.* New York: Guilford.

Linehan, M. M., Armstrong, H. E., Suarez, A., Allmon, D., & Heard, H. L. (1991). Cognitive-behavioral treatment of chronically parasuicidal borderline patients. *Arch. Gen. Psychiat., 48,* 1060–64.

Linehan, M. M., Heard, H. L., & Armstrong, H. E. (1993) Naturalistic follow-up of a behavioral treatment for chronically parasuicidal borderline patients. *Arch. Gen. Psychiat., 50,* 971–74.

Link, B. G., Cullen, F. T., Frank, J., & Wozniak, J.F. (1987). The social rejection of former mental patients: Understanding why labels matter. *American Journal of Sociology, 92,* 1461–1500.

Linszen, D. H., Dingemans, P. M., & Lenior, M. E. (1994). Cannabis abuse and the course of recent-onset schizophrenic disorders. *Arch. Gen. Psychiat., 51*(4), 273–79.

Lion, J.R. (1978). Outpatient treatment of psychopaths. In W. H. Reid (Ed.), *The psychopath: A comprehensive study of antisocial disorders and behaviors.* New York: Brunner/Mazel.

Lipowski, Z. J. (1988). Somatization: The concept and its clinical application. *Amer. J. Psychiat., 145,* 1358–68.

Lipton, D. N., McDonel, E. C., & McFall, R. M. (1987) Hetersocial perception in rapists. *J. Cons. Clin. Psychol., 55,* 17–21.

Lipton, E. L., Steinschneider, A., & Richmond, J. B. (1966). Psychophysiologic disorders in children. In L. W. Hoffman & M. L. Hoffman (Eds.), *Review of child development research* (pp. 169–220). Russell Sage Foundation.

Lisak, D., & Roth, S. (1988). Motivational factors in nonincarcerated sexually aggressive men. *J. Pers. Soc. Psychol., 55,* 795–802.

Lishman, W. A. (1990). Alcohol and the brain. *Brit. J. Psychiat., 156,* 635–44.

Lishman, W. A., Jacobson, R. R., & Acker, C. (1987). Brain damage in alcoholism: Current concepts. *Acta Medica Scandinavica* (Suppl. 717), 5–17.

Lissau, I., & Sorensen, T. I. A. (1994). Parental neglect during childhood and increased risk of obesity in young adulthood. *Lancet, 343,* 324–27.

Litwack, T. R., & Schlesinger, L. B. (1987). Assessing and predicting violence: Research, law, and applications. In A. Hess & I. Weiner (Eds.), *Handbook of forensic psychology.* New York: Wiley.

Livesley, W. J. (1991). Classifying personality disorders: Ideal types, prototypes, or dimensions? *J. Personal. Dis., 5,* 52–59.

Livesley, W. J., & Jackson, D. N. (1991). Construct validity and classification of personality disorders. In J. M. Oldham (Ed.), Personality disorders: *New perspectives on diagnostic validity.* Washington, DC: American Psychiatric Press.

Livesley, W. J., Jackson, D. N., & Schroeder, M. L. (1992). Factorial structure of traits delineating personality disorders in clinical and genereal population samples. *J. Abnorm. Psychol., 101,* 432–40.

Livesley, W. J., Jang, K. L., Jackson, D. N., & Vernon, P. A. (1993). Genetic and environmental contributions to dimensions of personality disorder. *Amer. J. Psychiat., 150,* 1826–31.

Livesley, W. J., Schroeder, M. L., Jackson, D. N., & Jang, K. L. (1994). Categorical distinctions in the study of personality disorder: Implications for classification. *J. Abnorm. Psychol., 103,* 6–17.

Livesley, W. J., West, M., & Tanney, A. (1985). Historical comment on the DSM III schizoid and avoidant personality disorders. *Amer. J. Psychiat., 142,* 1344–47.

Livingston, J. (1974, Mar.). Compulsive gamblers: A culture of losers. *Psych. Today,* 51–55.

Lizardi, H., Klein, D. N., Ouimette, P. C., Riso, L. P., Anderson, R. L., & Donaldson, S. K. (1995). Reports of the childhood home environment in early-onset dysthymia and episodic major depression. *J. Abnorm. Psychol. 104,* 132–39.

Lobitz, W. C., & Lobitz, G. K. (1978). Clinical assessment in the treatment of sexual dysfunctions. In J. LoPiccolo & L. LoPiccolo (Eds.), *Handbook of sex therapy* (pp. 85–102). New York: Plenum.

Lobovits, D. A., & Handel, P. (1985). Childhood depression: Prevalence using DSM III criteria and validity of parent and child depression scales. *J. Pediat. Psychol., 10*(1), 45–54.

Loeber, R., Green, S. M., Lahey, B. B., Crist, M. A., & Frick, P. J. (1992). Developmental sequences in the age of onset of disruptive child behaviors. *Journal of Child and Family Studies, 1,* 21–41.

Loftus, E. F. (1993). The reality of repressed memories. *Amer. Psychol., 48*(5), 518–537.

Loftus, E. F., Feldman, J., & Dashiell, R. (in press) The reality of illusory memories. In D. Schacter, J. Coyle, L. Sullivan, M. Mesulam, & G. Fischbach (Eds.), *Memory distortions: Interdisciplinary perspectives.* Cambridge: Harvard University Press.

Lombardo, V. S., & Lombardo, E. F. (1991). The link between learning disabilities and juvenile delinquency: Fact or fiction? *The Correctional Psychologist, 23,* 1–3.

Lomranz, J., Hobfoll, S., Johnson, R., Eyla, N., & Tzemach, M. (1994). A nation's response to attack: Israeli's depressive reactions to the Gulf War. *J. Traum. Stress, 7,* 59–73.

Long, J.V.F., & Valliant, G.E. (1984). Natural history of male psychological health, XI: Escape from the underclass. *Amer. J. Psychiat., 141,* 341–346.

Loosen, P. T. (1986). Hormones of the hypothalmic-pituitary thyroid axis: A psychoneuroendocrine perspective. *Pharmacopsychiatry, 19,* 401–15.

LoPiccolo, J. (1978). Direct treatment of sexual dysfunction. In J. LoPiccolo & L. LoPiccolo (Eds.), *Handbook of sex therapy* (pp. 1–17). New York: Plenum.

LoPiccolo, J., & LoPiccolo, L. (Eds.). (1978). *Handbook of sex therapy.* New York: Plenum.

LoPiccolo, J., & Stock, W. E. (1986). Treatment of sexual dysfunction. *J. Cons. Clin. Psychol., 54,* 158–67.

Loranger, A. W., Oldham, J. M., & Tulis, E. H. (1982). Familial transmission of DSM-III borderline personality disorder. *Arch. Gen. Psychiat., 39*(7), 795–99.

Lorenz, V. C., & Shuttlesworth, D. E. (1983). The impact of pathological gambling on the spouse of the gambler. *J. Comm. Psychol., 11,* 67–76.

Lorion, R. P. (1990). *Protecting the children: Strategies for optimizing emotional and behavioral development.* New York: Haworth.

Lorr, M., & Klett, C. J. (1968). Cross-cultural comparison of psychotic syndromes. *J. Abnorm. Psychol., 74*(4), 531–43.

Los Angeles Times. (1973, Sept. 30). A transvestite's plea for understanding and tolerance. IV, 7.

Lovaas, O. I. (1977). *The autistic child: Language development through behavior modification.* New York: Holsted Press.

Lovaas, O. I. (1987). Behavioral treatment of normal educational and intellectual functioning in young autistic children. *J. Cons. Clin. Psychol., 44,* 3–9.

Lovett, S. (1985). Microelectronic and computer-based technology. In A. M. Clarke, A. D. B. Clarke, & J. M. Berg (Eds.), *Mental deficiency: The changing outlook* (4th ed., pp. 549–83). London: Methuen.

Lovibond, S. H., & Caddy, G. R. (1970). Discriminated aversive control in the moderation of alcoholics' drinking behavior. *Behav. Ther. 1,* 437–44.

Lozoff, B. (1989). Nutrition and behavior. Special issue: Children and their development: Knowledge base, research agenda, and social policy application. *Amer. Psychol., 44,* 231–236.

Lubin, B. (1976). Group therapy. In I. Weiner (Ed.), *Clinical methods in psychology.* New York: Wiley.

Lubin, B., Larsen, R. M., & Matarazzo, J. (1984). Patterns of psychological test usage in the United States, 1935–1982. *Amer. Psychol., 39,* 451–54.

Lubin, B., Larsen, R. M., Matarazzo, J. D., & Seever, M. F. (1985). Psychological test usage patterns in five professional settings. *Amer. Psychol., 40,* 857–61.

Lucas, A. R., Duncan J. W., & Piens, V. (1976). The treatment for anorexia nervosa. *Amer. J. Psychiat., 133,* 1034–38.

Luchins, A. S. (1991). Moral treatment in asylums and general hospitals in 19th Century America. *J. Psychol., 123,* 585–607.

Luckasson, R., Coulter, D. L., Polloway, E. A., Reiss, S., Schalock, R. L., Snell, M. E., Spitalnik, D. M., & Stark, J. A. (1992). *Mental retardation: Definition, classification, and systems of supports* (9th ed.). Washington, DC: American Association on Mental Retardation.

Lukas, C., & Seiden, H. M. (1990). *Silent grief: Living in the wake of suicide.* New York: Bantam Books.

Lund, S. N. (1975). *Personality and personal history factors of child abusing parents.* Unpublished doctoral dissertation, University of Minnesota.

Lunsing, R. J., Hadders Algra, M., Touwen, B. C., & Huisjes, H. J. (1991). Nocturnal enuresis and minor neurological dysfunction at 12 years: A follow-up study. *Develop. Med. Child Neurol., 33,* 439–45.

Luntz, B. K., & Widom, C. S. (1994). Antisocial personality disorder in abused and neglected children grown-up. *Amer. J. Psychiat., 151,* 670–74.

Lusznat, R. M., Murphy, D. P., & Nunn, C. M. H. (1988). Carbamazepine vs. lithium in the treatment and prophylaxis of mania. *Brit. J. Psychiat., 153,* 198–204.

Luten, A., Ralph, I., & Mineka, S. (1995). *Pessimistic attributional style: Is it specific to depression versus anxiety versus negative affect?* Submitted for publication.

Lutz, D. J., & Snow, P. A. (1985). Understanding the role of depression in the alcoholic. *Clin. Psychol. Rev., 5,* 535–51.

Lykken, D. T. (1957). A study of anxiety in the sociopathic personality. *J. Abnorm. Soc. Psychol., 55*(1), 6–10.

Lynam, D., Moffitt, T. E., & Stouthamer-Loeber, M. (1993). Explaining the relation between IQ and delinquency: Class, race, test motivation, school failure, or self-control. *J. Abnorm. Psychol., 102,* 187–96.

Lynch, J. J. (1977). *The broken heart.* New York: Basic Books.

Lyness, S. A. (1993). Predictors of differences between Type A and B individuals in heart rate and blood pressure reactivity. *Psychol. Bull., 114*(2), 266–95.

Lyon, M., Barr, C. E., Cannon, T. D., Mednick, S. A., & Shore, D. (1989). Fetal neural development and schzophrenia. *Schizo. Bull., 15,* 149–61.

Lytton, H. (1980). *Parent-child interaction: The socialization process observed in twin and singleton families.* New York: Plenum.

Maccoby, E.E., & Martin, J.A. (1983) Socialization in the context of the family: Parent-child interaction. In E.M. Hetherington (Ed.), *Socialization, personality, and social development: Vol. 4. Handbook of child psychology.* New York: Wiley.

MacDonald, M. R., & Kuiper, N. A. (1983). Cognitive-behavioral preparations for surgery: Some theoretical and methodological concerns. *Clin. Psychol. Rev., 3,* 27–39.

Mackay, L. E. (1994). Benefits of a formalized traumatic brain injury program within a trauma center. *J. Head Trauma Rehab., 9*(1), 11–19.

MacLeod, C., & Cohen, I. L. (1993). Anxiety and the interpretation of ambiguity: A text comprehension study. *J. Abnorm. Psychol., 102* (2), 238–47.

MacLeod, C., & Mathews, A.M. (1991). Cognitive-experimental approaches to the emotional disorders. In P. Martin (Ed.), *Handbook of behavior therapy and psychological science: An integrative approach* (pp. 116–50). New York: Pergamon.

MacMillan, D. L., Gresham, F. M., & Siperstein, G. N. (1993). Conceptual and psychometric concerns about the 1992 AAMR definition of mental retardation. *Amer. J. Ment. Retard., 98*(3), 325–35.

Maddi, S. R., Bartone, P. T., & Puccetti, M. C. (1987). Stressful events are indeed a factor in physical illness: Reply to Schroeder and Costa. *J. Pers. Soc. Psychol., 52,* 833–43.

Maddux, J. F., Vogtsberger, K. N., Prihoda, T. J., Desmond, D. F., Watson, D. D., & Williams, M. L. (1994). Illicit drug injectors in three Texas cities. *Intern. J. Addict., 29,* 179–94.

Magnus, K., Diener, E., Fujita, F., & Pavot, W. (1993). Extraversion and neuroticism as predictors of objective life events: A longitudinal analysis. *J. Pers. Soc. Psychol., 65*(5), 1046–53.

Mahler, M. (1976). *On human symbiosis and the vicissitudes of individuation.* New York: Library of Human Behavior.

Mahoney, G., Glover, A., & Finger, I. (1981). Relationship between language and sensorimotor development of Down's syndrome and nonretarded children. *Amer. J. Ment. Def., 86,* 21–27.

Mahoney, M., & Arnkoff, D. (1978). Cognitive and self-control therapies. In S. Garfield & A. Bergin (Eds.), *Handbook of psychotherapy and behavior change: An empirical analysis.* New York: Wiley.

Maida, C. A., Gordon, N. S., & Farberow, N. L. (1989). *The crisis of competence.* New York: Brunner/Mazel.

Maier, S. F., Seligman, M., & Solomon, R. (1969). Pavlovian fear conditioning and learned helplessness. In B. A. Campbell & R. M. Church (Eds.), *Punishment and aversive behavior.* New York: Appleton-Century-Crofts.

Maier, S. F., Watkins, L. R., & Fleshner, M. (1994). Psychoneuroimmunology: The interface between behavior, brain, and immunity. *Amer. Psychol., 49*(12), 1004–17.

Main, M.B., & Weston, D.R. (1981). Security of attachment to mother and father: Related to conflict behavior and the readiness to establish new relationships. *Child Develop., 52,* 932–940.

Maisch, H. (1972). *Incest.* New York: Stein & Day.

Maj, M., Satz, P., Janssen, R., Zaudig, M., Starace, F., D'Elia, L., Sughondhabirom, B., Mussa, M., Naber, D., Ndetei, D., Schulte, G., & Sartorius, N. (1994). WHO neuropsychiatric AIDS study, cross sectional Phase II: Neuropsychological and neurological findings. *Arch. Gen. Psychiat., 51*(1), 51–61.

Makita, K. (1973). The rarity of "depression" in childhood. *Acta Psychiatr. Scandin. 40,* 37–44.

Malamud, N. (1975). Organic brain disease mistaken for psychiatric disorder: A clinicopathologic study. In D. F. Benson & D. Blumer (Eds.), *Psychiatric aspects of neurological disease* (pp. 287–307). New York: Grune & Stratton.

Malatesta, V. J., & Adams, H. (1993) The sexual dysfunctions. In P. Sutker & H. Adams (Eds.), *Comprehensive textbook of psychopathology.* New York: Plenum.

Malatesta, V. J., Sutker, P. B., & Treiber, F. A. (1981). Sensation seeking and chronic public drunkenness. *J. Cons. Clin. Psychol., 49,* 292–94.

Malec, J. F., Smigielski, J. S., DePompolo, R. W., & Thompson, J. M. (1993). Outcome evaluation and prediction in a comprehensive-integrated post-acute outpatient brain injury rehabilitation programme. *Brain Injury, 7*(1), 15–29.

Malinosky-Rummell, R., & Hansen, D.J. (1993). Long-term consequences of childhood physical abuse. *Psychol. Bull., 114,* 68–79.

Malinowski, B. (1927). *Sex and repression in savage society.* New York: Humanities.

Manderscheid, R. W., Witkin, M. J., Rosenstein, M. J., Milazzo-Sayre, L. J., Bethel, H. E., & MacAskill, R. L. (1985). In C. A. Taube & S. A. Barrett (Eds.), *Mental Health, United States, 1985.* Washington, DC: National Institute of Mental Health.

Mandler, G. (1964). The interruption of behavior. In D. Levine (Ed.), *Nebraska symposium on motivation: 1964.* Lincoln, Nebraska: University of Nebraska Press.

Mandler, G. (1972). Helplessness: Theory and research in anxiety. In C. Spielberger (Ed.), *Anxiety: Current trends in theory and research.* (pp. 359–74). New York: Academic Press.

Manglesdorff, D. (1985). Lessons learned and forgotten: The need for prevention and mental health interventions in disaster preparedness. *J. Comm. Psychol., 13,* 239–57.

Mann, J. (1973). *Time-dated psychotherapy.* Cambridge, MA: Harvard University Press.

Mann, L. M., Chassin, L., & Sher, K. J. (1987). Alcohol expectancies and risk for alcoholics. *J. Cons. Clin. Psychol., 55,* 411–17.

Mann, P. A. (1978). *Community psychology: Concepts and applications.* New York: Free Press.

Mannuzza, S., Gittelman, R., Bonagura, N., Konig, P. H., & Shenker, R. (1988). Hyperactive boys almost grown up. *Arch. Gen. Psychiat., 45,* 13–18.

Mannuzza, S., Klein, R., Bessler, A., Malloy, P., & LaPadula, M. (1993). Adult outcome of hyperactive boys: Educational achievement, occupational rank, and psychiatric status. *Arch. Gen. Psychiat., 50,* 565–76.

Marcourakis, T., Gorenstein, C., & Gentil, V. (1993). Clomipramine, a better reference drug for panic/agoraphobia: II Psychomotor and cognitive effects. *J. Psychopharm., 7,* 325–30.

Marcus, E. R., & Bradley, S. S. (1990). Combination psychotherapy and psychopharmacotherapy with treatment-resistent inpatients with dual disorder. *Psychiat. Clin. N. Amer., 13,* 209–14.

Marcus, J., Hans, S. L., Auerbach, J. G., & Auerbach, A. G. (1993). Children at risk for schizophrenia: The Jerusalem infant development study: II. Neurobehavioral deficits at school age. *Arch. Gen. Psychiat., 50*(10), 797–809.

Marcus, J., Hans, S. L., Mednick, S. A., Schulsinger, F., & Michelson, N. (1985). Neurological dysfunctioning in offspring of schizophrenics in Israel and Denmark: A replication analysis. *Arch. Gen. Psychiat., 42,* 753–61.

Marcus, M. D., Wing, R. R., & Hopkins, J. (1988). Obese binge eaters: Affect, cognitions, and response to behavioral weight control. *J. Cons. Clin. Psychol., 56,* 433–39.

Marder, S. R., Ames, D., Wirshing, W. C., & Van Putten, T. (1993). Schizophrenia. *Psychiat. Clin. N. Amer., 16,* 567–88.

Margolin, G., & Wampold, B. E. (1981). Sequential analysis of conflict and accord in distressed and non-distressed marital partners. *J. Cons. Clin. Psychol., 49*(4), 554–67.

Margraf, J., Ehlers, A., & Roth, W. T. (1986a). Sodium lactate infusions and panic attacks: A review and critic. *Psychosom. Med., 48,* 23–51.

Margraf, J., Ehlers, A., & Roth, W. (1986b). Biological models of panic disorder and agoraphobia—A review. *Behav. Res. Ther., 24,* 553–67.

Mariotto, M., Paul, G. L. & Licht, M. H. (1995). Assessing the chronically mentally ill patient. In J. N. Butcher (Ed.), *Clinical personality assessment: Practical considerations* New York: Oxford University Press.

Markovitz, P. J., & Schulz, S.C. (1993). Drug treatment of personality disorders. *Brit. J. Psychiat., 162,* 122.

Marks, I. M. (1969). *Fears and phobias.* New York: Academic Press.

Marks, I. M. (1982). Toward an empirical clinical science: Behavioral psychotherapy in the 1980's. *Behav. Ther., 13,* 63–81.

Marks, I. M. (1987). *Fear, phobias, and rituals: Panic, anxiety, and their disorders.* New York: Oxford University Press.

Marks, I., & Nesse, R. M. (1991). Fear and fitness: An evolutionary of anxiety disorders. Paper presented at the Eleventh National Conference on Anxiety Disorders. Chicago, IL.

Marlatt, G. A. (1985). Cognitive assessment and intervention procedures for relapse prevention. In G. A. Marlatt & J. R. Gordon (Eds.), *Relapse prevention.* New York: Guilford.

Marlatt, G. A. (1992). Substance abuse: Implications of a biopsychosocial model for prevention, treatment, and relapse prevention. In J. Grabowsik & G. R. VandenBos (Eds.), *Psychopharmacology: Basic mechanisms and applied interventions* (pp. 127–162). Washington, DC: American Psychological Association.

Marlatt, G. A., & Gordon, J. R. (1980). Determinants of relapse: Implications for the maintenance of behavior change. In P. Davidson & S. Davidson (Eds.), *Behavioral medicine: Changing health lifestyles.* New York: Brunner/Mazel.

Marmor, J., & Woods, S. M. (Eds.). (1980). *The interface between psychodynamic and behavior therapies.* New York: Plenum.

Marsella, A. J. (1980). Depressive experience and disorder across cultures. In H. C. Triandis & J. Draguns (Eds.), *Handbook of cross-cultural psychology* (Vol. 6). Boston: Allyn & Bacon.

Marsella, A. J., Sartorius, N., Jablensky, A., & Fenton, F. R. (1985). Cross-cultural studies of depressive disorders: An overview. In A. Kleinman & B. Good (Eds.), *Culture and depression.* Berkeley, CA: University of California Press.

Marshall, W. L. (1974). A combined treatment approach to the reduction of multiple fetish-related behaviors. *J. Cons. Clin. Psychol., 42*(4), 613–16.

Marshall, W. L. (1993). The treatment of sex offenders: What does the outcome data tell us? A reply to Quinsey, Harris, Rice, and Lalumiere. *J. Interpers. Viol., 8,* 524–30.

Marshall, W. L., & Barbaree, H. E. (1990a). An integrated theory of the etiology of sexual offending. In W. L. Marshall, D. R. Laws, & H. E. Barbaree (Eds.), *Handbook of sexual assault* (pp. 257–69). New York: Plenum.

Marshall, W. L., & Barbaree, H. E. (1990b). Outcome of comprehensive cognitive-behavioral treatment programs. In W. L. Marshall, D. R. Laws, & H. E. Barbaree (Eds.), *Handbook of sexual assault: Issues, theories, and treatment of the offender* (pp. 363–85). New York: Plenum.

Marshall, W. L., & Pithers, W. D. (1994). A reconsideration of treatment outcome with sex offenders. *Crim. Just. Behav., 21,* 10–27.

Marshall, W. L., Barbaree, H. E., & Christophe, D. (1986). Sexual offenders against female children: Sexual preferences for age of victim and type of behavior. *Canad. J. Behav. Sci., 18,* 424–39.

Marshall, W. L., Jones, R., Ward, T., Johnston, P., & Barbaree, H. E. (1991). Treatment outcome with sex offenders. *Clin. Psychol. Rev., 11,* 465–85.

Martell, D. A., & Dietz, P. E. (1992). Mentally disordered offenders who push or attempt to push victims onto subway tracks in New York City. *Arch. Gen. Psychiat., 49*(6), 472–75.

Martin, C. L. (1990). Attitudes and expectations about children with nontraditional and traditional gender roles. *Sex Roles, 22,* 151–65.

Martin, R. L., Cloninger, R., Guze, S. B., & Clayton, P. J. (1985). Mortality in a follow-up of 500 psychiatric outpatients: I. Total mortality. *Arch. Gen. Psychiat., 42,* 47–54.

Marvit, R. C. (1981). Guilty but mentally ill—an old approach to an old problem. *Clin. Psychol., 34*(4), 22–23.

Marx, J. (1991). Mutation identified as possible cause of Alzheimer's disease. *Science, 251,* 876–77.

Mash, E. J., Handy, L. C., & Hamerlynck, L. A. (1976). *Behavior modification approaches to parenting.* New York: Brunner/Mazel.

Maslow, A. H. (1962). *Toward a psychology of being.* New York: Van Nostrand.

Maslow, A. H. (1969). Toward a humanistic biology. *Amer. Psychol., 24*(8), 734–35.

Masten, A.S., Best, K., & Garmezy, N. (1990) Resilience and development: Contributions from the study of children who overcome adversity. *Develop. Psychopath., 2,* 425–444.

Masten, A.S., & O'Connor, M.J. (1989). Vulnerability, stress, and resilience in early development of a high risk child. *J. Amer. Acad. Child Adoles. Psychiat., 28,* 274–278.

Masters, J., Burish, T. Hollon, S., & Rimm, D. (1987). *Behavior therapy: Techniques and empirical findings* (3rd ed.). San Diego: Harcourt Brace Jovanovich.

Masters, W. H., & Johnson, V. E. (1966). *Human sexual response.* Boston: Little, Brown.

Masters, W. H., & Johnson, V. E. (1970). *Human sexual inadequacy.* Boston: Little, Brown.

Masters, W. H., & Johnson, V. E. (1975). *The pleasure bond: A new look at sexuality and commitment.* Boston: Little, Brown.

Masters, W. H., Johnson, V. E., & Kolodny, R. C. (1992). *Human sexuality*. New York: HarperCollins.

Masterson, J. (1987). Borderline and narcissistic disorders: An integrated developmental object-relations approach. In J. Grotstein, M. Solomon, & J. Lang (Eds.), *The borderline patient* (Vol. 1, pp. 205–17). Hillsdale, NJ: Analytic Press.

Matarazzo, J. D. (1986). Computerized clinical psychological test interpretations: Unvalidated plus all mean and no sigma. *Amer. Psychol., 41*, 14–24.

Matheny, A.P. Jr. (1989). Children's behavioral inhibition over age and across situations: Genetic similarity for a trait during change. *J. Personal., 57*, 215–235.

Mathew, R. J., Wilson, W. H., & Melges, F. T. (1992). Temporal disintegration and its psychological and physiological correlates: Changes in the experience of time after marijuana smoking. *Annals of Clinical Psychiatry, 4*, 235–45.

Mathews, A. M. (1993). Anxiety and the processing of emotional information. In L. Chapman, J. Chapman, & D. Fowles (Eds.), *Models and methods of psychopathology: Progress in experimental personality and psychopathology research*. New York: Springer.

Mathews, A. M., & MacLeod, C. (1994). Cognitive approaches to emotion and emotional disorders. *Ann. Rev. Psychol., 45*, 25–50.

Mathis, H. I. (1970). *Emotional responsivity in the antisocial personality*. (Doctoral dissertation, George Washington University), Ann Arbor, MI: University Microfilms, 1970, No, 71–12, 299. Cited in Hare (1978b).

Matier, K., Halperin, J. M., Sharma, V., & Newcorn, J. H. (1992). Methylphenidate response in aggressive and non-aggressive ADHD children: Distinctions on laboratory measures of symptoms. *J. Amer. Acad. Child Adoles. Psychiat., 31*, 219–25.

Matson, J. L. (1981). Use of independence training to teach shopping skills to mildly mentally retarded adults. *Amer. J. Ment. Def., 86*, 178–83.

Matsunaga, E., Tonomura, A., Hidetsune, O., & Yasumoto, K. (1978). Reexamination of paternal age effect in Down's syndrome. *Human Genet., 40*, 259–68.

Matt, G., Vazquez, C., & Campbell, W. (1992). Mood-congruent recall of affectively toned stimuli: A meta-analytic review. *Clin. Psychol. Rev., 12*, 227–255.

Mattes, J. A., & Gittelman, R., (1981). Effects of artificial food colorings in children with hyperactive symptoms: A critical review and results of a controlled study. *Arch. Gen. Psychiat., 38*(6), 714–18.

Mattia, J. I., Heimberg, R. G., & Hope, D. A. (1993). The revised Stroop color-naming task in social phobics: Diagnostic and treatment outcome implications. *Behav. Res. Ther., 31*, 305–13.

Mavissakalian, M. R., & Perel, J. M. (1989). Imipramine dose-response relationship in panic disorder with agoraphobia. *Arch. Gen. Psychiat., 46*, 127–31.

Max, W. (1993). The economic impact of Alzheimer's disease. *Neurology, 43*(8, Suppl. 4), S6–S10.

May, R. (1969). *Love and will*. New York: Norton.

Mays, D. T., & Franks, C. M. (Eds.). (1985). *Negative outcome in psychotherapy and what to do about it*. New York: Springer.

Mays, J. A. (1974, Jan. 16). High blood pressure, soul food. *Los Angeles Times*, II, 7.

Mazure, C. M., & Druss, B. G. (1995). A historical perspective on stress and psychiatric illness. In C. M. Mazure (Ed.), *Does stress cause psychiatric illness?* Washington, DC: American Psychiatric Association.

McAlister, A. L., Puska, P., Koskela, K., Pallonen, U., & Maccoby, N. (1980). Mass communication and community organization for public health education. *Amer. Psychol., 35*, 375–79.

McBride, W. J., Murphy, J. M., Gatto, G. J., et al. (1992). CNS mechanisms of alcohol drinking in genetically selected lines of rats. *Alcohol and Alcoholism, 27* (supplement 2).

McCall, L. (1961). Between us and the dark (originally published in 1947). Summary in W. C. Alvarez, *Minds that came back*.

McCann, I. L., Sakheim, D. K., & Abrahamson, D. J. (1988). Trauma and victimization: A model of psychological adaptation. *Counseling Psychologist, 16*, 531–94.

McCarthy, B. W. (1989). Cognitive-behavioral strategies and techniques in the treatment of early ejaculation. In S. R. Leiblum & R. C. Rosen (Eds.), *Principles and practice of sex therapy* (2nd ed., pp. 141–67). New York: Guilford.

McCarthy, P., & Foa, E. B. (1990). Treatment interventions for obsessive-compulsive disorder. In M. Thase, B. Edelstein, & M. Hersen (Eds.), *Handbook of outpatient treatment of adults*. New York: Plenum.

McClellan, J. M., & Wherry, J. S. (1992). Schizophrenia. *Psychiat. Clin. N. Amer., 15*, 131–48.

McClelland, D. C. (1979). Inhibited power motivation and high blood pressure in men. *J. Abnorm. Psychol., 88*(2), 182–90.

McCombie, S. L. (1976). Characteristics of rape victims seen in crisis intervention. *Smith College Studies in Social Work, 46*, 137–58.

McCord, J., & Tremblay, R. E. (1992). *Preventing antisocial behavior: Interventions from birth through adolescence*. New York: Guilford.

McCord, W., & McCord, J. (1964). *The psychopath: An essay on the criminal mind*. New York: Van Nostrand Reinhold.

McCutchan, J. A. (1990). Virology, immunology, and clinical course of HIV infection. *J. Cons. Clin. Psychol., 58*, 5–12.

McDonnell, J., Hardman, M. L., Hightower, J., & Keifer-O'Donnel, R. (1993). Impact of community-based instruction on the development of adaptive behavior of secondary-level students with mental retardation. *Amer. J. Ment. Retard., 97*(5), 575–84.

McFall, R. M. (1990). The enhancement of social skills: An information-processing analysis. In W. L. Marshall, D. R. Laws, & H. E. Barbaree (Eds.), *Handbook of sexual assault: Issues, theories, and treatment of the offender* (pp. 311–30). New York: Plenum.

McFarlane, A. C. (1988). The longitudinal course of posttraumatic morbidity: The range of outcomes and their predictors. *J. Nerv. Ment. Dis., 176*, 30–39.

McGlashan, T. H., & Fenton, W. S. (1992). The positive-negative distinction in schizophrenia: Review of natural history validators. *Arch. Gen. Psychiat., 49*(1), 63–72.

McGlashan, T. H., & Fenton, W. S. (1993). Subtype progression and pathophysiologic deterioration in early schizophrenia. *Schizo. Bull., 19*(1), 71–84.

McGue, M., & Lykken, D. T. (1992). Genetic influence on risk of divorce. *Psychological Science, 3*(6), 368–73.

McGuffin, P., & Gottesman, I.I. (1985). Genetic influences on normal and abnormal development. In M. Rutter & L. Hersov (Eds.), *Child and adolescent psychiatry: Modern approaches* (2nd ed.). Oxford: Blackwell Scientific.

McGuffin, P., Katz, R., & Rutherford, J. (1991). Nature, nurture and depression: A twin study. *Psychol. Med., 21*, 329–35.

McHugh, P. R. (1992). Psychiatric misadventures. *American Scholar, 61*, 497–510.

McIntosh, J. L. (1992). Suicide of the elderly. In B. Bongar (Ed.), *Suicide: Guidelines for assessment, management and treatment*. New York: Oxford University Press.

McKay, J. R., Alterman, A. I., McLellan, A. T., & Snider, E. C. (1994). Treatment goals, continuity of care, and outcome in a day hospital substance abuse rehabilitation program. *Amer. J. Psychiat., 151*, 254–59.

McLaughlin, A. M., & Peters, S. (1993). Evaluation of an innovative cost-effective programme for brain injury patients: Response to a need for flexible treatment planning. *Brain Injury, 7*(1), 71–75.

McLellan, A. T., Arndt, I. O., Metzger, D. S., Woody, G. E., & O'Brien, C. P. (1993). The effects of psychosocial services in substance abuse treatment. *JAMA, 269*, 1953–59.

McLellan, A. T., Luborsky, L., Woody, G. E., O'Brien, C. P., & Druley, K. A. (1993). Predicting response to alcohol and drug abuse treatments. *Arch. Gen. Psychiat., 40*, 620–25.

McMurran, M., & Hollin, C. R. (1993). *Young offenders and alcohol related crime*. New York: Wiley.

McNally, R. (1987). Preparedness and phobias: A review. *Psychol. Bull., 101*, 283–303.

McNally, R. J. (1990). Psychological approaches to panic disorder: A review. *Psychol. Bull., 108*(3), 403–419.

McNally, R. J. (1994). *Panic disorder: A critical analysis*. New York: Guilford.

McNeal, E. T., & Cimbolic, P. (1986). Antidepressants and biochemical theories of depression. *Psychol. Bull., 99*(3), 361–74.

McNeil, D. E., & Binder, R. L. (1986). Violence, civil commitment, and hospitalization. *J. Nerv. Ment. Dis., 174*(2), 107–11.

McWhirter, D. P., & Mattison, A. M. (1978). The treatment of sexual dysfunction in gay male couples. *J. Sex Marit. Ther., 4*, 213–18.

Mead, M. (1949). *Male and female*. New York: Morrow.

Mealiea, W. L., Jr. (1967). *The comparative effectiveness of systematic desensitization and implosive therapy in the elimination of snake phobia*. Unpublished doctoral dissertation, University of Missouri.

Mearns, J., & Lees-Haley, P. R. (1993). Discriminating of neuropsychological sequelae of head injury from alcohol-abuse-induced deficits: A review and analysis. *J. Clin. Psychol., 49*(5), 714–20.

Medea, A., & Thompson, K. (1974). *Against rape*. New York: Farrar, Straus & Giroux.

Mednick, S. A. (1978). Berkson's fallacy and high-risk research. In L. C. Wynne, R. L. Cromwell, & S. Matthysse (Eds.), *The nature of schizophrenia: New approaches to research and treatment* (pp. 442–52). New York: Wiley.

Mednick, S. A., & Schulsinger, F. (1968). Some premorbid characteristics related to breakdown in children with schizophrenic mothers. In D. Rosenthal & S. S. Kety (Eds.), *The transmission of schizophrenia* (pp. 267–91). Oxford: Pergamon.

Meehl, P. E. (1962). Schizotaxia, schizotypy, schizophrenia. *Amer. Psychol., 17*, 827–38.

Meehl, P. E. (1978). Theoretical risks and tabular asterisks: Sir Karl, Sir Ronald, and the slow progress of soft psychology. *J. Cons. Clin. Psychol., 46*, 806–34.

Meehl, P. E. (1989). Schizotaxia revisited. *Arch. Gen. Psychiat., 46*, 935–44.

Meehl, P. E. (1990a). Toward an integrated theory of schizotaxia, schizotypy, and schizophrenia. *J. Personal. Dis., 4*, 1–99.

Meehl, P. E. (1990b). Why summaries of research on psychological theories are often uninterpretable. *Psychol. Rep., 66*, 195–244.

Megargee, E. I. (1970). The prediction of violence with psychological tests. In C. D. Spielberger (Ed.), *Current topics in clinical and community psychology* (Vol. 2). New York: Academic Press.

Megargee, E. I. (1993). Aggression and violence. In P. B. Sutker & H. E. Adams (Eds.), *Comprehensive handbook of psychopathology* (2d ed. pp. 617–44). New York: Plenum.

Megargee, E. I. (1995). Assessing and understanding aggressive and violent patients. In J. N. Butcher (Ed.), *Clinical personality assessment: Practical considerations* (pp. 395–409). New York: Oxford University Press.

Mehlum, L., Friis, S., Irion, T., Johns, S., Karterud, S., Vaglum, P., & Vaglum (1991). Personality disorders 2–5 years after treatment: A prospective follow-up study. *Acta Psychiatr. Scandin., 84*, 72–77.

Meichenbaum, D. (1974). *Cognitive behavior modification*. General Learning Corporation, 16.

Meichenbaum, D. (1975). A self-instructional approach to stress management: A proposal for stress-inoculation training. In C. Spielberger & I. Sarason (Eds.), *Stress and anxiety* (Vol. 2). New York: Wiley.

Meichenbaum, D., & Cameron, R. (1982). Cognitive behavior therapy. In G. T. Wilson & C. M. Franks (Eds.), *Contemporary behavior therapy: Conceptual and empirical foundations*. New York: Guilford.

Meichenbaum, D., & Cameron, R. (1983). Stress inoculation training: Toward a general paradigm for training coping skills. In D. Meichenbaum & M. E. Jaremko (Eds.), *Stress reduction and prevention* (pp. 115–54). New York: Plenum.

Meichenbaum, D., & Jaremko, M. E. (1983). *Stress reduction and prevention*. New York: Plenum.

Meissner, W. W. (1978). *The paranoid process*. New York: Jason Aronson.

Meltzer, H. Y. (1993). New drugs for the treatment of schizophrenia. *Psychiat. Clin. N. Amer., 16*, 365–86.

Meltzer, H. Y. (1992). Treatment of the neuroleptic-nonresponsive schizophrenic patient. *Schizo. Bull., 18*(3), 515–42.

Mendels, J., & Frazer, A. (1974). Brain biogenic amine depletion and mood. *Arch. Gen. Psychiat., 30*, 447–51.

Mendelson, J. H., & Mello, N. (1992). Human laboratory studies of buprenorphine. In J. D. Blaine (Ed.), *Buprenorphine: An alternative treatment for opiate dependence* (pp. 38–60). Washington, DC: U.S. Department of Health and Human Services.

Mendlewicz, J. (1985). Genetic research in depressive disorders. In E. E. Beckham & W. R. Leber (Eds.), *Handbook of depression: Treatment, assessment and research* (pp. 795–815). Homewood, IL: Dorsey Press.

Mendlewicz, J., & Rainer, J. D. (1977). Adoption study supporting genetic transmission in manic-depressive illness. *Nature, 268*, 326–29.

Menninger, K. A. (1945). *The human mind* (3rd ed.). New York: Knopf.

Mental Health Law Project. (1987, October). Court decisions concerning mentally disabled people confined in institutions. *MHLP Newsletter*. Washington, DC.

Merbaum, M. (1977). Some personality characteristics of soldiers exposed to extreme war stress: A follow-up study of post-hospital adjustment. *J. Clin. Psychol., 33*, 558–62.

Merbaum, M., & Hefez, A. (1976). Some personality characteristics of soldiers exposed to extreme war stress. *J. Cons. Clin. Psychol., 44*(1), 1–6.

Merikangas, K. R. (1990). Comorbidity for anxiety and depression: Review of family and genetic studies. In J. D. Maser & C. R. Cloninger (Eds.), *Comorbidity of mood and anxiety disorders*. Washington, DC: American Psychiatric Press.

Merikangas, K. R., Spence, M. A., & Kupfer, D. J. (1989). Linkage studies of bipolar disorder: Methodologic and analytic issues. *Arch. Gen. Psychiat., 46*, 1137–41.

Merikangas, K. R., Wicki, W., & Angst, J. (1994). Heterogeneity of depression: Classification of depressive subtypes by longitudinal course. *Brit. J. Psychiat., 164*, 342–48.

Merson, S., & Tryer, P. (1991). Physical treatments for depression. In R. Horton & C. Katona (Eds.), *Biological aspects of affective disorders*. New York: Academic Press.

Metalsky, G. I., Abrason, L. Y., Seligman, M. E. P., Semmel, A., & Peterson, C. R. (1982). Attributional styles and life events in the classroom: Vulnerability and invulnerability to depressive mood reactions. *J. Pers. Soc. Psychol., 43*, 612–617.

Metalsky, G. I., Joiner, T. E., Hardin, T. S., & Abramson, L. Y. (1993). Depressive reactions to failure in a naturalistic setting: A test of the hopelessness and self-esteem theories of depression. *J. Abnorm. Psychol., 102*, 101–9.

Metz, J. T., Johnson, M. D., Pliskin, N. H., & Luchins, D. J. (1994). Maintenance of training effects on the Wisconsin Card Sorting Test by patients with schizophrenia or affective disorders. *Amer. J. Psychiat., 151*(1), 120–22.

Meyer, C. B., & Taylor, S. E. (1986). Adjustment to rape. *J. Pers. Soc. Psychol., 50*, 1226–34.

Meyer, R. E., & Mirin, S. M. (1979). *The heroin stimulus: Implications for a theory of addiction*. New York: Plenum.

Meyers, J., & Parsons, R. D. (1987). Prevention planning in the school system. In J. Hermalin & J. A. Morell (Eds.), *Prevention planning in mental health*. Beverly Hills, CA: Sage.

Meyerson, B. A., & Mindus, P. (1988). Capsulotomy as treatment of anxiety disorders. In L. D. Lunsford (Ed.), *Modern stereotactic neurosurgery* (p. 353). Boston: Nijhoff.

Michael, R. T., Gagnon, J. H., Laumann, E. O., & Kolata, G. (1994). *Sex in America: A definitive survey.* Boston: Little, Brown.

Miklowitz, D. J., Goldstein, M. J., & Falloon, I. R. (1983). Premorbid and symptomatic characteristics of schizophrenics from families with high and low levels of expressed emotion. *J. Abnorm. Psychol. 92,* 359–67.

Miklowitz, D. J., Goldstein, M. J., Nuechterlein, K. H., Snyder, K. S., & Mintz, J. (1988). Family factors and the course of bipolar affective disorder. *Arch. Gen. Psychiat., 45,* 225–31.

Miklowitz, D. J., Strachan, A. M., Goldstein, M. J., Doane, J. A., & Snyder, K. S. (1986). Expressed emotion and communication deviance in families of schizophrenics. *J. Abnorm. Psychol., 95,* 60–66.

Milby, J. B. (1988). Methadone maintenance to abstinency: How many make it? *J. Nerv. Ment. Dis., 176,* 409–22.

Miles, C. (1977). Conditions predisposing to suicide: A review. *J. Nerv. Ment. Dis., 164,* 232–46.

Millar, J. D. (1990). Mental health and the workplace: An interchangeable partnership. *Amer. Psychol., 45*(10), 1165–66.

Miller, E. (1992). Some basic principles of neuropsychological assessment. In J. R. Crawford, D. M. Parker, & W. W. McKinlay (Eds.), *A handbook of neuropsychological assessment* Hillsdale, NJ: Erlbaum.

Miller, F. T., Abrams, T., Dulit, R., & Fyer, M. (1993a). Psychotic symptoms in patients with borderline personality disorder and concurrent axis I disorder. *Hosp. Comm. Psychiat., 44,* 59–61.

Miller, F. T., Abrams, T., Dulit, R., & Fyer, M. (1993b). Substance abuse in borderline personality disorder. *Amer. J. Drug Alcoh. Abuse, 19,* 491–97.

Miller, H. L., Coombs, D. W., Leeper, J. D., & Barton, S. N. (1984). An analysis of the effects of suicide prevention facilities on suicide rates in the United States. *Amer. J. Pub. Hlth., 74,* 340–43.

Miller, J. P. (1975, Spring). Suicide and adolescence. *Adolescence, 10*(37), 11–24.

Miller, K. A. (1989). Enhancing early childhood mainstreaming through cooperative learning: A brief literature review. *Child Study Journal, 19,* 285–92.

Miller, N. S., & Gold, M. S. (1994). Criminal activity and crack addiction. *Inter. J. Addict., 29,* 1069–78.

Miller, R. (1970). Does Down's syndrome predispose children to leukemia? *Roche Report, 7*(16), 5.

Miller, R. C., & Berman, J. S. (1983). The efficacy of cognitive behavior therapies: A quantitative review of the research evidence. *Psychol. Bull., 94,* 39–53.

Miller, R. R., & Springer, A. D. (1974). Implications of recovery from experimental amnesia. *Psychol. Rev., 81*(5), 470–73.

Miller, W. R. (1978). Behavioral treatment of problem drinkers: A comparative outcome study of three controlled drinking therapies. *J. Cons. Clin. Psychol., 46,* 74–86.

Miller, W. R., & Caddy, G. R. (1977). Abstinence and controlled drinking in the treatment of problem drinking. *J. Stud. Alcoh., 38,* 986–1003.

Miller, W. R., & Hester, R. K. (1986). Inpatient alcoholism treatment: Who benefits? *Amer. Psychol., 41,* 794–805.

Miller, W. R., & Munoz, R. F. (1976). *How to control your drinking.* Englewood Cliffs, NJ: Prentice-Hall.

Miller, W. R., Leckman, A. L., Tinkcom, M., & Rubenstein, J. (1986). Long-term follow-up of controlled drinking therapies. Paper given at the Ninety-fourth Annual Meeting of the American Psychological Association, Washington, DC.

Millon, T. (1981). *Disorders of personality: DSM III, Axis II.* New York: Wiley.

Millon, T. (1991). Classification in psychopathology: Rationale, alternatives, standards. *J. Abnorm. Psychol., 100*(3), 245–61.

Mills, M. J. (1984). The so-called duty to warn: The psychotherapeutic duty to protect third parties from patients' violent acts. *Behavioral Sciences and the Law, 2,* 237–57.

Mills, M. J., Sullivan, G., & Eth, S. (1987). Protecting third parties: A decade after Tarasoff. *Amer. J. Psychiat., 144*(1), 68–74.

Milner, K. O. (1949). The environment as a factor in the aetiology of criminal paranoia. *J. Ment. Sci., 95,* 124–32.

Milns, R. D. (1986). Squibb academic lecture: Attitudes towards mental illness in antiquity. *Australian and New Zealand J. of Psychiat., 20,* 454–62.

Mindus, P., & Jenike, M. A. (1992). Neurosurgical treatment of malignant obsessive-compulsive disorder. *Psychiat. Clin. N. Amer., 15,* 921.

Mindus, P., Nyman, H., Lindquist, C., & Meyerson, B. A. (1993). *Neurosurgery for intractable obsessive-compulsive disorder, an update.* Paper presented at the International Workshop on Obsessive Disorder, Vail, CO.

Mineka, S. (1985a). Animal models of anxiety-based disorders: Their usefulness and limitations. In A. H. Tuma & J. D. Maser (Eds.), *Anxiety and the anxiety disorders.* Hillsdale, NJ: Erlbaum.

Mineka, S. (1985b). The frightful complexities of the origins of fears. In F. R. Brush & J. B. Overmier (Eds.), *Affect, conditioning, and cognition: Essays on the determinants of behavior.* Hillsdale, NJ: Erlbaum.

Mineka, S. (1992). Evolutionary memories, emotional processing and the emotional disorders. In D. Medin (Ed.), *The psychology of learning and motivation,* (Vol. 28, pp. 161–206). New York: Academic Press.

Mineka, S. (1993). Animal models of obsessive-compulsive disorder. In J. Greist & J. Jefferson (Eds.), *Proceedings of the Third International Workshop on Obsessive-Compulsive Disorder,* Vail, CO.

Mineka, S., & Cook, M. (1986). Immunization against the observational conditioning of snake fear in monkeys. *J. Abnorm. Psycho., 95,* 307–18.

Mineka, S., & Cook, M. (1993). Mechanisms underlying observational conditioning of fear in monkeys. *J. Exper. Psychol.: General, 122,* 23–38.

Mineka, S., & Kelly, K. A. (1989). The relationship between anxiety, lack of control and loss of control. In A. Steptoe & A. Appels (Eds.), *Stress, personal control and health.* Brussels-Luxembourg: J. Wiley.

Mineka, S., & Nugent, K. (in press). Mood-congruent memory biases in anxiety and depression. To appear in D. Schacter, J. Coyle, L. Sullivan, M. Mesulam, & G. Fischbach (Eds.), *Memory distortions: Interdisciplinary perspectives.* Cambridge: Harvard University Press.

Mineka, S., & Zinbarg, R. (1991). Animal models of psychopathology. In C.E. Walker (Ed.), *Clinical psychology: Historical and research foundations.* (pp. 51–86) New York: Plenum.

Mineka, S., & Zinbarg, R. (in press-a). Conditioning and ethological models of social phobia. In R. Heimberg, M. Liebowitz, D. Hope, & F. Schneier (Eds.), *Social phobia: Diagnosis, assessment, and treatment.* New York: Guilford.

Mineka, S., & Zinbarg, R. (in press-b). Conditioning and ethological models of anxiety disorders: Stress-in-Dynamic Context Anxiety Models. In D. Hope (Ed.), *Perspectives on Anxiety, Panic, and Fear: Nebraska Symposium on Motivation.* Lincoln: University of Nebraska Press.

Mineka, S., Davidson, M., Cook, M., & Keir, R. (1984). Observational conditioning of snake fear in Rhesus monkeys. *J. Abnorm. Psychol. 93*(4), 355–72.

Mineka, S., Gunnar, M., & Champoux, M. (1986). Control and early socioemotional development: Infant rhesus monkeys reared in controllable versus uncontrollable environments. *Child Develop. 57,* 1241–56.

Minuchin, S. (1974). *Families and family therapy.* Cambridge, MA: Harvard University Press.

Minuchin, S., Baker, L., Rosman, B., Liebman, R., Milman, L., & Todd, T. (1975). A conceptual model of psychosomatic illness in children. *Arch. Gen. Psychiat., 32,* 1031–38.

Miranda, J., & Persons, J. B. (1988). Dysfunctional attitudes are mood state dependent. *J. Abnorm. Psychol., 97,* 76–79.

Miranda, J., Persons, J. B., & Byers, C. N. (1990). Endorsement of dysfunctional beliefs depends on current mood state. *J. Abnorm. Psychol., 99,* 237–41.

Mirsky, A. F., DeLisi, L. E., Buchsbaum, M. S., Quinn, O. W., Schwerdt, P., Siever, L. J., Mann, L., Weingartner, H., Zec, R., et al. (1984). The Genain quadruplets: Psychological studies. *Psychiat. Res., 13,* 77–93.

Mirsky, A. F., Silberman, E. K., Latz, A., & Nagler, S. (1985). Adult outcomes of high-risk children. *Schizo. Bull., 11,* 150–54.

Mischel, W. (1973). Toward a cognitive social learning reconceptualization of personality. *Psychol. Rev., 80*(4), 252–83.

Mischel, W. (1990). Personality dispositions revisited and revised: A view after three decades. In L.A. Pervin (Ed.). *Handbook of personality: Theory and research* (pp. 111–134). New York: Guilford.

Mischel, W. (1993). *Introduction to personality,* 5th ed. Fort Worth, Texas: Harcourt, Brace & Jovanovich.

Mishler, E. G., & Waxler, N. E. (1968). *Interaction in families: An experimental study of family processes and schizophrenia.* New York: Wiley.

Mitchell, J. (1985). Healing the helper. In National Institute of Mental Health (Ed.), *Role stressors and supports for emergency workers* (pp. 105–18), DHHS Publication No. ADM 85–1408). Washington, DC: U.S. Government Printing Office.

Mitchell, J. E., Pyle, R. L., Eckert, E. D., Hatsukami, D., Pomeroy, C., & Zimmerman, R. (1990). A comparison study of antidepressants and structured intensive group psychotherapy in the treatment of bulimia nervosa. *Arch. Gen. Psychiat., 47,* 149–57.

Mitchell, J. T., & Resnik, H. L. P. (1981). *Emergency response to crisis.* Bowie, MD: Robert J. Brady.

Moats, L. C., & Lyon, G. R. (1993). Learning disabilities in the United States: Advocacy, science, and the future of the field. *J. Learn. Dis., 26*(5), 282–94.

Moffitt, T. E. (1993a). "Life-course persistent" and "adolescence-limited" antisocial behavior: A developmental taxonomy. *Psychol. Rev, 100,* 674–701.

Moffitt, T. E. (1993b). The neuropsychology of conduct disorder. *Development and Psychopathology, 5,* 135–51.

Moffitt, T. E. (1994a). *Juvenile delinquency: Seed of a career in violent crime, just sowing wild oats or both?* Science and public policy seminars: Federation of behavioral, psychological and cognitive sciences.

Moffitt, T. E. (1994b). Adolescence-limited and life-course-persistent antisocial behavior: A developmental taxonomy. *Psychol. Rev., 100,* 674–701.

Moffitt, T. E., & Lynam, D. (1994). The neuropsychology of conduct disorder and delinquency: Implications for understanding antisocial behavior. In D. C. Fowles, P. Sutker, & S. H. Goodman (Eds.), *Progress in experimental personality and psychopathology research.* New York: Springer.

Mohr, D. C., & Beutler, L. E. (1990). Erectile dysfunction: A review of diagnostic and treatment procedures. *Clin. Psychol. Rev., 10,* 123–50.

Mohr, J. W., Turner, R. E., & Jerry, M. B. (1964). *Pedophilia and exhibitionism: A handbook.* Toronto: University of Toronto Press.

Mohs, R. C., Breitner, J. C., Silverman, J. M., & Davis, K. L. (1987). Alzheimer's disease: Morbid risk among first-degree relatives approximates 50% by 90 years of age. *Arch. Gen. Psychiat., 44,* 405–8.

Mollica, R. F., Wyshak, G., Lavelle, J., Truong, T., Tor, S., & Yang, T. (1990). Assessing symptom change in Southeast Asian refugees. *Amer. J. Psychiat., 147,* 83–88.

Monahan, J. (1981). *Predicting violent behavior: An assessment of clinical techniques.* Beverly Hills, CA: Sage.

Monahan, J. (1992). Mental disorder and violent behavior: Perceptions and evidence. *Amer. Psychol., 47*(4), 511–21.

Money, J. (1985). *The destroying angel.* (pp. 17–31, 51–52, 61–68, 83–90, 107–20, 137–48). Buffalo, NY: Prometheus Books.

Money, J. (1986). *Lovemaps: Clinical concepts of sexual/erotic health and pathology, paraphilia, and gender transposition.* New York: Irvington.

Money, J. (1988). *Gay, straight, and in-between* (p. 77). New York: Oxford University Press.

Money, J., & Ehrhardt, A. A. (1972). *Man & woman, boy & girl: Differentiation and dimorphism of gender identity from conception to maturity.* Baltimore: Johns Hopkins University Press.

Monroe, S. M., & Simons, A. D. (1991). Diathesis-stress theories in the context of life stress research: Implications for the depressive disorders. *Psychol. Bull., 110,* 406–25.

Monroe, S. M., & Steiner, S. C. (1986). Social support and psychopathology: Interrelations with preexisting disorder, stress, and personality. *J. Abnorm. Psychol., 95,* 29–39.

Montgomery, S. A. (1994). Antidepressants in long-term treatment. *Ann. Rev. Med., 45,* 447–57.

Moolchan, E. T., & Hoffman, J. A. (1994). Phases of treatment: A practical approach to methadone maintenance treatment. *Inter. J. Addict., 151,* 165–68.

Mora, G. (1967). Paracelsus' psychiatry. *Amer. J. Psychiat., 124,* 803–14.

Moreno, J. L. (1959). Psychodrama. In S. Arieti, et al. (Eds.), *American handbook of psychiatry* (Vol. 2). New York: Basic Books.

Morey, L. C. (1988a). Personality disorders in DSM-III and DSM-III-R: Convergence, coverage, and internal consistency. *Amer. J. Psychiat., 145,* 573–77.

Morey, L. C. (1988b). The categorical representation of personality disorder: A cluster analysis of DSM-III-R personality features. *J. Abnorm. Psychol., 97,* 314–21.

Morey, L. C., Skinner, H. A., & Blashfield, R. K. (1984). A typology of alcohol abusers: Correlates and implications. *J. Abnorm. Psychol., 93,* 408–17.

Morlock, L. L. (1989). Recognition and treatment of mental health problems in the general health care sector. In C. A. Taube, D. Mechanic, & A. A. Hohmann (Eds.), *The future of mental health services research* (pp. 39–62). Washington, DC: U.S. Department of Health and Human Services.

Morrison, J. (1980). Adult psychiatric disorders in parents of hyperactive children. *Amer. J. Psychiat., 137*(7), 825–27.

Morrison, J. (1989). Childhood sexual histories of women with somatization disorder. *Amer. J. Psychiat., 146,* 239–41.

Morrison, T. L., Edwards, D. W., & Weissman, H. N. (1994). The MMPI and MMPI-2 as predictors of psychiatric diagnosis. *J. Pers. Assess., 62,* 17–30.

Morton, T. L., & Ewald, L. S. (1987). Family-based interventions for crime and delinquency. In E. K. Morris & C. J. Braukmann (Eds.), *Behavioral approaches to crime and delinquency: A handbook of application, research, and concepts* (pp. 271–94). New York: Plenum.

Mosbascher, D. (1988). Lesbian alcohol and substance abuse. *Psychiat. Ann., 18,* 47–50.

Mott, F. W. (1919). *War neuroses and shell shock.* Oxford: Oxford Medical Publications.

Mowbray, R. M. (1959). Historical aspects of electric convulsant therapy. *Scott Medical Journal, 4,* 373–78.

Mowrer, O. H. (1947). On the dual nature of learning: A reinterpretation of "conditioning" and "problem solving." *Harvard Educational Review, 17,* 102–148.

Mucha, T. F., & Reinhardt, R. F. (1970). Conversion reactions in student aviators. *Amer. J. Psychiat., 127,* 493–97.

Mueser, K. T., Bellack, A. S., & Blanchard, J. B. (1992). Comorbidity of schizophrenia and substance abuse: Implications for treatment. *J. Cons. Clin. Psychol., 60,* 845–56.

Mueser, K. T., Yarold, P. R., & Bellack, A. S. (1992). Diagnostic and demographic correlates of substance abuse in schizophrenia and major affective disorders. *Acta Psychiatr. Scandin., 85,* 48–55.

Mufson, L., Weissman, M. M., & Warner, V. (1992). Depression and anxiety in parents and children: A direct interview study. *J. Anxiety Dis., 6,* 1–13.

Mukherjee, S., Sackeim, H. A., & Schnur, D. B. (1994). Electroconvulsive therapy of acute manic episodes: A review of 50 years' experience. *Amer. J. Psychiat., 151,* 169–76.

Munro, J. F., & Duncan, L. J. P. (1972). Fasting in the treatment of obesity. *The Practitioner, 208,* 493–98.

Murphy, G. E. (1988). Suicide and substance abuse. *Arch. Gen. Psychiat., 45,* 593–94.

Murphy, G. E., & Wetzel, R. D. (1982). Family history of suicidal behavior among suicide attempters. *J. Nerv. Ment. Dis., 170,* 86–90.

Murphy, G. E., & Wetzel, R. D. (1990). The lifetime risk of suicide in alcoholism. *Arch. Gen. Psychiat., 47,* 383–92.

Murphy, G. E., Simons, A. D., Wetzel, R. D., & Lustman, P. J. (1984). Cognitive therapy and pharmacotherapy: Singly and together in the treatment of depression. *Arch. Gen. Psychiat., 41,* 33–41.

Murphy, H. B. (1968). Cultural factors in the genesis of schizophrenia. In D. Rosenthal & S. S. Kety (Eds.), *The transmission of schizophrenia* (pp. 137–52). Elmsford, NY: Pergamon.

Murphy, J. M. (1976). Psychiatric labeling in cross-cultural perspective. *Science, 191* (4231), 1019–28.

Murphy, S., & Irwin, J. (1992). "Living with the dirty secret": Problems of disclosure for methadone maintenance clients. *J. Psychoact. Drugs, 24,* 257–64.

Murphy, W. D. (1990). Assessment and modification of cognitive distortions in sex offenders. In W. L. Marshall, D. R. Laws, & H. E. Barbaree (Eds.), *Handbook of sexual assault: Issues, theories, and treatment of the offender* (pp. 331–42). New York: Plenum.

Murray, D. C. (1973). Suicidal and depressive feelings among college students. *Psychol. Rep., 33* (1), 175–81.

Myers, J. K., Weissman, M. M., Tischler, G. L., Holzer, C. E., Leaf, P. J., & Stoltzman, R. (1984). Six-month prevalence of psychiatric disorders in three communities: 1980 to 1982. *Arch. Gen. Psychiat., 41,* 959–67.

Myers, M. B., Templer, D. I., & Brown, R. (1985). Reply to Wieder on rape victims. Vulnerability does not imply responsibility. *J. Cons. Clin. Psychol., 53,* 431.

Nace, E. P., Orne, M. T., & Hammer, A. G. (1974). Posthypnotic amnesia as an active psychic process. *Arch. Gen. Psychiat., 31* (2), 257–60.

Nagaraja, J. (1974). Somnambulism in children: Clinical communication. *Child Psychiatry Quarterly, 7* (1), 18–19.

Nanson, J. L., & Hiscock, M. (1990). Attention deficits in children exposed to alcohol prenatally. *Alcoholism: Clin. Exper. Res., 14,* 656–661.

Narby, J. (1982). The evolution of attitudes towards mental illness in pre-industrial England. *Orthomolecular Psychiatry, 11,* 103–10.

Narrow, W. E., Regier, D. A., Rae, D. S., Manderscheid, R. W., & Locke, B. Z. (1993). Use of services by persons with mental and addictive disorders: Findings from the National Institute of Mental Health Epidemiologic Catchment Area Program. *Arch. Gen. Psychiat., 50,* 95–107.

Nash, M. R., Hulsey, T. L., Sexton, M. C., Harralson, T. L., & Lambert, W. (1993). Long-term sequelae of childhood sexual abuse: Perceived family environment, psychopathology, and dissociation. *J. Cons. Clin. Psychol., 61* (2), 276–83.

National Advisory Mental Health Council. (1990). *National plan for research on child and adolescent mental disorders.* Washington, DC: National Institute of Mental Health.

National Association for Mental Health. (1979, Mar. 23). *Bulletin* No. 103.

National Center for Health Statistics. (1982). Washington, DC: U.S. Government Printing Office.

National Institute of Drug Abuse. (1981). *Trend report: January 1978–September 1980.* Data from Client Oriented Data Acquisition Program (CODAP) (Series E, No. 24). Washington, DC: U.S. Department of Health and Human Services.

National Institute of Drug Abuse. (1990). Washington, DC: U.S. Department of Health and Human Services.

National Institute of Mental Health. (1971). Amphetamines approved for children. *Sci. News, 99* (4), 240.

National Institute of Mental Health. (1976, Apr. 20). Rising suicide rate linked to economy. *Los Angeles Times,* VIII, 2, 5.

National Institute of Mental Health. (1978a, Oct.). *Third report on alcohol and health.* Washington, DC: U.S. Government Printing Office.

National Institute of Mental Health. (1978b). *Indirect services* (Statistical Note No. 147). Washington, DC: U.S. Government Printing Office.

National Institute of Mental Health. (1985a). *Electroconvulsive therapy Consensus Development Conference statement.* Bethesda, MD: U.S. Department of Health and Human Services.

National Institute of Mental Health. (1985b). *Mental Health, United States, 1985.* Washington, DC: U.S. Government Printing Office.

National Transportation Safety Board. (1977). *Human factors specialist's factual report of investigation. Accident to Capitol Airways DC8.* Washington, DC: NTSB (NTSB-DCA-77-A-A008).

Navia, B. A., Jordan, B. D., & Price, R. W. (1986). The AIDS dementia complex: I. Clinical features. *Ann. Neurol., 19,* 517–24.

Neale, J. M., & Oltmanns, T. F. (1980). *Schizophrenia.* New York: Wiley.

Nee, L. F., Eldridge, R., Sunderland, T., Thomas, C. B., et al. (1987). Dementia of the Alzheimer type: Clinical and family study of 22 twin pairs. *Neurology, 37,* 359–63.

Neisser, U. (1967) *Cognitive Psychology.* New York: Appleton Century Crofts.

Neisser, U. (Ed.) (1982) *Memory observed: Remembering in natural contexts.* San Francisco: Freeman.

Nelson, F. L. (1984). Suicide: Issues of prevention, intervention, and facilitation. *J. Clin. Psychol., 40,* 1328–33.

Nelson, H. (1971, Jan. 26). County suicide rate up sharply among young. *Los Angeles Times,* II, 1.

Nelson, H. (1973, Mar. 27). High blood pressure found in third of adults in survey. *Los Angeles Times,* II, 1, 3.

Nelson, Z. P., & Mowry, D. D. (1976). Contracting in crisis intervention. *Comm. Ment. Hlth. J., 12,* 37–43.

Nemiah, J. C. (1961). *Foundations of psychopathology.* Cambridge: Oxford University Press.

Nemiah, J. C. (1975). Obsessive-compulsive neurosis. In A.M. Freedman, H.I. Kaplan, & B.J. Sadock (Eds.), *Comprehensive textbook of psychiatry* (2nd ed., Vol 1). Baltimore: Williams & Wilkins.

Nestor, P. G., Shenton, M. E., McCarley, R. W., Haimson, J., Smith, S., O'Donnell, B., Kimble, M., Kikinis, R., & Jolesz, F. A. (1993). Neuropsychological correlates of MRI temporal lobe abnormalities in schizophrenia. *Amer. J. Psychiat., 150* (12), 1849–55.

Neufeld, R. W. (1990). Coping with stress, coping without stress, and stress with coping: In inter-construct redundencies. *Stress Medicine, 6,* 117–25.

Neugarten, B. L. (1977). Personality and aging. In J. E. Birren & K. W. Schaie (Eds.), *Handbook of the psychology of aging.* New York: Van Nostrand.

Newman, B., Selby, J. V., Quesenberry, C. P., King, M., Friedman, G. D., & Fabsitz, R. P. (1990). Nongenetic influences of obesity on other cardiovascular disease risk factors: An analysis of identical twins. *Amer. J. Pub. Hlth., 80,* 675–78.

Newman, J. P., & Kosson, D. S. (1986). Passive avoidance learning in psychopathic and nonpsychopathic offenders. *J. Abnorm. Psychol., 95,* 252–56.

Newman, J. P., Kosson, D. S., & Patterson, C. M. (1992). Delay of gratification in psychopathic and nonpsychopathic offenders. *J. Abnorm. Psychol., 101,* 630–36.

Newman, L., Henry, P. B., DiRenzo, P., & Stecher, T. (1988–89). Intervention and student assistance: The Pennsylvania model. Special Issue: Practical approaches in treating adolescent chemical dependency: A guide to clinical assessment and intervention. *J. Chem. Depen. Treat., 2* (1), 145–62.

Newman, M. G., & Cates, M. S. (1977). *Methadone treatment in narcotic addiction.* New York: Academic Press.

NIAAA Eighth Special Report to the U.S. Congress. (1994). *Comorbidity of alcohol use disorders with other psychopathology.* Washington, DC: U.S. Government Printing Office.

Niccols, G. A. (1994). Fetal alcohol syndrome: Implications for psychologists. *Clin. Psychol. Rev., 14,* 91–112.

Nicholson, R. A., & Berman, J. S. (1983). Is follow-up necessary in evaluating psychotherapy? *Psychol. Bull., 93,* 261–78.

Niederland, W. G. (1968). Clinical observations of the survivor syndrome. *Inter. J. Psychoanal., 49,* 313–16.

Nietzel, M. T., & Harris, M. J. (1990). Relationship of dependency and achievement/autonomy to depression. *Clin. Psychol. Rev., 10,* 279–97.

Nigg, J. T., & Goldsmith, H. H. (1994). Genetics of personality disorders: perspectives from personality and psychopathology research. *Psychol. Bull., 115,* 346–80.

NIH Consensus Statement on Treatment of Panic Disorder. (1991). In B. E. Wolfe & J. D. Maser (Eds.) (1994), *Treatment of panic disorder. A consensus development conference.* Washington, DC: American Psychiatric Press.

NIMH Psychopharmacology Service Center Collaborative Study Group. (1964). Phenothiazine treatment in acute schizophrenia: Effectiveness. *Arch. Gen. Psychiat., 10,* 246–61.

Nisbett, R. E., & Wilson, T. D. (1977). Telling more than we can know: Verbal reports on mental processes. *Psychol. Rev., 84,* 231–59.

Noble, E. P. (Ed.). (1979). *Alcohol and health: Technical support document.* Third special report to the U.S. Congress (DHEW Publication No. ADM79–832). Washington, DC: U.S. Government Printing Office.

Noble, P., & Rodger, S. (1989). Violence by psychiatric inpatients. *Brit. J. Psychiat., 155,* 384–90.

Noia, G., De Santis, M., Fundaro, C., Mastromarino, C., Trivellini, C., Rosati, P., Caruso, A., Segni, G., & Mancuso, S. (1994). Drug addiction in pregnancy: 13 years of experience. *Fetal Diagnosis and Therapy, 9,* 116–24.

Nolen-Hoeksema, S. (1987). Sex differences in unipolar depression: Evidence and theory. *Psychol. Bull., 101,* 259–82.

Nolen-Hoeksema, S. (1990). *Sex differences in depression.* Stanford, CA: Stanford University Press.

Noll, K. M., Davis, J. M., & DeLeon-Jones, F. (1985). Medication and somatic therapies in the treatment of depression. In E. E. Beckham & W. R. Leber (Eds.), *Handbook of depression: Treatment, assessment, and research* (pp. 220–315). Homewood, IL: Dorsey Press.

Norcross, J. C., & Goldfried, M. R. (Ed.). (1992). *Handbook of psychotherapy integration.* New York: Basic Books.

Norris, F. H., & Kaniasty, K. (1994). Psychological distress following criminal victimization in the general population: Cross-sectional, longitudinal, and prospective analyses. *J. Cons. Clin. Psychol., 62,* 111–23.

North, C. S., Smith, E. M., & Spitznagel, E. L. (1994). Posttraumatic stress disorders in survivors of a mass shooting. *Amer. J. Psychiat., 151,* 82–88.

Novaco, R. W. (1977). A stress inoculation approach to anger management in the training of law enforcement officers. *Am. J. Community Psychol., 5,* 327–46.

Novaco, R. W. (1979). The cognitive regulation of anger and stress. In P. Kendall & S. Hollon (Eds.), *Cognitive-behavioral intervention: Theory, research, and procedures.* New York: Academic Press.

Novaco, R. W. (1977). Stress inoculation: A cognitive therapy for anger and its application to a case of depression. *J. Cons. Clin. Psychol., 45,* 600–8.

Noyes, R., Jr., Clarkson, C., Crowe, R. R., Yates, W. R., & McChesney, C. M. (1987). A family study of generalized anxiety disorder. *Amer. J. Psychiat., 144,* 1019–24.

Noyes, R., Jr., Crowe, R. R., Harris, E. L., Hamra, B. J., & McChesney, C. M. (1986). Relationship between panic disorder and agoraphobia: A family study. *Arch. Gen. Psychiat., 43,* 227–32.

Noyes, R., Kathol, R. G., Fisher, M. M., Phillips, B. M., Suelzer, M. T., & Holt, C. S. (1993). The validity of DSM-III-R hypochondriasis. *Arch. Gen. Psychiat., 50*(12), 961–70.

Nurnberger Jr., J. I., & Gershon, E. S. (1992). Genetics. In E. S. Paykel (Ed.), *Handbook of affective disorders* (2nd ed.). New York: Guilford.

Nurnberger, J., Roose, S. P., Dunner, D. S., & Fieve, R. R. (1979). Unipolar mania: A distinct clinical entity? *Amer. J. Psychiat., 136,* 1420–23.

O'Brien, D. (1979, Mar.). Mental anguish: An occupational hazard. *Emergency,* 61–64.

O'Connell, M., Cooper, S., Perry, J. C., & Hoke, L. (1989). The relationship between thought disorder and psychotic symptoms in borderline personality disorder. *J. Nerv. Ment. Dis., 177,* 273–78.

O'Connell, P. (1976, Nov.). Trends in psychological adjustment: Observations made during successive psychiatric follow-up interviews of returned Navy–Marine Corps POWs. In R. Spaulding (Ed.), *Proceedings of the 3rd annual joint meeting concerning POW/MIA matters* (pp. 16–22). San Diego.

O'Dell, S. (1974). Training parents in behavior modification: A review. *Psychol. Bull., 81*(7), 418–33.

O'Hara, M., Schlecte, J., Lewis, D., & Varner, M. (1991). Controlled prospective study of postpartum mood disorders: Psychological, environmental, and hormonal variables. *J. Abnorm. Psychol., 100,* 63–73.

O'Hara, M., Zekoski, E., Phiolipps, L., & Wright, E. (1990). Controlled prospective study of postpartum mood disorders: Comparison of childbearing and nonchildbearing women. *J. Abnorm. Psychol., 99,* 3–15.

O'Leary, A. (1985). Self-efficacy and health. *Behav. Res. Ther., 23,* 437–51.

O'Leary, D., & Wilson, G. T. (1987). *Behavior therapy* (2nd ed.). Englewood Cliffs, NJ: Prentice-Hall.

O'Leary, K. D., & Beach, S. R. H. (1990). Marital therapy: A viable treatment for depression and marital discord. *Amer. J. Psychiat., 147,* 183–86.

O'Malley, S., Adamse, M., Heaton, R. K., & Gawin, F. H. (1992). Neuropsychological impairment in chronic cocaine abusers. *Amer. J. Drug Alcoh. Abuse, 18,* 131–44.

O'Malley, S. S., Foley, S. H., Rounsaville, B. J., Watkins, J. T., Sotsky, S. M., Imber, S. D., & Elkin, I. (1988). Therapist competence and patient outcome in interpersonal psychotherapy of depression. *J. Cons. Clin. Psychol., 56,* 496–501.

Oetting, E. R., & Beauvais, F. (1990). Adolescent drug use: Findings of national and local surveys. *J. Cons. Clin. Psychol., 58,* 385–94.

Office of Technology Assessment, U.S. Congress. (1986, Dec.) *Children's mental health: Problems and services.* (OTA Publication No. OTA-BP-H-33). Washington, DC: U.S. Government Printing Office.

Office of Technology Assessment. (1993). *Biological components of substance abuse and addiction.* Washington, DC: United States Congress, Office of Technology Assessment.

Ogata, S. N., Silk, K. R., Goodrich, S., Lohr, N. E., & Hill, E. M. (1990). Childhood sexual and physical abuse in adult patients with borderline personality. *Amer. J. Psychiat., 147,* 1008–13.

Ogloff, J. R. P. (1995). The legal basis of forensic applications of the MMPI-2. In Y. S. Ben-Porath, J. R. Graham, G. C. Hall, R. D. Hirschman, & M. S. Zargoza (Eds.), *Forensic applications of the MMPI-2.* Newbury Park, CA: Sage.

Öhman, A. (1986). Face the beast and fear the face: Animal and social fears as prototypes for evolutionary analyses of emotion. *Psychophysiology, 23,* 123–45.

Öhman, A., & Soares, J. (1993). On the automatic nature of phobic fear: Conditioned electrodermal responses to masked fear-relevant stimuli. *J. Abnorm. Psychol., 102,* 121–32.

Öhman, A., Dimberg, U., & Esteves, F. (1989). Preattentive activation of aversive emotions. In T. Archer & L. G. Nilsson (Eds.), *Aversion, avoidance, and anxiety: Perspectives on aversively motivated behavior* (pp. 169–99). Hillsdale, NJ: Erlbaum.

Öhman, A., Dimberg, U., & Öst, L. G. (1985). Animal and social phobias: Biological constraints on learned fear responses. In S. Reiss & R. Bootzin (Eds.), *Theoretical issues in behavior therapy* (pp. 123–75). New York: Academic Press.

Okura, K. P. (1975). Mobilizing in response to a major disaster. *Community Health Journal, 2*(2), 136–44.

Oldenburg, B., Perkins, R. J., & Andrews, G. (1985). Controlled trial of psychological intervention in myocardial infarction. *J. Cons. Clin. Psychol., 53,* 852–59.

Oldham, J. M. (1991). *Personality disorders: New perspectives on diagnostic validity.* Washington, DC: American Psychiatric Press.

Oldham, J. M., Skodol, A. E., Kellman, H. D., Hyler, S. E., Rosnick, L., & Davies, M. (1992). Diagnosis of DSM-III-R personality disorders by two structured interviews: Patterns of comorbidity. *Amer. J. Psychiat., 149,* 213–20.

Olds, S. (1970). Say it with a stomach ache. *Today's Health, 48*(11), 41–43, 88.

Oles, B. (1994). *Psychosocially-imposed homosexuality: Institutionalized mate-guarding in Melanesia.* Paper presented at the sixth annual meeting of the Human Behavior and Evolution Society, June 15–19, Ann Arbor, Michigan.

Olfson, M. (1993). Trends in the prescription of antidepressants by office-based psychiatrists. *Amer. J. Psychiat., 150,* 571–77.

Olivera, A. A., Kiefer, M. W., & Manley, M. K. (1990). Tardive dyskinesia in psychiatric patients with substance use disorders. *Amer. J. Drug Alcoh. Abuse, 16,* 57–66.

Ollendick, T. H. (1981). Self-monitoring and self-administered overcorrection: The modification of nervous tics in children. *Behav. Mod., 5*(1), 75–84.

Oltmanns, T. F., & Maher, B. A. (Eds.). (1988). *Delusional beliefs.* New York: Wiley.

Opler, M. K., & Singer, J. L. (1959). Ethnic differences in behavior and psychopathology. *Inter. J. Soc. Psychiat., 2,* 11–23.

Oppenheim, J. (1991). *Shattered nerves.* New York: Oxford University Press.

Orford, J. (1985). Excessive appetites: A psychological view of addiction. New York: Wiley.

Orleans, C. T., Kristeller, J. L., & Gritz, E. R. (1993). Helping hospitalized smokers quit: New directions for treatment and research. *J. Cons. Clin. Psychol., 61,* 778–89.

Orne, M. T., Dinges, D. F., & Orne, E. C. (1984). On the differential diagnosis of multiple personality in the forensic context. *Int. J. Clin. Exp. Hypn., 32,* 118–69.

Oros, C. J., & Koss, M. P. (1978, Aug.). *Women as rape victims.* Paper presented at the American Psychological Association Annual Meeting, Toronto.

Osborn, A. F. (1992). Social influences on conduct disorder in mid-childhood. *Studia Psychologica, 34,* 29–43.

Osler, W. (1892). *Lectures on angina pectoris and allied states.* New York: Appleton-Century-Crofts.

Öst, L. G. (1987). Age of onset of different phobias. *J. Abnorm. Psychol., 96,* 223–9.

Öst, L. G., & Hugdahl, K. (1981). Acquisition of phobias and anxiety response patterns in clinical patients. *Behav. Res. Ther., 19,* 439–47.

Öst, L. G., & Hugdahl, K. (1985). Acquisition of blood and dental phobia and anxiety response patterns in clinical patients. *Behav. Res. Ther., 23*(1), 27–34.

Otto, R. M., Poythress, N., Starr, C. B., & Darkes, J. (1993). An empirical study of the Reports of APAs Peer Review Panel in the Congressional Review of the *U.S.S. Iowa* incident. *J. Pers. Assess., 61,* 425–42.

Overall, J. E., & Hollister, L. E. (1982). Decision rules for phenomenological classification of psychiatric patients. *J. Cons. Clin. Psychol., 50*(4), 535–45.

Overmier, J. B., & Seligman, M. E. P. (1967). Effects of inescapable shock upon subsequent escape and avoidance learning. *Journal of Comparative and Physiological Psychology, 63,* 23–33.

Owen, F. W. (1978). Dyslexia—genetic aspects. In A. L. Benton & D. Pearl (Eds.), *Dyslexia: In appraisal of current knowledge* (pp. 267–84). New York: Oxford University Press.

Ozdemir, V., Bremner, K. E., & Naranjo, C. A. (1994). Treatment of alcohol withdrawal syndrome. *Annals of Medicine, 26,* 101–6.

Palace, E. M., & Gorzalka, B. B. (1990). The enhancing effects of anxiety on arousal in sexually dysfunctional and functional women. *J. Abnorm. Psychol., 99,* 403–11.

Palmer, C. T. (1988). Twelve reasons why rape is not sexually motivated: A skeptical examination. *J. Sex Res., 25,* 512–30.

Papp, L., & Gorman, J. M. (1990). Suicidal preoccupation during fluoxetine treatment. *Amer. J. Psychiat., 147,* 1380.

Paris, J., Zweig-Frank, H., & Guzder, J. (1994). Risk factors for borderline personality disorders in male outpatients. *J. Nerv. Ment. Dis., 182,* 375–80.

Parker, G., Johnston, P., & Hayward, L. (1988). Parental "expressed emotion" as a predictor of schizophrenic relapse. *Arch. Gen. Psychiat., 45,* 806–13.

Parker, R. I. (1993). Comments on Ellis's Integrative Strategy Instruction model. *J. Learn. Dis., 26*(7), 443–47.

Parkes, C. M., Benjamin, B., & Fitzgerald, R. G. (1969). Broken heart: A statistical study of increased mortality among widowers. *Brit. Med. J., 1,* 740–43.

Parkin, M. (1974). Suicide and culture in Fairbanks: A comparison of three cultural groups in a small city of interior Alaska. *Psychiatry, 37*(1), 60–67.

Pasewark, R. A., Pantle, M. L., & Steadman, H. J. (1982). Detention and rearrest rates of persons found not guilty by reason of insanity and convicted felons. *Amer. J. Psychiat., 139*(7), 892–97.

Paternite, C. E., & Loney, J. (1980). Childhood hyperkinesis: Relationships between symptomatology and home environment. In C. K. Whelan & B. Henker (Eds.), *Hyperactive children: The social ecology of identification and treatment.* New York: Academic Press.

Paterson, R. J., & Neufeld, R. W. (1987). Clear danger: Situational determinants of the appraisal of threat. *Psychol. Bull., 101,* 404–16.

Patrick, C. J., Bradley, M. M., & Lang, P. J. (1993). Emotion in the criminal psychopath: Startle reflex modulation. *J. Abnorm. Psychol., 102*(1), 82–92.

Patrick, C. J., Cuthbert, B. N., & Lang, P. J. (1994). Emotion in the criminal psychopath: Fear image processing. *J. Abnorm. Psychol., 103,* 523–34.

Patterson, C. H. (1989). Eclecticism in psychotherapy: Is integration possible? *Psychotherapy, 26,* 157–61.

Patterson, C. M., & Newman, J. P. (1993) Reflectivity and learning from aversive events: Toward a psychological mechanism for the syndromes of disinhibition. *Psychol. Rev., 100,* 716–36.

Patterson, G. R. (1979). Treatment for children with conduct problems: A review of outcome studies. In S. Feshbach & A. Fraczek (Eds.), *Aggression and behavior change: Biological and social processes.* New York: Praeger.

Patterson, G.R., Capaldi, D., & Bank, L. (1991). An early starter model for predicting delinquency. In D. Pepler & K.H. Rubin (Eds.), *The development and treatment of childhood aggression* (pp. 139–168). Hillsdale, NJ: Erlbaum.

Patterson, G. R., DeBarsyshe, B. D., & Ramsey, E. (1989). A developmental perspective on antisocial behavior. *Amer. Psychol., 44,* 329–35.

Patterson, G. R., Reid, J. B., & Dishion, T. J. (1991). *Antisocial boys.* Eugene, OR: Castalia.

Paul, G. L. (1979). New assessment systems for residential treatment, management, research and evaluation: A symposium. *J. Behav. Assess., 1*(3), 181–84.

Paul, G. L. (1982). *The development of a "transportable" system of behavioral assessment for chronic patients.* Invited address. University of Minnesota, Minneapolis.

Paul, G. L., & Lentz, R. J. (1977). *Psychosocial treatment of chronic mental patients: Milieu versus social-learning programs.* Cambridge, MA: Harvard University Press.

Paul, G. L., & Menditto, A. A. (1992). Effectiveness of inpatient treatment programs for mentally ill adults in public psychiatric facilities. *Applied and Preventive Psychology: Current Scientific Perspectives, 1,* 41–63.

Paul, N. (1971, May 31). The family as patient. *Time,* 60.

Pauls, D. L., Raymond, C. L., & Robertson, M. (1991). The genetics of obsessive-compulsive disorder: A review. In J. Zohar, T. Insel, & S. Rasmussen (Eds.), *The psychobiology of obsessive-compulsive disorder.* New York: Springer.

Pauls, D. L., Towbin, K. E., Leckman, J. F., Zahner, G. E., & Cohen, D. J. (1986). Gilles de la Tourette's Syndrome and obsessive-compulsive disorder. *Arch. Gen. Psychiat., 43,* 1180–2.

Pausnau, R. O., & Russell, A. T. (1975). Psychiatric resident suicide. An analysis of five cases. *Amer. J. Psychiat., 132*(4), 402–6.

Pavlov, I. P. (1927). *Conditioned reflexes.* London: Oxford University Press.

Pavone, L., Meli, C., Nigro, F., & Lisi, R. (1993). Late diagnosed phenylketonuria patients: Clinical presentation and results of treatment. *Developmental Brain Dysfunction, 6*(1–3), 184–87.

Paykel, E. S. (Ed.). (1982a). *Handbook of affective disorders.* New York: Guilford.

Paykel, E. S. (1982b). Life events and early environment. In E. S. Paykel (Ed.), *Handbook of affective disorders.* New York: Guilford.

Paykel, E. S., Brayne, C., Huppert, F. A., Gill, C., Barkley, C., Gehlhaar, E., Beardsall, L., Girling, D. M., Pollitt, P., & O'Connor, D. (1994). Incidence of dementia in a population older than 75 years in the United Kingdom. *Arch. Gen. Psychiat., 51*(4), 325–32.

Paykel, E. S., Hallowell, C., Dressler, D. M., Shapiro, D. L., & Weissman, M. M. (1974). Treatment of suicide attempters. *Arch. Gen. Psychiat., 31*(4), 487–91.

Payne, R. L. (1975). Recent life changes and the reporting of psychological states. *J. Psychosom. Res., 19*(1), 99–103.

Pearlson, G. D., Kim, W. S., Kubos, K. L., Moberg, P. J., Jayaram, G., Bascom, M. J., Chase, G. A., Goldfinger, A. G., & Tune, L. E. (1989). Ventricle-brain ratio, computed tomographic density, and brain area in 50 schizophrenics. *Arch. Gen. Psychiat., 46,* 690–97.

Peck, M. A., & Schrut, A. (1971). Suicidal behavior among college students. *HSMHA Health Reports, 86*(2), 149–56.

Pelham, W. E., Carlson, C., Sams, S. E., Vallano, G., Dixon, M. J., & Hoza, B. (1993). Separate and combined effects of methylphenidate and behavior modification on boys with attention-deficit hyperactivity disorder in the classroom. *J. Cons. Clin. Psychol., 61,* 506–15.

Pelham, W. E., Murphy, D. A., Vannatta, K., Milich, R., Licht, B. G., Gnagy, E. M., Greenslade, K. E., Greiner, A. R., & Vodde-Hamilton, M. (1992). Methylphenidate and attributions in boys with attention-deficit hyperactivity disorder. *J. Cons. Clin. Psychol., 60,* 282–92.

Pelham, W. E., Schnedler, R. W., Bologna, N. C., & Contreras, J. A. (1980). Behavioral and stimulant treatment of hyperactive children. A therapy study with methylphenidate probes in a within subject design. *J. Appl. Beh. Anal., 13*(2), 221–36.

Penk, W. E., Charles, H. L., & Van Hoose, T. A. (1978). Comparative effectiveness of day hospital and inpatient psychiatric treatment. *J. Cons. Clin. Psychol., 46,* 94–101.

Penna, M. W. (1986). Classification of personality disorders. In J. R. Lion (Ed.), *Personality disorders: Diagnosis and management* (pp. 10–31). Malabar, FL: Robert F. Kreiger.

Pennisi, E. (1994). One team, two clues in Alzheimer's puzzle. *Sci. News, 146*(20), 308–9.

Penrose, L. S. (1963). *Biology of mental defect* (3rd ed.). New York: Grune & Stratton.

Pentz, M. A. (1983). Prevention of adolescent substance abuse through social skill development. *National Institute on Drug Abuse Research Monograph Series, 47,* 195–232.

Perlberg, M. (1979, Apr.). Adapted from Trauma at Tenerife: The psychic aftershocks of a jet disaster. *Human Behav.,* 49–50.

Perls, F. S. (1967). Group vs. individual therapy. *ETC: A Review of General Semantics, 34,* 306–12.

Perls, F. S. (1969). *Gestalt therapy verbatim.* Lafayette, CA: Real People Press.

Perris, C. (1979). Recent perspectives in the genetics of affective disorders. In J. Mendlewicz & B. Shopsin (Eds.), *Genetic aspects of affective illness.* New York: SP Medical & Scientific Books.

Perris, C. (1982). The distinction between bipolar and unipolar affective disorders. In E. S. Paykel (Ed.), *Handbook of affective disorders.* New York: Guilford.

Perris, C. (1992). Bipolar-unipolar distinction. In E. S. Paykel (Ed.), *Handbook of affective disorders* (2nd ed.). New York: Guilford.

Perry, C. L., & Murray, D. M. (1985). The prevention of adolescent drug abuse: Implications from etiological, developmental, behavioral, and environmental models. *J. Prim. Prevent., 6*(1), 31–52.

Perry, C. L., Williams, C. L., Forster, J. L., Wolfson, M., Wagenaar, A. C., Finnegan, J. R., McGovern, P. G., Veblen-Mortensen, S., Komro, K. A., & Anstine, P. S. (1993). Background, conceptualization, and design of a community-wide research program on adolescent alcohol use: Project Northland. *Health Education Research: Theory and Practice, 8*(1), 125–36.

Perry, T. (1970). The enigma of PKU. *The Sciences, 10*(8), 12–16.

Pert, C. B., & Snyder, S. H. (1973, Mar. 9). Opiate receptor: Demonstration in nervous tissue. *Science, 179*(4077), 1011–14.

Peters, R. H., & Kearns, W. D. (1992). Drug abuse history and treatment needs of jail inmates. *Amer. J. Drug Alcoh. Abuse, 18,* 355–66.

Petersen, A. C., Compas, B. E., Brooks-Gunn, J., Stemmler, M., Ey, S., & Grant, K. E. (1993). Depression in adolescence. *Amer. Psychol., 48,* 155–68.

Peterson, C., & Seligman, M. E. P. (1987). Explanatory style and illness. *J. Personal., 55,* 237–65.

Peterson, C., Maier, S. F., & Seligman, M. E. P. (1993). *Learned helplessness: A theory for the age of personal control.* New York: Oxford University Press.

Petito, C. K. (1988). Review of central nervous system pathology in human immunodeficiency virus infection. *Ann. Neurol., Suppl., 23,* 54–57.

Petronko, M. R., Harris, S. L., & Kormann, R. J. (1994). Community-based behavioral training approaches for people with mental retardation and mental illness. *J. Cons. Clin. Psychol., 62*(1), 49–54.

Pfeffer, C. R. (1981). The family system of suicidal children. *Amer. J. Psychother., 35,* 330–41.

Pfeffer, C. R., Hurt, S. W., Kakuma, T., Peskin, J., Siefker, C. A., & Nagbhairava, S. (1994). Suicidal children grow up: Suicidal episodes and effects of treatment during follow-up. *J. Amer. Acad. Child Adoles. Psychiat., 33,* 225–30.

Phares, V., & Compas, B.E. (1992). The role of fathers in child and adolescent psychopathology: Make room for daddy. *Psychol. Bull., 111,* 387–412.

Phifer, J. F., & Murrell, S. A. (1986). Etiologic factors in the onset of depressive symptoms in older adults. *J. Abnorm. Psychol., 95,* 282–91.

Piccinelli, M., & Wilkinson, G. (1994). Outcome of depression in psychiatric settings. *Brit. J. Psychiat., 164,* 297–304.

Pillard, R. C. (1988). Sexual orientation and mental disorder. *Psychiatr. Ann., 18,* 52–56.

Piotrowski, C., & Keller, J. W. (1992). Psychological testing in applied settings: A literature review from 1982–1992. *Journal of Training and Practice in Professional Psychology, 6,* 74–82.

Piotrowski, C., & Zalewski, C. (1993). Training in psychodiagnostic testing in APA aproved PsyD and PhD clinical psychology programs. *J. Pers. Assess., 61*, 394–405.

Pitman, R. K. (1993). Biological findings in posttraumatic stress disorder. In J.R. Davidson & E. B. Foa (Eds.), *Post-Traumatic Stress Disorder: DSM IV and Beyond* (pp. 173–189). Washington, DC: American Psychiatric Press.

Pitman, R. K., van der Kolk, B. A., Orr, S. P., Bessel, A., Manchester, N. H., & Greenberg, M. S. (1990). Naloxone-reversible analgesic response to combat related stimuli in post traumatic stress disorder. *Arch. Gen. Psychiat., 47*, 541–44.

Pitt, B. (1982). Depression and childbirth. In E. S. Paykel (Ed.), *Handbook of affective disorders.* New York: Guilford.

Plato. (n.d.). *The laws* (Vol. 5). (G. Burges, Trans.). London: George Bell & Sons.

Platt, S. D. (1984). Unemployment and suicidal behaviour: A review of the literature. *Social Science and Medicine, 19,* 93–115.

Pliner, P. L., & Cappell, H. D. (1974). Modification of affective consequences of alcohol: A comparison of social and solitary drinking. *J. Abnorm. Psychol., 83*(4), 418–25.

Pliszka, S. R. (1991). Antidepressants in the treatment of child and adolescent psychopathology. Special issue: Child psychopharmacology. *J. Clin. Child Psychol., 20*, 313–20.

Plomin, R. (1986). *Development, genetics and psychology.* Hillsdale, NJ: Erlbaum.

Plomin, R. (1989). Environment and genes: Determinants of behavior. *Amer. Psychol., 44*, 105–111.

Plomin, R. (1990). The role of inheritance in behavior. *Science, 248*, 183–188.

Plomin, R. (1991). Genetic risk and psychosocial disorders: Links between the normal and abnormal. In M. Rutter & P. Casaer (Eds.), *Biological risk factors for psychosocial disorders.* Cambridge: Cambridge University Press.

Plomin, R., & Daniels, D. (1987). Why are children in the same family so different from one another? *Behavioral and Brain Sciences, 10,* 1–15.

Plomin, R., & McClearn, G. E. (Eds.). (1993). *Nature, nurture, and psychology.* Washington, DC: American Psychological Association.

Plotkin, R. (1981). When rights collide: Parents, children and consent to treatment. *J. Pediat. Psychol., 6*(2), 121–30.

Polich, J. M., Armor, D. J., & Braiker, H. B. (1981). *The course of alcoholism: Four years after treatment.* New York: Wiley Interscience.

Politzer, R. M., Yesalis, C. E., & Hudak, C. J. (1992). The epidemiologic model and the risks of legalized gambling: Where are we headed? *Health Values, 16,* 20–27.

Polivy, J., Zeitlin, S., Herman, P., & Beal, L. (1994) Food restriction and binge eating: A study of former prisoners of war. *J. Abnorm. Psychol., 103,* 409–411.

Pollack, J. M. (1979). Obsessive-compulsive personality: A review. *Psychol. Bull. 86*(2), 225–41.

Pollard, C. A., Pollard, H. J., & Corn, K. J. (1989). Panic onset and major events in the lives of agoraphobics: A test of contiguity. *J. Abnorm. Psychol., 98,* 318–21.

Polvan, N. (1969). Historical aspects of mental ills in Middle East discussed. *Roche Reports, 6*(12), 3.

Pope, H. G., Jr., Mangweth, B., Negrao, A. B., Hudson, J. I., & Cordas, T. A. (1994). Childhood sexual abuse and bulimia nervosa: A comparison of American, Austrian, and Brazilian women. *Amer. J. Psychiat., 151*(5), 732–37.

Pope, K. S., & Vetter, V. A. (1991). Prior therapist-patient sexual involvement among patients seen by psychologists. *Psychotherapy, 28,* 429–38.

Pope, K. S., Butcher, J. N., & Seelen, J. (1993). *MMPI/MMPI-2/MMPI-A in court: A practical guide for expert witnesses and attorneys.* Washington, DC: American Psychological Association.

Pope, K. S., Sonne, J. L., & Holroyd, J. (1993). *Sexual feelings in psychotherapy: Explorations for therapists and therapists-in-training.* Washington, DC: American Psychological Association.

Popkin, J. (1994, Sept. 19). Sexual predators. *U.S. News and World Report,* 65–73.

Porter, B., & O'Leary, D. (1980). Marital discord and child behavior problems. *J. Abnorm. Child Psychol., 8,* 287–295.

Posener, J. A., Le Haye, A., & Cheifetz, P. N. (1989). Suicide notes in adolescence. *Canad. J. Psychiat., 34,* 171–76.

Post, R. M. (1975). Cocaine psychoses: A continuum model. *Amer. J. Psychiat., 132*(3), 225–31.

Post, R. M. (1992). Anticonvulsants and novel drugs. In E. S. Paykel (Ed.), *Handbook of affective disorders* (2nd ed.). New York: Guilford.

Powell, G. E., & Wilson, S. L. (1994). Recovery curves for patients who have suffered very severe brain injury. *Clinical Rehabilitation, 8*(1), 54–69.

Powers, M. (1992). Early intervention for children with autism. In D.E. Berkell (Ed.). *Autism* (pp. 225–72). Hillsdale, NJ: Erlbaum.

Prasher, V. P., & Kirshnan, V. H. (1993). Age of onset and duration of dementia in people with Down syndrome: Integration of 98 reported cases in the literature. *International Journal of Geriatric Psychiatry, 8*(11), 915–22.

President's Commission on Mental Health. (1978). *Report to the President.* Washington, DC: U.S. Government Printing Office.

Pribor, E. F., Yutzy, S. H., Dean, J. T., & Wetzel, R. D. (1993). Briquet's syndrome, dissociation, and abuse. *Amer. J. Psychiat., 150*(10), 1507–11.

Price, R. W., Brew, B., Sidtis, J., Rosenblum, M., Scheck, A. C., & Cleary, P. (1988a). The brain in AIDS: Central nervous system HIV-1 infection and the AIDS dementia complex. *Science, 239,* 586–92.

Price, R. W., Sidtis, J., & Rosenblum, M. (1988b). The AIDS dementia complex: Some current questions. *Ann. Neurol.,* Suppl., *23,* 27–33.

Prichard, J. C. (1835). *A treatise on insanity.* London: Sherwood, Gilbert, & Piper.

Prien, R. F. (1992). Maintenance treatment. In E.S. Paykel (Ed.), *Handbook of affective disorders* (2nd ed.). New York: Guilford.

Prien, R. F., & Potter, W. Z. (1990). Report on the treatment of bipolar disorder. *Psychopharm. Bull., 26,* 409–27.

Prien, R. F., Kupfer, D. J., Mannsky, P. Q., Small, J. G., Tuason, V. B., Voss, C. B., Johnson, W. E. (1984). Drug therapy in the prevention of recurrences in unipolar and bipolar affective disorders. *Arch. Gen. Psychiat., 41,* 1096–104.

Prigatano, G. P. (1992). Personality disturbances associated with traumatic brain injury. *J. Cons. Clin. Psychol., 60*(3), 360–68.

Prior, M., & Wherry, J. S. (1986). Autism, schizophrenia, and allied disorders. In H. C. Quay & J. S. Wherry (Eds.), *Psychopathological disorders of childhood* (3rd ed., pp. 156–210). New York: Wiley.

Pritchard, W. S. (1986). Cognitive event-related potential correlates of schizophrenia. *Psychol. Bull., 100*(1), 43–66.

Prizant, B. M. (1983). Language acquisition and communicative behavior in autism: Toward an understanding of the "whole" of it. *J. Speech Hear. Dis., 46,* 241–49.

Prizant, B. M., & Duchan, J. F. (1981). The functions of immediate echolalia in autistic children. *J. Speech Hear. Dis., 465*(3), 241–49.

Project DAWN Drug Enforcement Agency. (1988). Drug Abuse Warning Newtwork: Project DAWN.

Provence, S., & Lipton, R. C. (1962). *Infants in institutions.* New York: International Universities Press.

Pryor, J. C., & Sulser, F. (1991). Evolution of the monoamine hypothesis of depression. In R. Horton & C. Katona (Eds.), *Biological aspects of affective disorders.* San Diego, CA: Academic Press.

Puig-Antich, J., Goetz, D., Davies, M., Kaplan, T., Davies, S., Ostrow, L., Asnis, L., Twomey, J., Iyengar, S., & Ryan, N. D. (1989). A controlled family history study of prepubertal major depressive disorder. *Arch. Gen. Psychiat., 46,* 406–18.

Puig-Antich, J., Lukens, D., Davies, M., Goetz, D., & Brennan-Quattrock, J. (1985). Psychosocial functioning in prepubertal major depressive disorders: I. Interpersonal relationships during the depressive episode. *Arch. Gen. Psychiat., 42,* 500–57.

Puska, P. (1983, Feb./Mar.). Television can save lives. *World Health.* Geneva, Switzerland: Magazine of the World Health Organization, 8–11.

Puska, P., Tuomqwehto, J., Salonen, J., Neittaanmaki, L., Maki, J., Virtamo, J., Nissinen, A., Koskela, K., & Takalo, T. (1979). Changes in coronary risk factors during a comprehensive five-year community programme to control cardiovascular diseases (North Karelia Project). *Brit. Med. J., 2,* 1173–78.

Putallaz, M., & Gottman, J. M. (1983). Social relationship problems in children: An approach to intervention. In B. B. Lahey & A. E. Kazdin (Eds.), *Advances in clinical child psychology* (Vol. 6). New York: Plenum.

Putnam, F.W. (1989). *Diagnosis and treatment of multiple personality disorder.* New York: Guilford.

Putnam, F. W., Guroff, J. J., Silberman, E. K., Barban, L., & Post, R. M. (1986). The clinical phenomenology of multiple personality disorder: Review of 100 recent cases. *J. Clin. Psychiat., 47,* 285–93.

Pynoos, R. S., Frederick, C., Nader, K., Arroyo, W., Steinberg, A., Eth, S., Nunez, F., & Fairbanks, L. (1987). Life threat and posttraumatic stress in school-age children. *Arch. Gen. Psychiat., 44,* 1057–63.

Quay, H. C. (1965). Psychopathic personality as pathological stimulation seeking. *Amer. J. Psychiat., 122*(2), 180–83.

Quinsey, V. L., & Earls, C. M. (1990). The modification of sexual preferences. In W. L. Marshall, D. R. Laws, & H. E. Barbaree (Eds.), *Handbook of sexual assault: Issues, theories, and treatment of the offender* (pp. 279–95). New York: Plenum.

Quinsey, V. L., Harris, G. T., Rice, M. E., & Lalumiere, M. L. (1993). Assessing treatment efficacy in outcome studies of sex offenders. *J. Interpers. Viol., 8,* 512–23.

Quinton, D., & Rutter, M. (1988). *Parenting breakdown: The making and breaking of intergenerational links.* Aldershot, Hants: Avebury.

Quinton, D., Rutter, M., & Liddle, C. (1984) Institutional rearing, parenting difficulties, and marital support. *Psychol. Med., 14,* 102–124.

Rabin, A. I., Doneson, S. L., & Jentons, R. L. (1979). Studies of psychological functions in schizophrenia. In L. Bellak (Ed.), *The schizophrenic syndrome.* New York: Basic Books.

Rabinowitz, D. (1990, May). From the mouths of babes to a jail cell. *Harper's Magazine,* pp. 52–63.

Rabiner, D. & Coie, J. (1989). Effect of expectancy induction on rejected children's acceptance by unfamiliar peers. *Develop. Psychol., 25,* 450–457.

Rabkin, J. (1972). Public attitudes about mental illness: A review of the literature. *Schizo. Bull., 10,* 9–33.

Rachman, S. J., & Hodgson, R. (1980). *Obsessions and compulsions.* Englewood Cliffs, NJ: Prentice-Hall.

Rachman, S. J. (1990). *Fear and courage.* New York: Freeman.

Rachman, S. J., & De Silva, P. (1978). Abnormal and normal obsessions. *Behav. Res. Ther., 16,* 233–48.

Rado, S. (1956). *Psychoanalysis and behavior.* New York: Grune & Stratton.

Rado, S. (1962). *Psychoanalysis of behavior II* (p. 96). New York: Grune & Stratton.

Ragland, D. R., & Brand, R. J. (1988). Type A behavior and mortality from coronary heart disease. *New Engl. J. Med., 318,* 65–69.

Rahe, R. H. (1974). Life changes and subsequent illness reports. In K. E. Gunderson & R. H. Rahe (Eds.), *Life stress and illness.* Springfield, IL: Thomas.

Rahe, R. H., & Arthur, R. J. (1978). Life changes and illness studies: Past history and future directions. *Journal of Human Stress, 4,* 3–15.

Ramey, C. T., & Haskins, R. (1981). The causes and treatment of school failure: Insights from the Carolina Abecedarian Project. In M. J. Begab, H. C. Haywood, & H. L. Garber (Eds.), *Psychosocial influences in retarded performance* (Vol. II). Baltimore: University Park Press.

Ramirez, L. F., McCormick, R. A., & Russo, A. M. (1984). Patterns of substance abuse in pathological gamblers undergoing treatment. *Addictive Behavior, 8,* 201–03.

Rao, U., Weissman, M. M., Martin, J. A., & Hammond, R. W. (1993). Childhood depression and risk of suicide: A preliminary report of a longitudinal study. Special section: Longitudinal studies of depressive disorders in children. *J. Amer. Acad. Child Adoles. Psychiat., 32,* 21–27.

Rapaport, K., & Burkhart, B. R. (1984). Personality and attitudinal characteristics of sexually coercive college males. *J. Abnorm. Psychol., 93,* 216–21.

Rapee, R. M., & Barlow, D. H. (1993). Generalized anxiety disorder, panic disorder, and the phobias. In P. B. Sutker, & H. E. Adams (Eds.), *Comprehensive handbook of psychopathology* (2nd ed.). New York Plenum.

Rapoport, J. L. (1989). *The boy who couldn't stop washing: The experience and treatment of obsessive-compulsive disorder.* New York: Penguin.

Rapoport, J. L., & Wise, S. P. (1988). Obsessive-compulsive disorder: Evidence for basil ganglia dysfunction. *Psychopharm. Bull., 24,* 380–4.

Raskin, A., Pelchat, R., Sood, R., Alphs, L. D., & Levine, J. (1993). Negative symptom assessment of chronic schizophrenia patients. *Schizo. Bull., 19*(3), 627–35.

Raskin, V. D. (1993). Psychiatric aspects of substance use disorders in childbearing populations. *Psychiatr. Clin. N. Amer., 16,* 157–65.

Rasmussen, S. A., & Eisen, J. L. (1991). Phenomenology of OCD: Clinical subtypes, heterogeneity and coexistence. In J. Zohar, T. Insel, & S. Rasmussen (Eds.), *The psychobiology of obsessive-compulsive disorder.* New York: Springer.

Rasmussen, S. A., & Tsuang, M. T. (1986). Clinical characteristics and family history in DSM-III obsessive-compulsive disorder. *Amer. J. Psychiat., 143,* 317–22.

Rauh, V.A., Achenbach, T.M., Nurcombe, B., Howell, C.T., Teti, D.M. (1988). Minimizing adverse effects of low birthweight: Four-year results of an early intervention program. *Child Develop., 59,* 544–553.

Rawson, H. E., & Tabb, C. L. (1993). Effects of therapeutic intervention on childhood depression. *Child and Adolescent Social Work Journal, 10,* 39–52.

Raz, S. (1993). Structural cerebral pathology in schizophrenia: Regional or diffuse? *J. Abnorm. Psychol., 102*(3), 445–52.

Razran, G. (1961). The observable unconscious and the inferable conscious in current Soviet psychophysiology: Interoceptive conditioning, semantic conditioning, and the orienting reflex. *Psychol. Rev., 68,* 81–147.

Realmuto, G., M., & Wescoe, S. (1992). Agreements among professionals about a child's sexual abuse status: Interviews with sexually anatomically correct dolls as indicators of abuse. *Child Ab. Negl., 16,* 719–25.

Realmuto, G. M., Jensen, J. B., & Wescoe, S. (1990). Specificity and sensitivity of sexually anatomically correct dolls in substantiating abuse: A pilot study. *J. Amer. Acad. Child Adoles. Psychiat., 29,* 743–46.

Redmond, D. E., Jr. (1985). Neurochemical basis for anxiety and anxiety disorders: Evidence from drugs which decrease human fear of anxiety. In A. H. Tuma & J. D. Maser (Eds.), *Anxiety and the anxiety disorders.* Hillsdale, NJ: Erlbaum.

Reed, S. D., Katkin, E. S., & Goldband, S. (1986). Biofeedback and behavioral medicine. In F. H. Kanfer & A. P. Goldstein (Eds.), *Helping people change: A textbook of methods* (3rd ed.). Elmsford, NY: Pergamon.

Rees, T. P. (1957). Back to moral treatment and community care. *J. Ment. Sci., 103,* 303–13. In H. B. Adams, "Mental illness" or interpersonal behavior? *Amer. Psychologist,* 1964, *19,* 191–97.

Regier, D. A., Boyd, J. H., Burke, J. D., Rae, D. S., Myers, J. K., Kramer, M., Robins, L. N., George, L. K., Karno, M., & Locke, B. Z. (1988). One-month prevalence of mental disorders in the United States. *Arch. Gen. Psychiat., 45,* 877–986.

Regier, D. A., Narrow, W. E., Rae, D. S., Manderscheid, R. W., Locke, B. Z., & Goodwin, F. K. (1993). The de facto US mental and addictive disorders service system: Epidemiologic Catchment Area prospective 1-year prevalence rates of disorders and services. *Arch. Gen. Psychiat., 50,* 85–94.

Rehm, L. P., & Tyndall, C. I. (1993). Mood disorders: Unipolar and bipolar. In P. B. Sutker & H. E. Adams (Eds.), *Comprehensive handbook of psychopathology* (2nd ed.). New York: Plenum.

Reich, J. H., & Green, A. I. (1991). Effects of personality disorders on outcome of treatment. *J. Nerv. Ment. Dis., 179,* 74–82.

Reich, J., Noyes, R., & Troughton, E. (1987). Dependent personality disorder associated with phobic avoidance in patients with panic disorder. *Amer. J. Psychiat., 144,* 323–6.

Reid, A. H. (1985). Psychiatric disorders. In A. M. Clarke, A. B. D. Clarke, & J. M. Berg (Eds.), *Mental deficiency: The changing outlook,* (4th ed., pp. 291–325). London: Methuen.

Reisman, J. M. (1991). *A history of clinical psychology.* New York: Hemisphere Press.

Reiss, S., & McNally, R. J. (1985). Expectancy model of fear. In S. Reiss & R. R. Bootzin (Eds.), *Theoretical issues in behavior therapy* (pp. 107–121). San Diego, CA: Academic Press.

Reitan, R. M., & Wolfson, D. (1985). *The Halstead-Reitan Neuropsychological Test Battery: Theory and clinical interpretation.* Tucson, AZ: Neuropsychology Press.

Renvoize, E. B., Mindham, R. H., Stewart, M., McDonald, R., et al. (1986). Identical twins discordant for presenile dementia of the Alzheimer type. *Brit. J. Psychiat., 149,* 509–12.

Rescorla, R. A. (1974). Effect of inflation of the unconditioned stimulus value following conditioning. *Journal of Comparative and Physiological Psychology, 86,* 101–6

Rescorla, R.A. (1988). Pavlovian Conditioning: It's not what you think it is. *Amer. Psychol., 43,* 151–160.

Resnick, H. S., Kilpatrick, D. G., Dansky, B. S., Saunders, B., & Best, C. L. (1993). Prevalence of civilian trauma and posttraumatic stress disorder in a representative national sample of women. *J. Cons. Clin. Psychol., 61,* 984–991.

Rhoades, L. J. (1981). *Treating and assessing the chronically mentally ill: The pioneering research of Gordon L. Paul.* U.S. Department of Health and Human Services. Public Health Service. (Library of Congress Catalog #81-600097). Washington, DC: U.S. Government Printing Office.

Rhue, J. W., Lynn, S. J., & Kirsch, I. (Eds.). (1993). *Handbook of clinical hypnosis.* Washington: American Psychological Association.

Ricciuti, H. N. (1993). Nutrition and mental development. *Curr. Dir. Psychol. Sci., 2*(2), 43–46.

Rice, M. E., Quinsey, V. L., & Harris, G. T. (1991). Sexual recidivism among child molesters released from a maximum security psychiatric institution. *J. Cons. Clin. Psychol., 59,* 381–86.

Rich, B. E., Paul, G. L., & Mariotto, M. J. (1988). Judgmental relativism as a validity threat to standardized psychiatric relating scales. *J. Psychopath. Behav. Assess., 10,* 241–57.

Rich, C. L., Fowler, R. C., Fogarty, L. A., & Young, D. (1988). San Diego suicide study: III. Relationships between diagnoses and stressors. *Arch. Gen. Psychiat., 45,* 589–92.

Rich, C. L., Young, D., & Fowler, R. C. (1986). San Diego suicide study: I. Young vs. old subjects. *Arch. Gen. Psychiat., 43,* 577–82.

Richardson, S. A., Koller, H., & Katz, M. (1985). Relationship of upbringing to later behavior disturbance of mildly mentally retarded young people. *Amer. J. Ment. Def., 90,* 18.

Richelson, E. (1993). Treatment of acute depression. *Psychiat. Clin. N. Amer., 16,* 461–78.

Rickels, K., Schweizer, E., Weiss, S., & Zavodnick, S. (1993). Maintenance drug treatment for panic disorder: II. Short and long-term outcome after drug taper. *Arch. Gen. Psychiat., 50*(1), 61–68.

Rieder, R. O. (1979). Children at risk. In L. Bellak (Ed.), *The schizophrenic syndrome.* New York: Basic Books.

Rifkin, L., & Gurling, H. (1991). Genetic aspects of affective disorders. In R. Horton & C. Katona (Eds.), *Biological aspects of affective disorders.* San Diego: Academic Press.

Riggs, D. S., & Foa, E. B. (1993). Obsessive compulsive disorder. In D. H. Barlow (Eds.), *Clinical handbook of psychological disorders* (pp. 189–239). New York: Guilford.

Rimm, D. C., & Lefebvre, R. C. (1981). Phobic disorders. In S. M. Turner, K. S. Calhoun, & H. E. Adams (Eds.), *Handbook of clinical behavior therapy.* New York: Wiley.

Ritvo, E. R., & Freeman, B. J. (1978). Current research on the syndrome of autism. *J. Amer. Acad. Child Psychiat., 17,* 565–75.

Ritvo, E. R., & Ornitz, E. (1970). A new look at childhood autism points to CNS disease. *Roche Report, 7*(18), 6–8.

Ritvo, E. R., Brothers, A. M., Freeman, B. J., & Pingree, J. C. (1988). Eleven possibly autistic parents. *J. Autism Devel. Dis., 18,* 139–43.

Ritvo, E. R., Freeman, B. J., Pingree, C., Mason-Brothers, A., Jorde, L., Jenson, W. R., McMahon, W. M., Peterson, P. B., Mo, A., & Ritvo, A. (1989). The UCLA-University of Utah epidemiologic survey of autism: Prevalence. *Amer. J. Psychiat., 146,* 194–99.

Ritzler, B. A. (1981). Paranoia—prognosis and treatment: A review. *Schizo. Bull., 7,* 710–28.

Roberts, M. C., & Peterson, L. (1984). *Prevention of problems in childhood.* New York: Wiley Interscience.

Robins, C. J., & Hayes, A. M. (1993). An appraisal of cognitive therapy. *J. Cons. Clin. Psychol., 61*(2), 205–14.

Robins, L. N. (1978). Aetiological implications in studies of childhood histories relating to antisocial personality. In R.D. Hare & D. Schalling (Eds.), *Psychopathic behavior: Approaches to research* (pp. 255–71). Chichester, UK: Wiley.

Robins, L. N. (1991). Conduct disorder. *J. Child Psychol. Psychiat., 32,* 193–212.

Robins, L. N., & Price, R. (1991). Adult disorders predicted by childhood conduct problems: Results from the NIMH Epidemiologic Catchment Area Project. *Psychiatry, 54,* 116–32.

Robins, L. N., & Regier, D. A. (Eds.). (1991). *Psychiatric disorders in America.* New York: Free Press.

Robins, L. N., Helzer, J. E., Weissman, M. M., Orvaschel, H., Gruenberg, E., Burke, J. D., & Regier, D. (1984). Lifetime prevalence of specific psychiatric disorders in three sites. *Arch. Gen. Psych., 41,* 949–58.

Robinson, N. M., & Robinson, H. B. (1976). *The mentally retarded child* (2nd ed.). New York: McGraw-Hill.

Robinson, R. G., Kubos, K. L., Starr, L. B., Rao, K., & Price, T. R. (1984). Mood disorders in stroke patients: Importance of location of lesion. *Brain, 107,* 81–93.

Rogers, C. R. (1951). *Client-centered therapy.* Boston: Houghton Mifflin.

Rogers, C. R. (1959). A theory of therapy, personality, and interpersonal relationships as developed in the client-centered framework. In S. Koch (Ed.), *Psychology: A study of a science,* (Vol. 3, pp. 184–256). New York: McGraw-Hill.

Rogers, C. R. (1961). *On becoming a person: A client's view of psychotherapy.* Boston: Houghton Mifflin.

Rogers, C. R. (1966). Client-centered therapy. In S. Arieti et al. (Eds.), *American handbook of psychiatry* (Vol. 3). New York: Basic Books.

Rohde, P., Lewinsohn, P. M., Seeley, J. R. (1990). Are people changed by the experience of having an episode of depression? A further test of the scar hypothesis. *J. Abnorm. Psychol., 99,* 264–71.

Roiphe, K. (1993). *The morning after: Sex, fear, and feminism on campus.* Boston: Little, Brown.

Rolf, J., Masten, A.S., Cicchetti, D., Nuechterlein, K., & Weintraub, S. (Eds.) (1990) *Risk and protective factors in the development of psychopathology.* New York: Cambridge University Press.

Rolfs, R. T., Goldberg, M., & Sharrar, R. G. (1990). Risk factors for syphillis: Cocaine use and prostitution. *Amer. J. Pub. Hlth., 80*, 853–57.

Ronningstam, E., & Gunderson, J. G. (1989). Descriptive studies on narcissistic personality disorder. *Psychiat. Clin. N. Amer., 12*, 585–601.

Rooth, G. (1974). Exhibitionists around the world. *Human Behav., 3*(5), 61.

Rorvik, D. M. (1970, Apr. 7). Do drugs lead to violence? *Look*, 58–61.

Rosen, A. J. (1986). Schizophrenic and affective disorders: Rationale for a biopsychosocial treatment model. *Integr. Psychiat., 4*, 173–85.

Rosen, D. H. (1970). The serious suicide attempt: Epidemiological and follow-up study of 886 patients. *Amer. J. Psychiat., 127*(6), 64–70.

Rosen, R. C., & Leiblum, S. R. (1989). Assessment and treatment of desire disorders. In S. R. Leiblum & R. C. Rosen (Eds.), *Principles and practice of sex therapy*, (2nd ed., pp. 19–50). New York: Guilford.

Rosenbaum, G., Shore, D. L., & Chapin, K. (1988). Attention deficit and schizotypy: Marker versus symptom variables. *J. Abnorm. Psychol., 97*, 41–47.

Rosenblatt, A. (1984). Concepts of the asylum in the care of the mentally ill. *Hosp. Comm. Psychiat., 35*, 244–50.

Rosenman, R. H. (1978). The interview method of assessment of the coronary-prone behavior pattern. In T. P. Dembroski, S. M. Weiss, J. L. Shields, S. G. Haynes, & M. Feinleib (Eds.), *Coronary-prone behavior*. New York: Springer-Verlag.

Rosenman, R. H., Brand, R. J., Jenkins, C. D., Friedman, M., & Straus, R. (1975). Coronary heart disease in the Western Collaborative Group Study: Final follow-up experience of 8 1/2 years. *JAMA, 233*, 872–77.

Rosenthal, D. (Ed.). (1963). *The Genain quadruplets*. New York: Basic Books.

Rosenthal, D., Wender, P. H., Kety, S. S., Schulsinger, F., Welner, J., & Ostergaard, L. (1968). Schizophrenics' offspring reared in adoptive homes. In D. Rosenthal & S. S. Kety (Eds.), *The transmission of schizophrenia* (pp. 377–92). New York: Pergamon.

Rosenthal, N. E., Sack, D. A., Gillin, J. C., Lewry, A. J., Goodwin, F. K., Davenport, Y., Mueller, P. S., Newsome, D. A., & Wehr, T. A. (1984). Seasonal affective disorder: A description of the syndrome and preliminary findings with light therapy. *Arch. Gen. Psychiat., 41*, 72–80.

Rosenthal, R. J. (1992). Pathological gambling. *Psychiat. Ann., 22*, 72–78.

Ross, C. A. (1989). *Multiple personality disorder: Diagnosis, clinical features, and treatment*. New York: Wiley.

Ross, C. A., Norton, G. R., & Wozney, K. (1989). Multiple personality disorder: An analysis of 236 cases. *Canad. J. Psychiat., 34*, 413–18.

Ross, M. (1974). This doctor will self-destruct. . . . *Human Behav., 3*(2), 54.

Rossi, P. H. (1990). The old homeless and the new homelessness in historical perspective. *Amer. Psychol., 45*, 954–59.

Rosten, R. A. (1961). *Some personality characteristics of compulsive gamblers*. Unpublished dissertation, UCLA.

Roth, M. E. (1993). Advances in Alzheimer's disease: A review for the family physician. *J. Fam. Pract., 37*(6), 593–607.

Roth, S., & Lebowitz, L. (1988). The experience of sexual trauma. *J. Trauma. Stress, 1*, 79–107.

Rothbart, M.K., & Ahadi, S.A. (1994). Temperament and the development of personality. *J. Abnorm. Psychol., 103*, 55–66.

Rounsaville, B. J., Dolinsky, Z. S., Babor, T. F., & Meyer, R. E. (1987). Psychopathology as a predictor of treatment outcome in alcoholics. *Arch. Gen. Psychiat., 44*, 505–13.

Rounsaville, B. J., Weissman, M. M., & Prusoff, B. A. (1981). Psychotherapy with depressed outpatients: Patient and process variables as predictors of outcome. *Amer. J. Psychiat., 138*, 67–74.

Rovner, S. (1990, Nov.). Dramatic overlap of addiction, mental illness. *Washington Post Health*, 14–15.

Roy, A. (1985). Early parental separation and adult depression. *Arch. Gen. Psychiat., 42*, 987–91.

Rubenstein, J. L., Heeren, T., Houseman, D., Rubin, C., & Stechler, G. (1989). Suicidal behavior in "normal" adolescents: Risk and protective factors. *Amer. J. Orthopsychiat., 59*, 59–71.

Rubin, R. T., Reinisch, J. M., & Haskett, R. F. (1981). Postnatal gonadal steroid effects on human behavior. *Science, 211*, 1318–24.

Rush, A. J., & Hollon, S. D. (1991). Depression. In B. D. Beitman & G. L. Klerman (Eds.). *Integrating pharmacotherapy and psychotherapy* (pp. 121–142). Washington, DC: American Psychiatric Press.

Rush, A. J., Beck, A. T., Kovacs, M., & Hollon, S. (1977). The comparative efficacy of cognitive therapy and imipramine in the treatment of depressed out-patients. *Cog. Ther. Res., 1*(1), 17–37.

Rush, A. J., Beck, A. T., Kovacs, M., Weissenburger, J., & Hollon, S. D. (1982). Comparison of the effects of cognitive therapy and pharmacotherapy on hopelessness and self-concept. *Amer. J. Psychiat., 139*, 862–66.

Rush, A. J., Khatami, M., & Beck, A. T. (1975). Cognitive and behavior therapy in chronic depression. *Behav. Ther., 6*, 398–404.

Rush, A. J., Kovacs, M., Beck, A. T., Weissenburger, J., & Hollon, S. D. (1981). Differential effects of cognitive therapy and pharmacotherapy on depressive symptoms. *J. Affect. Dis., 3*, 221–29.

Russ, M. J., Roth, S. D., Kakuma, T., Harrison, K., & Hull, J. (1994). Pain perception in self-injurious borderline patients: Naloxone effects. *Biol. Psychiat., 35*, 207–9.

Russ, M. J., Roth, S. D., Lerman, A., Kakuma, T., et al. (1992). Pain perception in self injurious patients with borderline personality disorder. *Biol. Psychiat., 32*, 501–11.

Russell, D. E. H. (1983). The incidence and prevalence of intrafamilial and extrafamilial sexual abuse of female children. *Child Ab. Negl., 7*, 133–46.

Russell, D. E. H. (1984). *Sexual exploitation: Rape, child sexual abuse, and workplace harassment*. Beverly Hills, CA: Sage.

Russell, D. E. H. (1986). *The secret trauma: Incest in the lives of girls and women*. New York: Basic Books.

Russell, S. (1975). *The development and training of autistic children in separate training centres and in centres for retarded children*. Special Publication No. 6. Victoria: Mental Health Authority.

Russo, D. C., Carr, E. G., & Lovaas, O. I. (1980). Self-injury in pediatric populations. In J. Ferguson & C. R. Taylor (Eds.), *Comprehensive handbook of behavioral medicine, Vol. 3: Extended applications and issues*. Holliswood, NY: Spectrum.

Russo, J., Vitaliano, P. P., Brewer, D. D., Katon, W., & Becker, J. (1995). Psychiatric disorders in spouse caregivers of care recipients with Alzheimer's disease and matched controls: A diathesis-stress model of psychopathology. *J. Abnorm. Psychol., 104*, 197–204.

Rutter, M. (1971). Parent-child separation: Psychological effects on the children. *J. Child Psychol. Psychiat., 12*, 233–60.

Rutter, M. (1979). Maternal deprivations. 1972–1978: New findings, new concepts, new approachs. *Child Develop., 50*, 283–305.

Rutter, M. (1981). Stress, coping and development: Some issues and some questions. *J. Child Psychol. Psychiat., 22*, 323–356.

Rutter, M. (1982). Epidemiological-longitudinal approaches to the study of development. In W.A. Collins (Ed.), *The concept of development. Minnesota Symposia on Child Psychology, vol. 15*. Hillsdale, NJ: Erlbaum.

Rutter, M. (1985). The treatment of autistic children. *Journal of Child Psychiatry, 26*(2), 193–214.

Rutter, M. (1987a) Psychosocial resilience and protective mechanisms. *Amer. J. Orthopsychiat., 51*, 316–331.

Rutter, M. (1987b). Continuities and discontinuities from infancy. In J.D. Osofsky (Ed.), *Handbook of infant development*, 2nd ed. (pp. 1256–1296). New York: Wiley.

Rutter, M. (1988). Epidemiological approaches to developmental psychopathology. *Arch. Gen. Psychiat., 45*, 486–500.

Rutter, M. (1990). Psychosocial resilience and protective mechanisms. In J. Rolf, A.S. Masten, D. Cicchetti, K.H. Nuechterlein, & S. Weintraub (Eds.), *Risk and protective factors in the development of psychopathology.* Cambridge University Press: New York.

Rutter, M. (1991a). Nature, nurture, and psychopathology: A new look at an old topic. *Develop. Psychopath., 3,* 125–136.

Rutter, M. (1991b). Autism as a genetic disorder. In P. McGuffin & R. Murray (Eds.), *The new genetics of mental illness* (pp. 225–244). Oxford: Heinmann Medical.

Rutter, M., & Quinton, D. (1984a). Long term follow-up of women institutionalized in childhood: Factors promoting good functioning in adult life. *British Journal of Developmental Psychology, 18,* 225-234.

Rutter, M., & Quinton, D. (1984b). Parental psychiatric disorder: Effects on children. *Psychol. Med., 14,* 853–80.

Rutter, M., Tizard, J., & Whitmore, K. (1970). *Education, health and behavior: Psychological and medical study of childhood development.* New York: Wiley.

Ryan, N. D. (1992). The pharmacologic treatment of child and adolescent depression. *Psychiat. Clin. N. Amer., 15,* 29–40.

Ryan, N. D., Puig-Antich, J., Ambrosini, P., Rabinovich, H., Robinson, D., Nelson, B., Iyengar, S., & Twomey, J. (1987). The clinical picture of major depression in children and adolescents. *Arch. Gen. Psychiat., 44,* 854–61.

Sachar, E. J., Gruen, P. H., Altman, N., Langer, G., & Halpern, F. S. (1978). Neuroendocrine studies of brain dopamine blockade in humans. In L. C. Wynne, R. L. Cromwell, & S. Matthysse (Eds.), *The nature of schizophrenia: New approaches to research and treatment* (pp. 95–104). New York: Wiley.

Sack, D. A., Rosenthal, N. E., Perry, B. L., & Wehr, T. A. (1987). Biological rhythms in psychiatry. In H.Y. Meltzer (Ed.), *Psychopharmacology: The third generation of progress.* New York: Raven Press.

Sack, R. L., & Miller, W. (1975). Masochism: A clinical and theoretical overview. *Psychiatry, 38*(3), 244–57.

Sack, R. L., Lewry, A. J., White, D. M., Singer, C. M., Fireman, M. J., & Vandiver, R. (1990). Morning vs. evening light treatment for winter depression: Evidence that the therapeutic effects of light are mediated by circadian phase shifts. *Arch. Gen. Psychiat., 47,* 343–51.

Safer, D. J., & Krager, J. M. (1988). A survey of medication treatment for hyperactive/inattentive students. *JAMA, 260,* 2256–58.

Safran, J. D. (1990a). Towards a refinement of cognitive therapy in light of interpersonal theory: I. Theory. *Clin. Psychol. Rev., 10,* 87–105.

Safran, J. D. (1990b). Towards a refinement of cognitive therapy in light of interpersonal theory: II. Practice. *Clin. Psychol. Rev., 10,* 107–21.

Saghir, M. T., & Robins, E. (1973). *Male and female homosexuality: A comprehensive investigation.* Baltimore: William & Wilkins.

Salkovskis, P. M., & Harrison, J. (1984). Abnormal and normal obsessions: A replication. *Behav. Res. Ther., 22,* 549–52.

Salter, A. (1949). *Conditioned reflex therapy.* New York: Creative Age Press.

Samborn, R. (1994, Jul. 4). Priests playing hardball to battle abuse charges. *National Law Journal, 16,* A1.

Sameroff, A., Seifer, R., & Zax, M. (1982). Early development of children at risk for emotional disorders. *Monogr. Soc. Res. Child Develop., 47,* (7 No. 199).

Sameroff, A., Seifer, R., Zax, M., & Barocas, R. (1987). Early indicators of developmental risk: Rochester longitudinal study. *Schizo. Bull., 13,* 383–94.

Samson, H. H., & Harris, R. A. (1992). Neurobiology of alcohol abuse. *Trends in Pharmacological Science, 13,* 206–11.

Sanders, B., & Giolas, M. H. (1991). Dissociation and childhood trauma in psychologically disturbed adolescents. *Amer. J. Psychiat., 148,* 50–54.

Sanders, M. R., Shepherd, R. W., Cleghorn, G., & Woolford, H. (1994). The treatment of recurrent abdominal pain in children: A controlled comparison of cognitive-behavioral family intervention and standard pediatric care. *J. Cons. Clin. Psychol., 62*(2), 306–14.

Sanderson, W. C., & Barlow, D. H. (1990). A description of patients diagnosed with DSM-III-Revised generalized anxiety disorder. *J. Nerv. Ment. Dis., 178,* 588–91.

Sanderson, W. C., & Wetzler, S. (1991). Chronic anxiety and generalized anxiety disorder: Issues in comorbidity. In R. M. Rapee & D. H. Barlow (Eds.), *Chronic anxiety: Generalized anxiety disorder and mixed anxiety-depression* (pp. 119–35). New York: Guilford.

Sanderson, W. C., Rapee, R. M., & Barlow, D. H. (1989). The influence of an illusion of control on panic attacks induced via inhalation of 5.5%-carbon dioxide-enriched air. *Arch. Gen. Psychiat., 46,* 157–62.

Sandford, J. L. (1966). Electric and convulsive treatments in psychiatry. *Dis. Nerv. Sys., 27,* 333–38.

Sandhu, H. S., & Cohen, L. M. (1989). Endocrine disorders. In S. Cheren (Ed.), *Psychosomatic medicine: Theory, physiology, and practice,* (Vol. 2, pp. 661–706). Madison, CT: International Universities Press.

Santiago, J. M., McCall-Perez, F., Gorcey, M., & Beigel, A. (1985). Long-term psychological effects of rape in 35 rape victims. *Amer. J. Psychiat., 142,* 1338–40.

Sanua, V. D. (1969). Sociocultural aspects. In L. Bellak & L. Loeb (Eds.), *The schizophrenic syndrome.* New York: Grune & Stratton.

Saracoglu, B., Minden, H., & Wilchesky, M. (1989). The adjustment of students with learning disabilities to university and its relationship to self-esteem and self-efficacy. *J. Learn. Dis., 22,* 590–92.

Sarbin, T. R., & Juhasz, J. B. (1967). The historical background of the concept of hallucination. *J. Hist. Behav. Sci., 3,* 339–58.

Sargent, M. (1982a, Jul. 16). Schizophrenic quads not identically ill, studies show. *ADAMHA News, 8*(13), 4–5.

Sargent, M. (1982b, Dec. 3), Researcher traces Alzheimer's disease eight generations back in one family. *ADAMHA News, 8*(23), 3.

Sartorius, N., Kaelber, C. T., Cooper, J. E., Roper, M. T., Rae, D. S., Gulbinat, W., Ustun, T. B., & Regier, D. A. (1993). Progress toward achieving a common language in psychiatry: Results from the field trial of the clinical guidelines accompanying the WHO classification of mental and behavioral disorders in ICD-10. *Arch. Gen. Psychiat., 50,* 115–24.

Sarvis, M. A. (1962). Paranoid reactions: Perceptual distortion as an etiological agent. *Arch. Gen. Psychiat., 6,* 157–62.

Sasaki, M., & Hara, Y. (1973). Paternal origin of the extra chromosome in Down's syndrome. *Lancet, 2*(7840), 1257–58.

Satir, V. (1967). *Conjoint family therapy* (rev. ed.). Palo Alto, CA: Science and Behavior Books.

Satterfield, J. H., Satterfield, B. T., & Cantwell, D. P. (1981). Three year multimodal treatment study of 100 hyperactive boys. *Journal of Pediatrics, 98,*(4), 650–55.

Sauter, S. L., Murphy, L. R., & Hurrell, J. J., Jr. (1990). Prevention of work-related psychological disorders: A national strategy proposed by the National Institute for Occupational Safety and Health (NIOSH). *Amer. Psychol., 45*(10), 1146–58.

Savacir, I., & Erol, N. (1990). The Turkish MMPI: Translation, standardization, and validation. In J. N. Butcher & C. D. Spielberger (Eds.), *Advances in personality assessment* (Vol. 8). Hillsdale, NJ: Erlbaum.

Sawyer, J. B., Sudak, H. S., & Hall, S. R. (1972, Winter). A follow-up study of 53 suicides known to a suicide prevention center. *Life-Threatening Behavior, 2*(4), 227–38.

Saxe, G. N., Chinman, G., Berkowitz, R., Hall, K., Lieberg, G., Schwartz, J., & van der Kolk, B. A. (1994). Somatization in patients with dissociative disorders. *Amer. J. Psychiat., 151*(9), 1329–34.

Sayette, M. A. (1994). Effects of alcohol on self–appraisal. *Inter. J. Addictions, 29,* 127–33.

Saykin, A. J., Shtasel, D. L., Gur, R. E., Kester, D. B., Mozley, L. H., Stafiniak, P., & Gur, R. C. (1994). Neuropsychological deficits in neuroleptic naive patients with first-episode schizophrenia. *Arch. Gen. Psychiat., 51*(2), 124–31.

Scalf-McIver, L., & Thompson, K. J. (1989). Family correlates of bulimic characteristics in college females. *J. Clin. Psychol., 45,* 467–72.

Scarr, S. (1992). Developmental theories for the 1990s: Development and individual differences. *Child Develop., 63,* 1–19.

Schaar, K. (1974). Suicide rate high among women psychologists. *APA Monitor, 5*(7), 1, 10.

Schaefer, J. M. (1977, Aug. 30). *Firewater myths revisited: Towards a second generation of ethanol metabolism studies.* Paper presented at Cross-cultural Approaches to Alcoholism. Physiological variation: Invited Symposium. NATO Conference, Bergen, Norway.

Schaefer, J. M. (1978). Alcohol metabolism reactions among the Reddis of South India. *Alcoholism: Clin. Exper. Res., 2*(1), 61–69.

Schalling, D. (1978). Psychopathy-related personality variables and the psychophysiology of socialization. In R. D. Hare & D. Schalling (Eds.), *Psychopathic behavior: Approaches to research* (pp. 85–106). Chichester, UK: Wiley.

Schalock, R. L., Harper, R. S., & Carver, G. (1981). Independent living placement: Five years later. *Amer. J. Ment. Def., 86,* 170–77.

Schapiro, M. B., & Rapoport, S. I. (1987). "Pathological similarities between Alzheimer's disease and Down's syndrome: Is there a genetic link?": Commentary. *Integr. Psychiat., 5,* 167–69.

Schapiro, M. B., Haxby, J. V., & Grady, C. L. (1992). Nature of mental retardation and dementia in Down syndrome: Study with PET, CT, and neuropsychology. *Neurobiol. of Aging, 13*(6), 723–734.

Scharfman, M., & Clark, R. W. (1967). Delinquent adolescent girls: Residential treatment in a municipal hospital setting. *Arch. Gen. Psychiat., 17*(4), 441–47.

Scheff, T. J. (1984). *Being mentally ill: A sociological theory* (2nd ed.). New York: Aldine.

Scheier, M. F., & Carver, C. S. (1987). Dispositional optimism and physical well-being: The influence of generalized outcome expectancies on health. *J. Personal., 55,* 169–210.

Scheier, M. F., & Carver, C. S. (1992). Effects of optimism on psychological and physical well-being: Theoretical overview and empirical update. *Cog. Ther. Res., 16*(2), 201–28.

Scheiffelin, E. (1984). *The cultural analysis of depressive affect: An example from New Guinea.* Unpublished manuscript. University of Pennsylvania.

Schildkraut, J. J. (1965). The catecholamine hypothesis of affective disorders: A review of supporting evidence. *Amer. J. Psychiat., 122,* 509–22.

Schilling, R. F., & McAlister, A. L. (1990). Preventing drug use in adolescents through media interventions. *J. Cons. Clin. Psychol., 58,* 416–24.

Schleifer, S. J., Keller, S. E., & Stein, M. (1985). Central nervous system mechanisms and immunity: Implications for tumor responses. In S. M. Levy, *Behavior and cancer* (pp. 120–33). San Francisco: Jossey-Bass.

Schleifer, S. J., Keller, S. E., Bond, R. M., Cohen, J., & Stein, M. (1989). Major depressive disorder and immunity: Role of age, sex, severity, and hospitalization. *Arch. Gen. Psychiat., 46,* 81–87.

Schmalz, J. (1993, Mar. 5). Poll finds an even split on homosexuality's cause. *New York Times,* p. 11.

Schneider, S. (1978). Attitudes toward death in adolescent offspring of holocaust survivors. *Amer. J. Orthopsychiat., 13,* 575–83.

Schneider-Rosen, K., & Cicchetti, D. (1984). The relationships between affect and cognition in maltreated infants: Quality of attachment and the development of self-recognition. *Child Develop., 55,* 648–658.

Schoeneman, T. J. (1984). The mentally ill witch in textbooks of abnormal psychology: Current status and implications of a fallacy. *Profess. Psychol., 15*(3), 299–314.

Schofield, W. (1964). *Psychotherapy: The purchase of friendship.* Englewood Cliffs, NJ: Prentice-Hall.

Schopler, E. (1978). Changing parental involvement in behavioral treatment. In M. Rutter & E. Schopler (Eds.), *Autism: A reappraisal of concepts and treatment.* New York: Plenum.

Schopler, E. (1983). New developments in the definition and diagnosis of autism. In B. B. Lahey & A. E. Kazdin (Eds.), *Advances in clinical child psychology* (Vol. 6, pp. 93–127). New York: Plenum.

Schopler, E., Mesibov, G., & Baker, A. (1982). Evaluation of treatment for autistic children and their parents. *J. Amer. Acad. Child Psychiat., 21,* 262–67.

Schowalter, J. E. (1980). Tics. *Pediatrics in Review, 2,* 55–57.

Schreiber, F. R. (1973). *Sybil.* New York: Warner Paperback.

Schreibman, L., & Koegel, R. L. (1975). Autism: A defeatable horror. *Psych. Today, 8*(10), 61–67.

Schreibman, L., & Pierce, K. (1993). Achieving greater generalization of treatment effects in children with autism: Pivotal response training and self-management. *Clin. Psychol., 46,* 184–91.

Schreiner-Engel., P., Schiavi, R., White, D., & Ghizzani, A. (1989). Low sexual desire in women: The role of reproductive hormones. *Hormones and Behavior, 23,* 221–34.

Schuckit, M. A., & Gould, R. O. (1988). A simultaneous evaluation of multiple markers of ethanol/placebo challenges in sons of alcoholics and controls. *Arch. Gen. Psychiat., 45,* 211–16.

Schudson, M. (in press). Collective memory and modes of distortion. In D. Schachter, J. Coyle, L. Sullivan, M. Mesulam, & G. Fishbach (Eds.), *Memory distortion: Interdisciplinary perspectives.* Cambridge: Harvard University Press.

Schulsinger, F. (1972). Psychopathy: Heredity and environment. *Inter. J. Ment. Hlth., 1,* 190–206.

Schulsinger, F. (1980). Biological psychopathology. *Annu. Rev. Psychol., 31,* 583–606.

Schulsinger, F., Knop, J., Goodwin, D. W., Teasdale, T. W., & Mikkelsen, U. (1986). A prospective study of young men at high risk for alcoholism. *Arch. Gen. Psychiat., 43,* 755–60.

Schumm, J. S., & Vaughn, S. (1992). Planning for mainstreamed special education students: Perceptions of general classroom teachers. *Except., 3*(2), 81–98.

Schwalberg, M. D., Barlow, D. H., Alger, S. A., & Howard, L. J. (1992). Comparison of bulimics, obese binge eaters, social phobics, and individuals with panic disorder on comorbidity across DSM III-R anxiety disorders. *J. Abnorm. Psychol., 101,* 675–81.

Schwartz, C. C., & Myers, J. K. (1977). Life events and schizophrenia: I. Comparison of schizophrenics with a community sample. *Arch. Gen. Psychiat., 34,* 1238–41.

Schwartz, D. A. (1963). A review of the "paranoid" concept. *Arch. Gen. Psychiat., 8,* 349–61.

Schwartz, E. D., & Perry, B. D. (1994). The post-traumatic response in children and adolescents. *Psychiat. Clin. N. Amer., 17,* 311–26.

Schwartz, G. E. (1978). Psychobiological foundations of psychotherapy and behavior change. In S. L. Garfield & A. E. Bergin (Eds.), *Handbook of psychotherapy and behavior change* (2nd ed., pp. 63–99). New York: Wiley.

Schwartz, G. E. (1989). Disregulation theory and disease: Toward a general model for psychosomatic medicine. In S. Cheren (Ed.), *Psychosomatic medicine: Theory, physiology, and practice* (Vol. 1, pp. 91–118). Madison, CT: International Universities Press.

Schwartz, G. E., & Weiss, S. M. (1978). Behavioral medicine revisited: An amended definition. *J. Behav. Med., 1,* 249–51.

Schwartz, L., Slater, M. A., & Birchler, G. R. (1994). Interpersonal stress and pain behaviors in patients with chronic pain. *J. Cons. Clin. Psychol., 62*(4), 861–64.

Schwartz, R. C., Barrett, M. J., & Saba, G. (1983, Oct.). *Family therapy for bulimia*. Paper presented at American Association for Marriage and Family Therapy, Washington, DC.

Schwartz, S., & Johnson, J. H. (1985). *Psychopathology of childhood: A clinical-experimental approach* (2nd ed.). New York: Pergamon.

Schwarzwald, J., Weisenberg, M., Waysman, M., Soloman, Z., & Klingman, A. (1993). Stress reaction of school-age children to bombardment by SCUD missles. *J. Abnorm. Psychol., 102,* 404–10.

Schwitzgebel, R. L., & Schwitzgebel, R. K. (1980). *Law and psychological practice.* New York: Wiley.

Scovern, A. W., & Kilmann, P. R. (1980). Status of electron-convulsive therapy: A review of the outcome literature. *Psychol. Bull., 87,* 260–303.

Seaman, B., Roberts, P., Gilewski, M., & Nagai, J. (1993). Clinic to the real world: Community reintegration of head injured patients. *J. Cogn. Rehab., 11*(2), 6–17.

Searles, J. S. (1991). The genetics of alcoholism: Impact on family and sociological models of addiction. *Family Dynamics of Addiction Quarterly, 1,* 8–21.

Sears, R. R. (1961). Relation of early socialization experiences to aggression in middle childhood. *J. Abnorm. Soc. Psychol., 63,* 466–92.

Sedvall, G., Farde, L., Persson, A., & Wiesel, F. A. (1986). Imaging of neurotransmitter receptors in the living human brain. *Arch. Gen. Psychiat., 43,* 995–1005.

Segal, D. S., Yager, J., & Sullivan, J. L. (1976). *Foundations of biochemical psychiatry.* Boston: Butterworth.

Segal, S. (1978). Attitudes toward the mentally ill: A review. *Social Work, 23,* 211–17.

Segal, Z. V., & Stermac, L. E. (1990). The role of cognition in sexual assault. In W. L. Marshall, D. R. Laws, & H. E. Barbaree (Eds.), *Handbook of sexual assault* (pp. 161–75). New York: Plenum.

Seidl, F. W. (1974). Community oriented residential care: The state of the art. *Child Care Quarterly, 3*(3), 150–63.

Seligman, M. E. P. (1971). Phobias and preparedness. *Behav. Ther., 2,* 307–20.

Seligman, M. E. P. (1974). Depression and learned helplessness. In R.J. Friedman & M. M. Katz (Eds.), *The psychology of depression: Contemporary theory and research.* Washington, DC: Hemisphere.

Seligman, M. E. P. (1975). *Helplessness: On depression, development, and death.* San Francisco: Freeman.

Seligman, M. E. P. (1990). Why is there so much depression today? The waxing of the individual and the waning of the commons. In R. E. Ingram (Ed.), *Contemporary psychological approaches to depression.* New York: Plenum.

Seligman, M. E. P., & Binik, Y. (1977). The safety signal hypothesis. In H. Davis & H. M. B. Hurwitz (Eds.), *Operant-Pavlovian interactions* (pp. 165–88). Hillsdale, NJ: Erlbaum.

Selkin, J. (1975). Rape. *Psych. Today, 8*(8), 70–72.

Selkoe, D. J. (1986). Altered structural protein in plaques and tangles: What do they tell us about the biology of Alzheimer's disease? *Neurobiol. Aging, 7,* 425–32.

Selling, L. S. (1943). *Men against madness.* New York: Garden City Books.

Selye, H. (1956). *The stress of life.* New York: McGraw-Hill.

Selye, H. (1976a). *Stress in health and disease.* Woburn, MA: Butterworth.

Selye, H. (1976b). *The stress of life* (2nd ed.). New York: McGraw-Hill.

Serrano, A. C., Zuelzer, M. B., Howe, D. D., & Reposa, R. E. (1979). Ecology of abusive and nonabusive families, *J. Amer. Acad. Child Psychiat., 18,* 167–75.

Sewell, D. W., Jeste, D. V., Atkinson, J. H., Heaton, R. K., Hesselink, J. R., Wiley, C., Thal, L., Chandler, J. L., & Grant, I. (1994). HIV-associated psychosis: A study of 20 cases. *Amer. J. Psychiat., 151*(2), 237–42.

Shadish, W. R., Montgomery, L. M., Wilson, P., Wilson, M. R., Bright, I., & Okwumabua, T. (1993). Effects of family and marital psychotherapies: A meta-analysis. *J. Cons. Clin. Psychol., 61*(6), 992–1002.

Shaffer, H. J. & LaSalvia, T. A. (1992). Patterns of substance use among methadone maintenance patients: Indicators of outcome. *Journal of Substance Abuse Treatment, 9,* 143–47.

Shakow, D. (1969). On doing research in schizophrenia. *Arch. Gen. Psychiat., 20*(6), 618–42.

Shapiro, A. K., & Morris, L. A. (1978). The placebo effect in medical and psychological therapies. In S. L. Garfield & A. E. Bergin (Eds.), *Handbook of psychotherapy and behavior change* (2nd ed., pp. 369–410). New York: Wiley.

Shaw, E. D., Stokes, P. E., Mann, J. J., & Manevitz, A. Z. A. (1987). Effects of lithium carbonate on the memory and motor speed of bipolar outpatients. *J. Abnorm. Psychol., 96,* 64–69.

Shaw, J. A. (1990). Stress engendered by military action on military and civilian populations. In J. D. Noshpitz & R. D. Coddington (Eds.), *Stressors and the adjustment disorders.* New York: Wiley Intersciences.

Shea, M. T., Elkin, I., Imber, S. D., Sotsky, S. M., Watkins, J. T., Collins, J. F., Pilkonis, P. A., Beckham, E., Glass, D. R., Dolan, R. T., & Parloff, M. B. (1992). Course of depressive symptoms over follow-up: Findings from the National Institute of Mental Health Treatment of Depression Collaborative Research Program. *Arch. Gen. Psychiat., 49*(10), 782–87.

Shedler, J., & Block, J. (1990). Adolescent drug use and psychological health: A longitudinal inquiry. *Amer. Psychol., 45,* 612–30.

Shedler, J., Mayman, M., & Manis, M. (1993). The *illusion* of mental health. *Amer. Psychol., 48*(11), 1117–31.

Sheehan, D. Z. (1982). Panic attacks and phobias. *New Engl. J. Med., 307,* 156–8.

Sheehan, D. Z. (1983). *The anxiety disease.* New York: Bantam Books.

Shelton, R. C., Hollon, S. D., Purdon, S. E., & Loosen, P. T. (1991). Biological and psychological aspects of depression. *Behav. Ther., 22,* 201–28.

Shephard, M. (1974). The psycho-historians: A psychiatrist's scepticism. *Encounter,* March, 36.

Shepher, J. (1971). Mate selection among second generation kibbutz adolescents and adults. *Arch. Sex. Behav., 1,* 293–307.

Sher, K. J., & Trull, T. J. (1994). Personality and disinhibitory psychopathology: Alcoholism and antisocial personality disorder. *J. Abnorm. Psychol., 103,* 92–102.

Sher, K. J., Frost, R. O., Kushner, M., Crews, T. M., & Alexander, J. E. (1989). Memory deficits in compulsive checkers: A replication and extension in a clinical example. *Behav. Res. Ther., 27,* 65–69.

Sher, K. J., Frost, R. O., & Otis, R. (1983). Cognitive deficits in compulsive checkers: An exploratory study. *Behav. Res. Ther., 21,* 357–64.

Sherrod, B. (1968). *Dallas Times Herald* (n.d.). Quoted in D. Bolen & W. H. Boyd, Gambling and the gambler. *Arch. Gen. Psychiat., 18*(5), 617–30.

Sherwin, I., & Geschwind, N. (1978). Neural substrates of behavior. In A. M. Nicholi (Ed.), *The Harvard guide to modern psychiatry* (pp. 59–80). Cambridge, MA: Harvard University Press.

Shore, J. H., Vollmer, W. M., & Tatum, E. L. (1989). Community patterns of posttraumatic stress disorders. *J. Nerv. Ment. Dis., 177,* 681–85.

Shrout, P. E., Link, B. G., Dohrenwend, B. P., Skodol, A. E., Stueve, A., & Mirotznik, J. (1989). Characterizing life events as risk factors for depression: The role of fateful loss events. *J. Abnorm. Psychol., 89,* 460–67.

Sidtis, J. J., Gatsonis, C., & Price, R. W. (1993). Zidovudine treatment of the AIDS dementia complex: Results of a placebo-controlled trial. *Ann. Neurol., 33,* 343–49.

Siegel, J. M., & Kuykendall, D. H. (1990). Loss, widowhood, and psychological distress among the elderly. *J. Cons. Clin. Psychol. 58,* 519–24.

Siegel, R. K. (1984). Hostage hallucinations: Visual imagery induced by isolation and life-threatening stress. *J. Nerv. Ment. Dis., 172*(5), 264–72.

Siegelman, M. (1979). Adjustment of homosexual and heterosexual women: A cross-national replication. *Arch. Sex. Behav., 8,* 121–26.

Siever, L. J. (1985). Biological markers in schizotypal personality disorder. *Schizo. Bull., 11,* 564–75.

Siever, L. J. (1986). Schizoid and schizotypal personality disorders. In J. R. Lion (Ed.), *Personality disorders: Diagnosis and management.* (pp. 32–64). Malabar, Fl: Robert F. Kreiger.

Siever, L. J., & Davis, K. L. (1985). Overview: Toward a dysregulation hypothesis of depression. *Amer. J. Psychiat., 142,* 1017–31.

Siever, L. J., & Davis, K. L. (1991). A psychobiological perspective on the personality disorders. *Amer. J. Psychiat., 148,* 1647–58.

Siever, L. J., Silverman, J. M., Horvath, T. B., Klar, H., Coccaro, E., Keefe, R. S. E., Pinkham, L., Rinaldi, P., Mohs, R. C., & Davis, K. L. (1990). Increased morbidity risk for schizophrenia-related disorders in relatives of schizotypal personality disordered patients. *Arch. Gen. Psychiat., 47,* 634–40.

Sifneos, P. E. (1973). The prevalence of "alexithymic" characteristics in psychosomatic patients. *Psychotherapy and Psychosomatics, 22,* 255–62.

Sigal J. J., Silver, D., Rakoff, V., & Ellin, B. (1973, Apr.). Some second-generation effects of survival of the Nazi persecution. *Amer. J. Orthopsychiat., 43*(3), 320–27.

Sigerist, H. E. (1943). *Civilization and disease.* Ithaca, NY: Cornell University Press.

Sigman, M., Kasari, C., Kwon, J., & Yirmiya, N. (1992). Responses to the negative emotions of others by autistic, mentally retarded, and normal children. *Child Develop., 63,* 796–807.

Sigvardsson, S., Von Knorring, A. L., Bohman, M., & Cloninger, C. R. (1984). An adoption study of somatoform disorders: I. The relationship of somatization to psychiatric disability. *Arch. Gen. Psych., 41,* 853–59.

Silberman, E. K., & Tassone, E. P. (1985). The Israeli high-risk study: Statistical overview and discussion. *Schizo. Bull., 11,* 138–45.

Silverman, W. H., & Silverman, M. M. (1987). Comparison of key informants, parents, and teenagers for planning adolescent substance abuse prevention programs. *Psychology of Addictive Behaviors, 1*(1), 30–37.

Silverman, W. H., & Wallander, J. L. (1993). Bridging research and practice in interventions with children: Introduction to the special issue. *Clin. Psychol., 46,* 165–168.

Silverstein, A. B., Legutki, G., Friedman, S. L., & Takayama, D. L. (1982). Performance of Down's syndrome individuals on the Stanford-Binet Intelligence Scale. *Amer. J. Ment. Def., 86,* 548–5.

Silverton, L., Finello, K. M., Schulsinger, F., & Mednick, S. A. (1985). Low birth weight and ventricular enlargement in a high-risk sample. *J. Abnorm. Psychol., 94,* 405–9

Simon, W. (1975). Male sexuality: The secret of satisfaction. *Today's Health, 53*(4), 32–34, 50–52.

Simons, A. D., Angell, K. L., Monroe, S. M., & Thase, M. E. (1993). Cognition and life stress in depression: Cognitive factors and the definition, rating, and generation of negative life events. *J. Abnorm. Psychol., 102,* 584–91.

Simons, A. D., Murphy, G. E., Levine, J. L., & Wetzel, R. D. (1986). Cognitive therapy and pharmacotherapy for depression: Sustained improvement over one year. *Arch. Gen. Psychiat., 43,* 43–48.

Simons, R. C. (1987). Applicability of the DSM-III to psychiatric education. In G. L. Tischler (Ed.), *Diagnosis and classification in psychiatry: A critical appraisal of DSM-III* (pp. 510–29). New York: Cambridge University Press.

Simons, R. C., & Hughes, C. C. (Eds.). (1985). *The culture bound syndromes.* Boston: Reidel.

Singer, J. E. (1980). Traditions of stress research: Integrative comments. In I. G. Sarason & C. D. Spielberger (Eds.), *Stress and anxiety* (Vol. 7, pp. 3–10). Washington, DC: Hemisphere.

Singer, J., & Singer, I. (1978). Types of female orgasm. In J. LoPiccolo & L. LoPiccolo (Eds.), *Handbook of sex therapy* (pp. 175–86). New York: Plenum.

Singer, M. T., & Wynne, L. C. (1963). Differentiating characteristics of the parents of childhood schizophrenics, childhood neurotics and young adult schizophrenics. *Amer. J. Psychiat., 120,* 234–43.

Singer, M. T., & Wynne, L. C. (1965a). Thought disorder and family relations of schizophrenics. III. Methodology using projective techniques. *Arch. Gen. Psychiat., 12,* 182–200.

Singer, M. T., & Wynne, L. C. (1965b). Thought disorder and family relations of schizophrenics. IV. Results and implications. *Arch. Gen. Psychiat., 12,* 201–12.

Singer, M. T., Wynne, L. C., & Toohey, M. L. (1978). Communication disorders and the families of schizophrenics. In L. C. Wynne, R. L. Cromwell, & S. Matthysse (Eds.), *The nature of schizophrenia: New approaches to research and treatment* (pp. 499–511). New York: Wiley.

Skinner, B. F. (1990). Can psychology be a science of mind? *Amer. Psychol. 45,* 1206–10.

Skodol, A. E., Rosnick, L., Kellman, H. D., Oldham, J. M., & Hyler, S. E. (1991). Development of a procedure for validating structured assessments of Axis II. In J. Oldham (Ed.), *Personality disorders: New perspectives on diagnostic validity.* Washington DC: American Psychiatric Press.

Slap, G. B., Vorters, D. F., Chaudhuri, S., & Centor, R. (1989). Risk factors for attempted suicide during adolescence. *Pediatrics, 84,* 762–72.

Slater, E., with the assistance of J. Shields. (1953). *Psychotic and neurotic illness in twins.* Special Report Series No. 278. Medical Research Council (Great Britain).

Slater, J. F., & Depue, R. A. (1981). The contribution of environmental events and social support to serious suicide attempts in primary depressive disorder. *J. Abnorm. Psychol., 90,* 275–85.

Sloan, S. J., & Cooper, C. L. (1984). Health-related lifestyle habits in commercial airline pilots. *British Journal of Aviation Medicine, 2,* 32–41.

Sloane, R. B., Staples, F. R., Cristol, A. H., Yorkston, N. J., & Whipple, K. (1975). *Psychotherapy versus behavior therapy.* Cambridge, MA: Harvard University Press.

Sloman, L. (1991). Use of medication in pervasive developmental disorders. *Psychiat. Clin. N. Amer. 14,* 165–82.

Sloper, P., Turner, S., Knussen, C., & Cunningham, C. C. (1990). Social life of school children with Down's syndrome. *Child: Care, Health, and Development, 16,* 235–51.

Slovenko, R. (1994). Legal aspects of post-traumatic disorder. *Psychiat. Clin. N. Amer., 17,* 439–46.

Smalley, S. L. (1991). Genetic influences in autism. *Psychiat. Clin. N. Amer., 14,* 125–39.

Smith, D. (1982). Trends in counseling and psychotherapy. *Amer. Psychol., 37*(7), 802–9.

Smith, G., & Smith, D. (1985). A mainstreaming program that really works. *J. Learn. Dis., 18,* 369–72.

Smith, G. F., & Berg, J. M. (1976). *Down's anomaly.* New York: Churchill Livingstone (Distributed by Longman).

Smith, G. T., Goldman, M. S., Greenbaum, P. E., & Christiansen, B. A. (1995). Expectancy for social facilitation from drinking: The diveregent paths of high-expectancy and low-expectancy adolescents. *J. Abnorm. Psychol., 104,* 32–40.

Smith, M. L., Glass, G. V., & Miller, T. I. (1980). *The benefits of psychotherapy.* Baltimore: Johns Hopkins University Press.

Smith, R. J. (1978). *The psychopath in society.* New York: Academic Press.

Smith, R. J. (1979). Study finds sleeping pills overprescribed. *Science, 204,* 287–88.

Smith, R. S. (1976). Voyeurism: A review of the literature. *Arch. Sex. Behav., 5,* 585–608.

Smith, S. S., & Newman, J. P. (1990). Alcohol and drug abuse dependence disorders in psychopathic and nonpsychopathic criminal offenders. *J. Abnorm. Psychol., 99,* 430–39.

Smith, W. (1989). *A profile of health and disease in America.* New York: Facts on File.

Smithyan, S. D. (1978). *The undetected rapist*. Ph.D. Dissertation, Claremont Graduate School. University Microfilms International: Ann Arbor, MI.

Snow, D. L., & Kline, M. L. (1995). Preventive interventions in the work site to reduce negative psychiatric consequences of work and family stress. In C.M. Mazure (Ed.), *Does stress cause psychiatric illness?* Washington, DC: American Psychiatric Association.

Snowden, K. R., & Cheung, F. K. (1990). Use of inpatient mental health services by members of ethnic minority groups. *Amer. Psychol., 45*, 347–55.

Snyder, D. K., & Wills, R. M. (1989). Behavioral versus insight-oriented marital therapy: Effects on individual and interspousal functioning. *J. Cons. Clin. Psychol. 57*, 39–46.

Snyder, S. H. (1978). Dopamine and schizophrenia. In L. C. Wynne, R. L. Cromwell & S. Matthysse (Eds.), *The nature of schizophrenia: New approaches to research and treatment* (pp. 87–94). New York: Wiley.

Sokol, M. S., & Pfeffer, C. R. (1992). Suicidal behavior of children. In B. Bongar (Ed.), *Suicide: Guidelines for assessment, management and treatment*. New York: Oxford University Press.

Soloff, P. H., Cornelius, J., George, A. (1991). The depressed borderline: One disorder or two? *Psychopharma. Bull., 27*, 23–30.

Soni, S. D., & Rockley, G. J. (1974). Socio-cultural substrates of folie à deux. *Brit. J. Psychiat., 125*(9), 230–35.

Sonnenberg, S. M. (1988). Victims of violence and post-traumatic stress disorder. *Psychiat. Clin. N. Amer., 11*, 581–90.

Sorenson, S. B., Rutter, C. M., & Aneshensel, C. S. (1991). Depression in the community: An investigation into age of onset. *J. Cons. Clin. Psychol., 59*, 541–46.

Soroka v. Dayton-Hudson, Corp., 753 Cal.App.3d 654,1 Cal Rptr.2d77 (Cal.App.1. Dist.1991) (1991).

Spanos, N. P. (1986). Hypnosis, nonvolitional responding, and multiple personality. In B. Maher & W. Maher (Eds.), *Progress in experimental personality research* (pp. 1–62). New York: Academic Press.

Spanos, N. P. (1994). Multiple identity enactments and multiple personality disorder: A sociocognitive perspective. *Psychol. Bull., 116*, 143–65.

Spanos, N. P., & Burgess, C. (1994). Hypnosis and multiple personality disorder: A sociocognitive perspective. In S. J. Lynn & J. W. Rhue (Eds.), *Dissociation: Clinical and theoretical perspectives* (pp. 136–58). New York: Guilford.

Spanos, N. P., Weekes, J. R., & Bertrand, L. D. (1985). Multiple personality: A social psychological perspective. *J. Abnorm. Psychol., 94*, 362–76.

Speed, N., Engdahl, B., Schwartz, J., & Eberly, R. (1989). Posttraumatic stress disorder as a consequence of the POW experience. *J. Nerv. Ment. Dis. 177*, 147–53.

Speer, D. C. (1992). Clinically significant change: Jacobson and Truax (1991) revisited. *J. Cons. Clin. Psychol., 60*(3), 402–8.

Spencer, G. (1989). *Projections of the population of the United States, by age, sex, and race: 1988–2080*. U.S. Department of Commerce, Bureau of Census. Washington, DC: U. S. Government Printing Office.

Spielberger, C. D., Johnson, E. H., Russell, S. F., Crane, R. J., & Worden, T. J. (1985). The experience and expression of anger. In M. A. Chesney & R. H. Rosenman (Eds.), *Anger and hostility in cardiovascular and behavioral disorders*. New York: Hemisphere.

Spiess, W. F. J., Geer, J. H., & O'Donohue, W. T. (1984). Premature ejaculation: Investigation of factors in ejaculatory latency. *J. Abnorm. Psychol., 93*, 242–45.

Spitz, R. A. (1945). Hospitalization: An inquiry into the genesis of psychiatric conditions of early childhood. In R. S. Eissler, A. Freud, H. Hartman, & E. Kris (Eds.), *The psychoanalytic study of the child* (Vol. 1). New York: International Universities Press.

Spitz, R. A. (1946). Anaclitic depression. In *Psychoanalytic study of the child* (Vol. 2). New York: International Universities Press.

Spitzer, R. L., Gibbon, M., Skodol, A. E., Williams, J. B. W., & First, M. B. (1989). *DSM-III-R casebook*. Washington, DC: American Psychiatric Press.

Spitzer, R. L., Gibbon, M., Skodol, A. E., Williams, J. B. W., & First, M. B. (Ed.). (1994). *DSM-IV casebook* (4th ed.). Washington: American Psychiatric Press.

Spitzer, R. L., Skodol, A. E., Gibbon, M., & Williams, J. B. W. (1981). *DSM-III case book*. Washington, DC: American Psychiatric Association.

Spitzer, R. L., Skodol, A. E., Gibbon, M., & Williams, J. B. W. (1983). *Psychopathology: A case book*. New York: McGraw-Hill.

Spring, B. J., & Zubin, J. (1978). Attention and information-processing as indicators of vulnerability to schizophrenic episodes. In L. C. Wynne, R. L. Cromwell, & S. Matthysse (Eds.), *The nature of schizophrenia: New approaches to research and treatment* (pp. 166–175). New York: Wiley.

Spunt, B., Goldstein, P., Brownstein, H., & Fendrich, M. (1994). The role of marijuana in homicide. *Inter. J. Addict., 29*, 195–213.

Squire, L. R. (1977). ECT and memory loss. *Amer. J. Psychiat., 134*, 997–1001.

Squire, L. R., & Slater, P. C. (1978). Bilateral and unilateral ECT: Effects on verbal and nonverbal memory. *Amer. J. Psychiat., 135*, 1316–20.

Squire, L. R., Slater, P. C., & Chase, P. M. (1975). Retrograde amnesia: Temporal gradient in very long-term memory following electroconvulsive therapy. *Science, 187*, 77–79.

Stabenau, J. R. (1984). Implications of family history of alcoholism, antisocial personality, and sex differences in alcohol dependence. *Amer. J. Psychiat., 141*(10), 1178–82.

Stabenau, J., & Pollin, W. (1968). Comparative life history differences of families of schizophrenics, delinquents and "normals." *Amer. J. Psychiat., 124*, 1526–34.

Stabenau, J. R., Tupin, J., Werner, M., & Pollin, W. (1965). A comparative study of families of schizophrenics, delinquents, and normals. *Psychiatry, 28*, 45–59.

Stacy, A. W., Widaman, K. F., & Marlatt, G. A. (1990). Expectancy models of alcohol use. *J. Pers. Soc. Psychol., 58*, 918–28.

Stafford, K. P., & Ben-Porath, Y. S. (1995). Assessment of criminal responsibility. In J. N. Butcher (Ed.), *Foundations of clinical personality assessment: Practical considerations*. New York: Oxford University Press.

Stafford, S. H., & Green, V. P. (1993). Facilitating preschool mainstreaming: Classroom strategies and teacher attitude. *Early Child Development & Care, 91*, 93–98.

Stampfl, T. G., (1975). Implosive therapy: Staring down your nightmares. *Psych. Today, 8*(9), 66–68, 72–73.

Stanley, E. J., & Barter, J. T. (1970). Adolescent suicidal behavior. *Amer. J. Orthopsychiat., 40*(1), 87–96.

Stanton, M. D., & Todd, T. C. (1976, June). *Structural family therapy with heroin addicts: Some outcome data*. Paper presented at the Society for Psychotherapy Research. San Diego.

Stare, F. J., Whelan, E. M., & Sheridan, M. (1980). Diet and hyperactivity: Is there a relationship? *Pediatrics, 6*(4), 521–25.

Stark, L. J., Spirito, A., Lewis, A. V., & Hart, K. J. (1990). Encopresis: Behavioral parameters associated with children who fail medical management. *Child Psychiat. Human Develop., 20*, 169–79.

Stattin, H., & Klackenberg-Larsson, I. (1993). Early language and intelligence development and their relationship to future criminal behavior. *J. Abnorm. Psychol., 102*(3), 369–78.

Steadman, H. J., McGreevy, M. A., Morrissey, J. P., Callahan, L. A., Robbins, P. C., & Cirincione, C. (1993). *Before and after Hinckley: Evaluating insanity defense reform*. New York: Guilford.

Steffenberg, S., & Gillberg, C. (1986). Autism and autistic-like conditions in Swedish rural and urban areas: A population study. *Brit. J. Psychiat. 149*, 81–87.

Stein, J. (1970). *Neurosis in contemporary society: Process and treatment*. Belmont, CA: Brooks/Cole.

Stein, S. (1987). Computer-assisted diagnosis for children and adolescents. In J. N. Butcher (Ed.), *Computerized psychological assessment: A practitioner's guide*. New York: Basic Books.

Steinhausen, H.C., Williams, J., & Spohr, H.-L. (1993). Long-term psychopathological and cognitive outcome of children with fetal alcohol syndrome. *J. Amer. Acad. Child Adoles. Psychiat., 32,* 990–994.

Steinmann, A., & Fox, D. J. (1974). *The male dilemma: How to survive the sexual revolution.* New York: Jason Aronson.

Steketee, G., & Foa, E. B. (1985). Obsessive-compulsive disorder. In D. H. Barlow (Ed.), *Clinical handbook of psychological disorders.* (pp. 69–144) New York: Guilford.

Stelmachers, Z. T. (1995). Assessing suicidal patients. In J. N. Butcher (Ed.), *Clinical personality assessment: Practical considerations* New York: Oxford University Press.

Stelmack, R. M., Houlihan, M., & McGarry-Roberts, P. A. (1993). Personality, reaction time, and event-related potentials. *J. Pers. Soc. Psychol., 65*(2), 399–409.

Stene, J., Stene, E., Stengel-Rutkowski, S., & Murken, J. D. (1981). Paternal age and Down's syndrome, data from prenatal diagnoses (DFG). *Human Genet., 59,* 119–24.

Stephens, R., & Cottrell, E. (1972). A follow-up study of 200 narcotic addicts committed for treatment under the narcotic addiction rehabilitation act. *Brit. J. Addict., 67,* 45–53.

Stephens, R. S., Roffman, R. A., & Simpson, E. E. (1994). Treating adult marijuana dependence: A test of the relapse prevention model. *J. Cons. Clin. Psychol., 62,* 92–99.

Stermac, L. E., Hall, K., & Henskens, M. (1989). Violence among child molesters. *J. Sex Res., 26,* 450–59.

Stermac, L. E., Segal, Z. V., & Gillis, R. (1990). Social and cultural factors in sexual assault. In W. L. Marshall, D. R. Laws, & H. E. Barbaree (Eds.), *Handbook of sexual assault* (pp. 143–60). New York: Plenum.

Stern, D. B. (1977). Handedness and the lateral distribution of conversion reactions. *J. Nerv. Ment. Dis., 164,* 122–28.

Sternberg, K. J., Lamb, M. B., Greenbaum, C., & Cicchetti, D. (1992). Effects of domestic violence on children's behavior problems and depression. *Develop. Psychol., 29,* 44–52.

Stevens, J. R., & Hallick, L. M. (1992). Viruses and schizophrenia. In S. Specter, M. Bendinelli, & H. Friedman (Eds.), *Viruses and immunity* (pp. 303–16). New York: Plenum.

Stewart, J. B., Hardin, S. B., Weinrich, S., & McGeorge, S. (1992). Group protocol to mitigate disaster stress and enhance social support in adolescents exposed to Hurricane Hugo. *Issues in Mental Health Nursing, 13,* 105–19.

Stewart, S. H., Finn, P. R., & Pihl, R. O. (1990, Mar.). The effects of alcohol on the cardiovascular stress response in men at high risk for alcoholism: A dose response study. Paper presented at the annual meeting of the Canadian Psychological Association, Ottawa.

Stiles, W. B., & Shapiro, D. A., (1989). Abuse of the drug metaphor in psychotherapy process-outcome research. *Clin. Psychol. Rev., 9,* 521–43.

Stiles, W. B., Shapiro, D. A., & Elliott, R. (1986). "Are all psychotherapies equivalent?" *Amer. Psychol., 41,* 165–80.

Stokes, P. E., & Sikes, C. R. (1987). Hypothalamic-pituitary-adrenal axis in affective disorders. In H. Y. Meltzer (Ed.), *Psychopharmacology: A third generation of progress* (pp. 589–607). New York: Raven Press.

Stoller, R. U. (1977). Sexual deviations. In F. Beach (Ed.), *Human sexuality in four perspectives.* Baltimore, MD: Johns Hopkins University Press.

Stone, G. C., Weiss, S. M., Matarazzo, J. D., Miller, N. E., Rodin, J., Belar, C. D., Follick, M. J., & Singer, J. E. (Eds.), (1987). *Health psychology: A discipline and a profession.* Chicago: University of Chicago Press.

Stone, L. J., & Hokanson, J. E. (1969). Arousal reduction via self-punitive behavior. *J. Pers. Soc. Psychol., 12,* 72–79.

Stone, S. (1937). Psychiatry through the ages. *J. Abnorm. Soc. Psychol., 32,* 131–60.

Strack, S., & Coyne, J. C. (1983). Social confirmation of dysphoria: Shared and private reactions to depression. *J. Pers. Soc. Psychol., 44,* 798–806.

Strakowski, S. M. (1994). Diagnostic validity of schizophreniform disorder. *Amer. J. Psychiat., 151*(6), 815–24.

Strang, J. P. (1989). Gastrointestinal disorders. In S. Cheren (Ed.), *Psychosomatic medicine: Theory, physiology, and practice* (Vol. 2, pp. 427–502). Madison, CT: International Universities Press.

Strange, R. E., & Brown, D. E., Jr. (1970). Home from the wars. *Amer. J. Psychiat., 127*(4), 488–92.

Strauman, T. J., Lemieux, A. M., & Coe, C. L. (1993). Self-discrepancy and natural killer cell activity: Immunological consequences of negative self-evaluation. *J. Pers. Soc. Psychol., 64*(6), 1042–52.

Strauss, T. S. (1979). Social and cultural influences on psychopathology. *Annu. Rev. Psychol., 30*(4), 397–415.

Strayer, R., & Ellenhorn, L. (1975). Vietnam veterans: A study exploring adjustment patterns and attitudes. *Journal of Social Issues, 31,* 81–93.

Strean, H. S. (1985). *Resolving resistances in psychotherapy.* New York: Wiley Interscience.

Streissguth, A. P. (1976). Maternal alcoholism and the outcome of pregnancy: A review of the fetal alcohol syndrome. In M. Greenblatt & M. A. Schuckit (Eds.), *Alcoholism: Problems in women and children.* New York: Grune & Stratton.

Strine, G. (1971, Mar. 30). Compulsive gamblers pursue elusive dollar forever. *Los Angeles Times,* III, 1–6.

Strober, M. (1986). Anorexia nervosa: history and psychological concepts. In K. D. Brownell & J. P. Foreyt (Eds.), *Handbook of eating disorders* (pp. 231–46). New York: Basic.

Stroebe, M. S., & Stroebe, W. (1983). Who suffers more? Sex differences in health risks of the widowed. *Psychol. Bull., 93*(2), 279–301.

Strupp, H. H. (1981). Toward a refinement of time-limited dynamic psychotherapy. In S. H. Budman (Ed.), *Forms of brief therapy.* New York: Guilford.

Strupp, H. H. (1993). The Vanderbilt psychotherapy studies: Synopsis. *J. Cons. Clin. Psychol., 61*(3), 431–33.

Strupp, H. H., & Binder, J. L. (1984). *Psychotherapy in a new key: A guide to time-limited dynamic psychotherapy.* New York: Basic Books.

Strupp, H. H., Hadley, S. W., & Gomes-Schwartz, B. (1977). *Psychotherapy for better or worse: An analysis of the problem of negative effects.* New York: Jason Aronson.

Stuart, R. B. (1967). Behavioral control of overeating. *Behav. Res. Ther., 5,* 357–65.

Stuart, R. B. (1971). A three-dimensional program for the treatment of obesity. *Behav. Res. Ther., 9,* 177–86.

Stunkard, A. J., Harris, J. R., Pedersen, N. L., & McClearn, G. E. (1990). A separated twin study of the body mass index. *New Engl. J. Med., 322,* 1483–87.

Sturgis, E. T. (1993). Obsessive-compulsive disorders. In P. B. Sutker & H. E. Adams (Eds.), *Comprehensive handbook of psychopathology* (2nd ed.). New York: Plenum.

Sturmey, P., & Sevin, J. (1993). Dual diagnosis: An annotated bibliography of recent research. *J. Intell. Dis. Res., 37*(5), 437–48.

Sturt, E. (1986). Application of survival analysis to the inception of dementia. *Psychol. Med., 16,* 583–93.

Stuss, D. T., Gow, C. A., & Hetherington, C. R. (1992). "No longer Gage": Frontal lobe dysfunction and emotional changes. *J. Cons. Clin. Psychol., 60*(3), 349–59.

Suddath, R. L., Christison, G. W., Torrey, E. F., Casanova, M. F., & Weinberger, D. R. (1990). Anatomical abnormalities in the brains of monozygotic twins discordant for schizophrenia. *New Engl. J. Med., 322,* 789–94.

Sue, D., & Sue, S. (1987). Cultural factors in the clinical assessment of Asian Americans. *J. Cons. Clin. Psychol., 55,* 479–87.

Suedfeld, P., & Landon, P. B. (1978). Approaches to treatment. In R. D. Hare & D. Schalling (Eds.), *Psychopathic behavior: Approaches to research* (pp. 347–76). New York: Wiley.

Sulkunen, P. (1976). Drinking patterns and the level of alcohol consumption: An international overview. In R. I. Gibbons et al. (Eds.), *Research advances in alcohol and drug problems* (Vol. 3). New York: Wiley.

Sullivan, H. S. (1953). In H. S. Perry & M. L. Gawel (Eds.), *The interpersonal theory of psychiatry.* New York: Norton.

Sultzer, D. L., Levin, H. S., Mahler, M. E., High, W. M., & Cummings, J. L. (1993). A comparison of psychiatric symptoms in vascular dementia and Alzheimer's disease. *Amer. J. Psychiat., 150*(12), 1806–12.

Summers, F. (1979). Characteristics of new patient admissions to aftercare. *Hosp. Comm. Psychiat., 30*(3), 199–202.

Sundberg, N. D., & Tyler, L. E. (1962). *Clinical psychology.* New York: Appleton-Century-Crofts.

Surwit, R. S., Shapiro, D., & Good, M. L. (1978). Comparison of cardiovascular biofeedback, neuromuscular biofeedback, and meditation in the treatment of borderline essential hypertension. *J. Cons. Clin. Psychol., 46,* 252–53.

Susser, E., Moore, R., & Link, B. (1993). Risk factors for homelessness. *Amer. J. Epidemiol., 15,* 546–66.

Suter, B. (1976). Suicide and women. In B. B. Wolman & H. H. Krauss (Eds.), *Between survival and suicide* (pp. 129–61). New York: Gardner.

Sutker, P. B. & Allain, A. N. (1995). Psychological assessment of aviators captured in World War II. *Psychol. Assess., 7,* 66–68.

Sutker, P. B., Allain, A. N., Johnson, J. J., & Butters, N. M. (1992). Memory and learning performances in POW survivors with history of malnutrition and combat veteran controls. *Archives of Clinical Neuropsychology, 7,* 431–44.

Sutker, P. B., Archer, R. P., & Kilpatrick, D. G. (1979). Sociopathy and antisocial behavior: Theory and treatment. In S. M. Turner, K. S. Calhoun, & H. E. Adams (Eds.), *Handbook of clinical behavior therapy.* New York: Wiley.

Sutker, P. B., Bugg, F., & West, J. A. (1993). Antisocial personality disorder. In P. B. Sutker & H. E. Adams (Eds.), *Comprehensive handbook of psychopathology* (2nd ed.). New York: Plenum.

Sutker, P. B., Galina, H., & West, J. A. (1990). Trauma-induced weight loss and cognitive deficits among former prisoners of war. *J. Cons. Clin. Psychol., 58,* 323–28.

Sutker, P. B., Uddo, M., Brailey, K., Vasterling, J. J., & Errera, P. (1994). Psychopathology in war-zone deployed and non-deployed Operation Desert Storm troops assigned to graves registration duties. *J. Abnorm. Psychol., 103,* 383–90.

Svanum, S., & Schladenhauffen, J. (1986). Lifetime and recent alcohol consumption among male alcoholics. *J. Nerv. Ment. Dis., 174*(4), 214–20.

Swadi, H., & Zeitlin, H. (1988). Peer influence and adolescent substance abuse: A promising side? *Brit. J. Addiction, 83*(2), 153–57.

Swain, R. A., Armstrong, K. E., Comery, T. A., Humphreys, A. G., Jones, T. A., Klein, J. A., & Greenough, W.T. (in press). Speculations on the fidelity of memories stored in synaptic connections. In D. Schactern, J. Coyle, L. Sullivan, M. Mesulam, & G. Fischbach (Eds.), *Memory distortions: Interdisciplinary perspective.* Cambridge: Harvard University Press.

Swanson, D. W., Bohnert, P. J., & Smith, J. A. (1970). *The paranoid.* Boston: Little, Brown.

Swedo, S. E., Pietrini, P., Leonard, H. L., Schapiro, M. B., Rettew, D. C., Goldberger, E., Rapoport, S., Rapoport, J., & Grady, C. (1992). Cerebral glucose metabolism in childhood-onset obsessive-compulsive disorder. *Arch. Gen. Psychiat., 49,* 690–4.

Swedo, S. E., Rapoport, J. L., Leonard, H., Lenane, M., & Cheslow, D. (1989). Obsessive-compulsive disorder in children and adolescents: Clinical phenomenology of 70 consecutive cases. *Arch. Gen. Psychiat., 46,* 335–41.

Sweeney, J. A., Clementz, B. A., Haas, G. L., Escobar, M. D., Drake, K., & Frances, A. J. (1994). Eye tracking dysfunction in schizophrenia: Characterization of component eye movement abnormalities, diagnostic specificity, and the role of attention. *J. Abnorm. Psychol., 103*(2), 222–30.

Sweeney, P. D., Anderson, K., & Bailey, S. (1986). Attributional style in depression: A meta-analytic review. *J. Pers. Soc. Psychol., 50,* 974–91.

Sweet, W. H. & Meyerson, B. A. (1990). Neurosurgical aspects of primary affective disorders. In J. R. Youmans (Ed.). *Neurological surgery* (pp. 335). Philadelphia: Saunders.

Swenson, C. C., Powell, P., Foster, K. Y. & Saylor, C. E. (1991). *The long-term reactions of young children to natural disaster.* Paper presented at the annual convention of the American Psychological Association, San Francisco.

Swenson, C. R., & Wood, M. J. (1990). Issues involved in combining drugs with psychotherapy for the borderline patient. *Psychiat. Clin. N. Amer. 13,* 297–306.

Symonds, M. (1976). The rape victim. Psychological patterns of response. *Amer. J. Psychoanal., 36*(1), 27–34.

Symons, D. (1979). *The evolution of human sexuality.* New York: Oxford University Press.

Szapocznik, J., Perez-Vidal, A., Brickman, A. L., Foote, F. H., Santisteban, D., Hervis, O., & Kurtines, W. M. (1988). Engaging adolescent drug abusers and their families in treatment: A strategic structural systems approach. *J. Cons. Clin. Psychol., 56,* 552–57.

Szasz, T. (1974). *The myth of mental illness* (rev. ed., pp. 17–80). New York: Harper & Row.

Szmukler, G. I., & Russell, G. F. M. (1986). Outcome and prognosis of anorexia nervosa. In K. D. Brownell & J. P. Foreyt (Eds.), *Handbook of eating disorders* (pp. 283–300). New York: Basic Books.

Tacke, U. (1990). Fluoxetine: An alternative to the tricyclics in the treatment of major depression. *Amer. J. Med. Sci., 298,* 126–29.

Takei, N., Sham, P., O'Callaghan, E., Murray, G. K., Glover, G., & Murray, R. M. (1994). Prenatal exposure to influenza and the development of schizophrenia: Is the effect confined to females? *Amer. J. Psychiat., 151*(1), 117–19.

Talamini, J. T. (1982). *Boys will be girls: The hidden world of the heterosexual male transvestite.* Washington, DC: University Press of America.

Talbott, J. A. (1985). Community care for the chronically mentally ill. *Psychiat. Clin. N. Amer., 8,* 437–48.

Talley, P. F., Strupp, H. H., & Morey, L. C. (1990). Matchmaking in psychotherapy: Patient-therapist dimensions and their impact on outcome. *J. Cons. Clin. Psychol., 58,* 182–88.

Tardiff, K., Marzuk, P. M., Leon, A. C., Hirsch, C. S., Stajic, M., Portera, L., & Hartwell, N. (1994). Homicide in New York City: Cocaine use and firearms. *JAMA, 272,* 43–46.

Tarjan, G., & Eisenberg, L. (1972). Some thought on the classification of mental retardation in the United States of America. *Amer. J. Psychiat., Suppl., 128*(11), 14–18.

Tarler-Beniolo, L. (1978). The role of relaxation in biofeedback training: A critical review of the literature. *Psychol. Bull., 85*(4), 727–55.

Tarrier, M., & Barrowclough, C. (1990) Family interventions for schizophrenia. *Behav. Mod., 14,* 408–40.

Tarter, R. E. (1988). Are there inherited behavioral traits that predispose to substance abuse? *J. Cons. Clin. Psychol., 56,* 189–196.

Tasto, D. L., & Hinkle, J. E. (1973). Muscle relaxation treatment for tension headaches. *Behav. Res. Ther., 11,* 347–50.

Tavel, M. E. (1962). A new look at an old syndrome: Delirium tremens. *Arch. Int. Med., 109,* 129–34.

Taves, I. (1969). Is there a sleepwalker in the house? *Today's Health, 47*(5), 41, 76.

Taylor, A. J. W. (1989). *Disasters and disaster stress.* New York: AMS Press.

Taylor, S. E., & Brown, J. (1988). Illusion and well-being: A social psychological perspective on mental health. *Psychol. Bull., 103,* 193–210.

Teasdale, J. D. (1988). Cognitive vulnerability to persistent depression. *Cognition and Emotion, 2,* 247–74.

Telch, M. J. (1981). The present status of outcome studies: A reply to Frank. *J. Cons. Clin. Psychol., 49*(3), 472–75.

Tellegen, A. (1985). Structures of mood and personality and their relevance to assessing anxiety, with an emphasis on self-report. In A. H. Tuma & J. Maser (Eds.), *Anxiety and the anxiety disorders*. Hillsdale, NJ: Erlbaum.

Tennen, H., & Affleck, G. (1987). The costs and benefits of optimistic explanations and dispositional optimism. *J. Pers., 55*, 377–93.

Teri, L., & Wagner, A. (1992). Alzheimer's disease and depression. *J. Cons. Clin. Psychol., 60*(3), 379–91.

Thacher, M. (1978, Apr.). First steps for the retarded. *Human Behav.*

Thackwray, D. E., Smith, M. C., Bodfish, J. W., & Meyers, A. W. (1993). A comparison of behavioral and cognitive-behavioral interventions for bulimia nervosa. *J. Cons. Clin. Psych., 61*(4), 639–45.

Thase, M. E., Frank, E., & Kupfer, D. J. (1985). Biological processes in major depression. In E. E. Beckham & W. R. Leber (Eds.), *Handbook of depression: Treatment, assessment, and research* (pp. 816–913). Homewood, IL: Dorsey Press.

Thase, M. E., Simons, A. D., Cahalane, J. F., & McGeary, J. (1991). Cognitive behavior therapy of endogenous depression: Part 1: An outpatient clinical replication series. *Behav. Ther., 22*, 457–68.

The Medical Letter. (1990). Sudden death in children treated with a tricyclic antidepressant. *Medical Letter Drug Therapy, 32*, 53.

Theodor, L. H., & Mandelcorn, M. S. (1973). Hysterical blindness: A case report and study using a modern psychophysical technique. *J. Abnorm. Psychol., 82*(3), 552–53.

Thibaut, J. W., & Kelley, H. H. (1959). *The social psychology of groups*. New York: Wiley.

Thompson-Pope, S. K., & Turkat, I. D. (1993). Schizotypal, schizoid, paranoid, and avoidant personality disorders. In P. B. Sutker & H. E. Adams (Eds.), *Comprehensive handbook of psychopathology* (2nd ed.). New York: Plenum.

Thoreson, C. E., & Powell, L. H. (1992). Type A behavior pattern: New perspectives on theory, assessment, and intervention. *J. Cons. Clin. Psychol., 60*(4), 595–604.

Tiefer, L., & Melman, A. (1989). Comprehensive evaluation of erectile dysfunction and medical treatments. In S. R. Leiblum & R. C. Rosen (Eds.), *Principles and practice of sex therapy* (2nd ed., pp. 207–36). New York: Guilford.

Tien, A. Y., & Anthony, J. C. (1990). Epidemiological analysis of alcohol and drug use as risk factors for psychotic experiences. *J. Nerv. Ment. Dis., 178*, 473–80.

Tien, A. Y., & Eaton, W. W. (1992). Psychopathologic precursors and sociodemographic risk factors for the schizophrenia syndrome. *Arch. Gen. Psychiat., 49*(1), 37–46.

Tienari, P. (1991). Interaction between genetic vulnerability and family environment: The Finnish adoptive family study of schizophrenia. *Acta Psychiatr. Scandin., 84*, 460–65.

Tienari, P., Lahti, I., Sorri, A., Naarala, M., Moring, J., Wahlberg, K.-E., & Wynne, L. C. (1987). The Finnish adoptive family study of schizophrenia. *J. Psychiat. Res., 21*, 437–45.

Tienari, P., Sorri, A., Lahti, I., Naarala, M., Wahlberg, K.-E., Pohjola, J., & Moring, J. (1985). Interaction of genetic and psychosocial factors in schizophrenia. *Acta Psychiatr. Scandin.* (Suppl. No. 319), *71*, 19–30.

Tillman, J. G., Nash, M. R., & Lerner, P. M. (1994). Does trauma cause dissociative pathology? In S. J. Lynn & J. W. Rhue (Eds.), *Dissociation: Clinical and theoretical perspectives* (pp. 395–414). New York: Guilford.

Timbrook, R. E, & Graham, J. R. (1994). Ethnic differences on the MMPI-2? *Psychol. Assess., 6*, 212–17.

Time. (1966, June 17). From shocks to stop sneezes, p. 72.

Time. (1974, Apr. 22). Alcoholism: New victims, new treatment, pp. 75–81.

Time. (1983, Apr. 18). Ailing schoolgirls, p. 52.

Tizard, J. (1975). Race and IQ: The limits of probability. *New Behaviour, 1*, 6–9.

Tizard, B. & Hodges, J. (1978). The effect of early institutional rearing on the development of eight-year-old children. *J. Child Psychol. Psychiat., 19*, 99–118.

Tobler, N. S. (1986). Meta-analysis of 143 adolescent drug prevention programs: Quantitative outcome results of program participation compared to a control or comparison group. *Journal of Drug Issues, 16*, 537–68.

Tollison, C. D., & Adams, H. E. (1979). *Sexual disorders*. New York: Gardner Press.

Tomarken, A. J., Mineka, S., & Cook, M. (1989). Fear-relevant selective associations and covariation bias. *J. Abnorm. Psychol., 98*, 381–94.

Tomarken, A. J., Simien, C., & Garber, J. (1994). Resting frontal brain asymmetry discriminates adolescent children of depressed mothers from low-risk controls. *Psychophysiology, 31*, 97–98.

Torgersen, S. (1983). Genetic factors in anxiety disorders. *Arch. Gen. Psychiat., 40*, 1085–1089.

Torgerson, S. (1984). Genetic and nosological aspects of schizotypal and borderline personality disorders. *Arch. Gen. Psychiat., 41*, 546–54.

Torgersen, S. (1993). Genetics. In A.S. Bellack & M. Hersen (Eds.), *Psychopathology in adulthood*. Needham Heights, MA: Allyn and Bacon.

Torrey, E. F. (1973). Is schizophrenia universal? An open question. *Schizo. Bull., 7*, 53–59.

Torrey, E. F. (1979). Epidemiology. In L. Bellak (Ed.), *Disorders of the schizophrenic syndrome*. New York: Basic Books.

Torrey, E. F. (1987). Prevalence studies in schizophrenia. *Brit. J. Psychiat., 150*, 598–608.

Torrey, E. F., Bower, A. E., Taylor, E. H., & Gottesman, I. I. (1994). *Schizophrenia and manic-depressive disorder: The biological roots of mental illness as revealed by the landmark study of identical twins*. New York: Basic Books.

Torrey, E. F., Bowler, A. E., Rawlings, R., & Terrazas, A. (1993). Seasonality of schizophrenia and stillbirths. *Schizo. Bull., 19*(3), 557–62.

Toth, S. L., Manly, J. T., & Cicchetti, D. (1992). Child maltreatment and vulnerability to depression. *Develop. Psychopath., 4*, 97–112.

Townsley, R. M. (1992). Social phobia: Identification of possible etiological factors. University of Georgia, unpublished doctoral dissertation.

Trasler, G. (1978). Relations between psychopathy and persistent criminality-methodological and theoretical issues. In R. D. Hare & D. Schalling (Eds.), *Psychopathic behavior: Approaches to research*. New York: Wiley.

Tremble, J., Padillo, A., & Bell, C. (1994). *Drug abuse among ethnic minorities, 1987:* Washington, DC: U.S. Department of Health and Human Services.

Trickett, P. K., & Putnam, F. W. (1993). Impact of child sexual abuse on females: Toward a developmental, psychobiological integration. *Psychological Science, 4*(2), 81–87.

Tripp, C. A. (1975). *The homosexual matrix*. New York: McGraw-Hill.

Tronick, E. Z., & Cohn, J. F. (1989). Infant-mother face-to-face interaction: Age and gender differences in coordination and miscoordination. *Child Develop., 59*, 85–92.

Trull, T. J., Widiger, T. A., & Frances, A. (1987). Covariation of criteria sets for avoidant, schizoid, and dependent personality disorders. *Amer. J. Psychiat., 144*, 767–71.

Tsai, L. Y., & Ghaziuddin, M. (1992). Biomedical research in autism. In D. M. Berkell (Ed.), *Autism* (pp. 53–76). Hillsdale: Erlbaum.

Tseng, W. S. (1973). The development of psychiatric concepts in traditional Chinese medicine. *Arch. Gen. Psychiat., 29*(4), 569–75.

Tseng, W., Asai, M., Kitanishi, K., McLaughlin, D. G., & Kyomen, H. (1992). Diagnostic patterns of social phobia: Comparison in Tokyo and Hawaii. *J. Nerv. Ment. Dis., 180*, 380–5.

Tuckman, J., Kleiner, R., & Lavell, M. (1959). Emotional content of suicide notes. *Amer. J. Psychiat. 116*, 59–63.

Tulving, E. (1993). What is episodic memory? *Curr. Dir. Psychol. Sci., 2*(3), 67–70.

Turk, D., Meichenbaum, D., & Genest, M. (1983). *Pain and behavioral medicine: A cognitive-behavioral perspective.* New York: Plenum.

Turkheimer, E. (1991). Individual and group differences in adoption studies of IQ. *Psychol. Bull., 110*(3), 392–405.

Turner, S. M., Beidel, D. C., & Costello, A. (1987). Psychopathology in the offspring of anxiety disorder patients. *J. Cons. Clin. Psychol., 55,* 229–35.

Turner, S. M., Beidel, D. C., & Townsley, R. M. (1992). Social phobia: A comparison of specific and generalized subtypes and avoidant personality disorder. *J. Abnorm. Psychol., 101,* 326–31.

Tyor, P. L., & Bell, L. V. (1984). *Caring for the retarded in America: A history.* Westport, CT: Greenwood Press.

Tyrer, P. (1988). What's wrong with DSM III personality disorders? *J. Personal. Dis., 2,* 281–91.

U.S. Bureau of the Census (1989). *Statistical abstract of the United States* (109th ed.), Washington DC: Author.

U.S. Department of Health and Human Services. (1988). *The health consequences of smoking: Nicotine addiction.* Public Health Service, Office on Smoking and Health, Maryland.

U.S. Department of Health and Human Services. (1989). *Reducing the consequences of smoking: 25 years of progress.* Public Health Service, Office on Smoking and Health, Maryland.

Uchida, I. A. (1973). Paternal origin of the extra chromosome in Down's syndrome. *Lancet, 2*(7840), 1258.

Udry, J. R. (1993). The politics of sex research. *J. Sex Res., 30,* 103–10.

Uhde, T. W. (1990). Caffeine provocation of panic: A focus on biological mechanisms. In J. C. Ballenger (Ed.), *Neurobiology of panic disorder* (pp. 219–242). New York: Wiley-Liss.

Uecker, A., Mangan, P. A., Obrzut, J. E., & Nadel, L. (1993). Down syndrome in neurobiological perspective: An emphasis on spatial cognition. *J. Clin. Child Psychol., 22*(2), 266–76.

Ullmann, L. P., & Krasner, L. (1975). *Psychological approach to abnormal behavior* (2nd ed.). Englewood Cliffs, NJ: Prentice-Hall.

Umana, R. F., Gross, S. J., & McConville, M. T. (1980). *Crisis in the family.* New York: Gardner Press.

Uniform Crime Reports, (1989). *Federal Bureau of Investigation.* Washington, DC: U.S. Government Printing Office.

Uniform Crime Reports. (1992). *Federal Bureau of Investigation.* Washington, DC: U.S. Government Printing Office.

United Press International. (1982, Oct. 24). "Tylenol hysteria" hits 200 at football game. *Chicago Tribune,* Sec. 1, p. 4.

Ursano, R. J., Boydstun, J. A., & Wheatley, R. D. (1981). Psychiatric illness in U.S. Air Force Vietnam prisoners of war: A five-year follow-up. *Amer. J. Psychiat., 138*(3), 310–14.

USDHHHS. (1981). Surgeon General's Advisory on alcohol and pregnancy. *FDA Drug Bulletin,* 11, 9–10.

USDHHS. (1994). Preventing tobacco use among young people: A report of the Surgeon General. *U.S. Department of Health and Human Services.*

Vaillant, G. E. (1975). Sociopathy as a human process: A viewpoint. *Arch. Gen. Psychiat., 32*(2), 178–83.

Vaillant, G. E. (1978). The distinction between prognosis and diagnosis in schizophrenia: A discussion of Manfred Bleuler's paper. In L. C. Wynne, R. L. Cromwell, & S. Matthysse (Eds.), *The nature of schizophrenia: New approaches to research and treatment* (pp. 637–40). New York: Wiley.

Vaillant, G. E. (1983). Natural history of male alcoholism V: Is alcoholism the cart or the horse to sociopathy? *Brit. J. Addict., 711,* 317–26.

Vaillant, G. E. (1987). A developmental view of old and new perspectives of personality disorders. *J. Personal. Dis., 1,* 146–56.

Vaillant, G. E., & Schnurr, P. (1988). What is a case? *Arch. Gen. Psychiat., 45,* 313–19.

Valenstein, E. S. (1986). *Great and desperate cures.* New York: Basic Books.

Valenstein, E. S. (Ed.) (1980). *The psychosurgery debate: Scientific, legal, and ethical perspectives.* San Francisco: Freeman.

Vallacher, R. R., Wegner, D. M., & Hoine, H. (1980). A postscript on application. In D. Megner & R. R. Vallacher (Eds.), *The self in social psychology.* New York: Oxford University Press.

Van Broeckhoven, C., Genthe, A. M., Vandenberghe, A., Horsthemke, B., et al. (1987). Failure of familial Alzheimer's disease to segregate with the A4-amyloid gene in several European families. *Nature, 329,* 153–55.

van den Boom, D.C. (1989). Neonatal irritability and the development of attachment. In G.A. Kohnstamm, J.E. Bates, & M.K. Rothbart (Eds.), *Temperament in childhood* (pp. 299–318). Chichester, England: Wiley.

van den Hout, M. A. (1988). The explanation of experimental panic. In S. Rachman, & J. D. Maser (Eds.), *Panic: Psychological perspectives.* Hillsdale, NJ: Erlbaum.

VandenBos, G. R. (1986). Psychotherapy research: A special issue. *Amer. Psychol., 41,* 111–12.

VandenBos, G. R. (1993). U. S. Mental Health Policy: Proactive evolution in the midst of health care reform. *Amer. Psychol., 48*(3), 283–90.

van der Kolk, B.A. (1987). *Psychological trauma.* Washington, DC: American Psychological Association Press.

Vandereycken, W. (1982). Paradoxical strategies in a blocked sex therapy. *Amer. J. Psychother., 36,* 103–8.

Vargas, M. A., & Davidson, J. R. (1993). Posttraumatic stress disorder. *Psychiat. Clin. N. Amer., 16,* 737–48.

Vasiljeva, O. A., Kornetov, N. A., Zhankov, A. I., & Reshetnikov, V. I. (1989). Immune function in psychogenic depression. *Amer. J. Psychiat., 146,* 284–85.

Vaughn, C. E., & Leff, J. P. (1976). The influence of family and social factors on the course of psychiatric illness: A comparison of schizophrenic and depressed neurotic patients. *Brit. J. Psychiat., 129,* 125–37.

Vaughn, C. E., Snyder, K. S., Jones, S., Freeman, W. B., & Fallon, I. R. H. (1984). Family factors in schizophrenic relapse: Replication in California of British research on expressed emotion. *Arch. Gen. Psychiat., 41,* 1169–77.

Vega, W. A., & Rumbaut, R. G. (1991). Reasons of the heart: Ethnic minorities and mental health. *Annual Review of Sociology, 17.*

Vega, W. A., Zimmerman, R. S., Warheit, G. J., Apospori, E., & Gil, A. G. (1993). Risk factors for early adolescent drug use in four ethnic and racial groups. *Amer. J. Pub. Hlth., 83,* 185–89.

Veith, I. (1977). Four thousand years of hysteria. In M. J. Horowitz (Ed.), *Hysterical personality* (pp. 7–93). New York: Jason Aronson.

Velez, C. N., & Cohen, P. (1987). Suicidal behavior and ideation in a community sample of children: Maternal and youth reports. *J. Amer. Acad. Child Adoles. Psychiat., 27,* 349–56.

Vellutino, F. R. (1987). Linguistic and cognitive correlates of learning disability: Review of three reviews. In S. J. Ceci (Ed.), *Handbook of cognitive, social and neuropsychological aspects of learning disabilities* (Vol. 1, pp. 317–35). Hillsdale, NJ: Erlbaum.

Verhulst, F. C., & Koot, H. M. (1992). *Child psychiatric epidemiology: Concepts, methods, and findings.* Beverly Hills, CA: Sage.

Verhulst, J. H., Van Der Lee, J. H., Akkerhuis, G. W., Sanders-Woudstra, J. A. R., Timmer, F. C., & Donkhorst, I. D. (1985). The prevalence of nocturnal enuresis: Do DSM-III criteria need to be changed? A brief research report. *J. Child Psychol. Psychiat., 26*(6), 983–93.

Viney, W., & Bartsch, K. (1984). Dorthea Lynde Dix: Positive or negative influence on the development of treatment for the mentally ill. *Social Science Journal, 21,* 71–82.

Vitousek, K. B., & Manke, F. (1994). Personality variables and disorders in anorexia and bulimia nervosa. *J. Abnorm. Psychol., 103*(1), 137–47.

Vogel, E. M., & Vogel, J. M. (1993). Interventions with children after disasters. *J. Clin. Child Psychol., 22,* 485–98.

Vogel, J. M., & Vernberg, E. M. (1993). Children's psychological responses to disaster. *J. Clin. Child Psychol., 22,* 485–98.

Volberg, R. A. (1990). Estimating the prevalence of pathological gambling in the United States. Paper presented at the Eighth International Conference on Risk and Gambling (August).

Volberg, R. A. (1994). The prevalence and demographics of pathological gamblers: Implications for public health. *Amer. J. Pub. Hlth., 84,* 237–41.

Volberg, R. A., & Steadman, H. J. (1989). Prevalence estimates of pathological gambling in New Jersey and Maryland. *Amer. J. Psychiat., 146,* 1618–19.

Volkmar, F. R., Hoder, E. L., & Cohen, D. J. (1985). Compliance, "negativism," and the effects of treatment structure in autism: A naturalistic behavioral study. *J. Child Psychol. Psychiat., 26*(6), 865–77.

Von Korff, M., Ormel, J., Katon, W., & Lin, E. H. B. (1992). Disability and depression among high utilizers of health care: A longitudinal analysis. *Arch. Gen. Psychiat., 49*(2), 91–100.

Vredenbrug, K., Flett, G. L., & Krames, L. (1993). Analogue versus clinical depression: A critical reappraisal. *Psychol. Bull., 113* (2), 327–44.

Wachtel, P. L. (1977). *Psychoanalysis and behavior therapy: Toward an integration.* New York: Basic Books.

Wachtel, P. L. (1982). What can dynamic therapies contribute to behavior therapy? *Behav. Ther., 13,* 594–609.

Wachtel, P. L. (1993). *Therapeutic communication: Principles and effective practice.* New York: Guilford.

Wadden, T. A., Foster, G. D., & Letizia, K. A. (1994). One-year behavioral treatment of obesity: Comparison of the moderate and severe caloric restriction and the effects of weight maintenance procedures. *J. Cons. Clin. Psychol., 62,* 165–71.

Wadden, T. A., Luborsky, L., Greer, S., & Crits-Christopher, P. (1985). The behavioral treatment of essential hypertension: An update and comparison with phanamacological treatment. *Clin. Psychol. Rev., 4,* 403–29.

Wagner, G. (1981). Methods for differential diagnosis of psychogenic and organic erectile failure. In G. Wagner & R. Green (Eds.), *Impotence: Physiological, psychological, surgical diagnosis and treatment.* New York: Plenum.

Wagner, G., & Green, R. (Eds.). (1981). *Impotence: Physiological, psychological, surgical diagnosis and treatment.* New York: Plenum.

Wahler, R. G. (1980). The insular mother: Her problems in parent-child treatment. *J. Appl. Beh. Anal., 13,* 207–19.

Wahler, R. G., Hughey, J. B., & Gordon, J. S. (1981). Chronic patterns of mother-child coercion: Some differences between insular and noninsular families. *Analysis and Intervention in Developmental Disorders, 1,* 145–56.

Wakefield, J. C. (1992a). Disorder as harmful dysfunction: A conceptual critique of DSM-III-R's definition of mental disorder. *Psychol. Rev, 99*(2), 232–247.

Wakefield, J. C. (1992b). The concept of mental disorder: On the boundary between biological facts and social values. *Amer. Psychol., 47*(3), 373–388.

Walker, E. F., Grimes, K. E., Davis, D. M., & Smith, A. J. (1993). Childhood precursors of schizophrenia: Facial expressions of emotion. *Amer. J. Psychiat., 150*(11), 1654–60.

Walker, E. F., Katon, W., Harrop-Griffiths, J., Holm, L., Russo, J., & Hickok, L. R. (1988). Relationship of chronic pelvic pain to psychiatric diagnoses and childhood sexual abuse. *Amer. J. Psychiat., 145,* 75–80.

Walker, E. F., Savoie, T., & Davis, D. (1994). Neuromotor precursors of schizophrenia. *Schizo. Bull., 20*(3), 441–51.

Waller, G. (1994). Childhood sexual abuse and borderline personality disorder in the eating disorders. *Child Ab. Negl., 18,* 97–101.

Wallerstein, J. S. (1991). The long-term effects of divorce on children: A review. *J. Amer. Acad. Child Adoles. Psychiat., 30,* 349–60.

Wallerstein, J. S., & Kelly, J. B. (1980). *Surviving the breakup: How children and parents cope with divorce.* New York: Basic Books.

Wallerstein, R. S. (1989). The psychotherapy research project of the Menninger Foundation: An overview. *J. Cons. Clin. Psychol., 57,* 195–205.

Wallin, A., & Blennow, K. (1993). Heterogeneity of vascular dementia: Mechanisms and subgroups. *Journal of Geriatric Psychiatry and Neurology, 6*(3), 177–88.

Walsh, D. (1969). Mental illness in Dublin: First admissions. *Brit. J. Psychiat., 115,* 449–56.

Walsh, D., O'Hare, A., Blake, B., Halpenny, J. V., & O'Brien, P. F. (1980). The treated prevalence of mental illness in the Republic of Ireland: The three county case register study. *Psychol. Med., 10,* 465–70.

Walsh, J. (1993). The promise and pitfalls of Integrated Strategy Instruction. *J. Learn. Dis., 26*(7), 438–42.

Walsh, T. B. (1980). The endocrinology of anorexia nervosa. *Psychiat. Clin. N. Amer., 3*(2), 299–312.

Walters, J. A., & Croen, L. G. (1993). An approach to meeting the needs of medical students with learning disabilities. *Teaching and Learning in Medicine, 5*(1), 29–35.

Ward, N. G. (1991). Psychosocial approaches to pharmacotherapy. In B.D. Beitman & G. Klerman (Eds.). *Integrating pharmacotherapy and psychotherapy* (pp. 69–104). Washington, DC: American Psychiatric Press.

Warnes, H. (1973). The traumatic syndrome. *Ment. Hlth. Dig., 5*(3), 33–34.

Warrington, E. K., & Weiskrantz, L. (1973). An analysis of short-term and long-term memory defects in man. In J. A. Deutsch (Ed.), *The psychological basis of memory.* New York: Academic Press.

Wasserman, D. R., & Leventhal, J. M. (1993). Maltreatment of children born to cocaine-dependent mothers. *Archives of Pediatrics and Adolescent Medicine, 147,* 1324–28.

Watanabe, H., Kawauchi, A., Kitamori, T., & Azuma, Y. (1994). Treatment system for nocturnal enuresis according to an original classification system. *European Urology, 25,* 43–50.

Watkins, B., & Bentovim, A. (1992). The sexual abuse of male children and adolescents: A review of current research. *J. Child Psychol. Psychiat., 33,* 197–248.

Watson, D., & Pennebaker, J. W. (1989). Health complaints, stress, and distress: Exploring the central role of negative affectivity. *Psychol. Rev., 96*(2), 234–54.

Watson, D., Clark, L.A., Harkness, A.R. (1994). Structures of personality and their relevance to psychopathology. *J. Abnorm. Psychol., 103,* 18–31.

Watson, D., Clark, L. A., Weber, K., Assenheimer, J. S., Strauss, M. E., & McCormick, R. A. (1995a). Testing a tripartite model: I. Evaluating the convergent and discriminant validity of anxiety and depression symptom scales. *J. Abnorm. Psychol., 104,* 3–14.

Watson, D., Clark, L. A., Weber, K., Assenheimer, J. S., Strauss, M. E., & McCormick, R. A. (1995b). Testing a tripartite model: II. Exploring the symptom structure of anxiety and depression in student, adult, and patient samples. *J. Abnorm. Psychol., 104,* 15–25.

Watson, J. (1924). *Behaviorism.* The People's Institute Publishing Co., Inc.

Watt, N. F., Anthony, E. J., Wynne, L. C., & Rolf, J. E. (Eds.). (1984). *Children at risk for schizophrenia: A longitudinal perspective.* Cambridge: Cambridge University Press.

Weary, G., & Mirels, H. L. (1982). *Integrations of clinical and social psychology.* New York: Oxford University Press.

Weatherby, N. L., Shultz, J. M., Chitwood, D. D., & McCoy, H. V. (1992). Crack cocaine use and sexual activity in Miami, Florida. *J. Psychoact. Drugs, 24,* 373–80.

Webster-Stratton, C. (1991). Annotation: Strategies for helping families with conduct disordered children. *J. Child Psychol. Psychiat., 32,* 1047–62.

Wechsler, D. (1981). *Manual for the Wechsler Adult Intelligence Scale*. New York: Psychological Corporation.

Weddington, W. W. (1993). Cocaine: Diagnosis and treatment. *Psychiat. Clin. N. Amer., 16,* 87–95.

Weekes, J. R., Lynn, S. J., Green, J. P., & Brentar, J. T. (1992). Pseudomemory in hypnotized and task-motivated subjects. *J. Abnorm. Psychol., 101*(2), 356–60.

Wegner, D. M. (1989). *White bears and other unwanted thoughts*. New York: Viking.

Wegner, D. M., Schneider, D. J., Carter, S. R., & White, T. L. (1987). Paradoxical effects of thought suppression. *J. Pers. Soc. Psychol., 53*(1), 5–13.

Wehr, T. A., & Goodwin, F. K. (1987). Can antidepressants cause mania and worsen the course of affective illness? *Amer. J. Psychiat., 144,* 1403–11.

Wehr, T. A., Jacobsen, F. M., Sack, D. A., Arendt, J., Tamarkin, L., & Rosenthal, N. E. (1986). Phototherapy of seasonal affective disorder. *Arch. Gen. Psychiat., 43,* 870–75.

Weinberg, M. S., Williams, C. J., & Pryor, D. W. (1994). *Dual Attraction*. New York: Oxford University Press.

Weinberger, D. R. (1984). Brain disease and psychiatric illness: When should a psychiatrist order a CAT scan? *Amer. J. Psychiat., 141,* 1521–27.

Weinberger, D. R., DeLisi, L. E., Perman, G. P., Targum, S., & Wyatt, R. J. (1982). Computed tomography in schizophreniform disorder and other acute psychiatric disorders. *Arch. Gen. Psychiat., 39,* 778–83.

Weiner, H. (1977). *Psychobiology and human disease*. New York: Elsevier.

Weiner, H., & Fawzy, F. I. (1989). An integrative model of health, disease, and illness. In S. Cheren (Ed.), *Psychosomatic medicine: Theory, physiology, and practice* (Vol. 1, pp. 9–44). Madison, CT: International Universities Press.

Weiner, R. D., & Krystal, A. D. (1994). The present use of electroconvulsive therapy. *Annu. Rev. Med., 45,* 273–81.

Weinstein, A. S. (1983). The mythical readmissions explosion. *Amer. J. Psychiat., 140*(3), 332–35.

Weisenberg, M. (1977). Pain and pain control. *Psychol. Bull., 84,* 1008–44.

Weisman, A., Lopez, S. R., Karno, M., & Jenkins, J. (1993). An attributional analysis of expressed emotion in Mexican-American families with schizophrenia. *J. Abnorm. Psychol., 102*(4), 601–6.

Weiss, B., Weisz, J. R., & Bromfield, R. (1986). Performance of retarded and nonretarded persons on information-processing tasks: Further tests of the similar structure hypothesis. *Psychol. Bull., 100,* 157–75.

Weiss, G., & Hechtman, L. (1979). The hyperactive child syndrome. *Science, 205,* 1348–54.

Weiss, G., Hechtman, L., Perlman, T., Hopkins, J., & Wener, A. (1979). Hyperactives as young adults: A controlled prospective ten-year follow-up of 75 children. *Arch. Gen. Psychiat., 36,* 675–81.

Weiss, J. M. (1984). Behavioral and psychological influences on gastrointestinal pathology: Experimental techniques and findings. In W. D. Gentry (Ed.), *Handbook of behavioral medicine* (pp. 174–221). New York: Guilford.

Weiss, S. M., Herd, J. A., & Fox, B. H. (1981). *Perspectives on behavioral medicine*. New York: Academic Press.

Weiss, T., & Engel, B. T. (1971). Operant conditioning of heart rate in patients with premature ventricular contractions. *Psychosom. Med., 33,* 301–21.

Weisse, C. S. (1992). Depression and immunocompetence: A review of the literature. *Psychol. Bull., 111*(3), 475–89.

Weissman, M. M. (1990). Evidence for comorbidity of anxiety and depression: Family and genetic studies of children. In J. D. Maser & C. R. Cloninger (Eds.), *Comorbidity of mood and anxiety disorders*. Washington, DC: American Psychiatric Press.

Weissman, M. M. (1993). The epidemiology of personality disorders: A 1990 update. *J. Personal. Dis., Supplement,* 44–62.

Weissman, M. M., Fendrich, M., Warner, V., & Wickramaratne, P. (1992). Incidence of psychiatric disorder in offspring at high and low risk for depression. *J. Amer. Acad. Child Adoles. Psychiat., 31,* 640–48.

Weissman, M. M., Gammon, D., John, K., Merikangas, K. R., Warner, V., Prusoff, B. A., & Sholomskas, D. (1987). Children of depressed parents. *Arch. Gen. Psychiat., 44,* 847–53.

Weissman, M. M., Klerman, G. L., Markowitz, J. S., & Ouellette, R. (1989). Suicidal ideation and suicide attempts in panic disorder and attacks. *New Eng. J. Med., 321*(18), 1209–14.

Weissman, M. M., Leaf, P. J., Blazer, D. G., Boyd, J. H., & Florio, L. (1986). The relationship between panic disorder and agoraphobia: An epidemiologic perspective. *Psychopharm. Bull., 43,* 787–91.

Weissman, M. M., Pottenger, M., Kleber, H., Ruben, H. L., Williams, D., & Thompson, D. (1977). Symptom pattern in primary and secondary depression. *Arch. Gen. Psychiat., 34,* 854–62.

Weisz, J.R., Suwanlert, S., Chaiyasit, W., & Walter, B.R. (1987). Over and undercontrolled clinic-referral problems among Thai and American children and adolescents: The wat and wai of cultural differences. *J. Cons. Clin. Psychol., 55,* 719–726.

Weisz, J.R., Suevanlert, S., Chaiyasit, W., Weiss, B., Achenbach, T.M., & Eastman, K.L. (1993). Behavior and emotional problems among Thai and American adolescents: Parent reports for ages 12-16. *J. Abnorm. Psychol., 102,* 395–403.

Weisz, J. R., Weiss, B., Alicke, M. D., & Klotz, M. L. (1987). Effectiveness of psychotherapy with children and adolescents: A meta-analysis for clinicians. *J. Cons. Clin. Psychol., 55,* 542–49.

Weisz, J. R., Weiss, B., & Donenberg, G. R. (1992). The lab versus the clinic: Effects of child and adolescent psychotherapy. *Amer. Psychol., 47,* 1578–85.

Weizman, A., Zohar, J., & Insel, T. (1991). Biological markers in obsessive-compulsive disorder. In J. Zohar, T. Insel, & S. Rasmussen (Eds.), *The psychobiology of obsessive-compulsive disorder*. New York: Springer.

Weizman, R., Laor, N., Barber, Y., Selman, A., Schujovizky, A., Wolmer, L., Laron, Z., & Gil-Ad, I. (1994). Impact of the Gulf war on the anxiety, cortisol, and growth hormone levels of Israeli civilians. *Amer. J. Psychiat., 151,* 71–75.

Wekstein, L. (1979). *Handbook of suicidology: Principles, problems, and practice*. New York: Brunner/Mazel.

Welch, S. L., & Fairburn, C. G. (1994). Sexual abuse and bulimia nervosa: Three integrated case control comparisons. *Amer. J. Psychiat., 151*(3), 402–7.

Wenar, C. (1990). *Developmental psychopathology: From infancy through adolescence* (2nd ed.). New York: McGraw-Hill.

Wender, P. H., Kety, S. S., Rosenthal, D., Schulsinger, F., Ortmann, J. & Lunde, I. (1986). Psychiatric disorders in the biological and adoptive families of adopted individuals with affective disorders. *Arch. Gen. Psychiat., 43,* 923–29.

Wender, P. H., Reimherr, F. W., & Wood, D. R. (1981). Attention deficit disorder (minimal brain dysfunction) in adults. *Arch. Gen. Psychiat., 38,* 449–56.

Wender, P. H., Rosenthal, D., Kety, S. S., Schulsinger, F., & Weiner, J. (1974). Cross-fostering: A research strategy for clarifying the role of genetic and experimental factors in the etiology of schizophrenia. *Arch. Gen. Psychiat., 30*(1), 121–28.

Wennerholm, M., & Lopez-Roig, L. (1983). *Use of the MMPI with executives in Puerto Rico*. Paper given at the Eighth Annual Conference on Personality Assessment, Copenhagen, Denmark.

Wenzlaff, R. M., Wegner, D. M., & Klein, S. B. (1991). The role of thought suppression in the bonding of thought and mood. *J. Pers. Soc. Psychol., 60*(4), 500–8.

Werner, E.E., & Smith, R.S. (1982). *Vulnerable but invincible: A study of resilient children*. New York: McGraw-Hill.

Werry, J. S. (1979). The childhood psychosis. In H. C. Quay & J. S. Werry (Eds.), *Psychopathological disorders of childhood*. New York: Wiley.

Wester, P., Eriksson, S., Forsell, A., Puu, G., & Adolfsson, R. (1988). Monoamine metabolite concentrations and cholinesterase activities in cerebrospinal fluid of progressive dementia patients: Relation to clinical parameters. *Acta Neurol. Scandin., 77*, 12–21.

Westermeyer, J. (1982a). Bag ladies in isolated cultures, too. *Behav. Today, 13*(21), 1–2.

Westermeyer, J. (1982b). *Poppies, pipes and people: Opium and its use in Laos.* Berkeley, CA: University of California Press.

Westermeyer, J., (1987). Public health and chronic mental illness. *Amer. J. Pub. Hlth., 77*(6), 667–68.

Westermeyer, J., Neider, J., & Callies, A. (1989). Psychosocial adjustment of Hmong refugees during their first decade in the United States. A longitudinal study. *J. Nerv. Ment. Dis., 177*, 132–39.

Westermeyer, J., Williams, C. L., & Nguyen, N. (Eds.). (1991). *Mental health and social adjustment: A guide to clinical and prevention services.* Washington, DC: U.S. Government Printing Office.

Wetherby, A. M., & Prizant, B. M. (1992). Facilitating language and communication development in autism: Assessment and intervention guidelines. In D. E. Berkell (Ed.), *Autism* (pp. 107–34). Hillsdale, NJ: Erlbaum.

Wethington, E., Brown, G. W., & Kessler, R. C. (1994). Interview measurement of stressful life events. In S. Cohen, R. Kessler & L. Underwood-Gordon (Eds.), *Measuring stress.* New York: Oxford University Press.

Whalen, C. K., Henker, B., Buhrmester, D., Hinshaw, S. P., Huber, A., & Laski, K. (1989). Does stimulant medication improve the peer status of hyperactive children? *J. Cons. Clin. Psychol., 57*, 545–49.

Whiffen, V. E. (1992). Is postpartum depression a distinct diagnosis? *Clin. Psychol. Rev., 12*, 485–508.

Whiffen, V. E., & Gotlib, I. H. (1989). Infants of postpartum depressed mothers: Temperament and cognitive status. *J. Abnorm. Psychol., 98*, 274–79.

Whitaker, L. C. (1992). *Schizophrenic disorders: Sense and nonsense in conceptualization, assessment, and treatment.* New York: Plenum.

White, A. D. (1896). *A history of the warfare of science with theology in Christendom.* New York: Appleton.

White, J., Moffitt, T. E., & Silva, P. A. (1989). A prospective replication of the protective effects of IQ in subjects at high risk for juvenile delinquency. *J. Cons. Clin. Psychol., 57*, 719–24.

Whitehouse, P. J. (1993). Cholinergic therapy in dementia. *Acta Neurol. Scandin., 88* (Suppl. 149), 42–45.

Whitehouse, P. J., et al. (1982). Alzheimer's disease and senile dementia: Loss of neurons in the basal forebrain. *Science, 215*, 1237–39.

Whitman, B. Y., & Munkel, W. (1991). Multiple personality disorder: A risk indicator, diagnostic marker and psychiatric outcome for severe child abuse. *Clin. Pediat., 30*, 422–28.

Wickizer, T., Maynard, C., Atherly, A., Frederick, M., Koepsell, T., Krupski, A., & Stark, K. (1994). Completion rates of clients discharged from drug and alcohol treatment programs in Washington State. *Amer. J. Pub. Hlth., 84*, 215–21.

Widiger, T. A. (1992). Categorical versus dimensional classification: Implications from and for research. *J. Personal. Dis., 6*, 287–300.

Widiger, T. A. (1993). The DSM-III-R categorical personality disorder diagnoses: A critique and alternative. *Psychol. Inq., 4*, 75–90.

Widiger, T. A., & Chat, L. (1994). The DSM-IV personality disorders: Changes from DSM-III-R. In P. Wilner (Ed.), *Psychiatry* (Chap. 14.2, pp. 1–13). B. Lippincott: Phildelphia.

Widiger, T. A., & Corbitt, E.M. (1993). Antisocial personality disorder: Proposals for DSM-IV. *J. Personal. Dis., 7*, 63–77.

Widiger, T. A., & Costa, P. T. (1994). Personality and personality disorders. *J. Abnorm. Psychol., 103*, 78–91.

Widiger, T. A., & Frances, A. (1985). Axis II personality disorders: Diagnostic and treatment issues. *Hosp. Comm. Psychiat., 36*, 619–27.

Widiger, T. A., & Rogers, J. (1989). Prevalence and comorbidity of personality disorders. *Psychiat. Ann., 19*, 132–36.

Widiger, T. A., & Trull, T. J. (1993) Borderline and narcissistic personality disorders. In P. B. Sutker & H. E. Adams (Eds.), *Comprehensive handbook of psychopathology* (2nd ed.). New York: Plenum.

Widiger, T. A., Frances, A. J., Pincus, H. A., Davis, W. W., & First, M. B. (1991). Toward an empirical classification for the DSM-IV. *J. Abnorm. Psychol., 100* (3), 280–88.

Widiger, T. A., Frances, A., & Trull, T. J. (1987). A psychometric analysis of social-interpersonal and cognitive-perceptual items for the schizotypal personality disorder. *Arch. Gen. Psychiat., 44*, 741–45.

Widiger, T. A., Frances, A., Warner, L., & Bloom, C. (1986). Diagnostic criteria for the borderline and schizotypal personality disorders. *J. Abnorm. Psychol., 95*(1), 43–51.

Widom, C. S. (1977). A methodology for studying noninstitutionalized psychopaths. *J. Cons. Clin. Psychol., 45*, 674–83.

Widom, C.S. (1989). Does violence beget violence? A critical examination of the literature. *Psychol. Bull., 106*, 3–28.

Wiggins, J. S. (1982). Circumplex models of interpersonal behavior in clinical psychology. In P. C. Kendall & J. N. Butcher (Eds.), *Handbook of research methods in clinical psychology.* New York: Wiley Interscience.

Wilbur, R. S. (1973, June 2). In S. Auerbach (Ed.), POWs found to be much sicker than they looked upon release. *Los Angeles Times,* Part I, p. 4.

Wilcox, B. L. & Naimark, H. (1991). The rights of the child: Progress toward human dignity. *Amer. Psychol., 46*, 49–52.

Wilczenski, F. L. (1993). Comparison of academic performances, graduation rates, and timing of drop out for LD and nonLD college students. *Coll. Stud. J., 27*(2), 184–94.

Wilfley, D. E., Agras, W. S., Telch, C. F., Rossiter, E. M., Schneider, J. A., Cole, A. G., Sifford, L., & Raeburn, S. D. (1993). Group cognitive-behavioral and group interpersonal psychotherapy for the nonpurging bulimic individual: A controlled comparison. *J. Cons. Clin. Psychol., 61*(2), 296–305.

Williams, C. L., Perry, C. L., Dudovitz, B., Veblen-Mortenson, S., Anstine, P. S., Komro, K. A., & Toomey, T. L. (1995). A home-based prevention program for sixth grade alcohol use: Results from Project Northlands. *J. Prim. Preven, 16*, 125–147.

Williams, C. L., Solomon, S. D., & Bartone, P. (1988). Primary prevention in aircraft disasters: Integrating research and practice. *Amer. Psychol., 43*, 724–39.

Williams, J. A., Koegel, R. L., & Egel, A. L. (1981). Response-reinforcer relationships and improved learning in autistic children. *J. Appl. Beh. Anal., 14*(1), 53–60.

Williams, L. M., & Finkelhor, D., (1990). The characteristics of incestuous fathers: A review of recent studies. In W. L. Marshall, D. R. Laws, & H. E. Barbaree (Eds.), *Handbook of sexual assault* (pp. 231–56). New York: Plenum.

Williams, R. B., Jr. (1977). Headache. In R. B. Williams, Jr., & W. D. Gentry (Eds.), *Behavioral approaches to medical treatment* (pp. 41–53). Cambridge, MA: Ballinger.

Williams, R. B., Jr., & Gentry, W. D. (Eds.). (1977). *Behavioral approaches to medical treatment.* Cambridge, MA: Ballinger.

Williams, R. B., Jr., Barefoot, J. C., & Shekelle, R. B. (1985). The health consequences of hostility. In M. A. Chesney, S. E. Goldston, & R. H. Rosenman, (Eds.), *Anger, hostility, and behavioral medicine* (pp. 173–85). New York: Hemisphere/McGraw-Hill.

Williams, R. B., Jr., Haney, T. L., Lee, K. L., Kong, V., & Blumenthal, J. A. (1980). Type A behavior, hostility, and coronary atherosclerosis. *Psychosom. Med., 42*, 529–38.

Williams, S. L., & Zane, G. (1989). Guided mastery and stimulus exposure treatments for severe performance anxiety in agoraphobics. *Behav. Res. Ther., 27*, 237–45.

Williams, S. L., Turner, S. M., & Peer, D. F. (1985). Guided mastery and performance desensitization treatments for severe acrophobia. *J. Cons. Clin. Psychol., 53*, 237–47.

Wilson, G. T., & Fairburn, C. G. (1993). Cognitive treatments for eating disorders. *J. Cons. Clin. Psychol., 61*(2), 261–69.

Wilson, M. (1993). DSM-III and the transformation of American psychiatry: A history. *Amer. J. of Psychiat., 150,* 399–410.

Wincze, J. P., & Carey, M. P. (1991). *Sexual dysfunction: A guide for assessment and treatment.* New York: Guilford.

Wing, L. (1980). Childhood autism and social class: A question of selection. *Brit. J. Psychiat., 137,* 410–17.

Wing, L. K. (1976). Diagnosis, clinical description and prognosis. In L. Wing (Ed.), *Early childhood autism.* London: Pergamon.

Wing, S., & Manton, K. G. (1983). The contribution of hypertension to mortality in the U.S.: 1968, 1977. *Amer. J. Pub. Hlth., 73*(2), 140–44.

Winick, M. (Ed.). (1976). *Malnutrition and brain development.* New York: Oxford University Press.

Winokur, G. (1985). The validity of neurotic-reactive depression: New data and reappraisal. *Arch. Gen. Psychiat., 42,* 1116–22.

Winslow, J. T., & Insel, T. R. (1991). Neuroethological models of obsessive-compulsive disorder. In J. Zohar, T. Insel, & S. Rasmussen (Eds.), *The psychobiology of obsessive-compulsive disorder.* New York: Springer.

Winston, A., Laikin, M., Pollack, J., Samstag, L.W., McCullough, L., & Muran, C. (1994). Short-term psychotherapy of personality disorders. *Amer. J. Psychiat., 151,* 190–94.

Winters, K. C., & Neale, J. M. (1985). Mania and low self-esteem. *J. Abnorm. Psychol., 94,* 282–90.

Wolf, A. P. (1970). Childhood association and sexual attraction: A further test of the Westermarck hypothesis. *American Anthropologist, 72,* 503–15.

Wolf, M., Risley, T., & Mees, H. (1964). Application of operant conditioning procedures to the behavior problems of an autistic child. *Behav. Res. Ther., 1,* 305–12.

Wolf, S. L., Nacht, M., & Kelly, J. L. (1982). EMG feedback training during dynamic movement for low back pain patients. *Behav. Ther., 13,* 395–406.

Wolfe, B. E., & Maser, J. D. (1994). Treatment of panic disorder: Consensus statement. In B. E. Wolfe & J. D. Maser (Eds.), *Treatment of panic disorder. A consensus development conference* (pp. 237–255). Washington, DC: American Psychiatric Press.

Wolfe, D. A., & Wekerle, C. (1993). Treatment strategies for child physical abuse and neglect: A critical progress report. *Clin. Psychol. Rev., 13,* 473–500.

Wolfe, D. A., Edwards, B., Manion, I., & Koverola, C. (1988). Early intervention for parents at risk of child abuse and neglect: A preliminary investigation. *J. Cons. Clin. Psychol., 56,* 34–39.

Wolfe, V. V., Gentile, C., & Wolfe, D. A. (1989). The impact of sexual abuse on children: A PTSD formulation. *Behav. Ther., 20,* 215–28.

Wolff, H. G. (1950). Life stress and cardiovascular disorders. *Circulation, 1,* 187–203.

Wolff, H. G. (1960). Stressors as a cause of disease in man. In J. M. Tanner (Ed.), *Stress and psychiatric disorder.* London: Oxford University Press.

Wolff, P. H. (1972). Ethnic differences in alcohol sensitivity. *Science, 175,* 449–50.

Wolff, W. M., & Morris, L. A. (1971). Intellectual personality characteristics of parents of autistic children. *J. Abnorm. Psychol., 77*(2), 155–61.

Wolkin, A., Sanfilipo, M., Wolf, A. P., Angrist, B., Brodie, J. D., & Rotrosen, J. (1992). Negative symptoms and hypofrontality in chronic schizophrenia. *Arch. Gen. Psychiat., 49*(12), 959–65.

Wolpe, J. (1958). *Psychotherapy by reciprocal inhibition.* Stanford, CA: Stanford University Press.

Wolpe, J. (1969a). For phobia: A hair of the hound. *Psych. Today, 3*(1), 34–37.

Wolpe, J. (1969b). *The practice of behavior therapy.* New York: Pergamon.

Wolpe, J. (1988). *Life without fear: Anxiety and its cure.* Oakland, CA: New Harbinger Publications, Inc.

Wolpe, J. & Rachman, S. J. (1960). Psychoanalytic evidence: A critique based on Freud's case of Little Hans. *J. Nerv. Ment. Dis., 131,* 135–45.

Wood, C. (1986). The hostile heart. *Psych. Today, 20,* 10–12.

Wood, J. M., Bootzin, R. R., Rosenhan, D., Nolen-Hocksema, S., & Jourden, F. (1992). Effects of the 1989 San Francisco earthquake on frequency and content of nightmares. *J. Abnorm. Psychol., 101,* 219–24.

Woods, B. T., Kinney, D. K., & Yurgelun-Todd, D. (1986). Neurologic abnormalities in schizophrenic patients and their families: I. Comparison of schizophrenic, bipolar, and substance abuse patients and normal controls. *Arch. Gen. Psychiat., 43,* 657–63.

Woods, S. W., Charney, D. S., Goodman, W. K., & Heninger, G. R. (1987). Carbon dioxide-induced anxiety: Behavioral, physiologic, and biochemical effects of 5% CO2 in panic disorder patients and 5 and 7.5% CO2 in healthy subjects. *Arch. Gen. Psychiat., 44,* 365–75.

Woodworth, R. S. (1920). *The personal data sheet.* Chicago: Stoelting Press.

Woody, G. E., Luborsky, L., McLellan, L., O'Brien, C. P., Beck, A. T., Blaine, J., Herman, I., & Hole, A. (1983). Psychotherapy for opiate addicts: Does it help? *Arch. Gen. Psychiat., 40,* 639–45.

Woody, G. E., McLellan, A. T., Luborsky, L., & O'Brien, C. P. (1985). Sociopathy and psychotherapy outcome. *Arch. Gen. Psychiat., 42,* 1081–86.

Woody, G. E., McLellan, A. T., Luborsky, L., & O'Brien, C. P. (1987). Twelve month follow-up of psychotherapy for opiate dependence. *Amer. J. Psychiat., 144,* 590–96.

Worden, P. E. (1986). Prose comprehension and recall in disabled learners. In S. J. Ceci (Ed.), *Handbook of cognitive, social and neuropsychological aspects of learning disabilities* (Vol. 1, pp. 241-62). Hillsdale, NJ: Erlbaum.

Workman, E. A., & La Via, M. F. (1987). T-lymphocyte polyclonal proliferation: Effects of stress and stress response style on medical students taking national board examinations. *Clinical Immunology and Immunopathology, 43,* 308–13.

World Health Organization. (1978a, Apr.). *Report of the director-general.* Geneva: Author.

World Health Organization. (1978b). *Mental disorders: Glossary and guide to their classification in accordance with the ninth revision of the International Classification of Diseases.* Geneva: Author.

World Health Organization. (1989). *Lexicon of psychiatric and mental health terms.* Geneva: Author.

World Health Organization. (1992). *ICD-10 classification of mental and behavioral disorders: Clinical descriptions and diagnostic guidelines.* Geneva: Author.

World Health Organization. (1993). *A lexicon of alcohol and drug terms.* Geneva: Author.

Worthington, E. R. (1978). Demographic and pre-service variables as predictors of post-military adjustment. In C. R. Figley (Ed.), *Stress disorders among Vietnam veterans.* New York: Brunner/Mazel.

Wortman, C. B., & Silver, R. C. (1989). The myths of coping with loss. *J. Cons. Clin. Psychol., 57,* 349–57.

Wright, L. (1994). *Remembering Satan.* New York: Knopf.

Wynne, L. C., Toohey, M. L., & Doane, J. (1979). Family studies. In L. Bellak (Ed.), *The schizophrenic syndrome.* New York: Basic Books.

Yablonsky, L. (1975). Psychodrama lives. *Human Behav., 4,* 24–29.

Yager, J., Grant, I., & Bolus, R. (1984). Interaction of life events and symptoms in psychiatric patient and nonpatient married couples. *J. Nerv. Ment. Dis., 171*(1), 21–25.

Yanok, J. (1993). College students with learning disabilities enrolled in developmental education programs. *Coll. Stud. J., 27*(2), 166–74.

Yap, P. M. (1951). Mental diseases peculiar to certain cultures: A survey of comparative psychiatry. *J. Ment. Sci., 97*(3), 313.

Yapko, M. D. (1994). *Suggestions of abuse: True and false memories of childhood sexual trauma.* New York: Simon & Schuster.

Young, M. A., Fogg, L. F., Scheftner, W. A., Keller, M. B., & Fawcett, J. A. (1990). Sex differences in the lifetime prevalence of depression: Does varying the diagnostic criteria reduce the female/male ratio? *J. Affect. Dis., 18,* 187–92.

Youth Suicide in the United States, 1970–1980. (1986). Atlanta, GA: Centers for Disease Control.

Yule, W., & Rutter, M. (1985). Reading and other learning difficulties. In M. Rutter & L. Hersov (Eds.), *Child and adolescent psychiatry: Modern approaches* (2nd ed., pp. 444–64). Oxford, UK: Blackwell.

Zakowski, S., Hall, M. H., & Baum, A. (1992). Stress, stress management, and the immune system. *Applied & Preventive Psychology, 1,* 1–13.

Zanarini, M. C., Gunderson, J. G., Marino, M. F., Schwartz, E. O., & Frankenburg, F. R. (1989). Childhood experiences of borderline patients. *Comp. Psychiat., 30,* 18–25.

Zasler, N. D. (1993). Mild traumatic brain injury: Medical assessment and intervention. *J. Head Trauma Rehab., 8*(3), 13-29.

Zborowski, M. J., & Garske, J. P. (1993). Interpersonal deviance and consequent social impact in hypothetically schizophrenia-prone men. *J. Abnorm. Psychol., 102*(3), 482–89.

Zeidner, M. (1993). Coping with disaster: The case of Israeli adolescents under threat of missile attack. *Journal of Youth and Adolescence, 22,* 89–108.

Zeitlin, H. (1986). *The natural history of psychiatric disorder in childhood.* New York: Oxford University Press.

Zelikovsky, N., & Lynn, S. J. (1994). The aftereffects and assessment of physical and psychological abuse. In S. J. Lynn & J. W. Rhue (Eds.), *Dissociation: Clinical and theoretical perspectives* (pp. 190–214). New York: Guilford.

Zetlin, A., & Murtaugh, M. (1990). Whatever happened to those with borderline IQs? *Amer. J. Ment. Retard., 94,* 463–69.

Zheng, Y. P., & Lin, K. M. (1994). A nationwide study of stressful life events in Mainland China. *Psychosom. Med., 56,* 296–305.

Zigler, E., & Muenchow, S. (1992). *Head Start: The inside story of America's most successful educational experiment.* New York: Basic Books.

Zigler, E., & Styfco, S. J. (1994). Head Start: Criticisms in a constructive context. *Amer. Psychol., 49*(2), 127–32.

Zigler, E., Abelson, W. D., Trickett, P. K., & Seitz, V. (1982). Is an intervention program necessary in order to improve economically disadvantaged children's IQ scores? *Child Develop., 53,* 340–48.

Zilbergeld, B., & Evans, M. (1980, Jan.). The inadequacy of Masters and Johnson. *Psych. Today,* 29–43.

Zilbergeld, B., & Kilmann, P. R. (1984). The scope and effectiveness of sex therapy. *Psychotherapy, 21,* 319–26.

Zilboorg, G., & Henry, G. W. (1941). *A history of medical psychology.* New York: Norton.

Zill, N., & Schoenborn, G. A. (1990). Developmental, learning, and emotional problems: Health of our nation's children. *Advance data: National Center for Health Statistics* (Number 190).

Zimmerman, M. (1983). Methodological issues in the assessment of life events: A review of issues and research. *Clin. Psychol. Rev., 3,* 339–70.

Zimmerman, M., & Coryell, W. (1989). DSM-III personality disorder diagnoses in a nonpatient sample: Demographic correlates and comorbidity. *Arch. Gen. Psychiat., 46,* 682–89.

Zimmerman, M., & Coryell, W. (1990). Diagnosing personality disorders in the community. A comparison of self report and interview measures. *Arch. Gen. Psychiat., 47,* 527–31.

Zimring, F. (1979). *American youth violence.* Chicago: University of Chicago Press.

Zinbarg, R. E., Barlow, D. H., Brown, T. A., & Hertz, R. M. (1992). Cognitive-behavioral approaches to the nature and treatment of anxiety disorders. *Annu. Rev. Psychol., 43,* 235–67.

Zoccolillo, M., Pickles, A., Quinton, D., & Rutter, M. (1992). The outcome of conduct disorder: Implications for defining adult personality disorder and conduct disorder. *Psychol. Med., 22,* 971–86.

Zohar, J., Mueller, E. A., Insel, T. R., Zohar-Kadouch, R., & Murphy, D. L. (1987). Serotonergic responsivity in obsessive-compulsive disorder: Comparison of patients and healthy controls. *Arch. Gen. Psychiat., 44,* 946–51.

Zola, I. K. (1966). Culture and symptoms—An analysis of patients' presenting complaints. *American Sociological Review, 31,* 615–30.

Zubin, J., & Spring, B. J. (1977). Vulnerability: A new view of schizophrenia. *J. Abnorm. Psychol., 86,* 103–26.

Zuckerman, M. (1972). *Manual and research report for the Sensation Seeking Scale (SSS).* Newark, DE: University of Delaware.

Zuckerman, M. (1978). Sensation seeking and psychopathy. In R. D. Hare and D. Schalling (Eds.), *Psychopathic behavior: Approaches to research.* New York: Wiley.

Zuckerman, M. (1990). The psychophysiology of sensation seeking. *J. Personal., 58,* 313–45.

Zuger, B. (1984). Early effeminate behavior in boys: Outcome and significance for homosexuality. *J. Nerv. Ment. Dis., 172,* 90–972.

Zung, W. W. K. (1969). A cross-cultural survey of symptoms in depression. *Amer. J. Psychiat., 126*(1), 116–21.

Zweben, J. E., & O'Connell, K. (1992). Strategies for breaking marijuana dependence. *J. Psychoact. Drugs, 24,* 165–71.

Zwelling, S. S. (1985). *Quest for a cure.* Williamsburg, VA: The Colonial Williamsburg Foundation.

ACKNOWLEDGMENTS

Unless otherwise acknowledged, all photographs are the property of Scott, Foresman & Company. Page abbreviations are as follows: (T)top, (B)bottom, (L)left, (R)right.

Page 2: Berlinische Galerie Museum for Moderne Knust, Photographie und Architektur; page 4: Deborah Davis/Photo Edit; page 6: Tate Gallery, London/Art Resource, New York; page 8T: Rick Smolan/Against All Odds; page 8B: Bob Daemmrich/Stock Boston; page 9: American Heritage Publishing; page 12: Larry Mulvehill/Photo Researchers; page 16: AP/Wide World; page 18: Christopher Morrow/Stock Boston; page 19: Bill Davis (c) 1988/NEWSDAY; page 20: M. Siluk/The Image Works; page 22: Robert Brenner/Photo Edit; page 23: Hank Morgan/Rainbow; page 30: Courtesy of Ricco/Maresca Gallery; page 33: The Granger Collection, New York; page 35L: The Granger Collection, New York; page 35: The Granger Collection, New York; page 37: The Granger Collection, New York; page 38: Sven Nackstrand/Gamma-Liaison; page 39: The Granger Collection, New York; page 40: Mary Evans Picture Library; page 42: James Karales/Peter Arnold, Inc; page 43: Ets J. E. Bulloz; page 44: Mary Evans Picture Library; page 45L: The Granger Collection, New York; page 45R: The Granger Collection, New York; page 46: Courtesy of the Psychiatric Museum, St. Joseph, MO; page 47: Wade Davis; page 49L: Historical Pictures/Stock Montage, Inc.; page 49R: Brown Brothers; page 52R: Historical Pictures/Stock Montage, Inc.; page 53: Wellcome Institute Library, London; page 54: Bettmann Archive; page 56: Bettmann Archive; page 57: Bettmann Archive; page 58L: Bettmann Archive; page 58C: The Granger Collection, New York; page 58R: Courtesy, B.F.Skinner; page 64: Adolf-Wolfli-Stiftung Kunstmuseum; page 65: Robert Brenner/Photo Edit; page 66: Mike Mazzaschi/Stock Boston; page 73L: D. Gorton/TIME Magazine; page 73R: D. Gorton/TIME Magazine; page 77: Wallace Kirkland LIFE MAGAZINE (c)/Life Magazine/(c) 1945 Time Warner Inc; page 81: Laura Dwight/Peter Arnold, Inc.; page 82L: Bettmann Archive; page 82R: Courtesy of Margaret Mahler; page 87R: Courtesy Rockefeller University; page 88L: Photos courtesy of Dr. Albert Bandura; page 88C: Courtesy Aaron T. Beck M.D./Center for Cognitive Therapy; page 88R: Bettmann Archive; page 91L: Bettmann Archive; page 91C: Bettmann Archive; page 91R: AP/Wide World; page 92: Courtesy of the William Alanson White Psychiatric Institute; page 93L: Courtesy of New York University; page 93C: Association for the Advancement of Psychoanalysis of the Karen Horney Psychoanalytic Institute and Center, New York; page 93R: Jon Erickson; page 96: Chuck Savage/Uniphoto; page 98: Charles Gupton/Stock Boston; page 100: Mark Elias/AP/Wide World; page 102: Larence Migdale/Stock Boston; page 106: J.Greenberg/The Im-

age Works; page 107: Theodore Schwartz; page 112: Michael O'Brien; page 118: Collection De L'Art Brut, Lausanne/Photo: Germond; page 120L: Jean-Claude LeJeune; page 120R: Baldev/Sygma; page 121: M.Granitsas/The Image Works; page 124: Valery Zufarov/SOVFOTO; page 125T: (c) 1994 Rick Rickman/Matrix; page 125B: Ellis Herwig/Stock Boston; page 127: R. Maiman/Sygma; page 130: Reuters/Bettmann; page 133: Reuters/Bettmann; page 134: Reuters/Bettmann; page 137: AP/Wide World; page 140: Sidney/Monkmeyer Press Photo Service; page 141: United States Coast Guard; page 143: Larry Burrows LIFE MAGAZINE (c)/TIME Magazine (1965 Time Warner Inc.); page 146: U. S. Army Photo Center of Military History; page 147: Ledru/Sygma; page 151: R. Maiman/Sygma; page 156: Collection De L'Art Brut, Lausanne/Photo: Germon; page 159: PhotoFest; page 160: Rick Friedman/Black Star; page 161: J.Griffin/The Image Works; page 162: David Wells/The Image Works; page 164L: Susan Mineka; page 164R: Michael Newman/Photo Edit; page 166: Bill Horsman/Stock Boston; page 168: Bob Daemmrich/Stock Boston; page 172: Robert Brenner/Photo Edit; page 192: Insight Magazine; page 198: Janice & Mickey Cartin; page 203: Bob Daemmrich/Stock Boston; page 204: Robert Brenner/Photo Edit; page 207: Robert McElroy/Woodfin Camp & Associates; page 212L: Bettmann Archive ; page 212R: Harcourt Brace Jovanovich, Inc.; page 213: UCLA/Courtesy of Drs. Michael E.Phelps and John C.Mazziotta; page 217: J. Griffin/The Image Works; page 218: Lauren Freudmann/Rainbow; page 227: Brent Jones/Stock Boston; page 230: Snider/The Image Works; page 232L: With permission of Constance Weil/Kevin Horan; page 232R: David R. Frazier Photolibrary; page 232C: Kevin Horan; page 233: Courtesy of Drs. Michael E.Phelps and John C.Mazziotta Positron Emission Tomograph: "Human Brain Function and Biochemistry," Science 228: 799-809, 1985; page 242L: Reuters/Bettmann; page 242R: Mike Urban-Seattle PI/Sygma; page 248: Mary Kate Denny/Photo Edit; page 249: Reuters/Bettmann; page 252: Collection De L'Art Brut, Lausanne/Photo: Germon; page 255: Martin/Custom Medical Stock Photo; page 258: Merrim/Monkmeyer Press Photo Service; page 259: United States Signal Corp; page 265: Susan Greenwood/Gamma-Liaison; page 269: Dennis Budd/Stock Boston; page 271: Carolyn Brown; page 278: Galerie Karsten Greve Koln; page 281: Leinwand/Monkmeyer Press Photo Service; page 283: Jim Olive/Peter Arnold, Inc.; page 284: THE INCREDIBLE MACHINE/Boehringer Ingelheim Zentrale GmbH; page 287: David Lissy/The Picture Cube; page 289: Robert Frerck/Odyssey Productions, Chicago; page 291: Lou Lainey/Discover Magazine/Discover Syndication/Walt Disney Publications; page 293: William

Thompson/The Picture Cube; page 298: Bob Daemmrich/The Image Works; page 299: Peter Southwick/Stock Boston; page 302: J.Berndt/Stock Boston; page 304: Bill Gallery/Stock Boston; page 305: Burbank/The Image Works; page 307: Dan McCoy/Rainbow; page 313: Courtesy of Ricco/Maresca Gallery; page 318: M. Antman/The Image Works; page 320: Joel Gordon Photography; page 322: Scala/Art Resource, New York; page 325: Mike Nazzachi/Stock Boston; page 331L: Courtesy of Otto Kernberg; page 331R: Norton Professional Books; page 339: UPI/Bettmann; page 343: J. Ross Baughman/Visions; page 345: Louis Fernandez/Black Star; page 347: Alon Reininger/Contact Press Images; page 354: Collection De L'Art Brut, Lausanne; page 357: Paul Conklin/Photo Edit; page 361: George Steinmetz; page 362: Focus On Sports; page 367: Das/Monkmeyer Press Photo Service; page 368: Robert Daemmrich/Tony Stone Images; page 370: Pedrick/The Image Works; page 378: D&I MacDonald/The Picture Cube; page 383: Sharon Guynup/The Image Works; page 387T: Leonard Lee Rue/Monkmeyer Press Photo Service; page 387B: Larry Mulvehill/Photo Researchers; page 391: Michael L.Abramson/Woodfin Camp & Associates; page 393: M.Granitsas/The Image Works; page 398: Courtesy of Ricco/Maresca Gallery; page 403: Ronald Sheridan/Ancient Art & Architecture Collection; page 404: Marcia Weinstein; page 409: Peter Yates/Mercury; page 412: Joel Gordon Photography; page 417L: AP/Wide World; page 417R: UPI/Bettmann; page 418: AP/Wide World; page 418: Mary Ellen Mark; page 423L: Courtesy, the survivors living and deceased of convicted pedophile, former priest James Porter; page 423R: Reuters/Bettmann; page 424ALL: U.S. Dept. of Health and Human Services; page 427: Bob Mahoney; page 435: Rhoda Sidney/Photo Edit; page 436: Jim Wilson/Woodfin Camp & Associates; page 442: Prinzhorn-Sammlung Collection; page 446: NIMH; page 449: Mary Ellen Mark; page 454: Al Vercoutere, Malibu, CA; page 456: Grunnitus/Monkmeyer Press Photo Service; page 458ALL: Al Vercoutere, Malibu, CA; page 461: Max Aguilera-Hellweg; page 463: Max Aguilera-Hellweg; page 465: NIMH; page 484: Courtesy of Ricco/Maresca Gallery; page 486: Custom Medical Stock Photo; page 491L: Dan McCoy/Rainbow; page 491R: Dan McCoy/Rainbow; page 493: Lynn Johnson/Black Star; page 497: Ira Wyman/Sygma; page 499: Philip-Lorca di-Corcia; page 503: Hank Morgan/Photo Researchers; page 505: Warren Anatomical Museum, Harvard Medical School; page 508: Lawrence Migdale/Stock Boston; page 512L: Elaine Rebman/Photo Researchers; page 512R: Custom Medical Stock Photo; page 516: Guy Gillette/Photo Researchers; page 518: Richard Hutchings/SS/Photo Researchers; page 521: Will & Deni McIntyre/Photo Researchers; page 526: Courtesy of Ricco/Maresca Gallery; page 530: David Young-Wolff/Photo Edit; page 532: Aurora; page 536: Frank Siteman/Stock Boston; page 540: John Maher/Stock Boston; page 541: Douglas Burrows/Gamma-Liaison; page 552: Abraham Menashe; page 556: Michael Newman/Photo Edit; page 557: Heron/Monkmeyer Press Photo Service; page 561: M. Siluk/The Image Works; page 566: Adolf Wolfli Foundation Museum of Fine Arts, Bern; page 571: J. Pickerell/The Image Works; page 572: Hank Morgan/Rainbow; page 578: Tony Freeman/Photo Edit; page 580: Bob Daemmrich/Stock Boston; page 581: Peter Vandermark/Stock Boston; page 582: Merrim/Monkmeyer Press Photo Service; page 595: Frank Siteman/Rainbow; page 600: Prinzhorn-Sammlung Collection; page 602L: Bakken Library of Electricity in Life; page 602R: Eastern State Hospital; page 605: Will McIntyre/Photo Researchers; page 608L: UPI/Bettmann Archive; page 608R: UPI/Bettmann Archive; page 609: Jerry Cooke/Photo Researchers; page 610: Michael Newman/Photo Edit; page 616: Tony Freeman/Photo Edit; page 624: Courtesy of Ricco/Maresca Gallery; page 629: S. Agricola/The Image Works; page 634: The Freud Museum, London; page 637: Jacques Chenet/Woodfin Camp & Associates; page 639: Courtesy of Dr. Joseph Wolpe; page 641: Alan Carey/The Image Works; page 649: Smith/Monkmeyer Press Photo Service; page 655: Wiley/Monkmeyer Press Photo Service; page 666: Private Collection; page 670: Alan Carey/The Image Works; page 672: Bob Daemmrich/Stock Boston; page 677: AP/Wide World; page 680: Christopher Morris/Black Star; page 684: AP/Wide World; page 687: Trippett/SIPA-Press; page 691: Joseph Schuyler/Stock Boston; page 692: Eric Roth/The Picture Cube; page 695: D. Goldberg/Sygma.

NAME INDEX

Abel, E. L., 361
Abel, G. G., 75, 413, 426, 428
Abell, T., 298
Abou-Saleh, M. T., 237, 617
Abraham, H. D., 386
Abraham, K., 222
Abrahamson, D. J., 64, 226, 436
Abrahamson, L. S., 436
Abramowitz, A. J., 533
Abrams, D. M., 581
Abrams, R., 605
Abramson, H., 549
Abramson, L. Y., 111, 221, 226, 401
Abramson, R. K., 554
Achenbach, T. M., 530
Acker, C., 356
Adam, B. S., 138
Adams, D. M., 356
Adams, H., 432, 433, 434, 435, 436
Adams, H. E., 271, 274, 415, 416, 432, 434–435, 437
Adams, M. S., 423
Ader, R., 286
Adler, A., 53, 91, 92, 94, 135
Adler, T., 499
Adrien, J. L., 552
Affleck, G., 281, 282
Agnew, J., 602
Agras, W. S., 306, 307, 649
Ahadi, S. A., 75, 100
Aiken, L. R., 303
Akhtar, S., 183, 315
Akiskal, H. S., 209, 211, 219, 234
Alander, R., 373
Albee, G. W., 669
Albin, J. B., 562
Alden, L., 325
Alessandri, M., 555
Alexander, A. B., 297
Alexander, B., 297
Alexander, F., 79, 283, 625
Alexander, J. F., 654, 656

Alexander, K., 517
Alexander the Great, 34
Alison, N. G., 361
Al-Issa, I., 107
Allain, A. N., 146
Allen, B., 575
Allerton, W. S., 141
Allgood, B. A., 636
Allodi, F. A., 147
Alloy, L. B., 64, 96, 229
Alterman, A. I., 367, 396
Alvares, B., 41
Alvarez, W., 125
Alzheimer, A., 50, 495
Aman, C., 421
Amato, P. R., 104, 563
Ambrosini, P. J., 547
Amcoff, S., 77
Anand, K. J. S., 379
Anderson, B. L., 287, 438
Anderson, G., 439
Anderson, J. C., 527, 531
Anderson, N. B., 297
Anderson, R. L., 328
Andrasik, F., 298, 299, 300, 307
Andreasen, N. C., 78, 210, 448, 452, 467, 468
Andrews, G., 287, 307, 644
Andrews, J. D. W., 626, 631
Angiulo, M. J., 271
Anthony, J. C., 387
Antoni, M. H., 285, 286
Apfelbaum, B., 433
Aponte, H., 657
Appelbaum, P. S., 153
Arana, G. W., 215
Arbitman-Smith, R., 517
Archer, R. P., 347
Aring, C. D., 42
Aristophanes, 31
Aristotle, 34, 59
Arkowitz, H., 658
Armstrong, H. E., 334
Armstrong, J., 271
Arndt, I. O., 383
Arnkoff, D., 644, 646
Arnold, J. H., 379

Arnold, M. B., 581
Aronoff, B., 395
Aronson, S. S., 557
Arthur, R. J., 126
Asarnow, J. R., 242
Ascione, F. R., 518
Asher, S. J., 104, 302, 669
Asken, M., 573
Atkeson, B. M., 140, 427, 557
Atkinson, J. W., 581
Atkinson, J. W., 581
Auerbach, S. M., 674
Averill, J. R., 123
Avicenna, 35–36, 59
Avison, W., 101
Ayllon, T., 641
Azari, N. P., 512
Azrin, N. H., 641

Bachrach, B., 36, 58, 60
Bachrach, L. L., 690
Baer, L., 327
Baer, R. A., 86
Bailey, J. M., 405, 406, 414
Baker, A., 555
Baker, J. C., 521
Baker, L. A., 73
Bakow, H., 549
Baldessarini, R. J., 215
Baldwin, A. L., 103
Baldwin, C., 103
Bales, R. F., 368
Ballenger, J. C., 617
Balshem, M., 382
Bamidele, R., 467
Bandura, A., 88, 97, 347, 540, 541, 640, 641, 646
Bannister, G., Jr., 395
Barbach, L. G., 411
Barbaree, H. E., 411, 422, 424, 426, 429
Barber, T. X., 633
Barchas, J., 219
Barefoot, J. C., 289
Barkley, R. A., 534
Barlow, D. H., 97, 111, 158, 159, 168, 169, 170, 171, 172, 173, 175, 176, 177, 178, 179, 180, 181, 183,

184, 191, 192, 193, 194, 195, 327, 432, 436, 614, 638
Barnard, K., 74
Barnes, D. M., 500
Barnes, G. E., 100, 221
Barnett, P. A., 226
Baron, I. S., 514
Barrett, M. J., 657
Barrington, C. C., 643
Barrowclough, C., 475
Barry, H., III, 369
Barry, R. J., 553
Barsky, A. J., 257
Bartak, L., 554, 555
Barter, J. T., 243
Bartholomew, K., 654
Bartone, P., 677
Bartone, P. T., 125, 287
Bartsch, K., 48
Başoğlu, M., 149
Bass, E., 273, 418, 419
Bassuk, E. L., 615, 617, 618, 689
Batchelor, I. R. C., 260
Bates, C. M., 664
Bates, D. E., 78
Bates, J. E., 99
Bateson, G., 471
Baucom, D. H., 111
Bauer, A. M., 500, 512
Baum, A., 123, 128, 131
Baumeister, R. F., 243, 244
Baumrind, D., 72, 102, 103
Baxter, L. R., Jr., 188, 189, 233
Bayer, R., 403
Bayle, A. L. J., 51
Beach, S. R. H., 240
Beardslee, W. R., 230
Beason-Hazen, S., 494
Beatrix, Queen of the Netherlands, 449
Beauvais, F., 671, 673
Bebbington, P., 218, 219
Beck, A. T., 88, 89, 97, 168, 177, 180, 193, 217, 218, 220, 221, 222, 223–225, 238,

Kupersmidt, J. B., 105, 106
Kupfer, D. J., 214, 612
Kushner, M., 306–307
Kutcher, S. P., 545, 615
Kuykendall, D. H., 123

Lachar, D., 592
Ladd, G. W., 105
Lahey, B. B., 535, 563
Lake, C. R., 215
Lakin, M., 663
Lamb, H. R., 692
Lambert, J., 148
Lambert, M. J., 109, 627, 629, 658, 659, 660, 661, 663
Landesman-Dwyer, S., 517
Landon, P. B., 347
Lang, A. R., 369, 371, 372
Lang, P. J., 158, 304, 342, 343
Lange, W. R., 375
Langevin, R., 424
Lansky, M. R., 613
Lanyon, R., 596
Lanyon, R. I., 643
Lapidus, L. B., 379
LaSalvia, T. A., 380
Last, C. G., 544
Laufer, R. S., 142
La Via, M. F., 131
Lavori, P., 212
Lawton, H., 60
Lazarus, A. A., 66, 193, 434, 658
Leahy, J., 511
Leal, J., 383
Leary, T., 94
Lease, C. A., 100
Lebedev, B. A., 301
Leber, W. R., 236, 621
Lebergott, S., 132
Lebowitz, L., 139
Lebra, W., 108
Lee, J. R., 18
Lees-Haley, P. R., 506
Lefebvre, R. C., 86
Leff, J. P., 471, 472
Lefkowitz, M. M., 540, 541, 545
Le Haye, A., 548
Lehmann, H. E., 108
Lehmann, L., 212
Lehrer, P. M., 300, 306
Leiblum, S. R., 432, 434, 435, 436, 437, 438
Leichtman, M., 578
Leichtman, M. D., 420
Lelliott, P., 171
Lemert, E. M., 480

Lemieux, A. M., 285
Lencz, T., 319
Lenox, K. F., 536
Lentz, R. J., 86, 475, 578, 641, 678, 679, 680
Lenzenweger, M. F., 468
Leon, G. L., 147
Leon, G. R., 294, 389, 390
Leonard, C., 244
Leong, G. B., 605
Lerman, P., 690
Lerner, P. M., 270, 580
Lester, D., 242
Letizia, K. A., 392
LeVay, S., 405
Levenson, A. J., 190, 615
Leventhal, H., 122
Leventhal, J. M., 382
Levin, H. S., 504
Levin, S., 468
Levine, L., 411
Levine, M., 562, 676
Levine, M. D., 549
Levitan, H., 300
Levor, R. M., 282, 300
Levy, D. L., 466
Lewinsohn, P. M., 201, 208, 219, 222–223, 545, 548
Lewis, C. E., 338
Lewis, J., 73
Lewis, J. M., 472
Lewis, J. W., 381
Lewis, M. S., 468
Lewis, N. D. C., 33
Lewis, R. J., 528
Lewis, W. C., 263
Lexow, G. A., 557
Liberman, R. P., 85, 86
Licht, M. H., 578
Liddle, P. F., 610
Lidz, T., 16, 471
Lie, N., 533
Lieberman, J. A., 465, 466, 467
Lieberman, L. M., 518
Liebman, J. M., 364, 365
Liebowitz, M. R., 172, 188, 189, 191, 614
Liem, J. H., 471
Lifton, R. J., 144
Liljefors, I., 300
Lin, K. M., 123
Lincoln, J., 518
Lindman, R. E., 369
Lindsay, D. S., 420
Lindsey, K. P., 473
Lindy, J. D., 137
Linehan, M. M., 86, 334, 649, 654

Link, B., 556
Link, B. G., 16
Linney, J. A., 673
Linszen, D. H., 474
Linton, R., 106
Lion, J. R., 347
Lipowski, Z. J., 271
Lipton, D. N., 428
Lipton, E. L., 303
Lipton, R. C., 98
Lisak, D., 427
Lishman, W. A., 356, 362, 363
Lissau, I., 391
Litman, R. E., 245
Litwack, T. R., 683
Livesley, W. J., 27, 315, 316, 325, 330, 350, 351
Livingston, J., 394
Lizardi, H., 221
Lloyd, S. A., 427
Lobitz, G. K., 436
Lobitz, W. C., 436
Lobovits, D. A., 545
Locke, S. E., 286
Locklear, E., 572, 573
Loeber, R., 535, 540
Loewenstein, D. A., 228
Loewenstein, R. J., 274
Loftus, E. F., 272, 273, 419, 421
Lombardi, D. N., 379
Lombardo, E. F., 540
Lombardo, V. S., 540
Lomranz, J., 142
Loney, J., 532
Long, J. V. F., 111
Loosen, P. T., 215
Lopez-Roig, L., 592
LoPiccolo, J., 433, 434, 437, 438
LoPiccolo, L., 434
Loranger, A. W., 330
Lorenz, V. C., 394
Lorion, R. P., 667
Lorr, M., 236
Lovaas, O. I., 555, 640
Lovett, S., 517
Lovibond, S. H., 371
Lozoff, B., 77, 99
Lubin, B., 333, 583, 674
Lucas, A. R., 308
Luchins, A. S., 45, 46
Luckasson, R., 507, 516, 517
Luecke, W. J., 559
Luepker, R. V., 291
Lukas, C., 250
Lund, S. N., 560
Lunsing, R. J., 548

Luntz, B. K., 559
Lusznat, R. M., 617
Luten, A., 222
Luther, M., 39, 59
Lutz, D. J., 366
Lykken, D. T., 342
Lyman, D., 345, 346, 535, 536, 540
Lynch, J. J., 303
Lyness, S. A., 291, 297
Lynn, S. J., 270, 272, 633
Lyon, G. R., 520
Lyon, M., 467
Lytton, H. 72

McAlister, A. L., 309, 673
McAnulty, R. D., 415
McBride, W. J., 364
McCall, L., 604
McCann, I. L., 139
McCarthy, B. W., 433, 435
McClelland, D. C., 298
McClelland, J. M., 618
Maccoby, E. E., 102
McCombie, S. L., 139
McConaghy, N., 394
McConaughy, S. H., 530
McConville, M. T., 675
McCord, J., 344, 349
McCord, W., 344
McCown, W. G., 374
McCoy, N. L., 432
McCrae, R. R., 271, 282
McCutchan, J. A., 494
MacDonald, M. R., 123, 152
McDonel, E. C., 428
McDonnell, J., 517, 518
McEvoy, L., 138
McEwen, B. S., 405
McFall, R. M., 428, 429
McFarlane, A. C., 138
MacFarlane, K., 419
McGarry-Roberts, P. A., 466
McGill, K. L., 282
McGlashan, T. H., 448, 449, 472, 474
McGuffin, P., 213, 214, 231
Machado, P. P., 629
McHugh, P. R., 416, 439
McIntosh, J. L., 241
McKay, J. R., 369
Mackay, L. E., 506
McKeon, P., 379
McKinley, J. C., 583
Mackintosh, D., 398, 526
Mackintosh, E., 398
Mackintosh, N., 84

SUBJECT INDEX

Alcohol withdrawal delirium, 362–63
Alexithymia, **274**
Algophobia, 161
Alienists, 47
ALI (American Law Institute) standard, 688, 689
All-or-none thinking, 194
All-or-nothing reasoning, 223
Alprazolam (Xanax), 614, 615, 638; for anxiety disorders, 181, 190–91
Alter personalities, **267**
Alzheimer's disease (see Dementia of the Alzheimer's type (DAT))
AMA (American Medical Association), 694; on masturbation, 402
Amenorrhea, eating disorders and, 296
American Association on Mental Retardation (AAMR): adaptive skills assessment of, 516; mental retardation defined by, 507–8
American Law Institute (ALI) standard, 688, 689
American Medical Association (AMA), 694; on masturbation, 402
American Psychiatric Association (APA), 694; on electroconvulsive therapy, 605; on homosexuality, 404; mental retardation defined by, 507–8
American Psychological Association (APA), 694
American Psychological Society (APS), 694
Amicus curiae, 694
Aminoketones, 613, 614
Amitriptyline (Elavil), 613; for posttraumatic stress disorder, 152
Amnesia: alcohol amnestic disorder and, 363; anterograde, 502; dissociative, 264–66; retrograde, 502
Amnestic syndrome, **492**
Amniocentesis, 510
Amok, 108
Amoxapine (Asendin), 613
Amphetamines: abuse and dependence on, 383–84;

for attention-deficit hyperactivity disorder, 532–33
Anaclitic depression, 201, 545
Anafranil (clomipramine): for obsessive-compulsive disorder, 189, 191, 614
Analgesia, in conversion disorder, 260
Analogue studies, **23**
Anal stage, 81
Androgyny, 111
Anesthesia, in conversion disorder, 260
Angina pectoris, 290
Animal magnetism, 53–54
Anorexia nervosa, 108, **292–93**, 294, 296; treatment for, 308
Anorexigenic drugs, for hyperobesity, 391
Antabuse (disulfiram), 370
Anterograde amnesia, 502
Antianxiety drugs, 614–16, 620; abuse and dependence on, 376–77; for antisocial personality disorder, 347; for anxiety disorders, 181, 190–91; side effects of, 614–15; for somatoform disorders, 274
Anticipatory anxiety, 173
Anticipatory phase, in coping with rape, 139
Antidepressant drugs, 612–14, 619–20; for anxiety disorders, 189, 191; MAOIs, 613; SSRIs, 613; for childhood depression, 547; for enuresis, 549; for mood disorders, 236–37; MAOIs, 613; SSRIs, 613; side effects of, 547; for somatoform disorders, 274; tricyclic, 612–13; for unipolar mood disorders, 214, 215
Antigens, **284**
Antimanic drugs, 233, 617, 620 (see also Lithium)
Antipsychotic drugs, **609–12**, 619; for schizophrenia, 448
Antisocial personality disorder, 317, **322–23**, 329, 335–49; causes of, 341–46; clinical picture in, 337–41; delinquency

and, 540; drug abuse and dependence and, 379; posttraumatic stress disorder and, 144; treatment for, 346–49
Anxiety, 156–97, **157** (see also Anxiety disorders); anticipatory, 173; behavioral techniques used with, 86; castration, 81; comorbidity of, 229; defense mechanisms and, 79–81; fear compared with, 158–59; free-floating, 176; moral, 79; neurotic, 79; reality, 79; sexual dysfunctions and, 435–36; uncontrollable and unpredictable frightening events as cause of, 97–98
Anxiety disorders, **159–95**; during childhood and adolescence, 543–45; generalized, 176–82; obsessive-compulsive, 182–90; obsessive-compulsive disorder with, 184; overanxious, 544; panic disorder and agoraphobia, 168–76; phobias, 160–76; separation anxiety disorder, 543–44; treatment for, 190–95, 637–38 (see also Antianxiety drugs); unresolved issues concerning, 195–96
Anxiety sensitivity, 175–76
Anxiolytics (see Antianxiety drugs)
Anxious apprehension, 158, 176
Anxious hyperarousal, 229
APA (see American Psychiatric Association (APA); American Psychological Association (APA))
Apathy, brain damage and, 487
Aphonia, 260
Apolipoprotein-E (ApoE), in Alzheimer's disease, 500, 501
Apprehension, anxious, 158, 176
Approach-approach conflicts, 120
APS (American Psychological Society), 694
Arapesh, 110

Arbitrary inference, 224
ARC (AIDS-related complex), **494**
Asendin (amoxapine), 613
Asians (see also China); alcohol abuse among, 365–66; gambling among, 395
Asphyxia, autoerotic, 412, 413–14
Assertiveness therapy, **642–43**
Assessment (see Clinical assessment)
Assessment interviews, 574–75, 576, 577
Assimilation, **96**
Association for the Advancement of Behavior Therapy (AABT), 694
Astasia-abasia, 260
Asthma, 296–97
Astraphobia, 161
Asylums, **41–42** (see also Hospitalization; Institutionalization; Mental hospitals; Sanatoriums)
Attention-deficit hyperactivity disorder (ADHD), 530, **531–33**; causes of, 531–32; clinical picture in, 531; nutritional deficiencies causing, 77; treatment for, 384, 532–33, 617–18
Attitudes, physical health and, 281–82
Attribution(s), **88–89**, **226**
Attributional style, 88–89; unipolar mood disorders and, 221
Attribution theory, 88–89
Aura, migraines and, 298–99
Australian aborigines, physical illness among, 304
Authoritarian parenting style, 102
Authoritative parenting style, 102
Authority, rejection of, in antisocial personality disorder, 338
Autism, 451, **551–55**; causes of, 554; clinical picture in, 552–54; treatment for, 554–55, 640
Autistic-savants, 553
Autoerotic asphyxia, 412, 413–14

Isolation: as defense mechanism, 80; in obsessive-compulsive disorder, 185–86
Israeli-NIMH High-Risk Study, 464
Italy, exaggeration of physical complaints in, 109

Jamaica, overcontrolled problems in, 109
Japan: physical illness in, 304; suicide in, 244
Jealous delusional disorder, 476
Jenkins Activity Survey for Health Prediction, 289
Journal of Abnormal Psychology, 23, 56, 226
Judgment, brain damage and, 487
Juvenile delinquency, **534;** early studies of, 56

Kaluli, depression among, 235
Kamikaze pilots, 244
Kenyans, depression among, 235
Kindling phenomena, 173
Kitsunetsuki, 108
Klinefelter's syndrome, 511
Koro, 108
Korsakoff's syndrome, 363

Labeling, 16–17
Language disturbances: brain damage and, 487; in schizophrenia, 449–50
Laotian Americans, gambling among, 395
Latah, 108
Latency stage, 81
Latent content, **633**
LCUs (life change units), 126
LD (*see* Specific learning disorders)
Learned helplessness, **225;** depression and, 23, 225–26
Learning (*see also* Classical conditioning; Conditioning; Operant conditioning); behavioral perspective and, 83–85; brain damage and, 487; childhood depression and, 547; of illnesses,

303–4; pathological gambling and, 394; in personality disorders, 330–31; of phobias, 163–64; sexual dysfunctions and, 434–35
Learning disabilities (LD) (*see* Specific learning disorders)
Least restrictive environment, 555
Legal counsel, right to, 682
Legal issues (*see* Court cases; Forensic psychiatry)
Lehrbuch der Psychiatrie (Kraepelin), 51
Lesbians (*see* Homosexuality)
Librium (chlordiazepoxide), 614; for alcohol withdrawal, 362–63; for anxiety, 181
Life changes, stress and, 125–26
Life change units (LCUs), 126
Life event(s): physical health and, 282; stress and, 218–19, 233–34
Life Event and Difficulty Schedule, 126
Life instincts, 79
Lifestyle, health maintenance and, 287–88, 307, 308–9
Life-support retarded individuals, 509
Lifetime prevalence, 17–18
Light therapy, for seasonal affective disorder, 216–17
Limbic lobe, 490
Limbic system: panic disorder and, 173; in schizophrenia, 468; in unipolar mood disorders, 217
Listening to Prozac (Kramer), 237, 621
Lithium: for antisocial personality disorder, 347; for bipolar disorder, 232–33, 237–38, 616–17
Litigation (*see* Court cases)
Little Hans, 163
Lobotomy, 606, 607, 608
Locus coeruleus, panic disorder and, 173
Loma Prieta earthquake, 135

Low birth weight, 74–75
LSD (lysergic acid diethylamide), abuse and dependence on, 385–86
Ludiomil (maprotiline), 613
Lunatic's Tower, 41
Luria-Nebraska battery, 573
Lycanthropy, **37**
Lysergic acid diethylamide (LSD), abuse and dependence on, 385–86

McKenna v. *Fargo*, 591
McMartin Preschool Case, 418, 419
Macrocephaly, **514**
Madhouses, 41
Mainstreaming, of mentally retarded individuals, 518
La Maison de Charenton asylum, 41
Major depressive disorder, 201, 206–9; recurrence and relapse in, 208–9
Major tranquilizers (*see* Antipsychotic drugs)
Maladaptive behavior (*see* Abnormal behavior)
Malaria, false, in conversion disorder, 262
Malarial treatment, for syphilis, 50, 51
Malaysia, schizophrenia in, 473
Male erectile disorder, **432**
Male orgasmic disorder, **433**
Malingering, **254,** 263, 698–99; conversion reactions versus, 262; dissociative identity disorder versus, 268
Malleus maleficarum, 40
Malnutrition, 76–77; eating disorders and, 296; mental retardation and, 510
Mania, **201;** in bipolar disorder, 210–11; dancing, 37, 40; treatment for, 233, 617, 620 (*see also* Lithium)
Manic-depressive insanity (*see* Bipolar disorder)
Manifest content, **633**
MAO (monoamine oxidase) inhibitors, 612, 613; for generalized anxiety dis-

order, 614; for personality disorders, 335; for social phobia, 191
Maprotiline (Ludiomil), 613
Marijuana, **386;** abuse and dependence on, 386–88
Marital discord, 103 (*see also* Divorce); alcohol abuse and, 367–68; depression and, 208–9, 230, 240; physical illness and, 302; schizophrenia and, 471; sexual dysfunctions and, 436–37; transvestic fetishism and, 408–9
Marital schism, **471**
Marital separation, stress from, 134
Marital skew, **471**
Marital status, depression and, 236
Marital therapy, **654–56;** for mood disorders, 240
Marplan (isocarboxazid), 612
Masculinity, role expectations and, 111
Masochism, **412, 413–14**
Mass hysteria, 37–38, 262
Mass murders, 137
Masturbation, 402; sexual behavior and, 401
MBD (minimal brain dysfunction), 521
MCLP (mesocorticolimbic dopamine pathway), psychoactive substance abuse and, 364, 365
Medical Inquiries and Observations upon the Diseases of the Mind (Rush), 44
Medical model (*see* Biological perspective; Biological therapy)
Medications (*see* Pharmacologic therapy)
Medroxyprogesterone acetate (MPA; Depo-Provera), for sex offenders, 430
Melancholic major depression, **207**
Melanesia, homosexuality in, 402
Mellaril (thioridazine), 610, 611
Memmel v. *Mundy*, 682

About the Artwork in This Book

In 1945, Jean Dubuffet began collecting *art brut* (literally, "raw art"), a term he used to describe art created by people who live outside the cultural mainstream—mental patients, spiritualists, innocents, maladjusted persons, loners, and those who exist at the fringes of society. Dubuffet wanted to exhibit an art in which "creation shines in its pure state, free of all the compromises which alter the mechanisms in professionals' productions." The collection that resulted—now housed in the Chateau de Beaulieu in Lausanne, Switzerland—provides an extraordinary glimpse into the inner lives and private visions of cultural outsiders and confirms Dubuffet's sense of the profound talents that often lie within those who are, for one reason or another, considered to be abnormal. We are grateful to the museum in Lausanne for allowing us to use selected works from the collection in this text.

We are also grateful to the proprietors of the Prinzhorn Collection of the Art of the Mentally Ill at the University of Heidelberg for allowing us to reprint works from that collection, which contains some 6000 works or objects that were created by 516 patients, almost all of whom were chronically ill and many of whom had been institutionalized for most of their lives. Finally, we would like to thank the Ricco/Maresca Gallery, the Adolf-Wölffli-Stiftung Kunstmuseum, Al Vercoutere, Janice and Mickey Cartin, Galerie Karsten Greve Köln, and for sharing with us the work of artists who, for one reason or another, were or are outside the cultural mainstream.

At the beginning of each chapter, we display a work by one of the artists, along with a capsule biography. Some of the artists are known to have suffered from disorders described in the text; in other cases we lack the information to know for sure what the nature of the artist's problem was. The creators of these artworks, whatever their "diagnostic status," offer us an intriguing look into disordered human psychology.

Feedback, please!

We need your reactions and ideas if *Abnormal Psychology and Modern Life* is to serve you and others better. What did you like best and least? What would you like to have more or less of? How could it have been handled better? Please jot down your suggestions, cut out this page, fold and tape or staple it, and mail it to us. No postage is needed.

Many thanks!
The authors

For every chapter that you read, please make a check mark on each line to indicate your evaluation of it. It is ideal if you can do this as soon as you finish reading each chapter.

Chapter	Informational Value			Interest		
	high	average	low	high	average	low
1. Abnormal Behavior in Our Times						
2. Historical Views of Abnormal Behavior						
3. Causal Factors and Viewpoints in Abnormal Psychology						
4. Stress and Adjustment Disorders						
5. Panic, Anxiety, and Their Disorders						
6. Mood Disorders and Suicide						
7. Somatoform and Dissociative Disorders						
8. Psychological Factors and Physical Illness						
9. Personality Disorders						
10. Substance-Related and Other Addictive Disorders						
11. Sexual Varients, Abuse, and Dysfunctions						
12. The Schizophrenias and Delusional Disorders						
13. Brain Disorders and Other Cognitive Impairments						
14. Disorders of Childhood and Adolescence						
15. Clinical Assessment						
16. Biologically Based Therapies						
17. Psychologically Based Therapies						
18. Contemporary Issues in Abnormal Psychology						

What did you like best/least about *Abnormal Psychology and Modern Life* ?

Your name and address (if you wish)

_____

_____

Size of your psychology class_____

Were you in a discussion section? _____

Besides the text, did you use:

Study Guide to accompany *Abnormal Psychology and Modern Life 10th* ? _____

Other supplementary material? _____

Male_____ Female_____ Age_____

Your course grade_____

Will you take more psychology? _____

Your probable major_____

School_____

·· *fold here* ··

How could *Abnormal Psychology and Modern Life* be improved?

All things considered, how does *Abnormal Psychology and Modern Life* compare to texts you have used in other courses?

much better	*better*	*about average*	*worse*	*much worse*

·· *fold here* ··

▌▌▌▌▌

BUSINESS REPLY MAIL
FIRST CLASS PERMIT NO.247 NEW YORK, NY

POSTAGE WILL BE PAID BY ADDRESSEE

⬛ HarperCollins*Publishers*
   Attn: Psychology Editor—Abn Psy 10
   College Division
   10 East 53rd Street
   New York, NY 10022-5299

NO POSTAGE
NECESSARY
IF MAILED
IN THE
UNITED STATES

cut page out